NETWORK OPERATING SYSTEMS

Windows Server 2003

Ikvinderpal Singh
Lecturer,
PG Deptt of Computer Sc. & Applications,
Khalsa College, Amritsar.

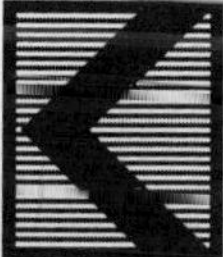

KHANNA BOOK PUBLISHING CO. (P) LTD.
Publisher of Science, Technology and Engineering Books
40/4344, Ansari Road, Darya Ganj, New Delhi-110002
Phone: 011-23244447-48 **Mobile:** +91-99109 09320
E-mail: contact@khannabooks.com
Website: www.khannabooks.com

Price : Rs. 425.00

Network Operating Systems
Ikvinderpal Singh

ISBN : 978-93-81068-19-9

Reprint : 2016

Published by:

KHANNA BOOK PUBLISHING CO. (P) LTD.
4C/4344, Ansari Road, Darya Ganj, New Delhi-1 10 002
Phone: 011-23244447-48 **Mobile:** +91-9910909320
E-mail: contact@khannabooks.com

Printed in India by:
India Book Printers & Binders, Delhi

NETWORK OPERATING SYSTEMS

Introduction of various Network Operating Systems: *Windows 2000/2003/XP, Unix/Linux.*

Overview of Network Operating System: *Introduction, Architecture, Shell, Kernel, File System, Hardware requirements, Active Directory, Clustering & Load Balancing, Storage Management, Editors, Networking and Communication features, Licensing*

Disk Management: *Terminology and Concepts, Managing Disks, Managing Basic and Dynamic Disks, Disk Quotas, Disk Fragmentation, Remote Storage, RAID and Mirroring.*

Servers: *Managing DHCP, IIS, WINS, DNS and Proxy servers.*

User, Group and Computer Accounts: *Creating and Managing user, Group and Computer Accounts, Managing Access Controls, Troubleshooting Accounts.*

Performance Monitoring and Security: *Task Management, System Monitoring, Performance Logs and Alerts, Monitoring Memory, Network and Process Objects, Auditing Security Events, Audit Policy and Event Viewer.*

Special Topics: *Introduction to E-Mail, Telnet and FTP, Distributed Systems.*

Case and Comparative Studies of Windows 2003 *server and Unix/Linux.*

Contents

CHAPTER 1

Introduction

1.1 INTRODUCTION

One of the most basic, low-level features of an operating system is its kernel. The kernel is usually responsible for I/O, and in much "monolithic" architecture it also deals with memory management, file systems, etc. The two extremes of contemporary kernel design are microkernel architectures, and monolithic kernels. Microkernel's themselves can offer several advantages over traditional, monolithic kernels. We want to look into the operating system from three view points:

1. **Users:** The services provided to users.
2. **Programmers:** The interface made available to programmers and how it is provided.
3. **Operating System Designers:** The methodologies for design.

1.2 OPERATING SYSTEM

Computers use low-level software called an operating system (O/S) to help people build and run their own programs. Operating system software runs not just on laptop computers but also on cell phones, network routers and other so-called embedded devices.

1.2.1 Types of Operating Systems

The best-known operating systems are those used on personal computers:

- Microsoft Windows
- Mac OS X
- Linux

Some operating systems are designed for certain types of equipment, such as

- Google Android (a variant of Linux), and Symbian - for cell phones

- Solaris, HP-UX, DG-UX, and other variants of Unix - for server computers
- DEC VMS (Virtual Memory System) - for mainframe computers

Other operating systems enjoyed a period of notoriety but are of only historical interest now:

- Novell Netware was a popular O/S for PCs in the 1990s
- IBM OS/2 was an early PC O/S that competed with Microsoft Windows for a time but had limited success
- Multics was an especially innovative operating system created in the 1960s for mainframes, that influenced the later development of Unix

1.2.2 Operating System Objectives and Functions

An OS is a program that controls the execution of application programs and acts as an interface between applications and the computer hardware. It can be thought of as having three objectives:

- **Convenience:** An OS makes a computer more convenient to use.
- **Efficiency:** An OS allows the computer system resources to be used in an efficient manner.
- **Ability to evolve:** An OS should be constructed in such a way as to permit the effective development, testing, and introduction of new system functions without interfering with service.

Let us examine these three aspects of an OS in turn.

1.2.3 The Operating System as a User/Computer Interface

The hardware and software used in providing applications to a user can be viewed in a layered or hierarchical fashion, as depicted in Figure 1.1.The user of those applications, the end user, generally is not concerned with the details of computer hardware. Thus, the end user views a computer system in terms of a set of applications. An application can be expressed in a programming language and is developed by an application programmer. If one were to develop an application program as a set of machine instructions that is completely responsible for controlling the computer hardware, one would be faced with an overwhelmingly complex undertaking. To ease this chore, a set of system programs is provided. Some of these programs are referred to as utilities. These implement frequently used functions that assist in program creation, the management of files, and the control of I/O devices. A programmer will make use of these facilities in developing an application, and the application, while it is running, will invoke the utilities to perform certain functions. The most important collection of system programs comprises the OS. The OS masks the details of the hardware from the programmer and provides the programmer with a convenient interface for using the system. It acts as mediator, making it easier for the programmer and for application programs to access and use those facilities and services.

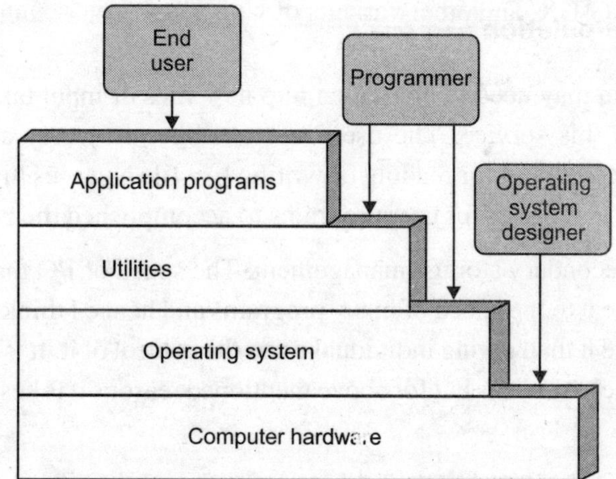

Figure 1.1 Layers and Views of a Computer System

1.2.4 Operating-system Functions

Following are the functions of an operating system:

1.2.4.1 Program Execution

The purpose of a computer system is to allow the user to execute programs. The system must be able to load a program into memory and to run that program, end execution, either normally or abnormally (indicating error).

So the operating systems provide an environment where the user can conveniently run programs. The user does not have to worry about the memory allocation or multitasking or anything. These things are taken care of by the operating systems.

Running a program involves the allocating and deallocating memory, CPU scheduling in case of multiprocessing. These functions cannot be given to the user-level programs. So user-level programs cannot help the user to run programs independently without the help from operating systems.

1.2.4.2 I/O Operations

Each program requires an input and produces output. A running program may require I/O, which may involve a file or an I/O device.

The operating systems hides the user the details of underlying hardware for the I/O. All the user sees is that the I/O has been performed without any details. So the operating systems by providing I/O make it convenient for the users to run programs.

For efficiently and protection users cannot control I/O so this service cannot be provided by user-level programs.

1.2.4.3 File-System Manipulation

The output of a program may need to be written into new files or input taken from some files. The operating system provides this service. The user does not have to worry about secondary storage management. User gives a command for reading or writing to a file and sees his her task accomplished. Thus operating system makes it easier for user programs to accomplished their task.

This service involves secondary storage management. The speed of I/O that depends on secondary storage management is critical to the speed of many programs and hence I think it is best relegated to the operating systems to manage it than giving individual users the control of it. It is not difficult for the user-level programs to provide these services but for above mentioned reasons it is best if this service s left with operating system.

The file system is of particular interest. Obviously, programs need to read and write files and directories, create and delete them, search them, list file Information, permission management.

1.2.4.4 Communications

There are instances where processes need to communicate with each other to exchange information. It may be between processes running on the same computer or running on the different computers. By providing this service the operating system relieves the user of the worry of passing messages between processes. In case where the messages need to be passed to processes on the other computers through a network it can be done by the user programs. The user program may be customized to the specifics of the hardware through which the message transits and provides the service interface to the operating system.

Processes may exchange information, on the same computer or between computers over a network. Communications may be via shared memory or through message passing (packets moved by the OS).

1.2.4.5 Error Detection

An error is one part of the system may cause malfunctioning of the complete system. To avoid such a situation the operating system constantly monitors the system for detecting the errors. This relieves the user of the worry of errors propagating to various part of the system and causing malfunctioning.

This service cannot allowed to be handled by user programs because it involves monitoring and in cases altering area of memory or deallocation of memory for a faulty process. Or may be relinquishing the CPU of a process that goes into an infinite loop. These tasks are too critical to be handed over to the user programs. A user program if given these privileges can interfere with the correct (normal) operation of the operating systems.

OS needs to be constantly aware of possible errors. Error may occur in the CPU and memory hardware, in I/O devices, in user program. For each type of error, OS should take the appropriate action to ensure correct and consistent computing. Debugging facilities can greatly enhance the user's and programmer's abilities to efficiently use the system. Another set of OS functions exists for ensuring the efficient operation of the system itself via resource sharing.

1.2.4.6 Resource Allocation

When multiple users or multiple jobs running concurrently, resources must be allocated to each of them. Many types of resources - Some (such as CPU cycles, main memory, and file storage) may have special allocation code, others (such as I/O devices) may have general request and release code.

1.2.4.7 Accounting

A good OS will collect usage statistics for various resources and monitor performance parameters such as response time. On any system, this information is useful in anticipating the need for future enhancements and in tuning the system to improve performance. On a multiuser system, the information can be used for billing purposes.

1.2.4.8 Protection and Security

The owners of information stored in a multiuser or networked computer system may want to control use of that information, concurrent processes should not interfere with each other.

Protection involves ensuring that all access to system resources is controlled. Security of the system from outsiders requires user authentication, extends to defending external I/O devices from invalid access attempts. If a system is to be protected and secure, precautions must be instituted throughout it. A chain is only as strong as its weakest link.

1.2.5 The Operating System as Resource Manager

A computer is a set of resources for the movement, storage, and processing of data and for the control of these functions. The OS is responsible for managing these resources. Can we say that it is the OS that controls the movement, storage, and processing of data? From one point of view, the answer is yes: By managing the computer's resources, the OS is in control of the computer's basic functions. But this control is exercised in a curious way. Normally, we think of a control mechanism as something external to that which is controlled, or at least as something that is a distinct and separate part of that which is controlled. (For example, a residential heating system is controlled by a thermostat, which is separate from the heat-generation and heat distribution apparatus.) This is not the case with the OS, which as a control mechanism is unusual in two respects:

- The OS functions in the same way as ordinary computer software; that is, it is a program or suite of programs executed by the processor.
- The OS frequently relinquishes control and must depend on the processor to allow it to regain control.

Like other computer programs, the OS provides instructions for the processor. The key difference is in the intent of the program. The OS directs the processor in the use of the other system resources and in the timing of its execution of other programs. But in order for the processor to do any of these things, it must cease executing the OS program and execute other programs. Thus, the OS relinquishes control for the processor to do some "useful" work and then resumes control long enough to prepare the processor to do the next piece of work. The mechanisms involved in all this should become clear as the chapter proceeds.

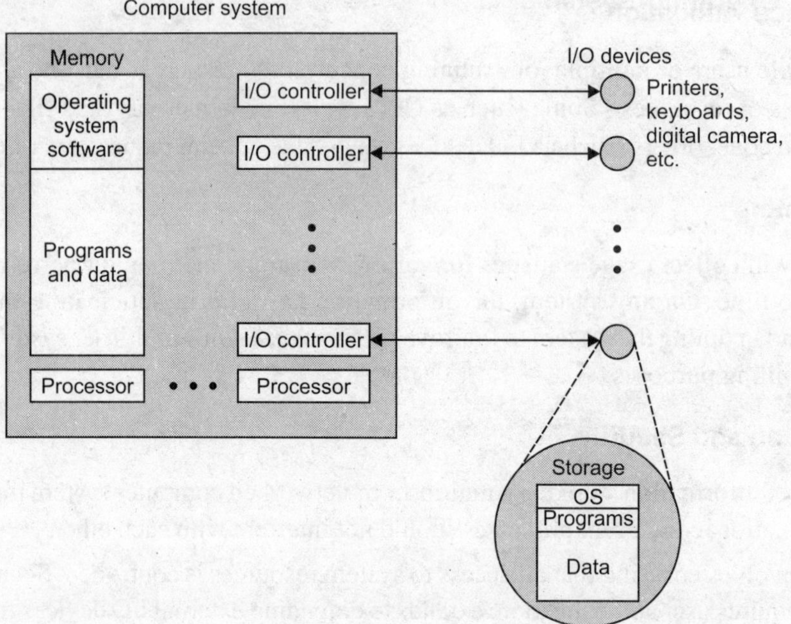

Figure 1.2 The Operating System as Resource Manager

Figure 1.2 suggests the main resources that are managed by the OS.A portion of the OS are in main memory. This includes the kernel, or nucleus, which contains the most frequently, used functions in the OS and, at a given time, other portions of the OS currently in use. The remainder of main memory contains user programs and data. The allocation of this resource (main memory) is controlled jointly by the OS and memory management hardware in the processor, as we shall see. The OS decides when an I/O device can be used by a program in execution and controls access to and use of files. The processor itself is a resource, and the OS must determine how much processor time is to be devoted to the execution of a particular user program. In the case of a multiple-processor system, this decision must span all of the processors.

1.3 NETWORK OPERATING SYSTEM

A modern O/S contains much built-in software designed to simplify networking of a computer. Typical O/S software includes an implementation of TCP/IP protocol stack and related utility programs like ping and trace route. This includes the necessary device drivers and other software to automatically enable a device's Ethernet interface. Mobile devices also normally provide the programs needed to enable Wi-Fi, Bluetooth, or other wireless connectivity.

The early versions of Microsoft Windows did not provide any computer networking support. Microsoft added basic networking capability into its operating system starting with Windows 95 and Windows for Workgroups. Microsoft also introduced its Internet Connection Sharing (ICS) feature in Windows 98 Second Edition (Win98 SE). Contrast that with Unix, which was designed from the beginning with networking in view. Nearly any consumer O/S today qualifies as a network operating system due to the popularity of the Internet.

1.3.1 Embedded Operating Systems

A so-called embedded system supports no or limited configuration of its software. Embedded systems like routers, for example, typically include a pre-configured Web server, DHCP server, and some utilities but do not allow the installation of new programs.

Examples of embedded operating systems for routers include:

- Cisco IOS (Internetwork Operating System)
- DD-WRT
- Juniper Junos

An embedded OS can also be found inside an increasing number of consumer gadgets including phones (iPhone OS), PDAs (Windows CE), and digital media players (ipodlinux).

1.3.2 Types of Network Operating Systems

Following are the various types of network operating systems:

		Windows NT releases		
Version	Marketing name	Editions	Release date	RTM build
NT 3.1	Windows NT 3.1	Workstation (named just Windows NT), Advanced Server	27 July 1993	528
NT 3.5	Windows NT 3.5	Workstation, Server	21 September 1994	807
NT 3.51	Windows NT 3.51	Workstation, Server	30 May 1995	1057
NT 4.0	Windows NT 4.0	Workstation, Server, Server Enterprise Edition, Terminal Server, Embedded	29 July 1996	1381
NT 5.0	Windows 2000	Professional, Server, Advanced Server, Datacenter Server, Advanced/Datacenter Server Limited Edition	17 February 2000	2195
NT 5.1	Windows XP	Home, Professional, 64-bit Edition (Itanium), Media Center (original, 2003, 2004 & 2005), Tablet PC (original and 2005), Starter, Embedded, Home N, Professional N	25 October 2001	2600
NT 5.2	Windows XP	64-bit Edition Version 2003 (Itanium)	28 March 2003	3790
NT 5.2	Windows Server 2003	Standard, Enterprise, Datacenter, Web, Storage, Small Business Server, Compute Cluster	24 April 2003	3790
NT 5.2	Windows XP	Professional x64 Edition	25 April 2005	3790
NT 5.2	Windows Home Server	N/A	16 July 2007	3790
NT 6.0	Windows Vista	Home Basic, Home Premium, Business, Enterprise, Ultimate, Home Basic N, Business N	Business: 30 November 2006	6000 6001(SP1)
NT 6.0	Windows Server 2008	Foundation, Standard, Enterprise, Datacenter, Web Server, HPC Server, Itanium-Based Systems	Consumer: 30 January 2007	6002(SP2) 6001
NT 6.1	Windows 7	Starter, Home Basic, Home Premium, Professional, Enterprise, Ultimate	27 February 2008	6002(SP2)
NT 6.1	Windows Server 2008 R2	Foundation, Standard, Enterprise, Datacenter, Web Server, HPC Server, Itanium-Based Systems	22 October 2009 22 October 2009	7600 7600

Windows NT 3.1 to 3.51 incorporated the Program Manager and File Manager from the Windows 3.x series. Windows NT 4.0 onwards replaced those programs with Windows Explorer (including a taskbar and Start menu), which originally appeared in Windows 95.

The first release was given version number 3.1 to match the contemporary 16-bit Windows; magazines of that era claimed the number was also used to make that version seem more reliable than a '.0' release. There were also some issues related to Novell IPX protocol licensing, which was apparently limited to 3.1 versions of Windows software.

1.3.3 Supported Platforms

NT was written in C and C++, and is reasonably portable, although (as of 2009) only three architectures are currently supported. That said, it proved far more difficult to port applications such as Microsoft Office which were sensitive to issues such as data structure alignment on RISC processors. Unlike Windows CE which routinely runs on a variety of processors, the lack of success of RISC-based systems in the desktop market has resulted in nearly all actual NT deployments being on x86 architecture processors.

In order to prevent Intel x86-specific code from slipping into the operating system by developers used to developing on x86 chips, Windows NT 3.1 was initially developed using non-x86 development systems and then ported to the x86 architecture. This work was initially based on the Intel i860-based Dazzle system and, later, the MIPS R4000-based Jazz platform. Both systems were designed internally at Microsoft.

Windows NT 3.1 was released for Intel x86 PC compatible, DEC Alpha, and ARC-compliant MIPS platforms. Windows NT 3.51 added support for the PowerPC processor in 1995, specifically PReP-compliant systems such as the IBM Power Series desktops/laptops and Motorola PowerStack series; but despite meetings between Michael Spindler and Bill Gates, not on the Power Macintosh as the PReP compliant Power Macintosh project failed to ship.

Intergraph Corporation ported Windows NT to its Clipper architecture and later announced intention to port Windows NT 3.51 to Sun Microsystems' SPARC architecture, but neither version was sold to the public as a retail product. Only two of the Windows NT 4.0 variants (IA-32 and Alpha) have a full set of service packs available. All of the other ports done by third parties (Motorola, Intergraph, etc.) have few, if any, publicly available updates.

Windows NT 4.0 was the last major release to support Alpha, MIPS, or PowerPC, though development of Windows 2000 for Alpha continued until August 1999, when Compaq stopped support for Windows NT on that architecture; and then three days later Microsoft also canceled their AlphaNT program, even though the Alpha NT 5 (Windows 2000) release had reached RC2 (build 2128).

Released versions of NT for Alpha were 32-bit only. The 64 bit port of Windows was originally intended to run on Itanium as well as on Alpha, and Alpha hardware was accordingly used internally at Microsoft during early development of 64-bit Windows. This continued for some time after Microsoft publicly announced that it was cancelling plans to ship 64-bit Windows for Alpha, because Itanium hardware was not yet available for development. Limited Editions of Windows 2000 Advanced Server and Datacenter Server, Windows XP 64-Bit, and Windows Server 2003 Enterprise and Datacenter support Intel's IA-64 processors. As of June 2010, Microsoft have released seventeen editions for the x64 processor architecture:

- Windows XP Professional x64 Edition
- Windows Server 2003 Standard x64 Edition

- Windows Server 2003 Enterprise x64 Edition
- Windows Server 2003 Datacenter x64 Edition
- Windows Vista Home Basic x64 Edition
- Windows Vista Home Premium x64 Edition
- Windows Vista Enterprise x64 Edition
- Windows Vista Ultimate x64 Edition
- Windows Server 2008 Web Server x64 Edition
- Windows Server 2008 Standard x64 Edition
- Windows Server 2008 Enterprise x64 Edition
- Windows Server 2008 Datacenter x64 Edition
- Windows 7 Home Basic x64 Edition
- Windows 7 Home Premium x64 Edition
- Windows 7 Professional x64 Edition
- Windows 7 Enterprise x64 Edition
- Windows 7 Ultimate x64 Edition.

According to Microsoft, it is a common misconception that the Xbox and Xbox 360 use a modified Windows 2000 kernel. They claim that the Xbox operating system was built from scratch but implements a subset of Windows APIs. The idea that it does, indeed, run a modified copy of the Windows kernel still persists in the community.

1.3.4 Hardware Requirements

The minimum hardware specification required to run each release of the professional workstation version of Windows NT has been fairly slow-moving until the 6.0 Vista release, which requires a minimum of 15 GB of free disk space, a 10-fold increase in free disk space alone over the previous version. Windows NT desktop (x86) minimum hardware requirements

NT version	CPU	RAM	Free disk space
NT3.1 NT 3.1 Advanced Server	386, 25 MHz	12MB 16MB	90MB
NT3.5Workstation NT 3.5 Server	386, 25 MHz	12MB 16MB	90MB
NT3.51Workstation NT 3.51 Server	386, 25 MHz	12MB 16MB	90MB
NT4.0Workstation NT 4.0 Server	486, 25 MHz	12MB 16MB	124MB
2000Professional 2000 Server	Pentium, 133 MHz	32MB 128MB	650MB
XP	Pentium, 233 MHz	64*MB	1.5GB
Server 2003	Pentium, 133 MHz	128MB	1.5GB
Vista	Pentium III, 800 MHz	512MB	15GB
Windows 7	Pentium III, 1 GHz	1GB	16GB

Windows XP can be run at 64 MB RAM. Some features require 128 MB RAM.

1.4 WINDOWS 2000

Windows 2000 (W2K) is a best commercial version of Microsoft's evolving Windows operating system. Previously called Windows NT 5.0, Microsoft emphasizes that Windows 2000 is evolutionary and "Built on NT Technology." Windows 2000 is designed to appeal to small business and professional users as well as to the more technical and larger business market for which the NT was designed.

The Windows 2000 product line consists of four products:

- Windows 2000 Professional, aimed at individuals and businesses of all sizes. It includes security and mobile use enhancements. It is the most economical choice.
- Windows 2000 Server, aimed at small-to-medium size businesses. It can function as a Web server and/or a workgroup (or branch office) server. It can be part of a two-way symmetric multiprocessing system. NT 4.0 servers can be upgraded to this server.
- Windows 2000 Advanced Server, aimed at being a network operating system server and/or an application server, including those involving large databases. This server facilitates clustering and load-balancing. NT 4.0 servers with up to eight-way SMP can upgrade to this product.
- Windows 2000 Datacenter Server, designed for large data warehouses, online transaction processing (OLTP), econometric analysis, and other applications requiring high-speed computation and large databases. The Datacenter Server supports up to 16-way SMP and up to 64 gigabytes of physical memory.

Windows 2000 is reported to be more stable (less apt to crash) than Windows 98/NT systems. A significant new feature is Microsoft's Active Directory, which, among other capabilities, enables a company to set up virtual private networks, to encrypt data locally or on the network, and to give users access to shared files in a consistent way from any network computer.

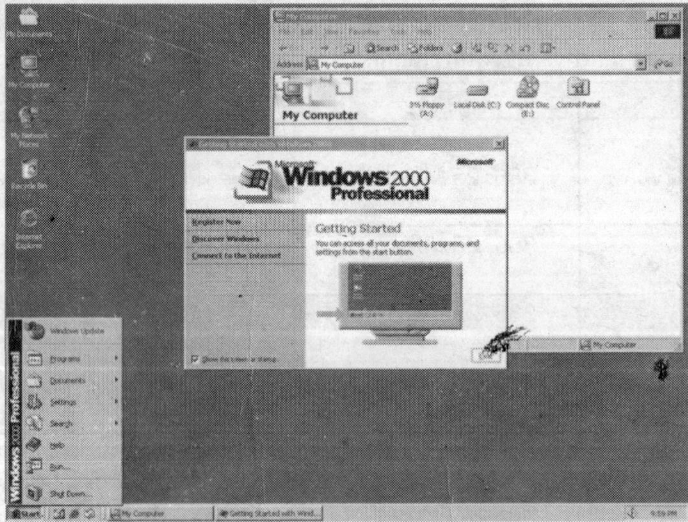

Figure 1.3: Windows 2000 professional

Windows 2000 is a line of operating systems produced by Microsoft for use on personal computers, business desktops, laptops, and servers. Released on 17 February 2000, it was the successor to Windows NT 4.0, and is the final release of Microsoft Windows to display the "Windows NT" designation. It was succeeded by Windows XP for desktop systems in October 2001 and Windows Server 2003 for servers in April 2003. Windows Me was released only a few months after Windows 2000 and one year before Windows XP, but Windows Me was not intended to be, nor did it serve as the successor to Windows 2000. Windows Me is designed for home use, while Windows 2000 is designed for business.

Four editions of Windows 2000 were released: Professional, Server, Advanced Server, and Datacenter Server. Additionally, Microsoft sold Windows 2000 Advanced Server Limited Edition and Windows 2000 Datacenter Server Limited Edition, which were released in 2001 and run on 64-bit Intel Itanium microprocessors. While each edition of Windows 2000 was targeted to a different market, they share a core set of features, including many system utilities such as the Microsoft Management Console and standard system administration applications.

Support for people with disabilities has been improved over Windows NT 4.0 with a number of new assistive technologies, and Microsoft increased support for different languages and locale information. All versions of the operating system support the Windows NT file system, NTFS 3.0, the Encrypting File System, as well as basic and dynamic disk storage. The Windows 2000 Server family has additional features, including the ability to provide Active Directory services (a hierarchical framework of resources), Distributed File System (a file system that supports sharing of files) and fault-redundant storage volumes. Windows 2000 can be installed through either a manual or unattended installation. Unattended installations rely on the use of answer files to fill in installation information, and can be performed through a bootable CD using Microsoft Systems Management Server, by the System Preparation Tool.

1.4.1 History of Windows 2000

Windows 2000 is a continuation of the Microsoft Windows NT family of operating systems, replacing Windows NT 4.0. Originally called Windows NT 5.0, then Windows NT 2000, Microsoft changed the name to Windows 2000 on 27 October 1998. It is also the first Windows version that has been released without a code name, though Windows 2000 Service Pack 1 was codenamed "Asteroid" and Windows 2000 64-bit was codenamed "Janus" (not to be confused with Windows 3.1, which had the same codename). The first beta for Windows 2000 was released in September 1997 and several further betas followed until Beta 3 which was released on 29 April 1999. During development, there was a build for the Alpha which was abandoned some time after RC1 after Compaq announced they had dropped support for Windows NT on Alpha. From here, Microsoft issued three release candidates between July and November 1999, and finally released the operating system to partners on 12 December 1999. The public could buy the full version of Windows 2000 on 17 February 2000. Three days before this event, which Microsoft advertised as "a standard in reliability", a leaked memo from Microsoft reported on by Mary Jo Foley revealed that Windows 2000 had "over 63,000 potential known defects". After Foley's article was published, Microsoft blacklisted her for a considerable time: InformationWeek summarized the release "our tests show the successor to NT 4.0 is everything we hoped it would be. Of course, it isn't perfect either." Wired News later described the results of the February launch as "lackluster". Novell criticized Microsoft's Active Directory, the new directory service architecture as less scalable or reliable than its own Novell Directory Services (NDS) alternative.

Windows 2000 was first planned to replace both Windows 98 and Windows NT 4.0. However, that changed later. Instead, an updated version of Windows 98 called Windows 98 Second Edition was released in 1999 and Windows Me was released in late 2000. Close to the release of Windows 2000 Service Pack 1, Microsoft released Windows 2000 Datacenter Server, targeted at large-scale computing systems with support for 32 processors, on 29 September 2000.

1.4.2 New and Updated Features

Windows 2000 introduced many of the new features of Windows 98 and Windows 98 SE into the NT line, such as the Windows Desktop Update, Internet Explorer 5, (Internet Explorer 6 which came in 2001 is also available for Windows 2000) Outlook Express, NetMeeting, FAT32 support, Windows Driver Model, Internet Connection Sharing, Windows Media Player, WebDAV support etc. Certain new features are common across all editions of Windows 2000, among them NTFS 3.0, the Microsoft Management Console (MMC), Automated System Recovery, UDF support, the Encrypting File System (EFS), Logical Disk Manager, Image Color Management 2.0, support for PostScript 3-based printers, OpenType (.OTF) and Type 1 PostScript (.PFB) font support, the Data protection API (DPAPI), an LDAP/Active Directory-enabled Address Book, usability enhancements and multi-language and locale support. Windows 2000 also introduced USB device class drivers for USB printers, Mass storage class devices, and Remote NDIS devices. Windows 2000 is also the first Windows version to support hibernation at the operating system level (OS-controlled ACPI S4 sleep state) unlike Windows 98 which required special drivers from the hardware manufacturer or driver developer.

A new capability designed to protect critical system files called Windows File Protection was introduced. This protects critical Windows system files by preventing programs other than Microsoft's operating system update mechanisms such as the Package Installer, Windows Installer and other update components from modifying them. The System File Checker utility provides users the ability to perform a manual scan the integrity of all protected system files, and optionally repair them, either by restoring from a cache stored in a separate "DLLCACHE" directory, or from the original install media.

Microsoft recognized that a serious error or a stop error could cause problems for servers that needed to be constantly running and so provided a system setting that would allow the server to automatically reboot when a stop error occurred. Also included is an option to dump any of the first 64 KB of memory to disk (the smallest amount of memory that is useful for debugging purposes, also known as a minidump), a dump of only the kernel's memory, or a dump of the entire contents of memory to disk, as well as write that this event happened to the Windows 2000 event log. In order to improve performance on servers running Windows 2000, Microsoft gave administrators the choice of optimizing the operating system's memory and processor usage patterns for background services or for applications. Windows 2000 also introduced core system administration and management features as the Windows Installer, Windows Management Instrumentation and Event Tracing for Windows (ETW) into the operating system.

1.4.2.1 Plug and Play

The most notable improvement from Windows NT 4.0 is the addition of Plug and Play with full ACPI and Windows Driver Model support. Similar to Windows 9x, Windows 2000 supports automatic recognition of installed hardware, hardware resource allocation, loading of appropriate drivers, PnP APIs and device notification events.

Windows Explorer

Windows Explorer has been enhanced in several ways in Windows 2000. It is the first Windows NT release to include Active Desktop, first introduced as a part of Internet Explorer 4.0 (specifically Windows Desktop Update), and only pre-installed in Windows 98 by that time. It allowed users to customize the way folders look and behave by using HTML templates, having the file extension HTT. This feature was abused by computer viruses that employed malicious scripts, Java applets, or ActiveX controls in folder template files as their infection vector. Two such viruses are VBS/Roor-C and VBS.Redlof.a.

The "Web-style" folders view, with the left Explorer pane displaying details for the object currently selected, is turned on by default in Windows 2000. For certain file types, such as pictures and media files, the preview is also displayed in the left pane. Until the dedicated interactive preview pane appeared in Windows Vista, Windows 2000 had been the only Windows release to feature an interactive media player as the previewer for sound and video files. However, such a previewer can be enabled in Windows Me and Windows XP through the use of third-party shell extensions, as the updated Windows Explorer allows for custom thumbnail previewers and tooltip handlers. The default file tooltip displays file title, author, subject and comments; this metadata may be read from a special NTFS stream, if the file is on an NTFS volume, or from an OLE structured storage stream, if the file is a structured storage document. All Microsoft Office documents since Office 4.0 make use of structured storage, so their metadata is displayable in the Windows 2000 Explorer default tooltip. File shortcuts can also store comments which are displayed as a tooltip when the mouse hovers over the shortcut. The shell introduces extensibility support through metadata handlers, icon overlay handlers and column handlers in Explorer Details view.

The right pane of Windows 2000 Explorer, which usually just lists files and folders, can also be customized. For example, the contents of the system folders aren't displayed by default, instead showing in the right pane a warning to the user that modifying the contents of the system folders could harm their computer. It's possible to define additional Explorer panes by using DIV elements in folder template files Other Explorer UI elements that can be customized include columns in "Details" view, icon overlays, and search providers: the new DHTML-based search pane is integrated into Windows 2000 Explorer, unlike the separate search dialog found in all previous Explorer versions. This degree of customizability is new to Windows 2000; neither Windows 98 nor the Desktop Update could provide it. The Indexing Service has also been integrated into the operating system and the search pane built into Explorer allows searching files indexed by its database.

1.1.2.2 NTFS 3.0

Microsoft released the version 3.0 of NTFS (sometimes incorrectly called NTFS 5 in relation to the kernel version number) as part of Windows 2000; this introduced disk quotas (provided by QuotaAdvisor), file-system-level encryption, sparse files and reparse points. Sparse files allow for the efficient storage of data sets that are very large yet contain many areas that only have zeros. Reparse points allow the object manager to reset a file namespace lookup and let file system drivers implement changed functionality in a transparent manner. Reparse points are used to implement volume mount points, junctions, Hierarchical Storage Management, Native Structured Storage and Single Instance Storage. Volume mount points and directory junctions allow for a file to be transparently referred from one file or directory location to another.

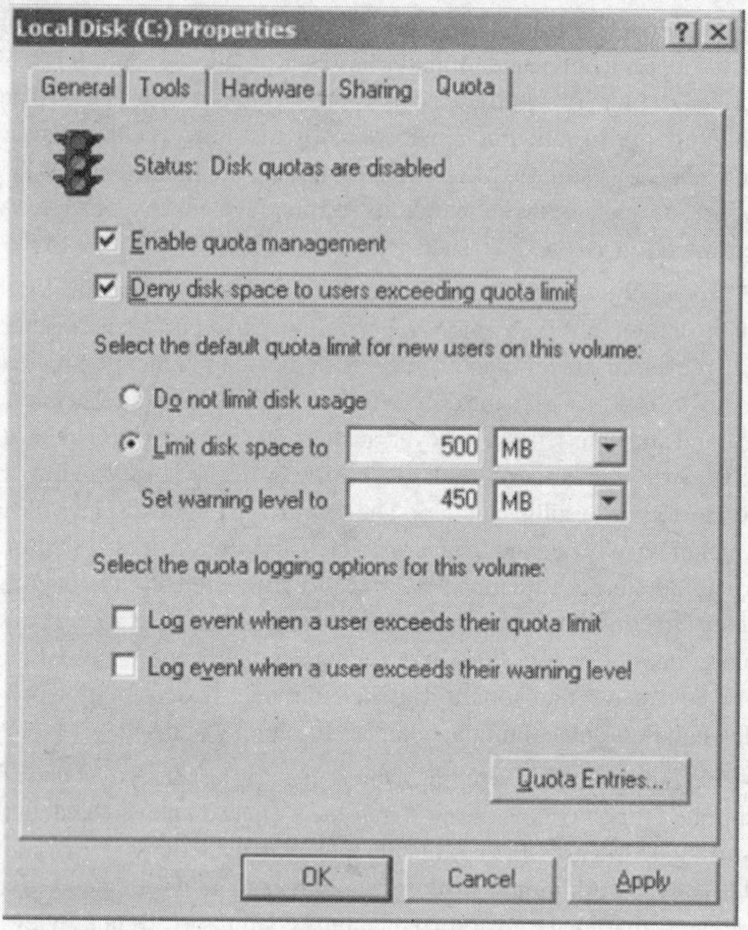

Figure 1.4: local disk properties of Windows 2000

1.4.2.3 Encrypting File System

The Encrypting File System (EFS) introduced strong file system-level encryption to Windows. It allows any folder or drive on an NTFS volume to be encrypted transparently by the user. EFS works together with the EFS service, Microsoft's CryptoAPI and the EFS File System Runtime Library (FSRTL). To date, its encryption has not been compromised.

EFS works by encrypting a file with a bulk symmetric key (also known as the File Encryption Key, or FEK), which is used because it takes less time to encrypt and decrypt large amounts of data than if an asymmetric key cipher were used. The symmetric key used to encrypt the file is then encrypted with a public key associated with the user who encrypted the file, and this encrypted data is stored in the header of the encrypted file. To decrypt the file, the file system uses the private key of the user to decrypt the symmetric key stored in the file header. It then uses the symmetric key to decrypt the file. Because this is done at the file system level, it is transparent to the user.

For a user losing access to their key, support for recovery agents that can decrypt files is built in to EFS. A Recovery Agent is a user who is authorized by a public key recovery certificate to decrypt files belonging to other users using a special private key. By default, local administrators are recovery agents however they can be customized using Group Policy.

1.4.2.4 Basic and Dynamic Disk Storage

Windows 2000 introduced the Logical Disk Manager for dynamic storage. All versions of Windows 2000 support three types of dynamic disk volumes (along with basic disks) : simple volumes, spanned volumes and striped volumes:

- Simple volume, a volume with disk space from one disk.
- Spanned volumes, where up to 32 disks show up as one, increasing it in size but not enhancing performance. When one disk fails, the array is destroyed. Some data may be recoverable. This corresponds to JBOD and not to RAID-1.
- Striped volumes, also known as RAID-0, store all their data across several disks in stripes. This allows better performance because disk reads and writes are balanced across multiple disks.

1.4.2.5 Accessibility

With Windows 2000, Microsoft introduced the Windows 9x accessibility features for people with visual and auditory impairments and other disabilities into the NT-line of operating systems.

These included:

- **StickyKeys:** makes modifier keys (ALT, CTRL and SHIFT) become "sticky": a user can press the modifier key, and then release it before pressing the combination key. (Activated by pressing Shift five times quickly.)
- **FilterKeys:** a group of keyboard-related features for people with typing issues, including:
  - *SlowKeys:* Ignore any keystroke not held down for a certain period.
  - *BounceKeys:* Ignore repeated keystrokes pressed in quick succession.
  - *RepeatKeys:* lets users slow down the rate at which keys are repeated via the keyboard's key-repeat feature.
- **ToggleKeys:** when turned on, Windows will play a sound when the CAPS LOCK, NUM LOCK or SCROLL LOCK key is pressed.
- **SoundSentry:** designed to help users with auditory impairments, Windows 2000 shows a visual effect when a sound is played through the sound system.
- **MouseKeys:** lets users move the cursor around the screen via the numeric keypad.
- **SerialKeys:** lets Windows 2000 support speech augmentation devices.
- **High contrast theme:** to assist users with visual impairments.
- **Microsoft Magnifier:** A screen magnifier that enlarges a part of the screen the cursor is over.

Additionally, Windows 2000 introduced the following new accessibility features:

- **On-screen keyboard:** displays a virtual keyboard on the screen and allows users to press its keys using a mouse or a joystick.
- **Microsoft Narrator:** Introduced in Windows 2000, this is a screen reader that utilizes the Speech API 5.

1.4.2.6 Games

Windows 2000 included version 7.0 of the DirectX API, commonly used by game developers on Windows 98. The last version of DirectX that Windows 2000 supports is DirectX 9.0c (Shader Model 3.0) that shipped with Windows XP Service Pack 2. Microsoft published quarterly updates to DirectX 9.0c through the February 2010 release after which support was dropped in the June 2010 SDK. These updates contain bug fixes to the core runtime and some additional libraries such as D3DX, XAudio 2, XInput and Managed DirectX components. The majority of games written for versions of DirectX 9.0c (up to the February 2010 release) can therefore run on Windows 2000.

1.4.2.7 System Utilities

Windows 2000 introduced the Microsoft Management Console (MMC), which is used to create, save, and open administrative tools. Each of these is called a console, and most allow an administrator to administer other Windows 2000 computers from one centralized computer. Each console can contain one or many specific administrative tools, called snap-ins. These can be either standalone (with one function), or an extension (adding functions to an existing snap-in). In order to provide the ability to control what snap-ins can be seen in a console, the MMC allows consoles to be created in author mode or user mode. Author mode allows snap-ins to be added, new windows to be created, all portions of the console tree to be displayed and consoles to be saved. User mode allows consoles to be distributed with restrictions applied. User mode consoles can grant full access to the user for any change, or they can grant limited access, preventing users from adding snapins to the console though they can view multiple windows in a console. Alternatively users can be granted limited access, preventing them from adding to the console and stopping them from viewing multiple windows in a single console.

The main tools that come with Windows 2000 can be found in the Computer Management console (in Administrative Tools in the Control Panel). This contains the Event Viewer-a means of seeing events and the Windows equivalent of a log file, a system information utility, a backup utility, Task Scheduler and management consoles to view open shared folders and shared folder sessions, configure and manage COM+ applications, configure Group Policy, manage all the local users and user groups, and a device manager. It contains Disk Management and Removable Storage snap-ins, a disk defragmenter as well as a performance diagnostic console, which displays graphs of system performance and configures data logs and alerts. It also contains a service configuration console, which allows users to view all installed services and to stop and start them, as well as configure what those services should do when the computer starts.

Windows 2000 comes with two utilities to edit the Windows registry, REGEDIT.EXE and REGEDT32.EXE. REGEDIT has been directly ported from Windows 98, and therefore does not support editing registry permissions. REGEDT32 has the older multiple document interface (MDI) and can edit registry permissions in the same manner that Windows NT's REGEDT32 program could. REGEDIT has a left-side tree view of the Windows registry, lists all loaded hives and represents the three components of a value (its name, type, and data) as separate columns of a table. REGEDT32 has a left-side tree view, but each hive has its own window, so the tree displays only keys and it represents values as a list of strings. REGEDIT supports right-clicking of entries in a tree view to adjust properties and other settings. REGEDT32 requires all actions to be performed from the top menu bar. Windows XP is the first system to integrate these two programs into a single utility, adopting the REGEDIT behavior with the additional NT features.

The System File Checker (SFC) also comes with Windows 2000. It is a command line utility that scans system files and verifies whether they were signed by Microsoft and works in conjunction with the Windows File Protection mechanism. It can also repopulate and repair all the files in the Dllcache folder.

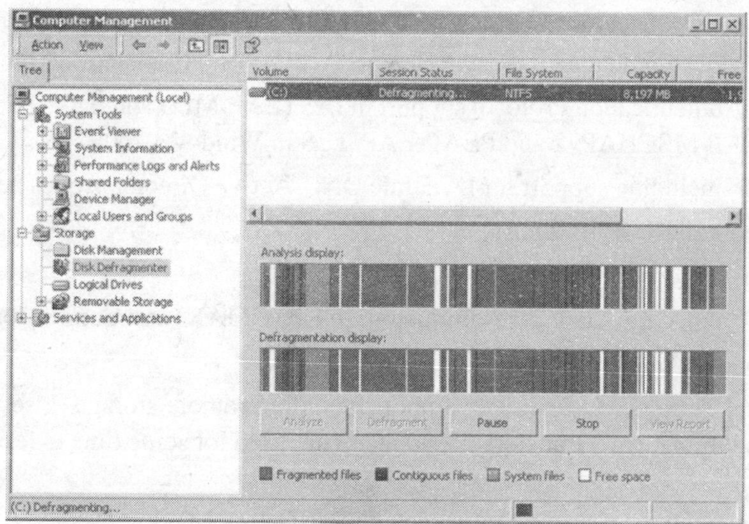

Figure 1.5: Computer management of Windows 2000

1.4.2.8 Recovery Console

The Recovery Console is run from outside the installed copy of Windows to perform maintenance tasks that can neither be run from within it nor feasibly be run from another computer or copy of Windows 2000. It is usually used to recover the system from problems that cause booting to fail, which would render other tools useless.

It has a simple command line interface, used to check and repair the hard drive(s), repair boot information (including NTLDR) , replace corrupted system files with fresh copies from the CD, or enable/ disable services and drivers for the next boot.

The console can be accessed in either of the two ways:

1. Booting from the Windows 2000 CD, and choosing to start the Recovery Console from the CD itself instead of continuing with setup. The Recovery Console is accessible as long as the installation CD is available.
2. Preinstalling the Recovery Console on the hard disk as a startup option in Boot.ini, via WinNT32.exe, with the /cmdcons switch. In this case, it can only be started as long as NTLDR can boot from the system partition.

1.4.3 Server Family Features

The Windows 2000 server family consists of Windows 2000 Server, Windows 2000 Advanced Server, and Windows 2000 Datacenter Server.

All editions of Windows 2000 Server have the following services and features built in:

- Routing and Remote Access Service (RRAS) support, facilitating dial-up and VPN connections using IPsec, L2TP or L2TP/IPsec, support for RADIUS authentication in Internet Authentication

Service, network connection sharing, Network Address Translation, unicast and multicast routing schemes.

- Remote access security features: Remote Access Policies for setup, verify Caller ID (IP address for VPNs), callback and Remote access account lockout
- Autodial by location feature using the Remote Access Auto Connection Manager service
- Extensible Authentication Protocol support in IAS (EAP-MD5 and EAP-TLS) later upgraded to PEAPv0/EAP-MSCHAPv2 and PEAP-EAP-TLS in Windows 2000 SP4
- DNS server, including support for Dynamic DNS. Active Directory relies heavily on DNS.
- IPsec support and TCP/IP filtering
- Smart card support
- Microsoft Connection Manager Administration Kit (CMAK) and Connection Point Services
- Support for distributed file systems (DFS)
- Hierarchical Storage Management support including remote storage, a service that runs with NTFS and automatically transfers files that are not used for some time to less expensive storage media
- Fault tolerant volumes, namely Mirrored and RAID-5
- Group Policy (part of Active Directory)
- IntelliMirror, a collection of technologies for fine-grained management of Windows 2000 Professional clients that duplicates users' data, applications, files, and settings in a centralized location on the network. IntelliMirror employs technologies such as Group Policy, Windows Installer, Roaming profiles, Folder Redirection, Offline Files (also known as Client Side Caching or CSC), File Replication Service (FRS), Remote Installation Services (RIS) to address desktop management scenarios such as user data management, user settings management, software installation and maintenance.
- COM+ and MTS
- MSMQ 2.0
- TAPI 3.0
- Integrated Windows Authentication (including Kerberos, Secure channel and SPNEGO (Negotiate) SSP packages for Security Support Provider Interface (SSPI)).
- MS-CHAP v2 protocol
- Public Key Infrastructure (PKI) and Enterprise Certificate Authority support
- Terminal Services and support for the Remote Desktop Protocol (RDP)
- Internet Information Services (IIS) 5.0 and Windows Media Services 4.1
- Network Quality of Service features
- A new Windows Time service which is an implementation of Simple Network Time Protocol (SNTP) as detailed in IETF RFC 1769. The Windows Time service synchronizes the date and time of computers in a domain running on Windows 2000 Server or later. Windows 2000 Professional includes an SNTP client.

The Server editions include more features and components, including the Microsoft Distributed File System (DFS) , Active Directory support and fault-tolerant storage.

1.4.3.1 Distributed File System

The Distributed File System (DFS) allows shares in multiple different locations to be logically grouped under one folder, or DFS root. When users try to access a network share off the DFS root, the user is really looking at a DFS link and the DFS server transparently redirects them to the correct file server and share. A DFS root can only exist on a Windows 2000 version that is part of the server family, and only one DFS root can exist on that server.

There can be two ways of implementing a DFS namespace on Windows 2000: either through a standalone DFS root or a domain-based DFS root. Standalone DFS allows for only DFS roots on the local computer, and thus does not use Active Directory. Domain-based DFS roots exist within Active Directory and can have their information distributed to other domain controllers within the domain - this provides fault tolerance to DFS. DFS roots that exist on a domain must be hosted on a domain controller or on a domain member server. The file and root information is replicated via the Microsoft File Replication Service (FRS).

1.4.3.2 Active Directory

A new way of organizing Windows network domains, or groups of resources, called Active Directory, is introduced with Windows 2000 to replace Windows NT's earlier domain model. Active Directory's hierarchical nature allowed administrators a built-in way to manage user and computer policies and user accounts, and to automatically deploy programs and updates with a greater degree of scalability and centralization than provided in previous Windows versions. It is one of the main reasons many corporations migrated to Windows 2000.] User information stored in Active Directory also provided a convenient phone book-like function to end users. Active Directory domains can vary from small installations with a few hundred objects, to large installations with millions. Active Directory can organise and link groups of domains into a contiguous domain name space to form trees. Groups of trees outside of the same namespace can be linked together to form forests.

Active Directory services could only be installed on a Windows 2000 Server, Advanced Server, or Datacenter Server computer, and cannot be installed on a Windows 2000 Professional computer. However, Windows 2000 Professional is the first client operating system able to exploit Active Directory's new features. As part of an organization's migration, Windows NT clients continued to function until all clients were upgraded to Windows 2000 Professional, at which point the Active Directory domain could be switched to native mode and maximum functionality achieved.

Active Directory requires a DNS server that supports SRV resource records, or that an organization's existing DNS infrastructure be upgraded to support this. There must be one or more domain controllers to hold the Active Directory database and provide Active Directory directory services.

1.4.3.3 Volume Fault Tolerance

Along with support for simple, spanned and striped volumes, the server family of Windows 2000 also supports fault-tolerant volume types. The types supported are mirrored volumes and RAID-5 volumes:

- **Mirrored volumes:** the volume contains several disks, and when data is written to one it is also written to the other disks. This means that if one disk fails, the data can be totally recovered from the other disk. Mirrored volumes are also known as RAID-1.
- RAID-5 volumes: a RAID-5 volume consists of multiple disks, and it uses block-level striping with parity data distributed across all member disks. Should a disk fail in the array, the parity blocks from the surviving disks are combined mathematically with the data blocks from the surviving disks to reconstruct the data on the failed drive "on-the-fly".

1.4.3.4 Editions

Microsoft released various editions of Windows 2000 for different markets and business needs: Professional, Server, Advanced Server and Datacenter Server. Each was packaged separately. Windows 2000 Professional was designed as the desktop operating system for businesses and power users. It is the client version of Windows 2000. It offers greater security and stability than many of the previous Windows desktop operating systems. It supports up to two processors, and can address up to 4 GB of RAM. The system requirements are a Pentium processor of 133 MHz or greater, at least 32 MB of RAM, 650 MB of hard drive space, and a CD-ROM drive (recommended: Pentium II, 128 MB of RAM, 2 GB of hard drive space, and CD-ROM drive).

Windows 2000 Server SKUs share the same user interface with Windows 2000 Professional, but contain additional components for the computer to perform server roles and run infrastructure and application software. A significant new component introduced in the server SKUs is Active Directory, which is an enterprise-wide directory service based on LDAP. Additionally, Microsoft integrated Kerberos network authentication, replacing the often-criticized NTLM authentication system used in previous versions. This also provided a purely transitive-trust relationship between Windows 2000 domains in a forest (a collection of one or more Windows 2000 domains that share a common schema, configuration, and global catalog, being linked with two-way transitive trusts). Furthermore, Windows 2000 introduced a Domain Name Server which allows dynamic registration of IP addresses. Windows 2000 Server supports up to 4 processors, requires 128 MB of RAM and 1 GB hard disk space, however requirements may be higher depending on installed components.

Windows 2000 Advanced Server is a variant of Windows 2000 Server operating system designed for medium-to-large businesses. It offers clustering infrastructure for high availability and scalability of applications and services, including main memory support of up to 8 gigabytes (GB) on Physical Address Extension (PAE) systems and the ability to do 8-way SMP. It supports TCP/IP load balancing and enhanced two-node server clusters based on the Microsoft Cluster Server (MSCS) in Windows NT Server 4.0 Enterprise Edition. Limited number of copies of an IA-64 version, called Windows 2000 Advanced Server, Limited Edition was made available via OEMs. System requirements are similar to those of Windows 2000 Server; however they may need to be higher to scale to larger infrastructure.

Windows 2000 Datacenter Server is a variant of Windows 2000 Server designed for large businesses that move large quantities of confidential or sensitive data frequently via a central server. Like Advanced Server, it supports clustering, failover and load balancing. Its minimum system requirements are normal, but it was designed to be capable of handing advanced, fault-tolerant and scalable hardware-for instance computers with up to 32 CPUs and 64 GBs RAM, with rigorous system testing and qualification, hardware partitioning, coordinated maintenance and change control. Limited number of copies of an IA-64 version, called Windows 2000 Datacenter Server, Limited Edition was made available via OEMs. System requirements are similar to those of Windows 2000 Advanced Server; however they may need to be higher to scale to larger infrastructure.

1.5 WINDOWS 2003

Windows Server 2003 (also referred to as Win2K3) is a server operating system produced by Microsoft, introduced on 24 April 2003. An updated version, Windows Server 2003 R2, was released to manufacturing on 6 December 2005. Its successor, Windows Server 2008, was released on 4 February 2008. According to Microsoft, Windows Server 2003 is more scalable and delivers better performance than its predecessor, Windows 2000

1.5.1 New and Updated Features

Following are the features of windows 2003:

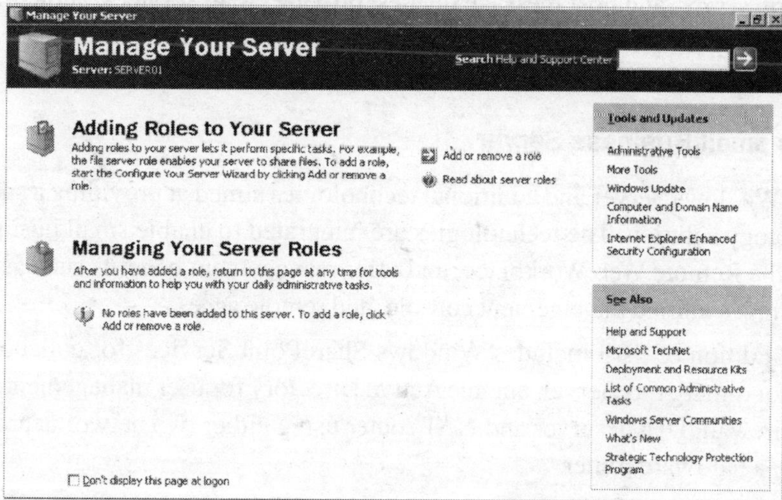

Figure 1.6: Manage Your Server

1.5.1.1 Manage your Server

- Internet Information Services (IIS) v6.0 - A significantly improved version of IIS.
- Increased default security over previous versions, due to the built-in firewall and having most services disabled by default.
- Significant improvements to Message Queuing.
- Manage Your Server - a role management administrative tool that allows an administrator to choose what functionality the server should provide.
- Improvements to Active Directory, such as the ability to deactivate classes from the scheme, or to run multiple instances of the directory server (ADAM)
- Improvements to Group Policy handling and administration
- Provides a backup system to restore lost files

- Improved disk management, including the ability to back up from shadows of files, allowing the backup of open files.
- Improved scripting and command line tools, which are part of Microsoft's initiative to bring a complete command shell to the next version of Windows.
- Support for a hardware-based "watchdog timer", which can restart the server if the operating system does not respond within a certain amount of time.

1.5.1.2 Removed Features

- The ability of creating rescue disk. Automated System Recovery (ASR) is used instead.

1.5.2 Editions

Windows Server 2003 comes in a number of editions, each targeted towards a particular size and type of business. In general, all variants of Windows Server 2003 have the ability to share files and printers, act as an application server, and host message queues, provide email services, authenticate users, act as an X.509 certificate server, provide LDAP directory services, serve streaming media, and to perform other server-oriented functions.

1.5.2.1 Windows small Business Server

SBS includes Windows Server and additional technologies aimed at providing a small business with a complete technology solution. The technologies are integrated to enable small business with targeted solutions such as the Remote Web Workplace, and offer management benefits such as integrated setup, enhanced monitoring, a unified management console, and remote access.

The Standard Edition of SBS includes Windows SharePoint Services for collaboration, Microsoft Exchange server for e-mail, Fax Server, and the Active Directory for user management. The product also provides a basic firewall, DHCP server and NAT router using either two network cards or one network card in addition to a hardware router.

The Premium Edition of SBS includes the above plus Microsoft SQL Server 2000 and Microsoft Internet Security and Acceleration Server 2004. SBS has its own type of Client Access License (CAL) that is different and costs slightly more than CALs for the other editions of Windows Server 2003. However, the SBS CAL encompasses the user CALs for Windows Server, Exchange Server, SQL Server, and ISA Server, and hence is less expensive than buying all other CALs individually. SBS server has the following design limitations:

- Only one computer in a domain can be running Windows Server 2003 for Small Business Server.
- Windows Server 2003 for Small Business Server must be the root of the Active Directory forest.
- Windows Server 2003 for Small Business Server cannot trust any other domains.
- Windows Server 2003 for Small Business Server is limited to 75 users or devices depending on which type of CAL.
- Windows Server 2003 for Small Business Server is limited to 4GB of RAM (Random Access Memory).

- A Windows Server 2003 for Small Business Server domain cannot have any child domains.
- Terminal Services only operates in remote administration mode on the server running SBS 2003, and only two simultaneous RDP sessions are allowed. (Change from SBS 2000 policy)
- To remove the limits from SBS server and upgrade from Small Business Server to regular Windows Server, Exchange Server, SQL and ISA server versions there is a Windows Small Business Server 2003 R2 Transition Pack.

1.5.2.2 Web Edition

Windows Server 2003, Web Edition is mainly for building and hosting Web applications, Web pages, and XML web services. It is designed to be used primarily as an IIS 6.0 Web server and provides a platform for rapidly developing and deploying XML Web services and applications that use ASP.NET technology, a key part of the .NET Framework. Terminal Server mode is not included on Web Edition. However, Remote Desktop for Administration is available on Windows Server 2003, Web Edition. Only 10 concurrent file-sharing connections are allowed at any moment. It is not possible to install Microsoft SQL Server and Microsoft Exchange software in this edition without installing Service Pack 1. Despite supporting XML Web services and ASP.NET, UDDI cannot be deployed on Windows Server 2003, Web Edition. The .NET Framework version 2.0 is not included with Windows Server 2003, Web Edition, but can be installed as a separate update from Windows Update.

Figure 1.7 Windows Server 2003 Standard Edition cover box

Windows Server 2003 Web Edition supports a maximum of 2 processors with support for a maximum of 2GB of RAM. Additionally, Windows Server 2003, Web Edition cannot act as a domain controller. It is the only edition of Windows Server 2003 that does not require Client Access Licenses when used as the internet facing server front end for Internet Information Services and Windows Server Update Services. When using it for storage or as a backend with another remote server as the frontend, CALs may still be required.

1.5.2.3 Standard Edition

Microsoft Windows Server 2003, Standard Edition is aimed towards small to medium sized businesses. Standard Edition supports file and printer sharing, offers secure Internet connectivity, and allows centralized desktop application deployment. The initial release of Windows Server 2003 was available solely for 32-

bit processors; a 64-bit version supporting the x86-64 architecture (AMD64 and EM64T, called collectively x64 by Microsoft) was released in April 2005. The 32-bit version will run on up to 4 processors with up to 4 GB RAM; the 64-bit version is capable of addressing up to 32 GB of RAM and also supports Non-Uniform Memory Access. The 32-bit version is available for students to download free of charge as part of Microsoft's DreamSpark program.

1.5.2.4 Enterprise Edition

Windows Server 2003, Enterprise Edition is aimed towards medium to large businesses. It is a full-function server operating system that supports up to 8 processors and provides enterprise-class features such as eight-node clustering using Microsoft Cluster Server (MSCS) software and support for up to 32 GB of memory through PAE (added with the /PAE boot string). Enterprise Edition also comes in 64-bit versions for the Itanium and x64 architectures. The 64-bit versions of Windows Server 2003, Enterprise Edition are capable of addressing up to 1 TB of memory. Both 32-bit and 64-bit versions support Non-Uniform Memory Access (NUMA). It also provides the ability to hot-add supported hardware. Enterprise Edition is also required to issue custom certificate templates.

1.5.2.5 Datacenter Edition

Windows Server 2003, Datacenter Edition is designed for infrastructures demanding high security and reliability. Windows Server 2003 is available for x86, Itanium, and x86-64 processors. It supports a maximum of up to 32 processors on 32-bit or 64 processors on 64-bit hardware. 32-bit architecture also limits memory addressability to 128 GB, while the 64-bit versions support up to 1 TB. Windows Server 2003, Datacenter Edition, also allows limiting processor and memory usage on a per-application basis.

Windows Server 2003 Datacenter Edition also supports Non-Uniform Memory Access. If supported by the system, Windows, with help from the system firmware will make use of NUMA kernel awareness, which is indicated by the presence of a firmware generatel ACPI Static Resource Affinity Table (SRAT) that defines the NUMA topology of the system. Windows then uses this table to optimize memory accesses, and provide NUMA awareness to applications, thereby increasing the efficiency of thread scheduling and memory management.

Windows Server 2003, Datacenter Edition has better support for Storage Area Networks (SAN). It features a service which uses Windows sockets to emulate TCP/IP communication over native SAN service providers, thereby allowing a SAN to be accessed over any TCP/IP channel. With this, any application that can communicate over TCP/IP can use a SAN, without any modification to the application.

Windows Server 2003, Datacenter Edition also supports 8-node clustering. Clustering increases availability and fault tolerance of server installations by distributing and replicating the service among many servers. Windows supports clustering with each cluster having its own dedicated storage, or with all clusters connected to a common storage area network (SAN). The SAN can be running on a Windows or non-Windows operating system and may be connected to other computers as well.

1.5.3 Windows Compute Cluster Server

Windows Compute Cluster Server 2003 (CCS), released in June 2006, is designed for high-end applications that require high performance computing clusters. It is designed to be deployed on numerous computers to be clustered together to achieve supercomputing speeds. Each Compute Cluster Server network comprises at least one controlling head node and subordinate processing nodes that carry out most of the work.

Compute Cluster Server uses the Microsoft Messaging Passing Interface v2 (MS-MPI) to communicate between the processing nodes on the cluster network. It ties nodes together with a powerful inter-process communication mechanism which can be complex because of communications between hundreds or even thousands of processors working in parallel.

The application programming interface consists of over 160 functions. A job launcher enables users to execute jobs to be executed in the computing cluster. MS MPI was designed to be compatible with the reference open source MPI2 specification which is widely used in High-performance computing (HPC). With some exceptions because of security considerations, MS MPI covers the complete set of MPI2 functionality as implemented in MPICH2, except for the planned future features of dynamic process spawn and publishing.

1.5.4 Windows Storage Server

Windows Storage Server 2003, a part of the Windows Server 2003 series, is a specialized server Operating System for Network Attached Storage (NAS). It is optimized for use in file and print sharing and also in Storage Area Network (SAN) scenarios. It is only available through Original equipment manufacturers (OEMs). Unlike other Windows Server 2003 editions that provide file and printer sharing functionality, Windows Storage Server 2003 does not require any Client access licenses.

Windows Storage Server 2003 NAS equipment can be headless, which means that they are without any monitors, keyboards or mice, and are administered remotely. Such devices are plugged into any existing IP network and the storage capacity is available to all users. Windows Storage Server 2003 can use RAID arrays to provide data redundancy, fault-tolerance and high performance. Multiple such NAS servers can be clustered to appear as a single device. This allows for very high performance as well as allowing the service to remain up even if one of the servers goes down.

Windows Storage Server 2003 can also be used to create a Storage Area Network, in which the data is transferred in terms of chunks rather than files, thus providing more granularities to the data that can be transferred. This provides higher performance to database and transaction processing applications. Windows Storage Server 2003 also allows NAS devices to be connected to a SAN.

Windows Storage Server 2003 R2, as a follow-up to Windows Storage Server 2003, adds file-server performance optimization, Single Instance Storage (SIS), and index-based search. Single Instance storage (SIS) scans storage volumes for duplicate files, and moves the duplicate files to the common SIS store. The file on the volume is replaced with a link to the file. This substitution reduces the amount of storage space required, by as much as 70%.

Windows Storage Server R2 provides an index-based, full-text search based on the indexing engine already built into Windows server. The updated search engine speeds up indexed searches on network shares. Storage Server R2 also provides filters for searching many standard file formats, such as .zip, AutoCAD, XML, MP3, and .pdf, and all Microsoft Office file formats.

Windows Storage Server 2003 R2 includes built in support for Windows SharePoint Services and Microsoft SharePoint Portal Server, and adds a Storage Management snap-in for the Microsoft Management

Console. It can be used to manage storage volumes centrally, including DFS shares, on servers running Windows Storage Server R2.

Windows Storage Server 2003 R2 can be used as an iSCSI target with standard and enterprise editions of Windows Storage Server 2003 R2, incorporating WinTarget iSCSI technology which Microsoft acquired in 2006 by from StringBean software. This will be an add-on feature available for purchase through OEM partners as an iSCSI feature pack, or is included in some versions of WSS as configured by OEMs. Windows Storage Server 2003 can be promoted to function as a domain controller, however this edition is not licensed to run directory services. It can be joined to an existing domain as a member server.

1.5.4.1 Features

- **Distributed File System (DFS):** DFS allows multiple network shares to be aggregated as a virtual file system.
- **Support for SAN and iSCSI:** Computers can connect to a Storage Server over the LAN, and there is no need for a separate fibre channel network. Thus a Storage Area Network can be created over the LAN itself. iSCSI uses the SCSI protocol to transfer data as a block of bytes, rather than as a file. This increases performance of the Storage network in some scenarios, such as using a database server.
- **Virtual Disc Service:** It allows NAS devices, RAID devices and SAN shares to be exposed and managed as if they were normal hard drives.
- **JBOD systems:** JBOD (Just a bunch of discs) systems, by using VDS, can manage a group of individual storage devices as a single unit. There is no need for the storage units to be of the same make and model.
- **Software and Hardware RAID:** Windows Storage Server 2003 has intrinsic support for hardware implementation of RAID. In case hardware support is not available, it can use software enabled RAID. In that case, all processing is done by the OS.
- **Multi Path IO (MPIO):** It provides an alternate connection to IO devices in case the primary path is down.

1.5.4.2 Editions

Windows Storage Server 2003 R2 is available in the following versions:

<table>
<tr><th></th><th>Express Edition</th><th>Workgroup Edition</th><th>Standard Edition</th><th>Enterprise Edition</th></tr>
<tr><td>Number of physical* CPUs</td><td colspan="2">1</td><td>1-4</td><td>1-64</td></tr>
<tr><td>32-bit and 64-bit versions available</td><td colspan="4">Yes</td></tr>
<tr><td>Numbers of disk drives</td><td>2</td><td>4</td><td colspan="2">Unlimited</td></tr>
<tr><td>NICS</td><td>1</td><td>2</td><td colspan="2">Unlimited</td></tr>
<tr><td>Print service</td><td>No</td><td colspan="3">Yes</td></tr>
<tr><td>CALS required</td><td colspan="4">No</td></tr>
<tr><td>iSCSI target support</td><td colspan="4">Optional</td></tr>
<tr><td>Clustering</td><td colspan="3">No</td><td>Yes</td></tr>
</table>

Windows Unified Data Storage Server is a version of Windows Storage Server 2003 R2 with ISCSI target support standard, available in only the standard and enterprise editions.

- Microsoft defines a physical CPU/processor as a single socket/node on the systemboard. For O/S licensing purposes, a dual-socket single-core (Intel Pentium/4 Xeon, AMD Athlon/64) system counts as a total of 2 processors, whereas a single-socket quad-core CPU (such as AMD's Opteron and Intel's Xeon) counts as 1 processor. Microsoft's policy has no bearing on how third-party software vendors (such as Oracle) administer CPU licensing for its server applications.

1.5.5 WINDOWS HOME SERVER

Windows Home Server is an operating system from Microsoft based on Windows Small Business Server 2003 SP2 (this can be seen in the directory listings of the install DVD). Announced on 7 January 2007 at the Consumer Electronics Show by Bill Gates, Windows Home Server is intended to be a solution for homes with multiple connected PCs to offer file sharing, automated backups, and remote access.

1.5.6 UPDATES

1.5.6.1 Service Pack 1

On 30 March 2005, Microsoft released Service Pack 1 for Windows Server 2003. Among the improvements are many of the same updates that were provided to Windows XP users with Service Pack 2.

Features that are added with Service Pack 1 include:

- **Security Configuration Wizard:** A tool that allows administrators to more easily research, and makes changes to, security policies.
- **Hot Patching:** This feature is set to extend Windows Server 2003's ability to take DLL, Driver, and non-kernel patches without a reboot.
- **IIS 6.0 Metabase Auditing:** Allowing the tracking of metabase edits.
- **Windows Firewall:** Brings many of the improvements from Windows XP Service Pack 2 to Windows Server 2003; also with the Security Configuration Wizard, it allows administrators to more easily manage the incoming open ports, as it will automatically detect and select default roles.
- Other networking improvements include support for Wireless Provisioning Services, better IPv6 support, and new protections against SYN flood TCP attacks.
- **Post-Setup Security Updates:** A default mode that is turned on when a Service Pack 1 server is first booted up after installation. It configures the firewall to block all incoming connections, and directs the user to install updates.
- **Data Execution Prevention (DEP):** Support for the No Execute (NX) bit which helps to prevent buffer overflow exploits that are often the attack vector of Windows Server exploits.
- Windows Media Player version 10
- Internet Explorer 6 SV1 (e.g. 'IE6 SP2')

- Support for fixed disks bearing data organized using the GUID Partition Table system A full list of updates is available in the Microsoft Knowledge Base.

1.5.7 WINDOWS SERVER 2003 R2

Windows Server 2003 R2, an update of Windows Server 2003, was released to manufacturing on 6 December 2005. It is distributed on two CDs, with one CD being the Windows Server 2003 SP1 CD. The other CD adds many optionally installable features for Windows Server 2003. The R2 update was released for all x86 and x64 versions. Windows Server 2003 R2 Enterprise Edition was not released for Itanium.

NEW FEATURES

- **Branch Office Server Management**
  - Centralized management tools for file and printers
  - Enhanced Distributed File System (DFS) namespace management interface
  - More efficient WAN data replication with Remote Differential Compression.
- **Identity and Access Management**
  - Extranet Single Sign-On and identity federation
  - Centralized administration of extranet application access
  - Automated disabling of extranet access based on Active Directory account information
  - User access logging
  - Cross-platform web Single Sign-On and password synchronization using Network Information Service (NIS)
- **Storage Management**
  - File Server Resource Manager (storage utilization reporting)
  - Enhanced quota management
  - File screening limits files types allowed
  - Storage Manager for Storage Area Networks (SAN) (storage array configuration)
- **Server Virtualization**
  - A new licensing policy allows up to 4 virtual instances on Enterprise Edition and Unlimited on Datacenter Edition
- **Utilities and SDK for UNIX-Based Applications add-on, giving a relatively full Unix development environment.**
  - Base Utilities
  - SVR-5 Utilities
  - Base SDK
  - GNU SDK
  - GNU Utilities

- Perl 5
- Visual Studio Debugger Add-in

1.6 WINDOWS XP

Windows XP is an operating system produced by Microsoft for use on personal computers, including home and business desktops, laptops, and media centers. It was first released in August 2001, and is currently one of the most popular versions of Windows. The name "XP" is short for "eXPerience."

Windows XP is the successor to both Windows 2000 and Windows Me, and is the first consumer-oriented operating system produced by Microsoft to be built on the Windows NT kernel and architecture. Windows XP was released for retail sale on October 25, 2001, and over 400 million copies were in use in January 2006, according to an estimate in that month by an IDC analyst. It was succeeded by Windows Vista, which was released to volume license customers on November 8, 2006, and worldwide to the general public on January 30, 2007. Direct OEM and retail sales of Windows XP ceased on June 30, 2008. Microsoft continued to sell XP through their System Builders (smaller OEMs who sell assembled computers) program until January 31, 2009. XP may continue to be available as these sources run through their inventory or by purchasing Windows 7 Ultimate, Windows 7 Pro, Windows Vista Ultimate or Windows Vista Business, and then downgrading to Windows XP.

The most common editions of the operating system are Windows XP Home Edition, which is targeted at home users, and Windows XP Professional, which offers additional features such as support for Windows Server domains and two physical processors, and is targeted at power users, business and enterprise clients. Windows XP Media Center Edition has additional multimedia features enhancing the ability to record and watch TV shows, view DVD movies, and listen to music. Windows XP Tablet PC Edition is designed to run stylus applications built using the Tablet PC platform.

Windows XP was eventually released for two additional architectures, Windows XP 64-bit Edition for IA-64 (Itanium) processors and Windows XP Professional x64 Edition for x86-64. There is also Windows XP Embedded, a component version of the Windows XP Professional, and editions for specific markets such as Windows XP Starter Edition. By mid 2009, a manufacturer revealed the first Windows XP powered cellular telephone.

The NT-based versions of Windows, which are programmed in C, C++, and assembly, are known for their improved stability and efficiency over the 9x versions of Microsoft Windows. Windows XP presents a significantly redesigned graphical user interface, a change Microsoft promoted as more user-friendly than previous versions of Windows. A new software management facility called Side-by-Side Assembly was introduced to ameliorate the "DLL hell" that plagues 9x versions of Windows. It is also the first version of Windows to use product activation to combat illegal copying, a restriction that did not sit well with some users and privacy advocates. Windows XP has also been criticized by some users for security vulnerabilities, tight integration of applications such as Internet Explorer 6 and Windows Media Player, and for aspects of its default user interface. Later versions with Service Pack 2, Service Pack 3, and Internet Explorer 8 addressed some of these concerns. During development, the project was codenamed "Whistler", after Whistler, British Columbia, as many Microsoft employees skied at the Whistler-Blackcomb ski resort.

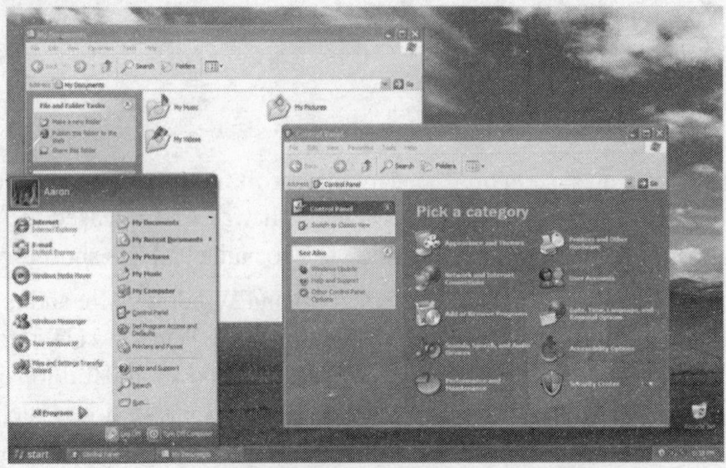

Figure 1.8: Windows XP Home Edition

The two major editions are Windows XP Home Edition, designed for home users, and Windows XP Professional, designed for business and power-users. XP Professional contains advanced features that the average home user would not use. However, these features are not necessarily missing from XP Home. They are simply disabled, but are there and can become functional. These releases were made available at retail outlets that sell computer software, and were preinstalled on computers sold by major computer manufacturers. As of mid-2008, both editions continue to be sold. A third edition, called Windows XP Media Center Edition was introduced in 2002 and was updated every year until 2006 to incorporate new digital media, broadcast television and Media Center Extender capabilities. Unlike the Home and Professional edition, it was never made available for retail purchase, and was typically either sold through OEM channels, or was preinstalled on computers that were typically marketed as "media center PCs".

Two different 64-bit editions were made available, one designed specifically for Itanium-based workstations, which was introduced in 2001 around the same time as the Home and Professional editions, but was discontinued a few years later when vendors of Itanium hardware stopped selling workstation-class machines due to low sales. The other, called Windows XP Professional x64 Edition supports the x86-64 extension of the Intel IA-32 architecture. x86-64 is implemented by AMD as "AMD64", found in AMD's Opteron and Athlon 64 chips, and implemented by Intel as "Intel 64" (formerly known as IA-32e and EM64T), found in Intel's Pentium 4 and later chips.

Windows XP Tablet PC Edition was produced for a class of specially designed notebook/laptop computers called tablet PCs. It is compatible with a pen-sensitive screen, supporting handwritten notes and portrait-oriented screens.

Microsoft also released Windows XP Embedded, an edition for specific consumer electronics, set-top boxes, kiosks/ATMs, medical devices, arcade video games, point-of-sale terminals, and Voice over Internet Protocol (VoIP) components. In July 2006, Microsoft released Windows Fundamentals for Legacy PCs, a thin client version of Windows XP Embedded which targets older machines (as early as the original Pentium). It is only available to Software Assurance customers. It is intended for corporate customers who would like to upgrade to Windows XP to take advantage of its security and management capabilities, but can't afford to purchase new hardware.

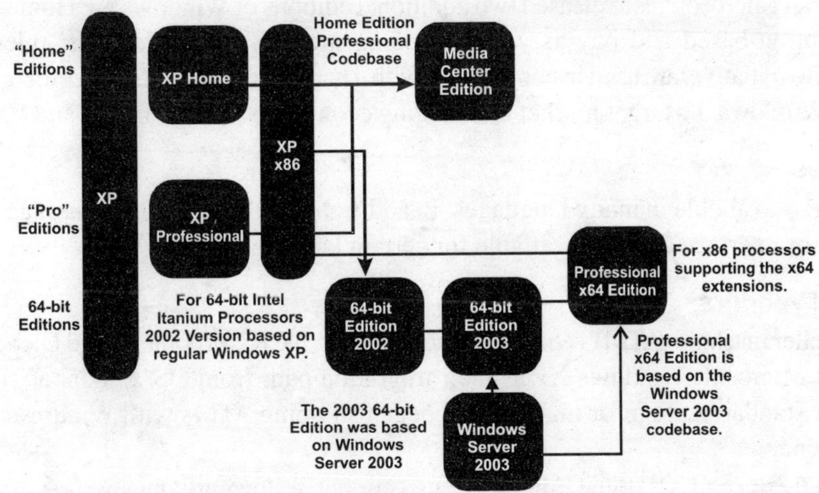

Figure 1.9: Editions of Windows XP

Windows XP Starter Edition is a lower-cost edition of Windows XP available in Thailand, Indonesia, Philippines, Russia, India, Colombia, Brazil, Argentina, Peru, Bolivia, Chile, Mexico, Ecuador, Uruguay and Venezuela. It is similar to Windows XP Home, but is limited to low-end hardware, can only run 3 programs at a time, and has some other features either removed or disabled by default. Each country's edition is also customized for that country, including desktop backgrounds of popular locations, localized help features for those who may not speak English, and other default settings designed for easier use than typical Windows XP installations. The Malaysian version, for example, contains a desktop background of the Kuala Lumpur skyline.

In March 2004, the European Commission fined Microsoft •497 million (US$603 million) and ordered the company to provide a version of Windows without Windows Media Player. The Commission concluded that Microsoft "broke European Union competition law by leveraging its near monopoly in the market for PC operating systems onto the markets for work group server operating systems and for media players". After unsuccessful appeals in 2004 and 2005, Microsoft reached an agreement with the Commission where it would release a court-compliant version, Windows XP Edition N. This version does not include the company's Windows Media Player but instead encourages users to pick and download their own media player. Microsoft wanted to call this version Reduced Media Edition, but EU regulators objected and suggested the Edition N name, with the N signifying "not with Media Player" for both Home and Professional editions of Windows XP. Because it is sold at the same price as the version with Windows Media Player included, Dell, Hewlett-Packard, Lenovo and Fujitsu Siemens have chosen not to stock the product. However, Dell did offer the operating system for a short time. Consumer interest has been low, with roughly 1,500 units shipped to OEMs, and no reported sales to consumers.

In December 2005, the Korean Fair Trade Commission ordered Microsoft to make available editions of Windows XP and Windows Server 2003 that do not contain Windows Media Player or Windows Messenger. Like the European Commission decision, this decision was based on the grounds that Microsoft had abused its dominant position in the market to push other products onto consumers. Unlike that decision, however, Microsoft was also forced to withdraw the non-compliant versions of Windows from the South Korean market. This decision resulted in Microsoft's releasing "K" and "KN" variants of the Home and Professional editions in August 2006.

That same year, Microsoft also released two additional editions of Windows XP Home Edition directed towards subscription-based and pay-as-you-go pricing models. These editions, released as part of Microsoft's FlexGo initiative, are used in conjunction with a hardware component to enforce time limitations on the usage of Windows. Its target market is emerging economies such as Brazil and Vietnam.

1.6.1 Languages

Windows XP is available in many languages. In addition, MUI packs and Language Interface Packs translating the user interface are also available for certain languages.

1.6.2 Atms and Vendors

Automated teller machine (ATM) vendors Wincor Nixdorf, NCR Corporation and Diebold Incorporated have all adopted Microsoft Windows XP as their migration path from OS/2. Wincor Nixdorf who has been pushing for standardization for many years, began shipping ATMs with Windows when they first arrived on the scene.

Diebold initially shipped XP Home Edition exclusively, but, following extensive pressure from customer banks to support a common operating system, switched to support XP Professional to match their primary competitor, NCR Corporation and Wincor Nixdorf. Redbox DVD Vending machines run a modified version of XP designed for the fullscreen User Interface of the Vending Touchscreen and the DVD vending itself.

1.6.3 New and Updated Features

Windows XP introduced several new features to the Windows line, including:

- Faster start-up and hibernation sequences
- The ability to discard a newer device driver in favor of the previous one (known as driver rollback), should a driver upgrade not produce desirable results
- A new, arguably more user-friendly interface, including the framework for developing themes for the desktop environment
- Fast user switching, which allows a user to save the current state and open applications of their desktop and allow another user to log on without losing that information
- The ClearType font rendering mechanism, which is designed to improve text readability on liquid crystal display (LCD) and similar monitors
- Remote Desktop functionality, which allows users to connect to a computer running Windows XP Pro from across a network or the Internet and access their applications, files, printers, and devices
- Support for most DSL modems and IEEE 802.11 connections, as well as networking over FireWire, and Bluetooth.

1.6.4 User Interface

Windows XP features a new task-based graphical user interface. The Start menu and Windows indexing service were redesigned and many visual effects were added, including:

- A translucent blue selection rectangle in Explorer
- Drop shadows for icon labels on the desktop
- Task-based sidebars in Explorer windows ("common tasks")

- The ability to group the taskbar buttons of the windows of one application into one button
- The ability to lock the taskbar and other toolbars to prevent accidental changes
- The highlighting of recently added programs on the Start menu
- Shadows under menus (Windows 2000 had shadows under mouse pointers, but not menus)

Windows XP analyzes the performance impact of visual effects and uses this to determine whether to enable them, so as to prevent the new functionality from consuming excessive additional processing overhead. Users can further customize these settings. Some effects, such as alpha compositing (transparency and fading), are handled entirely by many newer video cards. However, if the video card is not capable of hardware alpha blending, performance can be substantially hurt, and Microsoft recommends the feature should be turned off manually. Windows XP adds the ability for Windows to use "Visual Styles" to change the user interface.

However, visual styles must be cryptographically signed by Microsoft to run. Luna is the name of the new visual style that ships with Windows XP, and is enabled by default for machines with more than 64 MiB of RAM. Luna refers only to one particular visual style, not to all of the new user interface features of Windows XP as a whole. Some users "patch" the uxtheme.dll file that restricts the ability to use visual styles, created by the general public or the user, on Windows XP.

In addition to the included Windows XP themes, there is one previously unreleased theme with a dark blue taskbar and window bars similar to Windows Vista titled "Royale Noir" available for download, albeit unofficially. Microsoft officially released a modified version of this theme as the "Zune" theme, to celebrate the launch of its Zune portable media player in November 2006. The differences are only visual with a new glassy look along with a black taskbar instead of dark blue and an orange start button instead of green. Additionally, the Media Center "Energy Blue" theme, which was included in the Media Center editions, is also available to download for use on all Windows XP editions.

The default wallpaper, Bliss, is a BMP photograph of a landscape in the Napa Valley outside Napa, California, with rolling green hills and a blue sky with stratocumulus and cirrus clouds. The Windows 2000 "classic" interface can be used instead if preferred. Several third party utilities exist that provide hundreds of different visual styles. Microsoft licensed technology from WindowBlinds creator Stardock to create its visual styles in XP

1.6.5 System Requirements

System requirements for Windows XP Home and Professional editions as follows:

	Minimum	Recommended
Processor	233MHz	300 MHz or higher
Memory	64MB RAM	128 MB RAM or higher
Video adapter and monitor	Super VGA (800 x 600) or higher resolution	
Hard drive disk free space	1.5 GB or higher	
	(additional 1.8 GB in Service Pack 2 and additional 900 MB in Service Pack 3)	
Drives	CD-ROM drive or DVD drive	
Input devices	Keyboard. Microsoft Mouse or compatible pointing device	
Sound	Sound card. Speakers or headphones	

- *^1 Even though this is Microsoft's stated minimum processor speed for Windows XP, it is possible to install and run the operating system on early IA-32 processors such as a P5 Pentium without MMX instructions. Windows XP is not compatible with processors older than Pentium (such as 486) because it requires CMPXCHG8B instructions.*
- *^2 For many workloads that involve Web browsing, e-mail, and other activities, 64 MB of RAM will provide [the] user experience equivalent or superior to that of Windows Me running on the same hardware."*

1.6.6 Physical Memory Limits

Maximum limits on physical memory (RAM) that Windows XP can address vary depending on the both the Windows version and between 32-bit and 64-bit versions. The following table specifies the maximum physical memory limits supported:

Physical memory limits for Windows XP versions		
Version	**Limit in 32-bit Windows**	**Limit in 64-bit Windows**
Windows XP Professional	4 GB	128GB
Windows XP Home	4 GB	N/A
Windows XP Starter Edition	512 MB	N/A

1.6.7 Service Packs

Microsoft occasionally releases service packs for its Windows operating systems to fix problems and add features. Each service pack is a superset of all previous service packs and patches so that only the latest service pack needs to be installed, and also includes new revisions. However if you still have the earliest version of Windows XP on Retail CD (without any service packs included), you will need to install SP1a or SP2, before SP3 can be installed. Older service packs need not be manually removed before application of the most recent one. Windows Update "normally" takes care of automatically removing unnecessary files.

The service pack details below only apply to the 32-bit editions. Windows XP Professional x64 Edition was based on Windows Server 2003 Service Pack 1 and claimed to be "SP1" in system properties from the initial release. It is updated by the same service packs and hotfixes as the x64 edition of Windows Server 2003.

1.6.7.1 Service Pack 1

Service Pack 1 (SP1) for Windows XP was released on September 9, 2002. It contains post-RTM security fixes and hot-fixes, compatibility updates, optional .NET Framework support, enabling technologies for new devices such as Tablet PCs, and a new Windows Messenger 4.7 version. The most notable new features were USB 2.0 support and a Set Program Access and Defaults utility that aimed at hiding various middleware products. Users can control the default application for activities such as web browsing and instant messaging, as well as hide access to some of Microsoft's bundled programs.

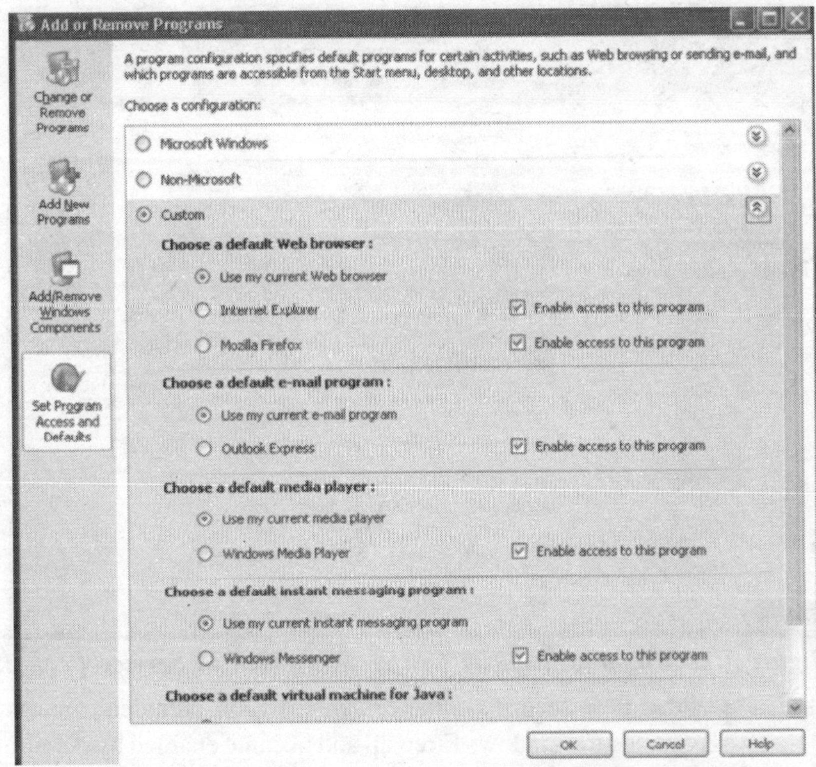

Figure 1.10 Set Program Access and Defaults was added in Service Pack 1.

This utility was first brought into the older Windows 2000 operating system with its Service Pack 3. This Service Pack supported SATA and hard drives that were larger than 137GB (48-bit LBA support) by default. The Microsoft Java Virtual Machine, which was not in the RTM version, appeared in this Service Pack. Support for IPv6 was also introduced in this Service Pack. On February 3, 2003, Microsoft released Service Pack 1a (SP1a). This release removed Microsoft's Java virtual machine as a result of a lawsuit with Sun Microsystems.

1.6.7.2 Service Pack 2

Service Pack 2 (SP2) (codenamed "Springboard") was released on August 25, 2004, with an emphasis on security. Unlike the previous service pack, SP2 added new functionality to Windows XP, such as WPA encryption compatibility and improved Wi-Fi support (with a wizard utility), a pop-up ad blocker for Internet Explorer 6, and Bluetooth support. The new welcome screen during the kernel boot removes the subtitles "Professional", "Home Edition" and "Embedded" since Microsoft introduced new Windows XP editions prior to the release of SP2. The green loading bar in Home Edition and the yellow one in Embedded were replaced with the blue bar, seen in Professional and other versions of Windows XP, making the boot-screen of operating systems resemble each other. Colors in other areas, such as Control Panel and the Help and Support tool, remained as before.

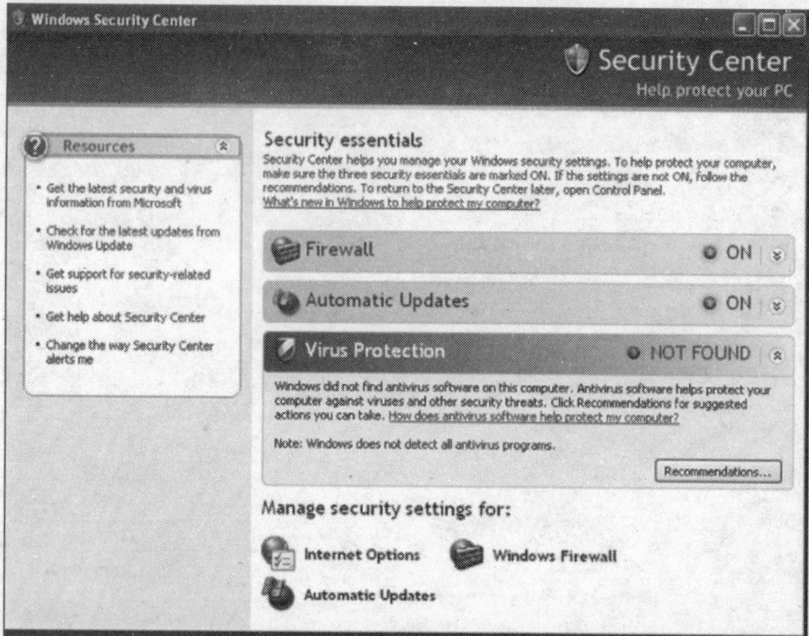

Figure 1.11 Windows Security Center was added in Service Pack 2.

Service Pack 2 also added new security enhancements, which included a major revision to the included firewall that was renamed to Windows Firewall and became enabled by default, Data Execution Prevention, which can be weakly emulated, gains hardware support in the NX bit that can stop some forms of buffer overflow attacks. Also raw socket support is removed (which supposedly limits the damage done by zombie machines). Additionally, security-related improvements were made to e-mail and web browsing. Windows XP Service Pack 2 includes the Windows Security Center, which provides a general overview of security on the system, including the state of antivirus software, Windows Update, and the new Windows Firewall. Third-party anti-virus and firewall applications can interface with the new Security Center.

1.6.7.3 Service Pack 3

Windows XP Service Pack 3 (SP3) was released to manufacturing on April 21, 2008, and to the public via both the Microsoft Download Center and Windows Update on May 6, 2008. It began being automatically pushed out to Automatic Update users on July 10, 2008. A feature set overview which details new features available separately as standalone updates to Windows XP, as well as backported features from Windows Vista has been posted by Microsoft. A total of 1,174 fixes have been included in SP3. Service Pack 3 can be installed on systems with Internet Explorer versions 6, 7 or 8. Internet Explorer 7 and 8 are not included as part of SP3.

A. NEW FEATURES IN SERVICE PACK 3

- Turns black hole router detection on by default
- Network Access Protection client
- Group Policy support for IEEE 802.1X authentication for wired network adapters.

- Credentials Security Service Provider
- Descriptive Security options in Group Policy/Local Security Policy user interface
- An updated version of the Microsoft Enhanced Cryptographic Provider Module (RSAENH) that is FIPS 140-2 certified (SHA-256, SHA-384 and SHA-512 algorithms)
- Installing without requiring a product key during setup for retail and OEM versions

B. PREVIOUSLY RELEASED UPDATES

Service Pack 3 also incorporated several previously released key updates for Windows XP, which were not included up to SP2 including:

- Windows Imaging Component
- IPSec Simple Policy Update for simplified creation and maintenance of IPSec filters
- Background Intelligent Transfer Service (BITS) 2.5
- MSXML 6.0 SP2 and XMLLite
- Microsoft Management Console 3.0
- Credential Roaming service (Digital Identity Management Service) update
- Remote Desktop Protocol 6.1
- Peer Name Resolution Protocol 2.1
- Network Diagnostics update
- WPA2 Update (KB893357)
- Windows Script 5.7
- Windows Installer 3.1 v2

Slipstreamed retail and OEM versions of Windows XP with SP3 can be installed and run with full functionality for 30 days without a product key, after which time the user will be prompted to enter a valid key and activate the installation. Volume license key (VLK) versions still require entering a product key before beginning installation.

XP SP3 is a cumulative update of all previous service packs for XP, the service pack installer checks HKLM\SYSTEM\CurrentControlSet\Control\Windows\CSDVersion registry key to see if has a value greater than or equal to 0x100, if it does it will allow the update to proceed, otherwise it will prompt to install either XP SP1 or SP2. Since SP1 is no longer available for full download, it would need to be downloaded using Windows Update. The other option is to manually change the registry key; in essence fool the installer into thinking SP1 is already installed.

However, it is possible to slipstream SP3 into the Windows XP setup files at any service pack level-including the original RTM version-without any errors or issues. Slipstreaming SP3 into Windows XP Media Center Edition 2005 is not supported. Service Pack 3 contains updates to the operating system components of Windows XP Media Center Edition (MCE) and Windows XP Tablet PC Edition, and security updates for .NET Framework version 1.0, which is included in these Windows XP SKUs. However, it does not include update rollups for the Windows Media Center application in Windows XP MCE 2005. SP3 also omits security updates for Windows Media Player 10, although the player is included in Windows XP MCE 2005. The Address Bar DeskBand on the Taskbar is no longer included due to legal restrictions. It also removed the Energy Star logo from the ScreenSaver tab of the Display properties, leaving a very noticeable blank space next to the link to enter the Power Management control panel.

C. USER COMPLAINTS

There have been various complaints regarding Service Pack 3's installation and performance reported by many users, ranging from conflicts with other software such as Symantec and other security applications, to internet connectivity and reboot loops.

Shortly after release, a large number of users with AMD processors reported that their PCs would not boot after installing Service Pack 3. The cause was established to be a result of OEMs who preinstalled (using Sysprep) a copy of Windows XP which had been created on a machine with an Intel processor. This resulted in the Intel SpeedStep driver (intelppm.sys) attempting to load on the AMD-based PC. Microsoft never supported this configuration.

1.6.8 Security Issues

Windows XP has been criticized for its susceptibility to malware, computer virus, trojan horses, and computer worms. Security issues are compounded by the fact that users, by default, receive an administrator account that provides unrestricted access to the underpinnings of the system. If the administrator's account is broken into, there is no limit to the control that can be asserted over the compromised PC.

Windows, with its large market share, has historically been a tempting target for virus creators. Security holes are often invisible until they are exploited, making preemptive action difficult. Microsoft has stated that the release of patches to fix security holes is often what causes the spread of exploits against those very same holes. Hackers exploit these holes by figuring out what problems the patches fix, and then proceed to launch attacks against unpatched systems. Microsoft recommends that all systems have automatic updates turned on to prevent a system from being attacked by an unpatched bug, but some business IT departments need to test updates before deployment across systems to predict compatibility issues with custom software and infrastructure. This deployment turn-around time also lengthens the time that systems are left unsecured in the event of a released software exploit.

When Windows XP was released in 2001, it came with Internet Explorer 6, which is now insecure and outdated. Since February 2010, Microsoft has urged all users to upgrade to Internet Explorer 8, which has better security.

1.6.9 Integration of Operating System Features

In light of the United States v. Microsoft case which resulted in Microsoft being found liable for abusing its operating system monopoly to overwhelm competition in other markets, Windows XP has drawn fire for integrating user applications such as Windows Media Player and Windows Messenger into the operating system, as well as for its close ties to the .NET Passport (now Windows Live ID) service.

1.6.10 Backward Compatibility

Migrating from Windows 9x to XP can be an issue for users dependent upon MS-DOS. Although XP comes with the ability to run DOS programs in a virtual DOS machine, it still has trouble running many old DOS programs. This is largely because it is a Windows NT system and does not use DOS as a base OS, and that the Windows NT architecture is different from Windows 9x. Some DOS programs that cannot run natively on XP, notably programs that do not rely on direct access to hardware, can be run in emulators, such as DOSBox or virtual machines, like VMware, Virtual PC, or VirtualBox. This also applies to programs that only require direct access to certain common emulated hardware components, like memory, keyboard, and serial ports.

1.6.11 Product Activation and Verification

Here we can explain the criteria for product activation and verification:

1.6.11.1 Product Activation

In an attempt to reduce piracy Windows XP introduced product activation. Activation requires the computer or the user to activate with Microsoft (either online or over the phone) within a certain amount of time in order to continue using the operating system. If the user's computer system ever changes - for example, if two or more relevant components of the computer itself are upgraded - Windows will return to the unactivated state and will need to be activated again within a defined grace period. If a user tries to reactivate too frequently, the system will refuse to activate online. The user must then contact Microsoft by telephone to obtain a new activation code.

However, activation only applies to retail and "system builder" (intended for use by small local PC builders) copies of Windows. "Royalty OEM" (used by large PC vendors) copies are instead locked to a special signature in the machine's BIOS (and will demand activation if moved to a system whose motherboard does not have the signature) and volume license copies do not require activation at all. Predictably, this led to pirates simply using volume license copies with volume license keys that were widely distributed on the Internet.

1.6.11.2 Product Key Testing

In addition to activation, Windows XP service packs will refuse to install on Windows XP systems with product keys known to be widely used in unauthorized installations. These product keys are either intended for use with one copy (for retail and system builder), for one OEM (for bios locked copies) or to one company (for volume license copies) and are included with the product. However a number of volume licence product keys (which as mentioned above avoid the need for activation) were posted on the Internet and were then used for a large number of unauthorized installations. The service packs contain a list of these keys and will not update copies of Windows XP that use them.

Microsoft developed a new key verification engine for Windows XP Service Pack 2 that could detect illicit keys, even those that had never been used before. After an outcry from security consultants who feared that denying security updates to illegal installations of Windows XP would have wide-ranging consequences even for legal owners, Microsoft elected to disable the new key verification engine. Service Pack 2 only checks for the same small list of commonly used keys as Service Pack 1. This means that while Service Pack 2 will not install on copies of Windows XP which use the older set of copied keys, those who use keys which have been posted more recently may be able to update their systems.

1.6.12 Windows Genuine Advantage

To try to curb piracy based on leaked or generated volume license keys, Microsoft introduced Windows Genuine Advantage (WGA). WGA comprises two parts, a verification tool which must be used to get certain downloads from Microsoft and a user notification system. WGA for Windows was followed by verification systems for Internet Explorer 7, Windows Media Player 11, Windows Defender, Microsoft Office 2007 and certain updates. In late 2007, Microsoft removed the WGA verification from the installer for Internet Explorer 7 saying that the purpose of the change was to make IE7 available to all Windows users.

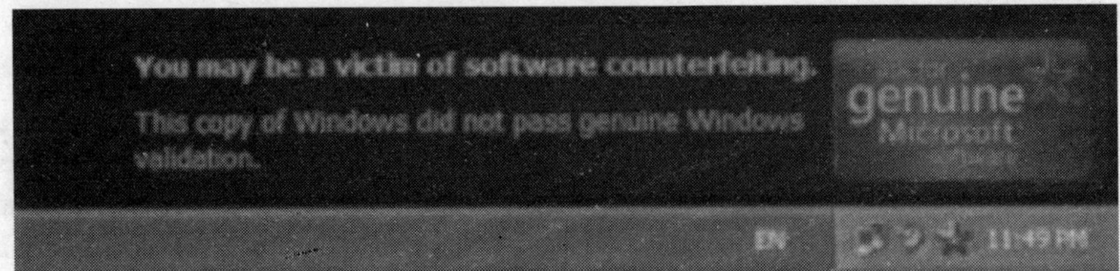

Figure 1.12 A Windows Genuine Advantage notification indicating a failed validation.

If the license key is judged not genuine, it displays a nag screen at regular intervals asking the user to buy a license from Microsoft. In addition, the user's access to Microsoft Update is restricted to critical security updates, and as such, new versions of enhancements and other Microsoft products will no longer be able to be downloaded or installed. As of August 26, 2008, Microsoft has released a new WGA activation program that displays a plain black desktop background for computers failing validation. The background can be changed, but reverts after 1 hour.

Common criticisms of WGA have included its description as a "Critical Security Update", causing Automatic Updates to download it without user intervention on default settings, its behavior compared to spyware of "phoning home" to Microsoft every time the computer is connected to the Internet, the failure to inform end users what exactly WGA would do once installed (rectified by a 2006 update), the failure to provide a proper uninstallation method during beta testing (users were given manual removal instructions that did not work with the final build), and its sensitivity to hardware changes which cause repeated need for reactivation in the hands of some developers. Also if the user has no connection to the internet or a phone, it will be difficult to activate it normally.

1.6.13 License and Media Types

There are three main types of Windows XP licenses: Retail, Volume (VLK), and Original Equipment Manufacturer (OEM). All three types of licenses are available for Windows XP Professional (32-bit and 64-bit). Windows XP Home Edition is limited to Retail and OEM licenses whereas Windows XP Media Center Edition and Windows XP Tablet PC Edition are exclusively available through VLK and OEM licenses.

Each type of license has a different installation CD. For customized or retail media, there is a small difference on each type of disc that will allow that installation disc to accept only one type of product key. Only retail and volume licenses include support for end-user installation scenarios from Microsoft. OEM software is preinstalled on systems and is supported by the system manufacturer rather than Microsoft. The price of such software is lower. There are two important restrictions on OEM licenses: Microsoft does not offer technical support, and the license cannot be transferred to another computer. The cost of OEM software products bundled with systems is not disclosed by Microsoft nor by its partners, as each system manufacturer will define its own bundling price.

Microsoft recommends that system manufacturers have their systems tested, for a fee, as part of the Windows Quality Online Services (Winqual) which includes extensive testing so that no component will cause instability in the Windows operating system due to incompatibility with the Windows operating system or with other system components or their respective drivers. Having a system tested and approved will allow the manufacturer to bear the "Certified for Windows" logo sticker on the exterior of the system, and there are additional benefits for having a tested product. This includes the product's being listed on the Windows Marketplace. Because of the fees and extensive requirements, Microsoft acknowledges that smaller system manufacturers may not opt in to the program until they produce computer systems at a modest rate and on recurring designs.

1.6.14 Retail

Retail licenses, those purchased from a retail store in full packaging, are of two sub-types: "Upgrade" and "Full Purchase Product", often abbreviated by Microsoft as FPP. FPP licenses are transferable from one computer to another, provided the previous installation is removed from the old computer. Although upgrade licenses are also transferable, a user must have a previous version of Windows even on the new computer to which they are moving the installation. Retail licenses include installation support for end-users, provided directly by Microsoft.

1.6.15 Volume License

A Volume License is the license given to a software version sold to businesses under a direct purchase agreement with Microsoft, and is sold as an upgrade license only, meaning that a previous license must be available for each new volume license. Volume license versions of Windows XP use a Volume License Key (VLK) which is a product key that does not require Windows Product Activation. The term "Volume License Key" refers to the ability to use one product key for multiple systems, depending on the type of agreement. Since Windows XP Volume License versions do not require product activation, this led to leaked copies of VLK media and product keys from businesses leading to piracy of Windows XP quickly spreading across the Internet upon early release. Beginning with Service Pack 1, Microsoft's active attempts to search out and blacklist known pirated VLK product keys became well known due to the inability to install the service pack on a system with one of the blacklisted keys. Later, this led to the Windows Genuine Advantage program.

1.6.16 Original Equipment Manufacturer (OEM)

Original equipment manufacturer (OEM) licenses are preinstalled on, and sold with, pre-assembled computers from system manufacturers. There are two types of OEM product types - those used for "direct OEMs" (major name brands that buy through a direct contract with Microsoft and produce and brand their own media from a Microsoft "Gold Master Copy" by using an authorized Microsoft duplication partner), and those used for "system builders" (local computer shops that buy generic, unbranded kits through authorized Microsoft distributors). Direct OEM product keys will often not activate with system builder installation media because direct OEMs are now required by Microsoft to pre-activate their copies in the factory using their own internal mechanism before delivery to the customer. It is recommended that system builders also pre-activate their systems before delivery, but this is not mandatory.

OEM installations can be customized using the Microsoft OEM Preinstallation Kit with branding, logos, additional applications, optional services, alternate applications for certain Windows components, Internet Explorer links, and various other customizations. All OEM customers must include support and contact information for the initial installation of Windows because it is the responsibility for the OEM to support the Windows installation, and is not provided by Microsoft to the end-user. Direct OEMs must create their own media, but have the option of creating their own custom recovery solution, which may or may not be similar to a generic installation. OEMs may provide a recovery partition on the hard drive as the custom recovery solution rather than providing disc-based media with the computer.

Some end-users have found this to be a troublesome option, because in the event of an out-of-warranty hard drive failure, they may not have access to any installation media in order to reinstall Windows onto a new hard drive. System builders are not allowed the option to create a custom recovery CD/DVD media. The only deliverable media available for a system builder to give to the end-user is the unbranded OEM system builder hologram media kit. Because of this, when end-users reformat their hard drives and re-install from the installation media, they lose all the custom branding and support information that the system builder would have included.

As a supplemental recovery method to a CD/DVD-based installation, a system builder may employ a fully customized recovery solution on the hard drive. Whether utilizing a recovery partition or not, a system builder must still include the original generic OEM system builder hologram CD/DVD media kit. OEM licenses are not transferable from one computer to another. Every computer sold/resold with an OEM license must include all of the original installation media or recovery solution, documentation, Certificate of Authenticity, and product key sticker with the sale. Microsoft requires that all OEM system manufacturers include as part of the configuration the Windows Out-of-Box Experience (OOBE), which is the initial setup wizard encountered the first time Windows boots up. It is also required that value-added resellers (VAR's), retailers, and general resellers not tamper with the OEM's customized OOBE mechanism unless under permission by the OEM, and it is a recommended configuration for systems that are privately resold so that a customer will have a like-new computer experience upon first boot-up.

OEM licenses are to be installed by professional system manufacturers only. Under Microsoft's OEM License Agreement, they are not to be sold to end-users under any circumstance, and are to be preinstalled on a computer using the OEM Preinstallation Kit (OPK) before shipment to the customer, and must include at the very least the manufacturer's support contact information. They are, therefore, designed for installation only on a single computer and are not transferable, even if the original computer is no longer in use. This is not usually an issue for users who purchase new computer systems, because most pre-assembled systems ship with a preinstalled operating system. There are few circumstances where Microsoft will allow the transfer of an OEM license from one non-functioning system to another, but the OEM System Builder License Agreement (SBLA), as well as the OEM End User License Agreement (EULA) do not contain any allowance for this, so it is entirely up to Microsoft's discretion, depending on the situation.

1.6.17 User Interface and Appearance

We can use GDI for interface and appearance as following:

1.6.17.1 Gdi+ Powered Graphics Architecture

With the introduction of Windows XP, GDI was deprecated in favor of its successor, the C++ based GDI+ subsystem. GDI+ adds anti-aliased 2D graphics, textures, floating point coordinates, gradient shading, and more complex path management, intrinsic support for modern graphics-file formats like JPEG and PNG, and support for composition of affine transformations in the 2D view pipeline. GDI+ uses ARGB values to represent color. Use of these features is apparent in Windows XP's user interface (drop shadows for icon labels on the desktop, shadows under menus, translucent blue selection rectangle in Windows Explorer, sliding task panes and taskbar buttons), and several of its applications such as Microsoft Paint, Windows Picture and Fax Viewer, Photo Printing Wizard, My Pictures Slideshow screensaver, and their presence in the basic graphics layer greatly simplifies implementations of vector-graphics systems such as Flash or SVG. The GDI+ dynamic library can be shipped with an application and used under older versions of Windows.

1.6.18 Start Menu and Taskbar

With Windows XP, the taskbar and the Start button have been updated to support Fitt's law. To help the user access a wider range of common destinations more easily from a single location, the Start menu was expanded to two columns; the left column focuses on the user's installed applications, while the right column provides access to the user's documents, and system links which were previously located on the desktop. Links to the My Documents, My Pictures and other special folders are brought to the fore. The My Computer and My Network Places (Network Neighborhood in Windows 95 and 98) icons were also moved off the Desktop and into the Start menu, making it easier to access these icons while a number of applications are open. Moreover, these links can be configured to expand as a cascading menu. Frequently used programs are automatically displayed in the left column, newly installed programs are highlighted, and the user may opt to "pin" programs to the start menu so that they are always accessible without having to navigate through the Programs folders. The default internet browser and default email program are pinned to the Start menu. The Start menu is fully customizable, links can be added or removed; the number of frequently used programs to display can be set. The All Programs menu expands like the classic Start menu to utilize the entire screen but can be set to scroll programs. The user account picture is also shown on the Start menu.

The taskbar now supports locking and unlocking to prevent itself from being accidentally resizes or elements such as Quick launch and other DeskBands from being moved inadvertently. The Taskbar grouping feature combines multiple buttons of the same application into a single button, which when clicked, pops up a menu listing all the grouped windows and their number. Advanced taskbar grouping options can be configured from the registry. The user can choose to always show, always hide or hide some or all notification area icons if inactive for some time. A button allows the user to reveal all the icons.

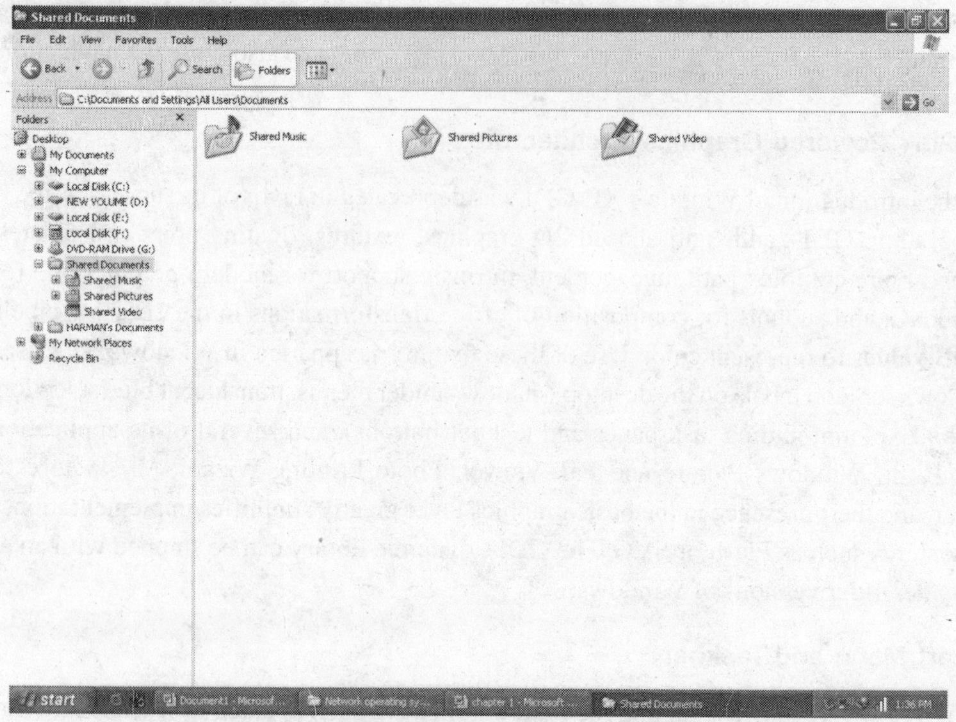

Figure 1.13 Windows Explorer in Windows XP

There are significant changes made to Windows Explorer in Windows XP, both visually and functionally. Microsoft focused especially on making Windows Explorer more discoverable and task-based, as well as adding a number of features to reflect the growing use of a computer as a "digital hub".

1.6.18.1 Task Pane and Navigation Pane

The task pane is displayed on the left side of the window instead of the traditional folder tree view when the navigation pane is turned off. It presents the user with a list of common actions and destinations that are relevant to the current directory or file(s) selected. For instance, when in a directory containing mostly pictures, a set of "Picture tasks" is shown, offering the options to display these pictures as a slide show, to print them, or to go online to order prints. Conversely, a folder containing music files would offer options to play those files in a media player, or to go online to purchase music.

Every folder also has "File and Folder Tasks", offering options to create new folders, share a folder on the local network, publish files or folders to a web site, and other common tasks like copying, renaming, moving, and deleting files or folders. File types that have identified themselves as being printable also have an option listed to print the file.

Underneath "File and Folder Tasks" is "Other Places", which always lists the parent folder of the folder being viewed and includes additional links to other common locations such as "My Computer", "Control Panel", and "My Documents" or previously navigated locations. These change depending on what folder the user was in.

Underneath "Other Places" is a "Details" pane which gives additional information when a file or folder is selected - typically the file type, file size and date modified, but depending on the file type, author, image dimensions, attributes, or other details. If the file type has a Thumbnail image handler installed, its preview also appears in the "Details" task pane. For music files, it might show the artist, album title, and the length of the song. The same information is also shown horizontally on the status bar.

The "Folders" button on the Windows Explorer toolbar toggles between the traditional navigation pane containing the tree view of folders, and the task pane. Users can also close the navigation pane by clicking the Close button in its right corner as well as turn off the task pane from Folder Options.

The navigation pane has been enhanced in Windows XP to support "simple folder view" which when turned on hides the dotted lines that connect folders and subfolders and makes folders browsable with single click while still keeping double clicking on in the right pane. Single clicking in simple folder view auto expands the folder and clicking another folder automatically expands that folder and collapses the previous one.

1.6.19 Search

Microsoft introduced animated "Search Companions" in an attempt to make searching more engaging and friendly; the default character is a puppy named Rover, with three other characters (Merlin the magician, Earl the surfer, and Courtney) also available. These search companions powered by Microsoft Agent technology, bear a great deal of similarity to Microsoft Office's Office Assistants, even incorporating "tricks" and sound effects. However, search companion can be turned off and the user can revert to using classic search.

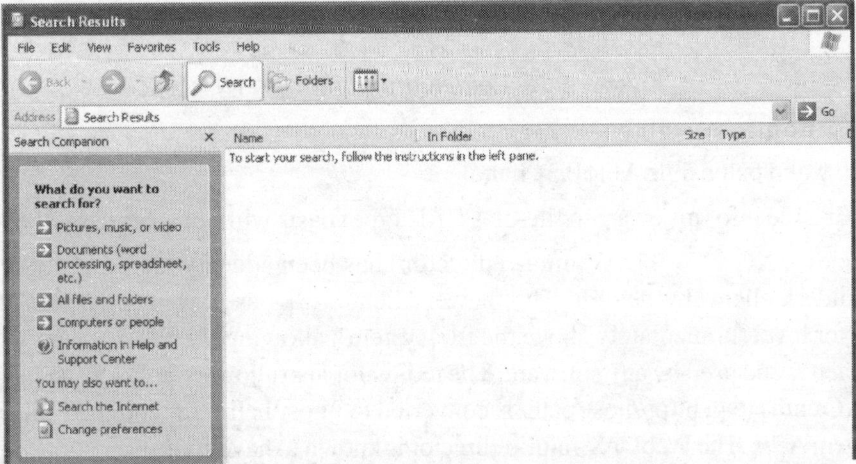

Figure 1.14 Windows Explorer's default Search Companion, Rover

The search capability itself is fairly similar to Windows Me and Windows 2000, with some important additions: Search can also be instructed to search only files that are categorically "Documents" or "Pictures, music and video"; this feature is noteworthy largely because of how Windows determines what types of files can be classified under these categories. Another important addition is that the "Look in" field accepts environment variables. Also, users can configure whether or not Windows XP searches for system and/or hidden files and folders.

1.6.20 Image Handling

Windows XP improves image preview by offering a Filmstrip view which shows images in a single horizontal row and a large preview of the currently selected image above it. "Back" and "Previous" buttons facilitate navigation through the pictures, and a pair of "Rotate" buttons offer 90-degree clockwise and counter-clockwise rotation of images. Filmstrip view like any other view can be turned on per folder. Aside from the Filmstrip view mode, there is a 'Thumbnails' view, which displays thumbnail-sized images in the folder and also displays images a subfolder may be containing (4 by default) overlaid on a large folder icon. A folder's thumbnail view can be customized from the Customize tab accessible from its Properties, where users can also change the folder's icon and specify a template type (pictures, music, videos, documents) for that folder and optionally all its subfolders. The size and quality of thumbnails in "Thumbnails" view can be adjusted using Tweak UI or the registry. Exif metadata stored in the image is also shown in the file's Properties -> Summary tab, in "Details" view and in any view on the status bar. Windows XP optionally caches the thumbnails in a "Thumbs.db" file in the same folder as the pictures so that thumbnails are generated faster the next time.

Figure 1.15 Folder thumbnail preview

Other shell improvements

- AutoPlay and extensible AutoPlay handlers
- Customizable info tips on a per-file-class (file type) basis without writing shell extensions
- In Windows XP, a "WebDAV mini-redirector" has been added which is preferred over the old Web folders client, by default. This newer client works as a system service at the network-redirector level (immediately above the file-system), allowing WebDAV shares to be assigned to a drive letter and used by any software. The redirector also allows WebDAV shares to be addressed via UNC paths (e.g. http://host/path/ is converted to \\host\path\) for compatibility with Windows filesystem APIs. The WebDAV mini-redirector is known to have some limitations in authentication support.
- Windows Explorer is content-dependent, that is, it attempts to detect the dominant type of files in a folder and then selects the most appropriate view for the user automatically unless the user manually sets the view.
- Windows XP introduced a large number of metadata categories which are shown as columns in the "Details" view of Explorer. Users also gain the ability to sort by any category which is turned on in "Details" view. Developers can write column handler shell extensions to further define their own metadata categories by which files can be sorted.
- The right pane of Windows Explorer has a "Show in Groups" feature which allows Explorer to separate its contents by headings based on any field which is used to sort the items. Items can thus be grouped by any detail which is turned on. "Show in Group" is available in Thumbnails, Tiles, Icons and Details views.

- A "Tiles" view was added, which displays the file's icon in a larger size (48 × 48), and places the file name, descriptive type, and additional information by which the items are sorted (typically the file size for data files, and the publisher name for applications) to the right.
- The toolbars can be locked to prevent them from being accidentally moved. This same capability was also added to Internet Explorer's toolbars.
- The sort order has changed compared to the one in Windows 2000. For file names containing numbers Windows Explorer now tries to sort based on numerical value rather than just comparing each number digit by digit for every character position in the file name. For instance, files containing "1", "2".."10" will be intuitively sorted with "10" appearing after "9" instead of appearing between "1" and "2".
- The "Line up icons" feature in the context menu has been replaced by an "Align to grid" feature which when turned on always lines up icons.
- For unknown/undefined file types which inexperienced users may get confused when double clicked, Windows XP can contact a web service which shows additional information about that file type and what program created or can open that file type.
- If an image named "Folder.jpg" is placed inside a folder, that image will be used as the thumbnail for that folder and as Album Art for media files in Windows Media Player.
- EFS-encrypted files can be shown in an alternate color beginning with Windows XP.
- File and folder size information is shown in tooltips upon mouse hover. For folders, size and partial folder contents are shown.
- When opening more than 15 files in a single operation, i.e. by selecting multiple files and pressing enter, Windows XP warns the user that Windows Explorer may become unresponsive, but still allows the user to do so.
- Windows Explorer supports a very basic form of mass renaming items.
- A hyperlink control in system supplied common controls.

Other usability improvements

- Windows XP includes a new set of visual themes or styles, known by its codename, Luna. Available in three color schemes, the interface is more task-based than the basic one included since Windows 95, with options available in Explorer windows to interact with each file. The user can however choose to fully revert to the pre-Windows XP "classic" user interface.

An example of the effects of ClearType. The top image example is with ClearType enabled, the bottom one is not.

- Windows XP's Display Properties allows users to save their customizations as Themes. This feature was previously available for earlier Windows operating systems by installing Microsoft Plus!.
- Windows XP includes ClearType sub-pixel font anti-aliasing, which makes onscreen fonts smoother and more readable on liquid crystal display (LCD) screens, although this causes minor performance degradation. Although ClearType has an effect on CRT monitors, its primary use is for LCD/TFT-based (laptop, notebook and modern 'flatscreen') displays.

- Icon support for 24-bit color depth with an 8-bit alpha channel.
- Use of black dots instead of asterisks in password fields of a TextBox control e.g. ??? instead of ***

1.6.21 Performance Improvements

The Windows XP kernel is completely different from the kernel of the Windows 9x/Me line of operating systems. Although an upgrade of the Windows 2000 kernel, there are major scalability, stability and performance improvements, albeit transparent to the end user.

1.6.21.1 Memory Management Improvements

The paged pool limit of 470 MB has been lifted from the Memory Manager in Windows XP, and data structures are allocated only for parts of a file that have active views, with unmapped views reusable by the memory manager depending on pool usage. Windows XP supports a larger system virtual address space (1.3 GB, of which the contiguous virtual address space that can be used by device drivers is 960 MB). The registry is reimplemented outside of the paged pool; the registry hives are memory mapped by the Cache Manager into the system cache, eliminating the registry size limit. The Configuration Manager has been updated to minimize the registry's memory footprint and lock contention, reduce fragmentation and speed up query processing.

The kernel page write protection limit in Windows XP is enabled on systems up to 256 MB of RAM (instead of 128 MB for earlier versions) beyond which large pages are enabled. Memory pages in working sets are trimmed more efficiently for multiprocessor systems depending on how recently they were accessed. Lock contention is reduced, as a number of unnecessary locks used in resource synchronizations (RAM allocation and mapping through Address Windowing Extensions, system page table entries, charging nonpaged/paged pool quotas, charging commitment of pages) have been removed. The dispatcher lock contention has been reduced and the Page Frame Number (PFN) lock has been optimized for increased parallelism and granularity. Windows XP uses push locks if there is no contention as they support shared and exclusive acquisition. Push locks are used to protect handle table entries, and in the Object Manager (to protect data structures and security descriptors) and Memory Manager (to protect AWE-related locks). Windows XP uses the SYSENTER/SYSEXIT mechanisms which require fewer clock cycles to transition to and from user mode to kernel mode to speed up system calls. Windows XP includes simultaneous multithreading support. Simultaneous multithreading is a processor's ability to process more than one data thread at a time.

1.6.21.2 Faster Boot and Logon

The ability to boot in 30 seconds was a design goal for Windows XP, and Microsoft's developers made efforts to streamline the system as much as possible; The Prefetcher is a significant part of this; it monitors what files are loaded during boot, optimizes the locations of these files on disk so that less time is spent waiting for the hard drive's heads to move and issues large I/O requests that can be overlapped with device detection and initialization. The prefetcher also uses the same algorithms to reduce application startup times. Activities such as system and service cleanup, and layout optimization of files and file metadata take place at idle time.

The Fast Logon Optimization feature performs logon asynchronously without waiting for the network to be fully initialized if roaming user profiles are not set up. Use of cached credentials avoids delays when logging on to a domain. Group Policy is applied in the background, and startup or logon scripts execute asynchronously by default.

1.6.22 Stability and Performance Improvements

Following are the stability and performance improvements of Windows XP:

1.6.22.1 Side-by-side (Sxs) Assemblies

A common issue in previous versions of Windows was that users frequently suffered from DLL hell, where more than one version of the same dynamically linked library (DLL) was installed on the computer. As software relies on DLLs, using the wrong version could result in non-functional applications, or worse. Windows XP solved this problem for native code by introducing side-by-side assemblies. The technology keeps multiple versions of a DLL in the WinSxS folder and runs them on demand to the appropriate application keeping applications isolated from each other and not using common dependencies.

1.6.22.2 Application Isolation

Windows XP also introduced a new mode of COM object registration called Registration-free COM. This makes it possible for applications that need to install COM objects to store all the required COM registry information in the application's directory, instead of in the global registry, where, strictly speaking, only a single application will ever use it. DLL hell can be substantially avoided using Registration-free COM, the only limitation being it requires at least Windows XP or later Windows versions and that it must not be used for EXE COM servers or system-wide components such as MDAC, MSXML, DirectX or Internet Explorer.

1.6.22.3 Application Compatibility

As Windows XP merged the consumer and enterprise versions of Windows, it was necessary to support applications developed for the popular and consumer oriented Windows 9x platform on the Windows NT kernel. Microsoft addressed this by going to great lengths to improve compatibility with application specific tweaks and shims and providing tools such as the Application Compatibility Toolkit to allow users to apply and automate these tweaks and shims on their own applications.

1.6.22.4 Device Support Improvements

Windows XP provides new and/or improved drivers and user interfaces for devices compared to Windows Me and 98.

1.6.22.5 CD Burning

Windows XP includes technology from Roxio which allows users to directly burn files to a compact disc through Windows Explorer. Previously, end users had to install CD burning software. In Windows XP, CD and DVD-RAM (FAT32 only for DVD-RAM) burning has been directly integrated into the Windows interface; user's burn files to a CD in the same way they write files to a floppy disk or to the hard drive. The burning functionality is also exposed as an API called the Image Mastering API. Windows XP's CD burning support does not do disk-to-disk copying or disk images, although the API can be used programmatically to do these tasks. Creation of audio CDs is integrated into Windows Media Player.

1.6.22.6 Device Driver Rollback

On old versions of Windows, when users upgrade a device driver, there is a chance the new driver is less stable, efficient or functional than the original. Reinstalling the old driver can be a major hassle and to avoid this quandary, Windows XP keeps a copy of an old driver when a new version is installed. If the new driver has problems, the user can return to the previous version. This feature does not work with printer drivers.

1.6.22.7 Power Management Improvements

- Support for the Simple Boot Specification
- Wake-on-Battery support so that the system has time to power off or hibernate
- LCD dimming when on battery power
- Processor power and performance control including C-state (run in lower power state when idle) and throttling
- USB selective suspend feature
- Significantly noticeable fast boot and resume from hibernation compared to previous Windows versions owing to the boot loader caching file and directory metadata sequentially and in large chunks in a most recently used manner, overlapping device initialization. Hibernation is faster as memory pages are compressed using an improved algorithm, unused memory pages are freed and DMA transfers are used during I/O.
- Faster resume from standby as the algorithm used by the Power Manager for notifying hardware and software of power state changes by dispatching power IRPs has been rewritten to maximize parallelism and important system drivers (PCMCIA, keyboard, and mouse) have been rewritten to eliminate blocking interactions.
- Built-in support for processor power management technologies such as Intel SpeedStep and AMD PowerNow!.

1.6.22.8 Other Hardware Improvements

- Windows XP's user interface for Plug and Play changed with all messages being shown in the notification area as balloon tips.
- Generic USB 2.0 EHCI drivers beginning with Windows XP SP1 and support for USB device classes such as Bluetooth, USB video device class, imaging (still image capture device class) and Media Transfer Protocol with Windows Media Player 10 USB audio devices support GFX filters FireWire (IEEE 1394) support for digital video cameras and audio video devices, MPEG-2 and S/PDIF across IEEE 1394 (IEC-61883 and AV/C protocols).
- The read-only attribute of files and folders is automatically removed when copying files from optical media using Windows Explorer.

- Improved mouse pointer ballistics.
- DualView for multi-monitor setups.
- The Scanner and Camera Wizard based on Windows Image Acquisition and other common dialogs for WIA devices have been improved in Windows XP to show the media information and metadata, rotate images as necessary, categorize them into subfolders, capture images and video in case of a still or video camera, crop and scan images to a single or multi-page TIFF in case of a scanner.
- Multichannel audio output and playback of additional audio formats. Volume can be set for each speaker in a multichannel configuration.
- Acoustic Echo Cancellation for USB microphones
- Global Effects (GFX) engine
- Support for reading UDF 2.01 upgradeable to UDF 2.50 by installing Windows Feature Pack for Storage.
- Sound Blaster 2.0 emulation support in NTVDM

1.6.23 System Administration Improvements

Following are the system administration improvements:

1.6.23.1 Remote Desktop

Users can log into Windows XP Professional remotely through the Remote Desktop service. It is built on Terminal Services technology (RDP), and is similar to "Remote Assistance", but allows remote users to access local resources such as printers.. Any Terminal Services client, a special "Remote Desktop Connection" client, or a web-based client using an ActiveX control may be used to connect to the Remote Desktop. (Remote Desktop clients for earlier versions of Windows, Windows 95, Windows 98 and 98 Second Edition, Windows Me, Windows NT 4.0, or Windows 2000 have been made available by Microsoft. This permits earlier versions of Windows to connect to a Windows XP system running Remote Desktop, but not vice-versa.)

There are several resources that users can redirect from the remote server machine to the local client, depending upon the capabilities of the client software used. For instance, "File System Redirection" allows users to use their local files on a remote desktop within the terminal session, while "Printer Redirection" allows users to use their local printer within the terminal session as they would with a locally or network shared printer. "Port Redirection" allows applications running within the terminal session to access local serial and parallel ports directly, and "Audio" allows users to run an audio program on the remote desktop and have the sound redirected to their local computer. The clipboard can also be shared between the remote computer and the local computer.

REMOTE ASSISTANCE

- Remote Assistance allows a Windows XP user to temporarily take over a remote Windows XP computer over a network or the Internet to resolve issues. As it can be a hassle for system administrators to personally visit the affected computer, Remote Assistance allows them to diagnose and possibly even repair problems with a computer without ever personally visiting it.

1.6.24 Fast User Switching and Welcome Screen

Windows XP introduces Fast User Switching and a more end user friendly Welcome Screen which replaces the Classic logon prompt. Fast user switching allows another user to log in and use the system without having to log out the previous user and quit his or her applications. Previously (on both Windows Me and Windows 2000) only one user at a time could be logged in (except through Terminal Services), which was a serious drawback to multi-user activity. Fast User Switching, like Terminal Services, requires more system resources than having only a single user logged in at a time and although more than one user can be logged in, only one user can be actively using their account at a time. This feature is not available when the Welcome Screen is turned off, such as when joined to a Windows Server Domain or with Novell Client installed.

1.6.24.1 Manageability Features

- Windows Disk Defragmenter was updated to alleviate some restrictions. It no longer relies on the Windows NT Cache Manager, which prevented the defragmenter from moving pieces of a file that cross a 256KB boundary within the file. NTFS metadata files can also be defragmented. A command-line tool, defrag.exe, has been included, providing access to the defragmenter from cmd.exe and Task Scheduler.
- Non-persistent Shadow Copy support
- NTBackup has a wizard-based interface for ease of use and supports backing up locked files using Shadow Copy.
- Windows Error Reporting
- Driver Verifier Manager, a GUI for Driver Verifier.
- Automated System Recovery
- Unified Registry editor
- Files and Settings Transfer Wizard and User State Migration Tool
- Several deployment tools improvements including enhancements to Sysprep, Setup Manager, introduction of WinPE
- Increased number of Group Policies and Resultant Set of Policy (RSoP) management console which allows administrators to see applied policies in logging mode or simulate policy settings that will be applied before committing to changes to objects in planning mode.
- A Desktop Cleanup Wizard was introduced to help users reduce clutter on their desktops, by looking at the shortcuts on the Desktop and moving any unused ones into a directory called "Unused Desktop Shortcuts". The Desktop Cleanup Wizard operates as a scheduled task that runs once a day to determine if it's been 60 days since the last time the wizard was run.

1.6.24.2 Networking and Communication Features

- IPv6 and Teredo tunneling through the Advanced Networking Pack later incorporated into Windows XP SP2, the combination of which helps traverse symmetric NATs.

- DHCP client alternate configuration to support more than one network or in the case when a DHCP server is not available
- Network bridging
- Internet Connection Firewall later upgraded to Windows Firewall in Windows XP Service Pack 2.
- Network Setup Wizard for setting up the network, an evolution of Windows Me's Home Networking Wizard.
- NAT Traversal APIs to abstract UPnP functions. UPnP IGD devices show up in Network Connections if the IGD Discovery and Control client is installed and double clicking their icon can initiate a connection to the Internet via the gateway device and show status information. NAT port mappings are also shown and can be set up.
- Internet Connection Sharing is integrated with UPnP and has a Quality of Service Packet Scheduler component
- Built-in PPPoE protocol
- Connection Manager supports favorites to save settings for multiple network locations, client side logging and callback features
- Peer-to-peer networking support later expanded with Advanced Networking Pack/Windows XP SP2 which introduced Peer Name Resolution Protocol that allows dynamic domain name publication and resolution of names to endpoints.
- Support for IP networking over the IEEE 1394 bus.
- Background Intelligent Transfer Service
- Wireless Zero Configuration for automatic wireless network configuration with re-authentication when necessary thus providing seamless roaming capability and setting the preferred order of connections
- IEEE 802.1X support for wireless and wired connections
- Ability to access hotspots created using Wireless Provisioning Services
- Ability to establish an ad hoc wireless network
- Native support for WPA and WPA2 in infrastructure networks
- Improved support for infrared including IrDA networking (IrCOMM modems, IrNET and P2P)
- Network connection status support tab which displays IP configuration and offers a 1-click "Repair" function to perform a series of steps that reset the network connection.
- Networking tab in Windows Task Manager
- Basic Network Diagnostics integrated into the Help and Support Center\
- Winsock has the ability to self-heal if a Winsock LSP uninstallation damages it. Also, users can manually reset and repair a corrupted Winsock stack using the netsh winsock reset command.
- Network Location Awareness APIs exposed through Winsock for determining network states and notifying Winsock client applications of changes

- Support for split tunneling (although not secure) for VPN connections so VPN clients may access the internet
- Support for PVC Encapsulation (RFC 2684)
- NDIS 5.1 has performance enhancements, Plug and Play and Power event notifications for miniport drivers, send cancellation and 64-bit statistic counters. Remote NDIS supports USB attached network devices.
- Wake on LAN can be configured to limit wake up packets to just magic packets.
- Expanded support for soft modems and HomePNA adapters.
- TAPI 3.1 exposes COM interfaces. H.323v2 based IP telephony and IP multicast AV conferencing Telephony Service Providers are included. TAPI 3.1 also includes File Terminals, Pluggable Terminals, USB Phone TSP and support for Auto Discovery of TAPI Servers. Several H.323 supplementary services have been implemented for richer call control features.
- Support for simple file sharing which disables the Security tab used to set ACLs/permissions and enables sharing of files and folders over the network without asking for a password. Simple file sharing also disables sharing permissions (shares the item with everyone on the network) but users can make folders in their user profile inaccessible.
- Native Bluetooth stack beginning with Windows XP Service Pack 2.
- Windows Messenger

1.6.24.3 Security Features

- Software Restriction Policies
- Credential Manager API with a Single Sign On mechanism
- Network logons disabled for user accounts with blank passwords.
- Several Encrypting File System improvements
- Digest SSP for HTTP and LDAP queries
- Smart Card login to terminal server sessions, using smart cards with system tools such as net.exe and runas.exe, auto-enrollment for smart cards
- Data Execution Prevention, Windows Security Center, Attachment Manager introduced in Windows XP SP2

1.6.24.4 Other Features

- Windows XP supports a total of 1 million card deals in its version of FreeCell.
- For computers in a workgroup, the Windows Time Service in Windows XP supports a new Internet Time feature (NTP client), which updates the clock on the user's computer by synchronizing with an NTP time server on the Internet. This feature is useful for computers whose real-time clock does not maintain the correct time.
- Video Mixing Renderer-7 (VMR-7) DirectShow renderer filters for video rendering. VMR-7 which can mix multiple streams and graphics with alpha blending, allowing applications to draw text and graphics over the video and support custom effects.

- Internet Information Services 5.1
- Microsoft Message Queuing 3.0 supports: Internet Messaging (referencing queues via HTTP, SOAP-formatted messages, MSMQ support for Internet Information Services), queue aliases, multicasting of messages, and additional support for programmatic maintenance and administration of queues and MSMQ itself. MSMQ 3 clients directly communicate with Active Directory using LDAP.
- COM+ 1.5
- Speech Application Programming Interface 5.1
- SAPI 5 support in Microsoft Narrator
- General improvements to international support such as more locales, languages and scripts, MUI support in Terminal Services, improved IMEs and National Language Support, Text Services Framework beginning with Windows XP SP1.
- Full Unicode support in the RichEdit control shipped in Windows XP and used by WordPad.
- Support for tablet and pen-sensitive screens, portrait-oriented screens in Windows XP Tablet PC Edition. It also includes speech recognition to control the operating system and for text dictation, handwriting recognition and digital ink support accessible through the Tablet PC Input Panel (TIP). Also included are applications to complement these features such as Windows Journal and Sticky Notes for note taking with additional downloadable applications and extras.

Microsoft Active Accessibility 2.0 API, adding support for Dynamic Annotation and MSAA Text.

1.7 WINDOWS NT

Windows NT is a family of operating systems produced by Microsoft, the first version of which was released in July 1993. It was originally designed to be a powerful high-level-language-based, processor-independent, multiprocessing, multiuser operating system with features comparable to Unix. It was intended to complement consumer versions of Windows that were based on MS-DOS. NT was the first fully 32-bit version of Windows, whereas its consumer-oriented counterparts, Windows 3.1x and Windows 9x, were 16-bit/32-bit hybrids. Windows 2000, Windows XP, Windows Server 2003, Windows Vista, Windows Home Server, Windows Server 2008 and Windows 7 are based on Windows NT, although they are not branded as Windows NT.

Although various Microsoft publications, including a 1998 question-and-answer session with Bill Gates, reveal that the letters 'NT' were expanded to 'New Technology' for marketing purposes, they originally stood for "N-Ten," the codename of the Intel i860 XR processor for which NT was initially developed. However, they no longer carry any specific meaning.

A main design goal of NT was hardware and software portability. Various versions of NT family operating systems have been released for a variety of processor architectures, initially Intel IA-32, MIPS R3000/R4000 and Alpha, with PowerPC, Itanium and AMD64 supported in later releases. The idea was to have a common code base with a custom Hardware Abstraction Layer (HAL) for each platform. However, support for MIPS, Alpha and PowerPC was later dropped after NT 4.0. Broad software compatibility was achieved with support for several API "personalities", including Win32, POSIX and OS/2 APIs - the latter two were phased out starting with Windows XP. Partial MS-DOS compatibility was achieved via an integrated DOS Virtual Machine - although this feature is being phased out in the x86-64 architecture. NT supported per-object (file, function, and role) access control lists allowing a rich set of security permissions to be applied to systems and services. NT supported Windows network protocols, inheriting the previous OS/2 LAN Manager networking, as well as TCP/IP networking (for which Microsoft would implement a TCP/IP stack derived from the BSD Unix stack).

Windows NT 3.1 was the first version of Windows to utilize 32-bit "flat" virtual memory addressing on 32-bit processors. Its companion product, Windows 3.1, used segmented addressing and switches from 16-bit to 32-bit addressing in pages. Windows NT 3.1 featured a core kernel providing a system API, running in supervisor mode, and a set of user-space environments with their own APIs which included the new Win32 environment, an OS/2 1.3 text-mode environment and a POSIX environment. The full preemptive multitasking kernel could interrupt running tasks to schedule other tasks, without relying on user programs to voluntarily give up control of the CPU, as in Windows 3.1 Windows applications (although MS-DOS applications were preemptively multitasked in Windows starting with Windows 1.0).

Notably, in Windows NT 3.x, several I/O driver subsystems, such as video and printing, were user-mode subsystems. In Windows NT 4, the video, server and printer spooler subsystems were integrated into the kernel. Windows NT's first GUI was strongly influenced by (and programmatically compatible with) that from Windows 3.1; Windows NT 4's interface was redesigned to match that of the brand new Windows 95, moving from the Program Manager to the Start Menu/Taskbar design.

NTFS, a journaled, secure file system, was created for NT. Windows NT also allows for other installable file systems, and with versions 3.1 and 3.51, NT could also be installed on DOS's FAT or OS/2's HPFS file systems. Later versions could be installed on a FAT32 partition, in select cases, including Vista versions. Windows Vista and Windows 7 require a FAT32 partition to boot on an EFI based system.

1.7.1 Architecture of Windows NT

Architecture of Windows NT, a line of operating systems produced and sold by Microsoft, is a layered design that consists of two main components, user mode and kernel mode. It is a preemptive, reentrant operating system, which has been designed to work with uniprocessor and symmetrical multi processor (SMP)-based computers. To process input/output (I/O) requests, they use packet-driven I/O, which utilizes I/O request packets (IRPs) and asynchronous I/O. Starting with Windows 2000, Microsoft began making 64-bit versions of Windows available-before this, these operating systems only existed in 32-bit versions.

Programs and subsystems in user mode are limited in terms of what system resources they have access to, while the kernel mode has unrestricted access to the system memory and external devices. The Windows NT kernel is known as a hybrid kernel. The architecture comprises a simple kernel, hardware abstraction layer (HAL), drivers, and a range of services (collectively named Executive), which all exist in kernel mode.

User mode in Windows NT is made of subsystems capable of passing I/O requests to the appropriate kernel mode software drivers by using the I/O manager. Two subsystems make up the user mode layer of Windows NT: the Environment subsystem (which runs applications written for many different types of operating systems), and the Integral subsystem (operates system specific functions on behalf of the environment subsystem). Kernel mode in Windows NT has full access to the hardware and system resources of the computer. The kernel mode stops user mode services and applications from accessing critical areas of the operating system that they should not have access to.

The Executive interfaces, with all the user mode subsystems, deals with I/O, object management, security and process management. The kernel sits between the Hardware Abstraction Layer and the Executive to provide multiprocessor synchronization, thread and interrupt scheduling and dispatching, and trap handling and exception dispatching. The kernel is also responsible for initializing device drivers at bootup. Kernel mode drivers exist in three levels: highest level drivers, intermediate drivers and low level drivers. Windows Driver Model (WDM) exists in the intermediate layer and was mainly designed to be binary and source compatible between Windows 98 and Windows 2000. The lowest level drivers are either legacy Windows NT device drivers that control a device directly or can be a PnP hardware bus.

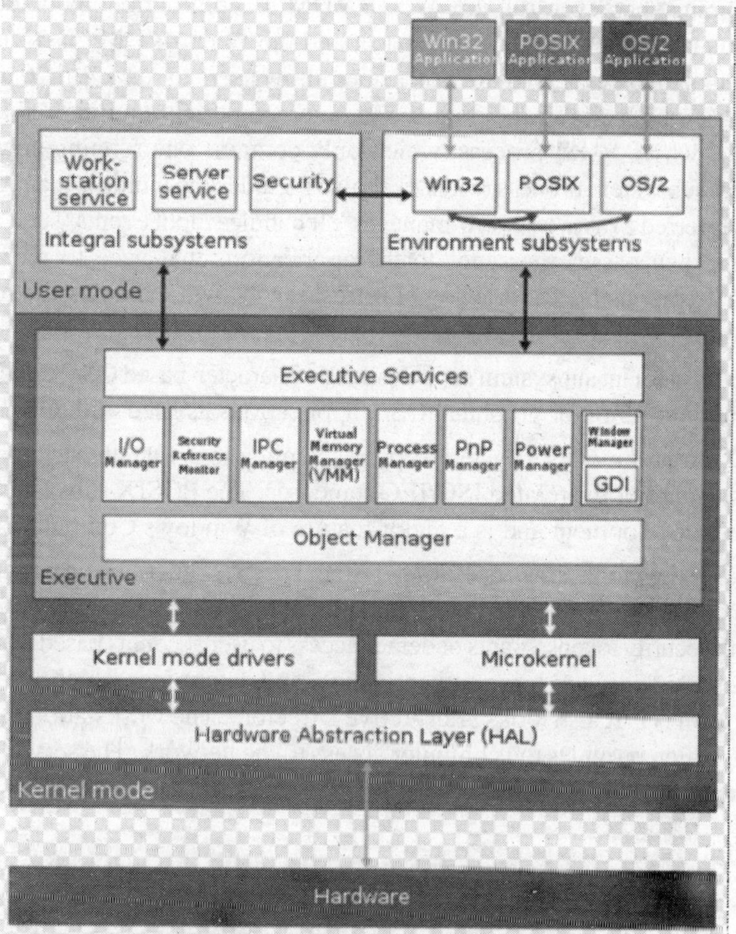

Figure 1.16: Architecture of Windows NT

1.7.2 User Mode

The user mode is made up of subsystems which can pass I/O requests to the appropriate kernel mode drivers via the I/O manager (which exists in kernel mode). Two subsystems make up the user mode layer of Windows NT: the Environment subsystem and the Integral subsystem.

The environment subsystem was designed to run applications written for many different types of operating systems. None of the environment subsystems can directly access hardware, and must request access to memory resources through the Virtual Memory Manager that runs in kernel mode. Also, applications run at a lower priority than kernel mode processes. There are three main environment subsystems: the Win32 subsystem, an OS/2 subsystem and a POSIX subsystem.

- The Win32 environment subsystem can run 32-bit Windows applications. It contains the console as well as text window support, shutdown and hard-error handling for all other environment subsystems. It also supports Virtual DOS Machines (VDMs), which allow MS-DOS and 16-bit Windows (Win16) applications to run on Windows NT. There is a specific MS-DOS VDM which runs in its own address space and which emulates an Intel 80486 running MS-DOS 5.0. Win16 programs, however, run in a Win16 VDM. Each program, by default, runs in the same process, thus using the same address space, and the Win16 VDM gives each program its own thread to run on. However, Windows NT does allow users to run a Win16 program in a separate Win16 VDM, which allows the program to be preemptively multitasked as Windows NT will pre-empt the whole VDM process, which only contains one running application. The Win32 environment subsystem process (csrss.exe) also includes the window management functionality, sometimes referred to as a "window manager". It handles input events (such as from the keyboard and mouse), then passes messages to the applications that need to receive this input. Each application is responsible for drawing or refreshing its own windows and menus, in response to these messages.
- The OS/2 environment subsystem supports 16-bit character-based OS/2 applications and emulates OS/2 1.x, but not 32-bit or graphical OS/2 applications as used with OS/2 2.x or later.
- The POSIX environment subsystem supports applications that are strictly written to either the POSIX.1 standard or the related ISO/IEC standards. The POSIX subsystem has been an area of recent active development and is a major feature of Windows Compute Cluster Server 2003.

The integral subsystem looks after operating system specific functions on behalf of the environment subsystem. It consists of a security subsystem, a workstation service and a server service. The security subsystem deals with security tokens, grants or denies access to user accounts based on resource permissions, handles login requests and initiates login authentication, and determines which system resources need to be audited by Windows NT. It also looks after Active Directory. The workstation service is an API to the network redirector, which provides the computer access to the network. The server service is an API that allows the computer to provide network services.

1.7.3 Kernel Mode

Windows NT kernel mode has full access to the hardware and system resources of the computer and runs code in a protected memory area. It controls access to scheduling, thread prioritization, memory management and the interaction with hardware. The kernel mode stops user mode services and applications from accessing critical areas of the operating system that they should not have access to; user mode processes must ask the kernel mode to perform such operations on their behalf.

While the x86 architecture supports four different privilege levels (numbered 0 to 3), only the two extreme privilege levels are used. Usermode programs are run with CPL 3, and the kernel runs with CPL

0. These two levels are often referred to as "ring 3" and "ring 0", respectively. Such a design decision had been done to achieve code portability to RISC platforms that only support two privilege levels, though this breaks compatibility with OS/2 applications that contain I/O privilege segments that attempt to directly access hardware. Kernel mode consists of executive services, which are it made up on many modules that do specific tasks, kernel drivers, a kernel and a Hardware Abstraction Layer, or HAL.

1.7.4 Executive

The Windows Executive services make up the low-level kernel-mode portion, and are contained in the file NTOSKRNL.EXE. It deals with I/O, object management, security and process management. These are divided into several subsystems, among which Cache Manager, Configuration Manager, I/O Manager, Local Procedure Call (LPC), Memory Manager, Object Manager, Process Structure and Security Reference Monitor (SRM). Grouped together, the components can be called Executive services (internal name Ex). System Services (internal name Nt), i.e., system calls, are implemented at this level, too, except very few that call directly into the kernel layer for better performance. The term "service" in this context generally refers to a callable routine, or set of callable routines. This is distinct from the concept of a "service process," which is a user mode component somewhat analogous to a daemon in Unix-like operating systems.

Each object in Windows NT exists in a global namespace. This is a screenshot from SysInternals WinObj.

1.7.5 Object Manager

The Object Manager (internal name Ob) is an executive subsystem that all other executive subsystems, especially system calls, must pass through to gain access to Windows NT resources-essentially making it a resource management infrastructure service. The object manager is used to reduce the duplication of object resource management functionality in other executive subsystems, which could potentially lead to bugs and make development of Windows NT harder. To the object manager, each resource is an object, whether that resource is a physical resource (such as a file system or peripheral) or a logical resource (such as a file). Each object has a structure or object type that the object manager must know about.

Object creation is a process in two phases, creation and insertion. Creation causes the allocation of an empty object and the reservation of any resources required by the object manager, such as an (optional) name in the namespace. If creation was successful, the subsystem responsible for the creation fills in the empty object. Finally, if the subsystem deems the initialization successful, it instructs the object manager to insert the object, which makes it accessible through its (optional) name or a cookie called a handle. From then on, the lifetime of the object is handled by the object manager, and it's up to the subsystem to keep the object in a working condition until being signaled by the object manager to dispose of it.

Handles are identifiers that represent a reference to a kernel resource through an opaque value. Similarly, opening an object through its name is subject to security checks, but acting through an existing, open handle is only limited to the level of access requested when the object was opened or created. Object types define the object procedures and any data specific to the object. In this way, the object manager allows Windows NT to be an object oriented operating system, as object types can be thought of as polymorphic classes that define objects. Most subsystems, though, with a notable exception in the I/O Manager, rely on the default implementation for all object type procedures.

Each instance of an object that is created stores its name, parameters that are passed to the object creation function, security attributes and a pointer to its object type. The object also contains an object close procedure and a reference count to tell the object manager how many other objects in the system reference that object and thereby determines whether the object can be destroyed when a close request is sent to it. Every named object exists in a hierarchical object namespace.

1.7.6 Cache Controller

Closely coordinates with the Memory Manager, I/O Manager and I/O drivers to provide a common cache for regular file I/O. Uniquely, the Windows Cache Manager operates on file blocks (rather than device blocks), for consistent operation between local and remote files, and ensures a certain degree of coherency with memory-mapped views of files, since cache blocks are a special case of memory-mapped views and cache misses a special case of page faults.

1.7.7 Configuration Manager

Implements the Windows registry.

1.7.7.1 I/O Manager

Allows devices to communicate with user-mode subsystems. It translates user-mode read and write commands into read or write IRPs which it passes to device drivers. It accepts file system I/O requests and translates them into device specific calls, and can incorporate low-level device drivers that directly manipulate hardware to either read input or write output. It also includes a cache manager to improve disk performance by caching read requests and write to the disk in the background.

1.7.7.2 Local Procedure Call (LPC)

Provides inter-process communication ports with connection semantics. LPC ports are used by user-mode subsystems to communicate with their clients, by Executive subsystems to communicate with user-mode subsystems, and as the basis for the local transport for MSRPC.

1.7.7.3 Memory Manager

Manages virtual memory, controlling memory protection and the paging of memory in and out of physical memory to secondary storage, and implements a general-purpose allocator of physical memory. It also implements a parser of PE executables that lets an executable be mapped or unmapped in a single, atomic step.

Starting from Windows NT Server 4.0, Terminal Server Edition, the memory manager implements a so-called session space, a range of kernel-mode memory that is subject to context switching just like user-mode memory. This lets multiple instances of the kernel-mode Win32 subsystem and GDI drivers run side-by-side, despite shortcomings in their initial design. Each session space is shared by several processes, collectively referred to as a "session".

To ensure a degree of isolation between sessions without introducing a new object type, the association between processes and sessions is handled by the Security Reference Monitor, as an attribute of a security subject (token), and it can only be changed while holding special privileges. The relatively unsophisticated and ad-hoc nature of sessions is due to the fact they weren't part of the initial design, and had to be developed, with minimal disruption to the main line, by a third party (Citrix) as a prerequisite for their terminal server product for Windows NT, called WinFrame. Starting with Windows Vista, though, sessions finally became a proper aspect of the Windows architecture. No longer have a memory manager constructed that creeps into user mode indirectly through Win32, they were expanded into a pervasive abstraction affecting most Executive subsystems. As a matter of fact, regular use of Windows Vista always results in a multi-session environment.

1.7.7.4 Process Structure

Handles process and thread creation and termination, and it implements the concept of Job, a group of processes that can be terminated as a whole, or be placed under shared restrictions (such a total maximum of allocated memory, or CPU time). Job objects were introduced in Windows 2000.

1.7.7.5 PNP Manager

Handles Plug and Play and supports device detection and installation at boot time. It also has the responsibility to stop and start devices on demand-this can happen when a bus (such as USB or FireWire) gains a new device and needs to have a device driver loaded to support it. Its bulk is actually implemented in user mode, in the Plug and Play Service, which handles the often complex tasks of installing the appropriate drivers, notifying services and applications of the arrival of new devices, and displaying GUI to the user.

1.7.7.6 Power Manager

Deals with power events (power-off, stand-by, hibernate, etc.) and notifies affected drivers with special IRPs (Power IRPs).

1.7.7.7 Security Reference Monitor (SRM)

The primary authority for enforcing the security rules of the security integral subsystem. It determines whether an object or resource can be accessed, via the use of access control lists (ACLs), which are they made up of access control entries (ACEs). ACEs contain a security identifier (SID) and a list of operations that the ACE gives a select group of trustees-a user account, group account, or login session-permission (allow, deny, or audit) to that resource.

1.7.8 GDI

The Graphics Device Interface is responsible for tasks such as drawing lines and curves, rendering fonts and handling palettes. The Windows NT 3.x series of releases had placed the GDI component in the user-mode Client/Server Runtime Subsystem, but this was moved into kernel mode with Windows NT 4.0 to improve graphics performance.

1.7.9 Kernel

The kernels sits between the HAL and the Executive and provides multiprocessor synchronization, thread and interrupts scheduling and dispatching, and trap handling and exception dispatching; it is also responsible for initializing device drivers at bootup that are necessary to get the operating system up and running. That is, the kernel performs almost all the tasks of a traditional microkernel; the strict distinction between Executive and Kernel is the most prominent remnant of the original microkernel design, and historical design documentation consistently refers to the kernel component as "the microkernel".

The kernel often interfaces with the process manager. The level of abstraction is such that the kernel never calls into the process manager, only the other way around (save for a handful of corner cases, still never to the point of a functional dependence).

1.7.10 Kernel-mode Drivers

Windows NT uses kernel-mode device drivers to enable it to interact with hardware devices. Each of the drivers has well defined system routines and internal routines that it exports to the rest of the operating system. All devices are seen by user mode code as a file object in the I/O manager, though to the I/O manager itself the devices are seen as device objects, which it defines as either file, device or driver objects. Kernel mode drivers exist in three levels: highest level drivers, intermediate drivers and low level drivers. The highest level drivers, such as file system drivers for FAT and NTFS, rely on intermediate drivers. Intermediate drivers consist of function drivers-or main driver for a device-those are optionally sandwiched between lower and higher level filter drivers. The function driver then relies on a bus driver-or a driver that services a bus controller, adapter, or bridge-which can have an optional bus filter driver that sits between itself and the function driver. Intermediate drivers rely on the lowest level drivers to function. The Windows Driver Model (WDM) exists in the intermediate layer. The lowest level drivers are either legacy Windows NT device drivers that control a device directly or can be a PnP hardware bus. These lower level drivers directly control hardware and do not rely on any other drivers.

1.7.11 Hardware Abstraction Layer

The Windows NT hardware abstraction layer, or HAL, is a layer between the physical hardware of the computer and the rest of the operating system. It was designed to hide differences in hardware and therefore provide a consistent platform on which the kernel is run. The HAL includes hardware-specific code that controls I/O interfaces, interrupt controllers and multiple processors.

However, despite its purpose and designated place within the architecture, the HAL isn't a layer that sits entirely below the kernel; the way the kernel sits below the Executive: all known HAL implementations depend in some measure on the kernel, or even the Executive. In practice, this means that kernel and HAL variants come in matching sets that are specifically engineered to work together.

In particular hardware abstraction does not involve abstracting the instruction set, which generally falls under the wider concept of portability. Abstracting the instruction set, when necessary (such as for handling the several revisions to the x86 instruction set, or emulating a missing math coprocessor), is performed by the kernel, or via platform virtualization.

1.8 UNIX

UNIX is an Operating System. It differs from other operating systems in several ways:

- It is multi-user.
- It is multi-tasking.

- It has been around for a long time, so is widely used and 'mature'.
- Because of the previous point, it is very stable. A UNIX operating system very rarely crashes.
- UNIX is like a 'tool kit'. It contains many small programs and tools, that can be used together to solve complex problems.
- Like all tool kits, it takes a little while to learn how to use each tool effectively. This tutorial will help you to take the first steps, then other areas of the web site will help you to expand your knowledge as and when you need to.

If you're completely new to UNIX, the first thing you'll need to do is learn how to log in and log out. Even if you already know how to do this, you may benefit from reading those sections before proceeding.

1.8.1 Multi-Tasking

This term describes an Operating System that can perform several tasks simultaneously. For example, on your computer you may browse the web, print a document, and perform several other tasks, all at once. Most computers only have one processor, so they perform multi-tasking by giving each task a short time on the processor in turn. Some computers have more than one processor, so can genuinely perform more than one task at time.

1.8.2 Multi-User

This term describes an Operating System that can have two or more concurrent users. Each one has their own 'space' within the operating system. For an individual user, it may appear that they are the only one using the operating system, even though there may be many others using it at the same time.

1.8.3 Operating System

An operating system is a piece of software. Its task is to manage the hardware resources of your computer, and make them available for useful tasks. Examples of tasks performed by an operating system are:

- Keep track of the memory and disk space in the computer. Keep a list of where everything is stored. If a user or another piece of software requests some memory or disk space, allocate some to it.
- Manage the main processor in the computer. If more than one task is running on the computer, make sure they all have access to the processor on a fair basis.
- Manage other hardware devices. For example, if the computer has a modem attached, the operating system keeps track of whether or not anyone is using it, and prevents more than one task from using it at a time.

UNIX®, Microsoft Windows, and MacOS are all different types of operating systems, and there are many others.

1.8.4 Single User

This term describes an Operating System that can be used by only one user at a time. Although the computer may be used by more than one person, they can not use it concurrently. Note that a single user operating system can still be multi-tasking.

The 'filesystem' is about the most important concept you must get used to in a UNIX system. It is as central to the work you will do in UNIX as, for example, your desk is probably central to your work now. Luckily, the UNIX filesystem is quite easy to learn to use - the following few segments will have you up to speed with the basics in no time.

1.8.5 What is the File System?

A UNIX system, like any other type of computer system, has some basic objectives: To store and process data. Of course, the exact type of data, and what processesing is done with it, will vary from system to system. On one system, there may a large accounting application, which will store details of financial transactions. At the other end of the scale, an individual may use a system to store private letters, or college notes. Someone else may store an address book, phone numbers, and their diary on the system. Of course, one system could be used for any or all of these applications, and endless others. They all have one thing in common: the need to store and retrieve data. The task of the filesystem is to provide a way to store data, in an organised structure, and retrieve it when requested. This is why it is so central to anything else you will ever do with a UNIX system.

1.8.6 Files

The basic 'unit' of the filesystem is, as you may guess, the 'file'. To understand the concept of a file, think of a blank piece of paper. At first, it contains nothing. However, you can write on it, and you can write anything. Similarly, a 'file' may be empty, or it may contain any amount of data. The data it contains can be anything, for example a list of phone numbers, a letter to a customer, or your company's accounts. In effect, a file is just like a piece of paper - the main difference is that it may store any amount of data.

The only other thing to note about files is that each one has a name. Think of this as the title at the top of the piece of paper. For example, one file may be named 'diary', while another may be named 'expenses'. This name is called the 'filename', and is simply used to determine one file from another.

Let's try an exercise now, to get to grips with the concept of files.

Exercise: Use the 'vi' editor to create a new file named 'diary'. (The command you will use for this is 'vi diary' - if you need help with vi, return to the vi tutorial and/or the vi reference guide). In the file, create a few lines which contain your schedule for the next few days, for example:

17th - AM - Continue learning Unix. PM - Draft report for new customers.

18th - AM - Get accounts up to date. PM - Organise payroll details.

When you have finished this, save the file and exit vi. Don't worry about the exact layout or contents of the file - the idea is just to get some text into a file for now!

You've just created a file called 'diary'. It contains some text, which in this case, is your schedule for the next day or two. Note however, that it could have been any text at all. You've given the file a label: 'diary'. This should help you to remember what the file is, and what it contains. Next time you need to see your schedule, you can look up that file. What you've just done is similar to taking a blank piece of paper, labeling it 'diary', and then writing on it.

How can I see what files I have?

In the previous exercise, we just created a new file. As well as that, there may (or may not) be several other files that you can access already. To list these files, use the UNIX command 'ls':

$ ls

Don't forget - the '$' is the prompt displayed by UNIX - you do not type that, but you do press ENTER or RETURN after each command.

The system will respond with a list of files, which should include your new file 'diary'. For example, the list may look a bit like this:

```
$ ls
diary expenses        www-files
dictionary todo
$
```

No matter how many other files is there, your file 'diary' that you created in the previous exercise should be visible. The only case where it may not be is if your list of files is so long that some of them scroll off the top of the screen!

We already know how to create a file, and edit it (both using vi).

Exercise: Using 'vi', load the file 'diary' again. Make a few changes, for example add a line at the start that says "My Schedule for this week". Then save it and exit vi.

For now, we will learn just one more command: If we want to look at a file, but not make any changes to it, we use the command 'cat'. (This is short for 'concatenate' - the reason the command is called this dates back decades, and need not concern us here!). The command 'cat' takes a paramater - the name of the file to view. In this case, let's use the command to look at our diary file:

$ cat diary

The system will respond by displaying the whole of the file 'diary' for you. Depending on what you entered in the file, it will look something like this:

```
$ cat diary
My Schedule for this week
17th - AM - Continue learning Unix.  PM - Draft report for new customers.
18th - AM - Get accounts up to date.  PM - Organise payroll details.
$
```

Ready to move on?

This has been a fairly long segment, but you've learned some of the most useful things you will ever learn about UNIX - it really is the equivalent of learning to read and write. You now know how to create a file, put some text into it, and save it. You know how to re-load it, and make changes, using vi. You know how to look to see what files are there, and how to look at the contents of an existing file. At this stage, have a quick practice by using the following exercise:

Exercise: Create a new file named 'contacts'. In the file, start a simple list of names of your colleagues or friends. Alongside each one, put their phone number or extension number. Don't do too many - just 5 or so will do for now. Then save the file and exit vi. Use the 'ls' command to see the file listed, alongside your 'diary' file, and maybe other files. Use the 'cat' command to look at your 'diary' file, and then use the 'cat' command again to look at your new 'contacts' file.

Why the need to 'log in'?

Many computers that you may have used before are single-user machines. As the name implies, only one user can use the computer at a time. You sit at the computer, do your work, and when you've finished, either someone else uses it, or you switch it off.

UNIX is a multi-user operating system. It can have any number of users all using it at once. To prevent this from causing chaos, each user has their own identification, called a 'user name' or 'user ID'. This identifies them to the system. It is allocated by a system administrator, and is often made up of the user's surname and first initial, such as 'smithj' or 'jsmith'.

Each user has their own 'space' within the system. For instance, they have their own area of disk space to use for storing files.

The process of 'logging in' is simply a way of saying to the operating system, "I am here, and I want to use the computer". It identifies you to the system, so that you may have access to your files, but not other peoples' files. To prevent other users from using your user ID, each user ID also has a password. Only the owner of the user ID should know the password. The system will ask you for the password, and if it is incorrect, you will be denied access to the system. For reference, see Choosing a Password.

How?

Before you log in, the system will only give you one choice: to log in. You cannot perform any other useful tasks on the system before you have done so. Before you log in, the system will display a prompt, which may give you details such as the machine name, and which will prompt you for your user ID. It will look something like what follows below:

london-pro v11.01
login:

In that example, 'london-pro' is the name of an imaginary UNIX system. v11.01 is the version number of this system. All login prompts are different, but yours will probably bear some resemblance to this. The important point is that we are being prompted for our user ID. We will now enter our user ID, which we'll assume is 'smithj', and hit 'RETURN' or 'ENTER' (we'll assume you hit 'RETURN' or 'ENTER' after every command, and we won't mention it again!)

london-pro v11.01

login: **smithj**

(Throughout this tutorial, text that the user enters is in bold, UNIX prompts and responses are not. On your screen, the text you enter will probably not be bold.) Assuming that this user ID has a password (and it should!), the system will prompt you for it now. The screen will look something like this:

london-pro v11.01

login: **smithj**

password:

You may now enter your password. Note that something unusual will happen here: when you enter your password, it will not be displayed on the screen. This is to prevent other users, who may be watching your screen, from seeing it. So even after you've typed it, the screen will still appear the same:

london-pro v11.01

login: **smithj**

password:

After you hit return, one of two things will happen. If you got the password wrong, you will get another go:

london-pro v11.01

login: **smithj**

password:

Incorrect login

london-pro v11.01

login:

When you get the password correct, you will be logged in to the system. This will cause some text to be displayed on your screen. The exact text is different on each system, and usually includes all manner of copyright messages, restricted rights legends, version numbers, etc. Finally, there may be a welcome message of some sort. An example is shown below:

london-pro v11.01

login: **smithj**

password:

Copyright 1986-2000 SomeVendor

This system is intended for the use of employees of SomeCompany.

$

In reality, your system may display more text than this, and the details will be different, but the overall idea will be similar.

The only thing likely to be drastically different is if you are using this user ID for the first time. In that case, you may be requested to changed your password before you will be fully logged on.

You should change your UNIX or Linux password regularly, and the system may even force you to change it from time to time. Also, is likely that it will ask you to change it when you first use your user ID (if so, you will go straight to step 4 below). You may like to read the tutorial choosing a password before continuing with this document.

To change your password on UNIX or Linux systems, follow these steps:

1. Log into the system using your old password, if you are not already logged in.
2. At the prompt, use the command:

   $ passwd

3. Usually, you will be asked to enter your old password first. This is a security measure, designed to help prevent someone else from changing your password:

   $ passwd

   Enter old password:

   Note that when you enter your old password, it will not be displayed.

4. (Note that, if you are being forced to change your password as part of logging in, you will come straight to this stage). You will be asked to enter your new password:

   $ passwd

   Enter old password:

   Enter new password:

   Note that when you enter your new password, it will not be displayed. Choosing a good password is not as simple as just thinking of a word - for a useful guide, have a look at Choosing a password.

5. You will then be asked to re-enter your new password. This is designed to make sure that you did not make any typing mistakes when typing your new password:

   $ passwd

   Enter old password:

   Enter new password:

   Re-enter new password:

6. You should then be informed that the change has been successful, and be returned to the prompt:

   $ passwd

   Enter old password:

   Enter new password:

   Re-enter new password:

   Password updated successfully.

   $

   (Note that if you are changing your password as part of the log on procedure, the log on procedure will continue now).

   If anything goes wrong (for instance, when you entered the password twice, there was a mismatch), you will be notified, and the password will remain unchanged. You may be given the option of trying again.

   If all went well, your new password is now in effect, and your old password will no longer work.

1.8.7 Logging Out

Normally, you won't log out until you have finished using the UNIX® system. However, we cover it here as it logically pairs up with the subject of logging in.

Why the need to 'log out'?

As we've already said, the reason for logging in in the first place, is to identify you to the system, so it knows which files and areas to give you access to. It allows you access to the areas you are supposed to have access to, and blocks users from each others' areas.

Logging out is the opposite - you are telling the system that you have finished using it for the time being, and that you no longer require access to your files at this time. It is very important that you log out when you have finished using the system, and preferably every time you leave your computer or terminal unattended. If you leave yourself logged in, then someone else may wander up to the terminal you have been using, and have access to all your files. They may read, modify, or delete them. They may send emails out from your user ID. They may even attempt to hack or damage the system from your user ID and this is your responsibility. By logging out, you prevent anyone else from using your user ID.

How?

There are several ways to log out. They all achieve the same thing - you will understand the difference between then later on, but for now you must simply make sure that you do log out every time you finish with the system.

The best way is to use the command 'logout' and any prompt. For example:

$ logout

The system will usually give you some sort of 'farewell' message, and then will return to the login screen to allow someone else to log in. Your exact 'farewell' message varies, and you may or may not get a message at all. For example:

$ logout

Thank you for using london-pro - you are now logging out.

london-pro v11.01

login:

Here you can see that the user has been logged out, and after a brief message, the system is prompting the next login request. At this stage, you may not access any of your files or programs - you are no longer logged into the system.

We said there were several ways to log out. We just saw the 'logout' command. Two other ways to log out are (1) - to use the 'exit' command, and (2) - to press 'CTRL D'. These both amount to the same thing. For now, the main point is to remember to log out when you are finished - leaving yourself logged in is the number one mistake to be avoided!

A filename can contain most keyboard characters. However, there are one or two restrictions, and a few things that should be avoided to make life easier:

- You may never use a slash (/) in a filename.
- Avoid using apostrophe ('), quotes (“), asterisk (*), plus (+), and spaces in a filename. Although valid, these characters make it more difficult to use the filename, for reasons we will see later on.

As a simple rule, it is best to use a mixture of letters and numbers, with spaces replaced by hyphens (-).

Also, the full-stop (.) is often used, and the part of the filename after the full stop (sometimes called the extension) is sometimes used to indicate the type of data. For example, a text file may have an extension of .text or .txt - however, don't worry too much about extensions for now. Look at the following, which are 'good' filenames, which don't use any illegal or difficult characters:

letter-to-John

report-14thMarch-2001.text

Website.html

Contacts

Note that filenames are case sensitive. This means that the upper case and lower case versions of any letter are considered to be different. So, you could have two files, one named 'contacts', and another named 'Contacts'. As far as the system is concerned, they are two different files. Of course, you should usually try not to have two files with such similar names, to avoid confusion!

1.8.8 Moving a File

Sometimes, it is useful to change the name of a file. For instance, if you have a file named 'diary', which was your schedule for last week, you may now want to rename it to 'old-diary' or 'diary-09-April-2001'.

Any file can be renamed by using the command 'mv' (short for 'move'). This command takes two parameters: the old (current) name of the file you wish to move, and its new name. For example:

$ mv diary old-diary

Exercise: Use the command 'ls', and make sure you can see your file 'diary' from the previous segment. Then use the command 'mv' to change the filename to 'old-diary' (without the apostrophes!). Then use the command 'ls' again, to make sure that the name has changed as expected. Use the 'cat' command to look at the file with the new name: The contents of the file should be completely un-changed, as the filename is just a label for the data - the data itself does not change. Then use the 'mv' command to rename the file back to its original name: 'diary'. Use 'ls' once more to make sure the file is back to its original name.

You have just renamed a file to a new name. You saw how the data itself stayed the same, only the filename changed. You then renamed the file again, to get it back to its original name.

1.8.9 Copying a File

When we renamed the file in the previous section, there was still only one copy of the file. Its name changed twice, but the data stayed the same. In this section, we'll find out how to take one file, and make a copy of it, which will be stored under a different filename.

The command to do this is 'cp' (short for 'copy'). This takes two parameters: The name of the file to copy, and the name of the new copy of the file. For example:

$ cp diary new-diary

This command would take the file 'diary', and create a new copy of the data in the file, this time stored with the name 'new-diary'.

Exercise: Use the command shown above to copy the file 'diary' to a new file named 'new-diary'. Use the 'ls' command to list the files in your directory. You should see the file 'new-diary' and the original file, 'diary'.

The difference between 'mv' and 'cp' is that 'mv' just renamed an existing file. In the end, there was still only one file, with a different name. In the case of 'cp', a new copy of the file was created, so that after the command, there are two files. The new file is an exact copy of the old file.

Exercise: Using vi, make some changes to the file 'new-diary'. Then save the file, and exit vi. Use the 'cat' command to view first the file 'new-diary', then the file 'diary'.

Note how you can now make changes to one file independently of the other. In other words, although the 'cp' command created an exact copy of the original, the new file is then a separate file like any other.

Project: A Simple (but useful) Electronic Diary

As an exercise, create an electronic diary, which you can use to store your schedule, one week at a time. This will use many of the skills you have learned so far, and will let you see how you already know enough to use UNIX to help with every day tasks. Follow these steps:

1. Use vi to create a file named 'weekly-diary-template'. The file should look something like this:

   My Schedule for Week Commencing:

Day	AM	PM	Evening
Mon			
Tue			
Wed			
Thur			
Fri			
Sat			
Sun			

2. Use the 'cp' command to make a new copy of the file, which should be named after the date of the Monday in the current week, for example '09-April-2001'. The command may be something like:

   $ cp weekly-diary-template diary-09-April-2001

   You should now have two files: the template, and the new copy of the template, which is named after the current week.

3. Use vi to fill in your schedule. Only make changes to the version of the file including the date. Leave the template as it is, ready to create next week's diary when you need it.

4. Whenever you need to start a new week's diary, use a similar 'cp' command. Again, copy the template file to a new file containing the date of the Monday in that week. For example, the following week, you may use:

   $ cp weekly-diary-template diary-16-April-2001

Start using the electronic diary on a regular basis. This will give you good practice in vi, and basic file management commands.

1.8.10 Using the Shell

Before starting this page of the tutorial, ensure that you are logged in. Refer to the section Logging In if you need guidance for this.

When you are logged in, you see a prompt. This may be a dollar sign, a hash sign, or even some text.

Examples are:

$

#

london-pro>

Throughout this tutorial, we'll use the dollar sign as the prompt. Whatever your prompt symbol is, it means the same thing: the system is prompting you to give it a command. First, just try hitting return a few times. You will see that each time you hit return, the prompt is displayed again:

$

$

$

We will now try some basic commands, just to get the feel of the way the system works. Let's start by asking the system for the current date and time. The command to do this is simply 'date'.

$ **date**

Tue Feb 20 11:28:18 GMT 2001

$

(As always in this tutorial, the command you enter is shown in bold. Everything else is the system's response). Don't worry about remembering the specific commands at this stage - we're just trying to get used to the way the system responds.

There are a few things to notice here. Firstly, when we typed 'date', it appeared on the screen just after the prompt. Nothing happened until after we pressed RETURN or ENTER after the 'date' command. The RETURN or ENTER key says to the system, "I've finished typing my command, now go and process it, and come back to me with a response". The system does just that. It checks to see if it recognises the command. If it does, it processes it. This is often known as 'running' the command. Many commands produce some sort of response (known as 'output' from the command). In this case, the 'date' command produces some output: the current date and time.

After you hit RETURN or ENTER, the system runs the command, and the output is displayed. Then, if the command has finished, the prompt is displayed again, ready for your next command.

If you run another command, your old command and its output will still be visible on the screen for a while. For example, run the 'date' command again. You will get a new date and time (which should be a few seconds or minutes later than the previous one, of course). You will still be able to see the previous 'date' command and its output on the screen. For example, your screen may now look like this:

$ **date**

Tue Feb 20 11:28:18 GMT 2001

$ **date**

Tue Feb 20 11:32:17 GMT 2001

$

Let's try a different command: 'hostname'. This command asks the system to tell us its name - this can be useful if you use more than one system, and get confused about which one you are using! If you run it, your screen will look something like this:

$ **date**

Tue Feb 20 11:28:18 GMT 2001

$ **date**

Tue Feb 20 11:32:17 GMT 2001

$ **hostname**

london-pro

$

The output of the 'hostname' command is the name of the system you are using, which will have been set up by your system administrators.

Your screen can only fit so many commands and their output on it. Eventually, old commands will start to 'scroll off' the top of the screen.

Let's try one more command: 'clear'. This command clears your screen, and removes all previous commands and their output, leaving you with just the prompt:

$

When you interact with the system in this way, you are actually interacting with the 'shell'. The shell's job is to take commands from you, and pass them onto the central part of the UNIX system. When the UNIX system responds to the command from the shell, the shell passes the response back to you, by displaying it on your screen. The shell is like an interpretter, translating commands you give it ready for use by the system, and translating the system's response back to you. This concept of a 'shell' can be difficult to understand at first, but for now it really doesn't matter. You have already learned how to make requests to the system, and see the responses.

By now, you will be ready to see some more useful commands, and learn about how the system can help you to store and organise your data.

This may be a good point at which to have a break. Bookmark this page in your browser, so you can come back to it later on. When you are ready, we will move on to look at some more useful commands.

1.8.11 Running vi

To run vi and create a new file, simply run the command 'vi' from any shell prompt:

$ vi

Alternatively, to load an existing text file into vi, run the command 'vi [filename]', from the shell prompt:

$ vi myfile.txt

Your file will be loaded into vi, and the cursor will be placed at the beginning of the first line. Note that an empty line is shown as a tilde (~).

1.8.12 Command Mode and Insert Mode

VI is different from many editors, in that it has two main modes of operation: command mode, and insert mode. This is the cause of much of the confusion when a new user is learning vi, but it is actually very simple to understand.

When you first load the editor, you will be placed into command mode. To switch into insert mode, simply press the 'i' key. Although nothing will change on the screen to indicate the new mode, any thing that you type from now on will appear in the screen - this is what you are used to if you have ever used any other editor, or word processor. Try typing a few lines of text. When you press 'return' or 'enter' a new line will be created, and you may continue typing.

When you have finished typing, you may return to command mode. This is done by pressing your 'Esc' key. In command mode, key presses do not appear on the screen, but instead are used to indicate various commands to vi.

At first, you may often mistake command mode and insert mode. For example, you may think you are in insert mode, and start typing your text, when in fact you are in command mode, and each keypress you make will issue a command to vi. Be careful - you may accidentally modify or delete parts of your file.

If you are unsure which mode you are in, press 'Esc'. If you were in insert mode, you will be returned to command mode. If you were already in command mode, you will be left in command mode (possibly with a 'beep', to indicate that you were already in command mode).

An Exercise

Try this simple exercise to get used to the two modes:

1. Load vi (if you haven't already), by typing:

$ **vi**

(don't forget - the $ is the system's prompt, and may be different on your system. You only type the 'vi' part, shown in bold.)

The screen should show a blank file, with each blank line represented by a tilde (~), for example:

~

~

~

~

~

By default you are in command mode.

2. Switch to insert mode, by pressing the 'i' key. Then type some text, using ENTER or RETURN to start new lines. For example:

Hello. This is my first session in the vi editor.

This is the second line of text.

~

~

~

3. When you have finished entering your sample text, press 'Esc' to return to command mode.
4. Now we will learn a useful command: to save the file. The command for this is ':w' (note the colon before the 'w'). After the 'w', put a space, and the name you want to store the file as. For example:

   :w firstfile

Type it now. Notice how the text ':w' appears at the bottom on the screen. When you have finished the command, press ENTER or RETURN. You should see a confirmation that the file has been saved, which may include the number of lines in the file, and possibly the file size.

5. To finish this simple introduction to the editor, we will learn one final command: How to close the editor. The command for this is ':q' (again, with a colon before the 'q'). Don't forget you need to be in command mode. If you're not already in command mode, or you're not sure which mode you're in, press 'Esc' now. Then issue the command:

   :q

   You should be returned to the UNIX prompt.

A FINAL NOTE:

Sometimes, you may have made changes to a file that you do not want to save. This may be because you have decided the changes are incorrect, or you have become confused using vi (not usual at first!), and incorrectly made some changes, maybe by typing into command mode instead of insert mode. To exit vi without saving, and ignoring any warnings about unsaved data, use a variation of the ':q' command, with an exclamation mark after it:

:q!

This will return you to the prompt, without saving any changes to the file, and with no warnings about unsaved data. Use this command carefully.

Ready to move on?

Before you move onto the next segment, it may be worth just playing with what you've already learned. Practice loading vi, either with an existing file, or with no filename so it creates a new file. Try going into insert mode, inserting some text, going back into command mode, saving the text, going back into insert mode, etc. You should be able to do the following:

- Load vi with no parameter, so it creates a new file.
- Load vi with a filename, so it loads that file. Try loading the file you saved in the exercise above.
- Switch into insert mode using the 'i' key, and insert some text.
- Switch into command mode using the 'Esc' key, and save the file using the ':w filename' command.
- Exit vi using the ':q' or ':q!' commands.

The cursor keys

Probably the most basic and most commonly used commands are those used to move the cursor around the screen. The cursor is the 'pointer' to the current position in the text, and is usually represented as a flashing underscore character.

To move the cursor around the screen, you must be in command mode. On some systems, you may use the standard 'cursor keys' on your keyboard to move the cursor. However, on many systems, this will not work. This mainly due to historical reasons, dating back to when not all terminals had cursor keys. If cursor keys do not work on your system, then use the following keys instead:

h - Cursor left

j - Cursor down

k - Cursor up

l - Cursor right

This may seem obscure at first, but you'll be surprised how quickly you get used to using these keys - you may even find yourself using them on terminals that do have working cursor keys!

Exercise: Load vi. Create a new file. Enter a few lines of text. Then go into command mode, and practice moving the cursor around the screen. Do your 'real' cursor keys work? Or do you have to use the other keys listed above? Try the keys above anyway. Go back into insert mode and insert some more text. Note that you can insert text wherever you put the cursor. Don't forget to go back into command mode before trying to move the cursor again. When you've finished, go into command mode, and use the ':q!' command to exit vi.

This exercise may also help you to understand the difference between command mode and insert mode better. When you are in insert mode, pressing any key, including h, j, k or l does what you'd expect:- it puts that character in the file in the current position. However, in command mode, the keys have a different function - to move the cursor. Nearly all keys have a different function in command mode - see our reference guide for the complete list. A common mistake for newcomers to the editor is to start typing when in command mode. Of course, the exact consequences of this depend on which keys you press, but this nearly always has undesirable results!

1.8.13 Deleting a Character

While you are in insert mode, you can delete a character that you have just typed by using the 'backspace' key - this is similar to most other editors and word processors. But there is a difference: You may only delete characters that you have entered in this session of insert mode. To understand this, try the following exercise:

Exercise: Load vi, and go into insert mode. Enter the following text: 'abcdefg'. Then press 'Esc' to return to command mode. Move the cursor back, using the left arrow or 'h' key, until the cursor points to the letter 'd'. Then press 'i' to go back into insert mode, and type 'hijklmn'. Now try to delete some of the characters using the backspace key. You will find that you can delete the characters that you have entered since being insert mode, but not those entered previously. So the 'abc' will remain undeleted. When you've finished, go into command mode, and use the ':q!' command to exit vi.

So how do we delete any characters that were entered in previous insert mode sessions? The answer is to go back into command mode, place the cursor over the character to be deleted, then press the 'x' key. This causes the character under the cursor to be deleted from the file. Any characters to the right of it will be shifted left one to take its place.

Exercise: Load vi, and go into insert mode. Enter the text '0123456789'. Then return to command mode, and use the cursor keys to go back until the cursor is pointing to the character '3'. Press 'x'. What happens? Press 'x' twice more. You can now see how to delete a character in any position. When you've finished, go into command mode, and use the ':q!' command to exit vi.

1.8.14 Repeating a Command

What if we wanted to delete a whole batch of characters? For example, if we had 20 characters to delete, it would take 20 keypresses. vi provides a simple way of performing this - in fact, many commands can automatically be run a given number of times.

To repeat a command, simply type the number of times to run the command before the command itself. For example, to delete 20 characters from a file, starting from the current position, using the command '20x'. Note that the command does not appear at the bottom of the screen, so you have to keep track of what you're typing yourself.

Exercise: Load vi, and go into insert mode. Enter a few lines of text, each containing at 30-40 characters, or more. Then return to command mode. Move the cursor to the beginning of the first line, then (still in command mode), type '20x'. Note what happens. Note that other commands, including cursor commands can be repeated in the same way. Go down the the second line in your file, and type '5l'. Notice how the cursor move 5 places to the right (or to the end of the line, whichever comes first). When you've finished, go into command mode, and use the ':q!' command to exit vi.

1.8.15 Deleting a Line

Just one more command to learn for now. We've seen how to delete a single character with the 'x' command. There is a quicker way to delete an entire line: with the 'dd' command.

Exercise: Load vi, and go into insert mode. Enter several lines of text, preferably at least 10. Each can just be a few characters long. Then return to command mode. Move the cursor up to the top of the screen (hint: use repeat commands like '20k' to make this easier.) Delete the line the cursor is on by pressing 'dd'. Then try the repeat version of that command - for example, type '5dd' to delete the next five lines. When you've finished, go into command mode, and use the ':q!' command to exit vi.

1.9 LINUX

Linux (commonly pronounced /•l•n•ks/ LIN-•ks in American English, also pronounced /•l•n•ks/ LIN-ooks in Europe and Canada) refers to the family of Unix-like computer operating systems using the Linux kernel. Linux can be installed on a wide variety of computer hardware, ranging from mobile phones, tablet computers and video game consoles, to mainframes and supercomputers. Linux is predominantly known for its use in servers; in 2009 it held a server market share ranging between 20-40%. Most desktop computers run either Microsoft Windows or Mac OS X, with Linux having anywhere from a low of an estimated 1-2% of the desktop market to a high of an estimated 4.8%. However, desktop use of Linux has become increasingly popular in recent years, partly owing to the popular Ubuntu, Fedora, Mint, and openSUSE distributions and the emergence of netbooks and smartphones running an embedded Linux.

The development of Linux is one of the most prominent examples of free and open source software collaboration; typically all the underlying source code can be used, freely modified, and redistributed, both commercially and non-commercially, by anyone under licenses such as the GNU General Public License. Typically Linux is packaged in a format known as a Linux distribution for desktop and server use. Linux distributions include the Linux kernel and all of the supporting software required to run a complete system, such as utilities and libraries, the X Window System, the GNOME and KDE desktop environments, and the Apache HTTP Server. Commonly used applications with desktop Linux systems include the Mozilla Firefox web-browser, the OpenOffice.org office application suite and the GIMP image editor.

The name "Linux" comes from the Linux kernel, originally written in 1991 by Linus Torvalds. The main supporting user space system tools and libraries from the GNU Project (announced in 1983 by Richard Stallman) are the basis for the Free Software Foundation's preferred name GNU/Linux

Figure 1.17: Linux

1.9.1 History

History of Linux began in 1991 with the commencement of a personal project by a Finnish student, Linus Torvalds, to create a new operating system kernel. Since then the resulting Linux kernel has been marked by constant growth throughout its history. Since the initial release of its source code in 1991, it has grown from a small number of C files under a license prohibiting commercial distribution to its state in 2009 of over 370 megabytes of source under the GNU General Public License

1.9.2 Events Leading to Creation

The Unix operating system was conceived and implemented in the 1960s and first released in 1970. Its availability and portability caused it to be widely adopted, copied and modified by academic institutions and businesses. Its design became influential to authors of other systems.

In 1983, Richard Stallman started the GNU project with the goal of creating a free UNIX-like operating system. As part of this work, he wrote the GNU General Public License (GPL). By the early 1990s there was almost enough available software to create a full operating system. However, the GNU kernel, called Hurd, failed to attract enough attention from developers leaving GNU incomplete.

Another free operating system project in the 1980s was the Berkeley Software Distribution (BSD). This was developed by UC Berkeley from the 6th edition of Unix from AT&T. Since BSD contained Unix code that AT&T owned, AT&T filed a lawsuit (USL v. BSDi) in the early 1990s against the University of California. This strongly limited the development and adoption of BSD.

MINIX, a Unix-like system intended for academic use, was released by Andrew S. Tanenbaum in 1987. While source code for the system was available, modification and redistribution were restricted. In addition, MINIX's 16-bit design was not well adapted to the 32-bit features of the increasingly cheap and popular Intel 386 architecture for personal computers.

These factors and the lack of a widely-adopted, free kernel provided the impetus for Torvalds's starting his project. He has stated that if either the GNU or 386BSD kernels were available at the time, he likely would not have written his own

In 1991, in Helsinki, Linus Torvalds began a project that later became the Linux kernel. It was initially a terminal emulator, which Torvalds used to access the large UNIX servers of the university. He wrote the program specifically for the hardware he was using and independent of an operating system because he wanted to use the functions of his new PC with an 80386 processor. Development was done on MINIX using the GNU C compiler, which is still the main choice for compiling Linux today (although the code can be built with other compilers, such as the Intel C Compiler).

Richard Stallman left, founder of the GNU Project, and Linus Torvalds right, principal author of the Linux Kernal

1.9.3 UNIX

The Unix operating system was conceived and implemented in 1969 at AT&T's Bell Laboratories in the United States by Ken Thompson, Dennis Ritchie, Douglas McIlroy, and Joe Ossanna. Unix derived its name as a joke and reference to an experimental operating system that was slow and ineffective called MULTICS. It was first released in 1971 and was initially entirely written in assembly language, a common practice at the time. Later, in a key pioneering approach in 1973, Unix was re-written in the programming language C by Dennis Ritchie (with exceptions to the kernel and I/O). The availability of an operating system written in a high-level language allowed easier portability to different computer platforms. With a legal glitch forcing AT&T to license the operating system's source code, Unix quickly grew and became widely adopted by academic institutions and businesses.

1.9.4 GNU

The GNU Project, started in 1983 by Richard Stallman, had the goal of creating a "complete Unix-compatible software system" composed entirely of free software. Work began in 1984. Later, in 1985, Stallman started the Free Software Foundation and wrote the GNU General Public License (GNU GPL) in 1989. By the early 1990s, many of the programs required in an operating system (such as libraries, compilers, text editors, a Unix shell, and a windowing system) were completed, although low-level elements such as device drivers, daemons, and the kernel were stalled and incomplete. Linus Torvalds has said that if the GNU kernel had been available at the time (1991), he would not have decided to write his own.

1.9.5 MINIX

MINIX was an inexpensive minimal Unix-like operating system, designed for education in computer science, written by Andrew S. Tanenbaum. Starting with version 3, MINIX is free and redesigned also for "serious" use.

Andrew S. Tanenbaum, author of the MINIX operating system

In 1991 while attending the University of Helsinki, Torvalds, curious about the operating systems and frustrated by the licensing of MINIX limiting it to educational use only (which prevented any commercial use) began to work on his own operating system which eventually became the Linux kernel.

Torvalds began the development of the Linux kernel on MINIX and applications written for MINIX were also used on Linux. Later Linux matured and it became possible for Linux to be developed under itself. Also GNU applications replaced all MINIX ones because, with code from the GNU system freely available, it was advantageous if this could be used with the fledgling operating system. Code licensed under the GNU GPL can be used in other projects, so long as they also are released under the same or a compatible license. In order to make the Linux available for commercial use, Torvalds initiated a switch from his original license (which prohibited commercial redistribution) to the GNU GPL. Developers worked to integrate GNU components with Linux to make a fully functional and free operating system.

1.9.6 Commercial and Popular Uptake

Today Linux distributions are used in numerous domains, from embedded systems to supercomputers, and have secured a place in server installations with the popular LAMP application stack. Use of Linux distributions in home and enterprise desktops has been expanding. They have also gained popularity with various local and national governments. The federal government of Brazil is well known for its support for Linux. News of the Russian military creating their own Linux distribution has also surfaced, and has come to fruition as the G.H.ost Project. The Indian state of Kerala has gone to the extent of mandating for all state high schools to run Linux on their computers. China uses Linux exclusively as the operating system for its Loongson processor family to achieve technology independence. In Spain some regions have developed their own Linux distributions, which are widely used in education and official institutions, like gnuLinEx in Extremadura and Guadalinex in Andalusia. Portugal is also using its own Linux distribution Caixa Mágica, used in the Magalhães netbook and the e-escola government program. France and Germany have also taken steps towards the adoption of Linux.

Linux distributions have also become popular with the newly founded netbook market, with many devices such as the ASUS Eee PC and Acer Aspire One shipping with customized Linux distributions installed.

1.9.7 Current Development

Torvalds continues to direct the development of the kernel. Stallman heads the Free Software Foundation, which in turn supports the GNU components. Finally, individuals and corporations develop third-party non-GNU components. These third-party components comprise a vast body of work and may include both kernel modules and user applications and libraries. Linux vendors and communities combine and distribute the kernel, GNU components, and non-GNU components, with additional package management software in the form of Linux distributions.

1.9.8 Design

A Linux-based system is a modular Unix-like operating system. It derives much of its basic design from principles established in Unix during the 1970s and 1980s. Such a system uses a monolithic kernel, the Linux kernel, which handles process control, networking, and peripheral and file system access. Device drivers are either integrated directly with the kernel or added as modules loaded while the system is running.

Separate projects that interface with the kernel provide much of the system's higher-level functionality. The GNU userland is an important part of most Linux-based systems, providing the most common implementation of the C library, a popular shell, and many of the common Unix tools which carry out many basic operating system tasks. The graphical user interface (or GUI) used by most Linux systems is built on top of an implementation of the X Window System.

1.9.9 User Interface

Users can control a Linux-based system through a command line interface (or CLI), a graphical user interface (or GUI), or through controls attached to the associated hardware (this is common for embedded systems). For desktop systems, the default mode is usually graphical user interface, where the CLI is available through terminal emulator windows or on a separate virtual console.

On desktop machines, KDE, GNOME, and Xfce are the most popular user interfaces, though a variety of additional user interfaces exist. Most popular user interfaces run on top of the X Window System (often simply called “X”), which provides network transparency, enabling a graphical application running on one machine to be displayed and controlled from another.

Other GUIs include X window managers such as FVWM, Enlightenment, and Window Maker. The window manager provides a means to control the placement and appearance of individual application windows, and interacts with the X Window System. This is a more minimalist goal than KDE, GNOME et al., which are termed desktop environments.

A Linux system typically provides a CLI through a shell, which is the traditional way of interacting with a Unix system. A Linux distribution specialized for servers may use the CLI as its only interface.

Most low-level Linux components, including the GNU userland, use the CLI exclusively. The CLI is particularly suited for automation of repetitive or delayed tasks, and provides very simple inter-process communication. A graphical terminal emulator program is often used to access the CLI from a Linux desktop.

1.9.10 Development

A summarized history of Unix-like operating systems showing Linux's origins. Note that despite similar architectural designs and concepts being shared as part of the POSIX standard, Linux does not share any non-free source code with the original Unix or MINIX.

The primary difference between Linux and many other popular contemporary operating systems is that the Linux kernel and other components are free and open source software. Linux is not the only such operating system, although it is by far the most widely used. Some free and open source software licenses are based on the principle of copyleft, a kind of reciprocity: any work derived from a copyleft piece of software must also be copyleft itself. The most common free software license, the GNU GPL, is a form of copyleft, and is used for the Linux kernel and many of the components from the GNU project.

Linux based distributions are intended by developers for interoperability with other operating systems and established computing standards. Linux systems adhere to POSIX, SUS, ISO, and ANSI standards where possible, although to date only one Linux distribution has been POSIX.1 certified, Linux-FT.

Free software projects, although developed in a collaborative fashion, are often produced independently of each other. The fact that the software licenses explicitly permit redistribution, however, provides a basis for larger scale projects that collect the software produced by stand-alone projects and make it available all at once in the form of a Linux distribution.

A Linux distribution, commonly called a "distro", is a project that manages a remote collection of system software and application software packages available for download and installation through a network connection. This allows the user to adapt the operating system to his/her specific needs. Distributions are maintained by individuals, loose knit teams, volunteer organizations, and commercial entities. A distribution is responsible for the default configuration of the installed Linux kernel, general system security, and more generally integration of the different software packages into a coherent whole. Distributions typically use a package manager such as Synaptic, YAST, or Portage to install, remove and update all of a system's software from one central location.

1.9.11 Community

A distribution is largely driven by its developer and user communities. Some vendors develop and fund their distributions on a volunteer basis, Debian being a well-known example. Others maintain a community version of their commercial distributions, as Red Hat does with Fedora.

In many cities and regions, local associations known as Linux Users Groups (LUGs) seek to promote their preferred distribution and by extension free software. They hold meetings and provide free demonstrations, training, technical support, and operating system installation to new users. Many Internet communities also provide support to Linux users and developers. Most distributions and free software / open source projects have IRC chatrooms or newsgroups. Online forums are another means for support, with notable examples being LinuxQuestions.org and the Gentoo forums. Linux distributions host mailing lists; commonly there will be a specific topic such as usage or development for a given list.

There are several technology websites with a Linux focus. Print magazines on Linux often include cover disks including software or even complete Linux distributions. Although Linux distributions are generally available without charge, several large corporations sell, support, and contribute to the development of the components of the system and of free software. An analysis of the Linux kernel showed 75 percent of the code from December 2008 to January 2010 was developed by programmers working for corporations, leaving about 18 percent to the traditional, open source community. Some of the major corporations that contribute include Dell, IBM, HP, Oracle, Sun Microsystems, Novell, and Nokia. A number of corporations, notably Red Hat, have built their entire business around Linux distributions.

The free software licenses, on which the various software packages of a distribution built on the Linux kernel are based, explicitly accommodate and encourage commercialization; the relationship between a Linux distribution as a whole and individual vendors may be seen as symbiotic. One common business model of commercial suppliers is charging for support, especially for business users. A number of companies also offer a specialized business version of their distribution, which adds proprietary support packages and tools to administer higher numbers of installations or to simplify administrative tasks. Another business model is to give away the software in order to sell hardware.

1.9.12 Programming on Linux

Most Linux distributions support dozens of programming languages. The most common collection of utilities for building both Linux applications and operating system programs is found within the GNU toolchain, which includes the GNU Compiler Collection (GCC) and the GNU build system. Amongst others, GCC provides compilers for Ada, C, C++, Java, and Fortran. Proprietary compilers for Linux include the Intel C++ Compiler, Sun Studio, and IBM XL C/C++ Compiler. BASIC is supported in such forms as Gambas, FreeBASIC, and XBasic.

Most distributions also include support for PHP, Perl, Ruby, Python and other dynamic languages. While not as common, Linux also supports C# via the Mono project, sponsored by Novell, C# via Vala and Scheme. A number of Java Virtual Machines and development kits run on Linux, including the original Sun Microsystems JVM (HotSpot), and IBM's J2SE RE, as well as many open-source projects like Kaffe.

The two main frameworks for developing graphical applications are those of GNOME and KDE. These projects are based on the GTK+ and Qt widget toolkits, respectively, which can also be used independently of the larger framework. Both support a wide variety of languages. There are a number of Integrated development environments available including Anjuta, Code::Blocks, Eclipse, KDevelop, Lazarus, MonoDevelop, NetBeans, Qt Creator and Omnis Studio while the long-established editors Vim and Emacs remain popular.

1.9.13 Uses

As well as those designed for general purpose use on desktops and servers, distributions may be specialized for different purposes including: computer architecture support, embedded systems, stability, security, localization to a specific region or language, targeting of specific user groups, support for real-time applications, or commitment to a given desktop environment. Furthermore, some distributions deliberately include only free software. Currently, over three hundred distributions are actively developed, with about a dozen distributions being most popular for general-purpose use.

Linux is a widely ported operating system kernel. The Linux kernel runs on a highly diverse range of computer architectures: in the hand-held ARM-based iPAQ and the mainframe IBM System z9, System z10 in devices ranging from mobile phones to supercomputers. Specialized distributions exist for less mainstream architectures. The ELKS kernel fork can run on Intel 8086 or Intel 80286 16-bit microprocessors, while the µClinux kernel fork may run on systems without a memory management unit. The kernel also runs on architectures that were only ever intended to use a manufacturer-created operating system, such as Macintosh computers (with both PowerPC and Intel processors), PDAs, video game consoles, portable music players, and mobile phones.

There are several industry associations and hardware conferences devoted to maintaining and improving support for diverse hardware under Linux, such as FreedomHEC.

The popularity of Linux on standard desktops (and laptops) has been increasing over the years. Currently most distributions include a graphical user environment. The two most popular such environments are GNOME and KDE, both of which are mature and support a wide variety of languages.

The performance of Linux on the desktop has been a controversial topic; for example in 2007 Con Kolivas accused the Linux community of favoring performance on servers. He quit Linux kernel development because he was frustrated with this lack of focus on the desktop, and then gave a "tell all" interview on the topic. Since then a significant effort has been expended improving the desktop experience. Projects such as upstart aim for a faster boot time. There are several companies that do port their own or other companies' games to Linux.

Many types of applications available for Microsoft Windows and Mac OS X are also available for Linux. Commonly, either a free software application will exist which does the functions of an application found on another operating system, or that application will have a version that works on Linux (such as Skype). Furthermore, the Wine project provides a Windows compatibility layer to run unmodified Windows applications on Linux. CrossOver is a proprietary solution based on the open source Wine project that supports running Windows versions of Microsoft Office, Intuit applications such as Quicken and QuickBooks, Adobe Photoshop versions through CS2, and many popular games such as World of Warcraft and Team Fortress 2. In other cases, where there is no Linux port of some software in areas such as desktop publishing and professional audio, there is equivalent software available on Linux.

Many popular applications are available for a wide variety of operating systems. For example Mozilla Firefox, and OpenOffice.org have downloadable versions for all major operating systems. Furthermore, some applications were initially developed for Linux (such as Pidgin, and GIMP) and, due to their popularity, were ported to other operating systems (including Windows and Mac OS X).

A growing number of proprietary desktop applications are also supported on Linux, see List of proprietary software for Linux. In the field of animation and visual effects, most high end software, such as AutoDesk Maya, Softimage XSI and Apple Shake, is available for Linux, Windows and/or Mac OS X.

The collaborative nature of free software development allows distributed teams to localize Linux distributions for use in locales where localizing proprietary systems would not be cost-effective. For example the Sinhalese language version of the Knoppix distribution was available significantly before Microsoft Windows XP was translated to Sinhalese. In this case the Lanka Linux User Group played a major part in developing the localized system by combining the knowledge of university professors, linguists, and local developers.

Installing new software in Linux is typically done through the use of package managers such as Synaptic Package Manager, PackageKit, and Yum Extender. While major Linux distributions have extensive repositories (tens of thousands of packages), not all the software that can run on Linux is available from the official repositories. Alternatively, users can install packages from unofficial repositories, download pre-compiled packages directly from websites, or compile the source code by themselves. All these methods come with different degrees of difficulty, compiling the source code is in general considered a challenging process for new Linux users, but it's hardly needed in modern distributions.

Servers, mainframes and supercomputers

Figure 1.18 Servers designed for Linux

Linux distributions have long been used as server operating systems, and have risen to prominence in that area; Netcraft reported in September 2006 that eight of the ten most reliable internet hosting companies ran Linux distributions on their web servers. (Since June 2008, Linux distributions represented five of the top ten, FreeBSD three of ten, and Microsoft two of ten; since February 2010, Linux distributions represented six of the top ten, FreeBSD two of ten, and Microsoft one of ten.

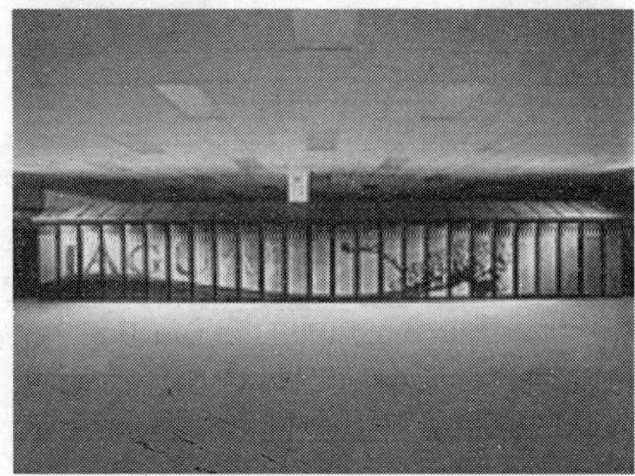

Figure 1.19: National Laboratory's Jaguar supercomputer

The Oak Ridge National Laboratory's Jaguar supercomputer, since November 2009 the world's fastest supercomputer. It uses the Cray Linux Environment as its operating system. Linux distributions are the cornerstone of the LAMP server-software combination (Linux, Apache, MySQL, Perl/PHP/ Python) which has achieved popularity among developers, and which is one of the more common platforms for website hosting.

Linux distributions have become increasingly popular on mainframes in the last decade due to pricing, compared to other mainframe operating systems. In December 2009, computer giant IBM reported that it would predominantly market and sell mainframe-based Enterprise Linux Server.

Linux distributions are also commonly used as operating systems for supercomputers: since June 2010, out of the top 500 systems, 455 (91%) run a Linux distribution. Linux was also selected as the operating system for the world's most powerful supercomputer, IBM's Sequoia which will become operational in 2011.

1.9.14 Embedded Devices

Due to its low cost and ease of modification, an embedded Linux is often used in embedded systems. Linux has become a major competitor of Symbian OS which is used in the majority of smartphones- 16.7% of smartphones sold worldwide during 2006 were using Linux-and it is an alternative to the proprietary Windows CE and Palm OS operating systems on mobile devices. Cell phones or PDAs running on Linux and built on open source platform became a trend from 2007, like Nokia N810, Openmoko's Neo1973, Motorola RAZR2 v8, Motorola ROKR E8, Motorola MING series, Motorola ZINE and Google Android. The popular TiVo digital video recorder uses a customized version of Linux. Several network firewall and router standalone products, including several from Cisco/Linksys, use Linux internally, using its advanced firewall and routing capabilities. The Korg OASYS and the Yamaha Motif XS music workstations, Yamaha S90XS/S70XS synthesizers, Yamaha Motif-Rack XS tone generator module, and Roland RD-700GX digital piano also run Linux. Furthermore, Linux is used in the leading stage lighting control system, FlyingPig/HighEnd WholeHogIII Console.

Figure 1.20: Embedded Device

1.9.15 Copyright and Naming

Linux and most GNU software are licensed under the GNU General Public License (GPL). The GPL requires that anyone who distributes Linux must make the source code (and any modifications) available to the recipient under the same terms. Other key components of a software system may use other licenses; many libraries use the GNU Lesser General Public License (LGPL), a more permissive variant of the GPL, and the X Window System uses the MIT License.

Torvalds states that the Linux kernel will not move from version 2 of the GPL to version 3. He specifically dislikes some provisions in the new license which prohibit the use of the software in digital rights management, and it would also be impractical to obtain permission from all the copyright holders, who number in the thousands.

A 2001 study of Red Hat Linux 7.1 found that this distribution contained 30 million source lines of code. Using the Constructive Cost Model, the study estimated that this distribution required about eight thousand man-years of development time. According to the study, if all this software had been developed by conventional proprietary means, it would have cost about $1.36 billion (2010 US dollars) to develop in the United States.

Most of the code (71%) was written in the C programming language, but many other languages were used, including C++, assembly language, Perl, Python, Fortran, and various shell scripting languages. Slightly over half of all lines of code were licensed under the GPL. The Linux kernel itself was 2.4 million lines of code, or 8% of the total.

In a later study, the same analysis was performed for Debian GNU/Linux version 4.0 (etch, which was released in 2007). This distribution contained close to 283 million source lines of code, and the study estimated that it would have cost US$7.53 billion (in 2010 dollars) to develop by conventional means.

In the United States, the name Linux is a trademark registered to Linus Torvalds. Initially, nobody registered it, but on 15 August 1994, William R. Della Croce, Jr. filed for the trademark Linux, and then demanded royalties from Linux distributors. In 1996, Torvalds and some affected organizations sued him to have the trademark assigned to Torvalds, and in 1997 the case was settled. The licensing of the trademark has since been handled by the Linux Mark Institute. Torvalds has stated that he trademarked the name only to prevent someone else from using it. LMI originally charged a nominal sublicensing fee for use of the Linux name as part of trademarks, but later changed this in favor of offering a free, perpetual worldwide sublicense.

1.10 UNIX, LINUX, AND VARIANT HISTORY

YEAR	EVENT
1957	Bell Labs found they needed an operating system for their computer center which at the time was running various batch jobs. The BESYS operating system was created at Bell Labs to deal with these needs.
1965	Bell Labs was adopting third generation computer equipment and decided to join forces with General Electric and MIT to create Multics (Multiplexed Information and Computing Service).
1969	By April 1969, AT&T made a decision to withdraw Multics and go with GECOS. When Multics was withdrawn Ken Thompson and Dennis Ritchie needed to rewrite an operating system in order to play space travel on another smaller machine (a DEC PDP-7 [Programmed Data Processor 4K memory for user programs). The result was a system which a punning colleague called UNICS (UNiplexed Information and Computing Service)--an 'emasculated Multics'.
1969	Summer 1969 Unix was developed.
1969	Linus Torvalds is born.
1971	First edition of Unix released 11/03/1971. The first edition of the "Unix PROGRAMMER'S MANUAL [by] K. Thompson [and] D. M. Ritchie." It includes over 60 commands like: b (compile B program); boot (reboot system); cat (concatenate files); chdir (change working directory); chmod (change access mode); chown (change owner); cp (copy file); ls (list directory contents); mv (move or rename file); roff (run off text); wc (get word count); who (who is one the system). The main thing missing was pipes.
1972	Second edition of Unix released 12/06/1972
1972	Ritchie rewrote B and called the new language C.
1973	Unix had been installed on 16 sites (all within AT&T/Western Electric); it was publically unveiled at a conference in October.
1973	Third edition of Unix released February 1973
1973	Forth edition of Unix released November 1973
1974	Fifth edition of Unix released June 1974
1974	Thompson went to UC Berkeley to teach for a year, Bill Joy arrived as a new graduate student. Frustrated with ed, Joy developed a more featured editor em.
1975	Sixth edition of Unix released May 1975
1975	Bourne shell is introduced begins being added onto.
1977	1BSD released late 1977
1978	2BSD released mid 1978
1979	Seventh edition of Unix released January 1979
1979	3BSD released late 1979
1979	SCO founded by Doug and Larry Michels as Unix porting and consulting company.

YEAR	EVENT
1980	4.0BSD released October 1980
1982	SGI introduces IRIX.
1983	SCO delivers its first packaged Unix system called SCO XENIX System V for Intel 8086 and 8088 processor-based PCs.
1984	Ultrix 1.0 was released.
1985	Eighth edition of Unix released February 1985
1985	The GNU manifesto is published in the March 1985 issue of Dr. Dobb's Journal. The GNU project starts a year and a half later.
1986	HP-UX 1.0 released.
1986	Ninth edition of Unix released September 1986
1987	Sun and AT&T lay the groundwork for business computing in the next decade with an alliance to develop Unix System V Release 4.
1988	HP-UX 2.0 released.
1988	HP-UX 3.0 released.
1989	SCO ships SCO Unix System V/386, the first volume commercial product licensed by AT&T to use the Unix System trademark.
1989	HP-UX 7.0 released.
1989	Tenth edition of Unix released October 1989
1990	AIX short for Advanced Interactive eXecutive was first entered into the market by IBM February 1990.
1991	Sun unveils Solaris 2 operating environment, specially tuned for symetric multiprocessing.
1991	Linux is introduced by Linus Torvalds, a student in Finland. Who post to the comp.os.minix newsgroup with the words:
	Hello everybody out there using minix -
	I'm doing a (free) operating system (just a hobby, won't be big and professional like gnu) for 386(486) AT clones.
1991	HP-UX 8.0 released.
1991	BSD/386 ALPHA First code released to people outside BSDI 12/xx/1991
1992	HP-UX 9.0 released.
1993	NetBSD 0.8 released 04/20/1993
1993	FreeBSD 1.0 released December of 1993
1994	Red Hat Linux is introduced.
1994	Caldera, Inc was founded in 1994 by Ransom Love and Bryan Sparks.
1994	NetBSD 1.0 released 10/26/1994

YEAR	EVENT
1995	FreeBSD 2.0 released 01/xx/1995
1995	SCO acquires Unix Systems source technology business from Novell Corporation (which had acquired it from AT&T's Unix System Laboratories). SCO also acquires UnixWare 2 operating system from Novell.
1995	HP-UX 10.0 released.
1995	4.4 BSD Lite Release 2 the true final distribution from the CSRG 06/xx/1995
1996	KDE is started to be developed by Matthias Ettrich
1997	HP-UX 11.0 released.
1997	Caldera ships OpenLinux Standard 1.1 May 5, 1997, the second offering in Caldera's OpenLinux product line
1998	IRIX 6.5 the fifth generation of SGI Unix is released July 6, 1998.
1998	SCO delivers UnixWare 7 operating system.
1998	Sun Solaris 7 operating system released.
1998	FreeBSD 3.0 released 10/16/1998
2000	FreeBSD 4.0 released 03/13/2000
2000	Caldera Systems Inc. announces that Caldera Systems has entered into agreement to acquire the SCO Server Software Division and the Professional Services Division.
2001	Linus Torvalds releases version 2.4 of the Linux Kernel source code on January 4th.
2001	Microsoft files a trademark suit against Lindows.com in December.
2004	Lindows changes it's name to Linspire April 14, 2004.

1.11 CASE STUDIES OF WINDOWS 2003 SERVER

1.11.1 Introductory Overviews

- **Active Directory Benefits for Smaller Enterprises**

  Read this white paper to understand quick and easy business advantages for small- and medium-sized organizations that can be realized through the use of Windows Server 2003 and Active Directory.

- **What's New in Active Directory**

  Read this article for an overview of benefits, new features, and improvements in Active Directory directory service.

- **Enterprise Management with the Group Policy Management Console**

  Find out how the Group Policy Management Console (GPMC) helps make Active Directory easier to use, by providing a single solution for managing all Group Policy-related tasks.

- **Popular Identity and Directory Services Features**

  Are you considering upgrading from Microsoft Windows NT Server 4.0 or from Windows 2000 Server? Explore the Feature Highlights Sorter to learn about new features in Windows Server 2003 that can benefit your enterprise.

- **Active Directory LDAP Compliance**

  Read this white paper to find out more about the origins of Lightweight Directory Access Protocol (LDAP) within Microsoft products and, specifically, the implementation of and conformance to the LDAPv3 Proposed Standard within Windows 2000 Server and Windows Server 2003.

- **Introduction to Active Directory Application Mode**

  Read this white paper for an introduction to Active Directory Application Mode (ADAM), one of the new capabilities of the fully integrated directory service available with Windows Server 2003. Organizations, independent software vendors, and developers who want to integrate their applications with a directory service now have an additional capability that provides unique benefits.

- **Active Directory Services in Windows Server 2003**

  Read this article by Professor Windows for a straightforward overview of deployment, domain renaming, security, and other Active Directory capabilities, as well as upgrade notes.

- **Active Directory Federation Services: A Path to Federated Identity and Access Management**

  Find out how federation technology enables the secure sharing of identity information across security boundaries. This white paper provides an overview of Active Directory Federation Services (ADFS)-a component of the upcoming Windows Server 2003 R2 release.

1.11.2 Technical Overviews

- **Windows Security and Directory Services for UNIX Guide v1.0**

  Just released, this prescriptive guide shows IT Pros how to use Microsoft Windows Server 2003 Active Directory for both authentication and identity storage within heterogeneous Microsoft Windows and UNIX environments.

- **Technical Overview of Active Directory**

  Read this TechNet article for an explanation of the basic concepts in Active Directory, as well as technical details about new features and improvements.

- **New Step-by-Step Guides Cover Key Active Directory Features**

  Use these guides to step through fundamentals of the Windows Server 2003 operating system, with an emphasis on features enabled by Active Directory. For small, medium, and large organizations, learn about common scenarios, including desktop and server management, using Group Policy Management Console, and using Active Directory to strengthen security.

- **Migrating Windows NT Server 4.0 Domains to Windows Server 2003 Active Directory**

  Read this white paper for an overview of the process for upgrading or migrating to Windows Server 2003 Active Directory, including an outline of basic decisions to be made during the process and a summary of Active Directory best practices.

- **Integrating Active Directory with an Existing DNS Infrastructure**

  View this online seminar to learn about installing and managing Domain Name System (DNS), Active Directory integration, DNS features and configuration, and DNS in federated forests.

- **Multiple Forest Considerations**

  Read this guide for descriptions of the features that can be deployed across forests and the effects on total cost of ownership of deploying each feature.

- **Scalable E-Commerce Solutions for Identity Management**

  Read this white paper about tests performed for a financial client that is deploying Active Directory to support nearly 18 million Internet-based customers.

- **Monitoring and Troubleshooting the File Replication Service**

  Find links to tools for managing File Replication Service (FRS), including continuous monitoring tools such as Ultrasound and Sonar and snapshot troubleshooting tools such as FRSDiag.

- **Index of Windows Server 2003 Technical Articles**

  See the complete list of all technical articles you'll find on the Windows Server 2003 Web site, organized by technology.

1.11.3 Planning and Deployment

- **Best Practices for Delegating Active Directory Administration**

  Delegation of administration, a key capability of Active Directory, provides a means to successfully manage an Active Directory environment. This document discusses in depth the issues involved in delegating administrative responsibilities, and can help you plan for and implement an administrative delegation model for more securely and efficiently managing Active Directory.

- **Active Directory Migration Tool 3.0**

  Download the Active Directory Migration Tool (ADMT) for an easy, secure, and fast way to either upgrade from Windows NT Server 4.0 to Windows Server Active Directory service or to restructure Active Directory domains between forests or within a forest. ADMT 3.0 includes new features, such as a new backend database, support for simultaneous migration tasks, multiple ADMT consoles with delegated tasks, agent enhancements, full object rename, to make migrations easier.

- **Identity Integration Feature Pack**

  Download the Identity Integration Feature Pack for Windows Server Active Directory to manage identities and coordinate user details across Active Directory, Active Directory Application Mode, Exchange 2000 Server, and Exchange Server 2003 implementations. The feature pack helps you combine identity information for a given user or resource into a single view and automates the provisioning of new and updated identity data.

- **Active Directory Performance for 64-bit Versions of Windows Server 2003**

  This white paper compares performance of the 64-bit Windows Server 2003 operating system and the 32-bit Windows Server 2003 operating system with Service Pack 1 (SP1) for Active

Directory operations. It also investigates workloads for which the 64-bit version of the operating system outperforms the 32-bit version.

- **Designing and Deploying Active Directory**

  Use this guide to help meet your organizations's Active Directory design and deployment goals, whether you are designing a new Active Directory logical structure, deploying Active Directory for the first time, upgrading an existing Windows environment to Windows Server 2003 Active Directory, or restructuring your current environment to a Windows Server 2003 Active Directory environment.

- **Windows Server 2003 Active Directory Branch Office Planning and Deployment Guide**

  This guide is aimed at network managers, system integrators, and consultants involved in Active Directory branch office implementations. The procedures in this document show how to deploy and maintain Active Directory in a large branch office environment (at least one data center attached to 100 or more branch offices).

- **Best Practice Guide for Securing Active Directory Installations**

  Targeted at IT professionals who participate in security planning for an Active Directory service deployment and who are running a secure Active Directory operation, this guide discusses the elements of a comprehensive plan for Active Directory security and provides best practice recommendations.

- **Migrating from Windows NT Server 4.0 to Windows Server 2003**

  Targeted at IT administrators who are responsible for network operations in a smaller organization, this guide provides a prescriptive migration path with step-by-step instructions for small- and medium-sized organizations planning a migration from Windows NT 4.0 to Windows Server 2003.

1.11.4 Administration and Configuration

- **Windows Server 2003 Active Directory Fast Recovery with Volume Shadow Copy Service and Virtual Disk Service**

  Learn how it is now possible to recover failed Active Directory servers in minutes rather than hours, using Volume Shadow Copy Service and Virtual Disk Service. This paper supplies a fast recovery demonstration designed to enable system administrators to implement fast recovery solutions in their own Active Directory environments.

1.11.5 Case Studies

- **Kimball Hill Homes**

  Find out how Kimball Hill Homes is using Active Directory to dramatically reduced the time that IT professionals spend on routine network management and allow Kimball Hill Homes to continue its rapid growth without frequent increases in IT head count.

- **Motorola**

  Read how Motorola migrated from Microsoft Windows NT Server 4.0 to Windows Server System, consolidated its infrastructure, and implemented a change and configuration management solution that they estimate saved them $11M.

- **Siemens**

  Learn how has deployed an Active Directory architecture that simplifies and facilitates management, saves tens of millions of dollars annually, and helps Siemens to add new business value that it couldn't otherwise consider.

- **Nancy's Specialty Foods**

  It took only six hours for Nancy's Specialty Foods to set the stage for future directory-enabled applications when it upgraded its computing platform to Microsoft Windows Server 2003 and Active Directory. Find out how its new directory service provides a central point of administration for IT staff, reducing desktop visits required and improving desktop management.

- **GameWorks**

  Learn how GameWorks improved the manageability and supportability of its IT infrastructure by deploying Microsoft Windows Server System integrated server software with the Active Directory directory service.

- **More Active Directory Case Studies**

  Browse over 200 case studies related to Active Directory that span a range of companies, industries, and solution types.

1.11.6 Partners

- **Automated Assessment and Deployment - Windows Server 2003 R2 & Active Directory**

  Take advantage of the Assessment and Deployment Solution for Midsize Businesses (ADS), designed to save Microsoft Partners time when assessing a prospective customer's network infrastructure, and help generate a detailed proposal for deployment project. In addition, if the project is approved, ADS can automate the deployment of Windows Server 2003 R2, Exchange 2003, Microsoft Operations Manager (MOM) 2005 Workgroup Edition with Active Directory and Windows Server Update Services (WSUS), saving you time, cost and risk. Download ADS today!

- **Active Directory Partners**

  Find third-party resources by browsing this compilation of partner descriptions.

1.11.7 Webcasts

- **Active Directory - Learn the Basics and Master Advanced Concepts**

  In this webcast series, Microsoft Active Directory experts provide you with a comprehensive tour of the technology, whether you are looking for information on Active Directory fundamentals, starting an Active Directory migration project, or seeking some advice for optimizing your existing deployment.

- **Liberate Your Infrastructure**

  Attend this series and become a dynamic IT organization and achieve operational effectiveness through delivering higher quality of service, e-mail availability, and a more secure Windows environment. Our technical experts will help guide you through step-by-step instructions on how to install, configure, automate, and mange a more secure and well managed infrastructure.

- **Active Directory Webcast Series**

  View live or on-demand webcasts featuring Active Directory experts from Microsoft. Learn basics and master advanced concepts.
- **To Active Directory and Beyond: Windows Migration Strategies**

  This series of webcasts for IT professionals outlines the planning, design, and implementation of a migration strategy from a legacy Windows environment to Windows Server 2003.
- **NT 4.0 and Windows 2003 Active Directory Interoperability**

  This webcast covers trust relationships, the Active Directory Sizer tool, name resolution methods, migrating accounts from Windows NT 4.0 to Windows Server 2003, directory and file replication in Windows NT 4.0 and Windows Server 2003, and interoperation of system and group policy.
- **Windows Server 2003 Active Directory Diagnostics, Troubleshooting, and Recovery**

  This webcast covers verifying Active Directory functionality, diagnosing and troubleshooting replication, locating Active Directory database files, backing up and recovering system state data, and seizing FSMO roles.
- **New Features of Windows Server 2003 Active Directory: Feature-Based**

  This webcast covers most aspects of Windows Server 2003 Active Directory operations, focusing on new features for deployment, administration, management, forest trusts, group policies, and application support.
- **New Features of Windows Server 2003 Active Directory: Scenario-Based**

  This webcast addresses pain points from Windows 2000 Active Directory deployments and shows how new features of Windows Server 2003 make management and deployment easier.
- **Automating Administration of Windows Server 2003**

  This webcast provides an overview of many Windows Server 2003 command-line tools and scripts. Scenarios demonstrate how command-line tools can automate administration of Active Directory, management of printers and print queues, and remote information-gathering by help desk personnel.
- **Migrating from Windows NT Server 4.0 to Windows Server 2003**

  This webcast covers migration from Windows NT 4.0 to Windows Server 2003. Topics include: choosing the migration path, the different paths available, and the aspects of each that require certain attention. The webcast also covers upgrading account domains and resource domains, restructuring domains, moving user and group accounts using ADMT, and the effects of migration on trust relationships, DNS, profiles, and scripts.

1.12 CASE STUDIES OF UNIX

UNIX is the eldest operating system still in use, having its roots in the 1960s Multics system. Not by chance its original name was Unics, later changed to its renowned denomination. It was designed and developed at the Bell Labs by Thompson, Ritchie and McIlroy, trying to avoid some complications its ancestor introduced, keeping the system small and simple. This philosophy, originated by complex systems engineering, gained fame under the acronym KISS, “keep it simple, stupid”, and dates back to the 14th century with the lex parsimoniae by the philosopher William of Ockham, who stated "entia non sunt multiplicanda praeter necessitatem", best known as Ockham's razor "entities should not be multiplied beyond necessity". We can easily recognize that the whole project followed this rule of thumb even from its first version. Small programs were preferred instead of big ones, developing programs that do a single task but very efficiently. To run complex jobs, these small applications could, and still are, connected by I/O redirection. After many years, and after many death prophecies, UNIX is still one of the most used operating systems. A question may arise, whether UNIX has observed in its history the KISS principle, or it has forgot this basic rule and followed other habits.

The operating system core is one of the major concerns. Microkernels have been developed during years of research, but the common understanding of them was poor. They were always addressed as neat and simple academic design projects, following the KISS principle, but with bad performances due to the number of context switches necessary to run an application. Even though there is commercial evidence that microkernels are not just academic proofs of concepts, with mission-critical real-time operating systems like QNX, and even end-user UNIX systems like MacOS X, the leitmotif of monolithic kernels being "better" never faded.

Dynamic linking was one of the features inherited by UNIX from its ancestor Multics. Reusing code through shared libraries is a common practice not only in the UNIX world, but in all modern operating systems. This praxis on one hand simplifies the developer's job, but on the other hand can add a high grade of complexity in a system if all softwares do actually share their code. Again, another common opinion is that sharing prevents a system to be overwhelmed by an ungovernable duplication of resources. However, this belief had never been proved right or wrong.

In this paper we address these issues from an historical and statistical point of view. We will evaluate the number of context switches with a set of tests, validating the results with state of the art statistical analyses. On the libraries side, we will take a survey of all shared resources present on our systems, inspecting the weight and impact of such libraries to corroborate or contradict the habit of sharing them. Finally, we will point out the historical heritage of UNIX, showing how the KISS philosophy had become less important than common habits. For our survey we chose Linux and MacOS X. This decision was taken to avoid biased results for any statistical analysis by choosing a niche OS. Thus, by selecting two UNIX (or UNIX-like) operating systems available to a general public, we achieve an impartial and fair comparison.

1.12.1 Kernel Wars

A kernel is the core of an operating system, giving the minimum abstraction layer for hardware handling, inter-process communication and memory management. Along with these, a kernel may provide other services like device management, sound and network control. On monolithic systems all services are implemented in kernel space, while on microkernels all these aspects are delegated to userland servers. A monolithic kernel is thus less adherent to the KISS principle, involving a high grade of complexity, evident even by the needed number of lines of code. By construction they have tight and often non-trivial dependencies between their components, affecting the whole system in case of bugs.

Microkernels on the other hand tend to keep all aspects simple and neat, commissioning all services to the servers. This quality affects microkernels on the design side by needing a great care in planning their features. In the history of operating systems the debate between the supporters of microkernel design, opposed to the monolithic approach, was one of the major discussion arguments. The most famous flaming discussion on the topic started between Andrew Tanenbaum and Linus Torvalds, the creators of Minix and Linux respectively. Much of the discussion between these two major schools is about performance.

A monolithic kernel should be more efficient than a microkernel because it requires less context switches for all tasks. This fact had always been addressed but never sufficiently investigated or statistically proved. We analyzed both MacOS X and Linux with a suite of tests to prove or confute this efficiency issue. All the tests have been then evaluated in their statistical significance to validate the results.

1.12.1.1 Test Suite

The suite consisted of 31 tests, divided into 7 categories. Each suite have been repeated fifty times on a freshly-rebooted machine in order to obtain a sufficient number of cases to achieve statistical significance (Casella and Berger, 2001; Freedman, 2005). The chosen tests are the following:

1. Multiplication of two randomly-generated integers with 1024, 2048, 5120, 10240, and 20480 digits;
2. Creation of a random file from /dev/random with sizes of 1024 KB, 2048 KB, 5120 KB, 10 MB, 20 MB, 50 MB, and 100 MB;
3. Conversion of images from PNG to JPEG, TIFF and PostScript;
4. Download of a 650 MB CD-ROM ISO image via the HTTP protocol;
5. Compression of random files with sizes of 1024 KB, 2048 KB, 5120 KB, and compression of the same random sequence repeated 15 times;
6. Behaviour of the Secure Shell daemon while uploading and downloading a 650 MB CD-ROM ISO image from a client, running on both high and low TCP ports;
7. Process generation with classical UNIX calls fork, wait, and exec, and thread spawning.

The chosen hardware models for a test have been an IBM IntelliStation M Pro running Linux Ubuntu 5.04 based on the Linux 2.6.10 kernel version m, and an Apple eMac PowerPC running Apple MacOS X 10.4.6 based on Darwin 8.6.0 kernel version. The test suite was designed to be independent of the underlying hardware, focusing exclusively on the context switch counts, and not on performances (e.g. execution times).

1.12.1.2 Statistical Analysis

A statistical analysis on the test suite has been conducted to check the validity of each test. The results are presented in Table 1.1 for both Linux and Darwin (MacOS X), where mean and standard deviation are shown in detail for each set of tests.

1. TEST RESULTS

As shown in Table 1 the Linux kernel has an overall number of context switches greater than MacOS

X. In one test, specifically the HTTP download, the number of context switches on the MacOS X system was less than the Linux counterpart with a significant difference. Apart from the number of context switches, the variance of MacOS X show that its kernel switches "irregularly" compared to Linux, which behaves smoothly with very sparse outliers. This fact was confirmed also by the confidence intervals and skewness of both the systems.

These results are a clear indication that the assertion that a microkernel has a number of context switches greater than a monolithic one has no real statistical evidence. As a matter of fact, a well-designed microkernel has a number of context switches less or at worst, comparable to its counterpart. Anyway, these results do not provide any performance comparisons between the two kernels, but they supply the important information that if a performance loss is present, is not due to the number of context switches.

Table 1.1 The statistical results of the test series

Test	Linux		MacOS X	
	Mean	Variance	Mean	Variance
bc 1024	87.46	5.58	0.38	0.85
bc 2048	158.20	9.15	0.44	1.01
bc 5120	381.14	21.27	1.96	4.72
bc 10240	779.44	50.65	1.54	3.47
bc 20480	1459.74	75.86	3.74	6.95
dd 1024 K	10.68	3.42	0.40	0.83
dd 2048 K	7.44	4.42	0.42	0.78
dd 5120 K	22.82	6.96	0.64	1.17
dd 10240 K	60.10	244.60	0.50	0.86
dd 20480 K	64.60	14.76	0.78	0.97
dd 51200 K	127.58	11.36	2.00	5.96
dd 102400 K	237.04	76.71	1.40	1.93
PNG to JPG (1)	121.42	10.90	2.64	4.28
PNG to TIFF (1)	4.26	0.90	0.52	0.50
PNG to PS (1)	8.68	1.36	0.52	0.54
PNG to JPG (2)	8.24	2.41	1.30	2.72
PNG to TIFF (2)	5.82	4.29	0.68	0.71
PNG to PS (2)	2.08	0.40	0.52	0.61
HTTP Download	454540.26	14104.41	466149.94	16854.00
zip 1024 K	6.96	1.64	1.84	2.06
zip 1024 K (15 times)	16.82	1.51	1.18	1.85
zip 2048 K	4.64	0.94	0.96	2.04
zip 2048 K (15 times)	27.18	3.38	3.62	13.86
zip 5120 K	5.00	0.83	0.68	1.36
zip 5120 K (15 times)	223.48	25.01	1.96	1.83
scp (Download, High)	121994.78	10812.82	89920.74	2868.35
scp (Download, Low)	158212.84	7542.38	88784.98	2774.65
scp (Upload, High)	273975.60	11675.82	85522.62	2026.85
scp (Upload, Low)	282313.78	8000.92	87982.98	2703.27
Processes (fork)	3.36	1.17	1.10	0.36
Processes (threads)	16.36	13.01	0.22	0.42

2. TEST VALIDATION

To validate the results we performed a standard t-Test (Hastie et al., 2003) in order to examine if the two series of results have statistically significant differences, in particular we conducted both 1- and 2-tailored t-Tests. In Table 1.2 we show the results for those tests that showed a non-significant difference in the 1-tailored test, sided by the corresponding 2-tailored study.

Table 1.2 The statistical results of the test series

Test	t-Test *p*-value 1-taliroed	2-tailored
dd 10240 K	0.05	0.09
PNG to PS (1)	0.02	$< 10^{-6}$
PNG to JPG (2)	0.45	$< 10^{-6}$
PNG to TIFF (2)	0.19	$< 10^{-6}$
HTTP Download	0.27	$< 10^{-4}$
zip 1024 K	0.71	$< 10^{-6}$
zip 1024 K (15 times)	0.87	$< 10^{-6}$
zip 2048 K	0.32	$< 10^{-6}$
zip 1024 K (15 times)	0.04	$< 10^{-6}$
zip 5120 K	0.17	$< 10^{-6}$
Processes (threads)	0.01	$< 10^{-6}$

All the tests have been proved being different in means and variances with statistical significance, having a p-value not exceeding the standard statistical limit of 0.05. In only one test, the creation of a 10 MB file from /dev/random has a higher p-value of 0.09, signifying that the two tests have no significant difference: an analysis of the data showed the presence of an outlier in the Linux system with a total context switches count of 1755. Applying an outlier filtering the test showed a p-value < 10-6.

Additionally a Sign test (Abdi, 2006) was performed in order to compare the performances in the overall contexts. In this case a positive match was given to MacOS X if the 1-tailored p-value of the t-Test was less than the standard threshold of 0.05. The sign test resulted in the probability of the two series not being statistically different of p < 2.94·10-3.

1.12.2 Shared Libraries

A common conduct in the UNIX world is to subdivide a complex program into small pieces, usually libraries. This approach is obviously conforming to the KISS principle, and of course is not limited to the UNIX world. During years of life, this procedure of using shared libraries have become so commonly spread, that there is the ongoing belief that a software using a shared library should install it system-wide, so that other softwares could use it as well. Another opinion is that using system-wide shared libraries would decrease the amount of disk space wasted by an "uncontrollable" duplication of resources. The consequence is that on a typical UNIX system we cannot recognize immediately who is a user of a library, and worse, if there are any. In the next section we analyze the shared library distribution and relative weight on a UNIX system, determining if the opinions about sharing system-wide libraries have a real foundation.

1.12.2.1 Statistical Analysis

We took a survey of all the shared libraries on our Linux system to find out if effectively those beliefs are supported by real evidence. We analyzed all the explicitly shared libraries present on the system, meaning that self-contained applications like VMWare or Matlab, were not taken into account, since they do not share their dynamic libraries. In order to obtain the total users of a library, we followed the linkage up to the second order, thus considering as users of a library, another shared library.

1. SELF AND NON-SELF

Roughly counting the number of shared libraries, we reach a total of 500 common resources present on a modern UNIX or UNIX-like system. A mere sorting by number of users shows which libraries can be counted as "self", and which ones should be classified as "non-self" on an operating system. An operating system by its very definition manages software and hardware resources, and on modern systems provides a minimal set of libraries for third-party software development. Softwares, other than the operating system itself, have no reason to be used a number of times comparable to a system resource. If this happens, the non-self classified library should then be taken into account to be included in the operating system.

In Table 1.3 we show the ten most used libraries on both operating systems. In the table we read the total count of users of each library along with the number of times they are dynamically linked by other applications and libraries. As expected, the most used libraries concern with low-level operations, graphic environment and dynamic libraries.

Table 1.3 The ten most used libraries with their respective linking count

Linux		MacOS X	
Library	Count	Library	Count
`ld-linux`	3294	`libSystem`	1159
`libc`	3291	`libiconv`	185
`libm`	1879	`libgcc_s`	127
`libdl`	1871	`CoreFoundation`	109
`libpthreads`	1561	`libncurses`	104
`libz`	989	`libcups`	92
`libX11`	804	`libsasl2`	83
`libglib`	781	`libssl`	78
`libgobject`	759	`DirectoryService`	75
`libXext`	749	`Kerberos`	70

2. LIBRARY WEIGHT

An interesting insight is given by the shared libraries distribution and relative weight on the Linux system. We divided the libraries into six main categories by number of users, and the results are shown in Figures 1 and 2. About half of the libraries present on the system are used less than 10 times, and the most used libraries (with more than 500 linkers) are actually about 2% of the total, as pictured in Figure 1. Shared libraries linked only once are about 28% of the total, and they can hardly classified as "shared". To better understand the importance of these shared objects, we focused on the weight of each libraries group. The weight of each library is the size that would have been occupied on a storage medium in case of static linkage. Figure 2 shows the weight of each group. The most used libraries linked more than 100 times, weight 85% of the total while they amount to 12% of the number of libraries. The least used libraries used less than 10 times, weight only for 2% but are 54% of the total.

This fact draws a shadow on the claim that shared libraries are a quasi-necessity, reducing disk space and of course helping the system to remain under the KISS principle. It happens that more than one fourth of the libraries are effectively shared just by name, and the half is shared less than 10 times. In this situation it is hard to classify a library as part of the operating system (the "self"), and adds confusion to the maintainability of a system keeping its structure not simple and certainly not stupid. To avoid this intrinsic disorganization, we can move the least used libraries from a system-wide location to the application itself, with a static linkage or bundling them into an application directory à la NeXT. The great benefit is evident: reducing the number of unknown libraries avoiding possible orphans, and having a better view of what is part of the system and what is not. The disk space overhead caused by the duplication of resources is clearly dependent on the limit we impose on the number of library users. For instance, if we had statically linked all libraries with less than 20 users on our system, we would add 450 MB of space removing 340 shared objects. Although the disk space evidently increases, it remains far under acceptable bounds: removing libraries used less than 20 times on a 40 GB hard drive, nowadays considered a small one, would add 1% of the disk space decreasing the number of shared objects by 68%.

We strongly stress the fact that we chose one of the cleanest and most coherent Linux distributions, having just one and only one desktop environment and so not adding other shared libraries for just a single application. Other UNIX systems that include more environments, such as Solaris that includes both CDE and JDE, or AIX including KDE as well as Gnome, have worse results. On MacOS X the number of shared libraries are far less than those present on other systems: since all applications bundle all their resources, there is no library installed system-wide by applications with few obvious exceptions (e.g. device drivers, kernel extensions).

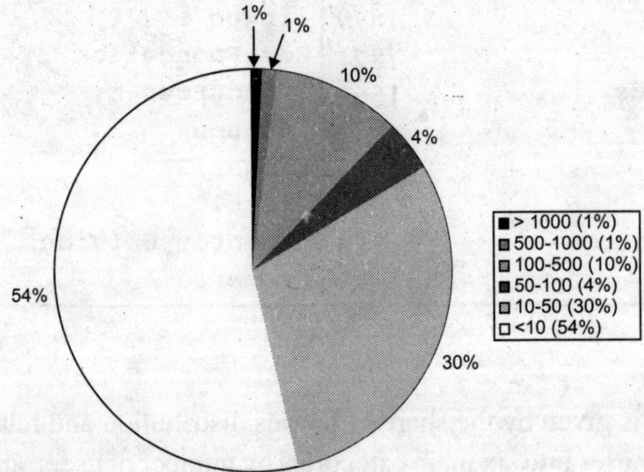

Figure 1.21 Number of libraries per number of linkers

1.12.3 Unix Heritage

As UNIX was developed, it followed the KISS principle in almost every aspect, although it was not a requirement. The "everything is a file" philosophy, which is characteristic to every UNIX system, was present from the very beginning. The first UNIX system already contained the dev directory with the special device files. This abstractive approach to devices, files and directories is clearly KISS-compliant, as it pursues an extreme simplicity and coherence in handling files, directories, devices and even IPC-related files with a simple API.

At its birth the directory structure on UNIX was also very simple, as we can see in (Thompson and Ritchie, 1971). In the first UNIX there were just few directories, bin, etc, and usr. The first two were integral part of the operating system, being respectively the place where the system binaries were stored, and where "other" things regarding the system were to be found (e.g. system libraries, configuration files). The usr directory was the place where users had their own personal space, thus properly the users directory. Reading the manual we can have the clear perspective of the author's intention: the clear distinction of roles between system and users, as the authors themselves say "user-maintained programs are not considered part of the UNIX system", referring to the Section 6 of the UNIX manual.

As UNIX grew, there were more additions to the system. A library directory was added moving the system-shared objects from the etc to a more meaningful location. The system administration services were also moved to another directory called sbin from their original location etc. We may notice as this choice has nothing to do with a privileged access to system binaries, but they were in etc "to lessen the probability of its being invoked by accident or from curiosity", as we can read in the boot command in (Thompson and Ritchie, 1971). This fact still holds in these days, being by default sbin not present in the path environment variable on many UNIX systems, but still accessible by users. We may recall that in the days when UNIX was conceived, many directories were mount points for storage mediums, making the swap between tapes easier to handle. The ongoing growth, and of course the lack of standardization in the early UNIX systems, led to the creation of a plethora of directories and mount points. While the habit of using many locations as mount points for different storage mediums was a necessary procedure in old times, nowadays had become just a habit: the sbin directory for example is there because we expect it to be there.

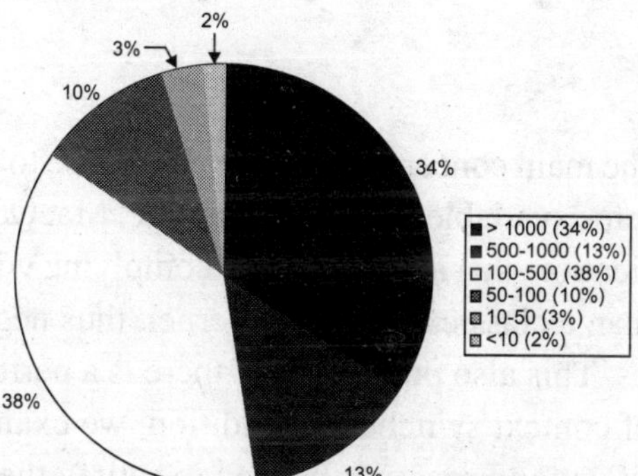

Figure 1.22 Library occupancy if statically linked (per number of linkers)

The usr directory is one of the notable examples of how a system can grow in complexity. From a user data storage location, this directory have been in years called with many acronyms, like User Shared Resources or UNIX System Resources, becoming full of locations with an unclear meaning. Originally a user directory was a shared resource, as we can see for example in the description of the cal program in the original UNIX manual. Over the years this location had been more and more used to store system binaries, like applications, graphic servers and UNIX commands. Apart from libraries, which have been analyzed in the previous section, this "shared" directory contains application resources such as translations, documentations, configurations, and even administrative commands. In fact, we may ask what is now the difference between an administrative commands stored in sbin from another one stored in usr/sbin. We can track the reason back to history, but none of the causes that originally drove this conduct hold today.

Focusing on the applications, we can ask ourselves why a translation file for particular software should reside in a directory different from the application itself. Moreover the question is whether or not these files can be classified as truly shared: by their very definition those resources are not certainly shared by any other software. Moreover, we find that almost any UNIX system contains a directory dedicated to the system header files. Although it might at first seem convincing, this habit is comparable to the practice of separating application resources from the application itself. A header by itself has almost no usage without the library it describes, so by their purpose they should not be stored in different places. As for applications, storing all the available header files in a single location does not help in keeping a resource simple and immediately recognizable. Bundling headers and respective binary library in a single location is again a possible solution, avoiding the spread of files in many directories and increasing the system simplicity.

Again a NeXT approach to software deployment gives a solution to this unreasonable complexity, which keeps a system not certainly simple and stupid to understand and maintain. We address NeXT in particular because it was a UNIX operating system, but bundles were actually not limited to the NeXT OS: for example BeOS applications were bundles even though it was not a UNIX. Bundling all the application-related files in a single location makes it simple to recognize an application resource from a system one. In the modern NeXT descendant, MacOS X, we can clearly see an effort in simplifying the system, by using application and library bundles. Moreover, it introduced locations with significant names like Applications, System, Library, and re-establishing the Users directory. Despite the efforts, the system still has common UNIX directories, which of course could have been easily avoided retaining a compatibility with the past.

1.12.4 Conclusion

We have analyzed some of the main concerns about the adherence to the KISS principle by two of the most used UNIX operating systems available to a general public, MacOS X and Linux. We have proved, with statistical evidence and validation, that a microkernel, complying with the KISS principle by design, has no more context switches than a classic monolithic kernel, thus negating the opposition to the first family of operating system cores. This also proves that if there is a performance difference between the two, is not due to the number of context switches. In addition, we examined the current shared library situation, showing that a simplification process is needed to satisfy the simplicity of maintenance that modern systems require.

Moreover, the spaces required by strictly limiting the number of libraries not only have an insignificant impact on modern storage media, but reduce the number of shared resources at least by 50%. Born following the KISS principle, UNIX had become a huge and habit-prone system. Vestigial heritages are still present, as in the MacOS X system, but have no reason to exist anymore. The KISS principle was of course present even in the first version of Bell Labs UNIX, but evidently it was swiftly replaced by habits that still in our times taint the simplicity and logic of the original intents

1.13 Case Studies of Linux

In 1991, Linus Torvalds studding Unix at the University, where he used special educational experimental purpose operating system called Minix (small version of Unix and used in Academic environment). But Minix had it's own limitations. Linus felt he could do better than the Minix. So he developed his own version of Minix, which is now known as Linux. Linux is Open Source From the start of the day.

1.13.1 Where I Can Use Linux?

You can use Linux as Server Os or as stand alone Os on your PC. (But it is best suited for Server.) As a server Os it provides different services/network resources to client. Server Os must be:

- Stable
- Robust
- Secure
- High Performance

Linux offers all of the above characteristics plus its Open Source and Free OS. So Linux can be used as:

1. On stand alone workstation/PC for word processing, graphics, software development, internet, e-mail, chatting, small personal database management system etc.
2. In network environment as:

   (a) File and Print or Application Server Share the data, Connect the expensive device like printer and share it, e-mail within the LAN/intranet etc are some of the application.

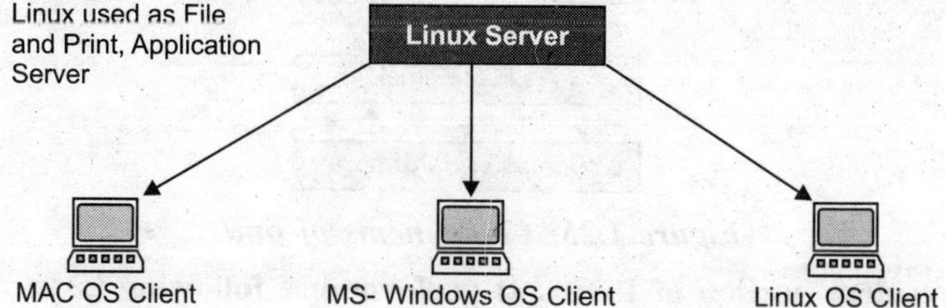

Figure 1.23 Linux Server with different Client Os

   (b) Linux sever cab be connected to Internet, So that PC's on intranet can share the internet/e-mail etc. You can put your web sever that run your web site or transmit the information on the internet.

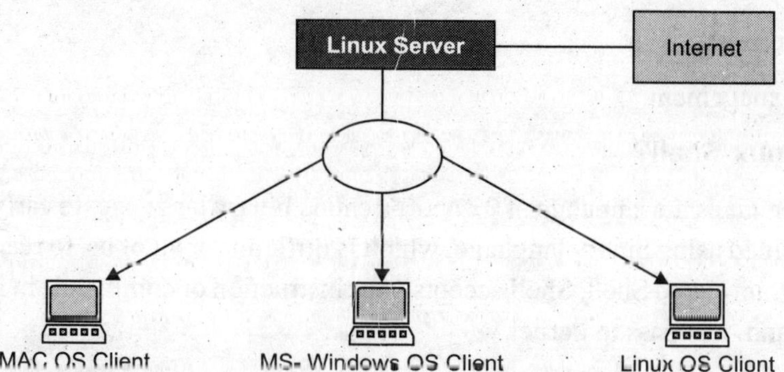

Figure 1.24 Linux Server can act as Proxy/Mail/WWW/Router Server etc.

So you can use Linux for:

- Personal Work
- Web Server

- Software Development Workstation
- Workgroup Server
- In Data Center for various server activities such as FTP, Telnet, SSH, Web, Mail, Proxy, Proxy Cache Appliance etc

1.13.2 What Kernel IS?

Kernel is hart of Linux Os. It manages resource of Linux Os. Resources mean facilities available in Linux. For e.g. Facility to store data, print data on printer, memory, file management etc. Kernel decides who will use this resource, for how long and when. It runs your programs (or set up to execute binary files). The kernel acts as an intermediary between the computer hardware and various programs/application/ shell.

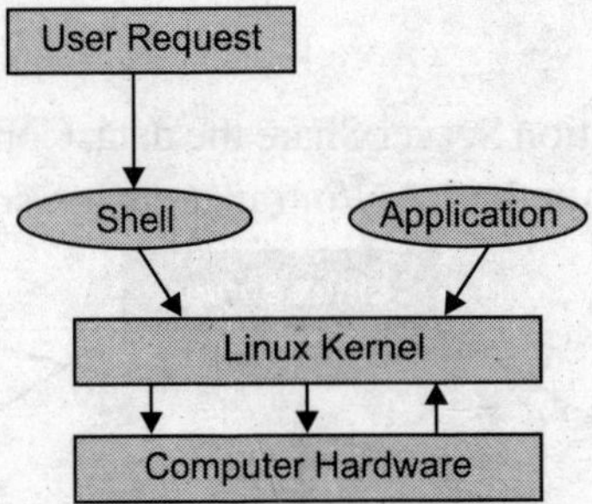

Figure 1.25: Components of linux

It's Memory resident portion of Linux. It performance following task:

- I/O management
- Process management
- Device management
- File management
- Memory management

1.13.3 What is Linux Shell?

Computer understands the language of 0's and 1's called binary language. In early days of computing, instruction are provided using binary language, which is difficult for all of us, to read and write. So in Os there is special program called Shell. Shell accepts your instruction or commands in English (mostly) and if its a valid command, it is pass to kernel.

Shell is a user program or it's environment provided for user interaction. Shell is an command language interpreter that executes commands read from the standard input device (keyboard) or from a file. Shell is not part of system kernel, but uses the system kernel to execute programs, create files etc. Several shells available with Linux including:

Shell Name	Developed by	Where	Remark
BASH (Bourne-Again SHell)	Brian Fox and Chet Ramey	Free Software Foundation	Most common shell in Linux. It's Freeware shell.
CSH (C SHell)	Bill Joy	University of California (For BSD) AT & T Bell Labs	The C shell's syntax and usage are very similar to the C programming language.
KSH (Korn SHell)	David Korn		--
TCSH	See the man page. Type $ man tcsh		TCSH is an enhanced but completely compatible version of the Berkeley UNIX C shell (CSH).

Tip: To find all available shells in your system type following command:

$ cat /etc/shells

Note that each shell does the same job, but each understand different command syntax and provides different built-in functions.

In MS-DOS, Shell name is COMMAND.COM which is also used for same purpose, but it's not as powerful as our Linux Shells are! Any of the above shell reads command from user (via Keyboard or Mouse) and tells Linux Os what users want. If we are giving commands from keyboard it is called command line interface (Usually in-front of $ prompt, This prompt is depend upon your shell and Environment that you set or by your System Administrator, therefore you may get different prompt).

Tip: To find your current shell type following command

$ echo $SHELL

1.13.4 What is Shell Script?

Normally shells are interactive. It means shell accept command from you (via keyboard) and execute them. But if you use command one by one (sequence of 'n' number of commands) , the you can store this sequence of command to text file and tell the shell to execute this text file instead of entering the commands. This is known as shell script. ***Shell script*** defined as:

*"Shell Script is **series of command** written **in plain text file.** Shell script is just like batch file is MS-DOS but have more power than the MS-DOS batch file."*

Why to Write Shell Script?

- Shell script can take input from user, file and output them on screen.
- Useful to create our own commands.
- Save lots of time.
- To automate some task of day today life.
- System Administration part can be also automated.

1.14 CASE STUDIES OF UNIX VS. LINUX

UNIX

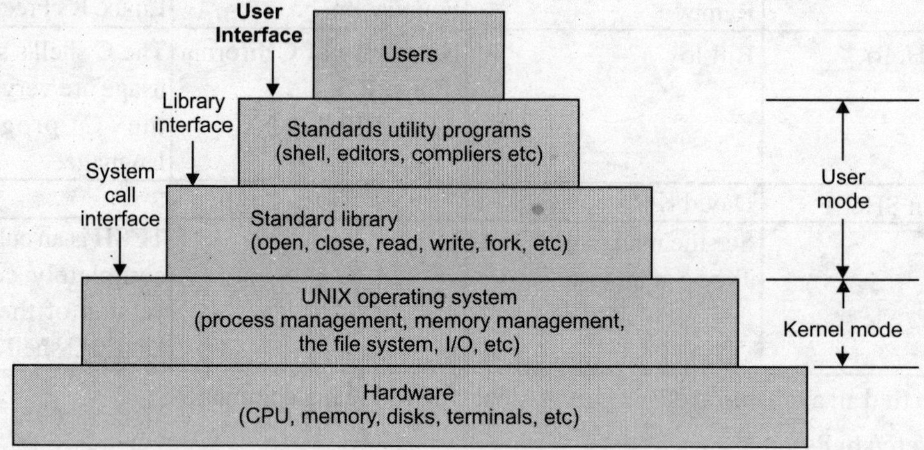

Figure 1.26: UNIX Architecture

UNIX Utility Programs

Program	Typical use
cat	Concatente multiple files to standard output
chmod	Change file protection mode
cp	Copy one or more files
cut	Cut columns of text from a file
grep	Search a file for some pattern
head	Extract the first lines of a file
ls	List directory
make	Compile files to build a binary
mkdir	Make a directory
od	Octal dump of file
paste	Paste columns of text into a file
pr	Format a file for printing
rm	Remove one or more files
rmdir	Remove a directory
sort	Sort a file of lines alphabetically
tail	Extract the last lines of file
tr	Translate between character sets

UNIX Kernel

System calls
Interrupts and traps
Terminal handing
Sockets
File naming
Map ping
Page faults
Signal handling
Process creation & termination
Raw tty
Cooked tty
Line disciplines
Network protocols
Routing
File systems
Buffer cache
Virtual memory
Page cache
Process scheduling
Character devices
Network device drivers
Disk device drivers
Process dispatching
Hardware

Processes in UNIX

```
pid = fork( );              /* if the fork succeeds, pid > 0 in the parent */
if (pid < 0) {
                            handle _error( ); /* fork failed (e.g., memory or some table is full) */
} else if (pid > 0) {
                                    /* parent code goes here. /*/
} else {
}
                                    /* child code goes here. /*/
}
```

POSIX

Signal	Cause
SIGABRT	Sent to abort a process and force a core dump
SIGALRM	The alarm clock has gone off
SIGFPE	A floating-point error has occurred (e.g., division by 0)
SIGHUP	The phone line the process was using has been hung up
SIGILL	The user has hit the DEL key to interrupt the process
SIGQUIT	The user has hit the key requesting a core dump
SIGKILL	Sent to kill a process (cannot be caught or ignored)
SIGPIPE	The process has written to a pip which has no readers
SIGSEGV	The process has referenced an invalid memory address
SIGTERM	Used to request that a process terminate gracefully
SIGUSR1	Available for application-defined purposes
SIGUSR2	Available for application-defined purposes

System Calls for Process Management

System call	Description
pid = fork()	Create a child process identical to the parent
pid = waitpid(pid, &statloc, opts)	Wait for a child to terminate
s = execve(name, argv, envp)	Replace a process' core image
esit(status)	Terminate process execution and return status
s = sigaction(sig, &act, &oldact)	Define action to take on signals
s = sigreturn(&context)	Return from a signal
s = sigprocmask(how, &set, &old)	Examine or change the signal mask
s = sigsuspend(set)	Get the set of blocked signals
s = sigpending(sigmask)	Replace the signal mask and suspend the process
s = kill(pid, sig)	Send a signal to a process
residual = alarm(seconds)	Set the alarm clock
s = pause( )	Suspend the caller until the next signal

s is an error code

pid is a process ID

residual is the remaining time from the previous alarm

POSIX Shell

```
while (TRUE) {                          /* repeat forever /*/
      type_prompt( );                   /* display prompt on the screen */
      read_command(command, params);    /* read input line from keyboard */
```

```
pid = form( );                          /* form off a child process */
if (pid < 0) {
        printf("Unable to fork0);       /* error condition */
        continue;                       /* repeat the loop */
}
if (pid ! = 0) {
        waitpid (–1, &status, 0);       /* parent waits for child */
} else {
        execve(command, params, 0);     /* child does the work */
        }
}
```

THREADS IN POSIX

Thread call	Description
pthread_create	Create a new thread in the caller's address space
pthread_exit	Terminate the calling thread
pthread_join	Wait for a thread to terminate
pthread_mutex_init	Create a new mutex
pthread_mutex_destroy	Destroy a mutex
pthread_mutex_lock	Lock a mutex
pthread_mutex_unlock	Unlock a mutex
pthread_cond_init	Create a condition variable
pthread_cond_destroy	Destroy a condition variable
pthread_cond_wait	Wait on a condition variable
pthread_cond_signal	Release one thread waiting on a condition variable

The *ls* Command

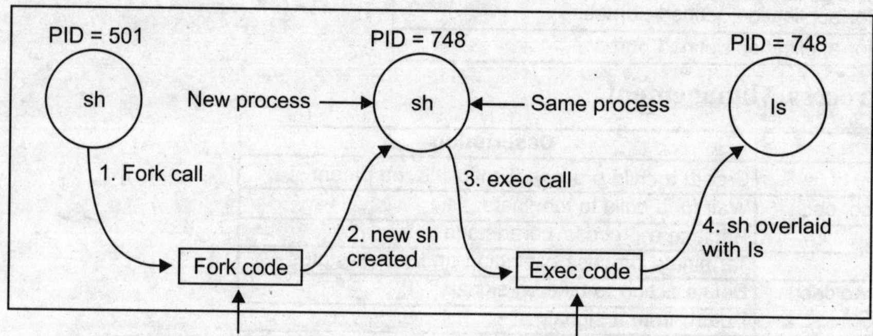

Allocate child's process table entry
Fill child's entry from parent
Allocate child's stack and user area
Fill child's user area from parent
Allocate PID for child
Set up child to share parent's text
Copy page tables for data and stack
Set up sharing of open files
Copy parent's registers to child

Find the executable program
Verify the execute permission
Read and verify the header
Copy arguments, environ to kernel
Free the old address space
Allocate new address space
Copy arguments, environ to stack
Reset signals
Initialize registers

Steps in executing the command ls type to the shell

Flags for Linux clone

Flag	Meaning when set	Meaning when cleared
CLONE_VM	Create a new thread	Create a new process
CLONE_FS	Share umask, root, and working dirs	Do not share them
CLONE_FILES	Share the file descriptors	Copy the file descriptors
CLONE_SIGHAND	Share the signal handler table	Copy the table
CLONE_PID	New thread gets old PID	New thread gets own PID

UNIX Scheduler

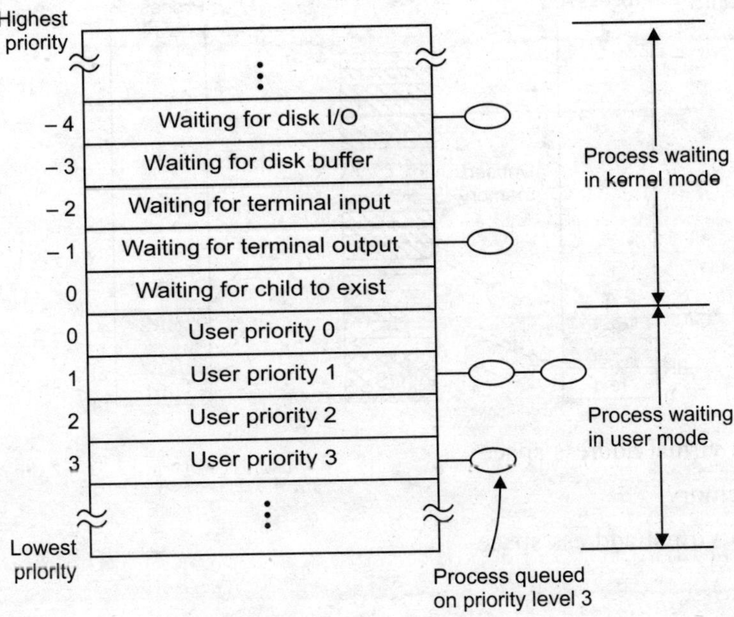

Figure 1.27 UNIX scheduler is based on a multilevel queue structure

Booting UNIX

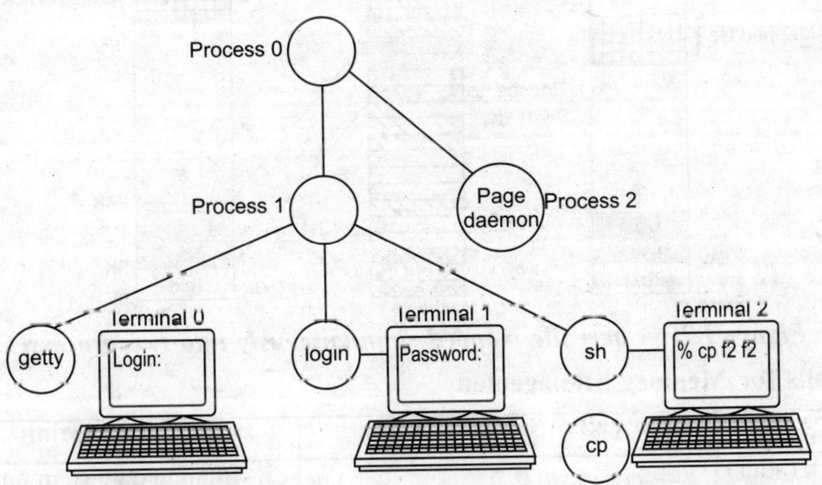

Figure 1.28 The sequences of processes used to boot some systems

Handling Memory

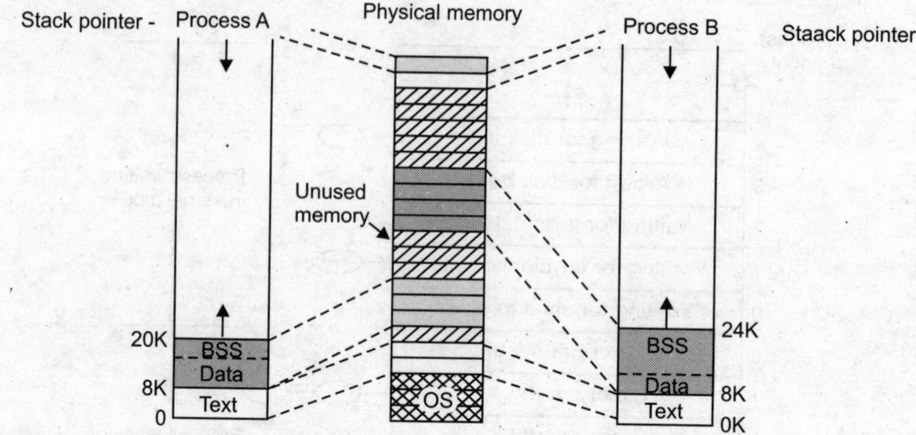

- Process A's virtual address space
- Physical memory
- Process B's virtual address space

Sharing Files

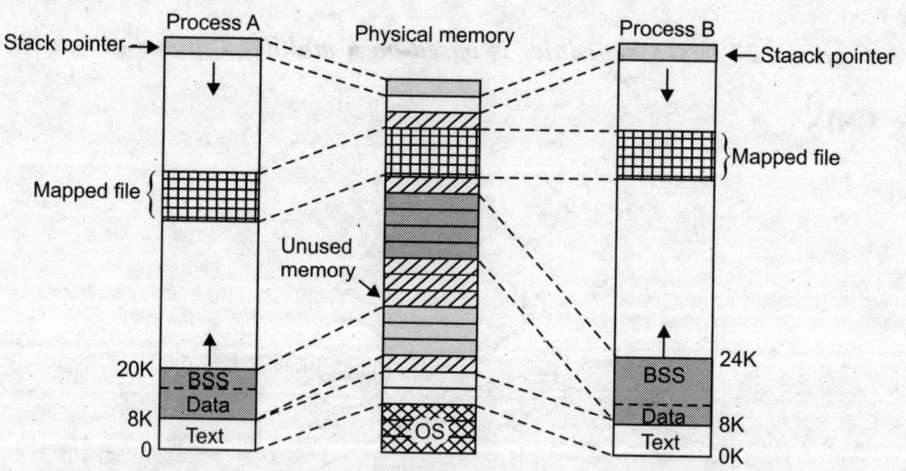

Figure 1.29 A new file mapped simultaneously into two processes

System Calls for Memory Management

System call	Description
s = brk (addr)	Change data segment size
a = mmap (addr, len, prot, flags, fd, offset)	Map a file in
s = unmap (addr, len)	Unmap a file

- **s** is an error code
- **b** and **addr** are memory addresses

- **len** is a length
- **prot** controls protection
- **flags** are miscellaneous bits
- **fd** is a file descriptor
- **offset** is a file offset

Paging in UNIX

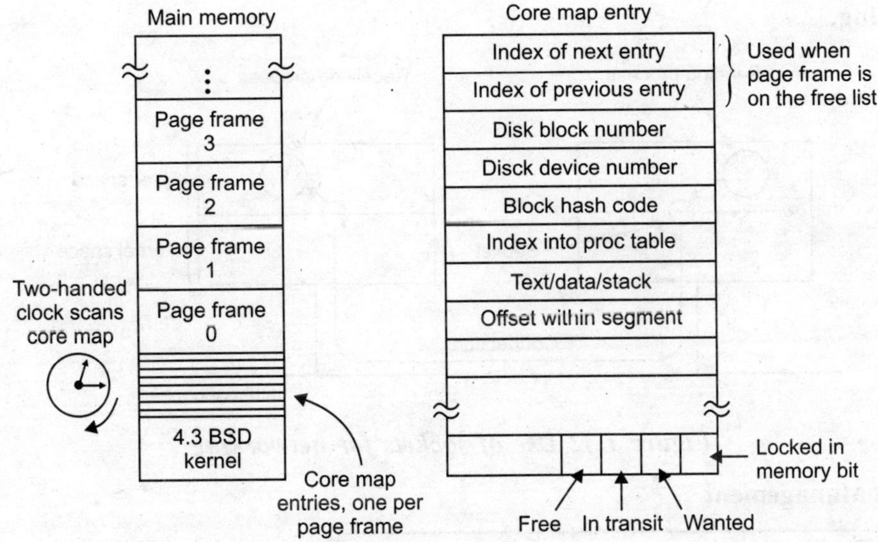

Figure 1.30 The core map has an entry for each page

Paging in Linux

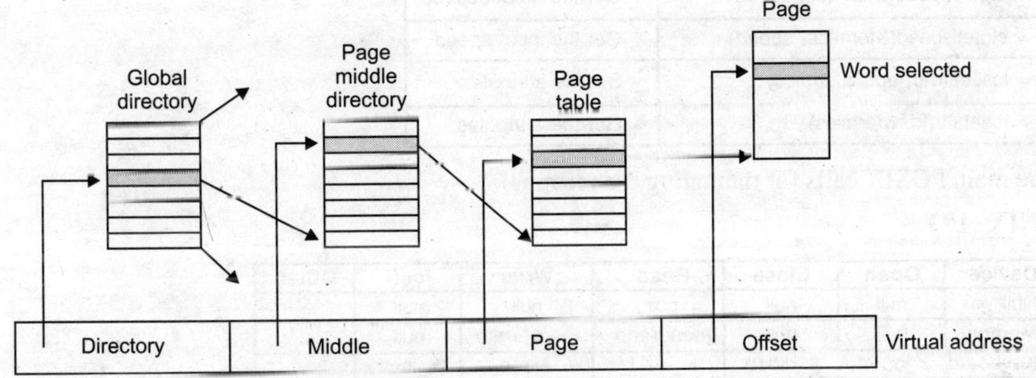

Figure 1.31 Linux uses three-level page tables

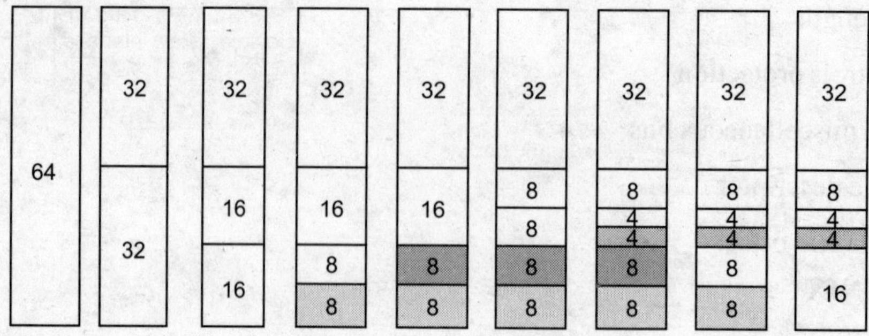

Networking

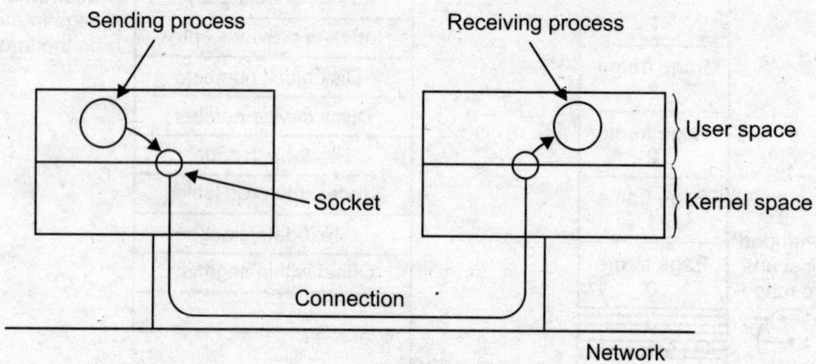

Figure 1.32 Use of sockets for networking

Terminal Management

Function call	Description
s = cfsetospeed(&termios, spped	Set the output speed
s = cfsetispeed(&termios, speed)	Set the input speed
s = cfgetospeed(&termios, speed)	Get the output speed
s = cfgtetispeed(&termios, speed)	Get the input speed
s = tcsetattr(fd, opt, &termios)	Set the attributes
s = tcgetattr(fd, &termios)	Get the attributes

The main POSIX calls for managing the terminal

UNIX I/O

Devlce	Open	Close	Read	Write	Ioctl	Other
Null	null	null	null	null	null	...
Memory	null	null	men_read	mem_write	null	...
Keyboard	k_open	k_close	k_read	error	k_ioctl	...
Tty	tty_open	tty_close	tty_read	tty_write	tty_ioctl	...
Printer	lp_open	lp_close	error	lp_write	lp_ioctl	...

Some of the fields of a typical cdevsw table

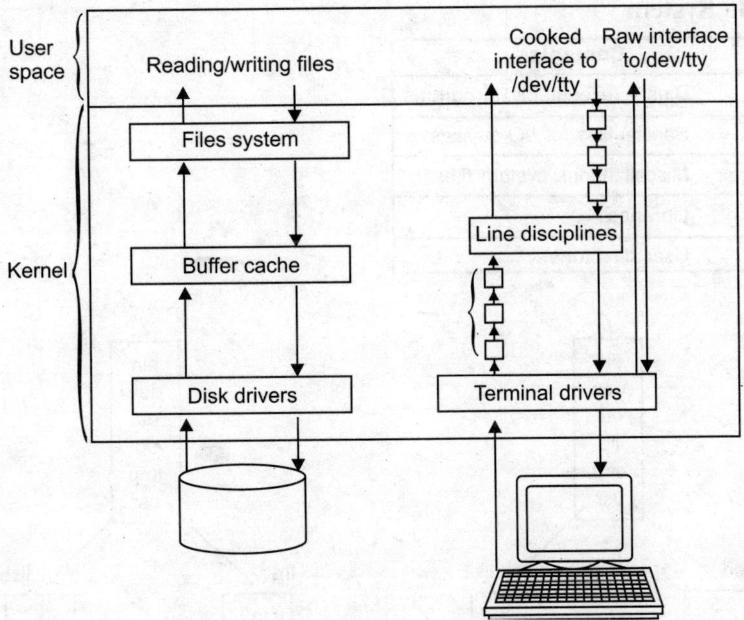

Figure 1.33 The UNIX I/O system in BSD

Streams

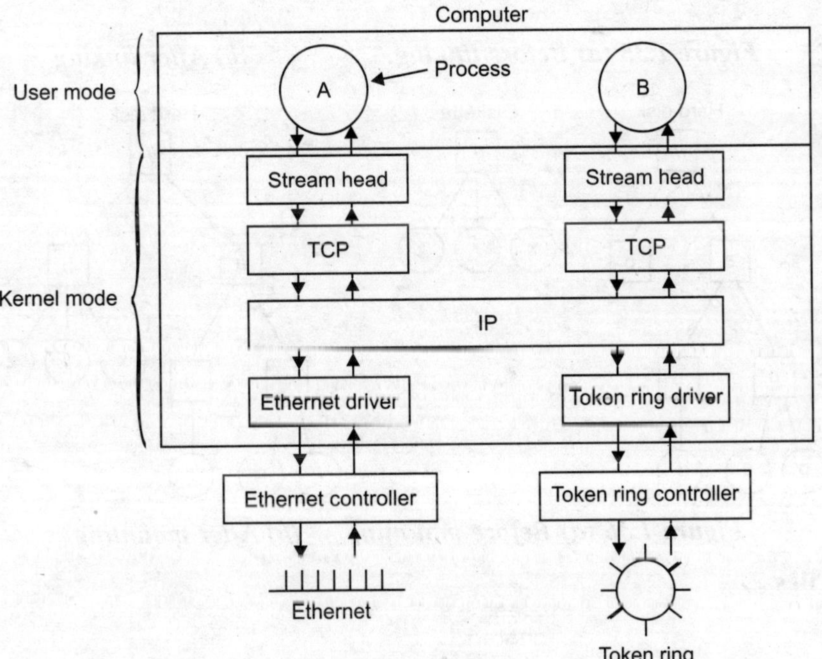

Figure 1.34 An example of streams in System V

The UNIX File System

Directory	Contents
bin	Binary (executable) programs
dev	Special files for I/O devices
etc	Miscellaneous system files
lib	Libraries
usr	User directories

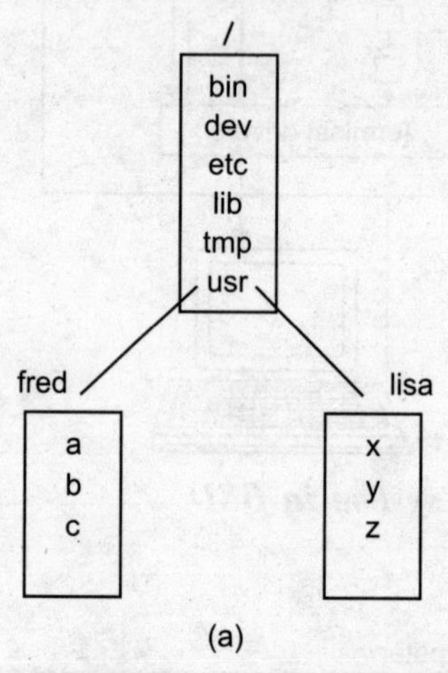

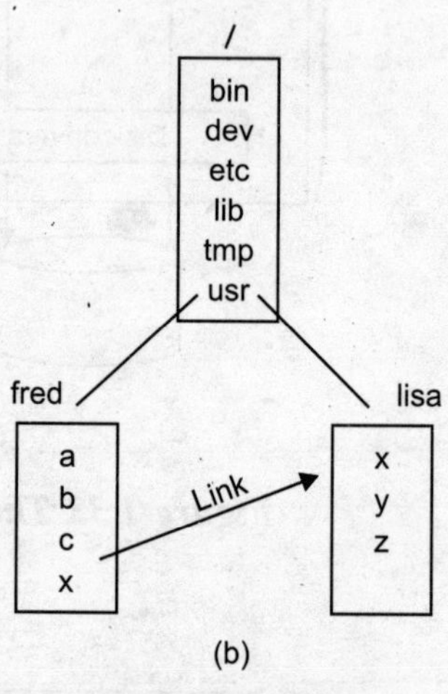

Figure 1.35 (a) Before linking. (b) After linking

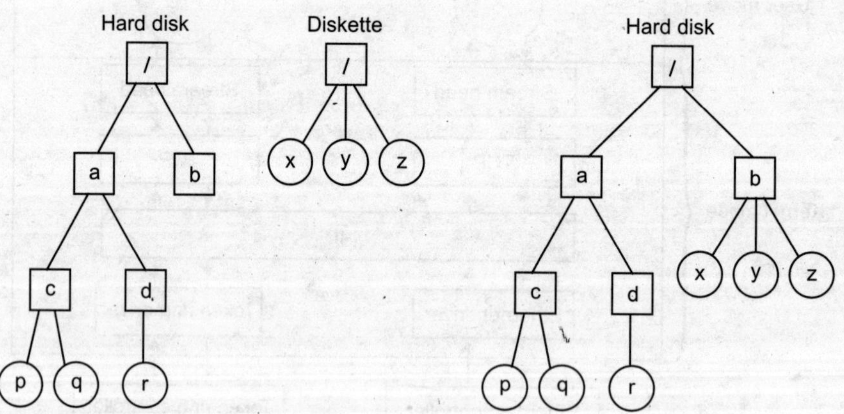

Figure 1.36 (a) Before mounting. (b) After mounting

Locking Files

Process A's shared lock

(a)	0	1	2	3	4	5	6	7	8	9	10	11	12	13	14	15

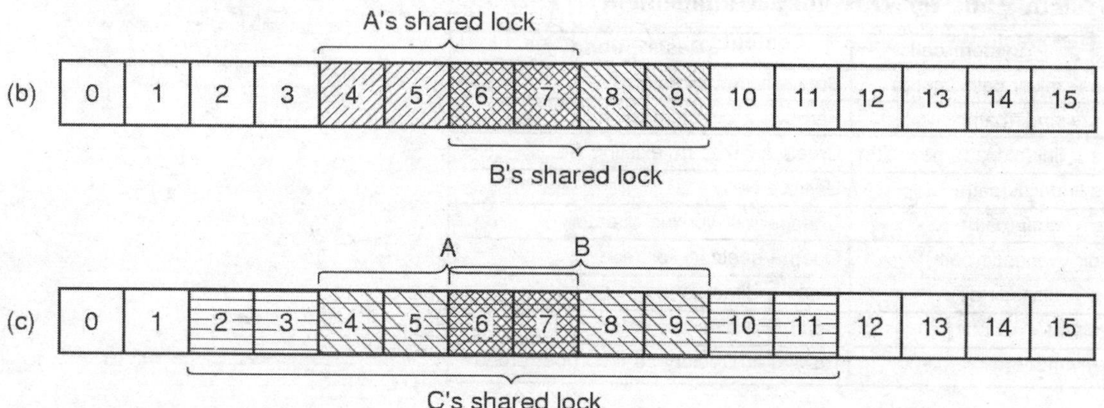

(a) File with one lock

(b) Addition of a second lock

(c) A third lock

System Calls for File Management

System call	Description
fd = creat(name, mode	One way to create a new file
fd = open(file, how,...)	Open a file for reading, writing or both
s = close(fd)	Close an open file
n = read(fd, buffer, nbytes)	Read data from a file into a buffer
n = write(fd, buffer, nbytes)	Write data from a buffer into a file
position = lseek(fd, offset, whence)	Move the file pointer
s = stat(name, &buf)	Get a file's status information
s = fstat(fd, &buf)	Get a file's status information
s = pipe(&fd[0])	Create a pipe
s = fcntl(fd, cmd,...)	File locking and other operations

- s is an error code
- fd is a file descriptor
- position is a file offset

The lstat System Call

Device the file is on
I-node number (which file on the device)
File mode (includes protection information)
Number of links to the file
Identity of the file's owner
Group the file belongs to
File size (in bytes)
Creation time
Time of last access
Time of last modification

Fields returned by the lstat system call.

System Calls for Directory Management

System call	Description
s = mkdir(path, mode)	Create a new directory
s = rmdir(path)	Remove a directory
s = link(oldpath, newpath)	Create a link to an existing file
s = unlink(path)	Unlink a file
s = chdir(path)	Change the working directory
dir = opendir(path)	Open a directory for reading
s = closedir(dir)	Close a directory
dirent = readdir(dir)	Read one directory entry
rewinddir(dir)	Rewind a directory so it can be reread

- **s** is an error code
- **dir** identifies a directory stream
- **dirent** is a directory entry

UNIX File System

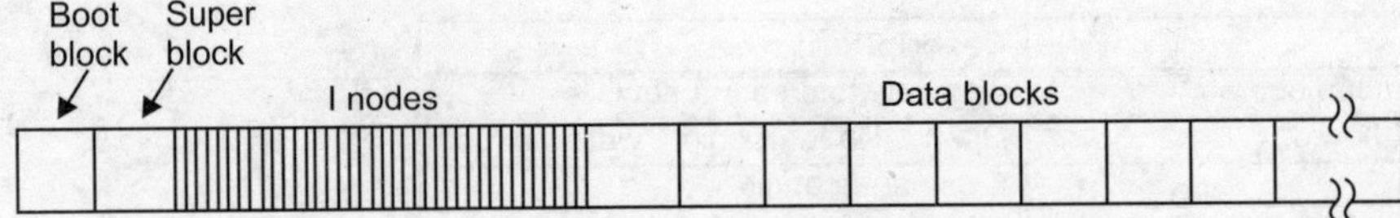

Figure 1.37 Disk layout in classical UNIX systems

Field	Bytes	Description
Mode	2	File type, protection bits, setuid, setgid bits
Nlinks	2	Number of directory entries pointing to this i-node
Uid	2	UID of the file owner
Gid	2	GID of the file owner
Size	4	File size in bytes
Addr	39	Address of first 10 disk blocks, then 3 indirect blocks
Gen	1	Generation number (incremented every time i-node is reused)
Atime	4	Time the file was last accessed
Mtime	4	Time the file was last modified
Ctime	4	Time the i-node was last changed (except the other times)

Structure of the i-node

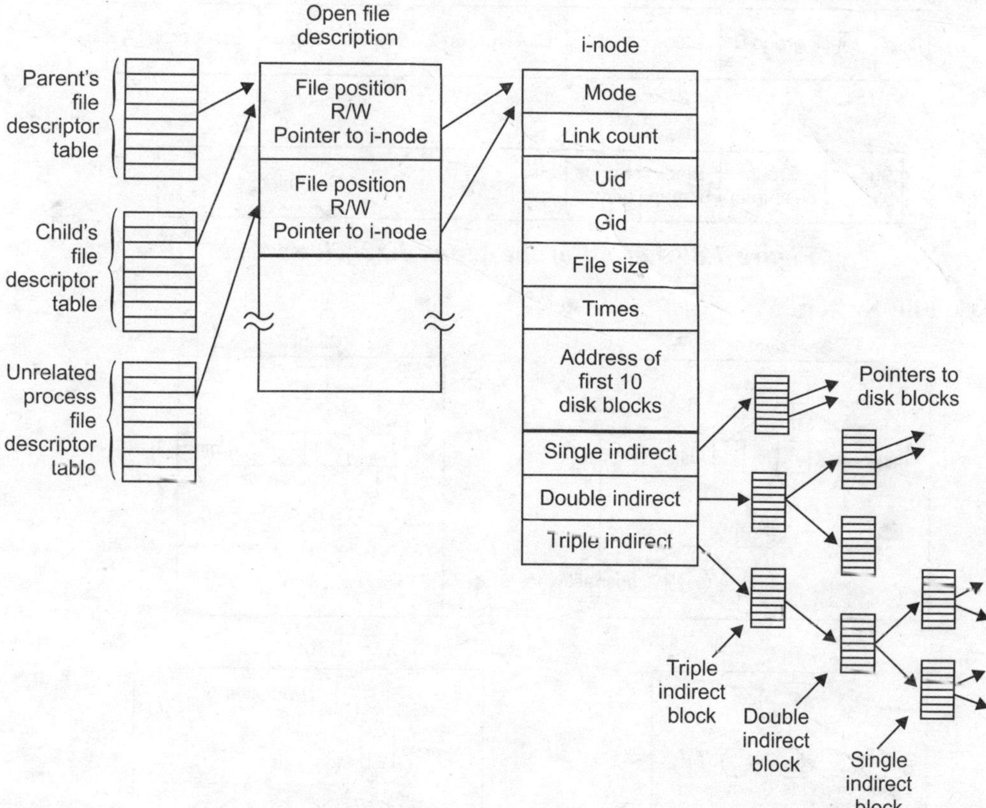

Figure 1.38 The relation between the file descriptor table, the open file description

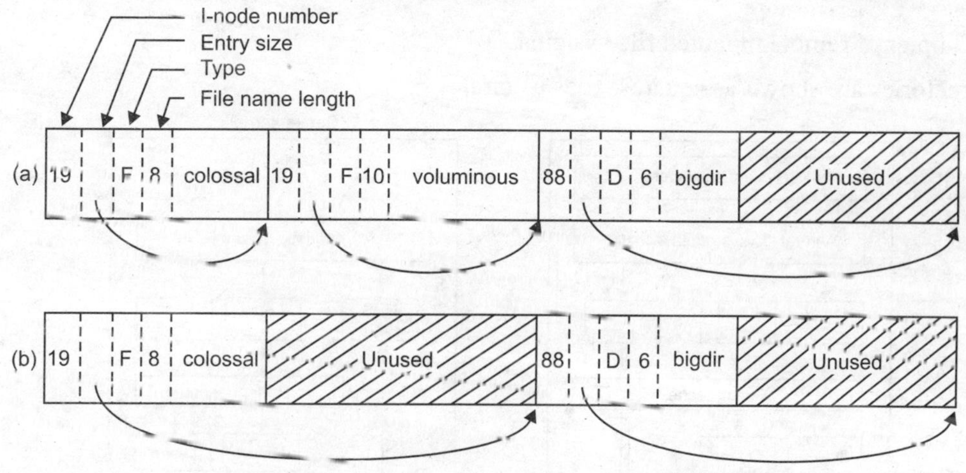

- A BSD directory with three files
- The same directory after the file voluminous has been removed

Linux File System

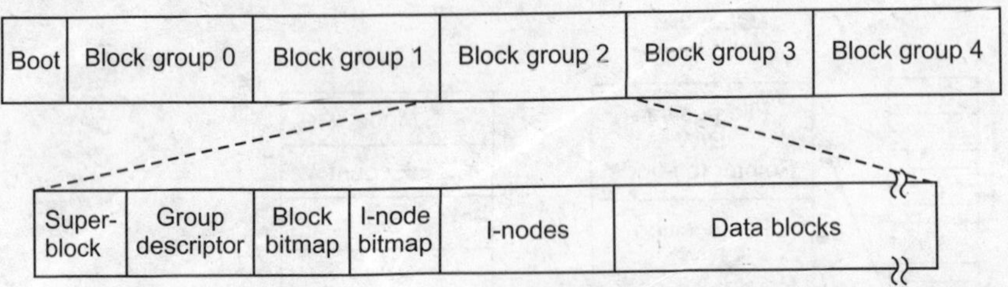

Figure 1.39 Layout of the Linux Ex2 file system.

Network File System

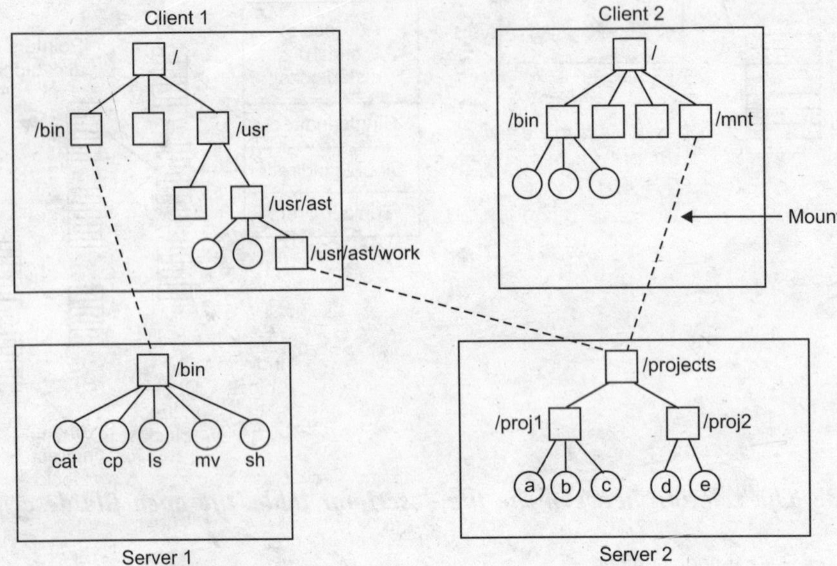

- o Examples of remote mounted file systems
- o Directories are shown as squares, files as circles

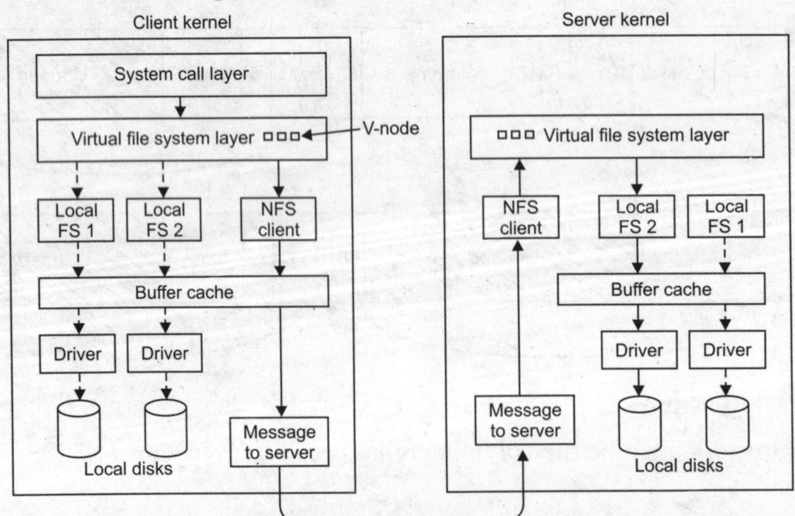

Figure 1.40 The NFS layer structure

Security in UNIX

Binary	Symbolic	Allowed file accesses
111000000	rwx-----------	Owner can read, write, and execute
111111000	rwxrwx------	Owner and group can read, write, and execute
110100000	rw–r--------	Owner can read and write; group can read
110100100	rw–r– –r– –	Owner can read and weite; all others can read
111101101	rwxr–xr–x	Owner can do everything, rest can read and execute
000000000	-------------	Nobody has any access
000000111	-----------rwx	Only outsiders have access (strange, but legal)

Some examples of file protection modes

System Calls for File Protection

System call	Description
s = chmod(path, mode)	Change a file's protection mode
s = access(path, mode)	Check access using the real UID and GID
udi = getuid( )	Get the real UID
uid = geteuid( )	Get the effective UID
gid = getgid( )	Get the real GID
gid = getegid( )	Get the effective GID
s = chown(path, owner, group)	Change owner and group
s = setgid(gid)	Set the GID
s = setgid(gid)	Set the GID

- s is an error code
- **uid** and **gid** are the UID and GID, respectively

1.15 COMPARATIVE STUDIES OF WINDOWS 2003 SERVER AND UNIX/LINUX

Windows has two main lines. The older flavors are referred to as "Win9x" and consist of Windows 95, 98, 98SE and Me. The newer flavors are referred to as "NT class" and consist of Windows NT3, NT4, 2000, XP and Vista. Going back in time, Windows 3.x preceded Windows 95 by a few years. And before that, there were earlier versions of Windows, but they were not popular. Microsoft no longer supports Windows NT3, NT4, all the 9x versions and of course anything older. Support for Windows 2000 is partial (as of April 2007).

The flavors of Linux are referred to as distributions (often shortened to "distros"). All the Linux distributions released around the same time frame will use the same kernel (the guts of the Operating System). They differ in the add-on software provided, GUI, install process, price, documentation and technical support. Both Linux and Windows come in desktop and server editions.

There may be too many distributions of Linux, it's possible that this is hurting Linux in the marketplace. It could be that the lack of a Linux distro from a major computer company is also hurting it in the marketplace. IBM is a big Linux backer but does not have their own branded distribution. Currently there seem to be many nice things said about the Ubuntu distribution.

Linux is customizable in a way that Windows is not. For one, the user interface, while similar in concept, varies in detail from distribution to distribution. For example, the task bar may default to being on the top or the bottom. Also, there are many special purpose versions of Linux above and beyond the full blown distributions described above. For example, NASLite is a version of Linux that runs off a single floppy disk (since revised to also boot from a CD) and converts an old computer into a file server. This ultra small edition of Linux is capable of networking, file sharing and being a web server.

1.15.1 Graphical User Interface

Both Linux and Windows provide a GUI and a command line interface. The Windows GUI has changed from Windows 3.1 to Windows 95 (drastically) to Windows 2000 (slightly) to Windows XP (fairly large) and is slated to change again with the next version of Windows, the one that will replace XP. Windows XP has a themes feature that offers some customization of the look and feel of the GUI.

Linux typically provides two GUIs, KDE and Gnome. See a screen shot of Lycoris and Lindows in action from the Wal-Mart web site. The lynucs.org web site has examples of many substantially different Linux GUIs. Of the major Linux distributions, Lindows has made their user interface look more like Windows than the others. Here is a screen shot of Linux made to look like Windows XP. Then too, there is XPde for Linux which really makes Linux look like Windows. Quoting their web site "It's a desktop environment (XPde) and a window manager (XPwm) for Linux. It tries to make easier for Windows XP users to use a Linux box."

Mark Minasi makes the point (Windows and .NET magazine, March 2000) that the Linux GUI is optional while the Windows GUI is an integral component of the OS. He says that speed, efficiency and reliability are all increased by running a server instance of Linux without a GUI, something that server versions of Windows can not do. In the same article he points out that the detached nature of the Linux GUI makes remote control and remote administration of a Linux computer simpler and more natural than a Windows computer.

Is the flexibility of the Linux GUI a good thing? Yes and No. While advanced users can customize things to their liking, it makes things harder on new users for whom every Linux computer they encounter may look and act differently.

1.15.2 Text Mode Interface

This is also known as a command interpreter. Windows users sometimes call it a DOS prompt. Linux users refer to it as a shell. Each version of Windows has a single command interpreter, but the different flavours of Windows have different interpreters. In general, the command interpreters in the Windows 9x series are very similar to each other and the NT class versions of Windows (NT, 2000, XP) also have similar command interpreters. There are however differences between a Windows 9x command interpreter and one in an NT class flavor of Windows. Linux, like all versions of Unix, supports multiple command interpreters, but it usually uses one called BASH (Bourne Again Shell). Others are the Korn shell, the Bourne shell, ash and the C shell (pun, no doubt, intended).

1.15.3 Cost

For desktop or home use, Linux is very cheap or free, Windows is expensive. For server use, Linux is very cheap compared to Windows. Microsoft allows a single copy of Windows to be used on only one computer. Starting with Windows XP, they use software to enforce this rule (Windows Product Activation at first, later Genuine Windows). In contrast, once you have purchased Linux, you can run it on any number of computers for no additional charge.

As of January 2005, the upgrade edition of Windows XP Home Edition sells for about $100, XP Professional is about $200. The "full" version of XP Home is about $200, the full version of XP Professional is $300. Windows Server 2003 Standard Edition with 10 Client licenses is about $1,100. Because they save $100 or so on the cost of Windows, Wal-Mart can sell a Linux based computer for $200 (without a monitor) whereas their cheapest Windows XP computer is $300 (as of January 2005).

The irony here is that Windows rose to dominance, way back when, in large part by undercutting the competition (Macs) on cost. Now Linux may do the same thing to Windows.

You can buy a Linux book and get the operating system included with the book for free. You can also download Linux for free from each of the Linux vendors (assuming your Internet connection is fast enough for a 600 MB file and you have a CD burner) or from www.linuxiso.org. Both these options however, come without technical support. All versions of the Ubuntu distribution are free.

You can purchase assorted distributions of Linux in a box with a CD and manuals and technical support for around $40 to $80 (some distributions may be less, others may be more). Regular updates and ongoing support range from $35 a year for a desktop version of Linux to $1,500 for a high-end server version. August 2004 Red Hat started selling a desktop oriented version of Linux for under $6 per user per year.

After the initial cost (or lack thereof) of obtaining software, there is the ongoing cost of its care and feeding. In October 2002, ComputerWorld magazine quoted the chief technology architect at Merrill Lynch & Co. in New York as saying that "the cost of running Linux is typically a tenth of the cost of Unix and Microsoft alternatives." The head technician at oil company Amerada Hess manages 400 Linux servers by himself. He was quoted as saying "It takes fewer people to manage the Linux machines than Windows machines." Microsoft commissioned a study that (no surprise) found it cheaper to maintain Windows than Linux. However, one of the authors of the study accused Microsoft of stacking the deck by selecting scenarios that are more expensive to maintain on Linux.

1.15.4 Installing the Operating System

There are three ways to install Windows XP: a clean install, an upgrade install and a repair install. Then, there is a "recovery" install, which is not an install in the true sense of the word but rather the restoration of a disk image backup.

- A clean install refers to starting with nothing (either an entirely empty hard disk or just an empty partition or just unallocated space on the hard disk) and ending up with just Windows.
- An upgrade install refers to starting with an older version of Windows and ending up with a newer version. Existing data files and applications should not be affected by the upgrade to the newer edition of Windows.
- A repair install refers to installing the same version of Windows on top of itself. This is used to fix a broken copy of Windows and existing data files and applications are not affected.
- A "recovery" is typically used to restore a computer to its factory fresh state. All data files are wiped out. All applications installed since the computer was new, are wiped out. All upgrades to

Windows itself (patches, service packs) are lost. Applications pre-installed by the computer manufacturer are restored. Originally this was done from CDs, then DVDs. Now it is normally done from a hidden area of the hard disk.

Then there is Windows Vista where much has changed. I'm not familiar with the install options for Vista. Andy Pennell, a Microsoft employee, wrote about his problems installing Vista on June 21, 2007. He is very familiar with Windows and installed Vista onto a second internal hard disk, leaving the existing hard disk with Windows XP unchanged. At least that was the plan. See Installing Vista: My Personal Hell. Installing Vista on a computer with an existing copy of Windows, with the intention of dual-booting, is much trickier than it used to be with earlier versions of Windows.

There is a huge variation in the Linux installation procedure. Different distributions of Linux have their own installation programs (which may even change with different versions of the same distribution). Installing Linux on a computer without an existing operating system is much easier than installing it on a machine with an existing OS that you want to preserve.

I'm sure that installing Linux is getting easier all the time. While I haven't done it all that often, I have seen it become easier over time. Is it easy enough for you?

- Ed Bott blogged about his experience installing Linux on July 31, 2006. Linux, XP, and my old PC
- In March 2007, he tried again with mixed success. Why does Linux hate me?
- A picture is worth a thousand words so this July 2007 picture show at ZDnet on Installing OpenSUSE 10.2 is instructive
- In June 2007, I installed Ubuntu v7.4 on an IBM NetVista machine that was about four years old. The system would only run at 640x480 and things went downhill from there. The problem may have been due to a KVM switch that prevented the system from querying the monitor. However, instead of asking me or telling me anything about a failure to detect the monitor, it just ran at 640x480 with no GUI based facility to increase the resolution.

When installing Linux on a machine where you don't need to preserve the existing operating system, there is likely to be an option to clobber the existing OS as part of the Linux installation procedure. Or, you can use a program to totally wipe everything off the hard disk before installing Linux. The free Darik's Boot and Nuke is fairly famous for this. Better yet, the hard disk vendor should have a free utility that not only wipes the hard disk but also can run diagnostics on the disk.

You can also buy a new computer without any operating system. A low end Dell server, the PowerEdge 840 sold for $600 in June 2007. You can buy an HP ProLiant server starting at $500 that is certified to run six Linux distributions. IBM is big on Linux, quoting their web site: "The entire IBM Systems product line is Linux enabled." They sell computers both with no operating system and with Linux pre-installed. Nothing there is cheap however. Wal-Mart used to sell Microtel machines without an OS, but no more.

Installing Linux for dual booting, that is, keeping the existing operating system in tact, is probably best left to techies. It is all too easy to lose the pre-existing OS. You need to be familiar with hard disk partitions and some Linux terminology. With Red Hat Linux 8, the booklet on how to install the OS was over a hundred pages.

1.15.5 Running Linux Without Installing IT

Added November 23, 2008: ZAReason sells a bootable copy of Ubuntu on a 4GB USB flash drive for $39.99. In general new computers can boot from a USB flash drive, however older computers may not be able to. According to the company, the drive is configured to support persistence, but it is not the default option. That is, by default it functions like a Live CD and throws away all record of your actions. However, at bootup you can select persistence if you want. That said, the company noted in an email that versions of Ubuntu prior to Intreped were "somewhat buggy with persistence".

Added July 10, 2008: From my CNET blog Why you want a Linux Live CD.

One thing that Linux can do that Windows can not, is run from a CD. To run Windows, it has to first be installed to your hard disk. Normally Linux also runs from a hard disk, but there are quite a few versions of Linux that run completely from a CD without having to be installed to a hard disk. The term for this is a "Live" CD.

Running a Live CD version of Linux is a great way for Windows users to experience Linux for the first time. Among the Linux distros that have a CD-only version are Knoppix, Ubuntu and Open SuSE). I tried SuSE Live Eval version 9 in October 2003 and had some gripes. FreeBSD, a version of Unix (rather than Linux), also has a LiveCD.

That said, if Windows is broken to the point that it can't start up, there is a free program called Bart's Preinstalled Environment (BartPE) that can run a few Windows programs from a bootable CD. However, this is not from Microsoft and is only intended to fix a broken copy of Windows; it is not for everyday use. BartPE can only run a handful of programs that have been set up ahead of time for use with it. BartPE fills an important need, but creating the CD is not trivial, it requires a Windows CD (not recovery CDs or DVDs) and it only works with Windows XP and 2003 (not sure about Vista). The main point stands, in and of itself, Windows can not run from a CD.

The CD based versions of Linux differ in their use of the hard disk. Some, such as Lindows, do not write anything at all to your hard disk, making it the safest and easiest way to experience Linux. The downside of this is speed (CDs are much slower than hard disks) and continuity (being able to save data between uses). Other versions, such as SuSE 9 (this is now up to v10.2), do use your hard disk (SuSE 9 creates over 200 MB worth of files). What you give up in safety, you gain in speed. For reviews of Linux distributions that run from a CD see A Taste of Linux by Jim Lynch at ExtremeTech January 23, 2004 and A Taste of Linux, Part Two by Jim Lynch March 5, 2004.

In addition to kicking the tires on Linux, a Live CD can also be used to insure that your hardware is supported by that specific version of Linux. Bootable Linux CDs are also used to recover files when Windows breaks to the point of not being able to start up. A recent Live Linux CD should be able to see all Windows files (they can read NTFS) and copy them to an external USB device or another computer on a LAN. Older CD based versions of Lindows and SuSE could not read files stored in an NTFS partition.

In October 2005 a whole new way of running Linux without installing it was introduced: Virtual Machines from VMware. Virtual machines let you run multiple operating systems on one computer at the same time. You can't beat it (virtual machines are used to run Windows on the Intel based Macs).

Using the free VMware Player you can download pre-built Linux virtual machines. Think of the VMware Player as analogous to the Adobe Acrobat Reader. Creating virtual machines costs money, but playing them does not.

VMware has been creating virtual machines on PCs for a long time. Running a virtual machine previously required their expensive software (VMWare Workstation was $200 in April 2007, only a couple years previously it cost almost twice that). Now it can be done for free. And prior to October 2005 there were no pre-built virtual machines available from VMWare, if you wanted to run Linux, you had to install it.

Now you can get a pre-installed virtual copy of Ubuntu v7.04 Server, OpenBSD 4.0 and CentOS 5.0. Even better, many pre-built Linux virtual machines come with pre-installed applications. Want to run the Apache web server and the MySQL database? Just download a VM with them installed.

For years you could have installed Linux into a new virtual machine. It is a great way to learn and experiment. However, creating a new virtual virtual machine required the somewhat expensive VMWare workstation. Now, the free VMware Server software can be used to create a new virtual machine into which you can install any operating system. You can also download new, empty virtual machines from EasyVMX.

VMWare Server has another big plus: it supports a checkpoint (a.k.a. restore point, synch point). You can take a checkpoint in your virtual machine, work on it a while and then revert the VM back to the checkpoint. All for free. How things change.

Microsoft also has free virtual machine software but there are no-prebuilt virtual machines for it. Needless to say, Microsoft is not going to provide Linux virtual machines and they make a lot of money selling Windows so they're not going to give it away. Also, their software is not as mature as VMware, not as robust and I've read that it runs slower.

VMware is not the only free virtual machine software. VirtualBox is free and open source. Yet another way to run Linux without installing it is from a flash drive (a.k.a thumb drive, USB drive, pen drive, memory stick, etc.).

In June 2006 David Pogue wrote about Linux distros can run from a thumb drive (A Handy Tip From a Reader on Flash Drives) where the two distros mentioned are 50MB (Damn Small Linux) and 70MB. In fact, Damn Small Linux does even more tricks. It can run from within Windows! And, if you have 128MB of ram to spare, it can run completely in ram, which has got to be fast.

In November 2005, you could have purchased a 3GB MicroDrive (1 inch hard disk) with Ubuntu Linux. The drive plugs into a USB port and is fully powered by the USB port.

1.15.6 Application Software

There is more application software available for Windows. Then again, there may be sufficient Linux software for your needs.

Obtaining application software: If you buy a copy of Windows on a CD-ROM, you get no application software with it. If you buy a copy of Linux on a CD-ROM (or two or three) it typically comes with gobs of free application software. Likewise, Linux ISO downloads usually include lots of application software. The exceptions are Linux distributions that are small on purpose such as Damn Small Linux or Pen Drive Linux.

A new computer with Windows pre-installed normally comes additional application software, exactly what to include is up to the PC vendor. On one extreme, I have seen a new Sharp laptop machine that came with no software other than Windows itself. This is rare. In contrast, Sony VAIOs, for example, are more mainstream and come with a lot of software. However, there are two problems with the pre-installed application software on Windows computers.

First, much of it is junk. So much, that a new term "crapware" is being used to describe it. The PC vendors make money by installing this software that many people consider worse than useless. In fact, the first thing many techies do is un-install this software, someone even came out with a PC de-crapifier program to automate the un-installs. Windows computers sold to businesses tend to have less undesirable application software pre-installed compared to computers sold to consumers. I have never heard of anyone complaining about the software that comes pre-installed in the normal, popular versions of Linux.

Second, important software is often missing or old. For example, the Adobe Acrobat reader, may not pre-installed by the PC vendor. In February 2008, I blogged about a new Lenovo computer that came with terribly old versions of application software.

On the Linux side, to get a feel for the application software that comes with Ubuntu version 8.04 see Adventures with open source apps on Linux - Part 1 by Adrian Kingsley-Hughes from May 23rd, 2008.

Application software installation: The installation of applications under Windows, while not standardized, is generally consistent and generally pretty easy. Installing software under Linux varies with each distribution and has not been nearly as simple, easy or obvious as Windows. A couple articles from 2004 griped about how hard it was to install software in Liunx: The May 20, 2004 issue of the Langa list newsletter and a July 4, 2004 review of Linux in the Washington Post (Linux, Still an Awkward Alternative) where Rob Pegoraro called application software installation "Linux's biggest embarrassment".

That said, current Linux distributions have an application somewhat akin to Windows update that can be used to install software. I don't have much experience doing this. However, in April 2008 I used one of the new $200 Walmart Linux gOS machines and found the application for installing software very confusing, and it failed every time I tried to install something.

1.15.7 Crossing the OS Boundary

A program written for Linux will not run under Windows and vice versa. For example, Microsoft makes a version of Office for Windows and another version for the Mac. They are two different products, each capable of only running on the operating system it was designed for. There is no version of Microsoft Office for Linux.

On the other hand, some programs, such as Firefox, are available for multiple operating systems. Firefox runs on Linux, Windows, Macs and more. Open Office competes with Microsoft Office and comes in versions for Windows (all the way from Windows 98 up to Vista), GNU/Linux ("Linux"), Sun Solaris, Mac OS X (under X11), and FreeBSD.

The process of making a new version of a program that will run on a different operating system is called "porting". But there are other ways to get a program to run on an operating system other than the one it was designed for.

1.15.8 Virtual Machines

The most ambitious approach is to install one operating system inside another. Perhaps the most popular example of this is with Intel based Macintosh computers. Software from Parallels (Parallels

Desktop 3.0 for Mac) and from VMware (Fusion) lets you run Windows at the same time as Mac OS X. In this example, the Mac OS X is referred to as the host or native operating system; it's the one that gets run when the computer is turned on. Windows is referred to as the guest operating system. This approach is called Virtual Machines. Assorted virtual machine software is available that lets Linux, Macs and Windows operate as either the host or guest operating system.

In a guest copy of Windows, running under either Linux or Mac OS X as the host OS, you can install any and all Windows programs. Somewhat like a split personality, one computer can run two (or more) operating systems at the same time. VMware was the first to market with a virtual machine product (also called VMware) for personal computers. Virtual PC, has competed with VMware for a long time. A parallel is a more recent competitor. VirtualBox is free and open source virtual machine software. Virtual Machine products from these companies differ in their supported host and guest operating systems.

Win4Lin is virtual machine software that only supports Linux as the host OS and only supports Windows (95, 98, Me, 2000 or XP) as the guest OS.

1.15.9 Specific Applications

Less ambitious than virtual machine products (which let you run any application in the guest OS) are approaches targeted at only running a handful of Windows applications under Linux.

The simplest example is probably IEs 4 Linux which lets you run Internet Explorer versions 6 and 5 under Linux. It's free. For more, see Run Internet Explorer on Linux by Brian Smith Oct 11, 2007.

Some distributions of Linux include commercial software called Crossover Office from CodeWeavers that runs Microsoft Office (versions 2003, XP, 2000 and 97) and some other Windows applications under Linux. While this approach does less, it does not require a Windows license. Codeweavers has a list of supported applications and a comparison of their approach vs. virtual machines.

Since Crossover Office is a commercial product, it is not included in the free distributions of Linux. As of October 2007 CodeWeavers sold it for $40 or $70 depending on the version.

CrossOver is based on the Wine project. Wine is free software and is included with many GNU/ Linux distributions. After 15 years of development, the first "finished" version of Wine was released in June 2008 (see Run Windows Software on Linux with Wine 1.0). Wine is, to a computer nerd, very interesting. It lets Windows applications run under Linux without a copy of Windows and without any virtualization. Windows applications talk to Windows using a specification known as the Windows API. Wine intercepts each Windows API command/request made by a Windows program and does, in Linux, the functions Windows does in response to the same command.

Wine does not, and will not, provide 100% compatibility; it will never run all Windows applications perfectly. Even applications that it runs well, may not have all their features and functions available. The Wine Project maintains a list of applications and how well they run under Wine. LifeHacker did a good intro to Wine in June 2008: Run Windows Apps in Linux with Wine 1.0.

Mary Jo Foley wrote that the Microsoft WGA (Windows Genuine Advantage) program looks for Windows programs running with Wine and purposely generates an error. See Microsoft Seeks to Bottle Up Open Source Wine (February 18, 2005).

As far as I know, the first Linux distribution that could run Windows applications was Lindows. As far back as October 2002, Xandros Linux Desktop v1.0 (previously Corel Linux) could run Windows applications. (ExtremeTech review). When SuSE Linux Office Desktop was released in January 2003, it too could run Microsoft Office applications thanks to Crossover Office.

TransGaming makes WineX which allows Linux users to run various Windows games that require OpenGL and DirectX. The combination of CrossOver Office and WineX should let you run many Windows programs under Linux. In July 2004 TransGaming gave WineX a new name, Cedega, and announced support some DirectX 9 games. (Linux Takes on Windows Gaming from ExtremeTech July 28, 2004) On yet another front, Ximian (owned by Novell) is developing Project Mono, which will allow Microsoft .Net applications to run on Linux.

On still another front, Adobe Air lets you run the same application on multiple Operating Systems. Interesting article on whether running Windows applications under Linux is a good idea: GNU/Linux Desktop: The Case Against Running Windows Apps by Bruce Byfield February 26, 2008.

1.15.10 Server Based Applications

There is yet another approach to crossing the operating system divide that goes by the names Terminal Services, Server Based Computing and Thin Client Computing. This approach runs applications on a server and sends a picture of the output to another (client) computer. From the client computer, keystrokes and mouse movements are sent back to the server. This approach is totally dependent on a network.

Windows applications are run by a server version of Windows and use the Terminal Services feature to communicate with a client computer. Depending on the software used, the client computer may be running Linux or Windows or a Mac. The all Microsoft solution can be supplemented with software from other companies (Citrix being the market leader) to provide advanced features. Years back, I used an earlier version of the Citrix software, then known as WinFrame, to provide Windows NT applications to client computers running Windows 95 and 98.

1.15.11 Security

The vast majority of malicious software (of all types) runs on Windows. I don't know the actual percentages, but it wouldn't surprise me if it was 98% or so. Windows users are burdened with the need for anti-virus and anti-spyware software

Linux [has] ... the notion of an administrative (root) user that maintains and operates the system, and desktop users who only run the software on the system, is completely ingrained in most Linux distributions. Now it's true that many Linux users ignore these features and run all their software from a root-level account anyway, but that's a choice that they've made. The system defaults to protecting the operating system components from its user's actions (intentional or otherwise). That feature alone must account in large degree for the dearth of viruses and other malicious vermin on Linux and UNIX platforms. Windows, on the other hand, started life as a single user system, with that single user being all-powerful. Although that's no longer the case, the general attitude can still be found in many Windows-based software products - many of which just can't be installed and/or run properly without desktop administrator privileges. This is all changing for the better, but it took Microsoft far too long to adopt this default-secure configuration practice.

1.15.12 Users and Passwords

Both Linux and Windows 2000/XP require a userid and password and boot time. That said, Windows XP supports users without a password (a very bad idea), I'm not sure if Linux does.

Windows can be configured to either ask for the userid/password at startup time or a default can be set instead. In Windows 2000 it is very easy to set a default userid/password, in Windows XP the method varies between the Home and Pro versions - in one it is straightforward, in the other it's a pain.

I've been told that in Linux the KDM and GDM login managers support automatic login. I've also been told that most versions of Linux do not allow the root user to login automatically. Windows, in contrast, is happy to let an Administrative user auto-login. Get started faster in Ubuntu explains how to configure Ubuntu to boot without asking for a userid/password.

A new Windows XP machine used by a home user is likely to not ask for a userid/password at start-up. However, this depends on the number of users defined to Windows. When you create a new user in XP the default is not to require a password (user friendly triumphs over security - the Microsoft way). Windows 98, never mind.

Windows XP, 2000 and Linux all support different types or classes of users. Windows XP Home Edition supports Administrator class users that have full and total access to the system and restricted users that, among other restrictions, can't install software. Windows XP Pro and Windows 2000 support additional levels of users.

Both Linux and Windows can group users into groups (finally, something well named) and assign privileges to the group rather than to each individual user. Windows XP and 2000 come with some pre-defined user groups (such as Power Users), I don't think Linux does (but I'm not sure). In XP and 2000 user "Administrator" is a member of the Administrators group.

Linux privileges are basically whether you can read, modify or execute a file. Files in Linux are always owned by a specific user and group. Windows has similar file-related privileges but only when using the NTFS file system. The earlier FAT and FAT32 file systems had no file level security.

I'm told that Windows NTFS permissions are a bit more functional than those in Linux, but that Linux distributions are starting to use extended Access Control Lists as a part of the file system, bringing them more on par with NTFS. (I won't swear by this)

Very often Windows users use an Administrator class userid which gives viruses total access to their system (see Why you should not run your computer as an administrator from Microsoft). This obviates the security rules discussed above. In contrast, Linux users often run as regular non-root users which not only means better security it also means that, if they get a virus, the operating system greatly restricts what the virus can do.

I have tried a couple times to set up a Windows XP computer for use by a family, creating Administrator class userids for the parents and restricted userids for children. Both cases failed because there were too many programs that did not function correctly when run by a restricted Windows user (more details here). While Linux has supported the concept of root and restricted users from the get-go, this is a relatively new thing to Windows. It will be a long time before all Windows software is designed to be used by a restricted user. Until then, viruses and malware will have free reign on Windows machines. Certainly software written for Windows 95, 98 and Me expects total system access and may not work when run from a restricted userid.

1.15.13 Supported Hardware Devices

While Linux itself runs on many more computers than Windows, when it comes to hardware peripherals, many work with Windows but not with Linux. The hardware vendors write drivers for Windows more often than they do for Linux. Market share and all that. Some hardware vendors will release technical specs so that someone in the Linux community can write a driver for the device, but other vendors aren't so open minded.

Everything isn't rosy in the Windows world however. When Windows XP was released, many existing peripherals would not work with it because XP required new drivers and the vendors had little motivation to write drivers for old hardware. The exact same scenario played out all over again when Vista was released. I think it's fair to say that hardware support was pretty lame when Vista was first released. This is not a knock on Microsoft.

The poor hardware support in Linux is drastically illustrated in an article by Fred Langa. He wrote about problems getting nine different Linux distributions (versions) to work correctly with two different sound cards (one real, one virtual) that all versions of Windows, even back to Windows 95, dealt with perfectly (see Linux's Achilles' Heel, Information Week magazine. April 19, 2004).

In Ten key differences between Linux and Windows (September 2008) Jack Wallen, a Linux devotee, about this: "One issue that is slowly becoming nonexistent is hardware support ... You can grab a PC (or laptop) and most likely get one or more Linux distributions to install and work nearly 100 percent. But there are still some exceptions; for instance, hibernate/suspend remains a problem with many laptops, although it has come a long way."

1.15.14 Hardware the OS Runs on

Linux runs on many different hardware platforms, not so with Windows. For example, Windows NT used to run on MIPS CPUs until Microsoft changed their mind. It also used to run on Alpha CPUs, again, until Microsoft changed their mind. No one gets to change their mind with Linux. It runs on a very wide range of computers, from the lowest of the low to the highest of the high. The supported range of computers is all but stunning.

Because of its ability to run without a GUI, and thus need less hardware horsepower than Windows, Linux can run on very old personal computers such as 486 based machines. I took a Linux class where the server the students used was a 100 MHz Pentium. To get more mileage out of old hardware, Papa John's converted 2,900 pizzerias to Linux. On the high end, Linux runs natively on IBM mainframes (the Z series) and on other high end IBM servers. eBay runs their web site on Linux as does Google. IBM's family of "Blue Gene" supercomputers, used by Lawrence Livermore National Laboratory for nuclear weapons simulations, run Linux. NASA uses it on supercomputers that run space-shuttle simulations. On the small side, the iPodLinux Project created a version of Linux that runs on Apple iPods. NEC is working on Linux-based cell phones and Motorola is going to make Linux its primary operating system for smart cell phones. Debian Linux can run on on a computer the size of a deck of playing cards (100mm by 55mm) with an ARM cpu. In the home, Sony and Matsushita (parent company of Panasonic) will use Linux to build increasingly 'smart' microwave ovens, TVs and other consumer gizmos. Likewise MontaVista Software will release a version of its embedded Linux for use in consumer electronics devices.

1.15.15 Clustering

Linux has an edge here. It has been used to make enormous clusters of computers. In October 2002, ComputerWorld magazine said: "Linux clusters provide supercomputer-type performance at a fraction of the expense." The same article reported that Merrill Lynch runs a cluster of 50 Linux computers. In March 2005, Forbes magazine reported that: "Linux now has become so technically powerful that it lays claim to a prestigious title--it runs more of the world's top supercomputers than any other operating system."(see Linux Rules Supercomputers by Daniel Lyons March 15, 2005).

1.15.16 Multiple Users

Linux is a multi-user system, Windows is not. That is, Windows is designed to be used by one person at a time. Databases running under Windows allow concurrent access by multiple users, but the Operating System itself is designed to deal with a single human being at a time. Linux, like all Unix variants, is designed to handle multiple concurrent users. Windows, of course, can run many programs concurrently, as can Linux. There is a multi-user version of Windows called Terminal Server but this is not the Windows pre-installed on personal computers.

1.15.17 Networking

They both do TCP/IP. Linux can do Windows networking, which means that a Linux computer can appear on a network of Windows computers and share its files and printers. Linux machines can participate on a Windows based network and vice versa. See Mixing Unix and Windows By Larry Seltzer (July 2002).

1.15.18 Hard Disk Partitions

Windows must be installed to and boot from a primary partition. There are a maximum of four primary partitions on a single hard disk (a computer with two hard disks can have eight primary partitions). Linux is better in this regard as it can be installed to and boot from either a primary partition or a logical partition. Logical partitions reside inside a special type of primary partition called an extended partition. There is no practical limit to the number of logical partitions that can exist on a single hard disk. Thus you can easily experiment with a dozen different Linux distributions by installing each one in a different logical partition.

Windows must boot from the first hard disk. Here too Linux is better, it can boot from any hard disk in the computer.

1.15.19 Swap Files

A swap file (a.k.a. page file) is used by the Operating System when the demands on RAM exceed the available capacity. Windows uses a hidden file for its swap file. By default, this file resides in the same partition as the OS, although you can put it in another partition, after Windows is installed. In Windows XP, the swap file resides initially on the C disk as a file called pagefile.sys. Linux likes to use a dedicated partition for its swap file, however advanced users can opt to implement the swap file as a file in the same partition as the OS. I'm not sure if this issue is clearly presented and explained when installing Linux.

Probably not. Xandros v4, for example, may use a separate swap partition or not, depending on the partition environment it finds at install time. Xandros 4 does not explain any of this.

Updated August 2006: With Windows XP the default size of the swap file is 1.5 times the amount of RAM in the machine at the time Windows was installed. I don't know how Linux chooses a default swap file size. In Windows XP you can change the swap file size and location with Control Panel -> System Properties -> Advanced tab -> Performance Settings -> Advanced tab again -> Change button, which opens the Virtual Memory window. Be aware that this window violates user interface standards. It is the only window I know of where clicking the OK button after making a change, does not activate the change. To change the size of the page/swap file, you must click the Set button. I don't know how to change the size of a Linux swap file.

1.15.20 File Systems

Windows uses FAT12, FAT16, FAT32 and/or NTFS with NTFS almost always being the best choice. The FATx file systems are older and have assorted limitations on file and partition size that make them problematical in the current environment. Linux also has a number of its own native file systems. The default file system for Linux used to be ext2, now it is typically ext3. Other supported file systems includes XFS, JFS, JFFS and Reiser3. Reiser4 is in development.

(Added December 2008: The ext3 file system is being replaced by ext4. Among the improvements in ext4 is an increase in the maximum filesystem size from 16 terabytes in ext3 to one exabyte. The largest file in ext3 is 2 terabytes, in ext4 it is 16 terabytes. OpenSolaris includes ZFS which seems like a drastic change in file system design.

File systems can be either journaled or not. Non-journaled systems are subject to problems when stopped abruptly. All the FAT variants and ext2 are non-journaled. After a crash, they should be examined by their respective health check utilities (Scan Disk or Check Disk or fsck). In contrast, when a journaled file system is stopped abruptly, recovery is automatic at the next reboot. NTFS is journaled. Linux supports several journaled file systems: ext3, ext4, reiserfs and jfs.

All the file systems use directories and subdirectories. Windows separates directories with a back slash, Linux uses a normal forward slash. Windows file names are not case sensitive. Linux file names are. For example "abc" and " aBC" are different files in Linux, whereas in Windows it would refer to the same file. Case sensitivity has been a problem for this very web page, the name of which is " Linux.vs.Windows.html". At times, people have tried to get to this page using " linux.vs.windows.html" (all lower case) which resulted in a Page Not Found error. Eventually, I created a new web page with the name in all lower case and this new page simply re-directs you to the real page, the one you are reading now (with a capital L and W).

Fragmentation: (Added January 2008) Windows file systems all suffer from fragmentation, which results in a file being scattered all over the hard disk. I'm told that Linux file systems are much less prone to this, but I don't know the details and whether it applies to all or some of the Linux file systems. With classic magnetic platter based hard disks, fragmentation can be a big deal as the disk is much slower than the RAM or CPU and having to walk all over the hard disk to get a file slows things down. How this will play out on newer SSDs I don't know. While there is no waiting for spinning platters, SSDs have to deal with wear leveling, a feature designed to extend their limited lifespan. Speaking of fragmentation, I've heard very good things about Raxco's PerfectDisk for Windows.

Crossing Over: (Last Updated: June 2007) As for supporting each others file systems, Linux can read/write FAT16 and FAT32. When I first wrote this topic, only some Linux distributions could read NTFS partitions. Now more can both read and update NTFS, a feature critical to using Linux as a Rescue CD for a broken copy of Windows.

Captive-NTFS was "the first free NTFS read/write filesystem for GNU/Linux". It is no longer being maintained. In its place is the NTFS-3G Read/Write Driver which the website describes as "an open source, freely available read/write NTFS driver for Linux, FreeBSD, OS X, and NetBSD." NTFS-3G is fairly new, being considered stable only since February 2007. It can deal with the multiple versions of NTFS used by Windows XP, Windows Server 2003, Windows 2000 and Windows Vista. At least 85 distributions support NTFS-3G in some manner, among them: Ubuntu, Red Hat, Debian, Knoppix and Mandriva.

In September 2005, PC Magazine reviewed a product called NTFS for Linux from the Paragon Software Group that gives Linux read/write access to NTFS partitions. For more information on Linux and NTFS, see the Linux NTFS Project. On its own, Windows can not read partitions formatted with any Linux file system. However, a number of products (I haven't tried any of them) enable this:

- Explore2fs by John Newbigin can be used to read Linux ext2 and ext3 partitions. Portable version
- Ext2Fsd claims to be an Ext2 File System Driver for Windows
- An open source project, the Ext2 File System Driver for Windows
- The free Linux Reader for Windows from Diskinternals can read the Ext2/Ext3 file systems (added September 2007) Portable version
- The Ext2 Installable File System For Windows is free and provides full read and write access to partitions and floppy disks formatted with either Ext2 or Ext3. It works with Windows NT4, 2000, XP, Server 2003, Vista and Server 2008 (last checked July 2009). It's also referred to as Ext2 IFS for Windows. If you are running a NAS device, it may very well be storing files using the Ext2 or Ext3 file system.

File Hierarchy: Windows and Linux use different concepts for their file hierarchy. Windows uses a volume-based file hierarchy, Linux uses a unified scheme. Windows uses letters of the alphabet to represent different devices and different hard disk partitions. Under Windows, you need to know what volume (C:, D:,...) a file resides on to select it, the file's physical location is part of it's name. In Linux all directories are attached to the root directory, which is identified by a forward-slash, "/". For example, below are some second-level directories:

/bin/ ---- system binaries, user programs with normal user permissions

/sbin --- executables that need root permission

/data/ --- a user defined directory

/dev/ ---- system device tree

/etc/ ---- system configuration

/home/ --- users' subdirectories

/home/{username} akin to the Windows My Documents folder

/tmp/ ---- system temporary files

/usr/ ---- applications software

/usr/bin - executables for programs with user permission

/var/ ---- system variables

/lib --- libraries needed for installed programs to run

Every device and hard disk partition is represented in the Linux file system as a subdirectory of the lone root directory. For example, the floppy disk drive in Linux might be /etc/floppy. The root directory lives in the root partition, but other directories (and the devices they represent) can reside anywhere. Removable devices and hard disk partitions other than the root are attached (i.e., "mounted") to subdirectories in the directory tree. This is done either at system initialization or in response to a mount command.

There are no standards in Linux for which subdirectories are used for which devices. This contrasts with Windows where the A disk is always the floppy drive and the C disk is almost always the boot partition.

Hidden Files: Both support the concept of hidden files, which are files that, by default, are not shown to the user when listing files in a directory. Linux implements this with a filename that starts with a period. Windows tracks this as a file attribute in the file metadata (along with things like the last update date). In both OSs the user can over-ride the default behavior and force the system to list hidden files.

Case: Case sensitivity is the same with commands as with file names. When entering commands in a DOS/command window under any version of Windows, "dir" is the same as "DIR". In Linux "dir" is a different command than "DIR".

1.15.21 Shutting Down

Both have to be told to shut down and for the same reason, to quiesce in-flight activity in an orderly manner. You shut down Windows thru the Start button, and then select Shutdown. In both the KDE and Gnome GUIs for Linux, you shut the system down by first logging out (equivalent to logging off in Windows). In Gnome, you select the Halt option, in KDE, the shutdown option. Linux can also be shut down from a command prompt using the shutdown command which can either shut the system down immediately or be told to shut it down at some time in the future. Windows XP also has a shutdown command; earlier versions of Windows did not

(Updated December 2005) The scheduler built into Windows XP is not able to schedule programs to run at shutdown time. I find this annoying, because it's an excellent time to schedule backups. Linux can schedule programs to run automatically at shutdown time. I haven't tried this but a quick glance at How Linux boots makes it seems complicated. I'm told to follow the instructions in this article but replace runlevel 5 with runlevel zero, which represents shutdown time.

EXERCISES

1. What do you mean by operating system?
2. Explain the various objectives of operating system?
3. How can operating system work as a user or computer interface?
4. Explain the various functions of operating-system?
5. How can operating system work as resource manager?
6. What do you understand by Network operating system?
7. Explain the concept of embedded operating systems?
8. Explain various types of network operating systems?
9. What are the hardware requirements of network operating system?
10. Explain the general study of Windows 2000 server?
11. Explain the various new and updated features of Windows 2000 server?
12. Explain the different versions of Windows 2000 server?
13. Explain the various editions of Windows 2000 server?
14. Explain the general study of Windows 2003 server?
15. Explain the various new and updated features of Windows 2003 server?
16. Explain the various editions of Windows 2003 server?
17. Explain the concept of Windows storage server 2003?
18. What do you understand by Windows server 2003 r2?
19. Explain the general study of Windows XP?
20. Explain the various new and updated features of Windows XP?
21. Write down the various system requirements of Windows XP?
22. Elaborate the different service packs of Windows XP?
23. Write down the procedure of product activation and verification?
24. Tell the advantage of genuine Windows?
25. Explain the working of start menu and taskbar?
26. Explain the search procedure of Windows XP?
27. Write down various performance improvements of Windows XP?
28. Explain the various system administration improvements of Windows XP?
29. Explain the concept of fast user switching and welcome screen?
30. Explain general study of Windows NT?

31. Explain the architecture of Windows NT?
32. Explain the role of kernel mode and user mode in Windows NT?
33. Explain the general study of UNIX?
34. Explain the various features of UNIX operating system?
35. Explain the concept of Logging out, using shell in UNIX?
36. Explain the general study of Linux?
37. Explain the development of Linux?
38. Explain the history of UNIX and Linux?
39. Explain the case studies of windows 2003 server?
40. Explain the case studies of UNIX?
41. Explain the case studies of Linux?
42. Differentiate between the operating systems UNIX vs. Linux?
43. Explain the comparative studies of windows 2003 server and Unix/Linux?

CHAPTER 2

Windows Server 2003

2.1 INTRODUCTION

A modern O/S contains much built-in software designed to simplify networking of a computer. Typical O/S software includes an implementation of TCP/IP protocol stack and related utility programs like ping and trace route. This includes the necessary device drivers and other software to automatically enable a device's Ethernet interface. Mobile devices also normally provide the programs needed to enable Wi-Fi, Bluetooth, or other wireless connectivity.

The early versions of Microsoft Windows did not provide any computer networking support. Microsoft added basic networking capability into its operating system starting with Windows 95 and Windows for Workgroups. Microsoft also introduced its Internet Connection Sharing (ICS) feature in Windows 98 Second Edition (Win98 SE). Contrast that with Unix, which was designed from the beginning with networking in view. Nearly any consumer O/S today qualifies as a network operating system due to the popularity of the Internet.

Windows Server 2003 (also referred to as Win2K3) is a server operating system produced by Microsoft, introduced on 24 April 2003. An updated version, Windows Server 2003 R2, was released to manufacturing on 6 December 2005. Its successor, Windows Server 2008, was released on 4 February 2008. According to Microsoft, Windows Server 2003 is more scalable and delivers better performance than its predecessor, Windows 2000.

2.2 WHAT'S NEW IN WINDOWS SERVER 2003?

Windows Server 2003 improves upon previous versions of Windows in the areas of availability, reliability, security, and scalability. Windows 2003 is designed to allow customers to do more with less. According to Microsoft, companies that have deployed Windows 2003 have been able to operate with up to 30 percent greater efficiency in the areas of application development and administrative overhead.

2.2.1 New Features

Microsoft has enhanced most of the features carried over from Windows 2000 Server and has added some new features for Windows Server 2003.

For example:

- Active Directory has been updated to improve replication, management, and migrations.
- File and Print services have been updated to make them more dependable and quicker.
- The number of nodes supported in clustering has been increased and new tools have been added to aid in cluster management.
- Terminal Server better supports using local resources when using the Remote Desktop Protocol.
- IIS 6.0, Media Services 9.0, and XML services have been added to Windows Server 2003.
- New networking technologies and protocols are supported, including Simple Object Access Protocol (SOAP), Web Distributed Authoring and Versioning (WebDAV), IPv6, wireless networking, fiber channel, and automatic configuration for multiple networks.New command-line tools have been added for easier administration.
- Software Restriction Policies allow administrators to control which applications can be run.
- All features of Windows have been updated to re?ect Microsoft's security initiative.

2.2.2 New Active Directory Features

Active Directory was first introduced in Windows 2000 and Microsoft has made improvements to AD in Windows Server 2003. Windows 2003 enhances the management of Active Directory. There are more AD management tools now and the tools are easier than ever to use. Microsoft has made it painless to deploy Active Directory in Windows 2003.The migration tools have been greatly improved to make way for seamless migrations.

In the corporate world where mergers and acquisitions are common, things change all the time. With Windows Server 2003, you can rename your domains, a feature missing from Windows 2000. You can also change the NetBIOS name, the DNS name, or both. Another problem with changes in the business environment is the need to configure trust relationships. With Windows 2000, if two companies merge and each has a separate Active Directory, they have to either set up manual nontransitive trusts between all of their domains or collapse one forest into the other. Neither of these is an ideal choice and is prone to error. The trusts are easy enough to set up, but then you lose the benefits of being in a single forest. Collapsing forests can require a lot of work, depending on the environment.

Windows Server 2003 Active Directory now supports forest-level trusts. By setting the trusts at the forest roots, you enable cross-forest authentication and cross-forest authorization. Cross-forest authentication provides a single sign-on experience by allowing users in one forest to access machines in another forest via NTLM or Kerberos (Kerberos is the preferred method, if all systems support it). Cross-forest authorization allows assigning permissions for users in one forest to resources in another forest. Permissions can be assigned to the user ID or through groups.

Not all improvements have to do with mergers and multiple forests. In the past, it was common practice for companies with many offices spread out geographically to build their domain controllers locally and ship them to the remote offices. This was because of replication issues. When a new domain controller is created, it must pull a full copy of the Active Directory database from another domain controller. This full replication can easily over saturate a slow network link. However, with Server 2003, you can create a new domain controller and pull the Active Directory information from your backup media. The newly created domain controller now only has to replicate the changes that have occurred since the backup was made. This usually results in much less traffic than replicating the entire database.

The Active Directory Users and Computers tool (ADUC) has been improved to include a new query feature that allows you to write filters for the type of objects you want to view. These queries can be saved and used multiple times. For example, you might want to create a query to show you all of the users with mailboxes on a specified Exchange server. By creating a query, you can easily pull up a current list with one click of the mouse. ADUC also now supports the following:

- Multi-object selection
- Drag-and-drop capabilities
- The ability to restore permissions back to the defaults
- The ability to view the effective permissions of an object

Group policy management has also been enhanced in Server 2003.The Microsoft Group Policy Management Console (GPMC) makes it easy to troubleshoot and manage group policy. It supports drag-and-drop capabilities, backing up and restoring your group policy objects (GPOs), and copying and importing GPOs. Where the GPMC really shines is in its reporting function. You now have a graphical, easy-to-use interface that, within a few clicks, will show you all of the settings configured in a GPO. You can also determine what a user's effective settings would be if he or she logged on to a certain machine. The only way you could do this in Windows 2000 was to actually log the user on to the machine and run gpresult (a command-line tool for viewing effective GPO settings).

In Windows Server 2003, the schema can now be redefined. This allows you to make changes if you incorrectly enter something into the schema. In Windows 2000, you can deactivate schema attributes and classes, but you cannot redefine them. You still need schema admin rights to modify the schema, but now it is more forgiving of mistakes.

The way objects are added to and replicated throughout the directory has been improved as well. The Inter-Site Topology Generator (ISTG) has been improved to support a larger number of sites. Group membership replication is no longer "all or nothing" as it was in Windows 2000. In Windows Server 2003, as members are added to groups, only those members are replicated to your domain controllers and global catalog (GC) servers, rather than the entire group membership list. No more worrying about the universal group replication to your GC servers.

Every domain controller caches credentials provided by GC servers. This allows users to continue to log on if the GC server goes down. It also speeds up logons for sites that do not have a local GC server. No longer is the GC server a single point of failure. In fact, you no longer are required to have one at each site.

Active Directory now supports a new directory partition called the application partition. You can add data to this partition and choose which domain controllers will replicate it. This is useful if you have information you want to replicate to all domain controllers in a certain area, but you do not want to make the information available to all domain controllers in the domain.

2.2.3 Improved File and Print Services

Practically every organization uses file and print services, as sharing files and printers was the original reason for networking computers together. Microsoft has improved the tools used to manage your file system by making the tools run faster than before; this allows users to get their jobs done in less time and requires less downtime from your servers. The Distributed File System (Dfs) and the File Replication Service (FRS) have also been enhanced for Windows Server 2003, and Microsoft has made printing faster and easier to manage.

2.2.3.1 Enhanced File System Features

Windows 2003 supports WebDAV, which was first introduced in Exchange 2000. It allows remote document sharing. Through standard file system calls, clients can access files stored on Web repositories. In other words, clients think they are making requests to their local file systems, but the requests are actually being ful?lled via Web resources.

Microsoft made it easier to manage disks in Windows Server 2003 by including a command line interface. From the command line, you can do tasks that were only supported from the GUI in Windows 2000, such as managing partitions and volumes, configuring RAID, and defragmenting your disks. There are also command-line tools for extending basic disk, file system tuning, and shadow copy management.

Disk fragmentation is a problem that commonly plagues file servers. This occurs when data is constantly written to and removed from a drive. Fragmented drives do not perform as well as defragmented drives. Although Windows 2000 (unlike NT) included a disk defragmentation tool, it was notoriously slow. To address this, Microsoft beefed up the defragmenter tool in Windows Server 2003 so that it is much faster than before. In addition, the new tool is not limited to only speci?c cluster sizes that it can defrag, and it can perform an online defragmentation of the Master Fat Table.

The venerable CHKDSK (pronounced "check disk") tool, which is used to ?nd errors on Windows volumes, has been revamped as well. Microsoft studies show that Windows Server 2003 runs CHKDSK 20 to 35 percent faster than Windows 2000. However, since Windows 2003 (like Window 2000) uses NTFS-which is less prone to errors than FAT file systems-you shouldn't have to run CHKDSK often.

Both the Dfs and the FRS have been improved. Dfs allows you to create a single logical tree view for multiple servers, so that all directories appear to be on the same server. However, they are actually on separate servers. Dfs works hand in hand with Active Directory to determine site locations for clients requesting data, thereby allowing clients to be directed to a server closest to them in physical proximity. FRS is used to replicate Dfs file share data. FRS now allows administrators to configure its replication topology and compress replication traffic.

One of the best file system improvements in Windows 2003 is shadow copies. After you enable shadow copies on the server and install the shadow copy client software on the desktop computer, end users can right-click on a file and view previous versions that were backed up via shadow copies. They can then keep the current version of the file or roll back to an early version. This will remove the burden (to some extent) of simple file restores from your IT staff and allow the users to handle it themselves.

2.2.3.2 Improved Printing Features

Even though we rely more on electronic communications than ever before, printing is still an important requirement for most companies. One of the more common reasons for small companies to put in a network is for the purpose of sharing printers (a shared Internet connection and e-mail are two other reasons). Microsoft has taken many steps to improve the printing experience in Windows Server 2003. Users who print long documents should notice a performance boost over Windows 2000, because 2003 does a better job of file spooling, print jobs should get to the printer faster.

Microsoft has also made printing easier to manage. Windows Server 2003 has command-line utilities for managing printer configuration; including print queues, print jobs, and driver management. System Monitor has counters for managing print performance. Installing printers is easy in Windows 2003 because of plug-and-play (PnP) functionality. This allows you to physically connect the printer to the machine and have Windows set it up for you automatically (as long as the printer itself supports PnP). Windows 2003 supports over 3800 new print drivers.

2.2.4 Revised IIS Architecture

Internet Information Services (IIS) is Microsoft's Web server product. IIS 6.0 is included with all versions of Windows Server 2003. With this new version, Microsoft has made great leaps in the area of IIS reliability, availability, management, and security. IIS 6.0 was designed so a problem with one application won't cause the server or other applications running on the server to crash. It provides health monitoring and disables Web sites and applications that fail too frequently within a defined period of time. IIS 6.0 can stop and restart Web sites and applications based on customized criteria (such as disk, CPU, or memory utilization). IIS 6.0 allows changing the configuration of your Web server without having to restart it. It is the most scalable version of IIS to date, supporting more Web sites on a single server than IIS 5.0.The actual IIS services stop and start much faster than before, helping to decrease Web site downtime.

Management of your Web server is easier in Server 2003, thanks to command-line scripting. The metabase is now stored in a plain-text XML configuration file. This improves backing up, restoring, recovering, troubleshooting, and directly editing the metabase. IIS 6.0 supports ASP .NET, .NET Framework, and a wide variety of languages. Since the .NET Framework doesn't depend on a speci?c language, almost any programming language will do.

One common complaint about Windows 2000 was that IIS installed by default; thereby creating an instant vulnerability on servers that were never intended to be Web servers. Microsoft recommends that you only install IIS when needed and lock it down so it only offers the services that your organization requires. In Windows Server 2003, IIS is not installed by default and is locked down by default when you do install it. This means that it will only deliver static content, unless you specifically configure it for dynamic content. IIS 6.0 requires an administrator to add necessary dynamic extensions to the Web services extensions list. Until they are added to this list, IIS will not support them; this will stop attackers from calling unsecured dynamic pages.

2.2.5 Enhanced Clustering Technology

A cluster is a group of servers that work together like one computer. Clusters can be used for performance reasons (to balance the load across two or more computers) or for fault tolerant reasons (to provide failover if one computer fails). Microsoft added clustering support to its OS line in 1997 with Windows NT 4.0 Enterprise Edition. At that time, clustering was not commonly used. Only the really big IT shops could afford to put in clustered solutions because of the cost of the extra servers. Now that hardware has dropped in price, more and more customers are choosing to cluster their mission-critical systems. As Storage Area Networking (SAN) technology becomes more widespread, clusters are becoming fairly easy to set up. Like Windows 2000, Windows 2003 supports two types of clustering: Microsoft Cluster Service (MSCS) and Network Load Balancing (NLB).

2.2.5.1 Microsoft Cluster Service

MSCS uses two or more physically connected servers, called nodes that communicate with each other constantly. If a node detects that another node is offline, it will take over the services provided by the offline node. However, this happens behind the scenes, and end users are unaware of the process (other than experiencing a small initial delay).

MSCS is traditionally used with mail servers, database servers, and file and print servers. MSCS is supported in Windows Server 2003 Enterprise Edition and Windows Server 2003 Datacenter Edition. Some of the new features of Windows Server 2003 clustering include:

- The support of more nodes in a cluster. Enterprise Edition and Datacenter Edition both support eight nodes.
- Clustering now integrates with Active Directory and creates a computer account for the virtual cluster name.
- Clustered applications can now use Kerberos authentication.

2.2.6 Network Load Balancing

NLB is available in all versions of Windows Server 2003. Unlike MSCS, where only one server offers the services at a time, NLB nodes all offer services at the same time. The NLB cluster is accessed via a virtual name (a name that represents the group of servers as an entity), and whichever server is least busy answers the request (there is a little more to it, but this is good enough for now). If one server goes offline, there is no transferring of services because all servers offer the services already. When a server goes offline, it is removed from the rotation of servicing requests until it comes back online. NLB is generally used with Web servers, application servers, terminal servers, and streaming media servers NLB Manager is a new tool in Windows Server 2003 that provides a central point for managing and configuring NLB clusters.

There are many new features for NLB in Server 2003. NLB now supports multiple network interface cards (NICs), allowing a single server to host multiple NLB clusters. You can use virtual clusters to set up different port rules for each cluster IP address, so that each IP address represents a different resource (Web page, application, and so forth).The Internet Group Management Protocol (IGMP) is now supported when NLB is configured in multicast mode. Using IGMP limits cluster traffic on the switch to the ports that have NLB server connected to them. This helps prevent switch flooding. (Switch flooding occurs when every server in an NLB cluster sees every packet addressed to the cluster.) NLB now supports IPSec traffic.

2.2.7 Improved Security

You might have noticed that Microsoft is paying more attention to concerns about security. Many of the new features discussed thus far relate in one way or another to security. One of the key components of Windows Server 2003 security is the Common Language Runtime (CLR) software engine. It reduces the number of security vulnerabilities due to programming mistakes, and makes sure that applications have appropriate permissions to run and that they can run without any errors. EFS encrypt files that are stored on NTFS-formatted partitions so that it can only be decrypted by the person who encrypted the file, those with whom he or she shares the file, or a designated recovery agent. The sharing of encrypted files is new to Windows XP/Server 2003. In Windows 2000, this was not possible because only the person who encrypted the file had the correct keys to decrypt it. Now, the person who encrypts the file can choose to give other people the ability to decrypt the file as well, and the file encryption key (FEK) is protected by the public key of each additional person who is given authorization. Encrypted files appear just like normal files in Windows Explorer. However, only authorized users can access them. Anyone else will be denied access. EFS now support encrypting offline files and storing encrypted files in Web folders.

Microsoft provides a single sign-on environment for users via Credential Manager. Credential Manager provides a secure place for users to store their passwords and X.509 certificates. When a resource is accessed, the correct credentials will be pulled from Credential Manager without prompting the user for action. In large complex environments in which you can have three or four user accounts, this is a great benefit. No longer do you have to key in your domain, username, and password each time; you set it up once and then Credential Manager does all of the work. You can now control which software can run on a machine via software restriction policies.

These policies can be applied at the domain, site, OU, or locally. You de?ne a default security level that either allows or disallows software to run via the Group Policy Object Editor Snap-in. Among other things, software restriction policies can be used to prevent viruses and other harmful programs from running on your PC, and can also be used to limit end users to only running the programs needed for their job.

Windows Server 2003 supports the IEEE 802.1X protocols. This standard allows authorization and authentication of users connecting to Ethernet and wireless local area networks (WLANs). Windows Server 2003 supports authentication via Extensible Authentication Protocol (EAP) methods, such as smart cards. Auto-enrollment and auto-renewal of certificates makes it easier to quickly deploy smart cards. Certi?cate Services now supports incremental (a.k.a. delta) Certi?cate Revocation Lists (CRLs), which means that the server can just push down the changes to the client and not have to push the entire CRL every time.

Another new security feature of Windows Server 2003 is Passport Integration. Passport is integrated with Active Directory and supports mapping AD user accounts to Passport accounts. Users can use Passport for a single sign-on to all of the supported systems.

2.2.8 Better Storage Management

In an effort to keep up with the changing times, Microsoft has greatly increased the level of built-in

SAN support in Windows Server 2003.The Virtual Disk Service (VDS) provides a unified interface for multivendor storage devices. VDS discovers the storage devices in your network and gives you a single place to manage them. You can now create and mount a SAN volume from within Windows. In previous versions of Windows, you had to do this from within your SAN application. Also included in Windows 2003, via the driver development kit, is multipathing input/output (MPIO). MPIO allows up to 32 different paths to external storage (for example, SAN).

Microsoft has also put a lot of work into the backup features of Windows Server 2003.The Volume Shadow Copy Services allows you to create a snapshot (or an exact copy) of volumes on your SAN. Clients can then perform shadow copy restores on their own. In other words, clients can look at a list of shadow copies performed on their data and choose to restore their own data from a given snapshot. NTBackup also uses shadow copies to make sure that all open files are backed up.

2.2.9 Improved Terminal Services

Terminal Server allows client workstations to function as terminal emulators. Terminal Services client software is installed on the local workstation, allowing it to connect to the terminal server and receive its own desktop session. Multiple clients can run sessions simultaneously. All processing takes place on the server. The client machine is only responsible for managing the keystrokes and mouse clicks, which are passed over the network to the terminal server via the Remote Desktop Protocol (RDP). Although RDP is the native protocol for Microsoft Terminal Server and is used with clients running the Windows 2000 Terminal Services client or the XP/2003 Remote Desktop Connection (RDC) client, the Server 2003 terminal server can also be configured to accept connections from Citrix clients using the ICA protocol.

In Windows Server 2003, Remote Administration mode has been renamed to Remote Desktop for Administration and it is installed by default. This works like the Remote Desktop feature in Windows XP. As in Windows 2000, you are still limited to two simultaneous remote desktops at a time. However, there is one improvement: you can now take over the local console session. Terminal Services in Application Server mode is now simply called Terminal Server.

The Windows Server 2003 Terminal Server and Remote Desktop for Administration support more local client devices than in Windows 2000. Now the local client file system, audio output, printers, serial ports, smart cards, and clipboard are supported making it easier for clients to use their local resources while connected to the terminal server. RDP 5.1 is a much more robust client than RDP 5.0 (Windows 2000). It supports display configurations up to 24-bit color at up to 1600x1200 resolution. It also allows customizing the client experience based on available bandwidth. In other words, unnecessary features can be turned off when connecting over a slow link to optimize performance.

Terminal Server is one of the most used features of Windows 2000. It allows users to connect from their local machines and run desktop sessions off of the server. The local workstation at this point is functioning as a "thin client" because all processing is taking place on the server. One common complaint about Terminal Server in Windows 2000 is a lack of support for local resources. This has been improved in Windows Server 2003.You can now share information easily between your local disk and the server. You no longer must map a drive back to your local workstation. You can print to locally attached printers and use locally attached serial devices. You can redirect the sound from the terminal server to come out of your local speakers. All of these things make using Terminal Server an even more transparent process to the end user.

2.2.10 New Media Services

Microsoft has redesigned Media Services. The version of Media Services in Windows Server 2003 is version 9.0. It is managed via the Windows Media Services Microsoft Management Console (MMC). Media Services provides audio and video content to clients via the Web (Internet or intranet).According to Microsoft, Media Services has been improved in four areas:

- Fast streaming
- Dynamic content
- Extensibility
- Industrial strength

2.10.1.1 Fast Streaming

Media Services supports fast streaming to ensure the highest quality streaming experience possible even over unreliable networks (for example, wireless networks). Streaming refers to sending video and/ or audio in compressed form over the network and playing the data as it arrives. There are four parts that make up fast streaming:

- **Fast start:** Supplies instant-on playback without a buffering delay.
- **Fast cache:** Supplies always-on playback by streaming to cache as quickly as the network will support and by playing back the stream to the client from cache.
- **Fast recovery:** Sends redundant packets to wireless clients to ensure that no data is lost due to connectivity problems.
- **Fast reconnect:** Supplies undisturbed playback by restoring connections if the client is disconnected during a broadcast.

2.10.1.2 Dynamic Content

Media Services supports advertisements and server-side playlists. Advertising support is very fiexible, in that ads can be placed anywhere and used as often as wanted in the playlist. You can even use data gathering tools such as cookies to personalize your ads, and all ad data can be logged for further analysis. Server-side playlists are great for clients that don't support client-side playlists. Server-side playlists can contain live data or preexisting content. They allow you to customize the way your content is presented to clients and to make changes quickly and easily without any delay in service.

2.10.1.3 Extensibility

Microsoft has exposed over 60 Media Services interfaces and their properties, making Media Services a very open platform. Customization can be achieved by using the Microsoft supplied plug-ins or by using the SDK to create your own plug-ins. You can use scripting languages you already know (such as Perl, Visual Basic, Visual Basic Scripting Edition, C, Visual C++, and Microsoft JScript) to customize Media Services.

2.10.1.4 Industrial Strength

Microsoft boasts that Media Services is the most scalable, reliable, and secure solution on the market today. Media Services in Windows 2003 supports twice as many users per server as Windows 2000. It supports HTTP 1.0/1.1, RTP, RPSP, HTML v3.2, FEC, IPv4/6, IGMPv3, SNMP, WEBM/WMI, SMIL 2.0, SML, SML-DOM, and COM/DCOM. All Media Services plug-ins run in protected memory to guarantee reliability. Many common authorization and authentication methods are supported, such as digital rights management and HTTP Digest. Microsoft provides a Web-based interface, an MMC snap-in interface, and command-line support for administering your media servers.

2.2.11 XML WEB Services

XML Web Services are building-block applications that connect together via the Internet. These services provide reusable components that call functions from other applications. It doesn't matter how these applications were built, the types of devices used, or the OS on the devices used as long as they support XML, because XML is an industry standard. XML Web Services are made available in Windows Server 2003 because of the .NET framework. XML Web Services help provide effective business-to-business (b2b) and business-to-consumer (b2c) solutions.

2.3 WINDOWS SERVER 2003 FAMILY

The Windows Server 2003 family comes in four different editions: Web Edition, Standard Edition, Enterprise Edition, and Data Center Edition. It also comes in both 32-bit and 64-bit versions.

2.3.1 Why Four Different Editions?

Although all organizations are different, most would fall into one of three categories: small, medium, and large. The networking needs of organizations in each of these categories are different. Typically, small organizations are concerned with performance versus cost. They want good performance, but it can't cost a fortune. Large companies want the best performance possible. They aren't as concerned with cost, as long as the product performs as expected. Medium-sized companies fall somewhere in the middle. They sometimes need a little more out of an OS than what a small company will settle for, but they don't need the high-end equipment and features used by very large companies.

Microsoft has tried to create a different edition of Windows for each type of organization, so that all companies can use Windows Server 2003 without overpaying or sacri?cing performance. Companies should buy the minimum version of Windows that provides all of the needed features.

2.3.2 Members of the Family

As noted, there are four editions of Windows Server 2003: Web Edition, Standard Edition, Enterprise Edition, and Datacenter Edition. Each edition has its own benefits:

- Web Edition is the least expensive and least functional version. However, if your server is only used for hosting Web pages, then it is a perfect choice.
- Standard Edition is the next step up from Web Edition. Most of the features in Windows Server 2003 are supported in Standard Edition.

- If you need features not provided by Standard Edition or hardware not supported on Standard Edition, then Enterprise Edition would be the next logical choice. Almost every feature in Windows Server 2003 is supported in Enterprise Edition.
- If you need to use Windows System Resource Manager or you need super powerful hard-ware, then Datacenter Edition is your only choice.

Be sure to pick the version that most closely matches your needs. There are huge differences in price as your work your way up the chain. There is no reason to pay for more than what you need, but you don't want your organization hobbled by limited functionality.

2.3.2.1 WEB Edition

Prior to the release of Windows 2003, if you wanted to have a Windows server function only as a Web server, you would have to buy a copy of Windows 2000 Server and use IIS. This was a waste of money and functionality, because most of the features of Server would never be used. Now there is a version of Windows designed to function exclusively as a Web server, Windows Server 2003 Web Edition. This will save companies a great deal of money and possibly give Microsoft a larger share of the Web server market. There is a difference in price (list price) of around $700 to $800 between Web Edition and Standard Edition Server.

Web Edition is meant to host Web pages, Web applications, and XML services. It supports IIS 6.0, ASP.NET, and .NET Framework. Web Edition supports up to two processors and 2GB of RAM. Client access licenses (discussed later in the chapter) are not required when connecting to Web Edition. However, you are only allowed 10 inbound simultaneous SMB connections, to be used for content publishing (this limit does not apply to Web connections). Web Edition allows you to install third-party Web server software such as Apache, Web availability management software such as Microsoft Application Center, and database engine software such as Microsoft SQL Server 2000 Desktop Engine (MSDE). Web Edition does not support the following functions:

- Internet Authentication Services (IAS)
- Microsoft Metadirectory Services
- Domain controller functionality
- Universal Description, Discovery, and Integration Services (UDDI)
- Remote Installation Services

2.3.2.2 Standard Edition

Windows Server 2003 Standard Edition is the replacement for Windows 2000 Server. It is meant for small to medium-sized businesses and contains most of the features discussed thus far in the book. It is not limited in functionality like Web Edition and it supports up to four CPUs and 4GB of RAM. Standard Edition is a great choice for file and print servers, Web servers, and application servers that don't need to be clustered. It can also function as a domain controller. Microsoft expects Standard Edition to be the most widely used version of Windows Server 2003.

2.3.2.3 Enterprise Edition

Windows Server 2003 Enterprise Edition is the replacement for Windows 2000 Advanced Server. Enterprise Edition is meant for any sized business, but includes features most often desired by enterprise-level organizations. It provides high performance and reliability. All of the features supported in Standard Edition are supported in Enterprise Edition, as well as support for clustering up to eight nodes. It supports more powerful hardware than Standard Edition, and can use up to eight processors and up to 32GB of memory. There is a 64-bit version of Enterprise Edition for Intel Itanium machines. The 64-bit version supports up to eight processors and up to 64GB of RAM. Enterprise Edition is good for companies that need features or hardware not supported in Standard Edition.

2.3.2.4 Datacenter Edition

Datacenter Edition is Microsoft's high-end OS. It is meant for companies that need the most reliable and scalable platform available. You cannot buy the Datacenter Edition software and install it yourself; only approved equipment vendors can buy it and they must install it onto approved hardware. Datacenter Edition contains all of the features found in both Standard Edition and Enterprise Edition; in addition, it adds the Windows System Resource Manager to aid in system management. Datacenter Edition supports up to 32 processors and 64GB of memory in the 32-bit version. The 64-bit version supports up to 64 processors and 512GB of memory. If performance and reliability are at the top of your list (and cost is near the bottom), then Datacenter Edition is an excellent choice.

2.3.3 Licensing Issues

Microsoft based the Windows Server 2003 licensing structure on Windows 2000's structure. However, they have changed some things. This section is not the final word when it comes to Microsoft licensing. This section is meant to serve as a guide on the basics of Windows 2003 licensing.

There are a few rules that you need to know about Microsoft's licensing schemes:

- You have to purchase a product license for every copy of the OS you are going to install.
- Every network connection that is authenticated requires a Windows Client Access License (CAL).Anonymous connections do not require a CAL (for example, anonymous access to a Web page). Windows CALs are not required for Windows 2003 Web Edition, as it is meant to serve Web content only.
- Every Terminal Server session made by a user or device requires a Terminal Server Client Access License (TS CAL).TS CALs are not required for Windows Server 2003 Web Edition, as it is meant to serve Web content only.

The product license allows you to install the OS onto a machine. The CAL allows devices or users to connect to that machine. Microsoft's reasoning behind this is that everyone pays the same price for the base OS, but companies with more connections pay more than companies with fewer connections. This allows them to price according to usage.

There are two licensing modes supported in Windows 2003:

- Per Server mode requires a Windows CAL for each connection. These are assigned to each server and cannot be shared between servers. You are allowed one connection for each CAL assigned to the server. Once the maximum number has been reached, no more connections are allowed.

- Per Device or Per User mode (formerly called "Per Seat" mode) Requires that each device or user have its own Windows CAL. These allow the device or user to connect to an unlimited number of servers. With Per Device or Per User mode, the server will not limit the number of connections made as it does in Per Server mode.

Generally, Per Server mode will be most cost effective if you have only one or two servers, and clients that don't always connect at the same time. Per Device or Per User mode will be most cost effective if you have many servers to which your clients need to connect. Microsoft has two types of CALs, User CALs and Device CALs. User CALs are purchased for every user that makes a connection to a Windows 2003 server. Device CALs are purchased for every machine that makes a connection to a Windows 2003 server. Microsoft recommends that you use either User CALs or Device CALs, but not both at the same time. User CALs are best when you have more machines than users and your users log on to multiple machines to access the servers.

Device CALs are better when you have more employees than machines and your users share machines. User CALs and Device CALs are available for both Windows and Terminal Server. Device CALs and User CALs cost the same. Windows 2000 supported the System Equivalency license for Terminal Server. The System Equivalency license stated that if your client was running the same OS version as the terminal server, then you did not have to buy a Terminal Server CAL (thus, a Windows 2000 Pro machine connecting to a Windows 2000 terminal server did not need a TS CAL). Windows 2003 no longer supports System Equivalency licenses. However, Microsoft does have a Terminal Server licensing transition plan. You can receive a free TS CAL for every copy of Windows XP that you own at the time of the Windows 2003 launch (April 24, 2003). Check out the Microsoft licensing page for more information (www.microsoft.com/licensing).

New to Windows 2003 is the External Connector (EC) license. ECs enable external users to access your server without requiring that you buy CALs for them. External users are people who are not employed by your company. Terminal Server also has an EC license called the Terminal Server External Connector (TS-EC). The EC license is replacing the Internet Connector and TS Internet Connector licenses.

2.3.4 Product Activation

Starting with Windows XP, Microsoft requires OSs to be authorized before a specified number of days pass, after which you won't be able to log on to the OS. Failure to activate only prevents logging on. Services and remote administration are not affected. Windows Server 2003 allows a 30-day grace period for product activation (for retail and OEM products). Companies that use volume licensing do not have to activate their software.

Windows includes an activation wizard. You can activate over the Internet or by phone. One important thing to remember about product activation is that the activation process keeps track of the hardware in your machine. If the hardware changes dramatically, you will have to reactivate your software within three days in order to continue logging on to the server. Microsoft does this to prevent people from purchasing one copy of the OS, activating it, making an image of it, and deploying that image to many more machines.

2.4 ARCHITECTURE OF WINDOWS SERVER 2003

Microsoft Windows 2003 is composed of different layers that interact to present the user with a complete operating system. At the core of this architecture lies the kernel which has special rights over the hardware of the system.

The kernel is responsible for:

- Allocating memory to applications.
- Communicating with device drivers.
- Determining which processes run at any given time.

The kernel allows the operating system to scale higher, supporting up to 64 processors and 512 GB of RAM, depending on the edition of Windows Server 2003. It allows database applications like Microsoft SQL Server to take advantage of that larger hardware, and increases their performance by moving pieces of functionality into the kernel itself. Applications depend on the kernel to allocate memory, processor time, and hardware resources.

Microsoft has changed several aspects of the kernel:

- Windows Server 2003 scales much higher than was possible with older versions.
- Network applications are more reliable and will run more efficiently.
- Users in other countries will have an easier time using the operating system and its applications in their environments.

Features such as processor quotas and process accounting make Windows Server 2003 an extremely attractive platform for web hosting environments. Clustering features are built into the kernel, allowing for greatly improved uptime in networks where redundancy is available.

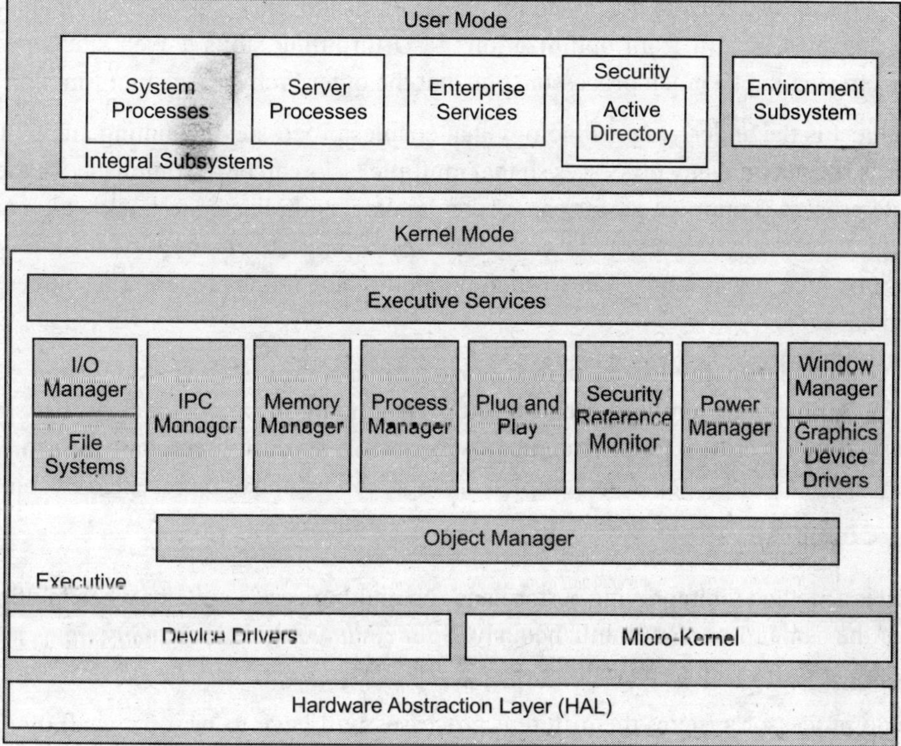

Figure 2.1 Architecture of Windows Server 2003

2.4.1 Process and Sessions

Windows 2003 launches a separate Win32 process for each user session. This ensures that applications do not communicate between user sessions, eliminating potential violations of a user*s privacy. These kernel changes will not affect administrators who choose not to use Terminal Services.

2.4.2 Windows 2003 WIN32 Architecture

The Windows 2003 Win32 subsystem is capable of handling multiple user sessions.

2.4.3 Kernel Facilities

Following are the kernel facilities:

2.4.3.1 Processor Quotas and Accounting

It is common practice for Internet Service Providers (ISPs) to share a single Web server between many customers.

Two features make multiuser environments more effective:

- Processor accounting.
- CPU throttling.

Processor accounting is used by IIS to record the number of processor cycles consumed by individual Web requests. This allows ISPs to bill based on processor usage, and enables developers to determine which pages can most benefit from optimization. CPU throttling stops a Web site*s out-of-process applications from stealing so much processor time that the other Web sites cannot function correctly.

The job object is the underlying technology that enables processor accounting and CPU throttling. Services such as IIS spawn many processes so that multiple tasks can be accomplished at the same time. While multiple processes improve performance, they make it complicated to track which processes are associated with which tasks. Because older versions of IIS supported many virtual servers sharing the same application space, it was impossible to audit or control how much processor resources each virtual server consumed.

Job objects allow the operating system to manage groups of processes as a single unit. This makes it much easier for applications to monitor and throttle the amount of processor time that separate tasks consume. This feature is critical for environments where multiple customers share the same server. One or more processes can work together to complete a single job, which is represented by a job object.

2.4.3.2 Spin Count

Spin count is a method for improving performance on multiprocessor systems when multiple programs need access to the same resources simultaneously. Spin count controls how many times a process will attempt to access a resource before waiting.

On a single processor system, the different processes will have to wait for each other to execute anyway, in which case repeated attempts to access the resource will not be successful until the other process has a chance to execute. Applications that use spin count on single processor systems will not hurt their performance; they just will not benefit.

2.4.3.3 Scatter/Gather I/O

Scatter/Gather I/O feature improves the performance of application servers on a network. Its use is entirely transparent to system administrators, because applications can make use of it without any special configuration.

The technology streamlines the process of moving data from discontinuous sections of the system*s RAM to a contiguous space on the disk drive. Applications must be written specifically to take advantage of it. Therefore, existing services will not realize any benefit.

2.4.3.4 Quantum

A quantum is a property of a thread that defines how long a thread will be allowed to execute before control is handed over to another thread. Since it takes time to switch the CPU between multiple threads, some applications will benefit from increasing the thread quantum length. The trade-off with this action is that increasing a thread*s time slice makes multitasking less smooth.

The quantum type can also be adjusted between fixed length and variable length. This can be configured from the Performance Options dialog box, which is acccssed from the advanced tab of the System Properties dialog box.

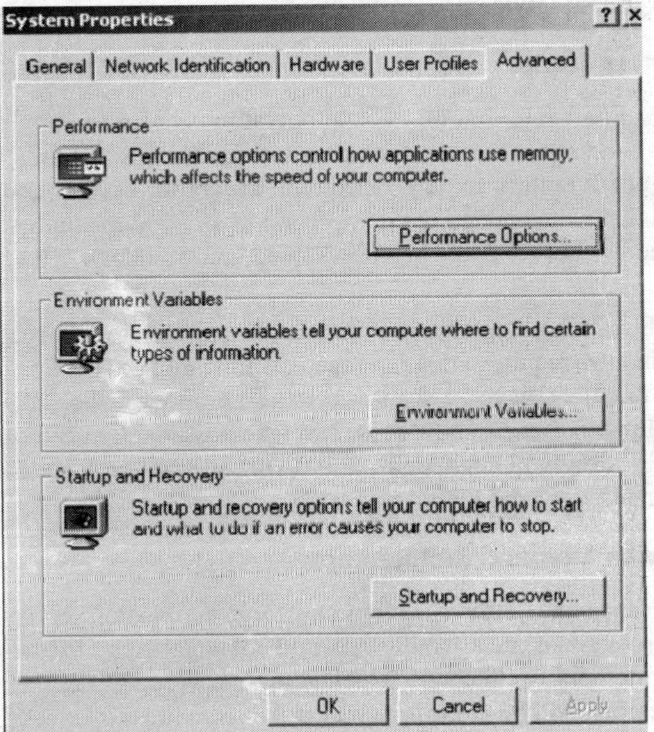

Figure 2.2 System properties of windows server 2003

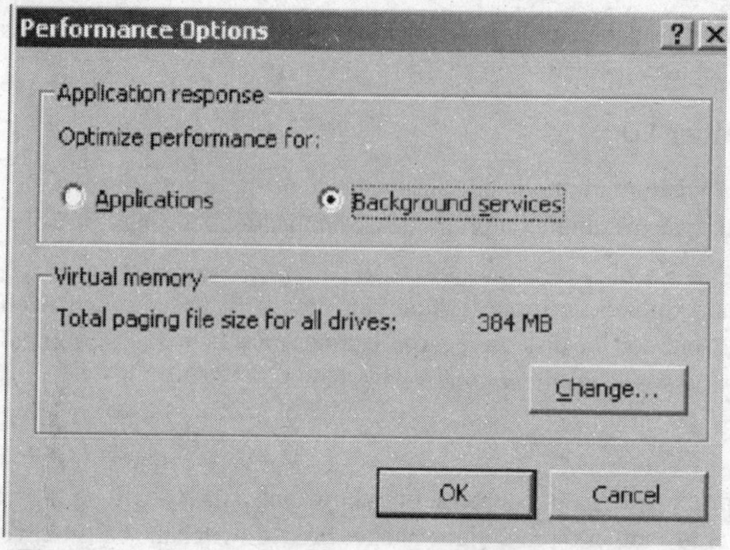

Figure 2.3 Performance options of windows server 2003

Administrators and developers have control over quantum type and length.

- Giving priority to applications allocates short, variable quanta, providing smoother multitasking.
- Giving priority to background services causes the operating system to use long, fixed quanta, which improves performance of network services. By default, Windows Server 2003 gives priority to background services.

2.4.3.5 Windows Driver Model

A driver is a piece of software that allows the operating system to communicate with a piece of hardware. All hardware accessories require drivers: network cards, SCSI cards, modems, scanners, and printers. Older versions of Windows required different drivers for each operating system. This was a burden to hardware vendors who created the drivers and to any administrators who managed multiple operating systems. Windows Server 2003, Windows 2002, and Windows XP systems can use the same drivers.

The WDM Kernel Streaming architecture improves the performance of real-time streaming media. Previous versions of Windows required streaming media applications to do the bulk of processing in user mode. Many of these functions have been moved to kernel mode, where they execute much faster. However, applications must be specifically written to take advantage of the WDM Kernel Streaming, however, so legacy applications will not benefit. The WDM Still Image Architecture provides operating system level support for scanners and digital cameras.

2.4.3.6 EMA: Enterprise Memory Architecture

Memory allocation can create bottlenecks for many large application servers and is particularly true for massive database servers that must handle hundreds of gigabytes of data. Windows Server 2003 incorporates Enterprise Memory Architecture which allows up to 512 GB of memory to be addressed by servers with 64-bit processors. Although most servers will not require this level of RAM, data warehouses will benefit because data can be manipulated faster in memory than on hard disks. Applications must be specifically coded to use the Very Large Memory APIs.

2.4.3.7 Multiprocessor Capabilities

Windows Server 2003 offers improved multiprocessor support. Multithreaded applications executing on multiprocessor systems will perform better; developers do not need to write special code to take advantage of the improved scalability.

- Windows Server 2003, Standard Edition supports 4 processors simultaneously.
- Windows 2003 Advanced Server, Enterprise Edition supports 8 simultaneous processors.
- Windows 2003 Advanced Server, Datacenter Edition supports 64 simultaneous processors.
- Windows 2003 Advanced Server, Web Edition supports 2 simultaneous processors.

Processes can be now be pinned to specific processors. Administrators can use the Task Manager to set the processor affinity of a process. This forces the process to use only that specific processor, which can improve performance by reducing the number of processor cache flushes as processes are swapped between processors. A potential drawback with this feature is that can also reduce performance by not allowing the process to move to the least busy processor.

2.4.3.8 I20 Support

I20 (Intelligent I/O Architecture) technology reduces the load on a system*s CPU and improves I/O performance. I20 works by adding a dedicated processor that is optimized for input and output operations. This technology is designed to streamline bandwidth-intensive activities such as realtime audio and video.

2.4.3.9 Clustering

Organizations that depend on their networks require extremely high uptime. Downtime is caused by several different events:

- Hardware failures.
- Application failures.
- Reboots as a result of configuration changes.
- Upgrades and patches.

The clustering features of Windows Server 2003 allow two servers to back each other up. When one server fails, a second server can automatically take over those services in less than a minute, in a process known as fail-over. The monitoring services will detect the failure and shift responsibility to the backup server.

For scheduled downtime events, one server can cover for the other server while it is taken offline. This process, called a rolling upgrade, reduces downtime to a minimum when applying patches. Clustering is designed to allow better scalability by load-balancing requests between multiple machines. In addition to improving uptime by providing fail-over capabilities, many aspects of the operating system are capable of being load balanced. Requests can be automatically distributed between two or more systems, and clients will automatically select a different server in the event one server in a cluster fails.

WINS	Windows Internet Name Service
DHCP	Dynamic Host Configuration Protocol
Dfs	Distributed File System

Figure 2.4 Servers

Clustering services are built into the operating system itself. Cluster-aware administration tools can be used for changing settings to multiple servers simultaneously. Windows Server 2003 clustering capabilities can be utilized/implemented without purchasing any special equipment. Servers in the cluster can have different hardware configurations. The following components have been improved to support fail-over between systems in a cluster:

2.4.3.10 Terminal Services

Terminal Services is built in to Windows Server 2003. Terminal services allow clients to run interactive applications on a remote server. The client system accepts input from and displays output to the user. The network infrastructure is used to carry the data between the client system and the server. All processing is done on the server.

Terminal services allow the use of thin clients. A thin client is a desktop system that has a bare minimum of hardware. Instead of requiring end-user systems to have fast processors, large amounts of RAM, and large hard drives, the network Terminal Services will do all the work. The thin client will forward requests to the server. The experience for the user is similar to that of having a fully equipped desktop system. While hardware requirements for the client are minimal, Terminal Services may be used with any type of desktop system.

The light requirements of the clients provide an added benefit to organizations with legacy hardware. Existing Windows for Workgroups 3.11 and Windows 95 systems can act as clients without upgrading the operating system. This allows an older piece of desktop hardware to run new 32-bit applications, increasing its lifetime. Terminal Services clients for Windows NT 4.0, Windows 95, Windows 98, and Windows 2003 Professional or Server are included with Windows Server 2003.

To allow multiple users to each have a session over the network, Windows Server 2003 incorporates a modified Win32 subsystem. The new Win32 subsystem can track different user sessions and keep them separate. Keyboard and mouse input are funneled not only to the proper application, but also to the proper session. Each user does work within his or her own security limitations. A separate Win32 process is launched for each user session. This ensures that applications do not communicate between user sessions.

2.5 SHELL

The Windows shell is the main graphical user interface in Microsoft Windows. The Windows shell includes well-known Windows components such as the Taskbar and the Start menu. The process that hosts the Windows shell is Explorer.exe. The Windows shell is not a "shell" in the usual sense of the term, and the word here is used more generally.

A shell is a piece of software that provides an interface for users of an operating system which provides access to the services of a kernel. However, the term is also applied very loosely to applications and may include any software that is "built around" a particular component, such as web browsers and email clients that are "shells" for HTML rendering engines. The name shell originates from shells being an outer layer of interface between the user and the internals of the operating system (the kernel).

Operating system shells generally fall into one of two categories: command-line and graphical. Command-line shells provide a command-line interface (CLI) to the operating system, while graphical shells provide a graphical user interface (GUI). In either category the primary purpose of the shell is to invoke or "launch" another program; however, shells frequently have additional capabilities such as viewing the contents of directories.

The relative merits of CLI- and GUI-based shells are often debated. CLI proponents claim that certain operations can be performed much faster under CLI shells than under GUI shells (such as moving files, for example). However, GUI proponents advocate the comparative usability and simplicity of GUI shells. The best choice is often determined by the way in which a computer will be used. On a server mainly used for data transfers and processing with expert administration.

In Windows 95 and later versions of Microsoft Windows, the Windows shell is by default explorer.exe (in the Windows folder or one of its subfolders, System32) which displays the icons on the desktop, the taskbar, the Start menu and the file browser. By default, explorer.exe runs automatically when Windows starts. Mostly the shell simply launches other programs on request.

Computer users with the desire can modify explorer.exe extensively. It is also possible to completely replace explorer.exe with another shell. Such a desktop shell replacement provides an alternative to the standard Windows shell. Alternatives such as those below can replace visual elements and windowing layout on a Microsoft Windows-based system. Many of these also provide more options for customization, or use fewer resources. The two most advanced and popular are Emerge Desktop and SharpE. Former versions of Windows relied on different default shells, which could also be replaced. In particular, this was a fairly common software enhancement in the days of Windows 3.x, due to the limitations of its default shell, Program Manager (progman.exe).

2.5.1 History

Given below the history of the Windows:

2.5.1.1 Windows 1.0 and 2.0: Early UI

Just after the IBM PC was marketed (August 1981), a project named "Interface Manager" started. It was renamed as "Windows" because the programmers often referred to zones called "windows" on the display screen. Rowland Hanson, the head of marketing at Microsoft, convinced the company that the name Windows would be a more appealing name to consumers. The first Windows pre-version was presented in November 1983. It used Word for DOS-like menus at the bottom of the screen. The first released version, Windows 1.01, released in November 1985, used pull-down menus like the early Macintosh System 1.x (Microsoft licensed GUI elements from Apple). The shell was a file manager (not a program manager) called "MS-DOS Executive". Applications could be launched from the MS-DOS Executive which minimized itself. The minimizing (called "iconing") was done by transforming the window into an icon which was placed at the bottom of the screen, in a special minimized windows zone. The maximizing (called "zooming") could extend the window over the minimized window zone. Windows could not be overlapped, but they were instead "tiled". As a result, two windows could not be "zoomed" at the same time.

Windows 2.0 was an interface-based release. New window controls were introduced with this release, along with the "minimize" and "maximize" terminology. Windows could be overlapped and the minimized window icons could be moved freely on the desktop.

2.5.1.2 Windows 3.x, NT 3.x: the First Revolution

Windows 3.0, introduced in May 1990, inherited the OS/2 GUI. The new "Program Manager" was a simple "front end" where the "groups" and icons had no relation to the actual file system. A background could be put on the desktop, and the window controls were redesigned. The buttons were all 3D in appearance but the windows weren't. The Windows 3.0 operating system was a success. Later versions of Windows 3.x introduced screensavers.

The new operating system from Microsoft, "Windows NT", featured the same GUI in the first version (3.1), like Windows 3.1x, although the color scheme was inherited from Windows 3.1, not the 3.0 version.

2.5.1.3 Windows 95

In Windows 95, the shell was redesigned. The taskbar was introduced, with an area consisting of buttons representing open windows, a digital clock, a "notifications area" for background processes and system notifications, and the Start button, which harbored the replacement for Program Manager, the Start menu. The desktop now linked to a folder, and also contained several system folders - My Computer, Network Neighborhood, and the Recycle Bin. The shell was now managed by Windows Explorer, which also served as the file browser, replacing File Manager.

2.5.1.4 Windows 95C, 98: "Nashville"

The growing popularity of the World Wide Web caused Microsoft to release its own browser, dubbed "Internet Explorer" which was based on technology licensed from Spyglass. In early 1996, Netscape announced that the next release of its browser, Netscape, would completely integrate with Windows and add a new shell, codenamed "Constellation". Microsoft started working on a similar Internet Explorer release, codenamed "Nashville". Internet Explorer 4.0 was redesigned and resulted in two products: the standalone IE4 and the Windows Desktop Update which replaced the Windows shell with a new "Active Desktop" shell. The Windows Desktop Update added rich shell functionality into earlier Windows 95 versions such as the Quick Launch bar on the taskbar, ability to minimize windows by clicking their button on the taskbar, Back and Forward navigation buttons and an address bar in Windows Explorer and HTML-based folder customization. Future Windows releases, like Windows 95C (OSR 2.5) and Windows 98 integrated Internet Explorer 4 and Active Desktop in the shell.

2.5.1.5 Georgia, Neptune and Tiger

Windows 2000 (NT 5.0) also integrated Internet Explorer into the shell and added new capabilities, such as personalized menus, ability to drag and sort menu items, customizable toolbars for Explorer, and comments in file shortcuts, a DHTML-based search pane and some eye candy. This interface was codenamed "Georgia" Windows Me also added these features. In the meantime, some new Windows versions were planned, "Neptune" and "Odyssey".

Neptune and Odyssey were cancelled in January 2000 and replaced with "Whistler". But before that, an early alpha release of "Neptune" appeared. It featured Activity Centers, which were also cancelled along with "Neptune" and "Odyssey". "Tiger" was a short-lived idea for continuing the DOS/9x platform.

2.5.1.6 Odyssey, Whistler: the Skinning Engine

"Odyssey" was designed to have a skinning engine similar to Stardock's WindowBlinds. It was later incorporated into "Whistler" (the "skin" name was changed to "visual style"). Two visual styles were developed: one "Professional" and one "Home". Early builds of "Whistler" (later named Windows XP) shipped only with the "Professional" visual style (later renamed to Watercolor), which was developed initially for Odyssey, but later Microsoft polls showed that consumers were interested in the "Home" visual style, which later replaced Professional/Watercolor.

2.5.1.7 XP, Server 2003: "Luna", "Royale"

The "home" skin became known as "Luna", and this refined version featured other UI elements, such as a reworked Start Menu and Control Panel and task panes in Windows Explorer, among other features. It was shipped with Windows XP. It received an update with Windows XP Media Center Edition 2005, called "Royale". Windows Server 2003 featured the same Luna UI, though it is disabled by default.

2.5.1.8 Longhorn: Plex, Slate and Jade

The future Longhorn operating system was designed to have a new interface called Aero. In the early alpha builds, Longhorn featured some interfaces called Plex, Slate and Jade, which were some interim steps between Luna and Aero. The Aero developments were at the beginning similar to Plex, but later transformed in the modern Aero.

2.5.1.9 Vista and 7: Aero

The Aero UI was introduced with Longhorn build 5048 and was developed along with the Vista builds, Beta 1 and the CTPs. It is currently included in most versions of Windows Vista (with the exception of Starter and Home Basic), as well as Windows Server 2008. The Aero UI is also incorporated in Windows 7. It introduced new UI gestures in Windows 7 such Aero Peek, Aero Snap, Aero Shake, thumbnail-based switching and Alt+Tab enhancements.

2.6 KERNEL

The kernel is the central component of most computer operating systems; it is a bridge between applications and the actual data processing done at the hardware level. The kernel's responsibilities include managing the system's resources (the communication between hardware and software components). Usually as a basic component of an operating system, a kernel can provide the lowest-level abstraction layer for the resources (especially processors and I/O devices) that application software must control to perform its function. It typically makes these facilities available to application processes through inter-process communication mechanisms and system calls.

Operating system tasks are done differently by different kernels, depending on their design and implementation. While monolithic kernels execute all the operating system code in the same address space to increase the performance of the system, microkernels run most of the operating system services in user space as servers, aiming to improve maintainability and modularity of the operating system

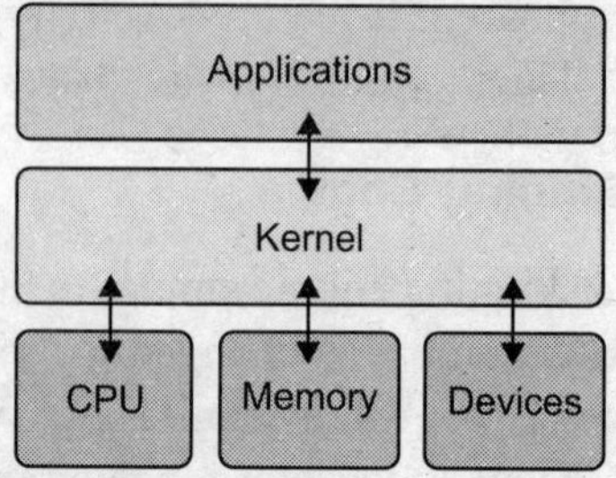

Figure 2.5 A kernel connects the application software to the hardware of a computer

The definition of "kernel", Jochen Liedtke said that the word is "traditionally used to denote the part of the operating system that is mandatory and common to all other software." Most operating systems rely on this concept of the kernel. The existence of a kernel is a natural consequence of designing a computer system as a series of abstraction layers, each relying on the functions of layers beneath it. The kernel, from this viewpoint, is simply the name given to the lowest level of abstraction that is implemented in software. In order to avoid having a kernel, one would have to design all the software on the system not to use abstraction layers; this would increase the complexity of the design to such a point that only the simplest systems could feasibly be implemented.

While it is today mostly called the kernel, originally the same part of the operating system was also called the nucleus or core, and was conceived as containing only the essential support features of the operating system. However the term core has also been used to refer to the primary memory of a computer system, because some early computers used a form of memory called core memory.

In most cases, the boot loader starts executing the kernel in supervisor mode. The kernel then initializes itself and starts the first process. After this, the kernel does not typically execute directly, only in response to external events (e.g., via system calls used by applications to request services from the kernel, or via interrupts used by the hardware to notify the kernel of events). Additionally, the kernel typically provides a loop that is executed whenever no processes are available to run; this is often called the idle process.

Kernel development is considered one of the most complex and difficult tasks in programming. Its central position in an operating system implies the necessity for good performance, which defines the kernel as a critical piece of software and makes its correct design and implementation difficult. For various reasons, a kernel might not even be able to use the abstraction mechanisms it provides to other software. Such reasons include memory management concerns (for example, a user-mode function might rely on memory being subject to demand paging, but as the kernel itself provides that facility it cannot use it, because then it might not remain in memory to provide that facility) and lack of reentrancy, thus making its development even more difficult for software engineers.

A kernel will usually provide features for low-level scheduling of processes (dispatching), inter-process communication, process synchronization, context switching, manipulation of process control blocks, interrupt handling, process creation and destruction, and process suspension and resumption.

2.6.1 Kernel Basic Facilities

The kernel's primary purpose is to manage the computer's resources and allow other programs to run and use these resources.

Typically, the resources consist of:

- **The Central Processing Unit (CPU, the processor):** This is the most central part of a computer system, responsible for running or executing programs on it. The kernel takes responsibility for deciding at any time which of the many running programs should be allocated to the processor or processors (each of which can usually run only one program at a time)
- **The computer's memory:** Memory is used to store both program instructions and data. Typically, both need to be present in memory in order for a program to execute. Often multiple programs will want access to memory, frequently demanding more memory than the computer has available. The kernel is responsible for deciding which memory each process can use, and determining what to do when not enough is available.
- **Any Input/Output:** (I/O) devices present in the computer, such as keyboard, mouse, disk drives, printers, displays, etc. The kernel allocates requests from applications to perform I/O to an appropriate device (or subsection of a device, in the case of files on a disk or windows on a display) and provides convenient methods for using the device (typically abstracted to the point where the application does not need to know implementation details of the device).

Key aspects necessary in resource managements are the definition of an execution domain (address space) and the protection mechanism used to mediate the accesses to the resources within a domain. Kernels also usually provide methods for synchronization and communication between processes (called inter-process communication or IPC).

A kernel may implement these features itself, or rely on some of the processes it runs to provide the facilities to other processes, although in this case it must provide some means of IPC to allow processes to access the facilities provided by each other. Finally, a kernel must provide running programs with a method to make requests to access these facilities.

2.6.1.1 Process Management

The main task of a kernel is to allow the execution of applications and support them with features such as hardware abstractions. A process defines which memory portions the application can access. (For this introduction, process, application and program are used as synonyms.) Kernel process management must take into account the hardware built-in equipment for memory protection. To run an application, a kernel typically sets up an address space for the application, loads the file containing the application's code into memory (perhaps via demand paging), sets up a stack for the program and branches to a given location inside the program, thus starting its execution.

Multi-tasking kernels are able to give the user the illusion that the number of processes being run simultaneously on the computer is higher than the maximum number of processes the computer is physically able to run simultaneously. Typically, the number of processes a system may run simultaneously is equal to the number of CPUs installed (however this may not be the case if the processors support simultaneous multithreading).

In a pre-emptive multitasking system, the kernel will give every program a slice of time and switch from process to process so quickly that it will appear to the user as if these processes were being executed simultaneously. The kernel uses scheduling algorithms to determine which process is running next and how much time it will be given. The algorithm chosen may allow for some processes to have higher priority than others. The kernel generally also provides these processes a way to communicate; this is known as inter-process communication (IPC) and the main approaches are shared memory, message passing and remote procedure calls (see concurrent computing).

Other systems (particularly on smaller, less powerful computers) may provide co-operative multitasking, where each process is allowed to run uninterrupted until it makes a special request that tells the kernel it may switch to another process. Such requests are known as "yielding", and typically occur in response to requests for interprocess communication, or for waiting for an event to occur. Older versions of Windows and Mac OS both used co-operative multitasking but switched to pre-emptive schemes as the power of the computers to which they were targeted grew.

The operating system might also support multiprocessing (SMP or Non-Uniform Memory Access); in that case, different programs and threads may run on different processors. A kernel for such a system must be designed to be re-entrant, meaning that it may safely run two different parts of its code simultaneously. This typically means providing synchronization mechanisms (such as spinlocks) to ensure that no two processors attempt to modify the same data at the same time.

2.6.1.2 Memory Management

The kernel has full access to the system's memory and must allow processes to safely access this memory as they require it. Often the first step in doing this is virtual addressing, usually achieved by paging and/or segmentation. Virtual addressing allows the kernel to make a given physical address appear to be another address, the virtual address. Virtual address spaces may be different for different processes; the memory that one process accesses at a particular (virtual) address may be different memory from what another process accesses at the same address. This allows every program to behave as if it is the only one (apart from the kernel) running and thus prevents applications from crashing each other.

On many systems, a program's virtual address may refer to data which is not currently in memory. The layer of indirection provided by virtual addressing allows the operating system to use other data stores, like a hard drive, to store what would otherwise have to remain in main memory (RAM). As a result, operating systems can allow programs to use more memory than the system has physically available. When a program needs data which is not currently in RAM, the CPU signals to the kernel that this has happened, and the kernel responds by writing the contents of an inactive memory block to disk (if necessary) and replacing it with the data requested by the program. The program can then be resumed from the point where it was stopped. This scheme is generally known as demand paging.

Virtual addressing also allows creation of virtual partitions of memory in two disjointed areas, one being reserved for the kernel (kernel space) and the other for the applications (user space). The applications are not permitted by the processor to address kernel memory, thus preventing an application from damaging the running kernel. This fundamental partition of memory space has contributed much to current designs of actual general-purpose kernels and is almost universal in such systems, although some research kernels (e.g. Singularity) take other approaches.

2.6.1.3 Device Management

To perform useful functions, processes need access to the peripherals connected to the computer, which are controlled by the kernel through device drivers. For example, to show the user something on the screen, an application would make a request to the kernel, which would forward the request to its display driver, which is then responsible for actually plotting the character/pixel.

A kernel must maintain a list of available devices. This list may be known in advance (e.g. on an embedded system where the kernel will be rewritten if the available hardware changes), configured by the user (typical on older PCs and on systems that are not designed for personal use) or detected by the operating system at run time (normally called plug and play). In a plug and play system, a device manager first performs a scan on different hardware buses, such as Peripheral Component Interconnect (PCI) or Universal Serial Bus (USB), to detect installed devices, then searches for the appropriate drivers.

As device management is a very OS-specific topic, these drivers are handled differently by each kind of kernel design, but in every case, the kernel has to provide the I/O to allow drivers to physically access their devices through some port or memory location. Very important decisions have to be made when designing the device management system, as in some designs accesses may involve context switches, making the operation very CPU-intensive and easily causing a significant performance overhead.

2.6.1.4 System Calls

To actually perform useful work, a process must be able to access the services provided by the kernel. This is implemented differently by each kernel, but most provide a C library or an API, which in turn invokes the related kernel functions. The method of invoking the kernel function varies from kernel to kernel. If memory isolation is in use, it is impossible for a user process to call the kernel directly, because that would be a violation of the processor's access control rules. A few possibilities are:

- **Using a software-simulated interrupt:** This method is available on most hardware, and is therefore very common.
- **Using a call gate:** A call gate is a special address stored by the kernel in a list in kernel memory at a location known to the processor. When the processor detects a call to that address, it instead redirects to the target location without causing an access violation. This requires hardware support, but the hardware for it is quite common.
- **Using a special system call instruction:** This technique requires special hardware support, which common architectures (notably, x86) may lack. System call instructions have been added to recent models of x86 processors, however, and some operating systems for PCs make use of them when available.
- **Using a memory-based queue:** An application that makes large numbers of requests but does not need to wait for the result of each may add details of requests to an area of memory that the kernel periodically scans to find requests.

2.6.2 Kernel Design Decisions

Following are the kernel design decisions:

2.6.2.1 Issues of Kernel Support for Protection

An important consideration in the design of a kernel is the support it provides for protection from faults (fault tolerance) and from malicious behaviors (security). These two aspects are usually not clearly distinguished, and the adoption of this distinction in the kernel design leads to the rejection of a hierarchical structure for protection.

The mechanisms or policies provided by the kernel can be classified according to several criteria, as: static (enforced at compile time) or dynamic (enforced at runtime); preemptive or post-detection; according to the protection principles they satisfy (i.e. Denning); whether they are hardware supported or language based; whether they are more an open mechanism or a binding policy; and many more.

2.6.2.2 Fault Tolerance

A useful measure of the level of fault tolerance of a system is how closely it adheres to the principle of least privilege. In cases where multiple programs are running on a single computer, it is important to prevent a fault in one of the programs from negatively affecting the other. Extended to malicious design rather than a fault, this also applies to security, where it is necessary to prevent processes from accessing information without being granted permission.

The two major hardware approaches for protection (of sensitive information) are Hierarchical protection domains (also called ring architectures, segment architectures or supervisor mode), and Capability-based addressing.

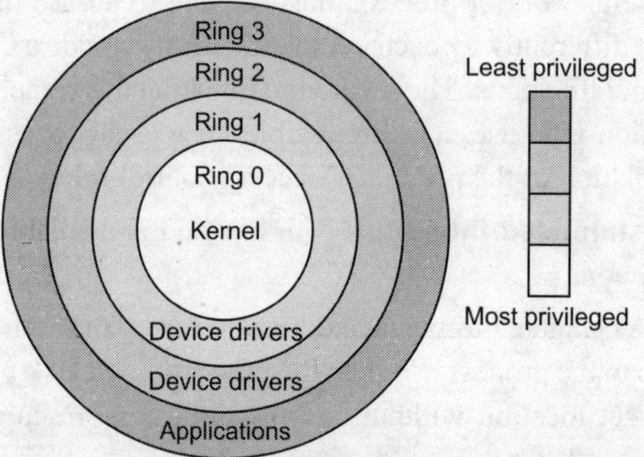

Figure 2.6 Privilege rings, such as in the x86, are a common implementation of Hierarchical protection domains used in many commercial systems to have some level of fault tolerance

Hierarchical protection domains are much less flexible, as is the case with every kernel with a hierarchical structure assumed as global design criterion. In the case of protection it is not possible to assign different privileges to processes that are at the same privileged level, and therefore is not possible to satisfy Denning's four principles for fault tolerance (particularly the Principle of least privilege). Hierarchical protection domains also have a major performance drawback, since interaction between different levels of protection, when a process has to manipulate a data structure both in 'user mode' and 'supervisor mode', always requires message copying (transmission by value). A kernel based on capabilities, however, is more flexible in assigning privileges, can satisfy Denning's fault tolerance principles, and typically doesn't suffer from the performance issues of copy by value.

Both approaches typically require some hardware or firmware support to be operable and efficient. The hardware support for hierarchical protection domains is typically that of "CPU modes." An efficient and simple way to provide hardware support of capabilities is to delegate the MMU the responsibility of checking access-rights for every memory access, a mechanism called capability-based addressing. Most commercial computer architectures lack MMU support for capabilities. An alternative approach is to simulate capabilities using commonly-supported hierarchical domains; in this approach, each protected object must reside in an address space that the application does not have access to; the kernel also maintains a list of capabilities in such memory. When an application needs to access an object protected by a capability, it performs a system call and the kernel performs the access for it. The performance cost of address space switching limits the practicality of this approach in systems with complex interactions between objects, but it is used in current operating systems for objects that are not accessed frequently or which are not expected to perform quickly. Approaches where protection mechanism are not firmware supported but are instead simulated at higher levels (e.g. simulating capabilities by manipulating page tables on hardware that does not have direct support), are possible, but there are performance implications. Lack of hardware support may not be an issue, however, for systems that choose to use language-based protection.

An important kernel design decision is the choice of the abstraction levels where the security mechanisms and policies should be implemented. Kernel security mechanisms play a critical role in supporting security at higher levels.

One approach is to use firmware and kernel support for fault tolerance (see above), and build the security policy for malicious behavior on top of that (adding features such as cryptography mechanisms where necessary), delegating some responsibility to the compiler. Approaches that delegate enforcement of security policy to the compiler and/or the application level are often called language-based security.

The lack of many critical security mechanisms in current mainstream operating systems impedes the implementation of adequate security policies at the application abstraction level. In fact, a common misconception in computer security is that any security policy can be implemented in an application regardless of kernel support.

2.6.2.3 Hardware-based Protection or Language-based Protection

Typical computer systems today use hardware-enforced rules about what programs are allowed to access what data. The processor monitors the execution and stops a program that violates a rule (e.g., a user process that is about to read or write to kernel memory, and so on). In systems that lack support for capabilities, processes are isolated from each other by using separate address spaces. Calls from user processes into the kernel are regulated by requiring them to use one of the above-described system call methods.

An alternative approach is to use language-based protection. In a language-based protection system, the kernel will only allow code to execute that has been produced by a trusted language compiler. The language may then be designed such that it is impossible for the programmer to instruct it to do something that will violate a security requirement.

Advantages of this approach include

- **No need for separate address spaces:** Switching between address spaces is a slow operation that causes a great deal of overhead, and a lot of optimization work is currently performed in order to prevent unnecessary switches in current operating systems. Switching is completely unnecessary in a language-based protection system, as all code can safely operate in the same address space.
- **Flexibility:** Any protection scheme that can be designed to be expressed via a programming language can be implemented using this method. Changes to the protection scheme (e.g. from a hierarchical system to a capability-based one) do not require new hardware.

Disadvantages include

- Longer application starts up time. Applications must be verified when they are started to ensure they have been compiled by the correct compiler, or may need recompiling either from source code or from bytecode.
- Inflexible type systems. On traditional systems, applications frequently perform operations that are not type safe. Such operations cannot be permitted in a language-based protection system, which means that applications may need to be rewritten and may, in some cases, lose performance.

1. PROCESS COOPERATION

Edsger Dijkstra proved that from a logical point of view, atomic lock and unlock operations operating on binary semaphores are sufficient primitives to express any functionality of process cooperation. However this approach is generally held to be lacking in terms of safety and efficiency, whereas a message passing approach is more flexible.

2. I/O DEVICES MANAGEMENT

The idea of a kernel where I/O devices are handled uniformly with other processes, as parallel co-operating processes, was first proposed and implemented by Brinch Hansen (although similar ideas were suggested in 1967). In Hansen's description of this, the "common" processes are called internal processes, while the I/O devices are called external processes.

2.6.3 Kernel-wide Design Approaches

Following are the various approaches for kernel designs:

2.6.3.1 Monolithic Kernels

In a monolithic kernel, all OS services run along with the main kernel thread, thus also residing in the same memory area. This approach provides rich and powerful hardware access. Some developers, such as UNIX developer Ken Thompson, maintain that it is "easier to implement a monolithic kernel" than microkernels. The main disadvantages of monolithic kernels are the dependencies between system components - a bug in a device driver might crash the entire system - and the fact that large kernels can become very difficult to maintain.

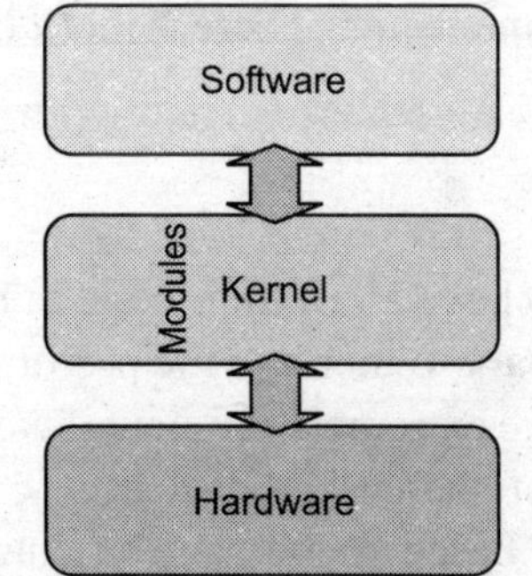

Figure 2.7 Monolithic Kernel

2.6.3.2 Microkernels

The microkernel approach consists of defining a simple abstraction over the hardware, with a set of primitives or system calls to implement minimal OS services such as memory management, multitasking, and inter-process communication. Other services, including those normally provided by the kernel, such as networking, are implemented in user-space programs, and referred to as servers. Microkernels are easier to maintain than monolithic kernels, but the large number of system calls and context switches might slow down the system because they typically generate more overhead than plain function calls.

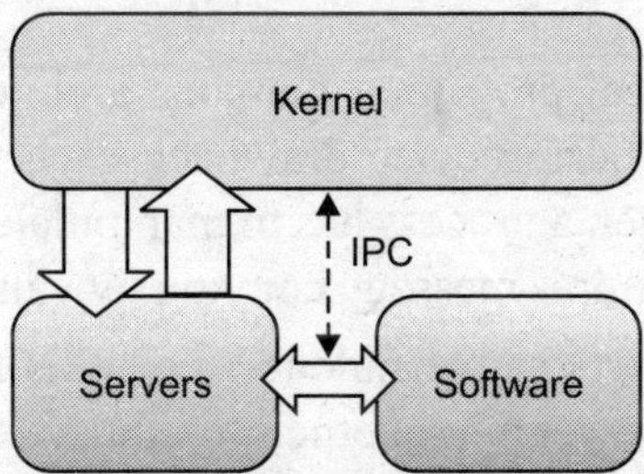

Figure 2.8 Microkernel's

A microkernel allows the implementation of the remaining part of the operating system as a normal application program written in a high-level language, and the use of different operating systems on top of the same unchanged kernel. It is also possible to dynamically switch among operating systems and to have more than one active simultaneously.

2.6.3.3 Monolithic Kernels VS Microkernels

As the computer kernel grows, a number of problems become evident. One of the most obvious is that the memory footprint increases. This is mitigated to some degree by perfecting the virtual memory system, but not all computer architectures have virtual memory support. To reduce the kernel's footprint, extensive editing has to be performed to carefully remove unneeded code, which can be very difficult with non-obvious interdependencies between parts of a kernel with millions of lines of code.

By the early 1990s, due to the various shortcomings of monolithic kernels versus microkernels, monolithic kernels were considered obsolete by virtually all operating system researchers. As a result, the design of Linux as a monolithic kernel rather than a microkernel was the topic of a famous flame war between Linus Torvalds and Andrew Tanenbaum. There is merit on both sides of the argument presented in the Tanenbaum-Torvalds debate.

1. PERFORMANCES

Monolithic kernels are designed to have all of their code in the same address space (kernel space), which some developers argue is necessary to increase the performance of the system. Some developers also maintain that monolithic systems are extremely efficient if well-written. The monolithic model tends to be more efficient through the use of shared kernel memory, rather than the slower IPC system of microkernel designs, which is typically based on message passing.

The performance of microkernels constructed in the 1980s and early 1990s was poor. Studies that empirically measured the performance of these microkernels did not analyze the reasons of such inefficiency. The explanations of this data were left to "folklore", with the assumption that they were due to the increased frequency of switches from "kernel-mode" to "user-mode", to the increased frequency of inter-process communication and to the increased frequency of context switches.

In fact, as guessed in 1995, the reasons for the poor performance of microkernels might as well have been: (1) an actual inefficiency of the whole microkernel approach, (2) the particular concepts implemented in those microkernels, and (3) the particular implementation of those concepts. Therefore it remained to be studied if the solution to build an efficient microkernel was, unlike previous attempts, to apply the correct construction techniques.

On the other end, the hierarchical protection domains architecture that leads to the design of a monolithic kernel has a significant performance drawback each time there's an interaction between different levels of protection (i.e. when a process has to manipulate a data structure both in 'user mode' and 'supervisor mode'), since this requires message copying by value.

By the mid-1990s, most researchers had abandoned the belief that careful tuning could reduce this overhead dramatically, but recently, newer microkernels, optimized for performance, such as L4 and K42 have addressed these problems.

2. HYBRID KERNELS

Hybrid kernels are a compromise between the monolithic and microkernel designs. This implies running some services (such as the network stack or the file system) in kernel space to reduce the performance overhead of a traditional microkernel, but still running kernel code (such as device drivers) as servers in user space.

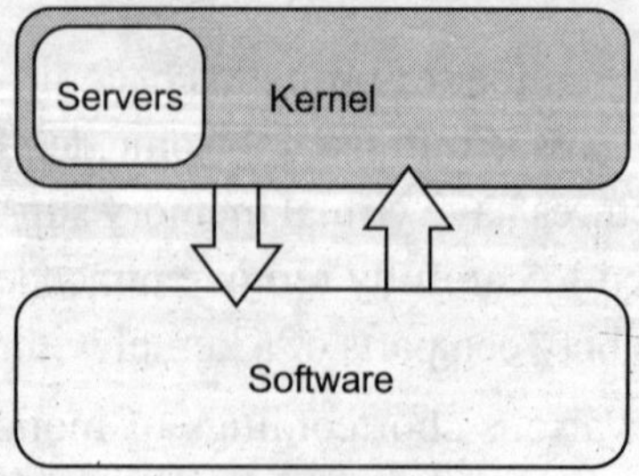

Figure 2.9 The hybrid kernel approach combines the speed and simpler design of a monolithic kernel with the modularity and execution safety of a microkernel.

3. NANOKERNELS

A nanokernel delegates virtually all services - including even the most basic ones like interrupt controllers or the timer - to device drivers to make the kernel memory requirement even smaller than a traditional microkernel.

4. EXOKERNELS

An exokernel is a type of kernel that does not abstract hardware into theoretical models. Instead it allocates physical hardware resources, such as processor time, memory pages, and disk blocks, to different programs. A program running on an exokernel can link to a library operating system that uses the exokernel to simulate the abstractions of a well-known OS, or it can develop application-specific abstractions for better performance.

2.7 FILE SYSTEM

Windows® 2003 supports the NTFS file system, two file allocation table (FAT) file systems (FAT16 and FAT32), the compact disc file system (CDFS), and the Universal Disk Format (UDF). The structures of the volumes formatted by each of these file systems, as well as the way each file system organizes data on the disk, are significantly different. The capabilities and limitations of these file systems must be reviewed to determine their comparative features. The version of NTFS included with Windows 2003 includes reparse points, the change journal, encryption, sparse file support, and several other new features.

2.7.1 Fat File System

The FAT file system has the file allocation table located at the beginning of a logical volume. FAT was designed for small disks and simple folder structures. Two copies of the file allocation table are stored on the volume. In the event that one copy of the file allocation table is corrupted, the other file allocation table is used.

2.7.1.1 Fat16 File System

FAT16 is included in Windows 2003 for the following reasons:

- It provides backward compatibility in the form of an upgrade path for earlier versions of Windows-compatible products.
- It is compatible with most other operating systems.

For Windows 2003 and Windows NT, the maximum size for a FAT16 volume is 4,095 megabytes (MB). A volume formatted with FAT16 is allocated in clusters. The default cluster size is determined by the volume size, and can be as large as 64 kilobytes (KB). The cluster size must be a power of 2 between 512 and 65,536 bytes. Table 2.1 shows the default cluster sizes for FAT16 volumes. You can specify a different cluster size if you format the volume with the format command from the command prompt. However, the size you specify must be listed in Table 2.1.

Table 2.1 FAT16 Cluster Sizes

Volume Size	Sectors Per Cluster	Cluster Size
0 MB-32 MB	1	512 bytes
33 MB-64 MB	2	1 KB
65 MB-128 MB	4	2 KB
129 MB-255 MB	8	4 KB
256 MB-511 MB	16	8 KB
512 MB-1,023 MB	32	16 KB
1,024 MB-2,047 MB	64	32 KB
2,048 MB-4,095 MB	128	64 KB

FAT16 is not recommended for volumes larger than 511 MB because, when relatively small files are placed on a FAT16 volume, FAT uses disk space inefficiently. You cannot use FAT16 on volumes larger than 4 gigabytes (GB), regardless of the cluster size.

On volumes with fewer than 32,680 sectors, the cluster sizes can be up to 8 sectors per cluster. The format program, whether you format the volume using Disk Management or by typing format at the command prompt, creates a 12-bit FAT. Volumes less than 16 MB are usually formatted for a 12-bit FAT, but the exact size depends on the disk geometry. The disk geometry also determines the point at which a larger cluster size is needed because the number of clusters on the volume must fit into 16 bits. Therefore, you might have a 33-MB volume that still has only 1 sector per cluster.

FAT12 is the original implementation of FAT and is intended for very small media. The file allocation table for FAT12 is smaller than the file allocation table for FAT16 and FAT32, because it uses less space for each entry. This leaves more space for data. All 5.25-inch floppy disks are formatted with FAT12, and 1.44-MB 3.5-inch floppy disks are generally formatted with FAT12. Volumes on Iomega Zip and Jaz drives are formatted with FAT16.

STRUCTURE OF A FAT16 VOLUME

Figure 2.6 illustrates how FAT maps out clusters on a volume. The file allocation table (areas FAT1 and FAT2 in Figure 2.10) identifies each cluster in the volume as one of the following:

- Unused
- Cluster in use by a file
- Bad cluster
- Last cluster in a file

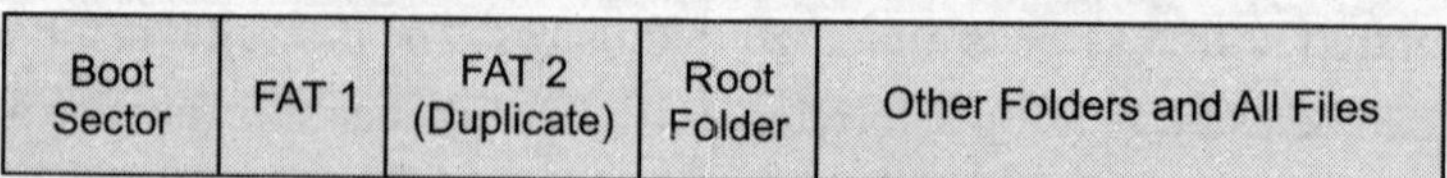

Figure 2.10 Organization of a FAT Volume

The only difference between the root folder and other folders is that the root folder is at a specified location and has a fixed number of entries (for a hard disk). The number of entries on a floppy disk depends on the size of the disk.

Each folder and file in the root folder uses one or more entries. For example, if the fixed number of entries is 512 and you have 100 folders, you can only create 412 files. Folders have a 32-byte entry for each file and folder contained in the folder. Assuming short file names are used, the entry includes the following information:

- Name (8.3) xxxxxxxx.yyy. (88 bits)
- Attribute byte (8 bits of information, described later in this section).
- One reserved byte.
- Create time (24 bits).
- Create date (16 bits).
- Last access date (16 bits).
- Two reserved bytes.
- Last modified time (16 bits).
- Last modified date (16 bits).
- Starting cluster number in the file allocation table (16 bits).
- File size (32 bits).

In a FAT folder structure, files are given the first available location on the volume. The starting cluster number is the address of the first cluster used by the file. Each cluster contains a pointer to the next cluster in the file, or an end-of-file (EOF) indicator at (0xFFFF) which indicates that this cluster is the end of the file. These pointers and end-of-file indicators are shown in Figure 2.11.

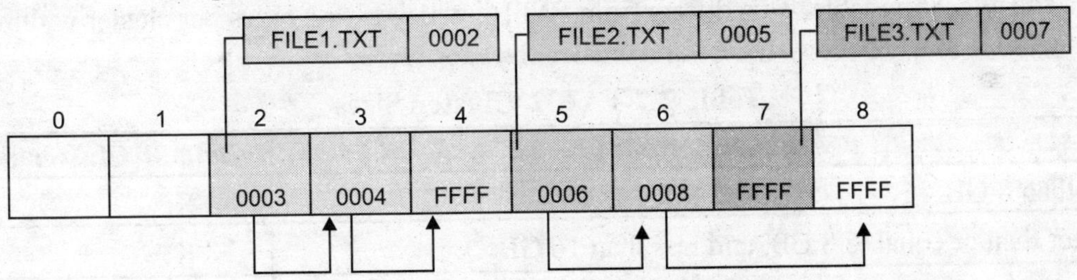

Figure 2.11 Files on a FAT Volume

Figure 2.11 shows three files in a folder. File1.txt is large enough to use three clusters. File2.txt is a fragmented file that also requires three clusters. The third file, File3.txt, fits completely in one cluster. In each case, the folder entry points to the first cluster of the file. The information in the folder is used by all operating systems that support FAT. Windows 2003 can store additional time stamps in a FAT folder entry. These time stamps show when the file was created or last accessed.

Because all entries in a directory are the same size, the attribute byte for each entry in a directory describes what kind of entry it is. For example, one bit indicates that the entry is for a subdirectory and another bit marks the entry as a volume. Typically, only the operating system controls the settings of these bits. The attribute byte includes four bits that can be turned on or off by the user - archive, system, hidden, and read-only.

2.7.1.2 FAT32 File System

Support for FAT32 is new in Windows 2003. FAT16 supports volumes up to 4 GB, whereas theoretically FAT32 can manage volumes up to 2 terabytes. The FAT32 on-disk format and features on Windows 2003 are similar to those on Windows 95 OSR2 and Windows 98.

The size of a FAT32 cluster can range in size from 1 sector (512 bytes) to 64 sectors (32 KB), incremented in powers of 2. Since FAT32 requires 4 bytes to store cluster values, many internal and on-disk data structures have been revised or expanded. Most programs are unaffected by these changes; however, disk utilities which read the on-disk format must be updated to support FAT32.

Two application programming interfaces (APIs) are disabled on FAT32. Since the BIOS parameter block (BPB) structure grows from 25 bytes on FAT16 to 53 bytes on FAT32, and FSCTL_QUERY_FAT_BPB is defined to return only as much of the boot sector as contains the 25 byte form of the BPB, it is disabled on FAT32. To retrieve the BPB on FAT32, applications should read the volume directly. This also works for FAT16. Extended attributes are disabled on FAT32 since increasing the cluster number to 4 bytes requires the use of the field previously used to index the extended attribute database.

STRUCTURE OF A FAT32 VOLUME

The main difference between FAT16 and FAT32 is the logical partition size. FAT32 breaks the 2-GB logical drive limitation of FAT16 volumes by extending a single logical drive capacity to at least 127 GB. If you have a 2-GB FAT16 drive, you must use a 32-KB cluster. With FAT32, the range for a 4-KB cluster, for example, includes drive sizes between 512 MB and 8 GB.

The largest possible file for a FAT32 drive is 4 GB minus 2 bytes. FAT32 uses 4 bytes per cluster within the file allocation table. This differs from FAT16, which uses 2 bytes per cluster within the file allocation table. Table 2.2 shows the default cluster sizes for FAT32.

Table 2.2 FAT32 Cluster Sizes

Partition Size	Default Cluster Size
Less than 8 GB	4 K
Greater than or equal to 8 GB, and less than 16 GB	8 K
Greater than or equal to 16 GB, and less than 32 GB	16 K
Greater than or equal to 32 GB	32 K

A FAT32 volume must have at least 65,527 clusters. Also, the cluster size on a FAT32 volume cannot be such that the file allocation table is greater than (16 MB - 64 KB)/4, or almost 4 million clusters.

FAT16 and FAT32 do not scale well. As the volume gets bigger, the file allocation table gets bigger, which dramatically increases the amount of time it takes Windows 2003 to compute how much free space is on the boot volume when the system is restarted.

For this reason, you may not create a FAT32 volume larger than 32 GB using the Format utility. However, the Windows 2003 Fastfat driver enables you to mount and fully support a FAT32 volume larger than 32 GB.

2.7.2 File Names on Fat Volumes

Files created or renamed on FAT volumes use attribute bits to support long file names in a way that does not interfere with how MS-DOS gains access to the volume. Whenever you create a file with a long file name, Windows 2000 creates a conventional 8.3 name for the file and one or more secondary folder entries for the file, one for each 13 characters in the long file name. Each secondary folder entry stores a corresponding part of the long file name in Unicode.

Windows 2003 marks the secondary folder entries as part of a long file name by setting the volume ID, read-only, system, and hidden attribute bits. MS-DOS generally ignores folder entries with all four of these attribute bits set, so these entries are invisible to these operating systems. MS-DOS accesses the file by using the conventional 8.3 file name contained in the folder entry for the file.

Figure 2.12 shows all of the folder entries for the file Thequi~1.fox, which has a long name of the quick brown. fox. The long name is in Unicode so each character in the name uses 2 bytes in the folder entry. The attribute field for the long-name entries has the value 0x0F. The attribute field for the short name has the value 0x20.

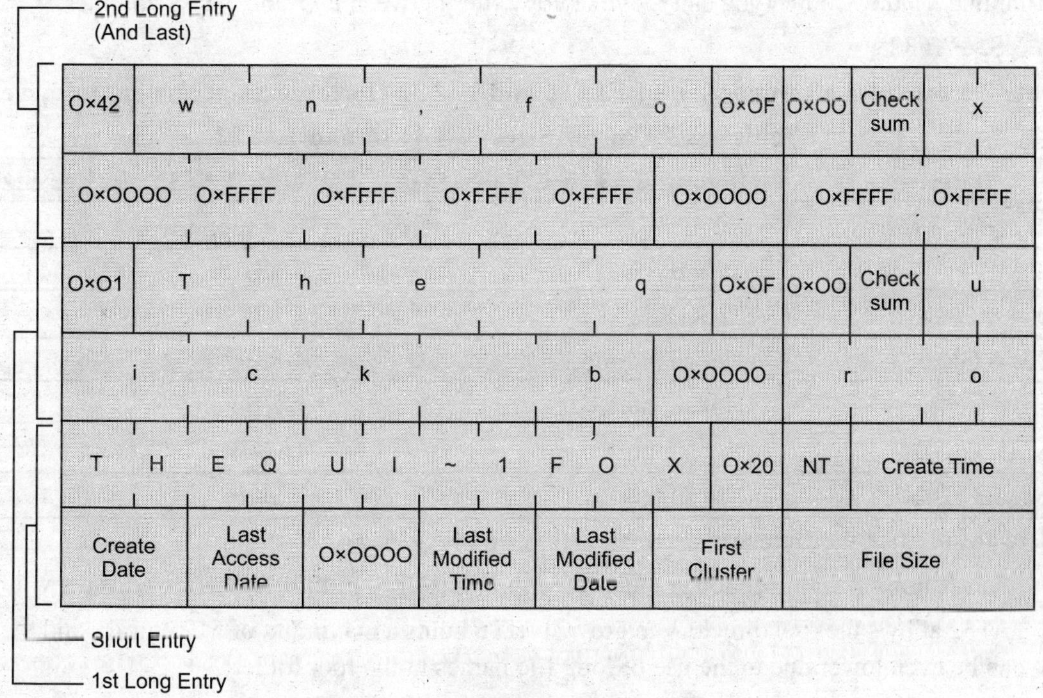

Figure 2.12 Long File Name on a FAT Volume

Windows NT and Windows 2003 do not use the same algorithm to create long and short file names as Windows 95 and Windows 98. However, on computers that multiple-boot these operating systems, files that you create when running one operating system can be accessed when running the other.

By default, Windows 2003 supports long file names on FAT volumes. You can prevent a FAT file system from creating long file names by setting the value of the Win31FileSystem registry entry (in HKEY_LOCAL_MACHINE\System \CurrentControlSet\Control\FileSystem\Win31FileSystem) to 1.

CAUTION

Do not use a registry editor to edit the registry directly unless you have no alternative. The registry editors bypass the standard safeguards provided by administrative tools. These safeguards prevent you from entering conflicting settings or settings that are likely to degrade performance or damage your system. Editing the registry directly can have serious, unexpected consequences that can prevent the system from starting and require that you reinstall Windows 2003. To configure or customize Windows 2003, use the programs in Control Panel or Microsoft Management Console (MMC) whenever possible. This value prevents Windows 2003 from creating new long file names on all FAT volumes, but it does not affect existing long file names.

2.7.3 Using Fat With Windows 2000

FAT16 works the same way in Windows 2000 as it does in MS-DOS, Windows 3. x , Windows 95, and Windows 98. FAT32 works the same way in Windows 2000 as it does in Windows 95 OSR2 and Windows 98. In fact, you can install Windows 2000 on an existing FAT primary partition or logical drive. When running Windows 2000, you can move or copy files between FAT and NTFS volumes.

FAT16 VS. FAT32

Table 2.3 provides a comparison of FAT16 and FAT32 cluster sizes according to drive size.

Table 2.3 Cluster Sizes of FAT16 and FAT32

Drive Size	Default FAT16 Cluster Size	Default FAT32 Cluster Size
260 MB-511 MB	8 KB	Not supported
512 MB-1,023 MB	16 KB	4 KB
1,024 MB-2 GB	32 KB	4 KB
2 GB-8 GB	Not supported	4 KB
8 GB-16 GB	Not supported	8 KB
16 GB-32 GB	Not supported	16 KB
> 32 GB	Not supported	32 KB

There are additional differences between FAT32 and FAT16:

- FAT32 allows finer allocation granularity (approximately 4 million allocation units per volume).
- FAT32 allows the root directory to grow (FAT16 holds a maximum of 512 entries, and the limit can be even lower due to the use of long file names in the root folder).

ADVANTAGES OF FAT16

Advantages of FAT16 are:

- MS-DOS, Windows 95, Windows 98, Windows NT, Windows 2000, and some UNIX operating systems can use it.
- There are many tools available to address problems and recover data.
- If you have a startup failure, you can start the computer with an MS-DOS bootable floppy disk.
- It is efficient, both in speed and storage, on volumes smaller than 256 MB.

DISADVANTAGES OF FAT16

Disadvantages of FAT16 are:

- The root folder can manage a maximum of 512 entries. The use of long file names can significantly reduce the number of available entries.
- FAT16 is limited to 65,536 clusters, but because certain clusters are reserved, it has a practical limit of 65,524. Each cluster is fixed in size relative to the logical drive. If both the maximum number of clusters and their maximum size (32 KB) are reached, the largest drive is limited to 4 GB on Windows 2000. To maintain compatibility with MS-DOS, Windows 95, and Windows 98, a FAT16 volume should not be larger than 2 GB.
- The boot sector is not backed up.
- There is no built-in file system security or file compression with FAT16.
- FAT16 can waste file storage space in larger drives as the size of the cluster increases. The space allocated for storing a file is based on the size of the cluster allocation granularity, not the file size. A 10-KB file stored in a 32-KB cluster wastes 22 KB of disk space.

ADVANTAGES OF FAT32

FAT32 allocates disk space much more efficiently than previous versions of FAT. Depending on the size of your files, there is a potential for tens and even hundreds of megabytes more free disk space on larger hard disk drives. In addition, FAT32 provides the following enhancements:

- The root folder on a FAT32 drive is now an ordinary cluster chain, so it can be located anywhere on the volume. For this reason, FAT32 does not restrict the number of entries in the root folder.
- It uses space more efficiently than FAT16. FAT32 uses smaller clusters (4 KB for drives up to 8 GB), resulting in 10 to 15 percent more efficient use of disk space relative to large FAT16 drives. FAT32 also reduces the resources necessary for the computer to operate.
- FAT32 is more robust than FAT16. FAT32 has the ability to relocate the root directory and use the backup copy of the FAT instead of the default copy. In addition, the boot record on FAT32 drives has been expanded to include a backup of critical data structures. This means that FAT32 volumes are less susceptible to a single point of failure than FAT16 volumes.

DISADVANTAGES OF FAT32

Disadvantages of FAT32 include:

- The largest FAT32 volume Windows 2000 can format is limited in size to 32 GB.
- FAT32 volumes are not accessible from any other operating systems other than Windows 95 OSR2 and Windows 98.
- The boot sector is not backed up.
- There is no built in file system security or compression with FAT32.

2.7.4 Compact Disk File System

Windows 2003 provides support for the ISO 9660-compliant CDFS, which supports long file names as listed in the ISO 9660 Level 2 standards. When creating a CD-ROM to be used on Windows 2003, you must adhere to the following standards:

- All directory and file names must have fewer than 32 characters.
- All directory and file names must be in capital letters.
- The directory tree cannot exceed 8 levels from the root.
- File name extensions are not mandatory.

2.7.5 Ntfs File System

Windows 2000 comes with a new version of NTFS. This newest version of NTFS provides performance, reliability, and functionality not found in FAT. Some new features in Windows 2000, such as Active Directory ™ directory service and the storage features based on reparse points are only available on volumes formatted with NTFS. NTFS also includes security features required for file servers and high-end personal computers in a corporate environment, and data access control and ownership privileges important for data integrity.

2.7.5.1 Multiple Data Streams

NTFS supports multiple data streams, where the stream name identifies a new data attribute on the file. A handle can be opened to each data stream. A data stream, then, is a unique set of file attributes. Streams have separate opportunistic locks, file locks, and sizes, but common permissions. This feature enables you to manage data as a single unit. The following is an example of an alternate stream:

myfile.dat:stream2

A library of files might exist where the files are defined as alternate streams, as in the following example:

library:file1

:file2

:file3

A file can be associated with more than one application at a time, such as Microsoft® Word and Microsoft® WordPad. For instance, a file structure like the following illustrates file association, but not multiple files:

program:source_file

:doc_file

:object_file

:executable_file

You can use the Win32 advanced programming interface (API) CreateFile to create an alternate data stream. Or, at the command prompt, you can type commands such as:

echo text>program:source_file

more <program:source_file

CAUTION

Because NTFS is not supported on floppy disks, when you copy an NTFS file to a floppy disk, data streams and other attributes not supported by FAT are lost without warning.

2.7.5.2 Reparse Points

Reparse points are new file system objects in the version of NTFS included with Windows 2000. Reparse points have a definable attribute containing user-controlled data and are used to extend functionality in the input/output (I/O) subsystem.

2.7.5.3 Change Journal

The change journal is used by NTFS to provide a persistent log of all changes made to files on the volume. For each volume, NTFS uses the change journal to track information about added, deleted, and modified files. The change journal is much more efficient than time stamps or file notifications for determining changes in a given namespace.

The change journal is implemented as a sparse stream in which only a small active range uses any disk allocation. The active range initially begins at offset 0 in the stream and moves monotonically forward. The unique sequence number (USN) of a particular record represents its virtual offset in the stream. As the active range moves forward through the stream, earlier records are deallocated and become unavailable. The size of the active range in a sparse file can be adjusted.

2.7.5.4 Encryption

File and directory-level encryption is implemented in the version of NTFS included with Windows 2000 for enhanced security in NTFS volumes. Windows 2000 uses Encrypting File System (EFS) to store data in encrypted form, which provides security when the storage media are removed from a system running Windows 2000.

2.7.5.5 Sparse File Support

Sparse files allow programs to create very large files, but to consume disk space only as needed. A sparse file is a file with an attribute that causes the I/O subsystem to allocate the file's meaningful (nonzero) data. All nonzero data is allocated on disk, whereas all non meaningful data (large strings of data composed of zeros) is not. When a sparse file is read, allocated data is returned as it was stored, and nonallocated data is returned, by default, as zeros in accordance with the C2 security requirement specification.

NTFS includes full sparse file support for both compressed and uncompressed files. NTFS handles read operations on sparse files by returning allocated data and sparse data. It is possible to read a sparse file as allocated data and a range of data without having to retrieve the entire data set, although, by default, NTFS returns the entire data set.

You can set a user-controlled file system attribute to take advantage of the sparse file function in NTFS. With the sparse file attribute set, the file system can deallocate data from anywhere in the file and, when an application calls, yield the zero data by range instead of storing and returning the actual data. File system APIs allow for the file to be copied or backed as actual bits and sparse stream ranges. The net result is efficient file system storage and access. Figure 2.13 shows how data is stored with and without the sparse file attribute set.

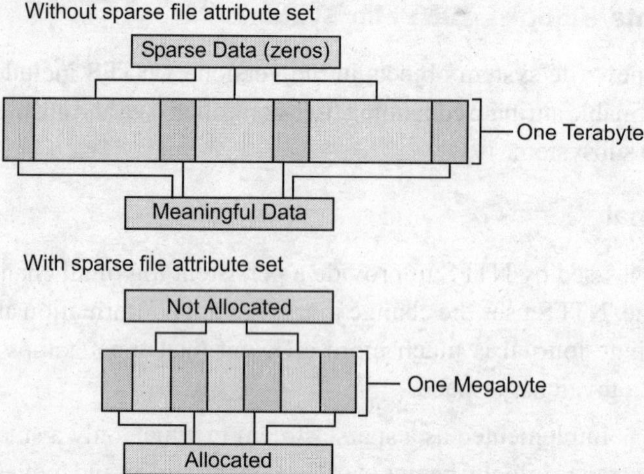

Figure 2.13 Sparse Data Storage

2.7.5.6 Disk Quotas

Disk quotas are a new feature in NTFS that provide more precise control of network-based storage. Disk quotas are implemented on a per-volume basis and enable both hard and soft storage limits to be implemented on a per-user basis. For more information about disk quotas, see "Data Storage and Management" in this book.

The introduction of distributed file system (Dfs), NTFS directory junctions, and volume mount points also creates situations where logical directories do not have to correspond to the same physical volume. Available disk space is based on user context, and the space reported for a volume is not necessarily representative of the space available to the user. For this reason, do not rely on space queries to make assumptions about the amount of available disk space in directories other than the current one.

2.7.5.7 Distributed Link-tracking

Windows 2000 provides a distributed link-tracking service that enables client applications to track link sources that have been moved locally or within a domain. Clients that subscribe to this link-tracking service can maintain the integrity of their references because the objects referenced can be moved transparently. Files managed by NTFS can be referenced by a unique object identifier. Link tracking stores a file's object identifier as part of its tracking information.

The distributed link-tracking service tracks shell shortcuts and OLE links within NTFS volumes on computers running Windows 2000. For example, if a shell shortcut is created to a text document, distributed link-tracking allows the shortcut to remain correct, even if the target file moves to a new drive or computer system. Similarly, in a Microsoft® Word document that contains an OLE link to a Microsoft® Excel spreadsheet, the link remains correct even if the Excel file moves to a new drive or computer system.

If a link is made to a file on a volume formatted with the version of NTFS included with Windows 2000, and the file is moved to any other volume with the same version of NTFS within the same domain, the file is found by the tracking service, subject to time considerations. Additionally, if the file is moved outside the domain or within a workgroup, it is likely to be found.

2.7.5.8 Converting to Windows 2000 File Systems

The on-disk format for NTFS has been enhanced in Windows 2000 to enable new functionality. The upgrade to the new on-disk format occurs when Windows 2000 mounts an existing NTFS volume. The upgrade is quick and automatic; the conversion time is independent of volume size. Note that FAT volumes can be converted to NTFS format at any time using the Convert.exe utility.

IMPORTANT

Performance of volumes that have been converted from FAT is not as high as volumes that were originally formatted with NTFS.

2.7.6 MULTIPLE BOOTING OF WINDOWS NT AND WINDOWS 2000

Your ability to access your NTFS volumes when you multiple-boot Windows NT and Windows 2000 depends on which version you are using. (Redirected clients using NTFS volumes on file and print servers are not affected.)

2.7.6.1 Windows NT Compatibility With the Version of NTFS Included with Windows 2000

When a Windows 2000 volume is mounted on a system running Windows NT 4.0 Service Pack 4, most features of the version of NTFS included with Windows 2000 are not available. However, most read and write operations are permitted if they do not make use of any new NTFS features. Features affected by this configuration include the following:

- **Reparse points:** Windows NT cannot use any features based on reparse points, such as Remote Storage and volume mount points.
- **Disk quotas:** When running Windows NT, Windows 2000 disk quotas are ignored. This allows you to allocate more disk space than is allowed by your quota.
- **Encryption:** Windows NT cannot perform any operations on files encrypted by Windows 2000.
- **Sparse files:** Windows NT cannot perform any operations on sparse files.
- **Change journal:** Windows NT ignores the change journal. No entries are logged when files are accessed.

2.7.7 Cleanup Operations on Windows NT Volumes

Because files on volumes formatted with the version of NTFS included with Windows 2000 can be read and written to by Windows NT, Windows 2000 may need to perform cleanup operations to ensure the consistency of the data structures of a volume after it was mounted on a computer that is running Windows NT. Features affected by cleanup operations are explained below.

Disk quotas: If disk quotas are turned off, Windows 2000 performs no cleanup operations. If disk quotas are turned on, Windows 2000 cleans up the quota information. If a user exceeds the disk quota while the NTFS volume is mounted by a Windows NT 4.0 system, all further disk allocations of data by that user will fail. The user can still read and write data to any existing file, but will not be able to increase the size of a file. However, the user can delete and shrink files. When the user gets below the assigned disk quota, he or she can resume disk allocations of data. The same behavior occurs when a system is upgraded from a Windows NT system to a Windows 2000 system with quotas enforced.

Reparse points: Because files that have reparse points associated with them cannot be accessed by computers that are running Windows NT 4.0 or earlier, no cleanup operations are necessary in Windows 2000.

Encryption: Because encrypted files cannot be accessed by computers that are running Windows NT 4.0 or earlier, no cleanup operations are necessary.

Sparse files: Because sparse files cannot be accessed by computers that are running Windows NT 4.0 or earlier, no cleanup operations are necessary.

Object identifiers: Windows 2000 maintains two references to the object identifier. One is on the file; the other is in the volume-wide object identifier index. If you delete a file with an object identifier on it, Windows 2000 must scan and clean up the leftover entry in the index.

Change journal: Computers that are running Windows NT 4.0 or earlier do not log file changes in the change journal. When Windows 2000 starts, the change journals on volumes accessed by Windows NT are reset to indicate that the journal history is incomplete. Applications that use the change journal must have the ability to accept incomplete journals.

2.7.8 Structure of an NTFS Volume

Like FAT, NTFS uses clusters as the fundamental unit of disk allocation. In the Disk Management snap-in, you can specify a cluster size of up to 4 KB. If you type format at the command prompt to format your NTFS volume, but do not specify an allocation unit size using the /A:<size> switch , the values in Table 2.4 will be used.

Table 2.4 Default Cluster Sizes for NTFS

Volume Size	Sectors Per Custer	Default Cluster Size
512 MB or less	1	512 bytes
513 MB-1,024 MB (1 GB)	2	1,024 bytes (1 KB)
1,025 MB-2,048 MB (2 GB)	4	2,048 bytes (2 KB)
Greater than 2,049 MB	8	4 KB

Windows 2000 like Windows NT 3.51 and Windows NT 4.0, supports file compression. Since file compression is not supported on cluster sizes above 4 K, the default NTFS cluster size for Windows 2000 never exceeds 4 K.

2.7.8.1 Boot Sector

The first information found on an NTFS volume is the boot sector. The boot sector starts at sector 0 and can be up to 16 sectors long.

It consists of two structures:

- The BIOS parameter block, which contains information on the volume layout and file system structures.

- Code that describes how to find and load the startup files for the operating system being loaded. For Windows 2000, this code loads the file Ntldr.

2.7.9 Master File Table and Metadata

When a volume is formatted with NTFS, a Master File Table (MFT) file and other pieces of metadata are created. Metadata are the files NTFS uses to implement the file system structure. NTFS reserves the first 16 records of the MFT for metadata files.

The data segment locations for both $Mft and $MftMirr are recorded in the boot sector. If the first MFT record is corrupted, NTFS reads the second record to find the MFT mirror file. A duplicate of the boot sector is located at the end of the volume. Table 2.5 lists and briefly describes the metadata stored in the MFT.

Table 2.5 Metadata Stored in the Master File Table

System File	File Name	MFT Record	Purpose of the File
Master file table	$Mft	0	Contains one base file record for each file and directory on an NTFS volume. If the allocation information for a file or directory is too large to fit within a single record, other file records are allocated as well.
Master file table 2	$MftMirr	1	A duplicate image of the first four records of the MFT. This file guarantees access to the MFT in case of a single-sector failure.
Log file	$LogFile	2	Contains a list of transaction steps used for NTFS recoverability. Log file size depends upon the volume size. It is used by Windows 2000 to restore consistency to NTFS in the event of a system failure. For more information about the log file, see "NTFS Recoverability" later in this chapter.
Volume	$Volume	3	Contains information about the volume, such as the volume label and the volume version.
Attribute definitions	$AttrDef	4	A table of attribute names, numbers, and descriptions.
Root file name index	$	5	The root directory.
Cluster bitmap	$Bitmap	6	A representation of the volume showing which clusters are in use.
Boot sector	$Boot	7	Includes the bootstrap for the volume if it is a bootable volume.
Bad cluster file	$BadClus	8	Contains bad clusters for the volume.

System File	File Name	MFT Record	Purpose of the File
Security file	$Secure	9	Contains unique security descriptors for all files within a volume.
Upcase table	$Upcase	10	Converts lowercase characters to matching Unicode uppercase characters.
NTFS extension file	$Extend	11	Used for various optional extensions such as quotas, reparse point data, and object identifiers.
		12-15	Reserved for future use.

The remaining records of the MFT contain the file and directory records for each file and directory on the volume. NTFS creates a file record for each file and a directory record for each directory created on an NTFS volume. The MFT includes a separate file record for the MFT itself. These file and directory records are stored on the MFT. The attributes of the file are written to the allocated space in the MFT. Besides file attributes, each file record contains information about the position of the file record in the MFT.

Each file usually uses one file record. However, if a file has a large number of attributes or becomes highly fragmented, it may need more than one file record. If this is the case, the first record for the file, called the base file record, stores the location of the other file records required by the file. Small files and directories (typically 1,500 bytes or smaller) are entirely contained within the file's MFT record.

Directory records contain index information. Small directories might reside entirely within the MFT structure, while large directories are organized into B-tree structures and have records with pointers to external clusters that contain directory entries that could not be contained within the MFT structure.

2.7.10 NTFS File Attributes

Every allocated sector on an NTFS volume belongs to a file. Even the file system metadata is part of a file. NTFS views each file (or folder) as a set of file attributes. Elements such as the file's name, its security information, and even its data, are all file attributes. Each attribute is identified by an attribute type code and, optionally, an attribute name.

When a file's attributes can fit within the MFT file record for that file, they are called resident attributes. Information such as file name and time stamp are always resident attributes. When the information for a file is too large to fit in its MFT file record, some of the file attributes are nonresident. Nonresident attributes are allocated one or more clusters of disk space and stored as an alternate data stream in the volume. NTFS creates the Attribute List attribute to describe the location of both resident and nonresident attribute records. Table 2.6 lists the file attributes defined by NTFS, although other file attributes might be defined in the future.

Table 2.6 NTFS File Attribute Types

Attribute Type	Description
Standard Information	Includes information such as time stamp and link count.
Attribute List	Lists the location of all the attribute records that do not fit in the MFT record.
File Name	A repeatable attribute for both long and short file names. The long name of the file can be up to 255 Unicode characters. The short name is the MS-DOS-readable, 8.3, case-insensitive name for the file. Additional names, or hard links, required by POSIX can be included as additional file name attributes.
Security Descriptor	Shows information about who owns the file and who can access the file.
Data	Contains file data. NTFS allows multiple data attributes per file. Each file typically has one unnamed data attribute. A file can also have one or more named data attributes, each using a particular syntax.
Object ID	A volume-unique file identifier. Used by the link tracking service. Not all files have object identifiers.
Logged Tool Stream	Similar to a data stream, but operations on a logged tool stream are logged to the NTFS log file just like NTFS metadata changes. Used by EFS.
Reparse Point	Used for directory junction points and volume mount points. They are also used by file system filter drivers to mark certain files as special to that driver.
Index Root	Used to implement folders and other indexes.
Index Allocation	Used to implement folders and other indexes.
Bitmap	Used to implement folders and other indexes.
Volume Information	Used only in the $Volume system file. Contains the volume version.
Volume Name	Used only in the $Volume system file. Contains the volume label.

2.8 HARDWARE REQUIREMENTS

Here we are given hardware requirements for network operating system:

Requirement	Standard Edition	Enterprise Edition	Datacenter Edition	Web Edition
Minimum CPU Speed	133 MHz	133 MHz for x86-based 733 MHz for Itanium-based computers*	400 MHz for x86-based computers 733 MHz for Itanium-based computers*	133 MHz

Requirement	Standard Edition	Enterprise Edition	Datacenter Edition	Web Edition
Recommended CPU Speed	550 MHz	733 MHz	733 MHz	550 MHz
Minimum RAM	128 MB	128 MB	512 MB	128 MB
Recommended Minimum RAM	256 MB	256 MB	1 GB	256 MB
Maximum RAM	4 GB	32 GB for x86-based computers 512 GB for Itanium-based computers*	64 GB for x86-based computers 512 GB for Itanium-based computers*	2 GB
Multiprocessor Support **	Up to 4	Up to 8	Minimum 8 required	Up to 2
Disk Space for Setup	1.5 GB	1.5 GB for x86-based computers 2.0 GB for Itanium -based computers*	1.5 GB for x86-based computers 2.0 GB for Itanium -based computers*	1.5 GB

* **Important:** The 64-bit versions of Windows Server 2003, Enterprise Edition and Windows Server 2003, Datacenter Edition are only compatible with 64-bit Intel Itanium-based systems. They cannot be successfully installed on 32-bit systems.

2.8.1 Windows 2003 Product Family

Following are hardware requirements for windows server 2003:

2.8.1.1 Feature Set

The hardware requirements for the Windows Server 2003 family are dependent upon the feature set and configuration.

Feature	Standard Edition	Enterprise Edition	Datacenter Edition	Web Edition
64-bit Support for Intel Itanium - Based Computrs	.Not supported	Supported	Supported	Not supported
Hot add memory[2,3]	Not supported	Supported	Supported	Not supported
Non-Uniform Memory Access (NUMA)[3]	Not supported	Supported	Supported	Not supported
Datacenter Program	Not supported	Not supported	Supported	Not supported
2 GB RAM Maximum	Not supported	N0t supported	Not supported	Supported
4 GB RAM Maximum	Supported	N0t supported	Not supported	Not supported
32 GB RAM Maximum	Not supported	Supported	Not supported	Not supported

Feature	Standard Edition	Enterprise Edition	Datacenter Edition	Web Edition
64 GB RAM Maximum	Not supported	Partially	Supported	Not supported
512 GB RAM Maximum	Not supported	N0t supported	Partially	Not supported
2-way SMP	Supported	Supported	Not supported	Not supported
4-way SMP	Supported	Supported	Not supported	Not supported
8-way SMP	Not supported	Supported	Supported	Not supported
32-way SMP	Not supported	Not supported	Supported	Not supported
64-way SMP	Not supported	Not supported	Supported	Not supported

2.8.1.2 Directory Services

Following are the various directory services:

Feature	Standard Edition	Enterprise Edition	Datacenter Edition	Web Edition
Active Directory	Supported	Supported	Supported	Partially
Metadirectory Services (MMS) Support	Not supported	Supported	Supported	Not supported

2.8.1.3 Security Services

Following are the various security services:

Feature	Standard Edition	Enterprise Edition	Datacenter Edition	Web Edition
Internet Connection Firewall[2]	Supported	Supported	Not supported	Not supported
Public Key Infrastructure, Certificate Services, and Smart Cards	Partially	Supported	Supported	Partially

2.8.1.4 Terminal Services

Following are the various terminal services:

Feature	Standard Edition	Enterprise Edition	Datacenter Edition	Web Edition
Remote Desktop for Administration	Supported	Supported	Supported	Supported
Terminal Server	Supported	Supported	Supported	Not supported
Terminal Server Session Directory	Not supported	Supported	Supported	Not supported

2.8.1.5 Clustering Technologies

Following are the various clustering services:

Feature	Standard Edition	Enterprise Edition	Datacenter Edition	Web Edition
Network Load Balancing	Supported	Supported	Supported	Supported
Cluster Service	Not supported	Supported	Supported	Not supported

2.8.1.6 Communications and Networking Services

Following are the various communication and networking services:

Feature	Standard Edition	Enterprise Edition	Datacenter Edition	Web Edition
VPN: Virtual Private Network Support	Supported	Supported	Supported	Partially
IAS: Internet Authentication Service	Supported	Supported	Supported	Not supported
Network Bridge[2]	Supported	Supported	Not supported	Not supported
ICS: Internet Connection Sharing	Supported	Supported	Not supported	Not supported
IPv6	Supported	Supported	Supported	Supported

2.8.1.7 File And Print Services

Following are the various file and print services:

Feature	Standard Edition	Enterprise Edition	Datacenter Edition	Web Edition
DFS: Distributed File System	Supported	Supported	Supported	Partially
EFS: Encrypting File System	Supported	Supported	Supported	Supported
Shadow Copies of Shared Folders	Supported	Supported	Supported	Supported
Removable Storage	Supported	Supported	Supported	Supported
Remote Storage	Not supported	Supported	Supported	Not supported
Fax Service	Supported	Supported	Supported	Not supported
Service for Macintosh	Supported	Supported	Supported	No supported

2.8.1.8 Management Services

Following are the various management services:

Feature	Standard Edition	Enterprise Edition	Datacenter Edition	Web Edition
IntelliMirror	Supported	Supported	Supported	Partially
Group Policy Results	Supported	Supported	Supported	Partially
WMI: Windows Management Instrumentation Command Line	Supported	Supported	Supported	Supported

Remote OS Installation	Supported	Supported	Supported	Supported
RIS: Remote Installation Services	Supported	Supported	Supported	Not supported
WSRM: Windows System Resource Manager	Not supported	Supported	Supported	Not Supported

2.8.1.9. Net Application Services

Following are the various .net services:

Feature	Standard Edition	Enterprise Edition	Datacenter Edition	Web Edition
.Net Framework[2]	Supported	Supported	Supported	Supported
Internet Information Services (IIS) 6.0	Supported	Supported	Supported	Supported
ASP .NET[2]	Supported	Supported	Supported	Supported
Enterprise UDDI Services	Supported	Supported	Supported	Not supported

2.8.1.10 Multimedia Services

Following are the various multimedia services:

Feature	Standard Edition	Enterprise Edition	Datacenter Edition	Web Edition
Windows Media Services	Supported	Supported	Supported	Not supported

- Applies to 64-bit versions only.
- Not supported in 64-bit versions of Windows Server 2003.
- May be limited by lack of support by OEM hardware.
- Both the 32-bit version of Datacenter Edition and the 64-bit version of Enterprise Edition support up to 64 GB RAM.
- The 64-bit versions of Datacenter Edition supports up to 512 GB RAM.

2.9 ACTIVE DIRECTORY

Active Directory was first introduced in Windows 2000 and Microsoft has made improvements to AD in Windows Server 2003. Windows 2003 enhances the management of Active Directory. There are more AD management tools now and the tools are easier than ever to use. Microsoft has made it painless to deploy Active Directory in Windows 2003.The migration tools have been greatly improved to make way for seamless migrations.

In the corporate world where mergers and acquisitions are common, things change all the time. With Windows Server 2003, you can rename your domains, a feature missing from Windows 2000. You can also change the NetBIOS name, the DNS name, or both. Another problem with changes in the business environment is the need to configure trust relationships. With Windows 2000, if two companies merge and each has a separate Active Directory, they have to either set up manual nontransitive trusts between all of their domains or collapse one forest into the other. Neither of these is an ideal choice and is prone to error. The trusts are easy enough to set up, but then you lose the benefits of being in a single forest. Collapsing forests can require a lot of work, depending on the environment.

Windows Server 2003 Active Directory now supports forest-level trusts. By setting the trusts at the forest roots, you enable cross-forest authentication and cross-forest authorization. Cross-forest authentication provides a single sign-on experience by allowing users in one forest to access machines in another forest via NTLM or Kerberos (Kerberos is the preferred method, if all systems support it). Cross-forest authorization allows assigning permissions for users in one forest to resources in another forest. Permissions can be assigned to the user ID or through groups.

Not all improvements have to do with mergers and multiple forests. In the past, it was common practice for companies with many offices spread out geographically to build their domain controllers locally and ship them to the remote offices. This was because of replication issues. When a new domain controller is created, it must pull a full copy of the Active Directory database from another domain controller. This full replication can easily oversaturate a slow network link. However, with Server 2003, you can create a new domain controller and pull the Active Directory information from your backup media. The newly created domain controller now only has to replicate the changes that have occurred since the backup was made. This usually results in much less traffic than replicating the entire database.

The Active Directory Users and Computers tool (ADUC) has been improved to include a new query feature that allows you to write filters for the type of objects you want to view. These queries can be saved and used multiple times. For example, you might want to create a query to show you all of the users with mailboxes on a specified Exchange server. By creating a query, you can easily pull up a current list with one click of the mouse. ADUC also now supports the following:

- Multi-object selection
- Drag-and-drop capabilities
- The ability to restore permissions back to the defaults
- The ability to view the effective permissions of an object

Group policy management has also been enhanced in Server 2003.The Microsoft Group Policy Management Console (GPMC) makes it easy to troubleshoot and manage group policy. It supports drag-and-drop capabilities, backing up and restoring your group policy objects (GPOs), and copying and importing GPOs. Where the GPMC really shines is in its reporting function. You now have a graphical, easy-to-use interface that, within a few clicks, will show you all of the settings configured in a GPO. You can also determine what a user's effective settings would be if he or she logged on to a certain machine. The only way you could do this in Windows 2000 was to actually log the user on to the machine and run gpresult (a command-line tool for viewing effective GPO settings).

In Windows Server 2003, the schema can now be redefined. This allows you to make changes if you incorrectly enter something into the schema. In Windôws 2000, you can deactivate schema attributes and classes, but you cannot redefine them. You still need schema admin rights to modify the schema, but now it is more forgiving of mistakes.

The way objects are added to and replicated throughout the directory has been improved as well. The Inter-Site Topology Generator (ISTG) has been improved to support a larger number of sites. Group membership replication is no longer "all or nothing" as it was in Windows 2000. In Windows Server 2003, as members are added to groups, only those members are replicated to your domain controllers and global catalog (GC) servers, rather than the entire group membership list. No more worrying about the universal group replication to your GC servers.

Every domain controller caches credentials provided by GC servers. This allows users to continue to log on if the GC server goes down. It also speeds up logons for sites that do not have a local GC server. No longer is the GC server a single point of failure. In fact, you no longer are required to have one at each site.

Active Directory now supports a new directory partition called the application partition. You can add data to this partition and choose which domain controllers will replicate it. This is useful if you have information you want to replicate to all domain controllers in a certain area, but you do not want to make the information available to all domain controllers in the domain.

2.10 CLUSTERING AND LOAD BALANCING

MICROSOFT CLUSTER SERVICE (MSCS) uses two or more physically connected servers, called nodes that communicate with each other constantly. If a node detects that another node is offline, it will take over the services provided by the offline node. However, this happens behind the scenes, and end users are unaware of the process (other than experiencing a small initial delay).

MSCS is traditionally used with mail servers, database servers, and file and print servers. MSCS is supported in Windows Server 2003 Enterprise Edition and Windows Server 2003 Datacenter Edition.

Some of the new features of Windows Server 2003 clustering include:

- The support of more nodes in a cluster. Enterprise Edition and Datacenter Edition both support eight nodes.
- Clustering now integrates with Active Directory and creates a computer account for the virtual cluster name.
- Clustered applications can now use Kerberos authentication.

2.10.1 Network Load Balancing

NLB is available in all versions of Windows Server 2003. Unlike MSCS, where only one server offers the services at a time, NLB nodes all offer services at the same time. The NLB cluster is accessed via a virtual name (a name that represents the group of servers as an entity), and whichever server is least busy answers the request (there is a little more to it, but this is good enough for now). If one server goes offline, there is no transferring of services because all servers offer the services already. When a server goes offline, it is removed from the rotation of servicing requests until it comes back online. NLB is generally used with Web servers, application servers, terminal servers, and streaming media servers. NLB Manager is a new tool in Windows Server 2003 that provides a central point for managing and configuring NLB clusters.

There are many new features for NLB in Server 2003. NLB now supports multiple network interface cards (NICs), allowing a single server to host multiple NLB clusters. You can use virtual clusters to set up different port rules for each cluster IP address, so that each IP address represents a different resource (Web page, application, and so forth).The Internet Group Management Protocol (IGMP) is now supported when NLB is configured in multicast mode. Using IGMP limits cluster traffic on the switch to the ports that have NLB server connected to them. This helps prevent switch flooding. (Switch flooding occurs when every server in an NLB cluster sees every packet addressed to the cluster.) NLB now supports IPSec traffic.

2.10.2 What is Cluster?

A cluster is a group of two or more computers functioning together to provide a common set of applications or services with a single apparent identity to clients. The computers are physically connected by hardware in the form of either a network or shared storage. The clustering software provides a common interface externally while managing the resources and load internally.

Windows Clustering provides the following benefits:

- **High availability:** When a clustered application or service fails or a computer in the cluster fails, the cluster responds by restarting the application or service on another member of the cluster or by distributing the load from the failed server to the rest of the cluster.
- **Scalability:** For cluster-aware applications, adding more machines to the cluster adds capabilities.
- **Manageability:** Administrators can move applications, services, and data from computer to computer within the cluster, allowing them to manually balance loads and to offload machines scheduled for maintenance.

2.10.3 Network Load Balancing Clusters

NLB-known as the Windows Load Balancing Service in Microsoft Windows NT 4-gives TCP/IP-based services and applications high availability and scalability by combining up to 32 servers running Windows Server 2003 in a single cluster. By combining NLB with round-robin DNS, NLB clustering can scale well beyond 32 servers. Client requests for applications and services provided by the cluster are distributed across the available servers in the cluster in a way that is transparent to the client. NLB clusters are supported in all versions of Windows Server 2003.

If a server fails or is taken offline, the cluster is automatically reconfigured and the client connections are redistributed across the remaining servers. If additional servers are added to the cluster, they are automatically recognized and the load is reconfigured and distributed.

2.10.4 Server Clusters

Server clusters distribute the workload among the servers in a cluster, with each server running its own workload. Like other types of clusters, server clusters are scalable and highly available. In the event of a failure, applications and services that can be restarted, such as print queues and file services, are restarted transparently. Ownership of shared resources passes to the remaining servers. When the failed server becomes available again, the workload is automatically rebalanced. Windows Server 2003 supports server clusters only in the Enterprise and Datacenter Editions. There are three basic types of server clusters supported by Windows Server 2003: single node clusters, single quorum device clusters, and majority node set clusters, as shown in Figure 2.14.

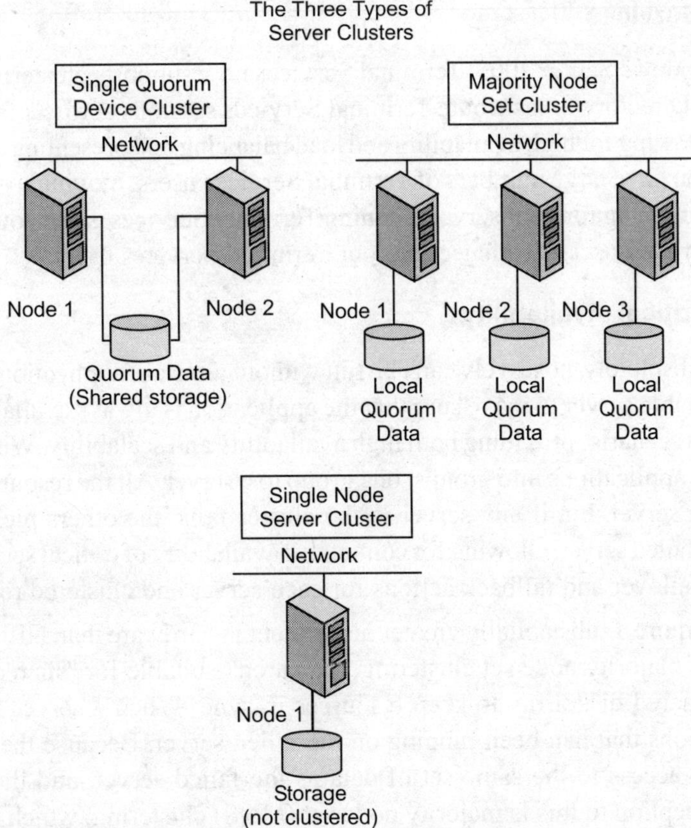

Figure 2.14 Windows Server 2003 supports three different server cluster models

2.10.5 Cluster Scenarios

In deciding whether and how to implement clustering, you first need to understand what problem is being solved and how best to solve it using the available technologies. Then you can make a business case for the particular solution or combination of solutions that best solves the particular problem. This section describes various scenarios and the type of clustering appropriate for each.

2.10.5.1 Intranet or Internet Functionality

An intranet or Internet server is a prime candidate for an NLB cluster. By enabling an NLB cluster across multiple servers, you provide your site with both redundancy and increased capacity. If a server should fail, the load is distributed transparently among the remaining servers.

Each Web server in the cluster runs its own Web server and accesses only local Web pages. This version is "shared nothing" clustering there are no shared disks and no shared applications or data, with the possible exception of a common back-end database. NLB clusters are an appropriate and relatively inexpensive way to achieve both redundancy and high availability for your Web site, whether it's internal or external. Clients that need access to the Web pages are distributed among the servers in the cluster according to the load at each server. What makes this work is that most Web pages change infrequently, allowing manual updates of all Web servers with the same information when you need to make changes.

2.10.5.2 Terminal Services

Starting with Windows Server 2003, Terminal Services now supports clustering using NLB clusters and the new Session Directory to distribute Terminal Services sessions across a farm of servers running Terminal Services, allowing for high availability and load balancing and presenting a single face to Remote Desktop clients. If you have large numbers of Terminal Services users, moving to Windows Server 2003 and enabling NLB clustering for your servers running Terminal Services gives you additional flexibility, redundancy, and improved user experience for your Terminal Services users.

2.10.5.3 Mission-critical Availability

If your business absolutely, positively can't be run without a certain application or set of applications, you need a highly reliable server to make sure that the application is always available. A server cluster is a good solution in this scenario, providing both high availability and scalability. With a server cluster, you organize your critical applications into groups, one group to a server. All the resources for each group are self-contained on the server, but if any server in the cluster fails, the others pick up the services and applications from the failed server, allowing for continuous availability of critical services and applications. You can control the failover and fallback actions for each server and clustered resource.

Server clusters require a substantially greater investment in hardware than NLB clusters. In addition, with the exception of majority node set clustering, they aren't suitable for "shared nothing" clustering, because they use a shared disk array to keep resources in sync. When a server fails, the other server picks up the applications that had been running on the failed server. Because the disks are shared, the remaining server has access to the same set of data as the failed server, and thus there is no loss of functionality. The exception to this is majority node set (MNS) clustering, which does not use a shared disk quorum resource but rather replicates data across the cluster to local quorum disks.

Majority node set clustering is appropriate for geographically diverse clusters and requires specialized support from original equipment manufacturers (OEMs) and independent software vendors (ISVs). For a TechNet support webcast on MNS clustering.

2.10.5.4 Requirements and Planning

Before you attempt to implement any form of clustering, you need to clearly understand the business reason for doing so. You also need to be aware of the costs and benefits of the implementation, as well as the resource requirements for a successful implementation. Treat the implementation of a Windows Server 2003 cluster as you would any other major project. Clearly state the business case for the cluster, and obtain a commitment from all levels before you expend substantial resources on the project.

2.10.5.5 Identifying and Addressing Goals

The first step in planning your cluster is to identify your goals for the implementation and the needs that using clusters will meet. This sounds obvious, but it is actually the part of the process that is most often overlooked. The implementation of any technology should always be first and foremost a business decision, not a technology decision. Creating and maintaining clusters is not a trivial task, and it requires both technological and financial resources. You'll have a hard time selling your project if you haven't clearly identified one or more needs that it will meet.

In identifying the needs to be met and the goals of your project, you need to be as objective as possible. Always keep in mind that what you might view as "cool" technology can look remarkably like scary, unproven gobbledygook to those in the organization who are less technically savvy than you are. This doesn't mean that those individuals won't support your project, but it does mean that you need to make the case for the project on a level that they can understand and identify with.

Start by clearly identifying the business goals that you're trying to accomplish. State the general goals, but provide enough detail to make the success of the project clearly measurable. Identify the specific gains you expect and how those gains will be measured. Be sure to clearly indicate how the needs you've identified are currently being met. This step is critical because it lets you point out both the costs of your suggested method and the risks associated with it.

2.10.5.6 Identifying a Solution

Once you know the business needs you're trying to meet, you can identify some solutions. If you've clearly laid out your goals and objectives for the project, the technology that achieves those goals will be driven by those needs, not the other way around. This is also the time to use your best political judgment. You need to identify not only the best way to meet the business needs, but also how much you can realistically sell and implement in a single shot. If you think that ultimately you will need a fully integrated, three tiered, multiple-cluster solution, you might want to build your plan around a phased approach that allows you to distribute the risks and costs over a broader period.

In addition, if you're proposing a clustering solution to the problem, spend some time and energy identifying methodologies that might be considered alternatives to clustering and clearly laying out the strengths and weaknesses of those alternatives. This effort will short-circuit objections and diversions as you build support for your project.

2.10.5.7 Identifying and Addressing Risks

As you plan your schedule, be sure to identify the risks at each step of the process and plan solid fallback positions if problems arise. Selling the project is also much easier if it's clear that you've actually thought about the risks. For example, if your goal is to replace an existing manual methodology, have you left yourself a way to fall back to it if there are problems? Or are the two mutually incompatible? If you're replacing an existing client/server application with a clustered, Web-based, distributed, n-tiered application, have you drawn a clear roadmap for how you will make the transition from one to the other? What are the risks of that transition?

Spend some time identifying failure points in your project. If you're building a server cluster to provide 24-hour, 7-day access to your Microsoft Exchange messaging, have you identified redundant network connections to the cluster? It does little good to create a highly available server if the network connection to it is questionable.

2.10.5.8 Making Checklists

Take the time to identify all the possible pieces of your cluster implementation ahead of time. Use this to build a checklist of steps that you need to take and the dependencies at each point. At each major step, identify the hardware, software, knowledge, and resources required, and create a checklist of the prerequisites for that step. Use the checklists in the Windows Help for Cluster Administrator as a starting point, but build onto them with the details for your implementation and your environment. The time you spend planning your clustering implementation will easily be saved in the actual installation and implementation, and it greatly reduces your risks of failure.

2.10.6 Network Load Balancing Clusters

NLB provides a highly available and scalable solution for TCP/IP-based network applications such as a Web server or FTP server. By combining the resources of two or more servers into a single cluster, NLB can provide for redundancy of information and resources while servicing far more clients than a single server alone could handle.

2.10.6.1 NLB Concepts

NLB is a Windows Server 2003 networking driver. It acts independently of the TCP/IP networking stack and is transparent to that stack. The NLB driver (Wlbs.sys) sits between the TCP/IP stack and the network card drivers, with the Windows Load Balancing Service (Wlbs.exe)-the necessary NLB control program-running on top, alongside the actual server application. (See Figure 2.15)

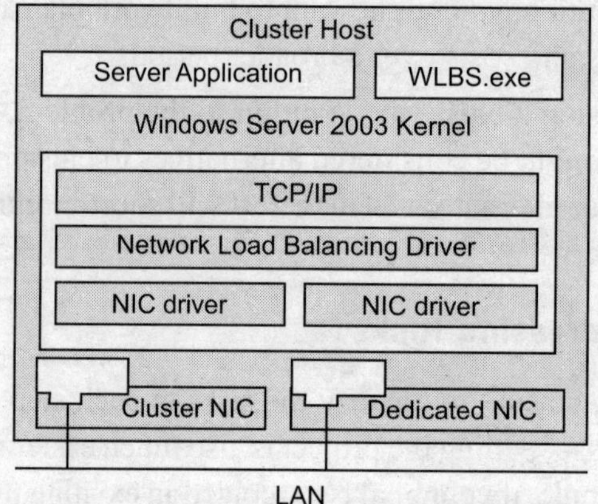

Figure 2.15 NLB as a network driver

Note: The Windows Load Balancing Service (Wlbs.exe) has been renamed in Windows Server 2003 to the Network Load Balancing Service (Nlb.exe). However, Wlbs.exe can continue to be used interchangeably with Nlbs.exe to provide full compatibility with existing scripts and applications. New scripts and applications should reference Nlb.exe to avoid future deprecation of Wlbs.exe.

Optimally, each server participating in an NLB cluster should have two network interface cards (NICs), although this is not an absolute requirement. Communications and management are materially improved with two NICs, however, especially in unicast mode. (Unicast mode, as opposed to multicast mode, allows each NIC to present only a single address to the network.) Overall network throughput is also improved, as the second network adapter is used to handle host-to-host traffic within the cluster. NLB clustering is not a place to try to cut costs on network cards. Server-grade NICs will provide full network throughput while minimizing the load on the servers.

NLB supports up to 32 computers per cluster. Each server application can be balanced across the entire cluster or can be primarily hosted by a single computer in the cluster, with another computer in the cluster providing directed failover redundancy. For fully distributed applications, the failure of any single host causes the load currently being serviced by that host to be transferred to the remaining hosts. When the failed server comes back online, the load among the other hosts is redistributed to include the restored server. While NLB clustering does not provide the failover protection appropriate for databases, it does provide for high availability and scalability of TCP/IP-based applications.

Note NLB is supported across the Windows Server 2003 family and requires that TCP/IP be installed. It works over Fiber Distributed Data Interface-based or Ethernet-based networks (including Wireless) from 10 megabits per second (Mbps) to 1 gigabit per second (Gbps). It uses from 250 KB to 4 MB of RAM and roughly 1 MB of disk space.

2.10.7 CHOOSING AN NLB CLUSTER MODEL

A host in an NLB cluster can use one of four models, each with its own merits and drawbacks.

These models are as follows:

- Single network adapter in unicast mode
- Single network adapter in multicast mode
- Multiple network adapters in unicast mode
- Multiple network adapters in multicast mode

The choice of model for a given host and cluster varies depending on the circumstances, requirements, and limitations imposed on the design of the cluster. The sections that follow provide details on each of the models.

Note: NLB in Windows Server 2003 does not support a mixed unicast mode and multicast mode environment. All hosts in the cluster must be either multicast or unicast. Some hosts, however, can have a single adapter, whereas others have multiple adapters. In addition, NetBIOS cannot be supported in a single-adapter only configuration.

2.10.7.1 Single Network Adapter in Unicast Mode

A single network adapter running in unicast mode is in some ways the easiest type of host to set up, and with only a single adapter, it is cheaper than one with multiple network adapters.

It does, however, impose significant limitations:

- Overall network performance is reduced.
- Ordinary communications among cluster hosts are disabled.
- NetBIOS support is not available within the cluster.

2.10.7.2 Single Network Adapter in Multicast Mode

Using multicast mode in clusters in which one or more hosts have a single network adapter means that normal communications are possible between hosts within the cluster. This capability overcomes one of the most awkward limitations of the single adapter in unicast mode.

However, there are still the following significant disadvantages:

- Overall network performance is reduced.
- Some routers do not support multicast media access control (MAC) addresses.
- NetBIOS support is not available within the cluster.

2.10.7.3 Multiple Network Adapters in Unicast Mode

Using multiple network adapters in unicast mode is generally the preferred configuration. It does impose the cost of a second network adapter per host, but given the relatively low cost of network adapters, including the per-port cost of hubs, this is a relatively minor price to pay for the resulting advantages:

- No limitations are imposed on ordinary network communications among cluster hosts.
- Ordinary NetBIOS support is available through the first configured adapter.
- No bottlenecks occur as a result of a single network adapter.
- The model works with all routers.

2.10.7.4 Multiple Network Adapters in Multicast Mode

If you are forced by circumstances to use some hosts within a cluster that have only a single network adapter and you must be able to maintain normal network communications among the hosts in the cluster, you must run all the hosts in multicast mode, even those with multiple adapters, because you can't run some hosts in unicast mode and some in multicast mode. This limitation could cause a problem with some routers, but otherwise it is a viable solution.

2.10.8 CREATING AN NLB CLUSTER

Creating an NLB cluster requires using the Network Load Balancing Manager, shown in Figure 2.12 This new manager simplifies the creation and management of NLB clusters, bringing all the pieces into a single management interface. You can connect to the NLB with the NLB Manager on any address in the cluster, including private addresses or the shared public address.

2.10.8.1 New NLB Cluster

To create a new NLB cluster, follow these steps:

1. Open the Network Load Balancing Manager from the Administrative Tools folder, as shown in Figure 2.16.

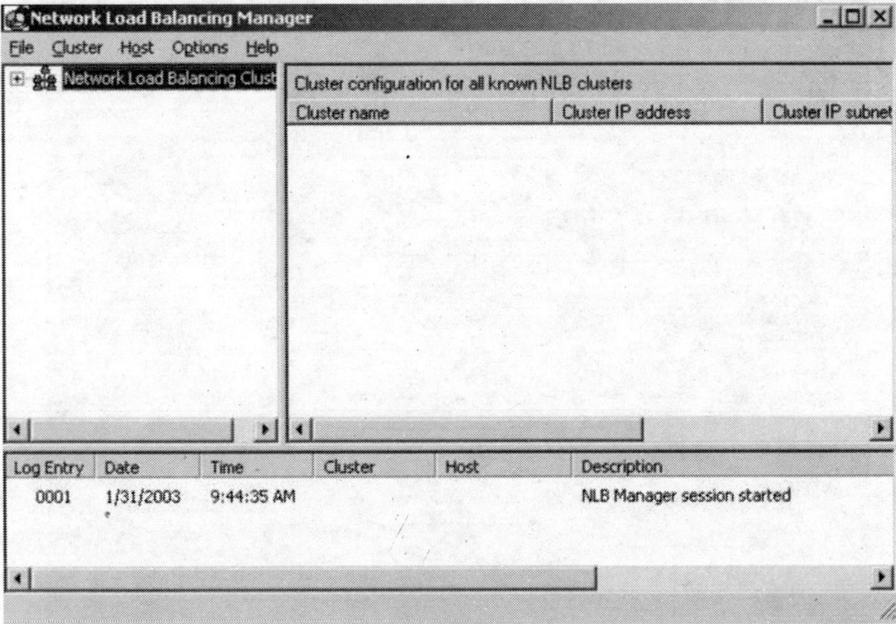

Figure 2.16 The Network Load Balancing Manager main screen

2. Right-click Network Load Balancing Clusters in the left pane and select New Cluster, as shown in Figure 2.17.

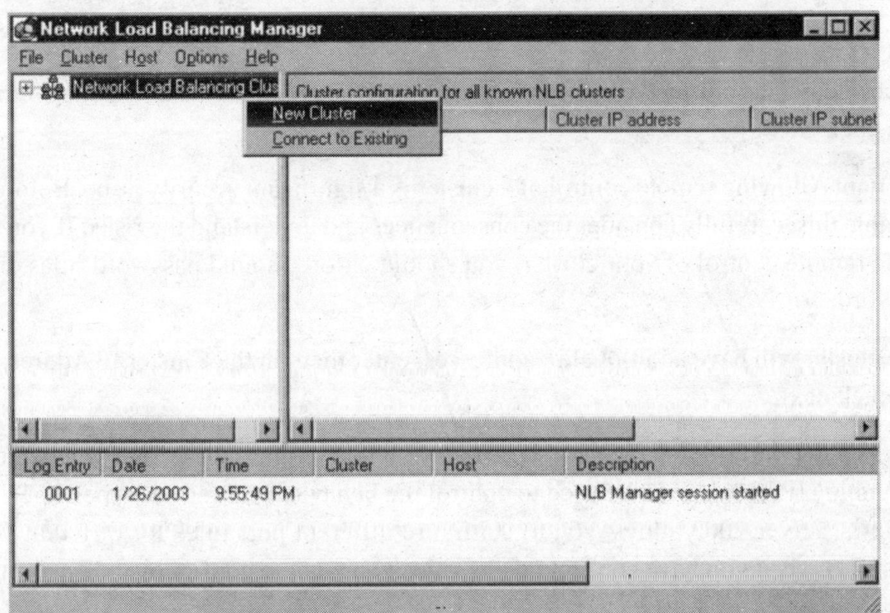

Figure 2.17 Select New Cluster to create a new NLB cluster

3. In the Cluster Parameters screen, shown in Figure 2.18, you need to enter an IP address, subnet mask, and the fully qualified domain name (FQDN) that the cluster will be known by. This IP address is a fixed IP address, so it can't be a DHCP address.

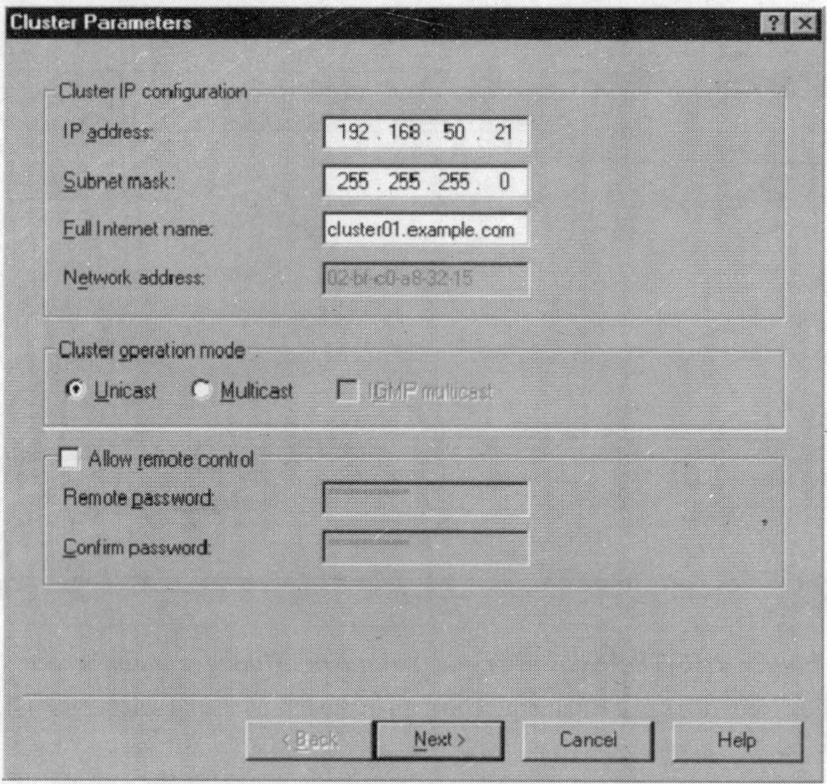

Figure 2.18 The Cluster Parameters screen

4. Select whether the cluster will be unicast or multicast and whether you will allow remote control. Then click Next.

   Important Allowing remote control of a cluster is a significant security issue. Before you decide to enable this, carefully consider the consequences and understand the risks. If you do decide to enable remote control of your cluster, you should enforce sound password rules on the remote password.

5. If the cluster will have additional IP addresses, enter them in the Cluster IP Address screen, and then click next.

6. You can enter port rules in the next screen, or wait to configure these after you get the cluster up and running. Port rules can be used to control the behaviour of various types of TCP/IP traffic. Windows Server 2003 allows you to configure different port rules for different IP addresses. Click Next when you have configured any rules you want to configure at this point.

7. Enter the name or IP address of the first host that will be joined to the cluster in the Connect screen, shown in Figure 2.19 Click Connect to connect to the server and bring up a list of network interfaces available. Highlight the interface that will host the public traffic of the cluster (as opposed to private, node-to-node traffic).

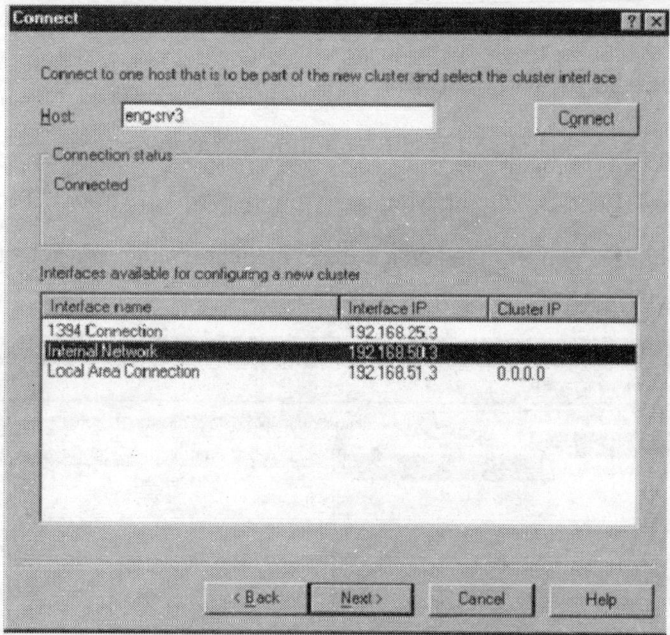

Figure 2.19 The Connect screen of the New NLB Cluster Wizard

8. Click Next to bring up the Host Parameters screen, shown in Figure 2.20. Here you set the priority for this host of the cluster and the dedicated IP address that will be used to connect to this specific server (as opposed to the cluster as a whole). This IP address must be a fixed IP address, not a DHCP address. Finally, set the initial state of this host when Windows is started.

Figure 2.20 The Host Parameters screen of the New NLB Cluster Wizard

9. Click Finish to start up the NLB service and configure the server into the new cluster.

2.10.8.2 Adding a Node to an NLB Cluster

To add another node to an existing NLB cluster, follow these steps:

1. Open the Network Load Balancing Manager from the Administrative Tools folder.
2. Right-click the cluster you want to add a node to in the left pane, and select Add Host To Cluster, as shown in Figure 2.21

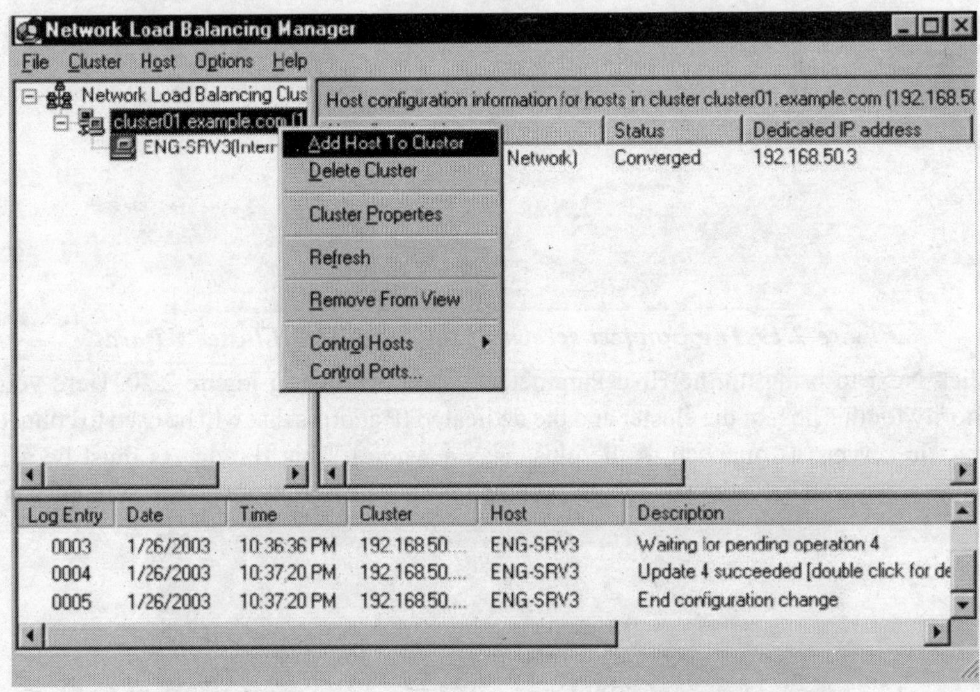

Figure 2.21 Adding a host to an existing cluster

3. Enter the name or IP address of the host that will be joined to the cluster in the Connect screen, shown previously in Figure 2.19 Click Connect to connect to the server and bring up a list of network interfaces available. Select the interface that will host the public traffic of the cluster (as opposed to private, node-to-node traffic).
4. Click Next to bring up the Host Parameters screen, shown earlier in Figure 2.20. Here you set the priority for this host of the cluster and the dedicated IP address that will be used to connect to this specific server (as opposed to the cluster as a whole). This IP address must be a fixed IP address, not a DHCP address. Finally, set the initial state of this host when Windows is started.
5. Click Finish to start up the NLB service on the new node and configure the server into the existing cluster. When the node is up and part of the cluster, it shows a status of Converged in the NLB Manager, as shown in Figure 2.22.

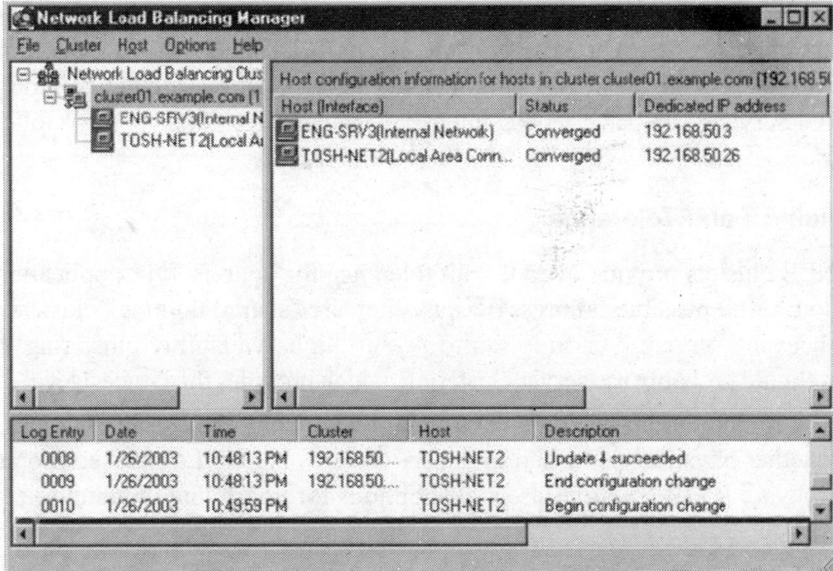

Figure 2.22 The NLB Manager shows the new node added with a status of Converged

2.10.8.3 Removing a Host From an NLB Cluster

To remove a host from an NLB cluster, follow these steps:

1. Open the Network Load Balancing Manager from the Administrative Tools folder.
2. Connect to the cluster you want to remove a node from by right-clicking Network Load Balancing Clusters in the left pane and selecting Connect to Existing.
3. Right-click the node you want to remove in the left pane, and select Delete Host.

2.10.9 Planning the Capacity of an NLB Cluster

In general, an NLB cluster should contain as many hosts as needed to handle the client load for the applications being run in the cluster. The exception to this would be cases in which the sole function of the cluster is to provide failover tolerance for a critical TCP/IP application-that is, when a single server can handle the load and the second server is there simply for fault tolerance.

The maximum number of hosts in a given cluster is 32. If your application requires more than 32 hosts, you can set up multiple clusters, using round-robin DNS to distribute the load among the clusters. The effective limitation, however, is likely to be the network saturation point. If you do run multiple clusters in a subnet, you should host each on its own network switch to minimize the network bottleneck.

Although fewer and more powerful servers might look cost-effective for a given application, you should consider how the failure of a server will affect the application and the remaining servers. If the remaining servers can't handle the resulting load, you could potentially have a cascading failure, bringing down the entire application. Always provide sufficient server capacity within the cluster to handle the expected load when a single server is down. Also consider ways to limit the load to the application when there has been a failure.

When determining the expected cluster capacity, you also need to consider the application being clustered and the type of load it imposes on the cluster. Plan your servers according to where the limitation and stress will be greatest. Web serving and FTP applications are input/output (I/O) intensive, whereas Terminal Services can be very CPU intensive, depending on the types of applications your user community uses.

2.10.9.1 Providing Fault Tolerance

Although NLB clusters provide overall fault tolerance for your TCP/IP application, they are not a complete solution for all possible failures. Because they are "shared nothing" clusters, there is always some data lag between servers. For fully fault-tolerant, high-availability clustering that can run any application, you should probably use server clustering, which provides the greatest level of fault tolerance.

One thing you can do to improve the overall fault tolerance of the cluster is to make the hard disks fault tolerant, whether physically attached to the server or as Network-Attached Storage (NAS). Both hardware and software RAID solutions are viable options for improving the fault tolerance of an NLB cluster.

2.10.9.2 Optimizing an NLB Cluster

Optimizing an NLB cluster calls for clearly understanding where the bottleneck in your clustered application is likely to be. An application such as a Web front end that is essentially a file server, for example, tends to be a heavy user of both disk I/O and network bandwidth, and such an application can be a RAM hog if you're going to do effective caching. Terminal Services, on the other hand, can put a heavy load on the CPU, and to a somewhat lesser extent, on RAM, depending on your user community. Focus your optimization efforts on the bottleneck and you'll get the most gain for your effort.

One area that can be a problem is running an NLB cluster in a switched environment without planning your network load carefully. If each of the servers in your cluster is connected to a different switched port, you can easily end up flooding your switched ports because every client request to the cluster passes through all switched ports to which a member of the cluster is attached. Running in multicast mode can exacerbate the problem. If you're running in a switched environment, you should follow these guidelines:

1. Use a top-quality hub to connect the servers in the cluster to one another, and uplink the hub to a single switched port. If you do use switches, separate each cluster onto its own VLAN.
2. Use unicast mode. If you enabled multicast mode during setup, change it. (You'll need to change this on all servers in the cluster.) It is possible to use multicast mode, but this requires enabling Internet Group Multicast Protocol (IGMP) support, introduced in Windows Server 2003. Given the other limitations multicast mode, however, unicast is preferred.
3. Edit the registry on each of the hosts in the cluster, changing the following key from the default parameter of 1 to 0:

HKEY_LOCAL_MACHINE\System\CurrentControlSet\Services\WLBS
\Parameters\MaskSourceMAC

This change allows the switch to tell which MAC address is really the source of traffic, helping it to do its switching job properly. You'll need to restart the servers after making this change.

2.10.10 Server Clusters

A server cluster is a group of independent nodes that work together as a single system. They share a common cluster database that enables recovery in the event of the failure of any node. A traditional server cluster uses a jointly connected resource, generally a disk array on a shared SCSI bus or Fibre Channel, which is available to all nodes in the cluster.

Each Windows Server 2003 Enterprise Edition node in the cluster must have access to the array, and each node in the cluster must be able to communicate at all times with the other nodes in the cluster. Windows Server 2003 supports server clusters only on machines running Enterprise Edition or Datacenter Edition. Both editions support up to eight node clusters and can be configured in three different models: single node clusters, single quorum device clusters, and majority node set clusters. Single node clusters are primarily used for creating virtual servers and for proof of concept and development of cluster-aware applications. Majority node set server clusters require specialized support from both the hardware and software vendors involved.

2.10.10.1 Server Cluster Concepts

To understand and implement server clusters, it is important to understand several new concepts and their ramifications, as well as specialized meanings for certain terms.

1. NETWORKS (INTERCONNECTS)

A cluster has two distinct types of networks: the private network that's used to maintain communications between nodes in the cluster and the public network that clients of the cluster use to connect to the services of the cluster. Each of these networks can share the same network card and physical network cabling, but it is a good practice to keep them separate. This gives you an alternate path for interconnection between the nodes of the cluster. Because the interconnect between the nodes of a cluster is a potential single point of failure, it should always be redundant. The cluster service uses all available networks, both private and public, to maintain communications between nodes.

2. NODES

A node is a member of a server cluster. It must be running Windows Server 2003, Enterprise Edition or Windows Server 2003, Datacenter Edition, and Windows Clustering. It must also be running TCP/IP, be connected to the shared cluster storage device, and have at least one network interconnect to the other nodes in the cluster.

3. GROUPS

Groups are the units of failover. Each group contains one or more resources. Should any of the resources within the group fail, all fail over together according to the failover policy defined for the group. A group can be owned by only one node at a time. All resources within the group run on the same node. If a resource within the group fails and must be moved to an alternate node, all other resources in that group must be moved as well.

When the cause of failure on the originating node is resolved, the group falls back to its original location, based on the failback policy for the group.

2.10.11 Resources

Any physical or logical entity that can be brought online or offline can be a server cluster resource. It must be able to be owned by only one node at a time and will be managed as part of the cluster. The quorum resource is a special resource that serves as the repository of the configuration data of the cluster and the recovery logs that allow recovery of the cluster in the event of a failure. The quorum resource must be able to be controlled by a single node, it must provide physical storage for the recovery logs and cluster database, and it must use the NTFS file system. The only resource type supported for a quorum resource in single quorum device clustering is the Physical Disk resource as shipped with Windows Server 2003 (which along with other resource types are described in the next section), but it is possible that other quorum resource types will be developed and certified by third parties.

2.10.11.1 Types of Resources

Windows Server 2003 Enterprise Edition includes several resource types; the sections that follow examine each of these resource types and the role they play in a server cluster. The available cluster resource types are as follows:

- Physical Disk
- Dynamic Host Configuration Protocol (DHCP)
- Windows Internet Naming Service (WINS)
- Print Spooler
- File Share
- Internet Protocol Address
- Local Quorum
- Majority Node Set
- Network Name
- Generic Application
- Generic Script
- Generic Service
- Volume Shadow Copy Service Task

1. PHYSICAL DISK

The Physical Disk resource type is the central resource type required as a minimum for all server clusters. It is used for the quorum resource that controls which node in the cluster is in control of all other resources. The Physical Disk resource type is used to manage a shared cluster storage device. It has the same drive letter on all cluster servers.

2. DHCP AND WINS

The DHCP service provides IP addresses and various other TCP/IP settings to clients, and WINS provides dynamic resolution of NetBIOS names to IP addresses. Both can be run as a resource of the cluster, providing for high availability of these critical services to network clients. For failover to work correctly, the DHCP and WINS databases must reside on the shared cluster storage.

3. PRINT SPOOLER

The Print Spooler resource type lets you cluster print services, making them fault tolerant and saving a tremendous number of help desk calls when the print server fails. It also ameliorates the problem of people simply clicking Print over and over when there's a problem, resulting in a long and repetitious print queue.

To be clustered, a printer must be connected to the server through the network. Obviously, you can't connect the printer to a local port such as a parallel or Universal Serial Bus (USB) port directly attached to one of the nodes of the cluster. The client can address the printer either by name or by IP address, just as it would a nonclustered printer on the network. In the event of a failover, all jobs that are currently spooled to the printer are restarted. Jobs that are in the process of spooling from the client are discarded.

4. FILE SHARE

You can use a server cluster to provide a high-availability file server using the File Share resource type. The File Share resource type lets you manage your shared file systems in three different ways:

- As a standard file share with only the top-level folder visible as a share name.
- As shared subfolders, where the top-level folder and each of its immediate subfolders are shared with separate names. This approach makes it extremely easy to manage users' home directories, for example.
- As a standalone Distributed file system (Dfs) root. You cannot, however, use a cluster server File Share resource as part of a fault-tolerant Dfs root.

5. INTERNET PROTOCOL ADDRESS AND NETWORK NAME

The Internet Protocol Address resource type is used to manage the IP addresses of the cluster. When an Internet Protocol Address resource is combined with a Network Name resource and one or more applications, you can create a virtual server. Virtual servers allow clients to continue to use the same name to access the cluster even after a failover has occurred. No client-side management is required because, from the client perspective, the virtual server is unchanged.

6. LOCAL QUORUM

The Local Quorum resource type is used to manage the system disk on the local node of a single node server cluster. The Local Quorum resource type cannot fail over to another node.

7. MAJORITY NODE SET

The Majority Node Set resource type is used to manage cluster configuration data that might or might not reside on a cluster storage device. It is used to ensure that the data remains consistent across nodes that may be geographically dispersed. Only a single Majority Node Set resource can exist in a server cluster.

8. GENERIC APPLICATION

The Generic Application resource type allows you to manage regular, cluster-unaware applications in the cluster.

A cluster-unaware application that is to be used in a cluster must, at a minimum:

- Be able to store its data in a configurable location
- Use TCP/IP to connect to clients
- Have clients that can reconnect in the event of an intermittent network failure

When you install a generic, cluster-unaware application, you have two choices: you can install it onto the shared cluster storage, or you can install it individually on each node of the cluster. The first method is certainly easier because you install the application only once for the whole cluster. However, if you use this method you won't be able to perform a rolling upgrade of the application, because it appears only once. (A rolling upgrade is an upgrade of the application in which the workload is moved to one server while the application on the other server is upgraded and then the roles are reversed to upgrade the first server.)

To give yourself the ability to perform rolling upgrades on the application, you need to install a copy onto each node of the cluster. You need to place it in the same folder and path on each node. This method uses more disk space than installing onto the shared cluster storage, but it permits you to perform rolling upgrades, upgrading each node of the cluster separately.

9. GENERIC SCRIPT

Similar to the Generic Application resource, the Generic Script resource type is used to manage operating system scripts as a cluster resource. The Generic Script resource type provides limited functionality.

10. GENERIC SERVICE

Finally, server clusters support one additional type of resource-the Generic Service resource. This is the most basic resource type, but it does allow you to manage your Windows Server 2003 services as a cluster resource.

11. VOLUME SHADOW COPY SERVICE TASK

The Volume Shadow Copy Service Task resource type allows you to create jobs in the Scheduled Task folder that will be run against whatever node is currently hosting a particular resource group, allowing the task to fail over with the resource. As shipped, this resource type is used only to support Shadow Copies of Shared Folders in a server cluster.

2.10.12 Defining Failover and Failback

Windows Server 2003 server clusters allow you to define the failover and failback (some-times referred to as fallback) policies for each group or virtual server. This ability enables you to tune the exact behaviour of each application or group of applications to balance the need for high availability against the overall resources available to the cluster in a failure situation. Also, when the failed node becomes available again, your failback policy determines whether the failed resource is immediately returned to the restored node, maintained at the failed-over node, or migrated back to the restored node at some predetermined point in the future. These options allow you to plan for the disruption caused when a shift in node ownership occurs, limiting the impact by timing it for off-hours.

2.10.13 Configuring a Server Cluster

When planning your server cluster, you'll need to think ahead to what your goal is for the cluster and what you can reasonably expect from it. Server clusters provide for extremely high availability and resource load balancing, but you need to make sure your hardware, applications, and policies are appropriate.

2.10.13.1 High Availability with Load Balancing

The most common cluster configuration is static load balancing. In this scenario, the cluster is configured so that some applications or resources are normally hosted on one node whereas others are normally hosted on another node. If one node fails, the applications or resources on the failed node fail over to another node, providing high availability of your resources in the event of failure and balancing the load across the cluster during normal operation. The limitation of this configuration is that in the event of a failure, your applications will all attempt to run on fewer nodes, and you need to implement procedures either to limit the load by reducing performance or availability, or to not provide some less critical services during a failure. Another possibility for managing the reduced load-carrying capacity during a failure scenario is to have "at risk" users and applications that can be shut off or "shed" during periods of reduced capacity, much like power companies do during peak load periods when capacity is exceeded.

It's important to quickly take steps to manage load during periods of failure when you configure your cluster for static load balancing. Failure to shed load can lead to catastrophic failure, or such extreme slowdown as to simulate it, and then no one will have access to the cluster's resources and applications.

2.10.13.2 Maximum Availability without Load Balancing

The cluster configuration with the highest availability and reliability for critical applications is to run one node of the cluster as a hot spare. This scenario requires that the hot spare node be sufficiently powerful to run the entire load of any other node in the cluster.

You then configure all the applications and resources to run on the other nodes, with the one node sitting idle. In the event of failure on one of the primary nodes, the applications fail over to the idle node and continue with full capability. After the primary node is back online it can continue as the new hot spare, or you can force the applications back to the primary node, depending on the needs of your environment.

This scenario provides full and complete fault tolerance in the event of the failure of one of the nodes, but it has the greatest hardware cost. It also does not provide for full and complete fault tolerance in the event of multiple node failures-that would take essentially one hot spare for each primary node. Use this clustering configuration only where your applications or resources are critical and you can afford the extra hardware expense far more than any limits to the load in case of a failure.

2.10.14 Partial Failover (Load Shedding)

Another cluster configuration is called load shedding or partial failover. In this configuration, critical applications and resources are designed to fail over to the other nodes in the cluster in the event of a failure, but noncritical applications and resources are unavailable until the cluster is back to full functionality. The critical resources and applications are thus protected in a failure situation, but noncritical ones simply run as though they were on a stand-alone server.

In this configuration, you might, depending on capacity and load conditions, have to configure the noncritical applications and resources on all nodes to be unavailable in the event of a failure on other nodes. This allows you to maintain a high level of performance and availability for your most critical applications while shedding the load from less critical applications and services when necessary. This strategy can be very effective when you must, for example, service certain critical applications or users under any and all circumstances but can allow other applications and users with a lower priority to temporarily fail.

2.10.14.1 Virtual Server only

You can create a server cluster that has only a single node, which allows you to take advantage of the virtual server concept to simplify the management and look of the resources on your network. For example, the File Share resource lets you create automatic subdirectory shares of your primary share and control their visibility, a perfect way to handle users' home directories. Having a single node doesn't give you any additional protection against failure or any additional load balancing over that provided by simply running a single standalone server, but it allows you to easily manage groups of resources as a virtual server.

This scenario is an effective way to stage an implementation. You create the initial virtual server, putting your most important resources on it in a limited fashion. Then, when you're ready, you add another node to the server cluster and define your failover and fail-back policies, giving you a high-availability environment with minimal disruption to your user community. In this scenario, you can space hardware purchases over a longer period while providing services in a controlled test environment.

2.10.14.2 Planning the Capacity of a Server Cluster

Capacity planning for a server cluster can be a complicated process. You need to thoroughly understand the applications that will be running on your cluster and make some hard decisions about exactly which applications you can live without and which ones must be maintained under all circumstances. You'll also need a clear understanding of the interdependencies of the resources and applications you'll be supporting.

The first step is to quantify your groups or virtual servers. Applications and resources that are in the same group will fail over together onto the same server. This means you'll need to plan out which applications are dependent on each other and will need to function together. Make a comprehensive list of all applications in your environment, and then determine which ones need to fail over and which ones can be allowed to simply fail but still should be run on a virtual server.

Next, determine the dependencies of the applications and the resources they need to function. This allows you to group dependent applications and resources in the same group or virtual server. Keep in mind that a resource can't span groups, so if multiple applications depend on a resource, such as a Web server, they must all reside in the same group or on the same virtual server as the Web server and thus share the same failover and failback policies.

A useful mechanism for getting a handle on your dependencies is to list all your applications and resources and draw a dependency tree for each major application or resource. This helps you visualize not only the resources that your application is directly dependent on, but also the second-hand and third-hand dependencies that might not be obvious at first glance. For example, a cluster that is used as a high-availability file server uses the File Share resource. And it makes perfect sense that this File Share resource is dependent on the Physical Disk resource. It's also dependent on the Network Name resource. However, the Network Name resource is dependent on the IP Address resource. Thus, although the File Share resource isn't directly dependent on the IP Address resource, when you draw the dependency tree you will see that they all need to reside in the same group or on the same virtual server. Figure 2.23 illustrates this dependency tree.

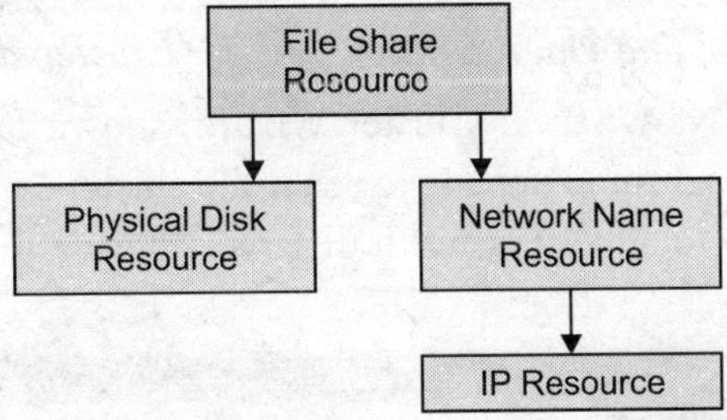

Figure 2.23 The dependency tree for a File Share resource

Finally, as you're determining your cluster capacity, you need to plan for the effect of a failover. Each server must have sufficient capacity to handle the additional load imposed on it when a node fails and it is required to run the applications or resources owned by the failed node.

The disk capacity for the shared cluster storage must be sufficient to handle all the applications that will be running in the cluster and to provide the storage that the cluster itself requires for the quorum resource. Be sure to provide enough RAM and CPU capacity on each node of the cluster so that the failure of one node won't overload the other node to the point that it too fails. This possibility can also be managed to some extent by determining your real service requirements for different applications and user communities and reducing the performance or capacity of those that are less essential during a failure.

However, such planned load shedding might not be sufficient and frequently takes a significant amount of time to accomplish, so give yourself some margin to handle that initial surge during failover.

2.10.15 Creating a Server Cluster

Once you've thoroughly researched and planned your implementation of server clusters, you're ready to actually create the cluster. The mechanism to create and manage server clusters is the Cluster Administrator application, part of the Administrative Tools folder.

2.10.15.1 New Server Cluster

To create a new server cluster, follow these steps:

1. Open the Cluster Administrator from the Administrative Tools folder. Select Create New Cluster from the drop-down list in the Open Connection To Cluster dialog box, as shown in Figure 2.24.

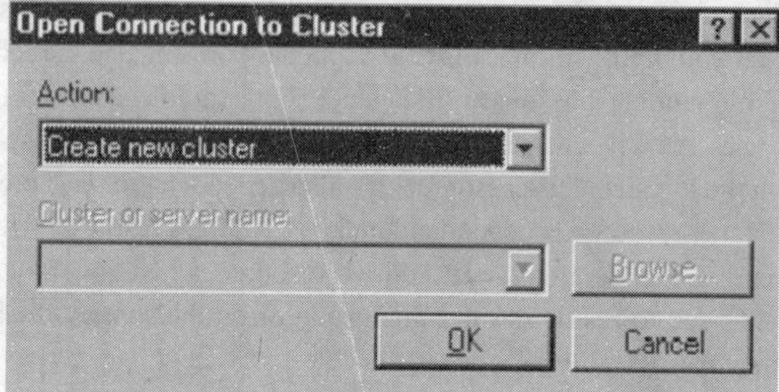

Figure 2.24 The Open Connection To Cluster dialog box

2. Click OK to launch the New Server Cluster Wizard, shown in Figure 2.25. The New Server Cluster Wizard walks you through testing to see if the cluster can be successfully created. It also gives you an opportunity to correct issues it discovers during the test, and then actually creates the cluster.

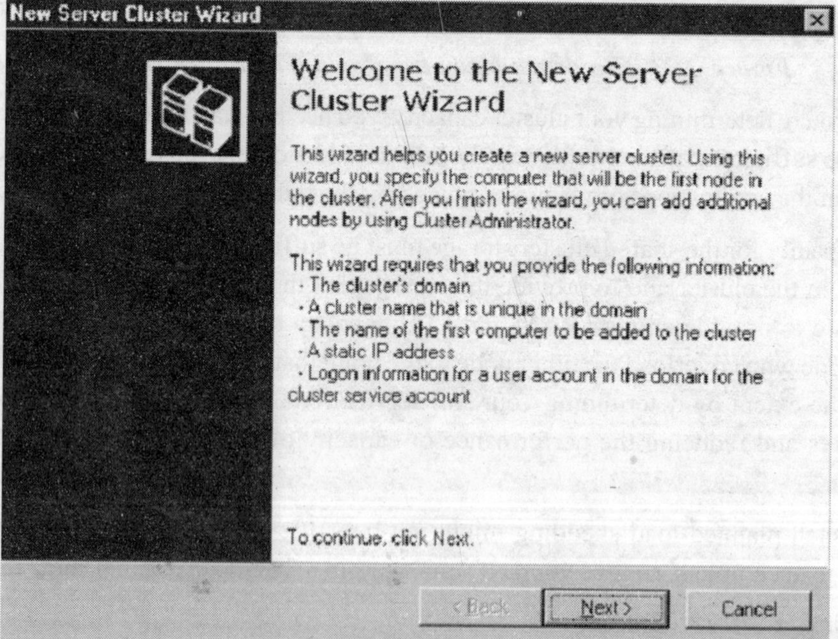

Figure 2.25 The New Server Cluster Wizard

3. Click Next to bring up the Cluster Name And Domain page, as shown in Figure 2.26. The domain is generally already filled in with the current domain. Fill in the name for the cluster. You can make this a name that means something to you, as opposed to your user community, because you'll likely be creating virtual servers for it.

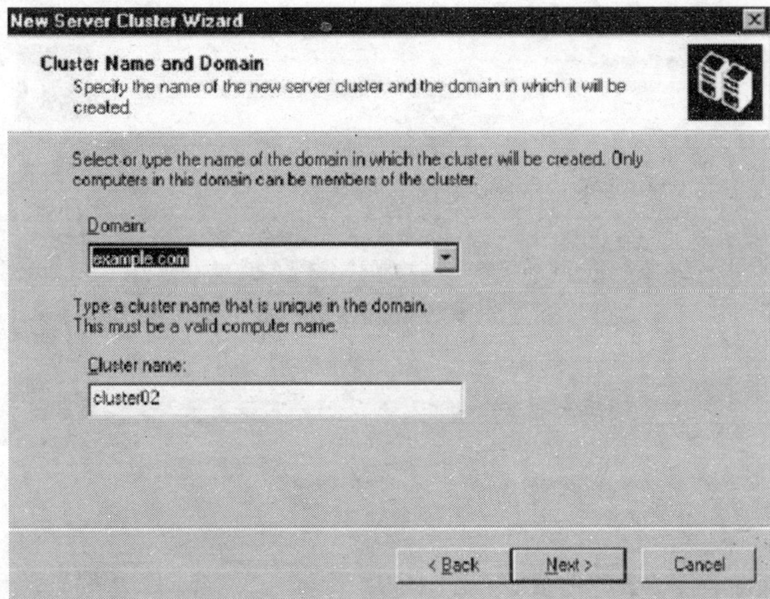

Figure 2.26 The Cluster Name And Domain page of the New Server Cluster Wizard

4. Click Next to bring up the Select Computer page, shown in Figure 2.27. Enter the name of the computer that will be the first computer in the new cluster in the Computer Name field.

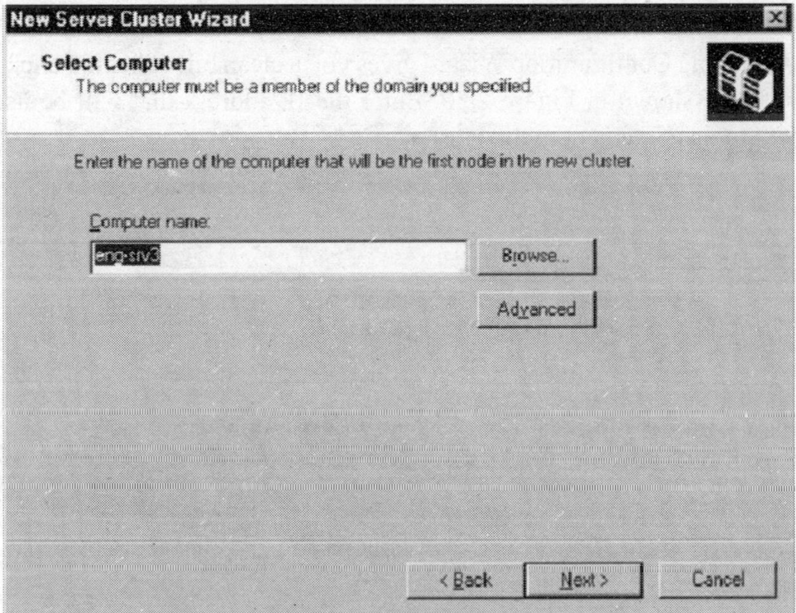

Figure 2.27 The Select Computer page of the New Server Cluster Wizard

5. Click Next to bring up the Analyzing Configuration page. The wizard automatically analyzes the configuration and highlights any problems, as shown in Figure 2.28. If the bar is green, the problems it found are nonfatal and you could go ahead and create the cluster. However, you should attempt to correct any problems before proceeding.

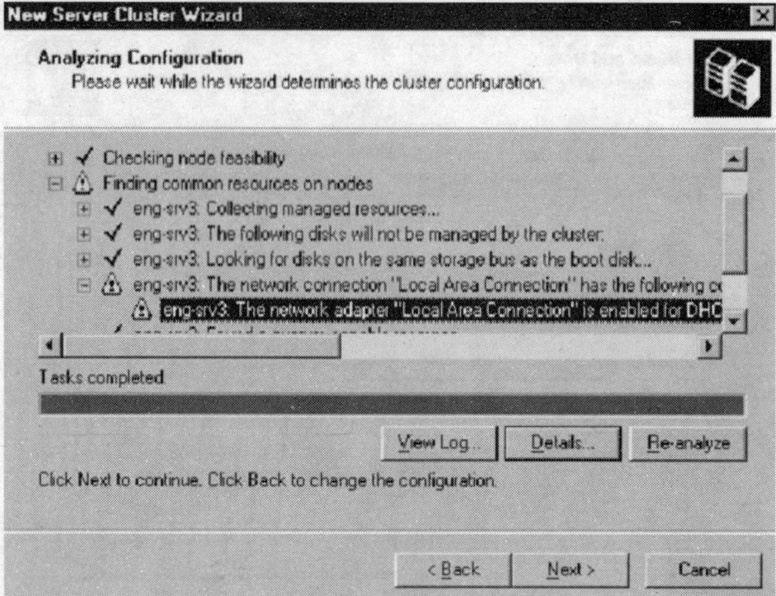

Figure 2.28 The Analyzing Configuration page of the New Server Cluster Wizard

6. To view details on the problems found, click View Log. A typical problem is shown in Figure 2.29. You can correct the problem (in this case, one of the network adapters was configured for DHCP, a non-recommended configuration) and then click Re-analyze to run the analysis again.
7. Once the Analyzing Configuration Wizard gives you a clean bill of health, click Next to open the IP Address page, shown in Figure 2.30. Enter the IP address that will be used by clustering management tools to connect to the cluster.

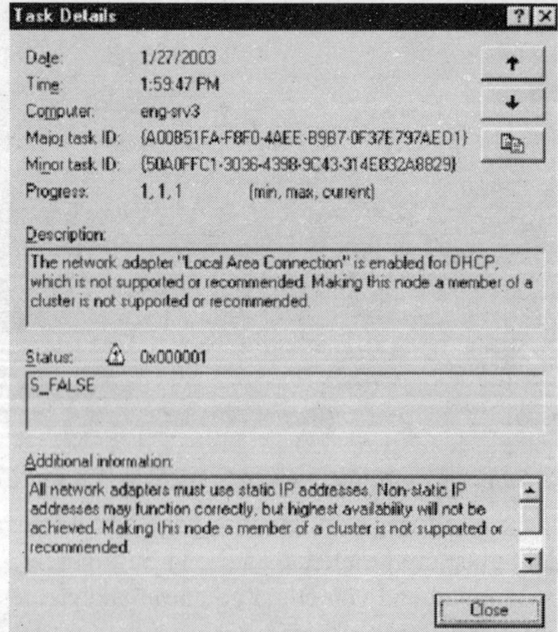

Figure 2.29 The Task Details page, showing that one adapter is configured for DHCP

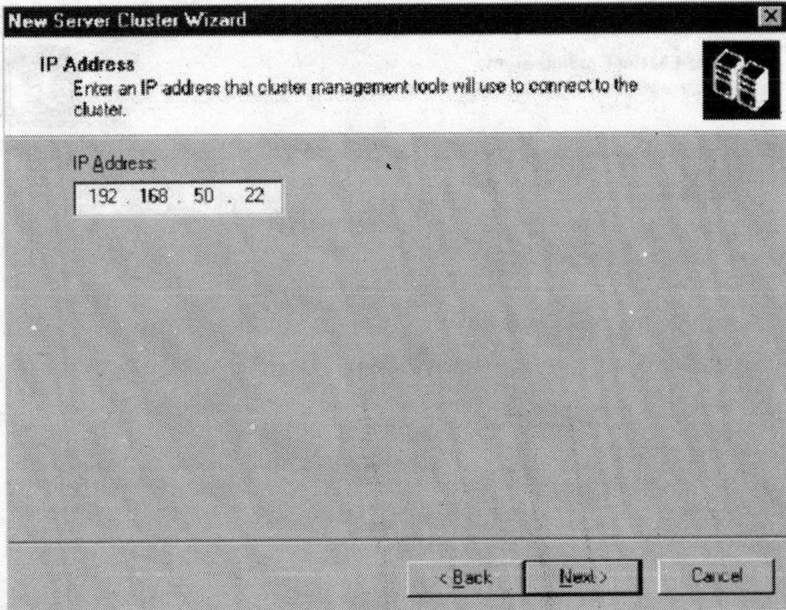

Figure 2.30 The IP Address page of the New Server Cluster Wizard

8. Click Next to bring up the Cluster Service Account page shown in Figure 2.31. This can be an existing account or a new account. The account will be given local administrative privileges on all nodes of the cluster. Click Next.

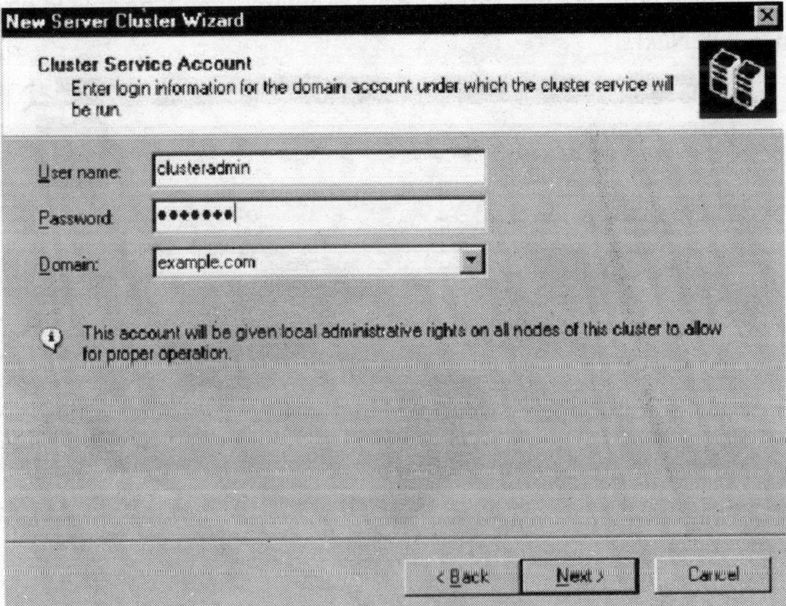

Figure 2.31 The Cluster Service Account page of the New Server Cluster Wizard

9. The final confirmation page is shown in Figure 2.32. Spend a moment here to verify that this is really what you want to do and that everything agrees with your checklist. You can go back and fix anything before continuing, if necessary, so take the time now.

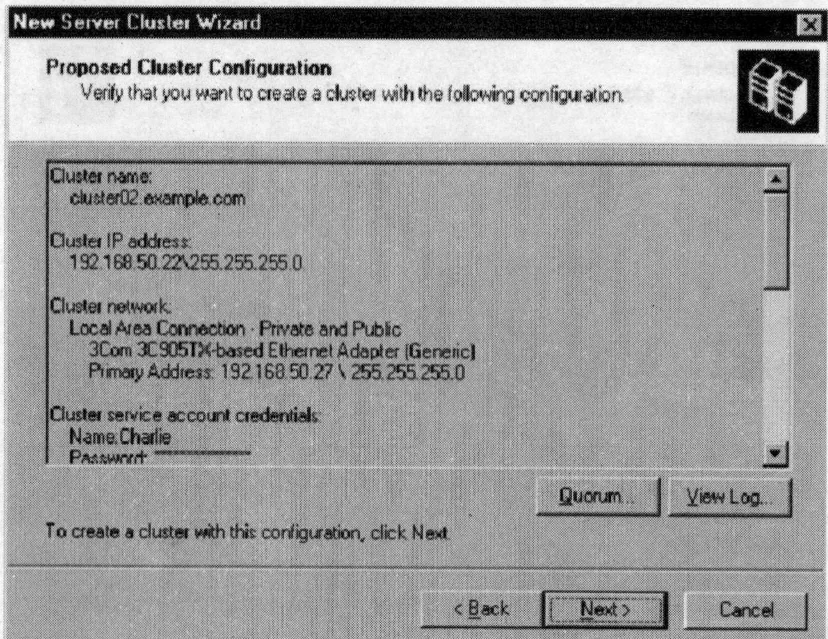

Figure 2.32 The Proposed Cluster Configuration page of the New Server Cluster Wizard

10. When you're ready, click Next to start creating the cluster. When the process is complete, you'll see a status page as shown in Figure 2.33. Click View Log to see a log of the process, or click Details to see more detailed steps than those shown. If there were problems, you'll be able to go back and correct them and try again. Click Next.

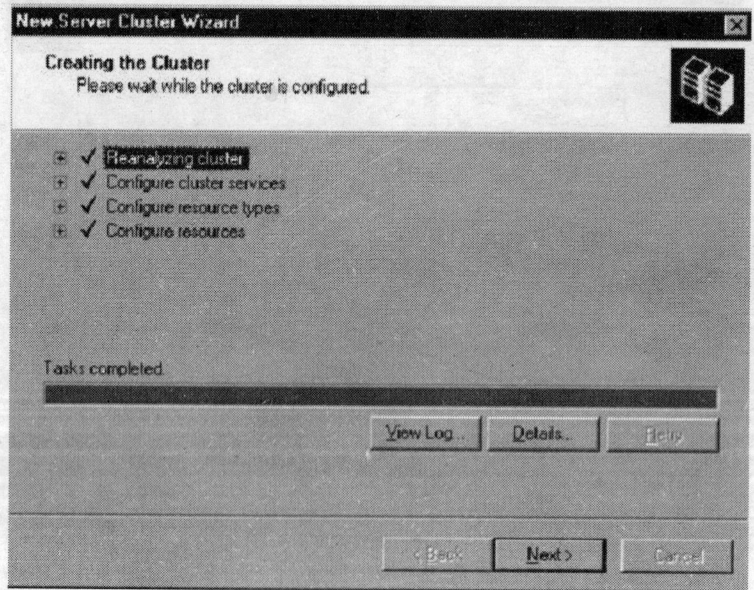

Figure 2.33 The Creating The Cluster page of the New Server Cluster Wizard

11. This brings you to the final page of the New Server Cluster Wizard. You can view the log from here by clicking View Log or change from Local Quorum to Majority Node Set by clicking the

Quorum button. Click Finish and the New Server Cluster Wizard exits, leaving you in the Cluster Administrator application, as shown in Figure 2.34.

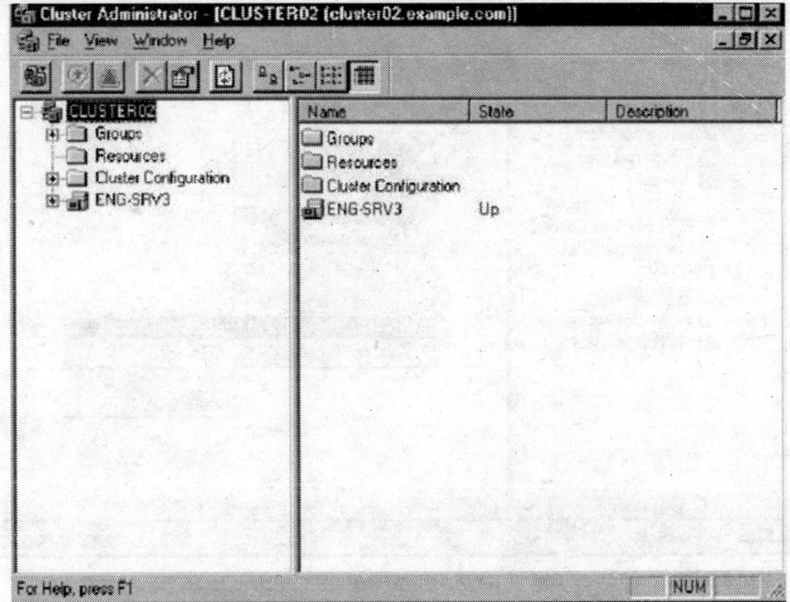

Figure 2.34 The Cluster Administrator application

2.10.15.2 Creating a Clustered Resource

Once you have your cluster created, you can take advantage of the management capabilities of Cluster Administrator to create cluster resources. We'll walk through the steps to create a File Share cluster resource in a new group on a virtual server called HOME. Although we could put these resources in the main Cluster group, we prefer to group items into more logical units, especially because failover policies are controlled at the group level. Therefore, to create our File Share resource, we'll need to do the following:

- Create a group to hold the necessary resources
- Create a Physical Disk resource
- Create an IP Address resource
- Create a Network Name resource
- Create the File Share resource

2.10.15.3 New Cluster Group

To create a new cluster group, follow these steps:

1. Open the Cluster Administrator from the Administrative Tools folder, and connect to the cluster where you will be creating the resource.
2. Right-click the Active Groups folder of the server that will host the File Share resource, and select Group from the New menu, as shown in Figure 2.35.

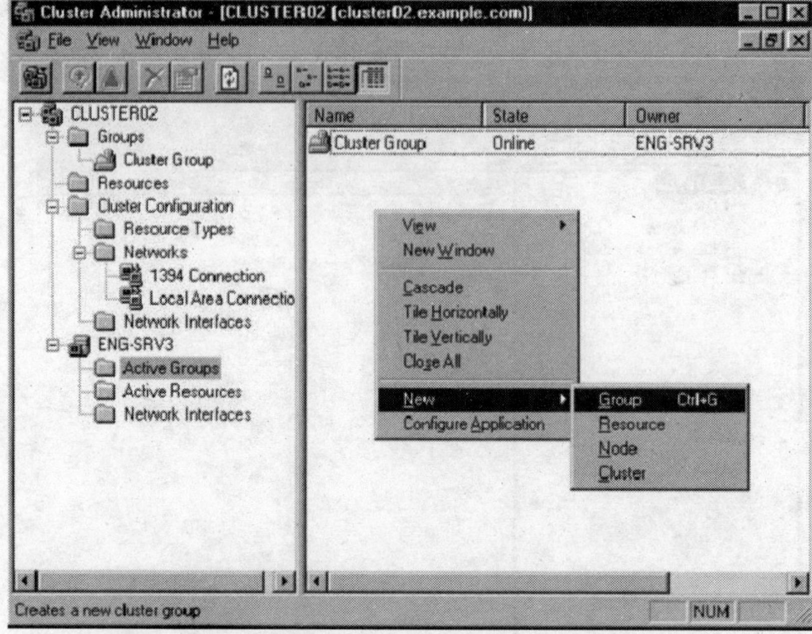

Figure 2.35 The shortcut menu to create a new group

3. This opens the New Group Wizard shown in Figure 2.36. Give your new cluster group an appropriate name and description.

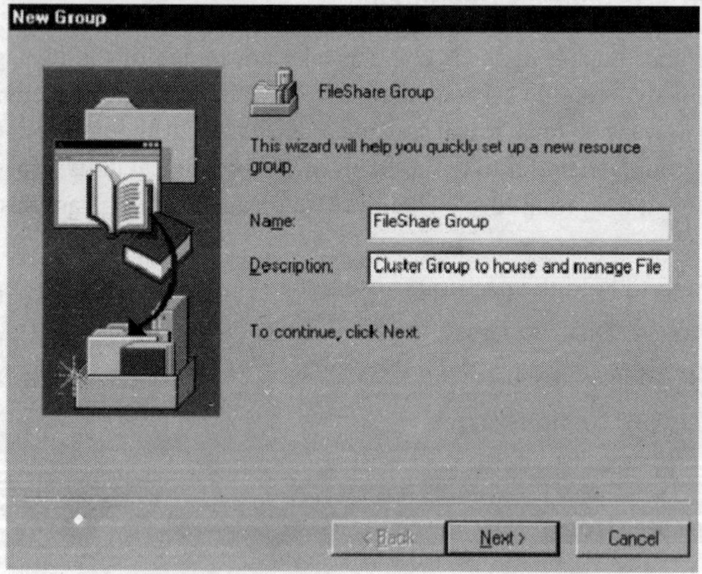

Figure 2.36 The New Group Wizard

4. Click Next to bring up the Preferred Owners dialog box shown in Figure 2.37. This allows you to control which nodes are the preferred owners of this share, and the order of preference. Select the nodes to be used for this group, and click Add to move them to the right pane. Use the Move Up and Move Down buttons to arrange their order of precedence.

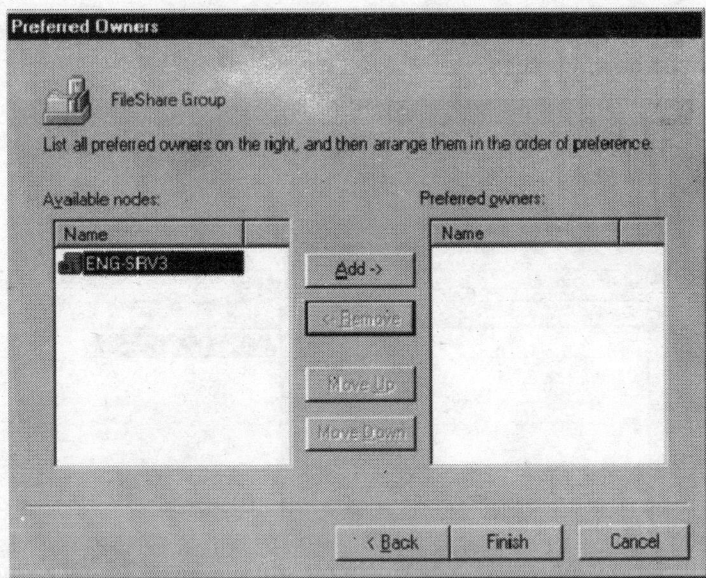

Figure 2.37 The Preferred Owners dialog box of the New Group Wizard

5. Click Finish to create the group. The group is created and is initially offline, because it has no active resources associated with it.

2.10.15.4 New Physical Disk Resource

To create a new Physical Disk resource, continue with the following steps:

1. Right-click the group just created and select Resource from the New menu to open the New Resource Wizard, shown in Figure 2.38.

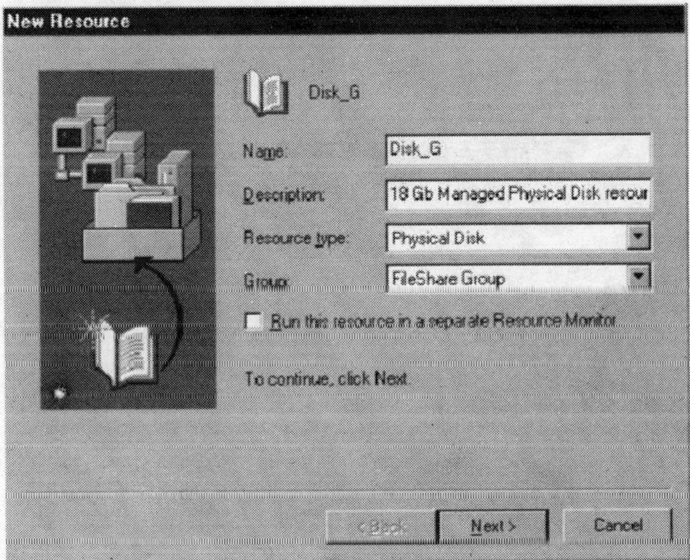

Figure 2.38 The New Resource Wizard

2. Fill in the Name and Description fields, and select Physical Disk from the Resource Type drop-down list. The Group should be the one you just created.

3. Click Next to open the Possible Owners page, as shown in Figure 2.39. Specify which machines in the cluster can host this resource.

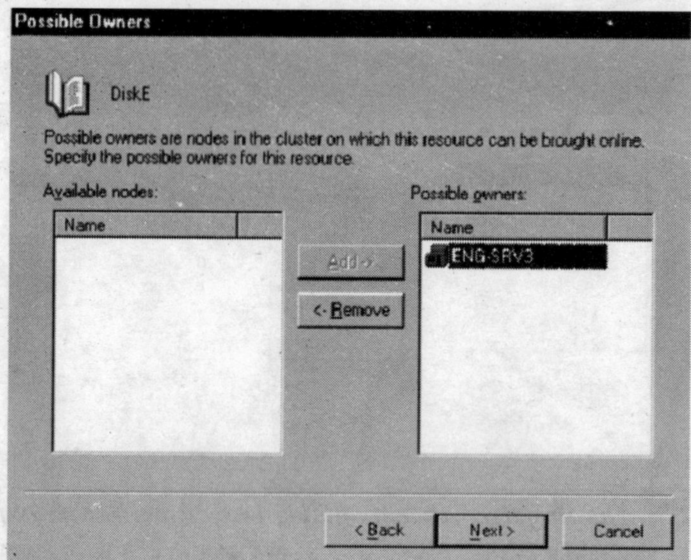

Figure 2.39 The Possible Owners page of the New Resource Wizard

4. Click Next to open the Dependencies page. This will be blank because this is the first resource in this group.
5. Click Next to open the Disk Parameters page, shown in Figure 2.40. The Disk drop-down list will include all Physical Disk resources that can be managed by the cluster service.

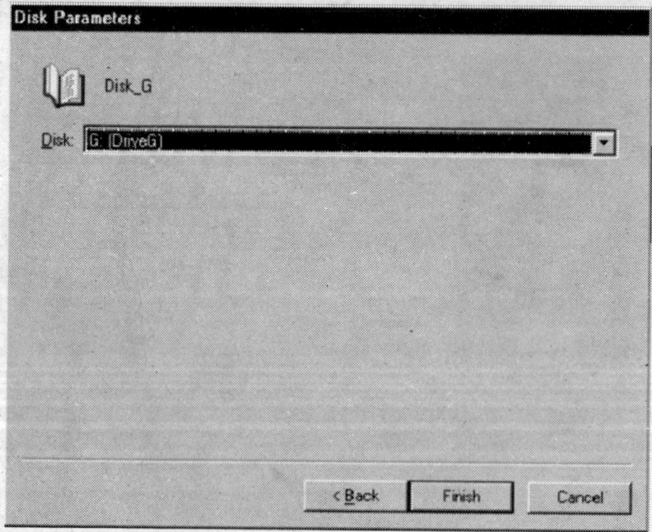

Figure 2.40 The Disk Parameters page of the New Resource Wizard

Note: The cluster service can manage only basic disks, not dynamic disks, and all partitions on the disk must be formatted with NTFS. Windows Server 2003 server clusters do support volume mount points.

6. Select the disk that will be the Physical Disk resource, and click Finish to create the resource.

2.10.15.5 New IP Address Resource

To add a new IP address resource, continue with the following steps:

1. Right-click the group just created and select Resource from the New menu to open the New Resource Wizard, shown earlier in Figure 2.40.
2. Fill in the Name and Description fields, and select File Share from the Resource Type drop-down list. The Group should be the one you just created.
3. Click Next to open the Possible Owners page, shown earlier in Figure 2.39. Specify which machines in the cluster can host this resource.
4. Click Next to open the Dependencies page. This will have the Physical Disk resource we just created, but referring to our dependency tree in the following box below, we see that there is no dependency for the IP Address resource type.

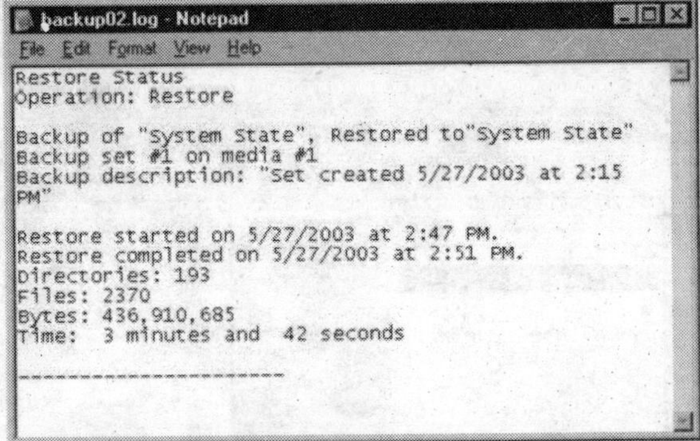

backup02.log - Notepad

File Edit Format View Help

```
Restore Status
Operation: Restore

Backup of "System State", Restored to"System State"
Backup set #1 on media #1
Backup description: "Set created 5/27/2003 at 2:15
PM"

Restore started on 5/27/2003 at 2:47 PM.
Restore completed on 5/27/2003 at 2:51 PM.
Directories: 193
Files: 2370
Bytes: 436,910,685
Time:  3 minutes and  42 seconds

----------------------
```

5. Click Next to open the TCP/IP Address Parameters page, shown in Figure 2.41. Fill in the IP address and parameters that will be used for this share.

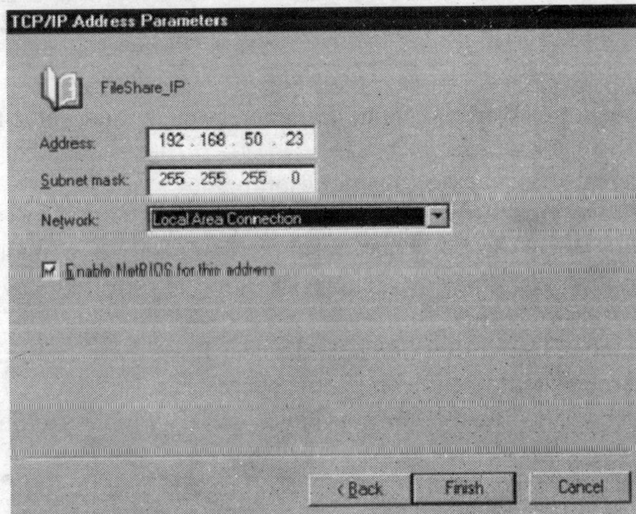

Figure 2.41 The TCP/IP Address Parameters page of the New Resource Wizard

6. Click Finish to create the IP Address resource.

2.10.15.6 New Network Name Resource

To add a new network name resource, continue with the following steps:

1. Right-click the group just created and select Resource from the New menu to open the New Resource Wizard shown earlier in Figure 19-25.
2. Fill in the Name and Description fields, and select Network Name from the Resource Type drop-down list. The Group should be the one you just created.
3. Click Next to open the Possible Owners page, shown earlier in Figure 19-26. Specify which machines in the cluster can host this resource.
4. Click Next to open the Dependencies page, shown in Figure 2.42. We'll now see both the Physical Disk and IP Address resources on the list of available resources. By looking at the dependency tree, we see that the Network Name resource has a dependency on the IP Address resource, so select the IP Address resource in the left plane and click Add to move it to the right dependencies pane.

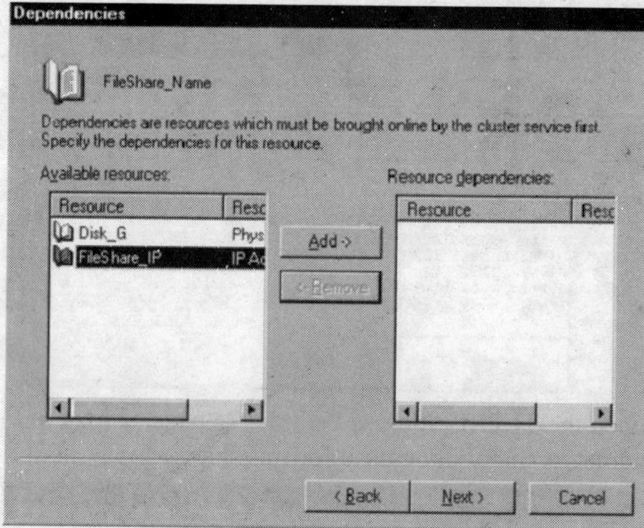

Figure 2.42 The Dependencies page

5. Click Next to open the Network Name Parameters page, and enter the name for the virtual server.
6. Click Finish to create the Network Name resource.

2.10.15.7 New File Share Resource

Finally, we're ready to create the File Share resource, because we've made all the dependencies.

1. Right-click the group just created and select Resource from the New menu to open the New Resource Wizard shown earlier.
2. Fill in the Name and Description fields, and select IP Address from the Resource Type drop-down list. The Group should be the one you just created.
3. Click Next to open up the Possible Owners page. Specify which machines in the cluster can host this resource.
4. Click Next to open the Dependencies page. We'll now see all three of the resources we've just created. We know that all of them are required for the File Share resource to work, so we'll move them all to the rightmost dependency pane.
5. Click Next to open the File Share Parameters page shown in Figure 2.43.

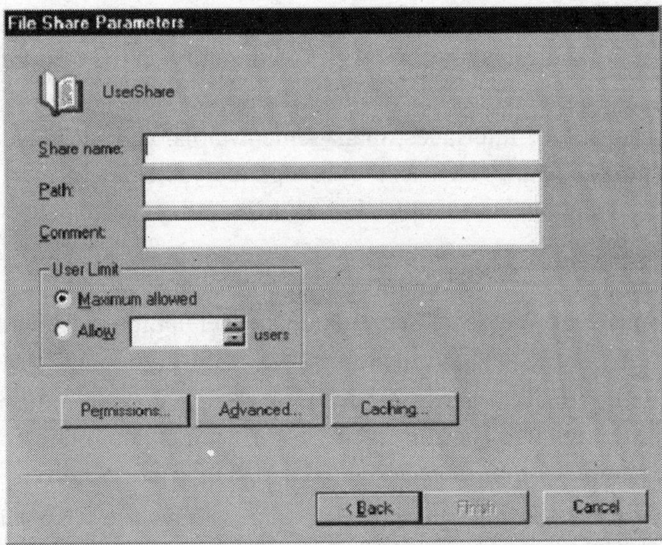

Figure 2.43 The File Share Parameters page

6. Fill in the Share Name and Path fields, and add a description in the Comment text box. If you click Finish now, you'll end up with a simple File Share.
7. Click Advanced to open the Advanced File Share Properties dialog box shown in Figure 2.44. Select Share Subdirectories and Hide Subdirectory Shares, and click OK.

Figure 2.44 Advanced File Share Properties dialog box

8. Click Finish to create the File Share resource, and click OK to acknowledge the success.
9. Finally, right-click the group you created and select Bring Online to make the resource actually online and available.

Note: The File Share resource will, by default, set the file system permissions to Read Only. Click Permissions in the File Share Parameters screen to change that as required.

2.10.16 Compute Clusters

As this edition of the book is being written, Microsoft is beta testing a new kind of Windows Server clustering-High Performance Computing (HPC) clusters, also called compute clusters. Unlike NLB or server clusters, compute clusters are not designed to provide high availability for critical applications, but rather to distribute highly parallel and complex computing tasks across multiple nodes. Windows Compute Cluster Server 2003 (CCS) enables super-computer functionality on the desktop.

CCS is a combination of a special version of Windows Server 2003 x64 Edition; the Compute Cluster Edition (CCE); and a package of interfaces, management tools, and utilities known as the Compute Cluster Pack. The Compute Cluster Pack is available separately and can be installed on any x64 Edition of Windows Server 2003, including R2 versions. CCE is at the SP1 level and does not support installation of R2.

Note Windows Compute Cluster Server 2003 is supported only on x64 Editions of Windows Server 2003. It is not available on 32-bit Windows Server 2003, nor on Itanium 64-bit editions.

CCS supports configurations that have one, two, or three NICs per node. The preferred configuration is a head node with a public (internal network LAN) interface, a private intra-cluster communications interface, and a high-speed Message Passing Interface (MPI). Each compute node in the cluster would have at least a private communications interface and the MPI interface. Figure 2.45 shows this topology.

CCS includes Remote Installation Services (RIS) that allows the easy setup and deployment of compute nodes on demand. Once the head node is created and configured, individual compute nodes are simply connected to the network and powered up. RIS then deploys Windows Server 2003 Compute Cluster Edition to the new node and configures it to be part of the compute cluster.

CCS includes the Microsoft Message Passing Interface (MS MPI), a highly compatible implementation of the Argonne National Labs MPICH2 specification. Because the MS MPI implementation is completely compatible with MPICH2 at the API level, existing HPC applications that use MPICH2 will easily migrate to CCS.

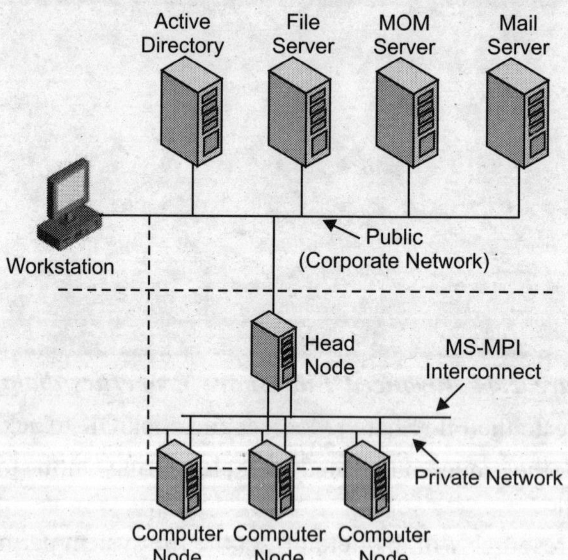

Figure 2.45 Windows Compute Cluster Server 2003 Topology

2.11 STORAGE MANAGEMENT

Generally speaking, systems have several levels of storage, including primary storage, secondary storage and cache storage. Instructions and data must be placed in primary storage or cache to be referenced by a running program. Because main memory is too small to accommodate all data and programs, and its data are lost when power is lost, the computer system must provide secondary storage to back up main memory. Secondary storage consists of tapes, disks, and other media designed to hold information that will eventually be accessed in primary storage (primary, secondary, cache) is ordinarily divided into bytes or words consisting of a fixed number of bytes. Each location in storage has an address; the set of all addresses available to a program is called an address space. The three major activities of an operating system in regard to secondary storage management are:

1. Managing the free space available on the secondary-storage device.
2. Allocation of storage space when new files have to be written.
3. Scheduling the requests for memory access.

Share and Storage Management provides a centralized location for you to manage two important server resources:

- Folders and volumes that are shared on the network
- Volumes in disks and storage subsystems

2.11.1 Shared Resources Management

You can share the content of folders and volumes on your server over the network using the Provision a Shared Folder Wizard, which is available in Share and Storage Management. This wizard guides you through the necessary steps to share a folder or volume and assign all applicable properties to it. With the wizard, you can:

- Specify the folder or volume that you want to share or create a new folder to share.
- Specify the network sharing protocol used to access the shared resource.
- Change the local NTFS permissions for the folder or volume you will be sharing.
- Specify the share access permissions, user limits, and offline access to files in the shared resource.
- Publish the shared resource to a Distributed File System (DFS) namespace.
- If Services for Network File System (NFS) has been installed, specify NFS-based access permissions for the shared resource.
- If File Server Resource Manager is installed on your server, apply storage quotas to the new shared resource, and create file screens to limit the type of files that can be stored in it.

Using Share and Storage Management, you can also monitor and modify important aspects of your new and existing shared resources. You can:

- Stop the sharing of a folder or volume.
- Change the local NTFS permissions for a folder or volume.

- Change the share access permissions, offline availability, and other properties of a shared resource.
- See which users are currently accessing a folder or a file and disconnect a user if necessary.
- If Services for Network File System (NFS) has been installed, change the NFS-based access permissions for a shared resource.

2.11.2 Share and Storage Management

With Share and Storage Management, you can provision storage on disks that are available on your server, or on storage subsystems that support Virtual Disk Service (VDS). The Provision Storage Wizard guides you through the process of creating a volume on an existing disk, or on a storage subsystem attached to your server. If the volume is going to be created on a storage subsystem, the wizard will also guide you through the process of creating a logical unit number (LUN) to host that volume. You also have the option of only creating the LUN, and using Disk Management to create the volume later.

Share and Storage Management also helps you monitor and manage the volumes that you have created, as well as any other volumes that are available on your server. Using Share and Storage Management you can:

- Extend the size of a volume.
- Format a volume.
- Delete a volume.
- Change volume properties like compression, security, offline availability and indexing.
- Access disk tools for error checking, defragmentation, and backup.

Data storage and management innovations in Microsoft® Windows® 2003 include Removable Storage and Remote Storage. The overall storage architecture changes provided with Windows 2003 allow users more manageable storage flexibility. They also allow users to take advantage of current storage concepts, including bulk media changers and libraries, data-vaulting managers, and fault-tolerant storage subsystems that are being introduced by a variety of vendors.

Significant changes have been made to the storage feature set in Windows 2003. These factors support growing storage requirements in large environments, scalability requirements of mission-critical applications, and support for innovation in the storage market. To address these needs, Windows 2000 features an improved NTFS file system and an extensive list of new storage features and applications.

2.11.3 Disk Management

Disk Management in Windows 2003 is responsible for creating, deleting, altering, and maintaining storage volumes in a system. Windows 2003 features significant improved manageability and recoverability of volumes in a Windows 2003 environment. This is achieved by the introduction of dynamic disks and a new snap-in. Windows 2003 supports two volume managers: basic disks and legacy Ftdisk volume sets are managed by FTDisk and the Ftdisk.sys driver; dynamic disks and all new volume sets are managed by Logical Disk Manager (LDM) and the Dmio.sys driver. Figure 2.46 shows the Disk Management architecture.

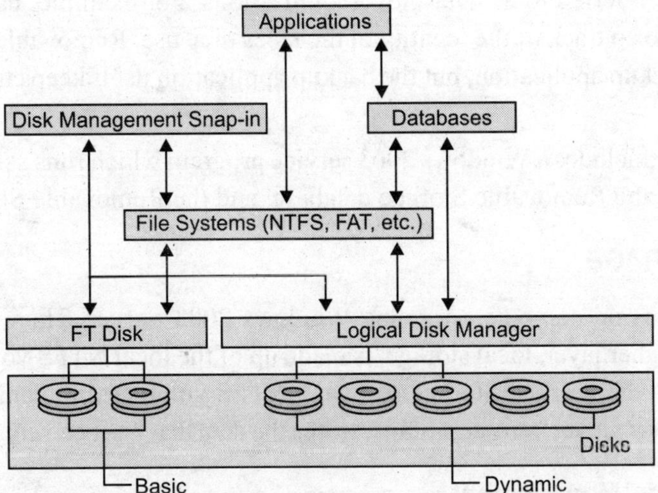

Figure 2.46 Disk Management Architecture

2.11.3.1 Fault-tolerant Disk Management

Ftdisk was used in Windows NT to manage partitions and all fault-tolerant volumes. In Windows 2003, FTDisk is used to manage basic partitions and fault-tolerant volumes from Windows NT 4.0. Ftdisk manages basic disks Basic disks can be partitioned with and recognized by Microsoft® MS-DOS®, Windows 95, Windows 98, and Windows NT. A basic partition does not provide fault tolerance or multiple disk volume functionality. Basic partition configuration is recorded in a few kilobytes of data at the beginning of the disk. Existing fault-tolerant volumes (Ftdisk sets) configured on Windows NT 4.0 can still be used on computers running Windows 2000 or converted to dynamic volumes.

2.11.4 DYNAMIC DISKS

As shown in Figure 2.46, Logical Disk Manager manages dynamic disks which can only be used on Windows 2003. Dynamic disk configuration uses a private database at the end of the disk in addition to the same kilobytes at the beginning of the disk that is used by basic disks. Any disk containing a volume managed by Disk Management contains this database. The database is replicated among all dynamic disks in the system. Dynamic disks can contain simple volumes, concatenated volumes, stripe volumes, mirrored volumes, and redundant array of independent disks (RAID) level 5 volumes. Dynamic volumes offer features, such as volume extension and fault tolerance configurations. Disk Management user interfaces, such as the Disk Management snap-in included with Windows 2003; interact with both Ftdisk and Disk Management functionality.

2.11.4 REMOVABLE STORAGE

Windows 2003 Removable Storage provides services to applications and system administrators that facilitate the use, sharing, and management of the removable media devices attached to a computer running Microsoft® Windows® 2003 Professional or Windows 2003 Server. Using Removable Storage services allows applications to share local robotic media libraries and tape and disk drives. Removable Storage is not in the media data path, so managing media content is left to Removable Storage client applications, which are referred to as data-mover applications. For example, backup applications use Removable Storage to keep track of the identity of the tapes they use. Removable Storage mounts tapes when needed by the backup application, but the backup application itself keeps track of the backup sets stored on that media.

Removable Storage includes a Windows 2003 service program which runs as part of the service host program (Svchost.exe), the Removable Storage database, and the Removable Storage snap-in.

2.11.5 REMOTE STORAGE

Remote Storage runs on computers running Windows 2003 Server. There are two layers to the storage hierarchy the higher layer, local storage, is made up of the local NTFS volumes of the Windows 2003 file server hosting the Remote Storage software. NTFS volumes are managed at the root of the physical volume. The lower layer, remote storage, stores the data that has been copied from local storage.

2.11.5.1 Local Storage Management

Remote Storage manages NTFS volumes on a computer that is running Windows 2000 Server. Remote Storage does not support clustering. Remote Storage manages free space on a logical volume. Management begins at the root of the physical volume.

NTFS volumes that reside on removable media can be managed. However, the placeholders on the removable media are not recallable if the volume is plugged into any computer other than the original computer being managed.

2.11.5.2 Remote Storage Engine

Remote storage is the part of the system that holds the copies of the data. The Remote Storage Engine consists of the media used to store the data, libraries, and drives. The Remote Storage Engine service runs on computers that are running Windows 2003 Server. Only one Remote Storage Engine can exist on a server. The Remote Storage Engine does not run on Windows 2000 Professional.

2.11.5.3 Flow Meter Capacity Metric

Remote Storage maintains a flow meter capacity metric monitoring the amount of data that is contained in remote storage, including overflowed and shelved data. Copying data from local storage to remote storage increases the value of the capacity metric. Removing local storage references to data in remote storage decreases the value of the capacity metric. The change in the capacity metric is immediate, but some operations are not immediately detected. Remote Storage increments the value of the flow meter capacity metric whenever one of the following occurs:

- A new file is managed.
- A previously deleted placeholder is restored to a volume and reconnected to remote storage.

Remote Storage decrements the value of the flow meter capacity metric whenever one of the following occurs:

- A premigrated file is modified.
- A placeholder or premigrated file is deleted.
- A file is unmanaged.

There might be a latency associated with the decrementing of the flow meter capacity metric since the detection of these conditions can happen at a later time.

2.11.5.4 Storage Pool

All remote storage in Remote Storage exists in a single storage pool there is no storage pool management required. Relocation is the movement of data from one remote storage pool to another. Since Remote Storage only supports a single remote storage pool, relocation is not supported in Remote Storage.

Remote Storage supports one storage library within the single tape storage pool. The library must have at least one drive, and two or more drives to support media copies. When multiple drives exist within a library, all drives must be identical in type (for example, density or firmware).

2.11.5.5 Handling of Physically full Remote Storage

Remote Storage provides the following options for handling physically full remote storage situations:

- Stop managing new files: Remote Storage becomes a recall-only system; this mode is invoked only after any possible space reclamation is performed.
- Shelf Storage: Remote Storage cycles removable media to "shelf"; recalls of files stored on shelved media require administrator interaction.

Remote storage is considered full either when there is not enough scratch media or when the scratch media are not online. In either case, the administrator must provide manual intervention. A notice is issued when physical remote storage utilization reaches the administrator-defined warning level.

2.11.5.6 Shelf Media

Shelf media for Remote Storage are media that are not currently accessible by the system. The medium with the data on it can be removed from the device and the media management subsystem tracks its location. Shelf media allow a system to have more data in remote storage than the device can physically contain.

For removable media, the administrator can remove media and optionally replace them with blank media. Remote Storage continues to premigrate data using the new media, and the removed media are considered shelf media. If a user needs access to data on shelf media, the administrator must place the shelf media in the library, and the new media become shelf media. Media do not need to be full to be shelf media.

2.11.5.7 Media Status and Location

When a medium is marked as having errors, the administrator is notified of the reason for the status change; the information is also kept in the Windows 2003 Event Log in later reference. Media within a library are not tied to specific locations or slots. The system adjusts to media being in different locations, so media can be shuffled in a library.

2.11.5.8 Upgrading Remote Storage Libraries

Removable Storage provides Remote Storage with the ability to replace a library with another library containing identical media and data read/write mechanisms. The administrator must physically move the media from the old library to the new library, that is, physically replace the library, and then use the user interface to register configuration changes within Remote Storage.

2.11.6 Disk Storage Options

Before you tackle the installation of a disk drive and the configuration of that drive, you must understand several important storage concepts.

2.11.6.1 Physical Disks

Physical disks are the conglomeration of plastic, metal, and silicon that enable users to store enormous quantities of useless data and MP3s, and the occasional business document. Of course I'm being sarcastic here, but it is important to understand the difference between the physical disk, and its logical volume(s), which are discussed in the next paragraph. It is also helpful to remember that an advanced disk subsystem, such as hardware-based redundant array of independent disks (RAID) system, may consist of several physical disks, but its dedicated hardware controllers abstract the physical composition of the disk set so that Windows Server 2003 perceives and represents the disk system as a single physical disk.

2.11.6.2 Logical Volumes

A logical volume is the basic unit of disk storage that you configure and manage. A logical volume may include space on more than one physical disk. Logical volumes (also called logical disks in the context of performance monitoring) are physically distinct storage units, allowing the separation of different types of information, such as the operating system, applications, and user data. Logical volumes have traditionally been represented by a single drive letter.

As you dig into disk-related terminology, you will learn about partitions, logical drives, and volumes. Many resources will use all these terms interchangeably, which is possible because the technical distinctions between the terms are minuscule, and the user interface and command-line tools guide you clearly by exposing only the appropriate type of logical volume based on the task you are performing. Don't get too hung up on the distinctions between the terms; they will become clear through experience if not through analysis.

2.11.6.3 Mounted Volumes

You noticed that we said, "Logical volumes have traditionally been represented by a single drive letter." That structure severely limited (to 26, says my kindergarten teacher) the number of volumes you could create on a system, and the flexibility with which those volumes could be used. Windows Server 2003's NTFS file system allows you to assign one or no drive letter to a volume. In addition, you can mount a volume to one or more empty folders on existing NTFS volumes. For example, you might create an empty folder Docs, on an existing volume with the drive letter X:, and mount a new 120 GB logical volume to that folder. When users navigate to X:\Docs, the disk subsystem redirects the input/output (I/O) requests to the new volume. All of this is transparent to the user.

The possibilities using this powerful feature are, as they say, "limitless." By mounting a volume to a folder path, you can extend the available drive space on an existing volume. If the existing volume is not fault-tolerant, but the new volume is fault-tolerant, the folder to which the volume is mounted, X:\Docs, represents a fault-tolerant portion of the existing volume's namespace. You could, theoretically, mount all logical volumes on a server to folders on the server's C or D drive and thereby unify enormous storage capacity under the namespace of a single drive letter.

2.11.7 Fault Tolerance

Fault tolerance refers to a system's ability to continue functioning when a component-in this case, a disk drive-has failed. Windows Server 2003 allows you to create two types of fault-tolerant logical volumes: mirrored (RAID-1) and striped with parity (RAID-5). You will learn more about the details of these configurations later in the chapter, but it is important to remember several facts about Windows Server 2003 fault tolerance, often called software RAID:

- In fault-tolerant disk configurations, two or more disks are used, and space is allocated to store data that will enable the system to recover in the event of a single drive failure.
- The fault tolerance options supported by Windows Server 2003 do not provide a means for a disk volume to continue functioning if two or more disks fail.
- The operating system allows you to use any two or more disk drives to create fault-tolerant volumes. You do not have to purchase any additional hardware or software to benefit immediately from fault-tolerant server configurations. However, if you use Windows Server 2003 mirrored or RAID-5 volumes, it is best practice to use similar or identical disk drives on the same bus. Combining a variety of disk hardware, or using drives connected to a variety of small computer systems interface (SCSI) or Integrated Device Electronics (IDE) buses can affect performance significantly.
- Speaking of performance, Windows Server 2003 fault tolerance is using processor cycles and other server resources to manage the volumes. RAID-5 can be particularly detrimental to server performance. It is possible and affordable these days, to purchase hardware-based fault-tolerant disk arrays, known as hardware RAID. Hardware RAID uses dedicated controllers to manage fault tolerance, and such systems are generally faster and more flexible in both management and recovery than is Windows Server 2003 RAID.
- Because hardware RAID controllers offload the management duties from the operating system, a hardware RAID array appears to Windows Server 2003 as a single disk.

2.11.8 Separation of Data

It is a good idea to analyze storage requirements carefully before configuring the disk subsystem of a server. Administrators typically elect to install the operating system on a logical volume separate from applications and data. By isolating the operating system, it is easier to secure the operating system volume and to manage disk space so that the volume does not run out of space. It is also usual to configure some kind of fault tolerance for the operating system.

Applications are generally stored in a separate volume, and user data and files in a third. Again, isolation of data types allows you to manage security, performance, and fault tolerance separately for each data type. If an application uses a transaction log to prepare entries into a database, as do Microsoft Active Directory directory service and Microsoft Exchange Server, it is typical to store those logs in volumes that reside on physical disks separate from the database itself, allowing the application to rebuild the database from the logs if the database fails.

Once you have thoroughly analyzed your storage requirements as they relate to the data type, security, performance, and fault tolerance, you can begin to determine how many disks you require and how those disks should be configured.

2.11.9 Basic and Dynamic Disks

An operating system must have a way to make sense of the physical space on a disk drive. There are two structures that Windows Server 2003 can apply to help it apportion and allocate drive space: basic and dynamic storage, also called basic and dynamic disks.

2.11.9.1 Basic Disks, Partitions, and Logical Drives

Basic disks maintain the structure with which you are probably most familiar. Each basic disk is partitioned, and each partition functions as a physically separate unit of storage. The information about the location and size of each partition is stored in the partition table of the Master Boot Record (MBR) on the drive. A basic disk can contain as many as four partitions, consisting of either four primary partitions or three primary partitions and one extended partition.

The logical volumes on a basic disk are primary partitions and logical drives. The logical volume, as mentioned, can be represented by zero or more drive letters and can be mounted to folders on an existing NTFS volume.

- **Primary partition:** Each primary partition maintains one logical volume on a basic disk. If a basic disk is used to start the operating system, one and only one primary partition on the disk must also be marked as active.
- **Extended partition:** A basic disk may also contain an extended partition. Unlike primary partitions, extended partitions are not formatted or assigned drive letters. Instead, extended partitions are further divided into logical drives. Logical drives are logical volumes on a basic disk.

In earlier versions of Microsoft operating systems, including Windows 95, Windows 98, and MS-DOS, the operating system could only "see" the primary partition on which it was installed, plus the extended partition on the drive, if one existed. If you wanted additional storage segments on the drive, you had to configure an extended partition and apportion it into one or more logical drives. Because Windows NT, Windows 2000, Windows XP, and Windows Server 2003 can access all partitions on a disk, you only need an extended partition if you want more than four logical drives on a single disk.

2.11.9.2 Dynamic Disks and Volumes

Microsoft Windows 2000, Windows XP, and the Windows Server 2003 family also support dynamic storage. The storage units on dynamic disks are called volumes, and the first distinctions between basic and dynamic storage are that dynamic disks support an unlimited number of volumes, and that the configuration information about the volumes is stored in a database controlled by the Logical Disk Manager (LDM) service. The logical volume of dynamic disks is the volume. Dynamic disks support simple volumes on a single disk. When a computer has more than one dynamic disk, you are provided more storage options from which to choose. Spanned, mirrored (RAID-1), striped (RAID-0), and striped with parity (RAID-5) volumes are logical volumes that utilize space on more than one physical disk. Each volume type uses disk space differently, and is characterized by a different level of fault tolerance. The list below summarizes the volume types; though each has nuances you will learn about as the chapter progresses.

- **Simple volume:** The equivalent to a basic disk partition is a dynamic disk simple volume. Simple volumes utilize space on a single physical disk, and correspond to a single logical volume. Simple volumes can be extended by appending unallocated space on other regions of the same disk, allowing you to adjust a volume's capacity with the growth of data stored in that volume. Because simple volumes exist on only one physical disk, they are not fault-tolerant.

- **Spanned volume:** A spanned volume includes space on more than one physical disk. Up to 32 physical disks can participate in a spanned volume, and the amount of space used on each disk can be different. Data is written to the volume beginning with the space on the first disk in the volume. When the space on the first disk fills, the second disk is written to, and so on. Spanned volumes provide an option for increasing drive capacity. If a simple or spanned volume is filling up, you can extend the volume onto additional new storage capacity.

But spanned volumes are not fault-tolerant, and cannot participate in any fault-tolerant configurations. Because their size tends to be greater, and because multiple physical disks are involved, the risk for failure increases. If any one disk in a spanned volume is corrupted or lost, data on the entire volume is lost as well. For these reasons, Windows Server 2003 will not allow the installation of the operating system on a spanned volume, nor can you extend or span the system volume.

Spanned volumes are recommended only as a stop-gap measure when an existing volume fills to capacity, or else in situations where tolerance for failure is high-for example, a large library of read-only data that can easily be restored from tape backup in the event of failure.

- **Striped volume:** A striped volume (RAID-0) combines areas of free space from multiple hard disks into one logical volume. Unlike a spanned volume, however, data is written to all physical disks in the volume at the same rate. Because multiple spindles are in use, read and write performance is increased almost geometrically as additional physical disks are added to the stripe. But like extended simple volumes and spanned volumes, if a disk in a striped volume fails, the data in the entire volume is lost.

- **Mirrored volume:** A mirrored volume (also known as RAID Level 1, or RAID-1) consists of two identical copies of a simple volume, each on a separate hard disk. Mirrored volumes provide fault tolerance in the event that one physical disk fails.

- **RAID-5 volume:** A RAID-5 volume is a fault-tolerant striped volume. Space on three or more physical disks is unified as a single volume. Data is written to all physical disks at the same rate, but unlike a striped volume, the data is interlaced with checksum information, called parity. Should a single disk in the volume fail, the data on that disk can be regenerated through calculations involving the remaining data and the checksum information. It is an interesting technical note that parity is distributed among all volumes in the RAID-5 set.

2.11.9.3 Basic VS. Dynamic Disks

So now that you know about basic and dynamic storage, and the types of partitions, logical drives, and volumes they support, which is better? The answer, as is frequently the case, is: "It depends." Dynamic disks that store data are easily transferred between servers, allowing you to move a disk from a failed server to a functioning server with little downtime. Dynamic disks flex their muscle when there is more than one dynamic disk in a computer. Each Windows 2000, Windows XP, and Windows Server 2003 computer can support one disk group, which itself can contain multiple dynamic disks. The LDM database is replicated among all disks in the disk group, which increases the resiliency of disk configuration information for all the group's disks. In addition, disks can be configured to work together to create a variety of flexible and powerful volume types including spanned volumes, striped volumes (RAID-0), mirrored volumes (RAID-1), and stripedwith-parity volumes (RAID-5).

Basic disks will continue to be used, however, for several reasons:

- Basic storage is the default in Windows Server 2003, so all new disks are basic disks until you convert them to dynamic-a simple process.

- Dynamic disks do not offer advantages over basic disks in a computer that will have only one disk drive.

- The behavior of the LDM database also makes it difficult to transfer a dynamic disk used for starting the operating system to another computer when the original computer fails.

- Dynamic disks are not supported for removable media, and are not supported on laptops.

- Basic storage is the industry standard, so basic drives are accessible from many operating systems, including MS-DOS, all versions of Microsoft Windows, and most non-Microsoft operating systems (there are a few). Therefore, dynamic disks cannot be used if you need to dual-boot an earlier operating system that requires access to the disks. Keep in mind that we are talking about local access only. When a client of any platform accesses files over the network, the underlying storage and volume type are transparent to the client.

2.11.10 Configuring Disks and Volumes

You will apply the concepts of disk storage to install, configure, and manage disk storage. You will learn how to use the Disk Management tool to direct the detection and initialization of newly installed disks, and to apportion that disk to partitions, logical drives, and volumes. In the event that a volume fills up, you will learn how to extend that volume's capacity. And you will explore the processes involved with moving disks between servers. Finally, you will uncover the powerful new DISKPART command, which allows you to manage storage from the command line.

2.11.10.1 Disk Management

Disk management activities are performed using the cleverly named Disk Management snap-in, which is part of the Computer Management console. Open the Disk Management snap-in in the Computer Management console, or add the snap-in to a custom console. Disk Management can manage disk storage on local or remote systems. The snap-in does not manipulate disk configuration directly; rather, it works in concert with Dmadmin, the Logical Disk Manager Administrative Service that is started on the computer you are managing when you start the Disk Management snap-in.

The Disk Management interface is shown in Figure 2.47. The top frame-the list view-displays information about each partition, logical drive, or volume. The bottom frame-the graphical view-depicts disk space allocation per physical disk, as perceived by Windows Server 2003. You can right-click the volumes in either frame to access a shortcut menu to format, delete, or assign a drive letter to the volume. If you right-click an area of unallocated disk space, you can create a partition or volume. By right-clicking the disk drive's status box, on the left of the disk's graphical view, you can initialize a new disk, convert between basic and dynamic disks, and access the disk's hardware properties dialog box.

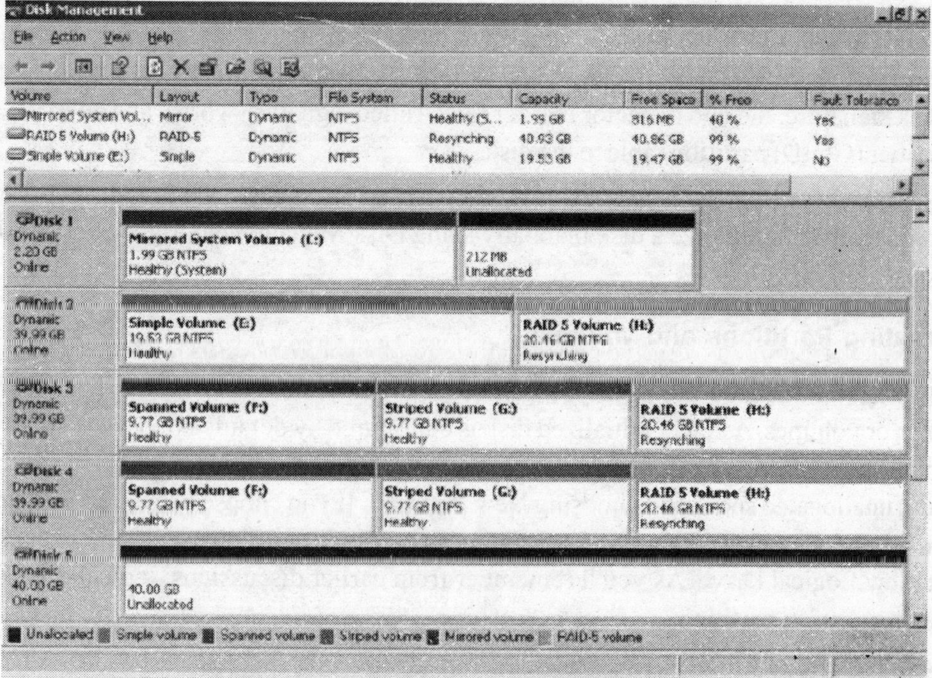

Figure 2.47 Disk Management console

2.11.10.2 Configuring Disks and Volumes

Configuring storage entails the following steps:

1. Physically installing the disk(s).
2. Initializing the disk.
3. On a basic disk, creating partitions and (if an extended partition) logical drives or, on a dynamic disk, creating volumes.
4. Formatting the volumes.
5. Assigning drive letters to the volumes, or mounting the volumes to empty folders on existing NTFS volumes.

You must be a member of the Administrators or Backup Operators group, or have been otherwise delegated authority, to perform these tasks, although only administrators can format a volume.

2.11.11 Installing the Disk

To add a new disk to a computer, install or attach the new physical disk (or disks). Open Disk Management and, if the drive has not been detected automatically, right click the Disk Management node and choose Rescan Disks. If a system must be taken offline to install a new disk, restart the computer, and then open Disk Management. If the new disks are not automatically detected, rescan the disks.

2.11.11.1 Initializing the Disk

When you add a disk to a server, you will need to initialize that disk before you can begin to allocate its available space to partitions, logical drives, and volumes. Initializing a disk allows the operating system to write a disk signature, the end of sector marker (also called signature word), and an MBR or globally unique identifier (GUID) partition table to the disk.

If you start the Disk Management console after installing a new disk, the Initialize Disk Wizard will appear automatically. To initialize a disk manually using Disk Management, right-click the disk's status box and choose Initialize Disk.

2.11.12 Creating Partitions and Volumes

After you have initialized the disk, you can begin to implement a storage structure of partitions, logical drives, or volumes. A newly initialized disk is configured by default as a basic disk. If you wish to maintain the disk as a basic disk, you can divide the basic disk into primary and extended partitions by right-clicking unallocated space and choosing New Partition. If you choose to create a primary partition, the partition becomes a logical volume. After creating an extended partition, right-click the partition again and choose New Logical Drive. As you'll remember from earlier discussions, logical drives are logical volumes on an extended partition.

If you want to configure the disk as a dynamic disk, right-click the disk's status box in Disk Management and choose Convert To Dynamic Disk. You can then right-click the unallocated space on the disk and choose New Volume. The New Volume Wizard will step you through the creation of supported volume types. The Select Volume Type page of the wizard is shown in Figure 2.48.

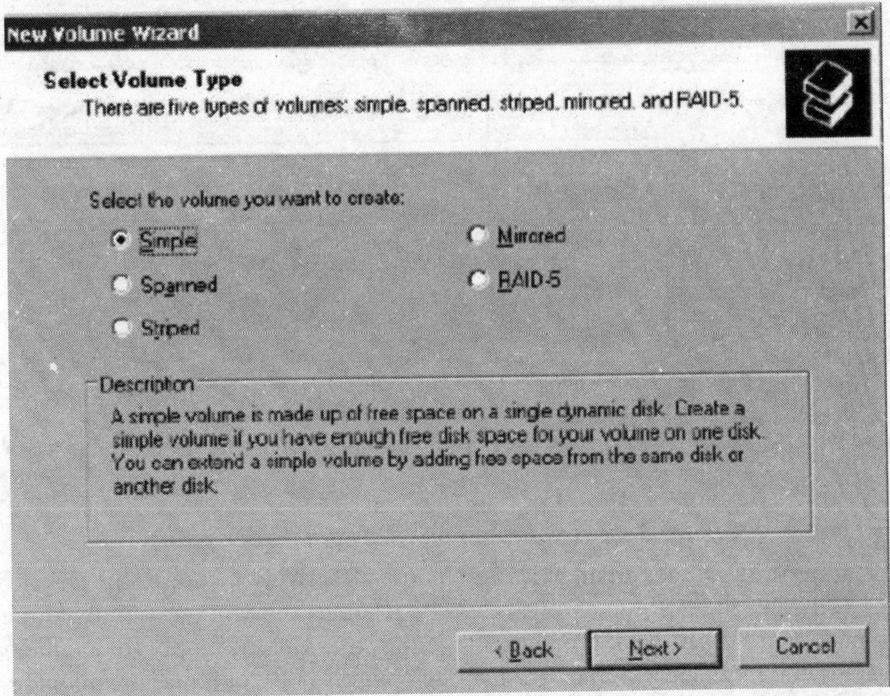

Figure 2.48 The Select Volume Type page of the New Volume Wizard

2.11.12.1 Formatting Volumes

Windows Server 2003 supports three file systems: FAT, FAT32, and NTFS. Let's keep this discussion simple: use FAT or FAT32 only when you have very specific reasons for doing so. Only NTFS gives you the level of stability, resiliency, scalability, flexibility and security required by most organizations. Many core components of Windows Server 2003, such as file security, and services, including Active Directory and Remote Installation Services (RIS), require NTFS. All advanced storage management tasks, including multidisk volumes and disk quotas require NTFS. If you think you need

FAT32, think again, and then think again.

2.11.12.2 Assigning Drive Letters or Mounting Volumes

When you create a volume, it defaults to the next available drive letter. The New Volume Wizard and New Partition Wizard give you a chance to specify an alternative representation for the new logical volume. You can also right-click an existing volume and choose Change Drive Letter and Paths.

A volume can be represented by only one drive letter, though you can configure a volume to have no drive letter. However, you can mount a volume in one or more empty folders on local NTFS volumes. In the Change Drive Letter And Paths dialog box, you can click Remove or Change to delete or modify an existing drive letter or folder mounting for the volume. Click Add to add a drive letter or mount point. Figure 2.49 shows a server in which the Docs folder on the X drive is a mount point to another volume. Note that the folder appears in the Explorer namespace exactly where it should, but displays a drive volume icon. When a user navigates to that folder, the user is transparently redirected to the volume.

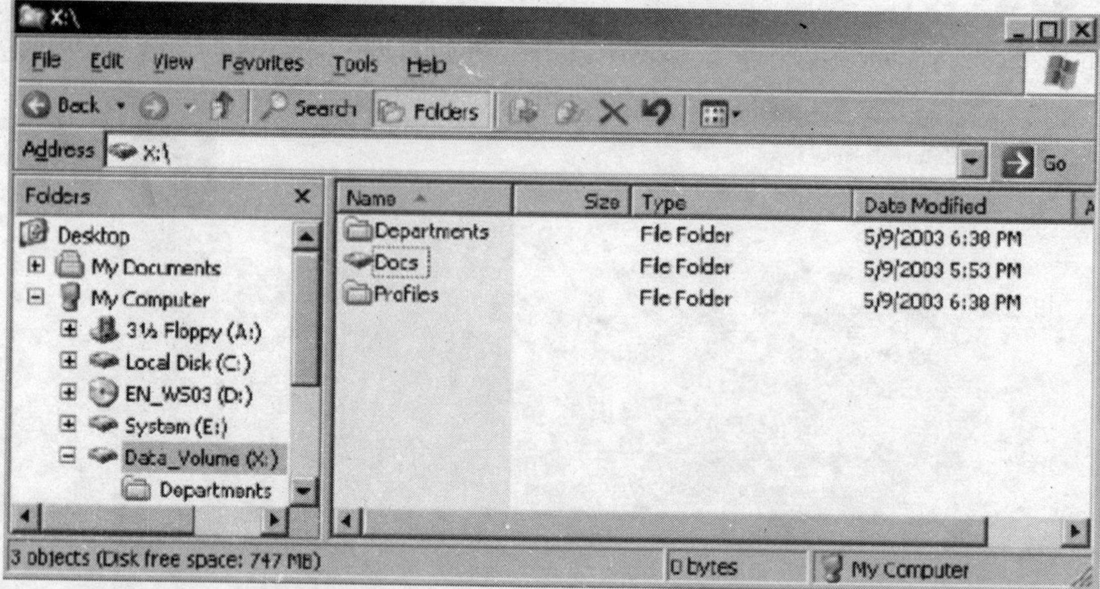

Figure 2.49 A volume mounted to a folder path

Mounting a volume in a folder on an existing volume effectively increases the target volume's size and free space. You can mount volumes regardless of whether the volumes involved are on basic or dynamic disks, and regardless of what type of volume they are. But the empty folder, the path of which becomes the path to the mounted volume, must reside on an NTFS volume. The mounted volume can, technically, be formatted as FAT or FAT32, but of course that is not the best practice.

2.11.12.3 Extending Volumes

Another way to increase a volume's capacity is to extend the volume. You can extend a simple or spanned volume on a dynamic disk so long as that volume is formatted as NTFS, and so long as the volume is not the system or boot volume. Right-click the volume and click Extend Volume. Follow the Extend Volume Wizard's instructions screen to select unallocated space on dynamic disks on which to extend the existing volume. If you extend a simple volume onto space on another physical disk, you create a spanned volume.

You can extend a partition on a basic disk using the DISKPART command. The basic partition must be formatted as NTFS, must not be the system or boot partition, and must be extended onto immediately contiguous space on the same physical disk that is either unallocated and unformatted, or formatted with NTFS.

2.11.13 Moving Disks Between Servers

It is possible to move disks between computers. If, for example, you plan to take a server offline, you might attach its physical disks to another server so that data can continue to be accessed. The process for doing so is the following:

1. Check the health of the disk while it is in the original server. It is recommended to open Disk Management and confirm that the disk status displays Healthy before moving the disk. If the disk is not healthy, repair the disk.
2. Uninstall the disk in the original computer. If the original server is online, uninstall the disk by right-clicking the disk in Device Manager and choosing Uninstall.

3. Remove a dynamic disk correctly. If the original server is online, open Disk Man-agement, right-click the dynamic disk and choose Remove. This step is not necessary or possible with basic disks.
4. Physically detach the disk. If the computer supports hot-swapping the drive, you may remove the drive. Otherwise, shut down the computer to remove the physical disk.
5. Attach the disk to the target server. Open Disk Management and, if the drive has not been detected automatically, right click the Disk Management node and choose Rescan Disks. Otherwise, shut down the target server before adding the physical disk.
6. Follow instructions in the Found New Hardware Wizard. If the wizard does not appear, open Device Manager and see if the drive was detected and installed automatically. If not, open Add Hardware from Control Panel.
7. Open Disk Management. Right-click Disk Management and choose Rescan Disks.
8. Right-click any disks marked Foreign and choose Import Foreign Disks. Importing a disk reconciles the LDM databases on a new dynamic disk with the existing disks.

Some important notes about moving physical disks:

- If an imported disk contains volumes that span to other physical disks, you must attach and import all physical disks before the volumes can be accessed.
- If you move drives from several computers to a single computer, move all drives from one computer before beginning to move drives from the next computer.
- A basic volume that is moved to a new computer receives the next available drive letter. Dynamic volumes retain the drive letter they had on the original computer. If a dynamic volume did not have a drive letter on the previous computer, it does not receive a drive letter when moved to another computer. If the drive letter is already used on the computer where they are moved, the volume receives the next available drive letter.
- Use the Mountvol /n or the DISKPART automount commands to prevent new volumes from being automatically mounted and assigned a drive letter. If these commands have been used, when you add a new disk you must manually mount the volumes and assign drive letters or paths.

2.11.14 Converting Disk Storage

You can convert a basic disk to a dynamic disk. If the disk already contains partitions and logical drives, those units will be converted to the equivalent units for a dynamic disk: simple volumes. The structure of data on the disk is not modified, so it is possible to convert a basic disk that already contains data, although it is always best practice to back up volumes before performing disk management tasks.

To convert a basic disk to a dynamic disk, right-click the disk's status box and choose Convert To Dynamic Disk. It's that simple. If you convert a disk that contains a system or boot partition, the computer must restart. Unfortunately, the reverse process is not as straightforward. Converting back to basic storage wipes out data on the drive. So you must first back up all data on the disk. Then you must delete all existing volumes on the dynamic disk before right-clicking the disk's status box in Disk Management and choosing Convert To Basic Disk. After recreating partitions and logical drives, restore the data onto the disk. Although you can convert from dynamic to basic from a technical perspective, you are actually wiping out the disk and starting over. Performing Disk Management Tasks from the Command Prompt Windows Server 2003 provides command-line alternatives for disk management, including the following:

- Chkdsk Scan a disk for errors and, optionally, attempt to correct those errors.
- Convert Convert a volume from FAT or FAT32 to NTFS.
- Fsutil Perform a variety of tasks related to managing FAT, FAT32, or NTFS volumes.
- Mountvol Manages mounted volumes and reparse points.

But the granddaddy of disk management command-line tools is DISKPART. Table 2.7 summarizes the DISKPART commands that achieve common disk management tasks. Diskpart can be used interactively or can call a script. To start Diskpart interactively, type diskpart at the command prompt. When the Diskpart command prompt (DISKPART >) appears, type? at any time for help. The command's built-in documentation will appear automatically when needed to help you achieve the tasks you perform. Diskpart is also well documented in the Help and Support Center.

Table 2.7 How to Complete Common Disk Management Tasks from the Command Prompt

Task	From DISKPART>	Description

List disk, partition, and volume information	`list disk`
	`list partition`
	`list volume`
		The first command lists disk information, the second command lists partition information for the current disk, and the third command lists volume and partition information for all disks.

Create a simple volume	`create volume simple size=500 disk=2`	Typed on one line, this taks creates a simple volume 500 MB in size on disk 2.
Assign a drive letter	`select volume 4` `assign letter j`	Assigns volume 4 as the J drive.
Extend a simple volume	`select volume 4` `extend size=250 disk=2`	Extends simple volume 4 (on disk 2) with an additional 250 MB on the same disk.
Create a spanned volume	`select volume 4` `extend size=250 disk=1`	Spans a simple volume 4 (on disk 2) with an additional 250 MB on disk 1.
Delete a spanned volume	`select volume 4` `delete volume`	Deletes spanned volume 4. If volume 4 was contained on disk 1 and disk 2, the space it occupied on the two disks becomes unallocated.
Create a volume mount point	`select volume 4` `assign mount=e:\Folder1`	Assigns a volume mount point to volume 4 that is accessed from E:\Folder1.
Create a striped volume	`create volume stripe size=500 disk=1,2`	Typed on one line, this task creates a striped volume which uses 500 MB on disks 1 and 2 for a total of 1 GB of storage space.
Create a mirrored volume	`create volume simple size= 00 disk=1 add disk 2`	Typed on one line, this task creates a mirrored volume which uses 500 MB on disks 1 and 2 for a total of 500 MB of fault-tolerant storage space.

Break a mirror	`select volume 5` `break disk 2`	Selects the mirror on volume 5 and break the mirror on disk 2.
Remove a mirror	`break disk 2 nokeep`	Deletes a mirror and remove the previously mirrored data on disk 2.
Create a RAID-5 stripe	`create volume raid size=500 disk=1,2,3`	Typed on one line, this task reates a RAID-5 volume which uses disks 1, 2, and 3 for a total of ~1 GB of fault-tolerant storage space.
Convert a disk from basic to dynamic storage	`select disk 2` `convert dynamic`	Converts disk 2 from basic storage to dynamic storage.
Convert a disk with unallocated space from dynamic to basic storage	`select disk 2` `convert basic`	Converts disk 2 from dynamic to basic.

2.11.15 Formatting Partitions

All drives must be formatted before information can be placed on them. Windows 2000 supports three kinds of file systems with which you can format drives: FAT, FAT32, and NTFS. In addition, Windows 2000 also supports CDFS for CD-ROMs, but you don't format drives with that file system. If you are planning to install more than one operating system on your computer (a plan that is ill-advised when talking about a server-unless it is a test machine), you will need to use FAT or FAT32. If you are not multi-booting, you should use NTFS.

FAT (File Allocation Table) was the original DOS file format. Is continues to be very popular for Windows and non-Windows operating systems alike. FAT uses a linked-list format to chain together files. A table contains pointers to the beginning of each list, and files are located through lookup to the table and navigation of the links that result.

FAT32 is simply an updated version of FAT that was implemented in Windows 95 OSR2, in Windows 98, and now in Windows 2000. Under FAT32, disk space is used more efficiently (the allocation units are smaller), which allows more information to be stored on hard drives. In addition, FAT32 also allows Windows 9x machines to create and use partitions larger than 2GB (something that was not possible under FAT).

Under Windows 2000, FAT/FAT32 supports long filenames and preserves case (although it does not recognize case sensitivity). FAT/FAT32 does not support local security-that is, not security as it pertains to users locally logging onto a system and accessing files. Under NT 4.0, a case could be made for creating at least one FAT partition to enable access to the drives to solve boot problems. However, now that the Recovery console is available, that is not necessary. Under Windows 2000, FAT and FAT32 are recommended as file formats only if you are planning to install more than one operating system on your Windows 2000 machine. If, for example, you want to dual-boot Windows 2000 Server with Windows 98, you will need to format the active partition with FAT/FAT32. If you do not, Windows 98 will not be able to read from the hard drive and will not boot.

All the partition types can be formatted with FAT or FAT32. However, it is pointless to format any of the dynamic volume types as FAT because no other local operating system can read from them anyway. NTFS is a proprietary file system that was introduced in the early days of NT. As a proprietary file system, it is readable by NT and Windows 2000 only. This means that in any multi-boot system, the non-NT or non-Windows 2000 operating system will not be able to read from a partition or volume formatted with NTFS. Under Windows 2000, the version of NTFS is 5. This version adds new features that were not present in Windows NT 4.0 (like file encryption). This means that not only does NTFS v.5 have advantages over FAT, but also has advantages over previous versions of NTFS.

NTFS has a number of advantages over FAT. One of the most signi?cant is that NTFS is capable of locally securing files and folders on a partition or volume; this means that you can control who has access to files even when accessed locally by logging onto the machine. Another feature that is signi?cant is that built-in compression can be implemented at the directory and file levels (this contrasts with FAT compression methods, which must be done on a volume level). This compression is intrinsic to the file system and does not need to be installed. It provides on-the-?y compression and decompression with little loss of performance.

NTFS is, by its nature, a more efficient file storage medium than FAT. Using binary tree sorting, it can quickly store and retrieve data. In addition, it can theoretically be configured for partitions and volumes up to 16 exabytes (an exabyte is one billion gigabytes or 264 bytes). Practically, however, a partition of 2 terabytes (TB) is its upper limit. It is impossible to format a 1.44MB disk with NTFS, and it is recommended that you do not use it on partitions or volumes smaller than 500MB.

NTFS supports sector sparing, also known as hot ?xing, on SCSI hard drives. If a sector fails on an NTFS partition of a SCSI hard drive, NTFS tries to write the data to a good sector (if the data is still in memory) and map out the bad sector so that it is not reused. NTFS also keeps a transaction log while it works. If the power fails, leaving NTFS in a possibly corrupt state, the CHKDSK command, which executes when the system boots, attempts to either redo the transaction (in the case of a deletion, for example) or undo the transaction (in the case of a file-write where the data is no longer in memory).

One other new feature of NTFS under Windows 2000 is the ability to implement disk quotas to prevent users from using more than a speci?c amount of disk space on a server. In addition, local encryption is also available under NTFS in Windows 2000. This feature is supported by security subsystem enhancements and allows for files to be secured in such a way as to allow only the user who secured them to access those files.

You must use NTFS if you want to preserve existing permissions when you migrate files and directories from a NetWare server to a Windows 2000 Server system. In addition, if you want to allow Macintosh computers to access files on the partition through Windows NT's Services for Macintosh, you must format the partition for NTFS. And if you want a Windows 2000 server to support Windows 2000 domains and/or the Active Directory, you must use NTFS.

COMPARISON BETWEEN FAT, FAT32, AND NTFS

Feature	FAT	FAT32	NTFS (v. 5)
Maximum filename length	255	255	255
8.3 filename compatibility	Yes	Yes	Yes
Maximum file size	4GB	2TB	16EB
Maximum partition size	4GB	2TB	16EB

Feature	FAT	FAT32	NTFS (v. 5)
Recommended volume size	<500MB	512MB-32GB	>500MB
Directory structure	Linked list	Linked list	B-tree
Intrinsic local security	No	No	Yes
Intrinsic local encryption	No	No	Yes
Intrinsic compression	No	Yes	Yes
Supports disk quotas	No	No	Yes
Transaction tracking	No	No	Yes
Hot fixing	No	No	Yes
Overhead	1MB	1MB	4.5-10MB
Locally accessible MS-DOS	Yes	No	No
Locally accessible Win 95 OSR2	Yes	Yes	No
Locally accessible Win 98	Yes	Yes	No
Locally accessible OS/2	Yes	No	No
Locally accessible Windows 2000	Yes	Yes	Yes
Locally accessible Windows NT 4.0	Yes	No	Limited
Locally accessible Windows NT 3.5x	Yes	No	No
Case-sensitive filenames	No	No	POSIX only
Case-preserving filenames	Yes	Yes	Yes
Fragmentation level	High	High	Low
Used on floppy disk	Yes	No	No

2.12 EDITORS

Windows Server 2003 comes in a number of editions, each targeted towards a particular size and type of business. In general, all variants of Windows Server 2003 have the ability to share files and printers, act as an application server, and host message queues, provide email services, authenticate users, act as an X.509 certificate server, provide LDAP directory services, serve streaming media, and to perform other server-oriented functions.

2.12.1 Windows Small Business Server

SBS includes Windows Server and additional technologies aimed at providing a small business with a complete technology solution. The technologies are integrated to enable small business with targeted solutions such as the Remote Web Workplace, and offer management benefits such as integrated setup, enhanced monitoring, a unified management console, and remote access.

The Standard Edition of SBS includes Windows SharePoint Services for collaboration, Microsoft Exchange server for e-mail, Fax Server, and the Active Directory for user management. The product also provides a basic firewall, DHCP server and NAT router using either two network cards or one network card in addition to a hardware router.

The Premium Edition of SBS includes the above plus Microsoft SQL Server 2000 and Microsoft Internet Security and Acceleration Server 2004. SBS has its own type of Client Access License (CAL) that is different and costs slightly more than CALs for the other editions of Windows Server 2003. However, the SBS CAL encompasses the user CALs for Windows Server, Exchange Server, SQL Server, and ISA Server, and hence is less expensive than buying all other CALs individually. SBS server has the following design limitations:

- Only one computer in a domain can be running Windows Server 2003 for Small Business Server.
- Windows Server 2003 for Small Business Server must be the root of the Active Directory forest.
- Windows Server 2003 for Small Business Server cannot trust any other domains.
- Windows Server 2003 for Small Business Server is limited to 75 users or devices depending on which type of CAL.
- Windows Server 2003 for Small Business Server is limited to 4GB of RAM (Random Access Memory).
- A Windows Server 2003 for Small Business Server domain cannot have any child domains.
- Terminal Services only operates in remote administration mode on the server running SBS 2003, and only two simultaneous RDP sessions are allowed. (Change from SBS 2000 policy)
- To remove the limits from SBS server and upgrade from Small Business Server to regular Windows Server, Exchange Server, SQL and ISA server versions there is a Windows Small Business Server 2003 R2 Transition Pack.

2.12.2 Web Edition

Windows Server 2003, Web Edition is mainly for building and hosting Web applications, Web pages, and XML web services. It is designed to be used primarily as an IIS 6.0 Web server and provides a platform for rapidly developing and deploying XML Web services and applications that use ASP.NET technology, a key part of the .NET Framework. Terminal Server mode is not included on Web Edition. However, Remote Desktop for Administration is available on Windows Server 2003, Web Edition. Only 10 concurrent file-sharing connections are allowed at any moment. It is not possible to install Microsoft SQL Server and Microsoft Exchange software in this edition without installing Service Pack 1. Despite supporting XML Web services and ASP.NET, UDDI cannot be deployed on Windows Server 2003, Web Edition. The .NET Framework version 2.0 is not included with Windows Server 2003, Web Edition, but can be installed as a separate update from Windows Update.

Figure 2.50 Windows Server 2003 Standard Edition cover box

Windows Server 2003 Web Edition supports a maximum of 2 processors with support for a maximum of 2GB of RAM. Additionally, Windows Server 2003, Web Edition cannot act as a domain controller. It is the only edition of Windows Server 2003 that does not require Client Access Licenses when used as the internet facing server front end for Internet Information Services and Windows Server Update Services. When using it for storage or as a backend with another remote server as the frontend, CALs may still be required.

2.12.3 Standard Edition

Microsoft Windows Server 2003, Standard Edition is aimed towards small to medium sized businesses. Standard Edition supports file and printer sharing, offers secure Internet connectivity, and allows centralized desktop application deployment. The initial release of Windows Server 2003 was available solely for 32-bit processors; a 64-bit version supporting the x86-64 architecture (AMD64 and EM64T, called collectively x64 by Microsoft) was released in April 2005. The 32-bit version will run on up to 4 processors with up to 4 GB RAM; the 64-bit version is capable of addressing up to 32 GB of RAM and also supports Non-Uniform Memory Access. The 32-bit version is available for students to download free of charge as part of Microsoft's DreamSpark program.

2.12.4 Enterprise Edition

Windows Server 2003, Enterprise Edition is aimed towards medium to large businesses. It is a full-function server operating system that supports up to 8 processors and provides enterprise-class features such as eight-node clustering using Microsoft Cluster Server (MSCS) software and support for up to 32 GB of memory through PAE (added with the /PAE boot string). Enterprise Edition also comes in 64-bit versions for the Itanium and x64 architectures. The 64-bit versions of Windows Server 2003, Enterprise Edition are capable of addressing up to 1 TB of memory. Both 32-bit and 64-bit versions support Non-Uniform Memory Access (NUMA). It also provides the ability to hot-add supported hardware. Enterprise Edition is also required to issue custom certificate templates.

2.12.5 Datacenter Edition

Windows Server 2003, Datacenter Edition is designed for infrastructures demanding high security and reliability. Windows Server 2003 is available for x86, Itanium, and x86-64 processors. It supports a maximum of up to 32 processors on 32-bit or 64 processors on 64-bit hardware. 32-bit architecture also limits memory addressability to 128 GB, while the 64-bit versions support up to 1 TB. Windows Server 2003, Datacenter Edition, also allows limiting processor and memory usage on a per-application basis.

Windows Server 2003 Datacenter Edition also supports Non-Uniform Memory Access. If supported by the system, Windows, with help from the system firmware will make use of NUMA kernel awareness, which is indicated by the presence of a firmware generatel ACPI Static Resource Affinity Table (SRAT) that defines the NUMA topology of the system. Windows then uses this table to optimize memory accesses, and provide NUMA awareness to applications, thereby increasing the efficiency of thread scheduling and memory management.

Windows Server 2003, Datacenter Edition has better support for Storage Area Networks (SAN). It features a service which uses Windows sockets to emulate TCP/IP communication over native SAN service providers, thereby allowing a SAN to be accessed over any TCP/IP channel. With this, any application that can communicate over TCP/IP can use a SAN, without any modification to the application.

Windows Server 2003, Datacenter Edition also supports 8-node clustering. Clustering increases availability and fault tolerance of server installations by distributing and replicating the service among many servers. Windows supports clustering with each cluster having its own dedicated storage, or with all clusters connected to a common storage area network (SAN). The SAN can be running on a Windows or non-Windows operating system and may be connected to other computers as well.

2.13 NETWORKING AND COMMUNICATION FEATURES

Windows Server 2003 adds a number of new networking technologies that enable it to grow with the needs of your business.

For example:

- It supports IPv6, which was created to overcome the limited number of addresses in IPv4 (previous versions of NT use IPv4). Windows Server 2003 supports IPv4/IPv6 coexistence through technologies such as Intra-site Automatic Tunnel Addressing Protocol (ISATAP) and 6to4. Internet and remote access functionality have been enhanced in Windows Server 2003.
- Point-to-Point Protocol over Ethernet (PPPoE) allows making broadband connections to an Internet Service Provider (ISP) without having to load any software.
- Windows can now use IPSec over NAT.
- Remote Authentication Dial-In User Service (RADIUS) has been improved to provide better control over network access and easier troubleshooting of authentication problems.
- Microsoft's implementation of RADIUS, Internet Authentication Service (IAS), can send its logs to a Microsoft SQL Server and it now supports 802.1X authentication and crossforest authentication.

In Windows 2000, IPSec was not supported through a NAT server. This was a serious drawback for some companies, as it meant they could not VPN through the NAT server using IPSec or the Layer Two Tunnelling Protocol (L2TP), which uses IPSec for encryption. This restriction has been removed in Windows Server 2003. Both IPSec connections and L2TP connections using IPSec are supported over NAT when you have a Server 2003 VPN server. This is done using a technology called NAT traversal, or NAT-T. On the client end, the Microsoft L2TP/IPSec VPN client supports NAT-T.

The Internet Connection Firewall (ICF) functions as a personal software-based ?rewall and provides protection for computers connected to the Internet or unsecured networks. ICF protects LAN, VPN, dial-up, and PPPoE connections by making it easier to secure your server against attacks. With ICF, only the services that you need to offer are exposed. For example, you can use ICF to ?lter the network connection of your DNS server so that only DNS requests are passed through. ICF is included with the 32-bit versions of the Standard and Enterprise Editions of Windows Server 2003. It is not included with the Web and Datacenter Editions, or with any of the 64-bit versions.

2.14 LICENSING

Microsoft based the Windows Server 2003 licensing structure on Windows 2000's structure. However, they have changed some things. This section is not the final word when it comes to Microsoft licensing.

This section is meant to serve as a guide on the basics of Windows 2003 licensing. To order licenses, contact your Microsoft Software Advisor. In the United States, call (800) 426-9400, or visit the Microsoft Licensing Program Reseller Web page (http://shop.microsoft.com/helpdesk/mvlref.asp). Outside of the United States and Canada, please review the Worldwide Microsoft Licensing Web site (www.microsoft.com/worldwide). There are a few rules that you need to know about Microsoft's licensing schemes:

- You have to purchase a product license for every copy of the OS you are going to install.
- Every network connection that is authenticated requires a Windows Client Access License (CAL).Anonymous connections do not require a CAL (for example, anonymous access to a Web page). Windows CALs are not required for Windows 2003 Web Edition, as it is meant to serve Web content only.
- Every Terminal Server session made by a user or device requires a Terminal Server Client Access License (TS CAL).TS CALs are not required for Windows Server 2003 Web Edition, as it is meant to serve Web content only.

The product license allows you to install the OS onto a machine. The CAL allows devices or users to connect to that machine. Microsoft's reasoning behind this is that everyone pays the same price for the base OS, but companies with more connections pay more than companies with fewer connections. This allows them to price according to usage. There are two licensing modes supported in Windows 2003:

- Per Server mode Requires a Windows CAL for each connection. These are assigned to each server and cannot be shared between servers. You are allowed one connection for each CAL assigned to the server. Once the maximum number has been reached, no more connections are allowed.
- Per Device or Per User mode (formerly called "Per Seat" mode) Requires that each device or user have its own Windows CAL. These allow the device or user to connect to an unlimited number of servers. With Per Device or Per User mode, the server will not limit the number of connections made as it does in Per Server mode.

Generally, Per Server mode will be most cost effective if you have only one or two servers, and clients that don't always connect at the same time. Per Device or Per User mode will be most cost effective if you have many servers to which your clients need to connect. Microsoft has two types of CALs, User CALs and Device CALs. User CALs are purchased for every user that makes a connection to a Windows 2003 server. Device CALs are purchased for every machine that makes a connection to a Windows 2003 server. Microsoft recommends that you use either User CALs or Device CALs, but not both at the same time. User CALs are best when you have more machines than users and your users log on to multiple machines to access the servers.

Device CALs are better when you have more employees than machines and your users share machines. User CALs and Device CALs are available for both Windows and Terminal Server. Device CALs and User CALs cost the same. Windows 2000 supported the System Equivalency license for Terminal Server. The System Equivalency license stated that if your client was running the same OS version as the terminal server, then you did not have to buy a Terminal Server CAL (thus, a Windows 2000 Pro machine connecting to a Windows 2000 terminal server did not need a TS CAL). Windows

2003 no longer supports System Equivalency licenses. However, Microsoft does have a Terminal Server licensing transition plan. You can receive a free TS CAL for every copy of Windows XP that you own at the time of the Windows 2003 launch (April 24, 2003). Check out the Microsoft licensing page for more information (www.microsoft.com/licensing).

New to Windows 2003 is the External Connector (EC) license. ECs enable external users to access your server without requiring that you buy CALs for them. External users are people who are not employed by your company. Terminal Server also has an EC license called the Terminal Server External Connector (TS-EC). The EC license is replacing the Internet Connector and TS Internet Connector licenses.

2.14.1 Product Activation

Starting with Windows XP, Microsoft requires OSs to be authorized before a specified number of days pass, after which you won't be able to log on to the OS. Failure to activate only prevents logging on. Services and remote administration are not affected. Windows Server 2003 allows a 30-day grace period for product activation (for retail and OEM products). Companies that use volume licensing do not have to activate their software.

Windows includes an activation wizard. You can activate over the Internet or by phone. One important thing to remember about product activation is that the activation process keeps track of the hardware in your machine. If the hardware changes dramatically, you will have to reactivate your software within three days in order to continue logging on to the server. Microsoft does this to prevent people from purchasing one copy of the OS, activating it, making an image of it, and deploying that image to many more machines.

2.14.2 Installation and Upgrade Issues

Unless your company is buying its first Windows server, you are going to have to decide between upgrading and performing a clean install. Each method has advantages and disadvantages:

- Upgrading preserves many of your existing settings, such as users and groups, permissions and rights, and applications.
- Performing a clean installation can improve the performance of your hard drive, as it will be reformatted during installation. This also gives you a chance to change the partition and volume sizes used on your drives. Clean installs ensure that you don't carry over any existing problems that you might have with your current OS. Some administrators (the authors of this book included) prefer clean installs because they have seen many problems related to OS upgrades in the past. There is something comforting about starting from scratch.

2.14.2.1 Common Installation Issues

The biggest problems with installing a new OS are hardware and software incompatibilities. It is important to adhere to the recommended hardware speci?cations for Windows Server 2003.At a minimum; you need the following hardware configuration:

- 133 MHz processor
- 128MB of RAM
- 1.5GB hard drive

Remember that these are the bare minimums on which Windows Server 2003 will run. Obviously, on such old hardware, performance will suffer. Microsoft recommends at least a 550 MHz processor and 256MB of RAM. The more RAM the better.

You should always verify hardware compatibility before you start your installation. There is a system compatibility check you can run from the Windows Server 2003 CD that will check out your hardware for you automatically via the System Compatibility wizard. Even if all of your hardware is supported, you should always update your machine's BIOS to the most recent version.

2.14.2.2 Common Upgrade Issues

As stated earlier, you should always verify hardware compatibility and BIOS versions. You should always back up your existing system before you start your upgrade. If you have applications on your server, you should read the release notes on application compatibility. These are found in the docs folder on the setup CD (relnotes.htm). When upgrading servers from NT 4.0 to Windows Server 2003, you must have Service Pack 5 or higher installed. You can perform upgrades from all server versions of NT 4.0 (Server, Enterprise Edition, and Terminal Server Edition). Upgrading Windows 2000 machines to Windows Server 2003 doesn't require any service packs to be installed first. Windows 2000 Server can be upgraded to Windows Server 2003 Standard Edition or Enterprise Edition. However, Windows 2000 Advanced Server can only be upgraded to Windows Server 2003 Enterprise Edition, and Windows 2000 Datacenter Server can only be upgraded to Windows Server 2003 Datacenter Edition. You must have at least 2GB of free hard drive space for all upgrades.

When upgrading Windows NT 4.0 domains to Windows Server 2003 domains, you must first make sure that DNS is installed and properly configured. You don't have to use a Microsoft DNS server, but your implementation of DNS must support service (SRV) records. Optionally, you might want it to support dynamic updates as well. If DNS does not support dynamic updates, you will have to manually create all of the needed SRV records. Before starting the upgrade, you should take one of your BDCs of?ine. This will allow you to roll back to your existing NT 4.0 environment if you should have problems with the upgrade. Always start your upgrades with the PDC, followed by the BDCs. After upgrading the PDC, you should set your forest functional level to Windows 2003 interim mode.

When upgrading Windows 2000 domains, you must first prepare the forest and the domain for Windows Server 2003 by using the ADPrep tool. You can prepare the forest by running adprep.exe / forestprep on the Schema Master, and you can prepare the domain by running adprep.exe /domainprep on the Infrastructure Master.ADPrep can only be run from the command line; there isn't an equivalent graphical tool. Unlike when you upgrade from NT 4.0 domains, you do not have to upgrade the PDC (technically the PDC Emulator) first. You can install a new Window 2003 domain controller into an existing Windows 2000 domain. When upgrading your domain controllers, you need to budget a little growing room for the Active Directory database. The database file (ntds.dit) might grow by up to 10 percent.

2.14.3 Windows Server 2003 Planning Tools and Documentation

Planning is the first step in building a reliable, secure, high-performance and highly available Windows Server 2003-based network. In this section, we'll begin with an overview of network infrastructure planning, introducing you to planning strategies and how to use planning tools. This section also looks at legal and regulatory considerations, how to calculate total cost of ownership (TCO), and how to plan for future growth. We discuss how to develop a test network environment and how to document the planning and network design process.

2.14.3.1 Overview of Network Infrastructure Planning

Proper planning of a network infrastructure is essential to ensuring high performance, availability, and overall satisfaction with your network operations. In order to create a viable network design, you'll need an understanding of both the business requirements of your organization and current and emerging networking technologies. Accurate network planning will allow your organization to maximize the efficiency of its computer operations, lower costs, and enhance your overall business processes. When planning for a new infrastructure or upgrading an existing network, you should take some or all of the following steps:

- Document the business requirements of your client or organization.
- Create a baseline of the performance of any existing hardware and network utilization.
- Determine the necessary capacity for the physical network installation, including client and server hardware, as well as allocating network and Internet bandwidth for network services and applications.
- Select an appropriate network protocol and create an addressing scheme that will provide for the existing size of the network and will allocate room for any foreseeable expansions, mergers, or acquisitions.
- Specify and implement the technologies that will meet the existing needs of your network while allowing room for future growth.
- Plan to upgrade and/or migrate any existing technologies, including server operating systems and routing protocols.

2.14.3.2 Planning Strategies

When designing a new network or significantly upgrading an existing one, you should first use the business requirements of your organization as the primary source of planning information. You'll need to create a network infrastructure that addresses the needs of your management structure, such as fault tolerance, security, scalability, performance, and cost. You'll need to balance these requirements with the types of services that your users and clients will expect from a modern network, including e-mail, calendaring, project collaboration, Internet access, file, print, and application services.

After you've determined the business requirements of your network, you should then analyze the technical requirements of your organization. These requirements may apply to any applications that are already in use or that you plan to implement, as well as to the associated hardware and operating system. You should carefully note all of these requirements so that you won't create any difficulties later on during the implementation process. Be sure to analyze and document the existing network, including any hardware, software, and network services that are already in place. This will make it easier to take the existing configuration into account when planning the new or upgraded network.

Finally, any well-formed network plan should make allowances for future changes to the organization, including support for new technologies and operating systems, as well as additional hardware and users. Your organization's business requirements can change-through a merger, an acquisition, or simple growth and expansion. Although it is impossible to foresee all possible changes of this nature, a good network design will be fiexible enough to accommodate as many adjustments as possible.

2.14.3.3 Using Planning Tools

There are a number of tools available to assist you in developing a plan for your network infrastructure. The first and best of these, however, might be the simplest: pencil and paper. As we discussed in the previous section, you should begin your planning by determining the requirements of the business that will be using the network. After you have a high-level understanding of your company's organizational structure and computing needs, you should inventory the hardware and software that is already in place. This is especially important to ensure existing hardware and software are supported in Windows Server 2003.

In a small office environment, you can accomplish this by simply taking a walk to determine the physical layout of network cables, routers, and the like. In a medium- to large-sized enterprise network, you will probably want to rely on automated inventory tools such as Microsoft's Systems Management Server (SMS) or a third-party equivalent. Take as detailed of an inventory as possible, including the hardware configuration of server and workstation machines, as well as vendor names and the version numbers of the operating system and business applications the systems are running.

You can use a network analyzer, such as the Network Monitor utility built into the Windows Server 2003 operating system or the more full-featured version of Network Monitor included in SMS, to create a baseline of the current utilization of your network bandwidth. If this utilization is already near capacity, you can use this baseline to justify and plan upgrades to your network infrastructure (moving from 10MB Ethernet to 100MB Ethernet, for example).

Windows Server 2003 has introduced new management features that will assist you in planning your network configuration, especially in the areas of user and computer management. The Resultant Set of Policy (RSoP) Microsoft Management Console (MMC) snap-in contains a Group Policy modeling function that will allow you to simulate changes to Group Policy Objects (GPOs) in an Active Directory (AD) environment before actually applying them to a production network.

For example, if you want to apply a new GPO to a departmental Organizational Unit (OU), the modeling report will indicate how the new GPO will affect the objects within the OU to which it's being applied. The Group Policy Management Console (GPMC) can also provide detailed configuration reports on existing GPO settings in place on a Windows 2000 or Windows Server 2003 AD installation.

2.14.3.4 Reviewing Legal and Regulatory Considerations

Depending on the business in which you are involved, your network design plan should address the legal issues associated with your industry, geographic location, and so on. Backup schedules and offsite data availability have become federally regulated matters, especially in the financial arena. Consult your Legal department during the design process, because like everything else in this venture, it's certainly best to get it right the first time. Don't forget to include your client workstations when making allowances for legal and regulatory matters. For example, if your corporate data-retention policy calls for maintaining e-mail data for twelve months, but some users have copies of every item they've sent or received in the last five years, that fact could come back to haunt you in a legal proceeding.

Some fields of business are subject to very detailed governmental regulations regarding data security. For example, healthcare providers now fall under strict laws regarding electronic patient information since the Health Insurance Portability and Accountability Act (HIPAA) went into effect in 2003. Regardless of your field, if you work on government projects, your network might be required to meet specified security criteria. Network communications can also subject your company to legal liability when employees misuse the network. For example, pornographic material on the company network can subject the company to charges of the "hostile workplace" de?nition of sexual harassment under Title VII of the federal Civil Rights Act of 1964 and various state laws. You should also consider intellectual property (copyright, trademark, and patent) laws in establishing your network policies.

Common factors that also need to be reviewed for legal compliance are any Service Level Agreements (SLAs) in place on your network. An SLA attempts to de?ne the scope of a service provider's responsibilities in maintaining applications or services on a network. This provider can be an external vendor to whom you've outsourced a critical service (your ISP, for example), or the SLA can be an internal document detailing the IT department's duties in maintaining network availability. The following are the major components of an external SLA, using an ISP as a real-world example:

- **Scope of services:** This spells out exactly which service or application that an SLA is referring to and the level of responsibility that the internal IT department will have in maintaining this service versus the external vendor. This includes outlining the hardware, software, and resources that comprise the particular service, such as the modems, network connectivity equipment, ISP help desk, and engineering personnel in the case of an ISP.
- **Roles and responsibilities:** Your ISP should establish a coverage schedule so that at least one primary and one backup support avenue is available to report any service outages. You'll also need to establish a system to escalate support calls if the scheduled support person is unavailable or cannot correct the problem. You can use this information to inform your users of the turnaround time they can anticipate in responding to and resolving any problems.

These are only a few of the legal considerations that are important in a corporate network environment. You should always include a legal advisor as a member of your network planning team.

2.14.3.5 Calculating TCO

"These upgrade proposals look interesting, but how will they impact our company's TCO?" Total Cost of Ownership (TCO) is a calculation that was designed to assist consumers and corporate managers in assessing the direct and indirect costs and benefits associated with the implementation of new or upgraded computer technology. The purpose of TCO is to quantify the financial bottom line associated with a computer or technology purchase decision.

TCO calculations do not rely on a single formula. For example, a high-end computer will have a higher initial purchase price, but will probably incur fewer repair bills during its active life cycle. TCO is balanced against the benefits created by the technology purchase, such as improved user efficiency or perceived happiness with improved performance, in attempting to make a final purchase decision.

The first part of calculating TCO is relatively simple: What is the initial purchase price of the new technology? Include the cost of hardware, software licensing, networking equipment, installation charges, and so on. Don't forget to factor in the necessary time to train your end users and IT staff in the use and administration of the new technology. Next, determine the ongoing costs for maintenance and support. These costs can include charges for vendor support, as well as in-house labor expended on interoperability issues with third-party and legacy software support. Try to estimate the total costs for the full anticipated life cycle of the proposed technology.

Determining the soft costs associated with a new technology are a bit more complicated. How much money will your company save by reducing the number of times your users are forced to reboot their computers each day? Conversely, how much money is lost when an account manager cannot access the order-entry application for 20 minutes, for an hour, and for a day? These costs are fairly difficult to quantify, but they can be critical when determining the total benefits afforded by a network upgrade. You can start investigating soft costs by talking to your users and reviewing TCO models from network analysts.

Your users can certainly tell you how much it aggravates them when their e-mail or order database is "running too slowly," even if they can't tell you what "too slowly" means in terms of actual response time. This can also point out performance bottlenecks that you may not have known about before. For example, a real estate lending office for a well-known bank shared a T1 line with the bank branch in the lobby of the office building. The real estate lenders encountered severe network performance degradation every day at around 4:30 P.M. Further investigation revealed that this time frame coincided with the bank tellers transmitting their daily totals to the bank's main headquarters when the branch closed each day.

Preconfigured TCO models from organizations like the Gartner Group, IDC, or other independent network analysts can walk you step-by-step through plugging in various budget figures to arrive at the TCO of a specific technology, hardware, or software package. However, remember that these models are not set in stone, and they should be modified as needed to meet the specific needs of your organization. These models will rely more on actual calculations, such as dividing a help desk analyst's salary by the number of support calls he or she is able to process in a day, or determining the "cost per e-mail message" of an e-mail server upgrade that increases the number of messages it can transmit in a day, week, or hour. You can then take these numbers and factor in the soft costs already mentioned. Using a combination of calculations and judgment calls will typically lead you to the most accurate assessment of TCO within your organization.

2.14.4 Developing a Windows Server 2003 Test Network Environment

When implementing a new network or computer solution, you should perform a thorough battery of testing before deploying it into production. Although not specific to Windows Server 2003, you should follow a systematic approach to designing a new or upgraded network. This typically includes developing a test environment in which you can test compatibility, usability, connectivity, security settings and more. You'll begin the test process in an isolated lab where new technologies will have no chance of adversely affecting the existing computing environment. After you are satisfied with the new technology's performance in the test lab, you can expand testing into a pilot deployment involving a few actual users, analyzing their input and reactions to make any necessary adjustments to your design. Only after you are satisfied with the pilot deployment should you perform a full-scale deployment in your production environment.

Depending on the total number of users you have, you might want to split your full-scale deployment schedule into stages. After each stage, you can verify that your system is accommodating the increased processing load from the additional users as expected, before you begin deploying the next group of users. The success of any network deployment depends heavily on your ability to develop an effective test environment. This test lab can consist of a single lab or several labs, each of which can test various pieces of the overall design without risking the integrity of your production environment. Working in the test lab will allow you to verify the effectiveness of your design, discover any potential deployment problems, and increase your staff's familiarity with the new technology before it "goes live." In short, a well-developed test environment will reduce the risk of errors during the deployment of a new technology, thus minimizing any potential downtime for your clients and users.

2.14.4.1 Planning the Test Network

Before you begin testing your Windows Server 2003 network design, you need to plan the test network itself. The first step is to determine the hardware resources required to set up the lab. This involves identifying the standard configurations of your existing or new client computers. (If you support diverse workstations, do your best to include a representative workstation from each supported configuration.) Be sure to include all components and peripherals, including the following:

- BIOS versions
- USB adapters
- CD and DVD drives
- Sound cards
- Video cards
- Network adapters
- Smart card readers
- Removable storage devices, such as Zip drives or external hard drives
- Small Computer System Interface (SCSI) adapters
- Removable storage devices
- Mouse or trackball devices
- Keyboards

Although using separate hardware devices for your test lab is the ideal, many small and medium-sized businesses simply cannot afford to buy dozens of computers for the test lab. Using a third-party product such as VMware (www.vmware.com) will allow you to simulate a multiple server/domain environment, as well as multiple desktop operations systems, fairly closely without the expense of multiple individual machines. VMware can run multiple operating systems-such as Microsoft Windows, Linux, and Novell NetWare-simultaneously on a single PC, including all networking and connectivity that you would need to perform your testing.

In addition to purchasing hardware or virtual PC environments for the test lab, you need to secure appropriate licensing for all necessary software, including operating systems, service packs, management utilities, and business applications. Make sure that you can obtain or duplicate the following configuration and information when creating a test lab for Windows Server 2003:

- **Network services:** Install the same services on a test server that will be used in the actual deployment. This can include Domain Name System (DNS), Dynamic Host Configuration Protocol (DHCP), Windows Internet Name Service (WINS), or any other Windows service.
- **User accounts:** Create a domain controller in your test environment to effectively simulate any upgrade procedures.
- **Domain structure:** Simulate the domain hierarchy of your proposed environment, including forests, trees, parent and child domains, and all necessary trust relationships. Configure sites as necessary to simulate any WAN testing considerations.
- **Network protocols and topology:** Re-create the network technologies that will be used in your production environment as completely as possible. For example, if your production environment will be using 100MB cabling, using Gigabit Ethernet will provide erroneous results when doing performance testing. You should also include routers to test for performance latency as well as replication across WAN links.
- **Domain authentication:** Use the appropriate authentication to mimic the desired production environment, including mixed mode versus native mode, and NTLM versus Kerberos client authentication. Selecting the appropriate authentication model will allow you to compare apples to apples during testing and avoid any unexpected behaviour later. Remember that Windows NT 4 workstations or servers cannot use Kerberos authentication. You will need to rely on either NTLM authentication or its stronger successor, NTLM version 2.
- **Group Policy Object (GPO) settings:** Create GPOs with the settings that you wish to deploy in your production environment. You can use the GPMC (discussed earlier) to test the potential behaviour of any policy objects on user and group objects.

  Although you usually want your test lab to mimic your production environment as closely as possible, there are exceptions to every rule. Some tests that you might wish to perform will affect an entire domain or forest, rather than a single machine. If you are testing this type of functionality, you might wish to create a separate domain within the test lab so that the remainder of the lab environment will not be adversely affected. Some of the tests for which you might wish to create a separate, isolated domain or forest are as follows:

- **Switching from mixed mode to native mode:** Changing from mixed mode to native mode will allow for much tighter security in a Windows 2000 or Windows Server 2003 environment, but it assumes that you have no Windows NT 4 backup domain controllers (BDCs) remaining in your domain. (After the switch to native mode, Windows NT 4 BDCs will no longer be able to replicate with Windows 2000 or 2003 domain controllers.) This change will affect an entire domain and cannot be reversed.
- **Upgrading the domain or forest functional level:** This feature was introduced in Windows 2000, where you had the ability to run a domain in mixed mode for backward compatibility or native mode for increased security and functionality. Windows Server 2003 expands on this by creating several levels of both forest and domain functionality that can expose different features

of the operating system for your use. For example, raising the functional level of a domain to Windows Server 2003 native will prevent any existing Windows NT 4 or Windows 2000 Server domain controllers from participating in domain replication. Like the swiich from mixed to native mode, this will affect the entire domain and/or forest in question and cannot be undone.

- **DNS settings:** Changes to a DNS server will affect all clients who use that server for name resolution. Although this does not involve the kinds of one-way changes described above, you should still proceed with caution before making changes that can affect other tests that might be running simultaneously in the lab environment.

One important (but often overlooked) step in the planning process is that of carefully selecting a location for your test lab. Too often, the test lab is relegated to a corner of a server room or what-ever room is available in a file or storage area. However, if you will be performing tests for an extended period of time, you should consider allocating a permanent or semi permanent location for the lab. Be sure to locate the test lab in an area with enough space for all necessary equipment and personnel. If you will be testing network equipment that will be deployed to multiple locations, you should consider deploying a test lab at each site to test WAN links, replication, and site configurations. Also, identify the personnel you'll need to perform testing, as well as whatever training they will need.

Finally, be sure to provide both physical and technological security measures for the equipment and resources of the test lab. This includes isolating the test lab topology from your corporate network using routers, switches, or firewalls, as appropriate. If you need to provide a connection from the test lab to the corporate network, decide in advance how you will control, secure and monitor that connection, and be sure to devise a way to quickly terminate the connection if something unexpected or adverse occurs.

2.14.4.2 Exploring the Group Policy Management Console (GMPC)

A prominent new feature of Windows Server 2003 that is helpful in planning and assessing network changes is the GPMC, which allows administrators to monitor, troubleshoot, and plan Group Policy settings across an entire enterprise from a single management console. Along with a console window that provides a graphical representation of GPO settings, the GPMC also includes a collection of scripts that you can run from the command line to streamline administration and planning tasks. You can download and install the GPMC from Microsoft's Web site. Once it's installed, you'll have a shortcut to it in the Administrative Tools folder, and it will be available as an MMC snap-in.

The scripts that are included with GPMC can greatly simplify your life when you attempt to take stock of an existing network environment (for example, when you begin to plan for an upgrade). Using GPMC, you can quickly perform the following tasks using its automated scripting function:

- List all GPOs that are present in a given domain
- List any disabled GPOs
- List GPOs at a backup location
- List GPOs by policy extension or security group
- List any orphaned GPOs (GPOs that are no longer linked to any AD object) that are still present in the SYSVOL directory

- List GPOs with duplicate names
- List GPOs without security filtering
- List unlinked GPOs in a domain

GPMC's reporting functions will also generate HTML-formatted reports in an easy-to-read format, which is always a hit when you're presenting the upgrade proposal to management or a budget committee. Additionally, the GPMC includes the Resultant Set of Policy Planning function to allow you to simulate changes to GPO settings for a user, computer, or container object. Both of these functions will greatly assist you with the administrative and technical aspects of a network design project.

2.14.4.3 Documenting the Planning and Network Design Process

The importance of documenting your computing environment after you have deployed a new network design such as Windows Server 2003 cannot be overemphasized. As you move through the network design and testing processes, you should also keep detailed documentation of each design, product, or vendor decision that you make, including your reasons for choosing one alternative over another. Personnel changes can occur without warning, and a well-maintained design document will quickly answer the question of "Why did we choose Vendor X over Vendor Y?" when it is posed by the new Vice President of IT, who just started last week. Knowing that Vendor Y's product proved incompatible after several hours of troubleshooting will save you from needing to waste time by repeating portions of the design process.

Because of the effects that ongoing changes can have in a production environment, many organizations use test equipment to test every patch and service pack that is released by their product vendors, so that any potential problems or bugs can be intercepted before the patch is applied globally. Whatever method you use to roll out ongoing updates and changes, you should include detailed documentation, not only of what update was rolled out on a given date, but also of how the change was applied to client machines or other devices on your network.

2.14.4.4 Creating the Planning and Design Document

When documenting both your test lab and your overall network design, there are a number of items that need to be discussed. Although maintaining network documentation is often relegated to a backseat behind the numerous fires that we must put out on a daily basis as network administrators, comprehensive records in this area will actually help you in whatever troubleshooting issues come up after the new network is placed into production. Include configuration information about the following components of your final network design (although a complete list is limited only by the amount of time you have in the day!):

- Windows Server 2003 domain structure information, including DNS hierarchy and replication information, AD hierarchy information (site configuration, forest, domains, and OUs), and GPO settings and where they are applied within the AD hierarchy. Be sure to include information about Enforce and Block Inheritance flags in Group Policy implementation. These affect how GPOs are inherited throughout the AD infrastructure.
- Trust relationships, both transitive and explicitly defined

- Network connectivity hardware (switches, routers, firewalls, and other LAN and WAN connectivity devices)
- Client computer configuration, both hardware and software
- Line-of-business application inventory and configuration
- Backup, restore, and disaster recovery procedures

Windows Server 2003, built upon the same technology as Windows 2000, has been upgraded and improved to address a variety of needs in today's networked environment. We've reviewed the new features in Windows Server 2003 and taken a quick look at some of the tools available to make installing, maintaining and repairing Windows Server 2003 a bit easier. We've also reviewed the basics of network design, planning and testing and we're now ready to jump into the specifics of Windows Server 2003.

2.15 SHARING FILE RESOURCES

Windows Server 2003 supports four kinds of file resource sharing:

- Shared Folders
- Network File System (NFS) Shared Folders
- Active Directory Shared Folders
- Distributed File System (DFS) Folders

2.15.1 Shared Folders

These are essentially the same old shared folders that we've all used and seen since at least Microsoft Windows for Workgroups. In Windows Server 2003 SP1 and later, there is an important change, however. The default share permissions for a folder are read-only for the everyone group. And in Windows Server 2003, the everyone group does not include anonymous users.

2.15.2 NFS Shared Folders

Starting in Windows Server 2003 R2, the Microsoft Services for NFS are an installable component of Windows. Services for NFS include NFS Server and NFS Client, along with the various supporting utilities, including the User Name Mapping Server. The NFS Server component allows you to share folders using the platform-independent NFS protocol. NFS Server supports both NFSv2 and NFSv3 protocols. The default permissions for an NFS share are read-only, with no anonymous access and no root access.

2.15.3 Active Directory Shared Folders

Active Directory Shared Folders are any shared folders that are published in Active Directory. To create an Active Directory Shared Folder, the underlying folder must first be shared on the host machine.

2.15.4 DFS Folders

DFS folders are another way to mask the underlying complexities of the network and file locations to simplify the user's view of file resources.

2.16 SHARE PERMISSIONS VS. FILE PERMISSIONS

Before we explain the details of how to manage and configure shares in Windows Server 2003, let's take a moment to understand how permissions work with shared folders. There are two kinds of permissions involved in any shared folder-those on the actual share, and those imposed by the underlying file system. These permissions are subtractive. This means that only the most restrictive permission will win. Managing permissions on both the share and the file system at the same time can often be quite confusing, and it's difficult to keep track of the details of both. We generally recommend using the underlying NTFS file permissions to control access and setting the share permissions to Full Control for everyone for most normal shares. The NTFS file permissions give much greater granularity and control over exactly what level of access is granted. However, there might be cases when using more restrictive share permission is useful. We suggest, however, that when you do that you indicate in the share name that the share is restricted.

2.16.1 Share Permissions

Shares can be entire volumes or a folder tree. Until a volume or folder is shared over the network, users can't see it or gain access to it. By default, the everyone group is granted read access to all files in the folder, to all subfolders of that folder, and so on, assuming they have sufficient file system permissions. After a volume or folder is shared, restrictions can be added or removed in the form of share permissions. These permissions apply only at the drive or folder level-not at the file level-and are limited to allowing or denying Full Control, Read, and Change, as shown in Table 2.8.

Table 2.8 Types of share permissions

Share Permission	Type of Access
Read	Allows viewing of file and subfolder names, viewing data in files, running programs
Change	Allows the access under Read, plus allows adding files and subdirectories to the shared folder, changing data in files, and deleting files and subdirectories
Full Control	Allows all the access under Change, plus allows changing file permissions (NTFS volumes only) and taking ownership (NTFS volumes only)

Share permissions determine the maximum access allowed over the network. They don't affect a user who logs on locally or a terminal server user of the computer. Share permissions are the only restrictions available for shares on a FAT volume (yet another reason to convert your FAT volumes to NTFS).

2.16.2 File Permissions

File permissions, unlike share permissions, control user access regardless of where it originates. Local users, Terminal Services users, and network users are all treated equally. Because FAT and FAT32 file systems don't support any restriction on access to files, you should always use NTFS file systems to protect sensitive information. NTFS uses access control lists (ACLs) to limit access to resources. NTFS permissions can be assigned to both files and folders, and they apply network-wide and locally.

On an NTFS volume, you can set permissions down to the file level. This means that for any file you can give individual users different types of access. Although you can set such detailed permissions, this way lies madness for all but the most meticulous control freaks (who are, arguably, already mad). Always try to operate with the simplest possible permissions. Set as few restrictions as possible. Assign permissions to groups, not individuals. Don't set file-by-file permissions unless doing so is unavoidable. Managing the minutiae of permissions can easily and quickly soak up all your time and much of your life's blood as well, unless you guard against it.

2.17 NTFS PERMISSIONS

As we noted earlier, the underlying ability to assign enforceable permissions to files and folders is part of the NTFS file system. As you work with files and folders on NTFS, you need to understand how the permissions work and how they are different for a file and for the folder that contains the file.

2.17.1 What Permissions Mean

Windows 2003 Server has a set of standard folder permissions that are combinations of specific kinds of access. The individual permissions are Full Control, Modify, Read & Execute, List Folder Contents, Read, and Write. Each of these permissions consists of a group of special permissions. Table 2.9 shows the special permissions and the standard permissions to which they apply.

Standard file permissions include Full Control, Modify, Read & Execute, Read, and Write. As with folders, each of these permissions controls a group of special permissions. Table 2.10 shows the special permissions associated with each standard permission.

Table 2.9 Special permissions for folders

Special Permission	Full	Modify	Read & Execute	List Folder	Read	Write
		Control			Contents	
Traverse Folder/Execute File	Yes	Yes	Yes	Yes	No	No
List Folder/Read Data	Yes	Yes	Yes	Yes	Yes	No
Read Attributes	Yes	Yes	Yes	Yes	Yes	No
Read Extended Attributes	Yes	Yes	Yes	Yes	Yes	No
Create Files/Write Data	Yes	Yes	No	No	No	Yes
Create Folders/Append Data	Yes	Yes	No	No	No	Yes
Write Attributes	Yes	Yes	No	No	No	Yes
Write Extended Attributes	Yes	Yes	No	No	No	Yes
Delete Subfolders and Files	Yes	No	No	No	No	No
Delete	Yes	Yes	No	No	No	No
Read Permissions	Yes	Yes	Yes	Yes	Yes	Yes
Change Permissions	Yes	No	No	No	No	No
Take Ownership	Yes	No	No	No	No	No
Synchronize	Yes	Yes	Yes	Yes	Yes	Yes

Standard file permissions include Full Control, Modify, Read & Execute, Read, and Write. As with folders, each of these permissions controls a group of special permissions. Table 2.10 shows the special permissions associated with each standard permission.

Table 2.10 Special permissions for files

Special Permission	Full	Modify Control	Read & Execute	Read	Write
Traverse Folder/Execute File	Yes	Yes	Yes	No	No
List Folder/Read Data	Yes	Yes	Yes	Yes	No
Read Attributes	Yes	Yes	Yes	Yes	No
Read Extended Attributes	Yes	Yes	Yes	Yes	No
Create Files/Write Data	Yes	Yes	No	No	Yes
Create Folders/Append Data	Yes	Yes	No	No	Yes
Write Attributes	Yes	Yes	No	No	Yes
Write Extended Attributes	Yes	Yes	No	No	Yes
Delete Subfolders and Files	Yes	No	No	No	No
Delete	Yes	Yes	No	No	No
Read Permissions	Yes	Yes	Yes	Yes	Yes
Change Permissions	Yes	No	No	No	No
Take Ownership	Yes	No	No	No	No

Important any user or group assigned Full Control on a folder can delete files and subfolders no matter what the permissions are on the individual files or subfolders. Any user or group assigned Take Ownership can become the owner of the file or folder and then change permissions and delete files or even entire subfolder trees, no matter what the permissions are before they become the owner.

2.17.2 How Permissions Work

If you take no action at all, the files and folders inside a shared folder have the same permissions as the share. Permissions for both directories and files can be assigned to the following:

- Groups and individual users on this domain
- Global groups, universal groups, and individual users from domains that this domain trusts\
- Special identities, such as Everyone and Authenticated Users

The important rules for permissions can be summarized as follows:

- By default, a folder inherits permissions from its parent folder. Files inherit their permissions from the folder in which they reside.
- Users can access a folder or file only if they were granted permission to do so or they belong to a group that has been granted permission.
- Permissions are cumulative, but the Deny permission trumps all others. For example, if the Technical Writers group has Read access to a folder, the Project group has Modify permission for the same folder, and Alex is a member of both groups, Alex has the higher level of permission, which is Modify. However, if the Technical Writers group permission is changed to explicitly Deny, Alex is unable to use the folder despite his membership-and ostensibly higher level of access-in the Project group.

- The user who creates a file or folder owns the object and can set permissions to control access.
- An administrator can take ownership of any file or folder.
- Members of the Administrators, Backup Operators, and Server Operators groups can take ownership and reassign ownership.

2.17.3 Considering Inheritance

Just to complicate matters a bit more, there are two types of permissions: explicit and inherited. Explicit permissions are the ones you set on files or folders you create. Inherited permissions are those that flow from a parent object to a child object. By default, when you create a file or a subfolder, it inherits the permissions of the parent folder.

If you don't want the child objects to inherit the permissions of the parent, you can block inheritance at the parent level or child level. Where you block inheritance is important. If you block at the parent level, no subfolders will inherit permissions. If you block selectively at the child level, some folders will inherit permissions and others will not. To block a file or folder from inheriting permissions, right-click the folder, select Properties, and then click the Security tab. Click Advanced, and clear the check box for Allow Inheritable Permissions from the Parent to Propagate to This Object and All Child Objects.

If the check boxes for permissions appear shaded, the permissions are inherited from a parent object. If the boxes are shaded and have a check mark (as shown in Figure 2.51), some permissions are inherited and others have been added. There are three ways to change this situation:

- Click Advanced, and clear the check box for Allow Inheritable Permissions from the Parent to Propagate to This Object and All Child Objects. When the check box is cleared, you can make changes to the permissions or change the users or groups in the list.
- Change the permissions of the parent folder.
- Select the opposite permission-Allow or Deny-to override the inherited permission.

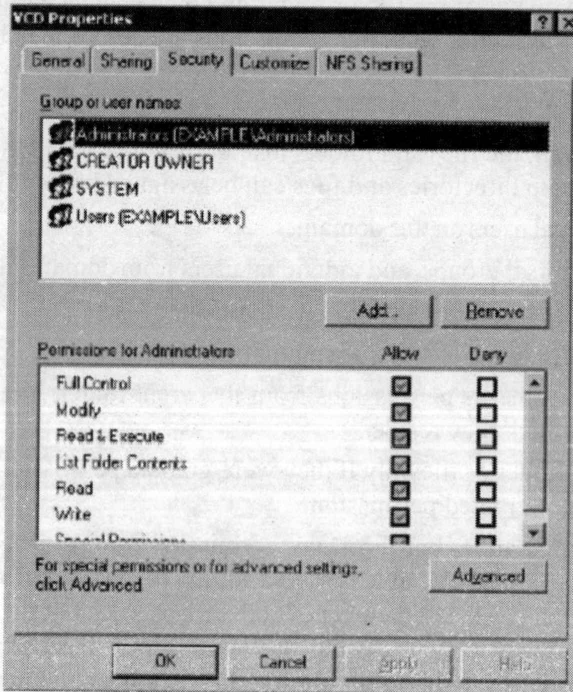

Figure 2.51 A folder with inherited and non-inherited permissions

2.17.4 Configuring Folder Permissions

Before sharing a folder on an NTFS volume, set all the permissions on the folder. When you set folder permissions, you're also setting permissions on all the files and subfolders in the folder. To set the permissions on the folder, perform one or more of the following actions:

- To assign permissions to a folder, right-click the folder in Explorer and choose Properties from the shortcut menu. Then click the Security tab.
- To remove an individual or group from the list, just select the name and click Remove.
- To add a user or group to the list of those with permissions, click Add. This opens the Select Users, Computers, Or Groups dialog box. Optionally, click Advanced to perform a more sophisticated search, as shown in Figure 2.52. Click OK when you're done.

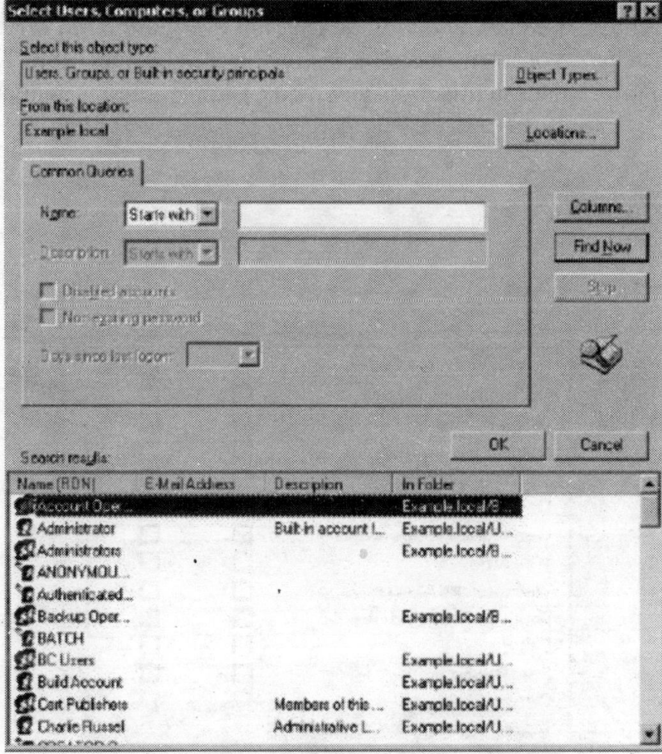

Figure 2.52 Selecting users and groups

2.17.5 Assigning Permissions to Files

Permissions for individual files are assigned in the same way as permissions for folders. There are, however, some special considerations:

- Remember to grant permissions to groups rather than to individuals.
- Create domain-based groups, and assign file permissions to them rather than assigning permissions directly to local groups.

2.17.6 Configuring Special Permissions

In some circumstances, you might find it necessary to set, change, or remove special permissions on either a file or folder. To access special permissions, follow these steps:

1. Right-click the file or folder, and choose Properties from the shortcut menu. For this example, we're working on a folder named VCD, which will appear in the various steps and screen shots. Your folder name will be different.
2. Click the Security tab, and then click Advanced.
   - To add a user or group, click Add. Double-click the user or group name to open the Permission Entry dialog box.
   - To view or modify existing special permissions, select the name of the user or group and click Edit.
   - To remove special permissions, select the name of the user or group and click Remove. If the Remove button is dimmed, clear the check box for Allow Inheritable Permissions from Parent to Propagate to This Object, and skip to step 6.
3. In the Permission Entry for VCD dialog box shown in Figure 2.53, select from the Apply Onto drop-down list where you want the permissions applied. (See Table 2.11 and Table 2.12 for explanations of the choices in this drop-down box.) Apply Onto is available for folders only.

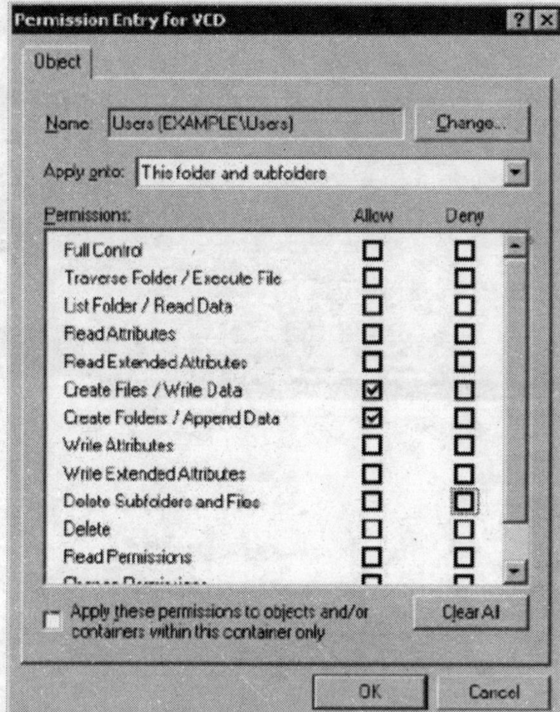

Figure 2.53 Setting special permissions for a folder

4. In Permissions, select Allow or Deny for each permission.
5. To prevent subfolders and files from inheriting these permissions, select Apply These Permissions to Objects and/or Containers within This Container Only.
6. Click OK to close the dialog box.

In the Permission Entry for VCD dialog box for folders, you can choose how and where the special permissions are applied. Table 2.11 and Table 2.12 demonstrate the application of the special permissions depending on whether Apply These Permissions to Objects and/or Containers within This Container Only is selected.

Table 2.11 Application of special permissions when Apply These Permissions To Objects And/Or Containers Within This Container Only is selected

Selected in Apply Onto	Applies to Current Folder?	Applies to Subfolders in Current Folder?	Applies to Files in Current Folder?	Applies to Subsequent Subfolders?	Applies to Files in Subsequent Subfolders?
This folder only	Yes	No	No	No	No
This folder, subfolders, and files	Yes	Yes	Yes	No	No
This folder and subfolders	Yes	Yes	No	No	No
This folder and files	Yes	No	Yes	No	No
Subfolders and files only	No	Yes	Yes	No	No
Subfolders only	No	Yes	No	No	No
Files only	No	No	Yes	No	No

Table 2.12 Application of special permissions when Apply These Permissions To

Selected in Apply Onto	Applies to Current Folder?	Applies to Subfolders in Current Folder?	Applies to Files in Current Folder?	Applies to Subsequent Subfolders?	Applies to Files in Subsequent Subfolders?
This folder only	Yes	No	No	No	No
This folder, subfolders, and files	Yes	Yes	Yes	Yes	Yes
This folder and subfolders	Yes	Yes	No	Yes	No
This folder and files	Yes	No	Yes	No	Yes
Subfolders and files only	No	Yes	Yes	Yes	Yes
Subfolders only	No	Yes	No	Yes	No
Files only	No	No	Yes	No	Yes

Objects And/Or Containers Within This Container Only is not selected

2.17.7 Ownership and how it Works

As you've seen, Administrators and members of a few other select groups are the only ones who can grant and change permissions. The exception is when a user is the owner of the folder or file in question. Every object on an NTFS partition has an owner, and the owner is the person who created the file or folder. The owner controls access to the file or folder and can keep out anyone he or she chooses.

Here's how it works. Let's say a user named Maxwell creates a folder on his computer named Max's Private Stuff. To check the settings on his new folder, Maxwell right-clicks the folder, chooses Properties, and then clicks the Security tab. (See Figure 2.54.)

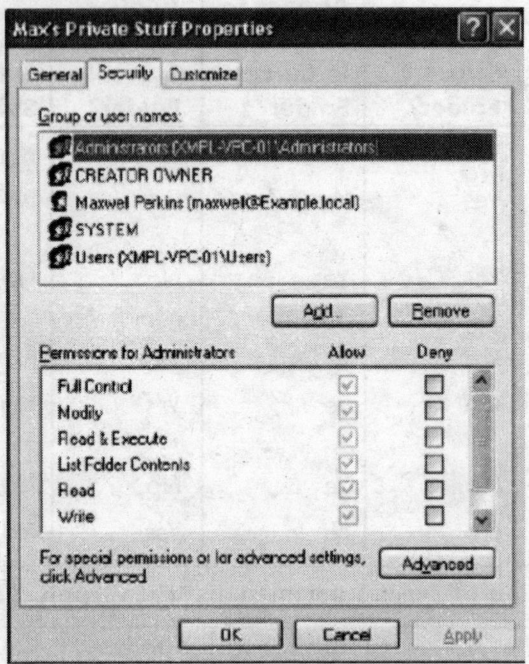

Figure 2.54 Viewing the NTFS permissions for a new folder

He sees that the Administrators group has full access to his folder, but because Maxwell is the owner of the folder, he can change the permissions so that he has the folder all to himself. To do so, he clicks Advanced to open the Advanced Security Settings dialog box and clears the Inherit from Parent option. (See Figure 2.55.)

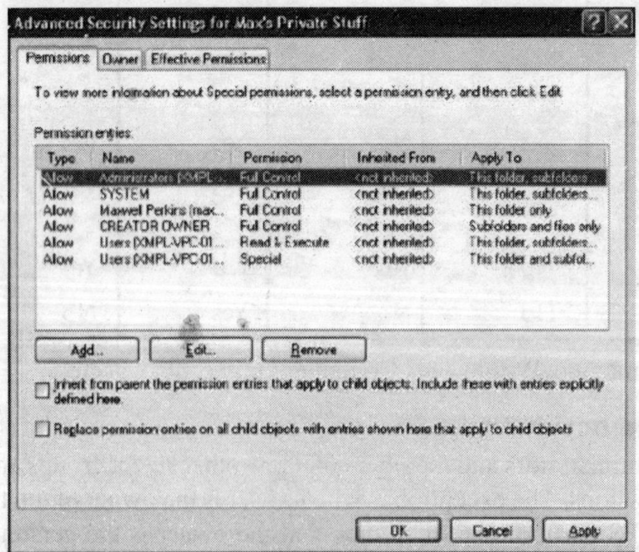

Figure 2.55 Removing inheritances from a permission entry

Maxwell gets a security warning, and he can choose to either copy the current (inherited) permissions to the folder, making them explicit, or remove all permissions from the folder. He clicks Copy and returns to the Security Properties dialog box, where he then highlights the Administrators group, and clicks Remove. After this is done, even the administrator sees an Access Denied message when trying to open the folder.

Of course, nothing on the network can be completely beyond the reach of administrators, so an administrator cans right-click the folder and choose Properties from the shortcut menu. When the administrator clicks the Security tab, the information box shown in Figure 2.56 opens.

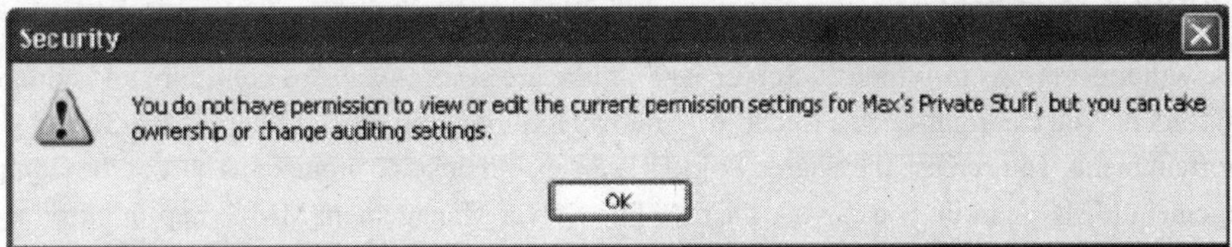

Figure 2.56 The administrator tries to view permissions for a folder owned by a user

In the Security Properties dialog box, no changes can be made. However, if the administrator clicks Advanced and then clicks the Owner tab (shown in Figure 2.57), he or she can change the owner of the folder to an administrator.

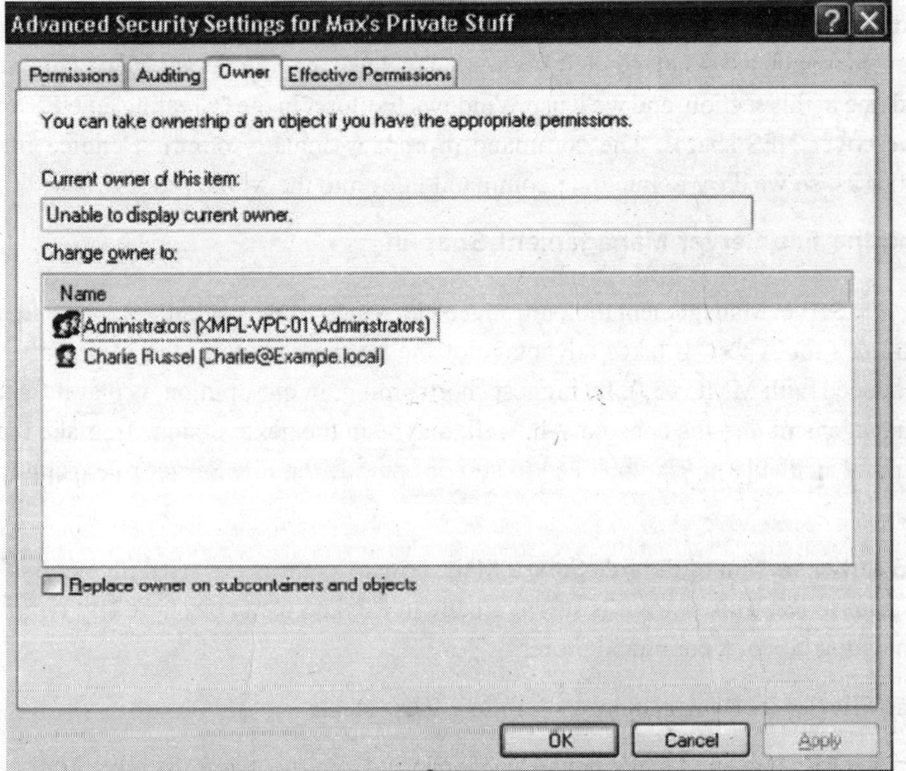

Figure 2.57 Changing the ownership of a folder

Regardless of the status of the folder, the administrator can take ownership. When Maxwell logs on the next time, he still has access to Max's Private Stuff, but when he clicks Advanced and then Owner, he sees that he's no longer the owner of the folder. Changing the ownership of the folder doesn't automatically give Administrators access to the contents of the folder, but ownership does grant the ability to read and change permissions. With that, an administrator can change permissions and attain access to the folder contents.

Note: The owner of a file or folder can also grant the Take Ownership special permission to others, allowing those users to take ownership at any time.

2.18 SHARED FOLDERS

As with most things in Windows Server 2003, there are several ways to configure and administer shared folders. You can right-click a folder in Windows Explorer and choose Sharing and Security from the shortcut menu; you can use the Shared Folders snap-in, either stand alone or as part of the Computer Management MMC snap-in; you can use the new File Server Management MMC snap-in introduced in R2; or you can use the command line.

Each approach has its advantages, but we recommend that you use the command line when you want to quickly create or modify a share, or that you use the File Server Management MMC snap-in when you want access to more management functions in a single place. The File Server Management snap-in not only gives you a place to create and manage shared folders, it provides quick access to the Disk Defragmenter and Disk Management snap-ins. We'll use the File Server Management snap-in and the command line in this section, and we'll use Windows Explorer in the "Creating an NFS Share" section and when we cover NFS shares. The command prompt is actually our first choice for most share management tasks, so we'll try to integrate command lines into the whole process.

2.18.1 Using the File Server Management Snap-in

The new File Server Management tool, introduced in Windows Server 2003 R2 is a useful addition to the administrator's tool chest. It takes advantage of the improvements in the Microsoft Management Console introduced with MMC v3.0. Its biggest shortcoming, in our opinion, is that it fails to integrate NFS share management into the console. Ah, well, maybe in the next version. To make the File Server Management tool available in R2, you need to add or upgrade the File Server role using Manage Your Server.

Note: An earlier version of the File Server Management snap-in was used in versions of Windows Server 2003 prior to R2. This snap-in is still available in R2, and it can be started by typing filesvr.msc from the Run dialog box or a command prompt.

To use the File Server Management tool, follow these steps:

1. Open the File Server Management MMC snap-in from the Administrative Tools folder on the Start menu, or type fs.msc in the Run dialog box or at a command prompt to open the File Server Management console shown in Figure 2.58.

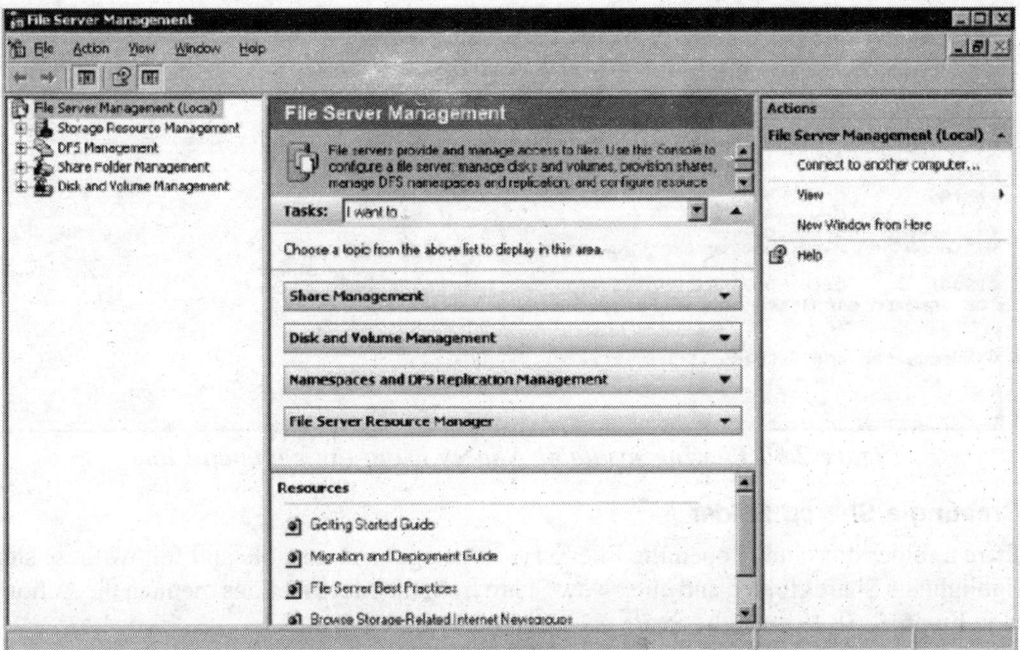

Figure 2.58 The File Server Management console in Windows Server 2003 R2

2. Expand Share Folder Management, and expand Shared Folders in the tree pane.
3. Use the Shares, Sessions, and Open Files folders to view the current file shares on the system you're managing and to see how much activity the shares are getting, as shown in Figure 2.59.

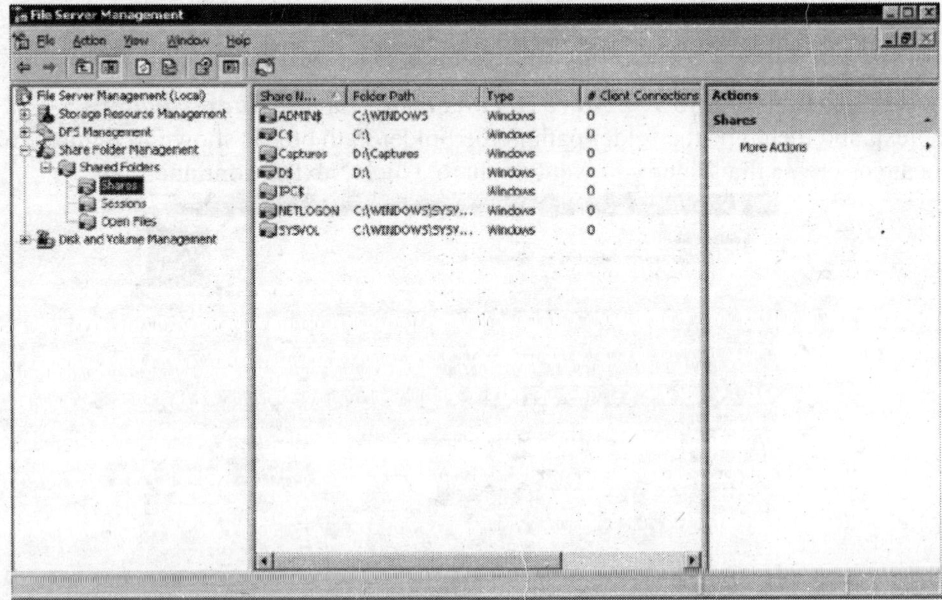

Figure 2.59 Viewing available Shares in the File Server Management console

4. To see the same information from the command line, open a command window and type the following command, as shown in Figure 2.60: net share.

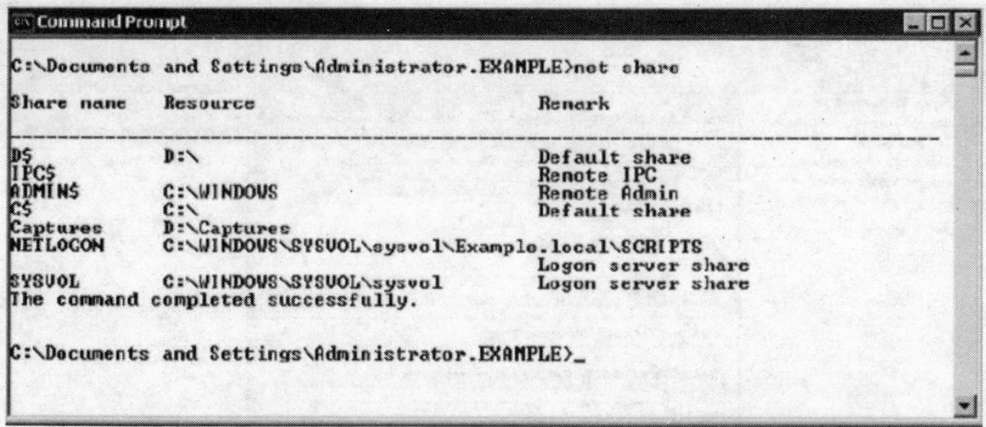

Figure 2.60 Viewing available Shares using the command line

2.18.2 Creating a Shared Folder

To share a folder or volume, open the File Server Management console and follow these steps:

1. Highlight the Shares folder, and click New Share from the More Actions menu in the Actions pane, as shown in Figure 2.61, to open the Share A Folder Wizard.

Figure 2.61 The More Actions menu for the Shares folder

2. Click Next, and then type the folder path in the Folder Path box as shown in Figure 2.62, or click Browse to locate or create the folder you want to share. Click Next to continue.

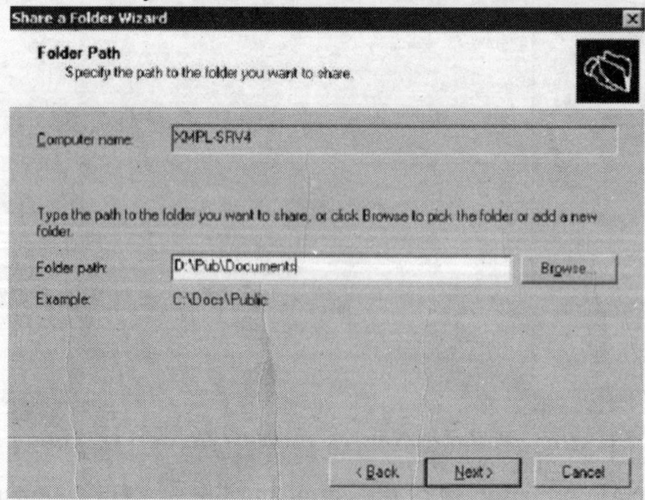

Figure 2.62 The Share A Folder Wizard

3. Type the name you want to give the file share. For the best interoperability with earlier versions of Windows and non-Microsoft clients, choose a name that is both DNS and NetBIOS compatible.
4. Type a description for the shared folder in the Share Description box.
5. Optionally, click Change to control whether clients should use the offline files feature with the shared folder, and then click Next.
6. Specify the Share Level permissions for the folder, and then click Finish. (You can also set NTFS permissions here by choosing the Use Custom Share And Folder Permissions option and clicking Customize.)
7. To create the same share from the command line, open a command window and type

net share Docs=D:\Pub\Documents /grant:Everyone, Full

/Remark:"Generally available documents" /cache:documents

as shown in Figure 2.63.

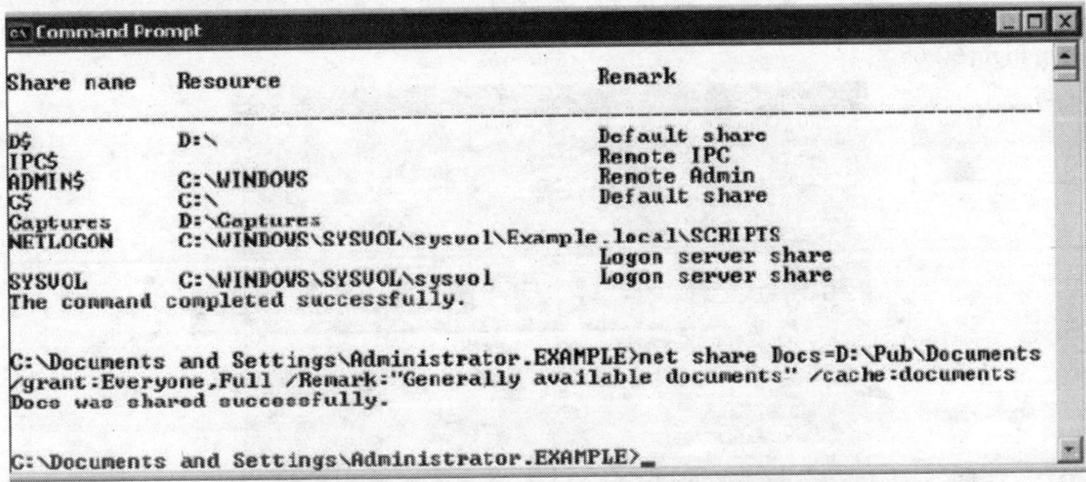

Figure 2.63 Creating a share from the command line

2.18.3 Removing a Folder Share

It's easy to stop sharing a folder without removing the underlying folder or files. From the File Server Management console, highlight the share, right-click, select Stop Sharing, and click Yes to confirm. Or, from the command line type

net share <sharename> /delete

From the command line, you won't even get prompted to confirm. Use caution when you remove a share. It will disconnect any open files that users might be using and potentially cause loss of data.

2.18.4 Disconnecting Users

If you need to disconnect users from the server for some reason-say, to close off the server while you update the files follow these steps:

1. Open the File Server Management console, and then open the Sessions subfolder.
2. Right-click the user you want to disconnect, and click Close Session from the short-cut menu.
3. To disconnect all sessions, click Disconnect All Sessions.
4. To close an open file, click the Open Files folder, select the file you want to close, and then click Close Open File.

5. To close all open files, click Disconnect All Open Files.
6. To close sessions from the command line, type net session /delete.
7. To see what files are open on the network prior to closing a session, type net file.

Important be kind to your users and warn them before disconnecting them. Disconnecting a user who is working on a file can cause data loss and ill feelings (and Help desk calls).

2.18.5 Limiting Simultaneous Connections

You can limit the number of simultaneous user connections you want to allow to a shared folder so that a given shared folder doesn't overburden the server with user connections. To do so, follow these steps:

1. Open the File Server Management console, and then open the Shares subfolder.
2. Right-click the shared folder you want to limit access to, and then choose Properties from the shortcut menu.
3. To place no limit on the number of connections you allow to the shared folder (other than the limit set by the number of licenses you have), select the Maximum Allowed option in the General tab, as shown in Figure 2.65.

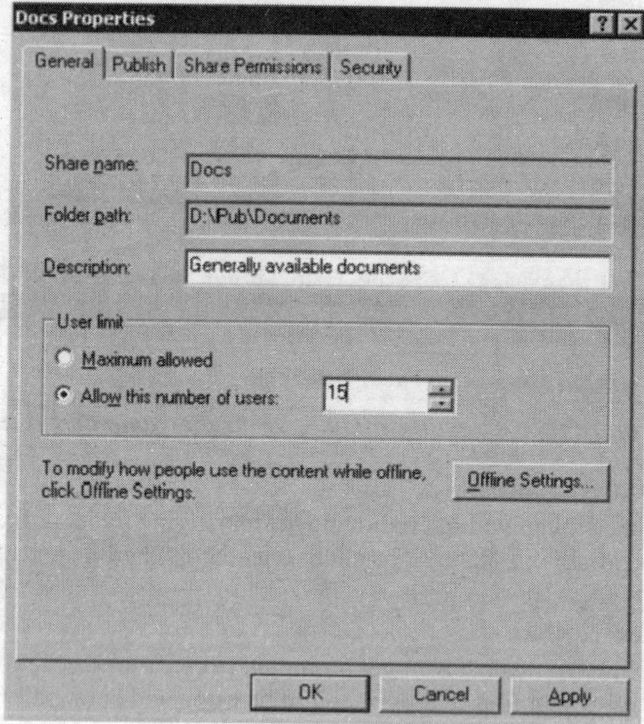

Figure 2.65 The General tab of a shared folder's Properties dialog box

4. To manually limit the number of connections you want to allow to the shared folder, type the maximum number of connections you want to allow in the Allow This Number of Users box and then click OK.
5. To do this from the command line, type net share /users:<number>.

2.18.6 Special Shares

In addition to shares created by a user or administrator, the system creates a number of special shares that shouldn't be modified or deleted. These include the administrative shares: the ADMIN$ share, and the hidden shares for each hard drive volume (C$, D$, E$, and so on). These shares allow administrators to connect to drives that are otherwise not shared. These shares are not visible by default and can be connected to only by an administrator.

Special shares exist as part of the operating system's installation. Depending on the computer's configuration, some or all of the following special shares might be present (and none of them should be modified or deleted):

- **ADMIN$:** Used during the remote administration of a computer. The path is always the location of the folder in which Windows was installed (that is, the system root). Only Administrators, Backup Operators, and Server Operators can connect to this share.
- **driveletter$:** The root folder of the named drive. Only Administrators, Backup Operators, and Server Operators can connect to these shares on Windows 2003 Server or a Windows 2000 server. On Microsoft Windows XP Professional and Windows 2000 Professional computers, only Administrators and Backup Operators can connect to these shares.
- **IPC$:** Used during remote administration and when viewing shared resources.This share is essential to communication and can't be deleted.
- **NETLOGON:** Essential to all domain controllers. Do not remove.
- **SYSVOL:** Required on all domain controllers. Do not remove.
- **PRINT$:** A resource that supports shared printers.

To connect to an unshared drive on another computer, you need to be logged on using an account with the necessary rights. Use the address bar in any window and type the address using the syntax \\computer_name\[driveletter]$

To connect to the system root folder (the folder in which Windows is installed) on another computer, use the syntax \\computer_name\admin$

Figure 2.66 shows a connection made to the Windows directory on a client machine (xmpl-vpc-01) using the special share admin$. Other special shares such as IPC$ and PRINT$ are created and used solely by the system.

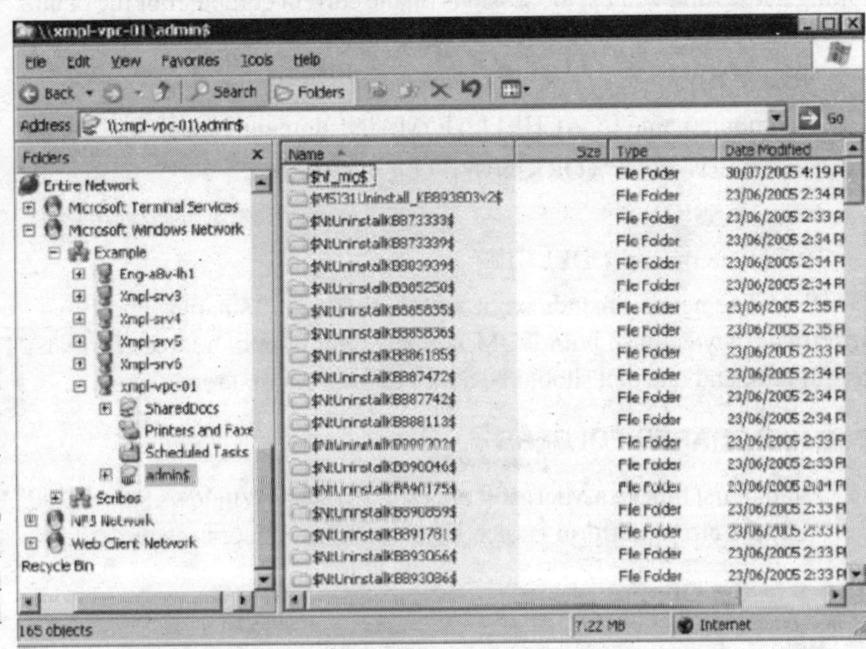

Figure 2.66 Connecting to an administrative share on a remote computer

NETLOGON is a special share on Windows Server 2003, Windows 2000, and Windows NT servers and is used while processing domain logon requests.

Note Adding a dollar sign ($) to the end of a share name hides the share from all users. To access a hidden share, you need to specify it explicitly; you can't browse the network for the share.

2.18.7 The Command Line-net Share

As we've seen throughout this chapter so far, it's easy to create and manage shares at the command line by using the net share command. The syntax of the net share command is

NET SHARE

sharename

sharename=drive:path [/GRANT:user,[READ | CHANGE | FULL]]

[/USERS:number | /UNLIMITED]

[/REMARK:"text"]

[/CACHE:Manual | Documents| Programs | None]

sharename [/USERS:number | /UNLIMITED]

[/REMARK:"text"]

[/CACHE:Manual | Documents | Programs | None]

{sharename | devicename | drive:path} /DELETE

Simply typing net share at the command line with no parameters will give you a list of currently shared folders. Typing net share <sharename> will give you the parameters in effect for the sharename. Two other useful net commands for dealing with shares are net view and net session. Typing net view will give you a list of computers on the network or the resources available on a particular computer, while typing net session will list the sessions on the current computer or the details of a session with a particular computer. The syntax for these two net commands are

NET VIEW

[\\computername [/CACHE] | /DOMAIN[:domainname]]

NET VIEW /NETWORK:NW [\\computername]

NET SESSION

[\\computername] [/DELETE]

Note The net commands work with both NetBIOS names and IP addresses, and where the user is specified, they can use both DOMAIN\User and e-mail address formats. This makes it a flexible and useful tool, and one that should be a part of your normal repertoire.

2.19 NFS SHARED FOLDERS

For the first time in a Microsoft operating system, Windows Server 2003 R2 includes built-in support for NFS, the cross-platform choice for sharing of network resources.

2.19.1 Initial Configuration

Before you can use Microsoft Server for NFS to share folders to NFS clients, you'll need to make several configuration changes on your server. You'll need to set up and specify a User Name Mapping server and open some ports on Windows Firewall if you're using it, at a minimum. Well, actually, you can go ahead and share folders without doing any of that, but no one will be able to use them. The graphical tool for configuring and administering NFS is the %windir%\msnfs\nfsmgmt.msc, and the command-line tool is %windir%\msnfs\nfsadmin.exe.

2.19.1.1 Specify a User Name Mapping Server

Windows Server 2003 supports direct mapping of UNIX user ID (UID) and group ID (GID) in Active Directory using RFC 2307, as well as the User Name Mapping service. You can specify the User Name Mapping server to use from the command line:

nfsadmin mapping mapsvr=<servername> To specify the User Name Mapping server graphically, open the MS NFS Administration console and follow these steps:

1. Right-click MSNFS Administration and select Properties, as shown in Figure 2.67.

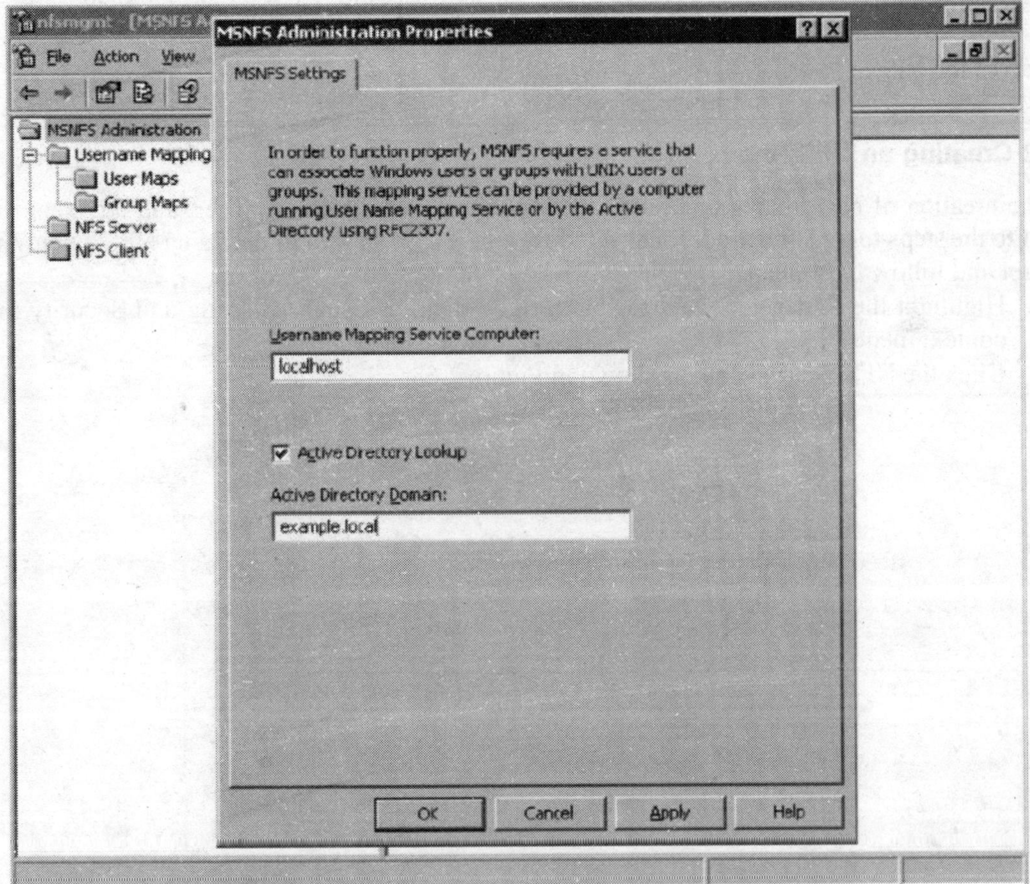

Figure 2.67 Using MSNFS Administration to specify the User Name Mapping server

2. Enter the name or IP address of the User Name Mapping server.
3. Optionally, select Active Directory Lookup and specify the Active Directory Domain to use.

2.19.1.2 Windows Firewall Configuration

To share folders using NFS on a computer that is protected by Windows Firewall, you must create port exceptions in the firewall. There is no automatic way to configure these exceptions, unfortunately. The ports that need to be opened for NFS are shown in Table 2.13.

Table 2.13 Open ports for NFS

NFS Component	Port to Open	Protocols Used	Port Number
Username Mapping Server and Server for NFS	Portmapper	TCP, UDP	111
Server for NFS	Network Status Manager	TCP, UDP	1039
Server for NFS	Nlockmgr (file locking manager)	TCP, UDP	1047
Server for NFS	Mountd (mounting daemon)	TCP, UDP	1048
Server for NFS	Server for NFS	TCP, UDP	2049

2.19.2 Creating an NFS Share

The creation of NFS shares is directly integrated into Windows Explorer, and the steps are very similar to the steps for creating traditional Windows shares. To share a folder using NFS, open Windows Explorer and follow these steps:

1. Highlight the folder you want to share, right-click, and select Sharing and Security from the context menu.
2. Click the NFS Sharing Tab, as shown in Figure 2.68.

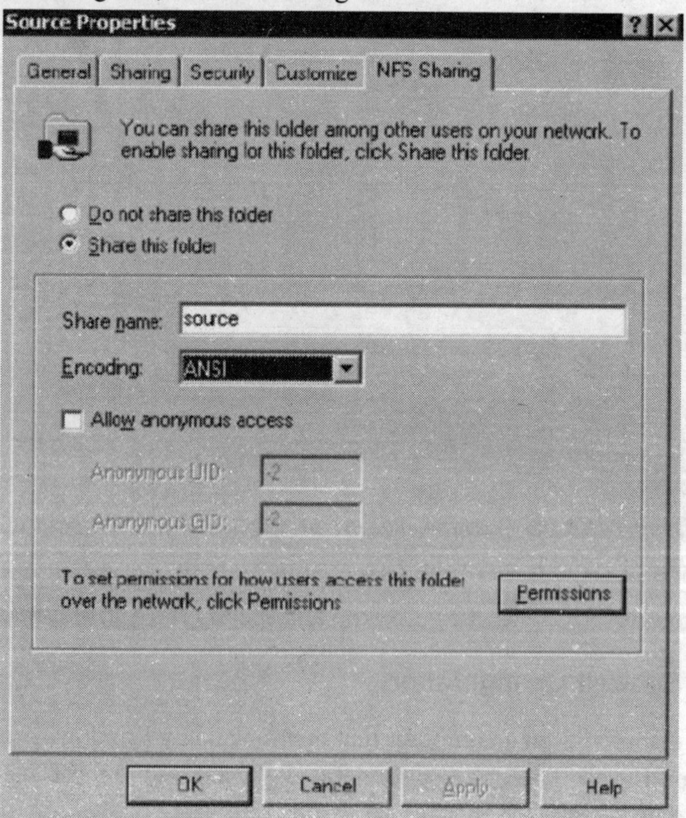

Figure 2.68 Creating the NFS Share from Windows Explorer

3. Click Share This Folder, and type in a share name to use for the folder.
4. Optionally, change the encoding used. The default is ANSI, which is appropriate for most situations.
5. Select Allow Anonymous Access if you want to allow unauthenticated users to access the share.
6. Click the Permissions button to set the share permissions on the new share, as shown in Figure 2.69.

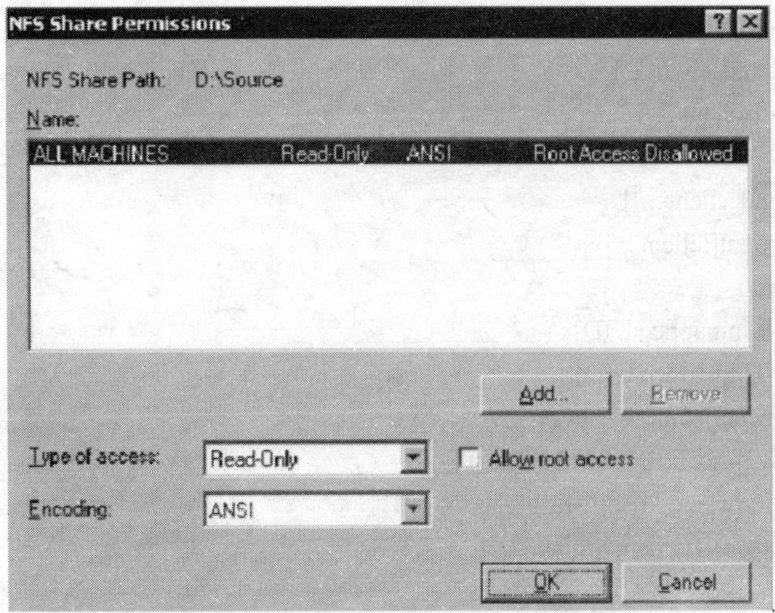

Figure 2.69 Setting share permissions

7. You can specify different permissions for each machine that accesses the share, or you can specify by groups of machines. The default permissions are Read-Only for all machines, with no root access.
8. Click your way out of the dialog boxes.
9. To configure the same share from the command line, open a command window and type nfsshare source=d:\Source -o ro -o noroot -o anon=yes as shown in Figure 2.70.

Figure 2.70 Creating an NFS share from the command line

2.19.3 Deleting or Modifying an NFS Share

Deleting or modifying an existing NFS share is essentially the same process as creating it in the first place. Open Windows Explorer, highlight the shared folder, and select Sharing and Security from the context menu. Make your changes on the NFS Sharing tab, and click OK the necessary number of times. You're done. Existing connections will not see the changes until the next time they connect to the share. The command line process is also the same. The full syntax of the nfsshare.exe command is

```
nfsshare
    sharename = drive:path
    [-o ro[=client[:client ...]]
    rw[=client[:client ...]]
    na
    root[=client[:client ...]]
    noroot[=client[:client ...]]
    anon=yes|no
    anonuid=[Unmapped UID]
    anongid=[Unmapped GID]
    encoding=euc-jp|euc-tw|euc-kr|
    shift-jis|big5|ksc5601|gb2312-80|ansi ]
    {euc-jp|euc-tw|euc-kr|shift-jis|big5|ksc5601
    |gb2312-80|ansi}=client1[:client2...]
sharename
    [-o ro[=client[:client ...]]
    rw[=client[:client ...]]
    na
    root[=client[:client ...]]
    noroot[=client[:client ...]]
    anon=yes|no
    anonuid=[Unmapped UID]
    anongid=[Unmapped GID]
    encoding={euc-jp|euc-tw|euc-kr|
    shift-jis|big5|ksc5601|gb2312-80|ansi} ]
    {euc-jp|euc-tw|euc-kr|shift-jis|big5|ksc5601
    |gb2312-80|ansi}=client1[:client2...]
    rem     oveclient=client[:client ...]
{sharename | drive:path} /delete
```

2.20 PUBLISHING SHARES IN ACTIVE DIRECTORY

You can publish relatively permanent file shares in Active Directory, making them easier for users to find in a large network. To do so, use the following steps:

1. Open the File Server Management console and then select Shares.
2. Right-click the shared folder for which you want to set permissions, and then choose Properties from the shortcut menu.
3. Click the Publish tab and then select the Publish This Share in Active Directory check box. (See Figure 2.71.)

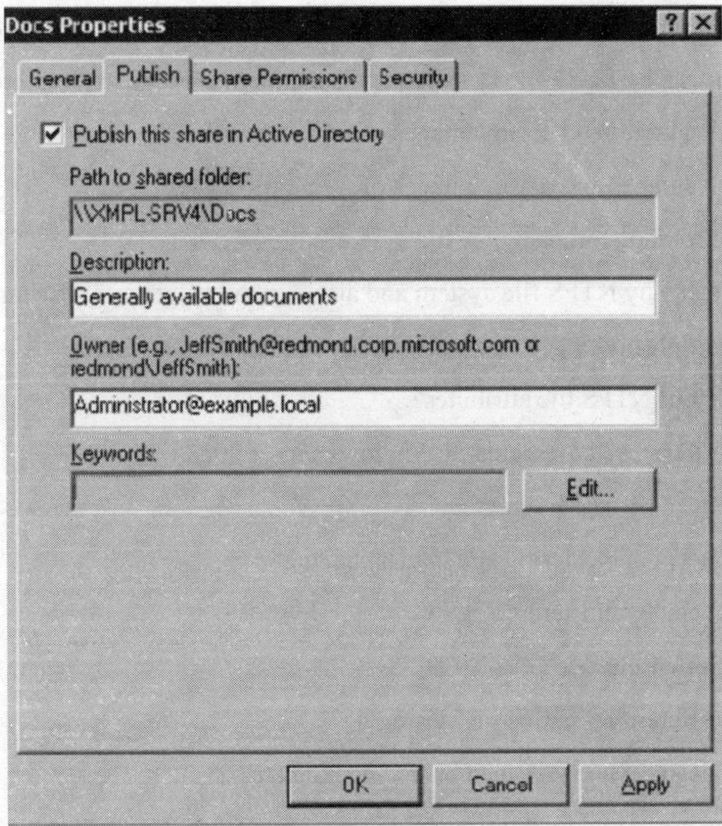

Figure 2.71 Publishing a share in Active Directory

4. In the Description box, type a description for the file share.
5. Type the e-mail address of the person responsible for the file share in the Owner box. (That would probably be you.) Click Edit, add any keywords relevant to the share, and then click OK.

EXERCISES

1. What do you mean by network operating system?
2. Explain the concept of Window server 2003?
3. Write down the new features of Window server 2003?
4. Explain the Windows server 2003 family?
5. Explain the general architecture of windows server 2003?

6. Explain the Shell system of windows server 2003?
7. What do you mean by kernel? Also explain the basic facilities of kernel.
8. Explain the various design approaches of kernel?
9. Explain in detail File system of windows server 2003?
10. What do you mean by Fat16 file system and also explain its general structure?
11. What do you mean by Fat32 file system and also explain its general structure?
12. Explain the advantages and disadvantages of fat16 file system?
13. Explain the advantages and disadvantages of fat 32 file system?
14. Explain the concept of compact disk file system?
15. What do you mean by NTFS file system and also explain its general structure?
16. Explain the multiple booting systems of Windows NT and windows 2000?
17. Explain the various NTFS file attributes?
18. Explain the hardware requirements of Windows server 2003?
19. What do you mean by active directory?
20. Explain the concept of clustering and load balancing?
21. What do you mean by cluster?
22. Why we use Server clusters?
23. What are the different scenarios of Cluster?
24. Explain the concept of network load balancing clusters?
25. Write down the procedure to choosing an NLB cluster model?
26. How can we create an NLB cluster?
27. How we can Plan the capacity of an NLB cluster?
28. How we can configure a server cluster?
29. Explain the various file sharing resources?
30. Differentiate between Share permissions and File permissions?
31. What are NTFS permissions?
32. Explain the configuring special permissions?
33. Explain how we can use permissions?
34. What are shared folders?

35. Explain in detail NFS shared folders?
36. How we can publish shares in active directory?
37. Explain the storage management of windows server 2003?
38. Explain the disk management of windows server 2003?
39. Explain the concept of fault tolerance in storage management?
40. Explain the basic and dynamic disks in detail?
41. Differentiate between basic and dynamic disks?
42. How we can configure disks and volumes?
43. Explain the comparison between FAT, FAT32, and NTFS?
44. Explain the various editors available in windows server 2003?
45. Explain the various features of networking and communication in windows server 2003?
46. Explain the concept of licensing?
47. Explain in detail windows server 2003 planning tools and documentation?
48. How we can develop a windows server 2003 test network environment?

CHAPTER 3

Disk Management

3.1 INTRODUCTION

Disk management is an important aspect of optimizing and maintaining any server and Windows Server 2003 includes a variety of tools that the administrator can use to format, partition, organize, and optimize disks. In this chapter, we take a look at how the operating system enables you to interface with the physical and logical disks in your machine, and how you can optimize disk performance to increase the overall performance of your server.

Like Windows 2000, Server 2003 supports two disk types: basic and dynamic. Upgrading your disks to dynamic status enables you to take advantage of the operating system's software RAID support, so that you can create fault-tolerant volumes. A regular schedule of defragmentation is another way you can enhance disk performance, and in this chapter, we will show you how to use both the graphical interface and the command-line tool to defragment your disks and perform other disk management tasks. You will also learn to configure disk quotas for better management of disk space on the file server, and we show you how to use the Remote Storage feature to manage volumes. Finally, we will discuss basic troubleshooting techniques for tracking down problems with disks and volumes.

3.2 TERMINOLOGY AND CONCEPTS

It is important for you to know the correct terminology relating to the various disk components in Windows Server 2003. There are two primary components to understand: physical disks and logical disks. Physical disks can be either basic or dynamic. Logically, they can be separated into either partitions or volumes. This section explains when and how each of these is used.

3.2.1 Physical VS Logical Disks

You must be able to distinguish between a physical disk and a logical disk. Physical refers to the actual, tangible hard disk itself. A physical disk is a piece of hardware, which can be organized into logical disks. A physical disk by itself is of no use to Windows. It is not until you format the physical disk and create a logical disk that it becomes a resource that is accessible from within Windows. Logical disks enable you to customize your physical disks to best fit your needs. Depending on the disk type used (basic or dynamic), logical disks consist of either partitions or volumes. These are units made up of all or part of one or more disks. Partitions are divisions of a single disk. Volumes can span multiple physical disks. Conversely, a single physical disk can contain multiple logical disks. The following illustrate a couple of real-world examples:

1. You have three physical disks installed in your server, each of which contains 30GB of disk space. However, you don't want to use them as three separate disks. In other words, you do not want the operating system to "see" these disks as a C drive, a D drive, and an E drive. Instead, you want to access all the space contained in the three disks as if it belonged to one 90GB physical disk. To accomplish this, you can create a spanned volume (covered later in this chapter) and combine all three physical disks into one logical disk. You can now access all the storage via one drive letter (e.g., D:).
2. Maybe you have the opposite scenario. You have one large 100 GB physical disk, but you don't want one large C: drive. You can create two or more partitions or logical drives to divide up the space. You can assign a separate drive letter for each logical disk and access the single physical disk as if it were multiple smaller physical disks.

3.2.2 Basic VS Dynamic Disks

Windows Server 2003 supports two types of physical disk configurations

1. Basic disks
2. Dynamic disks

By default, disks are initially configured as basic. Basic disks use the same disk structure used in Windows NT 4.0 and previous operating systems, all the way back to MS-DOS. That is, they are divided into primary and extended partitions, and logical drives can be created within extended partitions.

Dynamic disks use a new disk structure that was introduced in Windows 2000.The basic unit of a dynamic disk is the volume (rather than the partition). Dynamic disks support features that you don't get with basic disks and give you much more fiexibility in structuring your storage space. With dynamic disks, you can extend simple volumes (make them bigger without reformatting and losing data) to any empty space on any dynamic disk, create spanned volumes across multiple physical disks and create fault tolerant (RAID 1 and 5) volumes.

A single computer can contain both basic and dynamic disks. Each physical disk installed in the computer is separately identi?ed as either basic or dynamic. Basic disks and dynamic disks both support the same file systems (FAT16, FAT32, and NTFS). Basic disks can be upgraded to dynamic status at any time without losing data. You do not even have to reboot after upgrading to dynamic unless you are upgrading the system disk or the disk being upgraded is currently in use. As mentioned, basic disks are made up of partitions and logical drives. Basic disks do not support creating volume sets or fault-tolerant volumes. MS-DOS and all versions of Windows can use basic disks.

Although dynamic disks (unlike basic disks) support creating volumes that span multiple disks and creating fault-tolerant volumes, dynamic disks are not always the best solution. The following are some limitations of using dynamic disks:

- Dynamic disks are currently not supported on laptop computers.
- Removable media and disks attached via FireWire (IEEE 1394), Universal Serial Bus (USB), or shared SCSI buses cannot be converted to dynamic.
- You can install Windows Server 2003 only onto a dynamic volume that was converted from a basic boot or system partition. You cannot install onto a dynamic volume that was created from free space. This is because there must be an entry in the partition table for the setup program to recognize the volume, and such an entry does not exist on a newly created dynamic volume.
- Even though Windows 2000, XP Pro, and Server 2003 all use dynamic disks, you cannot convert a basic disk that holds multiple instances of these operating systems to dynamic. The operating systems installed on the disk will not start if you do this.
- Dynamic disks are not supported by Windows Cluster Service. If you need the features of dynamic disks on a clustered shared disk, you can use a third-party program called Veritas Volume Manager 4.0 to accomplish this.

3.2.3 Booting your Disk

Two disk sectors are vital to starting your computer, the master boot record (MBR) and the boot sector. The MBR is created when a disk is initially partitioned. The boot sector is created when a partition (or volume) is formatted. The MBR is located in the first sector on the physical hard disk. It contains the master boot code, the partition table, and the disk signature for the physical disk. The master boot code is responsible for booting the machine. The partition table identifies the type and location of partitions on the physical disk. The disk signature identifies the physical disk to the operating system. The MBR performs the following operations when a disk boots:

1. It scans the partition table (or disk configuration database) for an active partition.
2. It finds the starting sector for the active partition.
3. It loads a copy of the boot sector of the active partition into memory.
4. It passes control to the boot sector.

There is a boot sector for each partition on your physical disk. The boot sector (like the MBR) contains code that is required to boot. Among other things, it also contains information required by the file system to access the partition or volume. The boot sector loads NTLDR (the Windows startup file) into memory and gives it control of the boot process.

Unlike basic disks, dynamic disks do not use a partition table to store their configuration information. Instead, they use a private database that is stored at the end of the disk, called the Logical Disk Manager or LDM database. This database is exactly 1MB in size and is replicated to all the dynamic disks within a machine. This addresses the problem of the partition table as a single point of failure. The LDM database includes such information as volume types, offsets, memberships, and drive letters for each volume on the disk. The LDM replicates and synchronizes the databases across the disks, so that all dynamic disks on the system are aware of one another. There is a unique DiskID in the LDM header of each dynamic disk that enables LDM to identify each disk and distinguish it from the others.

3.2.4 Partitions VS Volumes

Both partitions and volumes enable us to divide one physical disk into sections so that each section appears as a separate disk. Each section is individually formatted (different sections can be formatted in different file systems) and can have its own drive letter. Basic disks contain partitions. Partitions cannot be configured to span disks and therefore cannot provide any fault tolerance. Dynamic disks contain volumes. Volumes can span disks and can provide fault tolerance.

3.2.4.1 Partition types and Logical Drives

There are two types of partitions:

1. Primary partitions
2. Extended partitions

Primary partitions are assigned drive letters and formatted as a whole; they cannot be subdivided. Extended partitions simply group free space so that it can be subdivided into logical drives, which can be individually formatted and used for storage.

1. PRIMARY PARTITIONS

After a primary partition is formatted and assigned a drive letter, it appears as a separate disk to the OS. Depending on the disk-partitioning method used, basic disks can have between four and 128 primary partitions. When using the 32-bit editions of Windows Server 2003, basic disks use the Master Boot Record (MBR) for partitioning and can have up to four primary partitions. The 64-bit editions of Windows Server 2003 can use the GUID partition table (GPT) for partitioning. The GPT utilizes primary and backup partitions for redundancy and allows for up to 128 partitions.

2. EXTENDED PARTITIONS

Extended partitions can be created only on an MBR-partitioned disk. Extended partitions enable you to have more than four drives on a basic disk. You can only have one extended partition per basic disk, but it can be divided into multiple logical drives. You do not format the extended partition itself. Creating an extended partition simply pools free space that can then be divided into logical drives. In other words, until you create a logical drive for your extended partition, you cannot access the space on that partition.

(I) LOGICAL DRIVES

Logical drives are created when you divide up the space contained within an extended partition. Logical drives are formatted and assigned a drive letter just like primary partitions. An extended partition can contain an unlimited number of logical drives. The Windows system partition cannot be stored on a logical drive.

3.2.4.2 Volume Types

Dynamic disks are made up of volumes. A single dynamic disk can hold up to 2,000 volumes, but Microsoft recommends that you limit the volumes per disk to 32.As with partitions, you can have multiple volumes per disk, but unlike partitions, volumes can span multiple disks. Some volume types are designed to increase performance and some types are designed to provide fault tolerance. Windows Server 2003 supports the following five volume types:

1. Simple
2. Spanned
3. Striped
4. Mirrored
5. RAID-5

1. SIMPLE VOLUMES

Simple volumes are made up of free space on a single dynamic disk. They function much like primary partitions on a basic disk. If you have only one physical disk, all the volumes you create on it will be simple volumes.

Simple volumes are not fault tolerant. However, you can mirror them (discussed below) to make them fault tolerant, in which case they become mirrored volumes. Simple volumes can be extended on a single disk as long as the disk is not the boot or system disk. Extending a simple volume involves taking free space on a disk and adding it to the existing volume. You can also extend a simple volume across multiple disks, but then it becomes a spanned volume. Note that you can't combine these operations (that is, you can't mirror a spanned volume).

Simple volumes provide almost 100 percent utilization of disk space. In other words, if you purchase two 100 GB disks and format them as simple volumes, you have a total of 200 GB total storage, minus the 1MB per disk overhead for the LDM database. You are able to use more of the purchased disks' space than is true with other types of volumes.

2. SPANNED VOLUMES

Spanned volumes support two to 32 disks. Each disk can be a different size (as shown in Figure 3.1). Creating a spanned volume is like extending a simple volume except that it spans multiple disks (hence the name, spanned volume). In fact, if you extend a simple volume across multiple disks, by definition it becomes a spanned volume. Spanned volumes are not fault tolerant and cannot be mirrored. Spanned volumes do not provide any performance improvements over simple volumes. They are used merely to increase the amount of space that can be accessed as a single unit. Like simple volumes, spanned volumes provide 100 percent drive utilization (minus the 1MB used for the LDM database). As data is written to the spanned volume, it is first written to the first disk in the set. When the first disk is full, the data is then written to the second disk, and so on.

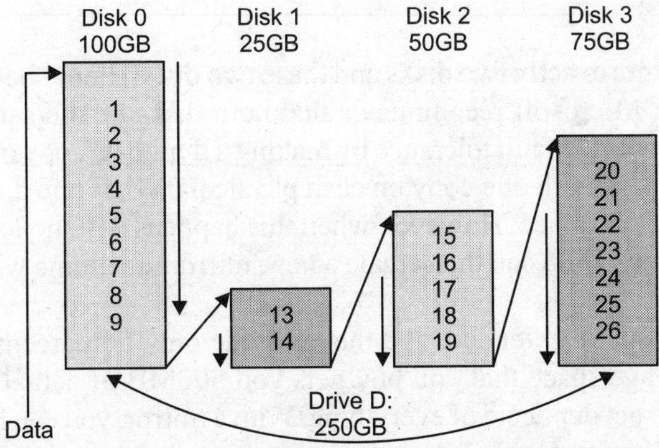

Figure 3.1 Understanding Spanning Volumes

You can extend a spanned volume to make it larger (if it is formatted with NTFS).This consists of adding unallocated space to the volume, like extending a simple volume, except that the unallocated space does not have to be contiguous and can be on any dynamic disk attached to the computer. No data is lost; the new space is formatted without any impact on the existing data.

3. STRIPED VOLUMES

Striped volumes are made up of two to 32 disks. Each disk should be the same size to efficiently use all space. It is possible to use different-sized disks, but the stripe size on every disk will be limited to the amount of free space on the smallest disk, so there will be space wasted on the larger disk(s).

In other words, if you created a striped volume with one 5 GB drive and two 10 GB drives, you would only be able to use 5 GB of each drive because that is the maximum amount that is available on all disks. This would create a 15 GB striped volume, wasting 10 GB of disk space (5 GB on each of the 10GB disks). If you use equal-sized disks, striped volumes provide 100 percent drive utilization (minus 1MB overhead for the LDM database).

Striped volumes cannot be mirrored or extended and they are not fault tolerant. However, striped volumes do provide performance advantage. Striping increases read and write access to the volume, because all the disks are working at the same time. In fact, striped volumes offer the best performance of all Windows Server 2003 volume types. This is because of the way data is stored (as shown in Figure 3.2). Data is written evenly across all disks in 64 KB chunks.

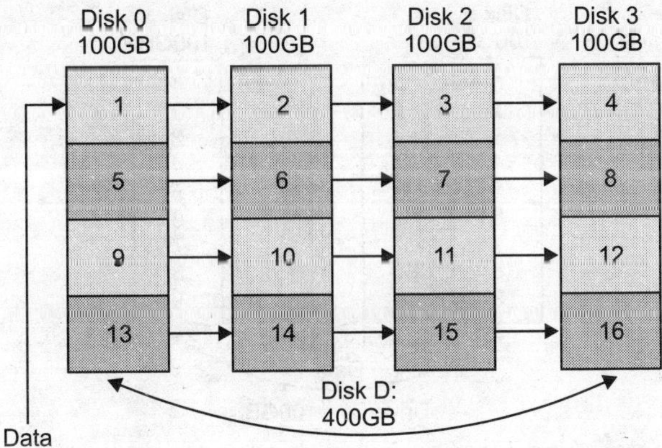

Figure 3.2 Understanding Striped Volumes

4. MIRRORED VOLUMES

Mirrored volumes require exactly two disks and these two disks should be identical. Not only should they be the same size, but Microsoft recommends that both disks be the same model, from the same vendor. Mirrored volumes provide fault tolerance by making a duplicate copy of everything that is written to the volume (see Figure 3.3), with one copy on each physical disk. If one disk in the mirrored volume fails, the other disk will take its place. However, when this happens, you no longer have fault tolerance. You need to break the mirror so you can then create a new, mirrored volume with another disk, to restore fault tolerance.

Mirrored volumes cannot be extended, and they provide only 50 percent disk utilization. In other words, every 1 GB of storage space that you buy gets you 500MB of actual storage. The benefit of a mirror is that you have an exact duplicate of everything. With a mirror, you can lose one disk and still have all your data intact. Only if you lost both disks at the same time would you lose your data. Because all the data is there on the duplicate disk, you can get back up and running after a failure much faster than with a RAID-5 volume, where the data must be regenerated from the parity information following a failure before it can be accessed.

Mirroring can have a negative impact on system performance, because of the overhead of writing to two disks at the same time. An even more fault-tolerant form of disk mirroring is called disk duplexing. Disk duplexing is the same as disk mirroring, except that each disk in the mirror is connected to a different disk controller. This eliminates the disk controller as a single point of failure. Duplexed disks appear to the operating system the same as mirrored disks; if you have duplexed disks, they will be shown as mirrored disks in the Disk Management console.

You can mirror any simple volume, including the boot and system volumes. Microsoft recommends that you use separate controllers (duplexing) if you mirror the system or boot volumes. The controllers should be identical (same model and vendor) to prevent problems with starting from the mirror if the primary disk fails. Always test a mirrored system or boot volume to ensure that the operating system will be able to start from a remaining mirror in case of failure.

There are several conditions that must be met in order for Windows to start from a remaining mirror. If the disks in a mirror are SCSI disks on separate controllers, both controllers must have translation enabled or disabled (one cannot be enabled while the other is disabled). If the disks are SCSI disks on the same controller and there are additional disks on the controller, the controller's BIOS have to support the capability to choose which device to boot from. If the disks are IDE disks, you must ensure that the remaining disk after a failure has its jumpers set to the "master" position.

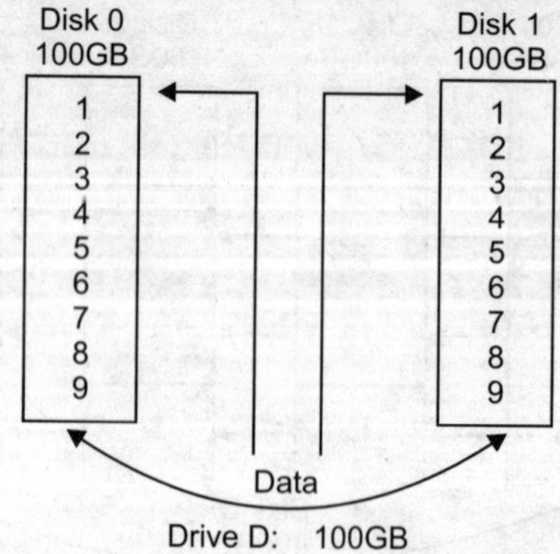

Figure 3.3 Understanding Mirrored Volumes

5. RAID-5 VOLUMES

RAID-5 volumes consist of three to 32 disks. RAID-5 volumes provide increased performance for read operations, as well as fault tolerance. The performance boost is due to the way RAID-5 volumes stripe data across all the disks and the fault tolerance is provided by parity information. As with a striped volume, data is written evenly across all disks in 64 KB chunks (see Figure 3.4). Unlike with disk striping, the available space (the stripe) on one disk is used for parity information. To increase performance, the parity information is split across all the disks in the volume, written in stripes like the data. Write performance is lower, because the parity must be calculated during the write operation. If most operations are read-oriented (for instance, users accessing files on a file server), RAID-5 provides signi?cant performance advantages.

Windows Server 2003's RAID-5 volumes cannot be extended or mirrored, and the boot and system partitions cannot be part of a RAID-5 volume. Disk utilization depends on how many disks are parts of the RAID array. The equivalent of one disk is used for writing the parity information. If you have three disks, one-third of the total disk space is used for parity information, so you are able to utilize two-thirds of the space you purchase for data. If you have 10 disks in the array, only one-tenth of the total space is used for parity. Thus, the more disks you have in the set, the more efficient disk usage becomes.

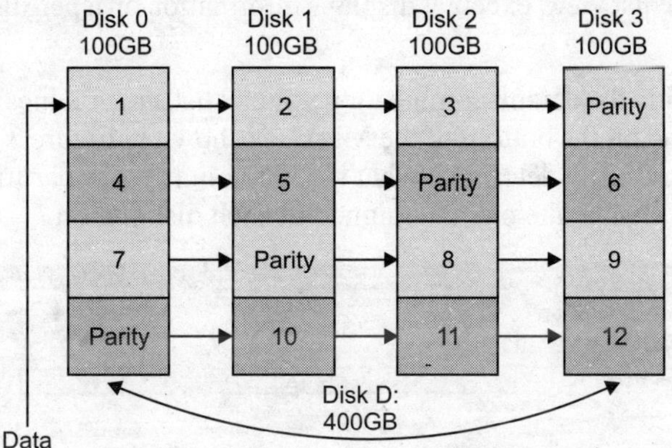

Figure 3.4 Understanding RAID-5 Volumes

3.3 MANAGING DISKS

Microsoft provides a variety of disk management tools in Windows Server 2003.These include command-line utilities such as diskpart.exe, fsutil.exe, and rss.exe. These tools support scripting, which enables you to automate many of your disk management responsibilities. You can also manage your disks through the graphical interface via the disk management MMC. This section will show you how to manage disks both from the GUI and from the command prompt.

3.3.1 Using the Disk Management MMC

You can access the disk management MMC, shown in Figure 3.5, in a couple of different ways:

1. You can get there via Computer Management, by clicking Start | Programs | Administrative Tools | Computer Management.

2. You can right-click the My Computer icon on the desktop or in the Start menu and select Manage from the context menu.
3. You can create a custom MMC console to use the Disk Management snap-in.

   Figure 3.5 shows the default view for the Disk Management MMC. Notice that the details pane is divided into two sections, a top section and a bottom section.

There are three different views that you can use for either section:

1. Disk list
2. Volume list
3. Graphical view

By default, the top section displays the volume list view and the bottom section displays the graphical view. You can change the view by clicking the View menu bar, choosing Top or Bottom, and selecting the view that you want.

In Figure 3.5, the top section is using the default volume list view. This view uses text in a table to show how your volumes and partitions are configured. The bottom section is using the graphical view. As the name implies, it provides a graphical representation of how your disks are configured. The third view (not shown by default) is the disk list view. It uses text to show you how your disks are configured. It looks similar to the volume list view, except it displays information on a per-disk basis instead of volume and partition information.

Most administrators' find the default combination volume list and graphical view to be most efficient. Notice that there is a legend on the bottom of the MMC, as shown in Figure 3.6. The color codes enable you to look at each disk and easily determine what type of volume(s) or partition(s) it contains. You can use the View menu bar to change the colors assigned to each disk region.

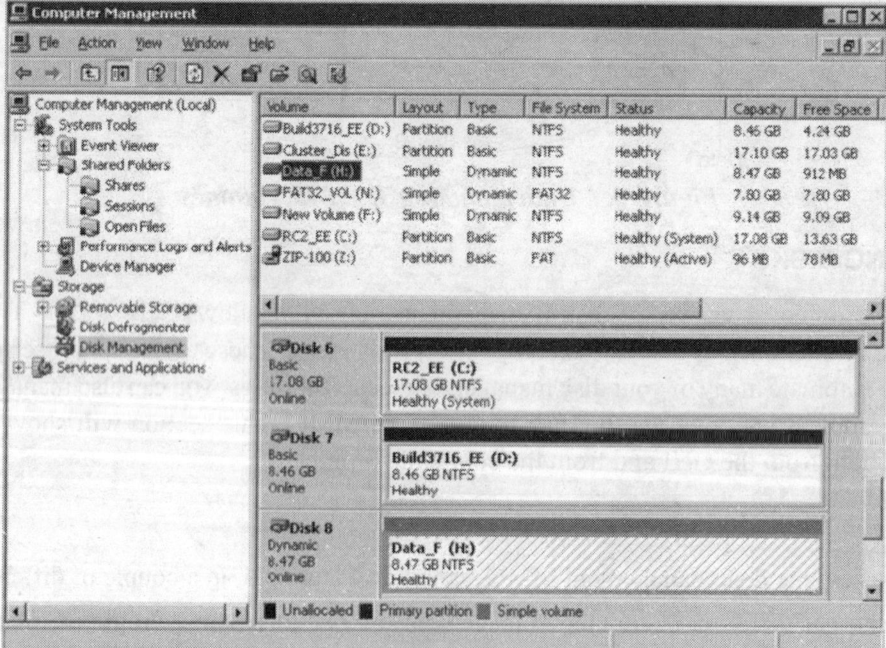

Figure 3.5 Using Disk Management from within Computer Management

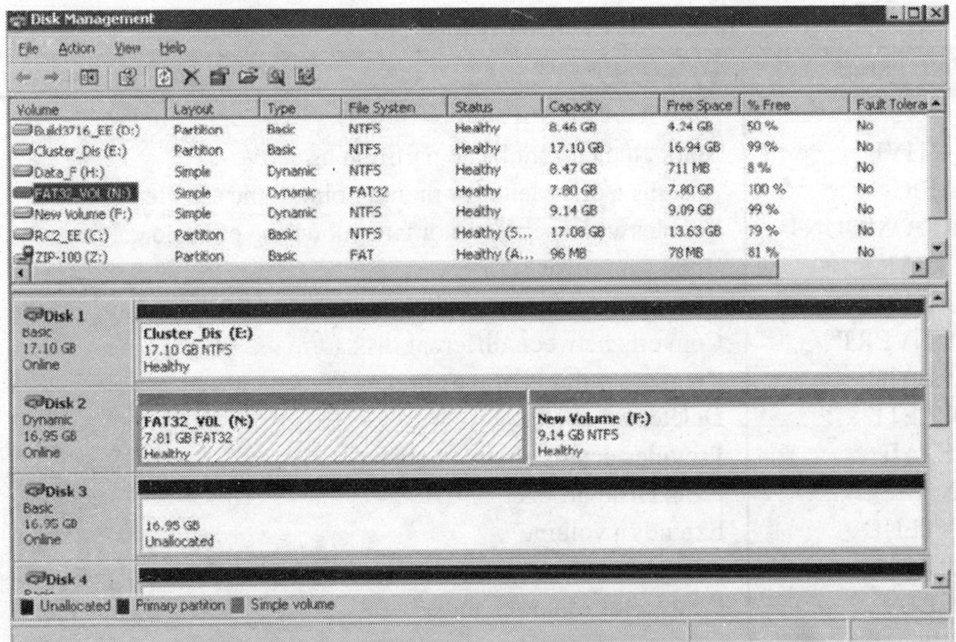

Figure 3.6 Using the Legend in the Disk Management MMC

3.3.2 Using the Command-line Utilities

Microsoft has increased the number of functions that administrators can perform from the command prompt in Windows Server 2003.This gives you more fiexibility in accomplishing administrative tasks. Windows Server 2003 includes the following command-line tools for performing disk-related tasks:

1. Diskpart.exe: for managing disks
2. Fsutil.exe: for managing the file system
3. Rss.exe: for managing remote storage

3.3.2.1 Using Diskpart.exe

Diskpart.exe enables you to manage disks, partitions, or volumes from the command prompt. You can type the commands directly at the command prompt via interactive mode or you can configure diskpart.exe to use a script for its input. Diskpart.exe scripting is beneficial if you are automating the deployment of Windows Server 2003 by using unattended setup files. Microsoft recommends that you put all your diskpart.exe commands into a single script to avoid confiicts between multiple scripts. If you must use separate scripts, you must allow at least 15 seconds after each script finishes before the next one starts to execute. Put the command timeout /t 15 at the beginning of each script to force a 15-second delay. The syntax for using diskpart.exe with scripts is:

diskpart [/s <script>]

If you want to use diskpart.exe in interactive mode, type diskpart.exe at the command prompt. This will take you to the DISKPART> prompt, shown in Figure 3.7. Whenever you see DISKPART>, you are in interactive mode and diskpart.exe is awaiting your input. Typing help in interactive mode will display all the utility's available commands, as shown in Table 3.1.

Table 3.1 Using Diskpart.exe Commands

Command	Description
ADD	Adds a mirror to a simple volume.
ACTIVE	Marks the current basic partition as active.
ASSIGN	Assigns a drive letter or mount point to the selected volume.
AUTOMOUNT	Enables and disables automatic mounting of basic volumes.
BREAK	Breaks a mirror set.
CLEAN	Clears the configuration information, or all information, off the disk.
CONVERT	Converts between different disk formats.
CREATE	Creates a volume or partition.
DELETE	Deletes an object.
DETAIL	Provides details about an object.
EXIT	Exits Diskpart.exe.
EXTEND	Extends a volume.
GPT	Assigns attributes to the selected GPT partition.
HELP	Prints a list of commands.
IMPORT	Imports a disk group.
INACTIVE	Marks the current basic partition as inactive.
LIST	Prints out a list of objects.
ONLINE	Onlines a disk that is currently marked as Offline.
REM	Does nothing. Used to comment scripts.
REMOVE	Removes a drive letter or mount point assignment.
REPAIR	Repairs a RAID
RESCAN	Rescans the computer looking for disks and volumes.
RETAIN	Places a retained partition under a simple volume.
SELECT	Moves the focus to an object.

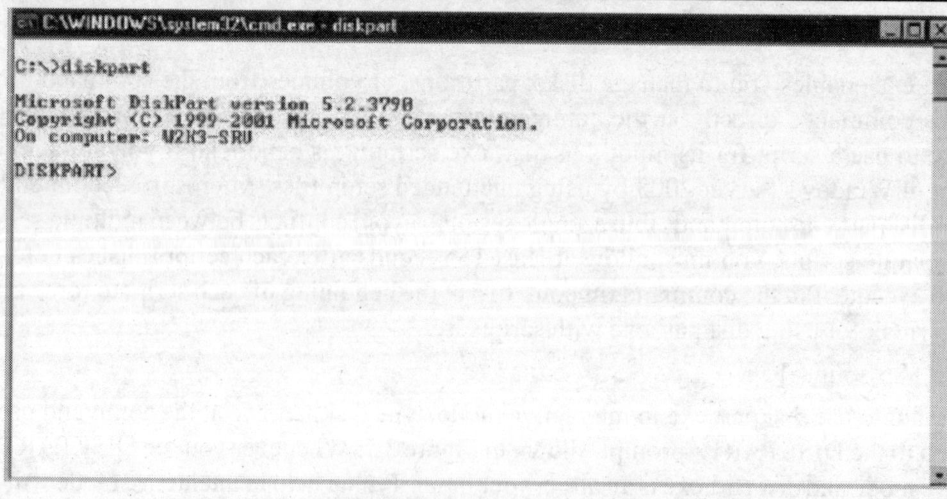

Figure 3.7 Using Diskpart.exe in Interactive Mode

Before you can use any of these commands, you must list all disk objects and then choose one on which diskpart.exe will carry out the command(s).After you place the focus on a particular object, all commands entered will target that object until you change the focus to a different object. Use the following steps to walk through the process of focusing diskpart.exe on a disk. Figure 3.8 shows these commands as entered in the command console.

1. Use the appropriate list command from the table to list the disk, volumes, or partitions on your system. For this example, we are going to list the disks. Type list disk and press Enter. The output is shown in Figure 3.8.
2. Now that you know which disks are available, select one for the focus of your commands. For this example, we select the first disk (disk 0).Type select disk 0 and press Enter.
3. You can now type list disk again and press Enter to verify that the correct disk was selected. The disk on which diskpart.exe is focused has an asterisk (*) to the left of it.

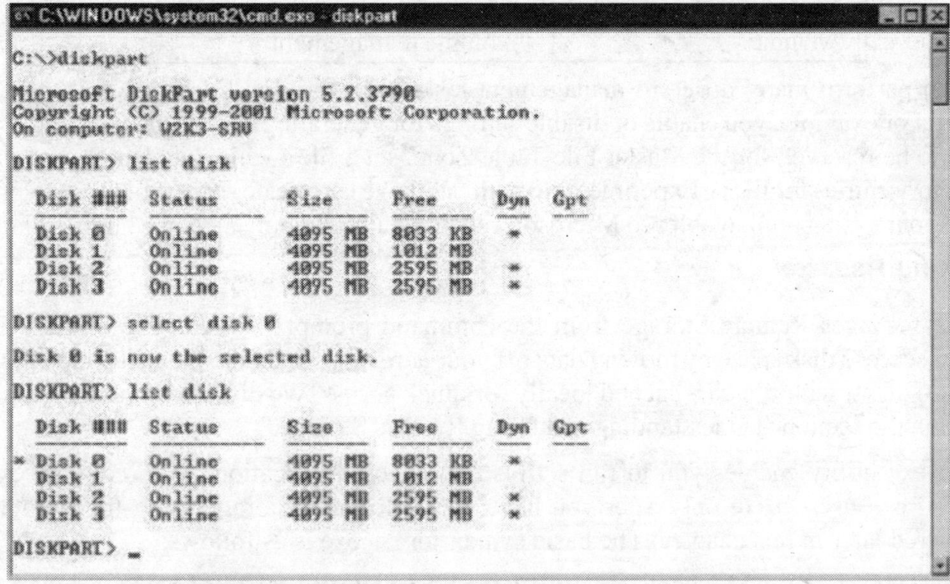

Figure 3.8 Focusing Diskpart.exe on Disk 0

Now you can use the desired command to perform an operation on the selected disk. For example, to change a basic disk to dynamic, you use the convert command with the following syntax:

DISKPART> convert dynamic

3.3.2.2 Using Fsutil.exe

You can use fsutil.exe to manage FAT and NTFS file systems from the command prompt. Some of the actions you can perform with this utility include the following:

1. Managing sparse files
2. Managing reparse points
3. Mounting and dismounting volumes
4. Viewing the amount of free space on a volume Fsutil.exe supports the commands shown in Table 3.2.

Table 3.2 Using Fsutil.exe Commands

Command	Description
behavior	File system behavior control
dirty	Volume dirty bit management
file	File-specific commands
fsinfo	File system information
Managing	Physical and Logical Disks
hardlink	Hardlink management
objectid	Object ID management
quota	Quota management
reparsepoint	Reparse point management
sparse	Sparse file control
usn	USN management
volume	Volume management

You can perform many different management tasks with these utilities that do not have a GUI counterpart. For example, you enable or disable settings for generating 8.3 file names, set the amount of disk space to be reserved for the Master File Table Zone, set a file's valid data length, and create hard links (directory entries for files). Experimenting with fsutil.exe can create serious file system problems or even make your system unbootable, so Microsoft recommends that only advanced users run this utility.

3.3.2.3 Using Rss.exe

Rss.exe manages Remote Storage from the command prompt. You can use Remote Storage to extend your server's disk space by moving data off your hard disks and onto magnetic tapes or magneto-optical (MO) disks, with file data cached locally for quick access. We discuss Remote Storage in much more detail in the section "Understanding and Using Remote Storage."

The rss.exe utility enables you to run scripts that enable applications to directly access Remote Storage. You can use rss.exe only after you have set up Remote Storage using the Remote Storage MMC (covered later in this chapter).The basic syntax for rss.exe is as follows:

RSS [ADMIN | VOLUME | MEDIA | FILE] [SET | SHOW | JOB | MANAGE | UNMANAGE| DELETE | SYNCHRONIZE | RECREATEMASTER | RECALL] <args> <switches>

3.4 MANAGING BASIC DISKS

It is important to understand the circumstances that make it desirable to use basic disks. You should not upgrade your disks to dynamic status without knowing all the consequences of that action. If you choose to stick with basic disks, you need to know how to create and delete partitions and logical drives. Basic disks can be managed via the Disk Management MMC or the diskpart.exe utility, and you can use scripts to automate many management tasks as discussed previously. In the following sections, we discuss the most important aspects of managing basic disks, including:

1. When to use basic disks instead of dynamic disks
2. How to create partitions and logical drives
3. How to assign a new drive letter
4. How to format a basic volume
5. How to extend a basic volume

3.4.1 When to Use Basic Disks

Basic disks are the default for Windows Server 2003.You should always use basic disk if you are going to dual-boot your machine with another operating system. MS-DOS, Windows 9x, Windows NT 4.0, and Windows XP Home Edition do not support dynamic disks. Windows 2000, Windows XP Professional, and Windows Server 2003 do support dynamic disks, but not when dual booting.

Use basic disk if you will be moving your disks between machines. If you use dynamic disks, you have to go into Disk Management and import dynamic disk every time you move them from one PC to another. With basic disks, you just install them and Windows automatically sees them. Laptop hard disks must be configured as basic disks as most removable storage media.

3.4.2 Creating Partitions and Logical Drives

When you install Windows Server 2003, setup will prompt you to create a primary partition to use as the boot partition for Windows. If you want to create more partitions afterwards, you will need to use the disk management MMC. This section will walk you through creating a primary partition, creating an extended partition, creating a logical drive, and assigning a new drive letter.

3.4.2.1 Creating a Primary Partition

1. Right-click the unallocated space on the disk on which you want to create a primary partition.
2. Click New partition on the pop-up menu. This will start the New Partition Wizard, as shown in Figure 3.9.
3. Click Next to continue.

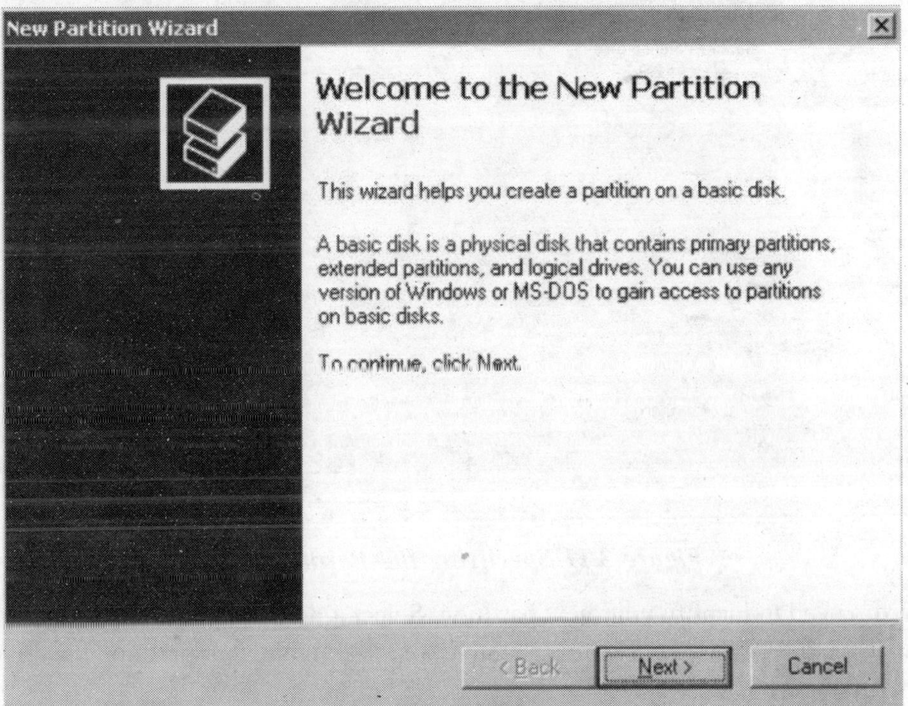

Figure 3.9 Creating a Primary Partition Using the New Partition Wizard

4. On the Select Partition Type window (Figure 3.10), select Primary partition.
5. Click Next to continue. You will now be prompted to specify the partition size as shown in Figure 3.11.
6. Specify the Partition size in MB and click Next to continue.

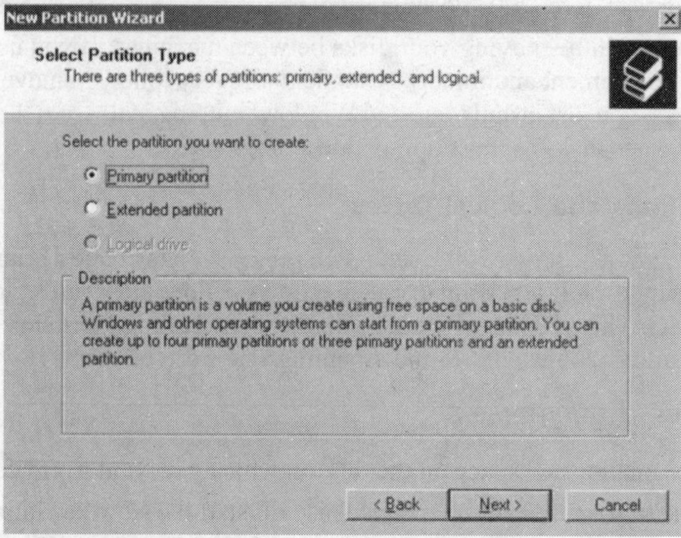

Figure 3.10 Selecting to Create a Primary Partition

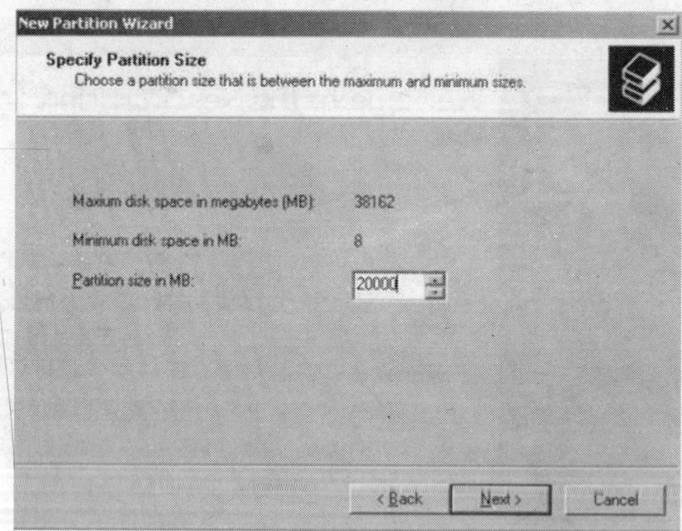

Figure 3.11 Specifying the Partition Size

7. Now you need to identify your new partition. Select a drive letter or choose to mount the new volume to an NTFS folder. For this example we are assigning our partition the drive letter F, as shown in Figure 3.12.

8. Click Next to continue.

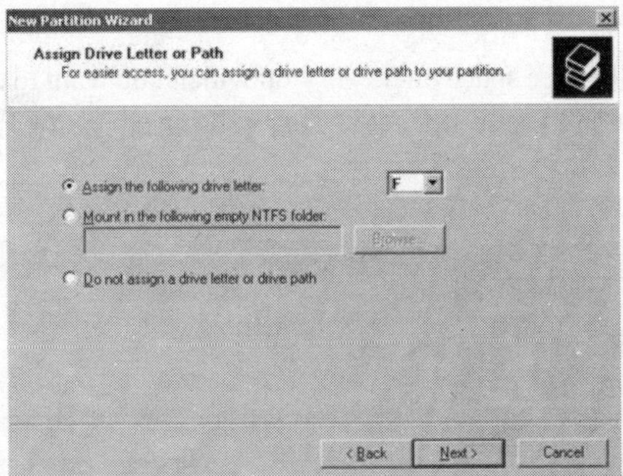

Figure 3.12 Assigning a Drive Letter or Path

9. You must now format your new partition. You can format partitions as FAT, FAT32, or NTFS. For this example, choose NTFS, as shown in Figure 3.13, and then click Next to continue.
10. You will now see the Completing the New Partition Wizard window, as shown in Figure 3.14. Read over the summary to verify that you made the correct selections and click Finish to complete the process.

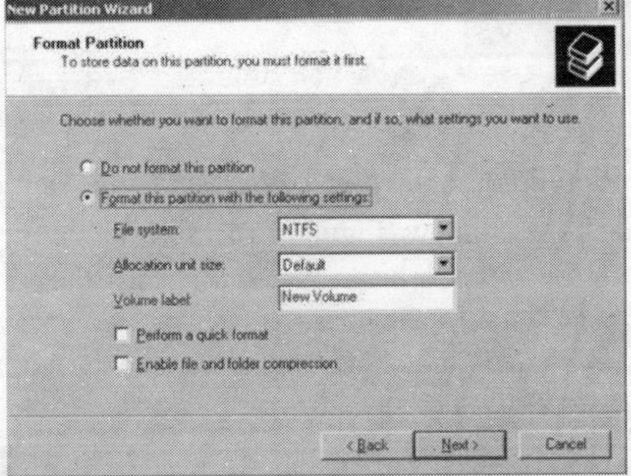

Figure 3.13 Formatting the Partition

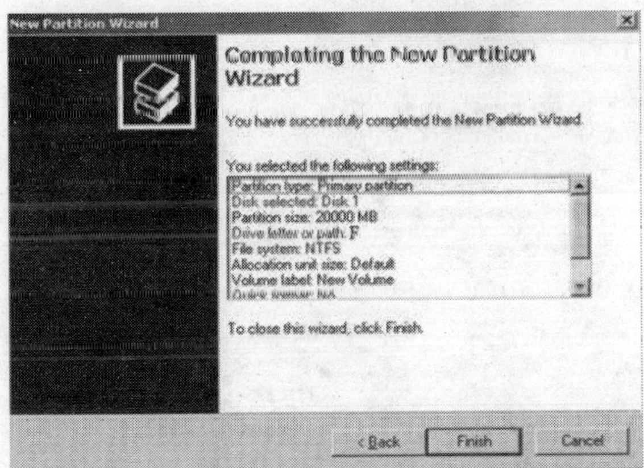

Figure 3.14 Completing the New Partition Wizard

3.4.2.2 Creating an Extended Partition

1. Right-click the unallocated space on the disk on which you want to create an extended partition.
2 Click New partition on the pop-up menu. This will start the New Partition Wizard as shown in Figure 3.15.
3. Click Next to continue.

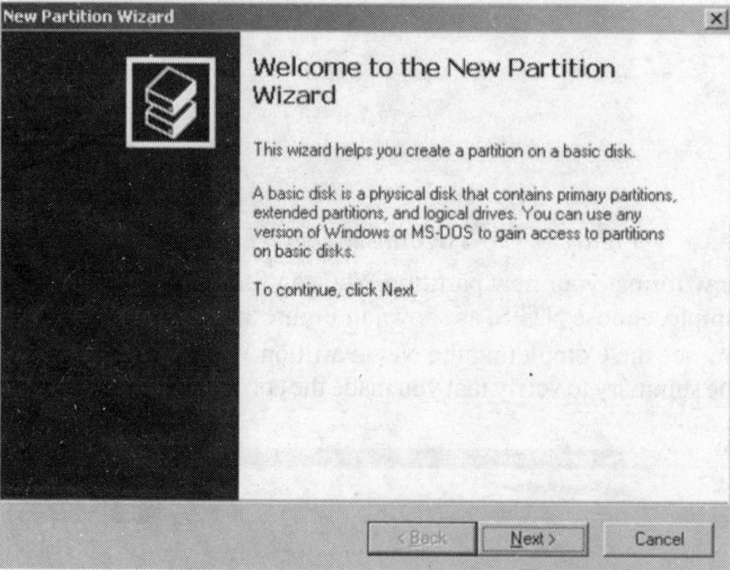

Figure 3.15 Creating an Extended Partition with the New Partition Wizard

4. On the Select Partition Type window (Figure 3.16), select Extended partition.
5. Click Next to continue. You will now be prompted to specify the partition size as shown in Figure 3.17.
6. Specify the Partition size in MB and click Finish to create the extended partition.

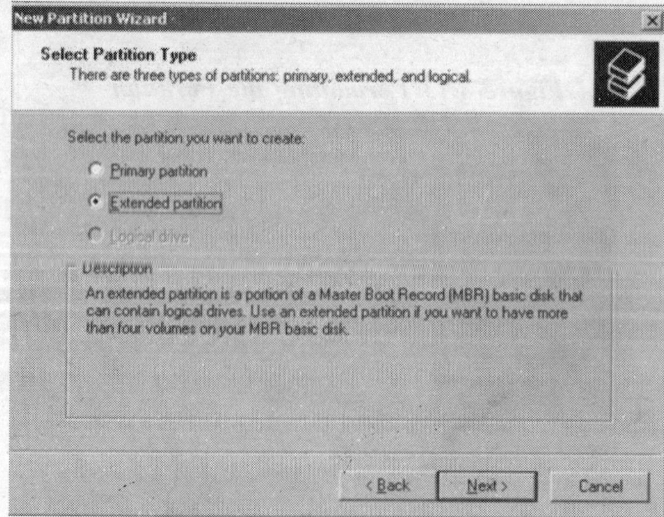

Figure 3.16 Selecting to Create an Extended Partition

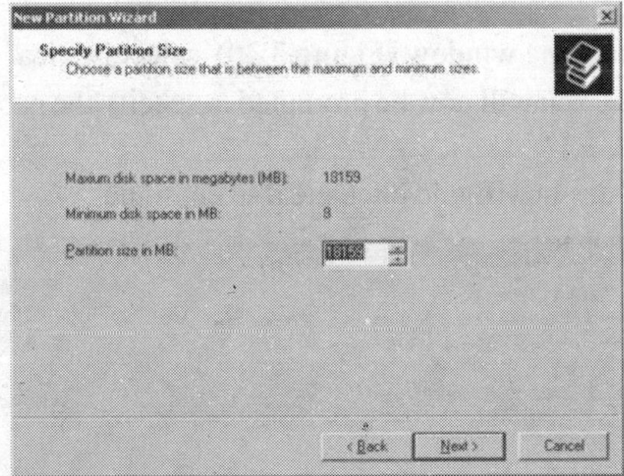

Figure 3.17 Specifying the Partition Size

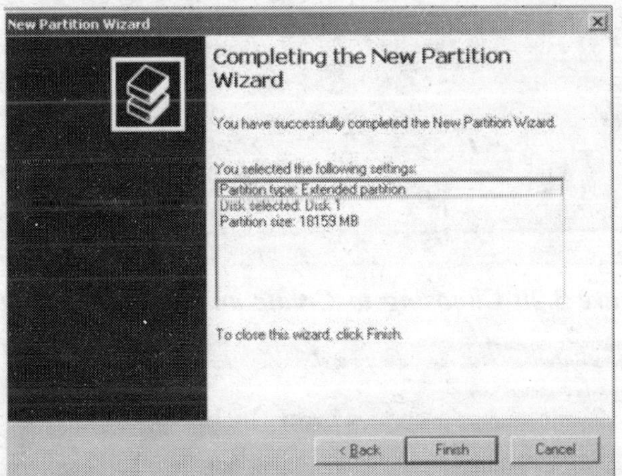

Figure 3.18: Completing the new partition wizard

3.4.2.3 Creating a Logical Drive

1. Right-click the Extended partition on the disk on which you want to create a logical drive.

2. Click New Logical Drive on the pop-up menu. This will start the New Partition Wizard, as shown in Figure 3.19.

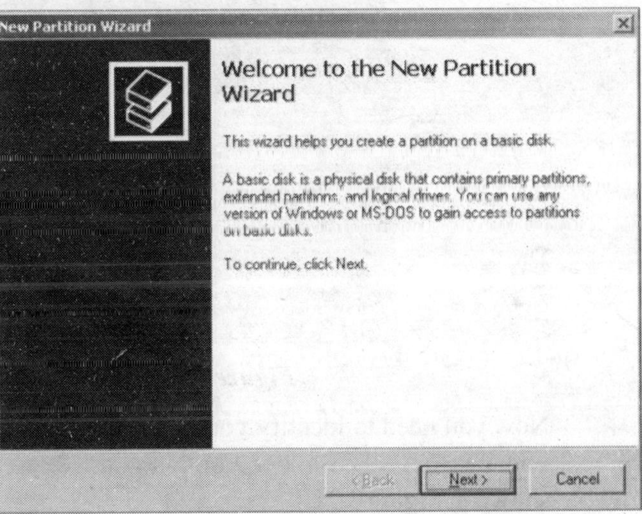

Figure 3.19 Using the New Partition Wizard to Create a Logical Partition

3. Click Next to continue.
4. On the Select Partition Type window (Figure 3.20), select Logical drive.
5. Click Next to continue. You will now be prompted to specify the partition size as shown in Figure 3.21.
6. Specify the Partition size in MB and click Next to continue.

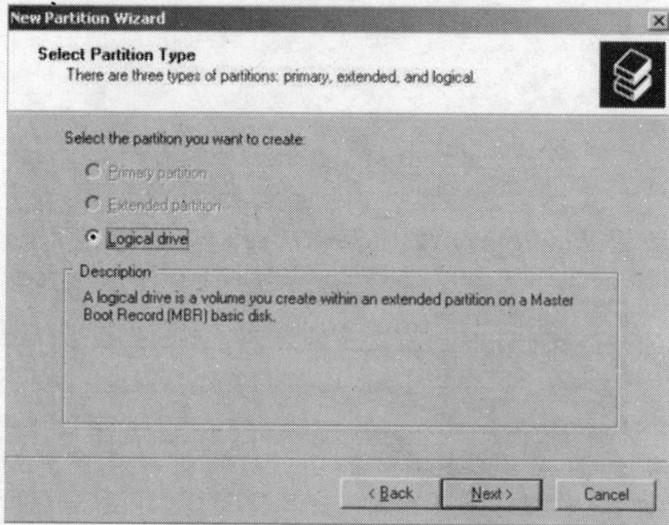

Figure 3.20 Choosing to Create an Extended Partition

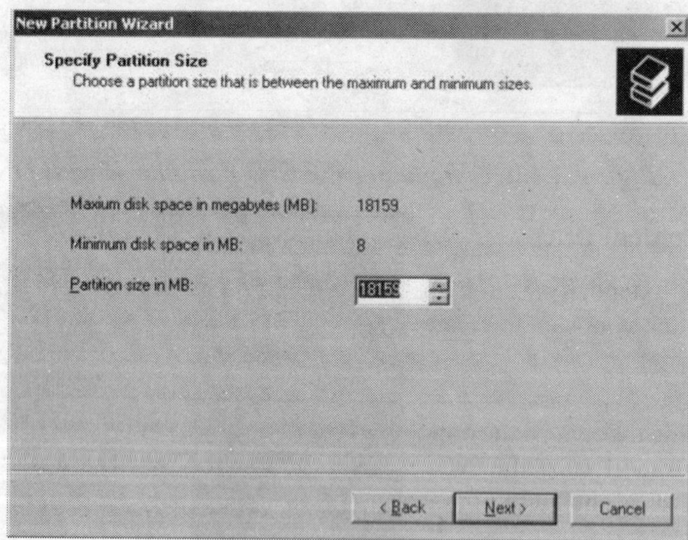

Figure 3.21 Specifying a Partition Size

7. Now you need to identify your new partition. Select a drive letter or choose to mount the new volume to an NTFS folder. For this example, we are assigning our partition the drive letter G, as shown in Figure 3.22.
8. Click Next to continue.

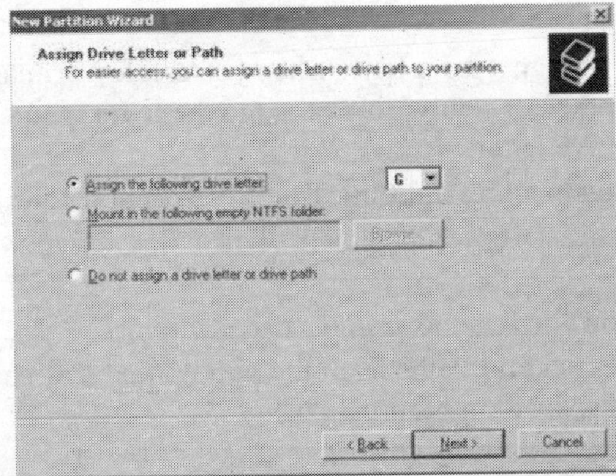

Figure 3.22 Assigning a Drive Letter or Path

9. You must now format your new partition. You can format partitions as FAT, FAT32, or NTFS. For this example, choose NTFS, as shown in Figure 3.23, and then click Next to continue.
10. You will now see the Completing the New Partition Wizard window, as shown in Figure 3.24. Read over the summary to verify that you made the correct selections and click Finish to complete the process.

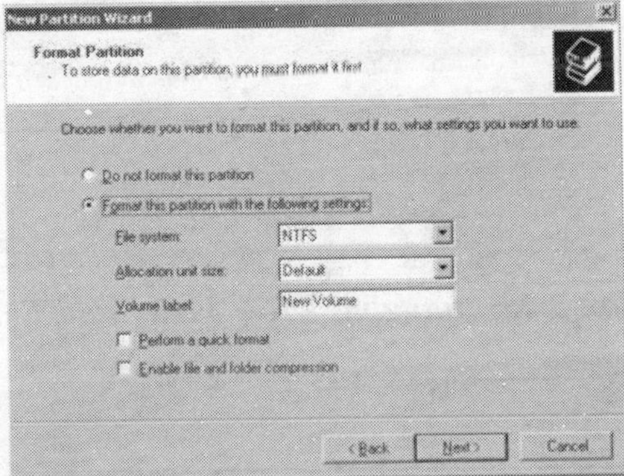

Figure 3.23 Formatting the New Partition

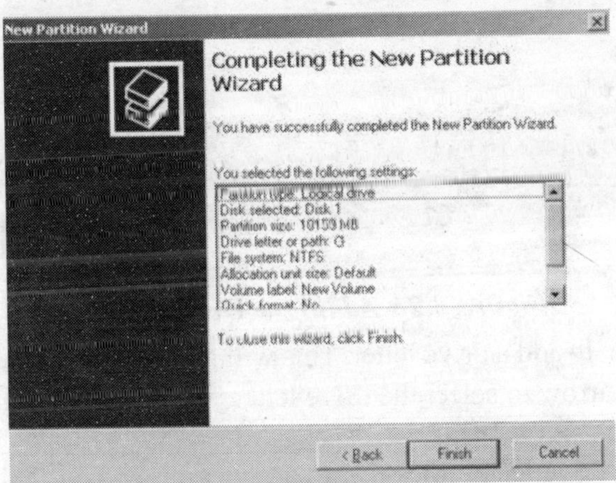

Figure 3.24 Finishing the New Partition Wizard

3.4.3 Assign a New Drive Letter

You are given the option to assign a drive letter when you create a primary partition or a logical drive. If you chose not to assign one then or you wish to change the letter, you can use Disk Management or diskpart.exe to assign a new drive letter.

1. Open Computer Management by right-clicking My Computer and choosing Manage.
2. Expand Storage and click Disk Management. This will give you the window shown in Figure 3.25.
3. Right-click the partition you want to assign a drive letter.
4. Select Change Drive Letter and Paths from the pop-up menu as shown in Figure 3.25.You will now see the window displayed in Figure 3.26.

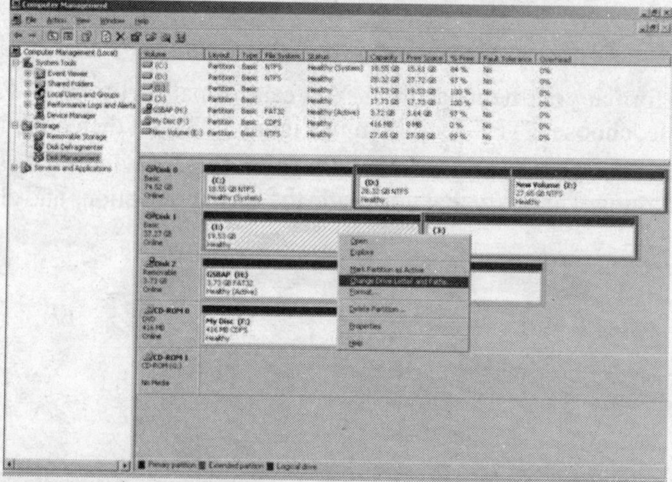

Figure 3.25 Changing Drive Letter and Paths

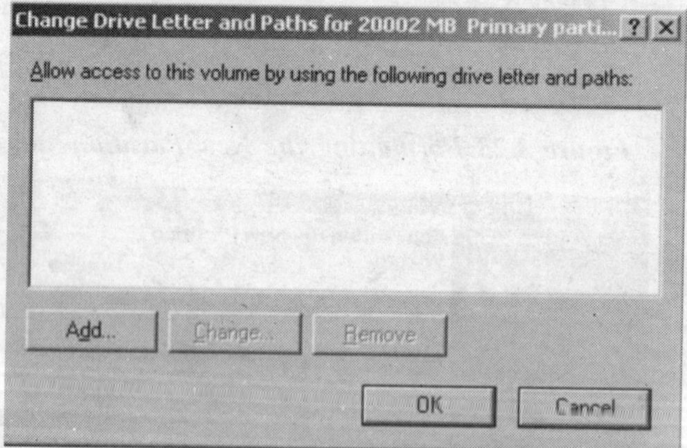

Figure 3.26 Adding a Drive Letter

5. Click the Add button to add a drive letter. This will give you the window shown in Figure 3.27
6. Use the drop-down arrow to select the drive letter you want to assign. For this example we are going to use E.
7. After you select the drive letter, click OK to accept your choice. This will apply your changes. Figure 3.28 shows that our partition now has the drive letter E.

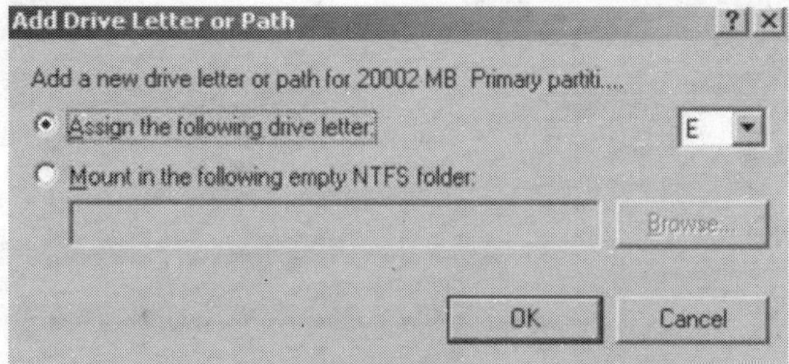

Figure 3.27 Selecting the Letter to Assign

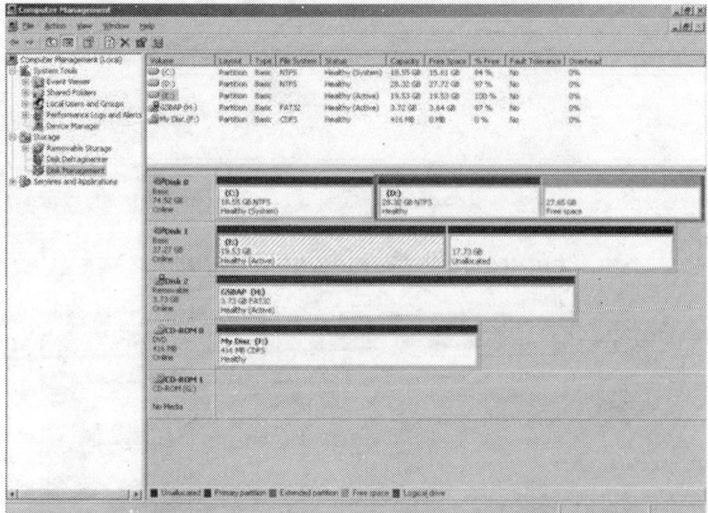

Figure 3.28 Seeing the New Drive Letter

3.4.4 Formatting a Basic Volume

Like assigning a drive letter, you are given the option to format a drive when you create a primary partition or a logical drive. If you do not format the volume during creation, you can use Disk Management or format.exe to format the volume afterwards.

3.4.4.1 Format a Volume

Use the following steps to format the first primary partition on Disk 2. Look at Figure 3.29 and you can see that this partition, unlike the C: and E: drives, has not been formatted. Here are the steps to format it with NTFS:

1. Open Computer Management by right-clicking My Computer and choosing Manage.
2. Expand Storage and click Disk Management. This will give you the window shown in Figure 3.29.
3. Right-click the partition you want to format.
4. Select Format from the pop-up menu, as shown in Figure 3.29.You will now see the window displayed in Figure 3.30.

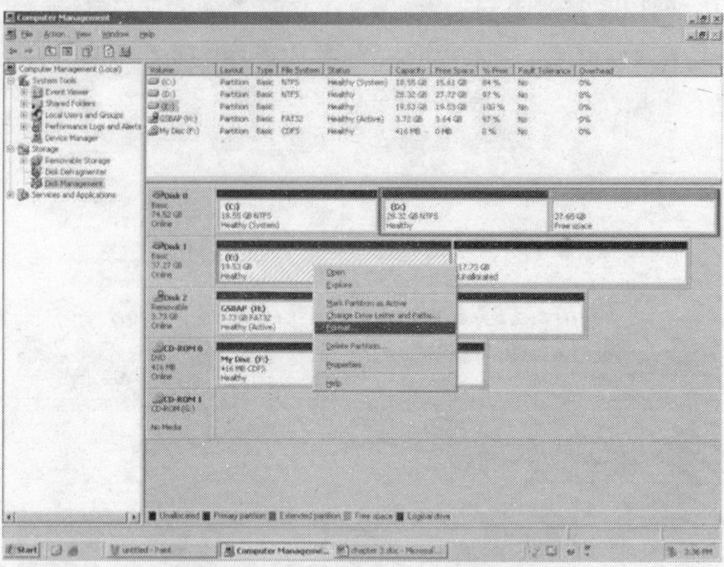

Figure 3.29 Formatting a Volume

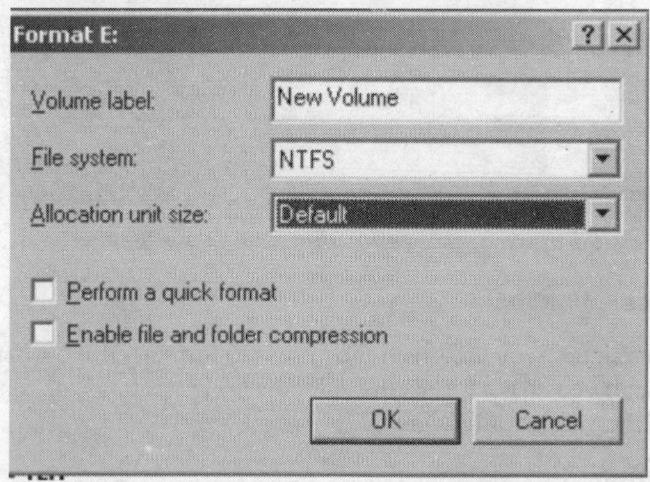

Figure 3.30 Choosing a Volume Label, File System, and Cluster Size

5. Enter the Volume label for the volume. For this example we are using New Volume.
6. Select the File system to use. In this example we are using NTFS.
7. Select the Allocation unit size (file system cluster). For this example we are using Default, which is 4 KB.
8. Optionally, you can choose to perform a quick format and to enable file and folder compression. After you make your choices, click OK to continue. You will now be warned that you are going to lose all data, as shown in Figure 3.31.
9. Click OK to start the format process. Figure 3.32 shows the volume being formatted and Figure 3.33 shows the volume after the format has completed.

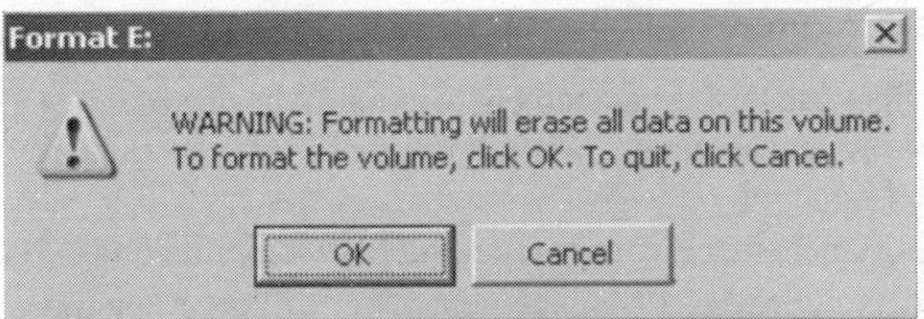

Figure 3.31 Acknowledging Formatting Warning

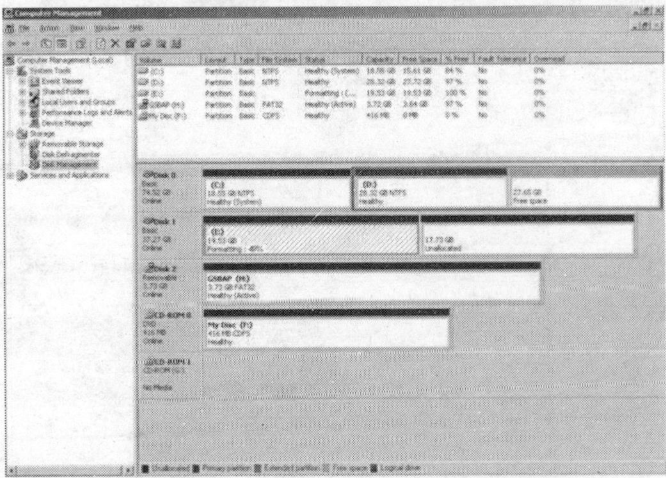

Figure 3.32 Watching the Drive Format

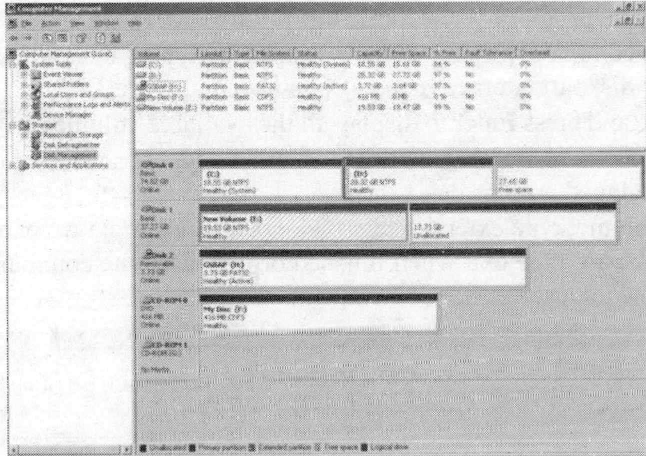

Figure 3.33 Seeing the Formatted Drive

3.4.5 Extending a Basic Volume

Extending a basic volume enables you to add more space to an existing volume without losing data. This is a new feature that was not available in Windows 2000.You can extend a basic volume only onto the same disk and only if it is followed by contiguous unallocated space. You cannot use Disk Management to extend a basic volume. The only way to do it is to use diskpart.exe from the command prompt.

3.4.5.1 Extend a Basic Volume

Even though you cannot use Disk Management to extend a basic volume, let's open it anyway so that we can see our volume as it gets extended. We will use diskpart.exe to actually do the extending of the primary partition (F:) on Disk 2.

1. Open Computer Management by right-clicking My Computer and choosing Manage.
2. Expand Storage and click Disk Management. This will give you the window shown in Figure 3.34. Use this window to see the before and after of extending your volume.

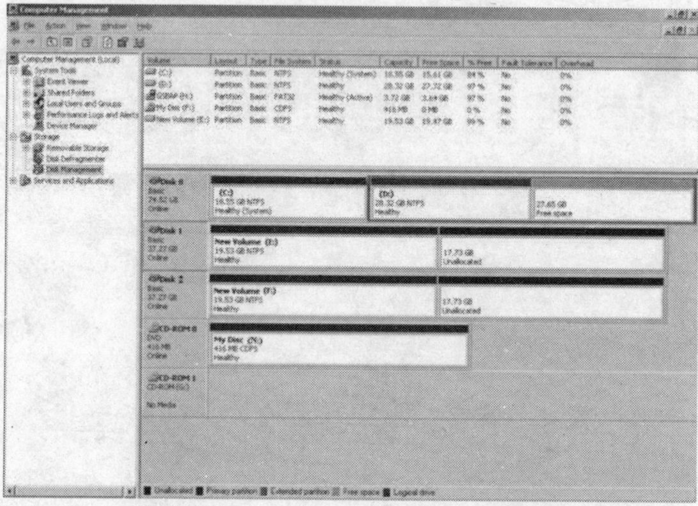

Figure 3.34 Extending a Basic Volume

3. Open the command prompt by selecting Start | Run | CMD | OK.
4. From within the command prompt, launch diskpart by typing diskpart and pressing Enter. This will put you into diskpart interactive mode, as shown in Figure 3.35.
5. Type list volume and press Enter to display all the available volumes on your system.
6. Focus diskpart onto the volume you wish to extend by typing select volume 3. For this example we choose to extended volume 3.
7. To extend the volume, type extend size=1024. For this example we extended the volume by 1 MB. To exit disk part, type exit when finished or just close the command prompt. Figure 3.36 shows the volume after it has been extended.

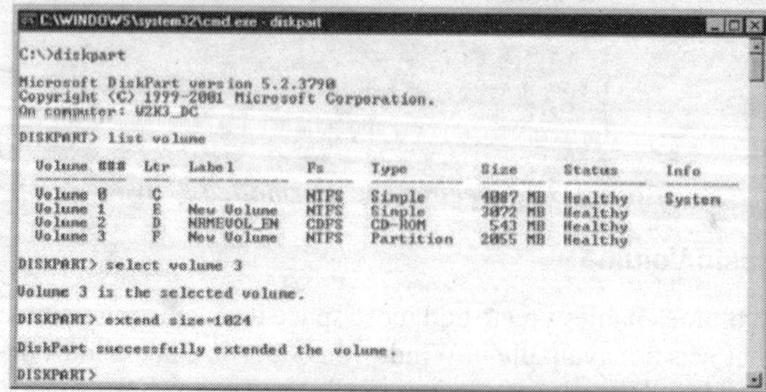

Figure 3.35 Using Diskpart

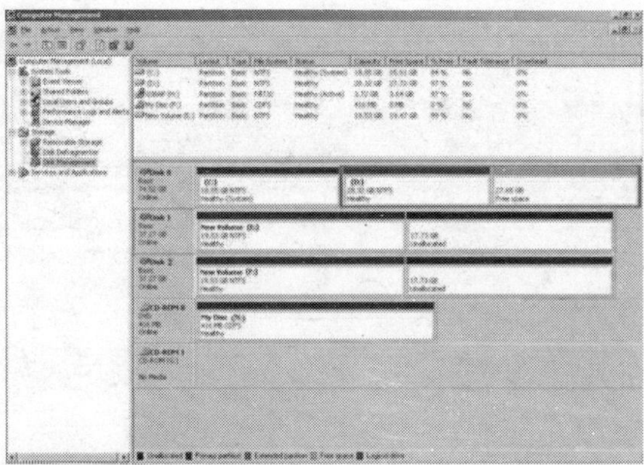

Figure 3.36 Seeing the Extended Volume

3.5 DYNAMIC DISKS

Dynamic disks are the required disk structure in Windows Server 2003 if you want to create fault tolerant volumes or increase read and write performance by spanning disks. Dynamic disks, like basic disks, can be managed via the Disk Management MMC or with the diskpart.exe utility. Managing dynamic disks is a little more complicated than managing basic disks, as you have more options from which to choose. This section discusses converting your disks from basic to dynamic and creating the various types of volumes supported in Windows Server 2003.

3.5.1 Converting to Dynamic Disk Status

By default, all disks are configured as basic disks. It is up to you to convert them to dynamic if you choose to do so. Remember to carefully assess your situation and determine whether you need the features of dynamic disks (and make sure your system is one of those that can use dynamic disks) before performing the conversion. If you convert a disk that is currently being accessed (such as the boot or system disks) then you must reboot in order to convert. Otherwise, you can convert without rebooting. Converting to dynamic does not erase any data.

3.5.1.1 Converting your System Disk to a Dynamic Disk

1. Right-click the disk that you want to upgrade to dynamic.
2. Select Convert to Dynamic Disk from the pop-up menu, as shown in Figure 3.37.This will give you the Convert to Dynamic Disk selection window, as shown in Figure 3.38.

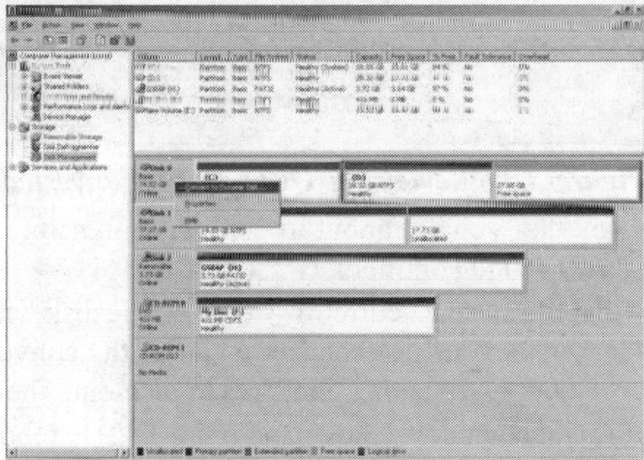

Figure 3.37 Converting to Dynamic Disk

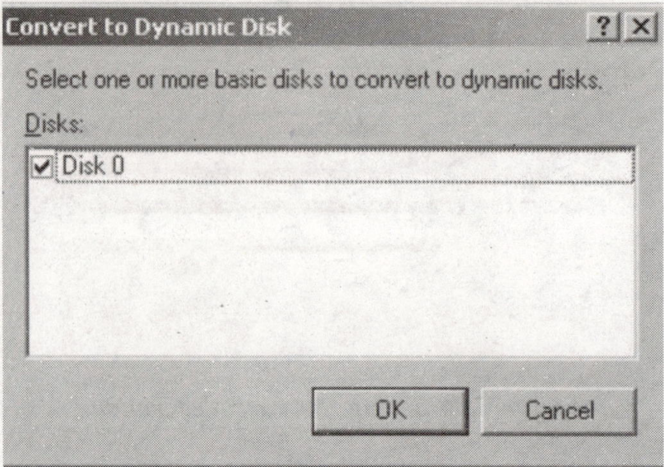

Figure 3.38 Selecting the Disk to Convert

3. The disk you want to upgrade should be checked by default. If not, check its check box and click OK to continue.
4. You are next shown a summary screen (Figure 3.39) that indicates which disk(s) will be converted. Click Convert to continue.

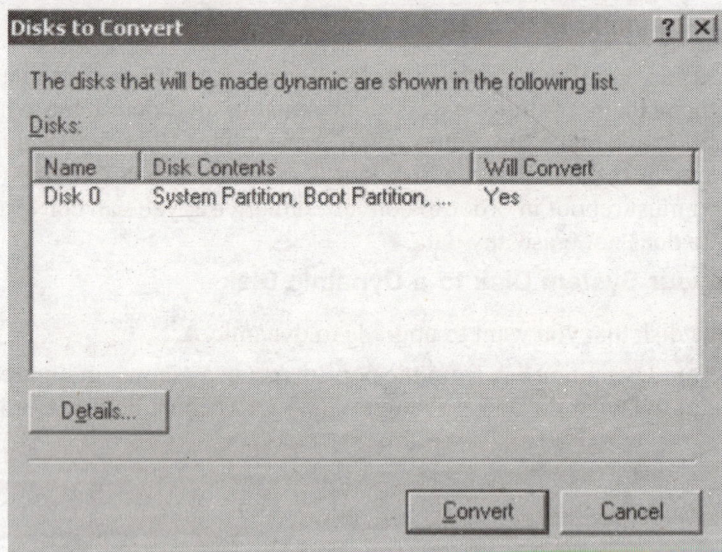

Figure 3.39 Reviewing Disks to be Converted

5. Windows will warn you that you are about to convert to dynamic. Click Yes on the warning screen (shown in Figure 3.40) to continue.
6. You are next warned that file systems currently in use on the disk will be dismounted during the upgrade (Figure 3.41).This is your last chance to cancel the conversion operation. If you are sure that you want to convert to dynamic, click Yes to dismount the file system.
7. Click OK on the confirmation window (shown in Figure 3.42) to reboot your PC. The disk(s) you selected will be upgraded when the computer is rebooted.

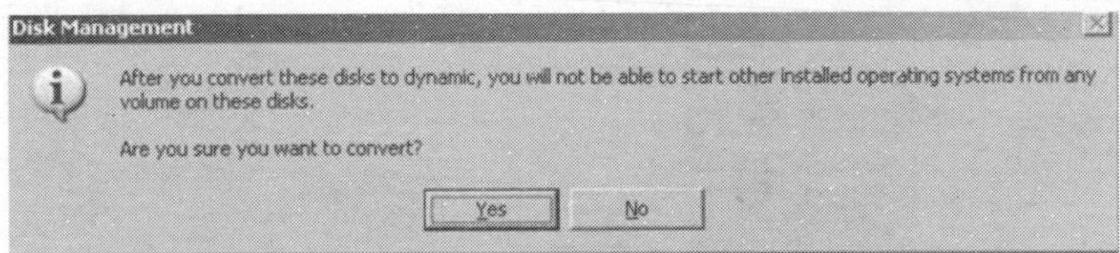

Figure 3.40 Con?rming the Conversion

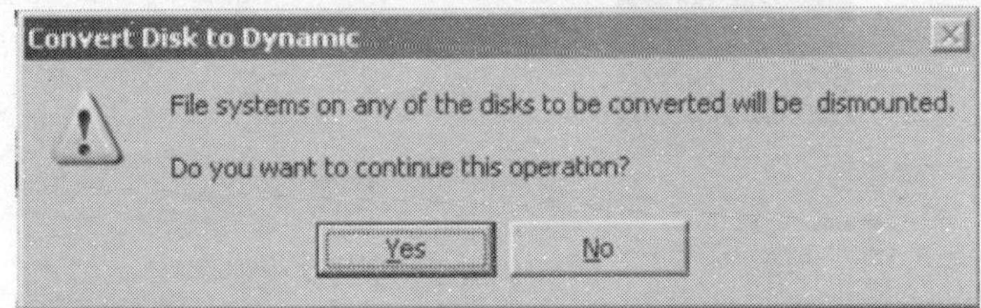

Figure 3.41 Dismounting Disk to be Converted

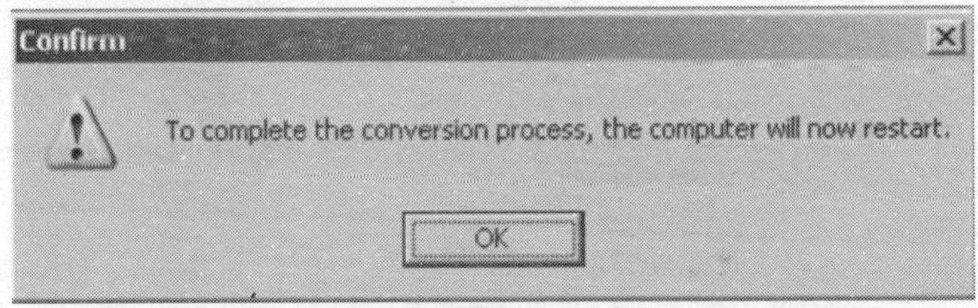

Figure 3.42 Completing the Conversion Creating and Using Dynamic Volumes

After you have converted your disk to dynamic, you can create volumes. Creating volumes is similar to creating partitions, except that there are some additional steps because, unlike partitions, volumes can span multiple disks. The type of volume you create depends on a variety of factors, such as the following:

1. How many disks do you have in your machine?
2. Do you want fault tolerance?
3. Do you want to increase read or write performance?
4. What is being stored (or will be stored) on the volume (e.g., database, system partition, print spooler, etc.)?

3.5.2 Creating and Using Simple Volumes

Simple volumes are the default volume type on a dynamic disk. Use simple volumes in the following situations:

- You only have one disk in a machine.
- You are not concerned with fault tolerance.
- You want the ability to dynamically extend the space used on a volume.

Use the following steps to create a simple volume

1. Right-click the unallocated space on the disk on which you want to create a simple volume.
2. Click New Volume on the context menu. This will start the New Volume Wizard, shown in Figure 3.43.
3. Click Next to continue.

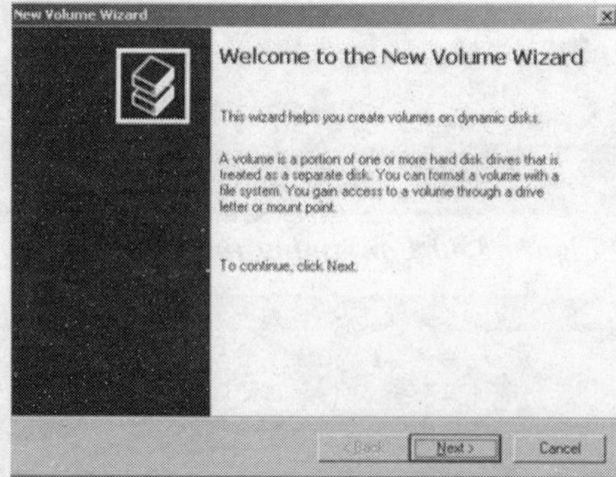

Figure 3.43 Creating Simple Volumes

4. On the Select Volume Type window (Figure 3.44), select Simple.
5. Click Next to continue.

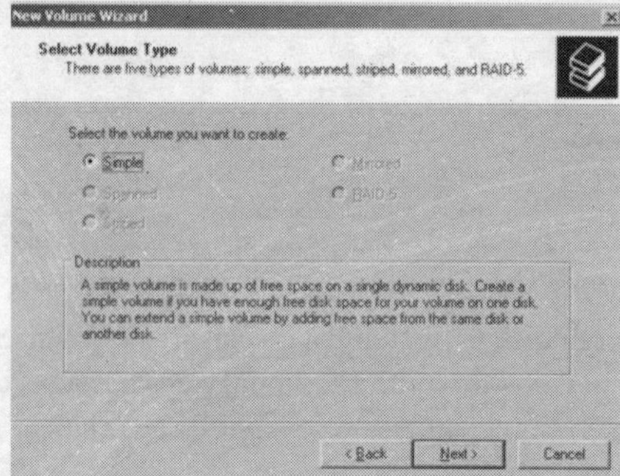

Figure 3.44 Selecting Volume Type

6. You will next be prompted to select the disk to use for the simple volume, as shown in Figure 3.45.The correct disk should already be selected. If not, select it.
7. Select the amount of space to be used for the simple volume and click Next to continue.

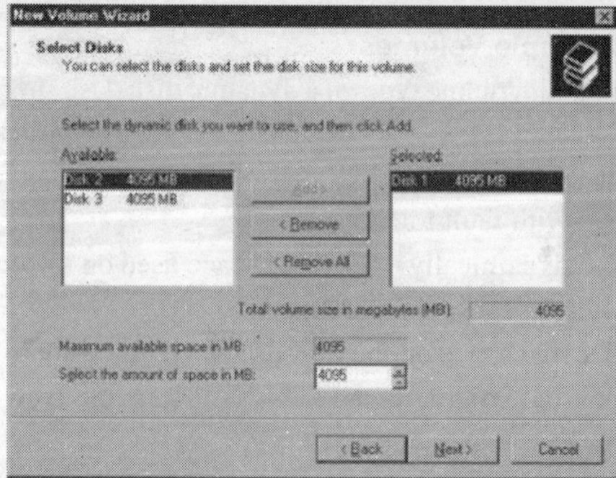

Figure 3.45 Selecting Disks to be Used in a Simple Volume

8. Next you need to identify your new volume. Select a drive letter or choose to mount the new volume to an NTFS folder. For this example, we assign the new volume the drive letter D, as shown in Figure 3.46

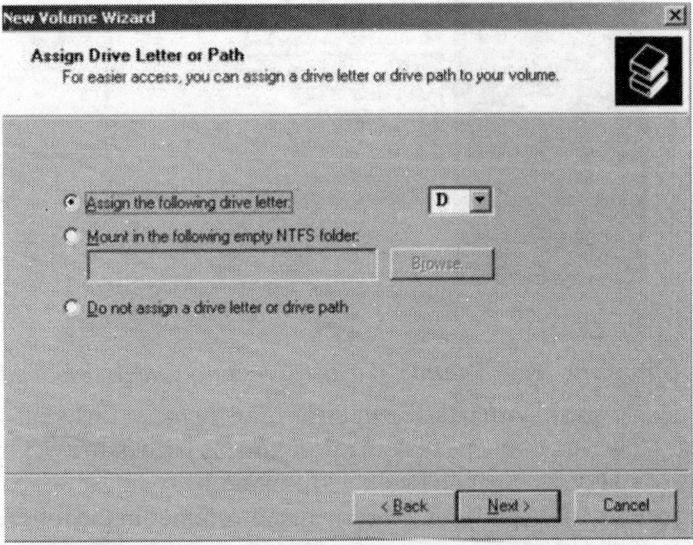

Figure 3.46 Assigning a Drive Letter or Path

9. Next, you can format your new volume. You can format the volume as FAT, FAT32, or NTFS, or you can choose not to format the volume now. For this example, choose NTFS, as shown in Figure 3.47, and click Next to continue.
10. You will now see the Completing the New Volume Wizard window, as shown in Figure 3.48. Read over the summary to verify that you made the correct selections and click Finish to complete the process.

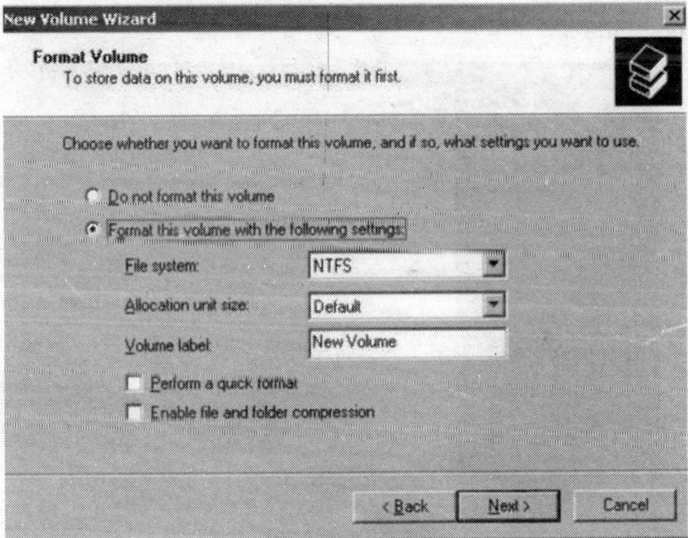

Figure 3.47 Formatting Your New Volume

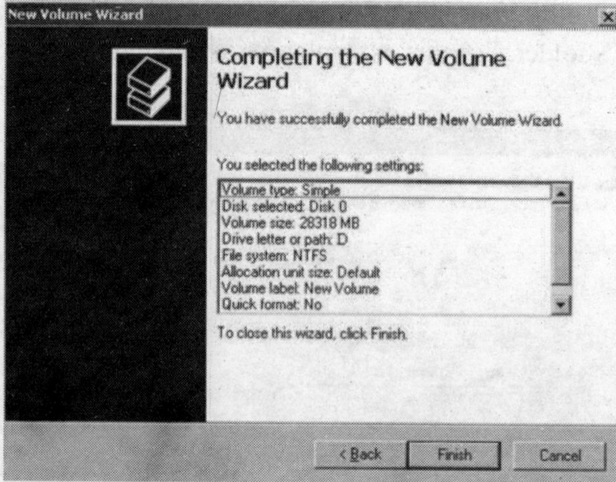

Figure 3.48 Finishing the New Volume Wizard Creating and Using Spanned Volumes

Spanned volumes enable you to group different disks of the same or different sizes and access them as if they were one disk. However, only one disk in the volume is written to at a time. Spanned volumes can be created using two to 32 disks. Spanned volumes provide 100 percent drive utilization (minus the 1MB per disk overhead for the LDM partition). Use spanned volumes in the following situations:

1. You want to access multiple disks as a single volume and you are not concerned about fault tolerance or increased read/write performance.
2. Your disks are different sizes and you want to achieve 100 percent drive utilization with a single volume.
3. You have a simple volume that is almost full and you need to expand it across multiple disks.

3.5.3 Create a Spanned Volume

1. Right-click the unallocated space on the disk on which you want to create a spanned volume.
2. Click New Volume on the context menu. This will start the New Volume Wizard, as shown in Figure 3.49.
3. Click Next to continue.

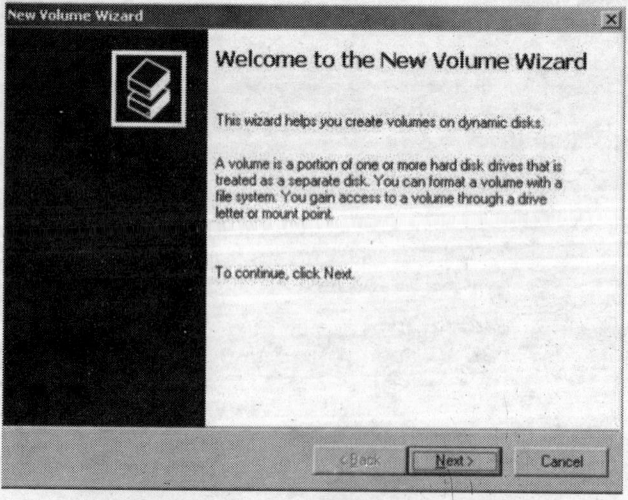

Figure 3.49 Creating a Spanned Volume

4. In the Select Volume Type window (Figure 3.50), select Spanned.
5. Click Next to continue.

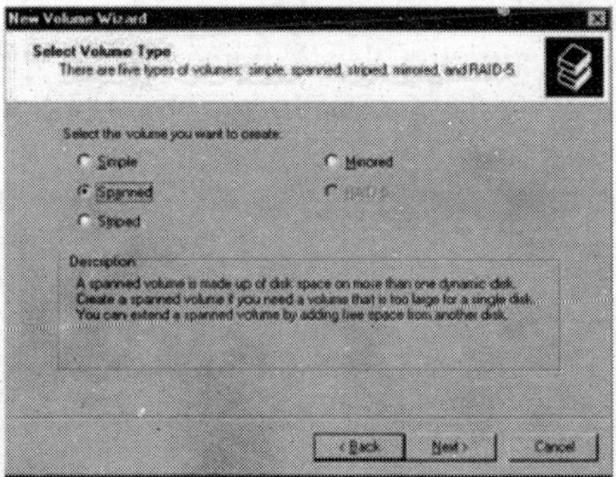

Figure 3.50 Selecting the Volume Type to be Created

6. You will next be prompted to select the disks to use for the spanned volume, as shown in Figure 3.51. Select the disks you want to use.
7. Select the amount of space to be used for simple volume and click Next to continue.

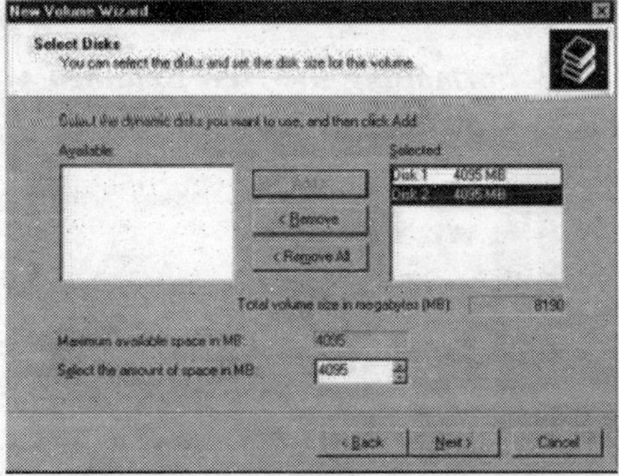

Figure 3.51 Selecting Disks to be used in Spanned Volume

8. Next you need to identify your new spanned volume. Select a drive letter or choose to mount the new volume to an NTFS folder. For this example, we assign the new volume the drive letter D, as shown in Figure 3.52.

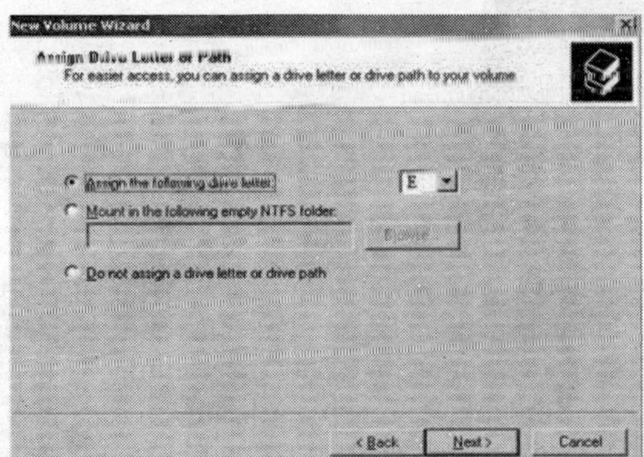

Figure 3.52 Assigning a Drive Letter or Path

9. Next you can format your new spanned volume. You can format the volume as FAT, FAT32, or NTFS, or you can choose not to format the volume at this time. For this example, choose NTFS, as shown in Figure 3.53, and then click Next to continue.
10. You will next see the Completing the New Volume Wizard window, as shown in Figure 3.54. Read over the summary to verify that you made the correct selections and click Finish to complete the process.

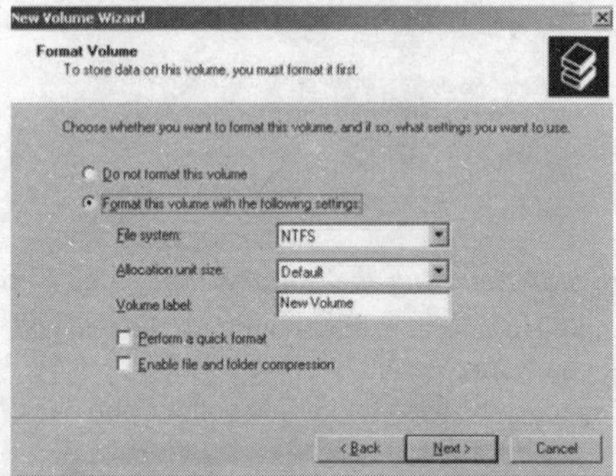

Figure 3.53 Formatting the New Spanned Volume

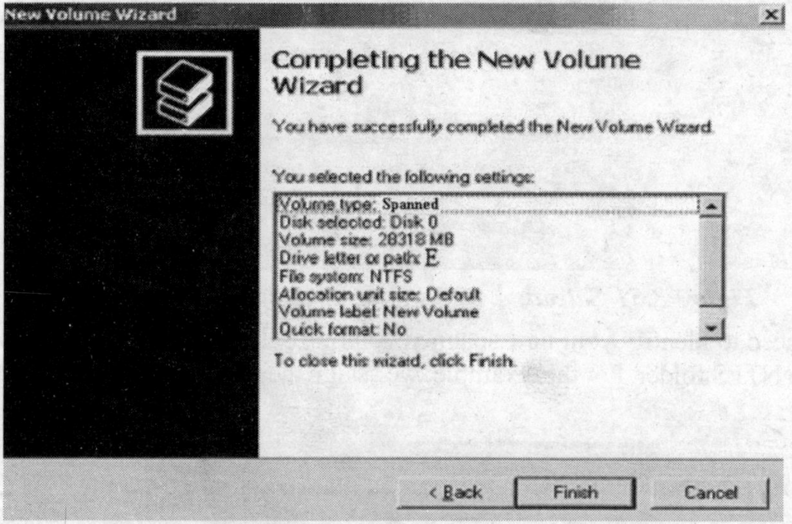

Figure 3.54 Completing the New Volume Wizard

3.5.4 Creating and Using Striped Volumes

Striped volumes require that you use an equal amount of unallocated space on each of the disks that is part of the volume. Ideally, your disks will all be the same size and all space on each will be unallocated. If not, some of the space will be wasted when you create the volume. Striped volumes increase both read and write performance when accessing the volume by utilizing all the disks at one time. Unlike spanned volumes, striped volumes cannot be extended. Striped volumes can be created using two to 32 disks. Use stripped volumes in the following situations:

1. The primary disk operation will be reading information from a large database such as SQL or Exchange.
2. The volume will be used to spool large print jobs.
3. You are not concerned with fault tolerance.
4. You plan to collect external data on the disk at very fast transfer rates.

3.5.4.1 Creating a Striped Volume

1. Right-click the unallocated space on the disk on which you want to create a striped volume.
2. Click New Volume on the context menu. This will start the New Volume Wizard, as shown in Figure 3.55.
3. Click Next to continue.

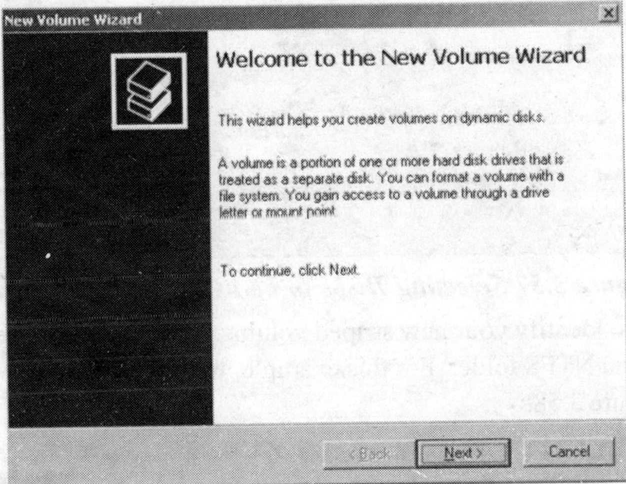

Figure 3.55 Creating a Striped Volume

4. On the Select Volume Type window (Figure 3.56), select Striped.
5. Click Next to continue.

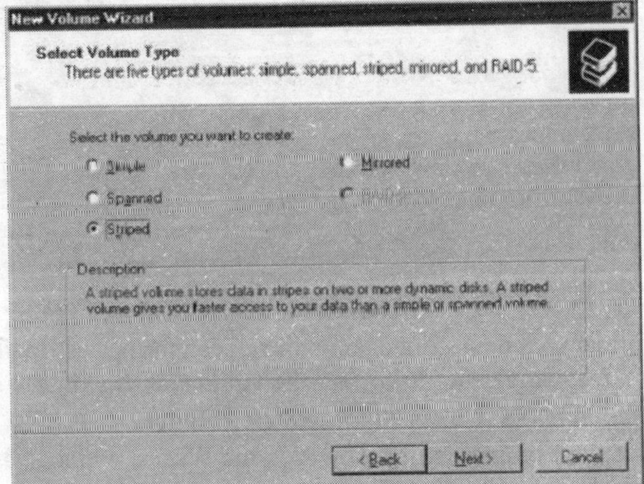

Figure 3.56 Selecting the Volume Type to be Created

6. You will next be prompted to select the disk to use for the striped volume, as shown in Figure 3.57. Select the disks you want to use.
7. Select the amount of space to be used for the striped volume and click Next to continue.

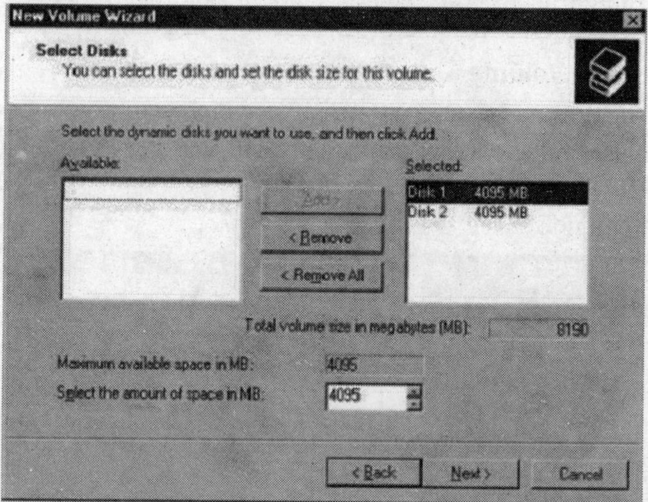

Figure 3.57 Selecting Disks to be used in Striped Volume

8. Next you need to identify your new striped volume. Select a drive letter or choose to mount the new volume to an NTFS folder. For this example, we assign the new volume the drive letter E, as shown in Figure 3.58.

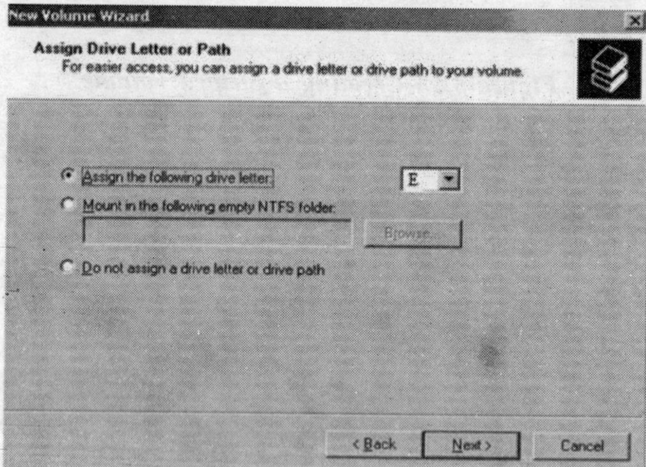

Figure 3.58 Assigning a Drive Letter or Path

9. Next, you can format your new striped volume. You can format a striped volume as FAT, FAT32, or NTFS, or you can choose not to format the volume at this time. For this example, choose NTFS, as shown in Figure 3.59, and click Next to continue.
10. You will next see the Completing the New Volume Wizard window, as shown in Figure 3.60. Read the summary to verify that you made the correct selections and click Finish to complete the process.

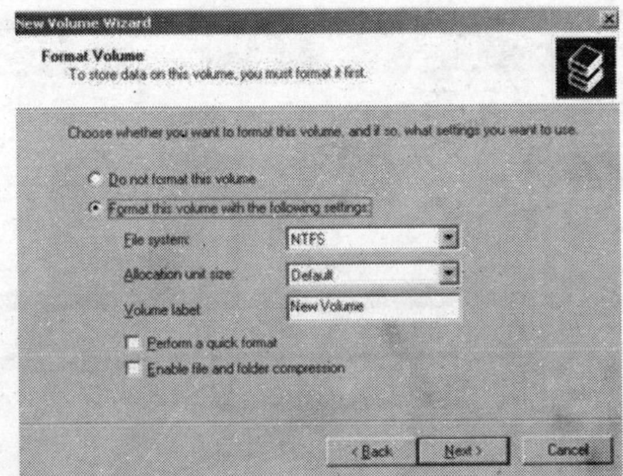

Figure 3.59 Formatting the New Striped Volume

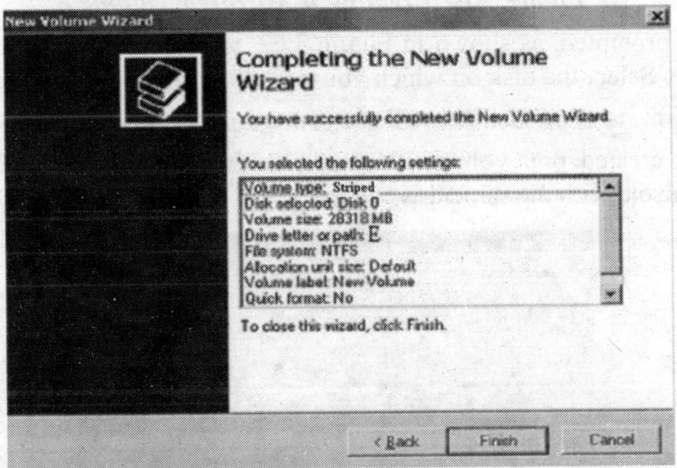

Figure 3.60 Ending the New Volume Wizard

3.5.5 Creating and Using Mirrored Volumes

Mirrored volumes require exactly two disks and both disks must be the same size. When you write information to the mirror, it is written twice - once to each disk. This provides complete redundancy for your data. Should one disk fail, you can use the mirrored copy. Mirrored volumes provide only 50 percent disk utilization (the least cost efficient of all volume types) and cannot be extended. However, they provide excellent fault tolerance. Use mirrored volumes in the following situations:

1. You want to provide fault tolerance for the boot and/or system partition.
2. You want an easy way to roll back failed operating system upgrades (break the mirror before the upgrade).
3. You need fault tolerance, but you only have two disks.
4. You want to be able to get the system up and running quickly after a disk failure.

3.5.5.1 Creating a Mirrored Volume

1. Right-click the simple volume you wish to mirror, as shown in Figure 3.61.
2. Choose Add Mirror from the context menu.

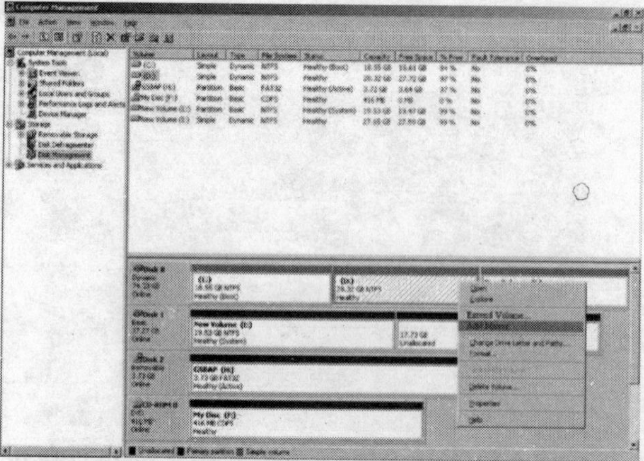

Figure 3.61 Creating a Mirrored Volume

3. You are next prompted, as shown in Figure 3.62, to select a location to hold a mirror of the selected drive. Select the disk on which you want to create the mirror copy.
4. Click Add Mirror to continue. You will see your mirror being created, as shown in Figure 3.63.

After the mirror is created, both volumes that make up the two parts of the mirror will appear in the Disk Management console with the same drive letter.

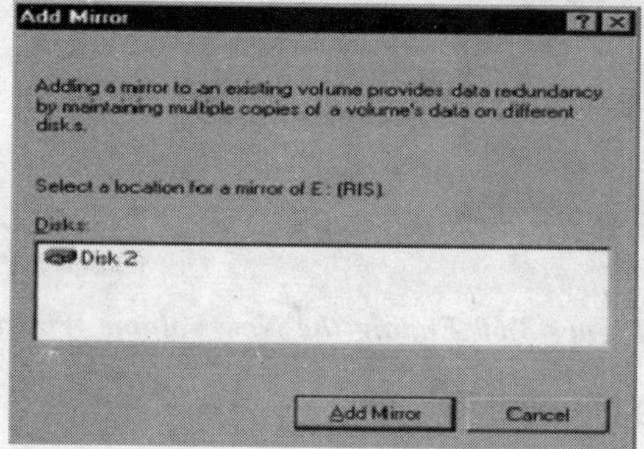

Figure 3.62 Selecting a Location for the Mirror

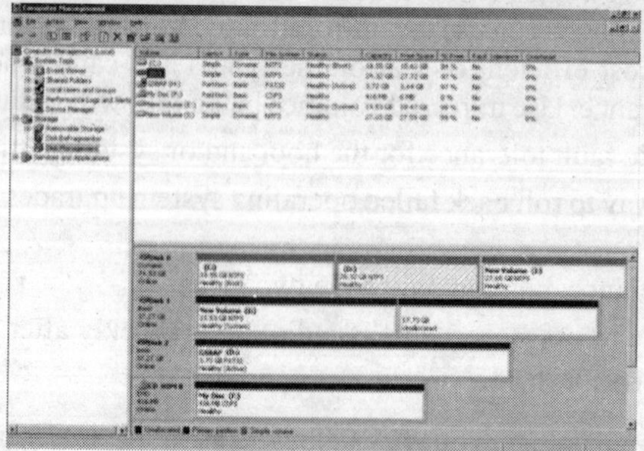

Figure 3.63 Synchronizing a Mirrored Volume

3.5.6 Creating and Using Raid-5 Volumes

RAID-5 volumes can be created using three to 32 disks. The parity information can be used to regenerate the missing data should one disk fail. If you lose more than one disk, however, all your data will be lost.

As with mirrored volumes, RAID-5 volumes cannot be extended. However, RAID-5 volumes offer more efficient disk utilization than mirrored volumes. You lose the storage space equivalent to one disk in the RAID-5 volume because it is used for parity information. For example, if you have five disks and you lose the storage space of one disk, you operate at 80 percent disk utilization. If you increase the number of disks in your RAID-5 volume, you will get even better disk utilization. For example, if you use 10 disks instead of five, you will operate at 90 percent utilization instead of 80 percent utilization. On the other hand, it takes longer to get your system back up and running after a disk failure with RAID-5, as opposed to mirrors, because you must go through the process of regenerating the data from parity. Use RAID-5 volumes in the following situations:

1. You need the boosted read performance of a striped volume, but you must have fault tolerance.
2. You want fault tolerance with the most efficient level of disk utilization possible.
3. You need fault tolerance, but you have too many disks to usc a mirror.

3.5.6.1 Creating a Raid-5 Volume

1. Right-click the unallocated space on the disk on which you want to create a RAID-5 volume.
2. Click New Volume on the context menu. This will start the New Volume Wizard, as shown in Figure 3.64.
3. Click Next to continue.

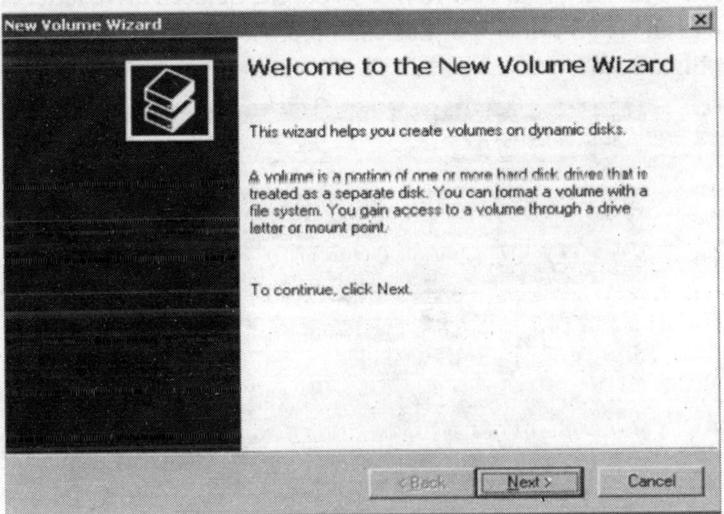

Figure 3.64 Using the New Volume Wizard to Create a RAID-5 Volume

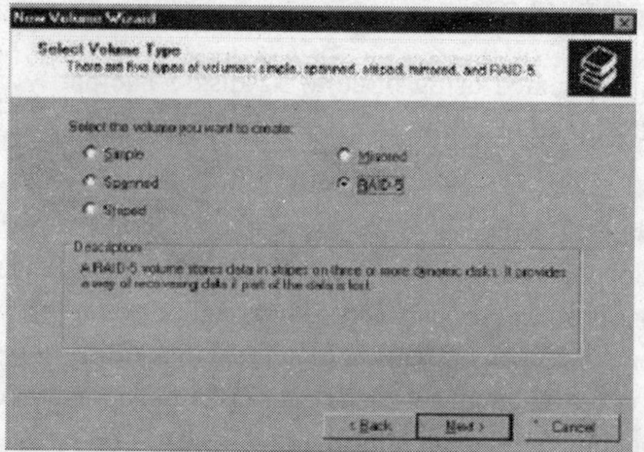

Figure 3.65 Selecting to Create a RAID-5 Volume

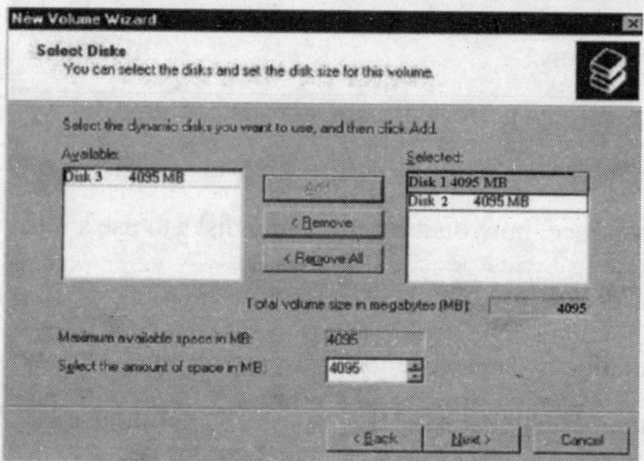

Figure 3.66 Adding Disks to the RAID-5 Volume

8. Next you need to identify your new RAID-5 volume. Select a drive letter or choose to mount the new volume to an NTFS folder. For this example, we assign the new volume the drive letter D, as shown in Figure 3.67.

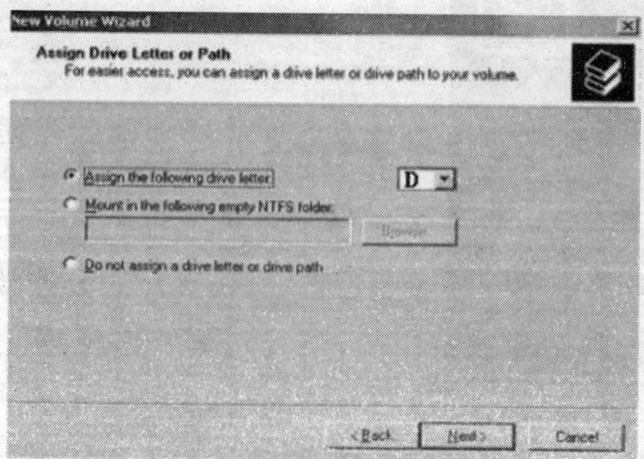

Figure 3.67 Assigning a Drive Letter or Path

9. Next, you can format your new RAID-5 volume.You can format a RAID-5 volume as FAT, FAT32, or NTFS, or you can choose not to format the volume at this time. For this example, choose NTFS, as shown in Figure 3.68, and click Next to continue.
10. You will next see the Completing the New Volume Wizard window, as shown in Figure 3.69. Read the summary to verify that you made the correct selections and click Finish to complete the process.

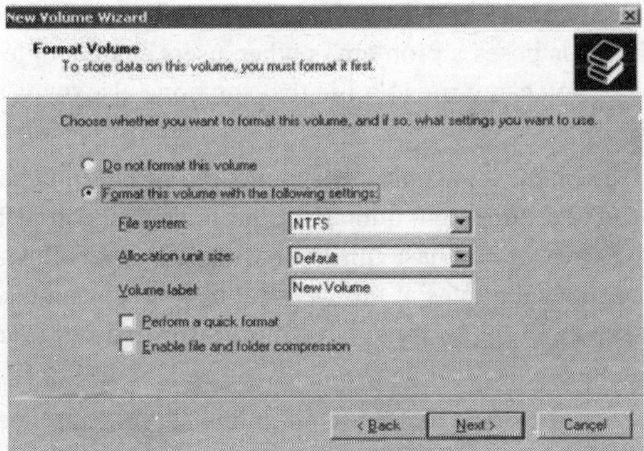

Figure 3.68 Formatting the RAID-5 Volume

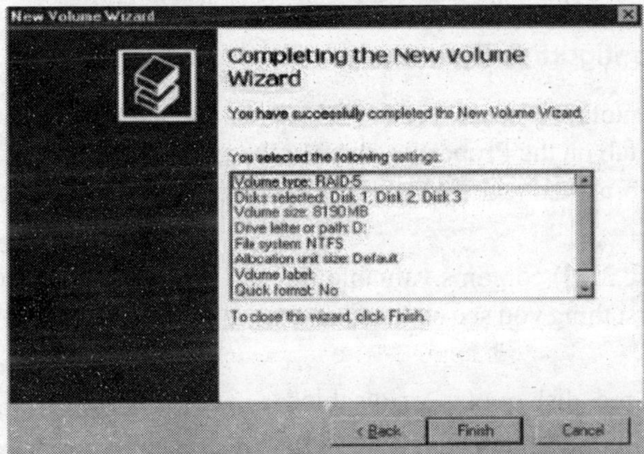

Figure 3.69 Finishing the New Volume Wizard

3.6 DISK QUOTAS

The capability to set disk quotas is a feature that was on the "wish list" of Windows NT administrators for a long time. Users tend to find a way of consuming every bit (and byte) of space that you offer them. Third-party products provided for setting quotas with NT, and built-in support for disk quotas was first introduced in Windows 2000. Disk quota support has been carried over to Windows XP and Windows Server 2003. In the following sections, we discuss how to enable, configure, and monitor disk quotas.

Disk quotas enable you to track and limit disk space usage on NTFS volumes. You can use disk quotas for two purposes:

1. To audit how much space your users are using (enabling quotas without limiting disk space)
2. To limit your users to a set amount of space (enabling quotas and setting limits on disk space)

Users are warned when they approach the specified limit. The administrator can set the level at which the warning occurs. After the limit is reached, a user can no longer save data to the volume without first deleting some files to create new space. You can also set the system to log an event to the event log when a user reaches either the warning level or the disk space limit.

Disk quota amounts are calculated based on file ownership. The size of the file is charged against its owner's limit. The only time this poses a problem is when users share single files. For example, if you have the correct permissions, you can write to a file that someone else owns and it would count against the other user's limit.

Disk quotas are set at the volume level only. You cannot create different quotas for individual folders within a volume. If you need to set different quotas for the same users on different folders, you can put those folders on separate volumes or purchase third-party software that allows for more granular setting of quotas. Likewise, you cannot set quotas at the physical disk level. If a disk has three volumes on it, each volume is managed separately. You must have administrative rights to assign quotas. Use disk quotas in the following situations:

1. You have limited shared storage available on public servers and need to ensure that the disks don't become full.
2. You want to keep a log of how much disk space is being consumed by each user.

3.6.1 Enabling and Configuring Disk Quotas

You can enable disk quotas by accessing the Properties sheet for a volume and using the Quota tab. If you do not see a Quota tab on the Properties sheet, either you do not have administrative rights on the machine or the volume is formatted with FAT or FAT32. Remember that disk quotas can only be configured on NTFS volumes.

The Quota tab (Figure 3.70) contains valuable information and you should be familiar with all the options on this tab. The first thing you see on the Quota tab is the "stop light." It indicates the status of disk quotas on the volume:

1. When the light is red, disk quotas are disabled.
2. When the light is yellow, the system is rebuilding disk quota information.
3. When the light is green, disk quotas are enabled and active.

When you select the check box next to Enable quota management, the light goes from red to yellow to green. However, the light may appear to go straight to green. This just means that the quota information was built very quickly and didn't register on the light.

After you enable disk quotas, you must configure how they will be used. By default, users are not denied disk space or warned about the amount of disk space they are using. This is the proper setting if you are only using disk quotas to track how much space each user is using, but if you want to limit the amount of space available to users, you must further configure the quotas feature. This is where the Deny disk space to users exceeding quota limit check box comes into play. When you check this checkbox, Windows will deny additional disk space to anyone who exceeds his or her limit.

You can either set limits for users individually by using the Quota Entries button or you can configure a default limit that will apply to everyone. You can also import quota settings from another volume. This is useful if you want to set the quotas identically on a number of different volumes. There are two settings to configure for each user (or for all users as the default): a limit level and a warning level:

1. Next to Limit disk space to, there are two boxes. The first box is a text field into which you can type a number. The second box is a drop-down box that contains a disk measurement unit (KB, MB, GB,TB, PB, EB). By entering a number in the first box and choosing a measurement from the second box, you can restrict each user to a disk space limit ranging from 1KB to 6 EB. The default limit is 1KB.
2. Directly under the limits boxes are identical Set warning level to boxes. Quota warnings are configured in the same ways as quota limits. You should set the warning level to a smaller number than the disk limit so that users will know they are approaching their limits before reaching them. Table 3.3 explains the different disk measurement options available for setting limits and warnings.

Table 3.3 Understanding Disk Measurements

Measurement	Description
KB	KB stands for kilobyte. One kilobyte equals one thousand bytes (1,024 bytes in decimal).
MB	MB stands for megabyte. One megabyte equals one million bytes (1,048,576 bytes in decimal).
GB	GB stands for gigabit. One gigabit equals one billion bytes (1,073,741,824 bytes in decimal).
TB	TB stands for terabyte. One terabyte equals one thousand billion bytes (1,099,511,627,776 bytes in decimal-that is a thousand gigabytes).
PB	PB stands for petabyte. One petabyte equals one thousand terabytes (1,125,899,906,842,624 bytes in decimal).
EB	EB stands for exabyte. One exabyte equals one quintillion bytes (a billion gigabytes-1,152,921,504,606,846,976 bytes in decimal).

Finally, you can configure the logging options. Under Select the quota logging options for this volume you have two options:

1. Log event when a user exceeds their quota limit
2. Log event when a user exceeds their warning level

Both options are disabled by default and either or both can be enabled by checking the corresponding check box (es). Both settings log events to the system log of the event viewer. Logging options are set only on a per-volume basis; there is no setting for logging on an individual user's Quota Settings page.

3.6.2 Enabling Disk Quotas and Setting Quota Limits

1. In Windows Explorer or My Computer, right-click the volume on which you want to set quotas and select Properties from the context menu. In this example, we enable quotas on the C drive. Note that to

manage quotas on a remote computer, you'll need to first map a network drive for the remote volume on which you want to set or manage quotas.

2. Click the Quota tab, as shown in Figure 3.70.
3. Check the check box next to "Enable quota management" to enable disk quotas for the C drive.
4. Check the check box next to "Deny disk space to users exceeding quota limit to enforce limits.
5. Click the Quota Entries button to open the Quota Entries console, as shown in Figure 3.71.

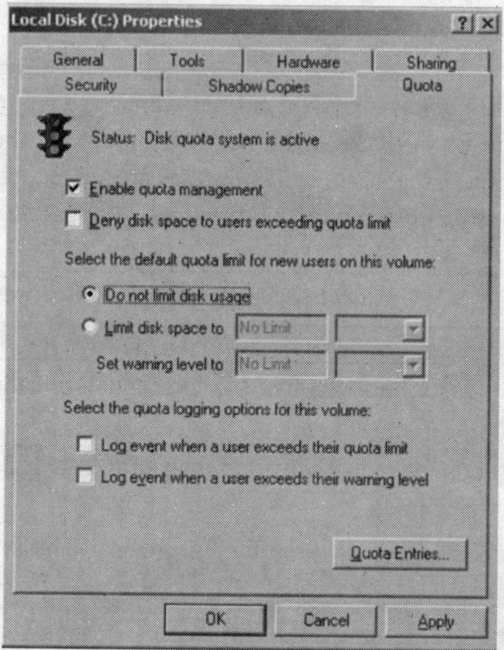

Figure 3.70 Enabling Disk Quotas

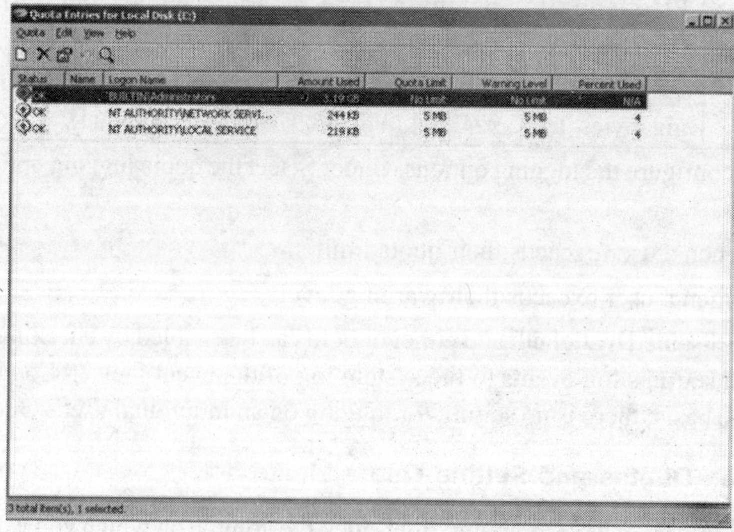

Figure 3.71 Viewing Quota Entries

6. Click the Quota menu bar.
7. Select New Quota Entry from the menu.
8. You are prompted to choose the users for which you want to add quotas, as shown in Figure 3.72.Type the user's name in the box and click Check Name to verify that the user exists in the account database.
9. If the name is veri?ed, click OK to continue. You next have to customize the quota entry for the user, as shown in Figure 3.73.

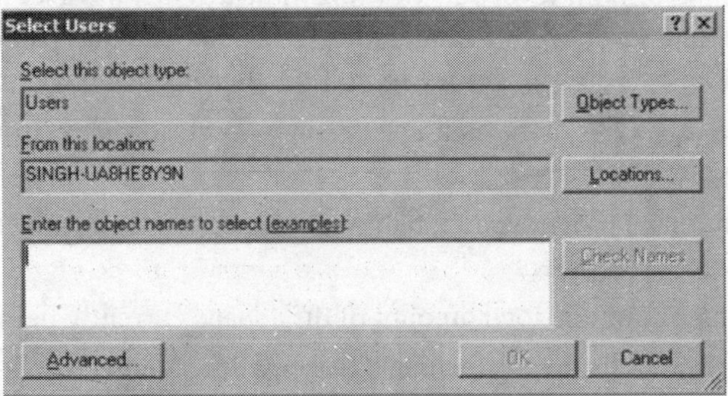

Figure 3.72 Choosing Users to Restrict

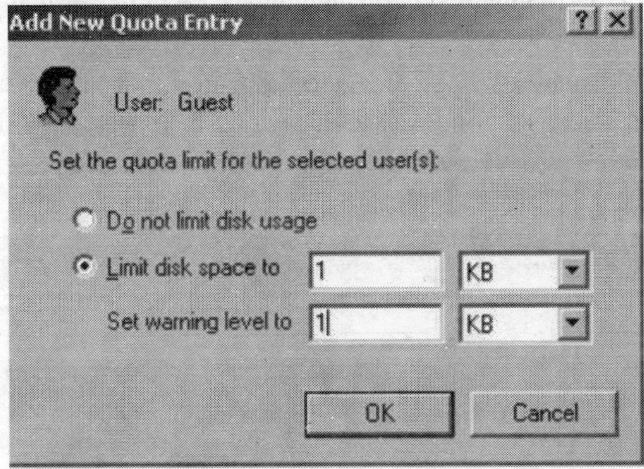

Figure 3.73 Configuring Limits and Warnings

10. Select "Limit disk space to" and enter the amount of space you wish to allow the user to use on the volume. Select a unit of measurement.
11. Set the warning level for your user in the same way.
12. Click OK to save the settings and add the user to the Quota Entries list.

3.6.3 Monitoring Disk Quotas

Now that you know how to enable disk quotas, we will discuss how to analyze the quota settings and monitor disk usage. Disk quota settings are accessed and disk usage is monitored via the Quota Entries console, as previously shown in Figure 3.71.

The Quota Entries console displays seven items in regard to each user. You can sort by the columns by clicking the corresponding section of the column title bar or by using the View menu (View | Arrange Items | by…). For example, if you want to sort by the amount of disk spaced used, click on the Amount Used bar. This will arrange the user accounts in order of least to greatest space used. Clicking the same column header again will rearrange the accounts in the opposite order (greatest to least).

1. **Status:** This indicates how well the user is complying with the quota limit. There are three possible settings: OK, Warning, or Above Limit. A status of OK indicates that the user hasn't reached the warning or limit level yet. Warning indicates that the user has reached the warning level, but not the limit level. Above Limit indicates that the user has passed both the warning and limit levels. Sorting by status makes it easy to find all users that have exceeded their limits.
2. Name This is the user's full name as it appears in Local Users and Groups or Active Directory Users and Computers.
3. Logon Name This is the user's account name as it appears in Local Users and Groups or Active Directory Users and Computers.
4. Amount Used This shows the total amount of disk space currently being used by the user.
5. Quota Limit This shows the level at which the user will no longer be allowed to save data to this volume.
6. Warning Level This shows the level at which the user will be warned when saving data to this volume.
7. Percent Used This displays the percentage of allocated space that has been used by the user. Sorting by Percent Used is a good way to discover which users may run out of space soon.

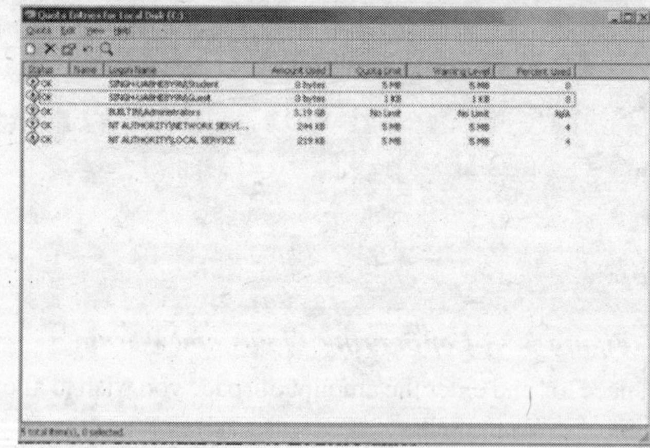

Figure 3.74 Resolving SIDs to Logon Names

3.7 EXPORTING AND IMPORTING QUOTA SETTINGS

If you have multiple volumes that contain users' data then you will probably want to apply the same quota settings to all volumes. Also, if you migrate your users' data from one volume to another, then you need an easy way to reapply all the disk quotas. There are a few different ways to copy disk quotas from one volume to another. If you open the Quota Entries window (as shown in Figure 3.75) for both volumes, you can drag and drop quota limits between the two windows. You can also export all quota settings to a file and import them to another volume. You can use the following steps to export quota settings and import quota settings.

3.7.1 Export Quota Settings

1. Open My Computer.
2. Right-click the volume you want to manage and choose Properties from the pop-up menu.
3. Click the Quota tab.
4. Click the Quota Entries button. This will give you a window similar to Figure 3.75.
5. Click the Quota menu bar and choose Export from the drop-down list. You will now be asked where to save the quota settings, as shown in Figure 3.76.
6. Type in a name and click the Save button to finish the export.

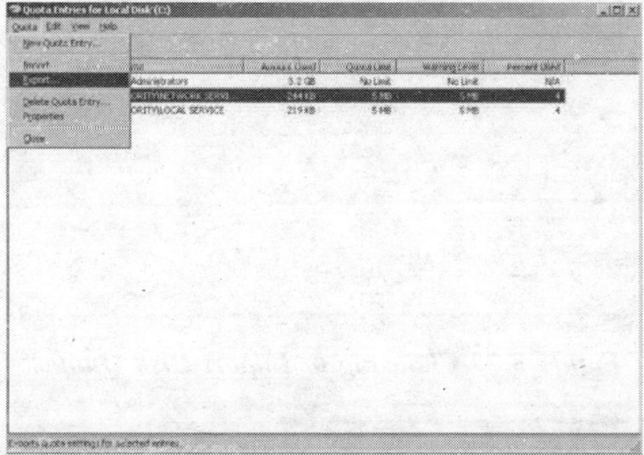

Figure 3.75 Choosing to Export Quota Settings

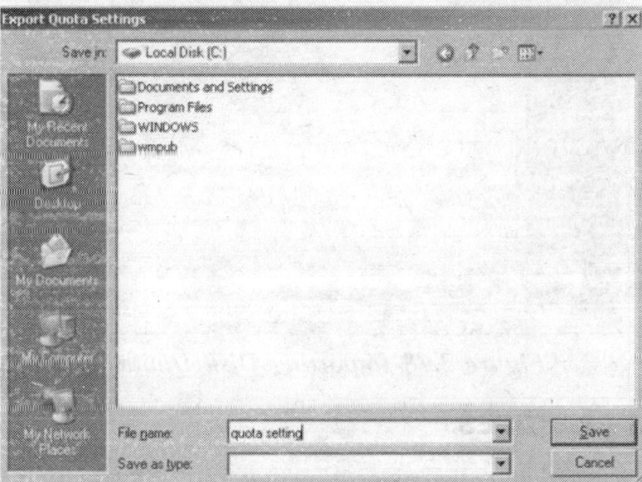

Figure 3.76 Exporting Quota Settings

3.7.2 Import Quota Settings

The steps for importing quota settings are very similar to the steps for exporting quota settings.

1. Open My Computer.
2. Right-click the volume you want to manage and choose Properties from the pop-up menu.
3. Click the Quota tab.
4. Click the Quota Entries button. This will give you a window similar to Figure 3.77.
5. Click the Quota menu bar and choose Import from the drop-down list. You will now be asked which quota settings file to import, as shown in Figure 3.78.
6. Navigate to the quota settings file and click Open to import the settings.

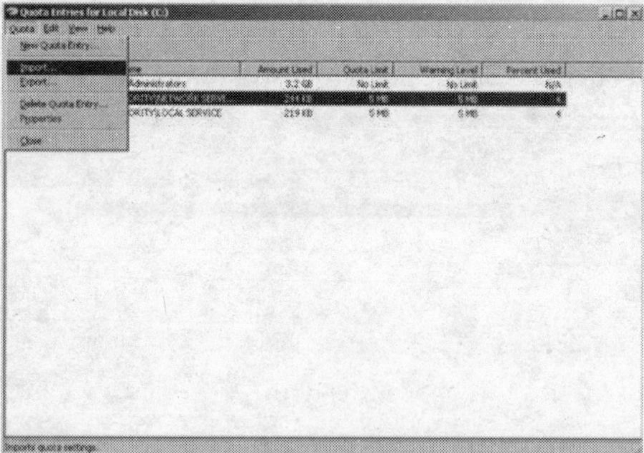

Figure 3.77 Choosing to Import Disk Quotas

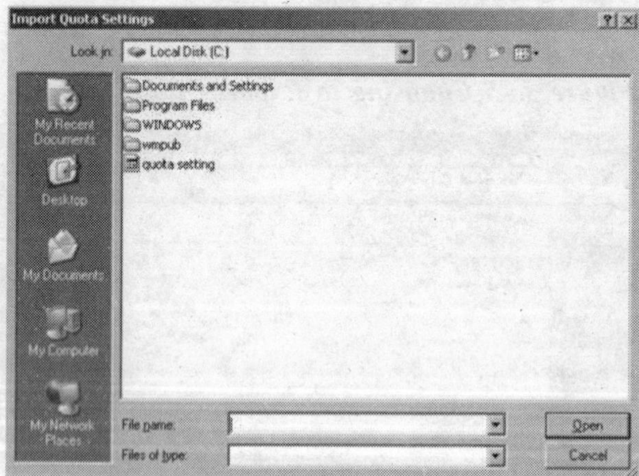

Figure 3.78 Importing Disk Quotas

3.8 DISK QUOTA BEST PRACTICES

Disk quotas are a powerful feature that gives Windows Server 2003 administrators fiexible control over disk usage. However, using them incorrectly car be disastrous. Don't let this keep you from using disk quotas - just learn to use them intelligently. Here are few guidelines that will ensure that enabling disk quotas makes your job as an administrator easier, not more difficult:

1. Set default limits so that all users are restricted in the amount of space they can use by default. Always make your default settings as restrictive as possible, while still providing users with enough space to do their work. It is easier to give users more space if needed than to take space away. Remember that this is only a default setting. It is not a mandatory setting for all your users; it only applies to those user accounts that do not have specific individual settings configured.
2. Use reasonable quota limits. Don't just take the amount of space available and divide it equally among your users. Sit down and calculate a fair limit, based on user needs. Not everyone needs the same amount of disk space. Power users may need more than standard users. Those who work with and save large graphic or video files need more space than those who work primarily with plain text files.
3. Be realistic in setting the quotas and stick to them unless/until there is a real need to change them. If you set the default limit at 50MB when you know most users are using 200MB, you are setting yourself up for trouble. Try not to get into the habit of setting quotas excessively low and then increasing them when users complain. It is better to give users the right amount of space up front, and be less fiexible about increasing the amount. If users know they can easily get their allocations increased by complaining, they will be less motivated to properly manage their files.
4. Delete quota entries for users who no longer need to store files on the volume. Delete or move their files to another volume, to free space for those who need to store data on the volume.
5. When calculating the amount of disk space available for allocating quotas, remember to take into account NTFS overhead. Files can contain up to 64KB of metadata (information about the file) that is not counted against a user's quota, but does take up space on the disk.

3.9 USING FSUTIL TO MANAGE DISK QUOTAS

If you prefer using a command-line tool instead of the graphical interface, you can perform many of the tasks involved in managing disk quotas with the command-line utility fsutil.exe. Use the command fsutil quota with one of the following parameters to perform quota-related tasks:

1. Fsutil quota disables <volumepathname> To disable quotas on the volume.
2. Fsutil quotas enforce <volumepathname > To enable quota enforcement on the volume.
3. Fsutil quotas modify <volumepathname> To create a new quota or change an existing one.
4. Fsutil quota query <volumepathname> To list existing quota entries.
5. Fsutil quota track <volumepathname> To track disk usage on the volume.
6. Fsutil quota violations To display detected quota violations.

The fsutil commands can be used in a script to automate quota tasks (for example, to set a specified quota limit each time you add a new user).

3.10 DISK FRAGMENTATION

Optimizing disk performance is an important part of managing a server. Consider the disk-oriented tasks that take place on a typical day on the typical server. Users save data to their home directories.

They send e-mail back and forth (which is saved in a database on the server).They print documents. They access shared files. All these tasks require good disk performance.

Two issues you will always run into when managing disks are disk fragmentation and insufficient disk space. Fragmentation problems are not as obvious as disk space problems; when you run out of disk space, you usually find out immediately. However, you may not notice that a disk is fragmented unless you take the time to check or you notice that performance has degraded. With Windows Server 2003, Microsoft provides ways to manage both of these concerns. The disk defragmentation utilities can ensure that your disk is performing at its peak and the disk quotas feature can ensure that you do not run out of disk space. In the following sections, we will discuss how to use these tools to keep your disks at optimum performance levels.

3.10.1 Defragmenting Volumes and Partitions

Defragmenting the disks on all your servers (especially file servers) can ensure optimal performance and enable you to get more use out of your disks. It is not something that you should do every day, but you de?nitely need to make it part of your server maintenance routine. Microsoft provides two tools for performing defragmentation. Both tools work with basic and dynamic disks that are formatted with the FAT, FAT32, or NTFS file systems.

These tools are:

1. Disk Defragmenter (graphical utility)
2. Defrag.exe (command-line tool)

You will learn how to use each of these tools to defragment your disks.

3.10.1.1 Using the Graphical Defragmenter

You can access the graphical defragmenter in several different ways:

1. Click Start | All Programs | Accessories | System Tools | Disk Defragmenter.
2. Right-click My Computer, select Manage, and click Disk Defragmenter in the left console pane.
3. Click Start | All Programs | Administrative Tools | Computer Management and click the Disk Defragmenter in the left console pane.

For our examples, we will access the Disk Defragmenter via Computer Management. Note that anyone can open the Disk Defragmenter tool, but only an administrator or someone with an account that has been delegated the authority, can analyze or defragment a volume.

3.10.1.2 Using the Disk Defragmenter

1. Open Computer Management (click Start | All Programs | Administrative Tools | Computer Management).
2. Click Disk Defragmenter as shown in Figure 3.79.
3. Click the Analyze button. This will analyze your disks and give you a report of how defragmented they are, as shown in Figure 3.80.

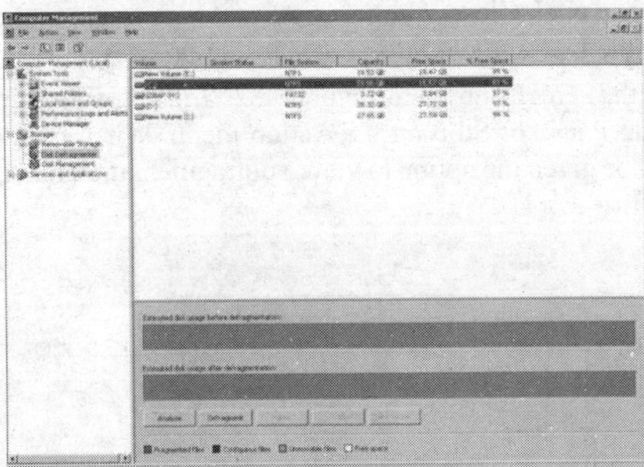

Figure 3.79 Using Disk Defragmenter from the GUI

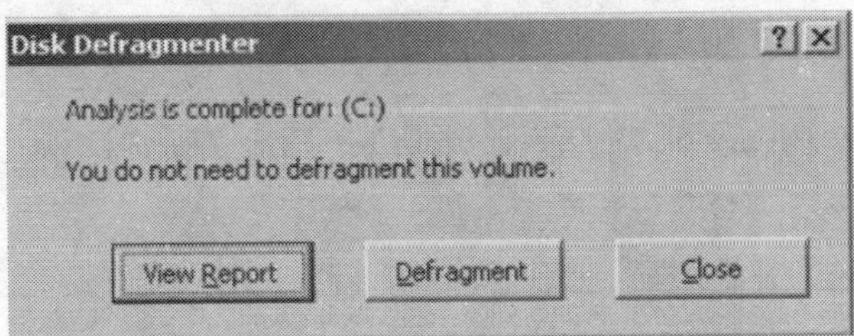

Figure 3.80 Analyzing Your Hard Disk for Defragmentation

4. Click the View Report button to see the status of your disk. This will give you a report similar to the one shown in Figure 3.81.

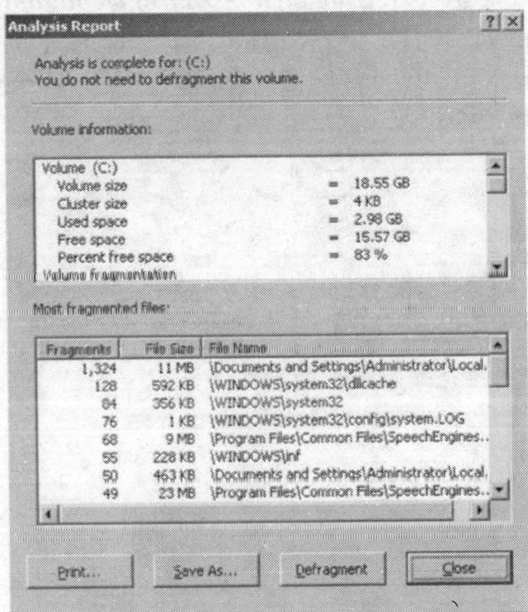

Figure 3.81 Viewing the Analysis Report

5. At this point, you can click Close if you do not want to defragment your disk. If you do want to defragment, click the Defragment button to start the process.
6. You will next see the screen shown in Figure 3.82. You can pause or stop the defragmentation process by clicking Pause or Stop on the Action menu. When the defragmentation process is complete, you will be given the option to view a defragmentation report, as shown in Figure 3.83. Click View Report.

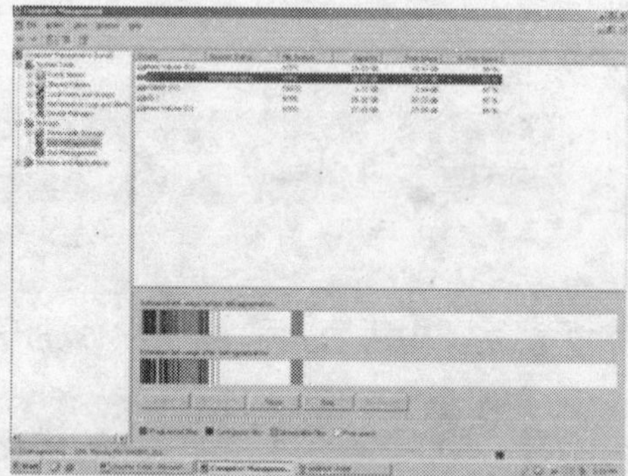

Figure 3.82 Defragmenting Your Hard Disk

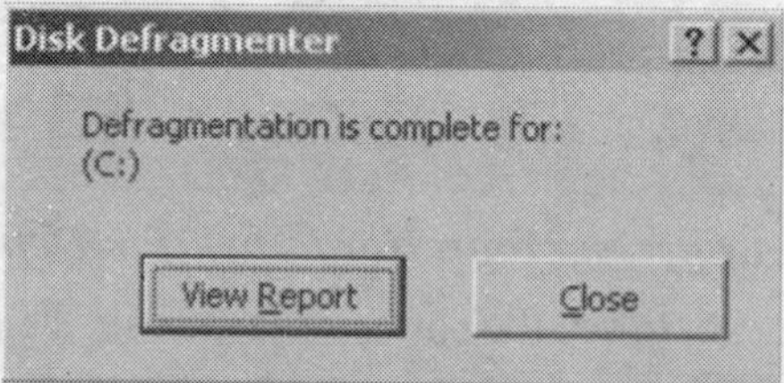

Figure 3.83 Completing Defragmentation

7. Compare the defragmentation report in Figure 3.84 with the analysis report in Figure 3.81.You should see a decrease in file fragmentation. You can print or save your report for later viewing. When finished, click Close.

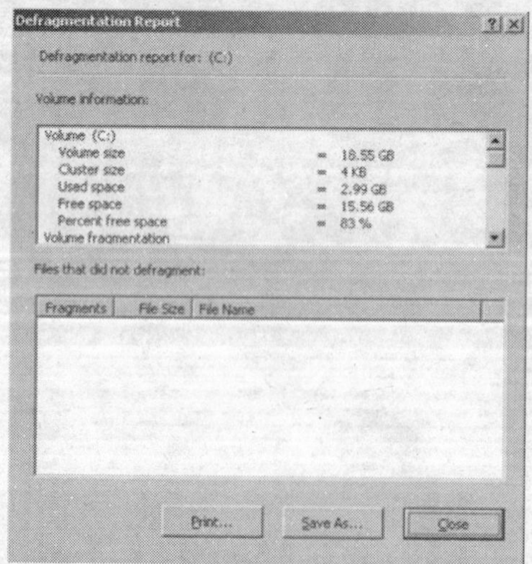

Figure 3.84 Viewing the Defragmentation Report

3.11 VIEWING THE ANALYSIS REPORT

You don't have to really understand the analysis report in order to defragment your disks. The software is smart enough to let you know whether or not you need to defrag. However, a lot of good information can be found in the analysis report.

This includes the following:

1. Fragmented files and folders Displays the paths and names of the most fragmented files on the volume.
2. Volume size
3. Amount of free space available
4. Average number of fragments per file You can use the average number of fragments per file to gauge how fragmented the volume is. Table 3.4 explains the possible averages.

Table 3.4 Describing the Average Number of Fragments per File

Average Number of Fragments per File	Description
1.00	Most or all files are contiguous.
1.10	Around ten percent of the files are fragmented into two or more sections.
1.20	Around twenty percent of the files are fragmented into two or more sections.
1.30	Around thirty percent of the files are fragmented into two or more sections.
2.00	Most or all of the files are fragmented into two or more sections.

3.12 UNDERSTANDING THE DISK DEFRAGMENTER INTERFACE

The Disk Defragmenter provides you with analysis reports and defragmentation reports to alert you to the fragmentation status of your disks. However, the graphical interface of the defragmenter tool also provides much of the same information if you know what to look for. The screenshot in Figure 3.85 was taken immediately after running the defragmentation utility. Let's analyze the display to determine the information that is available.

Notice that Disk Defragmenter runs in a standard MMC, which gives it a familiar feel, with the console tree in the left pane and the details pane on the right. On the right side, the pane is split into a top and a bottom section. The top section shows the volumes and partitions on the machine. The bottom section shows a graphical view of the fragmentation status of the selected volume. There are two bars in the bottom pane, which indicate the following:

1. Estimated disk usage before defragmentation
2. Estimated disk usage after defragmentation

By examining these bars, you can see the status of the disk before the defragmentation and the changes that have occurred afterward. These bars are obviously too small to list every cluster on the disk, but they do provide an accurate representation of how fragmented the volume is. Table 3.5 explains the color codes used in these two bars. After running Disk Defragmenter, the goal is to see most of the red in the top bar replaced with blue.

Table 3.5 Understanding the Estimated Disk Usage Bars in Disk Defragmenter

Color	Description
Red	Most of the clusters are fragmented files.
Blue	Most of the clusters are contiguous files.
Green	Most of the clusters are files that cannot be moved from their current location. This could include paging files, or files used by the file system.
White	Most of the clusters are free space.

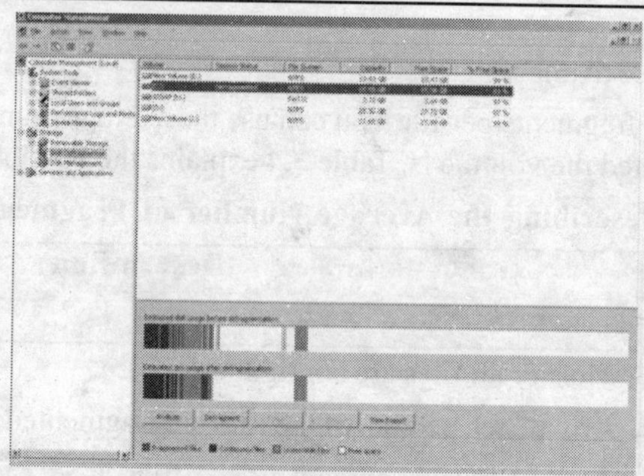

Figure 3.85 Viewing Your Disk After Defragmentation

USING DEFRAG.EXE

If you are comfortable with the Disk Defragmenter tool but prefer a character-based utility, you will feel right at home with defrag.exe, the command prompt equivalent of Disk Defragmenter. Defrag.exe does everything that Disk Defragmenter does and in addition, it supports scripting. You can use defrag.exe in a script to schedule analysis and defragmentation of your servers. Scripting is the primary reason to use defrag.exe instead of Disk Defragmenter. Table 3.6 explains the parameters for defrag.exe. Defrag.exe uses the following syntax:

defrag <volume> [-a] [-f] [-v] [-?]

Volume drive letter or mount point (d: or d:\vol\mountpoint)

Table 3.6 Understanding Defrag.exe Parameters

Parameters	Description
Volume	The drive letter or mount point to be defragmented.
A	Analyzes the volume and displays an analysis summary Indicating Whether you should defragment the volume.
F	Forces defragmentation of the volume when low on free space.
V	Displays the complete analysis and defragmentation reports (not just a summary). When used with the /a switch, it displays only the analysis report. When used alone, it displays both the analysis and defragmentation reports.
?	Displays help.

3.13 DEFRAGMENTATION BEST PRACTICES

As discussed, defragmenting your disks is a good thing. It speeds up access to your files and can make more free space available. However, for best results, here is a summary of the guidelines to follow when defragmenting your servers:

1. Make sure that you have at least 15 percent of your volume's total space free. Disk Defragmenter needs to have an area to sort fragments while it is rearranging your volume. If you can't meet this requirement due to low disk space, you will only get a partialde fragmentation.
2. Always try to schedule your defragmentations during non-production hours. You don't want your users accessing files while the volume is being defragmented. This can cause two problems: users' performance will suffer because of the resources being consumed by Disk Defragmenter and your defragmentation will take longer.
3. Always analyze before you defragment to make sure that you actually need to. You should analyze any time a large number of files are added to your server or after installing software on your server. Both of these actions tend to cause high levels of fragmentation.

3.14 REMOTE STORAGE

Windows Server 2003's Remote Storage provides fast access to data stored on disks and archival capabilities for data that isn't frequently used, and best of all, it handles switching between the two. It automates the archival process and makes accessing archived data easy for the end user. With Remote Storage the server backs up seldom-used files for you automatically, and then automatically restores them when you attempt to access them.

3.14.1 What is Remote Storage?

Remote Storage provides a means of extending the disk space on your servers without having to buy more hard disks. Instead, you use a tape or a magneto-optical (MO) disk library to archive less- frequently used files. It costs signi?cantly less per megabyte to buy a library full of tapes compared to equivalent storage space on hard disks. After it is set up, Remote Storage runs on autopilot. You tell Remote Storage which volume(s) to manage and you specify how much free space you want to remain available on your managed volume; when the amount of free space drops below that level, Remote Storage kicks in and moves enough files to the media library to bring the disk back within your predefined parameters. A managed volume refers to a disk volume in Windows whose files are monitored and managed by Remote Storage.

One big advantage of Remote Storage is that all the files on the server look the same to the end user. When a user needs to open a file, he simply double-clicks it. If the file has not yet been moved to tape, it is opened immediately. If the file has been moved to tape, Remote Storage retrieves it from storage and puts a copy on the local disk (a cached copy). Users might notice a delay while this takes place, but they do not have to take any extra steps to retrieve the file. After the file is cached, it will be automatically opened for the user.

3.14.2 Storage Levels

Remote storage has two de?ned storage levels. The levels exist in a hierarchical structure:

1. Local storage is the top level: It contains the NTFS disks of the computer that is running Remote Storage.
2. Remote storage is the bottom level: This is the library that is connected to the server running Remote Storage.

Remote Storage keeps as much information as possible in the top level for faster access. Only when this level is reaching its storage limit is the data moved to the bottom level.

3.15 RELATIONSHIP OF REMOTE STORAGE AND REMOVABLE STORAGE

Removable Storage is a feature of Windows Server 2003 that enables multiple programs to share the same storage media. It organizes all your available media into separate media pools. Microsoft defines a media pool as a logical collection of removable media that share the same management policies. Applications use media pools to control access to specific media within the library. Removable Storage requires that all data-management programs run on the computer connected to the library. In other words, Removable Storage provides a standard way for applications to access a media library. By having all applications access the library through Remote Storage, Microsoft has provided a level of compatibility between applications, including Remote Storage. Remote Storage uses Removable Storage to access the media stored in the library.

3.16 MEDIA POOLS

Media pools contain either media or other media pools. Using the capability to nest media pools inside each other enables you to create a hierarchical media pool structure for Removable Storage. You can group media pools together and manage them as a single unit. Media pools can span multiple libraries. There are two main types of media pools: system media pools and application media pools. System media pools hold media not currently being used by an application. Removable Storage creates one of each of the following system media pools (as shown in Figure 3.86) for each media type in your system:

1. **Free media pools:** These pools hold media not currently in use by applications. This media is readily available for use.
2. **Unrecognized media pools:** Blank media and media not recognized by Removable Storage go into the unrecognized media pool and are unusable until they are moved into a free media pool.
3. **Import media pools:** These pools are recognized by Removable Storage, but they have not been used by Remote Storage before. After they have been catalogued they can be used.

Application media pools contain media created and controlled by applications. For example, Backup and Remote Storage use application media pools for storage. Application media pools dictate which media can be accessed by any given application. An application can use more multiple media pools, and more than one application can use a single media pool.

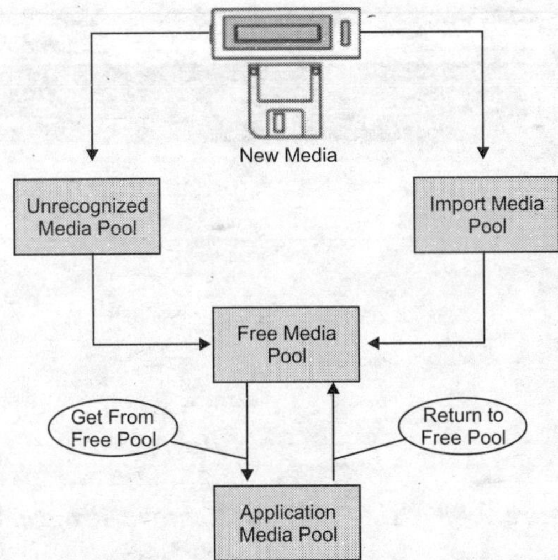

Figure 3.86 Understanding How Media Pools Work Together

3.17 SETTING UP REMOTE STORAGE

Remote Storage is not installed by default. You add it via the Add or Remove Programs applet in Control Panel. Before starting the installation, you must verify that enough tapes or disks have been moved to a free media pool in Removable Storage to hold all the files you wish to move to Remote Storage and that the local disks being managed are running Windows 2000's or Windows Server 2003's versions of NTFS (NTFS version 5). If you want compression and indexing on local disks, enable these before starting setup. You must be logged on with administrative rights to install Remote Storage. You cannot install Remote Storage into a clustered environment. Remote Storage will not fail over. Also, Remote Storage will not work with shared cluster disks but it will work with local disks that are not shared. Use the following steps to install and configure Remote Storage.

3.17.1 Installing Remote Storage

1. Open Control Panel by clicking Start | Control Panel. This will display a screen similar to that shown in Figure 3.87.
2. Double-click Add or Remove Programs. This will display the screen shown in Figure 3.88.

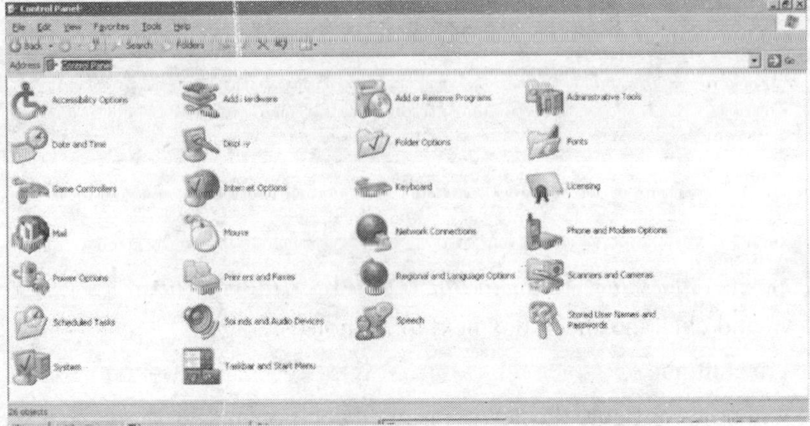

Figure 3.87 Opening Control Panel

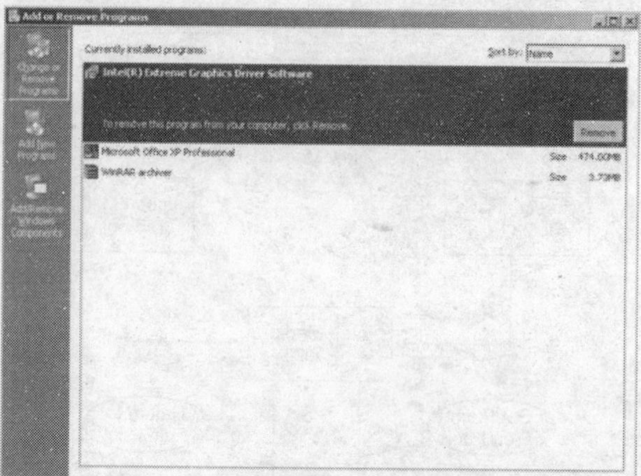

Figure 3.88 Using Add or Remove Programs

3. From the Add or Remove Programs window, click Add/Remove Windows Components. You should see a "Please wait…" message, as shown in Figure 3.89
4. You will next be presented with the Windows Components Wizard, as shown in Figure 3.90.

Figure 3.89 Waiting on Windows Setup

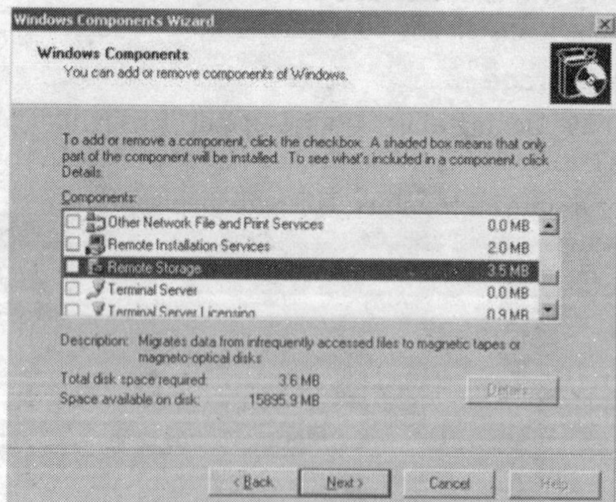

Figure 3.90 Adding Windows Components

5. Scroll down and click the check box next to Remote Storage.
6. Click Next to continue.
7. Windows will now configure the newly installed components, as shown in Figure 3.91.

8. Next you will see the Completing the Windows Components Wizard, as shown in Figure 3.92. Click Finish to close the wizard.

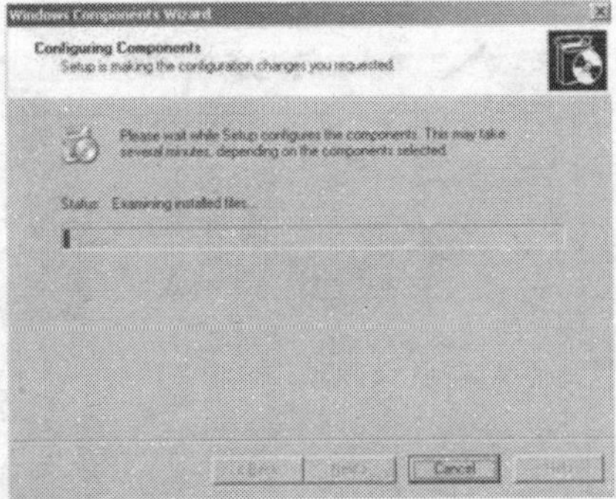

Figure 3.91 Waiting While Windows Configures Components

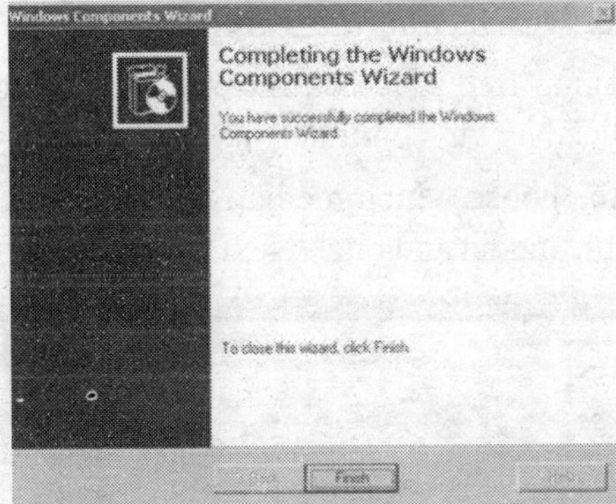

Figure 3.92 Completing the Components Wizard

3.17.2 Configuring Remote Storage

1. Open the Remote Storage MMC by clicking Start | All Programs | Administrative Tools | Remote Storage.
2. Because this is the first time you have opened the Remote Storage MMC, the Remote Storage Setup Wizard will automatically start, as shown in Figure 3.93. Click Next to continue.

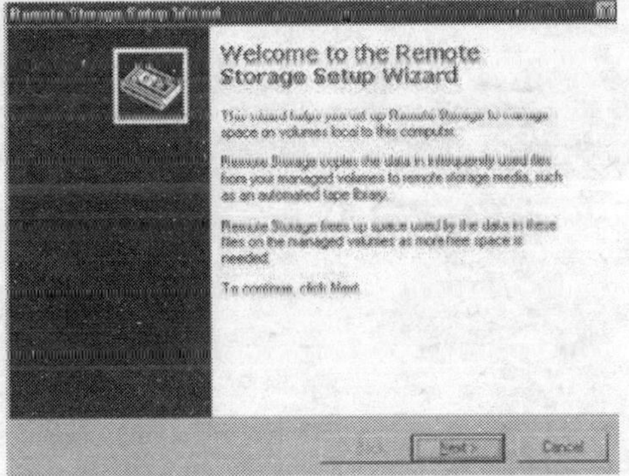

Figure 3.93 Running the Remote Storage Setup Wizard

3. You will next be asked which volumes you want Remote Storage to manage, as shown in Figure 3.94. For this example, we select the C drive. Select the disk(s) that you want to manage and click Next to continue.

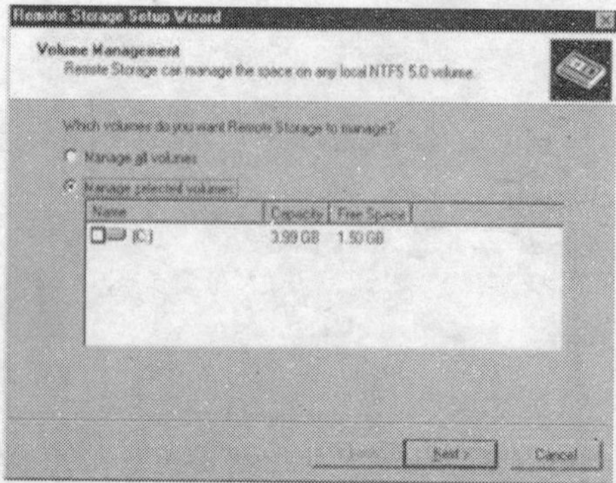

Figure 3.94 Selecting the Volumes to be Managed

4. Set the criteria for managing free space on the volume with the Volume Settings dialog box shown in Figure 3.95. Click Next to continue.
5. You will next be asked to choose which media type to use, as shown in Figure 3.96. For this example, select Removable media and click Next to continue.

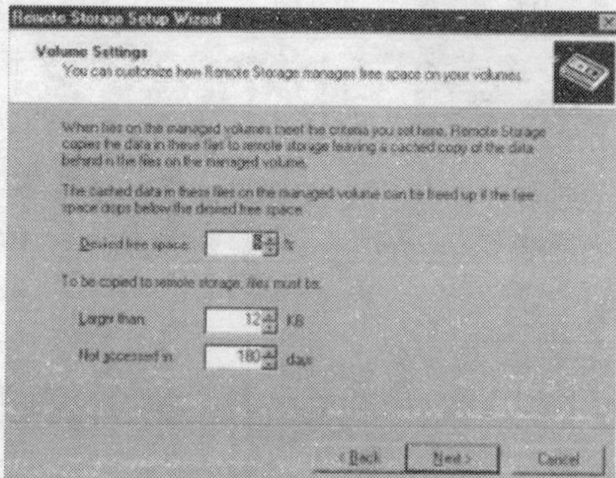

Figure 3.95 Managing Free Space on Your Volumes

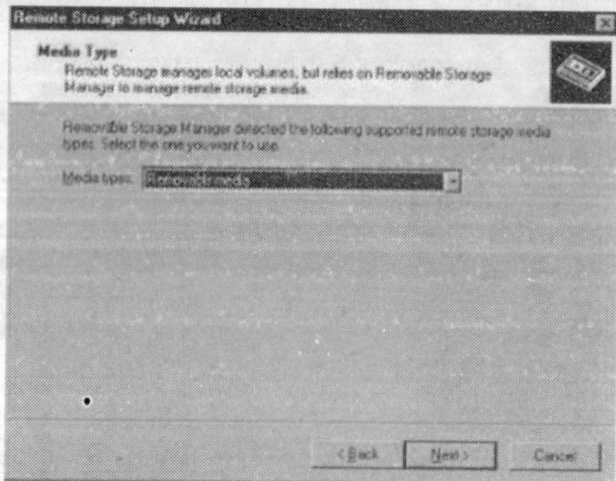

Figure 3.96 Selecting a Media Type

6. The last item to configure is the schedules for copying files, as shown in Figure 3.97. To accept the defaults, click Next and skip to step 9. To customize the schedule, click the Change Schedule button. This will display the Schedule window shown in Figure 3.98.
7. Set the schedule to copy files at a time that is least busy in your environment and click OK.
8. You will be returned to the screen shown in Figure 3.97. Click Next to continue.
9. On the Completing the Remote Storage Setup Wizard screen (3.99), review the settings to make sure they are correct, and then click Finish to complete the configuration of Remote Storage.

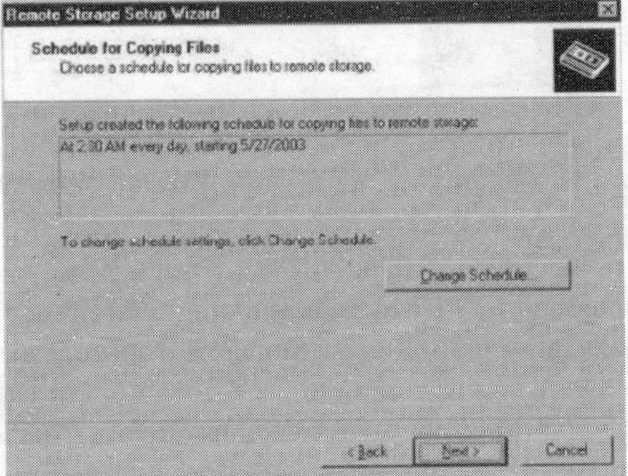

Figure 3.97 Verifying the Schedule for Copying Files

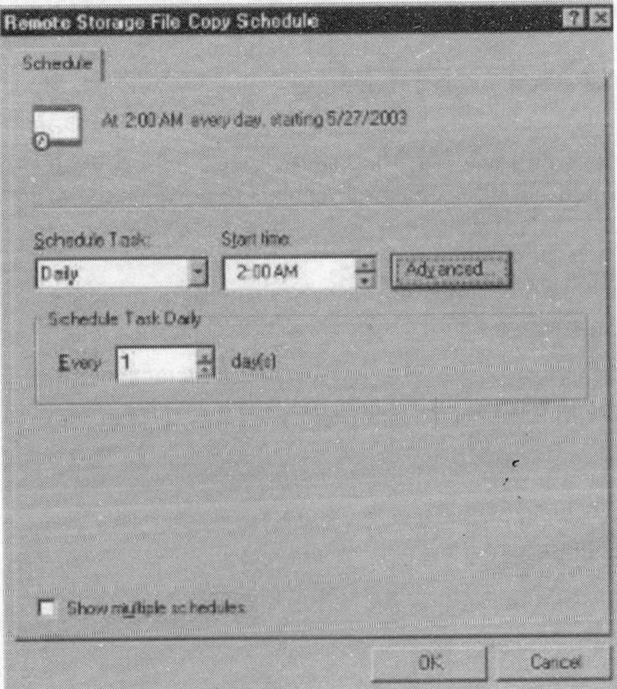

Figure 3.98 Customizing the Schedule for Copying Files

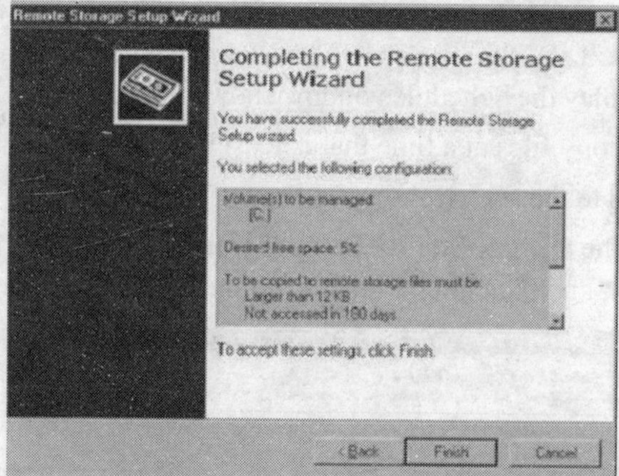

Figure 3.99 Completing the Remote Storage Setup Wizard

3.18 USING REMOTE STORAGE

Now that you have installed and configured Remote Storage, you need to know how to administer it. Like Microsoft's other administrative tools, Remote Storage is managed through an MMC snap-in. The Remote Storage MMC has two panes: the console pane on the left is used to navigate the various components of Remote Storage and the details pane on the right displays specifics of whichever component is selected in the left console pane.

The Remote Storage MMC (see Figure 3.100) that is accessed from the Administrative Tools menu also contains the snap-ins for Removable Storage and Event Viewer. However, Remote Storage itself has only two containers to manage: the Managed Volumes container and the Media container. We previously discussed storage levels within Remote Storage. We said the top level was for local storage and the bottom level was for remote storage. The Managed Volumes container is the top level of storage and is used for managing local storage. The Media container is the bottom level and is used for managing remote storage. The Managed Volumes container is used to perform the following tasks:

1. Set the desired free space.
2. Specify file-selection criteria and rules.
3. Change the file-copy schedule.
4. Set the maximum number of drives to access simultaneously.
5. Set the runaway recall limit.
6. Validate files.
7. Discontinue volume management.
8. Modify files on managed volumes.

The Media container is used to perform the following tasks:

1. Create media copies.
2. Synchronize media copies.
3. Recreate the media master.

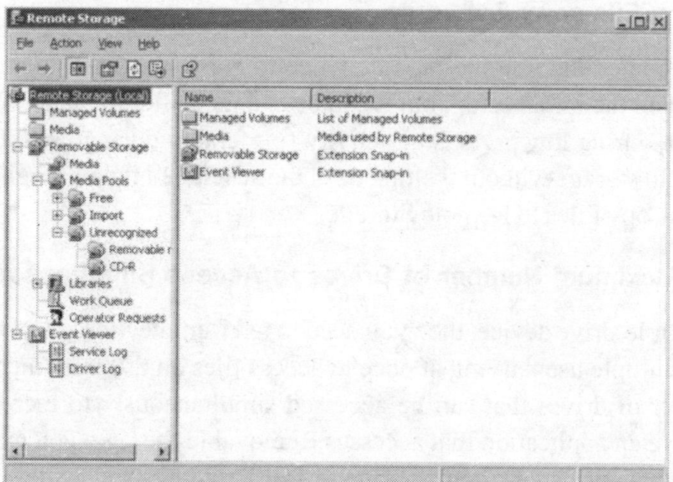

Figure 3.100 Using the Remote Storage MMC

3.18.1 Setting the Desired Free Space

You can configure how much free space you want available on your managed volume. If the volume falls below your specified threshold, then Remote Storage deletes cached files until the volume is back within acceptable limits. You can also tell Remote Storage to delete all cached files from the volume to create a large amount of available free space.

3.18.2 Specifying File-selection Criteria and Rules

You tell Remote Storage which files to manage on your volume. You set criteria that must be met in order for the file to be copied to remote storage. After the criteria have been met, the files are copied. Minimum files size and elapsed time since last use are the common criteria used by Remote Storage. In addition to using criteria to control which files get copied to Remote Storage, you can also create rules. There are two types of rules, inclusion and exclusion. Inclusion rules control which files are copied to Remote Storage and exclusion rules control which files are not copied to Remote Storage. Rules are processed in order and the first rule that matches is applied. Change the order of your rules to set their priority.

Remote Storage has a predefined list of rules available for use. You cannot modify these rules or change their order. You can create your own rules and order them however you see fit. By default, all system, hidden, encrypted, extended attribute, and sparse files are excluded from the file rule list as these files cannot be copied to remote storage.

Both types of rules are built on the same options:

1. A specified folder, including subfolders
2. A specified folder, excluding subfolders
3. File name extension
4. File name

3.18.3 Changing the File-copy Schedule

The file copy schedule tells Remote Storage when to copy files from the managed volume to the library. This is set during the initial setup, but it can be changed after the fact. You should always try to copy files into storage during low periods of activity (preferably during non-business hours).You can manually copy files into storage without waiting until the scheduled time by right-clicking the managed volume and choosing Copy Files to Remote Storage.

3.18.4 Setting the Maximum Number of Drives to Access Simultaneously

If you have a multiple-drive device, then you need to tell Remote Storage how many drives to utilize at once. If you have multiple users trying at once to access files on different media, then you may want to increase the number of drives that can be accessed simultaneously to increase your performance. Conversely, if you have an application that accesses Removable Storage, you may want to decrease the amount of disk utilized at once by Remote Storage so that Remote Storage doesn't access all the disks at once and prevent your application from working.

3.18.5 Setting the Runaway Recall Limit

The Runaway call limit defines the number of file recalls a user can make on a file within a single session. It stops Remote Storage from copying the same file from the library to the managed volume over and over. If a user recalls a file within 10 seconds of the original file recall, the runaway recall count is increased by one. After the runaway recall limit is reached, the file is still accessible; it just will be accessed from storage and not cached on the managed volume.

3.18.6 Validating Files

Validation is the process of verifying that the data in Remote Storage points to the correct file on the managed volume. Validation can determine if a file has been moved between volumes. You can manually perform file validation by right-clicking the managed volume, selecting All Tasks, and choosing Validate Files. Two hours after a backup program restores a file, Remote Storage automatically forces a file validation.

3.18.7 Discontinuing Volume Management

You can easily tell Remote Storage to stop managing a volume by right-clicking a managed volume and choosing Remove. If you do so, you have to decide if you want to leave the files on the library or if you want to copy them back to the original volume. If you leave the files in Remote Storage, it will recall them as normal. However, no new files created on the volume will be copied to Remote Storage.

3.18.8 Modifying Files on Managed Volumes

There are special considerations to be aware of when deleting files on managed volumes and moving files between managed volumes. If files on a managed volume are deleted, you must restore the file from backup. Do not think that because the file is stored in the library that it can be restored from there. When you delete a file from the managed volume it is also deleted from the library. If you move or copy files between managed volumes, the files are recalled. If you want to move files back and forth without causing a recall, then you must back up and restore the data to the new location and then run a volume validation.

3.18.9 Creating and Synchronizing Media Copies

You can create copies of your media to provide fault tolerance. These copies are called media copy sets and they provide redundancy for your data. If there is a problem with the master media set, the media copy set will be used. In order for Remote Storage to create media copy sets, there must be two or more drives in the library. When using media copy sets, you must make sure that the master set and the copies are in sync. To synchronize the media copies, right-click Media and select Synchronize Copies Now.

3.18.10 Recreating the Media Master

The media master is the tape that holds all the files required for Remote Storage. If the media master were to fail, you could create another one from a media copy set. However, you may lose any data that was created since the last time you synchronized the media copy set with the media master. Recreate the media master only if you get errors when recalling files.

Follow the steps below to recreate the media master:

1. Select Media.
2. Right-click the media you would like to recreate.
3. Select Properties.
4. Click the Recovery tab.
5. Click Recreate Master.

3.18.11 Remote Storage Best Practices

Microsoft provides some guidelines for you to follow when using Remote Storage. You should try to adhere to these best practices whenever possible:

1. Make multiple copies of your remote storage tapes and always keep a copy offsite.
2. Always configure Remote Storage through the GUI before using rss.exe to manage it.
3. Do not create File Replication service (FRS) replicas on a Remote Storage volume.
4. Regularly validate your managed volumes.
5. Stop managing all volumes before you uninstall Remote Storage.
6. Do not manage full volumes.
7. Do not format a managed volume.
8. Schedule your task to run during periods of low activity.
9. Do not change the drive letter of a managed volume.
10. Run a system state backup as an administrator to back up the Remote Storage database files.
11. Do not install Remote Storage on shared cluster disks.

3.19 RAID

There are several options for setting up a RAID environment. You can use either software-based RAID or hardware-based RAID. Software-based RAID is more cost effective because you don't have to purchase anything extra, but it works only in certain situations and performance is not as good. You cannot easily change from one RAID type to another. If you want to change you must do the following:

1. Back up your data.
2. Erase your existing RAID configuration.
3. Create a new RAID configuration.
4. Restore your data from backup.

This section covers the differences between hardware and software RAID and when it is best to use for a given environment.

3.19.1 Understanding Windows Server 2003 Raid

Windows Server 2003 RAID is software-based RAID. With software-based RAID, all the physical disks are presented to the operating system as they are and the operating system manages them in RAID configuration. The benefit is that software-based RAID is built into the operating system. The drawback is that the operating system incurs the entire overhead for maintaining the RAID volume. Additionally, there are limitations that apply to software-based RAID that do not apply to hardware-based RAID. You do not have as many RAID options with software-based RAID. Windows Server 2003 supports only three levels of RAID: RAID 0, RAID 1, and RAID 5.

3.19.1.1 Raid Level 0

RAID level 0 utilizes disk striping. A RAID level 0 volume in Windows Server 2003 is called a triped volume. This version of RAID does not provide any fault tolerance. Level 0 can be implemented as either a software or hardware solution and is supported by all controllers. Because the operating system must be loaded before the striped volume is initialized and made available, a level 0 array cannot be used for the boot or system partitions. RAID level 0 should be used when you are trying to get maximum performance from your drives. Level 0 is best for data that is not mission-critical or that is backed up regularly. It is good for audio/video streaming, gaming and other applications where performance is important. Windows Server 2003's RAID level 0 works with a minimum of two disks and up to a maximum of 32 disks.

3.19.1.2 Raid Level 1

RAID level 1 utilizes disk mirroring. A RAID level 1 volume in Windows Server 2003 is called a mirrored volume, and consists of two identical disks. This version of RAID does provide fault tolerance and is the only one of Windows Server 2003's software-based RAID levels that can be used for the boot and system partitions. Level 1 can be implemented as either a software or hardware RAID solution. RAID level 1 should be used when you want to provide fault tolerance for the boot and/or system partitions or if you need fault tolerance and have only two disks available. Level 1 is the most expensive form of Windows Server 2003 RAID because only 50% of the disk space that must be purchased is used for data.

3.19.1.3 Raid Level 5

RAID level 5 utilizes disk striping with parity. A RAID level 5 volume in Windows Server 2003 is called a RAID-5 volume. As with disk striping, a RAID-5 volume cannot be used for the boot or system partition because the operating system must be loaded first to initialize the volume and make it available. RAID-5 volumes require a minimum of three disks and work with up to 32 disks. You should use RAID level 5 when you need fault tolerance with better performance and drive utilization than RAID level 1 can provide. RAID 5 is one of the most popular RAID implementations.

However, software RAID 5 is considerably slower than its hardware counterpart, because of the overhead involved in calculating the parity information. It is better for read-intensive applications as opposed to write-intensive ones.

3.19.2 Hardware Raid

As the name implies, hardware-based RAID uses special hardware to create RAID volumes. A RAID controller is added to your server. The controller handles the overhead of managing the RAID volumes, and this improves performance by removing the processing burden from the operating system. This also removes many of the restrictions imposed by software-based RAID. Because the RAID controller presents the RAID volume to the OS as one disk, you can use hardware-based RAID 0 and RAID 5 volumes for the boot and system partitions. Hardware-based RAID provides you with many more RAID levels to choose from. You should refer to the hardware manufacturer's specification to determine the type of RAID supported and its compatibility with Windows Server 2003.The only real drawback to hardware-based RAID is the price. Server-grade RAID controllers typically cost $750 and up. This can add up quickly when you have a large number of servers.

3.19.3 Raid Best Practices

After you have made the decision to use a RAID volume, you need to determine which solution best fits your needs. Will it be hardware RAID or software RAID? Disk striping or disk mirroring? How should you set it up? There are no hard, fast rules, only recommendations, but the following provide some general guidelines to follow when setting up your RAID volumes:

1. Using Hardware RAID
2. Use hardware RAID whenever possible because it offers the best performance.
3. Try to use identical hardware for all your servers. This makes it easier to recover if you have a disaster.
4. Always keep spare disks on hand. When you lose one drive (with most RAID levels), you no longer have any fault tolerance. You need to be able to replace failed hardware as quickly as possible. (This also applies to software RAID).
5. Keep RAID controllers updated with the current firmware revision.
6. Always back up your data before updating the firmware on RAID controllers.
7. Using Software RAID
8. Use mirrored volumes for the boot and system partitions.
9. Use RAID-5 volumes for database disks (e.g., Exchange and SQL servers).

10. Use striped volumes on database servers' disks that contain transaction logs (e.g., Exchange and SQL servers).
11. Use striped volumes for disks that are used for printer spooling.

3.20 TROUBLESHOOTING DISKS AND VOLUMES

Thus far in this chapter, we have focused on how to enable and configure various disk-related features of Windows Server 2003. However, a large part of any administrator's job is dealing with problems and knowing what to do when things go wrong. In this section, we address some of the most common disk-related troubleshooting scenarios you're likely to encounter.

3.20.1 Troubleshooting Basic Disks

Many basic disk-troubleshooting scenarios involve a disk not being recognized by the operating system (and thus not showing up in the Disk Management console) or showing up in a problematic state. Remember the basic rules of troubleshooting any computer/network problem: begin at the physical level. This means you should always check the hardware first to make sure that it is functional.

In the following sections, we will cover these common situations:

1. New disks don't show up in the volume list view.
2. Disk status is not initialized or unknown.
3. Disk status is unreadable.
4. Disk status is failed.

3.20.1.1 New Disks are not Showing up in the Volume List View

New disks that fail to show up in the volume list view are a common concern. This is usually because there are no designators (drive letters) associated with the disk. If the disk is not mounted, you will need to use the diskpart and mountvol commands or use the Disk Management console to mount the volume and assign drive letters. The mountvol command enables you to mount a volume without a drive letter. This is useful if you have run out of drive letters.

You have to manually assign drive letters to each volume or partition on the disk before you can format them and use them for storage. Notice in Figure 3.101 that there are three disks shown online in the graphical view (bottom pane), but they do not have drive letters associated with them. Until they do, they will not show up in the volume list view (top pane).

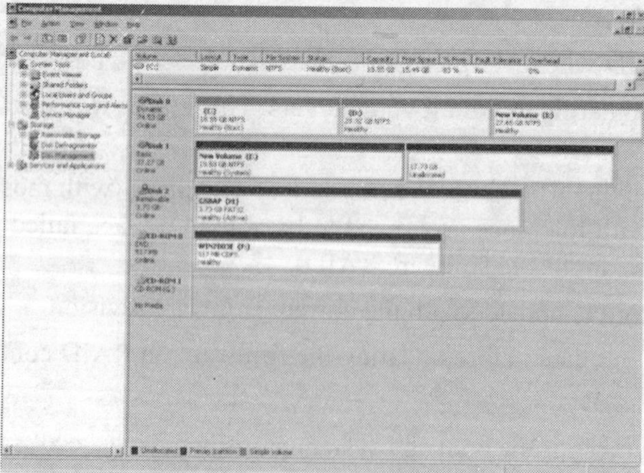

Figure 3.101 Understanding the Default State of Drives

3.20.1.2 Disk Status is not Initialized or Unknown

If your disks are showing up as unknown and not initialized, as shown in Figure 3.102, this is generally because no signature has been written to the disk by which Windows can identify it. You need to write a signature to a new disk when you install it, before you can use it. When Windows writes a signature to the disk, it also creates the master boot record (MBR) or GUID partition table. When you add a new disk and start Disk Management, the system automatically starts a wizard that prompts you to write a signature to the new disk. If you cancel the wizard, however, the disk will not have a signature and will be left in an uninitialized state.

To initialize a disk after the wizard has been cancelled, follow these steps:

1. Right-click the disk that needs to be initialized in the bottom graphical pane of the Disk Management console, and then select Initialize Disk from the context menu.
2. You will be prompted to select one or more disks to initialize. Ensure that the check box(es) of the appropriate disk(s) is checked and click OK.
3. The disk status in the graphical view will change from Unknown to Basic.

After the disk is initialized, you can create partitions.

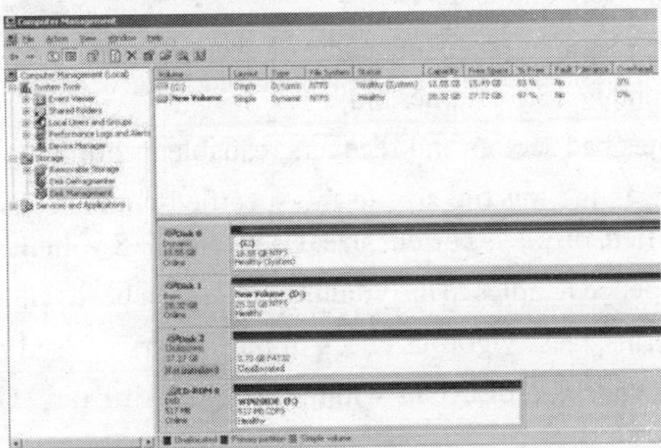

Figure 3.102 Troubleshooting Disks That Do Not Have a Signature

3.20.1.3 Disk Status is Unreadable

An unreadable disk indicates that you may have a hardware failure or corruption of the disk's copy of the disk configuration database. Unfortunately, there is generally no way to fix failed hardware other than to replace it. Sometimes you will get the "unreadable" message if the disks are still spinning up while you are viewing the Disk Management console. If this is the case, rescanning the computer for disks usually solves the problem. To rescan, click Action | Rescan Disks. If rescanning doesn't solve the problem, try rebooting the machine.

3.20.1.4 Disk Status is Failed

A failed disk indicates that the file system is corrupt, the disk is damaged, or for some other reason the volume could not start. Remember another rule of troubleshooting: always try the easy solutions first. Make sure that the disk has power and is plugged into the server. If your hardware is faulty, you will have to replace it and restore your data from backup. One of the most common causes of disk problems is a loose or bad IDE or SCSI cable. Try tightening or swapping out cables if you suspect this is the problem.

If the hardware is not faulty, we move on to troubleshooting the software. One possibility is that the file system is corrupt. If you can still access the volume, run chkdsk.exe against it. Chkdsk.exe may not be able to recover any lost data, but it can usually bring the file system back to a consistent state. Chkdsk.exe uses the following syntax.

CHKDSK [volume[[path]filename]]] [/F] [/V] [/R] [/X] [/I] [/C]

[/L[:size]]

Table 3.7 explains chkdsk.exe parameters.

Table 3.7 Understanding Chkdsk.exe Parameters

Parameter	Desription
volume	Speci?es the drive letter (followed by a colon), mount point, or volume name.
filename	Speci?es the files to check for fragmentation. Used on FAT and FAT32 volumes only.
/F	Fixes errors on the disk.
/V	Displays the full path and name of every file on the disk. Used on FAT and FAT32 volumes only.
/R	Locates bad sectors and recovers readable information (implies /F).
/L:size	Changes the log file size to the specified number of kilobytes. If size is not specified, displays current size. Used on NTFS volumes only.
/X	All opened handles to the volume would then be invalid (implies /F).
/I	Performs a less vigorous check of index entries. Used on NTFS volumes only.
/C	Skips checking of cycles within the folder structure. Used on NTFS volumes only.

3.20.2 Troubleshooting Dynamic Volumes

Dynamic disks can have the same problems as basic disk (discussed above). When troubleshooting dynamic disks, you should always run through the scenarios given for basic disks, as well. In addition to these problems that are common to both disk types, dynamic disks can have additional problems that do not apply to basic disks. In the following section, we will discuss these troubleshooting scenarios that are unique to dynamic disks:

1. Disk status is foreign.
2. Disk status is online (errors).
3. Disk status is offline or missing.
4. Disk status is data incomplete.
5. Disk status is Stale Data.
6. Disk status is Failed or Failed Redundancy.

3.20.2.1 Disk Status is Foreign

A disk status of Foreign, as shown in Figure 3.103, occurs when you move a dynamic disk from one machine to another. This happens because Windows stores all dynamic disk configurations in a private database in the last 1MB of disk space. This database is associated with the machine in which the disk is installed and is replicated to all the dynamic disks installed in that machine. If you connect the disk to a different machine, the second machine will detect that the database doesn't match anything in its database and the disk will be marked as foreign.

To make the new computer recognize the dynamic disk, you must import it. To do so, right- click the foreign disk and select Import Foreign Disks from the pop-up menu. This will make the volume visible and incorporate it into the new machine's dynamic disk database.

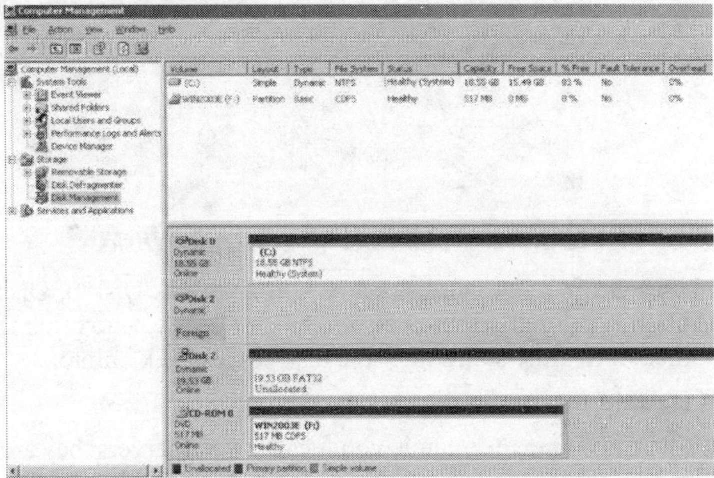

Figure 3.103 Importing a Foreign Disk

3.20.2.2 Disk Status is Online (Errors)

A disk status of Online (Errors) indicates that the disk is working, but is having problems. I/O errors are being detected somewhere on the disk. If this problem persists, you should replace the hardware. If the problem is temporary, you might be able to reactivate your volume to bring it back online. To do so, right-click the volume and choose Reactivate Disk from the pop-up menu. If the reactivation works, the disk will be marked as Online. You can also use the diskpart command with the online parameter to reactivate a disk (remember to first select the disk so that it is the focus).

3.20.2.3 Disk Status is Offline

A disk status of Ofline, where the disk name field indicates Missing (as shown in Figure 3.104) usually means that the disk is no longer physically connected to the server. Check to make sure that the disk is powered on and correctly connected to the server. After fixing a physical connectivity problem, right-click the volume and choose Reactivate Disk. This will bring the disk back online and make it usable by Windows again.

If this does not fix the problem, it is possible that your disk is corrupt beyond repair. If so, you must remove it from the server. Right-click the volume(s) contained on the disk and choose Remove Volume from the context menu. After all volumes have been removed, right-click the disk and choose Remove

Disk. At this point, all data is lost and the disk has been removed from your system. Do not do this unless you are sure that the disk is irreparably damaged.

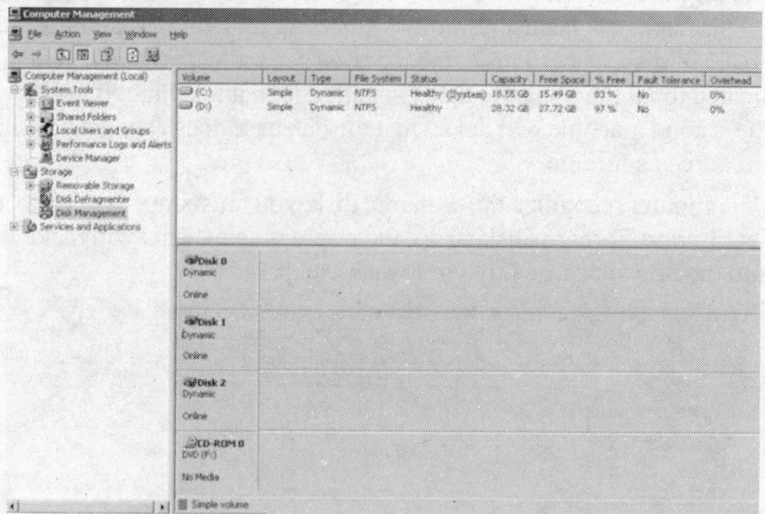

Figure 3.104 Troubleshooting Missing Disks

If the disk status shows Offline, but the disk name still shows as Disk 0, Disk 1, etc. (instead of "Missing"), you should be able to simply right-click and select Reactivate to bring the disk back online. Volumes should be returned to Healthy status after the disk comes back online.

3.20.2.4 Disk Status is Data Incomplete

As discussed earlier, when you move dynamic volumes between servers they are marked as foreign. You must import them in order for Windows to use them. If you have a volume that spans multiple disks (e.g., a spanned volume, striped volume, or RAID 5 volume) and you only import some of the disks, you will see the error message Data Incomplete, as shown in Figure 3.105. If this happens, cancel the import process until you can move all the disks in the volume at the same time. When all the disks have been physically installed in the new machine, import them together and Windows will recognize them as being part of the same volume.

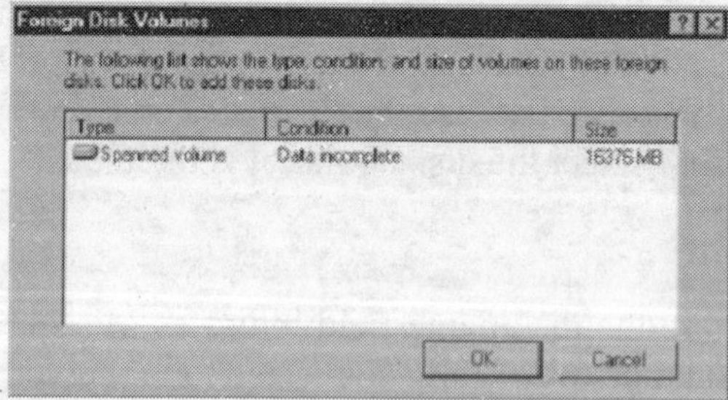

Figure 3.105 Importing Part of a Spanned Volume

3.20.3 Troubleshooting Fragmentation Problems

Disk fragmentation is inevitable if you ever delete files, install programs, or otherwise use the computer for normal tasks. To optimize disk performance, you should defragment your disks as often as needed.

This section covers some of the common problems that you might encounter related to disk fragmentation and the defragmentation process, including the following:

1. Computer is operating slowly.
2. The Analysis and Defragmentation reports do not match the display.
3. Volumes contain unmovable files.

3.20.3.1 Computer is Operating Slowly

This is a common complaint from computer users. This is often a sign of a highly fragmented disk and commonly occurs when applications are installed or removed or many new files are created. The solution is simple: use defrag.exe or Disk Defragmenter to defragment your disks.

3.20.3.2 The Analysis and Defragmentation Reports do not match the Display

The graphical display is designed to provide a quick look at the level of fragmentation of the volumes on your hard disk. The graphical representation is too small in scale to give a 100-percent accurate representation. The reports created by the defragmentation tools are much more detailed and are very accurate. When there are discrepancies between the display and reports, the information in the reports should be considered more reliable.

3.20.3.3 My Volumes Contain Unmovable Files

This is normal. Certain files cannot be moved during the defragmentation process. The page file is one of these files. Every volume containing a page file will appear as having files that cannot be moved. Also, on NTFS-formatted volumes, the NTFS Change journal and the NTFS log file cannot be moved.

3.20.4 Troubleshooting Disk Quotas

Disk quotas are a great feature. However, they can lead to trouble if they are improperly configured or not managed properly. This section covers some of the more common issues that appear when using disk quotas. Issues such as the following:

1. The Quota tab is not there.
2. Deleting a Quota entry gives you another window.
3. A user gets an "Insufficient Disk Space" message when adding files to a volume.

3.20.4.1 The Quota Tab is not There

Disk quotas are set via the quotas tab on the properties of a volume. If the tab does not appear (Figure 3.106), then one of three things is the cause. Either you do not have administrative rights on the machine, the volume is formatted as FAT or FAT32 and not as NTFS, or the volume is not shared from the volume's root directory.

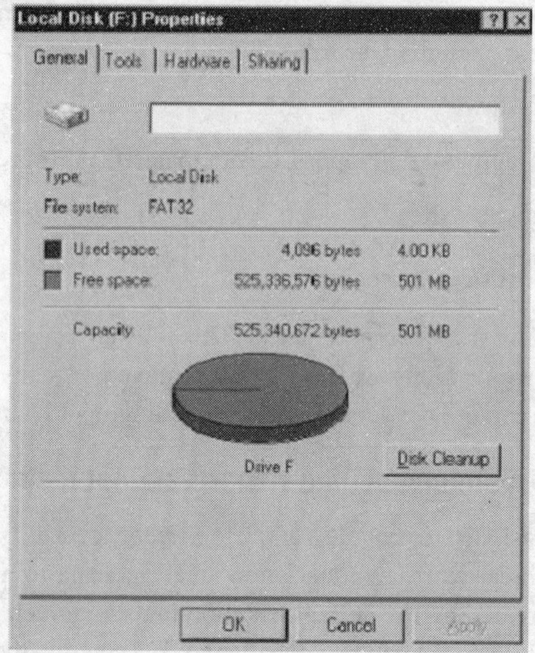

Figure 3.106 Missing the Quota Tab

3.20.4.2 Deleting a Quota Entry Gives you Another Window

Whenever you try to delete a quota entry for a user that still retains ownership of files, you are presented with the Disk Quota window shown in Figure 3.107. This is because you cannot delete a quota entry if the user still owns files. This keeps you from having files on your server that are not being managed by disk quotas because the owner is no longer around. You have three choices:

(1) Permanently delete all the files. (2) Take ownership of the files. (3) Move the files to another volume.

After doing so, you will be able to delete the quota entry for your user.

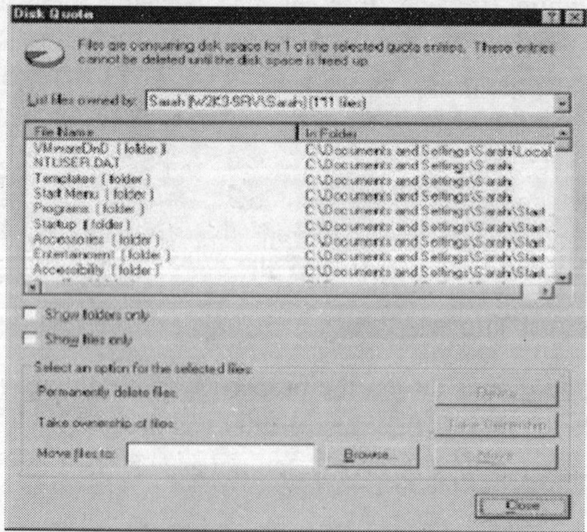

Figure 3.107 Cleaning Up Disk Quotas

3.20.4.3 A User Gets an "Insufficient Disk Space" Message When Adding Files to a Volume

The insufficient disk space message (see Figure 3.108) to be expected for any of your users that are over their quota limit. Usually this is a good thing because it means that disk quotas are working. The only way around it is to increase your users' quota limit or to stop denying users who exceed their disk space. If this is happening unexpectedly, verify that your users' limits are set correctly. A common error is to forget to change the quota measurement from KB to MB. You may think that your users have 150MB of available space when they only have 150KB of space.

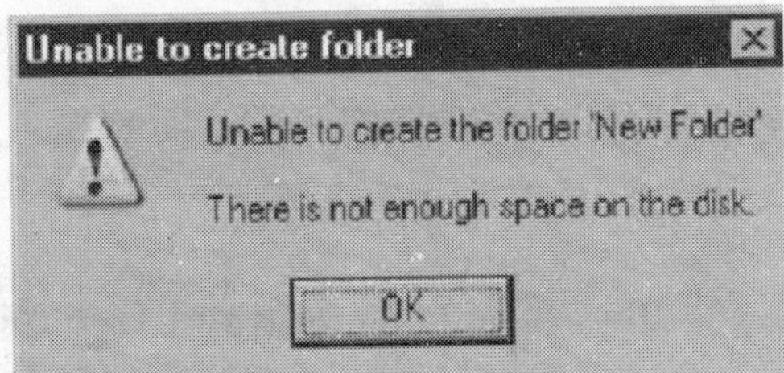

Figure 3.108 Exceeding Your Quota Limit

3.20.5 Troubleshooting Remote Storage

Remember when you are troubleshooting Remote Storage that you are writing data to backup media. This is going to be slower than writing to disks. This is not to say that your performance should be terrible. Just be realistic with your expectations. Here are some common Remote Storage troubleshooting issues:

1. Remote Storage will not install.
2. Remote Storage is not finding a valid media type.
3. Files can no longer be recalled from Remote Storage.

3.20.5.1 Remote Storage will not Install

Remote Storage is not installed by default. You must add it through Control Panel | Add or Remove Programs. You must have administrative rights on the machine on which you are installing Remote Storage. Without administrative rights, setup will not continue.

3.20.5.2 Remote Storage is not Finding a Valid Media Type

During initial setup, Remote Storage searches for an available media type. If Remote Storage is not finding one on your machine, you either has not waited long enough for Remote Storage to finish searching or you do not have a compatible library.

3.20.5.3 Files Can no Longer be Recalled from Remote Storage

Remote Storage has a runaway recall limit to deny recalling files from storage more than a specified number of times in a row. It is possible that you have an application that is making too many recalls. Once this threshold is crossed, future recalls are denied. If the recalls are legitimate, you can increase the threshold for the runaway recall limit. If they are not valid, then you need to terminate the application making the request.

3.20.6 Troubleshooting RAID

When troubleshooting RAID volumes, you must first troubleshoot the disk itself. So always start with the basic disk and dynamic disk checklist. However, there are times when the problem is with the RAID volume itself and not the underlying disk. This section covers the following:

1. Mirrored or RAID-5 volume's status is Data Not Redundant.
2. Mirrored or RAID-5 volume's status is Failed Redundancy.
3. Mirrored or RAID-5 volume's status is Stale Data.

3.20.6.1 Mirrored or Raid-5 Volume's Status is data not Redundant

A Data Not Redundant status indicates that your volume is not intact. This is due to moving disks from one machine to another without moving all the disks in the volume. Wait to import your disk until you have all the disks in the volume physically connected to the server. Then when you import them, Windows will see them as a complete volume and retain their configuration.

3.20.6.2 Mirrored or Raid-5 Volume's Status is Failed Redundancy

Failed Redundancy, occurs when one of the disks in a fault-tolerant volume fails. Your volume will continue to work, but it is no longer fault tolerant. If another disk fails, you will lose all your data on that volume. You should repair the failed disk as quickly as possible.

Your mirrored volume will need to be recreated after replacing the disk. Right-click the defective disk and select Remove Mirror. Then right-click the working disk and select Add Mirror, selecting the new disk as the mirror. To repair the RAID-5 volume, put in the disk and right-click the volume and choose Repair RAID-5 Volume.

3.20.6.3 Mirrored or Raid-5 Volume's Status is Stale Data

Stale data occurs when a volume's fault-tolerant information is not completely up to date. This happens in a mirrored volume if something has been written to the primary disk, but for whatever reason it hasn't made it to the mirror disk yet. This occurs in a RAID-5 volume when the parity information isn't up to date.

If you try to move a volume while it contains stale information, you will get a status of Stale Data when you try to import the disk. Move the disk back to the machine it was originally in and rescan the machine for new disk. After all the disks are discovered, wait until they say online and healthy before you try to move them again.

EXERCISES

1. Explain the terminology and concepts of disk management?
2. Differentiate between the following:
   - Physical and logical disks
   - Basic and dynamic disks
   - Partitions and volumes
3. Explain the various partition types and logical drives?
4. Explain the various volume types available in disk management?
5. How we can manage disks?
6. Explain the concept of using the disk management MMC?
7. Explain the concept of using the command-line utilities?
8. Elaborate the concept of managing basic disks?
9. Explain the concept of creating partitions and logical drives?
10. How we can assign a new drive letter?
11. How we can format a basic volume?
12. How we can extend a basic volume?
13. Explain the concept of dynamic disks?
14. Write a procedure to converting dynamic disk status?
15. Explain the procedure to creating and using simple volumes?
16. How we can create a spanned volume?
17. How we can create and use striped volumes?
18. Explain the concept of creating and using mirrored volumes?
19. Explain the concept creating and using raid-5 volumes?
20. Explain the various disk quotas?
21. How we can enable and configure disk quotas?
22. How we can enable disk quotas and setting quota limits?
23. Explain the concept of monitoring disk quotas?
24. Explain the concept of exporting and importing quota settings?
25. Explain the concept of disk fragmentation?
26. Explain the various defragmenting volumes and partitions?
27. How we can understanding the disk defragmenter interface
28. Explain the various practices of defragmentation?
29. What do you mean by remote storage?
30. Explain the various storage levels?

31. Explain the relationship of remote storage and removable storage?
32. How we can set up remote storage?
33. How we can use remote storage?
34. Explain the concept of raid and mirroring?
35. How we can understand windows server 2003 raid?
36. Explain the concept of hardware raid?
37. What do you mean by troubleshooting disks and volumes?
38. What do you mean by troubleshooting basic disks?
39. What do you mean by troubleshooting dynamic volumes?
40. Explain the various problems of troubleshooting fragmentation?
41. Explain the concept of troubleshooting disk quotas?
42. How we can troubleshoot remote storage?
43. Explain the concept of troubleshooting raid?

CHAPTER 4

Servers

4.1 INTRODUCTION

The three basic network features that virtually all TCP/IP-based networks need to use are:

- ***Dynamic Host Configuration Protocol (DHCP), to dynamically provide clients with IP addresses and configuration information***
- ***Domain Name System (DNS), to translate IP addresses into friendly names that are easier to deal with and vice versa***
- ***Windows Internet Naming Service (WINS), to translate NetBIOS names and IP addresses for clients that still use NetBIOS***

Although Active Directory and Microsoft Windows clients function with standards-based DHCP and DNS servers, such as those available for UNIX systems (nobody other than Microsoft makes WINS servers), Active Directory works best with the DHCP and DNS servers provided as a part of Microsoft Windows Server 2003 and Microsoft Windows 2000 Server. There are a few additional capabilities available when you deploy Active Directory in conjunction with DHCP and DNS servers running Windows Server 2003 or Windows 2000 Server, such as secure dynamic updates for legacy clients and multiple- master replication between DNS servers.

4.2 DHCP

Dynamic Host Configuration Protocol (DHCP): A Transmission Control Protocol/ Internet Protocol (TCP/IP) protocol used to automatically assign IP addresses and configure TCP/IP for network clients.

If you've ever managed more than a very small number of computers on a network, you've probably used DHCP. DHCP can provide both an IP address and all the essential configuration information that any client on the network needs to connect and communicate with other computers, both on the network and outside on the Internet. By providing a central location for address management and disbursement, the DHCP service of Windows Server 2003 makes it easy to configure and manage your TCP/IP network. The DHCP server provided with Microsoft Windows Server 2003 is truly excellent-it works predictably, reliably, and properly.

4.2.1 Designing DHCP Networks

It's important to design the deployment of DHCP servers in a way that fits the network. Small, non-routed networks can use a single DHCP server. If you have a larger network, consider the subnets and routers in use, and also split the address space between two servers or host your DHCP service on a cluster to improve fault tolerance. Use the following checklist as part of your planning:

- Draw a map of the network, showing each physical and logical subnet and the routers joining the subnets.
- If the network uses routers to subnet the network, determine whether the routers support forwarding DHCP broadcasts. (Most newer routers do, although this option usually needs to be turned on.)
- Plan on sectioning the IP address range between two DHCP servers to provide fault tolerance. (DHCP servers can't communicate with each other, so they can't share the same addresses.) Give 80 percent of the addresses to one server, and 20 percent to the other server. (This is called "the 80/20 rule.") If one server goes down, clients can still receive IP addresses from the other server. Alternatively, you can set up a DHCP server cluster to handle 100 percent of the addresses.
- If the link between the subnets is fast and reliable and the routers in between can be configured to forward DHCP broadcasts (or if you add a DHCP relay agent), you can place the second DHCP server on a different physical subnet. Otherwise, deploy a pair of DHCP servers to each physical subnet.
- Don't run a DHCP server on a domain controller if you plan on using the DHCP server to update DNS records for legacy clients. Doing so creates an additional security risk. (Consult the DNS Help topic in the Windows Server 2003 Help system for more information-specifically, check the Dynamic Updates topics.)
- Size the servers appropriately. A single DHCP server can service no more than 10,000 clients and 1000 scopes.
- Upgrade any Microsoft Windows NT 4 domain controllers to Windows Server 2003 or Windows 2000 Server. (See Chapter 6 for more information about upgrading.)
- Use a disk drive with fast access time, or better yet, use a redundant array of independent disks (RAID). DHCP servers frequently access the disk drives, and a fast storage subsystem means better DHCP performance.

4.2.2 DHCP Security Considerations

Although DHCP servers aren't high-value targets for hackers, there are nonetheless a number of vulnerabilities inherent to DHCP servers. Because the number of IP addresses in a scope is limited, an unauthorized user can launch a denial-of-service (DoS) attack on the network by acquiring a large number of IP addresses from the DHCP server. A DoS attack on the DNS server can also be initiated by performing a large number of DNS dynamic updates via DHCP. Similarly, a user with physical access to the network can easily use a non-Microsoft DHCP server to set up a rogue DHCP server that provides improper IP addresses to other clients.

To round off the list of DHCP security vulnerabilities, any user that obtains an IP address from the DHCP server will probably also obtain the addresses for company DNS and WINS servers. A hacker can then obtain further information about the network configuration from these servers or attack them.

To minimize these risks, limit physical access to your network. If a hacker can plug into your network, his or her job is immensely easier than trying to break through a firewall. The use of 802.1x across the entire physical network to control access can significantly reduce the risk. Also make sure to maintain and regularly review DHCP audit logs (stored by default in the %windir%\System32\Dhcp folder).

4.2.3 Plan the IP Address Range and Exclusions

Besides determining how to place the DHCP servers into the network structure, you also need to plan the IP address ranges you'll use, as well as which IP addresses to reserve or exclude from this pool of addresses. Use the following list to help plan the IP address ranges to use and exclude:

- Determine the range of IP addresses that the DHCP server will manage. Most likely, this will be a private address range such as 10.x.x.x or 192.168.x.x.
- Make a list of any IP addresses to exclude to support hosts with static IP addresses. Only DHCP servers and hosts that don't work as DHCP clients need static IP addresses, although you might want to use static addresses for DNS servers as well.
- Make a list of servers that need to have unchanging IP addresses, such as DNS and WINS servers, and then decide whether you can use a DHCP reservation or whether bona fide static addresses are needed.
- If the DHCP server will be using Internet-registered IP addresses (which it probably won't), register the IP addresses with the Internet service provider (ISP).

4.2.4 Installing the DHCP Service

The easiest way to set up the DHCP service is by using the Manage Your Server Wizard (also called the Configure Your Server Wizard) to install the DHCP server role and create a new scope. (The Configure Your Server Wizard is discussed in Chapter 7; creating scopes is covered in the next section.) However, you can also do this manually by installing the Dynamic Host Configuration Protocol (DHCP) component, accessible through the Add/Remove Programs tool

4.2.5 Real World DHCP Options

There are four levels at which you can configure DHCP options in a Windows Server 2003 DHCP server:

- **Server options:** These options apply to all clients of the DHCP server you're managing. Because of this, use server options sparingly-specify server options only for parameters common across all scopes on the server.

- **Scope options:** These are the most often used type of options-they apply to all clients within a scope and override any server options set on the DHCP server.
- **Client options:** These options are specified for individual clients. This is useful if specific computers need special options. Client options override all other options, including class options.
- **Class options:** These options provide DHCP parameters to clients based on the type of client they are either using vendor classes such as all Microsoft Windows 95 or Windows 98 clients, or with user classes that specify clients with particular needs, such as RRAS clients, "mobile clients," or any other user-defined class. For more information about creating and using class options, consult the Help system or the Microsoft Windows Server 2003 Resource Kit.

4.2.6 Creating a new Scope

After installing the DHCP service, the next thing you must do to get the DHCP server up and running is create a new scope of IP addresses for the DHCP server to manage. (A scope is a range of IP addresses that the DHCP server can manage.) Before you do this, make sure you know which range of IP addresses is approved, which IP addresses need to be excluded for systems with static IP addresses, and which IP addresses need to be reserved for DNS or WINS servers.

4.2.7 Scopes, Superscopes, and Multicast Scopes

A scope is simply the range of possible IP addresses on a network. To add more clients to a network where the scope is exhausted, you can add another scope as long as the scope doesn't overlap with an existing scope. An excellent source of information about the complex subject of choosing subnet masks and other TCP/IP issues is Microsoft Windows Server 2003 TCP/IP Protocols and Services Technical Reference by Thomas Lee and Joseph Davies (Microsoft Press, 2003).

When you create multiple scopes, it's important to understand that clients from one logical subnet aren't able to obtain IP addresses from a different scope than the one they currently belong to, because the other scope is in a different logical sub net. If this is the behaviour you want, great. However, if you want clients to be able to use addresses from other scopes, use a superscope. A superscope is a collection of scopes grouped together into a single administrative whole. There are three primary reasons you might want to use superscopes:

- One scope is running out of IP addresses.
- You need to renumber the IP network, and therefore move clients from one set of addresses to another.
- You want to use two DHCP servers on the same subnet for redundancy.

When you create a superscope, you enable clients to obtain or renew leases from any scope within the superscope, even if they contain addresses from a different logical subnet. A multicast scope is simply a scope of multicast addresses (class D addresses) that are then shared by many computers (members of the multicast group). To create the new scope, follow these steps (or if you're using the Configure Your Server Wizard to set up DHCP, you can jump to Step 4):

1. Launch DHCP from the Administrative Tools folder on the Start menu.
2. If the DHCP server you want to administer isn't listed in the DHCP console tree, choose the Add Server command from the Action menu to locate the server you want to administer.

3. Select the appropriate DHCP server in the console tree. Select the Action menu, and choose New Scope to launch the New Scope Wizard. 4. Click Next, and type a name and description for the scope to use for distinguishing this scope from others. (See Figure 4.1.) Click Next.

Figure 4.1 The Scope Name page of the New Scope Wizard

5. Type the IP address that the scope begins with in the Start IP Address field, and type the IP address that the scope ends with in the End IP Address field, as shown in Figure 4.2.

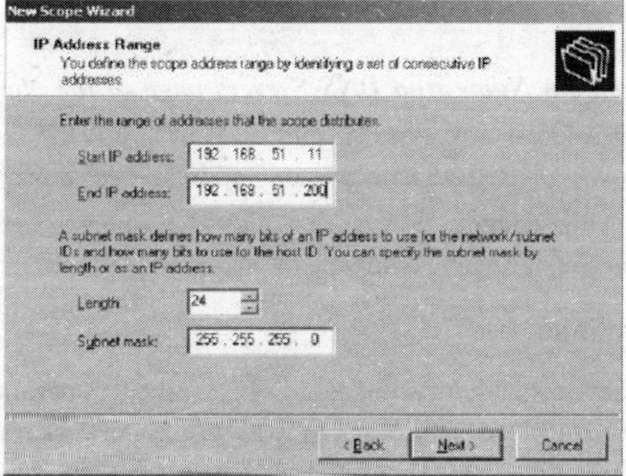

Figure 4.2 The IP Address Range page of the New Scope Wizard

6. Type the network's subnet mask in the Subnet Mask box, or use the Length box to adjust the length of the subnet mask. Then click Next.
7. To exclude a range of addresses from the scope, in the Start IP Address box, type the start IP address for the exclusion range; in the End IP Address box, type the end IP address for the exclusion range. (To add a single address, enter it in the Start IP Address box and then click Add.) Then click Add. Add as much exclusion as needed, and click Next when you're finished.
8. Specify the lease duration for the clients, and then click Next. For more information, see the "Setting Lease Durations" sidebar.

9. To configure DHCP options, choose Yes; otherwise, choose No, and then click Next. If you select No, click Finish to complete the setup of the scope.
10. If you chose to specify DHCP options for this scope, type the routers (default gate- ways) you want clients to use in the Router (Default Gateway) page, clicking Add after typing each one. When you're finished adding gateways, click Next.
11. Type the domain name of the domain in the Parent Domain box, and add the IP addresses for the DNS servers in the IP Address box, as shown in Figure 4.3, clicking Add after entering each one. Click Next when you're done.

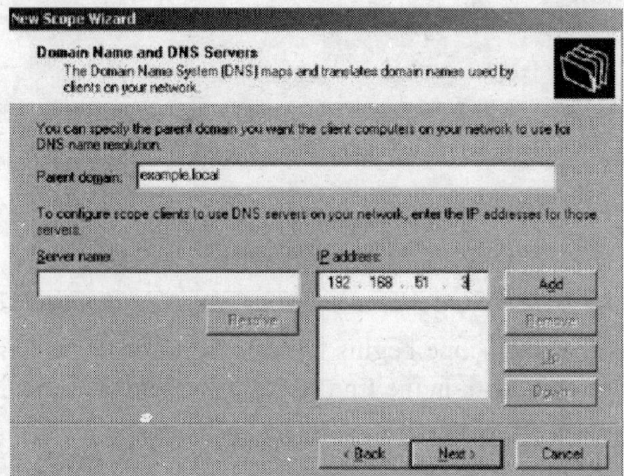

Figure 4.3 The Domain Name And DNS Servers page of the New Scope Wizard

12. In the WINS Server Address box, type the addresses of any WINS servers you configured on the network for resolving NetBIOS names into IP addresses for down level clients. Click Next.
13. To activate the scope immediately, choose Yes; otherwise, choose No to activate the scope later. Click Next, and then click Finish to complete the scope configuration.

4.2.8 Setting Lease Durations

Use longer leases for networks without redundant DHCP servers to permit more time to recover an offline DHCP server before clients lose their leases, or to minimize network traffic at the expense of less frequent address turnover. You can also use longer leases if scope addresses are plentiful (at least 20 percent available), the network is stable, and computers are rarely moved.

In contrast, scopes that support dial-up clients or mobile clients such as laptops or personal digital assistants (PDAs) can have shorter leases and therefore function well with fewer addresses. If you're planning a major network change, change the scope lease duration to be quite short. This will allow you to make the changes you need to the DHCP Scope properties and have them rapidly deployed to all clients. After the network change is made, don't forget to set the DHCP back to a more reasonable duration to minimize the amount of network traffic and resource utilization on the DHCP server. Lease durations are set in the scope's Properties dialog box. Scopes are listed in the DHCP administration console.

4.2.9 Authorizing the DHCP Server and Activating Scopes

After you set up the DHCP server and create the scopes, you must authorize the server to give leases and activate the scopes. DHCP servers that are also domain controllers are automatically authorized when added to the DHCP Manager console. Authorizing a DHCP server is an important step that Windows Server 2003 provides to reduce the occurrence of unauthorized (rogue) servers set up to hand out false IP addresses to clients. Although rogue DHCP servers that use UNIX or a hardware-based DHCP server can still be set up, Windows Server 2003-based and Windows 2000-based DHCP servers can't be used in a Windows domain without authorization.

To authorize the DHCP server after installing the service, select the server in the DHCP console and then choose Authorize from the Action menu. To manage the list of authorized servers, right-click DHCP at the root of the console tree and choose Manage Authorized Servers from the shortcut menu. To activate a scope, right-click the scope in the console tree, and then choose Activate from the shortcut menu. Don't activate a scope until you finish selecting all the options you want. When you activate a scope, the Activate command on the menu changes to Deactivate.

4.2.10 Under the Hood Scope Deactivation

When you deactivate a scope, the assumption is that those addresses are not being used by the network and the DHCP server will not accept those addresses as valid. Any existing clients will be unable to renew their addresses, and when they try, they'll cause DHCP negative acknowledgement messages to be sent from the server to the client. This is the correct method if your intent is to never use those addresses as part of a DHCP scope again, and you should deactivate a scope prior to deleting it. But if what you want to do is temporarily stop handing out addresses in a particular scope, the preferred method is to add an exclusion that covers the entire address range of the scope. This way, any existing addresses already given out are retained by the clients and are considered valid. When you're ready to re-enable the scope, you simply remove the exclusion.

4.2.11 Adding Address Reservations

Reservations are used to provide a consistent and unchanging IP address to servers and other hosts that need to be at a predictable IP address. The only servers that can't use a reservation are DHCP servers-they must be at a fixed IP address. Using reservations instead of static addresses guarantees that a server has a consistent IP address, while giving you the ability to easily change settings as required, and to recover the IP address in the future if the server is decommissioned or moved.

To add an address reservation to a scope, right-click the Reservations folder under the desired scope, and choose New Reservation from the shortcut menu. Walk through the wizard, and add the new reservation. You'll need to know the MAC address for the DHCP client you want a reservation for, and the IP address you want to assign to it.

4.2.12 Enabling Dynamic Updates to a DNS Server for Earlier Clients

Microsoft Windows Server 2003, Windows XP, and Windows 2000 clients automatically update their forward lookup records with the DNS server after obtaining a new IP address from a DHCP server, while explicitly requesting that the DHCP server update their reverse lookup (PTR) records on the DNS server. This second step requires communication between the DHCP server and the DNS server. Because legacy and non-Windows clients don't automatically update their own resource records, you can configure the DHCP server to update the legacy client's forward and reverse lookup records whenever the client obtains a new IP address. To enable legacy client support for DHCP and dynamic DNS, use the following procedure:

1. Select the scope or DHCP server on which you want to permit dynamic DNS updates.
2. From the Action menu, choose Properties, and then click the DNS tab.
3. Select the Enable DNS Dynamic Updates option, as shown in Figure 4.4.

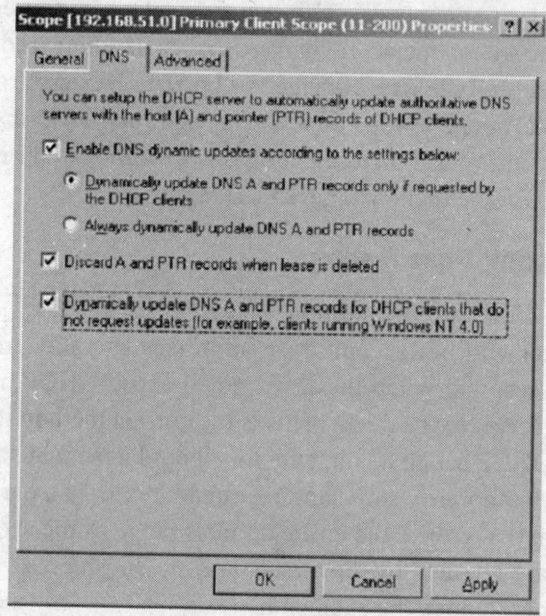

Figure 4.4 The DNS tab of the Properties dialog box for a DHCP scope

The other options available on the DNS tab are:

- Dynamically Update DNS A and PTR Records Only If Requested By The DHCP Clients This option allows Windows XP, Windows 2000, and other Windows clients to decide whether to update the DNS server themselves or have the DHCP server update their DNS address (A) and reverse lookup (PTR) records.
- Always Dynamically Update DNS A And PTR Records This option forces the DHCP server to update the A and PTR records for all DHCP clients, even if they request permission to update the DNS server themselves.
- Discard A and PTR Records When Lease Is Deleted This option forces the DHCP server to delete the A record as well as the PTR record of a client whose lease has expired or is deleted. (The PTR record is always deleted at lease expiration, regardless of this setting.)
- Dynamically Update DNS A And PTR Records For DHCP Clients That Do Not Request Updates This option enables the DHCP server to update the forward and reverse lookup records for clients that can't update their own forward lookup records (Windows Me and all other versions

of Windows prior to Windows 2000). If you don't select this check box, the DNS records of pre Windows 2000 clients aren't dynamically updated.

4.2.13 DHCP, Stale Records, and Secure Dynamic Updates

There is a problem that arises when using DHCP in combination with DNS zones that make use of secure dynamic updates. When DHCP creates a DNS record for a client running an earlier version of Windows, the DHCP server becomes the owner of the record. As the owner of the record in a zone with secure dynamic updates enabled, only thc DHCP server is allowed to update the record. This is usually fine; however, the DNS records of clients running earlier versions of Windows become stale (outdated) and orphaned (unable to be updated by anyone) under the following conditions:

- If the DHCP server is replaced by a backup server, or its scope is migrated to another server (in which case the records are still owned by the original server)
- If the client is upgraded to Windows 2000, Windows XP, or Windows Server 2003 (in which case the records are still owned by the DHCP server, which will no longer update the records because the client is now theoretically capablc of doing so).

The best solution is to upgrade all clients running earlier versions of Windows, but this is obviously impractical for some networks. Another solution is to add all DHCP servers to the DnsUpdateProxy group. When a member of this group creates or updates a DNS record, no security information is recorded. (The record is unsecured.) This prevents the record from becoming orphaned. When any other computer modifies one of these unsecured records, it then becomes the owner. (This is intended to allow upgraded clients to take possession of their DNS records.)

However, astute readers will notice that this means that all DNS records recorded by the DHCP servers are unsecured and can be modified by anyone who changes their DNS name to the name of an unsecured record. (They also acquire ownership in doing so.) This also includes the DNS record of the DHCP server itself. To protect against this risk, create a dedicated DHCP service account that is used exclusively for dynamic DNS updates.

To add a DHCP server to the DnsUpdateProxy group, in the Active Directory Users And Groups snap-in, right-click the DHCP server, and then choose Properties from the shortcut menu. Click the Member Of tab, click Add, type DnsUpdateProxy in the box, and then click OK. Windows Server 2003, Windows XP, and Windows 2000 clients are exempt from this issue. (They can directly communicate with the DNS server and securely update their DNS records.)

4.2.14 Using Multiple DHCP Servers for Redundancy

Computers don't lose network connectivity immediately when a DHCP server goes down, but new computers, returning laptops, or little-used systems that haven't recently logged on might not be able to obtain network access until a DHCP server is available. To ensure that there will continue to be an available DHCP server, even if the primary DHCP server is down, configure multiple DHCP servers. The traditional solution is to set up redundant servers with a split scope across the servers. Windows Server 2003 Enterprise Edition gives you the option of configuring DHCP onto a cluster for high availability.

Splitting the Address Space between Two Servers To employ two DHCP servers for load balancing and redundancy, use the following procedure:

1. Create identical scopes on each server for all valid IP addresses that the DHCP servers you're setting up will manage. This might mean creating a single scope (if you have a single subnet), or multiple scopes encompassing a number of subnets.
2. Set up exclusions so that the primary DHCP server handles 80 percent of the address pool and the secondary server handles the other 20 percent of the addresses. Thus, each server excludes the addresses available on the other server so that no address appears in both servers' address pools.
3. Create a superscope on both servers that contains all valid scopes for the physical subnet. To do so, select the appropriate DHCP server from the console tree, choose the New Superscope command from the Action menu, name the superscope, and then select the member scopes to include.

4.2.15 Best Practices

If you have a routed network with DHCP relay agents or routers that forward DHCP broadcasts between the physical subnets, you can use DHCP servers on other subnets as secondary servers. However, unless the DHCP server has at least one scope with available addresses from the client's own subnet, the client isn't able to obtain or renew an IP address lease. To make sure this doesn't happen, create two superscopes on each server, one for each logical subnet. Thus, each server owns 80 percent of the address pool for its local subnet, and 20 percent of the address pool for the other DHCP server's local subnet.

4.2.16 Setting up a Dhcp Server Cluster

Although splitting the address space between two DHCP servers is an adequate way to provide redundancy and load balancing, an even more powerful solution is to set up the DHCP service to run on a Windows Server 2003 cluster. The members of the cluster equally share the DHCP service workload, and if one of the servers fails, the other servers continue to provide addresses to clients as if nothing had happened. Instead of an address space split between servers, each server in the cluster has access to the complete address space.

Using the Windows Server 2003 Cluster service, but the basic steps to get a DHCP server up and running in a cluster are as follows:

1. Install DHCP (as described earlier in this chapter), and set up the server cluster.
2. Launch Cluster Administrator from the Administrative Tools folder on the Programs menu.
3. Select the cluster you want to use to host the DHCP service.
4. Choose the Configure Application command from the File menu to open the Configure Application Wizard.
5. Click Next in the first page, and then choose the Use An Existing Virtual Server option and select the appropriate group. If you haven't already created a virtual server, choose the Create A New Virtual Server option and use the wizard to create a new virtual server.

6. In the Create Application Cluster Resource page, choose the Yes, Create a Cluster Resource for My Application Now option, choose the DHCP resource type, and then click Next.
7. Type a name and, optionally, a description for the DHCP resource and then click Next.
8. Click Advanced Properties, click the Dependencies tab, and then click Modify.
9. Double-click the IP address, physical disk, and network name you want to use for the DHCP server cluster. These resources then appear as dependencies. Click OK when finished, optionally modify the properties of the resource, and then click OK.
10. Click Next in the Application Resource Name And Description page, specify where the DHCP database should be stored (most likely the physical disk you specified in Step 9), and then click Next. If you select a different disk, make sure that it belongs to the group and that a dependency has been created for it.
11. Review the settings, and click Finish to complete the wizard.
12. Verify that the resource is displayed in the correct group, and then right-click the resource and choose Bring Online from the shortcut menu to enable the DHCP server to begin servicing clients.
13. Authorize the DHCP server in Active Directory

4.2.17 Other DHCP Functions

The DHCP snap-in provides a single point from which to administer all the properties and functionality of the DHCP servers.

4.2.17.1 Modifying Scopes

Modify a scope's properties by right-clicking the scope in the console tree and choosing Properties from the shortcut menu. This displays the Scope Properties dialog box shown in Figure 4.5.

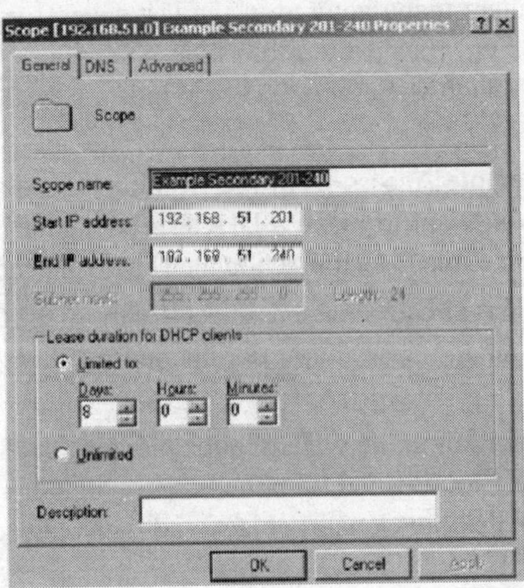

Figure 4.5 The General tab of the Properties dialog box for a DHCP scope

To deactivate a scope, right-click the scope in the DHCP console and choose Deactivate from the shortcut menu. To return the scope to use, right-click the scope again and choose Activate. To exclude a range of IP addresses from a scope, right-click the Address Pool folder under the appropriate scope and choose New Exclusion Range from the shortcut menu. Type the range of addresses you want to exclude, and then click Add.

4.2.17.2 Enabling Server-based Conflict Detection

The Windows Server 2003 DHCP server provides the ability to enable server-based conflict detection, which is a technique that pings an IP address before leasing it to a client to ensure that it's not already in use by a static IP client. Windows Server 2003, Windows XP, and Windows 2000 clients automatically verify that the IP address offered by the DHCP server is available before accepting it, so conflict detection is useful only for earlier clients. In the interest of conserving network bandwidth and reducing client startup times, leave this option disabled unless you're having problems with duplicate IP addresses, as might be the case if you have undocumented static IP addresses on the network.

To enable server-based conflict detection, right-click the DHCP server in the console tree and choose Properties from the shortcut menu. Click the Advanced tab, and then set the Conflict Detection Attempts number to 1. Don't increase this number beyond 2; this results in additional searches and needlessly increases the time it takes a client to obtain an IP address.

4.2.17.3 Setting up a Dhcp Relay Agent

If you have a routed network, deploy DHCP servers on both sides of routers to maximize reliability and minimize bandwidth usage. However, there are instances in which you want to allow DHCP to work across a router; for example, if the routed network is very reliable and fast, as might be the case with a partitioned local network or municipal area network (MAN), you might want to simply allow clients to cross the router to reach a DHCP server.

You can configure most routers manufactured in the last several years to pass DHCP broadcasts (because they're BOOTP-compliant), but if the router doesn't support forwarding DHCP broadcasts, you can set up a server running Windows Server 2003 or Windows 2000 Server as a DHCP relay agent using the following procedure:

1. Launch Routing and Remote Access from the Administrative Tools folder on the Programs menu. 2. If the server you want to make a DHCP relay agent isn't listed in the console tree, choose the Add Server command from the Action menu to locate the server you want to administer.
3. If the appropriate server isn't already enabled, select it, choose the Configure And Enable Routing And Remote Access command from the Action menu, and then click Next (otherwise, skip to Step 5).
4. Choose Custom Configuration in the wizard, click Next, select LAN Routing, click Next, and then click Finish. 5. In the Routing and Remote Access window, select the IP Routing object on the desired server, right-click the General object, and then choose New Routing Protocol from the shortcut menu.
6. Select DHCP Relay Agent and then click OK.

7. Right-click the DHCP Relay Agent object, and then choose New Interface from the shortcut menu.
8. Select the network adapter connected to the network with the wayward DHCP clients, and then click OK. As shown in Figure 4.6, change the Hop-Count Threshold and Boot Threshold values, if necessary, and then click OK. (The hop count determines the maximum number of relay agents a DHCP request can pass through, and the boot threshold introduces a forwarding delay so that local DHCP servers can get first crack at servicing clients.)

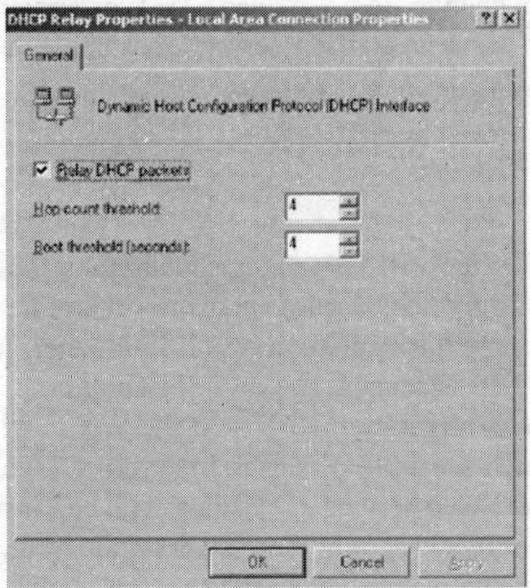

Figure 4.6 Setting up a DHCP relay agent

9. Right-click the DHCP Relay object again, and choose Properties from the shortcut menu.
10. Type the address of a DHCP server you want to forward DHCP requests to, and then click Add.

4.2.17.4 Backing up and Restoring the DHCP Database

Windows Server 2003 automatically backs up the DHCP database every 60 minutes to the \%Systemroot%\System32\Dhcp\Backup folder. Everything but registry and configuration settings (such as audit log settings) are saved during this backup. To manually force a backup, use the following procedure:

1. Select the DHCP server you want to back up from the console tree.
2. Choose Backup from the Action menu.
3. Select the folder you want to store the backup files in, and click OK.

To restore the DHCP database from a backup, either to the same system or a different one, use the following procedure:

1. Select the DHCP server you want to back up from the console tree.
2. Choose Restore from the Action menu.
3. Select the folder where the backup files are stored, and click OK.
4. Click Yes when asked whether you want to stop and restart the DHCP service. No clients are able to obtain or renew leases during this time.

4.2.17.5 DHCP Command-line Administration

The DHCP server in Windows Server 2003 provides full command-line administration capabilities with the rather unfriendly, but powerful, netsh command.

To use these capabilities, do the following:

1. Open a command prompt window.
2. Type netsh at the command prompt. The prompt changes to netsh>.
3. Type dhcp. The prompt changes to netsh dhcp>. 4. Type server followed by the server name or IP address to connect to the desired DHCP server-for example, server \\srv1 or server 192.168.0.1.
5. Type list to view a list of the available commands. To obtain help with a particular command, type the command name followed by /?.

4.3 IIS

The Internet Information Services (IIS) Manager, shown in Figure 4.7, is the primary tool used for administering IIS 6 on Windows Server 2003-based networks; therefore, it's the primary tool used for IIS 6 administration in this chapter and the next. To access IIS Manager, select Administrative Tools from the Start menu and then select IIS Manager. The basic installation of IIS includes the common files needed by IIS, documentation, configuration tools, and the World Wide Web service. To modify the settings of the installed components, use IIS Manager. In Figure 4.7, you see that you're able to manage application pools, Web sites, and Web service extensions. You can install the optional IIS services by opening Control Panel, Add/Remove Programs, and selecting the Add/ Remove Windows Components option. Select the Internet Information Services component, and click Details to make changes to the IIS configuration. Among the additional services available are the Background Intelligent Transfer Service (BITS), the FTP Service, Internet Printing, the NNTP Service, and the SMTP Service.

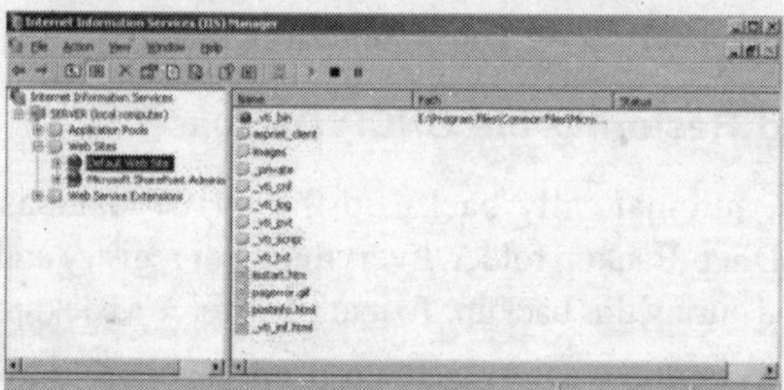

Figure 4.7 The Internet Information Services (IIS) Manager window

4.3.1 Remote Administration

The three primary methods of administering your IIS installation from another machine are the IIS Manager, the Remote Administration (HTML) Tool, and Remote Desktop.

- IIS Manager You can administer IIS on a remote machine using the IIS Manager. Start IIS Manager, and either select Connect from the Internet Information Services node's shortcut menu or click Add A Computer To The List in the IIS Manager toolbar.
- Remote Administration Tool You must install the Remote Administration (HTML) Tool to enable the administration options from a remote browser. Go to Control Panel, Add Or Remove Programs,

and select Add/Remove Windows Components. Select Internet Information Services and then click Details. Select the World Wide Web Publishing Service and click its Details button. Select the check box for the Remote Administration (HTML) option, and click OK. Acknowledge all choices to dismiss the cascade of dialog boxes and complete the installation. When the Remote Administration Tool is installed, you can use the address https://host- name:8098 (where hostname is the name of the computer name) to remotely administer the IIS Web server.

- Remote Desktop You can also use Remote Desktop to remotely administer IIS installations. Enable the Remote Desktop functionality by opening the System from Control Panel. Go to the Remote tab and select the Enable Remote Desktop On This Computer check box. Then you can configure the users you want to have this access.

4.3.2 Administration Scripts

To run administration scripts on Windows Server 2003, use the IIS Windows Management Instrumentation (WMI) interface or Active Directory Service Interfaces (ADSI). Either interface enables you to perform common administrative tasks such as creating new Web sites, configuring Web site security, creating virtual directories, stopping and starting Web sites, and so on. You can write these scripts in a number of COM-compatible languages, such as Visual Basic Scripting Edition (VBScript), Jscript, or Perl. WMI is the preferred interface to the programmatic controls of IIS. It offers a number of advantages over ADSI, including query support and object model GUI tools.

4.3.3 WWW Publishing Service

In this section, you'll learn about the steps you need to take to create your Web site and serve it to clients using IIS. You begin by examining the Default Web Site that is included as an example when you install Windows Server 2003 on a machine. Then you look at common tasks such as creating new Web sites and virtual directories. You also explore how to use Web sharing.

4.3.4 The Default Web Site

In Figure 4.7, you saw an administrator's view of the Default Web Site-a series of sample configuration files whose default location on the server's local file system is \Inetpub\wwwroot, the root directory for your Web site. The \Inetpub directory actually contains several important subdirectories, which are summarized in Table 32-1. Table 32-1 IIS-related subdirectories located within the default \Inetpub directory

Subdirectory	Description
Admin Scripts	Sample IIS administration scripts.
ftproot	Root directory of Default TP Site.
mailroot	Various folders used by the SMTP service.
nntpfile	Various folders used by the NNTP service
scripts	Default location for application scripts used by the Default Web Site. Includes samples and tools.
wwwroot	Root directory of the Default Web Site.

4.3.5 Connecting to a Web Site

On the server, you can access the home page of the Default Web Site (Figure 4.8) in various ways by using a Web browser. Try these methods:

- From the local console, click Start, point to Run, type http://127.0.0.1, and click OK. This opens Internet Explorer and accesses the home page by using the TCP/IP loopback address.
- From the local console, start Internet Explorer, type localhost in the Address bar, and press Enter.
- From IIS Manager, select the Default Web Site node and then do one of the following:
  - *(a)* Right-click and choose Browse from the shortcut menu
  - *(b)* Click Action on the toolbar, and select Browse from the drop-down menu

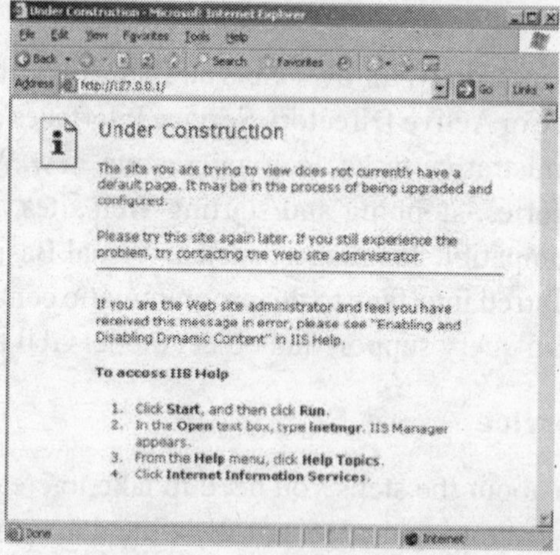

Figure 4.8 The home page of the Default Web Site

When you attempt access from a remote machine on the connected network, you see an "Under Construction" message, but that message actually tells you that the site is active and accessible. To connect, start Internet Explorer, press Ctrl+O to open the Open dialog box, type any of the items in the following list, and then click OK:

- The IP address of the Web server (for example, 192.168.1.128)
- The NetBIOS name of the Web server (for example, Server)
- The DNS name of the Web server (for example, server.example.com), provided either a name server is accessible or the Hosts file is configured on the client

4.3.6 Other Web Sites

The Default Web Site is only one small example of how you can deploy a Web site using IIS 6. In fact, you can create as many Web sites as you want using IIS 6, and you can host the content (pages, images, and other files) for these sites in a variety of locations. Each Web site acts as a separate entity, or virtual server-that is, it acts as if it were running on its own server and using the full resources available to it on that server. To illustrate this, let's create a new Web site on the server MyServer, create a simple home page for it, and then test it by connecting to it from another machine on the network.

4.3.7 Using the Web Site Creation Wizard

Before using the Web Site Creation Wizard to create a new Web site, you must decide how to name this site on the network. As you saw previously, when you use a Web browser such as Internet Explorer to connect to a Web site and view its home page, you can specify the URL of the site in a variety of ways, including using the site's IP address, NetBIOS name, or fully qualified DNS name. For this example, you bind a second IP address to the network interface card (NIC) on the Windows Server 2003 MyServer and establish a mapping between the new Web site you'll create and the new IP address you'll add. To add a second IP address, follow these steps:

1. Expand the Network Connections list in Control Panel and select the Local Area Connection icon.
2. On the General tab of the Local Area Connection Status dialog box, click Properties.
3. In the Local Area Connection Properties window, double-click Internet Protocol (TCP/IP).
4. In the Internet Protocol (TCP/IP) Properties window, click Advanced. 5. On the IP Settings tab in the Advanced TCP/IP Settings dialog box (Figure 4.9), click Add in the IP Addresses section. Then specify an additional IP address and subnet mask, and click Add.
6. Click OK until all dialog boxes have been closed.

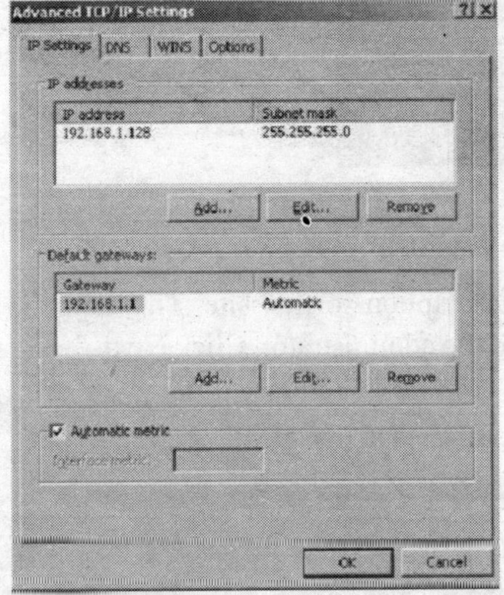

Figure 4.9 Adding IP addresses for Web site identities

Two more steps are required prior to creating the site. First, establish a new directory (for example, C:\Company) on the local server, which will store the content for the new site. Then create a simple home page called Default.htm within this site, using basic HTML. If you aren't familiar with HTML, type the following text into Notepad and save the file in the \Company directory as Default.htm, ensuring that your editor does not add a .TXT extension:

```
<HTML>
<HEAD><TITLE>The Company Site</TITLE></HEAD>
<BODY>
```

```
<H1>Welcome to the Company's Web Site</H1>
<HR>
This site is under construction!
</BODY>
</HTML>
```

Now create a new Web site called Company by following these steps:

1. Start IIS Manager on the machine acting as your Web server (or start it on a different server or workstation and connect to your Web server by clicking Action on the toolbar and selecting Connect from the drop-down menu), and select the server's name in the console tree. 2. Expand the server's node in the tree view, and right-click the Web Sites node. Point to New, and choose Web on the menu. The first page of the Web Site Creation Wizard appears (as shown in Figure 4.10). Click Next.

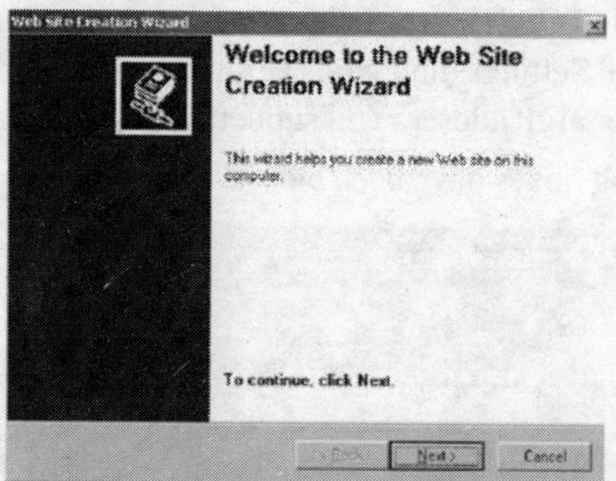

Figure 4.10 The first page of the Web Site Creation Wizard

3. Type Company as the description for the site. This name is displayed in IIS Manager, and identifies the new site for the administrator. Click Next.
4. Specify your second IP address as the one to be mapped to the site, leaving the remaining settings as they are (Figure 4.11). Click Next.

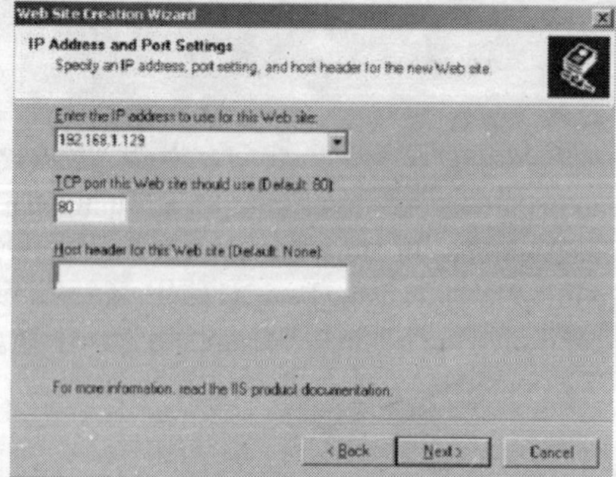

Figure 4.11 The IP Address And Port Settings page of the Web Site Creation Wizard

5. Specify the path to the home directory for the Web site as C:\Company. (Using the Browse button is the easiest way to do this.) Note that the home directory for your site can be either a local directory or a network share. Leave the check box selected to allow anonymous access to the Web site. (Because this is a public Web site, you want anyone to be able to access it.) Click Next.
6. Leave the access permissions set at their default settings.
7. Click Next, and then click Finish to complete the wizard. The new Company Web site should appear as a node under your server's node in IIS Manager, showing its single Web page Default.htm (as shown in Figure 4.12).

Figure 4.12 The new Web site

4.3.8 Testing the New Web Site

To test the IP address mapping (that is, Web site identity) for the new Web site, go to a different machine on the network, start Internet Explorer, and open the URL http:// 192.168.1.129, which specifies the new Web site using its associated IP address. The page Default.htm should load in the browser window. (See Figure 4.13.) Note that if a name server mapped this IP address to a DNS name such as www.example.com, you can access the Web site by using http://www.example.com instead of by using the IP address. As a further test, try opening http://192.168.1.128 or http://server instead.

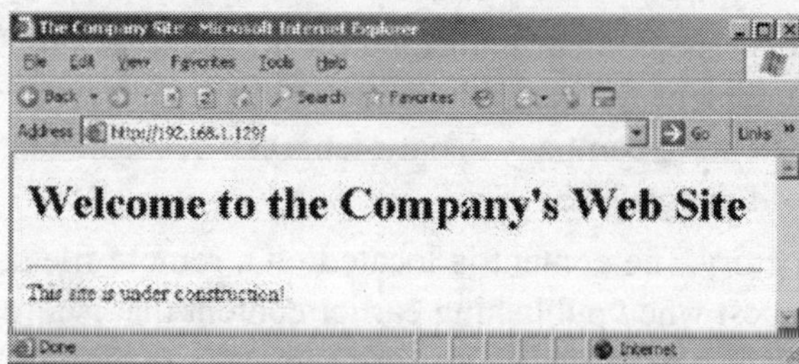

Figure 4.13 Testing the new Company Web site from a remote machine

Each of these URLs specifies an identity for the Default Web Site on the server and should open the default page for the site. (Remember, 192.168.1.129 was the IP address for the Company Web site.)

4.3.9 Virtual Directories

In the previous example, you created a new Web site called Company whose content was located in the home directory C:\Company on the server machine. To access content in this directory, you can use either of the following URLs:

- http://<IP_Address>, where <IP_Address> represents the IP address bound to the server's NIC that is mapped to that particular Web site

- http://<DNS_Name>, where <DNS_Name> is the fully qualified DNS name (such as servername.domainname.com) that is associated on the name server with the IP address mapped to that particular Web site Taking the first URL, you can associate or map a particular URL with the Web content stored in the site's home directory as represented here:

  C:\Company ↔ http://192.168.1.129

But what if you want to locate content for this Web site in a variety of locations and not just in the \Company directory on the server? You can do this by using something called a virtual directory. A virtual directory is a way of mapping an alias (a portion of a URL) to a physical directory containing additional Web site content not located in the home directory for the site. For example, say you want to store additional content in the directory C:\SalesData on the local server and associate it with the virtual directory /Sales. Note that the virtual directory uses a forward slash (/) instead of a backslash (\). The URL-to-directory map- ping is

C:\SalesData ↔ http://192.168.1.129/sales

Note that from the point of view of the client using the Web browser, the /sales content appears as a subdirectory of the home directory for Company. In other words, the content virtually appears as a subdirectory of the home directory http://192.168.1.129. But in fact, the content is physically located in an entirely separate part of the directory tree on the server's file system (instead of being located in \Company\sales, as you might expect from the URL). Virtual directories thus enable a kind of virtual file system specified by URLs that bears no direct relationship to the actual location of Web content for the site.

4.3.9.1 Local Virtual Directories VS. Remote Virtual Directories

The content that is mapped to the alias representing a virtual directory can be located in one of two places, resulting in two kinds of virtual directories:

- Local virtual directory The content is located on the local server. This solution might be the simplest because all content for the Web site is on the local server and can be backed up in a single operation. Content for company departments can be located in different directories on the server for security and integrity reasons.
- Remote virtual directory The content is located on a remote file server on the network. This solution is often the best when publishing earlier content that is already stored on network file servers. Security is enhanced because a user account is required to access the remote share, and suitable permissions can be assigned to this account. This remote placement of content also increases security by allowing content developers access only to file servers instead of to the Web servers themselves, and it reduces the processing load on the Web server. The only disadvantage is that the performance is slightly slower for content hosted on remote file servers, but this can be minimized by physically locating file servers close to the Web server on the network.

4.3.9.2 The Virtual Directory Creation Wizard

Now let's use the Virtual Directory Creation Wizard to create a virtual directory for the Company site. Here are the steps:

1. Start IIS Manager on your server (or start it on a different server or workstation, and connect to the IIS server by clicking Action on the toolbar and choosing Connect from the drop-down menu).
2. Select the Company entry in the console tree, click Action on the toolbar, point to New, and choose Virtual Directory from the drop-down menu (or right-click the Company node in the console, point to New, and choose Virtual Directory from the shortcut menu). The Virtual Directory Creation Wizard starts. Click Next.
3. Specify sales as the alias for the virtual directory. (You don't include the forward slash here.) Click Next.
4. Specify the path to the folder containing the pages you want access to, as seen in Figure 4.14. (If it's on another machine, specify the Uniform Naming Convention, or UNC, path.) You can also use the Browse button to navigate to the share folder. Click Next.

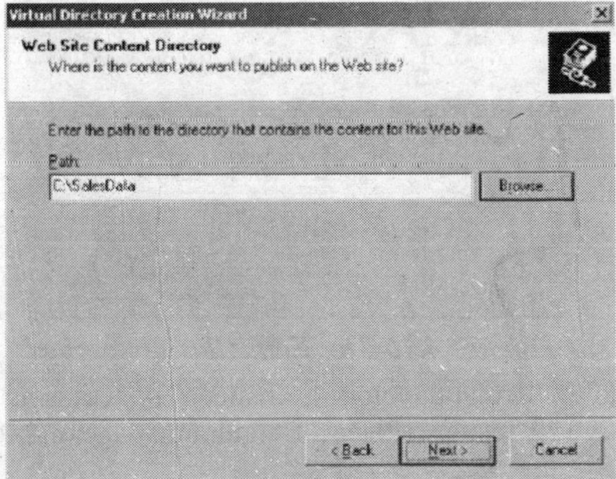

Figure 4.14 The Web Site Content Directory page of the Virtual Directory Creation Wizard

5. The Access Permissions dialog box allows you to change the security settings. For this example, they are left as is.
6. Click Next to reach the final dialog box. Click Finish to complete the wizard.

If you now examine the Company node in the Internet Information Services console tree, you notice a new node beneath it representing the new virtual directory. (See Figure 4.15.) Because you created the virtual directory under your Company site, you can access it via the URL http://192.168.1.129/sales. Of course, you must create content, including a Default.htm page, for the browser to render.

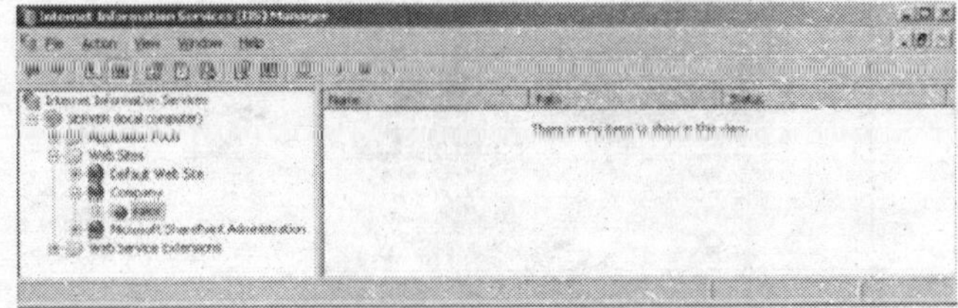

Figure 4.15 The sales virtual directory within the Company site

4.3.9.3 Web Sharing

Another way to create a new virtual directory is to use what's called Web sharing. For example, assume you have the directory C:\Testing located on the local Web server and you want to share this directory as a virtual directory of the Company. To do this, complete the following steps:

1. Right-click the \Testing directory in My Computer, and select Sharing And Security from the shortcut menu.
2. In the Testing Properties window, click the Web Sharing tab.
3. Select the Company site from the Share On drop-down box. This creates a new local virtual directory mapped to the \Testing directory for its content.
4. To open the Edit Alias dialog box (shown in Figure 4.16), select the Share This Folder option. You can specify an alias that is different from the name of the folder if you want.

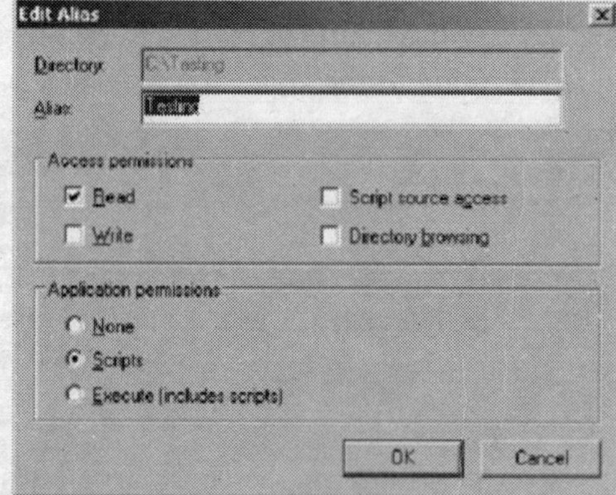

Figure 4.16 The Edit Alias dialog box

5. Click OK twice, and the virtual directory is created. Try accessing this directory by using the URL http://192.168.1.129/Testing. (Place a Default.htm page in the \Testing directory first.)

4.3.9.4 Virtual Directories, Physical Directories, and Icons

Virtual directories can be confusing for a couple of reasons. First, there are two icons you can use for nodes representing virtual directories in IIS Manager. Second, physical directories can behave like virtual directories if they're physically located as subfolders of the home directory or another virtual directory. Take a look at Figure 4.17 as an example.

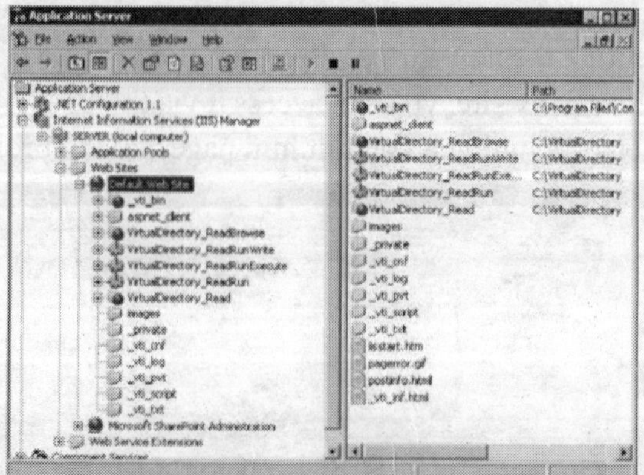

Figure 4.17 Confusion between virtual and physical directories

As you add a virtual directory, you can select among the five access permissions options: read, run scripts, execute, write, and browse. Looking at the various subnodes under the Default Web Site node in the console tree, you can easily see which have the run scripts or execute options set: they have the gear sprocket icon. Each of these-the starting directory for a Web application, typically developed by using ASP-creates dynamic content by running a script on your Web site.

In Figure 4.17, you see various virtual directories whose names start with "VirtualDirectory_". Each is named with the access permissions. The /VirtualDirectory_ReadBrowse virtual directory has an icon that looks like a folder with a globe attached to it. This is a virtual directory that doesn't create dynamic content, and therefore has neither the run scripts nor execute permission set. /VirtualDirectory_ReadRunExecute has the read, run scripts, and execute permission set; the sprocket icon is present because of the latter two. (You'll learn more about dynamic content in Chapter 33.) The /Images directory isn't a virtual directory at all, but rather a subdirectory of the Default Web Site's physical directory on the server's file system. As a result, it appears with an ordinary folder icon in the console tree. However, users can connect to it as if it were a physical directory by using the URL http://192.168.1.128/Images. Another icon you might see is the Error icon, which resembles a stop sign. This icon is used to indicate an error has occurred. For example, if a network device that contained the folder a node represents gets disconnected, that node will have the Error icon.

4.3.10 FTP Publishing Service

Now you look at concepts and tasks associated with the File Transfer Protocol Service. You begin by examining the Default FTP Site included as an example when you install the FTP service. Then you look at common tasks such as creating new FTP sites and virtual directories. These tasks are similar to ones you just learned for the World Wide Web service.

4.3.10.1 The Default FTP Site

As with the WWW service, installing the FTP service on Windows Server 2003 creates a new default site, called the Default FTP Site. Unlike the WWW service, the FTP service is not included in a default IIS installation. You can add it (and remove it later, if necessary) via Add/Remove Programs on Control Panel. Unlike the Default Web Site with its sample pages and numerous directories, however, the Default FTP Site is empty. This is singularly uninteresting, so let's move on!

4.3.10.2 Other FTP Sites

As with the WWW service, you can create as many FTP sites as you want using IIS 6 and you can host the content (pages, images, and other files) for these sites in either local directories or network shares. Each FTP site acts as a separate entity, or virtual server, and acts as if it were running on its own Windows Server 2003 using the full resources available to it on that server. To illustrate this, you will now create a new FTP site on the server, place a test file in its home directory, and then download the test file from another machine on the network.

4.3.10.3 Using the FTP Site Creation Wizard

As with Web sites, you can specify FTP sites on an internetwork in a variety of ways, including using the site's IP address, NetBIOS name, or fully qualified DNS name. For the present example, use a default private IP address, 192.168.1.128. You must create a home directory for the new FTP site. Start by creating a new folder on the C drive of the local server and naming it C:\ftphome. Then copy a bitmap file such as C:\Windows\Green stone.bmp to the C:\ftphome directory so that you have something to download from the client.

Follow these steps to create the new FTP site:

1. Start IIS Manager. Select the FTP Sites node in the tree.
2. On the toolbar, click Action, point to New, and choose FTP Site (or right-click the server's FTP Sites node in the console, point to New, and choose FTP Site from the shortcut menu). This starts the FTP Site Creation Wizard. Click Next.
3. Type Company FTP Site as the name for the site. This name is displayed in IIS Manager, and it identifies the new site for the administrator. Click Next.
4. Specify the IP address mentioned previously as the one to be mapped to the site, leaving the port number at its default setting of 21. Click Next.
5. Select the option most suitable for the limitations you want to place on users browsing folders on the server. The three options are to let users have free reign, isolate users to their own folder (and below), or use Active Directory to manage user permissions.
6. Specify the path to the home directory for the new FTP site as C:\ftphome and click Next. (Using the Browse button is the easiest way to do this.) 7. Make sure that both Read permissions and Write permissions are selected. This allows you to both download files from and upload files to your new FTP site.
8. Click Next, and then click Finish to complete the wizard. The new Company FTP Site should appear as a node under the server's FTP Sites node in the Internet Information Services console window (shown in Figure 4.18). Note that the Greenstone.bmp file within the home directory doesn't appear in the right pane of the console window. This is different from Web sites, where files in home directories and virtual directories are displayed in the console window. (You can see it by right-clicking the FTP site's node and selecting Explore from the menu.)

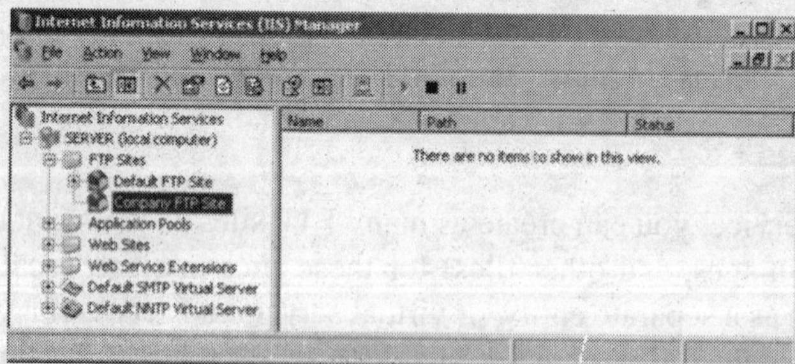

Figure 4.18 The new Company FTP Site shown in the Internet Information Services console window

4.3.10.4 Testing the New FTP Site

To test the new FTP site, go to a different machine on the network, start Internet Explorer 6, and open the URL ftp://192.168.1.128, which specifies the new FTP site using its associated IP address. The file Greenstone.bmp should be displayed in the browser window, along with the IP address you're connecting to and the user name Anonymous. (See Figure 4.19.)

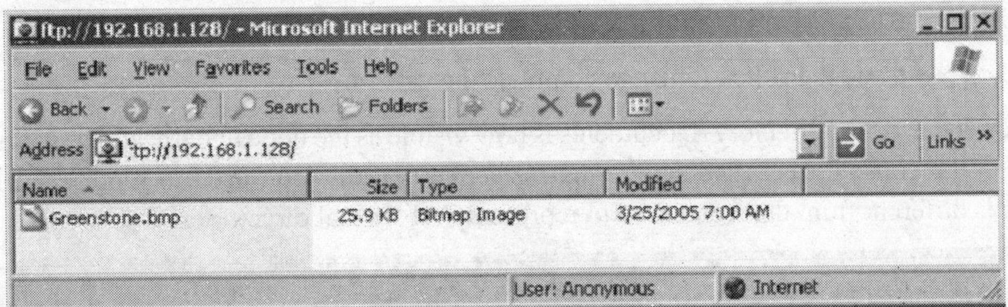

Figure 4.19 Connecting to the new Company FTP Site using Internet Explorer 6

After you connect to the FTP site, you can perform various actions in Internet Explorer including the following:

- Download the file to your machine by right-clicking its icon, choosing Copy To Folder, and specifying the destination folder on your machine (or anywhere else accessible on the network).
- Drag files from My Computer on your local machine into the browser window to upload them to the FTP site.
- Right-click the file icon, and choose Properties to display the type, location, size, and date modified of the original copy of the file on the FTP site.\
- Log on to the FTP site as a different user (if access is controlled by user names) by choosing the Login As command from the browser's File menu.
- View the FTP welcome message (if there is one) using the Help menu.

Now isn't that more fun than using the old text-based FTP command from the command prompt?

4.3.11 Virtual Directories

You can create virtual directories for FTP sites the same as you can for Web sites. Let's look at this briefly now.

4.3.11.1 Using the Virtual Directory Creation Wizard

You already saw the Virtual Directory Creation Wizard. It doesn't matter whether you create the virtual directory within a Web site or within an FTP site-the same wizard creates them. But just for variety, because you created a local virtual directory for the Company Web site last time, this time create a remote virtual directory for the Company FTP Site. (The following steps are compressed because you're already familiar with the wizard.)

1. Open IIS Manager. Right-click the Company FTP Site node, point to New, and choose Virtual Directory from the shortcut menu. Click Next. 2. Provide a name for the virtual directory. For this example, you're just sharing documents, so name the virtual directory "Documents." Type Documents as the alias for the virtual directory and click Next.
3. Specify the remote path for the location of the content directory that maps to the virtual directory being created. Here, you're connecting to a folder named Documents on the machine named Frog. Type \\Frog\Documents here and then click Next.

4. You're prompted for a user name and password in the Security Credentials dialog box. Type the information needed to connect to the remote folder and click Next.
5. Change the access permissions to enable write access and disable read access on the directory.
6. Click Next, and then click Finish to complete the wizard.

The new local virtual directory /Documents is now visible as the node underneath the Company FTP Site node in the console tree. (See Figure 4.20.) Notice that the icon used to represent FTP virtual directories is different from the icons used to represent Web virtual directories.

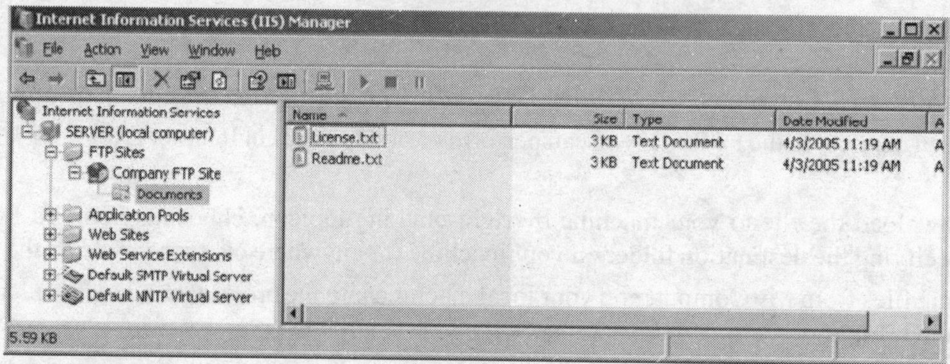

Figure 4.20 The /Documents virtual directory within the Company FTP Site

4.3.11.2 Testing the New Virtual Directory

Try accessing the new virtual directory from a remote machine by opening the URL ftp://192.168.1.128/ Documents virtual directory on the Company FTP Site using Internet Explorer. A message should appear in a dialog box saying, "An error occurred opening that folder on the FTP Server. Make sure you have permission to access that folder." Click OK to close the error message.

Now try dragging a file from My Computer into the browser window. Verify on the server that the file was indeed uploaded to the directory on the server. Now try refreshing the browser window. The same error message appears as before. Click OK to close the error message, and the browser window which is still open to the /Documents virtual directory-should appear empty. This verifies that anonymous users can upload files to the virtual directory, but can't view or download files from it, per the options you set in Step 5.

4.3.11.3 Basic Administrative Tasks

This chapter concludes with a look at some basic administrative tasks you can perform on Web sites and FTP sites by using the IIS Manager console. For now, the focus is on basic tasks such as configuring permissions, stopping and starting services, and enabling FrontPage Extensions on the server.

4.3.11.4 Configuring Permissions

Understanding permissions, and how they are configured and applied on IIS 6, is a part of the larger picture of understanding IIS security in general. This section covers the levels of security you can use to control access to content in Microsoft Server 2003 Web sites and FTP sites-and looks at the order in which these layers are applied.

4.3.11.5 Understanding Iis 6 Security

Administrators can control access to content on Web sites and FTP sites hosted on IIS 6 in four ways. These methods are applied in order each time a user tries to access a Web or FTP resource (an HTML or other file) on the server. The four-stage access control model is presented next, and only when all four of these rules have been applied and passed is the user granted access to the requested resource.

1. Is the user's IP address or domain name allowed access to the resource?

If not, access is denied and no further rules are applied. You can configure IP address and domain name restrictions using the Directory Security tab of the Properties window for the Web site, FTP site, or virtual or physical directory, or on the File Security tab of the Properties window for a file. Note that the Properties windows referred to here and in the next two steps apply to those accessed from the Internet Information Services console window.

2. Has the user been properly authenticated for accessing the resource?

If not, access is denied and no further rules are applied. You can configure authentication security settings on the Directory Security tab of the Properties window for a Web site or virtual or physical directory, on the Security tab of the Properties window for a file, or on the Security Accounts tab of the Properties window for an FTP site. Note that you can't configure this level of security on virtual directories that are located within FTP sites, only on those within Web sites.

3. Are the IIS access and application permissions configured to allow users access to the resource?

If not, access is denied and no further rules are applied. You can configure IIS access and application permissions on the Home Directory tab of the Properties window for a Web site or FTP site, on the Virtual Directory tab of the Properties window for a virtual directory, or on the Security tab of the Properties window for a physical directory or file.

4. Do NTFS permissions on the resource allow the user to access the resource?

If not, access to the resource is denied to the user. NTFS permissions are configured in the usual way by using the Security tab of the Properties window for the resource in My Computer.

5. Setting Permissions

Permissions settings are accessible by selecting Properties on the Action menu in IIS Manager. To change the security settings on the /Sales virtual directory created earlier within the Company Web site, follow these steps:

1. Select the Sales node under the Company Web site node.
2. On the Action menu, select Properties.
3. In the Properties dialog box, click the Directory Security tab, as shown in Figure 4.21.

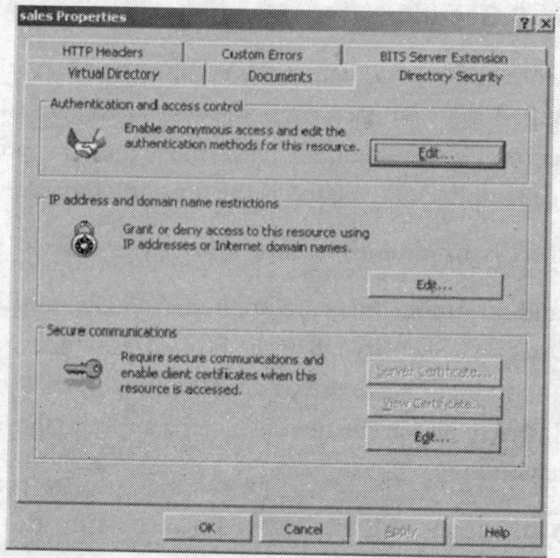

Figure 4.21 The Directory Security tab of the Virtual Directory's Properties dialog box

4. In the Authentication And Access Control section, click Edit to alter the authentication methods for /Sales.
5. In the Authentication Methods dialog box, you can enable or disable anonymous access, represented by the account IUSR_<MachineName>. (In Figure 4.22, IUSR_SERVER is the anonymous access account because your machine name is SERVER.) The Authenticated Access section also allows you to specify other authentication methods when anonymous access is not allowed or the NTFS security settings limit access. After making your selections, click OK to return to the Properties page.

Figure 4.22 The Authentication Methods dialog box

6. In the IP Address and Domain Name Restrictions section (see Figure 4.21), click Edit. In the IP Address And Domain Name Restrictions dialog box (shown in Figure 4.23), select one of the options to allow or prevent access from specific computers, groups of computers, and whole domains and then click OK to return to the Properties page.
   - To grant access to all machines except those in the list you create, select Granted Access.
   - To deny access to all machines except those in the list, select Denied Access.
   - To create the exception list, click Add. You can add single computers, a range of computers, or domains.

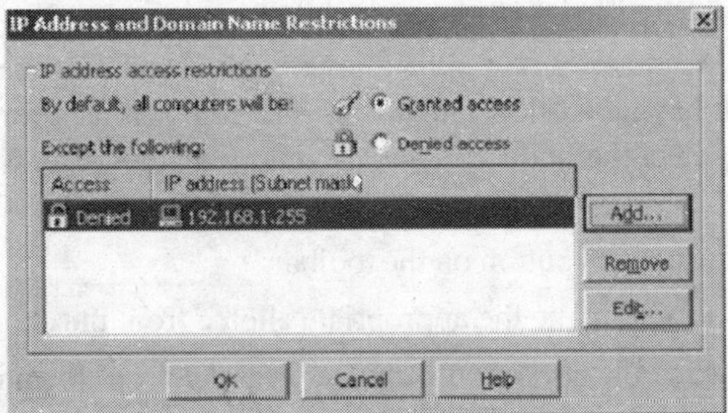

Figure 4.23 The IP Address And Domain Name Restrictions dialog box

7. In the Secure Communications section (Figure 4.21), click Edit to display the Secure Communications dialog box (Figure 4.24). You can specify that SSL is required, alter certificate acceptance settings, and enable client certificate mapping.

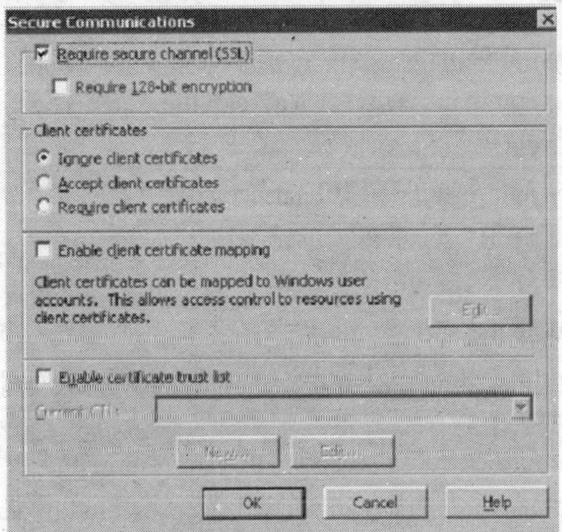

Figure 4.24 The Secure Communications dialog box

8. Make your selections and click OK.

4.3.12 Stopping, Starting, and Pausing Iis Services

Remember that individual Web sites and FTP sites that are created on IIS 6 are actually virtual servers-that is, they act and behave as if they were separate Windows Servers and had access to all the resources on the server. This allows Web sites for many companies to be hosted on a single Windows Server 2003 machine. Sometimes you might need to stop, start, or pause IIS services on these machines, however. For example, when files are being modified on a Web site, it's usually smart to pause the site so that no new user connections can be established with the site and to allow users who are currently connected a grace period before they're disconnected.

Another example is when you're testing a Web application developed by using ASP-you might need to stop and then restart the site during the testing process if the application hangs or becomes unresponsive. The trouble is, if you have multiple sites running on your server, you don't want to bring them all down just to deal with the problems of a particular site.

To solve this problem, Windows Server 2003 allows you to use IIS Manager to stop individual Web sites and FTP sites without having to stop the WWW and FTP services for all sites on the server. To pause, stop, or start a site, select the node in the console tree that represents the site and do one of the following:

- Click the appropriate control button on the toolbar.
- Right-click the node, and make the appropriate choice from the shortcut menu.
- Click Action, and select the appropriate choice from the drop-down menu.

Alternately, you can restart all Web and FTP sites on your server by selecting the node representing the server (the parent node of all the sites you've configured) in the console tree of IIS Manager. Then click Action on the toolbar, and select Restart IIS from the All Tasks menu. You might expect that you can stop all Web sites running on a machine by stopping the WWW service using the Services node under System Tools in Computer Management. Don't do it this way. IIS is implemented differently from other Windows Server 2003 services and should not be stopped or started in this fashion. Finally, if you want to control IIS from the command line, type iisreset<Computer_Name> /option. Table 32-2 lists the available control options. This command is useful in a batch file. Table 32-2 Control options for IISRESET

Command	Behavior
/restart	Stops and restarts all IIS services.
/start	Starts all IIS services.
/stop	Stops all IIS services.
/reboot	Reboots the server.
/rebootonerror	If starting, stopping, or restarting IIS services results in an error, reboots the server.
/noforce	If the service doesn't respond to a stop command, don't forcefully terminate it.
/timeout:val	Specifies the number of seconds (represented by val) to wait for a service to respond to a stop command. If /rebootonerror is also specified, the system restarts.
/status	Displays the current status of all running IIS services.
/enable	Enables the restarting of IIS services on the local server.
/disable	Disables the restarting of IIS services on the local server.

4.3.13 Using Frontpage Server Extensions

IIS 6 uses a set of proprietary server-side DLLs called FrontPage Extensions to support many of the advanced FrontPage features, such as its ability to create navigation bars, search tools, discussion Webs, and so on. Finally, let's look at installing FrontPage server extensions. In IIS 6, this is a basic Web server administration task for networks where developers use the popular Web content creation tool, Microsoft FrontPage. Content development isn't covered here, but you do examine how to enable the server to operate with FrontPage.

FrontPage Extensions are an optional component of IIS. Before you can enable FrontPage Extensions, you have to install them. Then you need to enable these extensions on the specific Web sites that your FrontPage content developers will be using.

To see how this works, use the Company Web site and follow these steps:

1. Right-click the Company Web site node in the Internet Service Manager console tree, point to All Tasks, and choose Configure Server Extensions 2002 from the shortcut menu and enter your credentials when requested. This generates and opens the Extend Virtual Server With FrontPage Server Extensions 2002 page.
2. Click Submit to enable FrontPage Server Extensions 2002. This opens to the Server Administration Web page, shown in Figure 4.25. The three options allow you to alter rights, set installation defaults, and reset user passwords. Below them are the virtual servers that you can administer.

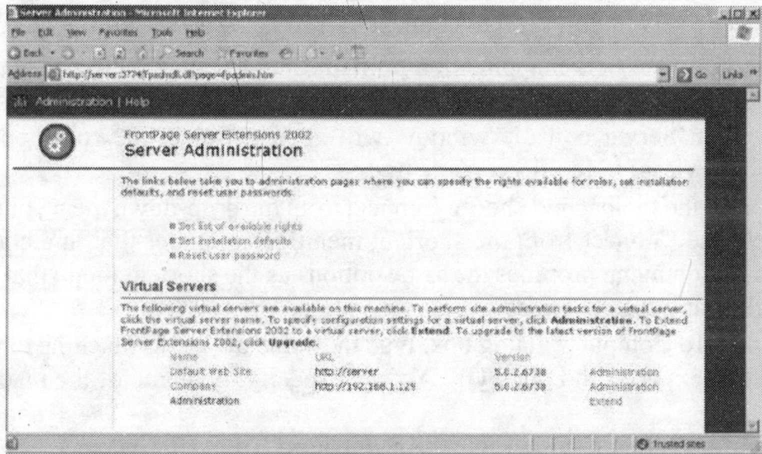

Figure 4.25 The Server Administration Web page

3. Click the Set List of Available Rights link to proceed to the Rights page. View the rights listed, and select the check boxes to enable those rights on the server. Navigate back to the previous page to examine the next option.
4. Click the Set Installation Defaults link to edit the mail and security settings. Mail Settings allows you to specify the SMTP server, From address, and Reply-To address for use in e-mail features of FrontPage Server Extensions. Security Settings allows you to log authoring activities, require SSL, and permit uploading executables by authors. Navigate to the previous page again to move to the last option.
5. Click the Reset User Password link. The Reset User Password page appears. You can specify the user name and new password you want to assign.

After the FrontPage Extensions are installed, you'll find that a number of new files and directories are created and added to your site. Don't delete any of these FrontPage files or directories, or the server extensions might fail to work properly!

4.3.13.1 Server-level Administration

Server-level administration involves the following tasks:

- Connecting to a machine running IIS to administer that machine
- Backing up and restoring the configuration of the machine
- Enabling global bandwidth throttling for all Web and FTP sites on the machine
- Configuring various master properties that apply globally to all Web and FTP sites created on the machine
- Compressing files by using HTTP compression
- Configuring the global Multipurpose Internet Mail Extensions (MIME) map
- Setting server extensions (if you have Microsoft FrontPage server extensions installed)

Let's begin with the general administration tasks and global settings you can configure for IIS on a Windows server. You can perform some common server-level administration tasks using the IIS Manager.

4.3.13.2 Connecting to an Iis Server

You can administer multiple servers running Windows Server 2003 and IIS from a single IIS console window. To administer a server, you need to connect to it first. To do so, follow these steps:

1. Start the Manage Your Server application from the Start Menu. 2. Select Manage this application server from the options available under the Application Server heading.
3. The Application Server console window will appear. Select the root node (called Internet Information Services) in the IIS console tree.
4. Click Action on the toolbar and choose Connect from the drop-down menu, or right-click the root node and choose Connect from the shortcut menu. (Remember that in a console window, the drop-down Action menu provides the same options as the shortcut menu that is displayed when you right-click any selected node.)
5. In the Connect To Computer dialog box, type the name of the IIS machine to which you want to connect in the text box, and click OK. You can specify the name of the machine as any of the following:
   - Network Basic Input/Output System (NetBIOS) name (for instance, the name "server")
   - Internet Protocol (IP) address (for instance, 192.168.1.128)
   - Fully qualified DNS name (for instance, server.example.com)
6. To disconnect from a server, select the node in the console tree that represents the server, click Action, and choose Disconnect.

4.3.14 Creating Configuration Backups

You can save the configuration settings for an IIS machine and all of its Web and FTP sites to a configuration backup file. Each backup file is stamped with a version number and its time and date of creation. You can create any number of backup files and restore these files if you want to restore your previous settings. This feature is quite useful-it allows you to take a snapshot of your IIS configuration before you start modifying permissions and other settings for the virtual servers, directories, and files on your machine.

4.3.14.1 Backing up a Server Configuration

To back up the configuration of your IIS machine, follow these steps:

1. Select the node in the console tree that represents your server.
2. Click Action, point to the All Tasks menu item, and when it is revealed, choose the Backup/ Restore Configuration menu item. 3. As Figure 4.26 shows, the Configuration Backup/Restore dialog box that appears displays the various backup files you created, their version numbers, and date/time of creation. Version numbers start with zero and increase sequentially.

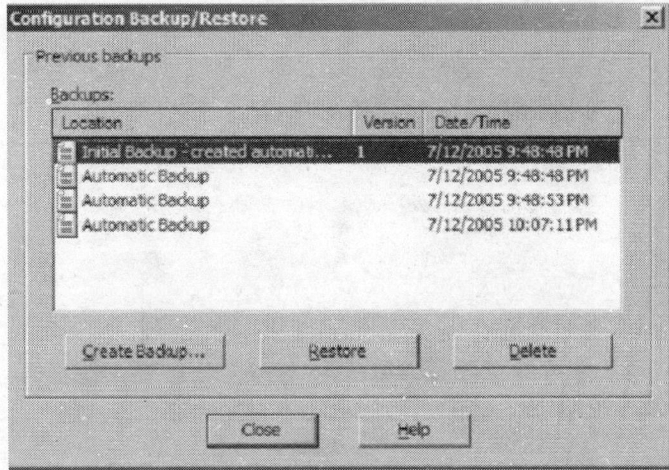

Figure 4.26 The Configuration Backup/Restore dialog box

4. To create a new backup file, click Create Backup and give the file a friendly name. The backup file is saved in the System32\inetsrv\MetaBack directory. The information is stored in binary format and is specific to the machine on which it has been created. If you reinstall Windows Server 2003 on the machine, you'll be unable to use previously created backup files to re-create your IIS configuration.

You can provide a password to encrypt the backup. You can read the backup information because only the secure properties are encrypted. Without the correct password, however, you are not able to restore the system with the backup files.

4.3.14.2 Restoring a Server Configuration

To restore the configuration of your server to a previous version, open the Configuration Backup/ Restore dialog box, select the backup file you want to restore to, and click Restore. Note that IIS must stop its services to perform a restore, so a restore takes longer than a backup.

4.3.14.3 Configuring Server Properties

Server-level properties for the WWW service are configured using the properties of the Web Sites node in IIS Manager. The configuration of IIS is stored in what's called the metabase. The metabase is a plain text file in XML (Extensible Markup Language) format named Metabase.xml. This file is in your system32\inetsrv directory. Metabase.xml is tied to a file called MBschema.xml that defines the schema of the metabase. It defines properties and specifies what properties can be written to what keys in the metabase configuration.

4.3.14.4 Editing the Metabase

Making the metabase a plain text file enables easy editing and viewing of your settings. You can edit the file in a text editor such as Notepad. You can view the file in a program that can render XML, such as Microsoft Internet Explorer. You can change the configuration of your server without having to stop IIS. If you right click the server node and select the Properties menu item, you can select the Enable Direct Metabase Edit option, which is shown in Figure 4.27.

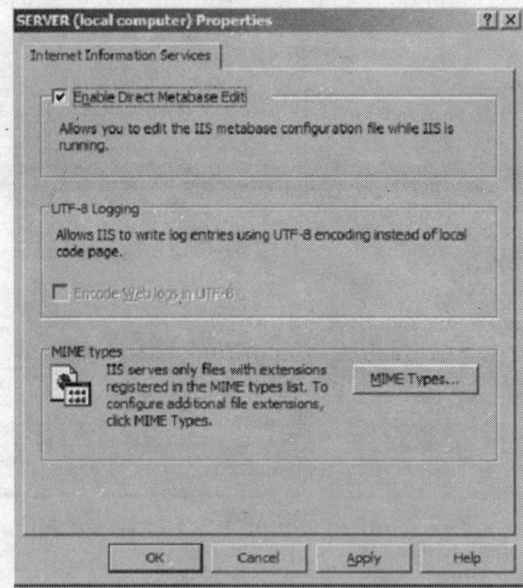

Figure 4.27 Enabling metabase changes without stopping IIS

The metabase schema consists of containers called collections. Each collection exists at the same hierarchical level; no collection can be contained in another collection. Properties represent a configurable facet of IIS. The IISConfigObject collection contains all properties in the metabase. Each property consists of ID, Type, UserType, Attributes, and Default Value. Some properties have other attributes; these include MetaFlags, MetaFlagsEx, StartingNumber, and EndingNumber.

4.3.14.5 Metabase History

If you have a basic grasp of the layout of the metabase file and a working knowledge of XML, you can begin to change the contents of the metabase. As you edit the metabase, the metabase history feature provides a level of safety. Changes are saved to disk in the system32\inetsrv\history directory.

By default, 10 metabase pairs (Metabase.xml and MBSchema.xml) are maintained in the history folder. If a new pair is being written and the history folder already contains 10 pairs, the oldest pair is deleted. The default number of versioned history pairs can be changed by editing the MaxHistoryFiles property.

4.3.15 Site-level Administration

Site-level administration of IIS differs considerably in its tasks depending on which of the four IIS services you are dealing with: WWW, FTP, SMTP, or NNTP. As a result, there is a detailed discussion of the various tasks involved in administering different kinds of sites (virtual servers) later in this chapter. (In other words, to learn how to administer WWW sites, go to the "Managing WWW Sites" section.)

Site-level settings for a newly created Web or FTP site are inherited from the server-level (Web Sites or FTP Sites node) properties. You can, however, modify settings at the site level and have those settings override the settings configured at the server level. Another important point to consider is that site-level settings are inherited by all virtual and physical directories and files within the site (that is, within the virtual server). This is true whether you are considering WWW, FTP, SMTP, or NNTP sites. A sample site-level settings dialog box is shown in Figure 4.28.

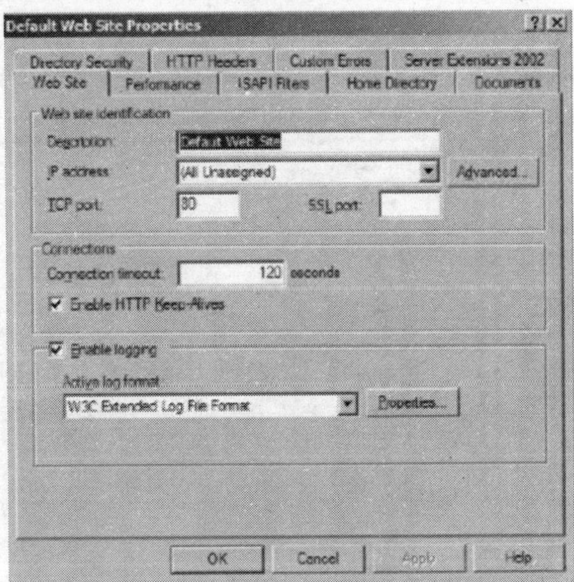

Figure 4.28 Editing site-level settings

4.3.16 Directory-level Administration

Directory-level settings are inherited by all files within the directory. They also override those configured at the site and server levels. Directory-level settings apply to both virtual and physical directories within a particular Web or FTP site. Directory-level properties are simply a subset of site-level properties. In fact, the WWW service master properties for a particular IIS machine are configured through a Master Properties page that has nine tabs: Web Site, Performance, ISAPI Filters, Home Directory, Documents, Directory Security, HTTP Headers, Custom Errors, and Service. Also, the Properties window for a particular Web site, such as the Default Web Site, has a set of tabs comparable to the set in the server's Master Properties window, replacing the Service tab with a Server Extensions 2002 tab.

Similarly, as Figure 4.29 shows, the Properties window for a particular virtual (or physical) directory within a Web site has a subset of the tabs in the Web site's Properties window: Directory (versus Home Directory), Documents, Directory Security, HTTP Headers, and Custom Errors. The following list summarizes the kinds of settings you can configure at the directory level:

- Location of content for the directory (local directory, network share, or redirection to a URL)
- Application settings (application name, starting point, execute permissions, and so on)
- Default documents and document footers

- Anonymous access and authentication control
- IP address and domain name restrictions
- Secure communications using SSL
- Content expiration
- Custom HTTP headers
- Content rating
- MIME mappings
- Custom HTTP errors

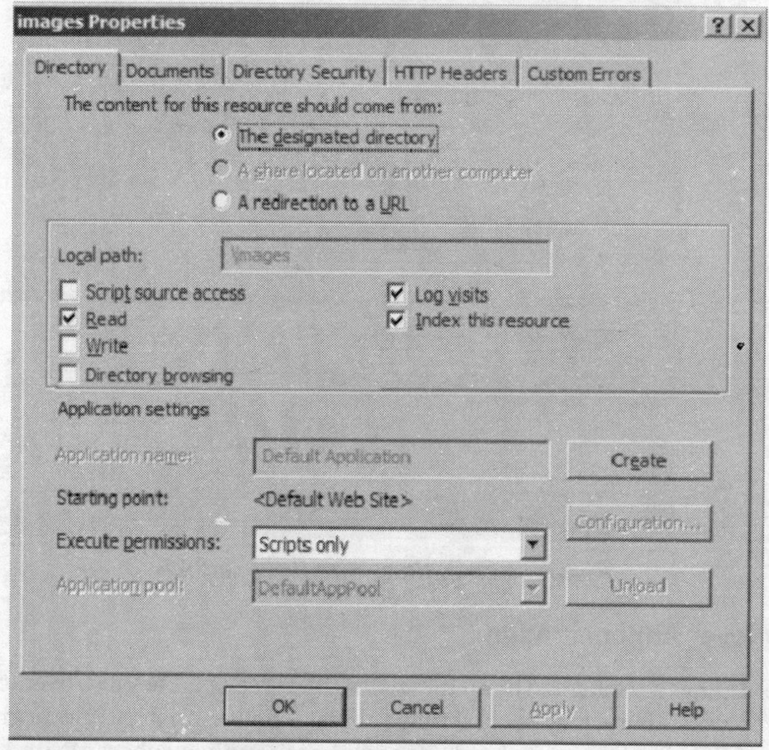

Figure 4.29 The Properties window of a directory within the Default Web Site

4.3.17 File-level Administration

File-level administration is the last of the four levels of IIS administration. At this level, you configure the properties of individual files within a Web or FTP site's home directory or other directories. For example, although a WWW service directory-level Properties window has five tabs, the Properties window for an individual Web page or other file has only four tabs: File, File Security, HTTP Headers, and Custom Errors, as you can see in Figure 4.30.

Configuring file-level properties is basically the same as configuring directory-level properties, except that a single file can't have a default document specified for it as a directory can, and you can't configure the following options at the file level: Directory Browsing, Index This Resource, and Enable Document Footer. Also, the location of the file can be either specified or redirected to a URL.

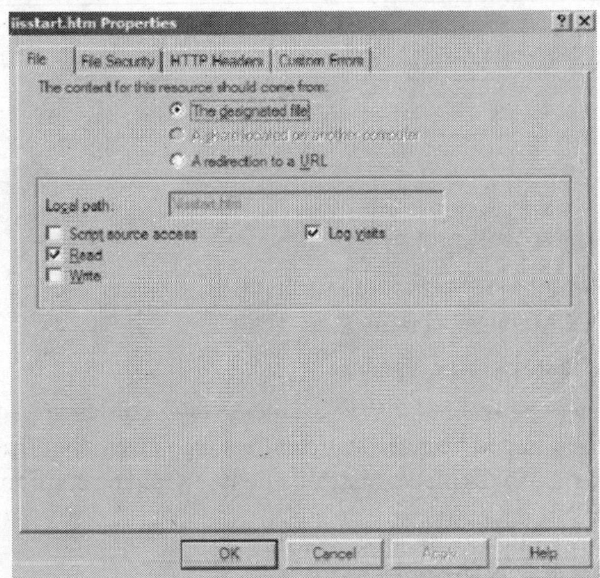

Figure 4.30 The Properties window for a file located within the home directory of the Default Web Site

4.4 WINS

WINS is an essential part of any large network with earlier Windows clients and network applications. It provides the equivalent function of a DNS server-except for the NetBIOS namespace. WINS servers resolve NetBIOS names into IP addresses by using the WINS dynamic database to call up the appropriate name records. If all your systems are Windows 2000 or later, it is possible for them to function without WINS.

4.4.1 Determining whether you need WINS

If you're asking yourself whether you need WINS at this point, the answer is probably yes. Most large networks need WINS to provide NetBIOS name resolution for their earlier Windows clients. There are two instances in which you don't need WINS servers (though you might still choose to use one):

- All clients on the network support name resolution through dynamic DNS. Windows XP, Windows 2000, and Windows Server 2003 are the only Microsoft operating systems that can rely exclusively on DNS for name resolution. If you have any down-level clients at all, you need WINS. If you have a mixed environment with other clients such as UNIX clients, make sure they're all configured to properly use DNS.
- The network is small (fewer than 50 clients) and not subnetted. If the entire network consists of a single network segment, clients that require NetBIOS name resolution can effectively resolve NetBIOS names by broadcast-a technique that doesn't work across routers or on large networks where the NetBIOS broadcasts would generate too much network traffic.

The following WINS clients are supported by WINS in Windows Server 2003:

- Windows Server 2003
- Windows XP

- Windows 2000
- Microsoft Windows NT 3.5 or later
- Windows Me
- Windows 98
- Windows 95
- Microsoft Windows for Workgroups 3.11
- MS-DOS with Microsoft Network Client version 3
- MS-DOS with LAN Manager version 2.2c
- Linux and UNIX clients running Samba

Non-WINS clients aren't resolvable by WINS unless static entries are added for them don't do it. This practice is strongly discouraged because static entries are extremely difficult to eliminate from the WINS database after replication takes place. Instead, clients should be configured to use DNS to resolve names that aren't in the WINS database.

4.4.2 Configuring the Server to Prepare for WINS

After you determine that you need WINS on your network, it's time to configure the server. The most common cause of WINS problems is improper TCP/IP configuration on the server. Follow these steps to properly configure the TCP/IP settings for the WINS server before you install the service:

1. Right-click the Local Area Connection icon in the Network Connections folder, and choose Properties from the shortcut menu.
2. Select the Internet Protocol (TCP/IP) component, and click Properties.
3. Configure the server to use a static IP address, or make sure that an address reservation for the server is configured on the DHCP server.
4. Click Advanced, and then click WINS.
5. Select any WINS servers listed on the tab, and click Remove. Failure to do this can cause the WINS server to register its own address with another WINS server instead of with itself, which you don't want.
6. Click Add, and type the IP address of your own server. Do not use the loopback address, 127.0.0.1; use the real address. Then click OK.

4.4.3 Installing WINS

After the TCP/IP settings are correct, you're ready to install the WINS component. Use the Windows Component Wizard, accessible either from the Configure Your Server tool or from Add/Remove Programs in Control Panel. If you installed WINS during Windows Setup, you can skip this section. Otherwise, use these steps to install WINS:

1. Open the Add/Remove Programs Control Panel tool, and click the Add/Remove Windows Components icon in the frame on the left (the Places bar) to launch the Windows Component Wizard. 2. Click Next, select Networking Services from the list of components, and click Details.
3. Select the Windows Internet Name Service (WINS) component check box, click OK, and then click Next.

4.4.4 Adding Replication Partners

WINS servers are easy to set up and require little management, except for replication partners. WINS replication is an important and somewhat delicate issue that you must examine closely before setting up. Deploy as few WINS servers as possible to minimize management migraines. For example, the entire Microsoft Corporation used only 12 WINS servers worldwide during the height of NetBIOS. Just about every enterprise can get by with a handful of WINS servers at most. A good rule of thumb is one WINS server for every 10,000 users, plus one WINS server for redundancy. To set up a replication partner and configure its settings after planning your WINS deployment, follow these steps:

1. Launch WINS from the Administrative Tools folder, and in the console tree expand the WINS server that you want to set up for replication.
2. Select the Replication Partners folder, and then choose New Replication Partner from the Action menu.
3. Type the IP address for the WINS server you want to enable replication with, and click OK.
4. To modify the replication parameters for the new replication partner, if necessary, double-click the server in the Replication Partners folder, and then click the Advanced tab. 5. To change the way you replicate with the server, choose an option from the Replication Partner Type drop-down list (Figure 4.31).

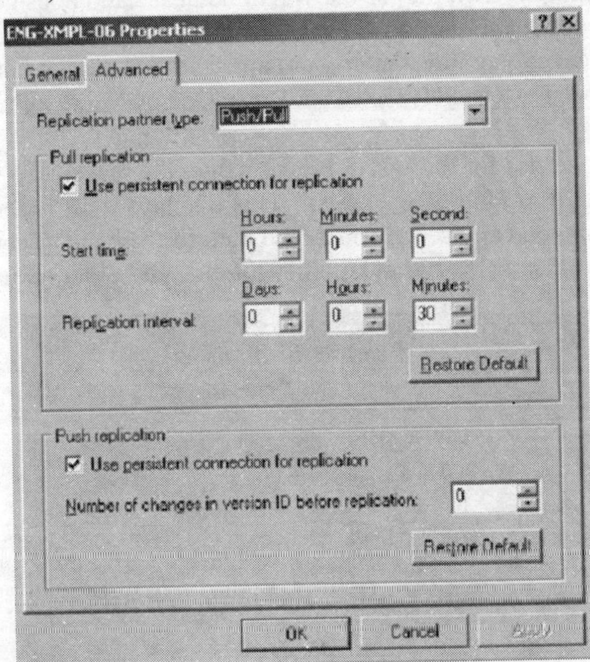

Figure 4.31 The Advanced tab of the Properties dialog box

6. To configure a permanent connection for pull or push replication, select the Use Persistent Connection For Replication check box in the Pull Replication section, the Push Replication section, or both.
7. In the Start Time fields, type the time you want pull replication to begin in hours, minutes, and seconds.
8. In the Replication Interval fields, type the frequency-days, hours, and minutes with which you want to replicate with the replication partner.

9. Use the Number of Changes in Version ID before Replication box to type the number of changes to the local copy of the WINS database that you will allow before the server pushes changes to the replication partner.

4.4.5 Miscellaneous WINS Functions

The WINS snap-in lets you manage all the functionality of WINS on multiple servers from the same application. The following are some functions you can perform with the WINS snap-in:

- To view the status of your WINS servers, click Server Status in the console tree. The status of your servers appears in the pane on the right.
- To view records in the WINS database, right-click the Active Registrations folder in the console tree under the desired server. Choose either Find By Name to search for a particular name or Find By Owner from the Action menu to display the Find By Owner dialog box, which shows all the records in the WINS database. When viewing records, you can use the Record Types tab of the Find By Owner dialog box to filter the type of records displayed.
- To add a static entry to the database, right-click the Active Registrations folder and choose New Static Mapping from the shortcut menu.
- To initiate scavenging, which purges the WINS database and does general cleanup on it, select the WINS server you want to scavenge and choose Scavenge Database from the Action menu. When initiating scavenging, don't attempt to alter the scavenging parameters for WINS. These parameters have been extensively tested and optimized by Microsoft. Any change you make will be for the worse.
- To modify the properties for the WINS server, select the server you want to work on, and then choose Properties from the Actions menu. This displays the Properties dialog box shown in Figure 4.32, which you can use to modify the path to the backup copy of the WINS database, change the length of name leases, and modify logging and other options.

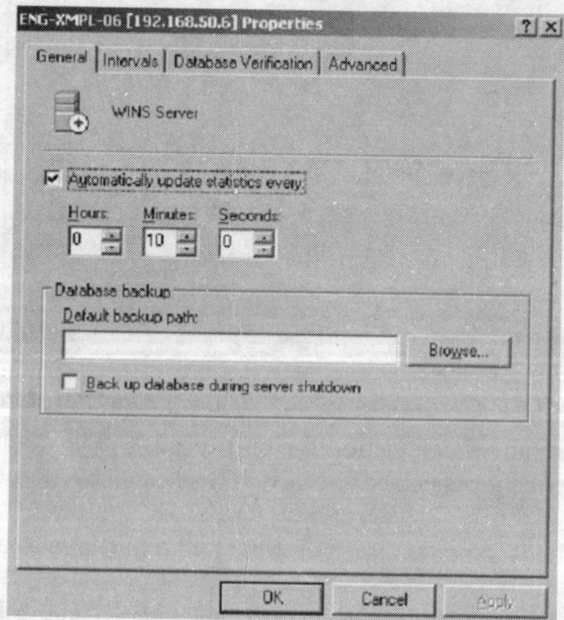

Figure 4.32 The Properties dialog box for a WINS server

4.4.6 Compacting the WINS Database

You should compact the WINS database whenever the database approaches 30 MB in size to maximize performance and stability.

To do so, follow these steps:

1. Open a command prompt window.
2. Type the following commands:

   cd %systemroot%\system32\wins

   net stop wins

   jetpack wins.mdb tmp.mdb

   netstartwins

4.4.7 Understanding WINS

In segmented network environments that use DHCP, the best solution to allow for proper NetBIOS name resolution is to use WINS servers. A WINS server provides a database that NetBIOS clients can use to register their NetBIOS names and resolve NetBIOS-to-IP address mappings.

Furthermore, WINS traffic is unicast-based. This means that, instead of relying on broadcasts to register and resolve names, WINS clients will send unicast messages directly to the WINS server, whether on the same or different subnet. The use of unicast helps to reduce the amount of broad cast traffic on the network that is the result of NetBIOS name resolution.

The ability for different WINS servers to replicate database information with each other is another significant advantage in that the replication of this information ensures that clients can resolve NetBIOS names regardless of their location or the WINS server they contact.

When a NetBIOS registration is successful, the WINS server stores the name mapping with the following information:

1. Record Name The NetBIOS name of the computer, group, or service registered in the database.
2. Type The resource type associated with the name. Common resource types are [00h] for the workstation service,[03h] for the messenger service,[020h] for the server service, and[1Ch] for the domain name.
3. IP Address The IP address for the registered name.
4. State The state of the registration, such as Active, Released, or Tomb stoned.
5. Static Indicates if record is a static mapping (column entry marked with an x).
6. Owner Indicates the owner (specific WINS server where the record was registered) of the record.
7. Version Indicates the version ID of the record.
8. Expiration Indicates the date and time the record will expire, if it is not refreshed.

NetBIOS clients that do not use a WINS server must constantly register and defend their NetBIOS names. However, the registration occurs by means of a broadcast and, thus, the registrations are local to the subnet. Whenever a computer attempts to register a duplicate name, it will receive a negative response from the computer that actively possesses the name. Whenever NetBIOS name registration fails, the computer receives an error message, and NetBT won't initialize on the computer until the problem is resolved.

Whenever a WINS client is gracefully shut down, it sends a name release request to the WINS server. The WINS server marks the entry as released and gives it a timestamp of the current time plus the extinction interval. This interval indicates the time that must elapse before the record is marked as extinct (or tomb stoned) and can be scavenged from the database. However, if the WINS server that receives the release request is not the original owner of the name registration, it will immediately mark the record as extinct. The reason for this is to prevent inconsistencies between primary and secondary servers configured as replication partners.

4.4.8 New for WINS in Windows Server 2003

The WINS service was significantly improved in Window 2000, which introduced a number of significant enhancements, such as enhanced filtering and searching for records display and burst handling of WINS registrations. The WINS service in Windows Server 2003 maintains these improvements and adds two more improvements.

1. Filtering records It is now possible to combine filters used to query the WINS database. The available filters include record owner, record type, NetBIOS name, and IP address with or without subnet mask. You can also cache the results of queries in the RAM of the local computer from which the query is performed, improving performance for subsequent queries and reducing network traffic.
2. Accepting replication partners For pull replication, you can configure the WINS server to either accept or reject only the name records that are owned by a list of predetermined WINS servers. (Figure 4.33 shows the advanced replication property page where accepting replication partners are configured.) In Windows 2000, it was possible to create only a list of replication partners to block.

4.4.9 Planning WINS Server Deployment

Clients can be configured to use multiple WINS servers (up to 12) to register and resolve computer names in the event that the primary WINS server is unavailable. WINS servers can be configured to replicate with one another to ensure both fault tolerance and the availability of records for name resolution in a distributed environment where WINS clients are registering with different WINS servers. The number of WINS servers that should be deployed depends on several complex factors, such as the number of WINS clients that will be registering and resolving names and the network topology (in particular, the presence, number, and capacity of WAN links). If you require WINS replication to meet the goals of fault tolerance and availability, the WINS replication topology needs to be designed to ensure optimal performance in the replication of WINS records and the currency of those records, as well as to ensure optimal query response times, given the constraints of the network topology.

4.4.9.1 Server Number and Placement

The number of WINS servers you deploy will be determined by the number of WINS clients and the network topology. In general, you should try to design the WINS infrastructure to minimize the number of WINS servers. Having too many WINS servers can complicate network problems, so Microsoft recommends a conservative approach in determining the number of WINS servers and further recommends one primary and one backup WINS server set up as replication partners to each other for every 10,000 clients.

The WINS traffic between clients and servers is relatively small, about 40 bytes, which is the average size of a WINS registration for a client. So, 10,000 WINS records would be approximately 400KB.Through a 56 Kbps WAN link, this amount of data would take a minute to transfer, assuming you could transfer at this rate. It is more likely, though, that the effective bandwidth is somewhat lower than 56 Kbps, and the transfer of 400KB of information would take longer. This delay might or might not be acceptable. However, it is unlikely that 10,000 WINS registrations or 10,000 updated WINS records would need to be transferred simultaneously across the WAN.

To determine the actual number of WINS servers to deploy, you will need to take into account server hardware, WAN links, the number of clients, and the need for redundancy and availability. You should also take into account peak-load conditions that could occur, for example, if the power to client computers were suddenly terminated and then resumed, resulting in a large number of simultaneous registration requests.

4.4.10 Planning for WINS Replication

Even in simple environments, it is a good idea to have two WINS servers configured as replication partners to provide greater fault tolerance and availability. This kind of replication is relatively easy to set up, for example by specifying automatic partner configuration, and requires little planning.

In larger and more complex networks, however, the replication topology will need to be carefully designed to ensure an optimal convergence time for the replication of WINS records, given the size, topology, and available bandwidth of the network. Convergence time refers to the maximum amount of time it takes for an updated record to be replicated to all WINS servers in the infrastructure. Generally, convergence time is a function of replication pull schedules and the number of hops in a given replication path that a changed object must travel.

In reality, the amount of time it will take for a record to be synchronized depends on a number of factors. For example, a WINS server configured to send push notifications immediately upon receiving an update will replicate the record faster than the time determined by the replication schedule of the WINS servers that have configured it as a pull partner. Factors that can affect convergence time include the following

1. The kind of replication partnership that is configured. A push/pull replication partnership is more efficient for replicating records than a limited partnership (push or pull only).
2. The settings for pull and push partnerships that determine the frequency of replication between servers.

3. The ability to use persistent connections for push and pull replication partners (this setting is the default and found in the Replication properties pages of the WINS server console.) The ability to use this setting depends on the presence of stable, high-speed links.
4. The particular replication model. The longer the replication path that a replicated object must travel, the longer the convergence time. In a complex replication environment involving multiple WINS servers, a hub-and-spoke replication topology provides the shortest replication paths.
5. The particular kind of update that occurs in the WINS database. For example, a name release update will not propagate as quickly as a name registration update, because it is more common for a name-to-IP address mapping to be reused by the same computer, even in an environment that uses DHCP. Since this kind of update is not as urgent as a new name registration, the WINS server provides it with a greater latency period for replication.

Along with these factors, you will need to take into account the network topology in planning for WINS replication. Your WINS replication design should, if possible, mirror your network topology. For example, if the organization has a centrally located head office that is connected by high-speed, persistent WAN links to satellite branch offices, you should consider a hub-and-spoke replication model with full push/pull partnerships. In this model, the WINS server in the head office receives replicated records through the push/pull partnership, and then propagates updates it receives from its own WINS clients and those changes it receives from the individual branch offices to the other branch offices. To plan for WINS replication, it is important to first understand partnership agreements and the settings that can be configured on them.

4.4.11 Replication Partnership Configuration

In order for WINS servers to replicate WINS records with each other, a replication partnership must be configured between them. There are three possible kinds of replication partnerships that can be configured between WINS servers: push/pull (also known as full), push-only, and pull-only (also known as limited). You can set up a replication partnership manually or implement it automatically.

4.4.11.1 Automatic Partner Configuration

Automatic partner configuration is an option that can be implemented on small networks to eliminate the administrative effort for configuring replication partnerships between WINS servers. When the automatic partner configuration is enabled, the WINS server will send announcements using the multicast Internet Group Messaging Protocol (IGMP) address at 224.0.1.24, which is the well known multicast address for WINS servers. When the WINS server discovers other WINS servers that are announcing themselves, the WINS server will automatically configure a partnership agreement between itself and the discovered WINS server. (Both must be enabled for automatic partner configuration.) When the WINS server discovers another WINS server, it will add the server to its list of replication partners, configure push/pull replication between the servers, and set the pull replication interval for every two hours. Figure 4.33 shows the Advanced tab of the Replication Partners Properties dialog box, which contains the Enable automatic partner configuration option. To view this page, you need to view the properties of the Replication Partners node in the WINS console.

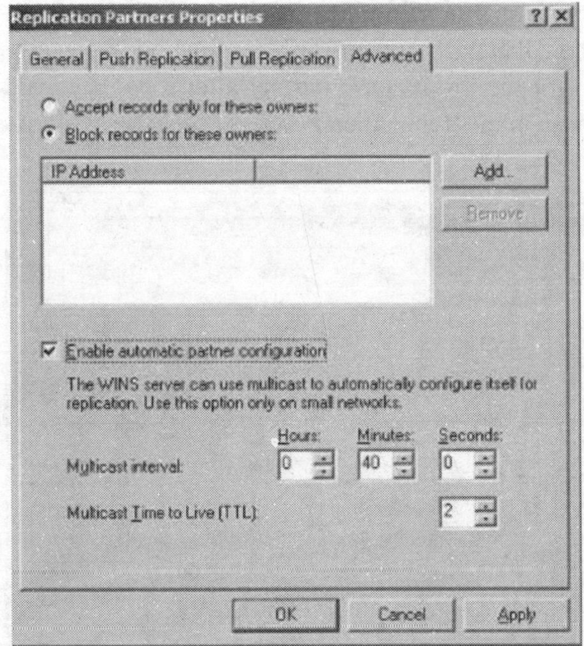

Figure 4.33 Enabling Automatic Partner Configuration

Normally, routers do not forward IGMP traffic, so this configuration is best used on small, unsegmented LANs. However, it is possible to configure routers to forward this traffic, allowing automatic partner configuration to be used in a routed environment. If there are only a few routers in the environment, the amount of multicast broadcast traffic should be minimal.

4.4.11.2 Push Partnerships

As the name implies, when a push partnership is configured, changes in the WINS database are pushed to the remote WINS server. More accurately, a WINS server with records to replicate sends a push notification to target servers (those configured to use it as a pull partner), alerting them that it has records to update on the target WINS servers. The push notification includes an owner table that lists the owner IDs and the highest version ID for each owner. The target servers compare this information with their own owner tables to determine which records to replicate. The target servers reply to the push notification with a pull request, and the transfer of records takes place.

Accordingly, since a transfer of records will not take place until a pull request has been received by the server that sent the push notification, pull replication is the single mechanism for replication.

The process for push replication occurs as follows

1. The source WINS server receives updates to its database and, based on a configurable threshold, sends a push notification to the destination WINS server (its push partner), indicating that it has updates to replicate.
2. The destination WINS server for the notification (the push partner) responds by initiating a pull request to its pull partner (the WINS server that sent the notification), and the replication is initiated between the replication partners.

Push replication is not schedulable according to an interval of time. Rather, the WINS administrator configures an update threshold that will trigger a push notification. For example, the WINS server could be configured to send a notification to its push partner after it has received 100 updates. Figure 4.34 shows the Push Replication tab of the Replication Partners Properties dialog box with the default settings for push replication.

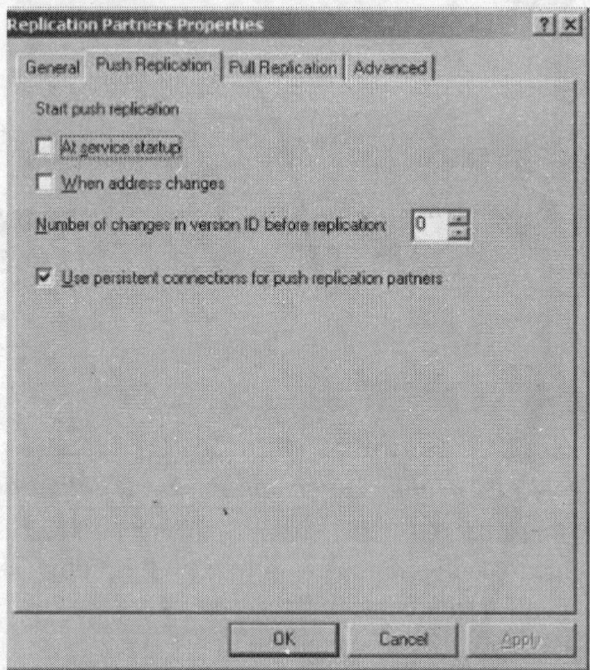

Figure 4.34 Push Replication Settings

The settings that you enter here will determine the threshold trigger for the push notification. In the configuration shown in Figure 4.34, a push notification is sent to the replication partner as soon as an update occurs in the WINS database. This is the result of setting the value for Number of changes in version ID before replication to 0. However, the value could be set to a higher number, such as 100. It is also possible to configure a push notification to occur when the service starts up or when there is an address change in a WINS registration.

The setting to Use persistent connections for push replication partners allows the connections between WINS servers to remain open. This is a useful feature when the WINS servers are connected by a high-speed LAN. Earlier versions of WINS would close the connection after each replication cycle. Opening the connection to initiate a new replication cycle could cause delays, however modest, that are not acceptable in an environment where records need to be synchronized as soon as possible.

It is also possible to manually initiate the push notification, as shown in Figure 4.35. When you manually initiate the push notification, you can choose to push the notification to the replication partner or to trigger the replication to send a notification to all of its partners as well. As an example, consider a replication topology where three WINS servers are configured as push replication partners. WINS-A replicates to WINS-B, which replicates to WINS-C. So, if you manually sent a push notification from WINS-A to its replication partner, WINS-B, you could force WINS-B to also send a push notification to its other replication partner, WINS-C.

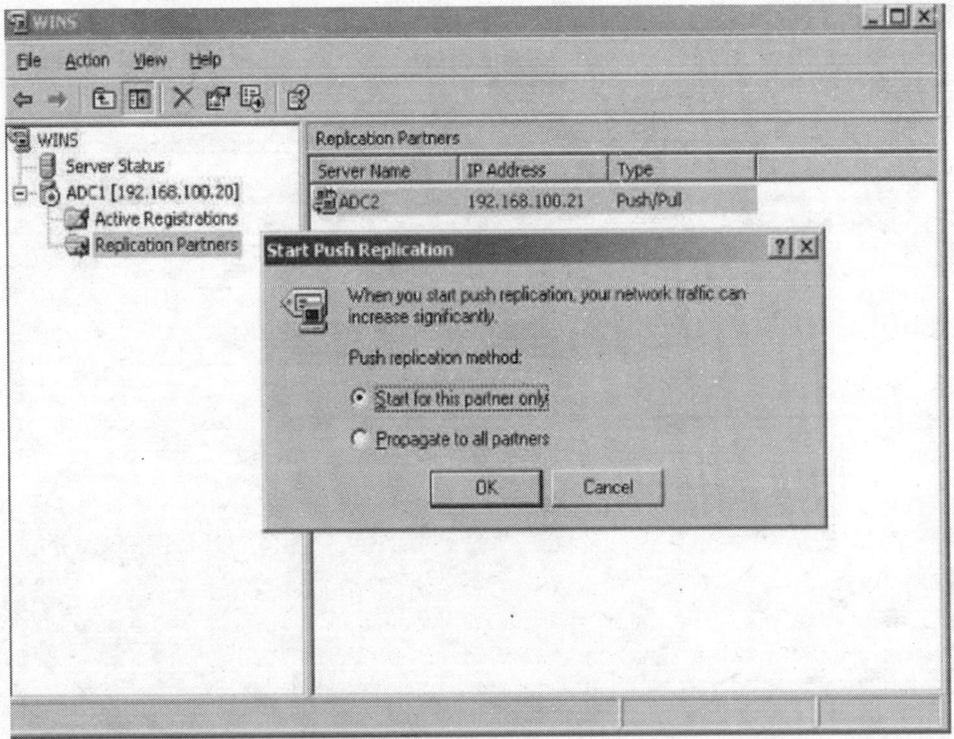

Figure 4.35 Manually Starting Push Notification

In certain rare situations, it might be desirable to use a push-only replication partnership for one way replication, for example, from a head office to a branch office. For example, suppose that WINS-A in the head office configures WINS-B in the branch office as its push-only partner. (WINS-B should also configure WINS-A as its pull-only partner.) When WINS-A receives updates to its records, it notifies WINS-B, which sends an update (pull) request to WINS-A for the changed records since the last replication cycle. In this scenario, WINS-B never sends its updated records to WINS-A.

Push partnerships are generally configured in LAN environments where bandwidth is not an issue, and it is not necessary to schedule replication to occur during off-peak hours. In general, you should use push replication partnerships in the following situations:

- There is ample bandwidth over LAN or WAN connections.
- There is a need to ensure that updates are replicated as soon as possible and the frequency of replication traffic is not a consideration.

4.4.11.3 Pull Partnerships

Pull replication differs from push replication in that the replication frequency is defined as an interval of time. At regularly scheduled intervals, a pull partner requests updates from other WINS servers (those configured to use it as a push partner) for updated records that have a higher version ID than the ones it currently has in its database.

Pull replication is configured similarly to push replication. The primary difference is that the WINS administrator schedules the times that the pull replication will take place. Figure 4.36 shows the settings for pull replication that an administrator can configure for individual replication partners.

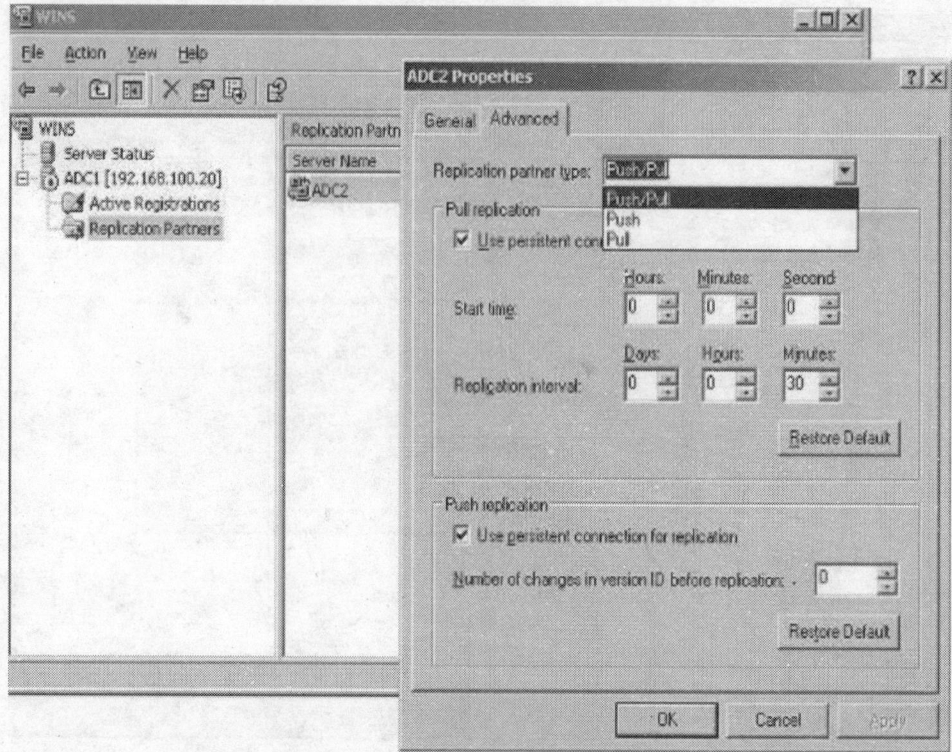

Figure 4.36 Choosing Replication Partnership Type and Push/Pull Settings

In some situations, it might be desirable to configure pull-only replication between replication partners. Usually, this configuration is implemented where WAN links are operating close to capacity and there is a need to schedule WINS replication during off-peak hours. Pull- only replication has an advantage over push-only replication in that the replication schedule can be known in advance. With push-only replication, replication is triggered by reaching a configured threshold of updates, and you can only estimate when this would occur based on experience with the network.

However, a disadvantage of pull-only replication is that the WINS server could potentially have acquired a large number of updates to replicate between cycles.

In general, you should use pull replication partnerships in the following situations:

- There is limited bandwidth between WINS servers that requires replication to be scheduled during off hours.
- There is a need to consolidate updates and reduce frequency and amount of replication traffic.
- There is a need to exercise finer control over the timing and frequency of replication traffic.

4.4.11.4 Push/Pull Partnerships

A push/pull partnership is the default when you configure replication between WINS servers. In fact, Microsoft recommends a push/pull partnership as a best practice and it further recommends that all WINS partnerships be set up this way, unless there is an overriding need to implement a limited partnership. The only need that Microsoft cites for a limited partnership is the presence of a large network connected by relatively slow WAN links. Microsoft often stresses the need for simplicity in a WINS environment.

With a push/pull partnership, a WINS server will be configured both to send push notifications and to make pull requests to its replication partner. The replication partner will also be configured in a similar way. Such a configuration helps to ensure that synchronization among WINS server is optimal, depending on the pull schedule and the configured threshold for push notifications, among other factors.

For example, suppose that a WINS server that suddenly experiences a large number of updates immediately sends a push notification to its push partner. The push partner would immediately request these updates, without waiting for the request to be triggered by its pull schedule. Conversely, a WINS server always pulls up-to-date records from its pull partner according to the replication schedule, regardless of how few records have been updated on the pull partner WIN server. You should always try to deploy a push/pull partnership, unless there is an overriding concern that requires the implementation of a limited partnership.

4.4.12 Replication Models

As we mentioned earlier, the replication model you design will have an effect on the convergence time for replicated WINS records and fault tolerance for replicated records. A replication model that is appropriate for your network topology will ensure the shortest convergence time for replicated WINS records. Where possible, it is recommended that your replication model mirror your network topology and that you keep this model as simple as possible.

In WINS environments where there are three or more WINS servers, you can employ either a ring replication model or a hub-and-spoke replication model. In more complex environments, these models can be combined to ensure optimal convergence time and fault tolerance for a given network topology.

4.4.12.1 Ring Model

In a ring model, three or more WINS servers are configured to replicate with one another in a circular fashion. The ring model provides for good convergence times for all replication partners when there are no more than four WINS servers. Figure 4.37 shows a ring replication model.

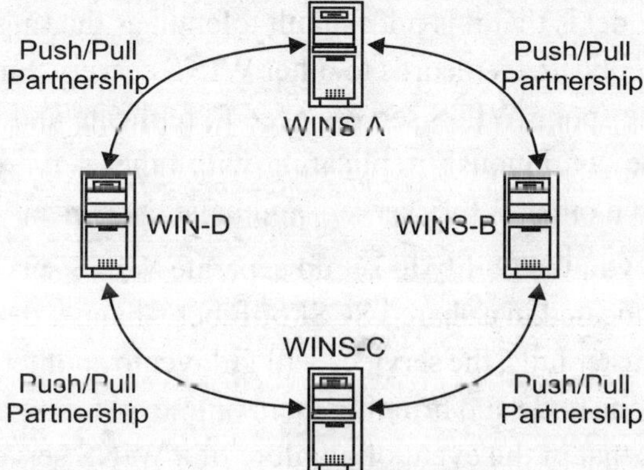

Figure 4.37: Ring model

In this model, fault tolerance for replication of WINS records is given priority. Imagine that a record is updated on WINS-A. The record must travel through either WINS-B or WINS-B before it is replicated to WINS-C. However, suppose that the WAN link connecting WINS-A and WINSD fails. The updated record can still arrive at WINS-C and WINS-D (via WINS-C). Conversely, a record created on WINS-D can still be replicated to WINS-A via WINS-C and WINS-B.

4.4.12.2 HUB-and-spoke Model

In the hub-and-spoke model, all WINS servers replicate with a centrally located hub WIN server. The hub-and-spoke model provides for the shortest convergence time in a replication environment that comprises five or more WINS servers, because it provides for the shortest replication paths between any two WINS servers. Furthermore, by implementing a hub-and-spoke model, you reduce the number of replication partnership agreements that you need to maintain. Figure 4.38 shows a typical hub-and-spoke implementation.

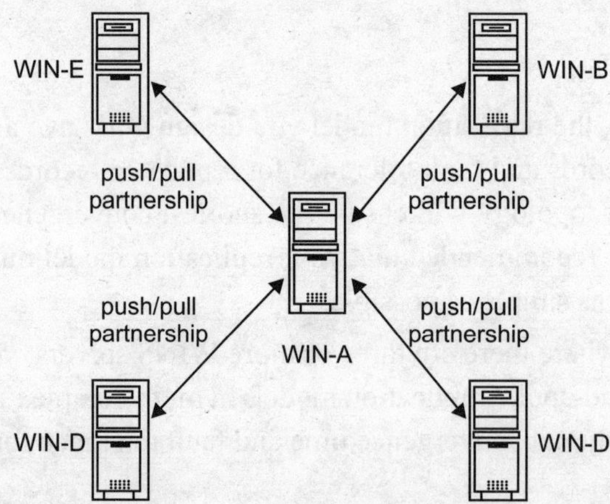

Figure 4.38 Hub-and-Spoke Replication Model for WINS Servers

Even though there are five WINS servers that replicate information, there are only four replication agreements to maintain. Furthermore, no server is more than two hops from any other server, regardless of the number of servers added to the topology.

A disadvantage of this model is that it is not as fault tolerant as the ring model. If WINS-A fails, no WINS server will be able to replicate its records to other WINS servers. Furthermore, depending on the average number of records the spoke WINS servers need to replicate and the settings for the push and pull triggers, WINS-A can be continuously replicating with other servers and processing updates. It should be well connected to the other WINS servers and have the capacity to handle the load.

A Windows cluster gives you the ability to set up separate WINS servers, known as cluster nodes, which use the same database located in a shared SCSI or Fiber Channel device. When the WINS server that is the active node in the cluster fails, the services will failover to another node. Failover is the process of taking resources offline in one node and bringing them online on a new node. The primary advantage of using a Windows cluster is that in the event of a failure of a WINS server, no subsequent replication needs to occur to synchronize records when the failed server is brought online, since only a single database is used. Windows Server 2003 Standard, Enterprise, and Datacenter editions support clustering. For more information about clustering, see the Windows Server 2003 help files.

4.4.12.3 Hybrid Replication Model

In many situations, it is desirable to combine replication models. As an example, consider a large organization that has three divisions in different geographic locations. Each of these divisions has a number of branch offices that are connected to their respective divisional offices. It might be advantageous to use a ring model of WINS replication among the divisional offices and use hub-and spoke replication for replication between the divisional offices and their respective branch offices.

Figure 4.39 shows a conceptual representation of a hybrid model. Many other variations are possible. A hybrid replication model can employ any mixture of full and limited replication partnerships, driven by the contingencies of the network topology.

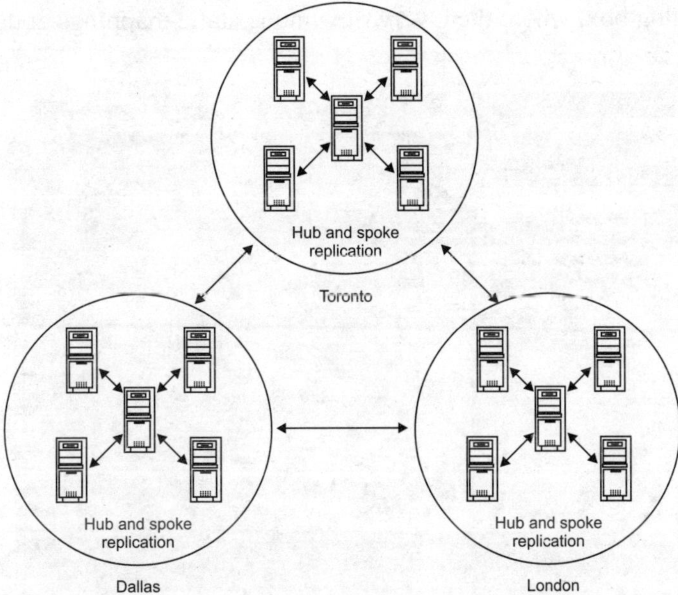

Figure 4.39 Hybrid Replication Model

4.4.13 WINS Issues

After establishing the need for WINS planning for the replication topology of the WINS infrastructure, the WINS servers need to be installed and configured. In this section, we will look at the various configuration issues that a WINS administrator needs to be familiar with to ensure an efficient and secure WINS infrastructure, such as handing static WINS entries, client configurations, database maintenance, and WINS infrastructure security.

4.4.13.1 Static WINS Entries

One of the advantages of using WINS is that it provides a way to dynamically register NetBIOS names, eliminating the need for static entries in LMHOSTS files. However, there are situations that require the use of static mappings in the WINS server database. For example, if you have non- WINS clients that are running NetBIOS applications, you might find it desirable to have entries for these clients in the WINS database, so that you can allow WINS clients to resolve the NetBIOS names of those clients. Static mappings are superior to entries in an LMHOSTS file because they can be replicated throughout the WINS infrastructure.

The use of static mappings can create problems on your network. Unlike dynamic mappings, static mappings stay in the WINS database until they are manually removed. (The expiration date for the static mapping entry in the WINS database is labeled as infinite.) Furthermore, unless the migrate on setting is enabled, static mappings are not overwritten by dynamic mappings. For example, a client computer might be given a static mapping in the WINS database, or an LMHOSTS file might be imported to the WINS database, creating a number of static WINS entries. If the clients that are associated with the static mappings were later configured as WINS clients, they would not be able to perform dynamic registration of their NetBIOS names, unless the migrate on setting was enabled. Figure 4.40 shows the Replication Partners Properties dialog box, where the Overwrite unique static mappings at this server (migrate on) setting is enabled.

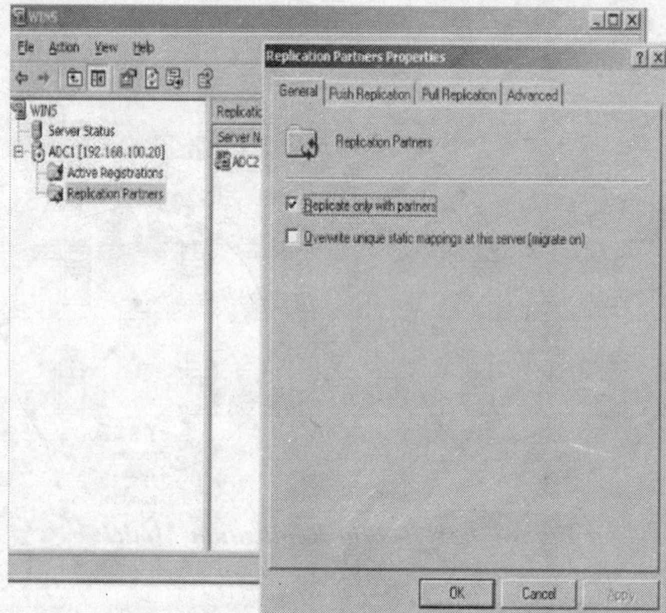

Figure 4.40 Configuring Static Entries to Be Overwritten

In general, static entries should never be created for WINS-capable client computers. However, it is sometimes desirable for security purposes to use static entries for mission-critical servers to prevent redirection.

1. USING STATIC ENTRIES TO PREVENT REDIRECTION

Unlike with Active Directory-integrated DNS zones, you cannot restrict clients from dynamically registering names according to Windows group memberships. The only mechanism by which WINS prevents clients from registering duplicate names is to send a challenge to the IP address of the active record. If the client responds to the challenge, the duplicate name registration is denied.

However, during periods when WINS clients are offline for maintenance or are being rebooted, a rogue computer could register the same name as the original computer, with the malicious intent of redirecting traffic to the rogue computer. In high-security environments, it might be desirable to enter static mappings for critical computers and to ensure that the Overwrite unique static mappings at this server (migrate on) setting is disabled.

2. MULTIHOMED WINS SERVERS

A multihomed WINS server is one that has more than one active network connection. You should avoid this configuration of a WINS server. Name resolution and replication problems are often the result of using a multihomed computer as a WINS server.

4.4.13.2 Client Configuration

WINS client configuration is accomplished either through a DHCP server or manually by configuring the settings in the WINS tab of the Advanced TCP/IP Settings property pages of the TCP/IP properties. Figure 4.41 shows these settings for a Windows XP client.

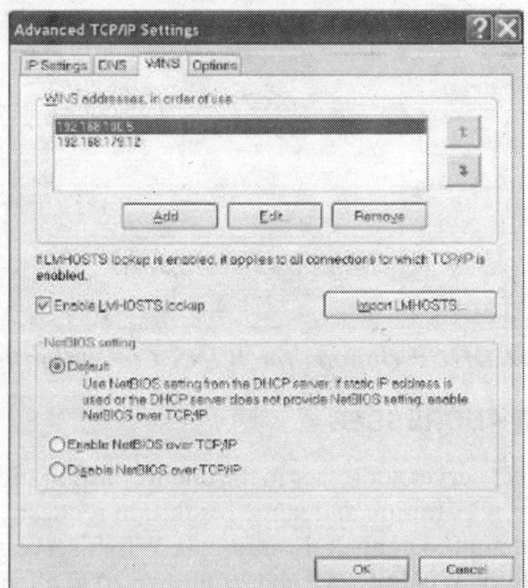

Figure 4.41 Advanced TCP/IP Settings for WINS Client Configuration

With the configuration shown in Figure 4.41, the client will use an LMHOSTS file if WINS name resolution fails. This is the default configuration. Also, the client is configured to get information about whether NetBT should be enabled from the DHCP server. (This information is provided by a special Microsoft-specific DHCP option.) If the client does not get this information from the DHCP server, it will default to enabling NetBT. You would disable NetBT only when you need to, such as on the Internet-facing interface of a multihomed server or if you have determined that the interface does not need to be able to provide access to NetBIOS applications.

If you are using a DHCP server, you do not need to specify static addresses for WINS servers in this dialog box. If you do configure WINS addresses here, these settings will override those that are supplied by the DHCP server. If you are using DHCP to supply the client settings, you will need to configure two DHCP options:

- Option 044 WINS/NBNS Servers You use this option to provide DHCP clients with the IP addresses of WINS servers to contact.
- Option 046 WINS/NBT Node Type This option governs the order of NetBIOS name resolution mechanisms that will be used.

The hybrid setting option (0x08) is the one most commonly used .With the hybrid node option specified, the WINS client will contact a WINS server before using broadcasts and other methods to resolve names. The mixed node setting option (0x04) forces WINS clients to use broadcasts before contacting the WINS server. This setting is useful in situations where there is a single subnet in a small branch office connected by a slow WAN link. In this case, you might want broadcasts to resolve local NetBIOS names before contacting the remote WINS server. Figure 4.42 shows the configuration of DHCP server options to support WINS client configurations.

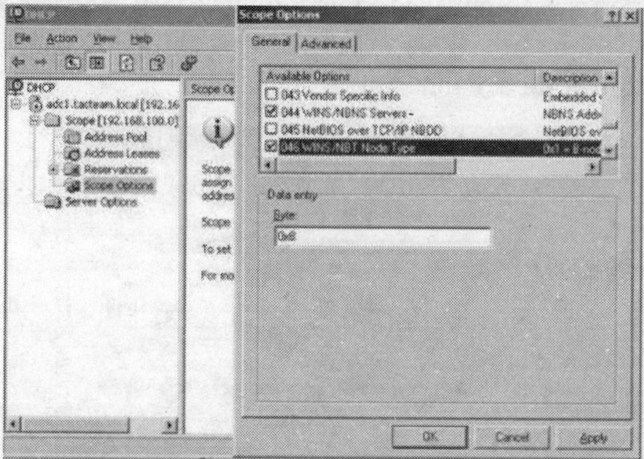

Figure 4.42 DHCP Options for WINS Client Configurations

1. MULTIPLE WINS SERVER ADDRESSES

If you specify multiple WINS server addresses in the client configuration, the client will try to use the first WINS server in the list for registration and name resolution requests. If the primary server fails to respond, the client will then attempt to contact the alternate WINS servers in the order listed. Up to 12 WINS servers can be specified for Windows XP and Windows 2000 clients.

2. WINS PROXY AGENT

For the rare case where you have a NetBIOS client that is not capable of querying a WINS server for NetBIOS name resolution, you can set up a WINS proxy agent. The WINS proxy agent is a WINS client that is set up on a subnet to provide limited WINS support for b-node and non-WINS NetBIOS clients. A WINS proxy agent listens for name registration and name query broadcasts, and it forwards these to its configured WINS server. This process ensures that the b-node client does not initialize with a duplicate name that is already registered in the WINS database and provides name resolution on behalf of the b-node client.

A common misconception is that a WINS proxy client will register the name on behalf of the non-WINS client. This is not the case. The WINS proxy merely contacts the WINS server to verify that the non-WINS client name does not exist. If there is a duplicate name in the WINS database, the WINS proxy client will send a negative response to the b-node client.

The proxy agent will use its NetBIOS name cache to temporarily store the results of responses to its queries to the WINS server. Performance of the WINS proxy agent could, therefore, be potentially improved by lengthening the amount of time an entry would persist in cache beyond the default 10 minutes.

4.4.14 Preventing Split WINS Registrations

A WINS server is also a WINS client to itself. A common configuration error is to specify a different WINS server to use as an alternate WINS server. The problem with doing this is that during startup of the WINS server, it will try to register its names with the WINS servers configured in the TCP/IP properties. Because the WINS server service won't start until NetBT has initialized, this causes the WINS server to attempt to register with the alternate or secondary WINS. However, it will continue to try to register these mappings in the local WINS database. Once the local WINS database is available, the WINS server will switch to it to register the remaining mappings. This results in what is known as a split registration, where name mappings are registered in and owned by two different WINS servers. A split registration for WINS servers can cause intermittent problems with WINS name resolution.

4.4.14.1 Performance Issues

As mentioned earlier in the chapter, a typical WINS server can handle WINS registrations and name resolution requests for up to 10,000 clients, even if the WINS server has only modest amounts of CPU power and RAM. WINS traffic for each registration and name resolution request is relatively small. However, a number of factors can affect the performance of WINS server. These factors include the presence of other services running on the WINS server, the performance of database maintenance on the WINS server, various WINS server settings, and the flooding of the network with NetBIOS name registration requests. In this section, we'll look at WINS server performance issues.

4.4.14.2 Hardware Considerations

Even a modestly powered computer can handle a large number of registrations and name resolution requests. However, WINS can generate intensive CPU and disk activity. WINS server performance is, therefore, significantly improved by using fast disks and multiple CPUs. For mission-critical WINS servers that handle large amounts of data, it is a good idea to use RAID arrays to enhance fault tolerance and performance. If you don't use a RAID array, you should consider placing the WINS database on a separate hard disk from the operating system.

If the organization requires a very high degree of fault tolerance and availability, you should consider using a Windows Server 2003 server cluster for the WINS service. This will require at least two WINS servers configured as cluster nodes to use a shared SCSI or Fibre Channel storage device. On large networks, adding more WINS servers to distribute the load will improve response times for WINS queries, but will add more replication traffic and require more administration.

4.4.14.3 Burst Handling

Since Windows NT 4.0 Service Pack 3, WINS servers have been capable of burst handling. Burst handling, which is enabled by default, allows the WINS server to handle a large volume of simultaneous registration requests. This situation can occur, for example, when power is suddenly returned to many computers after a power outage. With burst handling configured, the WINS server will respond positively to name registration and refresh requests before it writes them to the database.

However, it will supply the WINS clients with varied and short TTLs for the name registrations to stagger the load for subsequent WINS client refresh attempts. By default, burst handling occurs when the server has more than 500 requests in its queue. However, you can adjust this setting in the WINS console. As shown in Figure 4.43, the Advanced tab for the properties of the WINS server allows you to select a Low (300 requests), Medium (500), High (1000), or Custom (where you specify the number of requests). If the WINS server has more than 25,000 requests in its queue, it will start dropping queries.

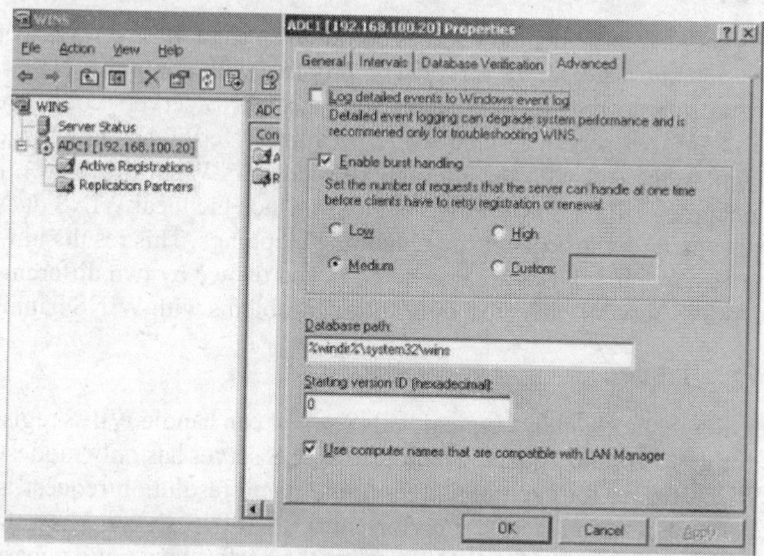

Figure 4.43 Configuring Burst Handling

It's a good idea to ensure that burst handling is enabled for reasons other than improving the performance of the WINS server under peak-load conditions. When burst handling is enabled, it writes events to the event log. The presence of burst handling events can provide an indication that the WINS server hardware is not adequate. Furthermore, the presence of burst handling events can indicate a possible DoS attack on the WINS server. You can use Network Monitor or some other tool for analyzing network traffic to capture packets and track down the possible causes of the presence of burst handling events.

4.4.14.4 Scavenging of WINS Records

Performance of a WINS server will be affected by the settings that are used to determine how frequently clients refresh their registrations, how long it takes for a released or deleted registration to be removed from the database, and how frequently the database verifies its records to ensure the integrity of data. Scavenging is the process by which WINS records are removed from the database.

More specifically, scavenging is a preset process that periodically runs on the WINS server and either deletes or changes the status of WINS records based on their timestamps and current state. The settings that control these intervals are found in the Intervals tab in the property pages of the WINS server. It might be useful to change these settings to improve the performance of the WINS server.

Renewal interval Governs the TTL of the client registration. WINS clients will attempt to renew registrations after half the renewal interval has elapsed. Increasing this interval will reduce the frequency of client renewal attempts and reduce the load on the WINS server. However, increasing the interval also makes the database less consistent with the network over time when computer names are changed.

The renewal interval should be the same for all WINS servers when they are replicating with one another.

Extinction interval Governs the period that must elapse from when a name is marked as released and when it is marked as tombstoned. Extinction timeout Governs the period that must elapse from when a name marked as tombstoned and is subsequently scavenged (removed) from the database.

Verification interval Dependent on the previous values and governs when a WINS server must validate active records it does not own; that is, records learned of via replication with other WINS servers. Figure 4.44 shows the Intervals tab with the default settings.

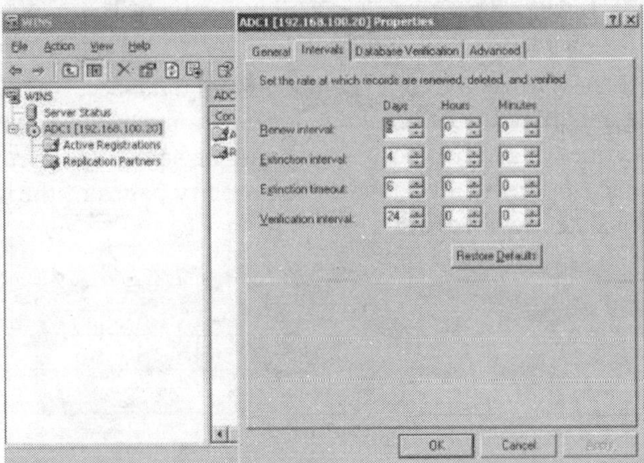

Figure 4.44 Interval Settings for Registration Renewal, Removal, and Verification

4.4.15 Database Compaction

When records are deleted from the WINS database, the space formerly occupied by them should be recovered to ensure optimal performance of the database. The process of recovering this space is referred to as compaction. The WINS service automatically and periodically performs online compaction of the WINS database. However, online compaction of the WINS database is not as efficient as offline compaction. It is, therefore, sometimes desirable for the WINS administrator to stop the WINS service (take the database offline) and perform a manual compaction of the database.

The WINS administrator can use Jetpack.exe, found in the System32 folder, for manual database compaction. The Jetpack utility works by creating a temporary database in which to compact the records, and then replacing the original database with the compacted one. To manually compact the database, the WINS administrator must first stop the WINS service and then issue the jetpack command, using the following syntax:

jetpack %systemroot%\system32\Wins\Wins.mdb [name_of_temp_database.mdb]

After running the jetpack command, the WINS administrator can start the WINS service again. Using the net stop and net start commands, the WINS administrator can automate offline compaction in a batch file. For example, you can create a simple batch file that contains the following

three lines:

net stop wins

jetpack %systemroot%\system32\Wins\Wins.mdb [name_of_temp_database.mdb]

net start wins

Once you have created the batch file, you can configure it to run at preconfigured intervals using the Task Scheduler or the AT command-line utility. For example, you could configure the batch file to run once a month during off hours to ensure that the database uses space optimally.

4.4.16 Scheduling Consistency Checking

In order to maintain database integrity in environments that employ replication, it is recommended that automatic periodic consistency checking be enabled. Consistency checking is the process whereby a local WINS server compares local entries that it has acquired by replication with the entries in WINS servers that own the record. If a WINS server detects that the records are identical between its locally stored copy and the remote database, it will update the record with a new timestamp.

However, if the record has a lower version ID in the local database, it will pull the updated record from its replication partner and mark the original one for deletion. Because consistency checking puts a significant load on the resources of a WINS server, it should be scheduled to run during off-peak hours. Figure 4.45 shows the Database Verification tab of the property pages of the WINS server, where you can set the schedule for consistency checking.

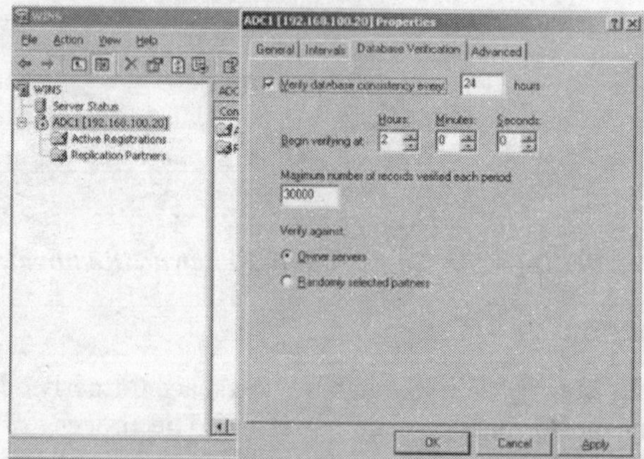

Figure 4.45 Enabling and Scheduling Consistency Checking

In Figure 4.45, consistency checking is enabled and scheduled to run every 24 hours at 2:00 A.M. Additional settings allow the WINS administrator to specify the maximum number of records to verify and to select randomly selected replication partners. Consistency checking can also be manually initiated from the context menu of the WINS server in the WINS server console.

4.4.17 Security Issues

As with any service that you implement on your servers and your network, it is important for you to understand the service and take measures that mitigate the risk to the service and the network as a whole. These measures include setting up restricted ACLs, logging, auditing, and monitoring, as well as using VPNs or IPSec to secure WINS replication traffic. In the next section, we briefly examine issues related to the security of the WINS service.

4.4.17.1 Netbios Security Issues

With regard to NetBIOS in general and the WINS service in particular, administrators need to be aware that NetBIOS is an unauthenticated protocol. That is, users are not required to submit credentials before using the services provided by a WINS server, such as name registration, renewal, release, and queries. This makes WINS susceptible to a number of different kinds of attacks, primarily DoS attacks and redirection attacks.

In a DoS attack, an attacker attempts to tie up the WINS service with a large number of requests that compromise the WINS server's ability to process legitimate requests. To mitigate the risk of DoS attacks, you should do the following:

- Secure the physical network from unauthorized access.
- Enable burst handling. When burst handling is enabled, burst handling events are recorded in Event Viewer, providing an alert to a possible DoS attack.
- Enable detailed WINS logging to provide more complete and specific logging of WINS events in the System log. (Also set in the Advanced tab for the properties of the WINS server, shown in Figure 4.42).
- Use a protocol-analysis tool, such as Network Monitor, to analyze traffic in the case of a suspected attack.

In a redirection attack, an attacker tries to register a rogue computer that has the same name mappings as a previously registered computer. If the previously registered computer is down for maintenance or is otherwise unable to respond to the challenge from the WINS server (for example, if it is also a victim of a specific DoS attack), the rogue computer will be able to register the name mappings with its own IP address. WINS clients will then subsequently be redirected to the rogue computer. To mitigate the risk of redirection attacks, you should do the following:

- Identify mission-critical systems and assign them static mappings in the WINS database.
- Ensure that the migrate on setting is disabled to prevent the WINS server from overwriting the static mappings with dynamic mappings. (This is controlled by the Overwrite unique static mappings at this server (migrate on) setting in the Replication Partners Properties dialog box, shown in Figure 4.40 earlier in this chapter.)

4.4.18 Protecting the WINS Database and Log Files

The WINS databases and log files contain important information about your network. The information in these files could be used by attackers to glean confidential information about your company.

For example, by an analysis of the number of computers, the attacker could learn the names of those computers, the NetBIOS applications running on the computers, and so on. Furthermore, the integrity and availability of the WINS database and the log files are critical to the operation of the network.

It is particularly important to note that, if you change the default location of the WINS database files, they will inherit the ACLs of the new destination folder, removing the effective security they inherited by virtue of being located in a subfolder of the System32 folder. Also, the WINS backup files inherit the ACL of the folder used to store the backup files. To mitigate the risks to the confidentiality, integrity, and availability of WINS databases, you should consider doing the following:

- Do not store WINS database files on anything except an NTFS formatted partition.
- Ensure that the ACLs for the WINS database, backup, and log files are restricted to allow access to only the Local System Account and the Administrators group.

- Enable file auditing on the WINS files to track attempts of objects that try to access these files.
- Ensure that the WINS server is physically secured from remote access.
- Do not transfer WINS database files over the network using FTP or other unsecured protocols.

4.4.19 WINS Users Group

Only members of the Administrators group can modify the settings for WINS servers. However, it is desirable, in some situations, to provide read-only access to the configuration and database information of WINS servers. To provide users with read-only access to the WINS server, you can use the special WINS Users group. Users who are members of this group are able to query the WINS server database to find records and to view configuration information.

4.4.19.1 Planning for WINS Database Backup and Restoration

Although it is possible to rely on replicated copies of WINS records to restore a corrupted database, you should only do so as a method of last resort. It is far better to back up the WINS database, either manually or automatically, and restore WINS records from the backup, if necessary. By default, the WINS database is not backed up automatically. To back up a WINS database automatically, you need to do the following:

1. Specify a backup directory in the General tab of the WINS server properties. (WINS will create a folder called Wins_bak under this folder to store the backups).
2. Perform a manual backup of the WINS database to the specified location. You can do this by choosing the Backup Up Database option from context menu of the WINS server object in the WINS console tree.

After you have performed these steps, backups will occur every 24 hours or upon service shutdown (if so configured). In the event that the WINS service detects a corrupt WINS database upon startup, it will automatically restore the backed up version from the location that you specified for the WINS backups. You cannot use a network drive for this location. Figure 4.46 shows the settings for configuring automatic backups.

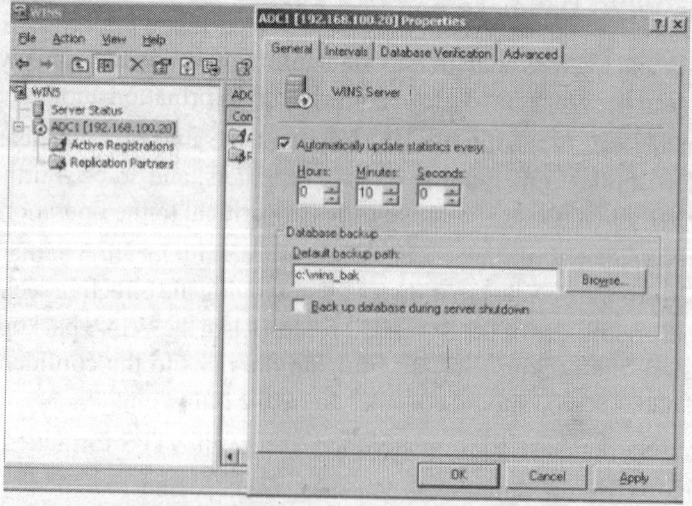

Figure 4.46 WINS Backup Configuration

4.5 DNS

Modern TCP/IP networks use DNS for name resolution, and DNS is a requirement for Active Directory. Active Directory supports the DNS server included with Windows 2000 Server and Windows Server 2003, either standalone or integrated directly into Active Directory, and it also supports BIND version 8.2.2 or later. . If you're using Active Directory-integrated DNS, you can skip the next section because DNS is automatically set up during the Active Directory Setup Wizard.

4.5.1 Installing DNS

To install DNS, use the Configure Your Server Wizard to set up Active Directory on the server and let Windows install DNS at the same time. This provides domain controller functionality and also lets DNS benefit from Active Directory integration. You can also use the Configure Your Server Wizard to set up DNS completely independent of Active Directory. If you want to set up DNS service the old-fashioned way (by installing the service), follow these steps:

1. Click Start, choose Control Panel, and then select Network Connections. Right click the connection you want, and choose Properties from the shortcut menu.
2. Select the Internet Protocol (TCP/IP) entry, and then click Properties. To specify a static IP address, type the IP address, subnet mask, and default gateway that you're using. Be sure the Use The Following DNS Server Addresses option is selected. In the Preferred DNS Sever box, type the computer's assigned IP address. 3. Click Start, choose Control Panel, and then click System.
4. In the Computer Name tab, click Change. In the Identification Changes box, click More. (You aren't able to perform this procedure on domain controllers.) 5. In the Primary DNS Suffix Of This Computer dialog box, type the DNS domain name and click OK. Reboot the server to implement the DNS suffix changes, if any. (Otherwise, no reboot is necessary.)
6. Open the Add/Remove Programs Control Panel tool, and then click Add/Remove Windows Components to launch the Windows Components Wizard.
7. Select Networking Services from the list of components, and then click Details.
8. Select the check box next to the Domain Name System (DNS) component, and then click OK.
9. Click Next to install the service. All the necessary files are copied to the hard disk.

4.5.2 Using the Configure DNS Server Wizard

Windows Server 2003 provides a handy wizard to help you set up a DNS server. The following sections guide you through the wizard, while later sections delve into more detail about individual tasks that the wizard accomplishes.

4.5.2.1 Setting up a DNS Server

Both large and small networks have similar DNS requirements, although many small networks will usually function well without Reverse Lookup zones. If your internal domain name is different from your public, Internet domain name (that is, internally you use "example.local" or "example.lan", but externally you use "example.com"), you must configure an internal DNS server to support your internal network.

If your DNS domain name is the same on your local network as it is on the Internet (that is, example.com is your Active Directory domain name as well as your Internet domain name), you could, theoretically, have only external DNS records, but this is a bad practice because it exposes your internal network topology and names to the world. In this case, it is better to maintain an internal DNS server that supports your internal network, while the publicly visible DNS server or servers for your domain should only have records for publicly visible servers.

4.5.2.2 Need (or Lack Thereof) for Secondary DNS Servers

Because of the pivotal role DNS plays in any TCP/IP-based network, it's vital for it to be reliable. Small networks can often make do with a single DNS server, but medium and large networks must have fault-tolerant DNS service.

One way of providing DNS redundancy is to set up secondary DNS servers using standard zone files to provide redundancy if the primary DNS server (of which there can be only one) doesn't respond to client queries. Secondary DNS servers can also be useful in reducing network traffic if placed in a location where the zone is heavily queried.

Another approach is to add another Active Directory-integrated DNS server. Because Active Directory uses a full multiple-master model, all DNS servers using Active Directory-integrated zones can be primary servers-no secondary zones are required. If you are going to use standard primary and secondary DNS servers, set up secondary DNS servers for both forward and reverse lookup zones. Fewer secondary servers are required for reverse lookup zones because of their infrequent use. They are usually placed outside the network and subnet that the reverse zone serves. The Configure DNS Server Wizard makes it easy to set up a DNS server.

To use the wizard, do the following:

1. Launch DNS from the Administrative Tools folder on the Programs menu.
2. Select the DNS server you want to configure. (Choose the Connect To Server command from the Action menu if the server isn't displayed in the console tree.)
3. Choose the Configure A DNS Server command from the Action menu.
4. Click Next in the first screen. (Optionally, click DNS Checklists to review background material about DNS and the DNS configuration process.)
5. Choose the Create Forward And Reverse Lookup Zones option in the Select Configuration Action page as shown in Figure 4.47, and then click Next.

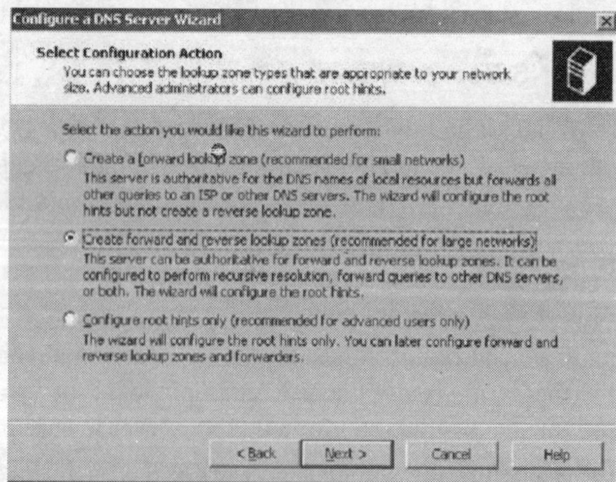

Figure 4.47 Choose what types of zones to create

6. Select Yes, Create A Forward Lookup Zone Now and then click Next.
7. In the Zone Type page shown in Figure 4.48, choose one of the following options, and then click Next to continue:
    - Primary zone Use this option if the DNS server is to be authoritative for the zone you want to create. Only authoritative servers can update the DNS database.
    - Secondary zone Use this zone if the DNS server is hosted on UNIX servers. Also, use it if this server is to have read-only privileges in the zone with all data obtained from the primary DNS server.
    - Stub zone Use this type of zone to create a pseudo-zone that allows the server to directly query DNS servers from a specific zone without having to locate the zone's DNS servers by querying the root servers or Internet DNS servers.

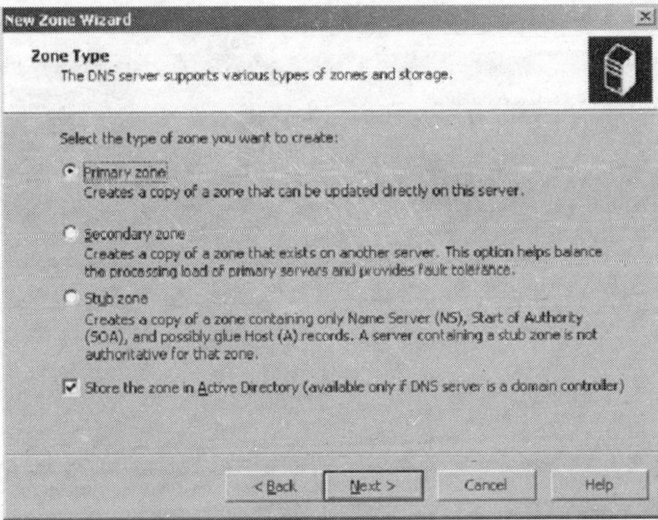

Figure 4.48 Choosing a zone type

8. If you're creating an Active Directory-integrated zone, specify with which servers the zone information should be replicated and then click Next. (You'll probably want to choose To All DNS Servers In The Active Directory Domain to reduce replication traffic.)
9. If you chose to create a secondary zone, type a name for the zone and then click Next. Then type the IP addresses of the master servers from which you want to copy the zone data. Click Add after typing or locating each one. Click Up and Down to arrange the IP addresses in the order you want to contact them. Click Next when you're done.
10. If you're creating a standard zone, type a filename for the zone file on the Zone File page. To use an existing file, copy the file to the %SystemRoot%\System32\Dns folder, select the Use This Existing File option, type the filename in the box provided, and then click Next.
11. On the Dynamic Update page (available only for primary zones), choose how you want to configure dynamic updates and then click Next. The options are:
    - Allow Only Secure Dynamic Updates This is the default for Active Directory integrated zones (and is available only for Active Directory-integrated zones), and it provides the best security. However, clients running earlier versions of Windows might end up with orphaned DNS records under certain circum stances.

- Allow Both Secure and Unsecure Dynamic Updates This is the recommended setting for standard zones.
- Do Not Allow Dynamic Updates This setting disables dynamic updates entirely.

12. To create a reverse lookup zone, click Next; otherwise, choose the No I Don't Want To option first and then click Next.
13. If you chose to create a reverse lookup zone, choose the type of zone to create and then click Next.
14. If you're creating an Active Directory-integrated zone, specify with which servers the zone information should be replicated and then click Next.
15. Type the address of the network in the Network ID box and then click Next. The wizard automatically creates the reverse lookup zone name for you from this information, as shown in Figure 4.49.

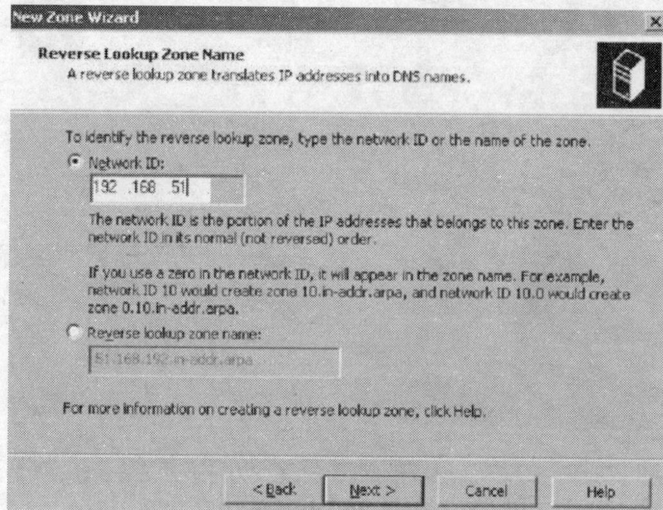

Figure 4.49 Creating a reverse lookup zone

16. If you're creating a standard zone, click Next to approve the filename provided.
17. On the Dynamic Update page, choose how you want to configure dynamic updates and then click Next.
18. To set up the server to forward unresolved DNS queries to another DNS server (which might either resolve the query from its cache or contact an external DNS server to resolve the query), type the IP address of the forwarding server and then click Next. Alternatively, choose the No, It Should Not Forward Queries option and then click Next.
19. Review the summary of the DNS server configuration, and then click Finish to complete the initial configuration of the DNS server.

4.5.3 Creating Zones

Zones allow you to store portions of the DNS namespace so that a single DNS server can serve a portion of the namespace. The two types of zones concerned are forward lookup zones and reverse lookup zones. Forward lookup zones are the types of zones normally associated with DNS servers; they return an IP address when given a DNS name. Reverse lookups are used less often, but they are still important. They provide the ability to resolve an IP address into a DNS name, something that Internet Information Services (IIS) can use for its log files. (Troubleshooting tools such as Nslookup rely on reverse lookup zones as well.)

When you first set up a DNS server, you'll probably want to use the Configure A DNS Server Wizard (discussed in the previous section), which guides you through creating the first forward lookup zone. However, if you didn't use the wizard to set up the zones or you need to create additional zones, use the following procedure:

1. Launch DNS from the Administrative Tools folder on the Programs menu.
2. Select the DNS server you want to configure. (Choose the Connect To Server command from the Action menu if the server isn't displayed in the console tree.) 3. Choose New Zone from the Action menu to start the New Zone Wizard. Click Next to start using the wizard. (See the "Setting Up a DNS Server" section for help with this.)

4.5.3.1 Creating Subdomains and Delegating Authority

In most large network environments, you need to create subdomains and delegate their management to other DNS zones hosted by other DNS servers. Doing so eliminates the undesirable situation of having a large namespace hosted in a single zone by a single server. Thus, you might have a zone containing the root domain example.local as well as the subdomain marketing.example.local; however, you might have the subdomain eng.example.local and its subdomains delegated to a separate zone managed by another DNS server, as shown in Figure 4.50.

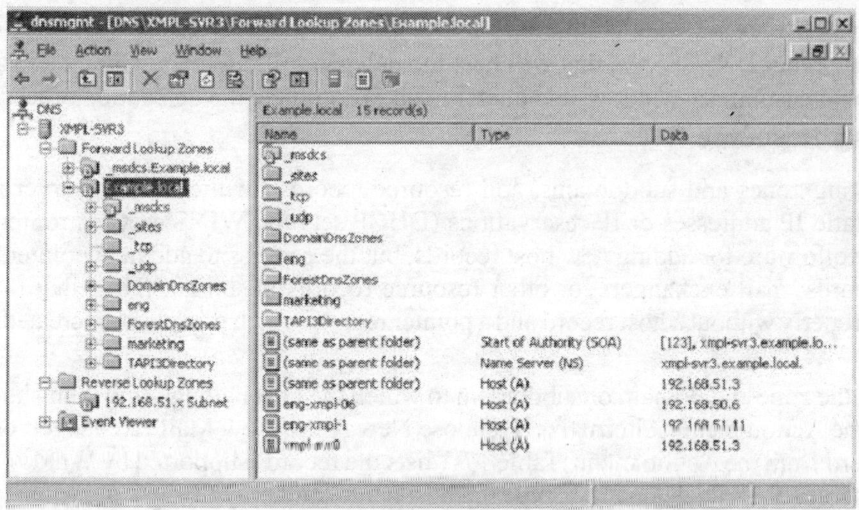

Figure 4.50 A domain tree with zones identified

To create a new subdomain in an existing zone and then delegate authority over the domain to another DNS server, perform the following steps:

1. Select the domain in which you want to create a new subdomain, and then choose New Domain from the Action menu.
2. Type the name of the subdomain in the dialog box that appears, and then click OK. This name must not be fully qualified. For example, if you were creating the subdomain eng.example.com under the domain example.com, type only eng in this dialog box.

3. To delegate authority over the subdomain, select the parent domain of the subdomain, choose New Delegation from the Action menu, and then click Next to start the New Delegation Wizard.
4. Type the name for the subdomain you want to delegate, as shown in Figure 4.51. Check that the fully qualified name of the subdomain displayed is correct and then click Next.

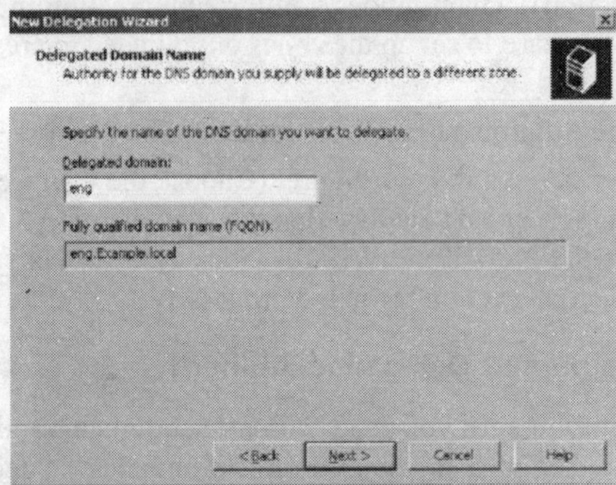

Figure 4.51 Delegating a subdomain

5. Click Add to specify the servers to which you want to delegate the subdomain. 6. Type the name of the server to which you want to delegate authority and then click Resolve, or click Browse to locate its resource record in the DNS server's zone files. Alternatively, type the IP address or addresses for the server, clicking Add after typing each one. Click OK when you're done.
7. Add any other DNS servers that will host the delegated subdomain. Click Next to continue. 8. Review the summary window, and click Finish to complete the delegation process.

4.5.3.2 Adding Resource Records

After creating zones and subdomains, add resource records for the domain server and any other servers with static IP addresses or IP reservations (DHCP servers, WINS servers, routers, and so on). The steps that follow are for adding new host records, but the process to add new pointer records, Alias (CNAME) records, mail exchangers, or other resource records is similar. (Note that the DNS server doesn't work properly without a host record and a pointer record, which might not be created automatically for you.)

1. Select the zone and domain or subdomain to which the host belongs, and then choose New Host from the Action menu. Alternatively, choose New Alias, New Mail Exchanger, or another type of record from the Action menu. Table 17-1 lists the records supported by Windows Server 2003 DNS server. 2. In the Name box, type the host name (and only the host name the name must not contain any periods), or leave the Name box blank to use the name of the parent domain. Type the host's IP address.
3. Select the Create Associated Pointer (PTR) Record to create a resource record for the host in the reverse lookup zone.
4. If you want to allow any authenticated user to update the resource record you're creating, select the Allow Any Authenticated User To Update DNS Records With The Same Owner Name check box.
5. Click Add Host, and then fill out the fields for any additional host records you want to create, or click Done.

4.5.3.3 Changing DNS Records

When you make a change to the DNS records, make sure you choose the Update Server Data Files command from the Action menu after making the changes. This option increment the serial numbers, letting other DNS servers know that you made a change and that they need to update their information.

If you're using conventional DNS zones, add or change DNS records only from the primary DNS server for a zone. If you're using Active Directory-integrated DNS, you can make the changes to any Active Directory-based DNS and it propagates correctly to the other Active Directory DNS servers and notifies secondary servers that there are updated records.

Table 4.1 Supported DNS record types

Record Type	Common Name	Function	RFC
A	Address record	Maps a fully qualified domain name (FQDN) to a 32-bit IPv4 address	
AAAA	IPv6 Host	Maps an FQDN to a 128-bit IPv6 address	1886
AFSDB	Andrews file system (AFS) or distributed computing environment (DCE) record	Maps a DNS domain name to a server subtype that is either an AFS version 3 volume or an authenticated name server (NS) using DCE or Network computing architecture (NCA)	1183
ATMS	Asynchrondus Transfer Mode (ATM address	Maps a host name to an ATM address	ATM Name System Specification Version 1.0
CNAME	Canonical name or alias record	Maps a virtual domain name (alias) to a real domain name	1035
HINFO	Host information record	Specifies the CPU and operating system type for the host	1700
ISDN	ISDN information record	Maps an FQDN to an ISDN telephone number	1183
KEY	Public key resource record	Contains a public key for a DNS zone	2535
MB	Mailbox name record	Maps a domain mail server name to the acutal host name of the mail server	1035
MG	Mail group record	Maps a domain mailing group to the actual mailbox (MB) resource records of its members	1035
MINFO	Mailbox information record	Specifies a mailbox for the person who maintains the person who maintain the mailbox or list, and can also specify a mailbox for related errors	1035
MR	Mailbox renamed record	Maps an old mailbox name to a new mailbox name for forwarding puroses	1035

Record Type	Common Name	Function	RFC
MX	Mail exchange record	Provides routing information to reach a given mailbox	974
NS	Name server record	Specifies that the name server listed has a zone starting with the owner name	1035
NXT	Next record	Specifies the nonexistance of the specified name	2035
OPT	Option resource recprd	Spefifies optional data with a DNS request or reply	2671
PTR	Pointer resource record	Points to another DNS resouce record–most often used in reverse lookup to point to the A record	1035
RP	Responsible person information record	Provides information about the peson responsible for a server	1183
RT	Route-through record	Provides routing information for hosts lacking a direct WAN address	1183
SIG	Signature resource record	Digitally signs a host name	2535
SOA	Start of authority	Specifies the beginning of a zone, and indicates the authoritative server	1034
SRV	Service locator record	Provides a way of locating multiple servers providing similar TCP/IP services	2052
TXT	Text record	Maps a DNS name to a string of descriptive text	1035
WKS	Well-known services record	Describes the most popular TCP/IP services supported by a protocol on a specific IP address	1035
X25	X.25 information	Maps a DNS address to a public switched data network (PSDN) address number	1083

4.5.3.4 Configuring Zone Transfers

Because the DNS service is so important to a modern TCP/IP-based network, and because it's essential to the operation of Active Directory, always configure multiple DNS servers in each zone to provide fault tolerance.

Windows Server 2003 supports several ways of achieving zone transfers between DNS servers managing a zone. If the DNS servers are using Active Directory to store their zone data, Active Directory handles the zone replication, allowing for a full multimaster model in which all servers are peers and any can make changes to the DNS database. Additionally, zone transfers are incremental so that only changed records are synchronized.

Windows Server 2003 also supports RFC 1995-compliant incremental zone transfers when using standard zone files. This incremental zone transfer method permits a secondary DNS server to pull only the zone changes that it needs to synchronize its copy of the zone data with the primary server's. If the serial number of the primary DNS server's zone file matches that of the secondary DNS server's serial number, no changes were made, so no zone transfer need take place.

Incremental zone transfers occur only if both servers support this feature. When performing zone transfers with Windows NT 4 DNS servers or other DNS servers that don't support this feature, a full zone transfer occurs. In a full zone transfer, the entire contents of the zone file are pulled from the primary DNS server by the secondary server.

4.5.4 Interoperating with other DNS Servers

Windows Server 2003 and Windows 2000 DNS servers perform fast zone transfers with data compression and multiple resource records sent in each message when transferring zones to other Windows DNS servers. This zone transfer method works with all Windows DNS servers, and BIND DNS servers version 4.9.4 or later. Note that Windows 2000 DNS servers must run Service Pack 3 or newer if receiving zone information from BIND 9.x servers.

4.5.4.1 Enabling WINS Resolution

WINS allows NetBIOS names to be resolved into IP addresses. This capability is important for networks that support large numbers of pre-Windows 2000 Microsoft clients. DNS can work with WINS to search the entire combined DNS and NetBIOS namespace, if necessary, when a client attempts to resolve a host name. In Windows NT 4, enabling WINS resolution within DNS was essential to successfully resolving hosts that might have recently changed IP addresses-the dynamic WINS database provided an up-to-date IP address when the static DNS zone file couldn't. However, with Windows Server 2003, Windows XP, and Windows 2000, dynamic updates to the DNS server have nearly eliminated the need to use WINS servers to keep the namespace up to date, and WINS is gradually being phased out. Not a moment too soon, in our opinion. To enable WINS resolution in a zone, follow these steps:

1. Select the zone in which you want to enable WINS resolution, and then choose Properties from the Action menu.
2. Click the WINS tab, and select the Use WINS Forward Lookup check box.
3. If you're not using Microsoft DNS servers as secondary servers, select the Do Not Replicate This Record check box to prevent compatibility problems. (Only Windows DNS servers support WINS records.)
4. Type the IP address of each WINS server you want to query, clicking Add after typing each one. You find more about setting up WINS in the "Setting Up a WINS Server".

4.5.4.2 Setting up a Forwarder

No name server is able to answer the queries of all clients; sometimes clients request a DNS name that isn't in a zone managed by the DNS server, let's say example.microsoft.com. The DNS server goes to the Internet to the top level of the DNS domain tree. The top-level DNS servers then provide the address of the DNS server for the first level (.com). This server in turn provides the address of the microsoft.com DNS server, which then provides the address of the example.microsoft.com DNS server.

This process is called recursion, and it takes time and a number of trips out to the Internet by the DNS server. In a network with multiple DNS servers and domains, it can be advantageous to have DNS servers forward their unresolved queries to another DNS server. This server then either replies with the desired record from its own DNS zone or hunts down the unresolved query and reports back to the DNS server that forwarded the request. This can reduce WAN link usage in two ways:

- If the server is authoritative for the zone containing the requested DNS record, the DNS server can reply directly without having to hunt for the appropriate DNS server.
- If the server isn't hosting the zone with the requested record, it still might be able to answer the quefy from its cache of recent DNS queries.

To configure the DNS server to forward unresolved queries to another DNS server, follow these steps:

1. In the console tree, select the DNS server on which you want to enable forwarding, and then choose Properties from the Action menu and then click the Forwarders tab.
2. To forward all unresolved queries to another DNS server, select All Other DNS Domains in the DNS domain box, and then type the IP addresses of the DNS server or servers to which you want to forward unresolved queries, clicking Add after typing each one.
3. To change the default timeout before DNS will try the next forwarder in the list, change the Number of Seconds before Forward Queries Time Out from the default of 5 seconds.
4. To disable recursion for a particular domain, select the domain and then select the Do Not Use Recursion for This Domain check box. If the DNS server that is the target of the forwarded queries doesn't respond and the Do Not Use Recursion For This Domain check box is selected, the DNS server fails the query, and the client fails over to a secondary DNS server if it's configured to do so. A DNS server that's configured to use forwarders and not perform recursion is called a slave server.

To enable forwarding queries for a specific domain to a specific DNS server (conditional forwarding) follow these steps:

1. In the console tree, select the DNS server on which you want to enable forwarding, choose Properties from the Action menu, and then click the Forwarders tab.
2. Click New in the DNS Domain, type the DNS domain for which to use conditional forwarding, and click OK.
3. With the domain highlighted, type the IP addresses of the DNS server or servers to which you want to forward unresolved queries, clicking Add after typing each one.
4. Click OK to close the dialog box and implement the changes.

4.5.4.3 Updating Root Hints

Root hints tell a DNS server where to look to find the DNS servers authoritative for the top level of the domain structure. Root hints for the Internet's root servers are automatically installed in the Cache.dns file located in the %SystemRoot%\System32\Dns folder. If the DNS server needs only to resolve names in the private network, you must provide the locations of the top-level DNS servers for the network, either through the DNS console (as described next) or by manually editing the Cache.dns file. Alternatively, you can import root hints from another server. To update root hints on the server, use the following procedure:

1. In the console tree, select the DNS server on which you want to update the root hints, and then choose Properties from the Action menu.
2. Click the Root Hints tab and then click Add to manually add a name server record for a root DNS server. Alternatively, click Copy From Server, type the IP address for the DNS server from which you want to copy root hints, and then click OK.

4.5.4.4 Setting up a Caching-only DNS Server

Caching-only servers are DNS servers that don't host any zones and aren't authoritative for any domains-they simply cache the queries that they perform on behalf of the clients that use the server. Caching-only servers are useful for sites that use a slow WAN link to other DNS servers. By simply caching queries instead of holding its own zone files, a caching-only server reduces network traffic because it never performs any zone transfers.

To set up a caching-only server, follow these steps:

1. Install the DNS service, using the Add/Remove Windows Components section of the Add/Remove Programs tool.
2. Configure the caching server with a static IP address.
3. Launch DNS from the Administrative Tools folder on the Programs menu, select The Following Computer in the Select Target Computer dialog box, type the name of the DNS server from which you want to cache, and click OK. (If this dialog box doesn't appear, choose Connect To Computer from the Action menu in the DNS window.)

The DNS server is added to the DNS console on the caching server. The caching server performs recursive queries on behalf of its clients and over time accumulates resource records for answering future queries. You can clear the cache on a caching server by right clicking the server's name in the DNS console and selecting Clear Cache from the short-cut menu.

4.6 PROXY SERVERS

A proxy server is a server (a computer system or an application program) that acts as an intermediary for requests from clients seeking resources from other servers. A client connects to the proxy server, requesting some service, such as a file, connection, web page, or other resource, available from a different server. The proxy server evaluates the request according to its filtering rules. For example, it may filter traffic by IP address or protocol. If the request is validated by the filter, the proxy provides the resource by connecting to the relevant server and requesting the service on behalf of the client. A proxy server may optionally alter the client's request or the server's response, and sometimes it may serve the request without contacting the specified server. In this case, it 'caches' responses from the remote server, and returns subsequent requests for the same content directly. A proxy server has a large variety of potential purposes, including:

- To keep machines behind it anonymous (mainly for security).
- To speed up access to resources (using caching). Web proxies are commonly used to cache web pages from a web server.

- To apply access policy to network services or content, e.g. to block undesired sites.
- To log / audit usage, i.e. to provide company employee Internet usage reporting.
- To bypass security/ parental controls.
- To scan transmitted content for malware before delivery.
- To scan outbound content, e.g., for data leak protection.
- To circumvent regional restrictions.

A proxy server that passes requests and replies unmodified is usually called a gateway or sometimes tunneling proxy. A proxy server can be placed in the user's local computer or at various points between the user and the destination servers on the Internet. A reverse proxy is (usually) an Internet-facing proxy used as a front-end to control and protect access to a server on a private network, commonly also performing tasks such as load-balancing, authentication, decryption or caching.

Figure 4.52 Schematic representation of a proxy server, where the computer in the middle acts as the proxy server between the other two

A proxy server is a computer that offers network and internet access services to the client computers in a network. A proxy is a stand-in for you - someone who does something on your behalf. A proxy server is a kind of stand in for your computer. In an enterprise that uses the Internet, a proxy server is a server that acts as an intermediary between a workstation user and the Internet so that the enterprise can ensure security, administrative control, and caching service.

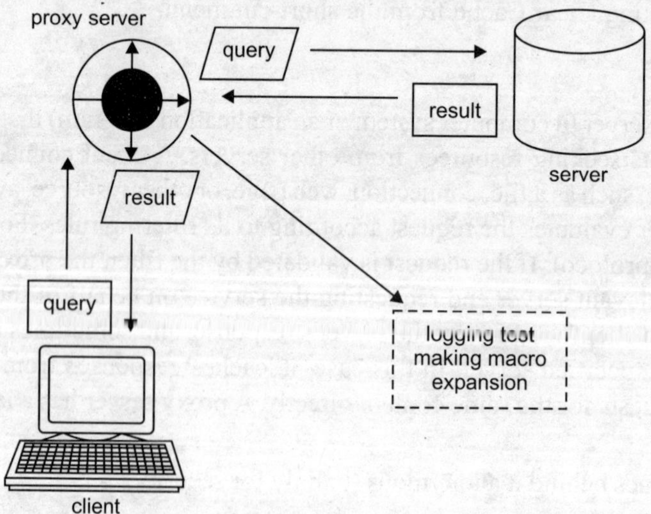

Figure 4.53 Queries of proxy server

By using the proxy server you can hide, conceal and make your network id anonymous by hiding your IP address. A proxy server is associated with or part of a gateway server that separates the enterprise network from the outside network and a firewall server that protects the enterprise network from outside intrusion. In short, a Proxy Server can be described as 'A server that sits between a client application, such as a Web browser, and a real server.' To get the anonymous status on the network or Internet, strong intermediate methods are employed like cryptography etc.

4.6.1 How Does Proxy Server Works?

A proxy server receives a request for an Internet service (such as a Web page request) from a user. If it passes filtering requirements, the proxy server, assuming it is also a cache server , looks in its local cache of previously downloaded Web pages. If it finds the page, it returns it to the user without needing to forward the request to the Internet. If the page is not in the cache, the proxy server, acting as a client on behalf of the user, uses one of its own IP addresses to request the page from the server out on the Internet. When the page is returned, the proxy server relates it to the original request and forwards it on to the user. A good example, and the one you probably see the most, is a web proxy. When configured to use a proxy, your web browser contacts the proxy server for each web access instead of going directly to the target server on the internet. The proxy server then turns around and makes the "real" request of the web server. The proxy server gets the response, and then passes it back to you.

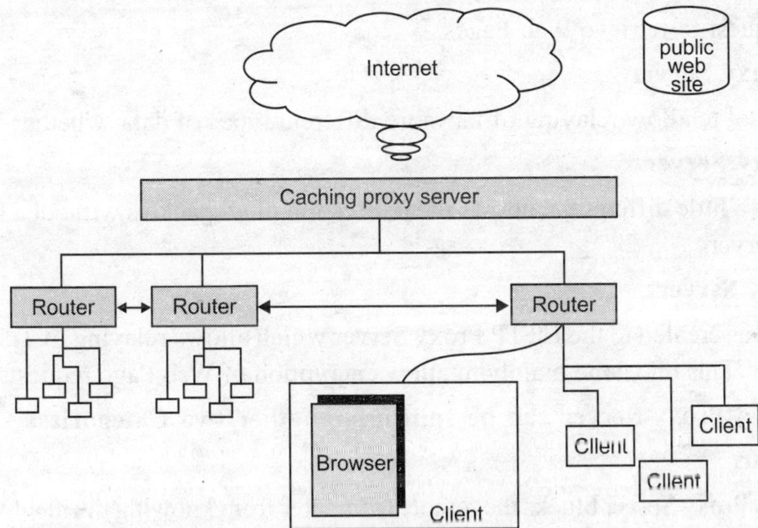

Figure 4.54 Caching proxy server

There is a large number of the software available that allows you to hide your IP address with the help of the proxy servers. The well known software for this purpose is Hide IP, Stealth surf, Netconceal, Anonymous surfing, Proxify and Ghost surf. To the user, the proxy server is invisible; all Internet requests and returned responses appear to be directly with the addressed Internet server. (The proxy is not quite invisible; its IP address has to be specified as a configuration option to the browser or other protocol program.)

4.6.2 Types of Proxy Servers

Many different types of Proxy Servers are available. Some common types are-

1. FTP
2. HTTP
3. Gopher
4. IRC
5. MSN
6. AIM
7. ICQ
8. VOIP
9. SSL

Depending on the purpose you can get Proxy Servers to route any of these common protocols, and many more. So out of the common types of Proxy Servers, you end up with the following:

1. FTP Proxy Server

Relays and caches FTP Traffic.

2. HTTP Proxy Server

A one way request to retrieve Web Pages.

3. Socks Proxy Server

A newer protocol to allow relaying of far more different types of data, whether TCP or UDP.

4. NAT Proxy Server

This one works a little different, it allows the redirection of all packets without a Program having to support a Proxy Server.

5. SSL Proxy Server

An extension was created to the HTTP Proxy Server which allows relaying of TCP data similar to a Socks Proxy Server. This one done mainly to allow encryption of Web Page requests.

Furthermore, a Proxy Server can be split into another two Categories:

1. Anonymous

An Anonymous Proxy Server blocks the remote Computer from knowing the identity of the Computer using the Proxy Server to make requests.

2. Transparent

A Transparent Proxy Server tells the remote Computer the IP Address of your Computer. This provides no privacy.

Anonymous Proxy Servers can further be broken down into two more categories, Elite and Disguised. An Elite Proxy Server is not identifiable to the remote computer as a Proxy in any way. A Disguised Proxy Server gives the remote computer enough information to let it know that it is a Proxy, however it still does not give away the IP of the Computer it is relaying information for.

4.6.3 Advantages of Proxy Server

Following are the advantages of the proxy server:

4.6.3.1 Improve Performance

Proxy servers can dramatically improve performance for groups of users. This is because it saves the results of all requests for a certain amount of time. Consider the case where both user X and user Y access the World Wide Web through a proxy server. First user X requests a certain Web page, which we'll call Page 1. Sometime later, user Y requests the same page. Instead of forwarding the request to the Web server where Page 1 resides, which can be a time-consuming operation, the proxy server simply returns the Page 1 that it already fetched for user X. Since the proxy server is often on the same network as the user, this is a much faster operation. Real proxy servers support hundreds or thousands of users. The major online services such as America Online, MSN and Yahoo, for example, employ an array of proxy servers.

4.6.3.2 Security Schemes

Proxy servers can also implement security schemes. For example, an FTP proxy server could be set up to allow files to be sent from the Internet to a computer on the intranet, but to block files from being sent from the corporate network out to the Internet-or vice versa. In this way, intranet administrators can block anyone outside the corporation from downloading vital corporate data. Or they can stop intranet users from downloading files which may contain viruses.

4.6.3.3 Logging

A proxy can also do logging.

4.6.3.4 Filter Requests

Proxy servers can also be used to filter requests. For example, a company might use a proxy server to prevent its employees from accessing a specific set of Web sites.

4.6.4 Types and Functions

Proxy servers implement one or more of the following functions:

4.6.4.1 Caching Proxy Server

A caching proxy server accelerates service requests by retrieving content saved from a previous request made by the same client or even other clients. Caching proxies keep local copies of frequently requested resources, allowing large organizations to significantly reduce their upstream bandwidth usage and cost, while significantly increasing performance. Most ISPs and large businesses have a caching proxy. Caching proxies were the first kind of proxy server. Some poorly-implemented caching proxies have had downsides (e.g., an inability to use user authentication). Some problems are described in RFC 3143 (Known HTTP Proxy/Caching Problems).

Another important use of the proxy server is to reduce the hardware cost. An organization may have many systems on the same network or under control of a single server, prohibiting the possibility of an individual connection to the Internet for each system. In such a case, the individual systems can be connected to one proxy server, and the proxy server connected to the main server.

4.6.4.2 Web Proxy

A proxy that focuses on World Wide Web traffic is called a "web proxy". The most common use of a web proxy is to serve as a web cache. Most proxy programs provide a means to deny access to URLs specified in a blacklist, thus providing content filtering. This is often used in a corporate, educational, or library environment, and anywhere else where content filtering is desired. Some web proxies reformat web pages for a specific purpose or audience, such as for cell phones and PDAs. Web Server is an intermediate server between client request and server resource.

4.6.4.3 Content-filtering web Proxy

A content-filtering web proxy server provides administrative control over the content that may be relayed through the proxy. It is commonly used in both commercial and non-commercial organizations (especially schools) to ensure that Internet usage conforms to acceptable use policy. In some cases users can circumvent the proxy, since there are services designed to proxy information from a filtered website through a non filtered site to allow it through the user's proxy.

Some common methods used for content filtering include: URL or DNS blacklists, URL regex filtering, MIME filtering, or content keyword filtering. Some products have been known to employ content analysis techniques to look for traits commonly used by certain types of content providers.

A content filtering proxy will often support user authentication, to control web access. It also usually produces logs, either to give detailed information about the URLs accessed by specific users, or to monitor bandwidth usage statistics. It may also communicate to daemon-based and/or ICAP-based antivirus software to provide security against virus and other malware by scanning incoming content in real time before it enters the network.

4.6.4.4 Anonymizing Proxy Server

An anonymous proxy server (sometimes called a web proxy) generally attempts to anonymize web surfing. There are different varieties of anonymizers. One of the more common variations is the open proxy. Because they are typically difficult to track, open proxies are especially useful to those seeking online anonymity, from political dissidents to computer criminals. Some users are merely interested in anonymity for added security, hiding their identities from potentially malicious websites for instance, or on principle, to facilitate constitutional human rights of freedom of speech, for instance. The server receives requests from the anonymizing proxy server, and thus does not receive information about the end user's address. However, the requests are not anonymous to the anonymizing proxy server, and so a degree of trust is present between the proxy server and the user. Many of them are funded through a continued advertising link to the user.

(a) Access control: Some proxy servers implement a logon requirement. In large organizations, authorized users must log on to gain access to the web. The organization can thereby track usage to individuals.

Some anonymizing proxy servers may forward data packets with header lines such as HTTP_VIA, HTTP_X_FORWARDED_FOR, or HTTP_FORWARDED, which may reveal the IP address of the client. Other anonymizing proxy servers, known as elite or high anonymity proxies, only include the REMOTE_ADDR header with the IP address of the proxy server, making it appear that the proxy server is the client. A website could still suspect a proxy is being used if the client sends packets which include a cookie from a previous visit that did not use the high anonymity proxy server. Clearing cookies, and possibly the cache, would solve this problem.

4.6.4.5 Hostile Proxy

Proxies can also be installed in order to eavesdrop upon the data-flow between client machines and the web. All accessed pages, as well as all forms submitted, can be captured and analyzed by the proxy operator. For this reason, passwords to online services (such as webmail and banking) should always be exchanged over a cryptographically secured connection, such as SSL.

4.6.4.6 Intercepting Proxy Server

An intercepting proxy combines a proxy server with a gateway or router (commonly with NAT capabilities). Connections made by client browsers through the gateway are diverted to the proxy without client-side configuration (or often knowledge). Connections may also be diverted from a SOCKS server or other circuit-level proxies.

Intercepting proxies are also commonly referred to as "transparent" proxies, or "forced" proxies, presumably because the existence of the proxy is transparent to the user, or the user is forced to use the proxy regardless of local settings.

***(a)* Purpose**

Intercepting proxies are commonly used in businesses to prevent avoidance of acceptable use policy, and to ease administrative burden, since no client browser configuration is required. This second reason however is mitigated by features such as Active Directory group policy, or DHCP and automatic proxy detection.

Intercepting proxies are also commonly used by ISPs in some countries to save upstream bandwidth and improve customer response times by caching. This is more common in countries where bandwidth is more limited (e.g. island nations) or must be paid for.

***(b)* Issues**

The diversion / interception of a TCP connection creates several issues. Firstly the original destination IP and port must somehow be communicated to the proxy. This is not always possible (e.g. where the gateway and proxy reside on different hosts). There is a class of cross site attacks which depend on certain behaviour of intercepting proxies that do not check or have access to information about the original (intercepted) destination. This problem can be resolved by using an integrated packet-level and application level appliance or software which is then able to communicate this information between the packet handler and the proxy.

Intercepting also creates problems for HTTP authentication, especially connection-oriented authentication such as NTLM, since the client browser believes it is talking to a server rather than a proxy. This can cause problems where an intercepting proxy requires authentication, then the user connects to a site which also requires authentication.

Finally intercepting connections can cause problems for HTTP caches, since some requests and responses become uncacheble by a shared cache. Therefore intercepting connections is generally discouraged. However due to the simplicity of deploying such systems, they are in widespread use.

***(c)* Implementation Methods**

Interception can be performed using Cisco's WCCP (Web Cache Control Protocol). This proprietary protocol resides on the router and is configured from the cache, allowing the cache to determine what ports and traffic is sent to it via transparent redirection from the router. This redirection can occur in one of two ways: GRE Tunneling (OSI Layer 3) or MAC rewrites (OSI Layer 2).

Once traffic reaches the proxy machine itself interception is commonly performed with NAT (Network Address Translation). Such setups are invisible to the client browser, but leave the proxy visible to the web server and other devices on the Internet side of the proxy. Recent releases of Linux and some BSD provide TPROXY (Transparent Proxy) which performs IP-level (OSI Layer 3) transparent interception and Spoofing of outbound traffic. Hiding the proxy IP address from other network devices.

***(d)* Detecting**

It is often possible to detect the use of an intercepting proxy server by comparing the client's external IP address to the address seen by an external web server, or sometimes by examining the HTTP headers received by a server. A number of sites have been created to address this issue, by reporting the user's IP address as seen by the site back to the user in a web page.

4.6.4.7 Transparent and Non-transparent Proxy Server

The term "transparent proxy" is most often used incorrectly to mean "intercepting proxy" (because the client does not need to configure a proxy and cannot directly detect that its requests are being proxied). However, RFC 2616 (Hypertext Transfer Protocol-HTTP/1.1) offers different definitions:

- A 'transparent proxy' is a proxy that does not modify the request or response beyond what is required for proxy authentication and identification".
- A 'non-transparent proxy' is a proxy that modifies the request or response in order to provide some added service to the user agent, such as group annotation services, media type transformation, protocol reduction, or anonymity filtering".

A security flaw in the way that transparent proxies operate was published by Robert Auger in 2009 and advisory by the Computer Emergency Response Team was issued listing dozens of affected transparent and intercepting proxy servers.

4.6.4.8 Forced Proxy

The term "forced proxy" is used was the user is being forced to use the proxy when they would prefer not to. This can be an "intercepting proxy" or a normal configured proxy where the direct (non-proxied) route is being blocked by a packet filter or similar.

It is also sometimes necessary (i.e. forced) to use a configured proxy due to issues with the interception of TCP connections and HTTP. For instance, interception of HTTP requests can affect the usability of a proxy cache, and can greatly affect certain authentication mechanisms. This is primarily because the client thinks it is talking to a server, and so request headers required by a proxy are unable to be distinguished from headers that may be required by an upstream server (esp authorization headers). Also the HTTP specification prohibits caching of responses where the request contained an authorization header.

4.6.4.9 Suffix Proxy

A suffix proxy server allows a user to access web content by appending the name of the proxy server to the URL of the requested content (e.g. "en.wikipedia.org.example.com"). Suffix proxy servers are easier to use than regular proxy servers. The concept appeared in 2003 in form of the IPv6Gate and in 2004 in form of the Coral Content Distribution Network, but the term suffix proxy was only coined in October 2008 by "6a.nl".

4.6.4.10 Open Proxy Server

Because proxies might be used to abuse, system administrators have developed a number of ways to refuse service to open proxies. Many IRC networks automatically test client systems for known types of open proxy. Likewise, an email server may be configured to automatically test e-mail senders for open proxies.

Groups of IRC and electronic mail operators run DNSBLs publishing lists of the IP addresses of known open proxies, such as AHBL, CBL, NJABL, and SORBS. The ethics of automatically testing clients for open proxies are controversial. Some experts, such as Vernon Schryver, consider such testing to be equivalent to an attacker portscanning the client host. Others consider the client to have solicited the scan by connecting to a server whose terms of service include testing.

4.6.4.11 Forward Proxy

The terms "forward proxy" and "forwarding proxy" are a general description of behaviour (forwarding traffic) and thus ambiguous. It is used to refer to a proxy able to retrieve from a wide range of sources (in most cases anywhere on Internet). Except for Reverse proxy, the types of proxies described on this article are more specialized sub-types of the general forward proxy concept.

4.6.4.12 Reverse Proxy Server

A reverse proxy is a proxy server that is installed in the neighborhood of one or more web servers. All traffic coming from the Internet and with a destination of one of the web servers goes through the proxy server. The use of "reverse" originates in its counterpart "forward proxy" since the reverse proxy sits closer to the web server and serves only a restricted set of websites.

There are several reasons for installing reverse proxy servers:

- Encryption / SSL acceleration: when secure web sites are created, the SSL encryption is often not done by the web server itself, but by a reverse proxy that is equipped with SSL acceleration hardware. See Secure Sockets Layer. Furthermore, a host can provide a single "SSL proxy" to provide SSL encryption for an arbitrary number of hosts; removing the need for a separate SSL Server Certificate for each host, with the downside that all hosts behind the SSL proxy have to share a common DNS name or IP address for SSL connections. This problem can partly be overcome by using the SubjectAltName feature of X.509 certificates.

- Load balancing: the reverse proxy can distribute the load to several web servers, each web server serving its own application area. In such a case, the reverse proxy may need to rewrite the URLs in each web page (translation from externally known URLs to the internal locations).
- Serve/cache static content: A reverse proxy can offload the web servers by caching static content like pictures and other static graphical content.
- Compression: the proxy server can optimize and compress the content to speed up the load time.
- Spoon feeding: reduces resource usage caused by slow clients on the web servers by caching the content the web server sent and slowly "spoon feeding" it to the client. This especially benefits dynamically generated pages.
- Security: the proxy server is an additional layer of defense and can protect against some OS and WebServer specific attacks. However, it does not provide any protection to attacks against the web application or service itself, which is generally considered the larger threat.
- Extranet Publishing: a reverse proxy server facing the Internet can be used to communicate to a firewalled server internal to an organization, providing extranet access to some functions while keeping the servers behind the firewalls. If used in this way, security measures should be considered to protect the rest of your infrastructure in case this server is compromised, as its web application is exposed to attack from the Internet.

4.6.4.13 Tunneling Proxy Server

A tunneling proxy server is a method of defeating blocking policies implemented using proxy servers. Tunneling proxy servers are used by people who have been blocked from viewing a particular web site. Most tunneling proxy servers are also proxy servers, of varying degrees of sophistication, which effectively implement "bypass policies".

A tunneling proxy server is a web-based page that takes a site that is blocked and "tunnels" it, allowing the user to view blocked pages. A famous example is elgooG, which allowed users in China to use Google after it had been blocked there. elgooG differs from most tunneling proxy servers in that it circumvents only one block.

A September 2007 report from Citizen Lab and BBC.co.uk recommended secure based proxies HTTP Tunnel, StupidCensorship, and CGIProxy. Alternatively, users could partner with individuals outside the censored network running Psiphon or Peacefire/tunneling proxy server. A more elaborate approach suggested was to run free tunneling software such as FreeGate, or pay services Anonymizer and Ghost Surf. Also listed were free application tunneling software PaperBus, Gpass and HTTP Tunnel, and pay application software Relakks and Guardster. Lastly, anonymous communication networks JAP ANON, Tor, and I2P offer a range of possibilities for secure publication and browsing. Other options include Garden and GTunnel by Garden Networks.

Students are able to access blocked sites (games, chatrooms, messenger, offensive material, internet pornography, social networking, etc.) through a tunneling proxy server. As fast as the filtering software blocks tunneling proxy servers, others spring up. However, in some cases the filter may still intercept traffic to the tunneling proxy server, thus the person who manages the filter can still see the sites that are being visited.

Another use of a tunneling proxy server is to allow access to country-specific services, so that Internet users from other countries may also make use of them. An example is country-restricted reproduction of media and webcasting. The use of tunneling proxy servers is usually safe with the exception that tunneling proxy server sites run by an untrusted third party can be run with hidden intentions, such as collecting personal information, and as a result users are typically advised against running personal data such as credit card numbers or passwords through a tunneling proxy server.

In some network configurations, clients attempting to access the proxy server are given different levels of access privilege on the grounds of their computer location or even the MAC address of the network card. However, if one has access to a system with higher access rights, one could use that system as a proxy server for which the other clients use to access the original proxy server, consequently altering their access privileges.

4.6.4.14 Content Filter

Many work places, schools, and colleges restrict the web sites and online services that are made available in their buildings. This is done either with a specialized proxy, called a content filter (both commercial and free products are available), or by using a cache-extension protocol such as ICAP, that allows plug-in extensions to an open caching architecture.

Requests made to the open internet must first pass through an outbound proxy filter. The web-filtering company provides a database of URL patterns (regular expressions) with associated content attributes. This database is updated weekly by site-wide subscription, much like a virus filter subscription. The administrator instructs the web filter to ban broad classes of content (such as sports, pornography, online shopping, gambling, or social networking). Requests that match a banned URL pattern are rejected immediately.

Assuming the requested URL is acceptable, the content is then fetched by the proxy. At this point a dynamic filter may be applied on the return path. For example, JPEG files could be blocked based on fleshtone matches, or language filters could dynamically detect unwanted language. If the content is rejected then an HTTP fetch error is returned and nothing is cached.

Most web filtering companies use an internet-wide crawling robot that assesses the likelihood that content is a certain type (e.g. "This content is 70% chance of porn, 40% chance of sports, and 30% chance of news" could be the outcome for one web page). The resultant database is then corrected by manual labor based on complaints or known flaws in the content-matching algorithms.

Web filtering proxies are not able to peer inside secure sockets HTTP transactions, assuming the chain-of-trust of SSL/TLS has not been tampered with. As a result, users wanting to bypass web filtering will typically search the internet for an open and anonymous HTTPS transparent proxy. They will then program their browser to proxy all requests through the web filter to this anonymous proxy. Those requests will be encrypted with https. The web filter cannot distinguish these transactions from, say, a legitimate access to a financial website. Thus, content filters are only effective against unsophisticated users.

As mentioned above, the SSL/TLS chain-of-trust does rely on trusted root certificate authorities; in a workplace setting where the client is managed by the organization, trust might be granted to a root certificate whose private key is known to the proxy. Concretely, a root certificate generated by the proxy is installed into the browser CA list by IT staff. In such scenarios, proxy analysis of the contents of a SSL/TLS transaction becomes possible. The proxy is effectively operating a man-in-the-middle attack, allowed by the client's trust of a root certificate the proxy owns.

A special case of web proxies is "CGI proxies". These are web sites that allow a user to access a site through them. They generally use PHP or CGI to implement the proxy functionality. These types of proxies are frequently used to gain access to web sites blocked by corporate or school proxies. Since they also hide the user's own IP address from the web sites they access through the proxy, they are sometimes also used to gain a degree of anonymity, called "Proxy Avoidance".

4.6.4.15 Risks Of Using Anonymous Proxy Servers

In using a proxy server (for example, anonymizing HTTP proxy), all data sent to the service being used (for example, HTTP server in a website) must pass through the proxy server before being sent to the service, mostly in unencrypted form. It is therefore a feasible risk that a malicious proxy server may record everything sent: including unencrypted logins and passwords.

By chaining proxies which do not reveal data about the original requester, it is possible to obfuscate activities from the eyes of the user's destination. However, more traces will be left on the intermediate hops, which could be used or offered up to trace the user's activities. If the policies and administrators of these other proxies are unknown, the user may fall victim to a false sense of security just because those details are out of sight and mind.

In what is more of an inconvenience than a risk, proxy users may find themselves being blocked from certain Web sites, as numerous forums and Web sites block IP addresses from proxies known to have spammed or trolled the site. Proxy bouncing can be used to maintain your privacy.

EXERCISES

1. What do you mean by DHCP?
2. How we can design DHCP networks?
3. Explain the various security considerations of DHCP?
4. Explain the various real world DHCP options?
5. How we can create a new scope?
6. How we can enable dynamic updates to a DNS server for earlier clients?
7. How we can set up a DHCP server cluster?
8. Explain the functions of DHCP?
9. What do you mean by IIS?
10. Explain the various methods to install IIS?
11. Explain the concept of virtual directories?
12. How IIS can connect to a web site?
13. Differentiate between local virtual directories and remote virtual directories?

14. Explain the concept of virtual directory creation wizard?
15. Explain the concept of FTP publishing service?
16. How we can understand by IIS 6 securities?
17. Explain the site-level administration for IIS?
18. Explain the directory-level administration?
19. Explain the file-level administration?
20. What do you mean by WINS?
21. Why we need WINS?
22. How we can configure the server to prepare for WINS?
23. How we can install WINS?
24. Explain the miscellaneous WINS functions?
25. How we can plan WINS server deployment?
26. How we can plan for WINS replication?
27. How we can configure replication?
28. Explain the various models of replication?
29. Explain the various issues of WINS?
30. How we can prevent split WINS registrations?
31. Explain the concept of database compaction?
32. Explain the various security issues of WINS?
33. Explain the WINS users group?
34. What do you mean by DNS?
35. How we can install DNS?
36. How we can configure DNS server wizard?
37. Explain the concept of creating zones?
38. How a DNS server interoperating with other DNS servers?
39. What do you understand by proxy servers?
40. How does proxy server works?
41. Explain the various types of proxy servers?
42. What are the advantages of proxy server?
43. Explain the various functions of proxy server?

CHAPTER 5

User, Group and Computer Accounts

5.1 INTRODUCTION

The central task of a network is to provide the customers (the users) with everything they need and clear away the clutter that hampers their progress. What they need includes access to the files, folders, applications, printers, and Internet connections that they require to do their jobs. What they don't need is any trouble getting at what they do need. The network administrator has additional needs, including shielding need-to-know material from those who don't need to know, protecting the network from malicious or otherwise dangerous users, and protecting the users from themselves. The key to meeting all these needs is the configuration of organizational units, groups, users, and Group Policies.

5.2 CREATING USER ACCOUNTS

Every person who has access to the network requires a user account. A user account makes it possible to do the following:

- Authenticate the identity of the person connecting to the network
- Control access to domain resources
- Audit actions performed using the account

Windows Server 2003 creates only two normal predefined accounts on a domain controller: the Administrator account, which is granted all rights and permissions, and the Guest account, which has limited rights. On domain controllers, there is also a KRBTGT key distribution account; on non-domain controllers, there are built-in special accounts for Help and Support and Remote Assistance. All other accounts are created by an administrator and are either domain accounts (which are valid throughout the domain by default) or local accounts (which are usable only on the machine on which they are created).

5.2.1 Naming User Accounts

In Active Directory, each user account has a principal name. The name consists of two parts, the security principal name and the principal name suffix. For existing Windows NT user accounts, the security principal name is by default the same as the name used to log on to the Windows NT domain. For new Windows Server 2003 user accounts, an administrator assigns the security principal name. The default principal name suffix is the DNS name of the root domain in the domain tree. So a user identified as EduardoP in a Windows NT domain has a principal name such as EduardoP@example.com in Windows Server 2003 (as well as Windows 2000 Server).

5.2.2 Account Options

Planning account options for users simplifies the process of creating accounts. Consider the following account options:

- Logon Hours By default, a user can log on at any hour of the day or night. For security reasons, you might want to restrict access by some or all users to certain times of the day or certain days of the week.
- Log On To By default, users can log on to all workstations. For security reasons, you can limit logon access to a particular machine or machines if you have the NetBIOS protocol installed in the domain. Without NetBIOS, Windows 2000 is unable to determine a specific logon location.
- Account Expiration You can decide whether you want to set accounts to expire.

For obvious reasons, it makes sense to set an expiration date for temporary employees to coincide with the end of their contracts. Other options-many other options-can be set in user accounts and are detailed in the section "Setting User Account Properties." The three options just listed are the most likely to be applied across large numbers of users.

5.2.3 Passwords

All your users must have well-chosen passwords and be required to change them periodically. Passwords should be chosen according to the guidelines in the Real World sidebar "Rules for Good Passwords." Set accounts to lockout when invalid passwords are entered. (Allow three attempts, to leave room for typographical errors by the user.)

5.2.3.1 Rules for good Passwords

A good password has the following characteristics:

- It is not a rotation or reuse of the characters in a logon name. (How many brain cells does it take to figure this one out?)
- It contains at least two alphabetic characters and one non-alphabetic character.
- It is at least seven characters long.
- It isn't the user's name or initials, the initials of his or her children or significant other, or any of these items combined with other commonly available personal data such as a birth date, telephone number, or license plate number.

Among the best passwords are alphanumeric acronyms of phrases that have a meaning to the user but are not likely to be known to others. This makes the password easy for the user to remember, while at the same time making it hard for an outsider to guess. Another good password isn't a word at all but a "passphrase"-an entire phrase or sentence, complete with spaces and punctuation. It pays to educate your users about passwords and password privacy, but most of all, it pays to heed your own advice: make sure the password you select for administration is a good password, and change it frequently. Doing so will help you avoid the consequences of having somebody break into your system and wreak havoc in your very own kingdom. If users dial in to the network from home or other remote sites, include more security than domain-level password authorization.

Administrators should have two accounts on the system: one administrative account and one normal user account. Use the normal user account unless you are performing administrative tasks like installing software or configuring accounts. Because of the privileges associated with administrative accounts, they are prime targets for intruders.

5.2.4 Creating A Domain User Account

Domain user accounts can be created in the default Users container, or you can make an OU to hold domain user accounts. The following steps describe how to add a domain user account:

1. Choose Active Directory Users and Computers from the Administrative Tools menu.
2. Right-click the container in which you want to create the account, point to New, and then choose User from the shortcut menu.
3. Provide the user's first and last name. The Full Name box is filled in automatically. The full name must be unique in the OU where the user account is created.
4. Provide the user logon name based on your naming convention. (See Figure 5.1.) This name must be unique in Active Directory. The pre-Windows 2000 logon name is filled in automatically. This is the name used to log on from computers running older Windows operating systems such as Windows NT. Click Next.

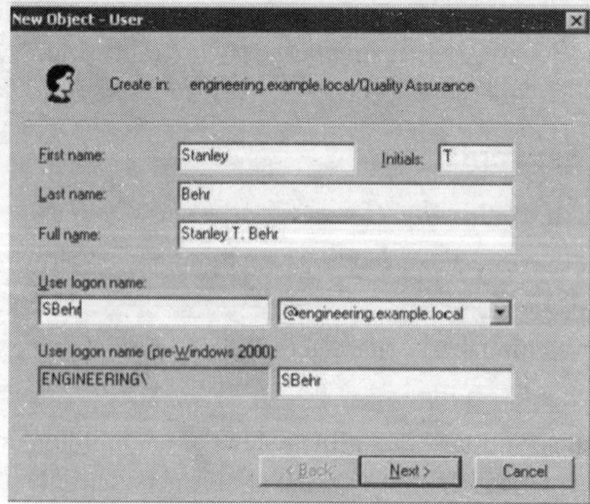

Figure 5.1 Creating a new user

5. Provide a password, and set password policies. Click Next. A confirmation screen appears.
6. If the details of the account you are about to create are correct, click Finish. Otherwise, click Back to make corrections.

At this point, the new user account is added to the OU with default settings. It's unlikely that the default settings are exactly what you want, so you need to adjust the properties of the new account, as described in the section "Setting User Account Properties."

5.2.5 Creating a Local User Account

A local account can't log on to the domain and therefore has access only to the resources on the computer where it's created and used. The following steps describe how to create a local user account:

1. Right-click My Computer, and choose Manage from the shortcut menu.
2. In the console tree, click Local Users And Groups. Right-click Users, and choose New User from the shortcut menu.
3. In the New User dialog box, supply the user name, full name, and description.
4. Provide a password, and set password policies. Click Create. At this point, the new user account is created with default settings. Local accounts can belong to locally created groups (on the single computer).

5.2.6 Setting User Account Properties

The Properties window for a domain user can have up to 13 tabs, depending on the domain's setup; Table 9-6 describes these tabs. Information entered in the Properties window can be used as the basis for a search in Active Directory. For example, you can find a user's telephone number or department by searching for the user's last name. The following steps describe how to set the properties for a domain user account:

1. Choose Active Directory Users And Computers from the Administrative Tools menu.
2. Open the OU where the domain user account was created.
3. Double-click the user account to open the Properties window.
4. Click the tab for the properties you want to set. Make the changes, and click OK when you're finished.

Table 5.1 Tabs in the Properties window for a domain user account

Tab	Description
General	Documents the unser's name, description, office location, telephone number, e-mail address, and Web address
Address	Documents the user's physical address
Account	Documents the logon name, logon restrictions, passward options, and whether the account expries
Profile	Shows the user's profile path, the path of any script that runs when the user logs on, the path to a home folder, any automatic drive connections
Telephones	Lists additional telephone numbers such as for a pager, cellular phone, or Internet phone
Organization	Documents the user's title, department, company, manager, and direct reports
Remote Control	Configures the degree to which an administrator can view or control the user's Terminal Services sessions

Tab	Description
Terminal Services Profile	Documents the user's Terminal Services profile
COM+	Documents the user's participation in COM+ partition sets
Member Of	Lists the user's group memberships
Dial-In	Documents the user's dial-in access
Environment	Settings for the user's Termianal Services environment
Sessions	Terminal Services disconnect and reconnect seetings

5.2.7 Testing User Accounts

As you develop different types of user accounts, it's advisable to test them. Create a dummy account with the memberships and restrictions you're planning on using. Then log on to a client machine and see whether the account produces the results you expect by doing the following:

- Test restrictions to logon hours and passwords by attempting to bypass them.
- Test home folders and profiles to see whether they are actually created.
- Test roaming profiles by logging on from various machines.
- Test group memberships by performing a task that membership in the group is supposed to allow (or deny), such as logging on to a server.

5.3 MANAGING USER ACCOUNTS

On a large, busy network, managing user accounts is a continual process of additions, deletions, and changes. Although these tasks aren't difficult, they can be time-consuming and need to be managed carefully.

5.3.1 Finding a User Account

On small networks, it's easy enough to locate a user under Active Directory Users and Computers. On a larger network, more advanced search techniques must be brought to bear. To search for a particular user account, choose Active Directory Users and Computers from the Administrative Tools menu and on the toolbar, click the Find icon, shown here:

This opens the Find Users, Contacts, And Groups dialog box. Click the drop-down arrow in the Find box and you see that you can also use this tool to search for computers, printers, shared folders, OUs, and more. (See Figure 5.2.)

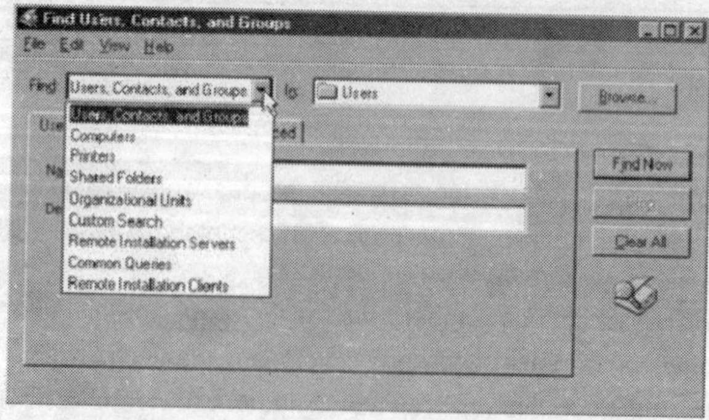

Figure 5.2 The Find tool allows for fairly specific searches

Select the scope of your search in the In box. Type a name or part of a name, and click Find Now. A search for a portion of a name returns all users, contacts, and groups with that element in their names.

Choose another option in Find and the possible search parameters adjust. For example, choose Common Queries in the Find list and you have an easy way to search for disabled accounts or users with non expiring passwords. For even more in-depth searches, click the Advanced tab and select criteria from the Field drop-down list. Searches can be made on virtually every bit of information in a user, contract, group, or other object record. Figure 5.3 shows a search for a printer that can print double-sided on legal-sized paper and can staple and can print at least four pages per minute and has a resolution of 600 dpi or greater. A tall order, but if it exists, it will be found.

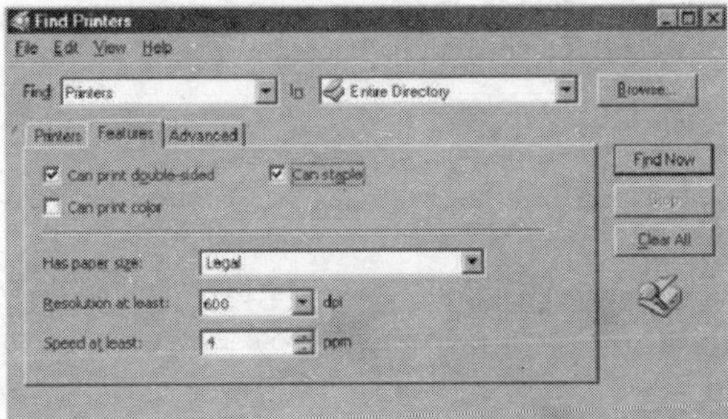

Figure 5.3 Searching for printers in Active Directory using specific criteria

5.3.2 Disabling and Enabling a User Account

If you need to deactivate a domain user account for some period of time but not delete it permanently, you can disable it. Find the user account, right-click the user name, and select Disable Account from the shortcut menu (as shown in Figure 5.4). An informational box opens telling you that the object has been disabled, and a red circle with an "X" appears over the user account's icon. Enable a disabled account by reversing the process, choosing Enable Account from the shortcut menu.

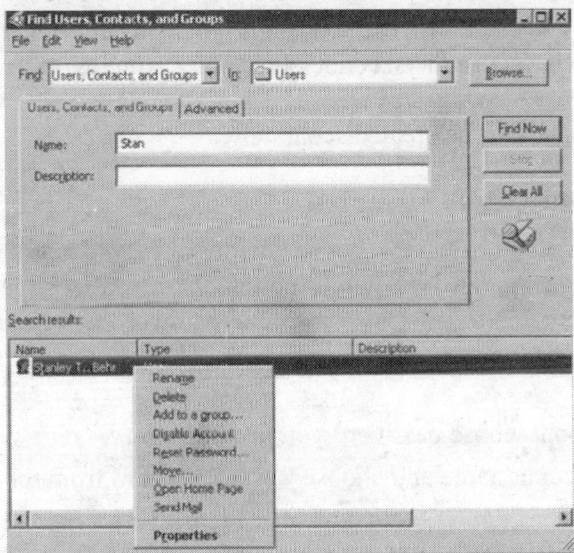

Figure 5.4 Disabling a user account

5.3.3 Deleting a User Account

Each user account in the domain has an associated SID that is unique and never reused, which means that a deleted account is completely deleted. If you delete Jeremy's account and later change your mind, you have to re-create not only the account but also the permissions, settings, group memberships, and other properties that the original user account had. For that reason, if there's any doubt about whether an account might be needed in the future, it's best to disable it and not perform the deletion until you're sure it won't be needed again.

However, accounts do have to be deleted at regular intervals. Just find the user account, right-click the user name, and select Delete from the shortcut menu. An Active Directory dialog box prompts you to confirm the deletion. Click Yes and the account is deleted.

5.3.4 Moving a User Account

Moving a user account from one container to another is similarly easy. Find the user account in Active Directory. Right-click and select Move from the shortcut menu. In the Move dialog box, select the destination container and click OK. Or just drag and drop the account into its new destination container.

Using the Ctrl and Shift keys, you can select multiple user accounts to move at once.

5.3.5 Renaming a User Account

On occasion, a user account might need to be renamed. For example, if you have an account configured with an assortment of rights, permissions, and group memberships for a particular position and a new person is taking over that position, you can change the first, last, and user logon names to fit the new person. The following steps describe how to rename an existing user account:

1. Find the existing user account. Right-click the user name, and choose Rename from the shortcut menu. (You can also slowly click the user name twice.)
2. Press the Delete key and then the Enter key to open the Rename User dialog box.
3. Type the changes, and click OK. The account is renamed, and all permissions and other settings remain intact. Other data in the account's Properties window-such as address, phone number, and so forth-have to be changed as well. If a home folder exists, it will not be renamed for the new user and will have to be created separately.

5.3.6 Resetting a User's Password

For passwords to be effective, they must not be obvious or easy to guess. However, when passwords are not obvious or easy to guess, they are often forgotten. When a user forgets his or her password, you can reset it. The best practice is to reset it to a simple password and require the user to change the password the next time he or she logs on to the network. The following steps describe how to reset a password:

1. Find the user account whose password you need to reset.
2. Right-click the account name and choose Reset Password from the shortcut menu.
3. In the Reset Password dialog box (shown in Figure 5.5), type the new password twice, and select the User Must Change Password At Next Logon option. Click OK to implement the change.

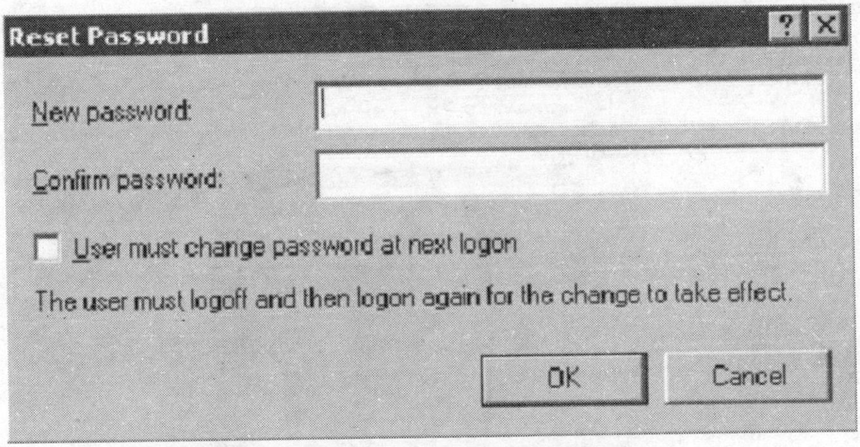

Reset Password

New password:

Confirm password:

☐ User must change password at next logon

The user must logoff and then logon again for the change to take effect.

OK Cancel

Figure 5.5 Resetting a user's password

5.3.7 Unlocking a User Account

If a user violates a group policy, such as exceeding the limit for bad logon attempts or failing to change an expired password, Active Directory locks the account. When an account is locked, it cannot be used to log on to the system. When the penitent comes pleading for reinstatement and after you deliver a few firm words on the importance of following rules, takes the following steps to unlock the user account:

1. Find the locked account in Active Directory. Right-click the account and choose Properties from the shortcut menu.
2. In the Properties window, click the Account tab.
3. Clear the check box next to Account Is Locked Out. Click OK. By default, Group Policy does not lock accounts because of failed logon attempts-you make this setting for security reasons.

5.4 USING HOME FOLDERS

Home directories or folders are repositories you can provide on a network server for users' documents. Placing home folders on a network file server has several advantages:

- Backup of user documents is centralized.
- Users can access their home folders from any client computer.
- Home folders can be accessed from clients running any Microsoft operating system (including MS-DOS and all versions of Windows)

The contents of home folders are not part of user profiles, so they don't affect network traffic when users log on. (A home folder can also be on a client computer, but that defeat much of its purpose.)

5.4.1 Creating Home Folders on a Server

The following steps describe how to create a home folder on a network file server:

1. On the server, create a new folder for the home folders. Name it Home Folders. Right- click the new folder, and choose Sharing And Security from the shortcut menu.
2. Click the Sharing tab, and select the Share This Folder option. 3. Click the Security tab, and assign Full Control to the Users group (as shown in Figure 5.6).

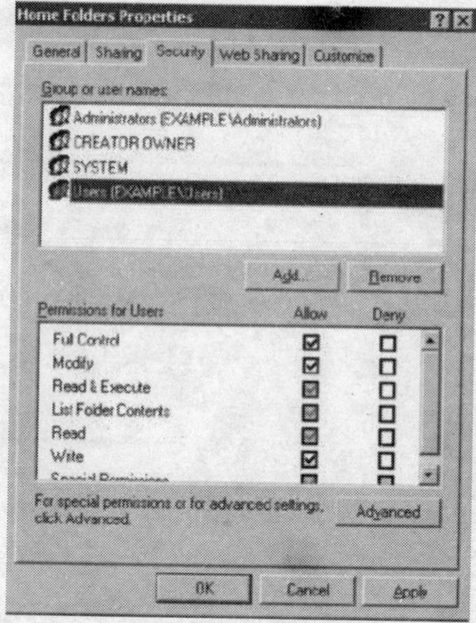

Figure 5.6 Giving full control to Users

5.4.2 Providing Home Folders to Users

To provide a user with a home folder, you must add the path for the folder to the user account's properties. Follow these steps to give a user access to a home folder:

1. Find the user account in Active Directory. Right-click the user name, and choose Properties from the shortcut menu.
2. Click the Profile tab. In the Home Folder area, click the Connect option and specify a drive letter to use to connect to the file server.
3. In the To box, specify the UNC name for the connection. For example, \\server_name\shared_folder\user_logon_name.

If you use the variable %username%, as shown in Figure 5.7, a home folder is given the user's logon name.

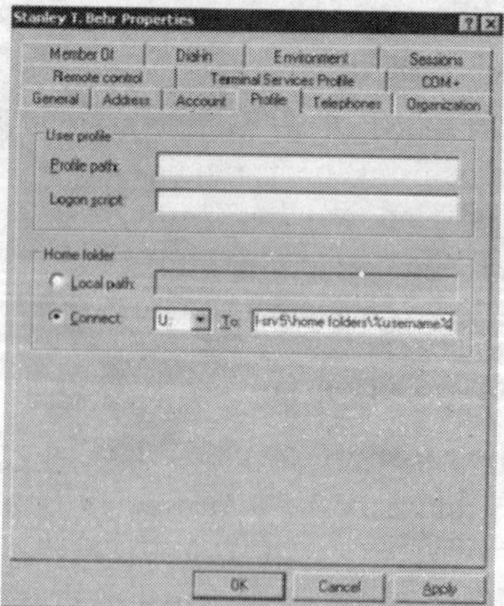

Figure 5.7 Specifying a home folder

5.5 MAINTAINING USER PROFILES

A profile is an environment specifically customized for a user. The profile contains the desktop and program settings for the user. Every user has a profile, whether the administrator configures one or not, because a default profile is automatically created for each user who logs on to a computer. Profiles offer a number of advantages:

- Multiple users can use the same computer, with the settings for each user restored at logon time to the same state as when he or she logged off.
- Desktop changes made by one user do not affect any other user.
- If user profiles are stored on a server, they can follow users to any computer on a network running Windows Server 2003, Windows XP Professional, Windows 2000, or Windows NT 4. From an administrator's standpoint, the information in the profile can be a valuable tool for setting up default user profiles for all users on the network or for customizing default profiles for different departments or job classifications. You can also set up mandatory profiles that allow a user to make changes to the desktop while logged on but not to save any of the changes. A mandatory profile always looks exactly the same every time a user logs on. There are three types of profiles:

  (a) **Local profiles:** Profiles made on a computer when a user logs on. The profile is specific to a user, local to that computer, and stored on the local computer's hard disk.

  (b) **Roaming profiles:** Profiles created by an administrator and stored on a server. These profiles follow a user to any computer on a network running Windows Server 2003, Windows XP Professional, Windows 2000, or Windows NT 4.

  (c) **Mandatory profiles:** Roaming profiles that can be changed only by an administrator.

5.5.1 What's Stored in a Profile?

All profiles start out as a copy of the Default User profile that is installed on every computer running Windows Server 2003, Windows XP Professional, Windows 2000, and Windows NT 4. Registry data for Default User is in the Ntuser.dat file contained in the Default User profile. Inside each profile are the following folders:

- Application Data Program-specific settings determined by the program manufacturer plus specific user security settings
- Cookies Messages sent to a Web browser by a Web server and stored locally to track user information and preferences (not in Windows NT 4)
- Desktop Desktop files, folders, shortcuts, and the desktop appearance
- Favorites Shortcuts to favorite locations, particularly Web sites
- Local Settings Application data, History, and Temporary files (not in Windows NT 4)
- My Documents User documents and My Pictures, which contains user graphics files (not in Windows NT 4)
- NetHood Shortcuts to My Network Places

- PrintHood Shortcuts to items in the Printers folder
- Recent Shortcuts to the most recently accessed folders and files
- SendTo Items on the Send To menu
- Start Menu Items on the user's Start menu
- Templates Application templates

By default, only the Cookies, Desktop, Favorites, My Documents, and Start Menu folders are visible in Microsoft Windows Explorer. The other folders are hidden; to see them select Folder Options, click the View tab, and select Show Hidden Files And Folders.

5.5.2 Local Profiles

Local profiles are created on computers when individual users log on. On a computer upgraded from Windows NT 4, the profile is stored in the Profiles folder on the system root partition. On a computer with a new installation of Windows Server 2003, Windows XP Professional, Windows 2000 Server, or Windows 2000 Professional, the user profile is in the Documents And Settings folder (as shown in Figure 5.8).

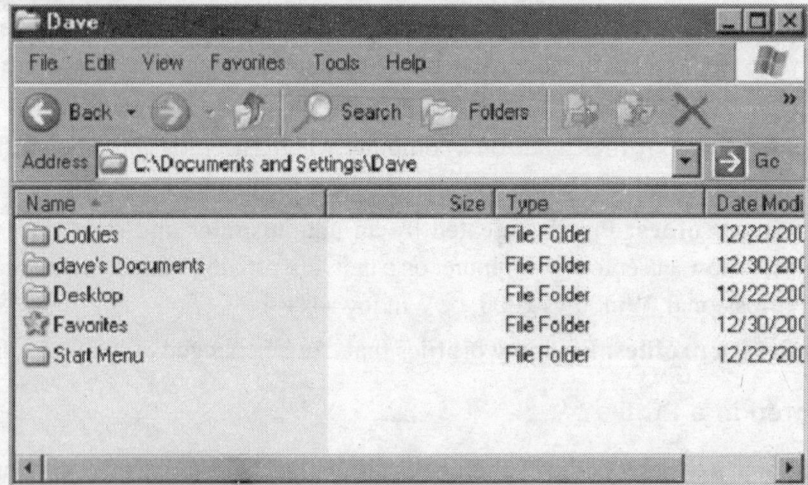

Figure 5.8 A user's local profile set up at the first logon event

The first time a user logs on to a computer, a profile folder is generated for the user, and the contents of the Default User folder are copied into it. Any changes made to the desktop by the user are saved in that user's profile when he or she logs off. If a user has a local account on the computer as well as a domain account and logs on at different times using both accounts, the user will have two profile folders on the local computer: one for when the user logs on to the domain using the domain user account and one for when the user logs on locally to the computer. The local profile is shown with the logon name. The domain profile is also shown with the logon name but has the domain name appended to it.

5.5.3 Roaming Profiles

Roaming profiles are a great advantage for users who frequently use more than one computer. A roaming profile is stored on a server and, after the user's logon attempt is authenticated in the directory service, the profile is copied to the local computer. This allows a user to have the same desktop, application configuration, and local settings at any machine running Windows Server 2003, Windows XP Professional, Windows 2000, or Windows NT 4.

Here's how it works. You assign a location on a server for user profiles and create a folder shared with users who are to have roaming profiles. You type a path to that folder in the user's Properties window. The next time the user logs on to a computer, the profile from the server are downloaded to the local computer. When the user logs off, the profile is saved both locally and in the user profile path location. Specifying the user profile path is all it takes to turn a local profile into a roaming profile, available anywhere in the domain.

When the user logs on again, the profile on the server is compared to the copy on the local computer, and the more recent copy is loaded for the user. If the server isn't available, the local copy is used. If the server isn't available and this is the first time the user has logged on to the computer, a user profile is created locally using the Default User profile. When a profile isn't downloaded to a local computer because of server problems, the roaming profile is not updated when the user logs off.

5.5.4 Setting Up Roaming Profiles

Setting up roaming profiles is easy-you assign a location on a server and complete the following steps:

1. Create a shared folder for the profiles on the server.
2. On the Profile tab in the user account Properties window, provide a path to the shared folder, such as \\server_name\shared_profile_folder\%username%.

Figure 5.9 shows an example of a path for a roaming profile. When you use the variable %username%, Windows Server 2003 automatically replaces the variable with the user account name.

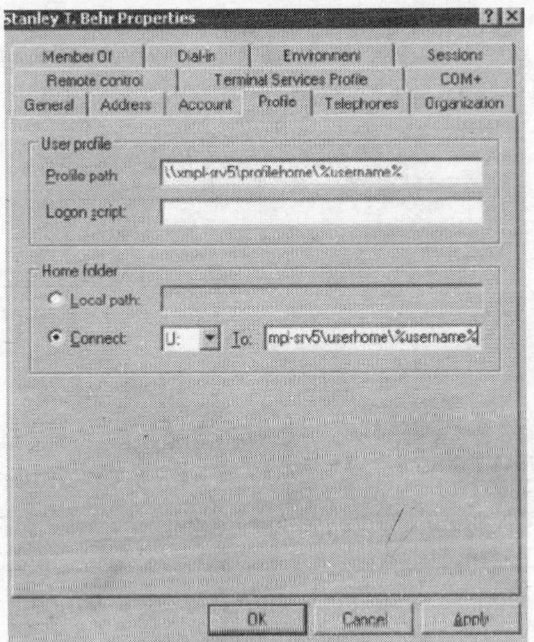

Figure 5.9 Setting a path for a roaming profile

After you create a shared profile folder on a server and supply a profile path in the user account, a roaming profile is enabled. The user's configuration of his or her desktop is copied and stored on the server and is available to the user from any computer. Most of the time, though, you don't want to send your users off to fend for themselves. Life is easer for them, and for you, if users are assigned a customized profile that is already set up with appropriate shortcuts, network connections, and Start menu items. For this, you need to set up customized profiles.

5.5.5 Creating Customized Roaming Profiles

Creating customized roaming profiles is a simple-albeit multistep-process:

1. Create a user account with a descriptive name such as District Managers or Sales Staff. This is just a "blank" user account that you use to create a template for the customized configuration.
2. Log on using the template account, and create the desktop settings you want, including applications, shortcuts, appearance, network connections, printers, and so forth.
3. Log off the template account. Windows Server 2003 creates a user profile on the system root drive in the Documents and Settings folder.
4. Log on again using an administrator account. Find the accounts that are going to have this customized roaming profile.
5. In each account, click the Profile tab, and in the Profile Path box, type \\server_name\profile_folder\%username%. Click OK.
6. In Control Panel, select System.
7. Click the Advanced tab, and then in the User Profiles section, click Settings. Highlight the template account-in this case Team Leaders-and click Copy To.
8. In the Copy To dialog box, type the path of the profiles folder on the server, \\server_name\roaming_profiles_folder\username. Note that this time you must use the actual name of the roaming profile or the profile will be stored under the name of whoever is logged on.
9. In the Permitted To Use area, click Change to give the appropriate group permission to use the profile. (See Figure 5.10.) Click OK to copy the template profile.

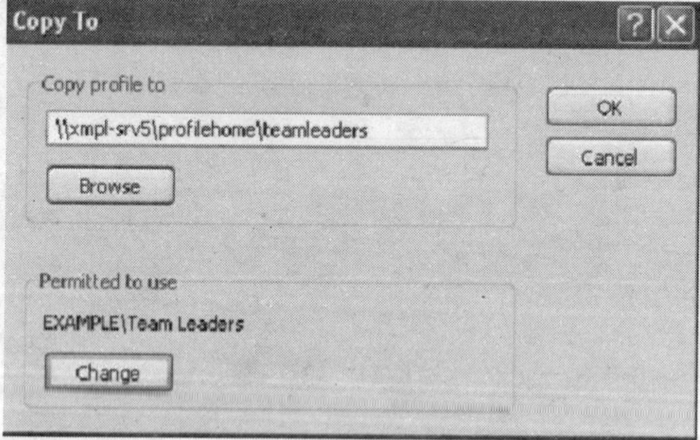

Figure 5.10 A template roaming profile is made available to all members of a Team Leaders group

5.5.6 Using Mandatory Profiles

If you're going to all the trouble of assigning customized profiles, you undoubtedly want to make the profiles mandatory. To change a profile into a mandatory profile, you need only rename the hidden file Ntuser.dat to Ntuser.man.

5.5.6.1 Assigning A Logon Script To A User Profile

Logon scripts can be assigned by profile or through Group Policy. The following steps describe how to assign a script to a profile:

1. Choose Active Directory Users And Computers from the Administrative Tools menu.
2. In the console tree, click Users. Right-click the user account, and choose Properties.
3. Click the Profile tab, and type the name of the logon script in the Logon Script box.
4. Click OK when you're finished.

Windows Server 2003 always looks for logon scripts in the same place-on the authenticating domain controller at the path %SystemRoot%\SYSVOL\sysvol\domain_ name\scripts. Scripts in this folder can be typed in the Logon Script path by name only, as shown in Figure 5.11. If you use folders inside the Scripts folder, you must show that part of the path in the Logon Script path. Table 5.1 shows the special variables that can be used when creating logon scripts. Logon scripts can also be created in VBScript and JScript. Replication of logon scripts to all domain controllers is automatic on NTFS volumes on servers running Windows Server 2003 and Windows 2000 Server. Scripts on FAT16 and FAT 32 partitions must be replicated manually.

Figure 5.11 A logon script that's located inside the Scripts folder

Table 5.1 Logon script variables

Variable	Description
%homedrive%	Letter of the drive containing the user's home directory on the user's local workstion
%homepath%	Full path of the user's home directory
%os%	User's operating system
%processor_architercture%	Processor type on the user's workstation
%processor_level%	Processor level of the user's workstation
%userdomain%	Domain where the user's account is defined
%username%	Account user name

5.5.7 Creating and Managing User Objects

Active Directory requires the verification of an individual's identity-a process called authentication-before that individual can access resources. The cornerstone of authentication is the user account, with its user logon name, password, and unique security identifier (SID). During logon, Active Directory authenticates the user name and password entered by the user. The security subsystem can then build the security access token that represents that user. The access token contains the user accounts SID, as well as the SIDs of groups to which the user belongs. That token can then be used to verify user rights assignments, including the right to log on locally to the system, and to authorize access to resources secured by access control lists (ACLs).

The user account is integrated into the Active Directory user object. The user object includes not just the user's name, password, and SID, but also contact information, such as telephone numbers and addresses; organizational information including job title, direct reports and manager; group memberships; and configuration such as roaming profile, terminal services, remote access, and remote control settings. This lesson will review and enhance your understanding of user objects in Active Directory.

5.5.7.1 Creating user objects with Active Directory users and Computers

You can create a user object with the Active Directory Users and Computers snap-in. Although user objects can be created in the domain or any of the default containers, it is best to create a user in an organizational unit, so that administrative delegation and Group Policy Objects (GPOs) can be fully leveraged. To create a user object, select the container in which you want to create the object, click the Action menu, then choose New and choose User. You must be a member of the Enterprise Admins, Domain Admins, or Account Operators groups, or you must have been delegated administrative permissions to create user objects in the container. If you do not have sufficient permissions to create user objects, the New User command will be unavailable to you.

The New Object-User dialog box appears, as shown in Figure 5.12. The first page of the New Object-User dialog box requests properties related to the user name. Table 5.2 describes the properties that appear on the first page of the dialog box.

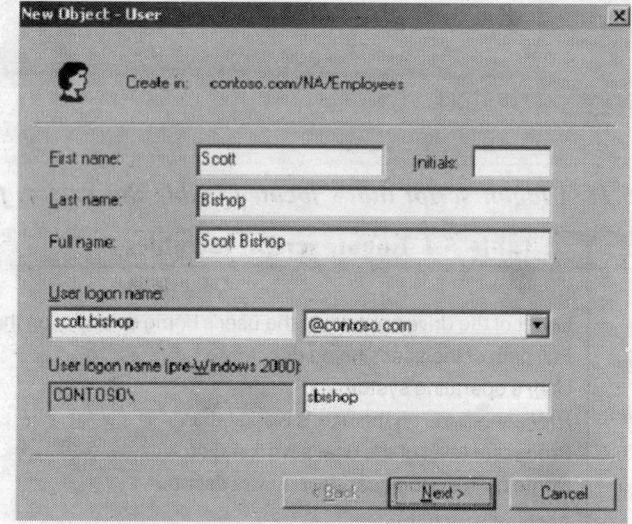

Figure 5.12 The New Object-User dialog box

Table 5.2 User Properties in the First Page of the New Object-User Dialog Box

Property	Description
First Name	The user's first name. Not required.
Initials	The middle initials of the user's name. Not required.
Last Name	The user's last name. Not required.
Full Name	The user's full name. If you enter values for the first or last name, the full name property is populated automatically. However, you can easily modify the suggested value. The field is required. The name entered here generates several user object properties, specifically CN (common name), DN (distinguished name), anme, and display Name.

Property	Description
	Because CN must be unique within a container, the name entered here must be unique relative to all other objects in the OU (or other container) in which you create the user object.
User Logon Name	The user principle name (UPN) consists of a logon name and a UPN suffix which is, by default, the DNS name of the domain in which you create the object. The property is required and the entire UPN, in the format *logon-name@UPN-suffix,* must be unique within the Active Director forest. A sample UPN would be *someone@contoso.come.* The UPN can be used to log on to any Microsoft Windows system running Window 2000, Windows XP, or Windows Server 2003.
User Logon Name (Pre-Windows 2000)	This logon name is used to log on from down-level clients, such as Microsoft Windows 95, Windows 98, Windows Millennium Edition (Windows Me), Windows NT 4, or Windows NT 3.51. This field is required and must be unique within the domain.

Once you have entered the values in the first page of the New Object-User dialog box, click Next. The second page of the dialog box, shown in Figure 5.13, allows you to enter the user password and to set account flags.

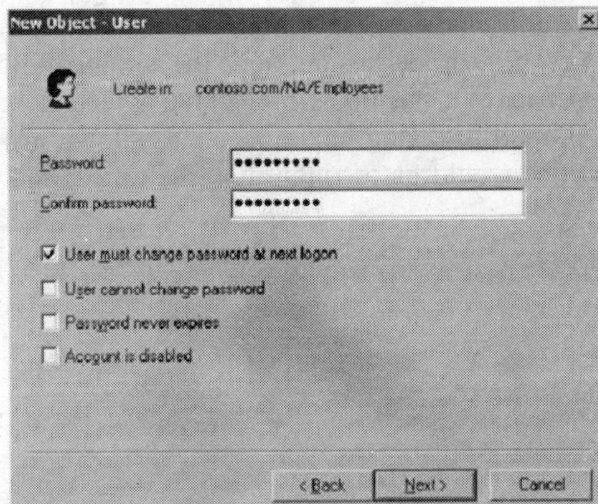

Figure 5.13 Second page of the New Object-User dialog box

The properties available in the second page of the New Object-User dialog box are summarized in Table 5.3.

Table 5.3 User Properties in the Second Page of the New Object-User Dialog Box

Property	Description
Password	The password that is used to authenticate the user. For security reasons, you should always assign a password. The password is masked as you type it.
Confirm Password	Confirm the password by typing it a second time to make sure you typed it correctly.
User Must Change Pass word At next Logon	Select this check box if you want the user to change the password you have entered the first time he or she logs on. You cannot select this option if you have selected Password Never Expires. Selecting this option will automatically clear the mutually exclusive option User Cannot Change Password.
User Cannot Change Password	Select this check box if you have more than one person using the smae domain user account (such as Guest) or to maintain control over user account passwords. This option is commonly used to manage service account passwords. You cannot select this option if you have selected User Must Change Password At Next Logon.

Property	Description
Password Never Expires	Select this check box if you never want the password to expire. This option will automatically clear the User Must Change Password At Next Logon setting, as they are mutually exclusive. This option is commonly used to manage service account passwords.
Account Is Disabled	Select this check box to disable the user account, for example, when creating an object for a newly hired employee who does not yet need access to the network.

Some of the account options listed in Table 5.3 have the potential to contradict policies set in the domain policies. For example, the default domain policy implements a best practice of disabling the storing of passwords using reversible encryption. However, in the rare circumstances that require reversible encryption, the user account property, Store Password Using Reversible Encryption, will take precedence for that specific user object. Similarly, the domain may specify a maximum password age, or that users must change password at next logon. If a user object is configured such that Password never expires, that configuration will override the domain's policies.

Managing User Objects with Active Directory Users And Computers When creating a user, you are prompted to configure the most common user properties, including logon names and password. However, user objects support numerous additional properties that you can configure at any time using Active Directory Users And Computers. These properties facilitate the administration of, and the searching for, an object. To configure the properties of a user object, select the object, click the Action menu, and then choose Properties. The user's Properties dialog box appears, as shown in Figure 5.14. An alternative way to view an object's properties would be to right-click the object and select Properties from the shortcut menu.

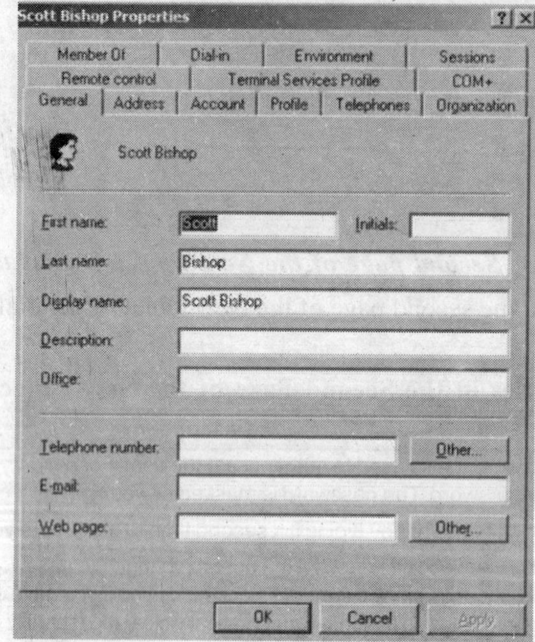

Figure 5.14 The user's Properties dialog box

The property pages in the Properties dialog box expose properties that fall into several broad categories:

- **Account properties:** the Account tab These properties include those that are configured when you create a user object, including logon names, password and account flags.

- **Personal information:** the General, Address, Telephones, and Organization tabs The General tab exposes the name properties that are configured when you create a user object.
- **User configuration management:** the Profile tab Here you can configure the user's profile path, logon script, and home folder locations.
- **Group membership:** the Member Of tab You can add and remove user groups, and set the user's primary group.
- **Terminal services:** the Terminal Services Profile, Environment, Remote Control, and Sessions tabs These four tabs allow you to configure and manage the user's experience when they are connected to a Terminal Services session.\
- **Remote access:** the Dial-in tab Allows you to enable and configure remote access permission for a user.
- **Applications:** the COM+ tab Assigns Active Directory COM+ partition sets to the user. This feature, new to Windows Server 2003, facilitates the management of distributed applications.

5.6 ACCOUNT PROPERTIES

Of particular note are the user's account properties, on the Account tab of the user's Properties dialog box. An example appears in Figure 5.15.

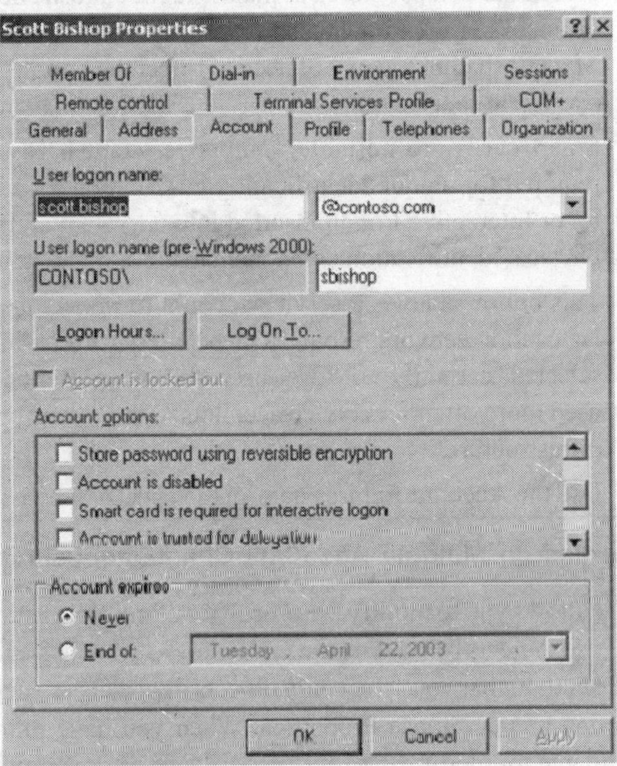

Figure 5.15 The user Account tab

Several of these properties were discussed in Table 5.3. Those properties were configured when creating the user object and can be modified, as can a larger set of account properties, using the Account tab. Several properties are not necessarily self-explanatory, and deserve definition in Table 5.4.

Table 5.4 User Account Properties

Property	Description
Logon Hours	Click Logon Hours to configure the hours during which a user is allowed to log on to the network.
Log On To	Click Log On To if you want to limit the workstations to which the user can log on. This is called Computer Restrictions in other parts of the user interface. You must have NetBIOS over TCP/IP enabled for this feature to restrict users because it uses the computer name, rather than the Media Access Control (MAC) address of its network card, to restrict logon.
Store Password	This option, which stores the password in Active Directory without using Using Reversible Active Directory's powerful, nonreversible encryption hashing algorithm,
Encryption	exists to support applications that require knowledge of the user password. If it is not absolutely required, do not enable this option because it weakens password security significantly. Passwords stored using reversible encryption are similar to those stored as plaintext. Macintosh clients using the AppleTalk protocol require knowledge of the user password. If a user logs on using a Macintosh client, you will need to select the option to Store password using reversible encryption.
Smart Card Is	Smart cards are portable, tamper-resistant hardware devices that store required for unique identification information for a user. They are attached to, or Interactive Logon inserted into, a system and provides an additional, physical identification component to the authentication process.
Account Is Trusted	This option enables a service account to impersonate a user to access For Delegation network resources on behalf of a user. This option is not typically selected, certainly not for a user object representing a human being. It is used more often for service accounts in three-tier (or multi-tier) application infrastructures.
Account Expires	Use the Account Expires controls to specify when an account expires.

5.6.1 Managing Properties on Multiple Accounts Simultaneously

Windows Server 2003 allows you to modify the properties of multiple user accounts simultaneously. You simply select several user objects by holding the CTRL key as you click each user, or using any other multiselection options. Be certain that you select only objects of one class, such as users. Once you have multiselected, on the Action menu, choose Properties. When you have multiselected user objects, a subset of properties is available for modification.

- General tab Description, Office, Telephone Number, Fax, Web Page, E-mail
- Account tab UPN Suffix, Logon Hours, Computer Restrictions (logon workstations), all Account Options, Account Expires

- Address Street, PO Box, City, State/Province, ZIP/Postal Code, Country/Region
- Profile Profile Path, Logon Script, and Home Folder
- Organization Title, Department, Company, Manager

5.7 GROUP AND COMPUTER ACCOUNTS

By definition, groups in the Microsoft Windows Server 2003 family are Active Directory directory service or local computer objects that can contain users, contacts, computers, or other groups. In general, though, a group is usually a collection of user accounts. The point of groups is to simplify administration by allowing the network administrator to assign rights and permissions to groups rather than individual users.

Windows Server 2003 allows two group types: security and distribution. Almost all groups used by Windows Server 2003 and Microsoft Windows 2000 Server are security groups because they're the only groups through which permissions can be assigned. Each security group is also assigned a group scope, which defines how permissions are assigned to the group's members. Programs that can search Active Directory can also use security groups for non-security purposes, such as sending e-mail to a group of users. Distribution groups, on the other hand, are not security-enabled and can be used only with e-mail applications to send e-mail to sets of users.

5.7.1 Group Scope

Group scope defines how permissions are assigned to the group members. Windows Server 2003 groups, both security and distribution groups, are classified into one of three group scopes: domain local, global, and universal.

5.7.1.1 Local Groups

Local groups (or machine local groups) are used primarily for backward compatibility with Windows NT 4. There are local users and groups on computers running Windows Server 2003 that are configured as member servers. Domain controllers do not use local groups.

- Local groups can include members from any domain within a forest, from trusted domains in other forests, and from trusted down-level domains.
- A local group has only machine wide scope; it can grant resource permissions only on the machine on which it exists.

5.7.1.2 Domain Local Groups

Domain local groups are used primarily to assign access permissions to global groups for local domain resources. Domain local groups:

- Exist in all mixed, interim and native functional level domains and forests.
- Are available domainwide only in Windows 2000 native or Windows Server 2003 domain functional level domains? Domain local groups function as a local group on the domain controllers while the domain is in mixed functional level.

- Can include members from any domain in the forest, from trusted domains in other forests, and from trusted down-level domains.
- Have domainwide scope in Windows 2000 native and Windows Server 2003 domain functional level domains, and can be used to grant resource permission on any Windows Server 2003 computer within, but not beyond, the domain in which the group exists.

5.7.1.3 Global Groups

Global groups are used primarily to provide categorized membership in domain local groups for individual security principals or for direct permission assignment (particularly in the case of a mixed or interim domain functional level domain). Often, global groups are used to collect users or computers in the same domain and share the same job, role, or function. Global groups:

- Exist in all mixed, interim, and native functional level domains and forests
- Can only include members from within their domain
- Can be made a member of machine local or domain local group
- Can be granted permission in any domain (including trusted domains in other forests and pre-Windows 2003 domains)
- Can contain other global groups (Windows 2000 native or Windows Server 2003 domain functional level only)

5.7.1.4 Universal Groups

Universal groups are used primarily to grant access to resources in all trusted domains, but universal groups can only be used as a security principal (security group type) in a Windows 2000 native or Windows Server 2003 domain functional level domain.

- Universal groups can include members from any domain in the forest.
- In Windows 2000 native or Windows Server 2003 domain functional level, universal groups can be granted permissions in any domain, including domains in other forests with which a trust exists.

5.7.2 Group Conversion

The scope of a group is determined at the time of its creation. However, in a Windows 2000 native or Windows Server 2003 domain functional level domain, domain local and global groups can be converted to universal groups if the groups are not members of other groups of the same scope. For example, a global group that is a member of another global group cannot be converted to a universal group. Table 5.5 summarizes the use of Windows Server 2003 domain groups as security principals (group type: security).

Table 5.5 Group Scope and Allowed Objects

Group Scope	Allowed Objects
Windows 2000 native or Windows Server 2003 functional level domain	
Domain Local	Computer accounts, users, global groups, and universal groups from any forest or trusted domain. Domain local groups from the same domain. Nested domain local groups in the same domain.
Global	Users, computers and global groups from same domain. Nested global (in same domain), domain local, or universal groups.
Universal	Universal groups, global groups, users and computers from any domain in the forest. Nested global, domain local, or universal groups.
Windows 2000 mixed or Windows Server 2003 interim functional level domain	
Domain Local	Computer accounts, users, global groups from any domain. Cannot be nested.
Global	Only users and computers from same domain. Cannot bc nested.
Universal	Not available.

5.7.3 Special Identities

There are also some special groups called special identities, which are managed by the operating system. Special identities cannot be created or deleted; nor can their membership be modified by administrators. Special identities do not appear in the Active Directory Users And Computers snap-in or in any other computer management tool, but can be assigned permissions in an ACL. Table 5.6 details some of the special identities in Windows Server 2003.

Table 5.6 Special Identities and Their Representation

Identity	Representation
Everyone	Represents all current network users, including guests and users from other domains. Whenever a user logs on to the network, that user is automatically added to the Everyone group.
Network	Represents users currently accessing a given resource over the network (as opposed to users who access a resource by logging on locally at the computer where the resource is located). Whenever a user accesses a given resource over the network, the user is automatically added to the Network group.
Interactive	Represents all users currently logged on to a particular computer and accessing a given resource located on that computer (as opposed to users who access the resource over the network). Whenever a user accesses a given resource on the computer to which they are logged on, the user is automatically added to the Interactive group.

Identity	Representation
Anonymous Logon	The Anonymous Logon group refers to any user who is using network resources, but did not go through the authentication process.
Authenticated	The Authenticated Users group includes all users who are authenticated into the Users network by using a valid user account. When assigning permissions, you can use the Authenticated Users group in place of the Everyone group to prevent anonymous access to resources.
Creator Owner	The Creator Owner group refers to the user who created or took ownership of the resource. For example, if a user created a resource, but the Administrator took ownership of it, then the Creator Owner would be the Administrator.
Dialup	The Dialup group includes anyone who is connected to the network through a dialup connection.

5.7.4 Assigning Group Scopes

When a group is created, it is assigned a group scope that in turn defines how permissions are assigned. The three possible group scopes-global, domain local, and universal-are defined in the following sections.

5.7.4.1 Global Scope

A group with a global scope is truly global in the sense that permissions can be granted for resources located in any domain. However, members can come only from the domain in which the group is created, and in that sense it is not global. Global groups are best used for directory objects that require frequent maintenance, such as user and computer accounts. Global groups can be members of universal and domain local groups in any domain, and they can have the following members:

- Other global groups in the same domain
- Individual accounts from the same domain

5.7.4.2 Domain Local Scope

A domain local group is the inverse of a global group in that members can come from any domain but the permissions can only be assigned for resources in the domain in which the group is created. The members of a domain local group have a common need to access certain resources in a particular domain. Domain local groups can have one or more of the following members:

- Other domain local groups in the same domain
- Global groups from any domain
- Universal groups from any domain
- Individual accounts from any domain

5.7.4.3 Universal Scope

A universal security group can have members from any domain and can be assigned permissions to resources in any domain. Although the universal scope sounds like an ideal solution in a multiple-domain enterprise, it's available only in domains that are running in Windows 2000 native domain functional level and higher. Universal groups can have the following members, which can be drawn from any domain:

- Other universal groups
- Global groups
- Individual accounts

Even in a Windows 2000 native or higher domain functional level, universal groups must be used with discretion because of the negative impact they can have on network performance, as described in the Real World sidebar, "How Groups Affect Network Performance."

5.7.5 How Groups Affect Network Performance

The importance of planning groups becomes even more apparent when you consider the negative effect your group organization can have on network performance. When a user logs on to the network, the domain controller determines the user's group memberships and assigns a security token to the user. The token includes the security identifiers (SIDs) of all the groups that the user belongs to, in addition to the user account ID. The more security groups the user belongs to, the longer it takes to assemble the token and the longer it takes the user to log on.

In addition, the security token, once assembled, is sent to every computer the user accesses. The target computer compares all the SIDs in the token against the permissions for all the shared resources available at that computer. A large number of users added to a large number of shared resources (including individual folders) can take up a lot of bandwidth and processing time. One solution is to limit membership in security groups. Use distribution groups for categories of users that don't require specific permissions or rights.

Groups with universal scope have a performance impact of their own because all such groups, along with their members, are listed in the global catalog. When there's a change to the membership in a group with universal scope, this fact must be relayed to every global catalog server in the domain tree, adding to the replication traffic on the network. New to Windows Server 2003 is the ability to enable universal group caching for remote domain controllers. This improves logon performance and limits replication traffic when changes are made to universal group membership on a remote domain controller. Groups with global or domain local scope are also listed in the global catalog, but their individual members are not, so the solution is to limit the membership of universal groups primarily to global groups.

5.7.6 Planning Organizational Units

Organizational units (OUs) are, as their name implies, organizing tools for collections of objects within a domain. An OU can contain any collection of Active Directory objects such as printers, computers, groups, and so forth. In the past, a domain that got very complicated was usually sorted out by splitting the domain into multiple domains. OUs provide an alternative administrative substructure that is infinitely more flexible. They can be arranged hierarchically within a domain, and administrative control can be delegated for functions in a single OU or an entire subtree of OUs. (An OU is the smallest entity over which you can delegate administrative control.) At the same time, OUs can be modified, moved, renamed, and even deleted easily. Another plus is that, unlike a domain, a subtree of OUs doesn't require a separate domain controller. OUs are containers only. They don't confer membership and aren't security principals. Rights and permissions are granted to users through group membership. After your groups are constructed, use OUs or organize group objects and assign Group Policy settings.

5.7.6.1 Creating Organizational Units

OUs are easily created and appear as folders in a domain structure. The following steps describe how to create an OU:

1. Choose Active Directory Users And Computers from the Administrative Tools menu.
2. Right-click the domain, and select New and then Organizational Unit to open the dialog box shown in Figure 5.16.
3. In the Organizational Unit dialog box, type the name for the unit and then click OK.

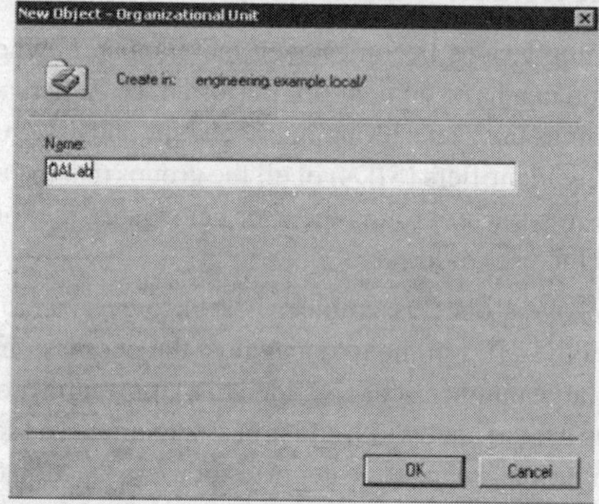

Figure 5.16 Creating a new organizational unit

5.7.6.2 Moving Organizational Units

One of the most useful aspects of OUs is that they can be moved from one container or even one domain to another. The following steps describe how to move an OU:

1. Choose Active Directory Users And Computers from the Administrative Tools menu.
2. Right-click the OU to be moved, and select Move from the shortcut menu.
3. In the Move dialog box, select the new location for the OU and click OK.

5.7.6.3 Deleting Organizational Units

OUs can also be deleted easily. However, exercise caution when deleting an OU because the contents of the OU are also removed. That means you can inadvertently delete all the resources and user accounts contained in an OU if you act too hastily. The following steps describe how to delete an OU:

1. Choose Active Directory Users and Computers from the Administrative Tools menu.
2. Right-click the OU, and select Delete.
3. Confirm the deletion by clicking Yes twice.

5.7.7 Planning a Group Strategy

Looking at your network and the various group types, and then factoring in your specific needs, you can end up feeling as though you're working on some infernal logic puzzle: Claire lives in a blue house, Luisa collects stamps, Sam drives a Toyota, and Ross eats cheese. Which one has red hair?

Nevertheless, as in so many other aspects of network administration, planning is the essential step. The domain mode determines the types of groups available to you. A domain having Windows 2000 mixed domain functional level, for example, can't support groups with universal scope. Thus, as long as you have Microsoft Windows NT backup domain controllers, you are limited to groups with global and domain local scopes.

5.7.7.1 Determining Group Names

In planning your groups, determine a naming scheme that is appropriate for your organization. Two factors have to be considered:

- Group names must be instantly recognizable: Administrators searching Active Directory don't have to guess at their meaning.
- Comparable groups must have similar names: In other words, if you have a group for engineers in each domain, give all the groups parallel names, such as NorAmer Engineers, SoAmer Engineers, and Euro Engineers.

5.7.7.2 Using Global and Domain Local Groups

Develop a strategy for using the different groups. For example, users with common job responsibilities belong in a global group. Thus, add user accounts for all graphic artists to a global group called Graphic Artists. Other users with common needs are assigned to other global groups. Then you must identify resources to which users need access and create a domain local group for that resource. If, for example, you have several color printers and plotters that are used by specific departments, you can make a domain local group called Printers & Plotters.

Next, decide which global groups need access to the resources you identified. Continuing the example, you add the global group Graphic Artists to the domain local group Printers & Plotters, along with other global groups that need access to the printers and plotters. Permission to use the resources in Printers & Plotters is assigned to the Printers & Plotters domain local group. Keep in mind that global groups can complicate administration in multiple-domain situations. Global groups from different domains must have their permissions set individually. Also, assigning users to domain local groups and granting permissions to the group does not give members access to resources outside the domain.

5.7.7.3 Using Universal Groups

When you're able to use universal groups (that is, when your domain is running in Windows 2000 native or higher domain functional level), keep the following guidelines in mind:

- Avoid adding individual accounts to universal groups, to keep replication traffic down.
- Add global groups from multiple domains to universal groups to give members access to resources in more than one domain.

- Universal groups can be members of domain local groups and other universal groups, but they can't be members of global groups.

5.7.8 Implementing the Group Strategy

After you plan your strategy and test it using a variety of scenarios, you're ready to begin putting the structure into place.

5.7.8.1 Creating Groups

Use Active Directory Users and Computers to create and delete groups. Create groups in the Users container or in an OU that you create for the purpose of containing groups. The following steps demonstrate how to create a group in the Quality Assurance OU:

1. Choose Active Directory Users and Computers from the Administrative Tools menu.
2. Expand the domain in which the group is to be created.
3. Right-click the Quality Assurance OU, point to New, and choose Group from the shortcut menu to open the dialog box shown in Figure 5.17.

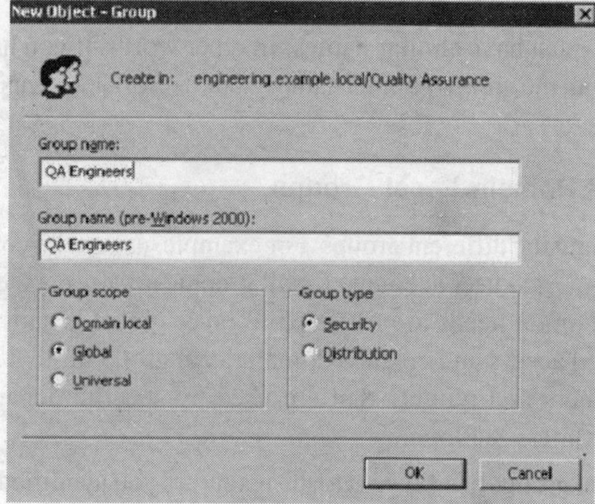

Figure 5.17 Creating a new group

4. Fill in the required information:
   - The group name must be unique in the domain.
   - The group name as it will be seen by pre-Windows 2000 operating systems is filled in automatically. (In Windows 2000 native and higher domain functional level, this field is Downlevel Name Of New Group, but it is still filled in automatically based on the name you provide as the group name.)
   - For Group Scope, click Domain Local, Global, or Universal.
   - For Group Type, click Security or Distribution.
5. Click OK when you're finished. The new group appears in the Quality Assurance OU. You might have to wait a few minutes for the group to be replicated to the global catalog before adding members.

5.7.8.2 Deleting Groups

Don't create groups you don't need, and when groups are no longer necessary be sure to promptly delete them from the system. Unnecessary groups are a security risk because it is all too easy to unintentionally grant permissions where you shouldn't. Each group, like each user, has a unique security identifier (SID). The SID is used to identify the group and the permissions assigned to the group. When the group is deleted, the SID is deleted and not used again. If you delete a group and decide later to re-create it, you have to configure the users and permissions as if for a new group.

To delete a group, right-click its name in Active Directory Users and Computers and choose Delete from the shortcut menu. Deleting a group deletes only the group and the permissions associated with the group. It has no effect on the accounts of users who are members of the group.

5.7.8.3 Adding Users to a Group

After you create a group, you need to add members to it. As was mentioned earlier in the chapter, groups can contain users, contacts, other groups, and computers.

The following steps show how to add members to a group:

1. Choose Active Directory Users and Computers from the Administrative Tools menu.
2. In the console tree, click the container that includes the objects you want to add to the group.
3. Highlight the accounts you want to add. (You can use the Shift and Ctrl keys to select multiple accounts.)
4. Right-click the highlighted accounts, and select Add To A Group from the shortcut menu. This opens the Select Group dialog box. Click Look For and Look In to narrow the search.
5. Type the first few letters of the group name and click OK. All matches are displayed. Highlight the correct group name and click OK.

You can also approach adding users to a group from another angle by following these steps:

1. Right-click a group name, and select Properties.
2. Click the Members tab and then click Add. Make sure the Object Types and Locations fields are pointing to the positions you want.
3. Click Advanced, and then click Find Now. All the potential group members appear in the lower pane.
4. Highlight the accounts to be added and click OK.

5.7.8.4 Changing the Group Scope

Over time, you might find that you need to change the scope of a particular group. For example, you might need to change a global group to a universal group so that users from another domain can be part of the group. However, the types of changes that can be made to a group scope are quite limited, and you might need to delete the group and create a new one to get the configuration you need.

To change a group scope, right-click the group name in Active Directory Users and Computers and choose Properties from the shortcut menu. Make the necessary changes on the General tab, and click OK when you're finished. There are several rules for changing a group scope, as described here:

- In Windows 2000 mixed domain functional level, a security group cannot have universal scope.
- A global group can be changed to a universal group if the global group is not already a member of another global group.
- A domain local group can be changed to a universal group if the domain local group does not already contain another domain local group.
- A universal group can be converted to a global group, as long as no other universal groups are members.

5.7.8.5 Creating Local Groups

A local group is a collection of user accounts on a single computer. The user accounts must be local to the computer, and members of local groups can be assigned permissions for resources only on the computer where the local group was created. Local groups can be created on any computer running Windows Server 2003 except a domain controller. In general, you don't want to use local groups on a computer that's part of a domain or, at least, you want to do so sparingly. Local groups don't appear in

Active Directory, so you must administer local groups separately on each computer. The following steps describe how to create a local group:

1. Right-click the My Computer icon on the desktop, and choose Manage from the shortcut menu.
2. In the console tree, expand System Tools and then Local Users and Groups.
3. Right-click the Groups folder, and select New Group from the shortcut menu.
4. In the New Group dialog box, type the group name. You can include a description if you want.
5. Click Add to add members to the group. (You can add members now or later.)
6. Click Create when you're finished, and the new group is added to the list of groups in the details pane.

5.7.9 Managing Built-in Groups and User Rights

When you create an Active Directory domain with one or more Windows Server 2003 domain controllers, built-in groups are automatically created in both the Users and Built - In containers. Many of these groups also have built-in rights that are automatically assigned to members of the group.

5.7.9.1 Built-in Local Groups

Member servers and standalone servers running Windows 2000 Server (Service Pack 3 or later) and computers running Microsoft Windows 2000 Professional (Service Pack 3 or later) or Microsoft Windows XP Professional (Service Pack 1 or later) have built-in local groups that give rights to perform tasks on a single computer. Install Adminpak.msi from the Windows Server 2003 installation disk on these computers as needed. Table 5.7 shows the built-in local groups on a standalone server. Many are common to clients and servers alike, but some, where noted, are only on member servers and standalone servers.

Table 5.7 Built-in local groups

Local Group	Description
Administrators	Members can perform all administrative tasks on the computer. The built-in Administrator account that's created when the operating system is installed is a member of the group. When a server (not a domain controller) or a client running Windos XP Professional or Windows 2000 Professional joins a domain, the Domain Admins group (described in Table 9-3) is made part of this group.
Backup Operators	Members can log on to the computer, back up and restore the computer's data, and shut down the computer. Members cannot change security settings but can override them for purposes of backup and restore. No default members.
DHCP Users (installed with DHCP Server service) *Servers or Domain Controllers only*	Members of this group can read DHCP information stored at a specific server for troubleshooting purposes. No default members.
DHCP Administrators (installed with DHCP Server service) Servers only	Members of this group can administer DHCP Server service but do not have access to other parts of the server. No default members.
Guests	Members can perform only tasks for which an administrator has granted rights. Members can use only resources for which an administrator has specifically granted permission. The guest account is a default memebr of this group.
Help Services Group	No users are assigned to this group. The oly memebr should be the account associated with support applications.
Network Configuration Operators	Memebrs can change TCP/IP settings, and renew and release addresses. No default members.
Performance Monitor Users *Servers only*	Members can monitor performance counters on a specific server locally and remotely. No default memebrs.
Performance Log Users *Servers only*	Members can administer performance logs, counters, and alerts on a specific server, locally or remotedly. No default memebrs.
Power User	Members can create and modify user accounts and install programs on the local computer but canot view other users' files. Members can create and delete local groups, and add or remove users from the groups they have created. Members can add or remove users from the Power Users, Users, and Guests groups. No default members.
Print Operators *Servers only*	Members can manage printers and print queues on a specific server. No default members.
Remote Desktop Users	Members are allowed to connect remotely. No default members.
Replicator	Do not add user accounts of actual users to this group. If necessary, you can add a "dummy" user account to this group to permit you to log on to Replicator services on a domain cantoroller to manage replication of files and directories.
Users	Members of this group can log on to the computer, access the network, save documents, and shut down the computer. Members cannot install programs or make system changes. When a member server, Windows 2000 Professional, or Windows XP Professional machine joins a domain, the Domain Users group is added to this group. The Interactive and Authenticated Users groups are also members of the users group, so all user accounts are automatically memebrs of the Users group.
WINS Users (installed with WINS) *Servers only*	Group memebrs have read-only access to information and properties stored at a specific WINS server. No default users.

5.7.9.2 Built-in Domain Local Groups

The Windows 2000 and Windows Server 2003 built-in domain local groups provide users with rights and permissions to perform tasks on domain controllers and in Active Directory. The domain local groups have predefined rights and permissions that are granted to users and global groups that you add as members. Table 5.8 shows the most commonly used built-in domain local groups.

Table 5.8 Commonly used built-in domain local groups

Domain Local Group	Description
Account Operators	Members can create, delete, and manage user accounts and groups. Members cannot modify the Administrators, Domain Admins, and Domain Controllers groups, or any of the Operators groups. Members can log on locally to domain controllers and shut them down. No default members.
Administrators	Members are automatically granted every right and permission on all domain controllers and the domain itself. The Administrator account, Enterprise Admins group, and Doamin Admins group are members.
Backup Operators	Members can back up and restore data on all domain controllers, and they can log on to domain controllers and shut them down. There are no default memebrs, and membership should be granted with care. This group is not the same as the Built-in Local Group Backup Operators.
Cert Publishers	Members can publish certificates for users and computers. Nio default members.
DnsAdmins (installed with DNS)	Members have administrative access to DNS servers. No default members.
Guests	Members can perform only tasks for which an administrator has granted rights. Members can use only resources for which an administrator has specifically granted permission. The Guest User and Domain Guests groups are members by default.
Incoming Forest Turst Builders (appears only) in forest root domain)	Members can allow an incoming forest trust to let users in another forest access resources in the home forest. No default members.
Network Configuration Operators	Members can change TCP/IP settings, and they can renew and release addresses on domain controllers. No default members.
Performance Monitor Users	Members cna monitor performance counters an domain controllers either locally or from remote clients wihout being Administrators or members of the Performance Log Users group. No default members.
Performance Log Users	Members can mange performance logs, counters, and alerts on domain controllers either locally or remotely without being Administrators. No default members.
Pre-Windows 2000 Compatible Access	Provided for backward compatibility for computers running Windows NT 4. Add user to this group only if they are running Windows NT 4 or earlier. No default members.
Print Operators	Members can manage all aspects of domain printer operation and configuration.
RAS and IAS Servers	Servers in this group have access to the remote access properties of users. No default members.
Remote Desktop Users	Members can remotely log on to domain controllers. No default members.
Server Operator	Members can parform most administrative tasks on domain controllers, except the manipulation of secutity options.
Users	Members can log on to the computer, access the network, save documents, and shut down the computer. Members cannot install programs or make system changes. The Domain Users group is a member by default.

5.7.9.3 Built-in Global Groups

Built-in global groups are created to encompass common types of accounts. By default, these groups do not have inherent rights; an administrator must assign all rights to the group. However, some members are added to these groups automatically, and you can add more members based on the rights and permissions you assign to the groups. Rights can be assigned directly to the groups or by adding the built-in global groups to domain local groups. Table 5.9 describes the built-in global groups that are commonly used.

Table 5.9 Commonly used built-in global groups

Global Group	Description
DnsUpdateProxy (installed with DNS)	Members are DNS clients that can provide dynamic updates to DNS on behalf of other clients. No default members.
Domain Admins	This group is automatically a member of the domain local Administrators group, so members of Damain Admins can perform administrative tasks on any computer in the domain. The Administrator account is a member of this group by default.
Domain Computers	All controllers and workstations in the domain are members.
Domain Controllers	All domain controllers in the domain are members.
Domain Guests	The Guest account is a member by default. This group is automatically a member of the domain local Guests group.
Domain Users	All domain users and the Administrator accounts are members. The Domain Users group is automatically a member of the domain local Users group.
Dnterprise Admins	This group is for users who are to have administrative rights for the entire network. Enterprise Admins is automatically a member of the Administrators group on all domain controllers in the forest.
Group PolicyCreator Owners	Members can create and modify group policy for the domain. The Administrator account is a default member of the group.
Schema Admins (appears only in forest root domain)	Members can alter the Active Directory Schema.

5.7.10 Defining User Rights

What users can and cannot do depends on the rights and permissions that have been granted to them. Rights generally apply to the system as a whole. The ability to back up files or to log on to a server, for example, is a right that the administrator giveth or taketh away. Rights can be assigned individually, but most often they are characteristics of groups, and a user is assigned to a particular group on the basis of the rights that the user needs. Permissions indicate the access that a user (or group) has to specific objects, such as files, directories, and printers. For example, the question of whether a user can read a particular directory or access a network printer is permission. Permissions are discussed at length later in this chapter.

Rights, in turn, are divided into two types: privileges and logon rights. Privileges include such functions as the ability to run security audits or force shutdown from a remote system-obviously not tasks that are done by most users. Logon rights are self-explanatory; they involve the ability to connect to a computer in specific ways. Rights are automatically assigned to the built-in groups in Windows Server 2003, although they can be assigned to individual users as well as groups. Assignment by group is preferred, so whenever possible, assign rights by group membership to keep administration simple. When membership in groups defines rights, rights can be removed from a user by simply removing the user from the group. Tables 5.10 and 5.11 list the logon rights and privileges and the groups to which they are assigned by default.

Table 5.10 Logon rights assigned to groups by default

Name	Description	Groups Assigned the Right on Domain Controllers	Groups Assigned the Right on Workstations and Servers
Access this computer from the network	Permits connection to the computer through the network	Administrators, Authenticated Users, Everyone	Administrators, Backup Operators, Power Users, Users, Everyone
Allow logon locally	Permits logging on to the computer interactively	Administrators, Account Operators, Backup Operators Print Operators, Server Operators	Administrators, Backup Operators, Power Users, Users, Guest
Allow logon through Terminal Services	Allows logging on as a Terminal Services client	Administrators	Administrators, Remote Desktop Users

Table 5.11 Privileges assigned to groups by default

Privilege	Description	Groups Assigned the Privilege by Default
Act as part of the operating system	Allows a process to authenticate as any user. A process that requires this privilege must use the LocalSystem account, which already includes this privillege.	None
Add worstations to domain	Allows a user to add new work-stations to an existing domain.	Authenticated Users on domain controllers
Adjust memory quotas for a process	Allows user to set the maximum amount of memory a process can use.	Administrators
Back up files and directories	Allows backing up the system; overrides specific file and folder permissions.	Administrators, Backup Operators
Bypass traverse checking	Allows a usr to go through directory trees (folder structures) even if the user doesn't have permission to access the directories being passed through.	Administrators and Authenticated Users on domain controllers; on servers and workstations. Administrators, Backup Operators, Power Users, Users, and Everyone
Change the system time	Allows the setting of the computer's internal clock.	Administrators and Server Operators on domain controllers; Administrators and Power Users on servers and workstations
Create a pagefile	Allows the creation and modification of a pagefile.	Administrators
Create global objects	Allows the creation of global objects in a Terminal Services session.	Administrators

Privilege	Description	Groups Assigned the Privilege by Default
Debug programs	Allows the user to attach a debugger to a process	Administrators
Enable computer and user accounts to be trusted for delegation	Permits a user to set the Trusted for Delegation setting on an object.	Administrators on domain controllers; not assigned on rember servers or workstations
Force shutdown from a remote system	Allows the shutdown of a computer from a remote location on the network.	Administrators and Server Operators on domain controllers; Administrators on member servers and workstations
Impersonate a client after authentication	Allows an account to impersonate another account	Administrators
Increase quotas	Allows a prcess with write property access to another process to increase the processor quota assigned to that process	Administrators
Increase scheduling priority	Allows the use of Task Manager to change the scheduling prionity of a process.	Administrators
Land and unload device drivers	install and remove device drivers.	Administrators
Manager auditing and security log	Allows a user to specify auditing options and to view and clear the security log in Event Viewr. Audit Directory Service Access must be turned on for object access auditing to be performed. (See Chapter 11) Administrators can always view and clear the security log.	Administrators
Modify firmware environment variables	Allows the configuration of nonvolatile RAM on oomputers that support such function.	Administrators
Profile a single process	Allows performance sampling on a process	Administrators and Power Users on member servers and work-stations; Administrators on domain controllers
Profile system performance	Allows performance sampling of the system	Administrators
Remove computer from docking station	Allows the removal of a laptop from a docking station using Eject PC on the Start menu.	Administrators Power Users, and Users (default setting for this is Disabled, not enforcing any limitations)

Privilege	Description	Groups Assigned the Privilege by Default
Restore files and directories	Allows restoring files and folders to a system; overrules specific file and folder permissions	Administrators. Backup Operators, and Server Operators on domain controllers; Administrators and Backup Operators on workstations and servers
Shout down the system	Shuts down the local computer.	Administrators Account Operators, Backup Operators, Print Operators, and Server Operators on domain controllers; Administrators Backup Operators, and Power Users on member servers; Administrators, Backup Operators, Power Users, and Users on workstations
Synchronize directory service data	Allows a user to initiate a synchronization of Active Directory.	None
Take ownership of files or other objects	Allows a user to take ownership of any security object, including files and folders, printers, registry keys, and processes.	Administrators

5.7.11 Assigning User Rights to a Group

Rights are assigned and removed most easily at a domain level using Group Policy. Suppose you have a group of users who should be able to log on locally to servers running Windows Server 2003 but you don't want them to be members of any groups that have this logon right by default. One way to approach this situation is to create a group called Logon Rights, add the users to the group, and assign the right to log on locally to the Logon Rights group. The following steps describe how to assign a right to a particular group:

1. Choose Active Directory Users And Computers from the Administrative Tools menu. Right-click the domain name, and select Properties.
2. Click the Group Policy tab, and then click Edit. Select Computer Configuration, and then choose Windows Settings.
3. Under Security Settings, click Local Policies and then click User Rights Assignment. (See Figure 5.18.) In the details pane, double-click Allow Log On Locally.
4. Select Define These Policy Settings and then click Add. 5. Type the name of the group to be granted this right (or click Browse to search for the group). Click OK twice, and close Default Domain Policy.

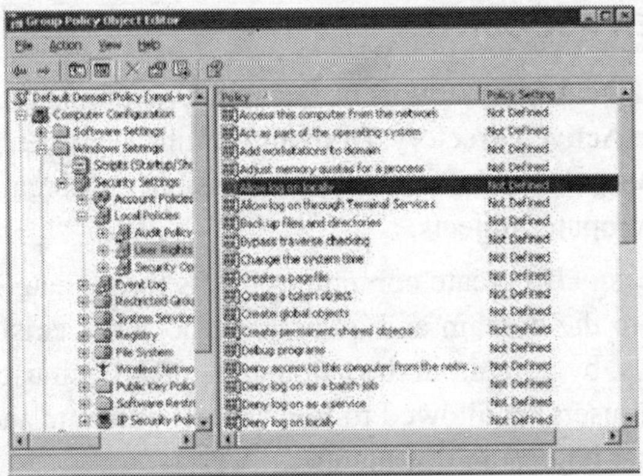

Figure 5.18 User rights listed under Group Policy

The same process can remove rights, except that you click Remove, rather than Add, in step 4. Rights can also be assigned to an individual user by using this method.

5.7.12 Assigning Rights Locally

Rights can be assigned or removed locally, though you must bear in mind that a defined domain-level policy overrides a local policy setting.

The following steps describe how to assign a policy locally:

1. Choose Local Security Policy from the Administrative Tools menu.
2. Under Security Settings, click Local Policies and then click User Rights Assignment.
3. In the detail pane, double-click the policy you want to assign to open the policy's properties window.
4. Click Add User Or Group to select an individual or a group in the Select Users Or Groups dialog box. Make sure the Look For and Look In fields are pointing to the locations you want. Click Advanced, and then click Find Now. All the potential group members appear in the lower pane.
5. Highlight the accounts to be added and click OK.

If the Add User Or Group and Remove buttons aren't available in the Properties window as shown in Figure 5.19, it means the policy has been set at the domain level and can't be overridden locally.

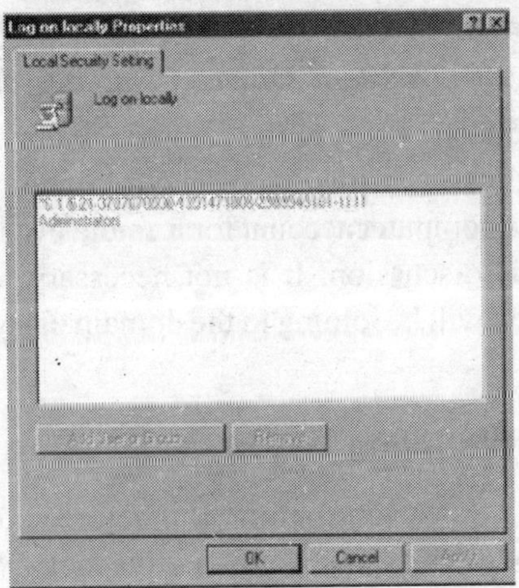

Figure 5.19: Local security settings

5.8 CREATING COMPUTER ACCOUNTS

You must be a member of the Administrators or Account Operators groups on the domain controllers to create a computer object in Active Directory. Domain Admins and Enterprise Admins are, by default, members of the Administrators group. Alternatively, it is possible to delegate administration so that other users or groups can create computer objects.

However, domain users can also create computer objects through an interesting, indirect process. When a computer is joined to the domain and an account does not exist, Active Directory creates a computer object automatically, by default, in the Computers OU. Each user in the Authenticated Users group (which is, in effect, all users) is allowed to join 10 computers to the domain, and can therefore create as many as 10 computer objects in this manner.

Creating Computer Objects Using Active Directory Users and Computers To create a computer object, or "account," open Active Directory Users And Computers and select the container or OU in which you want to create the object. From the Action menu or the right-click shortcut menu, choose the New-Computer command. The New Object-Computer dialog box appears, as illustrated in Figure 5.20.

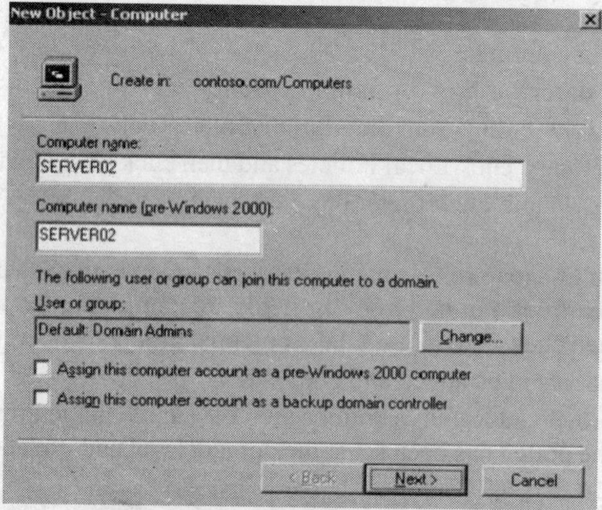

Figure 5.20 The New Object-Computer dialog box

In the New Object-Computer dialog box, type the computer name. Other properties in this dialog box will be discussed in the following lesson. Click Next. The following page of the dialog box requests a GUID. A GUID is used to prestage a computer account for Remote Installation Services (RIS) deployment, which is beyond the scope of this discussion. It is not necessary to enter a GUID when creating a computer account for a machine you will be joining to the domain using other methods. So just click Next and then click Finish.

5.8.1 Creating Computer Objects Using Dsadd

Chances are, this is something you've done before. But before you decide there's nothing new under the sun, Windows Server 2003 provides a useful command-line tool, DSADD, which allows you to create computer objects from the command prompt or a batch file.

"Administering Microsoft Windows Server 2003," you used DSADD to create user objects. To create computer objects, simply type dsadd computer ComputerDN, where ComputerDN is the distinguished name (DN) of the computer, such as

CN=Desktop123,OU=Desktops,DC=contoso,DC=com.

If the computer's DN includes a space, surround the entire DN with quotation marks. The ComputerDN… parameter can include more than one distinguished name for new computer objects, making DSADD Computer a handy way to generate multiple objects at once. The parameter can be entered in one of the following ways:

- By piping a list of DNs from another command, such as dsquery.
- By typing each DN on the command line, separated by spaces.
- By leaving the DN parameter empty, at which point you can type the DNs, one at a time, at the keyboard console of the command prompt. Press ENTER after each DN. Press CTRL+Z and ENTER after the last DN.

The DSADD Computer command can take the following optional parameters after the DN parameter:

- -samid SAMName
- -desc Description
- -loc Location

5.8.2 Creating a Computer Account with Netdom

The NETDOM command is available as a component of the Support Tools, installable from the Support\Tools directory of the Windows Server 2003 CD. The command is also available on the Windows XP and Windows 2000 CDs. Use the version that is appropriate for the platform. NETDOM allows you to perform numerous domain account and security tasks from the command line. To create a computer account in a domain, type the following command:

netdom add ComputerName /domain:DomainName /userd:User /PasswordD:UserPassword [/ou:OUDN]

This command creates the computer account for ComputerName in the domain DomainName using the domain credentials User and UserPassword. The /ou parameter causes the object to be created in the OU specified by the OUDN distinguished name following the parameter. If no OUDN is supplied, the computer account is created in the Computers OU by default. The user credentials must, of course, have permissions to create computer objects.

5.8.3 Joining a Computer to a Domain

A computer account alone is not enough to create the secure relationship required between a domain and a machine. The machine must join the domain. To join a computer to the domain, perform the following steps:

1. Right-click My Computer and choose Properties. Click the Computer Name tab.
    - Open Control Panel, select System, and in the System Properties dialog box, click the Computer Name tab.

- Open the computer's Computer Name properties. These properties can be accessed in several ways:

2. Open the Network Connections folder from Control Panel and choose the Network Identification command from the Advanced menu.
3. On the Computer Name tab, click Change. The Computer Name Changes dialog box, shown in Figure 5.21 allows you to change the name and the domain and workgroup membership of the computer.

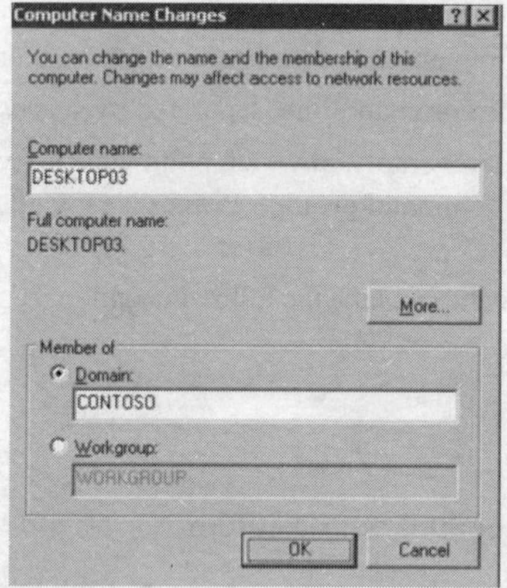

Figure 5.21 The Computer Name Changes dialog box

4. In the Computer Name Changes dialog box, click Domain and type the name of the domain. 5. Click OK. The computer contacts the domain controller. If there is a problem connecting to the domain, examine network connectivity and configuration, as well as DNS configuration.

When the computer successfully contacts the domain, you will be prompted, as in Figure 5.22, for a user name and password with privileges to join the domain. Note that the credentials requested are your domain user name and password.

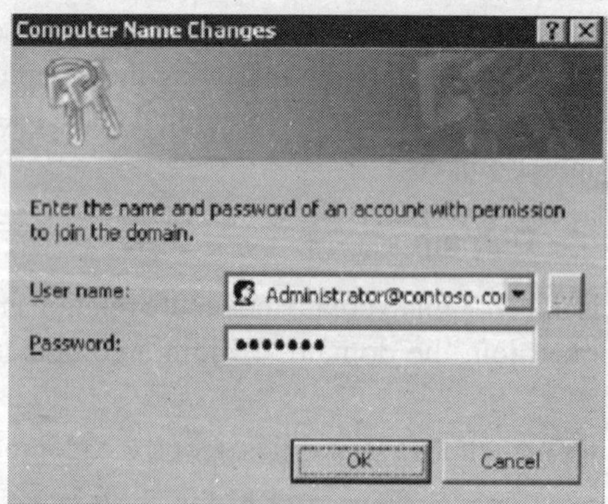

Figure 5.22 Prompt for credentials to join domain

If you have not created a domain computer account with a name that matches the computer's name, Active Directory creates an account automatically in the default Computers container. Once a domain computer account has been created or located, the computer establishes a trust relationship with the domain, alters its SID to match that of the account, and makes modifications to its group memberships. The computer must then be restarted to complete the process.

5.8.4 Computers Container Vs. OUs

The Computers container is the default location for computer objects in Active Directory. After a domain is upgraded from Windows NT 4 to Windows 2000, all computer accounts are found, initially, in this container. Moreover, when a machine joins the domain and there is no existing account in the domain for that computer, a computer object is created automatically in the Computers container.

Although the Computers container is the default container for computer objects, it is not the ideal container for computer objects. Unlike OUs, containers such as Computers, Users and Built-in cannot be linked to policies, limiting the possible scope of computer-focused group policy. A best-practice Active Directory design will include at least one OU for computers. Often, there are multiple OUs for computers, based on administrative division, region, or for the separate administration of laptops, desktops, file and print servers, and application servers. As an example, there is a default OU for Domain Controllers in Active Directory, which is linked to the Default Domain Controller Policy. By creating one or more OUs for computers, an organization can delegate administration and manage computer configuration, through group policy, more flexibly.

If your organization has one or more OUs for computers, you must move any computer objects created automatically in the Computers container into the appropriate OU. To move a computer object, select the computer and choose Move from the Action menu. Alternatively, use the new drag-and-drop feature of the MMC to move the object.

You can also move a computer object, or any other object, with the DSMOVE command. The syntax of DSMOVE is:

dsmove ObjectDN [-newname NewName] [-newparent ParentDN]

The -newname parameter allows you to rename an object. The -newparent parameter allows you to move an object. To move a computer named DesktopABC from the Computers container to the Desktops OU, you would type the following:

dsmove ?CN = DesktopABC, CN = Computers, DC = Contoso,DC = com? -newparent ?OU=Desktops,DC=Contoso,DC=com?

In this command you again see the distinction between the Computers container (CN) and the Desktops organizational unit (OU). You must have appropriate permissions to move an object in Active Directory. Default permissions allow Account Operators to move computer objects between containers including the Computers container and any OUs except into or out of the Domain Controllers OU. Administrators, which include Domain Admins and Enterprise Admins, can move computer objects between any containers, including the Computers container, the Domain Controllers OU, and any other OUs.

5.8.5 Managing Computer Accounts

The fundamental components of a computer's relationship with a domain: the computer's account, and joining the computer to the domain. This lesson looks more closely at the computer object in Active Directory. You will learn about the other properties and permissions that make computer objects "tick," and how to manage those properties and permissions using GUI and command line tools.

5.9 MANAGING COMPUTER OBJECT PERMISSIONS

You learned that you could join a computer to a domain by providing domain administrator credentials when prompted by the computer during the join process. Security concerns, however, require us to use the minimum necessary credentials to achieve a particular task, and it does seem like overkill to need a Domain Admins' account to add a desktop to the domain.

Fortunately, Active Directory allows you to control, with great specificity, the groups or users that can join a computer to a domain computer account. Although the default is Domain Admins, you can allow any group (for example, a group called "Installers") to join a machine to an account. This is most easily achieved while creating the computer object.

When you create a computer object, the first page of the New Object-Computer dialog box (previously shown in Figure 5.20) indicates The Following User or Group Can Join This Computer to a Domain. Click Change and you can select any user or group. This change modifies a number of permissions on the computer object in Active Directory.

The following page of the New Object-Computer dialog box prompts you for the globally unique identifier (GUID) of the computer, which is necessary if you install a system using Remote Installation Services (RIS). If the computer that is using the account that you are creating is running a version of Windows earlier than 2000, select the Assign This Computer Account as a Pre-Windows 2000 Computer check box. If the account is for a Windows NT backup domain controller, click Assign This Computer Account as a Backup Domain Controller.

5.9.1 Configuring Computer Properties

Computer objects have several properties that are not visible when creating a computer account in the user interface. Open a computer object's Properties dialog box to set its location and description, configure its group memberships and dial-in permissions, and link it to a user object of the computer's manager. The Operating System properties page is read-only. The information is published automatically to Active Directory, and will be blank until a computer has joined the domain using that account.

Several object classes in Active Directory support the Manager property that is shown on the Managed by property page of a computer. This linked property creates a crossreference to a user object. All other properties-the addresses and telephone numbers-are displayed directly from the user object. They are not stored as part of the computer object itself.

The DSMOD command, can also modify several of the properties of a computer object. You will see the DSMOD command in action in the following section regarding troubleshooting computer accounts.

5.9.2 Finding and Connecting to Objects in Active Directory

When a user calls you with a particular problem, you might want to know what operating system and service pack is installed on that user's system. You learned that this information is stored as properties of the computer object. The only challenge, then, is to locate the computer object, which may be more difficult in a complex Active Directory with one or more domains and multiple OUs.

The Active Directory Users and Computers snap-in provides easy access to a powerful, graphical search tool. This tool can be used to find a variety of object types. In this context, however, your search entails an object of the type Computer. Click the Find Objects In Active Directory button on the console toolbar. The resulting Find Computers dialog box is illustrated in Figure 5.23. You can select the type of object (Find), the scope of the search (In), and specify search criteria before clicking Find Now.

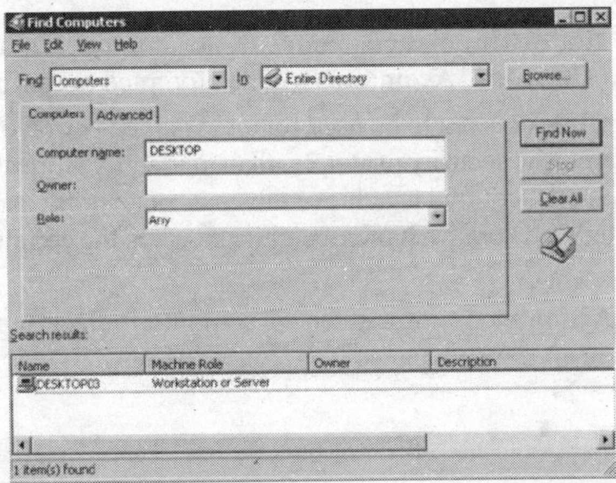

Figure 5.23 The Find Computers dialog box, as it appears after a successful search

The list of results allows you to select an object and, from the File menu or the shortcut menu, perform common tasks on the selected object. Many administrators appreciate learning that you can use the Manage command to open the Computer Management console and connect directly to that computer, allowing you to examine its event logs, device manager, system information, disk and service configuration, or local user or group accounts.

5.10 TROUBLESHOOTING ACCOUNTS

Active Directory domains treat computers as security principals. This means that a computer, just like a user, has an account-or, more specifically, properties within the computer object such as a name, a password, and a SID. Like user accounts, computer accounts require maintenance and, occasionally, troubleshooting. This lesson focuses on skills and concepts related to troubleshooting computer objects.

5.10.1 Deleting and Disabling and Resetting Computer Accounts

Computer accounts, like user accounts, maintain a unique SID, which enables an administrator to grant permissions to computers. Also like user accounts, computers can belong to groups. Therefore, like user accounts, it is important to understand the effect of deleting a computer account. When a computer account is deleted, its group memberships and SID are lost. If the deletion is accidental, and another computer account is created with the same name, it is nonetheless a new account, with a new SID. Group memberships must be re-established, and any permissions assigned to the deleted computer must be reassigned to the new account. Delete computer objects only when you are certain that you no longer require those security-related attributes of the object.

To delete a computer account using Active Directory Users and Computers, locate and select the computer object and, from the Action menu or the shortcut menu, select the Delete command. You will be prompted to confirm the deletion and, because deletion is not reversible, the default response to the prompt is No. Select Yes and the object is deleted.

The DSRM command-line tool allows you to delete a computer object from the command prompt. To delete a computer with DSRM, type:

DSRM ObjectDN

Where ObjectDN is the distinguished name of the computer, such as "CN=Desktop15, OU=Desktops,DC=contoso,DC=com." Again, you will be prompted to confirm the deletion.

If a computer is taken offline or is not to be used for an extended period of time, you may disable the account. Such an action reflects the security principle, that an identity store allow authentication only of the minimum number of accounts required to achieve the goals of an organization. Disabling the account does not modify the computer's SID or group membership, so when the computer is brought back online, the account can be enabled.

The context menu, or Action menu, of a selected computer object exposes the Disable Account command. A disabled account appears with a red "X" icon in the Active Directory Users And Computers snap-in, as shown in Figure 5.24.

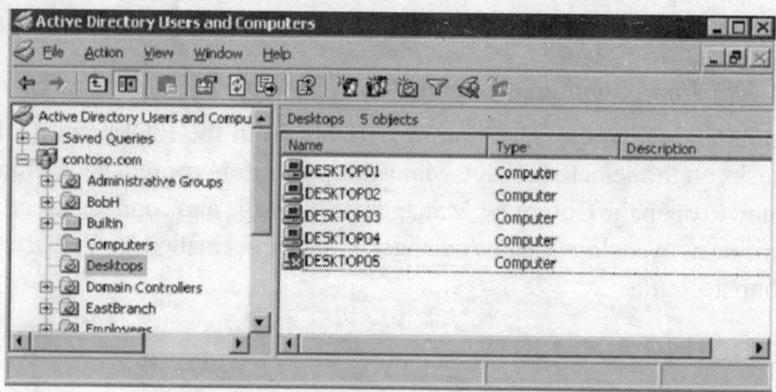

Figure 5.24 A disabled computer account

While an account is disabled, the computer cannot create a secure channel with the domain. The result is that users who have not previously logged on to the computer, and who therefore do not have cached credentials on the computer, will be unable to log on until the secure channel is re-established by enabling the account. To enable a computer account, simply select the computer and choose the Enable Account command from the Action or shortcut menus. To disable or enable a computer from the command prompt, use the DSMOD command. The DSMOD command modifies Active Directory objects. The syntax used to disable or enable computers is:

DSMOD COMPUTER ComputerDN -DISABLED YES

DSMOD COMPUTER ComputerDN -DISABLED NO

If a computer account's group memberships and SID, and the permissions assigned to that SID, are important to the operations of a domain, you do not want to delete that account. So what would you do if a computer was replaced with a new system, with upgraded hardware? Such is one scenario in which you would reset a computer account.

Resetting a computer account resets its password, but maintains all of the computer object's properties. With a reset password, the account becomes in effect "available" for use. Any computer can then join the domain using that account, including the upgraded system.

In fact, the computer that had previously joined the domain with that account can use the reset account by simply rejoining the domain. This reality will be explored in more detail in the troubleshooting lesson. The Reset Account command is available in the Action and context menus when a

computer object is selected. The DSMOD command can also be used to reset a computer account, with the following syntax:

dsmod computer ComputerDN -reset

The NETDOM command, included with the Windows Server 2003 Support Tools in the CD-ROM's Support\Tools directory, also enables you to reset a computer account.

5.10.2 Recognizing Computer Account Problems

Computer accounts, and the secure relationships between computers and their domain are robust. In the rare circumstance that an account or secure channel breaks down, the symptoms of failure are generally obvious. The most common signs of computer account problems are:

Messages at logon indicate that a domain controller cannot be contacted; that the computer account may be missing; or that the trust (another way of saying "the secure relationship") between the computer and the domain has been lost. An example is shown in Figure 5.25.

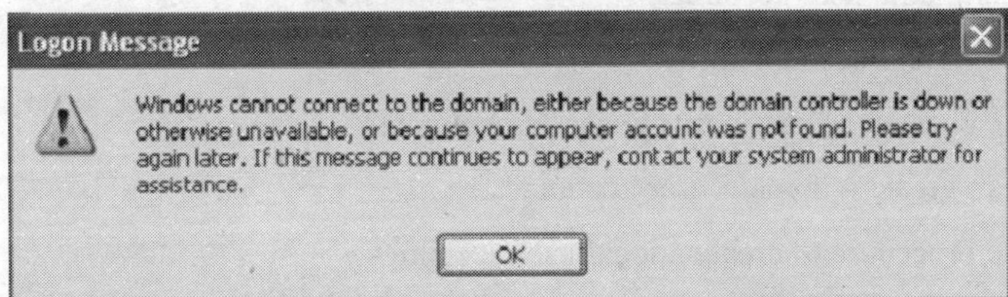

Figure 5.25 Logon message from a Windows XP client indicating a possible computer account problem

- Error messages or events in the event log indicating similar problems or suggesting that passwords, trusts, secure channels, or relationships with the domain or a domain controller have failed.
- A computer account is missing in Active Directory.

If one of these situations occurs, you must troubleshoot the account. You learned earlier how to delete, disable, and reset a computer account and, at the beginning of the chapter, how to join a machine to the domain.

The rules that govern troubleshooting a computer account are:

(a) If the computer account exists in Active Directory, it must be reset.

(b) If the computer account is missing in Active Directory, you must create a computer account.

(c) If the computer still belongs to the domain, it must be removed from the domain by changing its membership to a workgroup. The name of the workgroup is irrelevant. Best practice is to try and choose a workgroup name that you know is not in use.

(d) Rejoin the computer to the domain. Alternatively, join another computer to the domain; but the new computer must have the same name as the computer account.

To troubleshoot any computer account problem, apply all four rules. These rules can be addressed in any order, except that Rule D, involving rejoining the computer to the domain, must as always be performed as the final step. Let's examine two scenarios. In the first scenario, a user complains that when he or she attempts to log on, the system presents error messages indicating that the computer account might be missing. Applying Rule A, you open Active Directory Users And Computers and find that the computer account exists. You reset the account. Rule B does not apply-the account does exist. Then, using Rule C, you disjoin the system from the domain and, following Rule D, rejoin the domain.

In a second scenario, if a computer account is reset by accident, the first item that has occurred is Rule A. Although the reset is accidental, you must continue to recover by applying the remaining three rules. Rule B does not apply because the account exists in the domain. Rule C indicates that if the computer is still joined to the domain, it must be removed from the domain. Then, by Rule D, it can rejoin the domain. With these four rules, you can make an informed decision, on the job or on the certification exams, about how to address any scenario in which a computer account has lost functionality.

EXERCISES

1. How we can create a user account in windows server 2003?
2. How we can name user accounts?
3. Explain the various account options?
4. Explain the concept of passwords in server accounts?
5. How we can create a domain user account?
6. Explain the procedure to create a local user account?
7. Explain the properties of setting user account?
8. How we can test user accounts?
9. How we can manage user accounts?
10. Explain the concept of finding, renaming and deleting a user account?
11. How we can use home folders?
12. How we can maintain user profiles?
13. How we can use mandatory profiles?
14. Explain the concept of creating and managing user objects?
15. Explain the various account properties?

16. Explain in detail group and computer accounts?
17. What do you mean by group scope?
18. Explain the concept of group conversion?
19. How we can assign group scopes?
20. Explain the various group scopes in detail?
21. What are special identities?
22. How groups affect network performance?
23. Explain the concept of planning organizational units?
24. How we can plan a group strategy?
25. How we can implement the group strategy?
26. How we can manage built-in groups and user rights?
27. Define user rights?
28. How we can assign user rights to a group?
29. How we can assign rights locally?
30. Explain the creation of computer accounts?
31. How we can create computer objects using DSADD?
32. How we can create a computer account with NETDOM?
33. How we can join a computer to a domain?
34. Difference between computers container and organisational units?
35. How we can manage computer accounts?
36. How we can manage computer object permissions?
37. Explain the concept of troubleshooting accounts?

CHAPTER 6

Active Directory

6.1 INTRODUCTION

Active Directory is the foundation of an enterprise-level Windows network, and Windows Server 2003 includes a number of improvements and enhancements to its directory services that will make a network administrator's job easier. Windows Server 2003 administrators must understand the basics of how directory services work and the role they play in the network, and specifically how the directory services concept is implemented in Microsoft's Active Directory. we start with the basics by defining directory services and providing a brief background of the directory services standards and protocols. You'll learn how the Active Directory works, and be introduced to the terminology and concepts required to understand the Active Directory infrastructure.

We discuss how the directory is structured into sites, forests, domains, domain trees, and organizational units (OUs), and you'll learn about the components that make up the Active Directory, including both logical and physical components. These include the schema, the Global Catalog (GC), domain controllers (DCs), and the replication service. You'll learn to use the Active Directory administrative tools, and we discuss directory security and access control. Finally, we provide an overview of what's new for Active Directory in Windows Server 2003.

6.2 DIRECTORY SERVICES

As anyone familiar with networking knows, a network can be comprised of a vast number of elements, including user accounts, file servers, volumes, fax servers, printers, applications, databases, and other shared resources. Because the number of objects making up a network increases as an organization grows, finding and managing these accounts and resources becomes harder as the network gets bigger. To make a monolithic enterprise network more manageable, directory services are used to store a collection of information about users and resources, so they are organized and accessible across the network.

A directory allows accounts and resources to be organized in a logical, hierarchical fashion so that information can be found easily. By searching the directory, users can find the resources they need, and administrators are able to control and configure accounts and resources easily and effectively. Keeping this information in a centralized location ensures that users and administrators don't have to waste time looking at what's available on each server, they only have to refer to the directory. Any directory is a structured source of information, consisting of objects and their attributes. Those who have access to the directory can look up an object, and then view its attributes. If they have sufficient rights (as in the case of an administrator), the object can be modified. These attributes can be used to provide information that's accessible to users, or control security at a granular level.

Because a user can access account information from anywhere on the network, directory services allow a user to log on to multiple servers using a single logon. A single logon is an important feature to directory services, because without it, a user must log on to each server that provides needed resources. This is common on Windows NT networks, where the administrator must create a different account on each server the user needs to access. The user then needs to log on to each server individually. This is significantly different from the way Windows 2000/2003's directory services work, where a user logs on to the network once and can use any of the resources to which he or she has been given access.

Sophisticated directory services give administrators the ability to organize information, control security, and manage users and resources anywhere on the network. Information resides in a central repository that's replicated to different servers on the network. It allows the data to be accessed when needed and saves the administrator from having to visit each server to manage accounts. This lowers the amount of work needed to manage the network, while providing granular control over rights and permissions. The administrator only needs to modify a user account or other object once, and these security changes are replicated throughout the network.

Directory services have been used on different network operating systems for years, and have proven to be a useful and powerful technology. Following suit, Microsoft created its own implementation of directory services on Windows NT called NTDS, and then followed with Active Directory on newer versions of servers. NTDS used a fiat namespace, which provided limited functionality in comparison with Active Directory's hierarchical structure and feature set. Active Directory was first introduced in Windows 2000, and continues to provide directory services to the Windows Server 2003 family of servers. It can be installed on the Standard, Enterprise, and Datacenter Editions of Windows Server 2003, and provides a necessary foundation for any network using these servers.

6.3 TERMINOLOGY AND CONCEPTS

Before delving too far into the specifics of Active Directory, it is important to discuss a number of concepts and terms to appreciate the features and functionality of a directory service. As with anything dealing with technology, certain words and phrases associated with Active Directory and Windows Server 2003 are useful in identifying and defining specific components of the network. Some of the terms and concepts we discuss in the following subsections include:

- Directory data store
- Directory partitions
- Policy-based administration

- DAP and LDAP
- Naming schemes used in Active Directory

6.3.1 Directory Data Store

Active Directory isn't just a service that provides access to directory services; it's also a method of storing data about network elements. If you didn't have a place where configurations and directory data are saved, you'd lose this information every time you shut down your server. The data store contains a vast amount of information, including data dealing with users, groups, computers, the resources they can access, and other components of the network. Because the Active Directory data store is a database of all directory information, it is also referred to as the directory.

When you install the directory on a Windows Server 2003 server, the Active Directory data source is placed on the server's hard disk. The file used to store directory information is called NTDS.DIT, and is located in the NTDS folder in the systemroot (for example, C:\WINDOWS). Any changes made to the directory are saved to this file. The presence of Active Directory's data store on a Windows Server 2003 server has a major impact on that server's role in the network. As shown in Figure 6.1, the directory is stored on DCs, which are servers with writable copies of the data store. A DC is used to manage domains, which are groups of computers, users, and other objects that share (or are included in) the same directory.

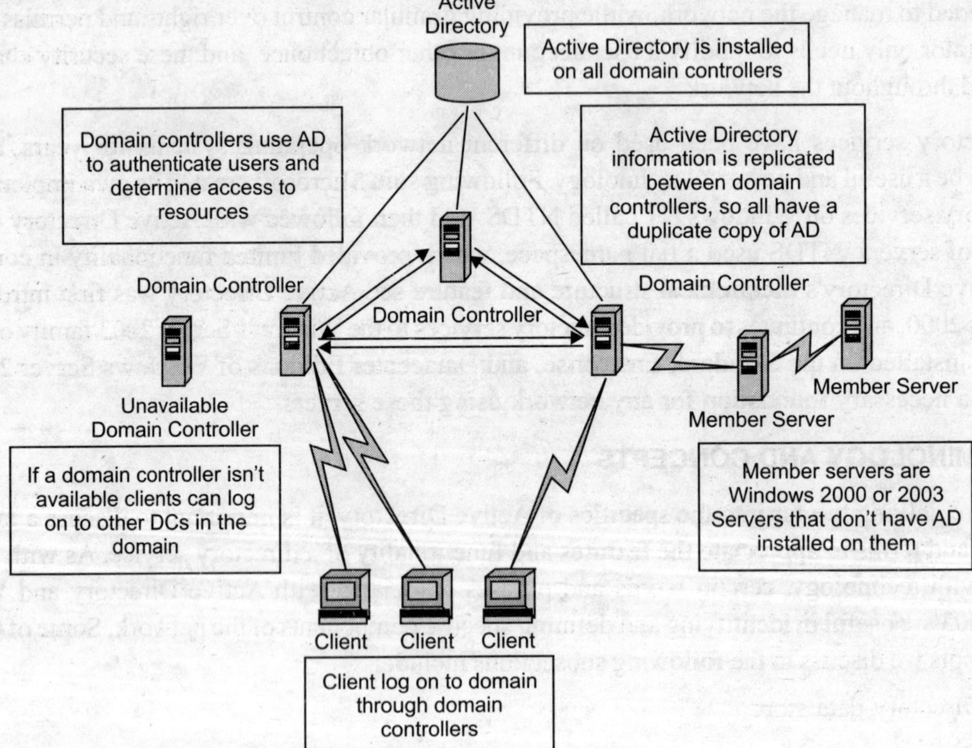

Figure 6.1 Relationship Between Active Directory, Domain Controllers, Member Servers and Clients

Domains that use different Active Directory data sources can still communicate with one another, but secure relationships between them must be configured. Each DC retains its own copy of the directory, containing information on the domain in which it is located. If one DC becomes unavailable, users and computers can still access the Active Directory data store on another DC in that domain. This allows users to continue logging on to the network even though the DC that's normally used is unavailable. It also allows computers and applications that require directory information to continue functioning while one of these servers is down.

Because a domain can have more than one DC, changes made to the directory on one DC must be updated on others. The process of copying these updates is called replication, and is used to synchronize information in the directory. Without replication, features in Active Directory would fail to function properly. For example, if you added a user on one DC, the new account would be added to the directory store on that server. This would allow the user to log on to that domain controller, but he or she still couldn't log on to other DCs until these changes to the directory were replicated. When a change is made on one DC, the changes need to be replicated quickly so that each DC continues to have an accurate duplicate copy of Active Directory.

Because replication is so important to making the directory consistent across the network, the data source is organized in a way to make replication more efficient. Not every piece of data is saved in the same location of the data source. As shown in Figure 6.2, information resides in different areas of the directory, called directory partitions. Because Active Directory is a logical, hierarchical structure, it has a treelike structure similar to that of the Windows Registry or folders on a hard disk.

Data is stored within subtrees of the directory; much like data on your hard disk is stored within folders that are nested within one another. Each contiguous subtree in the directory is a partition. Any data that changes within a directory partition is replicated as a single unit to other DCs.

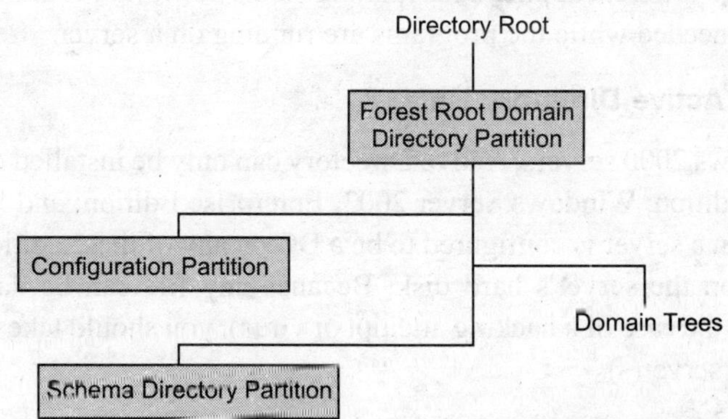

Figure 6.2 Active Directory Is a Hierarchical Structure

In Active Directory, three partitions exist on any DC and must be replicated, as these contain data that the Microsoft network needs to function properly:

- Domain partition
- Configuration partition
- Schema partition

The domain partition contains information about the domain. This includes information about users, computers, resources, and attributes associated with each. Without this data being replicated, any changes would be limited to the server on which the changes were made, and other servers would use older settings. For example, if the domain data wasn't replicated and you disabled a user's account on one DC, the user would still be able to log on to other DCs. The domain partition is important because it contains information about objects and their attributes, which are fundamental elements of your network.

Configuration data deals with the topology of Active Directory, and includes information about how the domains, domain trees, and forests within a network are configured. A domain tree is a structure of domains. If more than one domain is in a domain tree, trusts are set up between those domains so that they can share data and resources between them. A forest also consists of multiple domains that share directory data. It consists of one or more trees that are connected through trusts. The configuration partition also includes information about the locations of DCs and the GC, which is a subset of the data contained in Active Directory that is used to provide search and logon functionality across multiple domains.

Because Active Directory is made up of different objects, and each object has specific attributes, certain rules must be created to control what objects can exist in the directory, and the attributes of each. For example, a user account has attributes that include a password, an account name, and the first and last of the person to whom the account belongs. The types of objects that exist in Active Directory, and which attributes each type has, is determined by the schema. The schema partition contains information that defines object classes and attributes used within the domain. It determines what objects can exist within Active Directory, and what attributes each can have.

Windows Server 2003 servers can also create one or more application partitions, which are used to store data that is specific to different applications running on the network. Programs can use this partition to store settings that are needed while the programs are running on a server.

6.3.2 Protecting your Active Directory Data

In addition to Windows 2000 servers, Active Directory can only be installed on Microsoft Windows Server 2003, Standard Edition; Windows Server 2003, Enterprise Edition; and Windows Server 2003, Datacenter Edition. When a server is configured to be a DC on any of these editions, a writable copy of the directory is stored on the server's hard disk. Because any file can be damaged, destroyed, or compromised (such as in the case of a hacking attempt or virus), you should take steps to ensure that the directory is safe on your server(s).

If only one DC is used, then only one NTDS.DIT file will exist, meaning there is only one copy of the directory for that domain. Failure of this server or damage to the NTDS.DIT file will disable the network. Users will be unable to log on, computers will be unable to access needed information from the directory, and any configurations on your network could be lost. Rather than hoping that nothing ever happens to your one DC, it is wise to use multiple DCs on your network. If more than one DC exists in a domain, any updates to the NTDS.DIT will be replicated to other DCs. This will allow multiple copies of the directory to exist on the network, providing a level of fault tolerance if one server fails. If one fails, another can continue authenticating users, supplying services, and providing access to resources.

Because of the importance of the NTDS.DIT file, the drive on which it is stored should be formatted in NTFS format. NTFS is a file format that allows the best possible level of protection, allowing you to set permissions on who can access the directory and NTDS.DIT file locally and across the network. Such permissions cannot be set on hard disks that are formatted as FAT16 or FAT32. Limiting the access to this file lessens the chance that someone might accidentally or maliciously damage or delete the data source.

It is also important to remember that any measures you take to protect Active Directory from harm do not negate the need to perform regular backups. When backups are performed, the data on a computer is copied to other media (such as a tape, CD, or DVD), which can then be stored in another location. Should any problem occur, you can restore any files that were damaged or lost.

6.3.3 Policy-based Administration

There can be hundreds or thousands of users and computers in a large network. Having to go through each account and configure settings can be an arduous task. For example, imagine having to go to each computer to change the desktop so that it displays a company logo as the background image. Rather than visiting each computer, it would be far easier to make such changes in one location, and have these settings apply to everyone. This is why policy-based administration is such a bene?t to Active Directory: it makes managing accounts easier. Group policies allow you to apply default settings to groups of users and groups. Policies can be used to:

- Control desktop settings that determine the display properties of a computer.
- Assign scripts that run at logon, logoff, startup, and shutdown.
- Enforce password security, such as by setting minimum password lengths, maximum length of time before a password must be changed, and so on.
- Redirect folders from the local computer to a folder on a networked computer, such as when the My Documents folder is redirected to use specific folders on a server.
- Deploy applications, so that certain members have programs available to them to install or have them automatically installed.

As we'll see in the chapters that follow, these are just a few of the options available to administrators in managing users and computers on a network. When policies are created, they are stored as Group Policy Objects (GPOs) in Active Directory. The settings in a GPO can be applied to a site, domain, or OU. An OU is a container in Active Directory that can contain users, groups, computers, or other OUs. We'll discuss OUs in greater detail later in this chapter. Because GPOs can be applied at different levels, you can set different policies for different areas of your company. For example, you could create a group policy for users in Finance and another for the Sales department (by placing Finance users in one OU and Sales users in another). If you have different domains for different branch offices, you could have different settings for the Sales divisions in each domain. Using GPOs in this manner, you can configure which settings will be used for specific groups of users and computers.

6.3.4 Directory Access Protocol

For clients to search for objects, update information, and communicate with DCs when logging on to the network, a directory access protocol must be used. A protocol is a set of rules that dictate how data is sent over a network. A directory access protocol is used for the specific purpose of exchanging information with the directory service. Active Directory uses LDAP for communications between clients and directory servers. LDAP is a version of the X.500 Directory Access Protocol (DAP), and is considered lightweight because it uses less code than DAP does.

The Internet Engineering Task Force (IETF) established industry standards for LDAP, enabling LDAP to be used over local networks and the Internet by a variety of directory services. Many network operating systems that use directory services (including Novell NetWare, Windows 2000, and Windows Server 2003) implement LDAP for accessing the directory, while other products (such as Internet browsers) support it as a method for finding resources or managing the directory. Since its inception in 1994, there have been several versions of LDAP, with features being added to accommodate changing needs. Active Directory supports versions 2 and 3.

6.3.5 Naming Scheme

Active Directory supports several common formats for naming objects. By using different methods of naming objects, it allows objects to be accessed in a variety of ways. Providing different naming schemes also provides backward compatibility to older systems that might not support one or more of these formats. The naming schemes supported by Active Directory include:

- Domain Name System (DNS)
- User principal name (UPN)
- Universal Naming Convention (UNC)
- Uniform Resource Locator (URL)
- Lightweight Directory Access Protocol Uniform Resource Locator (LDAP URL)

In Active Directory, domains are usually given DNS names (such as syngress.com). Because Windows domains didn't use this naming scheme prior to Windows 2000, each domain is also given a name that's compatible with those used in Windows NT networks. These pre-Windows 2000 names are NetBIOS names, and are one-word names that users of older operating systems can use to log on to Active Directory. This allows clients to log on to domains by entering the domain name and username using the format: domain name\username.

UPNs are based on the IETF's RFC 822. Each user account in Active Directory has a logon name and UPN suffix. The logon name is the account name, and the UPN suffix is the domain that the user will log on to. The two are connected by the @ symbol, making the logon appear like an Internet e-mail address (username@domain). After entering a username, the user will generally be required to enter a password to prove that he or she is authorized to use this account.

When the UPN is created for a user account, it also suggests a pre-Windows 2000 logon name that is used by the Security Account Manager (SAM) to log on to a server. The SAM is a service that stores information about user accounts and groups to which they belong. Local computer accounts use the SAM to store accounts that are used to access the local computer, and Windows NT servers use it for allowing network users access to resources on the server. Although you can create your own logon name, Active Directory will suggest a pre-Windows 2000 user logon name that's based on the first 20 bytes of the Active Directory logon name.

Every computer account that is created in Active Directory also has multiple names, so that the account can be identified and accessed in a variety of ways. When a computer account is created in Active Directory, you need to enter a name for the computer, which will uniquely identify it in the domain. This is the host name for the machine, which can be used by DNS to indicate its place in the domain, and can be used to help find the computer when clients search for it and its resources on the network.

In DNS, the host name is combined with the domain name to create the computer's fully qualified domain name (FQDN).This combines the host name with the domain name, and separates the two with a period. For example, if you have a computer named COMP100 in the domain called knightware.ca, the FQDN for this computer would be comp100.knightware.ca. No two computers in a domain can have the same name, as this would create conflicts. When the computer account is created, it will also require the computer be given a pre-Windows 2000 name, so older clients and servers can identify and access it. As with user accounts, Windows Server 2003 will suggest a name, which is based on the first 15 bytes of the name used to create the account. If you don't want to use this default name, you can enter a new one at any time.

The UNC path is a tried-and-true method of accessing shared resources over a network. It uses the format of two backslashes, followed by the domain name or server name, the name of the share, and (where applicable) the name of the resource. The shared resource is often the name of a shared directory, and might be followed by the name of a file, application, or other resource on the server. In other words, the format would be \\domain name\share\filename or \\servername\share\filename. For example, if you were accessing a file named SPREADSHEET.XLS in a shared directory called XLS on a server named FS-GOTHAM, the UNC to access it would be \\fsgotham\xls\spreadsheet.xls.You can use UNC names in the address bar of browsers, from the Run command of the Windows Start menu, or any other place where UNC names are allowed.

Another common method of accessing resources through a browser is by using URLs. A URL generally begins with http (for HyperText Transfer Protocol), a colon, and two forward slashes, followed by a server name such as www, a domain name such as syngress.com, and a filename path (which can contain a directory name such as files, or just a filename such as file.htm or file.html for an HTTP document, file.asp for an Active Server Pages document, or file.jpg for a graphic in .JPG format). The final naming scheme we'll discuss is LDAP URL. This method is similar to using URLs, but uses the X.500 naming structure to locate a resource. An LDAP URL uses the format LDAP://domain name/CN=common name/OU=organizational unit/DC=domain component. In this format, the common name is the name of an object in Active Directory, OU is the organizational unit, and DC is the DNS domain name in which the object exists. This allows you to specify an object that is uniquely identified in the directory. As we'll see in the sections that follow, this information is built on X.500/LDAP standards.

6.3.6 X.500/LDAP Standards

Both the X.500 DAP and LDAP work by interacting with the directory. The directory is designed as a hierarchy, and has a tree-like structure called the directory information tree. Information in subtrees branch off the trunk, much as folders on the hard disk branch off a root directory. These subtrees contain objects that represent elements of the network, and are called directory service entries. Just as there can't be two files with the same name in a folder on your hard disk, each object must have a unique name in the directory structure.

6.3.6.1 Distinguished Name

To accommodate the need for each object being identified with a unique name in the directory, objects have a distinguished name (DN).A DN represents the exact location of an object within the directory. This is comparable to a file being represented by the full path, showing where it is located on the hard disk. With an object in the directory, several components are used to create this name:

- CN The common name of the object, and includes such things as user accounts, printers, and other network elements represented in the directory.
- OU The organizational unit. These are containers in the directory that are used to hold objects. To continue with our example of files on a hard disk, this would be comparable to a folder within the directory structure.
- DC A domain component. This is used to identify the name of the domain or server, and the DNS suffix (for example, .com, .net, .edu, and .gov).

When combined, these components of the DN are used to show the location of an object. Each DN can be used more than once to fully identify the object's place within the directory. For example, let's say a user account named BobSmith was stored in the Accounting OU in the syngress.com domain. In this case, the DN of this object would be:

CN=BobSmith, OU=Accounting, DC=syngress, DC=com

6.3.6.2 Relative Distinguished Name

An RDN is a portion of the DN, and is used to uniquely identify an object with a parent container. As each object must have a unique name with the directory structure, the RDN identi?es an object within a particular OU. This is comparable to a file in a folder, where you specify the name of the file and not the full path to it. Just as a file in one folder might have the same name as a file in another folder, an object in one OU might have the same name as another object in another OU.

While the RDN would be the same, the DN would indicate that each is in a different OU. To illustrate this, let's look at the previous example, which used the DN /CN=BobSmith, /OU=Accounting, / DC=syngress, /DC=com. In this case, CN=BobSmith is the RDN of the object. It is a subset of the DN, and the only one by that name in the Accounting OU. However, you could have a user account named BobSmith in the Sales OU. Even though the RDNs are identical, the full DNs are unique. DNS and RDNs apply to user accounts and any other objects within the directory. When a computer account is created, the name used for the computer is used by LDAP as the RDN. For example, if a computer were named COMP100, this would be its RDN.

6.3.6.3 Canonical Name

A canonical name is another way of showing the DN of an object. It contains the same information, but shows it in a way that is easier to read. Using the example of the BobSmith object, if we convert its DN to a canonical name, it would read:

syngress.com/Accounting/BobSmith

In the preceding example, the CN, OU, and DC components of the DN have been removed and replaced with slashes (similar to the way in which a pathname to a file on a DOS/Windows machine is notated with backslashes).The canonical format also reverses the information. Rather than beginning with the lowest level component of the DN (in other words, the object) and moving up through higher levels, it starts at the highest level of the directory structure and works its way down to the object's name. While it relates the DN of an object, it removes the extraneous notations in the name and makes it easier to read.

6.4 INSTALLING ACTIVE DIRECTORY TO CREATE A DOMAIN CONTROLLER

When Windows Server 2003 is installed on a computer, it doesn't mean that the directory is also installed. Active Directory is installed when you create a DC. It can be installed as part of the Windows Server 2003 installation, and can also be installed on member servers, which are computers running Windows Server 2003 that don't have Active Directory installed. A server without Active Directory installed on it can still deliver a variety of services, file storage, and access to other resources, but until Active Directory is installed, it can't authenticate users or provide the other functions of a DC. Once Active Directory is installed, the member server ceases to be a member server and becomes a DC.

To install Active Directory on a member server, the Active Directory Installation Wizard (DCPROMO) is used. DCPROMO is a tool that promotes a member server to DC status. Because a DC is a server with a writable copy of Active Directory installed on it, this tool will install a copy of the directory database on the server, and configure the structure of Active Directory based on your input. After Active Directory is installed, you can then perform other tasks that will allow users of your network to access resources on the domain. Use the following steps to install Active Directory on a Windows Server 2003 computer.

6.4.1 Install Active Directory

As with many of the example in this book, this example should not be performed on a production server. Moreover, while readers who have previous knowledge of Active Directory can perform these steps; those who are new to Active Directory might want to read the next section to understand how Active Directory works before attempting to install it.

1. From the Run command on the Windows Start menu, type DCPROMO and then click OK.
2. A welcome screen will appear that identi?es the program as the Active Directory Installation Wizard. Click Next to continue.
3. An information screen will appear, warning that clients running Windows 95 or Windows NT 4.0 SP3 and earlier won't be able to log on to Windows Server 2003 DCs or access domain resources. Click Next to continue.

4. The Domain Controller Type screen appears after this, allowing you to specify whether you want the server to be a DC for a new or existing domain (see Figure 6.3). Selecting the Domain controller for a new domain will allow you to create a new domain, while selecting Additional domain controller for an existing domain will add this server to a domain that already exists. Select the first of these options to create a new domain. Click Next to continue.

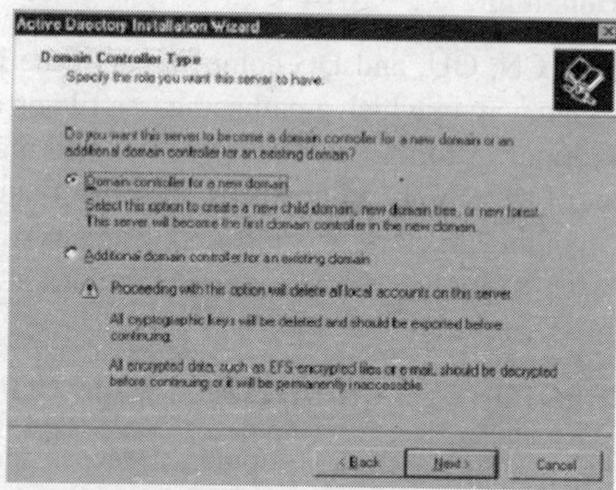

Figure 6.3 Domain Controller Type Screen of Active Directory Installation Wizard

5. The next screen allows you to configure or installs DNS on the server. If DNS is already running, then select Yes, I will configure the DNS client. If not, select No, just install and configure DNS on this computer. If you select Yes and DNS is not running, a warning screen will appear informing you of this. If DNS isn't running, select the second option (No), and click Next to continue.
6. Enter the DNS name for the new domain (for example, syngress.com). Click Next to continue.
7. As shown in Figure 6.4, the screen that appears next asks you to enter the NetBIOS name for this domain, which older versions of Windows will use to access the domain. Windows Server 2003 suggests a name based on your previously entered DNS name. Accept the default value, and click Next to continue.

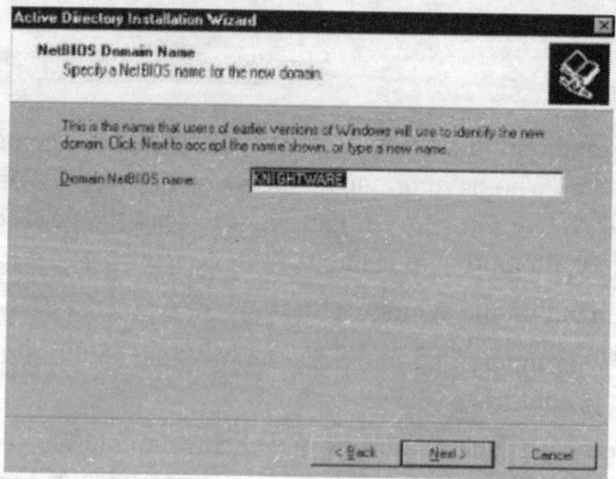

Figure 6.4 NetBIOS Domain Name Screen of the Active Directory Installation Wizard

8. The next screen, shown in Figure 6.5, allows you to specify where the Active Directory database and log files will be stored. By default, this will be a directory called NTDS in the systemroot folder. Accept the default values and click Next to continue.

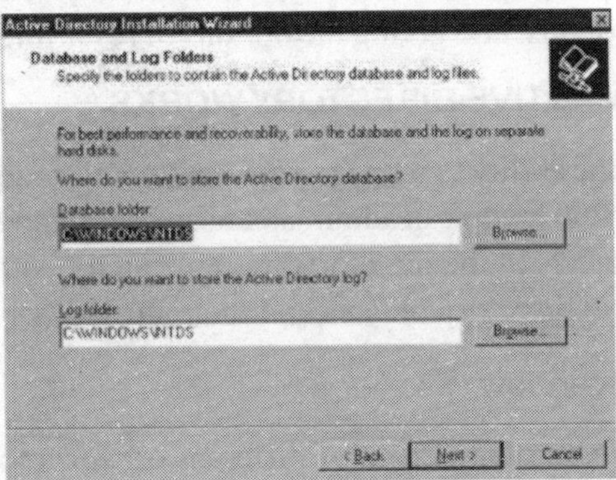

Figure 6.5 Database and Log Folders Screen of the Active Directory Installation Wizard

9. The next screen asks for the location of where public files that will be copied to other DCs will be stored. By default, this is stored in the SYSVOL directory in the systemroot folder. Accept the default value and click Next to continue.
10. The next screen is used to set proper permissions based on whether you will be running server programs that were designed for pre-Windows 2000 domains. If this were the case, you would select the first option Permissions compatible with pre-Windows 2000 Server operating systems. Selecting this will allow anonymous users to read information on the domain, so it is best to select Permissions compatible only with Windows 2000 or Windows Server 2003 operating systems whenever possible. Assuming you will not be running such software, select the second option, and click Next.
11. The following screen asks that you enter a password used when the server is started in Directory Services Restore mode. This mode is used to restore Active Directory after it has become damaged. Enter a password in the first field, and then enter it in the field below to confirm your password. Click Next to continue.
12. The screen that appears next displays all the settings you chose for your installation of Active Directory (see Figure 6.6). Review the summary information that's shown on this screen, and then click Next to continue.

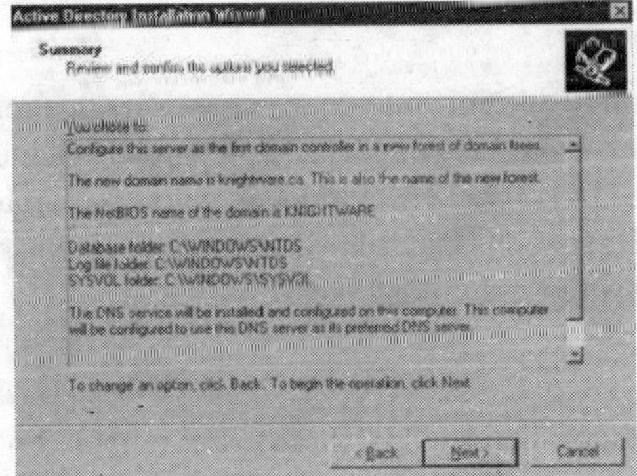

Figure 6.6 Summary Screen of the Active Directory Installation Wizard

13. The wizard will proceed to install and configure Active Directory based on your choices. Once this is done, click Finish.
14. To complete the installation, you will need to restart Windows Server 2003.A message box will appear informing you of this, and giving the options of restarting now or not. Click Restart Now.

6.5 UNDERSTANDING HOW ACTIVE DIRECTORY WORKS

Active Directory provides the ability to manage your network through a single source of information. Using tools in Windows Server 2003, you can administer users, computers, printers, and a variety of other resources. Changes made to objects in the directory are replicated to other DCs. This ensures that each DC has an up-to-date copy of all directory objects and their attributes.

6.5.1 Directory Structure Overview

When you compare the directory structure of different organizations, you will find that they are different. Active Directory is organized in a hierarchical structure that is built from a variety of different components that represent elements of your network. For example, there are user objects, computer objects, and various containers to organize them. The way you organize these elements will make the hierarchical structure of Active Directory in your company different from other companies.

The components that are part of this hierarchy include:

- Sites
- Domains
- Trees
- Forests
- Objects
- DCs

In addition to these, we will also look at the components of Active Directory that are used to organize and manage this hierarchy.

These components are:

- GC
- Schema

Active Directory allows you to administrate your network by dealing with the physical and logical structure. The physical structure of your network consists of tangible elements that make up your network, while the logical structure is used to organize components into a hierarchy that matches the structure of your company. As we'll see in the sections that follow, sites represent the physical structure of a network, while domains, trees, and forests represent the logical structure.

6.5.1.1 Sites

A site is one or more IP subnets connected by a fast and reliable link. The term subnet is short for "subnetwork," and refers to a group of neighboring computers that have been subdivided within the network. Computers in the subnet use a different network ID from those in other subnets, essentially becoming a smaller network within the network. Sites are used to store information about the topology of your network in Active Directory, so that the directory has information about the physical structure of the network.

Active Directory uses information about the physical elements of a network in a number of ways. It allows Active Directory to determine the fastest connections between sites, so that updates in the directory can be replicated to other DCs. Sites contain computer and connection objects, which are used to configure replication between sites, allowing this information to be copied in the fastest, most effective way to DCs in other sites. It is also useful to users, as it will allow each user to be authenticated by the DC that's closest to that user.

Although not required, it is a good idea to have a DC in each site. When a client logs on to a domain, a DC must be contacted. The client will search the local site for a DC and then, if one is not found, attempt to connect to DCs in other sites. If the client has to connect to a DC in a different site, it might take a long time for the user to be authenticated. Creating different sites will group computers together, so they will authenticate to the DC that's closest to them. An important feature of a site is that subnets are well connected. This means that the links between sites are reliable and fast. While determining what is fast can be subjective, Microsoft has traditionally defined a fast link as being at least 512 Kbps, whilc acknowledging that 128 Kbps or higher is sufficient. Because the bandwidth needed by an organization depends on the amount of data being transferred between sites, some companies will require a greater bandwidth to meet their needs.

As shown in Figure 6.7, there can be multiple domains in a site, or multiple sites in a domain. Because sites represent the physical structure, they are different from domains, trees, and forests (which we'll discuss next) that represent the logical structure. Sites are separate from these entities, and unfettered by issues that determine the logical structure of a Windows Server 2003 network.

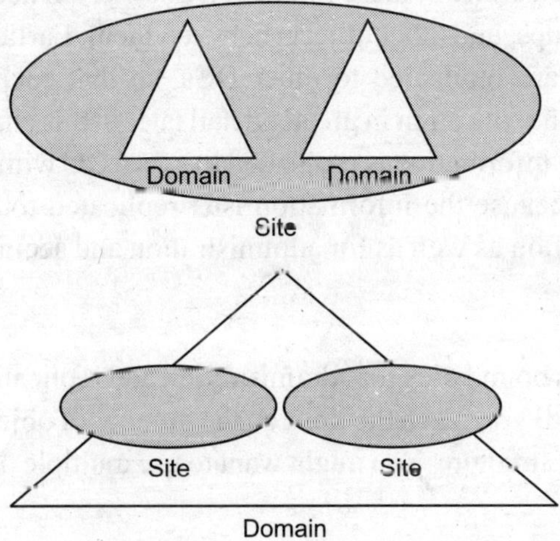

Figure 6.7 Sites Can Contain Multiple Domains, and Domains Can Contain Multiple Sites

6.5.1.2 Domains

Domains have been a cornerstone of a Microsoft network since the days of Windows NT. A domain is a logical grouping of network elements, consisting of computers, users, printers, and other components that make up the network and allow people to perform their jobs. Because domains group these objects in a single unit, the domain acts as an administrative boundary, in which you can control security on users and computers. In Windows Server 2003, a domain also shares a common directory database, security policies, and (when other domains exist in the network) relationships with other domains. They are important logical components of a network, because everything is built upon or resides within the domain structure.

Sites and domains are different structures, and aren't bound by one another. Just as a site can include users and computers from multiple domains, domains can include multiple sites. This allows you to have objects from different areas of your network in the same domain, even if they're in different subnets or geographical locations. In serving as an administrative boundary, each domain uses its own security policies. Group policies can be applied at a domain level, so that any users and computers within that domain are affected by it. This allows you to control access to resources, password policies, and other configurations to everyone within the domain. These security settings and policies only affect the domain, and won't be applied to other domains in the network. When a domain is created, a DNS domain name is assigned to identify it. DNS is used on the Internet and other TCP/IP networks for resolving IP addresses to user-friendly names. Because an Active Directory domain is integrated with DNS, this allows users, computers, applications, and other elements of the network to easily find DCs and other resources on the network.

As you can imagine, a significant number of objects can potentially exist within a domain. To allow for significant growth in a network, Microsoft designed Active Directory to support up to 10 million objects per domain. While Microsoft concedes this to be a theoretical estimate, the company provides a more practical estimate that each domain can support at least 1 million objects. In either case, chances are your domain will never reach either of these limits. If it does, you'll need to create additional domains, and split users, computers, groups, and other objects between them. Earlier in this chapter, we mentioned that updates to the directory are replicated to other DCs, so that each has an identical copy of the directory database. We'll explain replication in greater detail later in this chapter, but for now it is important to realize that Active Directory information is replicated to every DC within a domain. Each domain uses its own directory database. Because the information isn't replicated to other domains, this makes the domain a boundary for replication as well as for administration and security.

6.5.1.3 Domain Trees

Although domains serve as boundaries for administration and replication, this does not mean that you should only use one domain until you reach the limit on the number of objects supported per domain. That depends on your organizational structure. You might want to use multiple domains for any of the following reasons:

- To decentralize administration
- To improve performance

- To control replication
- To use different security settings and policies for each domain
- If you have an large number of objects in the directory

For example, your company might have branch offices in several countries. If there is only one domain, directory information will have to be replicated between DCs in each country, or (if no DCs resides in those locations) users will need to log on to a DC in another country. Rather than replicating directory information across a WAN, and having to manage disparate parts of the network, you could break the network into several domains. For example, you might create one domain for each country.

Creating separate domains does not mean there will be no relationship between these different parts of your network. Active Directory allows multiple domains to be connected together in a hierarchy. As shown in Figure 6.8, a domain can be created beneath an existing domain in the hierarchy. The pre-existing domain is referred to as a "parent domain," and the new domain created under it is referred to as a "child domain." When this is done, the domains share a common namespace. They also share a schema, configuration, and GC, as do all domains in the same forest, whether or not they have a parent-child relationship.

As seen in Figure 6.8, domains created in this parent-child structure and sharing a namespace belong to a domain tree. Trees follow a DNS naming scheme, so that the relationship between the parent and child domains is obvious and easy to follow. To conform to this naming scheme, a child domain appends its name to the parent's name. For example, if a parent domain used the domain name sygress.com, a child domain located in the United Kingdom might have the name uk.syngress.com. Names can also indicate the function of a domain, rather than its geographical location. For example, the child domain used by developers might use the name dev.syngress.com. Because domain trees use a contiguous namespace, it is easy to see which domains are child domains of a particular parent domain.

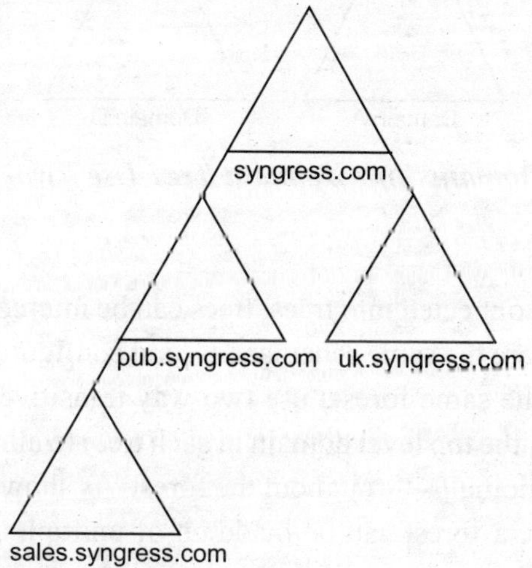

Figure 6.8 A Domain Tree Consists of Parent and Child Domains in a Contiguous

When a child domain is created, a two-way transitive trust relationship between the parent and child domains is automatically created. A trust relationship allows pass-through authentication, so users who are authenticated in a trusted domain can use resources in a trusting domain. Because the trust between a parent and child domain is bidirectional, both domains trust one another, so users in either domain can access resources in the other (assuming, of course, that the users have the proper permissions for those resources).

The other feature of the trust relationship between parent and child domains is that they are transitive. A transitive relationship means that pass-through authentication is transferred across all domains that trust one another. For example, in Figure 6.9, Domain A has a two-way transitive trust with Domain B, so both trust one another. Domain B has a two-way transitive trust with Domain C, so they also trust one another, but there is no trust relationship between Domain A and Domain C. With the two-way transitive trust, Domain C will trust Domain A (and vice versa) because both trust Domain B. This will allow users in each of the domains to access resources from the other domains. Trusts can also be manually set up between domains so that they are one-way and nontransitive, but by default, transitive bidirectional trusts are used in domain trees and forests. These trusts are also implicit, meaning that they exist automatically by default when you create the domains, unlike explicit trusts that must be created manually.

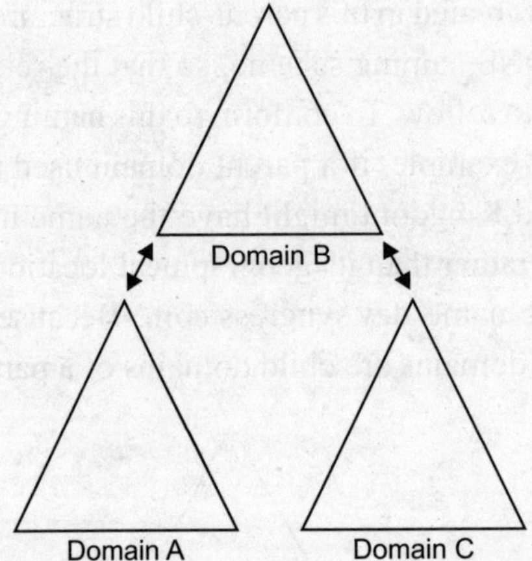

Figure 6.9 Adjoining Domains in a Domain Tree Use Two-Way Transitive Trusts

6.5.1.4 Forests

Just as domains can be interconnected into trees, trees can be interconnected into forests. A forest is one or more domain trees that share the same schema, GC, and configuration information. As is the case with domain trees, domains in the same forests use two-way transitive trusts between the roots of all domain trees in the forest (that is, the top level domain in each tree) to allow pass-through authentication, so users can access resources in domains throughout the forest. As shown in Figure 6.10, although trees require a contiguous namespace, a forest can be made up of multiple trees that use different naming schemes. This allows your domains to share resources across the network, even though they don't share a contiguous namespace.

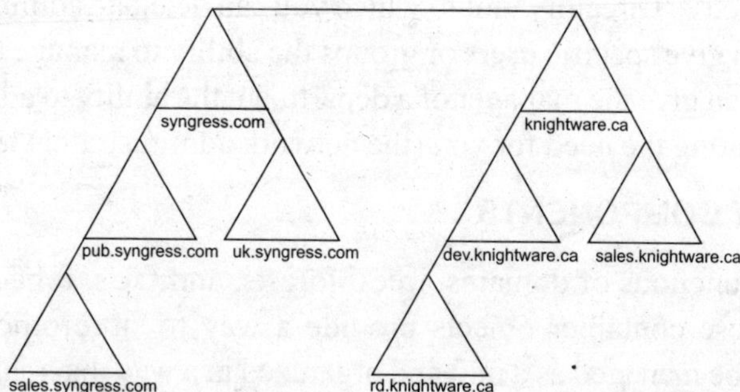

Figure 6.10 A Forest Allows Multiple Domain Trees to Be Connected and Share

Every Active Directory structure has a forest, even if it only consists of a single domain. When the first Windows Server 2003 DC is installed on a network, you create the first domain that's also called the forest root domain. Additional domains can then be created that are part of this forest, or multiple forests can be created. This allows you to control which trees are connected and can share resources with one another (within the same forest), and which are separated so that users can't search other domains sharing the GC (in separate forests).

6.5.1.5 Organizational Units

When looking at domain trees, you might think that the only way to create a directory structure that mirrors the organization of your company is to create multiple domains. However, in many companies, a single domain is all that's needed. To organize Active Directory objects within this single domain, OUs can be used. As we mentioned earlier, OUs are containers that allow you to store users, computers, groups, and other OUs. By placing objects in different OUs, you can design the layout of Active Directory to take the same shape as your company's logical structure, without creating separate domains. As shown in Figure 6.11, you can create OUs for different areas of your business, such as departments, functions, or locations. The users, computers, and groups relating to each area can then be stored inside the OU, so that you can find and manage them as a single unit.

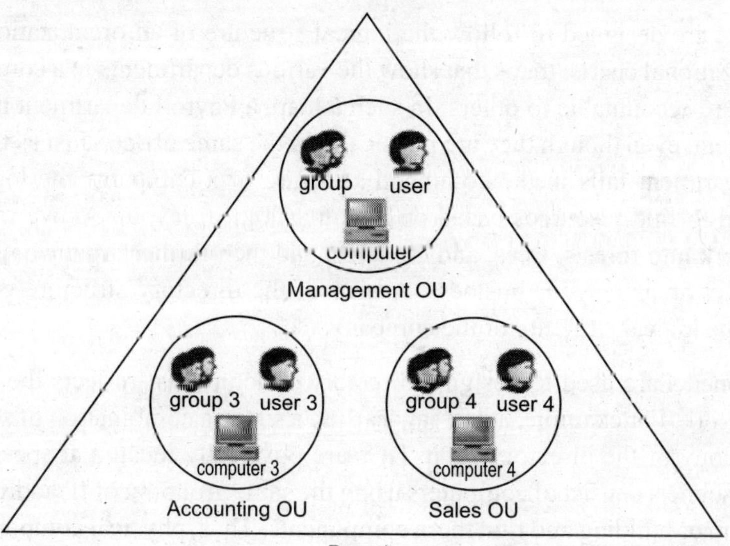

Figure 6.11 Organizational Units Can Contain Other Active Directory Objects

OUs are the smallest Active Directory unit to which you can delegate administrative authority. When you delegate authority, you give specific users or groups the ability to manage the users and resources in an OU. For example, you can give the manager of a department the ability to administer users within that department, thereby alleviating the need for you (the network administrator) to do it.

6.6 ACTIVE DIRECTORY COMPONENTS

When looking at the functions of domains, trees, forests, and OUs, it becomes apparent that each serves as a container. These container objects provide a way to store other components of Active Directory, so that they can be managed as a unit and organized in a way that makes administration easier. OUs also provide the added feature of allowing nesting, so that you can have one OU inside another.

The bulk of components in Active Directory, however, are objects that represent individual elements of the network (in Novell's NDS structure, these are called leaf objects, in keeping with the tree analogy, because they are at the end of the hierarchical "branch" and don't contain any other objects). Objects are divided into classes, and each object class includes a set of attributes, which are properties that hold data on characteristics and configurations. Just as people are defined by their characteristics (for example, eye and hair color, height, weight), attributes define an object. A printer object might have attributes that include the make, model, and configuration information related to that device, whereas a user object would include attributes such as username, password, and other data that defines the user.

6.6.1 Logical VS. Physical Components

The components making up Active Directory can be broken down into logical and physical structures. Logical components in Active Directory allow you to organize resources so that their layout in the directory reflects the logical structure of your company. Physical components in Active Directory are similarly used, but are used to reflect the physical structure of the network. By separating the logical and physical components of a network, users are better able to find resources, and administrators can more effectively manage them.

Many directories are designed to follow the logical structure of an organization. You're probably familiar with organizational charts; maps that show the various departments in a company, and illustrate which departments are accountable to others. In such a map, a Payroll department might appear below the Finance department, even though they are physically in the same office. Just as the chart allows you to find where a department falls in the command structure of a company, the logical structure of a directory allows you to find resources based on a similar logical layout. As we saw earlier, you can organize your network into forests, trees, and domains, and then further organize users and computers into OUs named after areas of your business. A map of the directory structure can be organized to appear identical to the logical structure of the company.

Physical components are used to design a directory structure that reflects the physical layout, or topology, of the network. For example, as we saw earlier, a site is a combination of subnets, and a DC is a server that has a copy of the directory on it. DCs are physically located at specific locations in an organization, while subnets consist of computers using the same grouping of IP addresses. In both cases, you could visit a room or building and find these components. Thus, physical components can be used to mirror the physical structure of an organization in the directory. As illustrated in Figure 6.12, this makes the physical structure considerably different from the logical structure of a network.

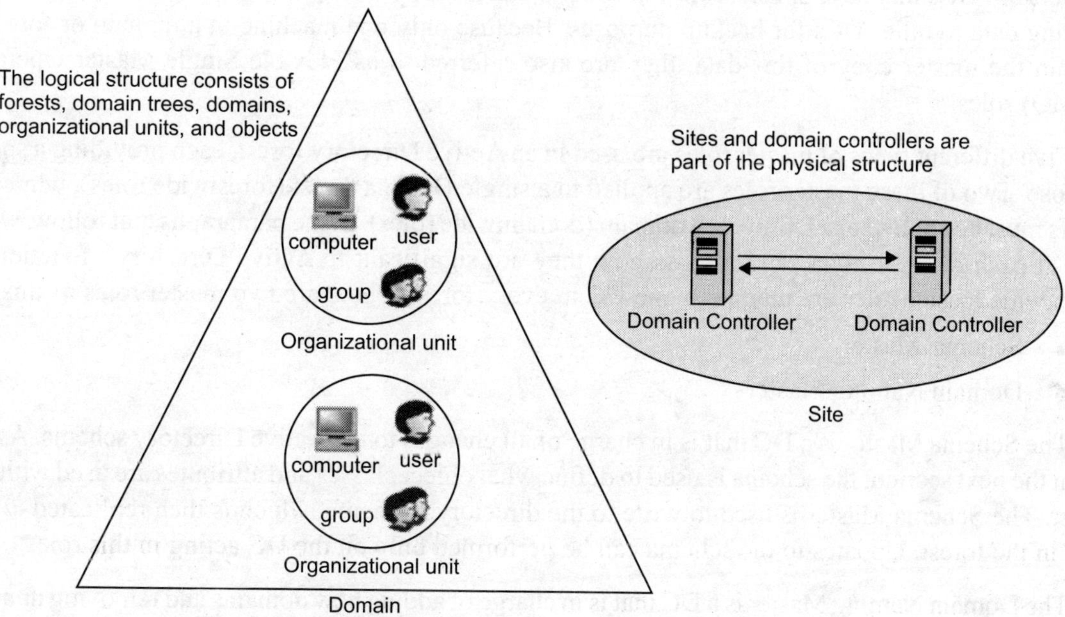

Figure 6.12 Logical Structure vs. Physical Structure

6.7 DOMAIN CONTROLLERS

DCs are used to manage domains. As mentioned, the directory on a DC can be modified, allowing network administrators to make changes to user and computer accounts, domain structure, site topology, and control access. When changes are made to these components of the directory, they are then copied to other DCs on the network. Because a DC is a server that stores a writable copy of Active Directory, not every computer on your network can act as a DC. Windows Server 2003 Active Directory can only be installed on Microsoft Windows Server 2003, Standard Edition; Windows Server 2003, Enterprise Edition; and Windows Server 2003, Datacenter Edition. Servers running other the Web Edition of Windows Server 2003 cannot be DCs, although they can be member servers that provide resources and services to the network.

When a DC is installed on the network, the first domain, forest, and site are created automatically. Additional domains, forests, and sites can be created as needed, just as additional DCs can be added. This allows you to design your network in a way that reflects the structure and needs of your organization. While only one DC is required to create a domain, multiple DCs can (and usually should) be implemented for fault tolerance and high availability. If more than one DC is used and one fails, users will be able to log on to another DC that is available. This will allow users to continue working while the DC is down. In larger companies, a number of DCs can be added to accommodate significant numbers of users who might log on and log off at the same time of day or need to access resources from these servers.

6.7.1 Master Roles

Certain changes in Active Directory are only replicated to specific DCs on the network. Operations Masters are DCs that have special roles, keeping a master copy of certain data in Active Directory and copying data to other DCs for backup purposes. Because only one machine in a domain or forest can contain the master copy of this data, they are also referred to as Flexible Single Master Operations (FSMO) roles.

Five different types of master roles are used in an Active Directory forest, each providing a specific purpose. Two of these master roles are applied to a single DC in a forest (forestwide roles), while three others must be applied to a DC in each domain (domainwide roles). In the paragraphs that follow, we will look each of these roles, and discuss how they are significant to Active Directory's functionality. Forestwide master roles are unique to one DC in every forest. There are two master roles of this type:

- Schema Master
- Domain Naming Master

The Schema Master is a DC that is in charge of all changes to the Active Directory schema. As we'll see in the next section, the schema is used to define what object classes and attributes are used within the forest. The Schema Master is used to write to the directory's schema, which is then replicated to other DCs in the forest. Updates to the schema can be performed only on the DC acting in this role.

The Domain Naming Master is a DC that is in charge of adding new domains and removing unneeded ones from the forest. It is responsible for any changes to the domain namespace. Such changes can only be performed on the Domain Naming Master, thus preventing conflicts that could occur if changes were performed on multiple machines. In addition to forestwide master roles, there are also domainwide master roles. There are three master roles of this type:

- Relative ID (RID) Master
- Primary domain controller (PDC) Emulator
- Infrastructure Master

The RID Master is responsible for creating a unique identifying number for every object in a domain. These numbers are issued to other DCs in the domain. When an object is created, a sequence of numbers that uniquely identi?es the object is applied to it. This number consists of two parts: a domain security ID (SID) and a RID. The domain SID is the same for all objects in that domain, while the RID is unique to each object. Instead of using the name of a user, computer, or group, this SID is used by Windows to identify and reference the objects. To avoid potential conflicts of DCs issuing the same number to an object, only one RID Master exists in a domain, to control the allocation of ID numbers to each DC, which the DC can then hand out to objects when they are created.

The PDC Emulator is designed to act like a Windows NT primary DC. This is needed if there are computers running pre-Windows 2000 and XP operating systems, or if Windows NT backup domain controllers (BDCs) still exist on the network. The PDC Emulator is responsible for processing password changes, and replicating these changes to BDCs on the network. It also synchronizes the time on all DCs in a domain so servers don't have time discrepancies between them. Because there can only be one Windows NT PDC in a domain, there can be only one PDC Emulator.

Even if there aren't any servers running as BDCs on the network, the PDC Emulator still has a purpose in each domain. The PDC Emulator receives preferred replication of all password changes performed by other DCs within the domain. When a password is changed on a DC, it is sent to the PDC Emulator. The PDC Emulator is responsible for this because it can take time to replicate password changes to all DCs in a domain. If a user changes his or her password on one DC and then attempts to log on to another, the second DC he or she is logging on to might still have old password information. Because this DC considers it a bad password, it forwards the authentication request to the PDC Emulator to determine whether the password is actually valid. Whenever a logon authentication fails, a DC will always forward it to the PDC Emulator before rejecting it.

The Infrastructure Master is in charge of updating changes made to group memberships. When a

user moves to a different domain and his or her group membership changes, it can take time for these changes to be reflected in the group. To remedy this, the infrastructure manager is used to update such changes in its domain. The DC in the Infrastructure Master role compares its data to the GC, which is a subset of directory information for all domains in the forest. When changes occur to group membership, it then updates its group-to-user references and replicates these changes to other DCs in the domain.

6.7.2 Schema

The schema is a database that is used to define objects and their attributes. Information in the schema is used to control the types of objects (classes) that can be created in Active Directory, and the additional properties (attributes) associated with each. In other words, the schema determines what you can create in Active Directory, and the data that can be used to configure these objects. The schema is made up of classes and attributes. Object classes define the type of object, and include a collection of attributes, which are used to describe the object. For example, the User class of object contains attributes made up of information about the user's home directory, first name, last name, address, and so on. While the object class determines the type of object that can be created in Active Directory, the attributes are used to provide information about it. An object's attributes are also known as its properties, and in most cases, you can configure its attributes by editing its properties sheet (usually accessed by right clicking the object and selecting Properties).

Active Directory comes with a wide variety of object classes, but additional ones can be created if needed. Because the schema is so important to Active Directory's structure, extensions (additions and modifications) to the schema can only be made on one DC in the forest. Modifications to the schema can only be made on the DC that's acting in the Schema Master role. Schema information is stored in a directory partition of Active Directory, and is replicated to all DCs in a forest. Attributes are created using the Active Directory Schema snap-in for the Microsoft Management Console (MMC) (which we'll discuss later in this chapter). When a new class or attribute is added to the schema, it cannot be deleted. If a class or attribute is no longer needed, it can only be deactivated, so it cannot be used anymore. Should the class or attribute be needed later, you can then reactivate it.

6.7.3 Global Catalog

As anyone who's tried to search a large database can attest, the more data that's stored in a database, the longer it will take to search. To improve the performance of searching for objects in a domain or forest, the GC is used. The GC server is a DC that stores a copy of all objects in its host domain, and a partial copy of objects in other domains throughout the forest. The partial copy contains objects that are most commonly searched for. Because the GC contains a subset of information in Active Directory, less information needs to be replicated, and increases performance when users search for specific attributes of an object.

In addition to being used for searches, the GC is also used to resolve UPNs that are used in authentication. As discussed earlier, the UPN has a format like an e-mail address. If a user logs on to a DC in a domain that doesn't contain the account, the DC will use the GC to resolve the name and complete the logon process. For example, if a user logged on with the UPN myname@us.syngress.com from a computer located in ca.syngress.com, the DC in ca.syngress.com would be unable to find the account in that domain. It would then use the GC to find and authenticate the user's account. The GC is also used to store information on Universal Group memberships, in which users from any domain can be added and allowed access to any domain. When a user who is a member of such a group logs on to a domain, the DC will retrieve his or her Universal Group membership from the GC. This is only done if there is more than one domain in a forest.

The GC is available on DCs that are configured to be GC servers. Creating a GC server is done by using the Active Directory Sites and Services snap-in for the MMC (which we'll discuss later in this chapter).After a GC server is configured, other DCs can query the GC on this server.

6.7.4 Replication Service

The Windows Server 2003 replication service is used to replicate Active Directory between DCs, so that each DC has an up-to-date copy of the directory database. Because each DC has an identical copy of the directory, they can operate independently, allowing users to be authenticated and use network resources if one of the DCs fails. This allows Windows Server 2003 DCs to be highly reliable and fault tolerant.

Multimaster replication is used to copy changes in the directory to other DCs. With multimaster replication, DCs work as peers to one another, so that any DC accepts and replicates these updates (with the exception of the special types of data for which an Operations Master is assigned). Rather than having to make changes on a primary DC, changes can be made to the directory from any DC. Replication occurs automatically between DCs, and generally, no additional configuration is required. However, because there are times when network traffic will be higher, such as when employees log on to DCs at the beginning of the workday, replication can be configured to occur at specific times. This will enable you to control replication traffic so it doesn't occur during peak hours.

To replicate the directory effectively, Windows Server 2003 uses the Knowledge Consistency Checker (KCC) to generate a replication topology of the forest. A replication topology refers to the physical connections used by DCs to replicate the directory to other DCs within the site and to DCs in other sites. After initially creating a replication topology, the KCC will review and modify the topology at regular intervals. This allows it to see if certain connections or DCs are unavailable, and if changes need to be made as to how replicated data will be transferred to other DCs.

Replication is handled differently within a site as opposed to when the directory is replicated to other sites. Intra-site replication (in which Active Directory is replicated within a site) is handled by using a ring structure. The KCC builds a bidirectional ring, in which replication data is passed between DCs in two directions. Because the data is only being transferred within the site, the replicated data isn't compressed.

The KCC creates at least two connections to each DC, so if one connection fails, the other can be used. For example, in Figure 6.13, connections that are functional are shown with a straight line, while broken connections are shown with dotted lines. Because one of the four servers in Figure 6.13 has failed, replication data cannot be passed through it, so another connection between the servers is used. Using multiple connections provides fault tolerance.

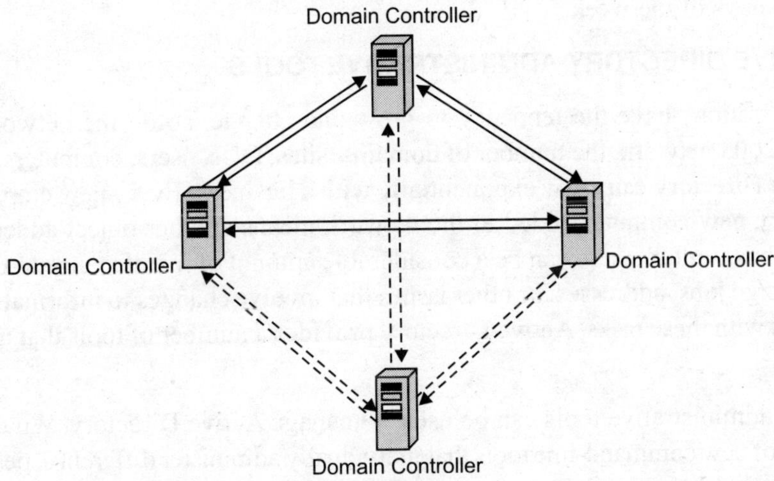

Figure 6.13 Replication Topology

Intra-site replication is automated to occur at regular intervals, and only occurs when DCs are notified of a change. By default, when a change is made on a DC, it will wait 15 seconds and then send notification to its closest replication partner. If it has more than one replication partner, it will send out notifications in three-second intervals to each additional partner. When a partner receives this notification, it will send out a request for updated directory information to the original DC, which then responds by sending the updated data. The exception to this process is when an account is locked out, the DC account is changed, or there are changes in account lockout policy or domain password policy. In these circumstances, there is no 15-second waiting period, and replication occurs immediately.

Replication between sites is called inter-site replication. Because the bandwidth between sites might be slower than that within a site, inter-site replication occurs less frequently and is handled differently. Rather than informing other DCs shortly after a change occurs, replication occurs at scheduled times. Information about site link objects is used to determine the best link to use for passing this data between sites.

Site links are used to define how sites replicate Active Directory information between one another. These objects store data controlling which sites are to replicate traffic between one another, and which should be used over others. For example, you might have an ISDN connection between your offices and one located overseas. If the overseas link were slower and more costly to use than others, you could configure the link so it is only used as a last resort. Through the site link object, the fastest and least expensive connection between sites is used for replication.

A DC acts in the role of an inter-site topology generator in each site, and serves the purpose of building this topology. It considers the cost of different connections, whether DCs are available, and whether DCs have been added to sites. By gathering this information, the KCC can then update the topology as needed, and provide the method of passing data between the sites. How often replication occurs is configurable, so that it occurs as frequently or infrequently as your needs dictate. By default, inter-site replication occurs every 180 minutes (three hours), and will use the site link to meet this schedule 24 hours a day, 7 days a week. The frequency of replications can be modified as needed to occur at certain times and days of the week.

6.8 USING ACTIVE DIRECTORY ADMINISTRATIVE TOOLS

Just as organizations have the tendency to grow and change, so do the networks they use. In a Windows Server 2003 network, the number of domains, sites, OUs, users, computers, and other objects populating Active Directory can grow exponentially with a business. Every new employee needs a new account, and every new computer added to the network means another object added to the directory. Even when growth is limited, there can be a considerable amount of maintenance to these objects, such as when users change jobs, addresses, or other issues that involve changes to information and access. To aid administrators with these tasks, Active Directory provides a number of tools that make management easier.

Two types of administrative tools can be used to manage Active Directory. Windows Server 2003 provides a variety of new command-line tools that individually administer different aspects of the directory and its objects. By clicking on the Windows Start menu and clicking Programs | Accessories | Command Prompt (or simply clicking Start | Run and typing cmd), a prompt will appear allowing you to enter these commands and control objects and elements of Active Directory. The other method of managing Active Directory is with tools using a graphical user interface (GUI).These tools allow you to point and click through objects, and modify them using a graphical display. Most of the graphical tools are available through the Start | Programs | Administrative Tools menu.

6.8.1 Graphical Administrative Tools/MMCS

A primary administrative tool for managing Windows Server 2003 and Active Directory is the Microsoft Management Console (MMC).The MMC isn't a management tool in itself, but an interface that's used to load snap-ins that provide administrative functionality. Snap-ins provides specific functionality, or a related set of functions. Because of the design of the MMC interface, you can load several snap-ins into one console, and create custom tools to deal with specific tasks. In addition, because these snap-ins run in the same environment, it becomes easier to learn how to use these tools because you don't have to learn a different interface for each.

MMCs can be started by opening pre-made consoles that are available under the Administrative Tools folder in the Windows Start menu. An empty MMC can be started by using the Run command in the Windows Start menu. By typing MMC in the Run command in the Windows Start menu, an empty MMC will start as shown in Figure 6.14.

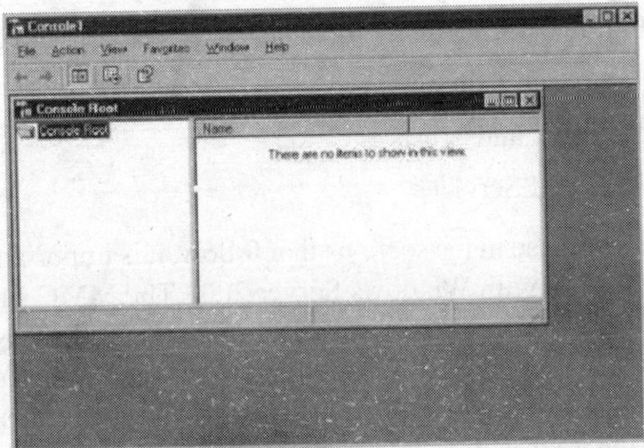

Figure 6.14 Microsoft Management Console

The windows appearing in the MMC are interfaces with individual snap-ins or custom console files. Each child window in the MMC has two panes. The left pane displays the console tree, which is a hierarchical display of tools available through the console. These can be multiple snap-ins that have been loaded into the MMC and saved as a custom console. The right pane is called the detail pane, and provides commands and information relating to what is selected in the console tree. You can add snap-ins for specific tasks by clicking on the File menu and selecting Add/Remove Snap-in. When this is done, a new dialog box will appear with two tabs:

6.8.1.1 Standalone and Extensions

The Standalone tab is used for standalone snap-ins, which are designed to run without any additional requirements. The Extensions tab is used to load a special type of snap-in, called an extension snap-in. These are used to add additional functions to a standalone snap-in that's already been installed. The Standalone tab is used to add or remove snap-ins from the console. As shown in Figure 6.15, clicking the Add button on this tab will display a list of available standalone snap-ins. After selecting the one you want to add, click the Add button on this dialog. Clicking Close will exit this screen, and return you to the previous one, which will now include your selected snap-ins in a list of ones to install in this console. Clicking OK confirms the selection, and installs them.

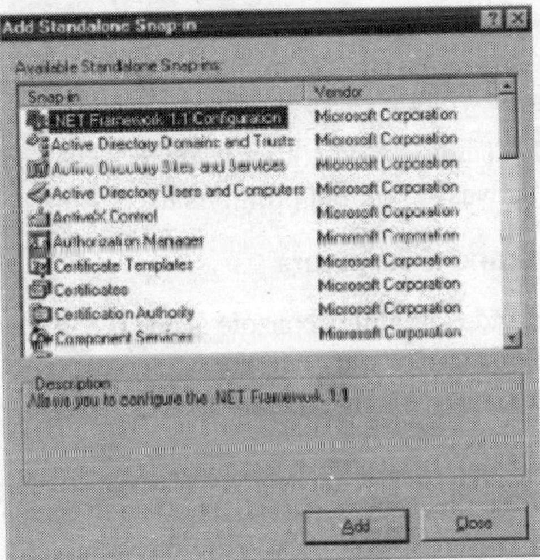

Figure 6.15 Add/Remove Snap-in Dialog Box

As you can see by in Figure 6.15, there are three snap-ins available for Active Directory:

- Active Directory Users and Computers
- Active Directory Domains and Trusts
- Active Directory Sites and Services

While we'll discuss each of these in the sections that follow, it is important to realize that these aren't the only snap-ins that you can use with Windows Server 2003.The MMC supplies these three snap-ins for use with Active Directory, but others are also available for specific purposes and management tasks. Each has an individual functionality or set of related functions for administering Windows Server 2003 and Active Directory. Note that although the three Active Directory-related snap-ins are available to be added to a custom MMC, each is already installed in a separate pre-con-?gured MMC available through the Administrative Tools menu.

Because multiple snap-ins can be added and configured in the MMC, you can create custom consoles to perform specific tasks. After setting up a console, you can save it to a file that has the .msc extension. The console can be saved in one of two modes:

6.8.1.2 Authoring and User

Authoring mode is used to provide full access to the functions of an MMC console. When saved in this mode, users who open the console can add and remove snap-ins, create new Windows, create Favorites and taskpads, view everything in the console tree, and save consoles. User mode is used to limit another user's ability to use certain functions of the console. If you were creating a console for users to perform a specific task, but didn't want them to access other functions, then User mode would be ideal.

There are three access levels for User mode:

- **Full Access:** The same as Author mode, except that snap-ins can't be added or removed, console settings can't be changed, and users can't create Favorites and taskpads.
- **Limited Access,** Multiple Windows Allows users to view parts of the console tree that were visible when the console was saved, and prohibits users from closing existing windows. Users can, however, create new windows.
- **Limited Access,** Single Window Also allows users to access parts of the console tree that were visible when the console was saved, but prohibits users from creating new windows.

6.8.2 Active Directory Users and Computers

The Active Directory Users and Computers console is one of the MMC snap-ins for use with Active Directory. It allows you to administer user and computer accounts, groups, printers, OUs, contacts, and other objects stored in Active Directory. Using this tool, you can create, delete, modify, move, organize, and set permissions on these objects.

As shown in Figure 6.16, when this tool is loaded, a node will appear in the console tree (left pane) showing the domain. Expanding this node will show a number of containers that are created by default. While additional containers can be created, the ones that appear here after creating a DC are:

- Built-in
- Computers
- Domain Controllers
- Users

These containers store objects that can be managed with this tool, and allow you to view and modify information related to these different objects.

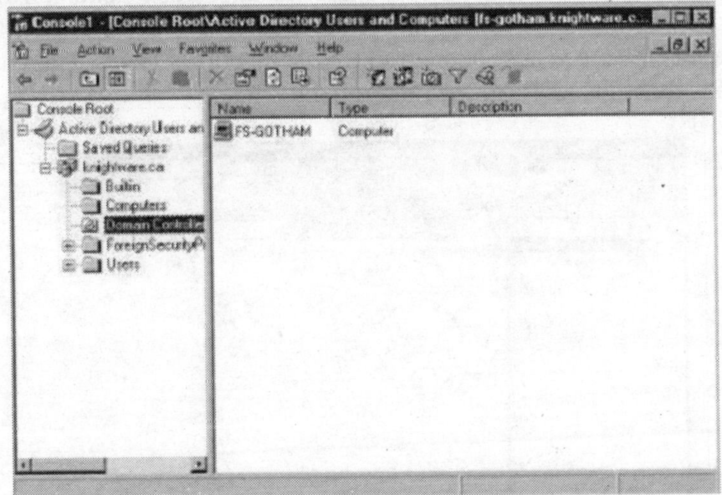

Figure 6.16 Active Directory Users and Computers

The Builtin container holds groups that were created by Windows Server 2003, and can be used to control access. You can add users to these Builtin groups to give them the ability to perform certain tasks. For example, rather than allowing everyone in the IT department to use the same Administrator account, users can be added to the built-in Administrators group. This gives them the ability to administer Windows Server 2003, but allows you to track which person with this level of security performed certain tasks.

The Computers container is used to store computer objects. These are (as the name implies) computers running on the network that have joined the domain and have accounts created in Active Directory. The Computers container can also include accounts used by applications to access Active Directory.

The Domain Controllers container contains objects representing DCs that reside in the domain. The ones shown in this container are ones running Windows 2000 Server and Windows Server 2003. Earlier versions are not displayed. The Users container is used to store user accounts and groups. Users and Groups that appear in this container are ones that were created using application programming interfaces (APIs) that can use Active Directory, and ones that were created in Windows NT prior to upgrading.

Additional containers can be displayed when Active Directory Users and Computers is running with Advanced Features activated. You can enable Advanced Features by clicking on the menu item with this name, found in the View menu. When Advanced Features have been activated, Lost And Found and System containers are displayed in the left console tree. The Lost And Found container is used to store stray objects whose containers no longer exist. If an object is created at the same time its container is deleted, or if it is moved to a location that's missing after replication, the object is placed in this container.

This allows you to manage the lost object, and move it to a container that does exist. The System container is used for system settings. These are built-in settings for containers and objects used by Active Directory and Windows Server 2003.

6.8.3 Active Directory Domains and Trusts

The Active Directory Domains and Trusts console is used to manage domains and the trust relationships between them. As shown in Figure 6.17, the console tree of this tool includes a node for domains making up the network. By selecting the Active Directory Domains and Trusts node, a listing of domains will appear in the right pane. Using this tool, you can create, modify, and delete trust relationships between domains, set the suffix for UPNs, and raise domain and forest functional levels. This enables administrators to control how domains function, and how they interoperate.

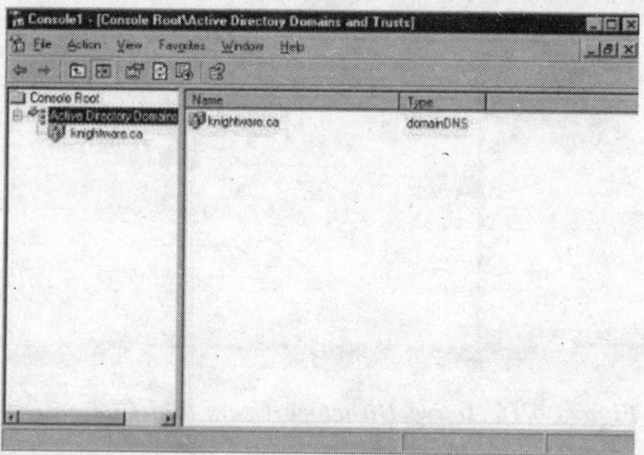

Figure 6.17 Active Directory Domains and Trusts

Using the Active Directory Domains and Trusts console, you can create a variety of different types of trusts between domains and forests. Earlier, we discussed how parent and child domains and domain trees use a two-way transitive trust to share resources between domains. The two-way transitive trust means that both domains trust one another, as well as any other domains with which they have similar trust relationships. In addition to this type of trust, additional trusts can be created:

- Shortcut trust
- Forest trust
- Realm trust
- External trust

A shortcut trust is transitive, and can be either one-way or two-way. This means that either one domain can trust another but not vice versa, or both domains can trust each other. This type of trust is used to connect two domains in a forest, and is particularly useful when the domains are in different trees. By creating a shortcut, one domain can connect with another quickly, improving logon times between domains. Connection is quicker because, when two domains in different trees connect via the implicit trusts that exist by default, the trust path must go all the way up the tree to the root domain, across to the other tree's root domain, and back down the second tree. A shortcut trust, as its name indicates, creates a direct trust between the two domains in different trees.

To illustrate this, let's look at the situation in Figure 6.18. If a user in DomainD wanted to use resources in Domain2, he or she would be authenticating to a domain that is located in a different tree. Without a shortcut trust, the connection would go through DomainA, across the trust between the two trees to Domain1, and then to Domain2. With a shortcut trust, DomainD and Domain2 would have a direct trust between them that could be used for authentication. As we can also see in Figure 6.18, multiple shortcut trusts can exist, allowing users to be authenticated to other domains that they commonly need to access.

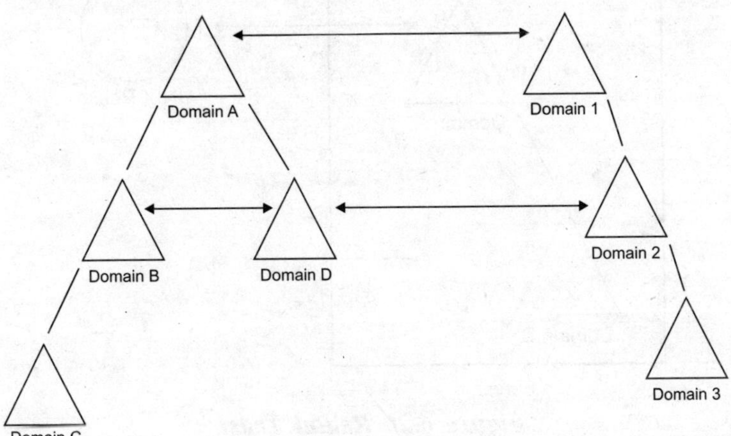

Figure 6.18 Shortcut Trusts

A forest trust is also transitive, and can be one-way or two-way. As shown in Figure 6.19, this type of trust is used to connect two different forests, so that users in each forest can use resources in the other. Using this type of trust, a user in a domain in one forest could be authenticated and access resources located in a domain that's in another forest. This allows different areas of the network to be interconnected, even though they are separated by administrative boundaries.

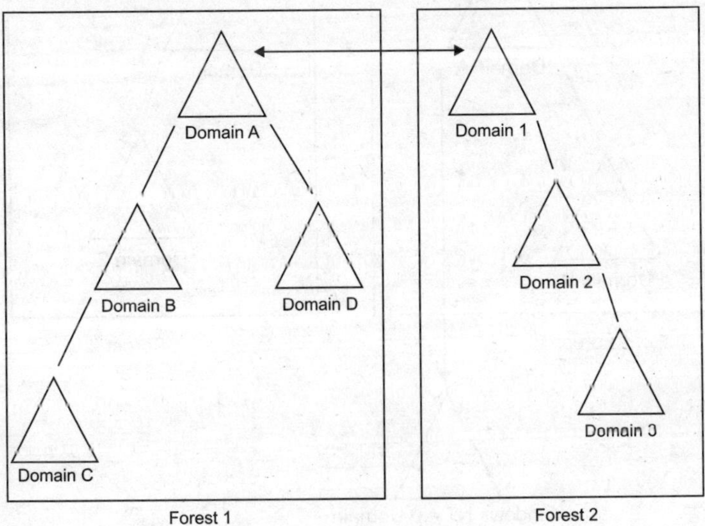

Figure 6.19 Forest Trust

A realm trust can be one-way or two-way, and can also be either transitive or nontransitive. Nontransitive means that the trust relationship doesn't extend beyond the two parties. For example, let's say DomainA trusts DomainB, and DomainB trusts DomainC. Because the trust is nontransitive, DomainA and DomainC don't trust one another because there isn't a trust relationship between them. As shown in Figure 6.20, the realm trust is used when a relationship needs to be created between a Windows Server 2003 domain and a non-Windows realm that uses Kerberos version 5 (such as one running UNIX).

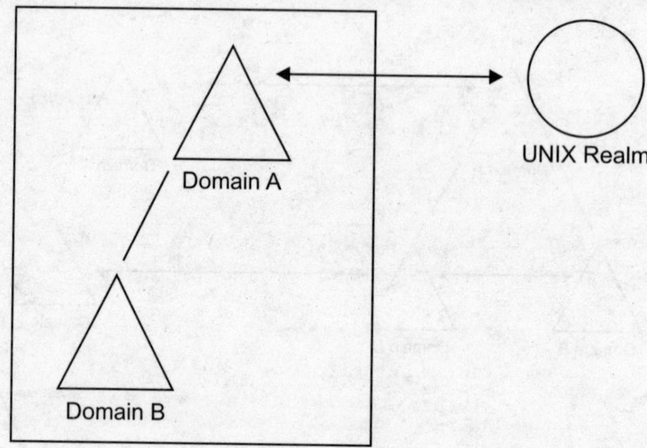

Figure 6.20 Realm Trust

The final type of trust that can be created is an external trust. An external trust is always nontransitive, and can be either one-way or two-way. As shown in Figure 6.21, this type of trust is used to create a relationship between a Windows Server 2003 domain and one running Windows NT 4.0. It can also be used to connect two domains that are in different forests, and don't have a forest trust connecting them.

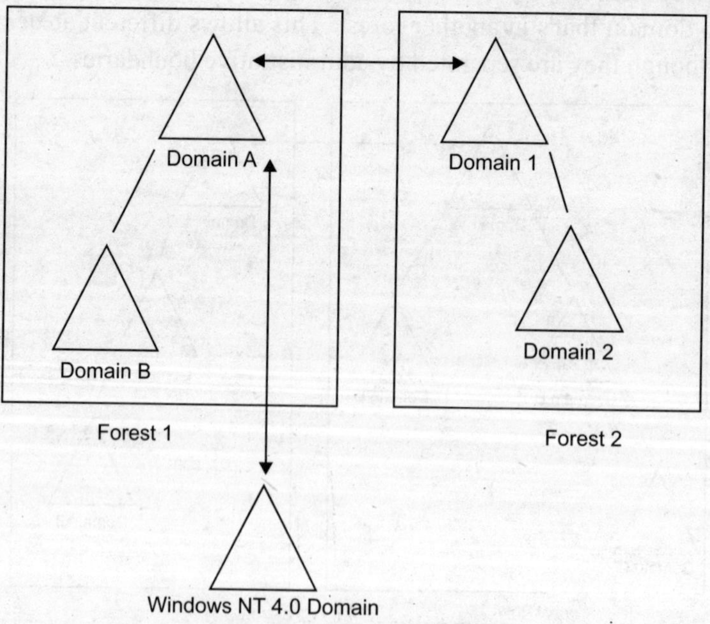

Figure 6.21 External Trust

The Active Directory Domains and Trusts console is also used for raising domain and forest levels, which enables additional features in Active Directory.

6.8.4 Active Directory Sites and Services

Earlier in this chapter, we discussed how sites represent the physical structure of your network, and are important to replicating information in Active Directory. The Active Directory Sites and Services console is used to create and manage sites, and control how the directory is replicated within a site and between sites. Using this tool, you can specify connections between sites, and how they are to be used for replication.

As shown in Figure 6.22, the Active Directory Sites and Services console has a number of containers that provide information and functions on creating and maintaining sites. When a domain is first installed on a DC, a site object named Default-First-Site-Name is created. This container can (and should) be renamed to something that is meaningful to the business. As mentioned earlier, additional sites can be created to improve replication between sites, or domains can be added to this existing site.

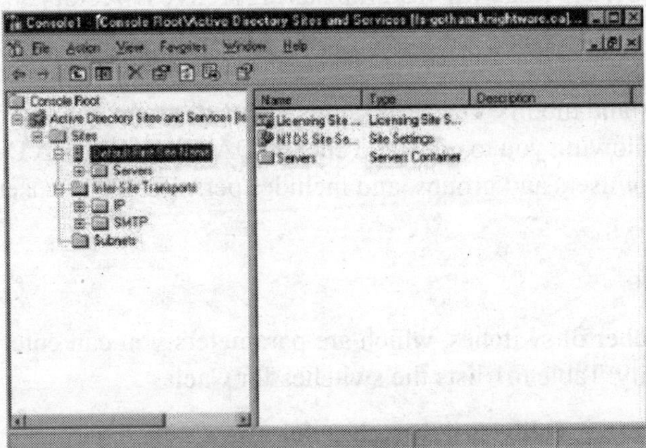

Figure 6.22 Active Directory Sites and Services

The Inter-Site Transports container is used to create and store site links. A site link is a connection between sites. Links created under the IP container use the Internet Protocol (IP) as their transport protocol, while those created under SMTP use the Simple Mail Transfer Protocol (SMTP). The Subnets container is used to create and store objects containing information about subnets on your network. Subnets are collections of neighboring computers that are subdivided within the network, using a common network ID. Using the Subnets container, you can group different subnets together to build a site.

6.8.5 Command-line Tools

Windows Server 2003 provides a number of command-line tools that you can use for managing Active Directory. These tools use commands typed in at the prompt, and can provide a number of services that are useful in administering the directory. The command-line tools for Active Directory include:

- Cacls Used to view and modify discretionary access control lists (DACLs) on files.
- Cmdkey Used to create, list, and delete usernames, passwords, and credentials.

- Csvde Used to import and export data from the directory.
- Dcgpofix Restores Group Policy Objects (GPOs) to the state they where in when initially installed.
- Dsadd Used to add users, groups, computers, contacts, and OUs.
- Dsget Displays the properties of an object in Active Directory.
- Dsmod Used to modify users, groups, computers, servers, contacts, and OUs.
- Dsmove Renames an object without moving it, or moves an object to a new location.
- Ldifde Used to create, modify, and delete objects from Active Directory.
- Ntdsutil Used for general management of Active Directory.
- Whoami Provides information on the user who's currently logged on.

In the sections that follow, we will brie?y discuss each of these tools, and show you how they can assist you in performing certain tasks when administering Active Directory.

6.8.5.1 Cacls

Cacls is used to view and modify the permissions a user or group has to a particular resource. Cacls provides this ability by allowing you to view and change DACLs on files. A DACL is a listing of access control entries (ACEs) for users and groups, and includes permissions the user has to a file. The syntax for using this tool is:

6.8.5.2 Cacls Filename

Cacls also has a number of switches, which are parameters you can enter on the command line to use a specific functionality. Table 6.1 lists the switches for Cacls.

Table 6.1 Switches for the Cacls Tool

Parameter	Description
/t	Change the DACLs of files in the current directory and all subdirectories.
/e	Edit the DACL.
/r	username revokes the users' rights.
/c	Ignore any errors that might occur when changing the DACL.
/g	username:permission Grants rights to a specified user. Rights that can be granted are: n (None), r (Read), w (Write), c (Change), and f (Full Control).
/p	username:permission Replaces the rights of a specified user. The rights that can be replaced are: n (None), r (Read), w (Write), c (Change), and f (Full Control).
/d	username Denies access to a specified user.

6.8.5.3 Cmdkey

Cmdkey is used to create, view, edit, and delete the stored usernames, passwords, and credentials. This allows you to log on using one account, and view and modify the credentials of another user. As with other command-line tools we'll discuss, cmdkey has a number of switches that provided needed parameters for the tool to function. Table 6.2 lists these parameters.

Table 6.2 Switches for the Cmdkey Tool

Parameter	Description
/add:targetname	Adds a username and password to the list, and specifies the computer or domain (using the targetname parameter) with which the entry will be associated.
/generic	Adds generic credentials to the list.
/smartcard	Instructs cmdkey to retrieve credentials from a smart card.
/user: username	Provides the username with which this entry is to be associated. If the username parameter isn't provided, you will be prompted for it.
/pass:password	Provides the password to store with this entry. If the password parameter isn't provided, you will be prompted for it.
/delete: {targetname | /ras}	Deletes the username and password from the list. If the targetname parameter is provided, the specified entry will be deleted. If /ras is included, the stored remote access entry is deleted.
/list: targetname	Lists the stored usernames and credentials. If the target-name parameter isn't provided, all of the stored usernames and credentials will be listed.

6.8.5.4 Csvde

Csvde is used to import and export data from Active Directory. This data is comma delimitated, so that a comma separates each value. Exporting data in this way allows you to then import it into other applications (for example, Microsoft Of?ce tools such as Access and Excel).Table 6.3 lists the parameters for this command.

Table 6.3 Switches for the Csvde Tool

Parameter	Description
-i	Used to specify the import mode.
-f	filename Specifies the filename to import or export data to.
-s	servername sets the DC that will be used to import or export data.
-c	string1 string2 replaces the value of string1 with string2. This is often used when importing data between domains, and the DN of the domain data is being exported from (string1) needs to be replaced with the name of the import domain (string2).

Parameter	Description
-v	Verbose mode.
-j path	Specifies the location for log files.
-t portnumber	The portnumber parameter is used to specify the LDAP port number. By default, the LDAP port is 389 and the GC port is 3268.
-d BaseDN	The BaseDN parameter is used to specify the DN of a search base for data export.
-p scope	Used to set the search scope. The value of the scope parameter can be Base, OneLevel, or SubTree.
-o LDAPAttributeList	Specifies a list of attributes to omit in an export query.
-g	Used to omit paged searches.
-m	Used to omit attributes that apply to certain objects in Active Directory.
-n	Specifies that binary values are to be omitted from an export.
-k	If errors occur during an import, this parameter specifies that csvde should continue processing.
-a	username password Specifies the username and password to be used when running this command. By default, the credentials of the user currently logged on are used.
-b username domain password	Specifies the username, domain, and password to use when running this command. By default, the credentials of the user currently logged on are used.

6.8.5.5 Dcgpofix

Dcgpofix is used to restore the default domain policy and default DC's policy to they way they were when initially created. By restoring these GPOs to their original states, any changes that were made to them are lost. This tool has only two switches associated with it:

- /ignoreschema Ignores the version number of the schema.
- /target: {domain | dc | both} Specifies the target domain, DC, or both.

When the /ignoreschema switch is used, Dcgpofix will ignore the version number of Active Directory's schema when it runs. This will allow it to work on other versions of Active Directory, as opposed to the one on the computer on which Dcgpofix was initially installed. You should use the version of Dcgpofix that was installed with your installation of Windows Server 2003, as GPOs might not be restored if versions from other operating systems are used.

6.8.5.6 Dsadd

Dsadd is used to add objects to Active Directory. The objects you can add with this command-line tool are users, computers, groups, OUs, contacts, and quota specifications. To add any of these objects, you would enter the following commands at the command prompt:

- dsadd user Adds a user to the directory
- dsadd computer Adds a computer to the directory
- dsadd group Adds a group to the directory
- dsadd ou Adds an OU to the directory
- dsadd contact Adds a contact to the directory
- dsadd quota Adds a quota specification to the directory

While the commands for this tool are straightforward, there is a variety of arguments associated with each. For full details on these arguments, type the command at the command prompt followed by /?.This will display a list of parameters for each command.

6.8.5.7 Dsget

Dsget is used to view the properties of objects in Active Directory. The objects you can view with dsget are users, groups, computers, servers, sites, subnets, OUs, contacts, partitions, and quota specifications. To view the properties of these objects, enter the following commands:

- dsget user Displays the properties of a user
- dsget group Displays the properties of a group and its membership
- dsget computer Displays the properties of a computer
- dsget server Displays the properties of a DC
- dsget site Displays the properties of a site
- dsget subnet Displays the properties of a subnet
- dsget ou Displays the properties of an OU
- dsget contact Displays the properties of a contact
- dsget partition Displays the properties of a directory partition
- dsget quota Displays the properties of a quota specification

While the commands for this tool are straightforward, there is a variety of arguments associated with each. For full details on these arguments, type the command at the command prompt followed by /?.This will display a list of parameters for each command.

6.8.5.8 Dsmod

Dsmod is used to modify existing objects in Active Directory. The objects you can modify using dsmod are users, groups, computers, servers, OUs, contacts, partitions, and quota specifications. Toedit these objects, enter the following commands:

- **dsmod user:** Modifies the attributes of a user in the directory
- **dsmod group:** Modifies the attributes of a group in the directory
- **dsmod computer:** Modifies a computer in the directory
- **dsmod server:** Modifies the properties of a DC
- **dsmod ou:** Modifies the attributes of an OU in the directory
- **dsmod contact:** Modifies the attributes of a contact in the directory
- **dsmod partition:** Modifies a directory partition
- **dsmod quota:** Displays the properties of a quota specification

While the commands for this tool are straightforward, there is a variety of arguments associated with each. For full details on these arguments, type the command at the command prompt followed by /?.This will display a list of parameters for each command.

6.8.5.9 Dsmove

Dsmove is used to either rename or move an object within a domain. Using this tool, you can rename an object without moving it in the directory, or move it to a new location within the directory tree. The dsmove tool can't be used to move objects to other domains.

Renaming or moving an object requires that you use the DN, which identi?es the object's location in the tree. For example, if you have an object called JaneD in an OU called Accounting, located in a domain called syngress.com, the DN is:

CN=JaneD, OU=Accounting, DC=syngress, DC=com

The -newname switch is used to rename objects using the DN. For example, let's say you wanted to change a user account's name from JaneD to JaneM. To do so, you would use the following command:

Dsmove CN=JaneD, OU=Accounting, DC=syngress, DC=com -newname JaneM

The -newparent switch is used to move objects within a domain. For example, let's say the user whose name you just changed was transferred from Accounting to Sales, which you've organized in a different OU container. To move the user object, you would use the following command:

Dsmove CN=JaneM, OU=Accounting, DC=syngress, DC=com -newparent OU=Sales, DC=syngress, DC=com

In addition to the -newname and -newparent switches, you can also use the parameters listed in Table 6.4 to control how this tool is used.

Table 6.4 Switches for Dsmove

Parameter	Description
{-s Server -d Domain}	Specifies a remote server or domain to connect to. By default, dsmove will connect to the DC in the domain you logged on to.

Parameter	Description
-u Username	Specifies the username to use when logging on to a remote server.
-p {Password | *}	Specifies the password to use when logging on to a remote server. If you type the * symbol instead of a password, you are then prompted to enter the password.
-q	Sets dsmove to suppress output.
{-uc | -uco | -uci}	Specifies dsmove to format input and output in Unicode.

6.8.5.10 Ntdsutil

Ntdsutil is a general-purpose command-line tool that can perform a variety of functions for managing Active Directory. Using Ntdsutil, you can:

- Perform maintenance of Active Directory
- Perform an authoritative restore of Active Directory
- Modify the Time To Live (TTL) of dynamic data
- Manage domains
- Manage data in the directory and log files
- Block certain IP addresses from querying the directory, and set LDAP policies
- Remove metadata from DCs that were retired or improperly uninstalled
- Manage Security Identifiers (SIDs)
- Manage master operation roles (Domain Naming Master, Schema Master, IinfrastructureMaster, PDC Emulator, and RID Master)

Typing ntdsutil at the command prompt will load the tool and the prompt will change to ntdsutil:.As shown in Figure 6.23, by typing help at the command line, you can view different commands for the tasks being performed. After entering a command, typing help again will provide other commands that can be used. For example, typing metadata cleanup after first starting ntdsutil, and then typing help will display a list of commands relating to metadata cleanup. This allows you to use the command as if you were navigating through menus containing other commands. You can return to a previous menu at any time, or exit the program by typing Quit.

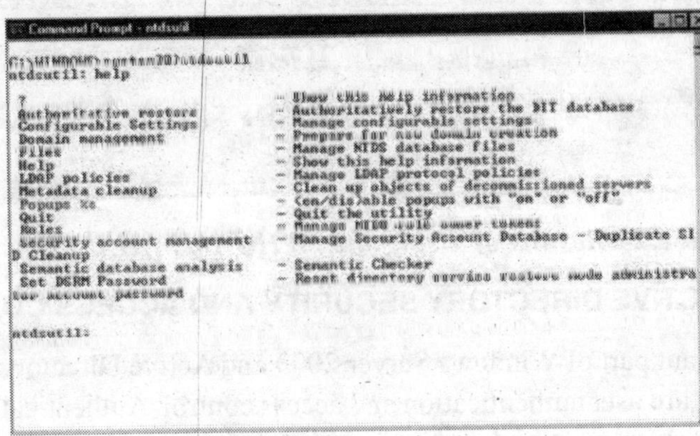

Figure 6.23 NTDSUTIL

6.8.5.11 Whoami

Whoami is a tool for displaying information about the user who is currently logged on. Using this tool, you can view your domain name, computer name, username, group names, logon identi?er, and privileges. The amount of information displayed depends on the parameters that are entered with this command. Table 6.5 lists the available parameters.

Table 6.5 Switches for Whoami

Parameter	Description
/upn	Displays the UPN of the user currently logged on.
/fqdn	Displays the FQDN of the user currently logged on.
/logonid	Displays the Logon ID.
/user	Displays the username of the user currently logged on.
/groups	Displays group names.
/priv	Displays privileges associated with the currently logged-on user.
/fo format	Controls the format of how information is displayed. The format parameter can have the value of: table (to show output in a table format), list (to list output), or csv to display in a comma-delimited format.
/all	Displays username, groups, SIDs, and privileges for the user currently logged on.

```
Command Prompt
C:\Documents and Settings\Administrator>whoami /all

USER INFORMATION
----------------

User Name                  SID
========================== ==============================================
knightware\administrator   S-1-5-21-2331013139-2269155295-1045398719-500

GROUP INFORMATION
-----------------

Group Name                                 Type             SID
                       Attributes
========================================== ================ ===============
====================== ===============================================
=========
Everyone                                   Well-known group S-1-1-0
                       Mandatory group, Enabled by default, Enabled group
BUILTIN\Administrators                     Alias            S-1-5-32-544
                       Mandatory group, Enabled by default, Enabled group, Gr
oup owner
BUILTIN\Users                              Alias            S-1-5-32-545
                       Mandatory group, Enabled by default, Enabled group
```

Figure 6.24 Results of Using the WHOAMI /ALL Command

6.9 IMPLEMENTING ACTIVE DIRECTORY SECURITY AND ACCESS CONTROL

Security is an important part of Windows Server 2003 and Active Directory. Two primary methods of implementing security are user authentication and access control. Authentication is used to verify the identity of a user or other objects, such as applications or computers. After it's been determined they are who or what they say they are, the process continues by giving them the level of access they deserve.

Access control manages what users (or other objects) can use, and how they can use them. By combining authentication and access control, a user is permitted or denied access to objects in the directory.

6.9.1 Access Control in Active Directory

In Active Directory, permissions can be applied to objects to control how these objects are used. Permissions regulate access by enforcing whether a user can read or write to an object, has full control, or no access. Active Directory permissions are separate from share permissions and NTFS permissions, and work in conjunction with both. Three elements determine a user's access, and define the permissions they have to an object:

- Security descriptors
- Object Inheritance
- Authentication

Objects in Active Directory use security descriptors to store information about permissions, and control who has access to an object. The security descriptor contains information that's stored in access control lists (ACLs), which define who can access the object and what they can do with it.

There are two different types of ACLs in the security descriptor:

- Security access control list (SACL)
- Discretionary access control list (DACL)

The SACL is used to track an object's security based on how a user or group accesses the object. For example, you can audit whether a user was able to access the object using a particular permission (such as Read, Write, or Full Control). Information about what to audit is kept in ACEs, which are stored within the SACL. These entries control what is audited, and contain information about the events to be logged. In doing this, records can be kept on the security of objects, and whether specific users or groups are able to successfully access them.

As we saw earlier, when we discussed command-line tools for Active Directory, a DACL is a listing of ACEs for users and groups, and includes information about the permissions that a user or group has to a file. The DACL controls whether a user is granted or denied access to an object. ACEs in the DACL explicitly identify individual users and groups, and the permissions granted to each. Because only users and groups identified in the DACL can access an object in Active Directory, any user or group that isn't specified is denied access.

Active Directory places the permissions you can apply to objects into two categories: standard permissions and special permissions. Standard permissions are those that are commonly applied to objects, whereas special permissions provide additional access control. For most objects in Active Directory, five permissions are available as standard permissions:

- **Full Control:** Allows the user to change permissions, take ownership, and have the abilities associated with all other standard permissions.
- **Read:** Allows the user to view objects, attributes, ownership, and permissions on an object.

- **Write:** Allows the user to change attributes on an object.
- **Create:** All Child Objects Allows the user to add objects to an OU.
- **Delete:** All Child Objects Allows the user to delete objects from an OU.

Permissions can be set on objects by using the Active Directory Users and Computers snap-in for the MMC.As shown in Figure 6.25, you can set permissions by using the Security tab of an object's Properties dialog box. The Security tab is hidden in the Properties dialog box, unless the Advanced Features menu item is toggled on the View menu first. After this is done, you can then bring up the Properties dialog box by selecting an object and clicking Properties on the Action menu, or right-clicking on the object and selecting Properties.

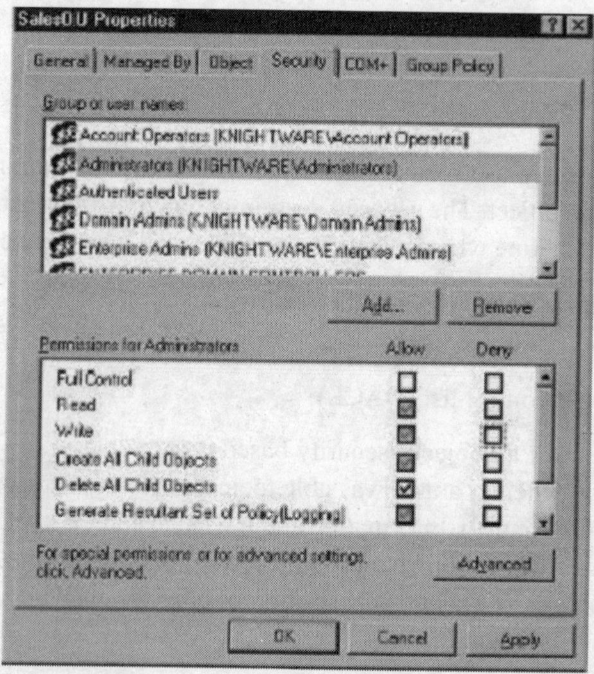

Figure 6.25 Permissions Are Set on the Security Tab of the Object's Properties

The top pane of the Security tab lists users and groups, and the lower pane lists the various permissions that can be applied to these users and groups. You can set permissions by selecting one of these users and groups, and checking the applicable permissions. Special permissions can be set for objects by clicking the Advanced button, which displays a dialog box where additional permissions can be applied.

Because it would take a while to assign permissions to every object in Active Directory, object inheritance can be used to minimize how often and where permissions are assigned. Object inheritance refers to how the permissions of a parent object are inherited by child objects. When permissions are applied to a container, they are propagated to objects within that container. For example, if a group had Full Control permissions on an OU, the group would also have Full Control of any of the printer objects within that OU. The permissions of one object flow down to any objects within the hierarchy, so child objects have the same permissions as their parents.

Since there might be times when you don't want the permissions from a parent to propagate to child objects, inheritance can be blocked. By clearing the Allow Inheritable Permissions from Parent to Propagate to This Object check box, the permissions from containers higher in the hierarchy are blocked. When this is done, any permissions that are modified on parent objects don't apply to the child. Permissions for the child object must be explicitly assigned. Use the following steps to set permissions on AD objects.

6.9.1.1 Set Permissions on ad Objects

1. Open Active Directory Users and Computers by clicking selecting Administrative Tools in the Windows Start menu, and then clicking on the Active Directory Users and Computers menu item.
2. When the MMC opens with this snap-in installed, expand the console tree so that your domain and the containers within it are visible.
3. Select your domain from the console tree. From the Action menu, select New and then click the Organizational Unit menu item. As shown in Figure 6.26, when the dialog box appears, name the new OU TestOU, and then click OK.A new OU with this name should now appear in the console tree beneath your domain.

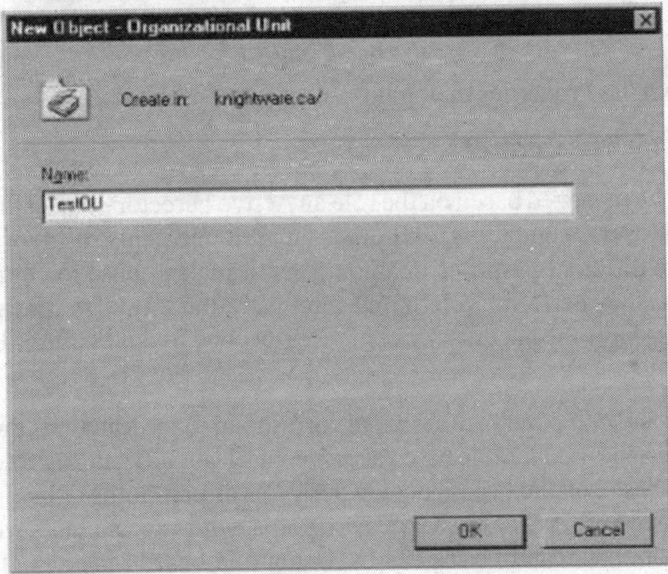

Figure 6.26 New Object Dialog Box

4. In the View menu, click Advanced Features.
5. Select the TestOU OU. From the Action menu, click Properties.
6. When the Properties dialog box appears, click the Security tab. In the list of usernames, select the name of the account you're currently logged on with.
7. In the pane below the list of usernames and groups, click the Full Control check box under Allow, so that a check mark appears in it. You now have full control of the OU.
8. Click the Advanced button to display the Advanced Security Settings dialog box. When the dialog box appears, click the Permissions tab. As shown in the Figure 6.27. Ensure that the Allow inheritable permissions from the parent to propagate to this object and all child objects check box is checked. This will allow inheritable permissions to be applied to this OU, and any within the container. Click OK to return to the previous screen.

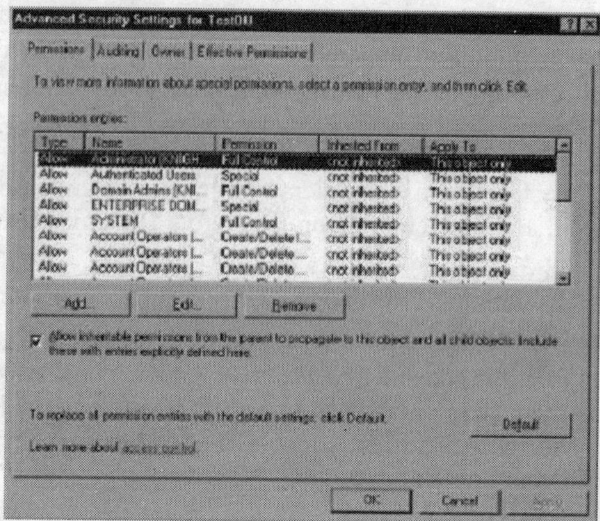

Figure 6.27 Advanced Settings Dialog Box

9. Click OK to exit the Properties dialog box.

6.9.1.2 Role-based Access Control

Access control can be managed based on the role an Active Directory object plays in an organization. Since objects represent users, computers, and other tangible elements of an organization, and these people and things serve different purposes in a company, it makes sense to configure these objects so that they reflect the tasks they perform. Role-based administration is used to configure object settings, so that computers and users have the necessary permissions needed to do their jobs based on the roles they fill.

The roles that users and computers are assigned correspond to the functions they serve in a company. Two categories of roles can be used for role based access control: authorization and computer configuration. Authorization roles are based on the tasks a person performs as part of his or her job. For example, Help Desk personnel would need the ability to change passwords, while accountants would need to be able to access financial information and audit transactions. Using role-based access control, you can give each person the access he or she needs to perform these tasks.

Authorization roles are similar to security groups, to which users can become members and acquire a level of security that gives them the ability to perform certain tasks. However, authorization roles differ in that they are used for applications. Role-based access can be applied to a single application, set of applications, or a scope within the application. Another important difference is that role based authorization can be dynamic, so that users become part of a group membership as an application runs. This is different from security groups that require membership to be set beforehand.

In the same way that users have different purposes in a company, so do computers. A business might have DCs, mail servers, file servers, Web servers, and any number of other machines providing services to users and applications in an organization. Computer configuration roles are used to control which features, services, and options should be installed and configured on a machine, based on the function it serves in the company.

6.9.1.3 Authorization Manager

Authorization Manager is a snap-in for the MMC that allows you to configure role-based access for applications. By using roles, you ensure that users only have access to the functions and resources they need to perform their jobs, and are prohibited from using other features and resources they're not authorized to use. For example, personnel in Payroll would need to view information on employees (so they can be paid), but wouldn't need to access administrative features that allow them to modify passwords.

In Authorization Manager, roles are designed based on the tasks that are supported by the application. After the role is developed, users and groups can then be assigned to the role so they have the access necessary to perform these tasks. The tasks that are available for users to use depend on the application, as the ability to support roles and the functions available are part of the software design.

6.10 ACTIVE DIRECTORY AUTHENTICATION

When you log on to a Windows Server 2003 domain, a single logon gives access to any resources you're permitted to use, regardless of their location on the network. A user doesn't need to re-enter a password every time the user accesses a server or other resources, because any authentication after initially logging on is transparent. Because only one logon is needed, the system needs to verify a person is who he or she claims to be, before any access is given.

Operating systems such as Windows NT, 2000, and Server 2003 store account information in the SAM database. The SAM stores credentials that are used to access the local machine. When a user logs on to a computer with a local user account that's stored in the SAM, the user is authenticated to the local machine. The user's access is limited to just that computer when logging on to the machine.

When users log on to the Windows Server 2003 domain, an account in Active Directory is used to access network resources located within the domain, or in other trusted domains. When a user logs on, the Local Security Authority (LSA) is used to log users on to the local computer. It is also used to authenticate to Active Directory. After validating the user's identity in Active Directory, the LSA on the DC that authenticates the user creates an access token and associates a SID with the user.

The access token is made up of data that contains information about the user. It holds information about the user's name, group af?liation, SID, and SIDs for the groups of which he or she is a member. The access token is created each time the user logs on. Because the access token is created at logon, any changes to the user's group membership or other security settings won't appear until after the user logs off and back on again. For example, if the user became a backup operator, he or she would have to log off and log back on before these changes affected the user's access.

6.10.1 Standards and Protocols

Authentication relies on standards and protocols that are used to confirm the identity of a user or object. Windows Server 2003 supports several types of network authentication:

- Kerberos
- X.509 certificates
- Lightweight Directory Access Protocol/Secure Sockets Layer (LDAP/SSL)
- Public Key Infrastructure (PKI)

As we'll see in the paragraphs that follow, some of these standards and protocols not only provide a method of authenticating users, but also the ability to encrypt data.

Kerberos: Kerberos version 5 is an industry standard security protocol that Windows Server 2003 uses as the default authentication service. It is used to handle authentication in Windows Server 2003 trust relationships, and is the primary security protocol for authentication within domains.

Kerberos uses mutual authentication to verify the identity of a user or computer, and the network service being accessed. Each side proves to the other that they are who they claim to be. Kerberos does this through the use of tickets.

X.509 Certificates: X.509 is a popular standard for digital certificates, published by the International Organization for Standardization (ISO). X.509 certificates are used to verify that the user is who he or she claims to be. Digital certificates work as a method of identifying the user, much as your birth certificate is used to identify you as a person. They can also be used to establish the identity of applications, network services, computers, and other devices.

LDAP/SSL: LDAP is used by Active Directory for communication between clients and directory servers. LDAP allows you to read and write data in Active Directory, but isn't secure by default. To extend security to LDAP communications, LDAP can be used over Secure Sockets Layer/Transport Layer Security.

Secure Sockets Layer (SSL) and Transport Layer Security (TLS) provide data encryption and authentication. TLS is the successor to SSL, and is more secure. It can be used by clients to authenticate servers, and by servers to authenticate clients. Communication using TLS allows messages between the client and server to be encrypted, so data being passed between the two isn't accessible by third parties.

PKI: PKI is a method of authentication that uses unique identifiers called "keys," which are mathematical algorithms used for cryptography and authentication. PKI uses two different types of keys: public keys and private keys.

6.11 WHAT'S NEW IN WINDOWS SERVER 2003 ACTIVE DIRECTORY?

A number of enhancements and new features in the Windows Server 2003 Active Directory weren't available in Windows 2000 Server. These improvements allow various tasks and network operations to be performed more efficiently. However, although there are many new features, the availability of a number of them depends on the environment in which DCs are running.

When a Windows Server 2003 DC is created on a network, Active Directory is installed with a basic set of features. Additional features can be enabled, but this is dependent on the operating systems running as DCs and the functional level (formerly called the mode) that's configured for the domain or forest.

There are four different levels of functionality for Active Directory:

- Windows 2000 mixed
- Windows 2000 native

- Windows 2003 interim
- Windows 2003

If you're upgrading from Windows 2000 Server on your network, you're probably familiar with the first two levels. Each of these appeared in Windows 2000, and provided backward compatibility to older operating systems such as Windows NT 4.0, and allowed control of what features were available in Active Directory. Windows Server 2003 interim and Windows Server 2003 functionality are new to Active Directory, and weren't available in previous versions.

Windows 2000 mixed allows domains to contain Windows NT BDCs that can interact with Windows 2000 and Windows Server 2003 servers. In this level, the basic features of Active Directory are available to use. However, you aren't able to nest groups within one another, use Universal Groups that allow access to resources in any domain, or use Security ID Histories (SIDHistory). Because it accommodates the widest variety of servers running on your network, this is the default level of functionality when a Windows Server 2003 DC is installed.

Windows 2000 native is the highest mode available for Windows 2000 and the next highest level for Windows Server 2003 DCs. Windows 2000 native removes support for replication to Windows NT BDCs, so these older servers are unable to function as DCs. In this level, only Windows 2000 and Windows Server 2003 DCs can be used in the domain, and support for Universal Groups, SIDHistory, and group nesting becomes available.

Windows 2003 interim is a new level that's available in Windows Server 2003.This level is used when your domain consists of Windows NT and Windows Server 2003 DCs. It provides the same functionality as Windows 2000 mixed mode, but is used when you are upgrading Windows NT domains directly to Windows Server 2003. If a forest has never had Windows 2000 DCs, then this is the level used for performing an upgrade.

The highest functionality level for Active Directory is Windows 2003.The Windows 2003 level is used when there are only Windows Server 2003 DCs in the domain. When this level is set for the domain, a considerable number of features are enabled. We discuss these features later in this chapter, when we discuss new features that are available with domain and forest functionality.

The number of features available for Active Directory is also dependent on whether the functionality level has been raised for the domain or the entire forest. With domain-level functionality, all servers in the domain are running Windows Server 2003. With this level, different domains in a forest can be set to use different functionality levels. With forest-level functionality, all domains in the forest are running Windows Server 2003 and have their domain functionality raised to Windows Server 2003.As stated previously, there are four different levels for Windows Server 2003 domain functionality. Forest functionality can also be raised to enable features that apply to all domains in the forest. With forest functionality, there are three different levels available:

- Windows 2000
- Windows 2003 interim
- Windows 2003

Windows 2000 level allows Windows NT, Windows 2000, and Windows Server 2003 DCs on the network, and is the default level for a forest. The other two levels are the same as the domain levels, in that Windows 2003 interim supports Windows Server 2003 DCs and NT BDCs, while Windows 2003 level supports only Windows Server 2003 DCs on the network. When the default level is raised to either of these other levels, additional features in Active Directory become available.

To raise the forest functionality, you must first raise the functionality of domains within the forest. Each domain in the forest must be raised to either Windows 2000 native or Windows 2003 before the forest functionality can be raised to Windows 2003. When the forest functional level is then raised to Windows 2003, any DCs in the forest's domains will have their domain functional level automatically raised to Windows 2003.

The tool used to raise domain and forest functional levels is Active Directory Domains and Trusts. Raising domain levels is done by right-clicking the domain in the left console pane and then clicking Raise Domain Functional Level from the menu that appears. As shown in Figure 6.28, you then select the level to which you want to raise the domain, and then click the Raise button. Raising forest functional levels is done similarly. To raise the forest level, right-click the Active Directory Domains and Trusts node, and then click Raise Forest Functional Level from the menu that appears (see Figure 9.28). Select the level to which you want to raise the forest, and click Raise to complete the task.

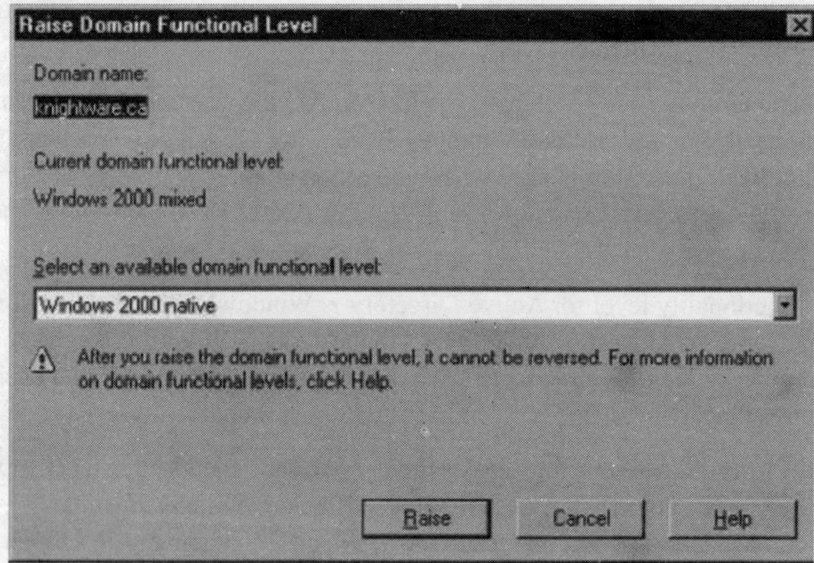

Figure 6.28 Raise Domain Functional Level Dialog Box

When raising the forest or domain functional levels, it is important to remember that it is a one-way change. After raising the level, you cannot lower it again later. For example, if you raise the domain from Windows 2000 mixed to Windows 2003, you cannot return the level to Windows 2000 mixed again. This means that you can't add Windows NT BDCs or Windows 2000 DCs to your domain after the upgrade, and any existing DCs need to be upgraded or permanently removed from service. If you attempt to change the domain or forest level after raising it to Windows 2003, a screen similar to Figure 6.29 will appear.

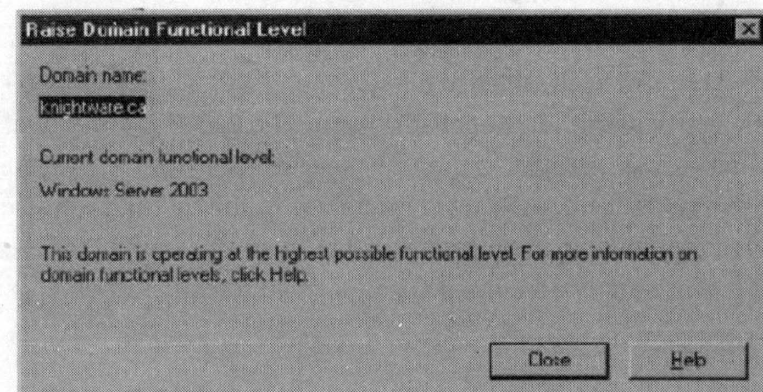

Figure 6.29 Raise Domain Functional Level Dialog Box After Raising the Domain Functional Level

6.11.1 New Features Available only with Windows Server 2003 Domain/Forest Functionality

The new features of Windows Server 2003 that apply to all computers running this latest OS. However, there are new features discussed in this section that are available only with Windows Server 2003 domain and forest functionality. When the domain or forest functional levels have been raised so that all DCs are running Windows Server 2003, a number of new features become enabled. These features allow you to modify elements of both your domain and forest, and provide advanced functions that aren't available until functionality levels are raised. In the paragraphs that follow, we will look at the new features available in Active Directory when all DCs have been upgraded to Windows Server 2003, and the functionality has been raised to Windows 2003.

6.11.1.1 Domain Controller Renaming Tool

The DC renaming tool allows you to rename a DC without having to demote it first. This can be useful when you need to restructure the network, or simply want to use a more meaningful name for a particular DC. When this tool is used, the DC name changes, and any Active Directory and DNS entries are automatically updated.

6.11.1.2 Domain Rename Utility

Domains can also be renamed. Using the domain rename utility (rendom.exe), you can change the NetBIOS and DNS names of a domain, including any child, parent, domain-tree, or forest root domains (from which all others branch off in the hierarchy). By renaming domains in this manner, you can thereby move them in the hierarchy. For example, you can change the name of dev.web.syngress.com to dev.syngress.com, making the web.syngress.com and dev.syngress.com domains on the same level of the hierarchy. You could even rename the domain so that it becomes part of a completely different domain tree. The only domain that you can't reposition in this manner is the forest root domain.

6.11.1.3 Forest Trusts

As we saw earlier, forest trusts can also be created, so that a two-way transitive trust relationship exists between two different forests. In creating such a trust, the users and computers in each forest are able to access what's in both forests. This expands the network, so users are able to use services and resources in both forests.

6.11.1.4 Dynamically Links Auxiliary Classes

Additional features have also been added to the schema. Windows Server 2003 supports dynamically linked auxiliary classes, which allow additional attributes to be added to individual objects. For example, you can have an auxiliary class that has attributes that are used for the Accounting department and others that are useful for the Sales department. By applying the auxiliary classes to the objects, only those objects are affected. Rather than adding attributes to an entire class of objects, dynamically linking auxiliary classes allows you to apply additional attributes to a selection of objects.

6.11.1.5 Disabling Classes

Because certain objects in Active Directory might no longer be needed after a specific point, you can disable classes and attributes that are no longer needed in the schema. Classes and attributes can be disabled, but cannot be deleted. If schema objects are not longer required, you can deactivate them, and reactivate them later if the situation changes.

6.11.1.6 Replication

Improvements have also been made in how Active Directory replicates directory data. Rather than having the entire group membership replicated as a single unit, individual members of groups can now be replicated to other DCs. In addition, changes have been made to GC replication. When there is an extension of a partial attribute set, only the attributes that have been added are replicated. These improvements decrease the amount of network traffic caused by replication because less data is transmitted across the network. You can use the following steps to raise domain and forest functionality.

6.11.1.7 Raise Domain and Forest Functionality

This should not be performed on a production network. It assumes that all DCs in the domain are running Windows Server 2003.After raising the functional levels; you will NOT be able to roll back to a previous level.

1. From the Windows Start menu, select Administrative Tools, and then click the Active Directory Domains and Trusts menu item.
2. When Active Directory Domains and Trusts opens, expand the Active Directory Domains and Trusts node, and select your domain.
3. From the Action menu, click Raise Domain Functional Level.
4. When the Raise Domain Functional Level dialog box appears, select Windows Server 2003 from the drop-down list. Click the Raise button.
5. A warning message will appear, informing you that this action will affect the entire domain, and after you raise the domain functional level, it cannot be reversed. Click OK.
6. After you raise the level, a message box will inform you that the action was successful. Click OK to continue.
7. In the context pane of Active Directory Domains and Trusts, select the Active Directory Domains and Trusts node.

8. From the Action menu, click Raise Forest Functional Level.
9. When the Raise Forest Functional Level dialog box appears, select Windows Server2003 from the drop-down list. Click the Raise button.
10. A warning message will appear, informing you that this action will affect the entire forest, and after you raise the forest functional level, it cannot be reversed. Click OK.

After you raise the level, a message box will inform you that the action was successful. Click OK to continue.

EXERCISES

1. Explain the various directory services?
2. Explain the terminology and concepts of active directory?
3. Explain the concept of directory data store?
4. How we can protect our active directory data?
5. Explain the policy-based administration?
6. What do you mean by directory access protocol?
7. Explain the concept of naming scheme?
8. What are X.500/ldap standards?
9. How we can install active directory to create a domain controller?
10. How active directory works?
11. Explain the basic structure of directory?
12. Explain the various components of active directory?
13. What are domain controllers?
14. How we can use active directory administrative tools?
15. Explain the role of graphical administrative tools?
16. Explain in detail active directory users and computers?
17. Explain in detail active directory domains and trusts?
18. What are command-line tools?
19. How we can implement active directory security and access control?
20. How we can access control in active directory?
21. How can active directory authenticated?
22. What's new in windows server 2003 active directory?
23. Explain the new features available only with windows server 2003 domain/forest functionality?

CHAPTER 7

Performance Monitoring and Security

7.1 INTRODUCTION

Server Performance Advisor uses three types of data sources to collect data: performance counters (which are also used by System Monitor), trace providers (data from Event Tracing for Windows, or ETW), and configuration settings (registry settings). The Server Performance Advisor groups these data sources into one or more "data collector groups" that gather data and prepare reports. Server Performance Advisor creates one data collector group by default, the System Overview, but you can easily add other data collector groups by server role, or create your own.

The first monitoring steps for a new Microsoft Windows Server 2003 computer should include a thorough base lining of resource availability and performance data, which should be compared periodically with real-time data so that developing problems with applications or hardware can be solved or averted before they become serious. With the broad range of tools available in Windows Server 2003, no self-respecting system administrator should be caught unaware.

Performance monitoring and tuning are two tasks that administrators often overlook, but they play an important role in server operations. Many scenarios call for monitoring a server, including the following:

- ***Establishing a baseline of a server's performance to serve as a reference for future comparison***
- ***Monitoring servers to determine load and whether to upgrade the servers or reallocate workloads***
- ***Regularly checking for program or operating system errors that can indicate a problem or potential problem***
- ***Using a packet sniffer to perform in-depth network troubleshooting when authentication or other communications fail.***

7.2 TASK MANAGEMENT

Task Manager provides information about programs and processes running on your computer. It also displays several common process performance counters. Task Manager can be opened by right-clicking an open area of the taskbar and then choosing Task Manager, or by pressing CTRL+ALT+DEL and then choosing Task Manager. The Windows Server 2003 Task Manager interface, by default, presents five tabs on which its data is categorized: Applications, Processes, Performance, Networking, and Users.

7.2.1 Applications Tab

The Applications tab shows the status of the user-level programs running on the computer. Services and system applications running in a context different from the logged on user are not displayed. On the Applications tab you can also start a new program with New Task, end a program with End Task, or switch to another program using Switch To. By right-clicking on an application, you can also select Go to Process from the shortcut menu, which will take you to the corresponding process on the Process tab.

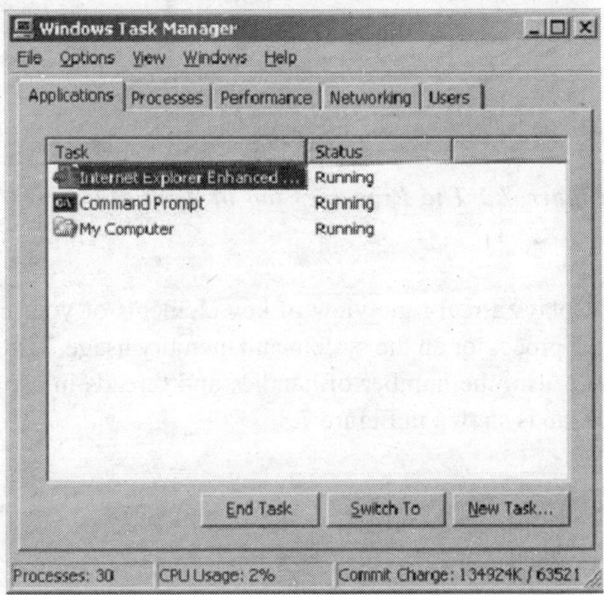

Figure 7.1 shows the Applications tab of Task Manager.

7.2.2 Processes Tab

The Processes tab shows information about all processes running on your computer, including user-level applications, services, and other system processes. By choosing Select Columns from the View menu, you can add or remove columns of data including memory usage changes (deltas), process IDs, and processor use. You can sort by any column by clicking on the column header.

By right-clicking on any process, you can change the priority of processor time that the process receives, set the processor affinity on multiple processor computers, and end a process. For processes that have child or related processes, you can end all related processes by choosing End Process Tree. If you needed to end a mail application, for example, you might also need to end the MAPI spooler; appropriately, you would right-click on the mail application and choose to End Process Tree. The Processes tab is shown in Figure 7.2.

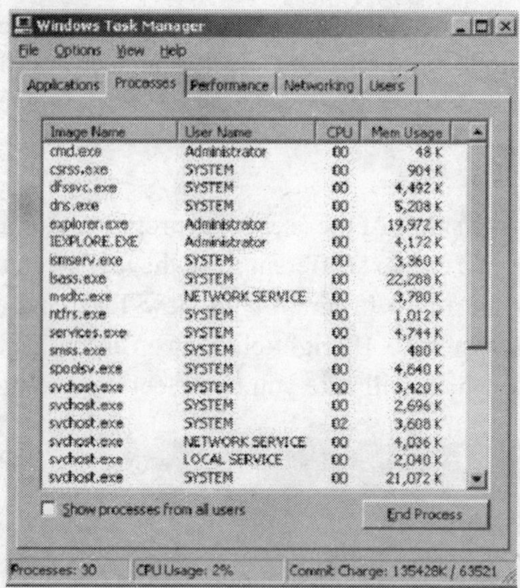

Figure 7.2 The Processes tab of Task Manager

7.2.3 Performance Tab

The Performance tab displays a real-time view of key elements of your computer's performance. Graphs are presented for each processor on the system and memory usage. Text displays show physical, kernel, and commit memory; also, the number of handles and threads in use by active processes are displayed. The Performance tab is shown in Figure 7.3.

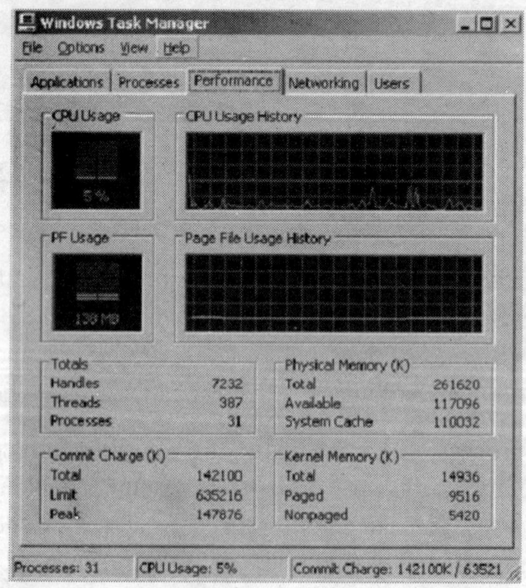

Figure 7.3 The Performance tab of Task Manager

7.2.4 Networking Tab

The Networking tab shows all active network connections by name, their connection speed, bandwidth usage, and status. The Networking tab is shown in Figure 7.4

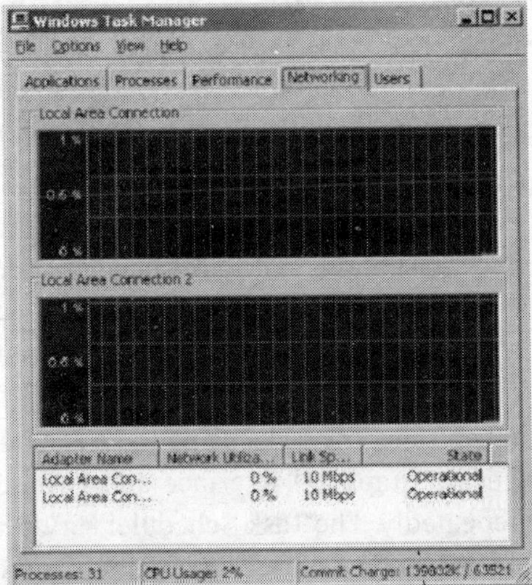

Figure 7.4 The Networking tab of Task Manager

7.2.5 Users Tab

The Users tab shows all users who are logged on, and allows for the logoff or forced disconnection of the user from the computer. Logged-on users may be local at the console, or remotely attached from the network. Network messages can be sent to remote users (it certainly is polite to tell them before you disconnect them) by selecting the users' session and then clicking Send Message. The Users tab is shown in Figure 7.5.

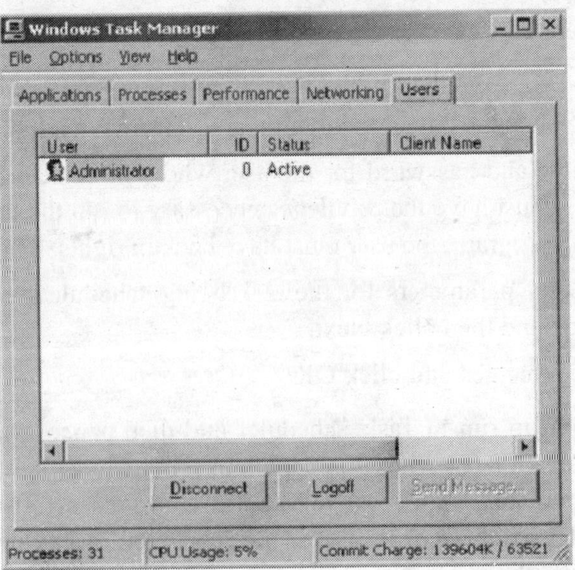

Figure 7.5 The Users tab of Task Manager

Example: **Task Manager**

In this practice, you will use Task Manager to start an application and identify its process.

1. Right-click an open section of the taskbar, and choose Task Manager from the shortcut menu.
2. On the Applications tab, click New Task. Type explorer, and then click OK. Windows Explorer will open focused on its default window (typically My Documents), and the My Documents (or other focus window) application name will appear in the Application tab of Task Manager.
3. Right-click the newly-opened application name, and choose Go To Process. The focus in Task Manager changes to the Processes tab, and the Explorer.exe process is highlighted. From this point, as a situation involving applications and Task Manager warrants, you can adjust the priority of the process or end it.

7.2.6 Task Scheduler

It's true that you could and still can schedule tasks using the AT command, as described later in this chapter, but Task Scheduler provides a graphical interface and is much easier to use. Tasks can be scheduled during off-hours to run repeatedly. The Task Scheduler service is started at bootup and runs in the background. To use Task Scheduler, open Control Panel, double-click the Scheduled Tasks folder, and then follow these steps:

1. In the Scheduled Tasks window, double-click the Add Scheduled Task entry. This starts the Scheduled Task Wizard. Click Next.
2. Select a program from the page, or click Browse to locate another program. Click Next.
3. Supply a name for the task, and then indicate how often you want it performed. Click Next.
4. Select the time of day you want the task performed. Depending on the timing you've selected, you'll also need to specify one of the following:
   - Daily Task Every day, every n days, or weekdays only.
   - Weekly Task Every n weeks; supply the day of the week.
   - Monthly Task Select the day of the month, and select which months.
5. Supply the user name and password for the user who will be scheduling tasks. Note that the account you specify must have the privileges necessary to run the task. For example, if you're scheduling a backup program, the user must have backup rights. Click Next.
6. If you need to specify parameters for the task being scheduled, select the Open Advanced Properties check box and then click Next.
7. Make the necessary changes and click OK.

Many programs will start to run in Task Scheduler and then pause, waiting for input that never comes-or input that comes much later, when someone looks at the machine to see what's going on. To make sure you have all the parameters for a task to be able to run successfully, open a command prompt and type program_name /?. Then right-click the task in the Scheduled Tasks window and choose Properties from the shortcut menu. Enter the necessary parameters in the Run text box and click OK.

You might want to schedule a task to run right away so that you can test its performance. If a task is scheduled by a user and that user isn't logged on at the scheduled time, the task still runs in the background and is not visible.

Note unfortunately, the Windows Server 2003 disk defragmenter utility doesn't support scheduled operation. To schedule a defrag operation, you can either purchase a commercial defrag program that supports scheduling, such as Raxco's PerfectDisk, which runs on both 32-bit and x64 versions of Windows Server 2003, or you can create a little batch file that runs the command-line version (Defrag.exe) and use the Windows Task Scheduler to run the batch file.

7.2.6.1 Changing a Schedule

Even the best schedule can run up against reality now and again, so you need to be able to adjust your planned events. Here are your options:

- To run a task immediately, right-click the task's icon in the Scheduled Tasks window and choose Run from the shortcut menu.
- To stop a task that's running, right-click the task's icon in the Scheduled Tasks window and choose End Task. If the scheduled task has been set up to start another task, the End Task command halts only the original scheduled task.
- To temporarily halt all Task Scheduler actions, open the Advanced menu in the Scheduled Tasks window and choose Pause Task Scheduler. Any tasks that do not start because Task Scheduler is paused will run again only at their next scheduled time. To start Task Scheduler again, click the same menu and choose Continue Task Scheduler.
- To stop using Task Scheduler, open the Advanced menu in the Scheduled Tasks window and choose Stop Using Task Scheduler. No scheduled tasks will run, and the Task Scheduler service no longer starts automatically when the system is rebooted.

7.2.6.2 Tracking Task Scheduler

The system maintains a detailed log of Task Scheduler's activities. To view the log, double-click Scheduled Tasks in Control Panel. From the Advanced menu, choose View Log. This opens a log, like the one shown in Figure 7.6, with the most recent entry at the bottom of the window. The Details view in the Scheduled Tasks window displays information about each task.

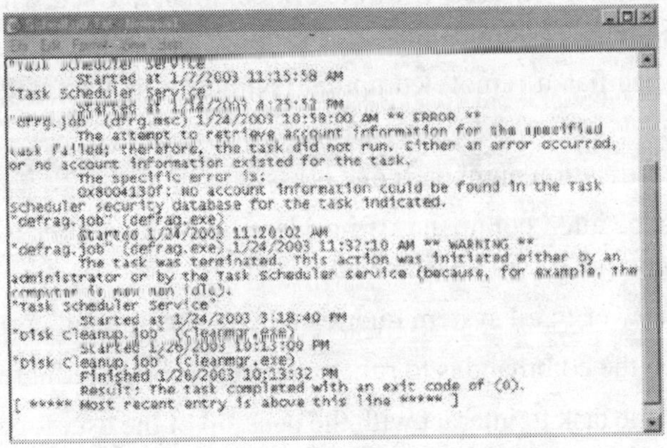

```
"Task Scheduler Service"
        Started at 1/7/2003 11:15:58 AM
"Task Scheduler Service"
        Started at 1/24/2003 4:25:52 PM
"drrg.job" (drrg.msc) 1/24/2003 10:58:00 AM ** ERROR **
        The attempt to retrieve account information for the specified
task failed; therefore, the task did not run. Either an error occurred,
or no account information existed for the task.
        The specific error is:
        0x8004130f: No account information could be found in the Task
Scheduler security database for the task indicated.
"defrag.job" (defrag.exe)
        Started 1/24/2003 11:20:02 AM
"defrag.job" (defrag.exe) 1/24/2003 11:32:10 AM ** WARNING **
        The task was terminated. This action was initiated either by an
administrator or by the Task Scheduler service (because, for example, the
computer is now non idle).
"Task Scheduler Service"
        Started at 1/24/2003 3:18:40 PM
"Disk Cleanup.job" (cleanmgr.exe)
        Started 1/26/2003 10:13:00 PM
"Disk Cleanup.job" (cleanmgr.exe)
        Finished 1/26/2003 10:13:32 PM
        Result: The task completed with an exit code of (0).
[ ***** Most recent entry is above this line ***** ]
```

Figure 7.6 The Task Scheduler log

If a scheduled task doesn't execute as expected, right-click that task in the Task Scheduler window and choose Properties from the shortcut menu. Verify that the task is in fact enabled. (The Enabled check box in the Task Properties dialog box should be selected.)

7.2.6.3 Viewing Tasks on a Remote Computer

If you are an administrator of a remote computer running Windows 2000 Server, Windows 2000 Professional, Windows XP Professional, Windows NT 4 Server, or Windows NT 4 Workstation, you can view and edit the Task Scheduler settings on that computer. Find the computer in the My Network Places window or in the Network Neighborhood window, right-click, and select Explore from the shortcut menu. In the left pane, open Control Panel and double-click Scheduled Tasks. To view and edit scheduled tasks, the remote computer must meet the following requirements:

- Have remote administration enabled
- Specify your user account as having remote administrative access
- Share the hard disk on which the Scheduled Tasks folder resides

7.2.7 Using the at Command

You can also use the AT command to schedule tasks. By default, the AT command is run using the Local System account, which requires administrative,privileges. To specify another account as the user of the AT command, follow these steps:

1. Open Control Panel and double-click Scheduled Tasks.
2. In the Scheduled Tasks window, open the Advanced menu and then choose AT Service Account.
3. Click This Account, and specify a particular user and password. Click OK.

The command structure for the AT command is as follows:

AT [\\computername][id] [[/delete]| /delete [/yes]]

AT [\\computername] time [/interactive] [/every:date[,...] |

/next:date[,...]] command

The following parameters can be used with the AT command. Used without parameters, the AT command returns a list of scheduled commands.

- \\computername Specifies a remote computer. Without this parameter, the local computer is assumed.
- id Indicates the identification number, if one is assigned.
- /delete Cancels a scheduled command. If no identification number is specified, all scheduled commands on the computer will be canceled.
- /yes Forces a yes answer to all system queries when canceling all commands.
- time Specifies when the command is to run, expressed as hours:minutes in 24-hour notation.
- /interactive Allows the task to interact with the desktop of the user logged on at the time the job is run.

- /every:date[,...] Runs the command on the date specified. The date can be specified as one or more days of the week (M, T, W, Th, F, S, Su) or as one or more days of the month (numbers 1 through 31). Separate multiple dates with commas. If this parameter is omitted, the current day of the month is assumed.
- /next:date[,...] Runs the command on the next occurrence of the specified day. If this parameter is omitted, the current day of the month is assumed.
- command Indicates the program, batch file, or command to be run. If a path is required, use the Uniform Naming Convention (UNC) path.

Here are some important facts to keep in mind about the AT command:

- The AT command doesn't automatically load Cmd, the command interpreter. Therefore, if the command parameter doesn't point to an executable file, you must explicitly specify Cmd, followed by the /c switch, at the beginning of the command.
- Commands scheduled using AT run as background processes, so there is no displayed output. To redirect output to a file, use the redirection symbol (>). The redirection symbol must be preceded by the escape symbol (^), so a sample command would be at retrieve.bat ^>c:\daylog.txt.

If you have to use a drive letter to connect to a shared directory, include an AT command to disconnect the drive when the task is completed. Otherwise, the assigned drive letter will be neither available nor seen at the command prompt.

7.3 SYSTEM MONITORING

The easiest way to monitor the performance of a single server running Windows Server 2003 is to use the Microsoft Windows Server 2003 Performance Advisor tool (Server Performance Advisor), which is available from the Microsoft Download center at http://www.microsoft.com/downloads. This program creates customizable reports that provide a summary of the overall performance of one or more servers running Windows Server 2003, with supplemental detail that simplifies further analysis and troubleshooting. Although Server Performance Advisor can monitor multiple servers, the setup process is complex, making it a less suitable solution for casual monitoring.

The Server Performance Advisor uses three types of data sources to collect data: performance counters (which are also used by System Monitor), trace providers (data from Event Tracing for Windows, or ETW), and configuration settings (registry settings). The Server Performance Advisor groups these data sources into one or more "data collector groups" that gather data and prepare reports. Server Performance Advisor creates one data collector group by default, the System Overview, but you can easily add other data collector groups by server role, or create your own.

Note Because reports use a large amount of disk space (approximately 20 MB per 100 seconds for the System Overview), the default data collector groups monitor for short periods of 100 to 300 seconds. Schedule or run data collector groups manually during periods that represent normal, heavy, and low usage to obtain a better overall understanding of a server's performance. The first time you open the Server Performance Advisor, the Start Page appears. Click Quick Tour to analyze the overall system performance of the server during the next 100 second period, or click Add/Repair Data Collector Groups to add data collector groups.

Choose Add/Repair Data Collector Groups from the File menu to add other data collector groups. Click the icon on the left of the Start Page to display the Scope Tree (console tree), which is shown in Figure 7.7. The console three has the following three nodes:

- Data Collectors And Reports Lists data collection groups, the data collectors for each group, and the reports generated by each group. Use this node to view reports generated by the System Overview data collection group or other data collection groups.
- Trace Providers Lists trace providers that you can drag into data collection groups to add them to the data sources included in reports.
- Performance Counters Lists performance counters that you can drag into data collection groups to add them to the data sources included in reports.

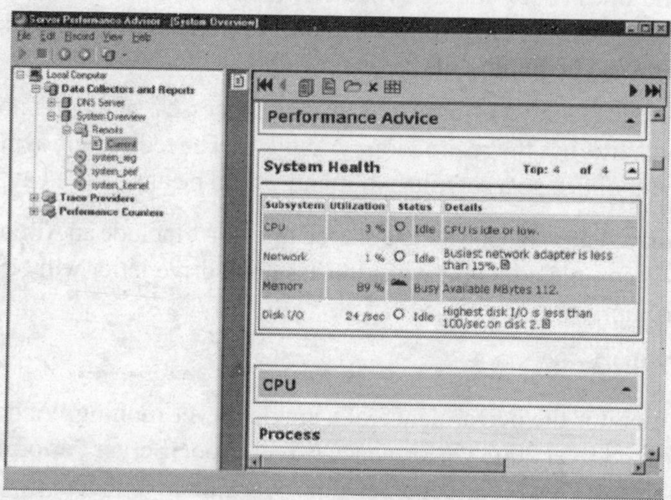

Figure 7.7 The System Overview report in Server Performance Advisor

Note: You can create and view customized groups of performance counters using Server Performance Advisor. To do so, first right-click Performance Counters in the console tree (also known as the Scope Tree), choose New, and then select Counter Group. Then drag counters from the All Counters group into the counter group you created. After adding the appropriate counters, drag the counter group into the main window to display System Monitor with the selected counters.

7.3.1 Recording and Viewing Data

To start recording data, select the appropriate data collection group, and then click the Start System Overview button (for example) on the toolbar. Server Performance Advisor collects data for the specified period and then generates a report from the data, as shown in Figure 7.7.

To view recorded data in System Monitor, click the Show System Monitor toolbar button. Even though the data in a report is static, you can add or remove counters from the System Monitor view, or use the System Monitor view to change the timeframe and then regenerate the report by clicking the Window Report toolbar button.

To schedule a data collection group, right-click the data collection group (for example, System Overview), choose Properties, and then click the Schedule tab, shown in Figure 7.8. Use the Duration box to change how long the data collection group gathers data, and click Change to schedule the data collection.

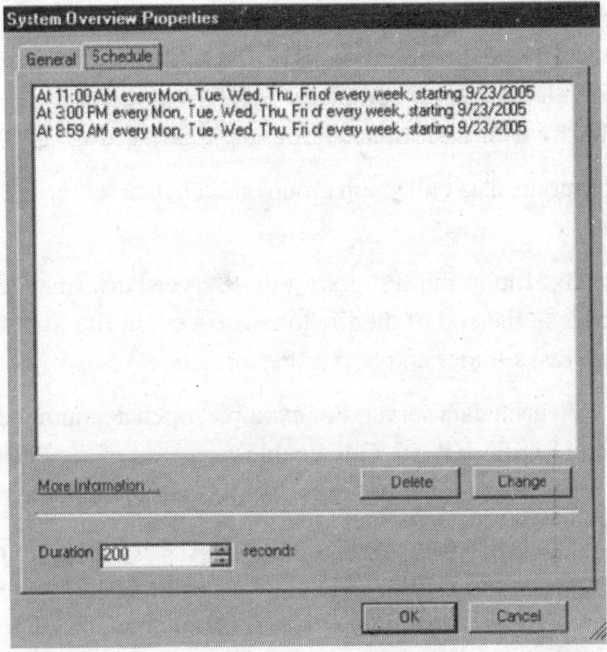

Figure 7.8 The Schedule tab of the System Overview Properties dialog box

7.3.2 Monitoring Multiple Servers

Server Performance Advisor can monitor multiple servers (data servers) from a single report server running Server Performance Advisor, thereby centralizing monitoring and reporting. Unfortunately, setup is complex. This is because the System Service account under which Server Performance Advisor runs does not have sufficient permissions to run the appropriate tasks and transfer data across the network. Running the Server Performance Advisor with an account that belongs to the Domain Admins group fixes this problem, but it poses a large security risk!

The best workaround is to run Server Performance Advisor on the data servers using an account that belongs to the local Performance Log Users group. To do this and set up a central report server to monitor multiple data servers, use the following steps:

1. Install Server Performance Advisor on the report server and all data servers. To deploy Server Performance Advisor to a large number of servers, use Group Policy.
2. Create a Global group called Server Performance Advisor Users (or another descriptive name).
3. Create a user account with a nonexpiring password, and add it to the Server Performance Advisor Users group. Limit the permissions given to the account, and deny the account dial-in rights by right-clicking the account in Active Directory Users and Computers, clicking Properties, clicking the Dial-In tab, and then selecting the Deny Access check box.
4. Add the Server Performance Advisor Users group to the Performance Log Users local group (or built-in group on domain controllers) on all data servers and the report server that generates reports.
5. Share the \PerfLogs\Transfer folder on the report server, or create a suitable DFS folder.

6. Set the Share permissions on the \Transfer share to give the Everyone group Full Control permissions, and set the NTFS permissions on the folder to give Write permissions to the group or groups to which all data server computers belong, as well as the Server Performance Advisor Users group or the built-in Performance Log Users group.

7. Schedule the appropriate data collection group on each data server as described in the "Recording and Viewing Data".

8. Open the Readme.txt file in the \Program Files\Server Performance Advisor\Data folder, and use the sample code at the end of the file to create a batch file that sets the proper permissions for the Scheduled Tasks folder and Server Performance Advisor jobs.

9. Run the batch file on each data server. For example, open a command prompt window and then type PerfLogUsersUseSPA.bat All /G to enable members of the Performance Log Users group to run all report jobs, where PerfLogUsersUseSPA.bat is the name of the batch file.

10. On the report server and each data server, right-click Local Computer in the System Performance Advisor console tree, choose Properties, and then use the Local Computer Properties dialog box to change the Transfer folder location to the \Transfer share or DFS folder.

11. On each data server, choose Data from the Role box in the Local Computer Properties dialog box.

12. On the report server, choose either Report from the Role box in the Local Computer Properties dialog box or Both to collect data from the report server as well as the data servers.

13. Right-click the appropriate data collection group on the report server, choose Properties, and then change the Generate property to Every 10 Minutes to force System Performance Advisor to check for new data from the data servers every 10 minutes.

14. Right-click the appropriate data collection group on each data server, choose Properties, and then under Run As type the username and password of the dedicated user account you created.

7.3.3 Using System Monitor

System Monitor is a utility designed to track various processes on a Windows Server 2003 system in real time, using a graphical display. Use the data from System Monitor to quickly evaluate a server's current performance. Use the Server Performance Advisor and/or Performance Logs And Alerts tools as described elsewhere in this chapter to perform long-term monitoring or create performance baselines.

When you launch the Performance (Perfmon.msc) MMC snap-in from the Administrative Tools folder, the main console (shown in Figure 7.9) appears, displaying the Pages/sec, Avg. Disk Queue Length, and % Processor Time counters.

Note: Save changes to the Performance console using a filename other than Perfmon.msc to avoid changing the default configuration of the performance tools on the computer.

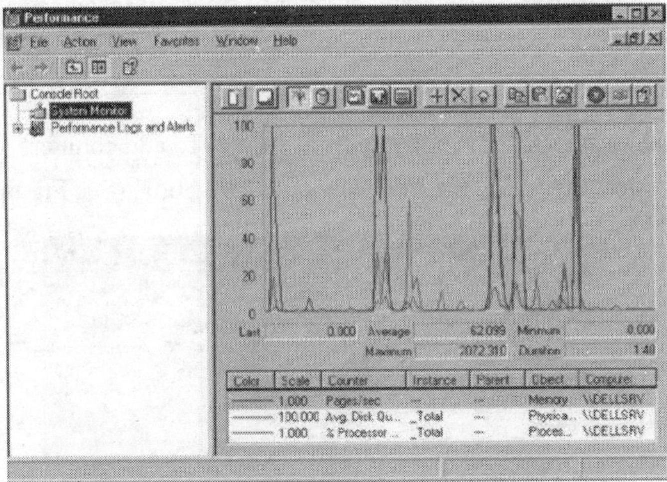

Figure 7.9 The System Monitor console

7.3.3.1 Objects, Counters, And Instances

System Monitor uses three types of items to monitor the system: objects, counters, and instances:

- Object A collection of counters associated with a resource or service that generates data. Each time an object performs a function, System Monitor updates its counters. Windows comes with a range of objects corresponding to major hardware and software components; programs add other components and their corresponding objects. Here is a listing of commonly used objects:
  1. Browser Monitors the Browser service for a domain or workgroup
  2. Cache Monitors disk cache usage
  3. Memory Monitors memory performance for physical and virtual memory
  4. Objects Monitors the number of events, mutexes, processes, sections, semaphores, and threads on the computer at the time of data collection
  5. Paging File Monitors page file usage
  6. Physical Disk Monitors hard disks with one or more partitions
  7. Process Monitors all processes running on a machine
  8. Processor Monitors each processor on the system
  9. Server Monitors bytes, sessions, certain system errors, pool nonpaged usage, and pool paged usage
  10. System Monitors the counters that affect all the hardware and software running on the system
  11. Thread Monitors all threads running in the system
- Counter A component within an object that represents data for a specific aspect of the system or service.
- Instance A single occurrence of multiple performance objects of the same type on a machine. If a particular object has multiple instances, you can track the statistics for each instance by adding

a counter for each. You can also add a counter to track all instances at once. An instance can also be an average of the last two values for a process over the period between samples.

1. ADDING COUNTERS

System Monitor can display dozens of counters at a time. To add counters, use the following steps:

1. Click Add Counters to display the Add Counters dialog box. (See Figure 7.10.)

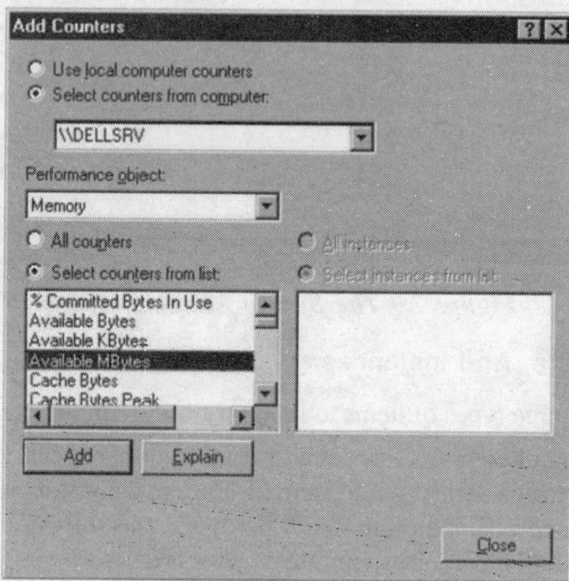

Figure 7.10 The Add Counters dialog box

2. Select the Select Counters From Computer option, and then type the name of the server to monitor. Note To minimize the performance impact of monitoring and maximize the accuracy of the performance data, monitor the server from a management computer, using an account with administrative permissions on the remote computer.
3. Choose an object to monitor from the Performance Object list.
4. Select the Select Counters From List option, and then choose a counter. Click Explain to obtain a description of the counter.

If you select a counter that has multiple instances, choose All Instances to monitor all instances of the selected counter, or choose Select Instances From List to specify the instances to monitor. Be aware that the instance index number assigned to a particular instance might change over time because whenever Windows starts or stops an instance, it might give the instance a different instance number.

Note To stop monitoring specific counters, select the name of a counter in the legend in the System Monitor details pane, and click Delete on the toolbar. To stop monitoring all counters, click New Counter Set on the toolbar.

2. MATCHING COUNTERS TO GRAPH LINES

There are two ways to determine which counter matches a line on the graph:

- Compare the color and bar thickness of each counter within the legend to the lines in the System Monitor graph.

- Double-click a line in the graph to select the corresponding counter in the legend located under the graph. If chart lines are close together, locate a position in the graph where they diverge.

Note: You can highlight a chart line by clicking the counter to highlight and then clicking the Highlight toolbar button. A black line replaces the colored data line if the background color of the chart is white or a light color; for all other background colors, the line is white. To highlight a different line double-click it. System Monitor highlights whatever line you click as long as the Highlight button is depressed.

7.3.3.2 Modifying the Display

You can change the way System Monitor displays information by using the System Monitor Properties dialog box. (See Figure 7.11.) To access this dialog box, click Properties on the toolbar or right-click in the details pane and choose Properties from the shortcut menu.

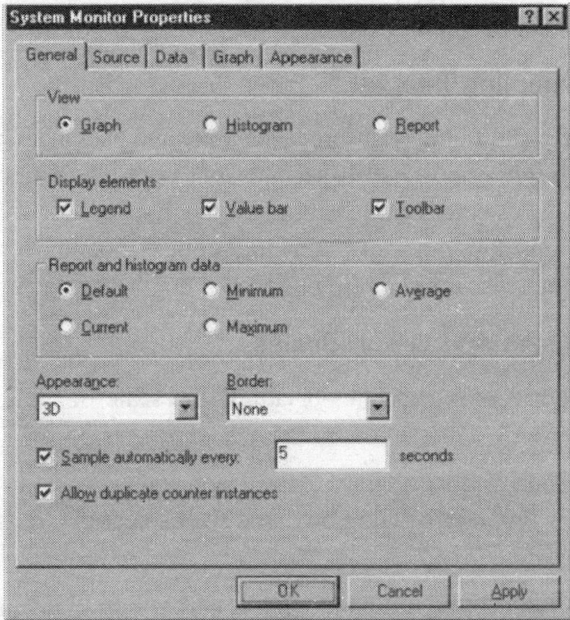

Figure 7.11 The System Monitor Properties dialog box

On the General tab the System Monitor Properties dialog box, you can choose to view the data in the form of a graph, histogram, or report:

- Graph view Presents information in a traditional line-graph format. System Monitor displays each of the counters and instances with a different color and line thickness, as shown in Figure 7.9. This view is the default, and it offers the greatest variety of options.
- Histogram view Presents information in a bar-graph format. As in graph view, System Monitor displays each of the counters and instances in a different color. You can easily track up to 100 counters using this view because System Monitor adjusts the bars to fit the display.
- Report view Presents the counter data in a report list format. System Monitor lists objects in alphabetical order, as is the case for each of the chosen counters. System Monitor displays the data itself numerically. Each object displays the total percentage of processor time in use for the chosen counters. This view works well for tracking a large number of counters.

Choose which display elements to view, as described in the following list:

- Legend Displays a legend at the bottom of the details pane that shows the data scale for each counter, the counter name, the instance, the parent object (if applicable), the object the counter belongs to, the computer being monitored, and the color used to draw the line for the counter. Display the legend to see the counter name associated with a data line.
- Value Bar Displays a value bar at the bottom of the details pane that provides a way to display the last, average, minimum, and maximum values recorded for the selected counter. System Monitor calculates the values from the number of samples and period displayed in the graph. The value bar also displays the total elapsed time displayed in the graph, which System Monitor derives from the sampling interval.
- Toolbar Displays the toolbar functions across the top of the details pane. The toolbar is the only way to do some tasks in System Monitor.

7.3.3.3 Choosing the Sampling Interval

System Monitor displays 100 samples onscreen at a time and uses a default sampling interval of one second, yielding 100 seconds (one minute and 40 seconds) of samples by default. To change how frequently System Monitor samples data, use the Sample Automatically Every n Seconds box on the General tab of the System Monitor Properties dialog box. To view longer periods and decrease the load placed on the server by System Monitor, increase the sampling interval.

7.3.3.4 Changing Grid Lines and Graph Scales

To enable vertical or horizontal grid lines or adjust the scale of the graph or histogram, use the following list:

- To add vertical and horizontal grid lines to the graph and histogram views, click the Graph tab of the System Monitor Properties dialog box, and then select the Vertical Grid and/or Horizontal Grid checkboxes.
- To change the maximum and minimum vertical scale values of the graph, use the Maximum and Minimum boxes on the Graph tab. The defaults are 100 for the maximum value and 0 for the minimum value. The highest value you can specify is 999999999, and the lowest value is 0. Both of these values must be a positive integer. To determine the vertical scale range, look at the range of values generated by the counters you are monitoring.
- To adjust the counter scale settings for a specific counter, click the Data tab, select the counter, and then use the Scale box. Counter scale values can range exponentially from 0.0000001 to 1000000.0. Adjusting the scale does not affect the statistics displayed in the value bar.

7.4 PERFORMANCE LOGS AND ALERTS

Performance Logs and Alerts is a useful tool for monitoring one or more servers over a long period. It can record counter logs and trace logs, as well as generate alerts when counters go over or under the values you specify. You can import the log files into spreadsheets or databases for analysis and report generation or into System Monitor for viewing. Performance Logs and Alerts runs as a service, obviating the need for a logged-on user. There are two types of data that Performance Logs and Alerts can collect: counter logs and trace logs, as discussed in the following list:

- **Counter logs:** Collects data from the specified object at a predefined interval. Counter logs are helpful for recording data about system services activities and hardware usage. You can log data on demand or schedule logging to start and stop automatically. The system can also perform continuous logging, depending on the file size and duration limits. You can view logged data through the System Monitor display or export it to spreadsheets or databases.

Note: To view data from a counter log in real-time, save the log settings as an HTML page, as discussed in the "Saving Log and Alert File Settings". The resulting page hosts the System Monitor ActiveX control that displays the counter data in real-time.

- **Trace Logs:** Monitors data continuously and waits for specific events, such as page faults, to occur. Trace logs record data into a trace log file. To interpret a trace log file, use a parsing tool.

Note: A parsing tool is software that reads the raw data and puts it into a form you can understand. Developers can create parsing tools by using the APIs provided at Microsoft's MSDN Online Library site at http://msdn.microsoft.com/library/default.asp or by using Log Parser 2.2, which is available from the Microsoft Download Center at http://www.microsoft.com/downloads.

7.4.1 Creating Counter and Trace Logs

To create a counter log or a trace log, perform the following steps:

1. Open the Performance (Perfmon.msc) MMC snap-in from the Administrative Tools folder, and then double-click Performance Logs and Alerts. Performance Logs and Alerts list existing logs in the details pane. A green icon indicates a log that is running; a red icon indicates a log that is not.

Note: You cannot run multiple trace logs concurrently that include the same provider attempting to run more than one generates an error message.

2. Right-click either Counter Logs or Trace Logs, and then choose New Log Settings.
3. In the New Log Settings dialog box, type a name for the log settings and then click OK.
4. Choose the objects and counters or trace log providers to monitor, as described in this list:
    - When creating a counter log, click Add Objects or Add Counters to collect data from entire objects or specific counters. (See Figure 7.12.) See the "Adding Counters" section earlier in this chapter for more information.
    - When creating a trace log, select Events Logged By System Provider and then select the appropriate system providers, or select Non-system Providers and then click Add to monitor trace providers not associated with the core operating system.

Important Always set a maximum log file size when creating trace log files that monitor page faults or file details-these providers generate a huge amount of data.

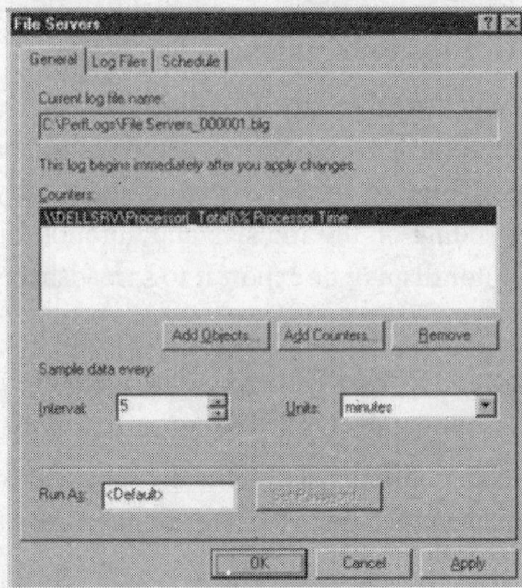

Figure 7.12 The General tab of a log's Properties dialog box

5. When creating a counter log, use the Interval box to specify the sampling interval.
6. Click the Log Files tab, choose a log file type (as described in the "Understanding Log File Parameters" sidebar), and specify the ending to use for log file names. (See Figure 7.13.)

Important To store the log file in a folder other than the PerfLogs folder on the system partition, or to limit the size of a log file, click Configure on the Log Files tab. Use the When The Log File Is Full option on the Schedule tab to run a command when the log file reaches its limit.

Figure 7.13 The Log Files tab of a counter log's Properties dialog box

7. Click the Schedule tab, and set the appropriate schedule for the log file.

7.4.2 Understanding Log File Parameters

The Log Files tab (shown in Figure 7.13) of a counter or trace log allows you to set a number of file parameters, such as the file type and whether to end the filename with a set of sequential numbers or a date.

For a counter log, choose from the following five file types:

- Text File- Comma Delimited Stores data in a comma-delimited text file that uses the file extension .CSV. Use this format to export data to a spreadsheet program.
- Text File- Tab Delimited Stores data in a tab-delimited text file that uses the file extension .TSV. Use this format to export data to a spreadsheet program or to view the data in a text editor.
- Binary File Stores data in a sequential binary file that uses the file extension .BLG. Use this format, which is the default format for counter logs, for intermittent instances (instances that stop and start after the log) and for later viewing in System Monitor.
- Binary Circular File Stores data in a binary file that overwrites the oldest records with the newest and that uses the file extension .BLG. Use this format to record data continuously to the same log file for later viewing in System Monitor.
- SQL Database Stores data in a SQL database. Use this format with networks that maintain a centralized SQL database for logs.

For a trace log, choose from the following two file types:

- Circular Trace File Stores data in a binary file that overwrites the oldest records with the newest and that uses the file extension .ETL. Use this format to record data continuously to the same log file.
- Sequential Trace File Stores data in a sequential binary file that uses the file extension .ETL. Use this format, which is the default format for trace logs, to collect data until the trace file reaches the user-defined limit. When the file reaches the limit, Performance Logs And Alerts closes the current file and starts a new one.

7.4.3 Saving Log and Alert File Settings

To save the settings for a log or an alert file, right-click the name of the log or alert file in the details pane, and then choose Save Settings As. Use the Save As dialog box to save the settings as an HTML file.

To use the saved settings for a new log or alert, right-click Counter Logs, Trace Logs or Alerts in the details pane, choose New Log Settings From, and then select the HTML that file contains the settings to use

Note: You can open settings files for counter logs or alerts in Internet Explorer to view the counter data in a System Monitor ActiveX control.

7.4.4 Using Alerts

Use the alerts feature of Performance Logs and Alerts to log entries in the application event log, start performance logs, send network messages, or run custom commands when counters fall below or rise above values you specify.

To create an alert, follow these steps:

1. Open the Performance (Perfmon.msc) MMC snap-in from the Administrative Tools folder and then double-click Performance Logs and Alerts. Performance Logs and Alerts list existing alerts in the details pane. A green icon indicates an alert that is running; a red icon indicates an alert that is not.
2. Right-click Alerts and choose New Alert Settings.
3. In the New Log Settings dialog box, type a name for the log settings and then click OK.
4. Click Add and then use the Add Counters dialog box to select a counter to monitor. See the "Adding Counters" section earlier in this chapter for more information.
5. Use the Alert When the Value Is and Limit boxes shown in Figure 7.14 to specify when to trigger an alert. Use System Monitor, Performance Logs and Alerts, or the Server Performance Advisor to determine an appropriate value.

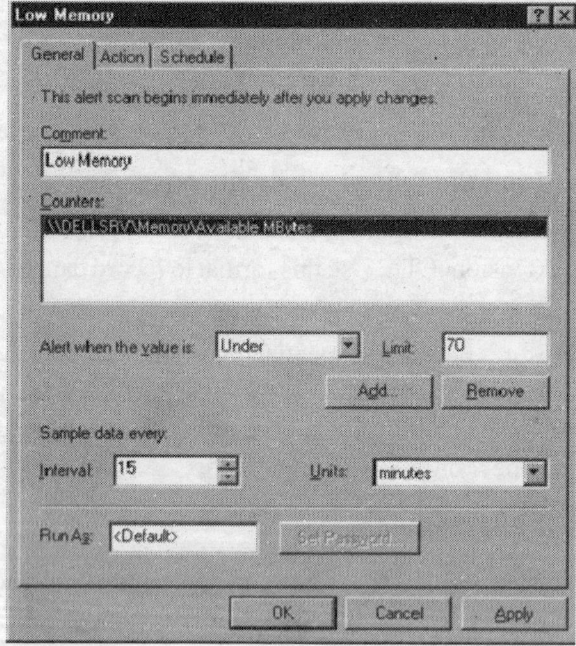

Figure 7.14 The Properties dialog box for an alert

Note: To create or modify a log or alert, you must have Full Control permission for the registry entry

KEY_LOCAL_MACHINE\SYSTEM\CurrentControlSet\Services\SysmonLog\LogQueries. Members of the local Administrators group have this permission by default.

6. Use the Interval box to specify the sampling interval. For guidelines about setting sampling intervals, see the "Determining How Often to Monitor".

7. Click the Action tab and then specify what actions to perform when the counter exceeds the specified threshold, as described in the following list:
   - Log An Entry In The Application Event Log Logs an entry in the application event log of Event Viewer
   - Send A Network Message To Sends an alert message to the specified computer using the Messenger service (if the service is not disabled on the target computer)
   - Start Performance Data Log Runs an existing counter or trace log
   - Run This Program Specifies a command file and command-line arguments to run when an alert occurs
8. Click the Schedule tab, and specify when to make the alert active.

Note: The Send A Network Message To option on the Action tab relies on the Messenger service, which is disabled by default on Windows Server 2003 and Windows Server XP Service Pack 2 to improve security by reducing the attack surface.

7.5 MONITORING MEMORY

There are numerous methods of monitoring servers running Microsoft Windows. To choose the most suitable method, use the following list.

- To quickly check the real-time processor and memory usage on a server, use the Windows Task Manager.
- To monitor a large number of servers, use Microsoft Operations Manager (MOM). To check for functionality or security-related problems, use Event Viewer.
- To observe performance in real-time, use a graph in System Monitor. Graphs are helpful for short-term monitoring of a remote or local computer.
- To perform long-term monitoring and record keeping, use the Microsoft Windows Server 2003 Performance Advisor, Performance Logs and Alerts, or both. Server Performance Advisor provides a simple way to collect counter data, trace data, and system settings and view reports for one or more servers. Performance Logs and Alerts provides a more granular way to collect the counter and trace data, and it enables you to create alerts when specific counters go over or under the specified values.
- To monitor data sent over the network to and from a server, usually to troubleshoot network communication, use Network Monitor.
- To compare Microsoft Exchange or Microsoft SQL Server installations with a list of best practices, use the Exchange Server Best Practices Analyzer or the SQL Server Best Practices Analyzer.
- To prioritize applications to maximize server utilization on a server running Windows Server 2003 Enterprise Edition or Datacenter Edition while ensuring that business critical applications always have sufficient resources, use the Windows System Resource Manager.

To determine how often to monitor servers or what counters to use when monitoring specific performance aspects such as memory usage, use the following sections.

7.5.1 Real World Monitoring and Tuning Strategies

When monitoring or tuning a system, use the following strategies:

- Make one change at a time. Bottlenecks can be the fault of several components. Do not confuse the issue by making too many changes at once, which can make it impossible to assess the impact each change has on the system.
- Keep a record of each change, and repeat the monitoring process after every change. Tuning one resource can affect another and potentially necessitate additional changes.
- Retain logs for an extended period, and store the data in a database for trend analysis, performance assessment, and capacity planning.
- Pay attention to event logs. Operating system and application errors can have a huge impact on performance. (A failed server does not usually perform well.)
- Turn off any screen-saver programs, and stop any services that are not relevant or essential to monitoring the system.

7.5.2 Determining how often to Monitor

The appropriate sampling interval depends on the duration and goals of the monitoring session. For example, use an interval of 3 to 15 seconds for short monitoring sessions and when searching for brief performance impacts. Use a longer sampling interval for routine, long-term logging or to look for a slow memory leak-5 to 15 minutes usually provides enough detail in this situation while minimizing log file size and the load on the server. Decreasing the sampling interval causes the data rate to increase, producing larger log files and placing a heavier load on the system.

7.5.3 Reducing the Performance Impact of Monitoring

To reduce the performance impact of monitoring a server, use the following list:

- Limit the number of objects and counters you monitor-each object and counter increases overhead.
- Do not run System Monitor in graph view for long periods on the server you are monitoring. This view incurs the highest overhead. Use Performance Logs and Alerts instead.
- Increase the sampling interval to reduce overhead. Specify sampling intervals of three seconds or more for intense scrutiny, or 10 to 15 minutes for routine logging.
- Record logs to a disk subsystem not used for performance-critical applications or services.

7.5.4 Monitoring Memory Usage

Lack of sufficient memory is one of the most frequent performance issues on a server. To determine whether this is the case, verify that the system has the required amount of memory to run the operating system and all applications and services, and then use Server Performance Advisor, Performance Logs and Alerts, or System Monitor to monitor the counters in the following list.

1 **Memory\Available Mbytes:** Displays the amount of currently unused physical memory (RAM). Windows uses available memory to satisfy the memory requirements of programs. When available memory falls into short supply, Windows takes memory from the working sets of less active

programs, which can result in more paging and reduced performance as Windows transfers data to and from the hard disk subsystem. Adding RAM when less than 10 to 15 percent of the total physical memory is available usually improves the performance of a server.

- **Memory\ Pages/Sec:** Displays the number of pages written to or read from disk to resolve hard page faults. A hard page fault occurs when a process requires code or data that Windows has paged to disk and removed from physical memory. A high value for this counter does not always indicate lack of memory, but if this value is consistently above 20 per page file and the Available MBytes is below 10 to 15 percent of the physical memory in the system, the system probably would perform better with more RAM.
- **Memory\ Cache Bytes:** Displays the physical memory used by the file system cache and device drivers, as well as operating system and program code that Windows can page to disk when not in use.

To check for a memory leak, look for a steady increase in the following counters regardless of the load on the server:

- **Memory\ Committed Bytes:** Displays the number of committed bytes of virtual memory. Monitor this counter in conjunction with Memory\ Available Bytes.
- **Process\ Working Set, Process\ Virtual Bytes, and Process\ Handle Count:** The Process\ Working Set and Virtual Bytes counters display the amount of physical memory and total memory allocated to all threads in the process you suspect might have a memory leak. The Process\ Handle Count counter displays the number of handles used by the process.
- **Memory\ Pool Nonpaged Bytes:** Displays the number of bytes allocated to the nonpaged pool for objects that Windows must keep in physical memory as long as they are allocated. Use this counter in conjunction with Memory\ Pool Nonpaged Allocs if you suspect that a kernel-mode process (such as a device driver) is the cause of a memory leak.
- **Memory\ Pool Nonpaged Allocs:** Displays the number of calls to allocated space in the nonpaged pool.

To monitor paging, use these counters:

- **Paging File\ % Usage (all instances):** Displays the current percentage of used space in all page files on the system. If you suspect that paging is to blame for a bottleneck, review this value along with Memory\ Available Bytes and Memory\ Pages/Sec.Enlarge the page file(s) if the Paging File\ % Usage counter exceeds 70 percent.
- **Physical Disk\ Avg. Disk Sec/Transfer and Memory\Pages/Sec:** The Physical Disk\ Avg. Disk Sec/Transfer counter displays the average duration of each disk-transfer operation in seconds. The Memory\ Pages/Sec counter displays the number of pages written to or read from the disk when a process requires information that is no longer in its working set and must be retrieved from disk. To determine whether the system is paging excessively, multiply the values of these two counters. If the result exceeds 0.1, paging is taking up more than 10 percent of disk access time. If this condition persists over a long period, add RAM to reduce paging.

Important when the paging file reaches the maximum limit assigned to it, Windows displays a warning and increases the limit. Programs can become unstable during this time, and the system might crash if there is not enough disk space for additional virtual memory.

7.5.5 Monitoring Processor Activity

Two common causes of processor bottlenecks are excess demand placed on the processor by CPU-bound programs and excess interrupts generated by drivers or subsystem components, such as disk or network components. When a bottleneck occurs because a process's threads need more processor cycles than are available, processor queues build up, causing the system response to suffer.

To monitor processor activity, examine the server roles and applications in use on the server and then use Server Performance Advisor, Performance Logs and Alerts, or System Monitor to monitor the following counters:

- **Processor\ % Processor Time (all instances):** Displays the percentage of time all processors in the system are busy. If the counter consistently exceeds 85 percent, evaluate whether the server meets the performance priorities of the organization during periods of heavy load. If it does not, install additional processors, upgrade the processors, or transfer server roles to another server to reduce load.
- **Processor\ % User Time:** Displays the percentage of nonidle processor time that the server spends in user mode, where most applications and services run. To resolve a high rate, move workloads to another server, or upgrade or install additional processors. Use this counter in conjunction with Processor\ % Processor Time (all instances).
- **System\ Processor Queue Length (all instances):** Displays the number of threads waiting to execute. A sustained queue length of more than two to five items per processor or processor core indicates that the processors cannot keep up with the load.
- **Server Work Queues\ Queue Length:** Displays the number of Server service threads waiting to execute. A queue length of greater than four over a sustained period indicates possible processor congestion from the Server service.
- **Processor\ Interrupts/Sec:** Displays the number of hardware interrupts received and processed by the processor per second. Use this counter to determine whether interrupt activity is causing a bottleneck. A dramatic increase in this counter value without a corresponding increase in system activity indicates a possible hardware problem. To resolve this problem, find the network adapter or other device that is causing the interrupts. Refer to the manufacturer's specifications for the acceptable processor threshold; use 1000 interrupts per second as a starting point.
- **Processor\ % Interrupt Time:** Displays the percentage of time the processor spends receiving and servicing hardware interrupts during the sampling interval. This value gives you an indirect indication of the activities of devices that generate interrupts, such as disk drives, network adapters, and other peripheral devices. These devices interrupt the processor when they require attention or complete a task.
- **Processor\ % Privileged Time:** Displays the percentage of nonidle processor time designated for hardware-manipulating drivers and operating system components. A high rate indicates a

failing device or device driver. Use this counter in conjunction with Processor\ % Processor Time (all instances).

Note: Setting processor affinity on multiprocessor servers can prevent other program threads from migrating to the least-busy processor and can hurt overall system performance. In general, let Windows assign threads to processors.

7.5.6 Monitoring Disk Activity

Monitor disk activity using the Server Performance Advisor, Performance Logs and Alerts, or System Monitor to determine whether the disk subsystem of a server is performing acceptably. When used in combination with the Storage Reports feature of File Server Resource Manager (discussed in Chapter 20), the following counters present a good summary of the health of a server's storage subsystem:

Note Windows Server 2003 and Windows XP enable disk counters permanently. To enable disk counters for Windows 2000 or Windows NT, use the Diskperf command. (Type Diskperf -? at a command prompt for additional information.)

- **Physical Disk\ Current Disk Queue Length (all instances):** Displays the number of requests waiting for disk access. This number should remain steady at no more than 1.5 to 2 times the number of spindles that make up the disk subsystem. Most disks have one spindle; redundant array of independent disks (RAID) devices have two or more spindles.
- **Physical Disk\ % Disk Time:** Displays the percentage of time that a drive is active. If the value of this counter rises to more than 90 percent, check the Physical Disk\Current Disk Queue Length (all instances) counter to see how many disk requests are queued for disk access. RAID devices can cause the Physical Disk\ % Disk Time value to exceed 100 percent and thus give an incorrect reading.
- **Physical Disk\ Avg. Disk Sec/Transfer:** Displays the amount of time a disk takes to fulfill a request. A high value might indicate that the disk controller is continually trying to access the disk because of failures. For most systems, a value of 0.3 seconds or higher indicates a high average time for disk transfers.
- **Physical Disk\ Avg. Disk Bytes/Transfer:** Displays the average number of bytes transferred from or to a disk during read or write operations. A value less than 15 KB under load might indicate that an application is accessing the disk drive inefficiently or that the drive is fragmented.
- **Physical Disk\ Disk Transfers/Sec:** Displays the number of bytes transferred to and from the storage subsystem. If these counters indicate that actual usage is near the minimum sustained transfer rate of the physical disks, reduce the server's work load or upgrade to a RAID subsystem.

7.5.7 Monitoring Network Activity

There are two primary reasons to monitor network activity: to troubleshoot network issues such as authentication, or to observe network performance. To troubleshoot network issues, use Network Monitor, as discussed in the "Using Network Monitor" section of this chapter. To observe basic network performance, monitor the following counters using Server Performance Advisor, Performance Logs and Alerts, or System Monitor. Abnormal network counter values usually indicate a problem or shortcoming of the server's processor, memory, or storage subsystems, though they can occasionally be due to a saturated network segment or interface, a broadcast storm or a failed network card.

- **Server\ Bytes Total/Sec** Displays the number of bytes the Server service has sent to and received from the network. This value is helpful in providing an indication of how busy the server is. Segment the network if the sum of the Bytes Total/Sec for all servers is close to the maximum transfer rate of the network.
- **Server\ Work Item Shortages** Displays the number of times no work items are available to service incoming requests. Consider tuning InitWorkItems or MaxWorkItems in the registry key HKEY_LOCAL_ MACHINE\SYSTEM\CurrentControlSet\Services\LanmanServer if the values of the Server\ Work Item Shortages counter reaches or exceeds the threshold of 3.
- **Server\ Server Sessions and Server\ Logon/sec** Displays the number of connections to the Server service and the number of logons per second. A high number of sessions or logons can indicate a busy (and perhaps overloaded) server. Use Network Monitor to pinpoint traffic from individual computers.

7.6 NETWORK AND PROCESS OBJECTS

Before monitoring and tuning a server, it is important to gain an understanding of the context in which the server operates. To do so, review or create documentation of the network configuration and usage, and any organizational policies or procedures that relate to the performance of the server.

7.6.1 Documenting the Network

Accurate and up-to-date documentation of a network helps prioritize performance issues and identify potential bottlenecks in the network. Create or review the following documentation:

- **Performance Priorities** Applications and network services that are business critical, as well as optimal and minimum required levels of performance for noteworthy applications and services. For example, optimal printing performance might be two minutes to print a 10-page document, while the minimum level of performance during busy times might be 20 minutes to print the same document.
- **Usage Patterns** Estimates of when users use applications and services. Document daily usage patterns such as the morning logon and e-mail rush, weekly patterns such as end-of-the week report printing, and monthly and yearly patterns such as project deadlines and tax-preparation activities. The following list contains typical user tasks and the network components stressed by the tasks:

  1. Logon and Logoff events (domain controllers, DHCP, and DNS servers)
  2. Software updates (LAN and WAN bandwidth, software update servers)
  3. Accessing documents (file servers, LAN bandwidth)
  4. Database usage (database server)
  5. Internet usage (proxy and firewall servers, routers, and Internet connection)

6. E-mail usage (e-mail servers)
7. Wireless usage (access points, RADIUS servers, certificate servers, and domain controllers)

- **Network Design** The network topology and structure and location of each device. At a minimum, record the following items:
  1. Internet and WAN link speeds
  2. Firewall locations
  3. Router and switch locations and speeds
  4. Physical network topology map
  5. Subnets and Virtual LANs (VLANs)
  6. Domains and sites
  7. Location of client computers, servers, Network Attached Storage (NAS), printers, and other network devices

Note: Include with the network documentation a series of performance-monitoring logs or traces that establish a performance baseline for important servers (as discussed later in this chapter). You can also include simple network benchmarks by timing typical user tasks such as file copy operations, printing, database queries, and Intranet page loads.

7.6.2 Evaluating Policies and Procedures

Another important factor in performance monitoring is reviewing the organization's acceptable-use policy and network administrator procedures. Acceptable-use policies for employees might include provisions prohibiting or limiting the use of applications that consume large quantities of network bandwidth, such as Peer-to-Peer (P2P) applications, streaming radio or video, Voice Over Internet Protocol (VOIP) applications, and multiplayer network games. Examine and update administration procedures as necessary to minimize the performance impact of regularly scheduled tasks such as backup, downloading and installing software updates, and software deployment.

Network Monitor is a packet-sniffer included with Microsoft Windows Server 2003 that captures and displays frames received from the network. It provides a way to examine at a low-level data traversing the network, and it's invaluable for troubleshooting network issues such as authentication or connection problems.

Network Monitor consists of two components that you must install using the Windows Components Wizard or Sysocmgr.exe: Network Monitor, and the Network Monitor driver. The Network Monitor driver enables Network Monitor to receive frames from the network adapter and is compatible with Windows Server 2003, Windows XP, or Windows 2000.

Note: The Systems Management Server (SMS) version of Network Monitor adds a number of features, including the ability to put the network adapter in promiscuous mode. Promiscuous mode allows the adapter to read all the frames (packets) it receives over the network, instead of only packets addressed to the server. This mode does not work unless the network uses a hub or a switch with port mirroring activated.

7.6.3 Network Frames

A frame is a portion of information from the network data stream that networking software has divided into smaller pieces and sent onto the network. Network Monitor makes it possible to capture these frames and display, filter, save, or print the captured frames to help identify network traffic patterns and network problems.

A frame contains the following data:

- The source MAC address of the machine that sent the frame
- The destination MAC address of the machine that received the frame
- The header information for the protocol that sent the frame
- The actual data sent to the destination computer

To isolate a specific subset of frames, design a capture filter or create a capture trigger that starts a capture when Network Monitor locates a frame that matches the criteria you specify, as discussed later in this section.

7.6.4 Capturing Frames

To capture frames from the network, use the following steps:

1. Open Network Monitor from the Administrative Tools folder using an account with local Administrator permissions.
2. Click OK and then select the network to monitor in the Select A Network dialog box, as shown in Figure 7.15, and then click OK again. If this dialog box does not appear, choose Networks from the Capture menu to open it.

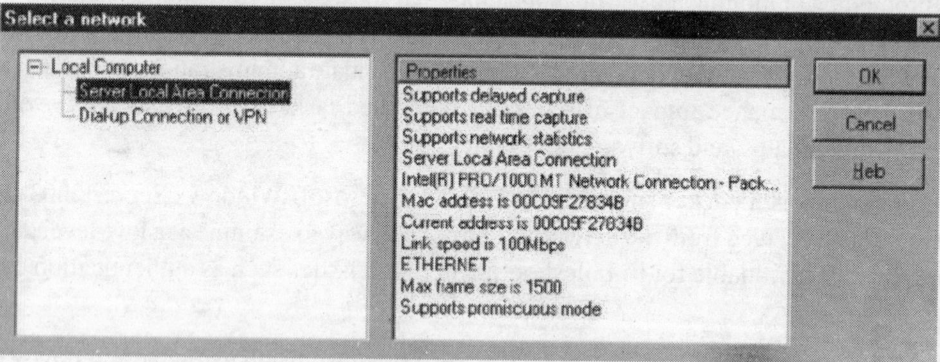

Figure 7.15 The Select A Network dialog box

3. Click Start Capture on the toolbar of the Capture window to begin capturing frames. For more information about the Capture window, see the "Viewing the Capture Window".
4. To halt the data capture temporarily, choose Pause from the Capture menu. To stop capturing data, click Stop and View Capture on the toolbar.

Note: Network Monitor displays network statistics while capturing all network packets to a temporary 1 MB capture file with the .CAP extension located in a subfolder of the \Documents and Settings\User\Local Settings\Temp folder.

7.6.5 Viewing the Capture Window

Network Monitor displays the Capture window when you open Network Monitor and during a capture. After a capture, use the Window menu to switch between the Capture window and the Frame Viewer window. The Capture window has four panes that display frame statistics, as discussed in the following list and shown in Figure 7.16:

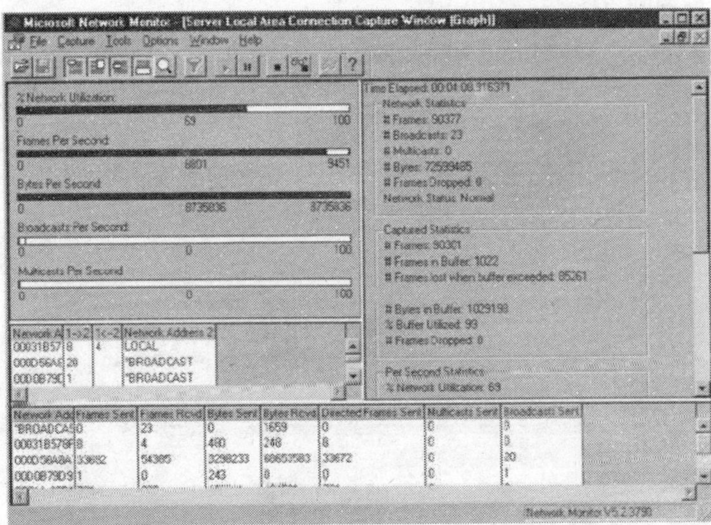

Figure 7.16 The Capture window in Network Monitor

- The graph pane (the upper leftmost pane in Figure 7.16) graphically displays the total capture statistics of current network activity.
- The session statistics pane (the middle left pane in the figure) displays statistics for current individual network sessions. Network Monitor identifies both participants in a session and the amount of information passed between them in either direction. Network Monitor displays only the first 128 unique addresses, so use a capture filter to identify a specific workstation on a busy network segment.
- The station statistics pane (the bottom pane in the figure) displays statistics about activities that occur from or to the local machine running Network Monitor. As with the session statistics pane, Network Monitor displays only the first 128 unique addresses.
- The total statistics pane (the rightmost pane in the figure) summarizes statistics about overall network activity detected by Network Monitor from the time the current capture process began. The total statistics pane consists of five panels:

1. Network Statistics displays statistics about the total amount of traffic that has occurred since the current capture on Network Monitor began. The status is always Normal on an Ethernet network and reflects the status of the ring on a token ring network.
2. Captured Statistics displays statistics regarding the current capture that is running.
3. Per Second Statistics displays averages of current activity. All frames, even those excluded by a filter, are included in these statistics.
4. Network Card (MAC) Statistics reflects the average activity detected by the network adapter from the time the current capture session began.

5. Network Card (MAC) Error Statistics displays network adapter card errors that have occurred from the time the current capture session began.

Note: Network Monitor displays the session statistics for only the first 100 unique network sessions. To view information for the next 100 unique network sessions, you must choose Clear Statistics from the Capture menu.

7.6.6 Viewing the Frame Viewer Window

Network Monitor displays captured frames in the Frame Viewer window (shown in Figure 7.17), which appears after you click Stop And View Capture. To return to the Capture window, select the appropriate capture from the Window menu.

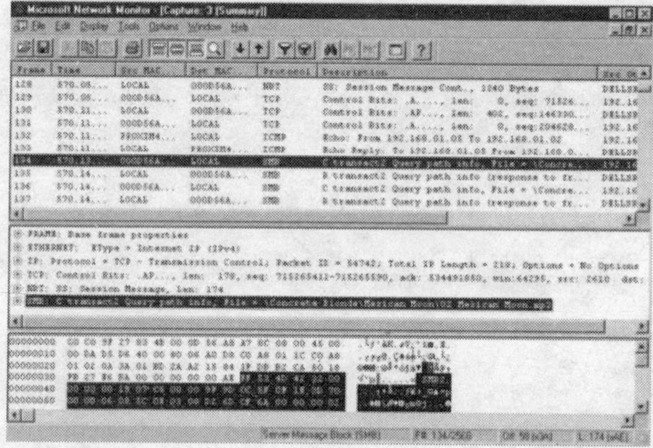

Figure 7.17 The Frame Viewer window

The Frame Viewer window has three panes, which you can toggle using the toolbar buttons:

- The Summary pane displays general information about the captured frames in the order in which Network Monitor captured them.
- The Detail pane displays the frames' contents, including the protocols used to send them.
- The Hex pane displays the ASCII and hexadecimal representation of the captured data. Double-click a frame to display the Detail and Hex panes for that frame; double-click the frame again to hide the detail and hex panes. If double-clicking a frame does not display a pane, select Zoom Pane and all windows from the Window menu.

Note: To change the Time column to display the actual time instead of the time elapsed, choose Options from the Display menu and then choose Time Of Day in the Display Options dialog box.

7.6.7 Configuring and Customizing Network Monitor

This section describes how to expand the capture buffer to capture more data, edit the address database, add comments to a capture, or print captured frames.

7.6.7.1 Modifying the Capture Buffer

By default, Network Monitor captures a maximum of 1 MB of data in its capture buffer (a binary file with the .CAP extension saved in the Windows Temp folder). When the buffer is full, Network Monitor overwrites the oldest data with the newest.

To adjust the size of the capture buffer in Network Monitor, choose Buffer Settings from the Capture menu and then use the Capture Buffer Settings dialog box to adjust the Buffer Size (MB) or Frame Size (Bytes) options. Network Monitor supports capturing and displaying up to 1 GB of data at a time.

7.6.7.2 Editing the Address Database

To make the Frame Viewer window easier to understand, you can replace IP addresses with computer names. To do so, choose Find All Names from the Display menu in the Frame Viewer window. Alternatively, you can right-click an IP address in the Frame Viewer window, choose Edit Address, and then use the Nslookup command at a command prompt to resolve the computer name for the appropriate IP address (provided that the network has a reverse lookup zone and that the host in question has a PTR record in the zone), and then type the host name in the Address Information dialog box.

To save this name in Network Monitor's local address database, select the Permanent Name checkbox. To display the address database (shown in Figure 7.18), choose Addresses from the Display menu of the Frame Viewer window. Click Save to export the database to a file, or click Load to import a previously saved address database.

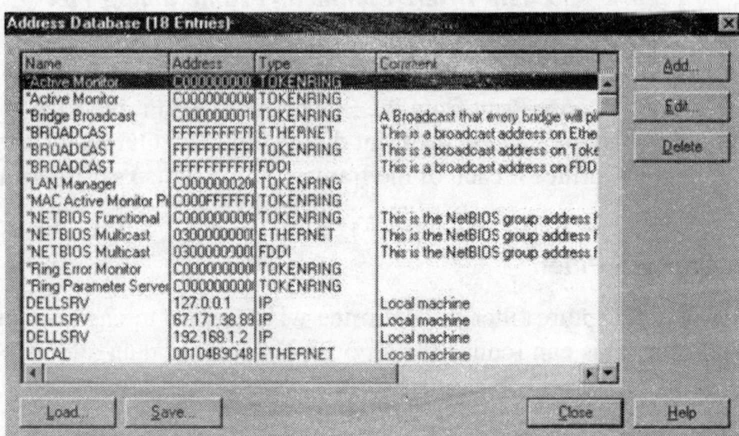

Figure 7.18 The Address Database dialog box

7.6.7.3 Adding a Comment Frame to a Capture

A comment frame is a helpful tool you can use to add comments or other information to a capture file within the Frame Viewer. For example, use comment frames to mark the beginning and ending points for a group of authentication frames. To add a comment frame, choose Insert Comment Frame from the Tools menu or right-click the Frame column at the point to insert the comment frame and choose Insert Comment from the shortcut menu. The Insert Comment Frame dialog box appears. (See Figure 7.19.) The options in this dialog box are as follows:

- **Frame Number:** The frame position where Network Monitor places the comment frame within the capture. Network Monitor lists the selected frame by default.
- **Type of Frame:** To Insert The Comment or Bookmark protocol parser used to process the comment frame. The default parser is Comment.
- **No Statistics:** Disables statistical generation for the comment frame.

- **Apply Current Filter:** To Statistics Calculates statistics using the current display filter.
- **Enter In A Comment:** For This New Frame Specifies the comment text to attach to the frame.

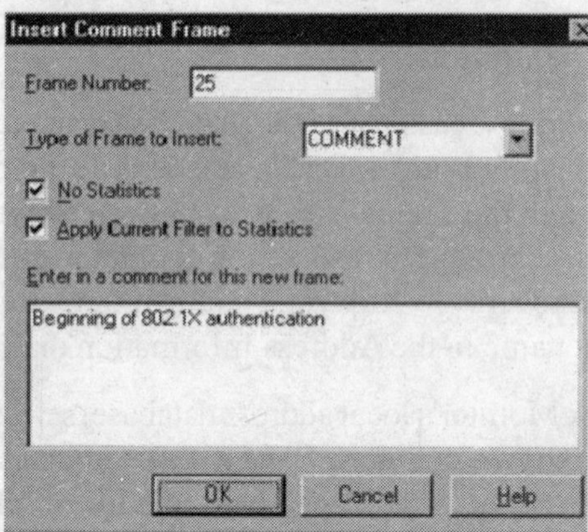

Figure 7.19 The Insert Comment Frame dialog box

7.6.7.4 Printing Captured Frames

To print captured frames, choose Print from the File menu in the Frame Viewer window. Select the desired output options on the Netmon tab in the Print dialog box. The Output Detail area enables you to specify the amount of detail to print for each of the frames. You can also set filters and add page breaks to the output.

7.6.8 Designing a Capture Filter

Network Monitor uses a capture filter to determine what frames to capture, and it ignores frames that do not match the filter. This can reduce the amount of captured data and make it easier to locate relevant frames.

To design a capture filter, stop any captures, choose Filter from the Capture menu of the Capture window, and then use the Capture Filter dialog box shown in Figure 7.20 to design the capture filter, as described in this section.

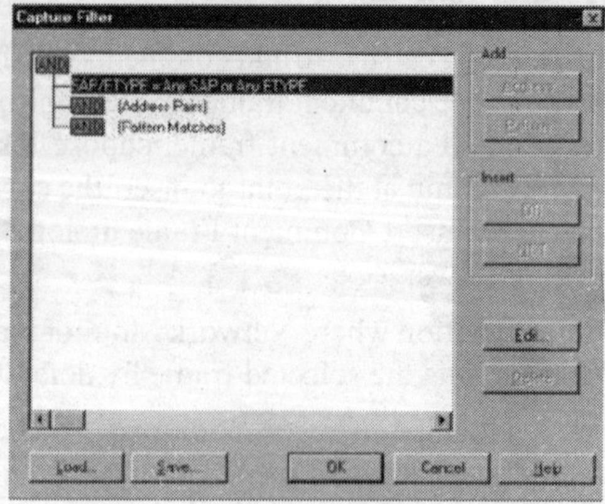

Figure 7.20 The Capture Filter dialog box

7.6.8.1 Specifying Capture Filter Protocols

Filter protocols capture frames sent using a specific protocol. To design filter protocols, double-click the default line SAP/ETYPE = Any SAP Or Any ETYPE in the decision tree of the Capture Filter dialog box shown in Figure 7.20. In the Capture Filter SAPs And ETYPEs dialog box (shown in Figure 7.21), select the protocols to omit from the capture and then click Disable. The default is to enable all the protocols.

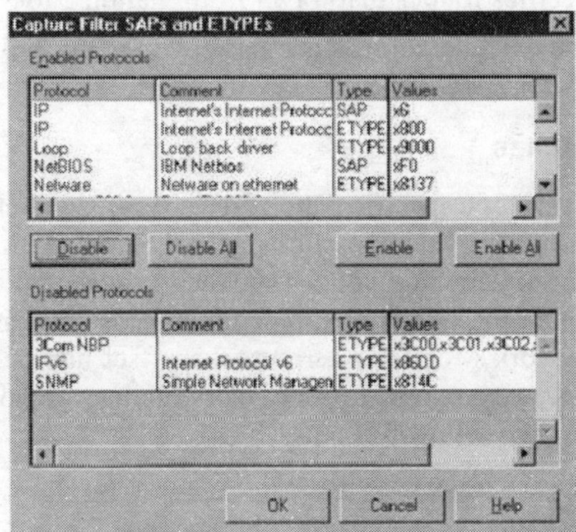

Figure 7.21 The Capture Filter SAPs And ETYPEs dialog box

7.6.8.2 Specifying Address Pairs

Address pairs capture or exclude traffic between the computer running Network Monitor and up to three other computers. To designate address pairs, double-click the AND (Address Pairs) line in the decision tree shown in Figure 7.20, and then specify address pair properties in the Address Expression dialog box shown in Figure 7.22 and described in the following list:

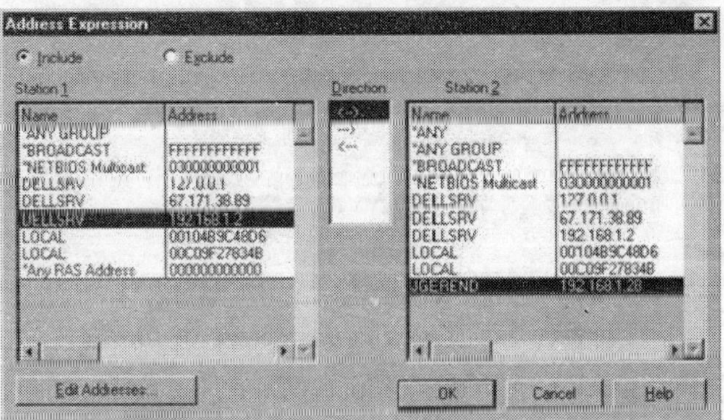

Figure 7.22 The Address Expression dialog box

1. Choose Include or Exclude to include or exclude data that travels between the members of the address pair.

2. Choose the first address from the Station 1 list and the second address from the Station 2 list.
3. Choose one of the three arrows from the Direction list to indicate the direction of the traffic to filter between the two addresses:
   - <-> This arrow specifies frames that travel in either direction between the Station 1 and Station 2 computers. This arrow is the default.
   - -> This arrow specifies frames that travel from Station 1 to Station 2.
   - <- This arrow specifies frames that travel from Station 2 to Station 1.
4. Optionally, modify the existing address database by clicking Edit Addresses and then adding, editing, or deleting information.

7.6.9 Defining Pattern Matches

To capture frames that consist of a specific pattern at a specified offset, create pattern matches. You can create up to four pattern matches by double-clicking the AND (Pattern Matches) line in the decision tree, and then using the Pattern Match dialog box. Type the hexadecimal or ASCII data pattern present in the frames to capture. Then, in the Offset box, type the hexadecimal number that specifies the byte where the pattern begins. Network Monitor interprets the offset number depending on whether you specify the From Start of Frame option or the From End of Topology Header option. To find a pattern to use in a pattern match filter, use the following steps:

1. Perform a capture, and open the capture in the Frame Viewer.
2. Double-click a frame to display the Details And Hex pane.
3. Select a portion of the frame in the Detail pane to obtain its pattern and offset. For example, select the SMB: NT status code = 0x0 text, as shown in Figure 7.23.

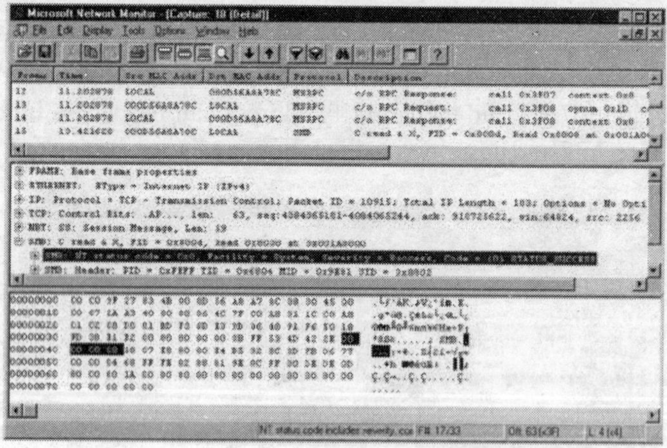

Figure 7.23 The Frame Viewer window

4. Write down the highlighted text in the left part of the Hex pane (this is the pattern) and the text in parentheses listed in the Off: section of the Status bar. (This is the offset from the beginning of the frame.) For example, Figure 7.23 shows the pattern 00 00 00 00 with an offset of x3F.
5. Remove any spaces from the pattern, type it in the Pattern box, and then select Hex, as shown in Figure 7.24.

6. Remove the leading "x" from the offset, type it in the Offset box and then select From Start Of Frame.

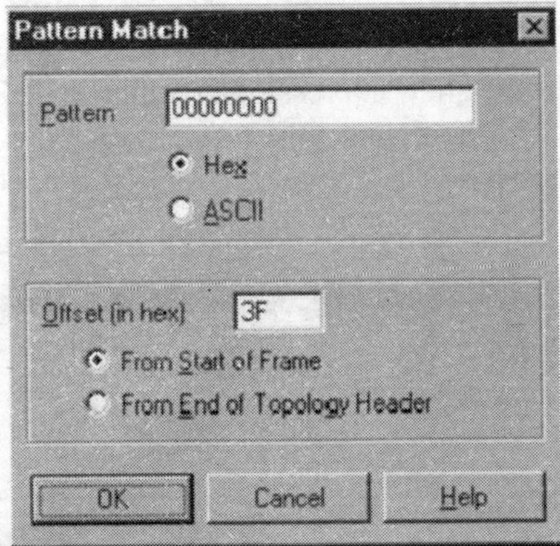

Figure 7.24 The Pattern Match dialog box

Note: The topology header is the section of the frame that the sender adds to identify the network type. Information such as the source and destination address of the frame is included in the topology header. For example, the sender adds 14 bytes to the frame at the Ethernet layer for an Ethernet network.

7.6.10 Designing a Display Filter

By default, Network Monitor displays all captured frames in the Frame Viewer, which can make it difficult to locate specific frames. To make it easier to locate frames of interest, create a display filter that tells Network Monitor to display only the frames that are of interest to you.

To create a display filter, perform a capture, choose Filter from the Capture menu of the Capture window, and then use the Capture Filter dialog box shown in Figure 7.25 to design the capture filter, as described in this section.

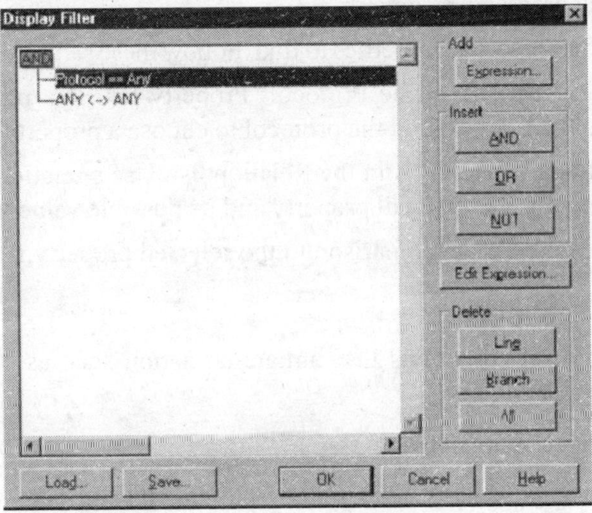

Figure 7.25 The Display Filter dialog box

There are two default branches on the decision tree, each with a single expression: the Protocol branch, which lists the protocols to display, and the Address Pairs branch, which lists the computer address pairs to display.

To add operators, use the AND, OR, and NOT buttons; to change an existing operator, select it and then click Change Operator. To create a new expression or edit an existing expression, click Expression or select an existing expression and then click Edit Expression. Use the Expression dialog box that appears to create or edit an expression. The Expression dialog box contains three tabs, as discussed below and shown in Figure 7.26.

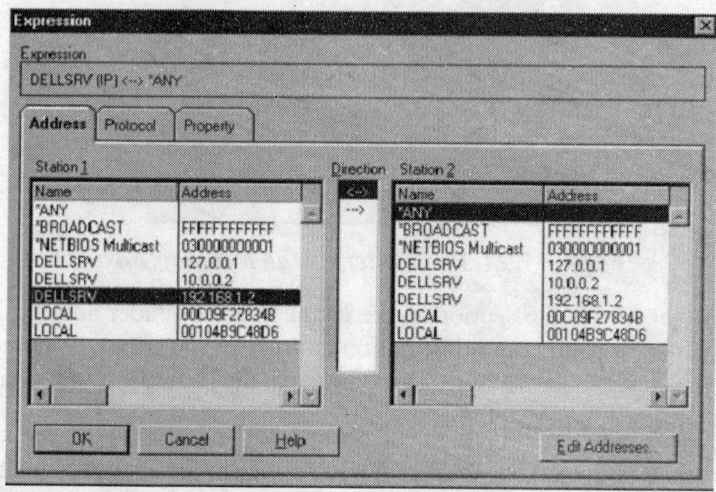

Figure 7.26 The Expression dialog box

- Address tab Specifies address pairs to display.
- Protocol tab Specifies protocols to display in the Frame Viewer. Choose protocols by selecting protocols and then clicking the Disable, Enable, Disable All, or Enable All buttons. Network Monitor enables all protocols by default.
- Property tab Specifies protocol properties to find. Follow these steps to design protocol properties:
    1. Choose the properties from the Protocol: Property list. If a plus sign appears next to a protocol name, you can expand the protocol to choose a property from its list.
    2. Choose a relational operator from the Relation list. Use a relational operator to specify the connection between the protocol property and its possible values.
    3. Type the value to use as a comparison to the selected property in the Value (Address) box.

7.6.11 Setting a Capture Trigger

Use a capture trigger to set conditions that initiate an action such as stopping data capture and executing a program or command.

To set a capture trigger, follow these steps:

1. Choose Trigger from the Capture menu of the Capture window. The Capture Trigger dialog box appears, as shown in Figure 7.27.

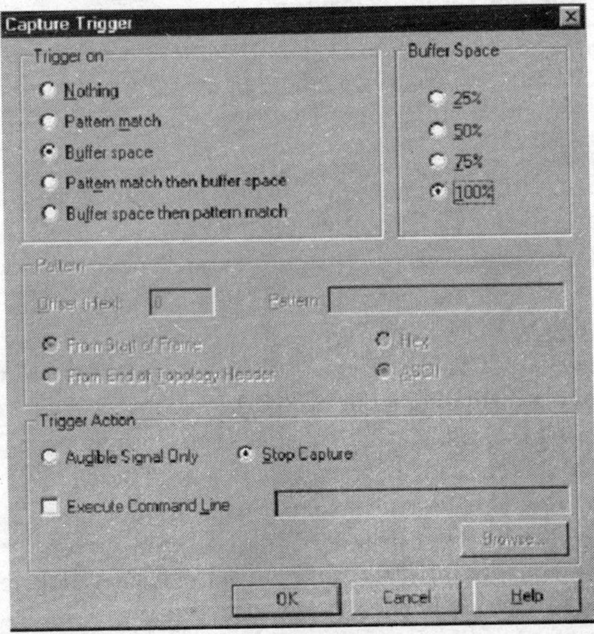

Figure 7.27 The Capture Trigger dialog box

2. Choose from the options in the Trigger On area:
   - Pattern Match Performs the trigger action when the specified hexadecimal or ASCII pattern match occurs.
   - Buffer Space Performs the trigger action when the capture fills the specified percentage of the capture buffer.
   - Pattern Match Then Buffer Space Monitors the capture for the specified data pattern, and then performs the trigger action when the capture fills the specified percentage of the capture buffer.
   - Buffer Space Then Pattern Match Monitors the capture buffer until the capture fills the specified percentage of the capture buffer, after which point Network Monitor monitors for the specified pattern. When the pattern match occurs, Network Monitor performs the trigger action.
3. In the Trigger Action area, choose the action to perform when the trigger criteria are met:
   - Audible Signal Only Beeps and continues to capture frames. This is the default option.
   - Stop Capture Ends the capture process.
   - Execute Command Line Executes a command line or opens a file. The command can be up to 259 characters.

7.6.12 Memory and Network Tuning

Windows Server 2003 is configured optimally for most workloads by default. If the default behaviour is not appropriate for your environment, you can improve performance by choosing the appropriate file system cache settings, optimizing the page file, and tuning network performance, as described in this section.

7.6.12.1 Changing File System Cache Settings

Windows Server 2003 favors the file system cache over running programs and processes by default, which is appropriate for file servers. However, the default settings can reduce the performance of database servers or other network applications. To change the way Windows Server 2003 allocates memory, use the following steps:

1. Click Start, choose Control Panel and then Network Connections, and then right-click the internal network connection and choose Properties.
2. Select File and Printer Sharing for Microsoft Networks and then click Properties.
3. Select the memory optimization method for the server to use and then click OK, as described here and shown in Figure 7.28:
   - Minimize Memory Used This setting uses the least amount of RAM for caching. Use it only when the server has a small amount of RAM.
   - Balance Balances the available RAM between the system cache and applications, and is inappropriate for servers with an adequate amount of RAM.
   - Maximize Data Throughput For File Sharing This is the default setting and is appropriate for most servers, especially those that act as file or print servers or have a large amount of memory. Also use this setting if the server is running a network application and memory is not a bottleneck, and the application does not have its own memory manager. The Maximize Data Throughput for File Sharing setting allocates the largest amount of RAM for the system cache (up to 960 MB), maximizing file-sharing performance but reducing the amount of available RAM for other programs.
   - Maximize Data Throughput For Network Applications Allocates a smaller amount of RAM for the system cache (up to 512 MB), making as much RAM available for server-based applications as possible while still ensuring good performance for clients. Use this setting for servers that run network applications that include their own memory managers, such as Microsoft SQL Server or Microsoft Exchange Server, and for servers that run network applications that require large amounts of free memory such as Internet Information Services (IIS).

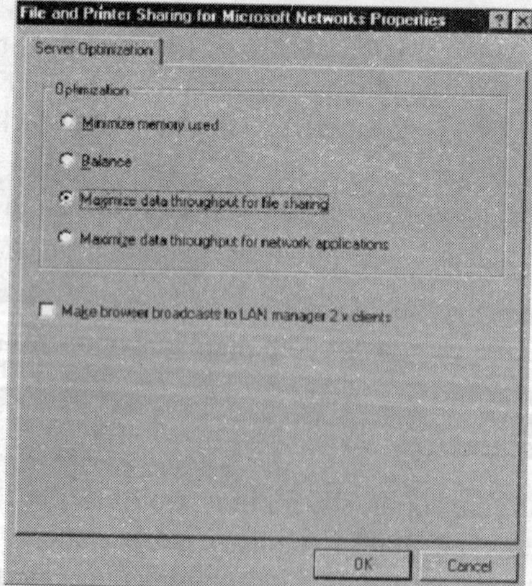

Figure 7.28 Optimizing memory usage for File and Printer Sharing

Note File and Printer Sharing optimization settings are not available on Windows Server 2003, Web Edition.

Table 7.1 shows the values of these keys.

Setting	LargeSystemCache Value	Size Value
Minimize Memory Used	0	1
Balance	0	2
Maximize Data Throughput For File Sharing	1	3
Maximize Data Throughput for Network Applications	0	3

7.6.12.2 Optimizing the Page File

There are a number of ways to optimize the Windows page file, and even more opinions about the best way to do so. Use the Advanced tab of the System tool in Control Panel and the following guidelines to optimize the Windows page file without a lot of debate:

- Remove any current page files on the partition, and defragment the partition before creating the page file to ensure that Windows allocates the page a contiguous area on the hard drive.
- Create a page file on the system (most likely C:\) partition with the initial size and maximum size set to slightly larger than the size of the crash dump file. To change the type of crash dump file the system creates in the event of a Stop Error (blue screen), click Settings in the Startup And Recovery section of the Advanced tab in the System Properties dialog box.
- In addition to the page file on the system partition, create a page file on a dedicated disk, RAID-0, RAID 0+1, or RAID-1 array. If this is impractical, allocate space for the page file on the fastest drive or drives in the system. Placing it on multiple physical drives improves performance, unless the drives are slow or heavily used (avoid these). Placing page files on multiple partitions on the same drive does not improve performance.
- Avoid RAID-5 volumes when possible because the data redundancy can reduce performance. Choose a simple volume, stripe set, mirror, or RAID 0+1 volume (a mirrored stripe set) for the page file.
- If you must place the page file on the same physical disk as the operating system, place it on the same partition as the operating system to minimize disk seek time and maximize disk performance.
- Use the Committed Bytes counter in Performance Monitor to determine how much virtual memory Windows consumes under the heaviest usage conditions. Set the initial size of the page file to a value significantly larger than the peak usage to allow for future growth or unusual conditions. This reduces page file fragmentation by reserving a block on the hard drive for the page file and eliminating the need to dynamically increase the file size.
- Set the maximum size to the maximum size you can imagine ever needing. This provides Windows the ability to increase the size of the page file in an emergency rather than deny memory requests.

7.6.12.3 Tuning Network Performance

To optimize network performance, use the following list:

- Unbind infrequently used protocols.
- Set the order in which the workstation and NetBIOS software bind to each protocol when using more than one protocol. Average connection time decreases when you list the most frequently used protocol first.
- Ensure that users and resources are located on the same subnet when possible.
- Install multiple network adapters to increase file-sharing throughput.
- Upgrade network adapters on heavily loaded servers to high-performance adapters designed for server loads.

7.7 AUDITING SECURITY EVENTS

The term security covers a lot of ground, and Windows Server 2003 uses a wide range of methods and mechanisms to implement security. But before you can evaluate those mechanisms, you need to know what a good security system is designed to accomplish. For all the protocols, passwords, and secret keys, security revolves around three basic concepts:

- **Authentication:** Confirming the identity of a person or entity before allowing access to a resource.
- **Data protection:** Ensuring the privacy and integrity of transmitted or stored data.
- **Access control:** Restricting the access of data and resources to privileged users.

In addition to these three security mainstays, two other security features are discussed in this section: auditing and non-repudiation.

7.7.1 Authentication

Authentication describes the process in which a person or entity identifies itself to a second party. In general terms, this can mean showing a driver's license to a bank teller or inserting a bank card into an ATM and typing a PIN. In computer language, authentication is a bit more deductive. Unlike the bank teller scenario, which has the luxury of personal contact, nearly all computer-related authentication scenarios are virtual. In a Windows Server 2003 environment, authentication involves two distinct processes: interactive logon and network authentication.

Interactive logon means logging on to either a domain account or a local computer. Before Windows 2000, the logon procedure was performed by password only; beginning with Windows 2000 and continuing with Windows Server 2003, the logon process allows smart-card authentication. After the user is logged on to the domain account, network authentication is required to identify the user to each network resource he or she requires.

7.7.1.1 Proof of Identity

Typically, proof of identity comes in the form of a shared secret-a password, a PIN, or an encryption key-between the requestor and the authenticator. The principal word here is "secret." The fulcrum of the entire authentication process is the authenticator's belief that the requestor-and only the requestor-has that secret. After this fails to be true, the system, to some degree or another, is compromised.

Depending on the protocol being used, the shared secret is communicated to the authenticator, who then either grants or denies access. Secure protocols protect the secret in transit; more elaborate schemes don't send the secret at all. Public-key technology uses a pair of encryption keys-a private key that is never exposed, and a public key that can be disseminated. The next section explores the types of protocols Windows Server 2003 uses to prove possession of identification credentials.

7.7.1.2 Authentication Protocols

Clearly, the effectiveness of an authentication process and the safety of your secret depend on the protocol being used. Countless books before this one have guided users through installations that require choosing a unique password and then warned them against the hazards of losing the password. Yet how many passwords leave fingerprints and slip unprotected through a network? Table 7.2 shows the Windows Server 2003 protocols that are designed to thwart would-be attackers and that authenticate both internal and external users. The Active Directory service maintains user accounts that hold security credentials for authentication purposes, such as passwords and public-key certificates, and it can store multiple security credentials for each of these protocols.

Table 7.2 Authentication protocols

Protocol	Used for
Kerberos version 5	Network authentication. Provides mutual authentication between user and resource.
Secure Socets Layer/Transport Layer Security (SSL/TLS)	Network authentication. Based on X.509 public-key certificates.
Microsoft Windows NT LAN Manager (NTLM)	Network authentication. Used for Microsoft Windows NT 4 compatibility.
NTLM 2	Authentication supporting lder versions of Windows (Windows 95 and newer). LAN Manager (LM) supported older versions of Windows, but it was not interoperable with Windows NT and newer. Because of additional features and improved security, NTLM 2 is recommended over NTLM even if your installed base includes no versions of Windows older than NT4 SP4 (which was the first to support NTLM 2).
Microsoft Challenge Handshake Authentication Protocol versions 2 (MS-CHAP v2)	Network and dial-up authentication. Uses separate encryption keys for sending and receiving.
Extensible Authentication Protocol (EAP)	Network and dial-up authentication. Provides support for additional authentication schemes, including smart cards.
Password Authentication Protocol (PAP)	Network and dial-up authentication. Sends passwords in clear text.
Extensible Authentication Protocol-Transport Layer Security (EAPTLS)	Provides authentication for wireless connections.
Digest Authentication	Credentials are transmitted as a message digest or MD5 hash.
Passport Authentication	Authentication mechanism offering a single sign-on capability.
Protected Extensible Authentication Protocol (PEAP)	Alternate authentication method for wireless connections.

7.7.1.3 Hardware-enabled Authentication

Hardware is used for authentication purposes to make it more difficult for someone to impersonate a requestor. By storing encryption keys on a smart card, a PC card, or any other cryptographic token, the logon process becomes more secure. It requires an extra level of possession that a mere password does not. It requires something you know-a PIN or password to access the smart card-and something you have-the smart card itself. An attacker might somehow obtain your PIN, but without the smart card, the PIN or password is useless. To decrease the vulnerability of secret keys, well-designed cryptographic tokens generate encryption keys directly on the token and prohibit extraction of encryption keys, except possibly in encrypted form.

There's also a lot of talk about the use of biometrics to facilitate authentication. Biometrics include such things as fingerprint identification, face recognition, and hand-geometry verification. Biometrics extends the logon requirements considerably, from something you know or have, to something you are.

7.7.1.4 Mutual Authentication

Authentication isn't necessarily a one-way street. Many times a requester wants proof of identity from the authenticating host. For instance, when you are creating a secure link to a restricted directory over which confidential data is to be exchanged, the identity of both the client and the server is important. Protocols such as SSL/TLS allow mutual authentication between client and server.

7.7.1.5 Single Sign-on

One of the additional Windows Server 2003 security features is the ability to authenticate to any computer or resource on the network by logging on to a single domain account. Through single sign-on, the user can log on to a domain account once, with a single password or smart card. The user's single-sign-on security credentials are stored in Active Directory, and each time a domain resource is required, a network authentication occurs transparently.

The advantages of single sign-on, as opposed to authenticating to each network resource when it's needed, are quite obvious. Users have fewer passwords to remember and fewer authentication screens to endure, and administrators find it easier to manage only one account per user.

7.7.2 Data Protection

Protecting passwords is critical to maintaining a secure system. Equally important is protecting the data you send after you're logged on. Whether it's a company's proprietary information or a personal credit card, the concerns are the same: keeping network information from being read by unauthorized persons, and preventing it from being modified.

Of course, sensitive information doesn't need to be on its way somewhere to be vulnerable. Although tools such as network sniffers can capture and read data packets, attacks can also occur on files on a hard disk. In addition to network security, Windows Server 2003 provides security for your stored data through Encrypting File System (EFS), which is discussed in the next section.

7.7.2.1 Data Confidentiality

The privacy of data-whether it's an e-mail message, input to a Web page or distinct IP packets-is jeopardized after the information is transmitted over nonsecure communication lines, such as the Internet. Using encryption algorithms and keys, data privacy can be protected. Without the appropriate decryption keys, unintended recipients intercepting the transmission receive nothing but encrypted garbage.

Note: Cryptographic operations use both an algorithm and a key. The algorithm is the specific mathematical process that performs the operation. The key is the input to the algorithm.

The strength of the encryption also depends on the algorithm used and the length of the key. With enough computing power, any encryption key can be broken. Windows Server 2003 supports a range of key lengths, from 40 to 256 bits. Typically, the bulk of data is encrypted using a cipher block algorithm (also known as a symmetric algorithm) and a key. The strength of this method lies in the cipher block chaining (CBC). Encrypting a block at a time, the output of one block is used as the input of the next. In this way, repeated patterns of data won't produce the same encrypted data. The input to the first block is a random number called an initialization vector (IV). The IV ensures that each time a message is encrypted, a unique result is produced.

For ensuring the integrity and confidentiality of transmitted data at the network level, Windows Server 2003 employs Internet Protocol security (IPSec). One aspect of IPSec, IPSec Authentication Header (IPSEC AH), allows you to verify the packet's integrity. IPSec Encapsulating Security Payload (IPSEC ESP) encrypts TCP/IP packets before transmission and decrypts them upon receipt.

Confidentiality of stored data is also a concern. Although access to stored files can be restricted for certain users through file permissions, intruders who gain unauthorized access to your hard disk can modify those permissions. To combat this problem, Windows Server 2003 uses a transparent encryption scheme called Encrypting File System (EFS). Files on NTFS volumes can be encrypted and decrypted with users' EFS public/private-key information. Users need only select the files to be encrypted. The actual encryption occurs behind the scenes.

7.7.2.2 Data Integrity

Windows Server 2003 supports digital signing, which guarantees the file's data integrity that is, that the file has not been modified or tampered with. Digital signing of a file, module, or other software component is somewhat like signing a contract on paper The signer is responsible for what he or she signs. Whoever subsequently views the document and signature can tell who signed it.

However, digital signatures offer a great deal of security beyond that. A digital signature is generated by creating a one-way hash of the document and encrypting the hash with the signer's private encryption key. This procedure produces a signature that is cryptographically tied to both the signer and the content of the document. Changing the content breaks the signature.

Upon verification, the digital signature is decrypted with the signer's public key. The resulting hash is compared against a newly computed hash of the message. As long as the original key has not been compromised, this process proves undeniably that the signer signed the message. His or her key was used to verify the signature.

In Windows Server 2003, digital signing has two meaningful purposes. First, it guarantees the integrity of data stored locally or being passed over a network. Second, it authenticates modules or other software components that are obtained from untrusted sources, such as the Internet. Validating the signature of a module verifies that the software hasn't been tampered with and that it was signed by a trusted software publisher. MD5 and SHA-1 cryptographic hash values are commonly used to verify file-level integrity. A useful tool for doing just that is the File Checksum Integrity Verifier (FCIV). The two most common digital signature algorithms are RSA and Digital Signature Algorithm (DSA). DSA signatures are 40 bytes (320 bits) long, while the length of RSA signatures depends on the key size. A key pair, consisting of a public key and a private key, with a 128-byte (1024-bit) public key typically produces a 128-byte signature.

7.7.3 Access Control

Authentication is the first layer of security in the protection of network objects and resources. The second layer is access control that is, controlling which resources can be accessed, by whom, and with which permissions. An authenticated user doesn't necessarily have authorization to access all files, printers, and registry keys. Access control is enforced by the manager for each object type, but it's up to the object owner to determine which access control restrictions to impose.

Access is controlled by assigning rights to users and by setting permissions for objects. Permissions specify which users can access a specific object and which type of access is allowed. For example, the owner of a quarterly finance spreadsheet might set permissions that allow read/write access to the head of finance, allow read-only access to everyone in finance, and deny access to everyone else. Groups of users have their own rights, and those can be specified when granting object permissions. In the previous example, establishing read-only permissions for everyone in finance probably means setting a group's rights, not setting users' rights individually.

Permissions can be explicitly set for an object, or for ease of administration they can be inherited from parent objects. However, the granularity of access control doesn't necessarily stop at objects. Permissions can even be set for attributes of an object, allowing access to some fields (such as the e-mail address of a user account), but denying access to other fields (such as the user's telephone number). Standard object permissions include the following:

- Reading an object
- Modifying an object
- Deleting an object
- Reading an object's permissions
- Modifying an object's permissions
- Changing an object's owner

Note: You cannot set permissions on a file's individual attribute, but you can set such permissions on an Active Directory object.

7.7.4 Auditing

Another Windows Server 2003 security feature is auditing, which allows an administrator to keep tabs on events that might possibly compromise the system. (If you're familiar with Windows server platforms tracing back to Windows NT, you're already accustomed to the auditing mechanisms available in the new versions.) Events such as logging on and logging off, access to files, and user-account management can all be audited. The administrator can choose which objects to audit, which events on that object to audit, and which users or groups using that object to audit. Both successful and unsuccessful access attempts can be audited.

Note: Viruses can leave trails of inappropriate writing of executables and dynamic-link libraries (DLLs). Auditing successful and failed write access to these files and monitoring the security log for unexpected occurrences gives you a head start at detecting viruses on your system.

In addition to auditing users' security-related events, Windows Server 2003 provides a means of tracking security management events because an audit trail reflects any changes in security policies. For instance, if an administrator changes the permissions of a particular object to deny access to a specific group, this change in permissions appears on the audit trail.

7.7.5 Nonrepudiation

Finally, let's take a look at nonrepudiation, another Windows Server 2003 security feature. Nonrepudiation is undeniable proof that a correspondence was sent or received and usually refers to security-enhanced e-mail messages. Proof that a message was sent is a property exhibited by digital signatures. For undeniable proof of receipt, the recipient of a signed or encrypted message responds to the sender with a signed receipt.

Important some e-mail packages allow for receipts of signed messages, but this doesn't necessarily demonstrate nonrepudiation. A signed receipt is undeniable proof that a message was received only if it is cryptographically tied to both the recipient and the original message.

7.7.6 Smart Cards

New to Microsoft Windows 2000 was the support of cryptographic smart cards. This support is maintained in Windows Server 2003. A smart card is a tamper-resistant, credit card-like hardware token that can be used to implement additional protection for security-enabled protocols and applications. Unlike credit cards, which have magnetic strips on the back, smart cards use metallic contacts as the hardware interface and require a card reader-Plug and Play (PnP) readers are recommended for use with Windows Server 2003. Manufacturers typically provide a software application interface, such as Crypto Service Provider, for use with Microsoft CryptoAPI, or they use a PKCS #11 module. Support for various smart cards-Gemplus GCR410P and GPR400, Litronic 220P, Rainbow Technologies 3531, and SCM Microsystems SwapSmart (for both the RS-232 and PC Card interface models-is included with the Windows Server 2003 installation.

Smart cards provide the strongest form of user authentication in Windows Server 2003. Either a PIN or password is required to access the card, which protects the user's credentials from both rogue parties and applications. In addition to storing public-key certificates and private keys, smart cards can also provide on-card functionality, such as digital signing, to ensure that a user's private key is never exposed.

Smart cards can be moved from computer to computer with ease, providing a high portability level for a user's credentials. Included in the list of security features is the ability to block a smart card from the system after a certain number of unsuccessful logon attempts, making dictionary attacks impractical. (A dictionary attack is a password attack in which a malicious user sends hundreds or thousands of credentials by using a list of passwords based on common words or phrases.)

Note: Smart cards aren't the only way you can have "mobile" credentials. The new Digital Identity Management Service allows credential roaming, enabling secure sharing of user credentials and private keys.

7.7.7 Public-key Infrastructures

Now that you have looked at more basic security concepts, let's examine some security-enabled protocols. In recent years, public-key infrastructures (PKIs) have been used increasingly in both commercial and government sectors. Based on public-key technology, a PKI describes a system of public-key certificate generation and management, including distribution and revocation. The important elements of this infrastructure are certificate authorities (CAs) that issue certificates, clients that use certificates and directories that store certificates. Many PKIs use a registration authority that ensures user identity and authorization before certificates are granted. Figure 7.29 shows a typical Microsoft Windows Server 2003 PKI.

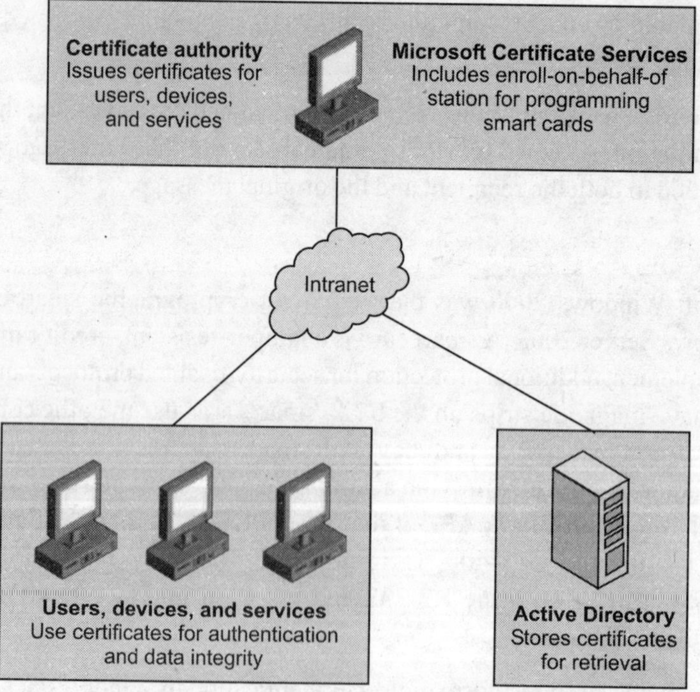

Figure 7.29 A typical public-key infrastructure

One of the distinct advantages of using public-key certificates for authentication is that server no longer need to store and maintain a password list for their individual users. Because identification is based on a trust relationship with the CAs, the servers need to trust only the authority that issued the requester's certificate. After the chain of trust is determined and the certificate is verified, authentication can be established.

RSA Laboratories maintains a list of public-key cryptography standards (PKCS) that define public-key-related formats. Table 7.3 contains four notable standards.

Table 7.3 important public-key cryptography standards

Standard	Subject
PKCS # 7	Cryptographic Measage Syntax Standard, the basis for Secure Multipurpose Internet Mail Extensions (S/MIME). Defines the format of signed and encrypted messages. The degenerate case allows the exchange of public-key certificates and certificate revocation lists (CRLs).
PKCS # 10	Certification Requests. Used by clients to request certificates from CAs.
PKCS # 11	Cryptographic Token Interface. Analogous to Microsoft CryptoAPI.
PKCS # 12	Personal Information Exchanges (PFX). Enables the encrypted transfer of private keys and associated certificates from one computer to another.

7.7.7.1 Public-key Encryption Vs. Symmetric-key Encryption

Although PKIs depend heavily on public-key technology, many functions performed by PKI entities combine public-key encryption and symmetric-key encryption. Symmetric key encryption has been around for hundreds of years. It involves the use of a single encryption key for both the encryption and decryption of data. Encrypting data this way is analogous to placing a document in a safe and locking it with a key. When the document needs to be retrieved, the same key is used to unlock the safe. Relatively speaking, this method is secure and fast. Unfortunately, this type of encryption doesn't lend itself well to encrypting data to a person. Because the key must remain private, the difficulty exists in transmitting the key. After all, if there's a secure means to send the key, why not send the message through that route to begin with?

Public-key encryption, also known as asymmetric encryption, emerged from the necessity to share encrypted data with people, where no secure path existed to pass an encryption key. Public-key encryption uses a pair of keys: a public key that is distributed, and a private key that remains secret. To encrypt a message to someone, the encryption algorithm uses the recipient's public key. The resulting encrypted message can be decrypted only by the recipient's private key. This method is analogous to a safe with an entry slot. Anyone can slip a document in, but only the person with the correct private key can retrieve it. This scheme works for self-encryption of files as well. The Windows Server 2003 EFS, for instance, protects data with the user's public key. To decrypt, the user's private key is accessed and used.

Unfortunately, public-key encryption algorithms are slow and are rarely used to encrypt large amounts of data. Instead, public keys are used to protect symmetric keys that encrypt large chunks of data. For example, suppose Rosemary wants to encrypt a portfolio to Harold. Rosemary encrypts the portfolio using a symmetric-key algorithm like the Advanced Encryption Standard (AES). She then encrypts the symmetric key with Harold's public key, producing an asymmetrically encrypted symmetric key. Harold, upon receiving the encrypted portfolio and key, decrypts the encrypted symmetric key with his private key and uses the resulting symmetric key to decrypt the message.

Public-key encryption extends to digital signatures as well. Digital signature algorithms actually reverse the encryption process. Encrypting the hash of a message with a user's private key generates a digital signature. The signature can be verified later by decrypting the hash with the user's public key.

7.7.7.2 Public-key Certificates And Private Keys

Most public-key infrastructures, including Windows Server 2003 PKI, revolve around the use of X.509 public-key certificates. PKI users have a private key and a circulated public key. A public-key certificate cryptographically binds a public key to the user who holds the corresponding private key. Certificates are issued and digitally signed by a CA. Table 7.4 lists the fields of an X.509 certificate.

Table 7.4 Public-key certificate fields

Certificate Field	Description
X.509 version	Windows Server 2003 supports X.509 version 3 certificates.
Serial number	Unique number that the CA assigns to a certificate.
Signature algorithm	ID of the algorithm that the CA uses to digitally sign the certificate.
Issuer	Name of the CA that issues the certificate.
Validity period	A pair of dates indicating when certificate validation begins and when it ends.
Subject	Name of the certificate user.
Public key	Public key that, with the corresponding private key, makes up a user's key pair.
Extensions	Additional information that a CA can include in the certificate. Examples of extensions are alternate names, such as the user's e-mail address; key usage, which indicates which operations a public key can be used for; and basic constraints, which show whether the certificate is a CA certificate.
Signature	Digital signature generated by the issuer.

When a certificate is used, it is validated by verifying the signature with the issuing authority's public key. As long as the issuing CA is trusted (or is within a trusted path), you can be certain that the user or entity named in the certificate holds the corresponding private key. Of course, certificates aren't issued solely to users. CAs have their own certificates. CAs can also issue certificates to services and devices that need to be accessed on the network.

A Web server that accepts SSL-encrypted transmissions and a directory that provides two-way authentication are both good examples of entities that use certificates. Even though certificates belong to users and other entities, that doesn't mean that a user or entity is limited to one certificate-or, for that matter, that a user can be a member of only one root hierarchy. Certificates are issued for many purposes-server authentication, file encryption, and code signing, to name a few. A user holds any number of certificates and private keys under different CAs or under the same CA; each might differ in usage, privilege, key size, and algorithm. For example, a security model might need multiple levels of access with separate CAs handling each level. On the other hand, a single user might hold Level 2 and Level 4 certificates; another might hold Level 1 and Level 3 certificates.

Having certificates under different root certificate authorities (root CAs) is common too. Consider the human resources director who has both an enterprise certificate, which allows her to access her company's human resources server, and a certificate from a commercial CA, which allows her to browse the company's 401(k) stock portfolio over the Internet.

At the very least, the functions of encryption and digital signatures must be split into separate certificates. Private keys used for encryption can be archived so that encrypted data of a lost key can be recovered. Because the integrity of digital signatures depends on sole possession of the private key, digital signature private keys must not be archived.

7.7.7.3 Certificate Authorities

Certificate authorities exist to issue certificates for entities-including users, services, devices, subordinate authorities, or the CA itself-which meet the policy set forth for the CA. The CA accepts and fulfills certificate requests and revocation requests and might also manage the policy-directed registration process that a user completes to get his or her certificate.

7.7.7.4 Root and Subordinate Certificate Authorities

Although CAs can issue and revoke certificates for a host of users, larger companies might be too big to administer with a single CA. In addition, enterprises might want to delegate authority of certain certificate types, or they might have divisions that manage their own resources and need to enforce separate certificate-issuing policies. Production, for instance, might want to issue certificates to anyone whose e-mail address is within the company domain. Engineering might require a picture ID for registration. On the other hand, by using autonomous CAs, users between the two divisions are cryptographically isolated. A digitally signed message sent from a user in production to a user in engineering has no common basis of trust.

To solve this dilemma, CAs can be stacked hierarchically. Root CAs use a certificate they issue to themselves (a self-signed certificate). They also issue certificates to subordinated authorities and in general do not issue user certificates. Subordinate authorities issue certificates to users and other end entities and might also issue certificates to other subordinate CAs. Root CAs is implicitly trusted-subordinate CAs and clients derive trust from the root.

Figure 7.30 shows an example of a CA hierarchy. By stacking CAs hierarchically, an enterprise can manage the certification system from a single authority while delegating control of policy decisions to discrete authorities.

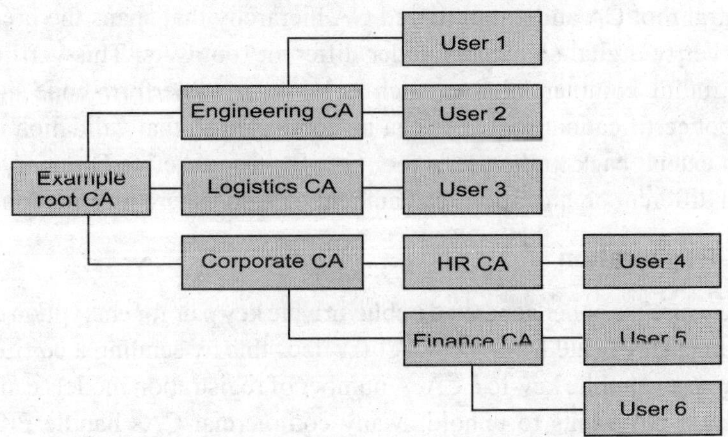

Figure 7.30 A certificate authority hierarchy

Windows Server 2003 also distinguishes between enterprise CAs and standalone CAs. The primary difference is that the enterprise CA uses Active Directory for user information and policy decisions and can publish certificates and CRLs to Active Directory. The standalone CA requires the certificate requestor to supply all user-identifying information.

1. CHAIN VERIFICATION AND TRUST

Before a received digital signature can be verified, the signer's certificate must be validated. This is true of any application, whether it's a service, device, or user performing the verification. Without a hierarchical chain back to a trusted root CA, the identity of the user in the certificate can't be confirmed.

Chain verification is a two-step process. The first step is to build the certificate chain from the signer's certificate to a trusted root CA. Consider the CA hierarchy in Figure 21-2. Suppose User 1 in engineering is trying to verify a signature from User 5 in finance. User 1 builds the certificate chain for User 5 back to the root CA; Netsolvers root CA, which is in User 1's trusted store. The certificate chain, built from the bottom up, is User 5: Finance CA: Corporate CA: Netsolvers root CA. The verifying entity obtains these certificates from the transmission protocol if they're included or from an accessible certificate store. The root CA certificate is the pivotal trust component in a certificate chain. It should be published only through a trusted method, such as Active Directory Group Policies.

The second step of chain verification is to verify the certificate chain from the top down. The verifying entity checks each certificate for validity, starting with the trusted root. Validity checking includes verifying the certificate's digital signature, checking the certificate's validity period, and ensuring that the certificate hasn't been revoked. Depending on policy, applications might also check any certificate extensions that the certificate contains.

Note: Currently, typical PKI implementations include two-tier or three-tier hierarchies. As the popularity of public-key infrastructure spreads, CA vendors will make more attempts to unite and centralize certificate authorities and root certificate authorities, which will result in longer certificate chains.

2. CROSS-ROOT CERTIFICATION

Even with a central root CA and a multitiered CA hierarchy that spans the breadth of a company, users might need to verify digital signatures under different root CAs. This verification is especially important when integrating commercial CAs, such as Verisign, to perform code signing, among other tasks. Using cross-root certification, root CAs can be connected so that validation paths of certificates under different roots extend back to the user's root CA. By using Active Directory Federated Forests, for example, users in different organizations can authenticate and share information securely.

7.7.7.5 Certificate Registration

Before being able to use his or her generated public/private key pair for encryption or digital signatures, a user must first obtain a certificate from a CA. A user does this by sending a certificate request-which includes his or her name and public key-to a CA. A number of registration models can exist depending on the registration policy a CA wants to uphold. Many commercial CAs handle PKCS #10 certificate requests and also allow Web based certificate generation.

For more secure needs, a registration authority can act as a certificate-requesting agent to ensure proper proof-of-identity procedures and to forward certificate requests to the CA. Microsoft Certificate Services includes an enroll-on-behalf-of station where administrators, using enrollment agent certificates, can program smart cards for users. Figure 7.31 shows two examples of certificate request scenarios.

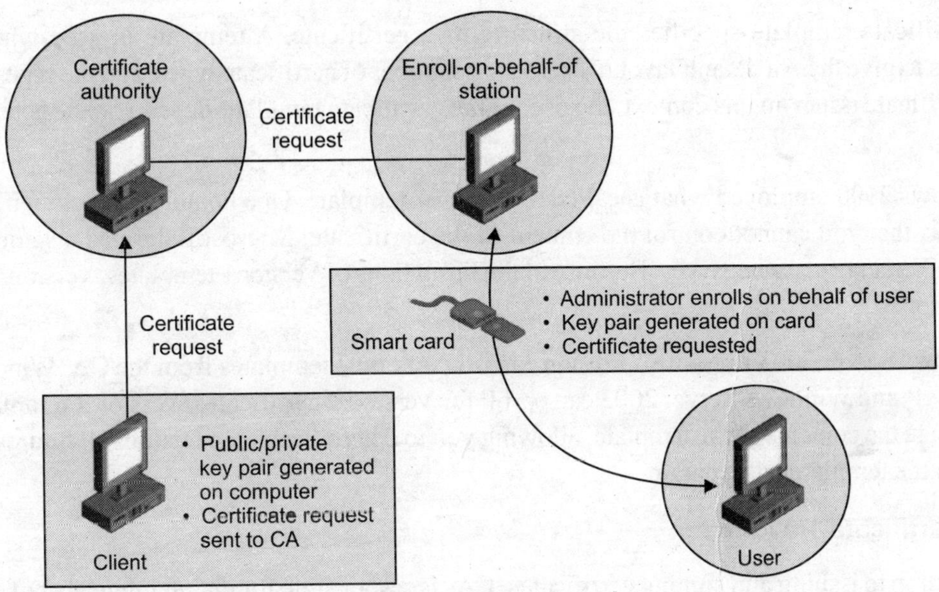

Figure 7.31 Two certificate request scenarios

In the first example, a client requests a certificate from an enterprise CA, perhaps using the Certificates snap-in Certificate Request Wizard. User information and certificate rights are obtained from Active Directory. The Certificate Request Wizard generates a public/private key pair for the user. The public key is included in the certificate request and sent to the CA. The private key is saved on the user's computer. Upon receipt of the certificate request, the CA issues and signs the certificate and pushes it to a directory where other users and entities can retrieve it.

The second example shows an administrator programming a smart card through the enroll-on-behalf-of station. In this case, the private key is written directly to the card. In neither scenario is the private key exposed to the CA or anyone else. Again, after the certificate is issued, it's written to a directory for public availability. The smart card is returned to the user and is ready for authentication.

7.7.7.6 Certificate Directories

An important piece of the PKI is the directory in which certificates are stored and from which they can be retrieved. To encrypt data to a user, you need the user's public-key certificate. Similarly, when verifying a digitally signed message, the certificate chain back to the verifier's root must be established.

In a Windows Server 2003 environment, Active Directory acts as a repository for certificates; any user or computer with appropriate rights can retrieve them. In addition, external users' certificates can be mapped to Active Directory user accounts.

Note: Typically, after a client application retrieves a given certificate, it caches the certificate locally to save the overhead of another retrieval. Use the Certificates snap-in to view stored certificates by purpose or by storage category, such as personal or trusted roots.

7.7.7.7 Certificate Templates

A certificate template specifies the structure of a certificate. A template is used when creating certificates to give them a default layout. There are a number of certificate types, and the types accessible by the certificate issuer-in this context, the user of the certificate template-depend on the access rights of the issuer.

Windows 2000 employed what is called a Version 1 template. One notable problem with Version 1 templates is that you cannot control the content of the certificate; Microsoft defined a static layout for each of the Version 1 template types. Because of the limitations of Version1 templates, Version 2 templates were developed.

Windows Server 2003 Enterprise Edition can use Version 2 templates from the CA. Windows 2000, Windows XP, and Windows Server 2003 can enroll for Version 2 certificates. Version 2 templates enable you to change the contents of the template, allowing you to determine which features all future certificates made from the template will contain.

7.7.7.8 Certificate Revocation

In addition to issuing and signing certificates, CAs is responsible for maintaining a list of certificates that are no longer valid. This list, called a certificate revocation list (CRL), is digitally signed by the issuing authority. Such a list is a necessary requirement for a public-key infrastructure (PKI). Consider a laptop user who dials in to his company's network to access a server that contains finance accounts. He uses his certificate and corresponding private key to authenticate himself to the finance server. Now suppose the laptop is stolen. In the past, a compromised password might have resulted in the administrator changing the user's password.

In a PKI, however, verification is based on possession of a private key. The finance server has no knowledge of a specific user, only the CAs that it trusts. By using the CRL as a revoking mechanism, the finance server can retrieve a current list of revoked certificates. After the stolen certificate is placed on the CRL and the CRL has been published and retrieved, verification of the certificate results in a failure and access is denied.

Like user certificates, a CRL is digitally signed by the issuing CA and can be verified with the CA's certificate. Table 7.5 describes the fields of an X.509 CRL.

Table 7.5 Certificate revocation list fields

CRL Field	Description
X.509 version	X.509 CRLs version. The current CRL version is X.509 version 2.
Signature algorithm	ID of the algorithm that the CA uses to digitally sign the CRL.
Issuer	Name of the CA that issues the CRL.
Last update	Date and time that the current CRL is issued.

CRL Field	Description
Next update	Date and time that the next CRL will be issued.
List of revoked certificates	Each entry in the list includes the certificate serial number and the date when the certificate was revoked. Optional extensions can be added, such as a reason flag.
Extensions Signature	Optional information that the CA can include in the CRL. Digital signature that the issuer generates.

Just as with the certificate registration and issuing procedures, policies are established for CAs that dictate certificate revocation. These policies should include such procedural decisions as how often CAs refresh their CRLs, which mandatory and discretional extensions CAs can include in their CRLs, and under what circumstances certificates get revoked. Under one policy, for instance, certificates of employees who leave the company are subject to revocation. Under another, a user merely being denied certain privileges is grounds for revoking his or her certificate.

Because certificates have a validity period, CRLs need to contain only revoked certificates that aren't yet expired. After a certificate expires (in other words, the Valid To date has passed), verifying entities refuse the certificate and it can be removed from the CRL. You must also consider CRL dispersal. The rate at which CRLs are issued, or "refreshed," is a policy decision made by the CA and can be as frequent as once a day. For highly secure domains, the refresh rate can be even more frequent; otherwise, a revoked certificate can continue to be used. To be current, verifying entities need to obtain the latest CRL. Microsoft Certificate Services allows CRLs to be published to Active Directory or to a URL for HTTP access.

7.7.7.9 Certificate Renewal

Another set of certificate policy decisions relates to the certificate renewal procedure specifically, whether certificates are allowed to be renewed, when certificates are renewed, and how certificates are renewed. Renewing certificates with the same key allows a user to extend the life of a public/private-key pair. In contrast, renewing a certificate with a different public key after a user's certificate expires can make it difficult to read previously encrypted messages.

7.7.7.10 Full CRLs and Delta CRLs

With Microsoft Windows 2000 Server, certificate authorities could publish CRLs at scheduled times or manually. Each update required the old CRL to be completely replaced by a new full CRL. With Windows Server 2003, the certificate authorities can use delta CRLs. These represent only the data that has changed since the last CRL update. Delta CRLs provide a number of benefits. Because the delta CRLs are smaller than the full CRLs, the delta CRLs can be updated more often without a large impact on the network or clients. These frequent updates reduce the time it takes for an entry to be published to the CRL. Delta CRLs have to be supported by the client as well; currently, only Windows XP and Windows Server2003 clients support using delta CRLs.

7.7.8 Security-enabled Protocols

Security in Windows Server 2003 exists at different levels-from the protection of entire messages at the application level, to secure channels, to the protection of data packets within IP. The security protocols residing at these different layers provide mechanisms not available at other layers.

S/MIME, for example, provides public-key-based encryption, integrity, and authentication of e-mail messages at the application level. SSL resides beneath the application layer, adding security to application protocols. IPSec, on the other hand, provides application independent data protection at the IP layer. The following sections examine Windows Server 2003 security protocols.

7.7.8.1 Secure Multipurpose Internet Mail Extensions

S/MIME is included with Microsoft Outlook and Outlook Express. It uses private-key certificates to secure e-mail messages and files in accordance with the PKCS #7 standard. It supports both encryption and digital signatures. When you nest single S/MIME contents, messages can also be signed and then encrypted, or signed multiple times.

1. SIGNED MESSAGES

A PKCS #7 digitally signed messages includes the message signature, the signature algorithm, and information about the signer. Optionally, the signer's certificate or certificate chain can be added, as well as any CRLs that the verifier might need. Authenticated attributes, which are protected by the digital signature, and unauthenticated attributes can also be added to the PKCS #7 content. The time at which a message is signed is an example of an authenticated attribute.

The content that is signed might or might not be included in the PKCS #7 message. If the content isn't included, the verifier needs both the PKCS #7 content and the original file that was signed to complete the verification. If the original file is easily available, this method saves the overhead of having redundant data.

2. ENCRYPTED MESSAGES

The current PKCS #7 standard requires the use of two algorithms for message encryption. Because public-key algorithms are slow, the message is first encrypted with a symmetric-key algorithm, such as DES. The small symmetric key is then encrypted to the recipient, using a public-key algorithm, such as RSA. In this way, a message can be encrypted to multiple recipients while the actual content has to be encrypted only once.

The PKCS #7 message includes the encrypted content and symmetric-key algorithm along with information for each recipient. This information contains the symmetric key encrypted to that specific recipient. Upon receipt, an application searches the list of recipients for one that matches the current user's certificate. It then decrypts the symmetric key with the user's private key and subsequently decrypts the message.

3. OTHER CONTENT TYPES

The degenerate case of the PKCS #7 message allows for the absence of the content and any signature information. This format provides a transport for certificates and CRLs. Table 7.6 shows the typical file extensions for different PKCS #7 files.

Table 7.6 Common PKCS #7 file extensions

Extension	Description
.P7M	PKCS # 7 encrypted file or signed file with content added
.P7B	PKCS # 7 file extension
.P7S	PKCS # 7 signature file (signed file without the content)
.P7C	PKCS # 7 certificate or CRL-only file

7.7.8.2 Kerberos Version 5

Kerberos is another authentication security protocol used by Windows 2000 Server and Windows Server 2003. It is used over a network to mutually identify the requestor (user) and authenticator (network resource). After they are identified, the user and network resource can encrypt transmissions to ensure privacy.

Kerberos works by issuing tickets to users for accessing resources on the network. Before exploring the high-level details of Kerberos, you need to understand some objects and services:

- **Ticket:** A packet of data that allows a client to access a resource. It includes an encrypted piece of client information that, when decrypted, confirms identity.
- **Ticket-granting ticket (TGT):** A special ticket that allows the client to obtain temporary tickets from the ticket-granting service for each authentication.
- **Key distribution center (KDC):** A service that runs as part of Active Directory and administers TGTs. Every domain controller is a KDC.
- **Ticket-granting service (TGS):** A service that is accessed by a client with a TGT and that administers tickets for network resources.

The use of a TGS keeps the user from having to log on for each resource request. Figure 7.32 shows the details of a client using Kerberos to authenticate to a server.

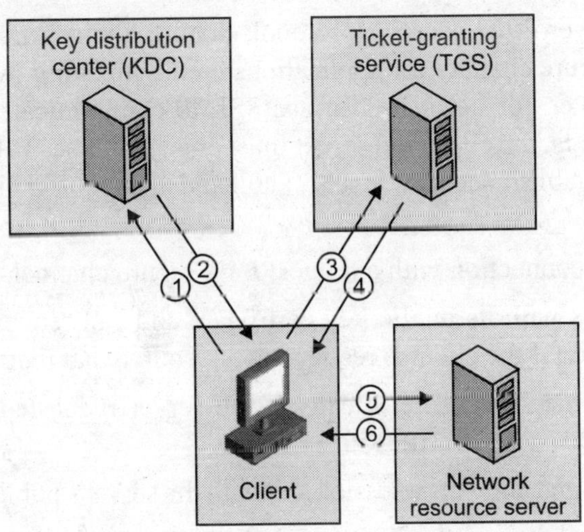

Figure 7.32 A client using Kerberos to authenticate to a server

The following steps describe the process a client goes through when using Kerberos to authenticate to a server:

1. A client authenticates once to the key distribution center by using a password or smart card.
2. The KDC issues a TGT to the client, for access to the TGS.
3. When the client wants to access a network resource, such as the corporate finance server, he or she requests a service ticket from the TGS, sending the TGT as proof of identity.
4. The TGS replies with a service ticket for use at the requested network resource server.
5. The client sends the service ticket to the network resource server for access.
6. To mutually authenticate, the network resource server replies with a packet that the client can decrypt.

After a client completes the first two steps, steps 3 through 6 can be repeated each time a user needs to access another resource.

Note: The advantage of this mechanism is that all Kerberos authentication occurs behind the scenes. The user needs to enter a password only once into the KDC-authentication to all other resources happens transparently.

7.7.8.3 Windows NT LAN Manager

Windows NT LAN Manager (NTLM) is the primary authentication mechanism for Windows NT 4. NTLM 2 is an extension that supports backward compatibility for previous versions of Windows. In Windows 2000 Server and later, NTLM and NTLM 2 are superceded by Kerberos as the default authentication protocol. NTLM is included as part of Windows Server 2003 for configurations that involve authentication between Windows NT and Windows Server 2003 machines or where the computers are not in a domain, like workgroups or standalone servers.

7.7.8.4 Secure Sockets Layer

Another Windows Server 2003 security protocol, Secure Sockets Layer (SSL), uses public-key technology to provide a secure channel for applications communicating over a non-secure network. A Web browser and Web server, for instance, can use SSL to communicate securely over the Internet. Before sending encrypted data, the client and server must engage in a security handshake to authenticate the parties involved and establish security levels. The handshake is a multipart process, as described here:

1. The client initiates connection with a request for a secure channel.
2. The server responds with its public-key certificate and can request the client's certificate for mutual authentication if the client is requesting a resource that requires authentication.
3. The client verifies the server's certificate. If the server requested the client's certificate, the client sends it and the server verifies it.
4. The client generates and encrypts a session key with the server's public key found in its certificate.
5. All communication between the server and client is symmetrically encrypted and decrypted using the session key.

Figure 7.33 illustrates the SSL handshake process. In addition to authentication, the SSL handshake allows the two parties to agree on security parameters. Because of SSL's positioning, it can add security to application protocols such as HTTP, LDAP, Telnet, FTP, Gopher, and Network News Transfer Protocol (NNTP).

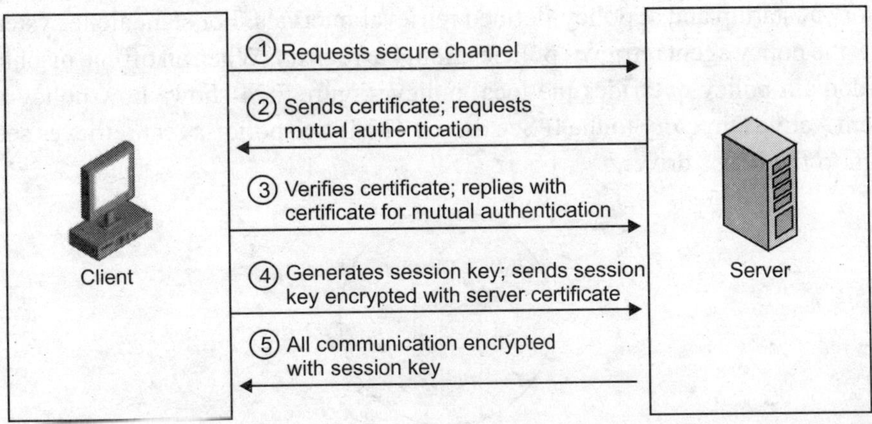

Figure 7.33 The SSL handshake process

7.7.8.5 Internet Protocol Security

Finally, the Windows Server 2003 IPSec security protocol provides end-to-end security of network data using encryption, digital signature, and hashing algorithms. The IPSec driver protects individual packets before they reach the network and unwraps the protection after they're received. Because the IPSec driver resides at the IP transport layer, individual applications don't need to handle the specifics of data security during transmission. Data passed though the network from applications without security features can still be protected. Because IPSec protects the packets of data-not the actual link-IPSec can provide security for transmissions on insecure networks, and only the two computers engaging in communications need to know about it. IPSec provides a number of security features:

- **Authentication:** Use of a digital signature verifies identity of sender
- **Integrity:** Use of hash algorithms ensures that data hasn't been altered
- **Privacy:** Use of encryption protects data from being read
- **Anti-replay:** Prevents packets from being re-sent by an attacker to gain unauthorized access
- **Nonrepudiation:** Use of public-key digital signatures proves message origin
- **Dynamic rekeying:** Ability to generate keys during communication so that parts of transmissions are protected with different keys
- **Key generation:** Diffie-Hellman key agreement algorithm allows two computers to agree on a key without ever exposing it
- **Key lengths:** Provides configurable key lengths for export restrictions or highly sensitive transmissions

1. IPSEC POLICY MANAGEMENT

An important component of IPSec is the policy agent. The policy agent begins during system startup and is responsible for retrieving IPSec policy information from either Active Directory or the registry and feeding it to the IPSec driver. For domain computers, the domain policy information is acquired from Active Directory at startup and at policy-defined retrieval intervals. For standalone systems or systems that are offline, the policy agent retrieves policies from the registry. When an offline machine reconnects, the retrieved domain policy overrides the local policy. Figure 7.34 shows how policy information is transferred from Active Directory to the IPSec driver. The IPSec policy agent retrieves security policies and feeds them to the IPSec driver.

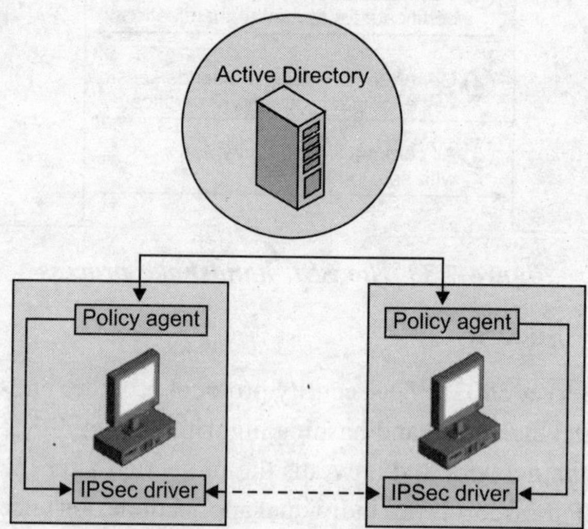

Figure 7.34 How policy information is transferred from Active Directory to the IPSec driver

Windows Server 2003 also provides predefined policies that can be customized to specific needs.

2. HOW IPSEC WORKS

Before data can be protected and transmitted between two IPSec-enabled machines, a negotiation must take place to agree on which keys, mechanisms, and security policies to use to protect the data. This negotiation produces a security association (SA).

For IPSec communications, an initial SA called Internet Security Association and Key Management Protocol (ISAKMP) is established between the two computers to provide a method of key exchange. Using the ISAKMP for protection, a second negotiation takes place to produce a pair of IPSec SAs and keys, one for inbound and one for outbound communications. Specifically, these SAs include an agreed algorithm for encryption and integrity and the agreed IPSec protocol to use. The two IPSec protocols are:

- **Authentication Header (AH):** Provides data authentication, integrity, and antire-play to IP packets
- **Encapsulating Security Payload (ESP):** Provides confidentiality along with data authentication, integrity, and antireplay to IP packets

The IPSec SAs and keys are loaded into the IPSec driver on their respective machines and are used to protect data during transmission.

7.7.9 Virtual Private Networks

Before you explore virtual private networks (VPNs), what they mean, and why they're useful, take a second to consider that acronym, VPN: "virtual," as in simulated; "private," as in secret and confidential; "network," as in a collection of computers.

Logically, a VPN is simply an extension of a private network. In reality, private networks are geographically isolated from remote users and other private networks by nonsecure communication lines such as the Internet. When you use a secure, network-level protocol such as IPSec, a private link can be emulated between two separate networks. Both requestor and authenticator perceive what actually the wrapping of data is before it passes through non-secure extranets or intranets as a private dedicated line. Because data packets are protected by encryption, any in-transit interception results in unreadable data.

IPSec enables the encryption of communications between peer machines; by design, no server is needed. Compare it with VPNs, which require the use of a dedicated server. That server is tied to the private network. By accepting connections from only VPN-authorized clients, the VPN server allows private traffic within the physical enclave to proceed normally without requiring additional internal security.

Before you can establish a VPN connection, VPN authorization must be confirmed for the client. Authorization is based on the remote access policies set by the network administrator and on the dial-in properties of the client requesting the connection. After a user is determined to be authorized and one-way or mutual authentication occurs, you can establish the VPN. Windows Server 2003 includes two protocols that are used to encapsulate data over the VPN:

- **Point-to-Point Tunneling Protocol (PPTP):** Provides data encryption using Microsoft Point-to-Point Encryption (MPPE)
- **Layer Two Tunneling Protocol (L2TP):** Provides data encryption, authentication, and integrity using IPSec

7.7.9.1 Remote Access VPNs

An authorized but isolated user can access the protected resources of a private or hidden network by authenticating to the network's VPN server and establishing a VPN connection. The remote user can at home or on the road need to connect through an ISP and the Internet, or the remote user can be part of the same intranet but detached from the secure or hidden network.

For example, suppose the engineering division of a company has a hidden enclave within an enterprise-wide network, complete with secret documents and alpha-version software. They want to grant access to the hidden network to the vice president of engineering but don't want to compromise the confidentiality of the information as it crosses the company's intranet. By providing a VPN server that blocks unauthorized users but allows the vice president to authenticate and establish a VPN connection, engineering's secret network is extended to one more user.

Note: Simply having a VPN connection to a private network does not mean you have full access. You still need the correct permissions to access specific resources.

After the client establishes a VPN connection with the VPN server, the user appears to be accessing the private network directly. Figure 7.35 shows remote access for an Internet-based VPN.

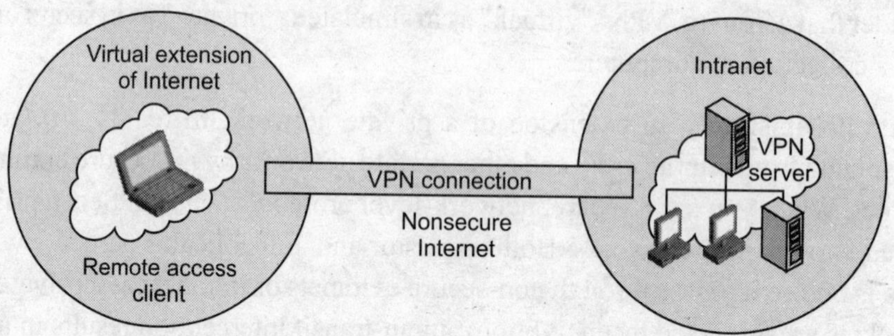

Figure 7.35 Remote access for an Internet-based VPN

7.7.9.2 Router-to-router VPNS

A VPN connection can also be established for two mutually exclusive private networks; the connection is also known as a VPN Tunnel. In this case, both the VPN client and VPN server are routers. Like remote access VPNs, router-to-router VPNs can involve enclaves that are part of the same intranet, or they can involve private networks that require the Internet infrastructure for communication. Figure 7.36 shows a router-to-router connection for an intranet-based VPN.

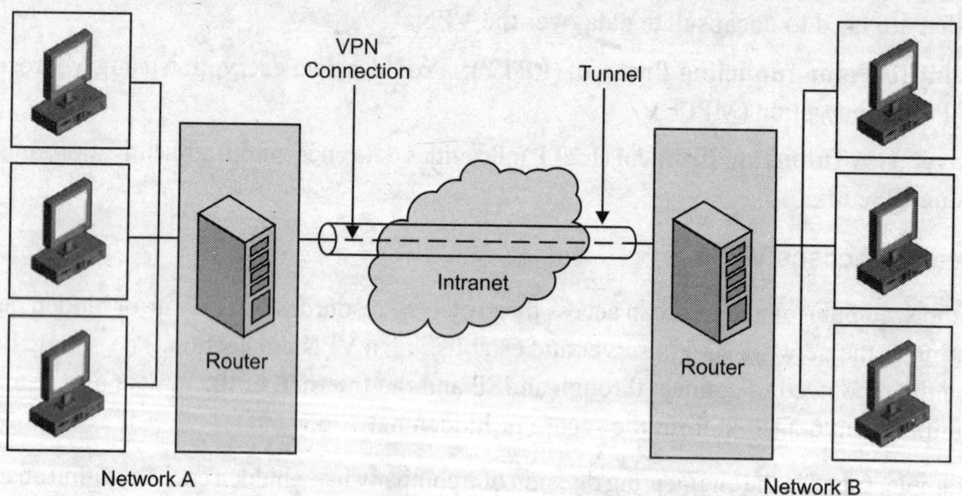

Figure 7.36 A router-to-router VPN connection

Here the VPN client authenticates itself to the VPN server, and a secure VPN connection is negotiated. Again, the logical appearance in both cases is that the private networks are physically connected.

7.7.10 Windows Rights Management Services

The Windows Rights Management Services (RMS) for Windows Server 2003 is a technology that allows users to protect information, from documents to e-mail. By using RMS, you can specify who else has access to protected content, and what that person can do with the protected content.

RMS consists of three components. The first is a trusted entity that issues a root certificate. The RMS server technologies perform the work required to protect data and authorize its use. RMS client software must be installed to allow users to participate in an RMS environment. Finally, RMS-enabled applications must be developed, using the RMS SDK, to provide the ability to create, distribute, and view protected content.

7.7.11 Security Modules

Interface that supports Windows cryptographic-enabled applications, such as Microsoft Certificate Services and Microsoft Internet Explorer.

7.7.11.1 Cryptographic Application Programming Interface

Microsoft CryptoAPI provides a standardized set of cryptographic functions-such as CryptGenKey, CryptVerifySignature, and CryptEncrypt-that allow applications to offer security without having to maintain their own cache of keys or certificates or know the particulars of the cryptographic device they're using. Because private keys are handled within the bounds of CryptoAPI, applications don't need to fumble around with unprotected private-key information.

When used, CryptoAPI passes each of its cryptographic calls off to one of a number of cryptographic service providers (CSPs) that actually perform the operation. Figure 7.37 shows the relationship between the API and the service providers.

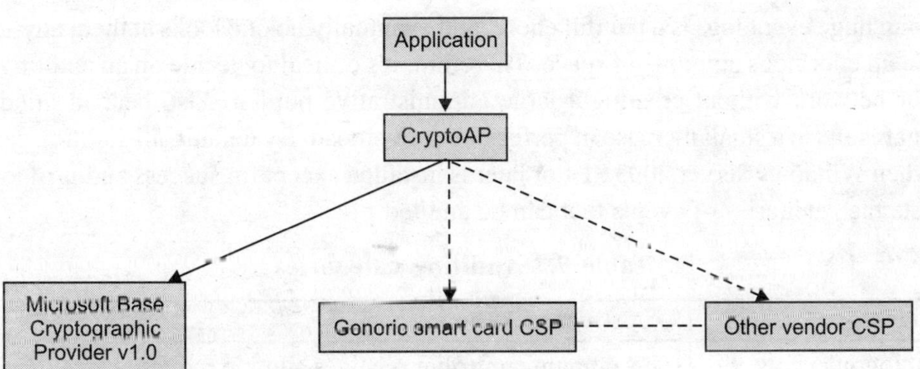

Figure 7.37 Cryptographic service providers "plugged in" to CryptoAPI

7.7.11.2 Cryptographic Service Providers

Cryptographic service providers (CSPs) vary according to the algorithms they use, the key lengths they support, and the cryptographic tokens with which they interface. A vendor introducing a new type of smart card, for instance, writes a CSP for its smart card that "plugs in" to the CryptoAPI. Being able to plug in allows applications to use myriad new and existing services without having to particularize their cryptographic calls to any one vendor-defined interface.

By displaying a list of available CSPs and allowing the user to choose, applications can take advantage of emerging technologies with little, if any, modification to their source code. Because CSPs provide the specific interface to the cryptographic device, whether it's software-based or hardware-based, they are responsible for any initialization required, such as PIN or password validation.

7.7.11.3 CAPICOM

CAPICOM is a COM (Component Object Model) client that wraps the details of CryptoAPI in a higher level package. Whereas CryptoAPI requires the developer to have a working knowledge of C/C++, CAPICOM allows users of COM-enabled languages, such as Visual Basic Scripting Edition and C#, to take a more abstract view of the details of CryptoAPI.

7.7.11.4 Data Protection API

The Data Protection API (DPAPI) is a pair of functions that, as part of the CryptoAPI, enable the developer to encrypt and decrypt data. It often uses the logon credentials to perform its encryption and decryption, but can optionally prompt for a password. DPAPI uses the 3DES algorithm and therefore provides strong encryption for end-user applications.

7.8 AUDIT POLICY

Auditing certain computers, users, and operating system events is a necessary part of network administration. You choose what is to be audited and then, by reviewing the event logs, track usage patterns, security problems, and network traffic trends. Beware of the impulse to audit everything, however. The more events you audit, the bigger the logs.

Reviewing huge event logs is a painful chore, and eventually no one looks at them any-more. These logs can take up enormous amounts of space. Therefore, it's critical to decide on an auditing policy that protects your network without creating a large administrative burden. Also bear in mind that every audited event results in a small increase in performance overhead. By default, all auditing categories are turned off when Windows Server 2003 SP1 or later is installed except for success audits of logon events. Table 7.7 lists the categories of events that can be audited.

Table 7.7 Auditing categories

Event Category	Activated When
Account logon events	A domain controller receives a logon request
Account management	A user account or group is created or changed
Directory service access	An Active Directory object is accessed
Logon events	A user logs on or logs off
Object access	An object is accessed
Policy change	A policy affecting security, user rights, or auditing is modified

Event Category	Activated When
Privilege use	A user right is used to perform an action
Process tracking	An application executes an action that is being tracked
System events	A computer is rebooted or shut down or another event occurs that affects security

Every audited event tells you something, but it's not always something you need to know. For example, auditing successful logons and logoffs might reveal the use of a stolen password, or it might just produce countless pages showing that your duly authorized users are logging on and off as expected. Auditing logon failures, however, will definitely be rewarding if someone is trying a random password hack.

Before you can audit access to Active Directory objects, you must turn on the Audit Policy setting by using Group Policy. To enable auditing of any of the categories in Table 7.7, open the Default Domain Policy MMC if you have one; otherwise, follow these steps to enable auditing for all computers in the domain:

1. Launch Active Directory Users and Computers.
2. Right-click the domain name in the console tree, and choose Properties from the shortcut menu.
3. Click the Group Policy tab and then click Edit.
4. In the console tree, click your way through Computer Configuration, Windows Settings, Security Settings, and Local Policies to reach Audit Policy, as shown in Figure 7.38.

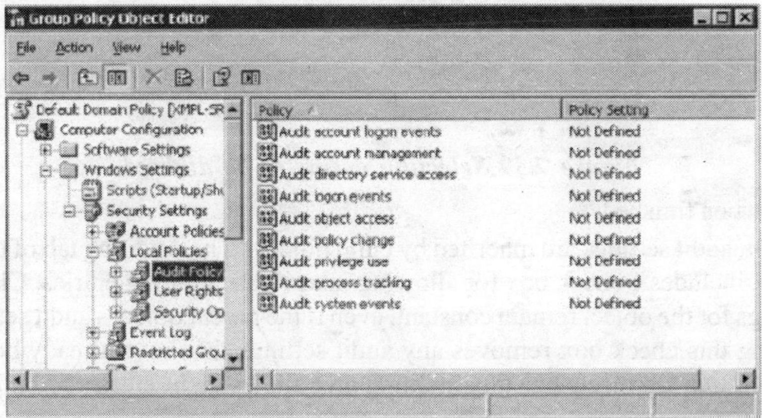

Figure 7.38 Categories of events for auditing

5. Right-click the event category you want to audit, and choose Properties from the shortcut menu.
6. In the dialog box that opens, select the check box to define the setting and select the option to audit successful attempts, failed attempts, or both.

7.8.1 Audit Settings for Objects

Assuming that you've turned on a policy setting for auditing an Active Directory object, create audit settings for objects by following these steps:

1. Right-click the object you want to audit, and choose Properties from the shortcut menu. Click the Security tab.
2. Click Advanced, and then click the Auditing tab.

3. Click Add to set up auditing for a new group or user. Make your selection and click OK.
4. Select the events you want to audit, as shown in Figure 7.39. Table 7.8 lists the options and their definitions.

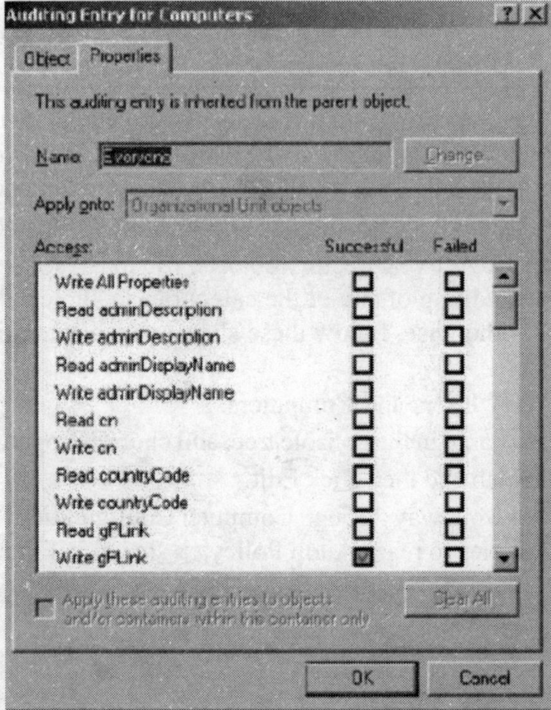

Figure 7.39 Selecting events to be audited

5. Click OK when finished.

Note By default, audit settings are inherited by child objects. The Auditing tab of the Access Control Settings dialog box includes a check box for allowing inheritable auditing entries. Clear this check box and the audit settings for the object remain constant, even if the parent object's audit settings are changed. In addition, clearing this check box removes any audit settings that have already been inherited. The second check box in this tab resets existing auditing and allows audit entries to be inherited from the parent object once again.

Table 7.8 File system events that can be audited

Event	Activated When
Traverse Folder/Execute File	A folder is traversed (that is, someone passes through the folder on the way to a parent folder or a child folder) or an application is run.
List Folder/Read Data	A folder is opened or data is viewed in files.
Read Attributes	The attributes of a file or folder are viewed.
Read Extended Attributes	Extended attributes (defined and created by programs) or a file or folder are viewed.
Create Files/Write Data	A file is created inside a folder or a file is changed, overwriting existing information in the file.
Create Folders/Append Data	A folder is created inside the folder being audited or information is added to an existing file.
Write Attributes	A file of folder attribute is changed.

Event	Activated When
Write Extended Attributes	Extended attributes (defined and created by programs) of a file or folder are changed.
Delete Subfolders and Files	A file or subfolder is deleted.
Delete	A specific file is deleted.
Read Permissions	Permissions for a file or folder are viewed.
Change Permissions	Permissions for a file or folder are modified.
Take Ownership	Ownership of a file or folder changes.

7.8.2 Auditing Advisory

Windows Server 2003 allows such granularity that it's possible-actually easy-to create a real morass when selecting audit settings. So many items can show up in the event log that really important issues might be lost in the crowd. Be very careful when deciding what events need to be audited, and audit as few as is reasonable.

7.8.2.1 Viewing Event Logs

Event logs must be viewed with regularity for auditing to have any effect. To view the security log, open Event Viewer from the Administrative Tools folder and then click Security. Double-click any entry to see more information about it. The security entries in Figure 7.40 occurred in the span of about a minute because the object being audited was set to audit successful events. Of course, you'll generally learn more from auditing failed events than from auditing successful ones, but this does demonstrate the need to choose your auditing battles carefully.

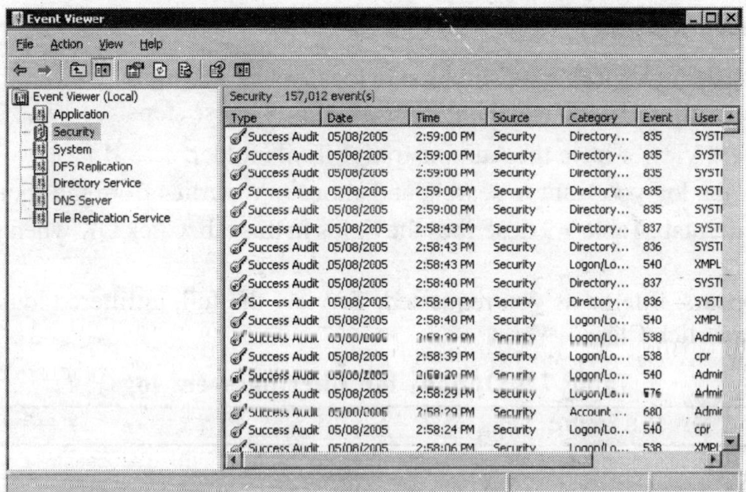

Figure 7.40 Viewing the security log

7.8.2.2 Searching Event Logs

No matter how selective you are, the event logs will mix all sorts of information together, making searches for specific information difficult. To search for a specific type of event, select the log in Event Viewer, and choose Find from the View menu. In the Find dialog box, shown in Figure 7.41, select the type or types of events you want returned. Table 7.9 describes the filtering options for the event logs.

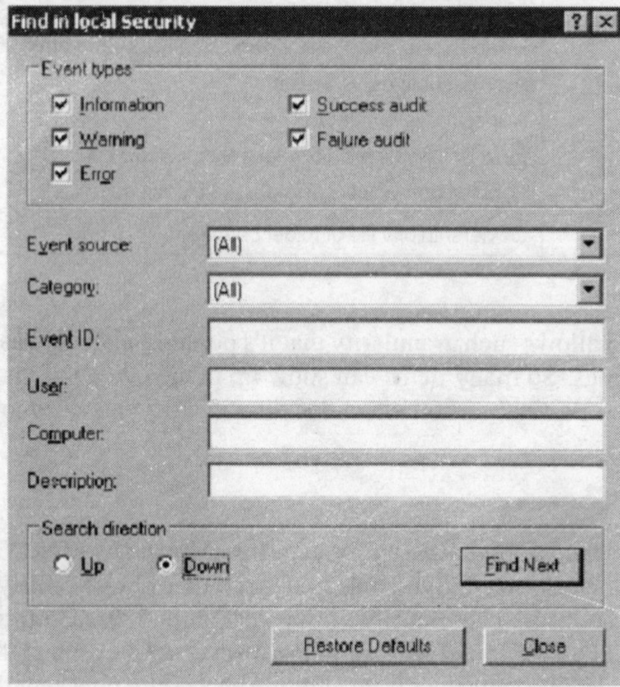

Figure 7.41 Searching for specific events in a log

7.8.2.3 Filtering Event Logs

If you don't have enough specific information to locate what you need, you can filter an event log for certain types of information. To use event log filtering, follow these steps:

1. Launch Event Viewer from the Administrative Tools folder.
2. Right-click the log you want to search, and choose Properties from the shortcut menu.
3. Click the Filter tab. Table 7.9 describes the fields in this tab. Click OK when you're ready to start filtering.
4. The log appears, filtered as you requested. To view the full, unfiltered log again, return to the Filter tab and click Clear.

Table 7.9 Options for filtering event logs

Option	Use to Search or Filter for
Information	Notification that some major operation has been performed successfully.
Warning	Notification of some problem or potential problem. Warnings might or might not be significant. For example, replication performed after repeated tries will generate a warning.
Error	Notification of an important event. Errors signify a loss of data or a loss of function. For example, failure of a service to start during bootup will generate an erroe.
Success Audit	Events audited for success.
Failure Audit	Events audited for failure.
Event Source	A source for an event, such as a system component or a program.
Category	Events by category, such as logon/logoff, policy change, or process tracking.

Option	Use to Search or Filter for
Event ID	The specific ID number assigned to each logged event.
User	A specific user.
Computer	A specific computer.
From	Events after a specific date. The default is the first date in the log. You can click the drop-down box to select events on a specific date.
To	Events before a specific date. The default is the last date in the file.

7.8.2.4 Setting the Size of Event Logs

When an event log is full, a dialog box pops up to notify you. If this happens often, you might want to reduce the number of items being reported or increase the size of the log. To set event log options, follow these steps:

1. Launch Event Viewer from the Administrative Tools folder.
2. Right-click the log you want to configure and choose Properties.
3. In the General tab, set the options you want. Under When Maximum Log Size Is Reached, there are three options:
   - If you don't archive this log, select Overwrite Events As Needed.
   - If you archive this log at regular intervals, you can select the Overwrite Events Older Than option. Fill in the appropriate number of days.
   - Do Not Overwrite Events, the last option, means that the log must be cleared manually. When the maximum log size is reached, new events are simply not recorded.
4. Click OK when you're finished.

Note: To set limits for a large number of machines-a department or a whole domain-use Group Policy.

7.8.2.5 Calling a Halt When the Log is Full

Maybe you are so security-conscious that none of the event log options are acceptable. If you absolutely, positively must not lose a single security event, you can set the computer to halt when the security log is full. A registry change is necessary to make this happen. First, set Event Log Wrapping to either Do Not Overwrite Events or Overwrite Events Older Than n Days.

Then start Regedit.exe, proceed to

HKEY_LOCAL_MACHINE\SYSTEM\CurrentControlSet\Control\Lsa\CrashOn AuditFail, and change the value to 1.

This setting takes effect after a reboot; then, when the log is full, the system simply stops. After restarting, only administrators are able to log on until the security log is cleared. This is obviously a drastic measure, but if you absolutely must retain an audit trail on a particular server, this is one way to ensure that.

7.8.3 Archiving Event Logs

If you will be using event logs to track system usage trends, you must save them. To archive an event log, launch Event Viewer from the Administrative Tools folder and click the log you want to archive. Then, from the Action menu, choose Save Log As. If you save the file in the event log format (.evt), it can be reopened in Event Viewer, and all the binary data for each event is retained. You can also save logs as .txt files or in comma-delimited format (.csv), but in those cases the binary data isn't saved.

7.8.4 Delegating Control

Obviously, one of the simplest ways to minimize your administrative chores is to delegate them. In a Windows NT network, the usual way to grant broad administrative rights was to make users members of the Domain Admins group. You could also parcel out administrative rights through some combination of other groups such as Print Operators or Server Operators.

These groups are still available, but Windows Server 2003 makes delegation even simpler, allowing you to assign responsibility for management of some portion of the namespace to another user or group. The recipient of the delegated authority can have complete administrative control within the area chosen but not the sweeping administrative rights inherent in being a member of the Domain Admins group.

Assign control by organizational unit (OU) whenever possible, because assigning permissions at the object level quickly becomes too complicated to be worthwhile. Records of security assignments are critical, so keep track of all delegations. To delegate control, use the Delegation of Control Wizard, which always assigns permissions at the OU level.

To use the wizard, follow these steps:

1. Launch Active Directory Users and Computers from the Administrative Tools folder.
2. Expand the domain node, right-click the container for which you want to delegate control, and choose Delegate Control from the shortcut menu. This starts the Delegation of Control Wizard. Click Next.
3. Click Add to select the user or group to be granted control. Make your selection from the Select Users, Computers, Or Groups page.
4. In the Tasks To Delegate page, shown in Figure 7.42, select the tasks that you want to delegate. Select predefined tasks, or click Create A Custom Task To Delegate. Click Next.
5. If you selected a predefined task, you're essentially finished. Review the summary and click Finished.

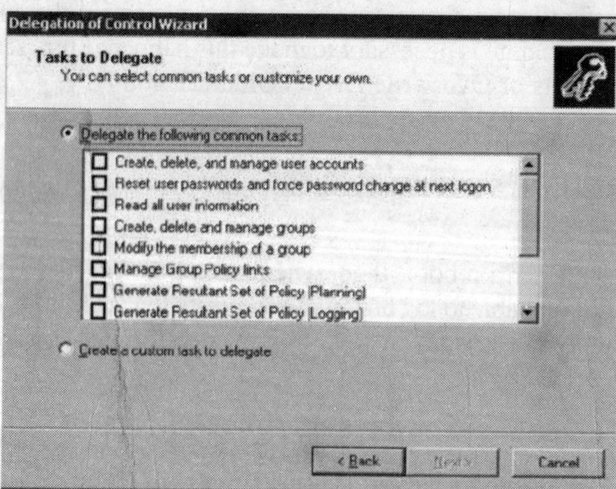

Figure 7.42 Choosing the tasks to be delegated

If you selected create a Custom Task to Delegate, you're presented with more specific choices about what objects you're delegating control on and the specific permissions to be granted. When those choices are made, you'll see a summary of the delegation. Click Finished.

7.9 EVENT VIEWER

Event Viewer is both a service and a Microsoft Management Console (MMC) snap-in that tracks and displays events recorded in the application, security, and system logs. It gathers information about software, hardware, and system problems and tracks security events. When you launch Event Viewer (Eventvwr.msc) from the Administrative Tools folder on the Programs menu, the Event Viewer console appears. (See Figure 7.43.)

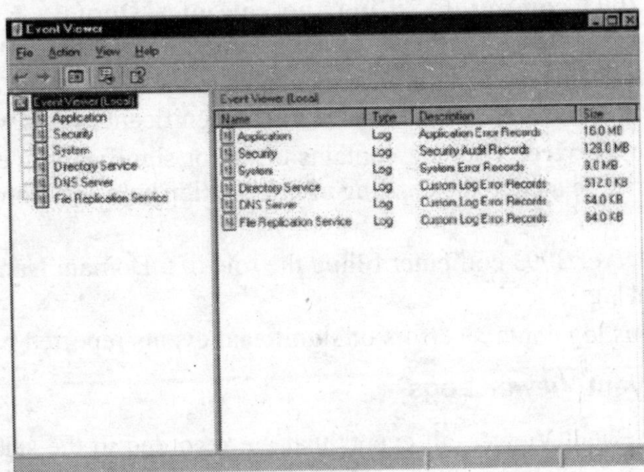

Figure 7.43 The Event Viewer console

7.9.1 Event Log Files

By default, Windows Server 2003 creates three event logs. As you assign additional roles to the server, these roles might create additional logs. The default logs are:

- **Application log:** Contains events logged by programs or applications. For example, a database program might log a file error in the program log. Application and program developers determine the events that programs log. All users can view this log, which is stored in the %WINDIR%\System32\Config\AppEvent.evt file by default.
- **Security log:** Records security events such as invalid and valid logon attempts and events related to resource use, such as creating, opening, or deleting files. Only administrators can view this log, which is stored in the %WINDIR%\System32\Config\SecEvent.evt file by default. You can also set an auditing policy in the registry to halt the system when the security log becomes full.
- **System log:** Contains events logged by the Windows Server 2003 system components. For example, services that fail during startup generate errors in the System log. All users can view this log, which is stored in the %WINDIR%\System32\Config\file by default.

Windows Server 2003 includes a set of log files that are configured and presented within the Event Viewer. By configuring the options on each of the logs to meet the requirements of your environment, you can collect data appropriate for troubleshooting hardware, application, system, and resource access.

7.9.1.1 Logs Available in Event Viewer

The Windows Server 2003 Event Log service, present and started automatically on all Windows Server 2003 computers, records events in one of three log files:

- Application Developers of an application can program their software to report configuration changes, errors, or other events to this log.
- System The Windows Server 2003 operating system will report events (service start or abnormal shutdown, device failures, and so on) to this log. The events reported to this log are preconfigured.
- Security Logon and resource access events (audits) are reported to this log. Configuration for most of these events is at the discrimination of the system administrator.

Windows Server 2003 computers filling the role of a Domain Controller contain two additional logs:

- **Directory Service:** This log contains events related to the Microsoft Active Directory directory service, such as irreconcilable object replication or significant events within the directory.
- **File Replication Service:** This log contains errors or significant events reported by the File Replication Service related to the copying of information between Domain Controllers during a replication cycle.

Lastly, a Windows Server 2003 computer filling the role of a Domain Name System (DNS) server will contain one additional log:

- **DNS Server:** This log contains errors or significant events reported by the DNS server.

7.9.1.2 Configuring Event Viewer Logs

When you first start Event Viewer, all events that are recorded in the selected log are displayed. Such a list may be lengthy, containing many entries of both informational and warning types. You can locate events by type using the Filter command on the shortcut menu's View menu for the log you want to view. The Filter properties page for the Security log is shown in Figure 7.44.

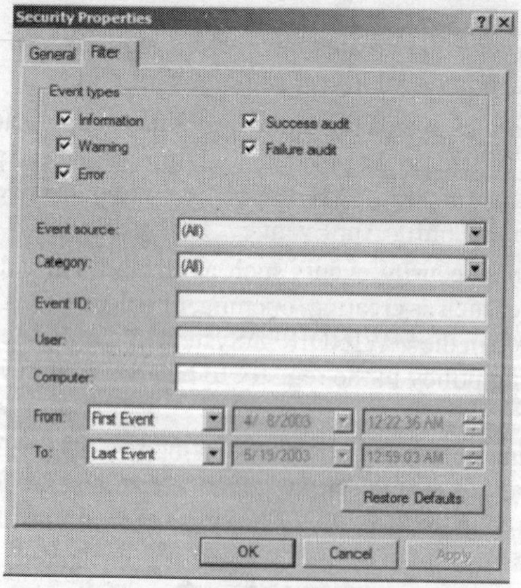

Figure 7.44 Filter settings for the Security log

Adjacent to the Filter tab in the properties of a log is the General tab, which provides access to the behaviours of the log, including

- The display name for the view of the log.
- The maximum size of the log.
- Whether the oldest events in the log should be overwritten when the maximum log size is reached. There are three overwrite options:

(a) **Overwrite Events As Needed (default):** This behaviour will overwrite the oldest entries in the log with newer ones when the log reaches the maximum size.

(b) **Overwrite Events Older Than n Days:** This configuration will overwrite events that exceed the age setting when the log reaches the maximum size.

(c) **Do Not Overwrite Events (Clear Log Manually):** This configuration will halt event logging when the log reaches the maximum size.

The General tab for the Security log is shown in Figure 7.45.

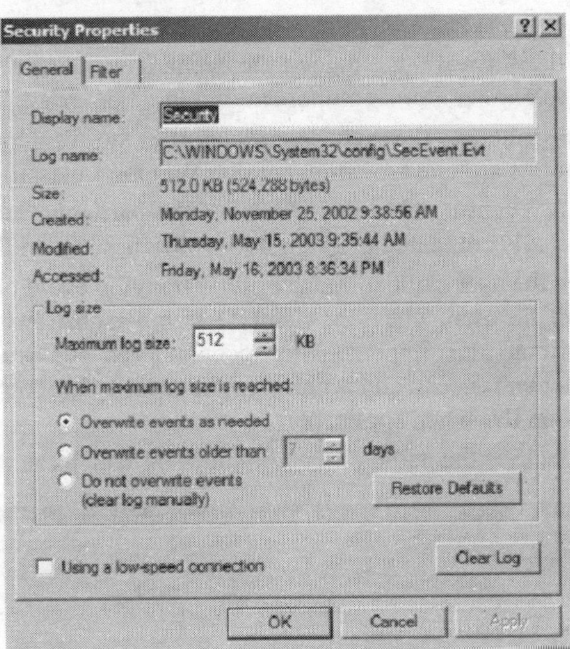

Figure 7.45 The General settings for the Security log

7.9.2 Components of an Event

The two key components in the interpretation of an event are the event header and the event description. The event description is the most useful piece of information because it indicates the significance of the event.

7.9.2.1 The Event Header

Windows displays event headers in columns in the Event Viewer console, as shown in Figure 7.46 and described in the following list:

- **Type:** Lists the severity of the event. Event Viewer classifies events in the application, system, and security logs using the following classifications, which are represented by symbols in the normal view:

1. **Information:** Describes the successful operation of a service, driver, or application. For example, when the Event Log service starts successfully, it records an Information event.
2. **Warning:** Indicates events that pose a possible future problem. For example, when Windows cannot renew its IP address, it generates a Warning event.
3. **Error:** Indicates that a significant problem has occurred, such as loss of functionality or loss of data. For example, if a service such as Net Logon fails to load, it generates an Error event.
4. **Failure:** Audit Lists a failed attempt to perform an audited security event. For example, if a user fails a logon attempt, Windows generates a Failure Audit event.
5. **Success:** Audit Lists a successful attempt to perform an audited security event. For example, when a user logs on successfully, Windows generates a Success Audit event.
    - **Date:** Indicates the date the event occurred.
    - **Time:** Indicates the (local) time the event occurred.
    - **Source:** Lists the software that logged the event. The software can be a program name, a component of the system, or a component of a large program, such as a driver name.
    - **Category:** Shows the way the event source classifies the event; primarily used in the security log. Security audits are one type of event that Windows classifies here.
    - **Event:** Lists the event number that identifies the particular event type. The name of the event type is usually contained in the first line of its associated description.
    - **User:** Indicates the user name of the user for whom the event occurred. If a server process caused the event, the user name is the client ID. If impersonation is not taking place, Windows displays the primary ID. Impersonation occurs when one process takes on the security attributes of another process, and is normal. The security log entry lists both the primary and the impersonation IDs when applicable.
    - **Computer:** Specifies the name of the computer on which the event took place.

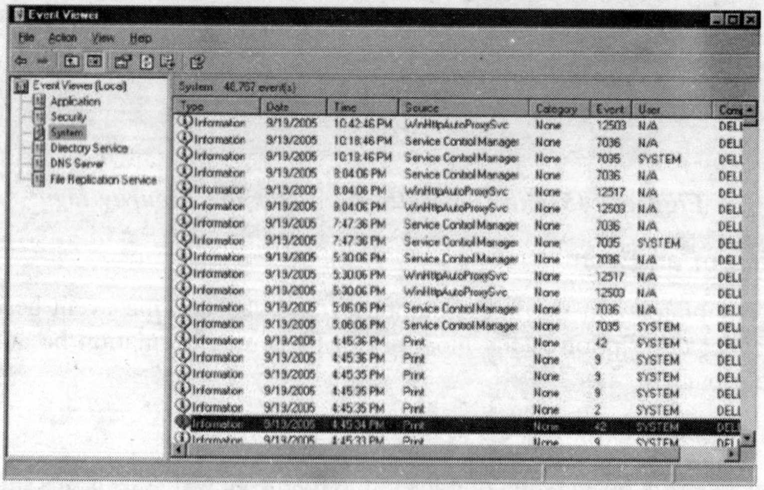

Figure 7.46 Event headers in the Event Viewer console

7.9.2.2 The Event Description

Double-clicking a specific event in Event Viewer displays the Event Properties dialog box shown in Figure 7.47. This dialog box describes the event and usually includes a link to more information about the event on the Microsoft Help and Support Center Web site. If the description is not helpful, select noteworthy text or the Event ID, press Ctrl+C to copy the text, and then perform a Web search for more information using the text you copied.

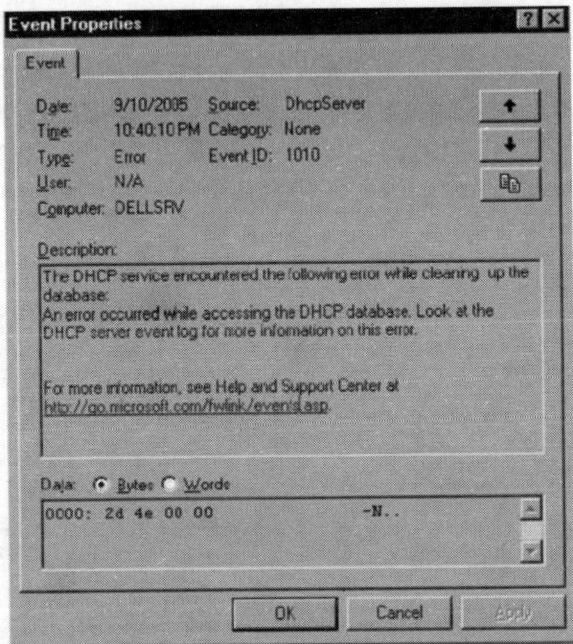

Figure 7.47 The Event Properties dialog box

7.9.2.3 Viewing an Event Log on Another Computer

Event Viewer can display the event log for remote machines running Windows Server 2003, Windows XP, Windows 2000, or Windows NT. To view the event log for another computer, right-click Event Viewer (Local) at the top of the tree and choose Connect to another Computer. In the Select Computer dialog box, type the name of the other computer, or click Browse to search for the desired computer.

To tune Event Viewer for a low-speed connection to the remote machine, right-click the log, choose Properties, and then select Low Speed Connection in the Properties dialog box.

7.9.2.4 Changing Event Log Settings

To change Event Log settings, right-click the log in Event Viewer, choose Properties, and then use the following list:

- To change the size of the event log, use the Maximum Log Size box to specify a new log size 4 GB in size or smaller. Before decreasing the size of the log file, clear the log of events by right-clicking the log and choosing Clear All Events. By default, the application, security, and system logs each have a maximum size of 16 MB in Windows Server 2003 (8 MB for Microsoft Windows XP Service Pack 1, and 512 KB for Windows XP and Windows 2000).

- To change the action Windows performs when a log file is full, choose one of the following options: Overwrite Events As Needed, Overwrite Events Older Than, or Do Not Overwrite Events. Windows overwrites events as needed by default. Logging stops if the log file is full and cannot overwrite itself.

7.9.2.5 Archiving an Event Log

To save an event log to a file, right-click the log in Event Viewer and then choose Save Log File As. You can archive event logs in one of the following three formats:

- **Event Log:** Allows you to view the log in Event Viewer. Its extension is .EVT.
- **Text (Tab delimited):** Enables you to view the data easily in any text editor or word processor. Its extension is .TXT.
- **CSV (Comma-delimited text):** Enables you to use the data in a spreadsheet or flat-file database. Its extension is .CSV.

To open an archived log file saved in the Event Log (.evt) format, right-click a log in Event Viewer, choose Open Log File, and then search for the log file in the Open dialog box.

Examples: **Event Monitor**

In this practice, you will configure the Security log for File and Object Access, and filter the data displayed in the Security log.

Exercise 1: Configuring the Security Log In this exercise, you will configure the auditing of File and Object Access.

1. Logged on to Server01 as an administrator, open Active Directory Users And Computers.
2. Right-click the Domain Controllers Organizational Unit (OU), and then choose Properties from the shortcut menu.
3. On the Group Policy tab, select the Default Domain Controllers Policy, and then click Edit.
4. Under the Computer Configuration node, expand Windows Settings, Security Settings, Local Policies, and then click Audit Policy.
5. In the details pane, right-click Audit Object Access, and then select Properties from the shortcut menu.
6. In the Audit Object Access Properties dialog box, select Audit These Attempts: Failure, and then click OK.
7. Close the Group Policy Object Editor, click OK to close the Domain Controllers Properties dialog box, and then close Active Directory Users And Computers.
8. Open a command window, type gpupdate, and then press Enter.
9. When the Computer Policy reports as refreshed, close the command window.

You have now enabled the auditing of failed Object Access attempts on Server01 (as part of the Domain Controllers OU), and refreshed Group Policy so that the settings take effect immediately.

Exercise 2: Setting File and Object Auditing

In this exercise, you will configure auditing on a folder that you will create. Permissions will be set so as to simulate a user attempting to gain unauthorized access to the resource.

1. On your desktop, create a folder called Data.
2. Right-click the folder and select Properties from the shortcut menu.
3. Select the Security tab, and then select your user account.
4. Select the check box indicating Deny: Full Control permissions for your user account, click Yes in the warning dialog box.
5. Click Advanced, and then select the Auditing tab. Add your user account to audit List Folder / Read Data: Failed, and then click OK to close all Property dialog boxes.
6. Double-click the Data folder to open it. You should receive an Access Denied warning message.

Exercise 3: Reading the Security Log

In this exercise, you will confirm the auditing of your failed access to the Data folder.

1. From Administratives Tools, open the Computer Management console.
2. Expand the Event Viewer node, and then click the Security log in the folder pane. Near the top of the list of events, you should see several Failure Audit events (with ID 560) indicating your failed attempt to access the Data folder.
3. Right-click the Security log in the folder pane, select View from the shortcut menu, and then choose Filter.
4. In the Filter dialog box, select each of the following:
   (a) **Event Source:** Security
   (b) **Category:** Object Access
   (c) **Event Types:** Failure selected, all others cleared
5. Click OK to apply the filter to the Security log. You have now filtered the Security log data to display only the events that apply to failed object access.

EXERCISES

1. Explain the concept of task management in detail?
2. Explain various tabs used in task management?
3. What do you mean by task scheduler?
4. Explain the use of at command?
5. Explain the concept of system monitoring: recording and viewing data, monitoring multiple servers and modifying the display etc.

6. Explain the concept of performance logs and alerts?
7. How we can create counter and trace logs?
8. How we can understand log file parameters?
9. How we can save log and alert file settings?
10. Explain the use of alerts?
11. What do you mean by monitoring memory?
12. Explain the various real world monitoring and tuning strategies?
13. How the performance impact of monitoring can reduced?
14. How can we use monitoring memory?
15. What is monitoring processor activity?
16. What is monitoring disk activity?
17. What do you mean by monitoring network activity?
18. What are network and process objects?
19. How we can document the network?
20. How we can evaluate policies and procedures?
21. What are network frames?
22. What are capturing frames?
23. How can we view the capture window?
24. How can we view the frame viewer window?
25. How can we configure and customize network monitor?
26. How we can design a capture filter?
27. Define pattern matches?
28. Write procedure to designing a display filter?
29. How can we setup a capture trigger?
30. Explain the concept of memory and network tuning?
31. What are the auditing security events?
32. Explain the data protection?
33. What do you understand by access control?

34. What is auditing?
35. Explain the concept of Non-repudiation and smart cards?
36. Explain in detail public-key infrastructures?
37. What are security-enabled protocols?
38. What are the virtual private networks?
39. Explain the various security modules?
40. Explain the concept of audit policy?
41. What are the audit settings for objects?
42. What is auditing advisory?
43. Explain the concept of event viewer?
44. Explain the concept of event log files?
45. Explain the various components of an event?

CHAPTER 8

Special Topics

8.1 INTRODUCTION

In this chapter we discuss the special topics like E-Mail, Telnet and FTP, Distributed Systems. Electronic mail, commonly called email or e-mail, is a method of exchanging digital messages across the Internet or other computer networks. TELNET is a network protocol used on the Internet or local area networks to provide a bidirectional interactive text-oriented communications facility via a virtual terminal connection.

File Transfer Protocol (FTP) is a standard network protocol used to copy a file from one host to another over a TCP/IP-based network, such as the Internet. Distributed Processing is the distribution of applications and business logic across multiple processing platforms. Distributed processing implies that processing will occur on more than one processor in order for a transaction to be completed.

8.2 E-MAIL

Electronic mail, commonly called email or e-mail, is a method of exchanging digital messages across the Internet or other computer networks. Originally, email was transmitted directly from one user to another computer. This required both computers to be online at the same time, a la instant messenger. Today's email systems are based on a store-and-forward model. Email servers accept, forward, deliver and store messages. Users no longer need be online simultaneously and need only connect briefly, typically to an email server, for as long as it takes to send or receive messages.

An email message consists of two components, the message header, and the message body, which is the email's content. The message header contains control information, including, minimally, an originator's email address and one or more recipient addresses. Usually additional information is added, such as a subject header field. Originally a text-only communications medium, email was extended to carry multi-media content attachments, a process standardized in RFC 2045 through 2049. Collectively, these RFCs have come to be called Multipurpose Internet Mail Extensions (MIME).

The history of modern, global Internet email services reaches back to the early ARPANET. Standards for encoding email messages were proposed as early as 1973 (RFC 561). Conversion from ARPANET to the Internet in the early 1980s produced the core of the current services. An email sent in the early 1970s looks quite similar to one sent on the Internet today.

Network-based email was initially exchanged on the ARPANET in extensions to the File Transfer Protocol (FTP), but is now carried by the Simple Mail Transfer Protocol (SMTP), first published as Internet standard 10 (RFC 821) in 1982. In the process of transporting email messages between systems, SMTP communicates delivery parameters using a message envelope separate from the message (header and body) itself.

8.2.1 History Of Email

Electronic mail, known commonly by its abbreviation 'email', is probably the most used medium of communication today. 50 years ago, had someone said that it would be possible to instantly deliver documents to a recipient sitting half way across the globe, he would have been a laughing stock. But, email came, saw and conquered the world wide web. Today, with email, there's so much more than just written text communication. Ability of the email to securely forward multimedia, photos, software, etc. has made it very popular. It's rightly said that 'necessity is the mother of all inventions', and we humans have always found a way whenever the need arose. The history of email communication is very interesting and intriguing. Let's go back to the days when the Cold War was at its peak.

Following the Cuban missile crisis of 1962, the Pentagon initiated a program to design a network whose main aim was to withstand a nuclear attack. Though, Pentagon insisted that this was not a military program and gave it a scientific angle. This network came to be known as the Advanced Research Projects Agency Network or ARPANET, after the program's completion by 1969. Evolution of email is said to have started much earlier than ARPANET, though.

In 1965, the Massachusetts Institute of Technology (MIT) was the first to demonstrate the use of the first email system, known as MAILBOX. This was before internetwork came into existence and therefore, this system was used to send messages to different users on the same computer.

In 1971, Ray Tomlinson, a former MITian, was working on TENEX operating system for BBN technologies as an ARPANET contractor. While using a local email program called SNDMSG, Tomlinson created the first email application when he patched a program called CPYNET to the existing SNDMSG. This introduced the capability to copy files through a network and Ray notified his colleagues by sending them the first email. It's said that the first message sent by Ray was 'QWERTYUIOP', which is formed by the entire first row characters of a standard keyboard. The history of email addresses can also be attributed to Tomlinson. He chose the '@' symbol to provide an addressing standard in the form of "user@host", which is in use till date. This is why Tomlinson is called the 'father of email' and is credited with its invention.

By 1974, email in its improved form was being used by the US military and became the savior of ARPANET, who's importance was continuously declining. From here on, things developed at a brisk pace. By 1975, efforts to organize the email bore fruit. A general operating area, known as email account, for a user who wants to avail the email service, was created. Access controlling was done by giving the user a secret password, which only he/she would know. Separate folders were created depending on the purpose. Inbox for incoming messages, outbox for outgoing messages, etc.

Year 1976 was a watershed year in the history of email marketing. Email service was being offered in commercial packages and per-minute charges were applicable to those using these services. This led to the requirement for offline reading, which meant that users could now download their emails on to their personal computers, and then read them leisurely without using and paying for the airtime. This led to the development of applications, which were similar to what Microsoft Outlook can do today.

Requirement for protocols was felt almost immediately, and in 1972, file transfer protocol (FTP) was put in use to send email messages. The main drawback here was that FTP created a separate mail for every recipient and then dispatched it, which resulted in loss of precious memory space. This prompted the creation of the more efficient SMTP (Simple Mail Transfer Protocol) in the early 1980s, which became a standard protocol to be used in sending email messages. But the initial versions of SMTP failed to control the cases of forgery and proved to be a naive protocol in the verification of the authenticity of a user. Email viruses, worms and spammers began exploiting these loopholes in SMTP and even though, many new and improved versions have been released, this problem continues to be addressed till date.

If SMTP is used to send messages, POP (post office protocol) was a standard for receiving emails. This protocol is used by email clients to retrieve messages from the mail server using a connection. Currently the third version, namely POP3 is in use. One drawback of POP is that it does not support offline retrieval of messages. This demerit has now been overcome, by the more capable IMAP (Internet message access protocol).

Talking of emails, we cannot do without mentioning email spam or bulk mail or commercial mail. With more than 85% of emails sent around the world being spam, it's very important to know the history of email spam. Most of us think that email spam is quite a recent phenomenon, but you will be surprised to know that the earliest documented spam was sent way back on May 3rd, 1978, by a DEC (Digital Equipment Corporation) employee using the SNDMSG application. He sent a marketing proposal to almost 400 ARPANET users, but the message was received by only 320 addresses, as that was the addressee limit of the application. Today, email spam is at its worst, with about 100 million spam mails being sent a day.

By the early 1990s, free and user-friendly email service providers had taken the industry by storm. Players like yahoo and hotmail were competing for the market share. It was this decade that not only saw the .com boom, but almost everyone wanted an email account. Today, there are more than 600 million email users across the globe and with newer players like google (gmail) and rediff entering the fray, the end user is set to be spoiled. Email is much older than ARPANet or the Internet. It was never invented; it evolved from very simple beginnings.

Early email was just a small advance on what we know these days as a file directory - it just put a message in another user's directory in a spot where they could see it when they logged in. Simple as that. Just like leaving a note on someone's desk.

Probably the first email system of this type was MAILBOX, used at Massachusetts Institute of Technology from 1965. Another early program to send messages on the same computer was called SNDMSG.

Some of the mainframe computers of this era might have had up to one hundred users -often they used what are called "dumb terminals" to access the mainframe from their work desks. Dumb terminals just connected to the mainframe - they had no storage or memory of their own, they did all their work on the remote mainframe computer.

Before internetworking began, therefore, email could only be used to send messages to various users of the same computer. Once computers began to talk to each other over networks, however, the problem became a little more complex - We needed to be able to put a message in an envelope and address it. To do this, we needed a means to indicate to whom letters should go that the electronic posties understood - just like the postal system, we needed a way to indicate an address.

This is why Ray Tomlinson is credited with inventing email in 1972. Like many of the Internet inventors, Tomlinson worked for Bolt Beranek and Newman as an ARPANET contractor. He picked the @ symbol from the computer keyboard to denote sending messages from one computer to another. So then, for anyone using Internet standards, it was simply a matter of nominating name-of-the-user@name-of-the-computer. Internet pioneer Jon Postel, who we will hear more of later, was one of the first users of the new system, and is credited with describing it as a "nice hack". It certainly was, and it has lasted to this day. Despite what the world wide web offers, email remains the most important application of the Internet and the most widely used facility it has. Now more than 600 million people internationally use email.

By 1974 there were hundreds of military users of email because ARPANET eventually encouraged it. Email became the saviour of Arpanet, and caused a radical shift in Arpa's purpose. Things developed rapidly from there. Larry Roberts invented some email folders for his boss so he could sort his mail, a big advance. In 1975 John Vital developed some software to organize email. By 1976 email had really taken off, and commercial packages began to appear. Within a couple of years, 75% of all ARPANET traffic was email. Email took us from Arpanet to the Internet. Here was something that ordinary people all over the world wanted to use. As Ray Tomlinson observed some years later about email, "any single development is stepping on the heels of the previous one and is so closely followed by the next that most advances are obscured. I think that few individuals will be remembered." That's true - to catalogue all the developments would be a huge task.

One of the first new developments when personal computers came on the scene was "offline readers". Offline readers allowed email users to store their email on their own personal computers, and then read it and prepare replies without actually being connected to the network - sort of like Microsoft Outlook can do today. This was particularly useful in parts of the world where telephone costs to the nearest email system were expensive. (often this involved international calls in the early days) With connection charges of many dollars a minute, it mattered to be able to prepare a reply without being connected to a telephone, and then get on the network to send it. It was also useful because the "offline" mode allowed for more friendly interfaces. Being connected direct to the host email system in this era of very few standards often resulted in delete keys and backspace keys not working, no capacity for text to "wrap around" on the screen of the users computer, and other such annoyances. Offline readers helped a lot.

The first important email standard was called SMTP, or simple message transfer protocol. SMTP was very simple and is still in use - however, as we will hear later in this series, SMTP was a fairly naïve protocol, and made no attempt to find out whether the person claiming to send a message was the person they purported to be. Forgery was (and still is) very easy in email addresses. These basic flaws in the protocol were later to be exploited by viruses and worms, and by security frauds and spammers forging identities. Some of these problems are still being addressed in 2004.

But as it developed email started to take on some pretty neat features. One of the first good commercial systems was Eudora, developed by Steve Dorner in 1988. Not long after Pegasus mail appeared. When Internet standards for email began to mature the POP (or Post Office Protocol) servers began to appear as a standard - before that each server was a little different. POP was an important standard to allow users to develop mail systems that would work with each other. These were the days of per-minute charges for email for individual dialup users. For most people on the Internet in those days email and email discussion groups were the main uses. These were many hundreds of these on a wide variety of topics, and as a body of newsgroups they became known as USENET.

With the World Wide Web, email started to be made available with friendly web interfaces by providers such as Yahoo and Hotmail. Usually this was without charge. Now that email was affordable, everyone wanted at least one email address, and the medium was adopted by not just millions, but hundreds of millions of people.

Email is a technology that includes passing and sending information from one place to another, using a computer and the Internet. It has proven beneficial in our personal as well as professional life. A majority of businesses around the globe use email as the most employed method of rapid and effective office communication. It is an important tool for corporate communication. From the time email has been used as a communication tool, businesses have experienced a rapid rise in productivity and reduction in expenses, and found new ways to improve their services. The advantages of email communication can be seen in large-scale as well as small-small industries and organizations. However, the advantages are not limited only to the business world. We also use emails in our day-to-day lives for sending and receiving messages from our friends and family members.

8.2.2 Operation

The diagram to the right shows a typical sequence of events that takes place when Alice composes a message using her mail user agent (MUA). She enters the e-mail address of her correspondent, and hits the "send" button.

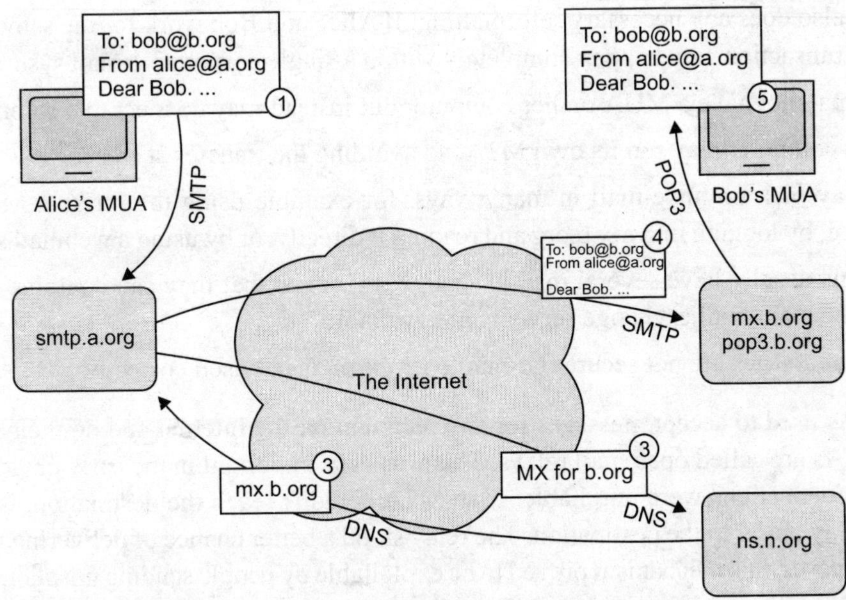

Figure 8.1 operation of Email

1. Her MUA formats the message in e-mail format and uses the Simple Mail Transfer Protocol (SMTP) to send the message to the local mail transfer agent (MTA), in this case smtp.a.org, run by Alice's internet service provider (ISP).
2. The MTA looks at the destination address provided in the SMTP protocol (not from the message header), in this case bob@b.org. An Internet e-mail address is a string of the form localpart@exampledomain. The part before the @ sign is the local part of the address, often the username of the recipient, and the part after the @ sign is a domain name or a fully qualified domain name. The MTA resolves a domain name to determine the fully qualified domain name of the mail exchange server in the Domain Name System (DNS).
3. The DNS server for the b.org domain, ns.b.org, responds with any MX records listing the mail exchange servers for that domain, in this case mx.b.org, a server run by Bob's ISP.
4. smtp.a.org sends the message to mx.b.org using SMTP, which delivers it to the mailbox of the user bob.
5. Bob presses the "get mail" button in his MUA, which picks up the message using the Post Office Protocol (POP3).

That sequence of events applies to the majority of e-mail users. However, there are many alternative possibilities and complications to the e-mail system:

- Alice or Bob may use a client connected to a corporate e-mail system, such as IBM Lotus Notes or Microsoft Exchange. These systems often have their own internal e-mail format and their clients typically communicate with the e-mail server using a vendor-specific, proprietary protocol. The server sends or receives e-mail via the Internet through the product's Internet mail gateway which also does any necessary reformatting. If Alice and Bob work for the same company, the entire transaction may happen completely within a single corporate e-mail system.

- Alice may not have a MUA on her computer but instead may connect to a webmail service.
- Alice's computer may run its own MTA, so avoiding the transfer at step 1.
- Bob may pick up his e-mail in many ways, for example using the Internet Message Access Protocol, by logging into mx.b.org and reading it directly, or by using a webmail service.
- Domains usually have several mail exchange servers so that they can continue to accept mail when the main mail exchange server is not available.
- E-mail messages are not secure if e-mail encryption is not used correctly.

Many MTAs used to accept messages for any recipient on the Internet and do their best to deliver them. Such MTAs are called open mail relays. This was very important in the early days of the Internet when network connections were unreliable. If an MTA couldn't reach the destination, it could at least deliver it to a relay closer to the destination. The relay stood a better chance of delivering the message at a later time. However, this mechanism proved to be exploitable by people sending unsolicited bulk e-mail and as a consequence very few modern MTAs are open mail relays, and many MTAs don't accept messages from open mail relays because such messages are very likely to be spam.

8.2.2.1 Message Format

The Internet e-mail message format is defined in RFC 5322 and a series of RFCs, RFC 2045 through RFC 2049, collectively called, Multipurpose Internet Mail Extensions, or MIME. Although as of July 13, 2005, RFC 2822 is technically a proposed IETF standard and the MIME RFCs are draft IETF standards, these documents are the standards for the format of Internet e-mail. Prior to the introduction of RFC 2822 in 2001, the format described by RFC 822 was the standard for Internet e-mail for nearly 20 years; it is still the official IETF standard. The IETF reserved the numbers 5321 and 5322 for the updated versions of RFC 2821 (SMTP) and RFC 2822, as it previously did with RFC 821 and RFC 822, honoring the extreme importance of these two RFCs. RFC 822 was published in 1982 and based on the earlier RFC 733. Internet e-mail messages consist of two major sections:

- Header - Structured into fields such as summary, sender, receiver, and other information about the e-mail.
- Body - The message itself as unstructured text; sometimes containing a signature block at the end. This is exactly the same as the body of a regular letter.

The header is separated from the body by a blank line.

8.2.2.2 Message Header

Each message has exactly one header, which is structured into fields. Each field has a name and a value. RFC 5322 specifies the precise syntax. Informally, each line of text in the header that begins with a printable character begins a separate field. The field name starts in the first character of the line and ends before the separator character ":". The separator is then followed by the field value (the "body" of the field). The value is continued onto subsequent lines if those lines have a space or tab as their first character. Field names and values are restricted to 7-bit ASCII characters. Non-ASCII values may be represented using MIME encoded words.

8.2.2.3 Header Fields

The message header should include at least the following fields:

- **From:** The e-mail address, and optionally the name of the author(s). In many e-mail clients not changeable except through changing account settings.
- **To:** The e-mail address(es), and optionally name(s) of the message's recipient(s). Indicates primary recipients (multiple allowed), for secondary recipients see Cc: and Bcc: below.
- **Subject:** A brief summary of the topic of the message. Certain abbreviations are commonly used in the subject, including "RE:" and "FW:".
- **Date:** The local time and date when the message was written. Like the From: field, many email clients fill this in automatically when sending. The recipient's client may then display the time in the format and time zone local to him/her.
- **Message-ID:** Also an automatically generated field; used to prevent multiple delivery and for reference in In-Reply-To: (see below).

Note that the To: field is not necessarily related to the addresses to which the message is delivered. The actual delivery list is supplied separately to the transport protocol, SMTP, which may or may not originally have been extracted from the header content. The "To:" field is similar to the addressing at the top of a conventional letter which is delivered according to the address on the outer envelope. Also note that the "From:" field does not have to be the real sender of the e-mail message. One reason is that it is very easy to fake the "From:" field and let a message seem to be from any mail address. It is possible to digitally sign e-mail, which is much harder to fake, but such signatures require extra programming and often external programs to verify.

Some ISPs do not relay e-mail claiming to come from a domain not hosted by them, but very few (if any) check to make sure that the person or even e-mail address named in the "From:" field is the one associated with the connection. Some ISPs apply e-mail authentication systems to e-mail being sent through their MTA to allow other MTAs to detect forged spam that might appear to come from them. RFC 3864 describes registration procedures for message header fields at the IANA; it provides for permanent and provisional message header field names, including also fields defined for MIME, netnews, and http, and referencing relevant RFCs. Common header fields for email include:

- **Bcc:** Blind Carbon Copy; addresses added to the SMTP delivery list but not (usually) listed in the message data, remaining invisible to other recipients.
- **Cc:** Carbon copy; Many e-mail clients will mark e-mail in your inbox differently depending on whether you are in the To: or Cc: list.
- **Content-Type:** Information about how the message is to be displayed, usually a MIME type.
- **In-Reply-To:** Message-ID of the message that this is a reply to. Used to link related messages together.

- **Precedence:** commonly with values "bulk", "junk", or "list"; used to indicate that automated "vacation" or "out of office" responses should not be returned for this mail, e.g. to prevent vacation notices from being sent to all other subscribers of a mailinglist.
- **Received:** Tracking information generated by mail servers that have previously handled a message, in reverse order (last handler first).
- **References:** Message-ID of the message that this is a reply to, and the message-id of the message the previous was reply a reply to, etc.
- **Reply-To:** Address that should be used to reply to the message.
- **Sender:** Address of the actual sender acting on behalf of the author listed in the From: field (secretary, list manager, etc.).

8.2.2.4 Message Body

E-mail was originally designed for 7-bit ASCII. Much e-mail software is 8-bit clean but must assume it will communicate with 7-bit servers and mail readers. The MIME standard introduced character set specifiers and two content transfer encodings to enable transmission of non-ASCII data: quoted printable for mostly 7 bit content with a few characters outside that range and base64 for arbitrary binary data. The 8BITMIME extension was introduced to allow transmission of mail without the need for these encodings but many mail transport agents still do not support it fully. In some countries, several encoding schemes coexist; as the result, by default, the message in a non-Latin alphabet language appears in non-readable form (the only exception is coincidence, when the sender and receiver use the same encoding scheme). Therefore, for international character sets, Unicode is growing in popularity.

8.2.2.5 Plain Text and HTML

Most modern graphic e-mail clients allow the use of either plain text or HTML for the message body at the option of the user. HTML e-mail messages often include an automatically-generated plain text copy as well, for compatibility reasons.

Advantages of HTML include the ability to include in-line links and images, set apart previous messages in block quotes, wrap naturally on any display, use emphasis such as underlines and italics, and change font styles. Disadvantages include the increased size of the email, privacy concerns about web bugs, abuse of HTML email as a vector for phishing attacks and the spread of malicious software.

Some web based Mailing lists recommend that all posts be made in plain-text for all the above reasons, but also because they have a significant number of readers using text-based e-mail clients such as Mutt. Some Microsoft e-mail clients allow rich formatting using RTF, but unless the recipient is guaranteed to have a compatible e-mail client this should be avoided.

In order to ensure that HTML sent in an email is rendered properly by the recipient's client software, an additional header must be specified when sending: "Content-type: text/html". Most email programs send this header automatically.

8.2.3 Servers and Client Applications

Messages are exchanged between hosts using the Simple Mail Transfer Protocol with software programs called mail transfer agents. Users can retrieve their messages from servers using standard protocols such as POP or IMAP, or, as is more likely in a large corporate environment, with a proprietary protocol specific to Lotus Notes or Microsoft Exchange Servers. Webmail interfaces allow users to access their mail with any standard web browser, from any computer, rather than relying on an e-mail client.

Mail can be stored on the client, on the server side, or in both places. Standard formats for mailboxes include Maildir and mbox. Several prominent e-mail clients use their own proprietary format and require conversion software to transfer e-mail between them. Accepting a message obliges an MTA to deliver it, and when a message cannot be delivered, that MTA must send a bounce message back to the sender, indicating the problem.

8.2.4 Filename Extensions

Upon reception of e-mail messages, e-mail client applications save message in operating system files in the file-system. Some clients save individual messages as separate files, while others use various database formats, often proprietary, for collective storage. A historical standard of storage is the mbox format. The specific format used is often indicated by special filename extensions:

eml Used by many e-mail clients including Microsoft Outlook Express, Windows Mail and Mozilla Thunderbird. The files are plain text in MIME format, containing the e-mail header as well as the message contents and attachments in one or more of several formats.

emlx

Used by Apple Mail.

msg

Used by Microsoft Office Outlook and Office Logic Groupware.

mbx

Used by Opera Mail, KMail, and Apple Mail based on the mbox format.

Some applications (like Apple Mail) leave attachments encoded in messages for searching while also saving separate copies of the attachments. Others separate attachments from messages and save them in a specific directory.

8.2.5 Problems

Email messages may have one or more attachments. Attachments serve the purpose of delivering binary or text files of unspecified size. In principle there is no technical intrinsic restriction in the SMTP protocol limiting the size or number of attachments. In practice, however, email service providers implement various limitations on the permissible size of files or the size of an entire message.

Furthermore, due to technical reasons, often a small attachment can increase in size when sent, which can be confusing to senders when trying to assess whether they can or cannot send a file by e-mail, and this can result in their message being rejected. As larger and larger file sizes are being created and traded, many users are either forced to upload and download their files using an FTP server, or more popularly, use online file sharing facilities or services, usually over web-friendly HTTP, in order to send and receive them.

8.2.5.1 Information Overload

A December 2007 New York Times blog post described information overload as "a $650 Billion Drag on the Economy", and the New York Times reported in April 2008 that "E-MAIL has become the bane of some people's professional lives" due to information overload, yet "none of the current wave of high-profile Internet start-ups focused on e-mail really eliminates the problem of e-mail overload because none helps us prepare replies". Technology investors reflect similar concerns. The email services are trying to provide maximum email inbox space to save the large size documents (attachments).

8.2.5.2 Spamming and Computer Viruses

The usefulness of e-mail is being threatened by four phenomena: e-mail bombardment, spamming, phishing, and e-mail worms. Spamming is unsolicited commercial (or bulk) e-mail. Because of the very low cost of sending e-mail, spammers can send hundreds of millions of e-mail messages each day over an inexpensive Internet connection. Hundreds of active spammers sending this volume of mail results in information overload for many computer users who receive voluminous unsolicited e-mail each day.

E-mail worms use e-mail as a way of replicating themselves into vulnerable computers. Although the first e-mail worm affected UNIX computers, the problem is most common today on the more popular Microsoft Windows operating system.

The combination of spam and worm programs results in users receiving a constant drizzle of junk e-mail, which reduces the usefulness of e-mail as a practical tool. A number of anti-spam techniques mitigate the impact of spam. In the United States, U.S. Congress has also passed a law, the Can Spam Act of 2003, attempting to regulate such e-mail. Australia also has very strict spam laws restricting the sending of spam from an Australian ISP, but its impact has been minimal since most spam comes from regimes that seem reluctant to regulate the sending of spam.

8.2.5.3 E-mail Spoofing

E-mail spoofing occurs when the header information of an email is altered to make the message appear to come from a known or trusted source. It is often used as a ruse to collect personal information.

8.2.5.4 E-mail Bombing

E-mail bombing is the intentional sending of large volumes of messages to a target address. The overloading of the target email address can render it unusable and can even cause the mail server to crash.

8.2.5.5 Privacy Concerns

E-mail privacy, without some security precautions, can be compromised because:

- e-mail messages are generally not encrypted.
- e-mail messages have to go through intermediate computers before reaching their destination, meaning it is relatively easy for others to intercept and read messages.
- many Internet Service Providers (ISP) store copies of e-mail messages on their mail servers before they are delivered. The backups of these can remain for up to several months on their server, despite deletion from the mailbox.
- the "Received:"-fields and other information in the e-mail can often identify the sender, preventing anonymous communication.

There are cryptography applications that can serve as a remedy to one or more of the above. For example, Virtual Private Networks or the Tor anonymity network can be used to encrypt traffic from the user machine to a safer network while GPG, PGP, SMEmail or S/MIME can be used for end-to-end message encryption, and SMTP STARTTLS or SMTP over Transport Layer Security/Secure Sockets Layer can be used to encrypt communications for a single mail hop between the SMTP client and the SMTP server.

Additionally, many mail user agents do not protect logins and passwords, making them easy to intercept by an attacker. Encrypted authentication schemes such as SASL prevent this. Finally, attached files share many of the same hazards as those found in peer-to-peer file sharing. Attached files may contain trojans or viruses.

8.2.5.6 Tracking of Sent Mail

The original SMTP mail service provides limited mechanisms for tracking a transmitted message, and none for verifying that it has been delivered or read. It requires that each mail server must either deliver it onward or return a failure notice (bounce message), but both software bugs and system failures can cause messages to be lost. To remedy this, the IETF introduced Delivery Status Notifications (delivery receipts) and Message Disposition Notifications (return receipts); however, these are not universally deployed in production. Many ISPs now deliberately disable non-delivery report (NDRs) and delivery receipts due to the activities of spammers:

- Delivery Reports can be used to verify whether an address exists and so is available to be spammed
- If the spammer uses a forged sender Email address (E-mail spoofing), then the innocent E-mail address that was used can be flooded with NDRs from the many invalid E-mail addresses the spammer may have attempted to mail. These NDRs then constitute spam from the ISP to the innocent user

There are a number of systems that allow the sender to see if messages have been opened.

8.2.6 Advantages of Email Communication for Business

Following are advantages of email communication for business:

8.2.6.1 Speedy Information Transfer

Email communication is certainly known for the rapid information transfer it provides. This speed enables businesses to operate at a faster pace and in an efficient manner. In larger companies, proper communication is very difficult to achieve. Email communication is definitely the correct resolution for this purpose. Corporates are able to receive accurate information in no time; as a result they can take well-informed decisions. Emails are generally used to let all company employees know about an occasion, announcement, event, or any such corporate information.

8.2.6.2 Low Cost

Cost savings is one of the most important advantages of email communication in business. The costs involved in maintaining an email system are generally very low. Small companies may use free online email services without spending on the expenses for incorporating separate email systems. They just need to pay the regular Internet connection charges. As companies mainly use emails, the expenses related to postage and telephones are low.

8.2.6.3 Security

Email communication is evidently the most secure method of communication compared to letters and faxes. If letters or paper documents fall in the wrong hands, they may be misused which might prove harmful to the business. If faxes containing confidential information are left unattended on the fax machine, they may also be used in an adverse manner. Emails ensure the security of information, records, and details.

8.2.6.4 Effective Marketing Tool

Email communication enables marketing businesses to reach a larger number of customers in a more economical and effective way. It also enables companies to quickly respond to consumer a query, which adds up to customer loyalty. Marketing advertisements can be sent to a specific customer base or prospective clients and consumers, which is known as email marketing. This results in rapid dispersal of product advertisements and marketing, which in turn has a positive effect on sales. It reduces the time between the commencement of the marketing campaign and consumer purchases.

8.2.6.5 Decreased Managerial Layers

Emails are a good way to approach anyone in an organization, be it the company vice president or just an executive. You do not need to go to the manager and confirm if you can contact the top management. You can just send an email to the person you want to contact. A CEO receiving feedback and suggestions from executives would certainly create a possibility of creativity and innovation.

8.2.6.6 Email is Inexpensive

Compared to telephone calls, faxes, or over night courier service, Email is less expensive.

8.2.6.7 Email Is Easy To Filter

The subject line on an Email makes it easy to prioritize messages. The reader can identify critical correspondence quickly and dealt with it immediately. Unlike regular mail which needs to be opened and reviewed, or voice mail which requires you to either listen to or scan all your messages for those that require immediate attention.

8.2.6.8 Transmission is Secure and Reliable

The level of security in transmitting Email messages is very high, and the industry continues to strive to develop even tighter security levels. Email is private. Often telephone and fax messages are not. If the address information is correct, rarely does an Email go astray. Fax machines can be out of order or out of paper and this prevents an important message from being delivered in a timely manner. Email is an Internet marketing tool that is fast, easy to use, inexpensive and effective. Email levels the playing field between the big corporations and small businesses. No longer is it just the big boys who have the resources to access the big advertising houses. Anyone can get their word out there using Email as the method of delivering the message.

8.2.7 Advantages Of Email

The benefits of e-mail are huge in number.

- **Easy to use:** E-mail frees us from the tedious task of managing data of daily use. It helps us to manage our contacts, send mails quickly, maintain our mail history, store the required information, etc.
- **Speed:** The e-mail is delivered instantly, anywhere across the globe. No other service matches the e-mail in terms of speed.
- **Easy to prioritize:** Since the mails have subject lines, it is easy to prioritize them and ignore unwanted mails.
- **Reliable and secure:** Constant efforts are being taken to improve the security in electronic mails. Thus making it one of the secured ways of communication.
- **Informal and conversational:** The language used in e-mails is generally simple and thus makes the communication informal. Sending and receiving e-mails takes less time, so it can be used as a tool for interaction.
- **Easier for reference:** When one needs to reply to a mail, there is a provision in the mailing system to attach the previous mails as references. This refreshes the recipient's knowledge, on what he is reading.
- **Automated e-mails:** It is possible to send automated e-mails using special programs like the autoresponders. The autoresponders reply back to the sender with generalized pre-written text messages.
- **Fast:** Message to send? Done, under a second! Email is by far the fastest form of written communication.
- **Global:** Web based email means you can access your messages anywhere online. Going oversees? Before you go, mail yourself a copy of your passport number, travel insurance details or your accommodation details.

- **Good for the planet:** Actually the advantages and disadvantages of email are clear here. Computers themselves aren't 'green', but email offsets some of the damage by reducing the environmental cost of contact.
- **Environment friendly:** Postal mails use paper as a medium to send letters. Electronic mail thus, saves a lot of trees from being axed. It also saves fuel needed in transportation.
- **Use of graphics:** Colorful greeting cards and interesting pictures can be sent through e-mails. This adds value to the e-mail service.
- **Advertising tool:** Many individuals and companies are using e-mails to advertise their products, services, etc.

8.2.8 Disadvantages of Email

The e-mails, though beneficial in our day-to-day life, has got its own drawbacks that are off late coming to the fore.

- **Viruses:** These are computer programs having the potential to harm a computer system. These programs copy themselves and further infect the computer. The recipient needs to scan the mails, as viruses are transmitted through them and have the potential to harm computer systems.
- **Spam:** E-mails when used to send unsolicited messages and unwanted advertisements create nuisance and is termed as Spam. Checking and deleting these unwanted mails can unnecessarily consume a lot of time, and it has become necessary to block or filter the unwanted e-mails by means of spam filters. Spamming includes, sending hoax e-mails. E-mail spoofing is another common practice, used for spamming. Spoofing involves deceiving the recipient by altering the e-mail headers or the addresses from which the mail is sent.
- **Hacking:** The act of breaking into computer security is termed as hacking. After the e-mail is sent and before it is received by the desired recipient, it "bounces" between servers located in different parts of the world. Hence, the e-mail can be hacked by a professional hacker.
- **Misinterpretation:** One has to be careful while posting any kind of content through an e-mail. If typed in a hurry, the matter could be misinterpreted.
- **Lengthy mails:** If the mail is too long and not properly presented the reader may lose interest in reading it.
- **Not suitable for business:** Since the content posted via e-mails is considered informal, there is a chance of business documents going unnoticed. Thus, urgent transactions and especially those requiring signatures are not managed through e-mails.
- **Crowded inbox:** Over a period of time, the e-mail inbox may get crowded with mails. It becomes difficult for the user to manage such a huge chunk of mails.
- **Need to check the inbox regularly:** In order to be updated, one has to check his e-mail account regularly.

8.3 TELNET

TELNET is a network protocol used on the Internet or local area networks to provide a bidirectional interactive text-oriented communications facility via a virtual terminal connection. User data is interspersed in-band with TELNET control information in an 8-bit byte oriented data connection over the Transmission Control Protocol (TCP).

Telnet was developed in 1969 beginning with RFC 15, extended in RFC 854, and standardized as Internet Engineering Task Force (IETF) Internet Standard STD 8, one of the first Internet standards. Historically, telnet provided access to a command-line interface (usually, of an operating system) on a remote host. Most network equipment and operating systems with a TCP/IP stack support a Telnet service for remote configuration (including systems based on Windows NT). Because of security issues with Telnet, its use for this purpose has waned in favor of SSH.

The term telnet may also refer to the software that implements the client part of the protocol. Telnet client applications are available for virtually all computer platforms. Telnet is also used as a verb. To telnet means to establish a connection with the Telnet protocol, either with command line client or with a programmatic interface. For example, a common directive might be: "To change your password, telnet to the server, login and run the passwd command." Most often, a user will be telnetting to a Unix-like server system or a network device such as a router and obtain a login prompt to a command line text interface or a character-based full-screen manager.

8.3.1 History and Standards

Telnet is a client-server protocol, based on a reliable connection-oriented transport. Typically this protocol is used to establish a connection to Transmission Control Protocol (TCP) port number 23, where a Telnet server application (telnet) is listening. Telnet, however, predates TCP/IP and was originally run over Network Control Program (NCP) protocols.

Before March 5, 1973, Telnet was an ad-hoc protocol with no official definition. Essentially, it used an 8-bit channel to exchange 7-bit ASCII data. Any byte with the high bit set was a special Telnet character. On March 5, 1973, a Telnet protocol standard was defined at UCLA with the publication of two NIC documents: Telnet Protocol Specification, NIC #15372, and Telnet Option Specifications, NIC #15373. Because of "negotiable options" protocol architecture, many extensions were made for it, some of which have been adopted as Internet standards, IETF documents STD 27 through STD 32.

8.3.2 Security

When Telnet was initially developed in 1969, most users of networked computers were in the computer departments of academic institutions, or at large private and government research facilities. In this environment, security was not nearly as much of a concern as it became after the bandwidth explosion of the 1990s. The rise in the number of people with access to the Internet, and by extension, the number of people attempting to crack other people's servers made encrypted alternatives much more of a necessity. Experts in computer security, such as SANS Institute, recommend that the use of Telnet for remote logins should be discontinued under all normal circumstances, for the following reasons:

- Telnet, by default, does not encrypt any data sent over the connection (including passwords), and so it is often practical to eavesdrop on the communications and use the password later for malicious purposes; anybody who has access to a router, switch, hub or gateway located on the network between the two hosts where Telnet is being used can intercept the packets passing by and obtain login and password information (and whatever else is typed) with any of several common utilities like tcpdump and Wireshark.
- Most implementations of Telnet have no authentication that would ensure communication is carried out between the two desired hosts and not intercepted in the middle.
- Commonly used Telnet daemons have several vulnerabilities discovered over the years.

These security-related shortcomings have seen the usage of the Telnet protocol drop rapidly, especially on the public Internet, in favor of the Secure Shell (SSH) protocol, first released in 1995. SSH provides much of the functionality of telnet, with the addition of strong encryption to prevent sensitive data such as passwords from being intercepted, and public key authentication, to ensure that the remote computer is actually who it claims to be. As has happened with other early Internet protocols, extensions to the Telnet protocol provide Transport Layer Security (TLS) security and Simple Authentication and Security Layer (SASL) authentication that address the above issues. However, most Telnet implementations do not support these extensions; and there has been relatively little interest in implementing these as SSH is adequate for most purposes. The main advantage of TLS-Telnet would be the ability to use certificate-authority signed server certificates to authenticate a server host to a client that does not yet have the server key stored. In SSH, there is a weakness in that the user must trust the first session to a host when it has not yet acquired the server key.

Telnet was developed in 1969 to aid in remote connectivity between computers over a network. Telnet can connect to a remote machine that on a network and is port listening. Most common ports to which one can connect to through telnet are:

Port 21 - File Transfer Protocol

Port 22 - SSH Remote Login Protocol

Port 23 - Telnet Server

Port 25 - Simple Mail Transfer Protocol (SMTP)

Port 53 - Domain Name Server (DNS)

Port 69 - Trivial File Transfer Protocol (TFTP)

Port 70 - Gopher

Port 80 - Hyper Text Transfer Protocol (HTTP)

Port 110 - Post Office Protocol 3 (POP3)

Telnet can be used to connect to virtually any machine that listens on ports. In other words, you can connect to any machine that has certain ports open. Once connected to a machine, you need to issue unix based commands to interact with the remote service. For example, a user don't need to login, check and send mails only through his email service provider's interface but this can be achieved using simple telnet commands. It is because of this reason that many hackers can send spoofed emails or access information such as which services are running on the remote machine. This is also called banner grabbing or daemon tracking. Black hat hackers can also use telnet to sniff network packets which might contain sensitive information such as usernames and passwords. This is achieved by using telnet and network utilities such as tcpdump and wireshark.

Telnet client and server functionality comes built-in in most operating systems. However, there are several third-party applications like putty client that enable remote connectivity. A user can connect to a remote machine through several access modes such as raw access, SSH access, etc. SSH mode offers encryption and security and hence can prevent eavesdropping by hackers. This is by far the most secure way of connecting to a machine. However, it is necessary that the remote machine supports SSH login to make use of the encryption and security features.

On windows machines, telnet client can simply be started by issuing the telnet command in windows command shell. The following example would help you connect to a remote machine on the HTTP Port 80 and issue a GET command which would fetch a file as your web browser does it behind scenes:

Command Prompt> Telnet

Command Prompt> open (somedomain.com or ip address) 80

At this stage, you would be connected to somedomain.com or ip address on port 80 and the daemon that is running on port 80 (most probably HTTP Server) would be waiting for HTTP requests.

GET / HTTP/1.1

host:

Issuing the command above would make the HTTP Server return the file requested; in this case it would be the default file at the root location. Most applications and embedded devices make use of the telnet technology to connect to remote server machines and provide end user functionality. The most common use of telnet stands to enable remote authentication and access.

8.3.3 Telnet Commands

The telnet commands allow you to communicate with a remote computer that is using the Telnet protocol. You can run telnet without parameters in order to enter the telnet context, indicated by the Telnet prompt (telnet>). From the Telnet prompt, use the following commands to manage a computer running Telnet Client.

The tlntadmn commands allow you to remotely manage a computer running Telnet Server. These commands are run from the command prompt. Used without parameters, tlntadmn displays local server settings.

To use telnet commands at the **Telnet** prompt

To start **Telnet** Client and to enter the Telnet prompt

Syntax

telnet [\\RemoteServer]

Parameters

\\ **RemoteServer :** Specifies the name of the server to which you want to connect.

/? **: Displays** help at the command prompt.

Remarks

- Used without parameters, telnet starts Telnet Client.
- When you are at the Telnet prompt, you must use Telnet commands.

To stop Telnet Client

Syntax

quit

Parameters

none

Remarks

- You can abbreviate this command to q.

To connect Telnet Client to a remote computer

Syntax

open [\\RemoteServer] [Port]

Parameters

\\ **RemoteServer:** Specifies the name of the server that you want to manage. If you do not specify a server, the local server is assumed.

Port: Specifies the port that you want to use. If you do not specify a port, the default port is assumed.

Remarks

- You can abbreviate this command to o.

Examples

To connect to remote server Redmond through port number 44, type:

- redmond 44

To disconnect Telnet Client from a remote computer

Syntax

close [\\RemoteServer]

Parameters

\\ **RemoteServer:** Specifies the name of the server that you want to manage. If you do not specify a server, the local server is assumed.

Remarks

- You can abbreviate this command to c.

Examples

To disconnect from remote server Redmond, type:

c redmond 44

To set Telnet Client options

Syntax

set [\\RemoteServer] [ntlm] [localecho] [term {ansi | vt100 | vt52 | vtnt}] [escape Character] [logfile FileName] [logging] [bsasdel] [crlf] [delasbs] [mode {console | stream}] [?]

Parameters

\\ **RemoteServer:** Specifies the name of the server that you want to manage. If you do not specify a server, the local server is assumed.

ntlm: Turns on NTLM authentication if it is available on the remote server.

localecho: Turns on local echo.

term { ansi | vt100 | vt52 | vtnt }: Sets the terminal to the specified type.

escape Character: Sets the escape character. The escape character can be a single character, or it can be a combination of the CTRL key plus a character. To set a control-key combination, hold down CTRL while you type the character that you want to assign.

logfile FileName: Sets the file to be used for logging Telnet activity. The log file must be on your local computer. Logging begins automatically when you set this option.

logging: Turns on logging. If no log file is set, an error message appears.

bsasdel: Sets **BACKSPACE** to be sent as delete.

crlf: Sets the new line mode, which causes the **ENTER** key to send 0x0D, 0x0A.

delasbs: Sets **DELETE** to be sent as backspace.

mode { console | stream }: Sets the mode of operation.

? : Allows you to view the complete syntax for this command.

Remarks

- To turn off an option that was previously set, at the Telnet prompt, type:

unset [Option]

- To set the escape character, type:

e Character

- On non-English versions of Telnet, the codeset Option is available. Codeset Option sets the current code set to an option, which can be any one of the following: Shift JIS, Japanese EUC, JIS Kanji, JIS Kanji (78), DEC Kanji, NEC Kanji. You should set the same code set on the remote computer.

To send Telnet Client commands

Syntax

send [\\RemoteServer] **[ao] [ayt] [esc] [ip] [synch] [?]**

Parameters

\\ RemoteServer : Specifies the name of the server that you want to manage. If you do not specify a server, the local server is assumed.

ao : Aborts output command.

ayt : Sends an "Are you there?" command.

esc : Sends the current escape character.

ip : Interrupts the process command.

synch : Performs the Telnet sync operation.

? : Allows you to view the complete syntax for this command.

To view the current settings for the Telnet client

Syntax

display

Parameters

none

Remarks

- The display command lists the currently operating parameters for the Telnet client. If you are in a Telnet session (in other words, if you are connected to a Telnet server), you can exit the Telnet session to modify the parameters by pressing CTRL+]. To return to the Telnet session, press ENTER.

To use tlntadmn commands at the command prompt

To administer a computer running Telnet Server

Syntax

tlntadmn [\\RemoteServer] [start] [stop] [pause] [continue]

Parameters

\\ **RemoteServer:** Specifies the name of the server that you want to manage. If you do not specify a server, the local server is assumed.

start : Starts Telnet Server.

stop : Stops Telnet Server.

pause : Interrupts Telnet Server.

continue : Resumes Telnet Server.

/? : Displays help at the command prompt.

Remarks

- You can remotely administer a computer running Telnet Server using the tlntadmn commands if both computers are running Windows XP. You can not use the tlntadmn commands to remotely administer a computer running Windows 2000 and Telnet Server from a computer that is running Windows XP.

To administer Telnet sessions

Syntax

tlntadmn [\\RemoteServer] [-s] [-k{SessionID | all}] [-m {SessionID | all} "Message"]

Parameters

\\ **RemoteServer :** Specifies the name of the server that you want to manage. If you do not specify a server, the local server is assumed.

-s : Displays active Telnet sessions.

-k { SessionID | all } : Terminates sessions. Type the session ID to terminate a specific session, or type all to terminate all sessions.

-m { SessionID | all } " Message " : Sends a message to one or more sessions. Type the session ID to send a message to a specific session, or type all to send a message to all sessions. Type the message that you want to send between quotation marks (that is, "Message").

/? : Displays help at the command prompt.

Remarks

- You can remotely administer a computer running Telnet Server using the tlntadmn commands if both computers are running Windows XP. You can not use the tlntadmn commands to remotely administer a computer running Windows 2000 and Telnet Server from a computer that is running Windows XP.

To set logging options on a computer running Telnet Server

Syntax

tlntadmn [\\RemoteServer] config [auditlocation={eventlog | file | both}] [audit=[{+|-}admin][{+|-}user][{+ | -}fail]]

Parameters

\\ RemoteServer : Specifies the name of the server that you want to manage. If you do not specify a server, the local server is assumed.

auditlocation= { eventlog | file | both } : Specifies whether to send event information to Event Viewer, to a file, or to both.

audit= [{ + | - } admin][{ + | - } user][{ + | - } fail] : Specifies which events you want to audit (administrative logon events, user logon events, or failed logon attempts). To audit events of a particular type, type a plus sign (+) before that event type. To stop auditing events of a particular type, type a minus sign (-) before that event type.

/? : Displays help at the command prompt.

Remarks

- You can remotely administer a computer running Telnet Server using the tlntadmn commands if both computers are running Windows XP. You can not use the tlntadmn commands to remotely administer a computer running Windows 2000 and Telnet Server from a computer that is running Windows XP.
- If you specify where to send event information without specifying which type or types of information to audit, only information about administrative logon events will be audited and sent to the location that you specified.

Examples

To send event information to Event Viewer, type:

tlntadmn config auditlocation=eventlog

To audit administrative logon events and failed logon attempts, type:

tlntadmn config audit=+admin +fail

To set the default domain on a computer running Telnet Server

Syntax

tlntadmn [\\RemoteServer] config [dom=DomainName]

Parameters

\\ RemoteServer : Specifies the name of the server that you want to manage. If you do not specify a server, the local server is assumed.

dom= DomainName : Specifies the domain that you want to make the default domain.

/? : Displays help at the command prompt.

Remarks

- You can remotely administer a computer running Telnet Server using the tlntadmn commands if both computers are running Windows XP. You can not use the tlntadmn commands to remotely administer a computer running Windows 2000 and Telnet Server from a computer that is running Windows XP.

Examples

To make Redmond the default domain on your local server, type:

tlntadmn config dom=Redmond

To map the Alt key on a computer running Telnet Server

Syntax

tlntadmn [\\RemoteServer] config [ctrlakeymap={yes | no}]

Parameters

\\ RemoteServer : Specifies the name of the server that you want to manage. If you do not specify a server, the local server is assumed.

ctrlakeymap= { yes | no } : Specifies whether you want Telnet Server to interpret CTRL+A as ALT. Type yes to map the shortcut key, or type no to prevent mapping.

/? : Displays help at the command prompt.

Remarks

- You can remotely administer a computer running Telnet Server using the tlntadmn commands if both computers are running Windows XP. You can not use the tlntadmn commands to remotely administer a computer running Windows 2000 and Telnet Server from a computer that is running Windows XP.
- If you do not map the ALT key, Telnet Server does not send the ALT key to applications that might rely on that key.

To set the maximum number of connections on a computer running Telnet Server

Syntax

tlntadmn [\\RemoteServer] config [maxconn=PositiveInteger]

Parameters

\\ RemoteServer : Specifies the name of the server that you want to manage. If you do not specify a server, the local server is assumed.

maxconn= PositiveInteger : Sets the maximum number of connections. You must specify this number with a positive integer that is smaller than 10 million.

/? : Displays help at the command prompt.

Remarks

- You can remotely administer a computer running Telnet Server using the tlntadmn commands if both computers are running Windows XP. You can not use the tlntadmn commands to remotely administer a computer running Windows 2000 and Telnet Server from a computer that is running Windows XP.

To set the maximum number of failed logon attempts on a computer running Telnet Server

Syntax

tlntadmn [\\RemoteServer] config [maxfail=PositiveInteger]

Parameters

\\ RemoteServer : Specifies the name of the server that you want to manage. If you do not specify a server, the local server is assumed.

maxfail= PositiveInteger : Sets the maximum number of failed logon attempts that a user is allowed. You must specify this number with a positive integer that is smaller than 100.

/? : Displays help at the command prompt.

Remarks

- You can remotely administer a computer running Telnet Server using the tlntadmn commands if both computers are running Windows XP. You can not use the tlntadmn commands to remotely administer a computer running Windows 2000 and Telnet Server from a computer that is running Windows XP.

To set the mode of operation on a computer running Telnet Server

Syntax

tlntadmn [\\RemoteServer] config [mode={console | stream}]

Parameters

\\ RemoteServer : Specifies the name for the server that you want to manage. If you do not specify a server, the local server is assumed.

mode= { console | stream } : Specifies the mode of operation.

/? : Displays help at the command prompt.

Remarks

- You can remotely administer a computer running Telnet Server using the tlntadmn commands if both computers are running Windows XP. You can not use the tlntadmn commands to remotely administer a computer running Windows 2000 and Telnet Server from a computer that is running Windows XP.

To set the Telnet port on a computer running Telnet Server

Syntax

tlntadmn [\\RemoteServer] config [port=IntegerValue]

Parameters

\\ RemoteServer : Specifies the name of the server that you want to manage. If you do not specify a server, the local server is assumed.

port= IntegerValue : Sets the Telnet port. You must specify the port with an integer smaller than 1,024.

/? : Displays help at the command prompt.

Remarks

- You can remotely administer a computer running Telnet Server using the tlntadmn commands if both computers are running Windows XP. You can not use the tlntadmn commands to remotely administer a computer running Windows 2000 and Telnet Server from a computer that is running Windows XP.

To set the methods of authentication on a computer running Telnet Server

Syntax

tlntadmn [\\RemoteServer] config [sec=[{+ | -}ntlm][{+ | -}passwd]]

Parameters

\\ RemoteServer : Specifies the name of the server that you want to manage. If you do not specify a server, the local server is assumed.

sec= [{ + | - } ntlm][{ + | - } passwd] : Specifies whether you want to use NTLM, a password, or both to authenticate logon attempts. To use a particular type of authentication, type a plus sign (+) before that type of authentication. To prevent using a particular type of authentication, type a minus sign (-) before that type of authentication.

/? : Displays help at the command prompt.

Remarks

- You can remotely administer a computer running Telnet Server using the tlntadmn commands if both computers are running Windows XP. You can not use the tlntadmn commands to remotely administer a computer running Windows 2000 and Telnet Server from a computer that is running Windows XP.
- NTLM is the authentication protocol for transactions between two computers where one or both computers is running Windows NT 4.0 or an earlier version. In addition, NTLM is the authentication protocol for computers that are not participating in a domain, such as stand-alone servers and workgroups.

To set the time-out for idle sessions on a computer running Telnet Server

Syntax

tlntadmn [\\RemoteServer] config [timeout=hh:mm:ss]

Parameters

\\ RemoteServer **:** Specifies the name of the server that you want to manage. If you do not specify a server, the local server is assumed.

timeout= hh : mm : ss **:** Sets the time-out period in hours, minutes, and seconds.

/? : Displays help at the command prompt.

Remarks

- You can remotely administer a computer running Telnet Server using the tlntadmn commands if both computers are running Windows XP. You can not use the tlntadmn commands to remotely administer a computer running Windows 2000 and Telnet Server from a computer that is running Windows XP.

Remarks

- To switch from Telnet Client to command mode, at the Telnet prompt, press CTRL+]. To switch back to Telnet Client, press ENTER.

COMMAND	DESCRIPTION
open	Use **open hostname portnumber** to establish a Telnet connection to a host.
close	Use the **close** command to close an existing Telnet connection.
display	Use the **display** command to view the current settings for the Telnet client. The display command lists the current operating parameters. If you are in a Telnet session (connected to a Telnet server), to modify the parameters, press CTRL+]. This escapes from the Telnet session. (To return to the Telnet session, press ENTER.) The following operating parameters are available:

COMMAND	DESCRIPTION
	• **WILL AUTH (NTLM Authentication)** • **WONT AUTH** • **WILL TERM TYPE** • **WONT TERM TYPE** • **LOCALECHO off** • **LOCALECHO on**
quit	Use the quit command to exit from Telnet.
set	Use the **set** command to set the terminal type for the connection, turn on local echo, set authentication to NTLM, set the escape character, and set up logging.
	• **SET NTLM turns on NTLM.** While you are using NTLM Authentication, you are not prompted for a logon name and password when connecting from a remote computer. • **SET LOCALECHO** turns on local echoing. • **SET TERM {ANSI|VT100|VT52|VTNT}** sets the terminal type to the appropriate terminal type. Use the VT100 terminal type if you are running normal command-line applications. Use the VTNT terminal type if you are running advanced command-line applications, such as **edit.** • **ESCAPE** Character sets the key sequence to use for switching from session to command mode. For example, to set CTRL+P as your escape character, type **set escape,** press CTRL+P, and then press ENTER. • **LOGFILE** FileName sets the file to be used for logging Telnet activity. The log file must be on your local computer. Logging begins automatically when you set this option. • **LOGGING** turns on logging. If no log file is set, an error message is displayed.
unset	Use unset to turn off local echo or to set authentication to logon/password prompt. • **UNSET NLM** turns off NLM. • **UNSET LOCALECHO** turns off local echoing.
status	Use the status command to determine whether the Telnet client is connected.
CTRL+]	Press CTRL+] to move to the Telnet command prompt from a connected session.
enter	Use the **enter** command from the command prompt to go to the connected session (if it exists).
?/help	Prints Help information.

CODE	COMMAND	DESCRIPTION
240	SE	End of subnegotiation parameters.
241	NOP	No operation.
242	Data Mark	The data stream portion of a Synch. This should always be accompanied by a TCP Urgent notification.
243	Break	NVT character BRK.
244	Interrupt Process	The function IP.
245	Abort output	The function AO.
246	Are You There	The function AYT.
247	Erase character	The function EC.
248	Erase Line	The function EL.
249	Go ahead	The GA signal.
250	SB	Indicates that what follows is subnegotiation of the indicated option.
251	WILL (option code)	Indicates the desire to begin performing, or confirmation that you are now performing, the indicated option.
252	WON'T (option code)	Indicates the refusal to perform, or continue performing, the indicated option.
253	DO (option code)	Indicates the request that the other party perform, or confirmation that you are expecting the other party to perform, the indicated option.
254	DON'T (option code)	Indicates the demand that the other party stop performing, or confirmation that you are no longer expecting the other party to perform, the indicated option.
255	IAC	Data Byte 255.

Telnet is the Internet protocol for connecting to a remote computer. It is a terminal emulator, a piece of software used to login from a local computer to a remote computer. It is a tool that allows you to remotely connect into other computers and access them just as if you were sitting directly in front of them. The majority of computers accessible via telnet are Unix-based systems. There are a few things you need to remember about them, in particular, and computer systems, in general:

- Unlike your PC, most Unix systems are case-sensitive so pay close attention to case, especially in file names.
- There's no way around it - you'll have to learn some basic Unix commands.

8.3.4 What are the Advantages of Telnet?

The big advantage of telnet is that it saves you are able to use another computer elsewhere in the world without actually being there. You are actually connected to that machine. You can use other computers, fix other people's computer problems, play games with other people (MUD games -- see your textbook for a discussion), etc.,all without leaving your seat.

8.3.5 Using Telnet

You need a special application to telnet from a Mac or a PC. You need to know is the hostname or the IP address of the computer that you want to connect to. Using telnet is as simple as launching the telnet application, and then opening a connection to a host (usually under the File menu). Once the connection is established, you can interact with the remote computer directly by typing commands.

Sometimes, when you connect to a remote computer, you will be asked for your "terminal type", or what sort of terminal you are emulating. The safest response to this is VT100, which is a type of dumb terminal made by DEC in the 1970s, and which almost all telnet applications support. Telnet connections can be expressed as URLs, as well. When Netscape sees a URL like this one:

telnet://pac.carl.org

..it will launch your telnet application. (provided you have one and Netscape has it listed in the Applications and Directories section of the Preferences). (check Browser)

Example 1: **Menu Driven Telnet**

```
pac.carl.org

WELCOME TO CSI.CARL.ORG (PORT $ZTCO *23 WINDOW $ZT2.*PTUFF7W)
TELSERV - T9553D40 - (20FEB98) - (IPMACT)


Available Services:

PAC       EXIT
Enter Choice> pac
Welcome to the CARL system
Please identify your terminal. Choices are:
1.ADM (all)
2.APPLE,IBM
3.TANDEM
4.TELE-914
5.VT100
6.WYSE 50
7.ZENTEC
8.HARDCOPY
9.IBM 316x
Use HARDCOPY if your terminal type isn't listed..
SELECT LINE #:
```

Example 2 - **Command Driven Telnet**

```
MC(A1)

     Authorized users are welcome to MC, Mesa's VAX 4000

Username: PETERSON_J
Password:

     Welcome to VAX/VMS V5.5-2H4

   Last interactive login on Sunday, 12-SEP-1999 20:30
   Last non interactive login on Wednesday,  4-NOV-1998 06:20

   The system has been up for 28 Days, 8 Hours, 27 Minutes.


  12-SEP-1999 21:08:54


MC $
```

Notice that Telnet is completely menu (example 1) or command driven (example 2) -- no graphics all text.

8.3.6 Types of Services Available Via Telnet?

Library catalogues are a very common one. You would also use telnet to access text-only databases, Internet-connected bulletin boards, and various text-based games and real-time services. There are two types of software that let you make a Telnet connection.

- NCSA Telnet, Better Telnet, MacSampson
- X-Window Software

With Telnet

- **Advantages**
  - Fast
  - Cheap
  - Can run on all computers (even Newton)
- **Disadvantages**
  - Only text and numbers displayed (VT100, VT220 connection)
  - no graphics, (limited Tektronix 4014 graphics)
  - no colors
  - no mouse (no menus, check boxes, etc)

Telnet is especially useful if you are dialing in over a modem. You are not sending lots of fancy graphics over the slow connection, so your response time is much faster. Many programs work perfectly well over a VT-100 Telnet connection. There are also many programs (Molecular Modeling) that require a more sophisticated connection, and for that, you need X-Windows

- **Advantages**
  - Mac/Windows-like user interface (mouse, menus, windows, etc)
  - Displays Graphics
- **Disadvantages**
  - slow over a modem
  - may not be free requires faster computer, more memory

8.4 FTP

File Transfer Protocol (FTP) is a standard network protocol used to copy a file from one host to another over a TCP/IP-based network, such as the Internet. FTP is built on client-server architecture and utilizes separate control and data connections between the client and server. FTP is used with user-based password authentication or with anonymous user access. Applications were originally interactive command-line tools with standardized command syntax, but graphical user interfaces have been developed for all desktop operating systems in use today

8.4.1 History

The original specification for the File Transfer Protocol was written by Abhay Bhushan and published as RFC 114 on 16 April 1971 and later replaced by RFC 765 (June 1980) and RFC 959 (October 1985), the current specification. Several proposed standards amend RFC 959, for example RFC 2228 (June 1997) proposes security extensions and RFC 2428 (September 1998) adds support for IPv6 and defines a new type of passive mode.

8.4.2 Protocol Overview

The protocol is specified in RFC 959. A client makes a TCP connection to the server's port 21. This connection, called the control connection, remains open for the duration of the session, with a second connection, called the data connection, opened by the server from its port 20 to a client port (specified in the negotiation dialog) as required to transfer file data. The control connection is used for session administration (i.e., commands, identification, passwords) exchanged between the client and server using a telnet-like protocol. For example "RETR filename" would transfer the specified file from the server to the client. Due to this two-port structure, FTP is considered an out-of-band, as opposed to an in-band protocol such as HTTP.

The server responds on the control connection with three digit status codes in ASCII with an optional text message, for example "200" (or "200 OK.") means that the last command was successful. The numbers represent the code number and the optional text represent explanations (i.e., <OK>) or needed parameters (i.e., <Need account for storing file>). A file transfer in progress over the data connection can be aborted using an interrupt message sent over the control connection.

FTP can be run in active or passive modes, which determine how the data connection is established. In active mode, the client sends the server the IP address and port number on which the client will listen and the server initiates the TCP connection. In situations where the client is behind a firewall and unable to accept incoming TCP connections, passive mode may be used, where the client sends a PASV command to the server and receives an IP address and port number in return, which the client uses to open the data connection to the server. Both modes were updated in September 1998 to add support for IPv6 and made some other changes to passive mode, making it extended passive mode. While transferring data over the network, four data representations can be used:

- **ASCII mode:** used for text. Data is converted, if needed, from the sending host's character representation to "8-bit ASCII" before transmission, and (again, if necessary) to the receiving host's character representation. As a consequence, this mode is inappropriate for files that contain numeric data in binary, floating point or binary coded decimal form.
- **Image mode (commonly called Binary mode):** the sending machine sends each file byte for byte and as such the recipient stores the byte stream as it receives it. (Image mode support has been recommended for all implementations of FTP).
- **EBCDIC mode:** use for plain text between hosts using the EBCDIC character set. This mode is otherwise like ASCII mode.
- **Local mode:** Allows two computers with identical setups to send data in a proprietary format without the need to convert it to ASCII

For text files, different format control and record structure options are provided. These features were designed to facilitate files containing Telnet or ASA formatting. Data transfer can be done in any of three modes:

- **Stream mode:** Data is sent as a continuous stream, relieving FTP from doing any processing. Rather, all processing is left up to TCP. No End-of-file indicator is needed, unless the data is divided into records.
- **Block mode:** FTP breaks the data into several blocks (block header, byte count, and data field) and then passes it on to TCP.
- **Compressed mode:** Data is compressed using a single algorithm (usually Run-length encoding).

8.4.3 Security

The original FTP specification has many security concerns. In May 1999, the following flaws were addressed:

- Bounce Attacks
- Spoof Attacks
- Brute Force Attacks
- Sniffing
- Username Protection
- Port Stealing

FTP has no encryption tools meaning all transmissions are in clear text; user names, passwords, FTP commands and transferred files can be read by anyone sniffing on the network. This is a problem common to many Internet protocol specifications written prior to the creation of SSL, such as HTTP, SMTP and Telnet. The common solution to this problem is to use either SFTP (SSH File Transfer Protocol), or FTPS (FTP over SSL), which adds SSL or TLS encryption to FTP as specified in RFC 4217.

8.4.4 Anonymous FTP

A host that provides an FTP service may additionally provide anonymous FTP access. Users typically log into the service with an 'anonymous' account when prompted for user name. Although users are commonly asked to send their email address in lieu of a password, no verification is actually performed on the supplied data; examples of anonymous FTP servers can be found here.

At times you may wish to copy files from a remote machine on which you do not have a loginname. This can be done using anonymous FTP. When the remote machine asks for your loginname, you should type in the word anonymous. Instead of a password, you should enter your own electronic mail address. This allows the remote site to keep records of the anonymous FTP requests.

Once you have been logged in, you are in the anonymous directory for the remote machine. This usually contains a number of public files and directories. Again you should be able to move around in these directories. However, you are only able to copy the files from the remote machine to your own local machine; you are not able to write on the remote machine or to delete any files there.

8.4.5 Remote FTP or Ftpmail

Where FTP access is restricted, a remote FTP (or FTPmail) service can be used to circumvent the problem. An e-mail containing the FTP commands to be performed is sent to a remote FTP server, which is a mail server that parses the incoming e-mail, executes the FTP commands, and sends back an e-mail with any downloaded files as an attachment. Obviously this is less flexible than an FTP client, as it is not possible to view directories interactively or to modify commands, and there can also be problems with large file attachments in the response not getting through mail servers. As most internet users these days have ready access to FTP, this procedure is no longer in everyday use.

8.4.6 Web Browser Support

Most recent web browsers can retrieve files hosted on FTP servers, although they may not support protocol extensions such as FTPS. When an FTP-rather than HTTP-URL is supplied, the accessible contents of the remote server is presented in a manner similar to that used for other Web content. Firefox has a full-featured FTP client in the form of an extension called FireFTP. FTP URL syntax is described in RFC1738, taking the form:

ftp://[<user>[:<password>]@]<host>[:<port>]/<url-path>

(The bracketed parts are optional.)

For example:

ftp://public.ftp-servers.example.com/mydirectory/myfile.txt

or:

ftp://user001:secretpassword@private.ftp-servers.example.com/mydirectory/myfile.txt

More details on specifying a user name and password may be found in the browsers' documentation, such as, for example, Firefox and Internet Explorer. By default, most web browsers use passive (PASV) mode, which more easily traverses end-user firewalls.

8.4.7 Nat and Firewall Traversal

FTP normally transfers data by having the server connect back to the client, after the PORT command is sent by the client. This is problematic for both NATs and firewalls, which do not allow connections from the Internet towards internal hosts. For NATs, an additional complication is the representation of the IP addresses and port number in the PORT command refer to the internal host's IP address and port, rather than the public IP address and port of the NAT.

There are two approaches to this problem. One is that the FTP client and FTP server use the PASV command, which causes the data connection to be established from the FTP client to the server. This is widely used by modern FTP clients. Another approach is for the NAT to alter the values of the PORT command, using an application layer gateway for this purpose.

8.4.8 FTP Over SSH (not SFTP)

FTP over SSH (not SFTP) refers to the practice of tunneling a normal FTP session over an SSH connection. Because FTP uses multiple TCP connections (unusual for a TCP/IP protocol that is still in use), it is particularly difficult to tunnel over SSH. With many SSH clients, attempting to set up a tunnel for the control channel (the initial client-to-server connection on port 21) will protect only that channel; when data is transferred, the FTP software at either end will set up new TCP connections (data channels), which bypass the SSH connection, and thus have no confidentiality, integrity protection, etc.

Otherwise, it is necessary for the SSH client software to have specific knowledge of the FTP protocol, and monitor and rewrite FTP control channel messages and autonomously open new forwarding for FTP data channels. Version 3 of SSH Communications Security's software suite, the GPL licensed FONC, and Co:Z FTPSSH Proxy are three software packages that support this mode. FTP over SSH is sometimes referred to as secure FTP; this should not be confused with other methods of securing FTP, such as with SSL/TLS (FTPS). Other methods of transferring files using SSH that are not related to FTP include SFTP and SCP; in each of these, the entire conversation (credentials and data) is always protected by the SSH protocol.

FTP (File Transfer Protocol) utility program is commonly used for copying files to and from other computers. These computers may be at the same site or at different sites thousands of miles apart. FTP is a general protocol that works on UNIX systems as well as a variety of other (non-UNIX) systems. For the purposes of this Web page, the local machine refers to the machine you are initially logged into, the one on which you type the ftp command. The remote machine is the other one, the one that is the argument of the ftp command.

A user interface for the standard File Transfer Protocol for ARPANET, FTP acts as an interpreter on the remote machine. The user may type a number of UNIX-like commands under this interpreter to perform desired actions on the remote machine.

Most operating systems and communication programs now include some form of an FTP utility program, but the commands differ slightly between them. The following explanations and alphabetical list of commands refers to the common FTP utility program as provided on a UNIX machine. Check the documentation for your own machine to determine the comparable commands. Most computers today include a windows-based type FTP program that is more PC-oriented and does not require full knowledge of these commands. You can also perform FTP through a browser. For example, bring up Internet Explorer and type in

ftp://yourLoginName@IPaddress

instead of a normal web page URL.

8.4.9 Getting Started

To connect your local machine to the remote machine, type

ftp machinename

where machinename is the full machine name of the remote machine, e.g., purcell.cs.colostate.edu. If the name of the machine is unknown, you may type ftp machinennumber

where machinennumber is the net address of the remote machine, e.g., 129.82.45.181. In either case, this command is similar to logging onto the remote machine. If the remote machine has been reached successfully, FTP responds by asking for a loginname and password. When you enter your own loginname and password for the remote machine, it returns the prompt

ftp>

and permits you access to your own home directory on the remote machine. You should be able to move around in your own directory and to copy files to and from your local machine using the FTP interface commands given on the following page.

8.4.10 FTP Command

Purpose

Transfers files between a local and a remote host.

Syntax

ftp [-d] [-D DataConnTimeOut] [-g] [-i] [-n] [-v] [-f] [-K] [-k realm] [-q[-C]][HostName [Port]]

DESCRIPTION

The **ftp** command uses the File Transfer Protocol (FTP) to transfer files between the local host and a remote host or between two remote hosts. Remote execution of the ftp command is not recommended.

The FTP protocol allows data transfer between hosts that use dissimilar file systems. Although the protocol provides a high degree of flexibility in transferring data, it does not attempt to preserve file attributes (such as the protection mode or modification times of a file) that are specific to a particular file system. Moreover, the FTP protocol makes few assumptions about the overall structure of a file system and does not provide or allow such functions as recursively copying subdirectories.

Note: If you are transferring files between systems and need to preserve file attributes or recursively copy subdirectories, use the rcp command.

8.4.10.1 Issuing Subcommands

At the ftp> prompt, you can enter subcommands to perform tasks such as listing remote directories, changing the current local and remote directory, transferring multiple files in a single request, creating and removing directories, and escaping to the local shell to perform shell commands. See the Subcommands section for a description of each subcommand.

If you execute the ftp command and do not specify the HostName parameter for a remote host, the ftp command immediately displays the ftp> prompt and waits for an ftp subcommand. To connect to a remote host, execute the open subcommand. When the ftp command connects to the remote host, the ftp command then prompts for the login name and password before displaying the ftp> prompt again. The ftp command is unsuccessful if no password is defined at the remote host for the login name. The ftp command interpreter, which handles all subcommands entered at the ftp> prompt, provides facilities that are not available with most file-transfer programs, such as:

- Handling file-name parameters to ftp subcommands
- Collecting a group of subcommands into a single subcommand macro
- Loading macros from a $HOME/.netrc file

These facilities help simplify repetitive tasks and allow you to use the ftp command in unattended mode. The command interpreter handles file-name parameters according to the following rules:

- If a - (hyphen) is specified for the parameter, standard input (stdin) is used for read operations and standard output (stdout) is used for write operations.
- If the preceding check does not apply and file-name expansion is enabled (see the -g flag or the glob subcommand), the interpreter expands the file name according to the rules of the C shell. When globbing is enabled and a pattern-matching character is used in a subcommand that expects a single file name, results may be different than expected.

For example, the append and put subcommands perform file-name expansion and then use only the first file name generated. Other ftp subcommands, such as cd, delete, get, mkdir, rename, and rmdir, do not perform file-name expansion and take the pattern-matching characters literally.

- For the get, put, mget, and mput subcommands, the interpreter has the ability to translate and map between different local and remote file-name syntax styles (see the case, ntrans, and nmap subcommands) and the ability to modify a local file name if it is not unique (see the runique subcommand). Additionally, the **ftp** command can send instructions to a remote **ftpd** server to modify a remote file name if it is not unique (see the sunique subcommand).
- Use double quotes (" ") to specify parameters that include blank characters.

Note: The ftp command interpreter does not support pipes. It also does not necessarily support all multibyte-character file names.

To end an **ftp** session when you are running interactively, use the quit or bye subcommand or the End of File (Ctrl-D) key sequence at the **ftp**> prompt. To end a file transfer before it has completed, press the Interrupt key sequence. The default Interrupt key sequence is Ctrl-C. The stty command can be used to redefine this key sequence.

The ftp command normally halts transfers being sent (from the local host to the remote host) immediately. The ftp command halts transfers being received (from the remote host to the local host) by sending an FTP ABOR instruction to the remote FTP server and discarding all incoming file transfer packets until the remote server stops sending them. If the remote server does not support the ABOR instruction, the ftp command does not display the ftp> prompt until the remote server has sent all of the requested file. Additionally, if the remote server does something unexpected, you may need to end the local ftp process.

8.4.11 Security and Automatic Login

The ftp command also handles security by sending passwords to the remote host and permits automatic login, file transfers, and logoff.

If you execute the ftp command and specify the host name (HostName) of a remote host, the ftp command tries to establish a connection to the specified host. If the ftp command connects successfully, the ftp command searches for a local $HOME/.netrc file in your current directory or home directory. If the file exists, the ftp command searches the file for an entry initiating the login process and command macro definitions for the remote host. If the $HOME/.netrc file or automatic login entry does not exist or if your system has been secured with the securetcpip command, the ftp command prompts the user for a user name and password. The command displays the prompt whether or not the HostName parameter is specified on the command line. Note: The queuing system does not support multibyte host names.

If the ftp command finds a $HOME/.netrc automatic login entry for the specified host, the ftp command attempts to use the information in that entry to log in to the remote host. The ftp command also loads any command macros defined in the entry. In some cases (for example, when the required password is not listed in an automatic login entry), the ftp command prompts for the password before displaying the ftp> prompt.

Once the ftp command completes the automatic login, the ftp command executes the init macro if the macro is defined in the automatic login entry. If the init macro does not exist or does not contain a quit or bye subcommand, the ftp command then displays the ftp> prompt and waits for a subcommand.

Note: The remote user name specified either at the prompt or in a $HOME/.netrc file must exist and have a password defined at the remote host. Otherwise, the ftp command fails.

The ftp command will use the extensions to ftp specifications as defined in IETF draft document "draft-ietf-cat-ftpsec-09.txt". The FTP security extensions will be implemented using the Generic Security Service API (GSSAPI) security mechanism. The GSSAPI provides services independent to the underlying security and communication mechanism. The GSSAPI is defined in rfc 1508 and 1509.

The ftp command will use the AUTH and ADAT commands to authenticate with the ftpd daemon. If both support Kerberos authentication, then they will use the local users DCE credentials to authenticate the user on the remote system. If this fails and Standard authentication is configured on both systems, the process described above will be used.

The HostName parameter is the name of the host machine to which files are transferred. The optional Port parameter specifies the ID of the port through which to transmit. (The /etc/services file specifies the default port.)

Flags

-C Allows the user to specify that the outgoing file sent using the send file command must be cached in the Network Buffer Cache (NBC). This flag cannot be used unless the -q flag is specified. This flag is only applicable when a file is being sent out in the binary mode with no protection.

-d Sends debugging information about ftp command operations to the syslogd daemon. If you specify the -d flag, you must edit the /etc/syslog.conf file and add one of the following entries:

user.info FileName

OR

user.debug FileName

Note: The syslogd daemon debug level includes info level messages.

If you do not edit the /etc/syslog.conf file, no messages are produced. After changing the /etc/syslog.conf file, run the refresh -s syslogd or kill -1 SyslogdPID command to inform the syslogd daemon of the changes to its configuration file. For more information about debug levels, refer to the /etc/syslog.conf file. Also, refer to the debug subcommand.

-D DataConnTimeOut Specifies the maximum number of seconds that the ftp command holds a data connection. The default value is 300 seconds and can range from 300 seconds to 3600 seconds.

-f Causes the credentials to be forwarded. This flag will be ignored if Kerberos 5 is not the current authentication method.

-g Disables the expansion of metacharacters in file names. Interpreting metacharacters can be referred to as expanding (sometimes called globbing) a file name. See the glob subcommand.

-i Turns off interactive prompting during multiple file transfers. See the prompt, mget, mput, and mdelete subcommands for descriptions of prompting during multiple file transfers.

-K Disables the SO_KEEPALIVE option defined in the sys/socket.h file on both the control and data connection.

-k realm Allows the user to specify the realm of the remote station if it is different from the local systems realm. For these purposes, a realm is synonymous with a DCE cell. This flag will be ignored if Kerberos 5 is not the current authentication method.

-n Prevents an automatic login on the initial connection. Otherwise, the ftp command searches for a $HOME/.netrc entry that describes the login and initialization process for the remote host. See the user subcommand.

-q Allows the user to specify that the send_file subroutine must be used for sending the file on the network. This flag is only applicable when a file is being sent out in the binary mode with no protection.

Displays all the responses from the remote server and provides data transfer statistics. This display mode is the default when the output of the ftp command is to a terminal, such as the console or a display.

-v If stdin is not a terminal, the ftp command disables verbose mode unless the user invoked the ftp command with the -v flag or issued the verbose subcommand.

8.4.12 Subcommands

The following **ftp** subcommands can be entered at the ftp> prompt. Use double quotes (" ") to specify parameters that include blank characters.

![Command [Parameters]] Invokes an interactive shell on the local host. An optional command, with one or more optional parameters, can be given with the shell command.

$ Macro [Parameters] Executes the specified macro, previously defined with the **macdef** subcommand. Parameters are not expanded.

?[Subcommand] Displays a help message describing the subcommand. If you do not specify a Subcommand parameter, the ftp command displays a list of known subcommands.

account [Password] Sends a supplemental password that a remote host may require before granting access to its resources. If the password is not supplied with the command, the user is prompted for the password. The password is not displayed on the screen.

Append

LocalFile [RemoteFile] Appends a local file to a file on the remote host. If the remote file name is not specified, the local file name is used, altered by any setting made with the ntrans subcommand or the nmap subcommand. The append subcommand uses the current values for form, mode, struct, and type subcommands while appending the file.

ascii Synonym for the type ascii subcommand.

bell Sounds a bell after the completion of each file transfer.

binary Synonym for the type binary subcommand.

block Synonym for the mode block subcommand.

bye Ends the file-transfer session and exits the ftp command. Same as the quit subcommand.

carriage-control Synonym for the form carriage-control subcommand.

case Sets a toggle for the case of file names. When the case subcommand is On, the ftp command changes remote file names displayed in all capital letters from uppercase to lowercase when writing them in the local directory. The default is Off (so the ftp command writes uppercase remote file names in uppercase in the local directory).

cd RemoteDirectory	Changes the working directory on the remote host to the specified directory.
cdup	Changes the working directory on the remote host to the parent of the current directory.
close	Ends the file-transfer session, but does not exit the ftp command. Defined macros are erased. Same as the disconnect subcommand.
copylocal	Toggles local copy. copylocal defaults to off. An effort is made by ftp to make sure you do not zero out a file by ftp'ing it to itself (eg. same hostname, same pathname). Turning copylocal ON bypasses this check.
cr	Strips the carriage return character from a carriage return and line-feed sequence when receiving records during ASCII-type file transfers. (The ftp command terminates each ASCII-type record with a carriage return and line feed during file transfers.) Records on remote hosts with operating systems other than the one you are running can have single line feeds embedded in records. To distinguish these embedded line feeds from record delimiters, set the cr subcommand to Off. The cr subcommand toggles between On and Off.
debug [0 | 1]	Toggles debug record keeping On and Off. Specify debug or debug 1 to print each command sent to the remote host and save the restart control file. Specify debug again, or debug 0, to stop the debug record keeping. The Ctrl-C key sequence also saves the restart control file. Specifying the debug subcommand sends debugging information about ftp command operations to the syslogd daemon. If you specify the debug subcommand, you must edit the /etc/syslog.conf file and add one of the following entries: user.info FileName OR user.debug FileName **Note:** The **syslogd** daemon debug level includes info level messages. If you do not edit the /etc/syslog.conf file, no messages are produced. After changing the /etc/syslog.conf file, run the refresh -s syslogd or kill -1 SyslogdPID command to inform the syslogd daemon of the changes to its configuration file. For more information about debug levels, refer to the /etc/syslog.conf file. Also, refer to the ftp -d flag.

delete RemoteFile	Deletes the specified remote file.
dir [RemoteDirectory] Append	Writes a listing of the contents of the specified remote directory (RemoteDirectory) to the specified local file (LocalFile). If the RemoteDirectory parameter is not specified, the dir subcommand lists the contents of the current remote directory. If the LocalFile parameter is not specified or is a - (hyphen), the dir subcommand displays the listing on the local terminal.
disconnect	Ends the file-transfer session but does not exit the ftp command. Defined macros are erased. Same as the close subcommand.
ebcdic	Synonym for the type ebcdic subcommand.
exp_cmd	Toggles between conventional and experimental protocol commands. The default is off.
file	Synonym for the struct file subcommand.
form [carriage-control | non-print | telnet]	Specifies the form of the file transfer. The form subcommand modifies the type subcommand to send the file transfer in the indicated form. Valid arguments are carriage-control, non-print, and telnet. **carriage-control** Sets the form of the file transfer to carriage-control. **non-print** Sets the form of the file transfer to non-print. **telnet** Sets the form of the file transfer to Telnet. Telnet is a Transmission Control Protocol/Internet Protocol (TCP/IP) protocol that opens connections to a system.
get RemoteFile [LocalFile]	Copies the remote file to the local host. If the LocalFile parameter is not specified, the remote file name is used locally and is altered by any settings made by the case, ntrans, and nmap subcommands. The ftp command uses the current settings for the type, form, mode, and struct subcommands while transferring the file.
glob	Toggles file-name expansion (globbing) for the mdelete, mget, and mput subcommands. If globbing is disabled, file-name parameters for these subcommands are not expanded. When globbing is enabled and a pattern-matching character is used in a subcommand that expects a single file name, results may be different than expected.

For example, the append and put subcommands perform file-name expansion and then use only the first file name generated. Other ftp subcommands, such as cd, delete, get, mkdir, rename, and rmdir, do not perform file-name expansion and take the pattern-matching characters literally.

Globbing for the mput subcommand is done locally in the same way as for the csh command. For the mdelete and mget subcommands, each file name is expanded separately at the remote machine and the lists are not merged. The expansion of a directory name can be different from the expansion of a file name, depending on the remote host and the ftp server.

To preview the expansion of a directory name, use the mls subcommand:

mls RemoteFile

To transfer an entire directory subtree of files, transfer a tar archive of the subtree in binary form, rather than using the mget or mput subcommand.

hash — Toggles hash sign (#) printing. When the hash subcommand is on, the ftp command displays one hash sign for each data block (1024 bytes) transferred.

help [Subcommand] — Displays help information. See the ? subcommand.

image — Synonym for the type image subcommand.

lcd [Directory] — Changes the working directory on the local host. If you do not specify a directory, the ftp command uses your home directory.

local M — Synonym for the type local M subcommand.

ls [RemoteDirectory] [LocalFile] — Writes an abbreviated file listing of a remote directory to a local file. If the RemoteDirectory parameter is not specified, the ftp command lists the current remote directory. If the LocalFile parameter is not specified or is a - (hyphen), the ftp command displays the listing on the local terminal.

macdef Macro — Defines a subcommand macro. Subsequent lines up to a null line (two consecutive line feeds) are saved as the text of the macro. Up to 16 macros, containing at most 4096 characters for all macros, can be defined. Macros remain defined until either redefined or a close subcommand is executed.

The $ (dollar sign) and \ (backslash) are special characters in ftp macros. A $ symbol followed by one or more numbers is replaced by the corresponding macro parameter on the invocation line (see the $ subcommand). A $ symbol followed by the letter i indicates that the macro is to loop, with the $i character combination being replaced by consecutive parameters on each pass.

The first macro parameter is used on the first pass, the second parameter is used on the second pass, and so on. A \ symbol prevents special treatment of the next character. Use the \ symbol to turn off the special meanings of the $ and \. (backslash period) symbols.

mdelete RemoteFiles Expands the files specified by the RemoteFiles parameter at the remote host and deletes the remote files.

mdir [RemoteDirectories LocalFile] Expands the directories specified by the RemoteDirectories parameter at the remote host and writes a listing of the contents of those directories to the file specified in the LocalFile parameter. If the RemoteDirectories parameter contains a pattern-matching character, the mdir subcommand prompts for a local file if none is specified. If the RemoteDirectories parameter is a list of remote directories separated by blanks, the last argument in the list must be either a local file name or a - (hyphen).

If the LocalFile parameter is - (hyphen), the mdir subcommand displays the listing on the local terminal. If interactive prompting is on (see the prompt subcommand), the ftp command prompts the user to verify that the last parameter is a local file and not a remote directory.

mget RemoteFiles Expands the RemoteFiles parameter at the remote host and copies the indicated remote files to the current directory on the local host. See the glob subcommand for more information on file-name expansion. The remote file names are used locally and are altered by any settings made by the case, ntrans, and nmap subcommands. The ftp command uses the current settings for the form, mode, struct, and type subcommands while transferring the files.

mkdir [RemoteDirectory] Creates the directory specified in the RemoteDirectory parameter on the remote host.

mls [RemoteDirectories LocalFile] Expands the directories specified in the RemoteDirectories parameter at the remote host and writes an abbreviated file listing of the indicated remote directories to a local file. If the RemoteDirectories parameter contains a pattern-matching character, the mls subcommand prompts for a local file if none is specified. If the RemoteDirectories parameter is a list of remote directories separated by blanks, the last argument in the list must be either a local file name or a - (hyphen).

If the LocalFile parameter is - (hyphen), the mls subcommand displays the listing on the local terminal. If interactive prompting is on (see the prompt subcommand), the ftp command prompts the user to verify that the last parameter is a local file and not a remote directory.

mode [stream | block]

Sets file-transfer mode. If an argument is not supplied, the default is stream.

block

Sets the file-transfer mode to block.

stream

Sets the file-transfer mode to stream.

modtime

Shows the last modification time of the specified file on the remote machine. If the ftp command is not connected to a host prior to execution, the modtime subcommand terminates with an error message. The ftp command ignores parameter beyond the first parameter. If the FileName parameter is not specified, the ftp command prompts for a file name. If no file name is given, the ftp command sends a usage message to standard output and terminates the subcommand.

If the name specified by the FileName parameter exists on the remote host, and the name specifies a file, then the ftp command sends a message containing the last modification time of the file to standard output and terminates the subcommand. If FileName specifies a directory, the ftp command sends an error message to standard output and terminates the subcommand.

Note: The modtime subcommand interprets metacharacters when allowed.

mput [LocalFiles]

Expands the files specified in the LocalFiles parameter at the local host and copies the indicated local files to the remote host. See the glob subcommand for more information on file-name expansion. The local file names are used at the remote host and are altered by any settings made by the ntrans and nmap subcommands. The ftp command uses the current settings for the type, form, mode, and struct subcommands while transferring the files.

nlist [RemoteDirectory] [LocalFile]

Writes a listing of the contents of the specified remote directory (RemoteDirectory) to the specified local file (LocalFile). If the RemoteDirectory parameter is not specified, the nlist subcommand lists the contents of the current remote directory. If the LocalFile parameter is not specified or is a - (hyphen), the nlist subcommand displays the listing on the local terminal.

nmap [InPattern OutPattern] Turns the file-name mapping mechanism On or Off. If no parameters are specified, file-name mapping is turned off. If parameters are specified, source file names are mapped for the mget and mput subcommands and for the get and put subcommands when the destination file name is not specified. This subcommand is useful when the local and remote hosts use different file-naming conventions or practices. Mapping follows the pattern set by the InPattern and OutPattern parameters.

The InPattern parameter specifies the template for incoming file names, which may have already been processed according to the case and ntrans settings. The template variables $1 through $9 can be included in the InPattern parameter. All characters in the InPattern parameter, other than the $ (dollar sign) and the \$ (backslash, dollar sign), are treated literally and are used as delimiters between InPattern variables. For example, if the InPattern parameter is $1.$2 and the remote file name is mydata.dat, the value of $1 is mydata and the value of $2 is dat.

The OutPattern parameter determines the resulting file name. The variables $1 through $9 are replaced by their values as derived from the InPattern parameter, and the variable $0 is replaced by the original file name. Additionally, the sequence [Sequence1,Sequence2] is replaced by the value of Sequence1, if Sequence1 is not null; otherwise, it is replaced by the value of Sequence2. For example, the subcommand:

nmap $1.$2.$3 [$1,$2].[$2,file]

would yield myfile.data from myfile.data or myfile.data.old, myfile.file from myfile, and myfile.myfile from .myfile. Use the \ (backslash) symbol to prevent the special meanings of the $ (dollar sign), [(left bracket),] (right bracket), and , (comma) in the OutPattern parameter.

non-print Synonym for the form non print subcommand.

ntrans **[InCharacters [OutCharacters]]** Turns the file-name character translation mechanism On and Off. If no parameters are specified, character translation is turned off. If parameters are specified, characters in source file names are translated for mget and mput subcommands and for get and put subcommands when the destination file name is not specified.

This subcommand is useful when the local and remote hosts use different file-naming conventions or practices. Character translation follows the pattern set by the InCharacters and OutCharacters parameter. Characters in a source file name matching characters in the InCharacters parameter are replaced by the corresponding characters in the OutCharacters parameter.

If the string specified by the InCharacters parameter is longer than the string specified by the OutCharacters parameter, the characters in the InCharacters parameter are deleted if they have no corresponding character in the OutCharacters parameter.

open HostName [Port]

Establishes a connection to the FTP server at the host specified by the HostName parameter. If the optional port number is specified, the ftp command attempts to connect to a server at that port. If the automatic login feature is set (that is, the -n flag was not specified on the command line), the ftp command attempts to log in the user to the FTP server.

You must also have a $HOME/.netrc file with the correct information in it and the correct permissions set. The .netrc file must be in your home directory.

passive

Toggles passive mode for file transfers. When a file transfer command (such as get, mget, put, or mput) is invoked with passive mode off, the ftp server opens a data connection back to the client. In passive mode, the client opens data connections to the server when sending or receiving data.

private

Sets the protection level to "private." At this level, data is integrity and confidentially protected.

prompt

Toggles interactive prompting. If interactive prompting is on (the default), the ftp command prompts for verification before retrieving, sending, or deleting multiple files during the mget, mput, and mdelete subcommands. Otherwise, the ftp command acts accordingly on all files specified.

protect

This command returns the current level of protection.

proxy [Subcommand]

Executes an ftp command on a secondary control connection. This subcommand allows the ftp command to connect simultaneously to two remote FTP servers for transferring files between the two servers. The first proxy subcommand should be an open subcommand to establish the secondary control connection. Enter the proxy ? subcommand to see the other ftp subcommands that are executable on the secondary connection.

The following subcommands behave differently when prefaced by the proxy subcommand:

- The open subcommand does not define new macros during the automatic login process.
- The close subcommand does not erase existing macro definitions.
- The get and mget subcommands transfer files from the host on the primary connection to the host on the secondary connection.
- The put, mput, and append subcommands transfer files from the host on the secondary connection to the host on the primary connection.
- The restart subcommand can be handled by the proxy command.
- The status subcommand displays accurate information.

File transfers require that the FTP server on the secondary connection must support the PASV (passive) instruction.

put LocalFile [RemoteFile] Stores a local file on the remote host. If you do not specify the RemoteFile parameter, the ftp command uses the local file name to name the remote file, and the remote file name is altered by any settings made by the ntrans and nmap subcommands. The ftp command uses the current settings for the type, form, mode, and struct subcommands while transferring the files.

pwd Displays the name of the current directory on the remote host.

quit Closes the connection and exits the ftp command. Same as the bye subcommand.

quote String Sends the string specified by the String parameter verbatim to the remote host. Execute the remotehelp or quote help subcommand to display a list of valid values for the String parameter.

Note: "Quoting" commands that involve data transfers can produce unpredictable results.

record Synonym for the struct record subcommand.

recv RemoteFile [LocalFile] Copies the remote file to the local host. Same as the get subcommand.

reinitialize Reinitializes an FTP session by flushing all I/O and allowing transfers to complete. Resets all defaults as if a user had just started an FTP session without logging in to a remote host.

remotehelp [Subcommand] Requests help from the remote FTP server

rename FromName ToName Renames a file on the remote host.

reset Clears the reply queue. This subcommand resynchronizes the command parsing.

restart get | put | append	Restarts a file transfer at the point where the last checkpoint was made. To run successfully, the subcommand must be the same as the aborted subcommand, including structure, type, and form. Valid arguments are get, put, and append.
rmdir RemoteDirectory	Removes the remote directory specified by the RemoteDirectory parameter at the remote host.
runique	(ReceiveUnique) Toggles the facility for creating unique file nâmes for local destination files during get and mget subcommands. If this facility is Off (the default), the ftp command overwrites local files. Otherwise, if a local file has the same name as that specified for a local destination file, the ftp command modifies the specified name of the local destination file with .1. If a local file is already using the new name, the ftp command appends the postfix .2 to the specified name. If a local file is already using this second name, the ftp command continues incrementing the postfix until it either finds a unique file name or reaches .99 without finding a unique file name. If the ftp command cannot find a unique file name, the ftp command reports an error and the transfer does not take place. Note that the runique subcommand does not affect local file names generated from a shell command.
safe	Sets the protection level to "safe." At this level, data is integrity protected.
send LocalFile [RemoteFile]	Stores a local file on the remote host. Same as the put subcommand.
sendport	Toggles the use of FTP PORT instructions. By default, the ftp command uses a PORT instruction when establishing a connection for each data transfer. When the use of PORT instructions is disabled, the ftp command does not use PORT instructions for data transfers. The PORT instruction is useful when dealing with FTP servers that ignore PORT instructions while incorrectly indicating the instructions have been accepted.
site Args	Displays or sets the idle time-out period, displays or sets the file-creation umask, or changes the permissions of a file, using the chmod command. Possible values for the Args parameter are umask and chmod.
size RemoteFile	Displays the size in bytes of the remote file specified by the RemoteFile parameter.
status	Displays the current status of the ftp command as well as the status of the subcommands.

stream	Synonym for the mode stream subcommand.
	struct [file | record] Sets the data transfer structure type. Valid arguments are file and record. **file** Sets the data-transfer structure type to file. **record** Sets the data-transfer structure type to record.
sunique	(Send/Store Unique) Toggles the facility for creating unique file names for remote destination files during put and mput subcommands. If this facility is off (the default), the ftp command overwrites remote files. Otherwise, if a remote file has the same name as that specified for a remote destination file, the remote FTP server modifies the name of the remote destination file. Note that the remote server must support the STOU instruction.
system	Shows the type of operating system running on the remote machine.
telnet	Synonym for the form telnet subcommand.
tenex	Synonym for the type tenex subcommand.
trace	Toggles packet tracing.
type [ascii | binary | ebcdic | image | local M | tenex]	Sets the file-transfer type. Valid arguments are ascii, binary, ebcdic, image, local M, and tenex. If an argument is not specified, the current type is printed. The default type is ascii; the binary type can be more efficient than **ascii**. **ascii** Sets the file-transfer type to network ASCII. This type is the default. File transfer may be more efficient with binary-image transfer. See the binary argument for further information. **binary** Sets the file-transfer type to binary image. This type can be more efficient than an ASCII transfer. **ebcdic** Sets the file-transfer type to EBCDIC. **image** Sets the file-transfer type to binary image. This type can be more efficient than an ASCII transfer.

local M

Sets the file-transfer type to local. The M parameter defines the decimal number of bits per machine word. This parameter does not have a default.

tenex

Sets the file-transfer type to that needed for TENEX machines.

user User [Password] [Account]

Identifies the local user (User) to the remote FTP server. If the Password or Account parameter is not specified and the remote server requires it, the ftp command prompts for the password or account locally. If the Account parameter is required, the ftp command sends it to the remote server after the remote login process completes.

Note: Unless automatic login is disabled by specifying the -n flag on the command line, the ftp command sends the User, Password, and Account parameters automatically for the initial connection to the remote server. You also need a .netrc file in your home directory in order to issue an automatic login.

verbose

Toggles verbose mode. When the verbose mode is on (the default), the ftp command displays all responses from the remote FTP server. Additionally, the ftp command displays statistics on all file transfers when the transfers complete.

8.4.13 Example of Regular FTP Session

```
% ftp nordsieck.cs.colorado.edu
Connected to nordsieck.cs.colorado.edu.
220 nordsieck FTP server (Version 5.53 Tue Aug 25 10:46:12 MDT 1992) ready.
Name (nordsieck.cs.colorado.edu:yourlogin): yourlogin
331 Password required for yourlogin.
Password:
230 User yourlogin logged in.
ftp> cd HPSC/exercises
250 CWD command successful.
ftp> ls
200 PORT command successful.
```

```
550 No files found.
ftp> put tmul.out
200 PORT command successful.
150 Opening ASCII mode data connection for tmul.out.
226 Transfer complete.
local: tmul.out remote: tmul.out
1882 bytes sent in 0.0095 seconds (1.9e+02 Kbytes/s)
ftp> ls
200 PORT command successful.
150 Opening ASCII mode data connection for file list.
tmul.out
226 Transfer complete.
9 bytes received in 0.0021 seconds (4.3 Kbytes/s)
ftp> mput *
mput Makefile? y
200 PORT command successful.
150 Opening ASCII mode data connection for Makefile.
226 Transfer complete.
local: Makefile remote: Makefile
1020 bytes sent in 0.0062 seconds (1.6e+02 Kbytes/s)
mput tmul.out? n
ftp> quit
221 Goodbye.
%  ls
  . . .
Makefile
tmul.out
  . . .
```

8.4.14 Common FTP Commands

Command	Description
!	Preceding a command with the exclamation point will cause the command to execute on the local system instead of the remote system.
?	Request assistance or information about the FTP commands. This command does not require a connection to a remote system.
ascii	Set the file transfer mode to ASCII (Note: this is the default and transmits seven bits per byte).
bell	Turns bell mode on / off. This command does not require a connection to a remote system.
binary	Set the file transfer mode to binary (Note: the binary mode transfers all eight bits per byte and must be used to transfer non-ASCII files).
bye	Exit the FTP environment (same as quit). This command does not require a connection to a remote system.
cd	Change directory on the remote system.
close	Terminate a session with another system.
debug	Sets debugging on/off. This command does not require a connection to a remote system.
delete	Delete (remove) a file in the current remote directory (same as rm in UNIX).
dir	Lists the contents of the remote directory.The asterisk (*) and the question mark (?) may be used as wild cards. For example: dir b* — This will display all entries that start with the letter "b". For example, the following will be displayed. bet, ben, bingo, born, boon, bipartisan, bandit, boy dir b*n* — This will display all entries that start with the letter "b" and have the letter "n" somewhere after the letter "b". For example, the following will be displayed. ben, bingo, born, boon, bipartisan, bandit The following will not be displayed. bet, boy dir b?n — This will display all entries that start with the letter "b", have the letter "n" in the 3rd position and have a three character name. For example, the following will be displayed. ben

		The following will not be displayed. bet, bingo, born, boon, bipartisan, bandit, boy
	dir b?n*	This will display all entries that start with the letter "b" and have the letter "n" in the 3rd position. For example, the following will be displayed. ben, bingo, bandit The following will not be displayed. bet, born, boon, bipartisan, boy
get	Copy a file from the remote system to the local system. get filename-1 — Copy (or replace) filename-1 from the current remote directory to a file with the same name in the current local directory. get filename-1 filename-2 — Copy (or replace) filename-1 from the current remote directory to filename-2 in the current local directory.	
help	Request a list of all available FTP commands. This command does not require a connection to a remote system.	
lcd	Change directory on your local system (same as CD in UNIX).	
ls	List the names of the files in the current remote directory.	
mget	Copy multiple files from the remote system to the local system. (Note: You will be prompted for a "y/n" response before copying each file).	
mget *	Copies all the files in the current remote directory to the current local directory, using the same filenames. Note the use of the asterisk (*) as a wild card character.	
mkdir	Make a new directory within the current remote directory.	
mput	Copy multiple files from the local system to the remote system. (Note: You will be prompted for a "y/n" response before copying each file).	
open	Open a connection with another system.	
put	Copy a file from the local system to the remote system.	
pwd	Find out the pathname of the current directory on the remote system.	
quit	Exit the FTP environment (same as "bye"). This command does not require a connection to a remote system.	
rmdir	Remove (delete) a directory in the current remote directory.	
trace	Toggles packet tracing. This command does not require a connection to a remote system.	

8.4.14.1 FTP Extended Command List

The following are additional commands that are used when transferring files between an IBM Mainframe and a Windows or UNIX client system. Also, the following includes commands required when working with files containing variable length records.

```
user
password
CD ..
PWD
VERBOSE
BINARY
LITERAL SITE RDW LRECL=80 RECFM=FB TRACKS PRIMARY=10 SECONDARY=5
PUT c:\SimoDemo\TestLib1\DataFtp1\CARDFILE.DAT SIMOTIME.DATA.CARDFILE
QUIT
```

Command	Description
literal	Will send an argument to the remote FTP Server. This statement is similar in purpose as the "QUOTE" statement.
locsite	LOCSITE This statement may be used at the mainframe for commands specific to the mainframe
quote	Will send an argument to the remote FTP Server. This statement is similar in purpose as the "LITERAL" statement.
site	This statement is used at the client system and is used to transfer a function (via the literal or quote) to the host site. The following is a summary of the commonly used SITE/LOCSITE Commands.
Command	Description
BLKSIZE	BLocKSIZE=nnnn where nnnn is the block size (BLKSIZE)
CYLINDERS	CYlinders To indicate that space should be allocated in cylinders
DIRECTORY	DIrectory=nnn where 'nnn' indicates the number of directory blocks to be allocated for the directory of a PDS
LRECL	LRecl=nnn where nnn is the logical record length (LRECL)
PRIMARY	PRImary=nnn where nnn indicates the number of primary space units (tracks or cylinders)

Command	Description
RDW	RDW will cause each record of a variable length record to be preceded with a four byte Record Descriptor Word (RDW) and possible four byte Block Descriptor Word (BDW).
RECFM	RECfm=format where format is: F, FA, FB, FBA, FBM, FM, U, V, VA, VB, VBA, VBM, or VBS
SECONDARY	SECondary=nnn where nnn indicates the number of secondary space units (tracks or cylinders)
TRACKS	TRacks To indicate that space should be allocated in tracks.

8.5 DISTRIBUTED SYSTEMS

Distributed systems involve the interaction between disparate independent entities, bounded by common language and protocols and working toward a common goal. Different types of distributed systems are found in real life. One of the biggest and perhaps the most complex distributed system is human society itself. In the digital world, the Internet has become a very important distributed environment for everybody.

8.5.1 Characteristics of Distributed Systems

If we look at any distributed system, for example the Internet, there are several mandatory characteristics, in addition to 'good-to-have' or desirable characteristics. Mandatory characteristics determine the basic nature of distributed systems, such as having multiple entities, heterogeneity, concurrency and resource sharing.

(1) Multiple entities: One of the key characteristics of a distributed system is the presence of multiple - in many cases a great many - entities participating in the system. The entities can be users or subsystems which compose the distributed system.

(2) Heterogeneity: Another key characteristic is the heterogeneous nature of the entities involved. The heterogeneity may lie in the type of system or user, underlying policies and/or the data/resources that the underlying subsystems consume. The heterogeneity of distributed systems can be best observed in the Internet, where multitudes of systems, protocols, policies and environments interact to create a scalable infrastructure.

(3) Concurrency: Another important characteristic that distinguishes any distributed system from a centralized one is concurrency. Different components of distributed systems may run concurrently as the components may be loosely coupled. Therefore there is a need to understand the synchronization issues during the design of distributed systems.

(4) Resource sharing: Sharing of resources is another key characteristic of distributed systems.

In addition to the above mandatory characteristics, there are several desirable characteristics for a distributed system.

(1) Openness: A desirable characteristic for a distributed system is openness of the underlying architecture, protocols, resources and infrastructure, where they can be extended or replaced without affecting the system behaviour. If we look at the Internet, this issue is nicely handled through the use of open standards: we can see the interplay between different protocols, standards, infrastructures and architectures without affecting the activities of the Internet as a whole.

(2) Scalability: One of the key motivations for going from a centralized system to a distributed one is to increase the overall scalability of the system. Hence to have a highly scalable system is desirable in any form of distributed system.

(3) Transparency: Another desirable characteristic is to have transparency in the operation. From the user's and the subsystem's point of view, the underlying systems should be transparent. Primarily, transparency can be of two types - location transparency and system transparency. The first type talks about the need to be transparent regarding the location disparity between different systems. The second talks about the need to be transparent about system issues like failure, concurrency, scaling, and migration and so on.

8.5.2 Types of Distributed System

Distributed systems can be divided into mainly three types: distributed computing systems, distributed information systems and distributed pervasive systems. The first type of system is mainly concerned with providing computations in a distributed manner. The second type of system is mainly concerned with providing information in a distributed manner, while the third type is the next-generation distributed system, which is ubiquitous in nature.

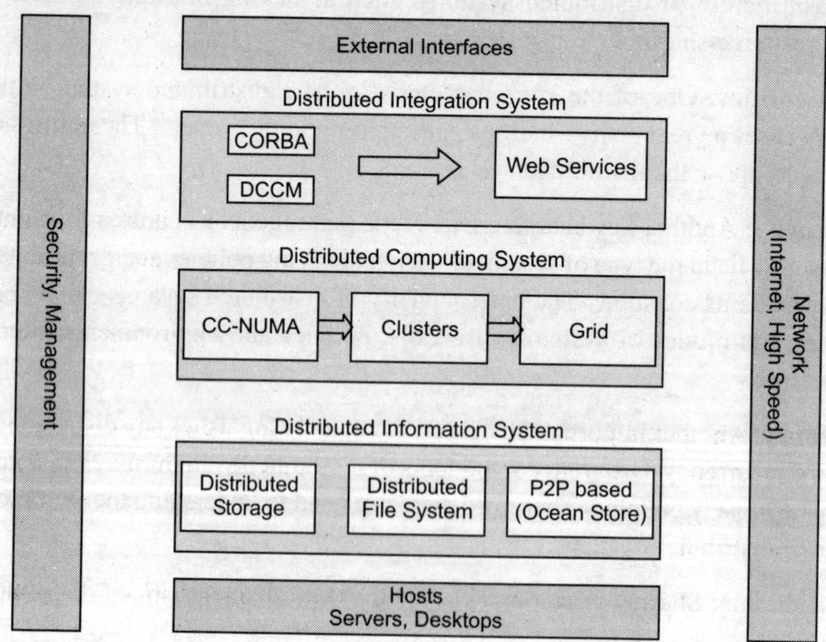

Figure 1.1 Distributed system landscape.

8.5.2.1 Distributed Computing Systems

Distributed computing systems provide computations in a distributed manner. Computing power is needed in many different industries, including banking and finance, life sciences, manufacturing and so on. If we look at the computing resources available, we shall find that the laptops of today are perhaps as powerful as servers a decade ago. Moore's law, which states that computing power doubles every 18 months, is valid even today and will probably be true for the next 5-6 years. With the growth of the multicore technologies, Moore's law can be extended even further. Computing power is increasing and so is demand.

In this rat race, researchers have found an able ally in the form of networking. Between 2001 and 2010, while processing power is supposed to increase 60 times, networking capabilities are supposed to increase by 4000 times. This means that at the same cost, 4000 times the same bandwidth will be available in 2010 as compared to 2001. Therefore, the computing architectures developed a decade back will probably require a rethink based on the technological progress in the fields of computers and networks. Last decade saw the development of a field called cluster computing, where different computing resources are connected together using a very-high-speed network like Gigabit Ethernet or more recently Infiniband. In addition to the technological progress and the huge requirement of computing power, the enterprises have also undergone a radical shift in IT operations in the last few years. Enterprises are now witnessing increasing collaboration and data sharing among the different participating entities, resulting in the need for and use of distributed resources and computing. Another important element that has increased the complexity of IT operations is the need for integration of different applications: middlewares developed on different platforms and by different vendors. We are also seeing a spurt of mergers and acquisitions that require integration of technologies across enterprises. Moreover, the enterprises are outsourcing the nonessential elements of the IT infrastructure. The dual pull of requiring more computing power and the integration of heterogeneous components into the IT infrastructure has led to the development of grid technology. This technology is seeing a classical evolution pattern. Initiated by the academic and research community to fulfill its needs, it is slowly being adopted by the enterprises, especially those who have high computing needs, such as the life sciences, finance and manufacturing industries. However, the promise of grid computing goes beyond that and the next few years should see a gradual adoption of grid as the natural choice among the other enterprises. But a widespread adoption of grid computing depends upon the ability of researchers and practitioners to reduce the pitfalls that lie along the way. One such pitfall is security, which is the focus of this book as a whole. In this chapter we will briefly talk about grid computing's evolution, benefits and concerns.

8.5.2.2 Distributed Information Systems

Distributed information systems are responsible for storing and retrieving information in a distributed manner. There are many manifestations of this type of distributed system. The underlying storage system can be distributed in the form of storage area networks (SANs). SANs have become de facto storage infrastructures in most enterprises. SAN is a high-speed data storage network that connects different types of storage device. One of the most popular modes of storage communication is the Fibre Channel fabric. Another paradigm of the distributed information system is the distributed file system (DFS). The first secure DFS in common use was atheos file system (AFS).

This file system was later followed by DFS. AFS servers store sub-trees of the file system and use Kerberos to provide authenticated access to the trees. Network file system (NFS) is another very popular DFS, which allows users distributed over the network to access distributed files. With the growth of peer-to-peer (P2P) technologies, highly-distributed storage is in vogue. Systems like OceanStore are becoming popular. This uses a large number of untrusted storage devices to store redundant copies of encrypted files and directories in persistent objects. Objects are identified by globally unique identifiers (GUID), which are generated in a similar fashion to the unique identifiers in SAN file system (SFS). Each identifier is a hash of the owner's public key and a name. Objects can point to other objects to enable directories. All objects are encrypted by the client. By replicating the objects among servers, clients can even avoid malicious servers deleting their data. The extensive use of replication and public keys makes revocation of access and deletion of data difficult to achieve, but it does provide a nice model for a completely decentralized DFS.

8.5.2.3 Distributed Integration Systems

Distributed integration systems are responsible for integrating applications, policies and interfaces across diverse distributed systems. The last couple of decades have seen numerous implementations of distributed computing, such as CORBA, Java RMI, DCOM and so on. None of these systems were taken up in a big way by the industries, mainly because of their tightly-coupled nature. Current trends in the application space suggest that enterprises are moving away from monolithic tightly-coupled systems toward loosely-coupled dynamically-bound components. With the growth of the Internet as a premier means of communication, a new paradigm called the Web Services emerged, facilitating a new style of architecting systems, termed as service-oriented architecture (SOA). Web Services can be thought of as reusable, loosely-coupled software components that are deployed over the network, or specifically the World Wide Web. There are some advantages that the experts claim as the major reasons for the adoption of Web Services as a de facto standard for application integration. These are:

(1) Simplicity: Implementation of Web Services is very simple from the point of view of programmers and as a result, easy and fast deployments are possible. All the underlying technologies and protocols are based on Extended Markup Language (XML), which is simple and intuitive.

(2) Loosely coupled: Since the very design of Web Services is based on loose coupling of its different components, they can be deployed on demand.

(3) Platform independent: Web Services architecture is platform- and language independent since it is based on XML technologies. Therefore, one can write a client in C++ running on Windows, while the Web Service is written in Java running on Linux.

(4) Transparent: Since most of the deployed Web Services use Hypertext Transfer Protocol (HTTP) [17] for transmitting messages, they are transparent to firewalls, which generally allow HTTP to pass through. This may not always be the case for CORBA, RMI and so on.

According to many experts, CORBA and RMI provide a much better alternative to Web Services because of the flexibility and features that CORBA provide. Moreover, performance-wise the CORBA/RMI combination may be better than protocol designed over HTTP. However, because of its simplicity and the backing of the big commercial vendors, Web Services is steadily becoming a standard which none can ignore. There are many forums where debates are being pursued as we move on to the different components which constitute the Web Services.

There are three main components of Web Services:

- **SOAP:** The Simple Object Access Protocol (SOAP) is a lightweight protocol for exchange of information between diverse and distributed computing environments. It combines the extensibility and portability of XML with the ubiquitous Web technology of HTTP. It provides a framework for defining how an XML message is structured, using rich semantics for indicating encoding style, array structure and data types.
- **WSDL:** The Web Service Description Language (WSDL) can be used to describe a Web Service, providing a standard interface. A WSDL document is written in XML and describes a service as a set of endpoints, each consisting of a collection of operations. XML input and output messages are defined for each operation and their structure and data types are described using an XML Schema in the WSDL document. The Web Description Services Language (WDSL) and XML Schema provide a complete definition for the service interface, allowing programmatic access to the Web Service in the manner of an API. Tasks like data requests or code executions can be performed by sending or receiving XML messages using, for example, SOAP.
- **UDDI:** The Universal Description, Discovery and Integration (UDDI) specification defines a way to publish and discover information about Web Services. It is collaboration between Ariba, IBM and Microsoft to speed interoperability and adoption of Web Services. The project includes a business registry (an XML document) and a set of operations on it. The registry can be used by programs to find and get information about Web Services and check compatibility with them, based on their descriptions. UDDI allows categorization of Web Services so that they can be located and discovered, and WSDL enables a programmatic interface to a service once it has been located.

8.5.3 Different Distributed Architectures

There are four different types of architecture that are used for designing distributed systems, namely client-server-based systems, Multinode systems, P2P systems and service-oriented systems. The first type of system is a client- and a server-based system, the second type of system distributes the data or the information across multiple nodes or systems, the third type of system is a P2P-based architecture where all components are peers or at the same level, and the last type of system is a federated model where interactions happen via standards-based messages.

8.5.3.1 Client-server-based Architecture

Client-server-based architecture is the most popular distributed system that has been used over the years. In this architecture, the server is responsible for providing service to the client or a set of clients. In a client server kind of environment, a client requests a service from the server, which the server provides over the network in a remote environment. The main advantage of a client-server system is that the business services are abstracted from the set of clients accessing them. Security is implemented at the link and the end server, while fault tolerance is applied at the server end by replicating the functionality. Though extremely popular, there are some inherent limitations in this type of architecture, which led practitioners and researchers to other models.

- **Scalability:** One of the primary limitations of this model is scalability. If the number of users increases significantly, the system fails to handle such a large load. There are two ways to handle this issue: scale up or scale out. Scaling up means moving to a higher end server to handle the same type of request. Though this may be an effective solution in some cases, it does not scale as there is a limitation to scaling up. The second approach, or scale-out approach, distributes the server into multiple servers, which improves scalability. We will talk about this approach later.
- **Flexibility:** Just having a client and a server reduces the overall flexibility of the system, the reason being that database management, application business logic and other processes are embedded in the server code and hence inflexible. Practitioners and designers slowly moved to three-tier architecture mainly to tackle this problem.

8.5.3.2 Multinode

One variation of the client-server technology distributes the server into multiple nodes that can be used for parallel processing. There are several advantages of such a multinode configuration, namely performance, fault tolerance and scalability. Performance can be improved, since the different nodes involved in the process provide part of the service a single node was supposed to perform. Different components of the multinode system are: processing nodes, scheduler or load balancer and clients. Having different nodes perform similar actions can result in improvement of fault tolerance. Moreover, multinode systems improve scalability since they can scale out instead of scaling up. However, the advantages of multimode systems come at a cost, which is complexity. Managing synchronization, security, load balancing and so on in such an environment is extremely challenging.

8.5.3.3 Peer-to-peer

The third type of architecture, which is becoming at the moment, is P2P. This type of system is different from client-server-based systems as, in P2P systems, all the nodes in the distributed system participate in the same hierarchy. This means that there is no concept of client and server, and each participant assumes the role of client and server based on need and requirement. Systems like Gnutella, Napster and so on are based on such principles. P2P systems have found significant applications in the area of file distribution and transfer. They are also being applied in the area of data and information storage. P2P systems have several advantages in terms of scalability and fault tolerance. Since the system is dependent on end systems and nodes, it scales infinitely. The scalability property is exhibited by all the P2P systems. Similarly, fault tolerance is also an important characteristic of such a system. However, several challenges exist, in the form of security and service level agreement (SLA). Since the end systems are responsible for performance, guaranteeing service is almost impossible. Management of security is also extremely difficult as maintaining security at the end systems is a challenge.

8.5.3.4 Service-oriented Architecture

SOA is the latest in the evolution of distributed architectures, which builds upon the client-server and other such distributed architecture models. SOA implementations revolve around the basic idea of a service. A service refers to a modular, self-contained piece of software, which has a well-defined functionality expressed in abstract terms independent of the underlying implementation. Basically, any implementation of SOA has three fundamental roles: service provider, service requestor and service registry, and three fundamental operations: publish, find and bind. The service provider publishes details pertaining to service invocation with a services registry. The service requestor finds the details of a service from the service registry. The service requestor then invokes (binds) the service on the service provider. Web Services, described earlier, represent the most popular form of implementation of SOA.

8.5.4 Challenges in Designing Distributed Systems

The challenges in designing a distributed system lie in managing the different disparate entities responsible for providing the end service. Synchronization between the different entities needs to be handled. Similarly, security and fault tolerance are extremely important and need to be handled as well.

8.5.4.1 Synchronization

One of the most complex and well-studied problem in the area of distributed systems is synchronization. The problem of synchronizing concurrent events also occurs in nondistributed systems. However, in distributed systems, the problem gets amplified many times. Absence of a globally-shared clock, absence of global shared memory in most cases and the presence of partial failures makes synchronization a complex problem to deal with. There are several issues, like clock synchronization, leader election, collecting global states, mutual exclusion and distributed transactions, which are critical and have been studied in detail in literature.

- **Clock synchronization:** Time plays a crucial role as it is sometimes necessary to execute a given action at a given time, timestamping data/objects so that all machines or nodes see the same global state. Several algorithms for clock synchronization have been proposed, which include synchronization of all clocks with a central clock or through agreement. In the first case, the time server or external clock periodically sends the clock information to all the nodes, either through a broadcast or through multicast mechanisms, and the nodes adjust the clock based on the received information and the round-trip time calculation. In the second mechanism, the nodes exchange information so that the time clock can be calculated in a P2P fashion. It is to be noted that clock synchronization is a major issue in distributed systems and clock skew always needs to be considered when designing such a system.
- **Leader election:** This is another critical synchronization problem used in many distributed systems. Many varieties of solution are available, ranging from the old leader forcing the new leader on the group members based on certain selection criteria, to polls or votes where the node receiving the maximum number of votes gets elected as the leader.
- **Collection global state:** In some applications, especially when debugging a distributed system, knowledge of the global states is especially useful. Global state in a distributed system is defined as the sum of the local states and states in transit. One mechanism is to obtain a distributed

snapshot which represents the consistent and global state in which the distributed system would have been. There are several challenges in moving a process to the consistent state.

- **Mutual exclusion:** In some cases, it is required that certain processes access critical sections or data in a mutually-exclusive manner. One way to tackle such a problem is to emulate the centralized system by having the server manage the process lock through the use of tokens. Tokens can also be managed in a distributed manner using a ring or a P2P system, which increases the complexity.

8.5.4.2 Fault Tolerance

If we look at the issue of fault tolerance from the distributed systems perspective, it is both an opportunity and a threat. It is an opportunity as distributed systems bring with them natural redundancy, which can be used to provide fault tolerance. However, it is a threat as the issue of fault tolerance is complex, and extensive research has been carried out in this area to tackle the problem effectively. One of the issues that haunts distributed systems designers is the source of many failures. Failures can happen in processing nodes and transmission media, and due to distributed agreement.

- **Processing sites:** The fact that the processing sites of a distributed system are independent of each other means that they are independent points of failure. While this is an advantage from the viewpoint of the user of the system, it presents a complex problem for developers. In a centralized system, the failure of a processing site implies the failure of all the software as well. In contrast, in a fault-tolerant distributed system, a processing site failure means that the software on the remaining sites needs to detect and handle that failure in some way. This may involve redistributing the functionality from the failed site to other, operational, sites, or it may mean switching to some emergency mode of operation.
- **Communication media:** Another kind of failure that is inherent in most distributed systems comes from the communication medium. The most obvious, of course, is a permanent hard failure of the entire medium, which makes communication between processing sites impossible. In the most severe cases, this type of failure can lead to partitioning of the system into multiple parts that are completely isolated from each other. The danger here is that the different parts will undertake activities that conflict with each other. Intermittent failures are more difficult to detect and correct, especially if the media is wireless in nature.
- **Errors due to transmission delays:** There are two different types of problem caused by message delays. One type results from variable delays (jitter). That is, the time it takes for a message to reach its destination may vary significantly. The delays depend on a number of factors, such as the route taken through the communication medium, congestion in the medium, congestion at the processing sites (e.g. a busy receiver), intermittent hardware failures and so on. If the transmission delay is constant then we can much more easily assess when a message has been lost. For this reason, some communication networks are designed as synchronous networks, so that delay values are fixed and known in advance. However, even if the transmission delay is constant, there is still the problem of out-of-date information. Since messages are used to convey information about state changes between components of the distributed system, if the

delays experienced are greater than the time required to change from one state to the next, the information in these messages will be out of date. This can have major repercussions that can lead to unstable systems. Just imagine trying to drive a car if visual input to the driver were delayed by several seconds.

- **Distributed agreement:** The problem of distributed agreement has been briefly touched upon in the previous subsection. There are many variations of this problem, including time synchronization, consistent distributed state, distributed mutual exclusion, distributed transaction commit, distributed termination, distributed election and so on. However, all of these reduce to the common problem of reaching agreement in a distributed environment in the presence of failures.

8.5.4.3 Security

Perhaps the most compelling challenge associated with distributed systems is the issue of security. The complexity of the issue arises from the different points of vulnerability that exist in a distributed system. The processing nodes, transmission media and clients are the obvious points that need to be secured. With the growth of heterogeneity in different layers of enterprise infrastructure, the complexity increases enormously.

8.5.5 Applications of Distributed Systems

There are two main reasons for using distributed systems and distributed computing. First, the very nature of the application may require the use of a communication network that connects several computers. For example, data is produced in one physical location and it is needed in another location.

Second, there are many cases in which the use of a single computer would be possible in principle, but the use of a distributed system is beneficial for practical reasons. For example, it may be more cost-efficient to obtain the desired level of performance by using a cluster of several low-end computers, in comparison with a single high-end computer. A distributed system can be more reliable than a non-distributed system, as there is no single point of failure. Moreover, a distributed system may be easier to expand and manage than a monolithic uniprocessor system.

Examples of distributed systems and applications of distributed computing include the following:

- **Telecommunication networks:**
  - Telephone networks and cellular networks.
  - Computer networks such as the Internet.
  - Wireless sensor networks.
  - Routing algorithms.
- **Network applications:**
  - World Wide Web and peer-to-peer networks.
  - Massively multiplayer online games and virtual reality communities.

- Distributed databases and distributed database management systems.
- Network file systems.
- Distributed information processing systems such as banking systems and airline reservation systems.

- **Real-time process control:**
  - Aircraft control systems.
  - Industrial control systems.
- **Parallel computation:**
  - Scientific computing, including cluster computing and grid computing and various volunteer computing projects; see the list of distributed computing projects.
  - Distributed rendering in computer graphics.

EXERCISES

1. What is E-mail? Also explain the history of email?
2. Explain the operation performed by email?
3. What are the advantages of email communication for business?
4. What are the advantages and disadvantages of email?
5. What do you mean by telnet?
6. Explain the history and standards of telnet?
7. What do you mean by telnet Security?
8. Explain the various telnet commands?
9. What are the advantages of telnet?
10. How we can use telnet?
11. Explain various types of services available via telnet?
12. What do you mean by FTP?
13. Explain the concept of FTP in detail?
14. Explain the security concerns of FTP?
15. What do you mean by anonymous FTP?
16. How we can use FTP?
17. Explain the various commands of FTP?

18. Explain the security and automatic login of FTP?
19. Explain the various subcommands of FTP?
20. Write an example of regular FTP session?
21. What are the common FTP commands?
22. What is distributed systems?
23. Explain the characteristics of distributed systems?
24. Explain the various types of distributed system?
25. Explain the different architectures of distributed systems?
26. Explain the various challenges in designing distributed systems?
27. Explain the various applications of distributed systems?

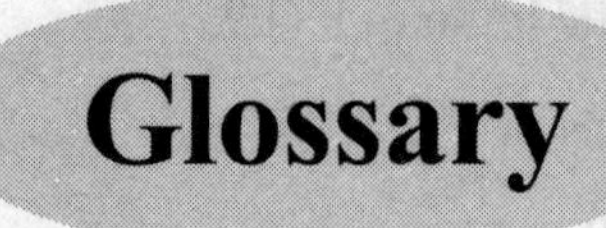

Glossary

A

access control entry (ACE) An entry in an access control list (ACL) that defines the level of access for a user or group.

access control list (ACL) A set of data associated with a file, directory, or other resource that defines the permissions users or groups have for accessing it. In Active Directory, the ACL is a list of access control entries (ACEs) stored with the object it protects. In Microsoft Windows NT, an ACL is stored as a binary value called a security descriptor.

access token or security access token A collection of security identifiers (SIDs) that represent a user and that user's group memberships. The security subsystem compares SIDs in the token to SIDs in an access control list (ACL) to determine resource access.

account lockout A security feature that disables a user account if failed logons exceed a specified number in a specified period of time. Locked accounts cannot log on and must be unlocked by an administrator.

Active Directory Beginning in Microsoft Windows 2000 Server and continuing in Windows Server 2003, Active Directory replaces the Windows NT collection of directory functions with functionality that integrates with and relies upon standards including Domain Name System (DNS), Lightweight Directory Access Protocol (LDAP), and Kerberos security protocol.

Active Directory-integrated zone A DNS (Domain Name System) zone stored in Active Directory so it has Active Directory security features and can be used for multimaster replication.

Active Directory Service Interface (ADSI) A programming interface that provides access to Active Directory.

ActiveX A loosely defined set of technologies that allows software components to interact with each other in a networked environment.

ActiveX component Reusable software component that adheres to the ActiveX specification and can operate in an ActiveX-compliant environment.

address A precise location where a piece of information is stored in memory or on disk. Also, the unique identifier for a node on a network. On the Internet, the code by which an individual user is identified. The format is username@hostname, where username is your user name, logon name, or account number, and host-name is the name of the computer or Internet provider you use. The host name might be a few words strung together with periods.

Address Resolution Protocol (ARP) A Transmission Control Protocol/Internet Protocol (TCP/IP) and AppleTalk protocol that provides IP-address-to-MAC (media access control) address resolution for IP packets.

Advanced Configuration Power Interface (ACPI) An industry specification, defining power management on a range of computer devices. ACPI compliance is necessary for devices to take advantage of Plug and Play and power management capabilities.

allocation unit The smallest unit of managed space on a hard disk or logical volume. Also called a cluster.

anonymous FTP A way to use an FTP program to log on to another computer to copy files when you do not have an account on that computer. When you log on, enter anonymous as the user name and your e-mail address as the password. This gives you access to publicly available files. See also File Transfer Protocol (FTP).

AppleTalk Local area network architecture built into Macintosh computers to connect them with printers. A network with a Windows Server 2003 server and Macintosh clients can function as an AppleTalk network with the use of AppleTalk network integration (formerly Services for Macintosh).

Archive (A) attribute An attribute of each file that is used by backup utilities to determine whether or not to back up that file. The Archive attribute is set to TRUE whenever a file is created or modified. Differential and incremental backup jobs will back up files only if their archive attribute is TRUE.

Associate To connect files having a particular extension to a specific program. When you double-click a file with the extension, the associated program is launched and the file you clicked is opened. In Windows, associated file extensions are usually called registered file types.

Asynchronous Transfer Mode (ATM) A network technology based on sending data in cells or packets of a fixed size. It is asynchronous in that the transmission of cells containing information from a particular user is not necessarily periodic.

attribute A characteristic. In Windows file management, it is information that shows whether a file is read-only, hidden, compressed, encrypted, ready to be backed up (archived), or should be indexed.

audit policy Defines the type of security events to be logged. It can be defined on a server or an individual computer.

authentication Verification of the identity of a user or computer process. In Windows Server 2003, Windows 2000, and Windows NT, authentication involves comparing the user's security identifier (SID) and password to a list of authorized users on a domain controller.

authoritative restore Specifies a type of recovery of Active Directory. When an authoritative restore is performed using the Backup Utility and Ntdsutil in the Directory Services Restore Mode, the directory or the specific object(s) in the directory that have been authoritatively restored are replicated to other domain controllers in the forest. See also non-authoritative restore.

Automated System Recovery (ASR) A feature of Windows Server 2003 that allows an administrator to return a failed server to operation efficiently. Using the ASR Wizard of the Backup Utility, you create an ASR set which includes a floppy disk with a catalog of system files, and a comprehensive backup. When a server fails, boot with the Windows Server 2003 CD-ROM and press F2 when prompted to start Automated System Recovery.

Automatic Updates A client-side component that can be used to keep a system up to date with security rollups, patches, and drivers. Automatic Updates is also the client component of a Software **Update Services** (SUS) infrastructure, which allows an enterprise to provide centralized and managed updates.

B

Background Intelligent Transfer Service (BITS) A service used to transfer files between a client and a Hypertext Transfer Protocol (HTTP) server. BITS intelligently uses idle network bandwidth, and will decrease transfer requests when other network traffic increases.

backup domain controller (BDC) In a Windows NT domain, a computer that stores a backup of the database that contains all the security and account information from the primary domain controller (PDC). The database is regularly and automatically synchronized with the copy on the PDC. A BDC also authenticates logons and can be promoted to a PDC when necessary. In a Windows Server 2003 or Windows 2000 domain, BDCs are not required; all domain controllers are peers, and all can perform maintenance on the directory.

backup media pool A logical set of backup storage media used by Windows Server 2003 and Windows 2000 Server Backup.

bandwidth On a network, the transmission capacity of a communications channel stated in megabits per second (Mbps). For example, Ethernet has a bandwidth of 10 Mbps. Fast Ethernet has a bandwidth of 100 Mbps.

basic disk A physical disk that is configured with partitions. The disk's structure is compatible with previous versions of Windows and with several non-Windows operating systems.

Basic Input/Output System (BIOS) The program used by a personal computer's microprocessor to start the system and manage data flow between the operating system and the computer's devices, such as its hard disks, CD-ROM, video adapter, keyboard, and mouse.

binding A software connection between a network card and a network transport protocol such as Transmission Control Protocol/Internet Protocol (TCP/IP).

BOOTP Used on Transmission Control Protocol/Internet Protocol (TCP/IP) networks to enable a diskless workstation to learn its own IP address, the location of a BOOTP server on the network, and the location of a file to be loaded into memory to boot the machine. This allows a computer to boot without a hard disk or a floppy disk. Stands for "Boot Protocol."

bottleneck Refers to the point of resource insufficiency when demand for computer system resources and services becomes extreme enough to cause performance degradation.

broadcasting To send a message to all computers on a network simultaneously. See also multicasting.

Browser service The service that maintains a current list of computers and provides the list to applications when needed. When a user attempts to connect to a resource in the domain, the Browser service is contacted to provide a list of avail-able resources. The lists displayed in My Network Places and Active Directory Users and Computers (among others) are provided by the Browser service. Also called the Computer Browser service.

C

Caching A process used to enhance performance by retaining previously-accessed information in a location that provides faster response than the original location. Hard disk caching is used by the File and Print Sharing for Microsoft Networks service, which stores recently accessed disk information in memory for faster retrieval. The Remote Desktop Connection client can cache previously viewed screen shots from the terminal server on its local hard disk to improve performance of the Remote Desktop Protocol (RDP) connection.

catalog An index of files in a backup set.

certificate A credential used to prove the origin, authenticity, and purpose of a public key to the entity that holds the corresponding private key.

certificate authority (CA) The service that accepts and fulfills certificate requests and revocation requests and that can also manage the policy-directed registration process a user completes to get a certificate.

certificate revocation list (CRL) A digitally signed list (published by a certificate authority) of certificates that are no longer valid.

child domain A domain located directly beneath another domain name (which is known as a parent domain). For example, Engineering.scribes.com is a child domain of scribes.com, the parent domain. Also called a subdomain.

child object An object inside another object. For example, a file is a child object inside a folder, which is the parent object.

Client Access License (CAL) The legal right to connect to a service or application. CALs can be configured per server or per device/per user.

cluster A set of computers joined together in such a way that they behave as a single system. Clustering is used for network load balancing as well as fault tolerance. In data storage, a cluster is the smallest amount of disk space that can be allocated for a file.

Cluster service The collection of software on each node that manages all cluster-specific activity.

codec Technology that compresses and decompresses data, particularly audio or video. Codecs can be implemented in software, hardware, or a combination of both.

common name (CN) The primary name of an object in a Lightweight Directory Access Protocol (LDAP) directory such as Active Directory. The CN must be unique within the container or organizational unit (OU) in which the object exists.

concurrent Simultaneous.

console tree The default left pane in a Microsoft Management Console (MMC) that shows the items contained in a console.

container An Active Directory object that has attributes and is part of the Active Directory namespace. Unlike other objects, it does not usually represent some-thing concrete. It is a package for a group of objects and other containers.

D

delegate Assign administrative rights over a portion of the namespace to another user or group.

Device Driver A program that enables a specific device, such as a modem, network adapter, or printer, to communicate with the operating system. Although a device might be installed on your system, Windows cannot use the device until you have installed and configured the appropriate driver. Device drivers load automatically (for all enabled devices) when a computer is started, and thereafter run transparently.

Device Manager An administrative tool that you can use to administer the devices on your computer. Using Device Manager, you can view and change device properties, update device drivers, configure device settings, and uninstall devices.

digital signature An attribute of a driver, application, or document that identifies the creator of the file. Microsoft's digital signature is included in all Microsoft-supplied drivers, providing assurance as to the stability and compatibility of the drivers with Windows Server 2003 and Windows 2000 Server.

directory service A means of storing directory data and making it available to net-work users and administrators. For example, Active Directory stores information about user accounts, such as names, passwords, phone numbers, and so on, and enables other authorized users on the same network to access this information.

disk quota A limitation set by an administrator on the amount of disk space available to a user.

distinguished name (DN) In the context of Active Directory, "distinguished" means the qualities that make the name distinct. The DN identifies the domain that holds the object, as well as the complete path through the container hierarchy used to reach the object.

Distributed file system (Dfs) A file management system in which files can be located on separate computers but are presented to users as a single directory tree.

DNS name servers Servers that contain information about part of the Domain Name System (DNS) database. These servers make computer names available to queries for name resolution across the Internet. Also called domain name servers.

domain A group of computers that share a security policy and a user account data-base. A Windows Server 2003 domain is not the same as an Internet domain. See also domain name.

domain controller A server in a domain that accepts account logons and initiates their authentication. In an Active Directory domain, a domain controller controls access to network resources and participates in replication.

domain functional level The level at which an Active Directory domain operates. As functional levels are raised, more features of Active Directory become avail-able. There are four levels: Windows 2000 mixed, Windows 2000 native, Windows Server 2003 interim, and Windows Server 2003.

domain local group A local group used on ACLs only in its own domain. A domain local group can contain users and global groups from any domain in the forest, universal groups, and other domain local groups in its own domain.

domain name In Active Directory, the name given to a collection of networked computers that share a common directory. On the Internet, the unique text name that identifies a specific host. A machine can have more than one domain name, but a given domain name points to only one machine. Domain names are resolved to IP addresses by DNS name servers.

Domain Name System (DNS) A service on Transmission Control Protocol/Internet Protocol (TCP/IP) networks (including the Internet) that translates domain names into IP addresses. This allows users to employ friendly names like FinanceServer or Adatum.com when querying a remote system, instead of using an IP address such as 192.168.1.10.

domain naming master The one domain controller assigned to handle the addition or removal of domains in a forest. See also Operations Master.

DWORD A data type consisting of four bytes in hexadecimal.

Dynamic Data Exchange (DDE) Communication between processes implemented in the Windows family of operating systems. When programs that support DDE are running at the same time, they can exchange data by means of conversations. Conversations are two-way connections between two applications that transmit data alternately.

dynamic disk A disk that is configured using volumes. Its configuration is stored in the Logical Disk Manager (LDM) database, and is replicated to other dynamic disks attached to the same computer. Dynamic disks are compatible only with Windows Server 2003, Windows XP, and Windows 2000.

Dynamic Host Configuration Protocol (DHCP) A Transmission Control Protocol/ Internet Protocol (TCP/IP) protocol used to automatically assign IP addresses and configure TCP/IP for network clients.

dynamic-link library (DLL) A program module that contains executable code and data that can be used by various programs. A program uses the DLL only when the program is active, and the DLL is unloaded when the program closes.

E

effective permissions The permissions that result from the evaluation of group and user permissions allowed, denied, inherited, and explicitly defined on a resource. The effective permissions determine the actual access for a security principal.

enterprise Term used to encompass a business's entire operation, including all remote offices and branches.

environment variable A string of environment information such as a drive, path, or filename associated with a symbolic name. The System option in Control Panel or the Set command from the command prompt can be used to define environment variables.

Ethernet A local area network (LAN) protocol. Ethernet supports data transfer rates of 10 Mbps and uses a bus topology and thick or thin coaxial, fiberoptic, or twisted-pair cabling. A newer version of Ethernet called Fast Ethernet supports data transfer rates of 100 Mbps, and an even newer version, Gigabit Ethernet, sup-ports data transfer rates of 1000 Mbps.

extended partition A nonbootable portion of a hard disk that can be subdivided into logical drives. There can be only a single extended partition per hard disk.

Extensible Authentication Protocol (EAP) An extension to the Point-to-Point Protocol (PPP) that allows the use of arbitrary authentication methods for validating a PPP Connection.

Extensible Markup Language (XML) An abbreviated version of the Standard Generalized Markup Language (SGML), it allows the flexible development of user-defined document types and provides a non-proprietary, persistent, and verifiable file format for the storage and transmission of text and data both on and off the Web.

external trust A one-way or two-way trust for providing access to a Windows NT 4 domain or a domain located in another forest that is not joined by a forest trust.

F

failover An operation that automatically switches to a standby database, server, or network if the primary system fails or is temporarily shut down for servicing. In server clusters, the process of taking resources off one node in a prescribed order and restoring them on another node.

fault tolerance The ability of a system to ensure data integrity when an unexpected hardware or software failure occurs. Many fault-tolerant computer systems mirror all operations-that is, all operations are done on two or more duplicate systems, so if one fails the other can take over.

File Replication Service (FRS) The service responsible for ensuring consistency of the SYSVOL folder on domain controllers. FRS will replicate, or copy, any changes made to a domain controller's SYSVOL to all other domain controllers. FRS can also be used to replicate folders in a Distributed File System (Dfs).

File Transfer Protocol (FTP) A method of transferring one or more files from one computer to another over a network or telephone line. Because FTP has been implemented on a variety of systems, it's a simple way to transfer information between usually incongruent systems such as a PC and a minicomputer.

firewall A protective filter for messages and logons. An organization connected directly to the Internet uses a firewall to prevent unauthorized access to its net-work. See also proxy server.

folder redirection An option in Group Policy to place users' special folders, such as My Documents, on a network server.

forest A group of one or more Active Directory trees that trust each other through two-way transitive trusts. All trees in a forest share a common schema, configuration, and Global Catalog (GC). When a forest contains multiple trees, the trees do not form a contiguous namespace. Unlike trees, a forest does not need a distinct name.

forest trust A transitive trust used to share resources between forests. Can be one-way or two-way.

fully qualified domain name (FQDN) A domain name that includes the names of all network domains leading back to the root to clearly indicate a location in the domain namespace tree. An example of an FQDN is Accts.finance.adatum.com or Sales.europe.microsoft.com.

G

gateway A device used to connect networks using dissimilar protocols so that information can be passed from one to another.

Global Catalog (GC) Contains a full replica of all Active Directory objects in its host domain plus a partial replica of all directory objects in every domain in the forest. A GC contains information about all objects in all domains in the forest, so finding information in the directory does not require unnecessary queries across domains. A single query to the GC produces the information about where the object can be found.

global group A group that can be used in its own domain and in trusting domains. However, it can contain user accounts and other global groups only from its own domain.

globally unique identifier (GUID) Part of the identifying mechanism generated by Active Directory for each object in the directory. If a user or computer object is renamed or moved to a different name, the security identifier (SID), relative distinguished name (RDN), and distinguished name (DN) will change, but the GUID will remain the same.

GUID partition table (GPT) The storage location for disk configuration information for disks used in 64-bit versions of Windows.

Group Policy Setting of rules for computers and users in Windows Server 2003 and Windows 2000 Server. Group Policy is able to store policies for file deployment, application deployment, logon/logoff scripts, startup/shutdown scripts, domain security, Internet Protocol security (IPSec), and so on.

Group Policy Object (GPO) A collection of policies stored in two locations: a Group Policy container (GPC) and a Group Policy template (GPT). The GPC is an Active Directory object that stores version information, status information, and other policy information (for example, application objects). The GPT is used for file-based data and stores software policy, script, and deployment information. The GPT is located in the system volume folder of the domain controller.

H

headless server A server without a monitor, keyboard, mouse, or video card, which is administered remotely.

hive One of five sections of the registry. Each hive is a discrete body of keys, sub-keys, and values that record configuration information for the computer. Each hive is a file that can be moved from one system to another but can be edited only by using the Registry Editor.

host Any device on the network that uses TCP/IP. A host is also a computer on the Internet you might be able to log on to. You can use FTP to get files from a host computer and use other protocols (such as Telnet) to make use of the host computer.

hosts file A local ASCII text file that maps host names to IP addresses. Each line represents one host, starting with the IP address, one or more spaces, and then the host's name.

hypertext A system of writing and displaying text that enables the text to be linked in multiple ways, available at several levels of detail. Hypertext documents can also contain links to related documents, such as those referred to in footnotes.

Hypertext Markup Language (HTML) A language used for writing pages for use on the Internet or an intranet. HTML allows text to include codes that define fonts, layout, embedded graphics, and hypertext links.

Hypertext Transfer Protocol (HTTP) The method by which Web pages are transferred over the network.

I

identity store A database of security identities, or security principals. Active Directory is the identity store for a Windows Server 2003 domain.

inheritance The process through which permissions are propagated from a parent object to its children. Inheritance is at work in Active Directory and on disk volumes formatted with NTFS.

instance The most granular level of performance counter. A performance object, such as LogicalDisk, has counters, such as % Free Space. That counter may have instances, representing specific occurrences of that counter, for example the free space on disk volume C:\ and disk volume D:\.

IntelliMirror A suite of technologies that allows a complete operating environment to follow the user to other computers, as well as offline. Components include the user's profiles, data, and applications.

Internet Authentication Service (IAS) The Microsoft implementation of Remote Authentication Dial-In User Service (RADIUS), an authentication and accounting system used by many Internet Service Providers (ISPs). When a user connects to an ISP using a username and password, the information is passed to a RADIUS server, which checks that the information is correct, and then authorizes access to the ISP system.

Internet Control Message Protocol (ICMP) A protocol used to report problems encountered with the delivery of data, such as unreachable hosts or unavailable ports. ICMP is also used to send a request packet to determine whether a host is available. The receiving host sends back a packet if it is available and functioning. See also ping.

Internet Printing Protocol (IPP) A protocol that allows a client to send a job to a printer over the Internet or an intranet. The communication between the client and the printer is encapsulated in HTTP.

Internet Protocol (IP) The inter-network layer protocol used as a basis of the Inter-net. IP enables information to be routed from one network to another in packets and then reassembled when they reach their destination.

Internet Protocol version 6 (IPv6) A new version of Internet Protocol supported in Windows Server 2003. The current version of IP is version 4, also known as IPv4. IPv6, formerly called IP-The Next Generation (IPng), is an evolutionary upgrade and will coexist with version 4 for some time.

Internetwork Packet Exchange/Sequenced Packet Exchange (IPX/SPX) Trans-port protocols used in Novell NetWare networks.

interrupt request (IRQ) One of a set of possible hardware interrupts, identified by a number. The number of the IRQ determines which interrupt handler will be used.

Internet Protocol security (IPSec) An Internet Engineering Task Force (IETF) standard that provides authentication and encryption over the Internet. IPSec is widely used with virtual private networks (VPNs).

IP address A 128-bit number, usually represented as a four-part decimal separated by periods (for example, 192.168.1.10) that uniquely identifies a machine on the Internet. Every machine on the Internet has a unique IP address.

K

Kerberos An identity-based security system developed at the Massachusetts Institute of Technology (MIT) that authenticates users at logon. It works by assigning a unique key, called a ticket, to each user who logs on to the network. The ticket is then embedded in messages to identify the sender of the message. The Kerberos security protocol is the primary authentication mechanism in Windows Server 2003 and Windows 2000 Server.

kernel The part of the executive (or operating system) that manages the processor. The kernel performs thread scheduling and dispatching, interrupt and exception handling, and multiprocessor synchronization.

L

Layer Two Tunneling Protocol (L2TP) An extension to the Point-to-Point Protocol (PPP) used in conjunction with IPSec to provide secure VPN connections.

license group A group of users or devices that shares one or more client access licenses (CALs). License groups are administered using the Licensing tool in the Administrative Tools folder.

Lightweight Data Interchange Format (LDIF) An ASCII file format used to transfer data between Lightweight Directory Access Protocol (LDAP) directory services.

Lightweight Directory Access Protocol (LDAP) A protocol used to access a directory service. LDAP is a simplified version of the Directory Access Protocol (DAP), which is used to gain access to X.500 directories. LDAP is the primary access protocol for Active Directory.

LISTSERV A family of programs that manage Internet mailing lists by distributing messages posted to the list, and adding and deleting members automatically.

Lmhosts An ASCII text file like Hosts but used to associate IP addresses to host names inside a network. To remember which is which, remember Lmhosts as LAN Manager Hosts.

local area network (LAN) A group of connected computers, usually located close to one another (such as in the same building or the same floor of the building) so that data can be passed among them.

log on The act of entering into a computer system; for example, "Log on to the net-work and read your e-mail."

Logical Disk Manager (LDM) The service responsible for maintaining configuration information for disks that are configured as dynamic disks.

logical printer The representation of a physical printer. A logical printer is created on a Windows computer and includes the printer driver, printer settings, print defaults, and other configuration information that controls when and how a print job is sent to the printer.

logon script Typically a batch file set to run when a user logs on or logs off a system. A logon script is used to configure a user's initial environment. A logoff script is used to return a system to some predetermined condition. Either script can be assigned to multiple users individually or through Group Policy.

M

master boot record (MBR) The first sector on a hard disk where the computer gets its startup information. Thc MBR contains the partition table for the computer and a small program called the master boot code.

master file table (MFT) A special system file on an NT file system (NTFS) volume that consists of a database describing every file and subdirectory on the volume.

media access control (MAC) address A unique 48-bit number assigned to network interface cards by the manufacturer. MAC addresses are used for mapping in TCP/ IP network communication.

media pool A logical collection of removable media sharing the same management policies.

member server A server that is part of a domain but is not a domain controller. Member servers can be dedicated to managing files or printer services or other functions. A member server does not verify logons or maintain a security database.

mirror 1. Two partitions on two hard disks (also called RAID-1) configured so that each will contain identical data to the other. If one disk fails, the other contains the data and processing can continue. 2. A File Transfer Protocol (FTP) server that provides copies of the same files as another server. Some FTP servers are so popular that other servers have been set up to mirror them and spread the FTP load to more than one site.

MMC (Microsoft Management Console) A framework for hosting administrative tools called snap-ins. A console might contain tools, folders, or other containers, Web pages, and other administrative items. These items are displayed in the left pane of the console, called a console tree. A console has one or more windows that can provide views of the console tree. See also snap-in.

multicasting Simultaneously sending a message to more than one destination on a network. Multicasting is distinguished from broadcasting in that multicasting sends to only selected recipients.

multilink dialing Combining two or more physical communication links into a single logical link to increase available bandwidth.

multimaster replication A feature of Active Directory, multimaster replication automatically propagates every object (such as users, groups, computers, domains, organization units, security policies, and so on) created on any domain controller to each of the other participating domain controllers. All domain controllers contain the same directory data, so the domain does not depend on a single source for directory information.

multitasking Computer legerdemain by which tasks are switched in and out of the processor so quickly that it appears they are all happening at once. The success of a multitasking system depends on how well the various tasks are isolated from one another.

multithreading The simultaneous processing of several threads inside the same program. Because several threads can be processed in parallel, one thread does not have to finish before another one can start.

N

name resolution The process of mapping a name to its corresponding IP address.

namespace A name or group of names defined according to a naming convention; any bounded area in which a given name can be resolved. Active Directory is primarily a namespace, as is any directory service. The Internet uses a hierarchical namespace that partitions names into categories known as top-level domains, such as .com, .edu, and .gov.

native mode In Windows 2000 domains, the condition of a domain when all domain controllers have been upgraded to Windows 2000 and the administrator has enabled native mode operation. In Windows Server 2003 domains, where there are no Windows 2000 or Windows NT 4 domain controllers, native mode is simply called Windows Server 2003 mode or functional level. See also domain functional level.

Net Logon service A service that accepts logon requests from any client and provides authentication from the Security Accounts Manager (SAM) database of accounts.

NetBIOS Enhanced User Interface (NetBEUI) A small and fast protocol that requires little memory but can be routed only by using token ring routing. Remote locations linked by routers cannot use NetBEUI to communicate.

network Two or more computers connected for the purpose of sharing resources.

Network Access Server (NAS) A server that accepts Point-to-Point Protocol connections and places them on the network served by NAS.

Network Address Translation (NAT) A technology that enables a local-area net-work (LAN) to use one set of Internet Protocol (IP) addresses for internal traffic and a second set of addresses for external traffic.

Network Load Balancing (NLB) A technology that allows for efficient utilization of multiple network cards.

Network News Transfer Protocol (NNTP) A protocol defined for distribution, inquiry, retrieval, and posting of news articles on the Internet.

newsgroup On the Internet, a distributed bulletin board system about a particular topic. USENET News (also known as Netnews) is a system that distributes thou-sands of newsgroups to all parts of the Internet.

node A location on a tree structure with links to one or more items below it. On a local area network (LAN), a device that can communicate with other devices on the network. In clustering, a computer that is a member of a cluster.

non-authoritative restore When a domain controller's system state is restored, Active Directory is restored. When the domain controller is restarted, the information in the directory, which is only as recent as the date of the backup set, is brought up to date through normal replication processes between the restored domain controller and its replication partners.

NTFS file system (NTFS) The native file system for Windows Server 2003, Windows 2000, and Windows NT. Supports long filenames, a variety of permissions for sharing files to manage access to files and folders, and a transaction log that allows the completion of any incomplete file-related tasks if the operating system is interrupted.

O

object A particular set of attributes that represents something concrete, such as a user, a printer, or an application. The attributes hold data describing the thing that is identified by the object. Attributes of a user might include the user's given name, surname, and e-mail address. The classification of the object defines which types of attributes are used. For example, the objects classified as users might allow the use of attribute types like common name, telephone number, and e-mail address, whereas the object class of organization allows for attribute types like organization name and business category. An attribute can take one or more values, depending on its type.

object identifier (OID) A globally unique identifier (GUID), which is assigned by the Directory System Agent (DSA) when the object is created. The GUID is stored in an attribute, the object GUID, which is part of every object. The object GUID attribute cannot be modified or deleted. When storing a reference to an Active Directory object in an external store (for example, a database), you should use the object GUID because, unlike a name, it will not change.

Operations Master A domain controller that has been assigned Active Directory operations that are single master-that is, operations that are not permitted to occur at different places in the network at the same time. Some single-master operations include schema modification, domain naming, and the relative identifier (RID) allocator.

organizational unit (OU) A container object in Active Directory used to separate computers, users, and other resources into logical units. An organizational unit is the smallest entity to which Group Policy can be linked. It is also the smallest scope to which administration authority can be delegated.

P

packet The basic unit of information sent over a network. Each packet contains the destination address, the sender's address, error-control information, and data. The size and format of a packet depend on the protocol being used.

page A document, or collection of information, available over the Web. A page can contain text, graphics, video, and sound files. Also can refer to a portion of memory that the virtual memory manager can swap to and from a hard disk.

paging A virtual memory operation in which pages are transferred from memory to disk when memory becomes full. When a thread accesses a page that's not in memory, a page fault occurs and the memory manager uses page tables to find the page on disk and then loads the page into memory.

PDC Emulator master The domain controller that services network clients that do not have Active Directory client software installed and replicates changes to any Windows NT backup controllers. The PDC emulator master also handles authentication requests for accounts with recently changed passwords, if the change has not been replicated yet to the entire domain.

Ping An Internet Protocol (IP) utility that checks to see whether another computer is available and functioning. It sends a short message to which the other computer automatically responds. If the other computer does not respond to the ping, it is often an indication that communications between the two computers cannot be established at the IP level.

point of presence (POP) A physical site in a geographic area where a network access provider, such as a telecommunications company, has equipment to which users connect. The local telephone company's central office in a particular area is also sometimes referred to as their POP for that area.

Point-to-Point Tunneling Protocol (PPTP) A protocol that provides router-to-router and host-to-network connections over a telephone line (or a network link that acts like a telephone line). See also Serial Line Internet Protocol (SLIP).

port From a computer system perspective, a physical connection point on a computer where you can connect devices that pass data into and out of a computer. For example, a printer is typically connected to a parallel port (also called an LPT port), and a modem is typically connected to a serial port (also called a COM port). From a network perspective, a port is a numbered communication channel through which information passes from one computer system to another. Terminal Services traffic, for example, communicates on port 3389.

Post Office Protocol (POP) A protocol by which a mail server on the Internet lets you access your mail and download it to a computer. Most people refer to this protocol with its version number (POP2, POP3, and so on) to avoid confusing it with points of presence (POPs).

primary domain controller (PDC) In a Windows NT domain, the server that authenticates domain logons and maintains the security policy and master data-base for a domain. In a Windows 2000 or Windows Server 2003 domain, running in mixed mode, one of the domain controllers in each domain is identified as the PDC emulator master for compatibility with down-level clients and servers.

primary partition A portion of the hard disk that's been marked as a potentially bootable logical drive by an operating system. MS-DOS can support only a single primary partition. Master boot record disks can support four primary partitions. Computers with the Intel Itanium processor use a GUID partition table that sup-ports up to 128 primary partitions.

profile Loaded by the system when a user logs on, the profile defines a user's environment, including network settings, printer connections, desktop settings, and program items.

proxy server A server that receives Web requests from clients, retrieves Web pages, and forwards them back to clients. Proxy servers can dramatically improve performance for groups of users by caching retrieved pages. Proxy servers also provide security by shielding the IP addresses of internal clients from the Internet.

public-key cryptography A method of secure transmission in which two different keys are used-a public key for encrypting data and a private key for decrypting data.

Q

Quality of Service (QoS) A set of standards for assuring the quality of data transmission on a network.

Queue Length A performance counter that measures the number of instructions that are waiting to be processed by an object such as the Processor or Physical Disk. If the Queue Length is greater than 2 or 3 for an extended period of time, it is a reflection that the system's resources are not sufficient for the demands being placed on that system.

R

realm trust Used to connect between a non-Windows Kerberos realm and a Windows Server 2003 domain. Realm trusts can be transitive or non-transitive, one-way, or two-way.

Recovery Console A command-line interface that provides limited access to the system for troubleshooting purposes. The Recovery Console can be launched by booting with the Windows Server 2003 CD-ROM and, when prompted, pressing R for Repair.

redundant array of independent disks (RAID) A range of disk management and striping techniques to implement fault tolerance.

relative distinguished name (RDN) Active Directory uses the concept of a relative distinguished name (RDN), which is the part of the distinguished name that is an attribute of the object itself.

relative identifier (RID) The part of the security identifier (SID) that is unique to each object.

Remote Access Service (RAS) Allows users to connect from remote locations and access their networks for file and printer sharing and e-mail. The computer initiating the connection is the RAS client; the answering computer is the RAS server.

Remote Assistance Allows for a novice user to use Windows Messenger to request personal, interactive help from an expert user. When the help request is accepted and the remote session negotiated, the expert is able to view and, if allowed by the novice, control the desktop.

Remote Authentication Dial-In User Service (RADIUS) A security authentication system used by many Internet service providers (ISPs). A user connects to the ISP and enters a user name and password. This information is verified by a RADIUS server, which then authorizes access to the ISP system.

Remote Desktop for Administration A technology based on Terminal Services that allows up to two remote connections to a server for remote administration purposes. In Windows 2000, this was known as Terminal Server in Remote Administration mode.

Remote Installation Services (RIS) Allows clients to boot from a network server and use special preboot diagnostic tools installed on the server to automatically install a client operating system.

Removable Storage Management (RSM) system A feature of Windows Server 2003 that interfaces with robotic changers and media libraries, enables multiple applications to share local libraries and tape or disk drives, and controls removable media within a single-server system.

replication On network computers, enables the contents of a directory, designated as an export directory, to be copied to other directories, called import directories. Active Directory changes are replicated to all domain controllers on a regular schedule.

Requests for Comments (RFCs) An evolving collection of information that details the functions within the TCP/IP family of protocols. Some RFCs are official documents of the Internet Engineering Task Force (IETF), defining the standards of TCP/IP and the Internet, whereas others are simply proposals trying to become standards, and others fall somewhere in between. Some are tutorial in nature, whereas others are quite technical.

roaming user profile A profile that is stored in a network-accessible location, thus allowing a user to access their desktop, application data, and settings when they log on to any computer. See also profile.

router A network hardware device (or computer-installed software package) that handles the connection between two or more networks. Routers look at the destination addresses of the packets passing through them and decide which route to use to send them.

S

schema A set of definitions of the object classes and attributes that can be stored in Active Directory. Like other objects in Active Directory, schema objects have an access control list (ACL) to limit alterations to only authorized users.

schema master The single domain controller assigned to track all updates to a schema within a forest.

scope In Dynamic Host Configuration Protocol (DHCP), the range of Internet Protocol (IP) addresses available to be leased to DHCP clients by the DHCP service. In groups, scope describes where in the network permissions can be assigned to the group.

Security Accounts Manager (SAM) A service used at logon that manages user account information, including group membership.

security descriptor An attribute of an object that contains ownership and access control information.

Security Identifier (SID) A unique number assigned to every computer, group, and user account on a Windows Server 2003, Windows 2000, or Windows NT network. Internal processes in the operating system refer to an account's SID, rather than a name. A deleted SID is never reused.

security principal An identity that can be given permission to a resource. A security principal is an object that includes a security identifier (SID) attribute. Windows Server 2003 supports four security principals: users, groups, computers, and the InetOrgPerson object.

Serial Line Internet Protocol (SLIP) A protocol used to run Internet Protocol (IP) over serial lines or telephone lines using modems. Rapidly being replaced by Point-to-Point Tunneling Protocol (PPTP). SLIP is part of Windows remote access for compatibility with other remote access software.

server A computer that provides a service to other computers on a network. A file server, for example, provides files to client machines.

Server Message Block (SMB) An application-layer protocol that allows a client to access files and printers on remote servers. Clients and servers that are configured to support SMB can communicate using SMB over transport- and network-layer protocols, including Transmission Control Protocol (TCP/IP).

Service locator (SRV) resource record A record in a DNS zone that specifies the computer (by name) that is hosting a particular service. SRV records allow clients to query DNS for services.

shortcut trust Used to reduce logon times between two domains in a Windows Server 2003 or Windows 2000 forest. This type of trust is transitive and can be one-way or two-way.

Simple Object Access Protocol (SOAP) An XML/HTTP-based protocol that provides a way for applications to communicate with each other over the Internet, independent of platform.

site In Active Directory, an area of one or more well-connected subnets. When users log on to a site, clients use Active Directory servers in the same site. See also well-connected.

smart card A credit card-sized device that securely stores user credentials such as pass-words, certificates, public and private keys, and other types of personal information.

snap-in A tool that can be added to a console supported by the Microsoft Management Console (MMC). You can add a snap-in extension to extend the function of a snap-in.

socket An endpoint to a connection. Two sockets form a complete path for a bidirectional pipe for incoming and outgoing data between networked computers. The Windows Sockets API is a networking application programming interface (API) for programmers writing for the Windows family of products.

Software Update Services (SUS) A server-based technology that centralizes the acquisition and approval of security rollups and critical updates for distribution to network clients running the Automatic Updates client.

subnet The portion of a Transmission Control Protocol/Internet Protocol (TCP/IP) network in which all devices share a common prefix. For example, all devices with an IP address that starts with 198 are on the same subnet. IP networks are divided using a subnet mask.

superscope A collection of scopes grouped into a single administrative whole. Grouping scopes together into a superscope makes it possible to have more than one logical subnet on a physical subnet.

SystemRoot The path and folder where the Windows system files are located. The value %SystemRoot% can be used in paths to replace the actual location. To identify the SystemRoot folder on a computer, type **%SystemRoot%** at a command prompt.

System State The collection of critical system files, such as the registry, COM+ registration database, and startup files that must be backed up regularly to provide for system recoverability.

SYSVOL The folder on a domain controller that contains group policies and logon scripts. SYSVOL is replicated between domain controllers by the file replication service (FRS).

T

Telnet The protocol and program used to log on from one Internet site to another. The Telnet protocol/program gets you to the logon prompt of another host.

terminal A device that allows you to send commands to another computer. At a minimum, this usually means a keyboard, a display screen, and some simple circuitry. You will usually use terminal software in a personal computer-the software pre-tends to be, or emulates, a physical terminal and allows you to type commands to another computer.

Terminal Services The underlying technology that enables Remote Desktop for Administration, Remote Assistance, and Terminal Server.

thread An executable entity that belongs to one (and only one) process. In a multi-tasking environment, a single program can contain several threads, all running at the same time.

token ring A type of computer network in which the computers connected in a ring. A token, which is a special bit pattern, travels around the ring. To communicate to another computer, a computer catches the token, attaches a message to it, and the token continues around the network, dropping off the message at the designated location.

transitive trust The standard trust between Windows Server 2003 domains in a domain tree or forest. Transitive trusts are always two-way trusts. When a domain joins a domain tree or forest, a transitive trust relationship is established automatically.

Transmission Control Protocol/Internet Protocol (TCP/IP) A suite of protocols that networks use to communicate with each other on the Internet.

tree A tree in Active Directory is just an extension of the idea of a directory tree. It's a hierarchy of objects and containers that demonstrates how objects are connected, or the path from one object to another. Endpoints on the tree are usually objects.

trust relationship A security term meaning that one workstation or server trusts a domain controller to authenticate a user logon on its behalf. It also means a domain controller trusts a domain controller in another domain to authenticate a logon.

U

Uniform Resource Locator (URL) The standard way to give the address of any resource on the Internet that is part of the Internet. For example, http://www.adatum.com. The most common way to use a URL is to enter it into a Web browser.

universal group A group that can be used anywhere in a domain tree or forest. Members can come from any domain, and rights and permissions can be assigned at any domain. Universal groups are available only when the domain is in native mode.

Universal Naming Convention (UNC) A PC format for indicating the location of resources on a network. UNC uses the following format: \\Server\Shared_ resource_path. To identify the Example.txt file in the Sample folder on the server named Ample, the UNC would be \\Ample\Sample\Example.txt.

Universal Plug and Play (UPnP) A standard that enables a network-attached device such as a PC, peripheral, or wireless device to acquire an Internet Protocol (IP) address and then, using Internet and Web protocols such as Hypertext Transfer Protocol (HTTP), to announce its presence and availability on the network.

universal serial bus (USB) An interface between a computer and add-on devices that enables simplified connection and Plug-and-Play detection of those devices. USB ports support multiple devices per port and usually allow a device to be added to the computer without powering the computer off.

UNIX An operating system designed to be used by many computer users at the same time (multiuser) with Transmission Control Protocol/Internet Protocol (TCP/IP) built in. A common operating system for servers on the Internet.

user account A user's access to a network. Each user account has a unique user name and security ID (SID).

User Principal Name (UPN) An attribute of every user object in Active Directory that uniquely identifies that user in the entire forest. The UPN includes the user logon name and a suffix, such as lsmithbates@contoso.com.

user profile Information about user accounts. See also profile.

user right A logon right or privilege that allows a user to perform a system task, such as logging on locally or restoring files and folders. Because user rights are system-specific, rather than resource-specific, they will override permissions on an individual resource. For example, users with the user right to Backup Files And Folders can back up a file to tape even if they are denied read permission for that file.

V

Virtual Private Network (VPN) A network constructed by using public wires to connect nodes. VPNs use encryption, such as Internet Protocol security (IPSec), and other security mechanisms to make sure only authorized users can access the network and that the data cannot be intercepted.

Voice over Internet Protocol (VoIP) A method for using the Internet as a transmission medium for telephone calls.

Volume Shadow Copy Service (VSS) A service that creates snapshot backups of files, allowing a backup utility to back up the snapshot regardless of whether the original file is locked or open.

W

Web-Based Enterprise Management (WBEM) A set of management and Internet standard technologies developed to unify the management of enterprise computing environments. Microsoft's implementation of WBEM is the Windows Management Instrumentation.

well-connected Being fast and reliable for the needs of Active Directory site communication. The definition of "sufficiently fast and reliable" for a particular net-work depends on the work being done on the specific network.

wide area network (WAN) Any Internet or network that covers an area larger than a single building or campus.

Windows Internet Name Service (WINS) A name resolution service that converts computer NetBIOS names to Internet Protocol (IP) addresses in a routed environment.

Windows Management Instrumentation (WMI) A programming interface that provides access to the hardware, software, and other components of a computer. WMI is the Microsoft implementation of Web-Based Enterprise Management (WBEM) to establish standards of data in Enterprise Management.

Windows Sockets (Winsock) Winsock is a standard way for Windows-based pro-grams to work with Transmission Control Protocol/Internet Protocol (TCP/IP). You can use Winsock if you use SLIP to connect to the Internet.

workstation In Windows NT, a computer running the Windows NT Workstation operating system. In a wider context, used to describe any powerful computer optimized for graphics or computer-aided design (CAD) or any of a number of other functions requiring high performance.

X

X.500 A standard for a directory service established by the International Telecommunications Union (ITU). The same standard is also published by the International Standards Organization/ International Electro-technical Commission (ISO/IEC). The X.500 standard defines the information model used in the directory service. All information in the directory is stored in entries, each of which belongs to at least one object class. The actual information in an entry is determined by attributes that are contained in that entry.

Z

zone A part of the Domain Name System (DNS) namespace that consists of a single

NOTES